Number 60485   Tuesday 23 April 2012   http://www.london-gazette.co.uk   1

Registered as a newspaper
Published by Authority
Established 1665

of Monday 22 April 2013
Supplement No. 2

List of Statutory Publications 2012

Contents

Preliminary Information	2
UK Legislation	**4**
Public general acts	4
Public general acts - explanatory notes	7
Local acts	7
Measures of the General Synod	8
Other statutory publications	8
Statutory Instruments, by subject heading	8
Statutory Instruments, by number	316
Subsidiary Numbers	355
Scottish Legislation	**361**
Acts of the Scottish Parliament	361
Acts of the Scottish Parliament - Explanatory notes	362
Other Scottish statutory publications	362
Scottish Statutory Instruments, by subject heading	362
Scottish Statutory Instruments, by number	399

Northern Ireland Legislation	**404**
Acts of the Northern Ireland Assembly	404
Acts of the Northern Ireland Assembly - explanatory notes	404
Other Northern Ireland statutory publications	404
Statutory Rules of Northern Ireland, by subject heading	405
Statutory Rules of Northern Ireland, by number	449
Welsh Assembly Legislation	**455**
Measures of the National Assembly for Wales	455
Measures of the National Assembly for Wales - Explanatory notes	455
Alphabetical Index	**456**

Preface

Content and Layout

This list contains details of the statutory publications and accompanying explanatory documents published during the year. It is arranged in three main sections that group the primary and delegated legislation of the United Kingdom, England & Wales, Scotland and Northern Ireland (Statutory Instruments made by the National Assembly for Wales are included within the UK section). Within each section the publications are listed in the same order:

Acts and their Explanatory Notes;

Statutory Instruments or Statutory Rules, arranged under subject headings. Each entry includes, where available or appropriate: the enabling power; the date when the instrument was issued, made and laid and comes into force; a short note of any effect; territorial extent and classification; a note of the relevant EU legislation; pagination; ISBN and price;

A numerical listing of the instruments, with their subject heading. This list also includes any subsidiary numbers in the series: C for commencement orders; L for instruments relating to court fees or procedure in England and Wales; NI for Orders in Council relating only to Northern Ireland; S for instruments relating only to Scotland; W for instruments made by the National Assembly for Wales;

There is a single alphabetical, subject index.

Unpublished Statutory Instruments

Although the majority of Statutory Instruments are formally published, some SIs of limited, local application are not printed but are available online at legislation.gov.uk and are listed in this publication.

Access to Documents

The full text of all legislation and delegated legislation (Statutory Instruments) is available from the The National Archives website, www.legislation.gov.uk on the day of publication. The website contains a complete dataset from 1988 for Acts and 1987 for Statutory Instruments and partial datasets for earlier years.

The full text of the general statutory instruments and statutory rules are also published in the respective annual editions of: Statutory Instruments, Scottish Statutory Instruments, Statutory Instruments made by the National Assembly for Wales and Statutory Rules of Northern Ireland.

Copies of legislation and published delegated legislation can be purchased from the addresses on the back cover.

Copies of non-print instruments unobtainable from The Stationery Office may be obtained from:

The National Archives, Kew, Richmond, Surrey, TW9 4DU (from 1922 onwards – except for the years 1942, 1950, 1951 and up to SI no. 940 of 1952). Please quote repository reference TS37

British Library, Official Publications and Social Sciences Service, 96 Euston Road, London, NW1 2DB (as before, up to 1980)

Belfast Statutory Publications Office, Castle Buildings, Stormont, Belfast, BT4 3SR (non-print Statutory Rules)

Standing Orders

Standing orders can be set up to ensure the receipt of all statutory publications in a particular subject area, without the need to continually scan lists of new publications or place individual orders. The subject categories used can be either broad or very specific. For more information please contact the TSO Standing Orders department on 0870 600 5522, or fax: 0870 600 5533.

Copyright

Legislation from official sources is reproducible freely under waiver of copyright. Full details can be found at: http://www.nationalarchives.gov.uk/doc/open-government-licence/

Most other TSO publications are Crown or Parliamentary copyright. Information about the licensing arrangements for Crown and Parliamentary copyright can be found at http://www.nationalarchives.gov.uk/doc/open-government-licence/, and
http://www.parliament.uk/site-information/copyright/open-parliament-licence/.

To find out more about licensing please contact:

Information Policy Team
The National Archives
Kew, Richmond, Surrey
TW9 4DU

psi@nationalarchives.gsi.gov.uk

List of Abbreviations

accord.	accordance
art(s).	article(s)
c.	chapter
C.	Commencement
CI.	Channel Islands
E.	England
EC	European Commission
EU	European Union
G.	Guernsey
GB.	Great Britain
GLA	Greater London Authority
IOM	Isle of Man
J.	Jersey
L.	Legal: fees or procedure in courts in E. & W.
NI.	Northern Ireland
para(s).	paragraph(s)
reg(s).	regulation(s)
s(s).	section(s)
S.	Scotland
sch(s).	schedule(s)
SI.	Statutory instrument(s)
SR.	Statutory rule(s) of Northern Ireland
SR & O.	Statutory rules and orders
SSI	Scottish Statutory Instrument
UK.	United Kingdom
W.	Wales

UK Legislation

Acts

Public General Acts 2003

Criminal Justice Act 2003: Elizabeth II. Chapter 44 (correction slip). - 1 sheet: 30 cm. - Correction slip (to ISBN 9780105444039) dated May 2012. - *Free*

Sexual Offences Act 2003: Elizabeth II. Chapter 42 (correction slip). - 1 sheet: 30 cm. - Correction slip (2nd to ISBN 0105442035), dated May 2012. - *Free*

Public General Acts 2004

Scottish Parliament (Constituencies) Act 2004: Elizabeth II. Chapter 13 (correction slip). - 1 sheet: 30 cm. - Correction slip (to ISBN 9780105413042) dated May 2012. - *Free*

Public General Acts 2006

Police and Justice Act 2006: Elizabeth II. Chapter 48 (correction slip). - 1 sheet: 30 cm. - Correction slip (to ISBN 9780105448068) dated May 2012. - *Free*

Racial and Religious Hatred Act 2006: Elizabeth II. Chapter 1 (correction slip). - 1 sheet: 30 cm. - Correction slip (to ISBN 9780108401063) dated May 2012. - *Free*

Public General Acts 2011

Energy Act 2011: Chapter 16. - vii, 102p.: 30 cm. - Royal assent, 18 October 2011. An Act to make provision for the arrangement and financing of energy efficiency improvements to be made to properties by owners and occupiers; about the energy efficiency of properties in the private rented sector; about the promotion by energy companies of reductions in carbon emissions and home-heating costs; about information relating to energy consumption, efficiency and tariffs; for increasing the security of energy supplies; about access to upstream petroleum infrastructure and downstream gas processing facilities; about a special administration regime for energy supply companies; about designations under the Continental Shelf Act 1964; about licence modifications relating to offshore transmission and distribution of electricity; about the security of nuclear construction sites; about the decommissioning of nuclear sites and offshore infrastructure; for the use of pipelines for carbon capture and storage; for an annual report on contribution to carbon emissions reduction targets; for action relating to the energy efficiency of residential accommodation in England; for the generation of electricity from renewable sources; about renewable heat incentives in Northern Ireland; about the powers of the Coal Authority; for an amendment of section 137 of the Energy Act 2004; for the amendment and repeal of measures relating to home energy efficiency. Explanatory notes to the Act are available separately (ISBN 9780105616115). Corrected reprint issued July 2012. Free to all known recipients of the original. - 978-0-10-541611-1 £16.00

Localism Act 2011: Chapter 20 (correction slip). - 1 sheet: 15 cm. - Correction slip (to ISBN 9780105420118) dated August 2012. - *Free*

Public General Acts 2012

Civil Aviation Act 2012: Elizabeth II. Chapter 19. - v, 121p.: 30 cm. - Royal assent, 19th December 2012. An Act to make provision about the regulation of operators of dominant airports; to confer functions on the Civil Aviation Authority under competition legislation in relation to services provided at airports; to make provision about aviation security; to make provision about the regulation of provision of flight accommodation; to make further provision about the Civil Aviation Authority's membership, administration and functions in relation to aviation. Explanatory notes have been produced to assist in the understanding of this Act and are available separately (ISBN 9780105619123). - 978-0-10-541912-9 £18.50

Civil Contingencies Act 2004: Elizabeth II. Chapter 36 (correction slip). - 1 sheet: 30 cm. - Correction slip (to ISBN 9780105436041) dated May 2012. - *Free*

Consumer Insurance (Disclosure and Representations) Act 2012: Chapter 6. - [16]p.: 30 cm. - Royal assent, 8 March 2012. An Act to make provision about disclosure and representations in connection with consumer insurance contracts. Explanatory notes have been produced to assist in the understanding of this Act and will be available separately. - 978-0-10-543111-4 £5.75

Domestic Violence, Crime and Victims (Amendment) Act 2012: Chapter 4. - [12]p.: 30 cm. - Royal assent, 8 March 2012. An Act to amend section 5 of the Domestic Violence, Crime and Victims Act 2004 to include serious harm to a child or vulnerable adult; to make consequential amendments to the Act. Explanatory notes have been produced to assist in the understanding of this Act and are available separately (ISBN 9780105604129). - 978-0-10-542911-1 £5.75

European Union (Approval of Treaty Amendment Decision) Act 2012: Chapter 15. - [4]p.: 30 cm. - Royal assent, 31st October 2012. An Act to make provision for the purposes of section 3 of the European Union Act 2011 in relation to the European Council decision on 25 March 2011 amending Article 136 of the Treaty on the functioning of the European Union with regard to a stability mechanism for Member States whose currency is the euro. Explanatory notes have been produced to assist in the understanding of this Act and are available separately (ISBN 9780105615125). - 978-0-10-541512-1 £4.00

Finance Act 2012: Chapter 14. - xiv, 687p.: 30 cm. - Royal assent, 17th July 2012. An Act to grant certain duties, to alter other duties, and to amend the law relating to the National Debt and the Public Revenue, and to make further provision in connection with finance. - 978-0-10-541412-4 £58.50

Financial Services Act 2012: Elizabeth II. Chapter 21. - vii, 376p.: 30 cm. - Royal assent, 19th December 2012. An Act to amend the Bank of England Act 1998, the Financial Services and Markets Act 2000 and the Banking Act 2009; to make other provision about financial services and markets; to make provision about the exercise of certain statutory functions relating to building societies, friendly societies and other mutual societies; to amend section 785 of the Companies Act 2006; to make provision enabling the Director of Savings to provide services to other public bodies. Explanatory notes have been produced to assist in the understanding of this Act and are available separately (ISBN 9780105621126). - 978-0-10-542112-2 £38.00

Health and Social Care Act 2012: Chapter 7. - xiii, 457p.: 30 cm. - Royal assent, 27 March 2012. An Act to establish and make provision about a National Health Service Commissioning Board and clinical commissioning groups and to make other provision about the National Health Service in England; to make provision about public health in the United Kingdom; to make provision about regulating health and adult social care services; to make provision about public involvement in health and social care matters, scrutiny of health matters by local authorities and co-operation between local authorities and commissioners of health care services; to make provision about regulating health and social care workers; to establish and make provision about a National Institute for Health and Care Excellence; to establish and make provision about a Health and Social Care Information Centre and to make other provision about information relating to health or social care matters; to abolish certain public bodies involved in health or social care; to make other provision about health care. Explanatory notes have been produced to assist in the understanding of this Act and are available separately (ISBN 9780105607120). - 978-0-10-540712-6 £44.75

Infrastructure (Financial Assistance) Act 2012: Chapter 16. - [8]p.: 30 cm. - Royal assent, 31st October 2012. An Act to make provision in connection with the giving of financial assistance in respect of the provision of infrastructure. Explanatory notes have been produced to assist in the understanding of this Act and are available separately (ISBN 9780105616122). - 978-0-10-541612-8 £4.00

Legal Aid, Sentencing and Punishment of Offenders Act 2012: Chapter 10. - viii, 302p.: 30 cm. - Royal assent, 1 May 2012. An Act to make provision about legal aid; to make further provision about funding legal services; to make provision about costs and other amounts awarded in civil and criminal proceedings; to make provision about referral fees in connection with the provision of legal services; to make provision about sentencing offenders, including provision about release on licence or otherwise; to make provision about the collection of fines and other sums; to make provision about bail and about remand otherwise than on bail; to make provision about the employment, payment and transfer of persons detained in prisons and other institutions; to make provision about penalty notices for disorderly behaviour and cautions; to make provision about the rehabilitation of offenders; to create new offences of threatening with a weapon in public or on school premises and of causing serious injury by dangerous driving; to create a new offence relating to squatting; to increase penalties for offences relating to scrap metal dealing and to create a new offence relating to payment for scrap metal; and to amend section 76 of the Criminal Justice and Immigration Act 2008. Explanatory notes have been produced to assist in the understanding of this Act and are available separately (ISBN 9780105610120). With correction slips dated July 2012 and October 2012 and November 2012. - 978-0-10-541012-6 £38.00

Live Music Act 2012: Chapter 2. - [12]p.: 30 cm. - Royal assent, 8 March 2012. An Act to amend the Licensing Act 2003 with respect to the performance of live music entertainment. Explanatory notes have been produced to assist in the understanding of this Act and are available separately (ISBN 9780105602125). - 978-0-10-542711-7 £5.75

Local Government Finance Act 2012: Chapter 17. - ii, 73p.: 30 cm. - Royal Assent, 31st October 2012. An Act to make provision about non-domestic rating; to make provision about grants to local authorities; to make provision about council tax; to make provision about the supply of information for purposes relating to rates in Northern Ireland. Explanatory notes have been produced to assist in the understanding of this Act are available separately (ISBN 9780105617129). - 978-0-10-541712-5 £13.75

Mental Health (Approval Functions) Act 2012: Chapter 18. - [4]p.: 30 cm. - Royal assent, 31st October 2012. An Act to authorise things done before the day on which this Act is passed in the purported exercise of functions relating to the approval of registered medical practitioners and clinicians under the Mental Health Act 1983. Explanatory notes have been produced to assist in the understanding of this Act and are available separately (ISBN 9780105618126). - 978-0-10-541812-2 £4.00

Police (Complaints and Conduct) Act 2012: Elizabeth II. Chapter 22. - [1], 4p.: 30 cm. - Royal assent, 19th December 2012. An Act to make provision about interviews held in certain investigations under schedule 3 to the Police Reform Act 2002; and about the application of Part 2 of that Act to matters occurring before 1 April 2004. Explanatory notes have been produced to assist in the understanding of this Act and are available separately (ISBN 9780105622123). - 978-0-10-542212-9 £5.75

Prisons (Interference with Wireless Telegraphy) Act 2012: Elizabeth II. Chapter 20. - [1], 5p.: 30 cm. - Royal assent, 19th December 2012. An Act to make provision about interference with wireless telegraphy in prisons and similar institutions. Explanatory notes have been produced to assist in the understanding of this Act and are available separately (ISBN 9780105620129). - 978-0-10-542012-5 £5.75

Protection of Freedoms Act 2012: Chapter 9. - viii, 215p.: 30 cm. - Royal assent, 1 May 2012. An Act to provide for the destruction, retention, use and other regulation of certain evidential material; to impose consent and other requirements in relation to certain processing of biometric information relating to children; to provide for a code of practice about surveillance camera systems and for the appointment and role of the Surveillance Camera Commissioner; to provide for judicial approval in relation to certain authorisations and notices under the Regulation of Investigatory Powers Act 2000; to provide for the repeal or rewriting of powers of entry and associated powers and for codes of practice and other safeguards in relation to such powers; to make provision about vehicles left on land; to amend the maximum detention period for terrorist suspects; to replace certain stop and search powers and to provide for a related code of practice; to make provision about the safeguarding of vulnerable groups and about criminal records including provision for the establishment of the Disclosure and Barring Service and the dissolution of the Independent Safeguarding Authority; to disregard convictions and cautions for certain abolished offences; to make provision about the release and publication of datasets held by public authorities and to make other provision about freedom of information and the Information Commissioner; to make provision about the trafficking of people for exploitation and about stalking; to repeal certain enactments. Explanatory notes have been produced to assist in the understanding of this Act and are available separately (ISBN 9780105609124). - 978-0-10-540912-0 £28.75

Public Services (Social Value) Act 2012: Chapter 3. - [8]p.: 30 cm. - Royal assent, 8 March 2012. An Act to require public authorities to have regard to economic, social and environmental well-being in connection with public services contracts. Explanatory notes have been produced to assist in the understanding of this Act and are available separately (ISBN 9780105603122). - 978-0-10-542811-4 £5.75

Scotland Act 2012: Chapter 11. - iii, 42p.: 30 cm. - Royal assent, 1 May 2012. An Act to amend the Scotland Act 1998 and make provision about the functions of the Scottish Ministers. Explanatory notes have been produced to assist in the understanding of this Act and are available separately (ISBN 9780105611127). - 978-0-10-541112-3 £9.75

Small Charitable Donations Act 2012: Elizabeth II. Chapter 23. - ii 15p.: 30 cm. - Royal assent, 19th December 2012. An Act to provide for the making of payments to certain charities and clubs in respect of certain gifts made to them by individuals. Explanatory notes have been produced to assist in the understanding of this Act and are available separately (ISBN 9780105623120). - 978-0-10-542312-6 £5.75

Sunday Trading (London Olympic Games and Paralympic Games) Act 2012: Chapter 12. - [8]p.: 30 cm. - Royal assent, 1 May 2012. An Act to suspend restrictions on Sunday trading hours for the period of the London Olympic Games and Paralympic Games. Explanatory notes have been produced to assist in the understanding of this Act and will be available separately. - 978-0-10-541212-0 £4.00

Supply and Appropriation (Anticipation and Adjustments) Act 2012: Chapter 1. - [1], 72p.: 30 cm. - Royal assent, 8 March 2012. An Act to authorise the use of resources for the years ending with 31 March 2012 and 31 March 2013; to authorise the issue of sums out of the Consolidated Fund for those years and for the year ending with 31 March 2011; and to appropriate the supply authorised by this Act for the years ending with 31 March 2011 and 31 March 2012. - 978-0-10-542611-0 £13.75

Supply and Appropriation (Main Estimates) Act 2012: Chapter 13. - 74p.: 30 cm. - Royal assent, 17th July 2012. An Act to authorise the use of resources for the year ending with 31 March 2013; to authorise both the issue of sums out of the Consolidated Fund and the application of income for that year; and to appropriate the supply authorised for that year by this Act and by the Supply and Appropriation (Anticipation and Adjustments) Act 2012. - 978-0-10-541312-7 £13.75

Water Industry (Financial Assistance) Act 2012: Chapter 8. - [8]p.: 30 cm. - Royal assent, 1 May 2012. An Act to make provision for the giving of financial assistance for the purpose of securing the reduction of charges for the supply of water and the provision of sewerage services and in connection with the construction of, and the carrying out of works in respect of, water and sewerage infrastructure. Explanatory notes have been produced to assist in the understanding of this Act and are available separately (ISBN 9780105608127). - 978-0-10-540812-3 £4.00

Welfare Reform Act 2012: Chapter 5. - viii, 177p.: 30 cm. - Royal assent, 8 March 2012. An Act to make provision for universal credit and personal independence payment; to make other provision about social security and tax credits; to make provision about the functions of the registration service, child support maintenance and the use of jobcentres; to establish the Social Mobility and Child Poverty Commission and otherwise amend the Child Poverty Act 2010. Explanatory notes have been produced to assist in the understanding of this Act and are available separately (ISBN 9780105605126). - 978-0-10-543011-7 £26.75

Public General Acts - Explanatory Notes 2012

Civil Aviation Act 2012: Chapter 19: explanatory notes. - 51p.: 30 cm. - These notes refer to the Civil Aviation Act 2012 (c. 19) (ISBN 9780105419129) which received Royal Assent on 19 December 2012. - 978-0-10-561912-3 £9.75

Domestic Violence, Crime and Victims (Amendment) Act 2012: Chapter 4: explanatory notes. - [12]p.: 30 cm. - These notes refer to the Domestic Violence, Crime and Victims (Amendment) Act 2012 (c. 4) (ISBN 9780105429111) which received Royal Assent on 8 March 2012. - 978-0-10-560412-9 £5.75

European Union (Approval of Treaty Amendment Decision) Act 2012: Chapter 15: explanatory notes. - [8]p.: 30 cm. - These notes refer to the European Union (Approval of Treaty Amendment Decision) Act 2012 (c.15) (ISBN 9780105415121) which received Royal Assent on 31 October 2012. - 978-0-10-561512-5 £4.00

Finance Act 2012: Chapter 14: explanatory notes. - [2], 500p.: 30 cm. - These notes refer to the Finance Act 2012 (c. 14) (ISBN 9780105414124) which received Royal assent on 17 July 2012. - 978-0-10-561412-8 £44.75

Health and Social Care Act 2012: Chapter 7: explanatory notes. - 259p.: 30 cm. - These notes refer to the Health and Social Care Act 2012 (c. 7) (ISBN 9780105407126) which received Royal Assent on 27 March 2012. - 978-0-10-560712-0 £28.75

Infrastructure (Financial Assistance) Act 2012: Chapter 16: explanatory notes. - [8]p.: 30 cm. - These notes refer to the Infrastructure (Financial Assistance) Act 2012 (c.16) (ISBN 9780105416128) which received Royal Assent on 31 October 2012. - 978-0-10-561612-2 £4.00

Legal Aid, Sentencing and Punishment of Offenders Act 2012: Chapter 10: explanatory notes. - 143p.: 30 cm. - These notes refer to the Legal Aid, Sentencing and Punishment of Offenders Act 2012 (c.10) (ISBN 9780105410126) which received Royal Assent on 1 May 2012. - 978-0-10-561012-0 £22.50

Live Music Act 2012: Chapter 2: explanatory notes. - [8]p.: 30 cm. - These notes refer to the Live Music Act 2012 (c. 2) (ISBN 9780105427117) which received Royal Assent on 8th March 2012. - 978-0-10-560212-5 £4.00

Local Government Finance Act 2012: Chapter 17: explanatory notes. - 19p.: 30 cm. - These notes refer to the Local Government Finance Act 2012 (c.17) (ISBN 9780105417125) which received Royal Assent on 31 October 2012. - 978-0-10-561712-9 £5.75

Mental Health (Approval Functions) Act 2012: Chapter 18: explanatory notes. - 3p.: 30 cm. - These notes refer to the Mental Health (Approval Functions) Act 2012 (c. 18) (ISBN 9780105418122) which received Royal Assent on 31st October 2012. - 978-0-10-561812-6 £4.00

Protection of Freedoms Act 2012: Chapter 9: explanatory notes. - 91p.: 30 cm. - These notes refer to the Protection of Freedoms Act (c.9) (ISBN 9780105409120) which received Royal Assent on 1 May 2012. - 978-0-10-560912-4 £15.50

Public Services (Social Value) Act 2012: Chapter 3: explanatory notes. - [8]p.: 30 cm. - These notes refer to the Public Services (Social Value) Act 2012 (c. 3) (ISBN 9780105428114) which received Royal assent on 8 March 2012. - 978-0-10-560312-2 £4.00

Scotland Act 2012: Chapter 11: explanatory notes. - 31p.: 30 cm. - These notes refer to the Scotland Act 2012 (c. 11) (ISBN 9780105411123) which received Royal Assent on 1 May 2012. - 978-0-10-561112-7 £9.75

Small Charitable Donations Act 2012: Chapter 23: explanatory notes. - 20p.: 30 cm. - These notes refer to the Small Charitable Donations Act 2012 (c. 23) (ISBN 9780105423126) which received Royal Assent on 19 December 2012. - 978-0-10-562312-0 £5.75

Water Industry (Financial Assistance) Act 2012: Chapter 8: explanatory notes. - 4p.: 30 cm. - These notes refer to the Water Industry (Financial Assistance) Act 2012 (c. 8) (ISBN 9780105408123) which received Royal Assent on 1 May 2012. - 978-0-10-560812-7 £4.00

Welfare Reform Act 2012: Chapter 5: explanatory notes. - 94p.: 30 cm. - These notes refer to the Welfare Reform Act 2012 (c. 5) (ISBN 9780105430117) which received Royal Assent on 8 March 2012. - 978-0-10-560512-6 £15.50

Local Acts 2012

Bank of Ireland (UK) plc Act 2012: Chapter i. - [12]p.: 30 cm. - Royal assent, 8th March 2012. An Act to provide that the statutory right of The Governor and Company of the Bank of Ireland to issue banknotes shall transfer and apply to Bank of Ireland (UK) plc. - 978-0-10-545010-8 £5.75

London Local Authorities Act 2012: Chapter ii. - ii, 47p.: 30 cm. - Royal assent, 27 March 2012. An Act to confer further powers upon local authorities in London. - 978-0-10-545598-1 £9.75

Measures of the General Synod

Measures of the General Synod 2012

1   **Church of England Marriage (Amendment) Measure 2012**
- [2], 3p.: 30 cm. - Royal Assent, 19th December 2012. A measure passed by the General Synod of the Church of England to amend the Church of England Marriage Measure 2008 to widen the conditions for establishing the qualifying connections of persons intending to be married in certain cases and to provide for the form of banns of matrimony where the form set out in the Book of Common Prayer is not used and for the time of the publication of banns. - 978-0-10-545638-4 £5.75

Other statutory publications

Her Majesty's Stationery Office.

Chronological table of the statutes [1235-2010]. - 3v. (xii, 2828p.): hdbk: 25 cm. - 3 vols. not sold separately. Part 1: Covering the acts of the Parliaments of England, Great Britain and the United Kingdom from 1235 to the end of 1955; Part 2: Covering the acts of the Parliaments of the United Kingdom from 1956 to the end of 1987; Part 3: Covering the Acts of the Parliaments of the United Kingdom from 1988 to the end of 2010, the acts of the Parliaments of Scotland from 1424 to 1707, the acts of the Scottish Parliament from 1999 to the end of 2010 and Measures of the National Assembly for Wales from 2008 to the end of 2010 and the Church Assembly measures and General Synod measures from 1920 to the end of 2010. - 978-0-11-840509-6 *£425.00 per set*

Chronological table of the statutes [1235-2011]. - 3v. (xii, 2910p.): hdbk: 25 cm. - 3 vols. not sold separately. Part 1: Covering the acts of the Parliaments of England, Great Britain and the United Kingdom from 1235 to the end of 1964; Part 2: Covering the acts of the Parliaments of the United Kingdom from 1965 to the end of 1988; Part 3: Covering the Acts of the Parliaments of the United Kingdom from 1989 to the end of 2011, the acts of the Parliaments of Scotland from 1424 to 1707, the acts of the Scottish Parliament from 1999 to the end of 2011 and Measures of the National Assembly for Wales from 2008 to the end of 2011 and the Church Assembly measures and General Synod measures from 1920 to the end of 2011. - 978-0-11-840523-2 *£435.00 per set*

The public general acts and General Synod measures 2011. - 4v. (various pagings): hdbk: 31 cm. - 4 parts not sold separately. Contents: Part 1: PGA chapters 1 - 11; Part 2: PGA chapters 12 - 20; Part 3: PGA chapters 21 - 25, General Synod Measures 1 - 3; Part 4: Table V of Origins and Destinations, Table VI - Effect of Legislation; General Index. - 978-0-11-840529-4 *£370.00 per set*

The public general acts and General Synod measures 2011: tables and index. - a-j, 490p.: 30 cm. - 978-0-11-840538-6 *£70.00*

Statutory instruments 2009

Part 2: Section 1 nos. 1122-1568; Section 2 nos. 1569-1885; Section 3 nos. 1886-2092; Section 4 nos. 2093-2344; 1st May to 31st August 2009. - 4v. (xxii, p. 4221-8642): hdbk: 31 cm. - 4 vols. not sold separately. Includes: Guide to the edition; General statutory instruments issued in the period; selected local instruments; selected instruments not registered as statutory instruments; index to parts 1 and 2. - 978-0-11-840517-1 *£530.00 per set*

Part 3: Section 1 nos. 2350-2715; Section 2 nos. 2720-3040; Section 3 nos. 3042-3344; Section 4 nos. 3345-3404; 1st September to 31st December 2009. - 4v. (xx, p. 8643-12584): hdbk: 31 cm. - 4 vols. not sold separately. Includes: Guide to the edition; General statutory instruments issued in the period; selected local instruments; selected instruments not registered as statutory instruments; classified list of local instruments; tables of effects; numerical and issue list; index to part 3. - 978-0-11-840525-6 *£518.00 per set*

Statutory Instruments

Arranged by Subject Headings

Agriculture

The Agriculture (Miscellaneous Amendments) Regulations 2012 No. 2012/66. - Enabling power: European Communities Act 1972, s. 2 (2). - Issued: 16.01.2012. Made: 10.01.2012. Laid: 16.01.2012. Coming into force: 13.02.2012. Effect: S.I. 2009/3263, 3365 amended. Territorial extent & classification: UK in respect of the amendment to S.I. 2009/3263 & to England in respect of amendments to S.I. 2009/3365. General. - This SI has been corrected by SI 2012/2897 (ISBN 9780111530894) which is being sent free of charge to all known recipients of 2012/66. - 4p.: 30 cm. - 978-0-11-151920-2 *£4.00*

The Uplands Transitional Payment Regulations 2012 No. 2012/114. - Enabling power: European Communities Act 1972, s. 2 (2). - Issued: 20.01.2012. Made: 16.01.2012. Laid: 20.01.2012. Coming into force: 13.02.2012. Effect: S.I. 2001/476; 2002/271; 2003/289; 2004/145; 2005/154 revoked. Territorial extent & classification: E for regs 2-8 but the instruments revoked in reg. 9 applied to E/S. General. - EC note: These regulations partially implement Council Regulation 1698/2005 on support for rural development by the European Agricultural Fund for Rural Development and Council Regulation 1257/1999 on support for rural development from the European Agricultural Guidance and Guarantee Fund (EAGGF) in relation to less favoured areas. - 12p.: 30 cm. - 978-0-11-151931-8 £5.75

Agriculture, England

The Common Agricultural Policy Single Payment and Support Schemes (Amendment) Regulations 2012 No. 2012/3027. - Enabling power: European Communities Act 1972, s. 2 (2). - Issued: 07.12.2012. Made: 03.12.2012. Laid: 07.12.2012. Coming into force: 01.01.2012. Effect: S.I. 2010/540 amended. Territorial extent & classification: E. General. - 2p.: 30 cm. - 978-0-11-153173-0 £4.00

The Nitrate Pollution Prevention (Amendment) Regulations 2012 No. 2012/1849. - Enabling power: European Communities Act 1972, s. 2 (2). - Issued: 17.07.2012. Made: 13.07.2012. Laid: 16.07.2012. Coming into force: 07.08.2012. Effect: S.I. 2008/2349 amended. Territorial extent & classification: E. General. - EC note: These Regulations revoke and replace certain provisions of S.I. 2008/2349 which relate to the designation of nitrate vulnerable zones. The principal regulations implement in England Council Directive 91/676/EEC concerning the protection of waters against pollution by nitrates from agricultural sources. - 4p.: 30 cm. - 978-0-11-152711-5 £4.00

The Specified Products from China (Restriction on First Placing on the Market) (England) (Amendment) Regulations 2012 No. 2012/47. - Enabling power: European Communities Act 1972, s. 2 (2). - Issued: 12.01.2012. Made: 09.01.2012. Laid: 11.01.2012. Coming into force: 12.01.2012. Effect: S.I. 2008/1079 amended. Territorial extent & classification: E. General. - EC note: These Regulations implement, in England, Commission Implementing Decision 2011/884/EU on emergency measures regarding the unauthorised genetically modified rice in rice products originating from China and repealing Decision 2008/289/EC. The Commission Implementing Decision provides for import restrictions that previously applied to Bt 63 genetically modified rice to apply, with modifications, to all unauthorised GM rice. - 4p.: 30 cm. - 978-0-11-151905-9 £4.00

Agriculture, Wales

The Beef and Pig Carcase Classification (Wales) (Amendment) Regulations 2012 No. 2012/948 (W.125). - Enabling power: European Communities Act 1972, s. 2 (2). - Issued: 11.04.2012. Made: 26.03.2012. Laid before the National Assembly for Wales: 28.03.2012. Coming into force: 18.04.2012. Effect: S.I. 2011/1826 (W. 198) amended. Territorial extent & classification: W. General. - In English and Welsh. Welsh title: Rheoliadau Dosbarthu Carcasau Eidion a Moch (Cymru) 2011. - 4p.: 30 cm. - 978-0-348-10591-9 £4.00

The Common Agricultural Policy Single Payment and Support Schemes (Wales) (Amendment) Regulations 2012 No. 2012/3093 (W.311). - Enabling power: European Communities Act 1972, s. 2 (2). - Issued: 23.01.2013. Made: 13.12.2012. Laid before the National Assembly for Wales: 13.12.2012. Coming into force: 03.01.2013. Effect: S.I. 2010/1892 (W.185) amended. Territorial extent & classification: W. General. - In English and Welsh. Welsh title: Rhwoliadau Cynllun Taliad Sengl a Chynlluniau Cymorth y Polisi Amaethyddol Cyffredin (Cymru) (Diwygio) 2012. - 4p.: 30 cm. - 978-0-348-10680-0 £4.00

The Nitrate Pollution Prevention (Wales) (Amendment) Regulations 2012 No. 2012/1238 (W.151). - Enabling power: European Communities Act 1972, s. 2 (2). - Issued: 24.05.2012. Made: 05.05.2012. Laid before the National Assembly for Wales: 09.05.2012. Coming into force: 01.06.2012. Effect: S.I. 2008/3143 (W.278) amended. Territorial extent & classification: W. General. - In English and Welsh. Welsh title: Rheoliadau Atal Llygredd Nitradau (Cymru) (Diwygio) 2012. - 8p.: 30 cm. - 978-0-348-10609-1 £5.75

The Red Meat Industry (Designation of Slaughterers and Exporters) (Wales) Order 2012 No. 2012/247 (W.40). - Enabling power: Red Meat Industry (Wales) Measure 2010, ss. 4 (3), 17. - Issued: 23.02.2012. Made: 01.02.2012. Laid before the National Assembly for Wales: 02.02.2012. Coming into force: 01.04.2012. Effect: None. Territorial extent & classification: W. General. - In English and Welsh: Welsh title: Gorchymyn Diwydiant Cig Coch (Dynodi Cigyddwyr ac Allforwyr) (Cymru) 2012. - 4p.: 30 cm. - 978-0-348-10695-4 £4.00

The Specified Products from China (Restriction on First Placing on the Market) (Wales) (Amendment) Regulations 2012 No. 2012/64 (W.15). - Enabling power: European Communities Act 1972, s. 2 (2). - Issued: 27.01.2012. Made: 11.01.2012. Laid before the National Assembly for Wales: 12.01.2012. Coming into force: 12.01.2012. Effect: S.I. 2008/1080 (W.114) amended. Territorial extent & classification: W. General. - EC note: These Regulations amend SI 2008/1080 (W.114) in order to implement Commission Implementing Decision 2011/884/EU on emergency measures regarding unauthorised genetically modified rice in rice products originating from China and repealing Decision 2008/289/EC. The Commission Decision provides for import restrictions that previously applied to Bt 63 genetically modified rice to apply, with modifications, to all unauthorised GM rice. - In English and Welsh: Welsh title: Rheoliadau Cynhyrchion Penodedig o Tsieina (Cyfyngiad ar eu Rhoi Gyntaf ar y Farchnad) (Cymru) (Diwygio) 2012. - 8p.: 30 cm. - 978-0-348-10545-2 £5.75

Animals

The Animals (Scientific Procedures) Act 1986 Amendment Regulations 2012 No. 2012/3039. - Enabling power: European Communities Act 1972, sch. 2, para. 2 (2). - Issued: 21.12.2012. Made: 18.12.2012. Coming into force: In accord. with reg. 1 (2) to (4). Effect: 1976 c. 38; 1986 c. 14; 2005 c. 15; 2006 c. 45; 2011 c. 16 (NI); S.I. 1986/1911; 1996/3090; 2004/1993 (NI 16); 2006/336, 2702, 2927; 2007/68; S.S.I. 2006/336 amended & S.I. 1993/2103; 1998/1974; 2006/2407 partially revoked & S.I. 1993/2102 revoked. Territorial extent & classification: E/W/S/NI. General. - Supersedes draft SI (ISBN 9780111530313) issued on 05.11.2012. EC note: Transposes Directive 2010/63/EU on the protection of animals used for scientific purposes. - 52p.: 30 cm. - 978-0-11-153275-1 £9.75

The Animals (Scientific Procedures) Act 1986 (Fees) Order 2012 No. 2012/3050. - Enabling power: Animals (Scientific Procedures) Act 1986, s. 8. - Issued: 11.12.2012. Made: 07.12.2012. Laid: 10.12.2012. Coming into force: 01.01.2013. Effect: S.I. 2000/480 revoked. Territorial extent & classification: E/W/S. General. - 2p.: 30 cm. - 978-0-11-153200-3 £4.00

Animals, England

The Local Policing Bodies (Consequential Amendments) Regulations 2012 No. 2012/61. - Enabling power: Police and Criminal Evidence Act 1984, s. 63B (6) & Animal Welfare Act 2006, ss. 6 (4) (5) (6) (8) (14) & Violent Crime Reduction Act 2006, ss. 15, 16 (7), 17 (6), 20 (5). - Issued: 17.01.2012. Made: 10.01.2012. Coming into force: 16.01.2012. Effect: S.I. 2001/2645; 2007/1120; 2008/1430 amended. Territorial extent & classification: E/W. General. - Supersedes draft SI (ISBN 9780111517130) issued on 22.11.2011. - 4p.: 30 cm. - 978-0-11-151915-8 £4.00

The Welfare of Wild Animals in Travelling Circuses (England) Regulations 2012 No. 2012/2932. - Enabling power: Animal Welfare Act 2006, s. 13 (2) (7) (10), sch. 1, parts 1, 3. - Issued: 26.11.2012. Made: 21.11.2012. Coming into force: In accord. with reg. 1. Effect: None. Territorial extent & classification: E. - Supersedes draft SI (ISBN 9780111527832) issued on 31.07.2012. - 12p.: 30 cm. - 978-0-11-153116-7 £5.75

The Zootechnical Standards (England) Regulations 2012 No. 2012/2665. - Enabling power: European Communities Act 1972, s. 2 (2), sch. 2, para. 1A. - Issued: 26.10.2012. Made: 16.10.2012. Laid: 25.10.2012. Coming into force: 30.11.2012. Effect: S.I. 1992/2370 revoked in relation to England; 2007/3167 revoked. Territorial extent & classification: E. General. - EC note: These Regulations transpose the following EU instruments in relation to cattle: Council Directives 87/328/EEC; 2009/157/EC and Commission Decisions 2006/427/EC; 2005/379/EC; 84/247/EEC; 84/419/EEC. In relation to pigs: Council Directives 88/661/EEC; 90/118/EEC; 90/119/EEC and Commission Decisions 89/501/EEC; 89/504/EEC; 89/502/EEC; 89/505/EEC; 89/503/EEC; 89/506/EEC; 89/507/EEC. In relation to sheep and goats: Council Directive 89/361/EEC and Commission Decisions 90/254/EEC; 90/255/EEC; 90/258/EEC; 90/256/EEC; 90/257/EEC. They also transpose Art. 4 of Council Directive 94/28/EC and amending Directive 77/504/EEC. - 8p.: 30 cm. - 978-0-11-152996-6 £5.75

Animals, England: Animal health

The African Horse Sickness (England) Regulations 2012 No. 2012/2629. - Enabling power: European Communities Act 1972, s. 2 (2). - Issued: 22.10.2012. Made: 15.10.2012. Laid before Parliament and the National Assembly for Wales: 19.10.2012. Coming into force: 21.11.2012. Effect: S.I. 1992/3159; 1996/2628 amended. Territorial extent & classification: E. General. - 24p.: 30 cm. - 978-0-11-152978-2 £5.75

The Bluetongue (Amendment) Order 2012 No. 2012/1977. - Enabling power: European Communities Act 1972, s. 2 (2). - Issued: 30.07.2012. Made: 25.07.2012. Laid: 30.07.2012. Coming into force: 24.08.2012. Effect: S.I. 2008/962 amended. Territorial extent & classification: E. General. - This SI has been corrected by SI 2012/2897 (ISBN 9780111530894) which is being sent free of charge to all known recipients of 2012/1977. - 4p.: 30 cm. - 978-0-11-152782-5 £4.00

The Cattle Compensation (England) Order 2012 No. 2012/1379. - Enabling power: Animal Health Act 1981, ss. 1, 32 (3). - Issued: 30.05.2012. Made: 16.05.2012. Laid: 30.05.2012. Coming into force: 01.07.2012. Effect: S.I. 2006/168 revoked with saving. Territorial extent & classification: E. General. - This Order will cease to have effect on 01.07.2019. - 8p.: 30 cm. - 978-0-11-152489-3 £5.75

The Individual Ascertainment of Value (England) Order 2012 No. 2012/1380. - Enabling power: Animal Health Act 1981, ss. 1, 32 (3), 34 (7). - Issued: 30.05.2012. Made: 16.05.2012. Laid: 30.05.2012. Coming into force: 01.07.2012. Effect: S.I. 2005/3434 revoked. Territorial extent & classification: E. General. - This Order, which will cease to have effect on 01.07.2019, should be read alongside the Cattle Compensation Order (SI 2012/1379, ISBN 9780111524893). - 4p.: 30 cm. - 978-0-11-152488-6 £4.00

The Tuberculosis (England) (Amendment) Order 2012 No. 2012/1391. - Enabling power: Animal Health Act 1981, ss. 1, 8 (1), 25. - Issued: 29.05.2012. Made: 14.05.2012. Coming into force: 01.07.2012. Effect: S.I. 2007/740 amended. Territorial extent & classification: E. General. - 4p.: 30 cm. - 978-0-11-152481-7 £4.00

Animals, England: Prevention of cruelty

The Spring Traps Approval (England) Order 2012 No. 2012/13. - Enabling power: Pests Act 1954, s. 8 (3) (7). - Issued: 09.01.2012. Made: 04.01.2012. Coming into force: 15.02.2012. Effect: S.I. 1995/2427; 2007/2708; 2009/2166; 2010/2882 revoked. Territorial extent & classification: E. General. - 8p.: 30 cm. - 978-0-11-151896-0 £5.75

The Welfare of Animals (Slaughter or Killing) (Amendment) (England) Regulations 2012 No. 2012/501. - Enabling power: European Communities Act 1972, s. 2 (2). - Issued: 28.02.2012. Made: 22.02.2012. Laid: 28.02.2012. Coming into force: 06.04.2012. Effect: S.I. 1995/731 amended. Territorial extent & classification: E. General. - 8p.: 30 cm. - 978-0-11-152064-2 £4.00

Animals, England and Wales: Animal health

The Agriculture, Animals, Environment and Food etc. (Miscellaneous Amendments) Order 2012 No. 2012/2897. - Enabling power: European Communities Act 1972, s. 2 (2) & Animal Health Act 1981, ss. 1, 8 (1). - Issued: 21.11.2012. Made: 15.11.2012. Laid: 21.11.2012. Coming into force: 24.12.2012. Effect: 45 SI's amended. Territorial extent & classification: E/W. General. - This Statutory Instrument has been made partly in consequence of defects in SI 2010/108, 2011/1543, 2011/2936, 2012/66 and 2012/1977, and is being issued free of charge to all known recipients of those Statutory Instruments. - 16p.: 30 cm. - 978-0-11-153089-4 £5.75

Animals, Wales

The Badger (Control Area) (Wales) (Revocation) Order 2012 No. 2012/1387 (W.168). - Enabling power: Animal Health Act 1981, ss. 1, 21 (2), (4) (5), 86 (1). - Issued: 19.06.2012. Made: 23.05.2012. Laid before the National Assembly for Wales: 25.05.2012. Coming into force: 15.06.2012. Effect: S.I. 2011/693 (W. 105) revoked. Territorial extent & classification: W. General. - In English and Welsh. Welsh language title: Gorchymyn Moch Daear (Ardal Reoli) (Cymru) (Dirymu) 2012. - 4p.: 30 cm. - 978-0-348-10624-4 £4.00

The Mink Keeping (Prohibition) (Wales) Order 2012 No. 2012/1427 (W. 177). - Enabling power: Destructive Imported Animals Act 1932, s. 10 (1). - Issued: 08.06.2012. Made: 08.05.2012. Laid before the National Assembly for Wales: 08.05.2012. Coming into force: 01.06.2012. Effect: None. Territorial extent & classification: W. General. - Approved by the National Assembly for Wales. Supersedes Unnumbered WSI (ISBN 9780348106053) issued 17.05.2012. With correction slip dated July 2012. - 4p.: 30 cm. - 978-0-348-10619-0 £4.00

The Spring Traps Approval (Wales) Order 2012 No. 2012/2941 (W.300). - Enabling power: Pests Act 1954, s. 8 (3) (7). - Issued: 14.12.2012. Made: 21.11.2012. Laid before the National Assembly for Wales: 20.11.2012 Coming into force: 17.12.2012. Effect: S.I. 2010/2447 (W.210) revoked in so far as it applies to Wales. Territorial extent & classification: W. General. - With correction slip dated February 2013. - In English and Welsh. Welsh title: Gorchymyn Cymeradwyo Trapiau Sbring (Cymru) 2012. - 12p.: 30 cm. - 978-0-348-10669-5 £5.75

Animals, Wales: Animal health

The Bluetongue (Wales) (Amendment) Regulations 2012 No. 2012/2403 (W.257). - Enabling power: European Communities Act 1972, s. 2 (2). - Issued: 15.10.2012. Made: 15.09.2012. Laid before the National Assembly for Wales: 19.09.2012. Coming into force: 10.10.2012. Effect: S.I. 2008/1090 (W.116) amended. Territorial extent & classification: W. General. - EC note: These Regulations amend the Bluetongue (Wales) Regulations 2008 (S.I. 2008/1090 (W.116)) ("the 2008 Regulations") by transposing Directive 2012/5/EU amending Council Directive 2000/75/EC as regards vaccination against bluetongue. - In English and Welsh. Welsh title: Rheoliadau'r Tafod Glas (Cymru) (Diwygio) 2012. - 8p.: 30 cm. - 978-0-348-10653-4 £4.00

Auditors

The Statutory Auditors (Amendment of Companies Act 2006 and Delegation of Functions etc) Order 2012 No. 2012/1741. - Enabling power: European Communities Act 1972, s. 2 (2) (a) (b) & Companies Act 2006, ss. 464 (1) (3), 504 (1) (b) (ii), 525 (1) (a) (ii), 1228 (1) (2) (6), 1231 (4), 1239, 1252 (1) (2) (b) (4) (a) (5) (6) (7) (8), 1253 (4), 1292 (1) (b) (c) (2), sch. 13, paras 7 (3), 11 (2) (3) (a). - Issued: 06.07.2012. Made: 02.07.2012. Coming into force: 02.07.2012. Effect: 2006 c.46 amended & S.I. 1996/1975; 2005/590, 672; 2007/865, 3494; 2008/629, 1911; 2009/209, 2436; 2011/99 amended & S.I. 2007/3534; 2008/496, 651 revoked. Territorial extent & classification: E/W/S/NI. General. - Supersedes draft (ISBN 97801111524404) issued 17.05.2012. EC note: Part 2 of the Order amends the 2006 Act, it re-implements obligations in Directive 2006/43/EC on statutory audits of annual accounts and consolidated accounts and makes provision for matters which arise out of or relate to these obligations. - 20p.: 30 cm. - 978-0-11-152631-6 £5.75

Bank levy

The Bank Levy (Double Taxation Relief Arrangements) (Federal Republic of Germany) Order 2012 No. 2012/459. - Enabling power: Finance Act 2011, s. 66 (8) (9). - Issued: 23.02.2012. Made: 21.02.2012. Laid: 22.02.2012. Coming into force: 14.03.2012. Effect: None. Territorial extent & classification: E/W/S/NI. General. - 8p.: 30 cm. - 978-0-11-152048-2 £5.75

The Bank Levy (Double Taxation Relief) Regulations 2012 No. 2012/458. - Enabling power: Finance Act 2011, sch. 19, para. 67. - Issued: 23.02.2012. Made: 21.02.2012. Laid: 22.02.2012. Coming into force: 14.03.2012. Effect: None. Territorial extent & classification: E/W/S/NI. General. - 8p.: 30 cm. - 978-0-11-152047-5 £5.75

The Bank Levy: International Tax Enforcement Arrangements (Federal Republic of Germany) Order 2012 No. 2012/2933. - Enabling power: Finance Act 2011, sch. 19, para. 67A (1). - Issued: 23.11.2012. Made: 22.11.2012. Laid: 23.11.2012. Coming into force: 15.12.2012. Effect: None. Territorial extent & classification: E/W/S/NI. General. - 2p.: 30 cm. - 978-0-11-153117-4 £4.00

The Double Taxation Relief (Bank Levy) (Federal Republic of Germany) Order 2012 No. 2012/432. - Enabling power: Finance Act 2011, sch. 19, para. 66 (1). - Issued: 23.02.2012. Made: 21.02.2012. Laid: 22.02.2012. Coming into force: 14.03.2012. Effect: None. Territorial extent & classification: E/W/S/NI. General. - 12p.: 30 cm. - 978-0-11-152049-9 £5.75

Betting, gaming and lotteries

The Gambling Act 2005 (Amendment of Schedule 6) Order 2012 No. 2012/1633. - Enabling power: Gambling Act 2005, s. 351. - Issued: 26.06.2012. Made: 21.06.2012. Coming into force: 22.06.2012. In accord. with art. 1. Effect: 2005 c.19 amended. Territorial extent & classification: E/W/S. General. - Supersedes draft SI (ISBN 9780111523926) issued on 03.05.2012. - 4p.: 30 cm. - 978-0-11-152575-3 £4.00

The Gambling (Licence Fees) (Miscellaneous Amendments) Regulations 2012 No. 2012/1851. - Enabling power: Gambling Act 2005, ss. 69 (2) (g) (5), 100 (2) (3), 104 (3) (4), 128, 132 (2) (3), 355 (1). - Issued: 17.07.2012. Made: 13.07.2012. Laid: 16.07.2012. Coming into force: 01.09.2012. Effect: S.I. 2006/3284, 3285 amended. Territorial extent & classification: E/W/S. General. - 4p.: 30 cm. - 978-0-11-152710-8 £4.00

The Gambling (Operating Licence and Single-Machine Permit Fees) (Amendment) Regulations 2012 No. 2012/829. - Enabling power: Gambling Act 2005, ss. 69 (2) (g) (5), 100 (2) (3), 103 (2), 104 (3) (4), 355 (1). - Issued: 23.03.2012. Made: 14.03.2012. Laid: 15.03.2012. Coming into force: 06.04.2012. Effect: S.I. 2006/3284 amended. Territorial extent & classification: E/W/S. General. - 40p.: 30 cm. - 978-0-11-152224-0 £9.75

British nationality

The British Nationality (General) (Amendment) Regulations 2012 No. 2012/1588. - Enabling power: British Nationality Act 1981, s. 41 (1) (3). - Issued: 25.06.2012. Made: 19.06.2012. Laid: 25.06.2012. Coming into force: 16.07.2012. Effect: S.I. 2003/548 amended. Territorial extent & classification: E/W/S/NI/Islands/British Overseas Territories. General. - 2p.: 30 cm. - 978-0-11-152566-1 £4.00

Broadcasting

The Broadcasting (Local Digital Television Programme Services and Independent Productions) (Amendment) Order 2012 No. 2012/1842. - Enabling power: Communications Act 2003, ss. 244 (1), 277 (2), 309 (2), 402 (3), sch. 12, paras. 1 (2), 7 (2). - Issued: 23.07.2012. Made: 11.07.2012. Coming into force: In accord. with art. 1. Effect: S.I. 1991/1408; 2012/292 amended. Territorial extent & classification: E/W/S/NI. General. - Supersedes draft SI (ISBN 9780111524695) issued on 24.05.2012. - 4p.: 30 cm. - 978-0-11-152714-6 £4.00

The Communications (Bailiwick of Guernsey) (Amendment) Order 2012 No. 2012/2688. - Enabling power: Communications Act 2003, ss. 402 (3) (c), 411 (6) (8). - Issued: 12.11.2012. Made: 07.11.2012. Coming into force: 05.12.2012. Effect: S.I. 2003/3195 amended. Territorial extent & classification: Guernsey. General. - 2p.: 30 cm. - 978-0-11-153072-6 £4.00

The Community Radio (Guernsey) Order 2012 No. 2012/2690. - Enabling power: Communications Act 2003, s. 262 (1) (3) (4). - Issued: 13.11.2012. Made: 07.11.2012. Coming into force: 05.12.2012. Effect: 1990 c. 42; 2003 c. 21 modified. Territorial extent & classification: Guernsey. General. - 12p.: 30 cm. - 978-0-11-153065-8 £5.75

The Local Digital Television Programme Services Order 2012 No. 2012/292. - Enabling power: Communications Act 2003, ss. 244, 402. - Issued: 17.02.2012. Made: 13.02.2012. Coming into force: 14.02.2012, in accord. with art. 1. Effect: 1996 c. 55; 2003 c. 21 modified. Territorial extent & classification: E/W/S/NI. General. - Supersedes draft SI (ISBN 9780111518212) issued on 16.12.2011. - 12p.: 30 cm. - 978-0-11-152025-3 £5.75

The Wireless Telegraphy Act 2006 (Directions to OFCOM) Order 2012 No. 2012/293. - Enabling power: Wireless Telegraphy Act 2006, ss. 5, 121 (3). - Issued: 17.02.2012. Made: 13.02.2012. Coming into force: 14.02.2012. Effect: None. Territorial extent & classification: E/W/S/NI. General. - Supersedes draft SI (ISBN 9780111518229) issued on 16.12.2011. - 4p.: 30 cm. - 978-0-11-152026-0 £4.00

Budget responsibility

The Budget Responsibility and National Audit Act 2011 (Appointed Day) Order 2012 No. 2012/727. - Enabling power: Budget Responsibility and National Audit Act 2011, s. 25 (3), sch. 4, paras 1 (11), 5 (4). Appointing 01.04.2012 as appointed day for various purposes of the Act. - Issued: 08.03.2012. Made: 07.03.2012. Effect: None. Territorial extent & classification: E/W/S/NI. General. - 2p.: 30 cm. - 978-0-11-152164-9 £4.00

The Budget Responsibility and National Audit Act 2011 (Consequential Amendments) Order 2012 No. 2012/725. - Enabling power: Budget Responsibility and National Audit Act 2011, s. 28 (1) (2). - Issued: 08.03.2012. Made: 07.03.2012. Laid: 08.03.2012. Coming into force: 01.04.2012. Effect: S.I. 1990/200; 1994/1986; 1998/2573; 1999/1549; 2000/432; 2001/2188; 2002/1889; 2004/1861; 2006/5; 2008/2551; 2010/2476; 2011/2260 amended. Territorial extent & classification: E/W/S/NI. General. - 4p.: 30 cm. - 978-0-11-152163-2 £4.00

Building and buildings

The Energy Act 2011 (Amendment) (Energy Performance of Buildings) Regulations 2012 No. 2012/3170. - Enabling power: European Communities Act 1972, s. 2 (2). - Issued: 02.01.2013. Made: 20.12.2012. Laid: 02.01.2012. Coming into force: 25.01.2013. Effect: 2011 c.16 amended. Territorial extent & classification: E/W/S. General. - EC note: The amendments made by this instrument ensure that section 11 of the 2011 Act is consistent with recent changes to the implementation in England and Wales and Scotland of article 7 of Directive 2002/91/EC on the energy performance of buildings. - 4p.: 30 cm. - 978-0-11-153287-4 £4.00

Building and buildings, England

The Building (Repeal of Provisions of Local Acts) Regulations 2012 No. 2012/3124. - Enabling power: Building Act 1984, s. 1 (1), sch. 1, paras 10, 11 (1) (c). - Issued: 19.12.2012. Made: 17.12.2012. Laid: 19.12.2012. Coming into force: 09.01.2013. Effect: 23 local acts partially repealed. Territorial extent & classification: E. General. - 8p.: 30 cm. - 978-0-11-153265-2 £4.00

Building and buildings, England and Wales

The Building (Amendment) Regulations 2012 No. 2012/718. - Enabling power: Building Act 1984, s. 1 (1), sch. 1, paras 1, 4, 4A, 7, 8, 10. - Issued: 13.03.2012. Made: 07.03.2012. Laid: 13.03.2012. Coming into force: 06.04.2012. Effect: S.I. 2010/2214 amended. Territorial extent & classification: E/W. General. - 2p.: 30 cm. - 978-0-11-152169-4 £4.00

The Building Regulations &c. (Amendment) Regulations 2012 No. 2012/3119. - Enabling power: Building Act 1984, ss. 1, 2A, 16 (9) (10), 17 (1) (6), 34, 47 (1) to (5), 49 (5), 50 (1) (4) (6), 51 (1) (2), 51A (2) (3) (6), 56 (1) (2), sch. 1, paras 1, 2, 4, 4A, 6, 7, 8, 9, 10. - Issued: 19.12.2012. Made: 17.12.2012. Laid: 19.12.2012. Coming into force: In accord. with reg. 1. Effect: S.I. 2010/404, 2214, 2215 amended. Territorial extent & classification: E/W. General. - With correction slip dated February 2013. This SI has been corrected by SI 2013/181 (ISBN 9780111534069) which is being sent free of charge to all known recipients of SI 2012/3119. - 24p.: 30 cm. - 978-0-11-153264-5 £5.75

The Energy Performance of Buildings (Certificates and Inspections) (England and Wales) (Amendment) Regulations 2012 No. 2012/809. - Enabling power: European Communities Act 1972, s. 2 (2). - Issued: 15.03.2012. Made: 13.03.2012. Laid: 15.03.2012. Coming into force: 05.04.2012 for regulation 12 & 06.04.2012 for the remainder in accord. with reg. 1 (2) (3). Effect: S.I. 2007/991; 2010/2214 amended & S.I. 2011/2452 partially revoked (05.04.2012). Territorial extent & classification: E/W. General. - Revoked by SI 2012/3118 (ISBN 9780111532614). EC note: These regulations ensure the continued implementation in England and Wales of art 7 of Directive 2002/91/EC on the energy performance of buildings. - 12p.: 30 cm. - 978-0-11-152207-3 £5.75

The Energy Performance of Buildings (England and Wales) Regulations 2012 No. 2012/3118. - Enabling power: European Communities Act 1972, s. 2 (2) & Energy Act 2011, s. 74. - Issued: 19.12.2012. Made: 17.12.2012. Laid: 19.12.2012. Coming into force: 09.01.2013. Effect: S.I. 2010/2214; 2011/1515 partially revoked & S.I. 2007/991, 1669, 3302; 2008/647, 2363; 2009/1900; 2010/1456; 2011/2452; 2012/809 revoked. Territorial extent & classification: E/W. General. - This SI has been corrected by SI 2013/181 (ISBN 9780111534069) which is being sent free of charge to all known recipients of SI 2012/3118. EC note: These regulations consolidate enactment in England and Wales of Directive 2002/91/EC and enact where necessary new requirements of Directive 2010/31/EU. - 28p.: 30 cm. - 978-0-11-153261-4 £5.75

Canals and inland waterways

The British Waterways Board (Transfer of Functions) Order 2011 No. 2012/1659. - Enabling power: Public Bodies Act 2011, ss. 5 (1) , 6 (1) to (3), 35 (2). - Issued: 04.07.2012. Made: 01.07.2012. Coming into force: 02.07.2012 in accord. with art. 1. Effect: 29 Acts and 9 statutory instruments amended & S.I. 2003/1545 revoked. Territorial extent & classification: E/W/S/NI. General. - Supersedes draft S.I. (ISBN 9780111521045) issued 02.03.2012. - 32p.: 30 cm. - 978-0-11-152621-7 £5.75

The Inland Waterways Advisory Council (Abolition) Order 2012 No. 2012/1658. - Enabling power: Public Bodies Act 2011, ss. 1 (1), 6 (1), 35 (2). - Issued: 04.07.2012. Made: 01.07.2012. Coming into force: 02.07.2012 in accord. with art. 1. Effect: 1995 c. i amended & partially revoked & 1968 c. 73; 1974 c. 24; 1983 c. ii; 2000 c. 36; 2006 c. 16 partially repealed & S.I. 1993/1119; 1999/1319; 2000/3251; 2006/1466; 2007/570 partially revoked. Territorial extent & classification: E/W/S. - Supersedes draft S.I. (ISBN 9780111521038) issued 02.03.2012. - 4p.: 30 cm. - 978-0-11-152620-0 £4.00

Canals and inland waterways, England

The Bridgewater Canal (Transfer of Undertaking) Order 2012 No. 2012/1266. - Enabling power: Transport and Works Act 1992, s. 3 (1) (a), 5, sch. 1, paras. 5, 7, 8, 12, 13, 15. - Issued: 18.05.2012. Made: 01.05.2012. Coming into force: 22.05.2012. Effect: None. Territorial extent & classification: E. General. - 8p.: 30 cm. - 978-0-11-152430-5 £5.75

Capital gains tax

The Authorised Investment Funds (Tax) (Amendment) Regulations 2012 No. 2012/1783. - Enabling power: Finance (No. 2) Act 2005, ss. 17 (3), 18 (5). - Issued: 10.07.2012. Made: 09.07.2012. Laid: 10.07.2012. Coming into force: 01.08.2012. Effect: S.I. 2006/964 amended. Territorial extent & classification: E/W/S/NI. General. - With correction slip dated November 2012. - 4p.: 30 cm. - 978-0-11-152648-4 £4.00

The Capital Gains Tax (Annual Exempt Amount) Order 2012 No. 2012/881. - Enabling power: Taxation of Chargeable Gains Act 1992, s. 3 (4). - Issued: 21.03.2012. Made: 20.03.2012. Coming into force: 20.03.2012. Effect: None. Territorial extent & classification: E/W/S/NI. General. - 2p.: 30 cm. - 978-0-11-152260-8 £4.00

The Double Taxation Relief and International Tax Enforcement (Bahrain) Order 2012 No. 2012/3075. - Enabling power: Taxation (International and Other Provisions) Act 2010, s. 2 & Finance Act 2006, s. 173 (1) to (3). - Issued: 17.12.2012. Made: 12.12.2012. Effect: None. Territorial extent & classification: E/W/S/NI. General. - Supersedes draft SI (ISBN 9780111527078) issued 17.07.2012. - 24p.: 30 cm. - 978-0-11-153244-7 £5.75

The Double Taxation Relief and International Tax Enforcement (Barbados) Order 2012 No. 2012/3076. - Enabling power: Taxation (International and Other Provisions) Act 2010, s. 2 & Finance Act 2006, s. 173 (1) to (3). - Issued: 17.12.2012. Made: 12.12.2012. Effect: None. Territorial extent & classification: E/W/S/NI. General. - Supersedes draft SI (ISBN 9780111527160) issued 17.07.2012. - 20p.: 30 cm. - 978-0-11-153242-3 £5.75

The Double Taxation Relief and International Tax Enforcement (Liechtenstein) Order 2012 No. 2012/3077. - Enabling power: Taxation (International and Other Provisions) Act 2010, s. 2 & Finance Act 2006, s. 173 (1) to (3). - Issued: 17.12.2012. Made: 12.12.2012. Effect: None. Territorial extent & classification: E/W/S/NI. General. - Supersedes draft SI (ISBN 9780111527092) issued 17.07.2012. - 24p.: 30 cm. - 978-0-11-153241-6 £5.75

The Double Taxation Relief and International Tax Enforcement (Singapore) Order 2012 No. 2012/3078. - Enabling power: Taxation (International and Other Provisions) Act 2010, s. 2 & Finance Act 2006, s. 173 (1) to (3). - Issued: 17.07.2012. Made: 12.12.2012. Effect: None. Territorial extent & classification: E/W/S/NI. General. - Supersedes draft SI (ISBN 9780111527153) issued 17.07.2012. - 12p.: 30 cm. - 978-0-11-153240-9 £5.75

The Finance Act 2010, Schedule 6, Part 1 (Further Consequential and Incidental Provision etc) Order 2012 No. 2012/735. - Enabling power: Finance Act 2010, sch. 6, para. 29 (1) (2). - Issued: 12.03.2012. Made: 08.03.2012. Laid: 09.03.2012. Coming into force: 01.04.2012. Effect: 2009 c.4 amended. Territorial extent & classification: E/W/S/NI. General. - 4p.: 30 cm. - 978-0-11-152181-6 £4.00

The Finance Act 2010, Schedule 6, Part 2 (Commencement) Order 2012 No. 2012/736 (C.18). - Enabling power: Finance Act 2010, sch. 6, para. 34 (1) (b) (2) (3). Bringing into operation various provisions of this Act on 01.04.2012. - Issued: 12.03.2012. Made: 08.03.2012. Effect: None. Territorial extent & classification: E/W/S/NI. General. - 8p.: 30 cm. - 978-0-11-152189-2 £5.75

The Finance Act 2012 (Enterprise Investment Scheme) (Appointed Day) Order 2012 No. 2012/1896 (C. 74). - Enabling power: Finance Act 2012, sch. 7, paras. 23 (1), 33 (1). Bringing into operation various provisions of the 2012 Act on 19th July 2012, in accord. with art. 2. - Issued: 20.07.2012. Made: 18.07.2012. Effect: None. Territorial extent & classification: E/W/S/NI. General. - 2p.: 30 cm. - 978-0-11-152747-4 £4.00

The Individual Savings Account (Amendment) (No. 2) Regulations 2012 No. 2012/1871. - Enabling power: Income Tax (Trading and Other Income) Act 2005, ss. 694 to 699, 701 & Taxation of Chargeable Gains Act 1992, s. 151. - Issued: 18.07.2012. Made: 16.07.2012. Laid: 17.07.2012. Coming into force: 08.08.2012. Effect: S.I. 1998/1870 amended. Territorial extent & classification: E/W/S/NI. General. - 16p.: 30 cm. - 978-0-11-152719-1 £5.75

The Individual Savings Account (Amendment) Regulations 2012 No. 2012/705. - Enabling power: Income Tax (Trading and Other Income) Act 2005, s. 694 & Taxation of Chargeable Gains Act 1992, s. 151. - Issued: 08.03.2012. Made: 06.03.2012. Laid: 07.02.2012. Coming into force: 06.04.2012. Effect: S.I. 1998/1870 amended. Territorial extent & classification: E/W/S/NI. General. - 2p.: 30 cm. - 978-0-11-152156-4 £4.00

The Taxation of Chargeable Gains (Gilt-edged Securities) Order 2012 No. 2012/1843. - Enabling power: Taxation of Chargeable Gains Act 1992, sch. 9, para. 1. - Issued: 16.07.2012. Made: 12.07.2012. Effect: None. Territorial extent & classification: E/W/S/NI. General. - 2p.: 30 cm. - 978-0-11-152706-1 £4.00

Channel Tunnel

The Channel Tunnel (International Arrangements) (Amendment) Order 2012 No. 2012/1264. - Enabling power: Channel Tunnel Act 1987, s. 11. - Issued: 15.05.2012. Made: 10.05.2012. Laid: 14.05.2012. Coming into force: In accord. with art. 1 (2). Effect: S.I. 1993/1813 amended. Territorial extent & classification: E/W/S/NI. General. - EC note: This Order amends the 1993 Order to implement the Agreement between the Government of the United Kingdom of Great Britain and Northern Ireland and the Government of the Republic of France on Implementation of the Cyclamen Device in the French Terminal of the Channel Tunnel Situated in Coquelles. - 4p.: 30 cm. - 978-0-11-152426-8 £4.00

Charging orders, England and Wales

The Tribunals, Courts and Enforcement Act 2007 (Commencement No. 8) Order 2012 No. 2012/1312 (C.46). - Enabling power: Tribunals, Courts and Enforcement Act 2007, s. 148 (5). Bringing into operation various provisions of the 2007 Act on 17.05.2012 & 01.10.2012 in accord. with arts. 2, 3. - Issued: 21.05.2012. Made: 16.04.2012. Effect: None. Territorial extent & classification: E/W. General. - 4p.: 30 cm. - 978-0-11-152458-9 £4.00

Charities

The Finance Act 2010, Schedule 6, Part 1 (Further Consequential and Incidental Provision etc) Order 2012 No. 2012/735. - Enabling power: Finance Act 2010, sch. 6, para. 29 (1) (2). - Issued: 12.03.2012. Made: 08.03.2012. Laid: 09.03.2012. Coming into force: 01.04.2012. Effect: 2009 c.4 amended. Territorial extent & classification: E/W/S/NI. General. - 4p.: 30 cm. - 978-0-11-152181-6 £4.00

The Finance Act 2010, Schedule 6, Part 2 (Commencement) Order 2012 No. 2012/736 (C.18). - Enabling power: Finance Act 2010, sch. 6, para. 34 (1) (b) (2) (3). Bringing into operation various provisions of this Act on 01.04.2012. - Issued: 12.03.2012. Made: 08.03.2012. Effect: None. Territorial extent & classification: E/W/S/NI. General. - 8p.: 30 cm. - 978-0-11-152189-2 £5.75

Charities, England and Wales

The Charitable Incorporated Organisations (Consequential Amendments) Order 2012 No. 2012/3014. - Enabling power: Charities Act 2006, ss. 74 (2), 75 (4) (5) & Charities Act 2011, ss. 324, 347 (3), sch. 8, para. 3 (3) (a). - Issued: 11.12.2012. Made: 05.12.2012. Coming into force: In accord. with art. 1. Effect: 1986 c. 46; 1996 c. 18; 2011 c. 25 amended. Territorial extent & classification: E/W. General. - Supersedes draft SI (ISBN 9780111530238) issued 31.10.2012. - 8p.: 30 cm. - 978-0-11-153188-4 £4.00

The Charitable Incorporated Organisations (General) Regulations 2012 No. 2012/3012. - Enabling power: Charities Act 2011, ss. 30 (2) (c), 42 (2) (c), 206 (3), 207 (2) (b), 223, 246, 347 (3). - Issued: 10.12.2012. Made: 05.12.2012. Laid: 10.12.2012. Coming into force: 02.01.2013. Effect: S.I. 1965/1056; 1966/965; 1992/1901; 1996/180; 2008/3268; 2010/502 amended. Territorial extent & classification: E/W. General. - 36p.: 30 cm. - 978-0-11-153183-9 £9.75

The Charitable Incorporated Organisations (Insolvency and Dissolution) Regulations 2012 No. 2012/3013. - Enabling power: Charities Act 2011, ss. 245, 347 (3). - Issued: 11.12.2012. Made: 05.12.2012. Coming into force: In accord. with reg. 1. Effect: 1986 c. 45 amended. Territorial extent & classification: E/W. General. - Supersedes draft SI (ISBN 9780111530146) issued on 30.10.2012. - 50p.: 30 cm. - 978-0-11-153201-0 £9.75

The Charities Act 2011 (Commencement No. 1) Order 2012 No. 2012/3011 (C.120). - Enabling power: Charities Act 2011, sch. 9, para. 29. Bringing into operation various provisions of the 2011 Act on 02.01.2013 in accord. with art. 2. - Issued: 10.12.2012. Made: 05.12.2012. Effect: None. Territorial extent & classification: E/W. General. - 2p.: 30 cm. - 978-0-11-153184-6 £4.00

The Charities (Exception from Registration) (Amendment) Regulations 2012 No. 2012/1734. - Enabling power: Charities Act 2011, ss. 30 (2) (c). - Issued: 09.07.2012. Made: 02.07.2012. Laid: 09.07.2012. Coming into force: 01.09.2012. Effect: S.I. 2007/2655 revoked. Territorial extent & classification: E/W. General. - 2p.: 30 cm. - 978-0-11-152638-5 £4.00

Children and young persons, England

The Childcare (Early Years Register) (Amendment) Regulations 2012 No. 2012/939. - Enabling power: Childcare Act 2006, ss. 35 (3) (b) (5), 36 (2) (a) (3) (b) (5), 104 (2). - Issued: 30.03.2012. Made: 26.03.2012. Laid: 27.03.2012. Coming into force: 01.09.2012. Effect: S.I. 2008/974 amended. Territorial extent classification: E. General. - 2p.: 30 cm. - 978-0-11-152296-7 £4.00

The Childcare (Fees) (Amendment) Regulations 2012 No. 2012/2168. - Enabling power: Childcare Act 2006, ss. 89 (1), 104 (2). - Issued: 29.08.2012. Made: 20.08.2012. Laid: 29.09.2012. Coming into force: 21.09.2012. Effect: S.I. 2008/1804 amended. Territorial extent & classification: E. General. - 2p.: 30 cm. - 978-0-11-152834-1 £4.00

The Childcare (General Childcare Register) (Amendment) Regulations 2012 No. 2012/1699. - Enabling power: Childcare Act 2006, ss. 54 (3) (b) (5), 55 (2) (a) (3) (b) (5), 59, 63 (2) (a) (4) (b) (6), 67, 104 (2). - Issued: 05.07.2012. Made: 28.06.2012. Laid: 05.07.2012. Coming into force: 01.09.2012. Effect: S.I. 2008/975 amended. Territorial extent & classification: E. General. - 4p.: 30 cm. - 978-0-11-152625-5 £4.00

The Childcare (Inspections) (Amendment and Revocation) Regulations 2012 No. 2012/1698. - Enabling power: Childcare Act 2006, ss. 49, 50, 61, 104 (2). - Issued: 05.07.2012. Made: 28.06.2012. Laid: 05.07.2012. Coming into force: 01.08.2012. Effect: S.I. 2008/1729 amended & S.I. 2009/1508 revoked. Territorial extent & classification: E. General. - 2p.: 30 cm. - 978-0-11-152624-8 £4.00

The Children Act 2004 Information Database (England) (Revocation) Regulations 2012 No. 2012/1278. - Enabling power: Children Act 2004, ss. 12 (4) (f) (h) (5) (6) (7) (f) (8) (e) (10) (11), 66 (1) (c). - Issued: 21.05.2012. Made: 14.05.2012. Coming into force: 15.05.2012 in accord. with reg. 1. Effect: S.I. 2008/912 amended & S.I. 2007/2182; 2010/1213 revoked. Territorial extent & classification: E. General. - Supersedes draft S.I. (ISBN 9780111519530) issued 01.02.2012. - 2p.: 30 cm. - 978-0-11-152437-4 £4.00

The Children (Secure Accommodation) (Amendment) (England) Regulations 2012 No. 2012/3134. - Enabling power: Children Act 1989, s. 25 (7) (b). - Issued: 21.12.2012. Made: 17.12.2012. Laid: 21.12.2012. Coming into force: 11.01.2013. Effect: S.I. 1991/1505 amended. Territorial extent & classification: E. General. - 2p.: 30 cm. - 978-0-11-153272-0 £4.00

The Early Years Foundation Stage (Exemptions from Learning and Development Requirements) (Amendment) Regulations 2012 No. 2012/2463. - Enabling power: Childcare Act 2006, ss. 46, 104 (2). - Issued: 01.10.2012. Made: 25.09.2012. Laid: 01.10.2012. Coming into force: 26.10.2012. Effect: S.I. 2008/1743 amended. Territorial extent & classification: E. General. - 4p.: 30 cm. - 978-0-11-152902-7 £4.00

The Early Years Foundation Stage (Learning and Development Requirements) (Amendment) Order 2012 No. 2012/937. - Enabling power: Childcare Act 2006, ss. 39 (1) (a), 42 (1) (2), 44 (1) to (4). - Issued: 30.03.2012. Made: 26.03.2012. Laid: 27.03.2012. Coming into force: 01.09.2012. Effect: S.I. 2007/1772 amended. Territorial extent & classification: E. General. - 2p.: 30 cm. - 978-0-11-152290-5 £4.00

The Early Years Foundation Stage (Welfare Requirements) Regulations 2012 No. 2012/938. - Enabling power: Childcare Act 2006, ss. 39 (1) (b), 43 (1) (3), 44 (1) to (4). - Issued: 30.03.2012. Made: 26.03.2012. Laid: 27.03.2012. Coming into force: 01.09.2012. Effect: S.I. 2007/1771; 2008/1953; 2009/1549 revoked. Territorial extent & classification: E. General. - 8p.: 30 cm. - 978-0-11-152295-0 £5.75

Her Majesty's Chief Inspector of Education, Children's Services and Skills (Fees and Frequency of Inspections) (Children's Homes etc.) (Amendment) Regulations 2012 No. 2012/511. - Enabling power: Care Standards Act 2000, ss. 16 (3), 118 (5) (6) & Education and Inspections Act 2006, s. 155 (1) (2) & Children Act 1989, ss. 87D (2), 104 (4) (a). - Issued: 01.03.2012. Made: 23.02.2012. Laid: 29.02.2012. Coming into force: 01.04.2012. Effect: S.I. 2007/694 amended. Territorial extent & classification: E. General. - With correction slip dated March 2012 - corrects the year in the number heading page 1 and back page immediately below the banner: so 2011 No. 511 should read 2012 No. 511. - 4p.: 30 cm. - 978-0-11-152067-3 *£4.00*

The Inspectors of Education, Children's Services and Skills Order 2012 No. 2012/2597. - Enabling power: Education and Inspections Act 2006, s. 114 (1). - Issued: 25.10.2012. Made: 17.10.2012. Coming into force: 18.10.2012. Effect: None. Territorial extent & classification: E. General. - 2p.: 30 cm. - 978-0-11-152973-7 *£4.00*

The Legislative Reform (Annual Review of Local Authorities) Order 2012 No. 2012/1879. - Enabling power: Legislative and Regulatory Reform Act 2006, s. 1. - Issued: 30.07.2012. Made: 17.07.2012. Coming into force: 18.07.2012 in accord. with art. 1. Effect: 2006 c. 40 amended. Territorial extent & classification: E. General. - Supersedes draft S.I. (ISBN 9780111524091) issued 10.05.2012. - 4p.: 30 cm. - 978-0-11-152739-9 *£4.00*

The Local Authority (Duty to Secure Early Years Provision Free of Charge) (Amendment) Regulations 2012 No. 2012/2488. - Enabling power: Childcare Act 2006 ss. 7, 104 (2). - Issued: 04.10.2012. Made: 27.09.2012. Laid: 04.10.2012. Coming into force: 01.09.2013. Effect: S.I. 2008/1724; 2010/301 revoked. Territorial extent & classification: E. General. - 4p.: 30 cm. - 978-0-11-152906-5 *£4.00*

Children and young persons, England and Wales

The Adoption Agencies (Panel and Consequential Amendments) Regulations 2012 No. 2012/1410. - Enabling power: Adoption and Children Act 2002, ss. 9 (1) (a), 84 (3), 140 (7) (8), 142 (5) & Adoption (Intercountry Aspects) Act 1999, s. 1 (1) (3) (a) (c) (d) (5). - Issued: 01.06.2012. Made: 28.05.2012. Laid: 01.06.2012. Coming into force: 01.09.2012. Effect: S.I. 2005/389, 392 amended. Territorial extent & classification: E/W. General. - 4p.: 30 cm. - 978-0-11-152492-3 *£4.00*

The Disclosure and Barring Service (Core Functions) Order 2012 No. 2012/2522. - Enabling power: Protection of Freedoms Act 2012, sch. 8, para. 8 (1) (d). - Issued: 09.10.2012. Made: 03.10.2012. Laid: 05.10.2012. Coming into force: 01.12.2012. Effect: None. Territorial extent & classification: E/W. General. - 4p.: 30 cm. - 978-0-11-152912-6 *£4.00*

The Legal Aid, Sentencing and Punishment of Offenders Act 2012 (Children Act 1989) (Children Remanded to Youth Detention Accommodation) Regulations 2012 No. 2012/2813. - Enabling power: Legal Aid, Sentencing and Punishment of Offenders Act 2012, ss. 104 (2), 106. - Issued: 14.11.2012. Made: 07.11.2012. Laid: 12.11.2012. Coming into force: 03.12.2012. Effect: S.I. 1991/1505 amended. Territorial extent & classification: E/W/S. General. - 4p.: 30 cm. - 978-0-11-153070-2 *£4.00*

The Legal Aid, Sentencing and Punishment of Offenders Act 2012 (Consequential and Saving Provisions) Regulations 2012 No. 2012/2824. - Enabling power: Legal Aid, Sentencing and Punishment of Offenders Act 2012, ss. 149 (1) (2). - Issued: 14.11.2012. Made: 08.11.2012. Laid: 12.11.2012. Coming into force: 03.12.2012. Effect: S.I. 1991/1505 amended. Territorial extent & classification: E/W but these Regs make provision in relation to the Armed Forces Act 2006 which extends to the UK. General. - 4p.: 30 cm. - 978-0-11-153076-4 *£4.00*

The Protection of Freedoms Act 2012 (Commencement No. 3) Order 2012 No. 2012/2234 (C.89). - Enabling power: Protection of Freedoms Act 2012, ss. 116 (1), 120 (1). Bringing into operation various provisions of the 2012 Act on 10.09.2012 & 01.10.2012 in accord. with arts 2 to 3. - Issued: 04.09.2012. Made: 28.08.2012. Effect: None. Territorial extent & classification: E/W/S/NI. General. - 8p.: 30 cm. - 978-0-11-152842-6 *£5.75*

The Protection of Freedoms Act 2012 (Commencement No. 4) Order 2012 No. 2012/2521 (C.100). - Enabling power: Protection of Freedoms Act 2012, s. 120 (1). Bringing into operation various provisions of the 2012 Act on 15.10.2012 & 01.12.2012 in accord. with arts 2 and 3. - Issued: 08.10.2012. Made: 03.10.2012. Effect: None. Territorial extent & classification: E/W/NI. General. - 4p.: 30 cm. - 978-0-11-152911-9 *£4.00*

The Protection of Freedoms Act 2012 (Disclosure and Barring Service Transfer of Functions) Order 2012 No. 2012/3006. - Enabling power: Protection of Freedoms Act 2012, ss. 88, 89. - Issued: 05.12.2012. Made: 29.11.2012. Coming into force: 01.12.2012. Effect: 13 Acts amended & 46 SI's and SR's amended & 1998 c.29 & SI 2007/1351 (NI.11) partially revoked. Territorial extent & classification: E/W/NI. General. - Supersedes draft SI (ISBN 9780111529409) issued 16.10.2012. - 24p.: 30 cm. - 978-0-11-153157-0 *£5.75*

The Safeguarding Vulnerable Groups Act 2006 (Commencement No. 8 and Saving) Order 2012 No. 2012/2231 (C.88). - Enabling power: Safeguarding Vulnerable Groups Act 2006, ss. 64 (1) (b) (2) (b), 65. Bringing into operation various provisions of the 2006 Act on the dates specified in the Order. - Issued: 04.09.2012. Made: 28.08.2012. Effect: None. Territorial extent & classification: E/W. General. - 8p.: 30 cm. - 978-0-11-152841-9 *£5.75*

The Safeguarding Vulnerable Groups Act 2006 (Controlled Activity and Prescribed Criteria) Regulations 2012 No. 2012/2160. - Enabling power: Safeguarding Vulnerable Groups Act 2006, ss. 23 (1), 61 (5), 64 (1) (a) (3), sch. 3, paras 1 (1), 2 (1), 7 (1), 8 (1), 24 (1) (2). - Issued: 21.08.2012. Made: 20.08.2012. Coming into force: In accord. with reg 1. Effect: S.I. 2009/37 amended & S.I. 2010/1146 partially revoked (03.09.2012). Territorial extent & classification: E/W. General. - Supersedes draft S.I. (ISBN 9780111524275) issued 16.05.2012. - 8p.: 30 cm. - 978-0-11-152830-3 £5.75

The Safeguarding Vulnerable Groups Act 2006 (Miscellaneous Provisions) Order 2012 No. 2012/2113. - Enabling power: Safeguarding Vulnerable Groups Act 2006, ss. 43 (7), 48 (6), 49 (6), sch. 4, para. 9, sch. 7, para. 2. - Issued: 20.08.2012. Made: 14.08.2012. Laid: 16.08.2012. Coming into force: 10.09.2012, in accord. art. 1. Effect: 2006 c. 47 amended. Territorial extent & classification: E/W. General. - 4p.: 30 cm. - 978-0-11-152823-5 £4.00

The Safeguarding Vulnerable Groups Act 2006 (Miscellaneous Provisions) Regulations 2012 No. 2012/2112. - Enabling power: Safeguarding Vulnerable Groups Act 2006, ss. 2 (5), 35 (1), 36 (1), 37 (2), 39 (1) (5), 41 (1), 42 (2), 45 (1) (5), 46 (1) (2), 50A (1) (d), 60 (1) (5), sch. 3, para. 15, sch. 4, para. 7 (1) (f) (g). - Issued: 20.08.2012. Made: 14.08.2012. Laid: 16.08.2012. Coming into force: 10.09.2012, in accord. with reg. 1 (2) (3). Effect: S.I. 2008/16, 474, 3265; 2009/1548 amended. Territorial extent & classification: E/W. General. - 8p.: 30 cm. - 978-0-11-152822-8 £5.75

The Safeguarding Vulnerable Groups (Miscellaneous Amendments) Order 2012 No. 2012/2157. - Enabling power: Safeguarding Vulnerable Groups Act 2006, ss. 59 (11), 64 (1) (2) (3), sch. 4, paras 6, 9. - Issued: 21.08.2012. Made: 20.08.2012. Coming into force: In accord. with art. 1. Effect: S.I. 2009/1797, 2610 amended & partially revoked (10.09.2012) & 1997 c. 50 modified. Territorial extent & classification: E/W. General. - Supersedes draft S.I. (ISBN 9780111524190) issued 16.05.2012. - 4p.: 30 cm. - 978-0-11-152829-7 £4.00

Children and young persons, Northern Ireland

The Protection of Freedoms Act 2012 (Commencement No. 2) Order 2012 No. 2012/2075 (C.82). - Enabling power: Protection of Freedoms Act 2012, ss. 116 (1), 120 (1). Bringing into operation various provisions of the 2012 Act on 10.08.2012, 01.10.2012 & 01.11.2012, 25.11.2012, in accord. with arts 2 to 5. - Issued: 10.08.2012. Made: 07.08.2012. Effect: None. Territorial extent & classification: E/W/S/NI. General. - 4p.: 30 cm. - 978-0-11-152805-1 £4.00

The Protection of Freedoms Act 2012 (Commencement No. 3) Order 2012 No. 2012/2234 (C.89). - Enabling power: Protection of Freedoms Act 2012, ss. 116 (1), 120 (1). Bringing into operation various provisions of the 2012 Act on 10.09.2012 & 01.10.2012 in accord. with arts 2 to 3. - Issued: 04.09.2012. Made: 28.08.2012. Effect: None. Territorial extent & classification: E/W/S/NI. General. - 8p.: 30 cm. - 978-0-11-152842-6 £5.75

The Protection of Freedoms Act 2012 (Commencement No. 4) Order 2012 No. 2012/2521 (C.100). - Enabling power: Protection of Freedoms Act 2012, s. 120 (1). Bringing into operation various provisions of the 2012 Act on 15.10.2012 & 01.12.2012 in accord. with arts 2 and 3. - Issued: 08.10.2012. Made: 03.10.2012. Effect: None. Territorial extent & classification: E/W/NI. General. - 4p.: 30 cm. - 978-0-11-152911-9 £4.00

The Protection of Freedoms Act 2012 (Disclosure and Barring Service Transfer of Functions) Order 2012 No. 2012/3006. - Enabling power: Protection of Freedoms Act 2012, ss. 88, 89. - Issued: 05.12.2012. Made: 29.11.2012. Coming into force: 01.12.2012. Effect: 13 Acts amended & 46 SI's and SR's amended & 1998 c.29 & SI 2007/1351 (NI.11) partially revoked. Territorial extent & classification: E/W/NI. General. - Supersedes draft SI (ISBN 9780111529409) issued 16.10.2012. - 24p.: 30 cm. - 978-0-11-153157-0 £5.75

Children and young persons, Wales

The Adoption Agencies (Wales) (Amendment) Regulations 2012 No. 2012/1905 (W.232). - Enabling power: Adoption and Children Act 2002, ss. 9 (1) (a), 140 (7) (8), 142 (4) (5). - Issued: 02.08.2012. Made: 18.07.2012. Laid: 19.07.2012. Coming into force: 01.09.2012. Effect: S.I. 2005/1313 (W.167) amended & S.I. 2007/1086 (W.115) partially revoked. Territorial extent & classification: W. General. - In English and Welsh. Welsh title: Rheoliadau Asiantaethau Mabwysiadu (Cymru) (Diwygio) 2012. - 8p.: 30 cm. - 978-0-348-10646-6 £5.75

The Breaks for Carers of Disabled Children (Wales) Regulations 2012 No. 2012/1674 (W.215). - Enabling power: Children Act 1989, sch. 2, para. 6 (2). - Issued: 19.07.2012. Made: 26.06.2012. Coming into force: 28.06.2012. Effect: None. Territorial extent & classification: W. General. - In English and Welsh. Welsh title: Rheoliadau Seibiannau i Ofalwyr Plant Anabl (Cymru) 2012. - 8p.: 30 cm. - 978-0-348-10633-6 £4.00

The Children and Families (Wales) Measure 2010 (Commencement No. 4) Order 2012 No. 2012/191 (W.30) (C.5). - Enabling power: Children and Families (Wales) Measure 2010, ss. 74 (2), 75 (3). Bringing into operation various provisions of the 2010 Measure on 27.01.2012, 31.01.2012, 28.02.2012, 31.03.2012 in accord. with arts. 2, 3, 4, 5. - Issued: 10.02.2012. Made: 26.01.2012. Effect: None. Territorial extent & classification: W. General. - In English and Welsh. Welsh title: Gorchymyn Mesur Plant a Theuluoedd (Cymru) 2010 (Cychwyn Rhif 4) 2012. - 8p.: 30 cm. - 978-0-348-10549-0 £5.75

The Children and Families (Wales) Measure 2010 (Commencement No. 5) Order 2012 No. 2012/2453 (W.267) (C.96). - Enabling power: Children and Families (Wales) Measure 2010, s. 75 (3). Bringing into operation various provisions of the 2010 Measure on 01.11.2012 in accord. with art. 1. - Issued: 22.10.2012. Made: 22.09.2012. Effect: None. Territorial extent & classification: W. General. - In English and Welsh. Welsh title: Gorchymyn Mesur Plant a Theuluoedd (Cymru) 2010 (Cychwyn Rhif 5) 2012. - 8p.: 30 cm. - 978-0-348-10657-2 £4.00

The Children and Young Persons Act 2008 (Commencement No. 7) (Wales) Order 2012 No. 2012/1553 (W.206) (C.58). - Enabling power: Children and Young Persons Act 2008, s. 44 (3) (5) (10) (b). Bringing into operation in relation to Wales various provisions of the 2008 Act on 19.06.2012 in accord. with art. 2. - Issued: 29.06.2012. Made: 16.06.2012. Effect: None. Territorial extent & classification: W. General. - In English and Welsh. Welsh title: Gorchymyn Deddf Plant a Phobl Ifanc 2008 (Cychwyn Rhif 7) (Cymru) 2012. - 8p.: 30 cm. - 978-0-348-10630-5 £5.75

The Integrated Family Support Teams (Composition of Teams and Board Functions) (Wales) Regulations 2012 No. 2012/202 (W.33). - Enabling power: Children and Families (Wales) Measure 2010, ss. 60 (1), 62 (2). - Issued: 23.02.2012. Made: 30.01.2012. Laid before the National Assembly for Wales: 31.01.2012. Coming into force: 28.02.2012. Effect: S.I. 2010/1690 (W.159) revoked. Territorial extent & classification: W. General. - In English & Welsh. Welsh title: Rheoliadau Timau Integredig Cymorth i Deuluoedd (Cyfansoddiad Timau a Swyddogaethau Byrddau) (Cymru) 2012. - 8p.: 30 cm. - 978-0-348-10690-9 £5.75

The Integrated Family Support Teams (Family Support Functions) (Wales) Regulations 2012 No. 2012/204 (W.34). - Enabling power: Children and Families (Wales) Measure 2010, s. 58 (2). - Issued: 16.02.2012. Made: 30.01.2012. Laid before the National Assembly for Wales: 31.01.2012. Coming into force: 28.02.2012. Effect: S.I. 2010/1701 (W.162); 2011/191 (W. 36) revoked. Territorial extent & classification: W. General. - In English & Welsh. Welsh title: Rheoliadau Timau Integredig Cymorth i Deuluoedd (Swyddogaethau Cymorth i Deuluoedd) (Cymru) 2012. - 8p.: 30 cm. - 978-0-348-10554-4 £5.75

The Integrated Family Support Teams (Review of Cases) (Wales) Regulations 2012 No. 2012/205 (W.35). - Enabling power: Children and Families (Wales) Measure 2010, ss. 63 (a), 74 (2) & Children Act 1989, ss. 26 (1) (2), 104 (4), 104A (1) (2). - Issued: 23.02.2012. Made: 30.01.2012. Laid before the National Assembly for Wales: 31.01.2012. Coming into force: 28.02.2012. Effect: S.I. 2010/1700 (W.161) partially revoked. Territorial extent & classification: W. General. - In English & Welsh. Welsh title: Rheoliadau Timau Integredig Cymorth i Deuluoedd (Adolygu Achosion) (Cymru) 2012. - 8p.: 30 cm. - 978-0-348-10691-6 £5.75

The Local Safeguarding Children Boards (Wales) (Amendment) Regulations 2012 No. 2012/1712 (W.222). - Enabling power: Children Act 2004, ss. 32 (2) (3), 34 (1), 66 (1). - Issued: 19.07.2012. Made: 30.06.2012. Laid before the National Assembly for Wales: 03.07.2012. Coming into force: 01.01.2013. Effect: S.I. 2006/1705 (W.167) amended/partially revoked. Territorial extent & classification: W. General. - In English and Welsh. Welsh title: Rheoliadau Byrddau Lleol ar gyfer Diogelu Plant (Cymru) (Diwygio) 2012. - 8p.: 30 cm. - 978-0-348-10639-8 £5.75

The Play Sufficiency Assessment (Wales) Regulations 2012 No. 2012/2555 (W.279). - Enabling power: Children and Families (Wales) Measure 2010, s. 11 (1). - Issued: 29.10.2012. Made: 06.10.2012. Laid before the National Assembly for Wales: 09.10.2012. Coming into force: 02.11.2012. Effect: None. Territorial extent & classification: W. General. - In English and Welsh. Welsh title: Rheoliadau Asesu Digonolrwydd Cyfleoedd Chwarae (Cymru) 2012. - 8p.: 30 cm. - 978-0-348-10659-6 £4.00

Child trust funds

The Child Trust Funds (Amendment) Regulations 2012 No. 2012/1870. - Enabling power: Child Trust Funds Act 2004, ss. 3 (2), 28 (1) to (4). - Issued: 18.07.2012. Made: 16.07.2012. Laid: 17.07.2012. Coming into force: 08.08.2012. Effect: S.I. 2004/1450 amended. Territorial extent & classification: E/W/S/NI. General. - 2p.: 30 cm. - 978-0-11-152718-4 £4.00

The Child Trust Funds, Registered Pension Schemes and Stamp Duty Reserve Tax (Consequential Amendments) Regulations 2012 No. 2012/886. - Enabling power: Child Trust Funds Act 2004, ss. 13, 28 (1) (2) & Finance Act 1986, s. 98 & Finance Act 2004, ss. ss. 267 (10), 268 (10). - Issued: 21.03.2012. Made: 21.03.2012. Laid: 21.03.2012. Coming into force: 06.04.2012. Effect: S.I. 1986/1711; 2004/1450; 2005/3452 amended. Territorial extent & classification: E/W/S/NI. General. - 4p.: 30 cm. - 978-0-11-152265-3 £4.00

Civil aviation

The Air Navigation (Amendment) Order 2012 No. 2012/1751. - Enabling power: Civil Aviation Act 1982, ss. 60 (1) (2) (b) (3) (b) (h) (j) (n), 61 (1) (a), 101 & European Communities Act 1972, s. 2 (2), sch. 2, para 1A. - Issued: 17.07.2012. Made: 10.07.2012. Laid: 17.07.2012. Coming into force: 10.08.2012 other than part 1; 17.09.2012 for part 1. Effect: S.I. 2009/3015 amended. Territorial extent & classification: E/W/S/NI. General. - 36p.: 30 cm. - 978-0-11-152688-0 £9.75

The Air Navigation (Dangerous Goods) (Amendment) Regulations 2012 No. 2012/3054. - Enabling power: S.I. 2009/3015, art. 132 (1). - Issued: 14.12.2012. Made: 05.12.2012. Coming into force: 01.01.2013. Effect: SI 2011/1454 revoked. Territorial extent & classification: E/W/S/NI. General. - 2p.: 30 cm. - 978-0-11-153202-7 £4.00

The Air Navigation (Restriction of Flying) (Abingdon Air and Country Show) Regulations 2012 No. 2012/74. - Enabling power: S.I. 2009/3015, art. 161. - Issued: 17.01.2012. Made: 11.01.2012. Coming into force: 05.05.2012. Effect: None. Territorial extent & classification: E. Local. - Available at http://www.legislation.gov.uk/uksi/2012/74/contents/made *Non-print*

The Air Navigation (Restriction of Flying) (Balado) Regulations 2012 No. 2012/790. - Enabling power: S.I. 2009/3015, art. 161. - Issued: 20.03.2012. Made: 09.03.2012. Coming into force: 05.07.2012. Effect: None. Territorial extent & classification: E. Local. - Available at http://www.legislation.gov.uk/uksi/2012/790/contents/made *Non-print*

The Air Navigation (Restriction of Flying) (Biggin Hill) Regulations 2012 No. 2012/1176. - Enabling power: S.I. 2009/3015, art. 161. - Issued: 02.05.2012. Made: 25.04.2012. Coming into force: 05.05.2012. Effect: None. Territorial extent & classification: E. Local. - Available at http://www.legislation.gov.uk/uksi/2012/1176/contents/made *Non-print*

The Air Navigation (Restriction of Flying) (Bournemouth) Regulations 2012 No. 2012/869. - Enabling power: S.I. 2009/3015, art. 161. - Issued: 23.03.2012. Made: 12.03.2012. Coming into force: 30.08.2012. Effect: None. Territorial extent & classification: E. Local. - Available at http://www.legislation.gov.uk/uksi/2012/869/contents/made *Non-print*

The Air Navigation (Restriction of Flying) (Breighton Airfield) Regulations 2012 No. 2012/1350. - Enabling power: S.I. 2009/3015, art. 161. - Issued: 24.05.2012. Made: 14.05.2012 at 17.56 hours. Coming into force: With immediate effect. Effect: None. Territorial extent & classification: E. Local. - Revoked by S.I. 2012/1351 (Non-print). - Available at http://www.legislation.gov.uk/uksi/2012/1350/contents/made *Non-print*

The Air Navigation (Restriction of Flying) (Breighton Airfield) (Revocation) Regulations 2012 No. 2012/1351. - Enabling power: S.I. 2009/3015, art. 161. - Issued: 24.05.2012. Made: 14.05.2012 at 23.10 hours. Coming into force: With immediate effect. Effect: S.I. 2012/1350 revoked. Territorial extent & classification: E. Local. - Available at http://www.legislation.gov.uk/uksi/2012/1351/contents/made *Non-print*

The Air Navigation (Restriction of Flying) (Brentwood) Regulations 2012 No. 2012/1174. - Enabling power: S.I. 2009/3015, art. 161. - Issued: 02.05.2012. Made: 25.04.2012. Coming into force: 05.05.2012. Effect: None. Territorial extent & classification: E. Local. - Available at http://www.legislation.gov.uk/uksi/2012/1174/contents/made *Non-print*

The Air Navigation (Restriction of Flying) (Burton Bradstock, Dorset) Regulations 2012 No. 2012/1974. - Enabling power: S.I. 2009/3015, art. 161. - Issued: 30.07.2012. Made: 24.07.2012 at 16.45 hours. Coming into force: With immediate effect. Effect: None. Territorial extent & classification: E. Local. - Revoked by S.I. 2012/1975 (Non-print). Available at http://www.legislation.gov.uk/uksi/2012/1974/contents/made *Non-print*

The Air Navigation (Restriction of Flying) (Burton Bradstock, Dorset) (Revocation) Regulations 2012 No. 2012/1975. - Enabling power: S.I. 2009/3015, art. 161. - Issued: 30.07.2012. Made: 25.07.2012 at 16.00 hours. Coming into force: With immediate effect. Effect: S.I. 2012/1974 revoked. Territorial extent & classification: E. Local. - Available at http://www.legislation.gov.uk/uksi/2012/1975/contents/made *Non-print*

The Air Navigation (Restriction of Flying) (Chelmsford) Regulations 2012 No. 2012/1172. - Enabling power: S.I. 2009/3015, art. 161. - Issued: 02.05.2012. Made: 25.04.2012. Coming into force: 06.05.2012. Effect: None. Territorial extent & classification: E. Local. - Available at http://www.legislation.gov.uk/uksi/2012/1172/contents/made *Non-print*

The Air Navigation (Restriction of Flying) (Cheltenham Festival) Regulations 2012 No. 2012/72. - Enabling power: S.I. 2009/3015, art. 161. - Issued: 17.01.2012. Made: 10.01.2012. Coming into force: 13.03.2012. Effect: None. Territorial extent & classification: E. Local. - Available at http://www.legislation.gov.uk/uksi/2012/72/contents/made *Non-print*

The Air Navigation (Restriction of Flying) (Cholmondeley Castle) Regulations 2012 No. 2012/151. - Enabling power: S.I. 2009/3015, art. 161. - Issued: 26.01.2012. Made: 19.01.2012. Coming into force: 15.06.2012. Effect: None. Territorial extent & classification: E. Local. - Available at http://www.legislation.gov.uk/uksi/2012/151/contents/made *Non-print*

The Air Navigation (Restriction of Flying) (Diamond Jubilee Concert) Regulations 2012 No. 2012/907. - Enabling power: S.I. 2009/3015, art. 161. - Issued: 26.03.2012. Made: 15.03.2012. Coming into force: 04.06.2012. Effect: None. Territorial extent & classification: E. Local. - Available at http://www.legislation.gov.uk/uksi/2012/907/contents/made *Non-print*

The Air Navigation (Restriction of Flying) (Dunsfold) Regulations 2012 No. 2012/156. - Enabling power: S.I. 2009/3015, art. 161. - Issued: 31.01.2012. Made: 23.01.2012. Coming into force: 26.08.2012. Effect: None. Territorial extent & classification: E. Local. - Available at http://www.legislation.gov.uk/uksi/2012/156/contents/made *Non-print*

Civil aviation

The Air Navigation (Restriction of Flying) (Duxford) (Amendment) Regulations 2012 No. 2012/1348. - Enabling power: S.I. 2009/3015, art. 161. - Issued: 24.05.2012. Made: 10.05.2012. Coming into force: 27.05.2012. Effect: S.I. 2012/150 amended. Territorial extent & classification: E. Local. - Available at http://www.legislation.gov.uk/uksi/2012/1348/contents/made *Non-print*

The Air Navigation (Restriction of Flying) (Duxford) Regulations 2012 No. 2012/150. - Enabling power: S.I. 2009/3015, art. 161. - Issued: 26.01.2012. Made: 20.01.2012. Coming into force: 27.05.2012. Effect: None. Territorial extent & classification: E. Local. - Available at http://www.legislation.gov.uk/uksi/2012/150/contents/made *Non-print*

The Air Navigation (Restriction of Flying) (Eastbourne) Regulations 2012 No. 2012/196. - Enabling power: S.I. 2009/3015, art. 161. - Issued: 01.02.2012. Made: 26.01.2012. Coming into force: 09.08.2012. Effect: None. Territorial extent & classification: E. Local. - Available at http://www.legislation.gov.uk/uksi/2012/196/contents/made *Non-print*

The Air Navigation (Restriction of Flying) (Elgin Offshore Installation) (Amendment No. 2) Regulations 2012 No. 2012/1016. - Enabling power: S.I. 2009/3015, art. 161. - Issued: 12.04.2012. Made: 30.03.2012 at 17.38 hours. Coming into force: With immediate effect. Effect: S.I. 2012/982 amended. Territorial extent & classification: E. Local. - Available at http://www.legislation.gov.uk/uksi/2012/1016/contents/made *Non-print*

The Air Navigation (Restriction of Flying) (Elgin Offshore Installation) (Amendment No. 3) Regulations 2012 No. 2012/1018. - Enabling power: S.I. 2009/3015, art. 161. - Issued: 12.04.2012. Made: 02.04.2012 at 16.31 hours. Coming into force: With immediate effect. Effect: S.I. 2012/982 amended. Territorial extent & classification: E. Local. - Available at http://www.legislation.gov.uk/uksi/2012/1018/contents/made *Non-print*

The Air Navigation (Restriction of Flying) (Elgin Offshore Installation) (Amendment) Regulations 2012 No. 2012/983. - Enabling power: S.I. 2009/3015, art. 161. - Issued: 04.04.2012. Made: 28.03.2012. Coming into force: With immediate effect. Effect: S.I. 2012/982 amended. Territorial extent & classification: E. Local. - Available at http://www.legislation.gov.uk/uksi/2012/983/contents/made *Non-print*

The Air Navigation (Restriction of Flying) (Elgin Offshore Installation) Regulations 2012 No. 2012/982. - Enabling power: S.I. 2009/3015, art. 161. - Issued: 04.04.2012. Made: 25.03.2012 at 17.00 hours. Coming into force: With immediate effect. Effect: None. Territorial extent & classification: E. Local. - Revoked by S.I. 2012/1402 (Non-print). - Available at http://www.legislation.gov.uk/uksi/2012/982/contents/made *Non-print*

The Air Navigation (Restriction of Flying) (Elgin Offshore Installation) (Revocation) Regulations 2012 No. 2012/1402. - Enabling power: S.I. 2009/3015, art. 161. - Issued: 01.06.2012. Made: 24.05.2012 at 12.20 hours. Coming into force: With immediate effect. Effect: S.I. 2012/982 revoked. Territorial extent & classification: E. Local. - Available at http://www.legislation.gov.uk/uksi/2012/1402/contents/made *Non-print*

The Air Navigation (Restriction of Flying) (Exeter) Regulations 2012 No. 2012/1177. - Enabling power: S.I. 2009/3015, art. 161. - Issued: 02.05.2012. Made: 25.04.2012. Coming into force: 02.05.2012. Effect: None. Territorial extent & classification: E. Local. - Available at http://www.legislation.gov.uk/uksi/2012/1177/contents/made *Non-print*

The Air Navigation (Restriction of Flying) (Fair Isle) Regulations 2012 No. 2012/2682. - Enabling power: S.I. 2009/3015, art. 161. - Issued: 30.10.2012. Made: 22.10.2012 at 16.40 hours. Coming into force: With immediate effect. Effect: None. Territorial extent & classification: E. Local. - Revoked by S.I. 2012/2689 [Non-print]. - Available at http://www.legislation.gov.uk/uksi/2012/2682/contents/made *Non-print*

The Air Navigation (Restriction of Flying) (Fair Isle) (Revocation) Regulations 2012 No. 2012/2689. - Enabling power: S.I. 2009/3015, art. 161. - Issued: 30.10.2012. Made: 23.10.2012 at 13.40 hours. Coming into force: With immediate effect. Effect: S.I. 2012/2682 revoked. Territorial extent & classification: E. Local. - Available at http://www.legislation.gov.uk/uksi/2012/2689/contents/made *Non-print*

The Air Navigation (Restriction of Flying) (Farnborough Air Show) (Amendment No. 2) Regulations 2012 No. 2012/1958. - Enabling power: S.I. 2009/3015, art. 161. - Issued: 30.07.2012. Made: 13.07.2012 at 14.55 hours. Coming into force: With immediate effect. Effect: S.I. 2012/194 amended. Territorial extent & classification: E. Local. - Available at http://www.legislation.gov.uk/uksi/2012/1958/contents/made *Non-print*

The Air Navigation (Restriction of Flying) (Farnborough Air Show) (Amendment) Regulations 2012 No. 2012/1946. - Enabling power: S.I. 2009/3015, art. 161. - Issued: 30.07.2012. Made: 10.07.2012. Coming into force: 11.07.2012. Effect: S.I. 2012/194 amended. Territorial extent & classification: E. Local. - Available at http://www.legislation.gov.uk/uksi/2012/1946/contents/made *Non-print*

The Air Navigation (Restriction of Flying) (Farnborough Air Show) Regulations 2012 No. 2012/194. - Enabling power: S.I. 2009/3015, art. 161. - Issued: 01.02.2012. Made: 26.01.2012. Coming into force: 02.07.2012. Effect: None. Territorial extent & classification: E. Local. - Available at http://www.legislation.gov.uk/uksi/2012/194/contents/made. - 2p., col. map *Non-print*

The Air Navigation (Restriction of Flying) (Fillingham) Regulations 2012 No. 2012/2375. - Enabling power: S.I. 2009/3015, art. 161. - Issued: 18.09.2012. Made: 06.09.2012 at 01.00 hours. Coming into force: With immediate effect. Effect: None. Territorial extent & classification: E. Local. - Revoked by SI 2012/2376 (Non-print). - Available at http://www.legislation.gov.uk/uksi/2012/2375/contents/made *Non-print*

The Air Navigation (Restriction of Flying) (Fillingham) (Revocation) Regulations 2012 No. 2012/2376. - Enabling power: S.I. 2009/3015, art. 161. - Issued: 18.09.2012. Made: 07.09.2012 at 10.20 hours. Coming into force: With immediate effect. Effect: S.I. 2012/2375 revoked. Territorial extent & classification: E. Local. - Available at http://www.legislation.gov.uk/uksi/2012/2376/contents/made *Non-print*

The Air Navigation (Restriction of Flying) (Folkestone) Regulations 2012 No. 2012/154. - Enabling power: S.I. 2009/3015, art. 161. - Issued: 26.01.2012. Made: 23.01.2012. Coming into force: 02.06.2012. Effect: None. Territorial extent & classification: E. Local. - Available at http://www.legislation.gov.uk/uksi/2012/154/contents/made *Non-print*

The Air Navigation (Restriction of Flying) (Frogham) (Amendment) Regulations 2012 No. 2012/1353. - Enabling power: S.I. 2009/3015, art. 161. - Issued: 24.05.2012. Made: 18.05.2012 at 14.15 hours. Coming into force: With immediate effect. Effect: S.I. 2012/1352 amended. Territorial extent & classification: E. Local. - Available at http://www.legislation.gov.uk/uksi/2012/1353/contents/made *Non-print*

The Air Navigation (Restriction of Flying) (Frogham) Regulations 2012 No. 2012/1352. - Enabling power: S.I. 2009/3015, art. 161. - Issued: 24.05.2012. Made: 18.05.2012 at 12.40 hours. Coming into force: With immediate effect. Effect: None. Territorial extent & classification: E. Local. - Revoked by S.I. 2012/1354 (Non-print). - Available at http://www.legislation.gov.uk/uksi/2012/1352/contents/made *Non-print*

The Air Navigation (Restriction of Flying) (Frogham) (Revocation) Regulations 2012 No. 2012/1354. - Enabling power: S.I. 2009/3015, art. 161. - Issued: 24.05.2012. Made: 18.05.2012 at 15.15 hours. Coming into force: With immediate effect. Effect: S.I. 2012/1352 revoked. Territorial extent & classification: E. Local. - Available at http://www.legislation.gov.uk/uksi/2012/1354/contents/made *Non-print*

The Air Navigation (Restriction of Flying) (Guildford) Regulations 2012 No. 2012/1401. - Enabling power: S.I. 2009/3015, art. 161. - Issued: 01.06.2012. Made: 23.05.2012. Coming into force: 23.06.2012. Effect: None. Territorial extent & classification: E. Local. - Available at http://www.legislation.gov.uk/uksi/2012/1401/contents/made *Non-print*

The Air Navigation (Restriction of Flying) (Her Majesty The Queen's Birthday Flypast) Regulations 2012 No. 2012/525. - Enabling power: S.I. 2009/3015, art. 161. - Issued: 01.03.2012. Made: 23.02.2012. Coming into force: 12.06.2012. Effect: None. Territorial extent & classification: E. Local. - Available at http://www.legislation.gov.uk/uksi/2012/525/contents/made *Non-print*

The Air Navigation (Restriction of Flying) (Her Majesty The Queen's Diamond Jubilee Flypast) Regulations 2012 No. 2012/984. - Enabling power: S.I. 2009/3015, art. 161. - Issued: 04.04.2012. Made: 29.03.2012. Coming into force: 19.05.2012. Effect: None. Territorial extent & classification: E. Local. - Available at http://www.legislation.gov.uk/uksi/2012/984/contents/made *Non-print*

The Air Navigation (Restriction of Flying) (Her Majesty The Queen's Diamond Jubilee Flypast Rehearsal) Regulations 2012 No. 2012/1014. - Enabling power: S.I. 2009/3015, art. 161. - Issued: 12.04.2012. Made: 29.03.2012. Coming into force: 15.05.2012. Effect: None. Territorial extent & classification: E. Local. - Available at http://www.legislation.gov.uk/uksi/2012/1014/contents/made *Non-print*

The Air Navigation (Restriction of Flying) (Jet Formation Display Teams) (No. 2) (Amendment) Regulations 2012 No. 2012/1231. - Enabling power: S.I. 2009/3015, art. 161. - Issued: 10.05.2012. Made: 02.05.2012. Coming into force: 21.05.2012. Effect: S.I. 2012/487 amended. Territorial extent & classification: E. Local. - Available at http://www.legislation.gov.uk/uksi/2012/1231/contents/made *Non-print*

The Air Navigation (Restriction of Flying) (Jet Formation Display Teams) (No. 2) Regulations 2012 No. 2012/487. - Enabling power: S.I. 2009/3015, art. 161. - Issued: 29.02.2012. Made: 16.02.2012. Coming into force: 21.05.2012. Effect: None. Territorial extent & classification: E. Local. - Available at http://www.legislation.gov.uk/uksi/2012/487/contents/made *Non-print*

The Air Navigation (Restriction of Flying) (Jet Formation Display Teams) (No. 3) Regulations 2012 No. 2012/978. - Enabling power: S.I. 2009/3015, art. 161. - Issued: 04.04.2012. Made: 21.03.2012. Coming into force: 02.06.2012. Effect: None. Territorial extent & classification: E. Local. - Revoked by S.I. 2012/1230 (Non-print). - Available at http://www.legislation.gov.uk/uksi/2012/978/contents/made *Non-print*

Civil aviation

The Air Navigation (Restriction of Flying) (Jet Formation Display Teams) (No. 4) (Amendment) Regulations 2012 No. 2012/1959. - Enabling power: S.I. 2009/3015, art. 161. - Issued: 30.07.2012. Made: 10.07.2012. Coming into force: 12.07.2012. Effect: S.I. 2012/1230 amended. Territorial extent & classification: E. Local. - Available at http://www.legislation.gov.uk/uksi/2012/1959/contents/made *Non-print*

The Air Navigation (Restriction of Flying) (Jet Formation Display Teams) (No. 4) Regulations 2012 No. 2012/1230. - Enabling power: S.I. 2009/3015, art. 161. - Issued: 10.05.2012. Made: 02.05.2012. Coming into force: 02.06.2012. Effect: S.I. 2012/978 revoked. Territorial extent & classification: E. Local. - Available at http://www.legislation.gov.uk/uksi/2012/1230/contents/made *Non-print*

The Air Navigation (Restriction of Flying) (Jet Formation Display Teams) (No. 5) (Amendment) Regulations 2012 No. 2012/2110. - Enabling power: S.I. 2009/3015, art. 161. - Issued: 17.08.2012. Made: 10.08.2012. Coming into force: 17.08.2012. Effect: S.I. 2012/1349 amended. Territorial extent & classification: E. Local. - Available at http://www.legislation.gov.uk/uksi/2012/2110/contents/made *Non-print*

The Air Navigation (Restriction of Flying) (Jet Formation Display Teams) (No. 5) Regulations 2012 No. 2012/1349. - Enabling power: S.I. 2009/3015, art. 161. - Issued: 24.05.2012. Made: 18.05.2012. Coming into force: 15.08.2012. Effect: None. Territorial extent & classification: E. Local. - Available at http://www.legislation.gov.uk/uksi/2012/1349/contents/made *Non-print*

The Air Navigation (Restriction of Flying) (Jet Formation Display Teams) (No. 6) Regulations 2012 No. 2012/1970. - Enabling power: S.I. 2009/3015, art. 161. - Issued: 30.07.2012. Made: 13.07.2012. Coming into force: 14.07.2012. Effect: None. Territorial extent & classification: E. Local. - Available at http://www.legislation.gov.uk/uksi/2012/1970/contents/made *Non-print*

The Air Navigation (Restriction of Flying) (Jet Formation Display Teams) Regulations 2012 No. 2012/71. - Enabling power: S.I. 2009/3015, art. 161. - Issued: 17.01.2012. Made: 10.01.2012. Coming into force: 06.03.2012. Effect: None. Territorial extent & classification: E. Local. - Available at http://www.legislation.gov.uk/uksi/2012/71/contents/made *Non-print*

The Air Navigation (Restriction of Flying) (Kemble) Regulations 2012 No. 2012/812. - Enabling power: S.I. 2009/3015, art. 161. - Issued: 20.03.2012. Made: 12.03.2012. Coming into force: 26.08.2012. Effect: None. Territorial extent & classification: E. Local. - Available at http://www.legislation.gov.uk/uksi/2012/812/contents/made *Non-print*

The Air Navigation (Restriction of Flying) (Kensington) (Amendment) Regulations 2012 No. 2012/2303. - Enabling power: S.I. 2009/3015, art. 161. - Issued: 11.09.2012. Made: 04.09.2012 at 13.00 hours. Coming into force: With immediate effect. Effect: S.I. 2012/2302 amended. Territorial extent & classification: E. Local. - Available at http://www.legislation.gov.uk/uksi/2012/2303/contents/made *Non-print*

The Air Navigation (Restriction of Flying) (Kensington) Regulations 2012 No. 2012/2302. - Enabling power: S.I. 2009/3015, art. 161. - Issued: 11.09.2012. Made: 04.09.2012 at 11.50 hours. Coming into force: With immediate effect. Effect: None. Territorial extent & classification: E. Local. - Revoked by SI 2012/2337 (Non-print). - Available at http://www.legislation.gov.uk/uksi/2012/2302/contents/made *Non-print*

The Air Navigation (Restriction of Flying) (Kensington) (Revocation) Regulations 2012 No. 2012/2337. - Enabling power: S.I. 2009/3015, art. 161. - Issued: 14.09.2012. Made: 05.09.2012 at 16.00 hours. Coming into force: With immediate effect. Effect: S.I. 2012/2302 revoked. Territorial extent & classification: E. Local. - Available at http://www.legislation.gov.uk/uksi/2012/2337/contents/made *Non-print*

The Air Navigation (Restriction of Flying) (London 2012 Olympic and Paralympic Games, Brands Hatch, Kent) Regulations 2012 No. 2012/1330. - Enabling power: S.I. 2009/3015, art. 161. - Issued: 23.05.2012. Made: 14.05.2012. Coming into force: 01.06.2012. Effect: None. Territorial extent & classification: E. Local. - Available at http://www.legislation.gov.uk/uksi/2012/1330/contents/made *Non-print*

The Air Navigation (Restriction of Flying) (London 2012 Olympic and Paralympic Games, City of Coventry Stadium, Coventry) Regulations 2012 No. 2012/1336. - Enabling power: S.I. 2009/3015, art. 161. - Issued: 23.05.2012. Made: 14.05.2012. Coming into force: 01.06.2012. Effect: None. Territorial extent & classification: E. Local. - Available at http://www.legislation.gov.uk/uksi/2012/1336/contents/made *Non-print*

The Air Navigation (Restriction of Flying) (London 2012 Olympic and Paralympic Games, Egham, Surrey) Regulations 2012 No. 2012/1335. - Enabling power: S.I. 2009/3015, art. 161. - Issued: 23.05.2012. Made: 14.05.2012. Coming into force: 01.06.2012. Effect: None. Territorial extent & classification: E. Local. - Available at http://www.legislation.gov.uk/uksi/2012/1335/contents/made *Non-print*

The Air Navigation (Restriction of Flying) (London 2012 Olympic and Paralympic Games, Eton Dorney, Buckinghamshire) Regulations 2012 No. 2012/1337. - Enabling power: S.I. 2009/3015, art. 161. - Issued: 23.05.2012. Made: 14.05.2012. Coming into force: 01.06.2012. Effect: None. Territorial extent & classification: E. Local. - Available at http://www.legislation.gov.uk/uksi/2012/1337/contents/made *Non-print*

The Air Navigation (Restriction of Flying) (London 2012 Olympic and Paralympic Games, Hadleigh Farm, Essex) Regulations 2012 No. 2012/1332. - Enabling power: S.I. 2009/3015, art. 161. - Issued: 23.05.2012. Made: 14.05.2012. Coming into force: 01.06.2012. Effect: None. Territorial extent & classification: E. Local. - Available at http://www.legislation.gov.uk/uksi/2012/1332/contents/made *Non-print*

The Air Navigation (Restriction of Flying) (London 2012 Olympic and Paralympic Games, Hampden Park, Glasgow) Regulations 2012 No. 2012/1334. - Enabling power: S.I. 2009/3015, art. 161. - Issued: 23.05.2012. Made: 14.05.2012. Coming into force: 01.06.2012. Effect: None. Territorial extent & classification: E. Local. - Available at http://www.legislation.gov.uk/uksi/2012/1334/contents/made *Non-print*

The Air Navigation (Restriction of Flying) (London 2012 Olympic and Paralympic Games, Lee Valley White Water Centre, Broxbourne, Hertfordshire) (Amendment) Regulations 2012 No. 2012/1940. - Enabling power: S.I. 2009/3015, art. 161. - Issued: 30.07.2012. Made: 11.07.2012. Coming into force: 12.07.2012. Effect: S.I. 2012/1339 amended. Territorial extent & classification: E. Local. - Available at http://www.legislation.gov.uk/uksi/2012/1940/contents/made *Non-print*

The Air Navigation (Restriction of Flying) (London 2012 Olympic and Paralympic Games, Lee Valley White Water Centre, Broxbourne, Hertfordshire) Regulations 2012 No. 2012/1339. - Enabling power: S.I. 2009/3015, art. 161. - Issued: 23.05.2012. Made: 14.05.2012. Coming into force: 01.06.2012. Effect: None. Territorial extent & classification: E. Local. - Available at http://www.legislation.gov.uk/uksi/2012/1339/contents/made *Non-print*

The Air Navigation (Restriction of Flying) (London 2012 Olympic and Paralympic Games, London Prohibited Zone EGP111) Regulations 2012 No. 2012/1340. - Enabling power: S.I. 2009/3015, art. 161. - Issued: 23.05.2012. Made: 14.05.2012. Coming into force: 01.06.2012. Effect: None. Territorial extent & classification: E. Local. - Available at http://www.legislation.gov.uk/uksi/2012/1340/contents/made *Non-print*

The Air Navigation (Restriction of Flying) (London 2012 Olympic and Paralympic Games, London Prohibited Zone EGP114) Regulations 2012 No. 2012/1341. - Enabling power: S.I. 2009/3015, art. 161. - Issued: 23.05.2012. Made: 14.05.2012. Coming into force: 01.06.2012. Effect: None. Territorial extent & classification: E. Local. - Available at http://www.legislation.gov.uk/uksi/2012/1341/contents/made *Non-print*

The Air Navigation (Restriction of Flying) (London 2012 Olympic and Paralympic Games, London Restricted Zone EGR112) Regulations 2012 No. 2012/1328. - Enabling power: S.I. 2009/3015, art. 161. - Issued: 23.05.2012. Made: 14.05.2012. Coming into force: 01.06.2012. Effect: None. Territorial extent & classification: E. Local. - Available at http://www.legislation.gov.uk/uksi/2012/1328/contents/made *Non-print*

The Air Navigation (Restriction of Flying) (London 2012 Olympic and Paralympic Games, Millennium Stadium, Cardiff) Regulations 2012 No. 2012/1331. - Enabling power: S.I. 2009/3015, art. 161. - Issued: 23.05.2012. Made: 14.05.2012. Coming into force: 01.06.2012. Effect: None. Territorial extent & classification: E. Local. - Available at http://www.legislation.gov.uk/uksi/2012/1331/contents/made *Non-print*

The Air Navigation (Restriction of Flying) (London 2012 Olympic and Paralympic Games, Old Trafford, Manchester) Regulations 2012 No. 2012/1329. - Enabling power: S.I. 2009/3015, art. 161. - Issued: 23.05.2012. Made: 14.05.2012. Coming into force: 01.06.2012. Effect: None. Territorial extent & classification: E. Local. - Available at http://www.legislation.gov.uk/uksi/2012/1329/contents/made *Non-print*

The Air Navigation (Restriction of Flying) (London 2012 Olympic and Paralympic Games, Road Cycle Event, Leatherhead, Surrey) (Amendment) Regulations 2012 No. 2012/1972. - Enabling power: S.I. 2009/3015, art. 161. - Issued: 30.07.2012. Made: 06.07.2012. Coming into force: 07.07.2012. Effect: S.I. 2012/1338 amended. Territorial extent & classification: E. Local. - Available at http://www.legislation.gov.uk/uksi/2012/1972/contents/made *Non-print*

The Air Navigation (Restriction of Flying) (London 2012 Olympic and Paralympic Games, Road Cycle Event, Leatherhead, Surrey) Regulations 2012 No. 2012/1338. - Enabling power: S.I. 2009/3015, art. 161. - Issued: 23.05.2012. Made: 14.05.2012. Coming into force: 01.06.2012. Effect: None. Territorial extent & classification: E. Local. - Available at http://www.legislation.gov.uk/uksi/2012/1338/contents/made *Non-print*

Civil aviation

The Air Navigation (Restriction of Flying) (London 2012 Olympic and Paralympic Games, St James' Park, Newcastle) Regulations 2012 No. 2012/1333. - Enabling power: S.I. 2009/3015, art. 161. - Issued: 23.05.2012. Made: 14.05.2012. Coming into force: 01.06.2012. Effect: None. Territorial extent & classification: E. Local. - Available at http://www.legislation.gov.uk/uksi/2012/1333/contents/made *Non-print*

The Air Navigation (Restriction of Flying) (London 2012 Olympic and Paralympic Games, Weymouth Restricted Zone EGR005) Regulations 2012 No. 2012/1342. - Enabling power: S.I. 2009/3015, art. 161. - Issued: 23.05.2012. Made: 14.05.2012. Coming into force: 01.06.2012. Effect: None. Territorial extent & classification: E. Local. - Available at http://www.legislation.gov.uk/uksi/2012/1342/contents/made *Non-print*

The Air Navigation (Restriction of Flying) (London Remembrance Commemorations) Regulations 2012 No. 2012/2330. - Enabling power: S.I. 2009/3015, art. 161. - Issued: 13.09.2012. Made: 06.09.2012. Coming into force: 10.11.2012. Effect: None. Territorial extent & classification: E. Local. - Available at http://www.legislation.gov.uk/uksi/2012/2330/contents/made *Non-print*

The Air Navigation (Restriction of Flying) (Lowestoft) Regulations 2012 No. 2012/153. - Enabling power: S.I. 2009/3015, art. 161. - Issued: 26.01.2012. Made: 19.01.2012. Coming into force: 23.06.2012. Effect: None. Territorial extent & classification: E. Local. - Available at http://www.legislation.gov.uk/uksi/2012/153/contents/made *Non-print*

The Air Navigation (Restriction of Flying) (Machynlleth) Regulations 2012 No. 2012/2603. - Enabling power: S.I. 2009/3015, art. 161. - Issued: 18.10.2012. Made: 02.10.2012 at 15.35 hours. Coming into force: With immediate effect. Effect: None. Territorial extent & classification: E. Local. - Revoked by S.I. 2012/2604 [Non-print]. - Available at http://www.legislation.gov.uk/uksi/2012/2603/contents/made *Non-print*

The Air Navigation (Restriction of Flying) (Machynlleth) (Revocation) Regulations 2012 No. 2012/2604. - Enabling power: S.I. 2009/3015, art. 161. - Issued: 18.10.2012. Made: 08.10.2012 at 15.15 hours. Coming into force: With immediate effect. Effect: S.I. 2012/2603 revoked. Territorial extent & classification: E. Local. - Available at http://www.legislation.gov.uk/uksi/2012/2604/contents/made *Non-print*

The Air Navigation (Restriction of Flying) (Northampton Sywell) (No. 2) Regulations 2012 No. 2012/910. - Enabling power: S.I. 2009/3015, art. 161. - Issued: 26.03.2012. Made: 16.03.2012. Coming into force: 31.08.2012. Effect: None. Territorial extent & classification: E. Local. - Available at http://www.legislation.gov.uk/uksi/2012/910/contents/made *Non-print*

The Air Navigation (Restriction of Flying) (Northampton Sywell) Regulations 2012 No. 2012/706. - Enabling power: S.I. 2009/3015, art. 161. - Issued: 14.03.2012. Made: 06.03.2012. Coming into force: 25.05.2012. Effect: None. Territorial extent & classification: E. Local. - Available at http://www.legislation.gov.uk/uksi/2012/706/contents/made *Non-print*

The Air Navigation (Restriction of Flying) (Northern Ireland International Air Show) Regulations 2012 No. 2012/1637. - Enabling power: S.I. 2009/3015, art. 161. - Issued: 29.06.2012. Made: 20.06.2012. Coming into force: 08.09.2012. Effect: None. Territorial extent & classification: E. Local. - Available at http://www.legislation.gov.uk/uksi/2012/1637/contents/made *Non-print*

The Air Navigation (Restriction of Flying) (Old Warden) Regulations 2012 No. 2012/2370. - Enabling power: S.I. 2009/3015, art. 161. - Issued: 18.09.2012. Made: 07.09.2012. Coming into force: 07.10.2012. Effect: None. Territorial extent & classification: E. Local. - Available at http://www.legislation.gov.uk/uksi/2012/2370/contents/made *Non-print*

The Air Navigation (Restriction of Flying) (Plymouth) Regulations 2012 No. 2012/1060. - Enabling power: S.I. 2009/3015, art. 161. - Issued: 16.04.2012. Made: 10.04.2012. Coming into force: 30.06.2012. Effect: None. Territorial extent & classification: E. Local. - Available at http://www.legislation.gov.uk/uksi/2012/1060/contents/made *Non-print*

The Air Navigation (Restriction of Flying) (Portsmouth) Regulations 2012 No. 2012/524. - Enabling power: S.I. 2009/3015, art. 161. - Issued: 01.03.2012. Made: 23.02.2012. Coming into force: 18.08.2012. Effect: None. Territorial extent & classification: E. Local. - Available at http://www.legislation.gov.uk/uksi/2012/524/contents/made *Non-print*

The Air Navigation (Restriction of Flying) (RNAS Yeovilton) Regulations 2012 No. 2012/155. - Enabling power: S.I. 2009/3015, art. 161. - Issued: 26.01.2012. Made: 23.01.2012. Coming into force: 22.06.2012. Effect: None. Territorial extent & classification: E. Local. - Available at http://www.legislation.gov.uk/uksi/2012/155/contents/made *Non-print*

The Air Navigation (Restriction of Flying) (Royal Air Force Cosford) Regulations 2012 No. 2012/730. - Enabling power: S.I. 2009/3015, art. 161. - Issued: 19.03.2012. Made: 06.03.2012. Coming into force: 15.06.2012. Effect: None. Territorial extent & classification: E. Local. - Available at http://www.legislation.gov.uk/uksi/2012/730/contents/made *Non-print*

The Air Navigation (Restriction of Flying) (Royal Air Force Leuchars) Regulations 2012 No. 2012/1691. - Enabling power: S.I. 2009/3015, art. 161. - Issued: 03.07.2012. Made: 27.06.2012. Coming into force: 14.09.2012. Effect: None. Territorial extent & classification: E. Local. - Available at http://www.legislation.gov.uk/uksi/2012/1691/contents/made *Non-print*

The Air Navigation (Restriction of Flying) (Royal Air Force Waddington) Regulations 2012 No. 2012/909. - Enabling power: S.I. 2009/3015, art. 161. - Issued: 26.03.2012. Made: 16.03.2012. Coming into force: 28.06.2012. Effect: None. Territorial extent & classification: E. Local. - Available at http://www.legislation.gov.uk/uksi/2012/909/contents/made *Non-print*

The Air Navigation (Restriction of Flying) (Royal International Air Tattoo RAF Fairford) (No. 2) (Amendment No. 2) Regulations 2012 No. 2012/1971. - Enabling power: S.I. 2009/3015, art. 161. - Issued: 30.07.2012. Made: 06.07.2012. Coming into force: 07.07.2012. Effect: S.I. 2012/1232 amended. Territorial extent & classification: E. Local. - Available at http://www.legislation.gov.uk/uksi/2012/1971/contents/made *Non-print*

The Air Navigation (Restriction of Flying) (Royal International Air Tattoo RAF Fairford) (No. 2) (Amendment) Regulations 2012 No. 2012/1403. - Enabling power: S.I. 2009/3015, art. 161. - Issued: 01.06.2012. Made: 24.05.2012. Coming into force: 07.07.2012. Effect: S.I. 2012/1232 amended. Territorial extent & classification: E. Local. - Available at http://www.legislation.gov.uk/uksi/2012/1403/contents/made *Non-print*

The Air Navigation (Restriction of Flying) (Royal International Air Tattoo RAF Fairford) (No. 2) Regulations 2012 No. 2012/1232. - Enabling power: S.I. 2009/3015, art. 161. - Issued: 10.05.2012. Made: 02.05.2012. Coming into force: 07.07.2012. Effect: None. Territorial extent & classification: E. Local. - Available at http://www.legislation.gov.uk/uksi/2012/1232/contents/made *Non-print*

The Air Navigation (Restriction of Flying) (Royal International Air Tattoo RAF Fairford) Regulations 2012 No. 2012/729. - Enabling power: S.I. 2009/3015, art. 161. - Issued: 19.03.2012. Made: 06.03.2012. Coming into force: 04.07.2012. Effect: None. Territorial extent & classification: E. Local. - Available at http://www.legislation.gov.uk/uksi/2012/729/contents/made *Non-print*

The Air Navigation (Restriction of Flying) (Saltburn-by-the-Sea, Durham) Regulations 2012 No. 2012/892. - Enabling power: S.I. 2009/3015, art. 161. - Issued: 26.03.2012. Made: 13.03.2012 at 16.45. Coming into force: With immediate effect. Effect: None. Territorial extent & classification: E. Local. - Revoked by S.I. 2012/895 (Non-print). - Available at http://www.legislation.gov.uk/uksi/2012/892/contents/made *Non-print*

The Air Navigation (Restriction of Flying) (Saltburn-by-the-Sea, Durham) (Revocation) Regulations 2012 No. 2012/895. - Enabling power: S.I. 2009/3015, art. 161. - Issued: 26.03.2012. Made: 14.03.2012 at 10.15. Coming into force: With immediate effect. Effect: S.I. 2012/892 revoked. Territorial extent & classification: E. Local. - Available at http://www.legislation.gov.uk/uksi/2012/895/contents/made *Non-print*

The Air Navigation (Restriction of Flying) (Shivering Sands) Regulations 2012 No. 2012/3051. - Enabling power: S.I. 2009/3015, art. 161. - Issued: 11.12.2012. Made: 24.11.2012 at 10.50 hours. Coming into force: With immediate effect. Effect: None. Territorial extent & classification: E. Local. - Revoked by S.I. 2012/3052 [Non-print]. - Available at http://www.legislation.gov.uk/uksi/2012/3051/contents/made *Non-print*

The Air Navigation (Restriction of Flying) (Shivering Sands) (Revocation) Regulations 2012 No. 2012/3052. - Enabling power: S.I. 2009/3015, art. 161. - Issued: 11.12.2012. Made: 24.11.2012 at 12.00 hours. Coming into force: With immediate effect. Effect: S.I. 2012/3051 revoked. Territorial extent & classification: E. Local. - Available at http://www.legislation.gov.uk/uksi/2012/3052/contents/made *Non-print*

The Air Navigation (Restriction of Flying) (Shoreham-by-Sea) (Amendment) Regulations 2012 No. 2012/1347. - Enabling power: S.I. 2009/3015, art. 161. - Issued: 24.05.2012. Made: 10.05.2012. Coming into force: 01.09.2012. Effect: None. Territorial extent & classification: E. Local. - Available at http://www.legislation.gov.uk/uksi/2012/1347/contents/made *Non-print*

The Air Navigation (Restriction of Flying) (Shoreham-by-Sea) Regulations 2012 No. 2012/871. - Enabling power: S.I. 2009/3015, art. 161. - Issued: 23.03.2012. Made: 12.03.2012. Coming into force: 01.09.2012. Effect: None. Territorial extent & classification: E. Local. - Available at http://www.legislation.gov.uk/uksi/2012/871/contents/made *Non-print*

The Air Navigation (Restriction of Flying) (Silverstone and Turweston) Regulations 2012 No. 2012/73. - Enabling power: S.I. 2009/3015, art. 161. - Issued: 17.01.2012. Made: 11.01.2012. Coming into force: 07.07.2012. Effect: None. Territorial extent & classification: E. Local. - Available at http://www.legislation.gov.uk/uksi/2012/73/contents/made *Non-print*

The Air Navigation (Restriction of Flying) (Southend-on-Sea) (Amendment) Regulations 2012 No. 2012/1208. - Enabling power: S.I. 2009/3015, art. 161. - Issued: 08.05.2012. Made: 30.04.2012. Coming into force: 26.05.2012. Effect: S.I. 2012/83 amended. Territorial extent & classification: E. Local. - Available at http://www.legislation.gov.uk/uksi/2012/1208/contents/made *Non-print*

The Air Navigation (Restriction of Flying) (Southend-on-Sea) Regulations 2012 No. 2012/83. - Enabling power: S.I. 2009/3015, art. 161. - Issued: 18.01.2012. Made: 11.01.2012. Coming into force: 26.05.2012. Effect: None. Territorial extent & classification: E. Local. - Available at http://www.legislation.gov.uk/uksi/2012/83/contents/made
Non-print

The Air Navigation (Restriction of Flying) (Southport) Regulations 2012 No. 2012/891. - Enabling power: S.I. 2009/3015, art. 161. - Issued: 26.03.2012. Made: 15.03.2012. Coming into force: 08.09.2012. Effect: None. Territorial extent & classification: E. Local. - Available at http://www.legislation.gov.uk/uksi/2012/891/contents/made
Non-print

The Air Navigation (Restriction of Flying) (State Opening of Parliament) Regulations 2012 No. 2012/906. - Enabling power: S.I. 2009/3015, art. 161. - Issued: 26.03.2012. Made: 19.03.2012. Coming into force: 09.05.2012. Effect: None. Territorial extent & classification: E. Local. - Available at http://www.legislation.gov.uk/uksi/2012/906/contents/made
Non-print

The Air Navigation (Restriction of Flying) (Stonehenge) Regulations 2012 No. 2012/152. - Enabling power: S.I. 2009/3015, art. 161. - Issued: 26.01.2012. Made: 20.01.2012. Coming into force: 20.06.2012. Effect: None. Territorial extent & classification: E. Local. - Available at http://www.legislation.gov.uk/uksi/2012/152/contents/made
Non-print

The Air Navigation (Restriction of Flying) (Stratford) Regulations 2012 No. 2012/1598. - Enabling power: S.I. 2009/3015, art. 161. - Issued: 26.06.2012. Made: 18.06.2012. Coming into force: 19.06.2012. Effect: None. Territorial extent & classification: E. Local. - Revoked by SI 2012/1632 (Non-print). - Available at http://www.legislation.gov.uk/uksi/2012/1598/contents/made
Non-print

The Air Navigation (Restriction of Flying) (Stratford) (Revocation) Regulations 2012 No. 2012/1632. - Enabling power: S.I. 2009/3015, art. 161. - Issued: 28.06.2012. Made: 19.06.2012 at 17.19 hours. Coming into force: With immediate effect. Effect: S.I. 2012/1598 revoked. Territorial extent & classification: E. Local. - Available at http://www.legislation.gov.uk/uksi/2012/1632/contents/made
Non-print

The Air Navigation (Restriction of Flying) (Sunderland) Regulations 2012 No. 2012/195. - Enabling power: S.I. 2009/3015, art. 161. - Issued: 01.02.2012. Made: 26.01.2012. Coming into force: 21.07.2012. Effect: None. Territorial extent & classification: E. Local. - Available at http://www.legislation.gov.uk/uksi/2012/195/contents/made
Non-print

The Air Navigation (Restriction of Flying) (The Thames Diamond Jubilee Pageant) Regulations 2012 No. 2012/908. - Enabling power: S.I. 2009/3015, art. 161. - Issued: 26.03.2012. Made: 15.03.2012. Coming into force: 03.06.2012. Effect: None. Territorial extent & classification: E. Local. - Available at http://www.legislation.gov.uk/uksi/2012/908/contents/made
Non-print

The Air Navigation (Restriction of Flying) (Tottenham Court Road, London) Regulations 2012 No. 2012/1209. - Enabling power: S.I. 2009/3015, art. 161. - Issued: 08.05.2012. Made: 27.04.2012 at 14.22 hours. Coming into force: With immediate effect. Effect: None. Territorial extent & classification: E. Local. - Revoked by S.I. 2012/1210 (Non-print). - Available at http://www.legislation.gov.uk/uksi/2012/1209/contents/made
Non-print

The Air Navigation (Restriction of Flying) (Tottenham Court Road, London) (Revocation) Regulations 2012 No. 2012/1210. - Enabling power: S.I. 2009/3015, art. 161. - Issued: 08.05.2012. Made: 27.04.2012 at 15.45 hours. Coming into force: With immediate effect. Effect: S.I. 2012/1209 revoked. Territorial extent & classification: E. Local. - Available at http://www.legislation.gov.uk/uksi/2012/1210/contents/made
Non-print

The Air Navigation (Restriction of Flying) (Trooping the Colour) (Amendment) Regulations 2012 No. 2012/1061. - Enabling power: S.I. 2009/3015, art. 161. - Issued: 16.04.2012. Made: 10.04.2012. Coming into force: 16.06.2012. Effect: None. Territorial extent & classification: E. Local. - Available at http://www.legislation.gov.uk/uksi/2012/1061/contents/made
Non-print

The Air Navigation (Restriction of Flying) (Trooping the Colour) Regulations 2012 No. 2012/490. - Enabling power: S.I. 2009/3015, art. 161. - Issued: 29.02.2012. Made: 23.02.2012. Coming into force: 16.06.2012. Effect: None. Territorial extent & classification: E. Local. - Available at http://www.legislation.gov.uk/uksi/2012/490/contents/made
Non-print

The Air Navigation (Restriction of Flying) (Wales Rally GB) Regulations 2012 No. 2012/1638. - Enabling power: S.I. 2009/3015, art. 161. - Issued: 29.06.2012. Made: 20.06.2012. Coming into force: 14.09.2012. Effect: None. Territorial extent & classification: E. Local. - Available at http://www.legislation.gov.uk/uksi/2012/1638/contents/made
Non-print

The Air Navigation (Restriction of Flying) (Weston Park) Regulations 2012 No. 2012/488. - Enabling power: S.I. 2009/3015, art. 161. - Issued: 29.02.2012. Made: 10.02.2012. Coming into force: 17.08.2012. Effect: None. Territorial extent & classification: E. Local. - Available at http://www.legislation.gov.uk/uksi/2012/488/contents/made
Non-print

The Air Navigation (Restriction of Flying) (West Wales) Regulations 2012 No. 2012/1207. - Enabling power: S.I. 2009/3015, art. 161. - Issued: 08.05.2012. Made: 30.04.2012. Coming into force: 03.07.2012. Effect: None. Territorial extent & classification: E. Local. - Available at http://www.legislation.gov.uk/uksi/2012/1207/contents/made *Non-print*

The Air Navigation (Restriction of Flying) (Wimbledon) Regulations 2012 No. 2012/708. - Enabling power: S.I. 2009/3015, art. 161. - Issued: 14.03.2012. Made: 06.03.2012. Coming into force: 25.06.2012. Effect: None. Territorial extent & classification: E. Local. - Available at http://www.legislation.gov.uk/uksi/2012/708/contents/made *Non-print*

The Civil Aviation (Air Travel Organisers' Licensing) (Amendment) Regulations 2012 No. 2012/1134. - Enabling power: Civil Aviation Act 1982, ss. 2 (3), 7 (1) (2), 71, 71A, sch. 1, para.15; sch. 13, part 2, part 3, paras 1, 2. - Issued: 30.04.2012. Made: 23.04.2012. Laid: 25.04.2012. Coming into force: 29.04.2012. Effect: S.I. 2012/1017 amended. Territorial extent & classification: E/W/S/NI. General. - This Statutory Instrument has been made in consequence of defects in S.I. 2012/1017 (ISBN 9780111523520) and is being issued free of charge to all known recipients of that Statutory Instrument. - 4p.: 30 cm. - 978-0-11-152377-3 £4.00

The Civil Aviation (Air Travel Organisers' Licensing) Regulations 2012 No. 2012/1017. - Enabling power: Civil Aviation Act 1982, ss. 2 (3), 7 (1) (2), 71, 71A, sch. 1, para.15; sch. 13, part 2, part 3, paras 1, 2. - Issued: 10.04.2012. Made: 02.04.2012. Laid: 04.04.2012. Coming into force: 30.04.2012 for all regs except reg 10 (f) & 30.04.2019 for reg 10 (f). Effect: S.I. 2007/2999 partially revoked & S.I. 1995/1054; 1996/1390; 1997/2912; 2003/1741 revoked (30.04.2012). Territorial extent & classification: E/W/S/NI. General. - With correction slip dated May 2012. - 32p.: 30 cm. - 978-0-11-152352-0 £5.75

Civil aviation: Aviation security

The Policing of Aerodromes (Belfast International Airport) Order 2012 No. 2012/837. - Enabling power: Aviation Security Act 1982, s. 25AA (2). - Issued: 22.03.2012. Made: 13.03.2012. Laid: 19.03.2012. Coming into force: 16.04.2012. Effect: S.I. 2010/575 revoked. Territorial extent & classification: NI. General. - This Statutory Instrument is being made for the same purposes as, and replaces, SI 2010/575 (ISBN 9780111494639) and is being issued free of charge to all known recipients of that instrument. - 2p.: 30 cm. - 978-0-11-152245-5 £4.00

Civil contingencies, England and Wales

The Civil Contingencies Act 2004 (Contingency Planning) (Amendment) Regulations 2012 No. 2012/624. - Enabling power: Civil Contingencies Act 2004, ss. 2 (3) (5), 6 (1), 17 (6). - Issued: 06.03.2012. Made: 29.02.2012. Laid: 06.03.2012. Coming into force: 01.04.2012. Effect: S.I. 2005/2042 amended. Territorial extent & classification: E/W/NI [though in relation to NI, the amendments do not alter the current effect of the Principal Regs]. General. - 8p.: 30 cm. - 978-0-11-152114-4 £4.00

Civil contingencies, Northern Ireland

The Civil Contingencies Act 2004 (Contingency Planning) (Amendment) Regulations 2012 No. 2012/624. - Enabling power: Civil Contingencies Act 2004, ss. 2 (3) (5), 6 (1), 17 (6). - Issued: 06.03.2012. Made: 29.02.2012. Laid: 06.03.2012. Coming into force: 01.04.2012. Effect: S.I. 2005/2042 amended. Territorial extent & classification: E/W/NI [though in relation to NI, the amendments do not alter the current effect of the Principal Regs]. General. - 8p.: 30 cm. - 978-0-11-152114-4 £4.00

Civil partnership

The Civil Partnership (Registration Abroad and Certificates) (Amendment) Order 2012 No. 2012/3063. - Enabling power: Civil Partnership Act 2004, ss. 210, 240, 241, 244. - Issued: 19.12.2012. Made: 12.12.2012. Laid: 19.12.2012. Coming into force: 09.01.2013. Effect: S.I. 2005/2761 amended. Territorial extent & classification: E/W/S/NI. General. - 2p.: 30 cm. - 978-0-11-153231-7 £4.00

The Civil Partnerships Act 2004 (Overseas Relationships) Order 2012 No. 2012/2976. - Enabling power: Civil Partnership Act 2004, s. 213. - Issued: 04.12.2012. Made: 21.11.2012. Laid: 03.12.2012. Coming into force: 31.01.2013. Effect: 2004 c. 33 amended. Territorial extent & classification: E/W/S/NI. General. - 8p.: 30 cm. - 978-0-11-153135-8 £5.75

Civil partnership, England and Wales

The Registration of Civil Partnerships (Fees) (Amendment) Order 2012 No. 2012/761. - Enabling power: Civil Partnership Act 2004, ss. 34 (1), 258 (2). - Issued: 13.03.2012. Made: 08.03.2012. Laid: 09.03.2012. Coming into force: 01.04.2012. Effect: S.I. 2005/1996, 3167 amended. Territorial extent & classification: E/W. General. - 4p.: 30 cm. - 978-0-11-152174-8 £4.00

Clean air, England

The Smoke Control Areas (Authorised Fuels) (England) (No.2) Regulations 2012 No. 2012/2281. - Enabling power: Clean Air Act 1993, s. 20 (6). - Issued: 10.09.2012. Made: 05.09.2012. Laid: 07.09.2012. Coming into force: 01.10.2012. Effect: S.I. 2012/814 revoked. Territorial extent & classification: E. General. - 16p.: 30 cm. - 978-0-11-152864-8 £5.75

The Smoke Control Areas (Authorised Fuels) (England) Regulations 2012 No. 2012/814. - Enabling power: Clean Air Act 1993, ss. 20 (6), 63 (1). - Issued: 16.03.2012. Made: 13.03.2012. Laid: 16.03.2012. Coming into force: 06.04.2012. Effect: S.I. 2008/514, 2342; 2009/2191; 2010/576; 2011/715, 2105 revoked. Territorial extent & classification: E. General. - Revoked by SI 2012/2281 (ISBN 9780111528648). - 16p.: 30 cm. - 978-0-11-152220-2 £5.75

The Smoke Control Areas (Exempted Fireplaces) (England) (No. 2) Order 2012 No. 2012/2282. - Enabling power: Clean Air Act 1993, s. 21. - Issued: 10.09.2012. Made: 05.09.2012. Laid: 07.09.2012. Coming into force: 01.10.2012. Effect: S.I. 2012/815 revoked. Territorial extent & classification: E. General. - 72p.: 30 cm. - 978-0-11-152865-5 £13.75

The Smoke Control Areas (Exempted Fireplaces) (England) Order 2012 No. 2012/815. - Enabling power: Clean Air Act 1993, s. 21. - Issued: 16.03.2012. Made: 13.03.2012. Laid: 16.03.2012. Coming into force: 06.04.2012. Effect: S.I. 2011/2106 revoked. Territorial extent & classification: E. General. - Revoked by SI 2012/2282 (ISBN 9780111528655). - 64p.: 30 cm. - 978-0-11-152223-3 £10.75

Clean air, Wales

The Smoke Control Areas (Exempted Fireplaces) (Wales) Order 2012 No. 2012/244 (W.38). - Enabling power: Clean Air Act 1993, s. 21. - Issued: 09.03.2012. Made: 01.02.2012. Laid before the National Assembly for Wales: 02.02.2012. Coming into force: 27.02.2012. Effect: S.I. 2011/38 (W.13) revoked. Territorial extent & classification: W. General. - In English and Welsh. Welsh title: Gorchymyn Ardaloedd Rheoli Mwg (Lleoedd Tân Esempt) (Cymru) 2012. - 132p.: 30 cm. - 978-0-348-10557-5 £20.00

Climate change

The Greenhouse Gas Emissions Trading Scheme (Amendment) (Charging Schemes) Regulations 2012 No. 2012/2788. - Enabling power: European Communities Act 1972, s. 2 (2). - Issued: 08.11.2012. Made: 06.11.2012. Laid: 12.11.2012. Coming into force: 03.12.2012. Effect: 1995 c. 25; 1999 c. 24; S.R. 2010/151 amended & S.I. 2005/925; 2011/2911; S.R. 2010/92 partially revoked. Territorial extent & classification: E/W/S/NI. General. - EC note: These regulations deal with matters arising from the duty to transpose into UK law Directive 2003/87/EC and amending Council Directive 96/61/EC as amended in particular by Directives 2008/101/EC and 2009/29/EC. Under the emissions trading system established by those Directives, an overall cap is set for emissions of greenhouse gases from specified activities. Under the amendments made by Directive 2008/101/EC the system covers emissions from aviation activities as well as from stationary installations. A new phase of the system (phase 3) begins on 1 January 2013. - 12p.: 30 cm. - 978-0-11-153056-6 £5.75

The Greenhouse Gas Emissions Trading Scheme Regulations 2012 No. 2012/3038. - Enabling power: Pollution Prevention and Control Act 1999, ss. 2, 7 (9), sch.1, & European Communities Act 1972, s. 2 (2). - Issued: 12.12.2012. Made: 05.12.2012. Laid: 10.12.2012. Coming into force: 01.01.2013. Effect: S.I. 2005/2903; 2010/1513; 2011/1506, 2911; S.R. 2010/92 partially revoked & S.I. 2005/ 925; 2006/737; 2007/465, 1096, 3433; 2009/3130; 2010/1996; 2011/765 revoked. Territorial extent & classification: E/W/S/NI. General. - EC note: These regulations implement Directive 2003/87/EC establishing a scheme for greenhouse gas emission allowance trading within the Community and amending Council Directive 96/61/EC. In particular, they implement the amendments to the Directive made by Directive 2009/29/EC. - 92p.: 30 cm. - 978-0-11-153186-0 £15.50

The Motor Fuel (Road Vehicle and Mobile Machinery) Greenhouse Gas Emissions Reporting Regulations 2012 No. 2012/3030. - Enabling power: European Communities Act 1972, s. 2 (2), sch. 2, para. 1A. - Issued: 12.12.2012. Made: 05.12.2012. Laid: 06.12.2012. Coming into force: 01.01.2013. Effect: None. Territorial extent & classification: E/W/S/NI. General. - EC note: These regulations transpose arts 7a to 7e and Annex IV of Directive 98/70/EC relating to the quality of petrol and diesel fuels as inserted by Directive 2009/30/EC. - 20p.: 30 cm. - 978-0-11-153174-7 £5.75

Climate change: Emissions trading

The CRC Energy Efficiency Scheme (Allocation of Allowances for Payment) Regulations 2012 No. 2012/1386. - Enabling power: Finance Act 2008, s. 21 (1) (2) (3). - Issued: 28.05.2012. Made: 23.05.2012. Coming into force: In accord. with reg. 1. Effect: None. Territorial extent & classification: E/W/S/NI. General. - Supersedes draft SI (ISBN 9780111522998) issued on 29.03.2012. - 8p.: 30 cm. - 978-0-11-152483-1 £5.75

Climate change levy

The Climate Change Agreements (Administration) Regulations 2012 No. 2012/1976. - Enabling power: Finance Act 2000, sch. 6, paras 52D to 52F, 146. - Issued: 06.08.2012. Made: 25.07.2012. Laid: 30.07.2012. Coming into force: 01.10.2012. Effect: None. Territorial extent & classification: E/W/S/NI. General. - 12p.: 30 cm. - 978-0-11-152785-6 £5.75

The Climate Change Agreements (Eligible Facilities) Regulations 2012 No. 2012/2999. - Enabling power: Finance Act 2000, sch. 6, paras 50 (3) to (5), 146. - Issued: 06.12.2012. Made: 29.11.2012. Laid: 04.12.2012. Coming into force: 01.01.2013. Effect: S.I. 2001/662; 2006/60, 1931; 2009/2458 revoked with saving. Territorial extent & classification: E/W/S/NI. General. - 12p.: 30 cm. - 978-0-11-153151-8 £5.75

The Climate Change Levy (General) (Amendment) (No. 2) Regulations 2012 No. 2012/3049. - Enabling power: Finance Act 2000, sch. 6, paras 22, 146 (7). - Issued: 10.12.2012. Made: 06.12.2012. Laid before the House of Commons: 07.12.2012. Coming into force: 01.01.2013. Effect: S.I. 2001/838 amended. Territorial extent & classification: E/W/S/NI. General. - 2p.: 30 cm. - 978-0-11-153199-0 £4.00

The Climate Change Levy (General) (Amendment) Regulations 2012 No. 2012/943. - Enabling power: Finance Act 2000, s. 30, sch. 6, paras 22, 43 (A) (8) (9), 62 (1) (ca) (cb), 125 (1), 146 (7) (c). - Issued: 28.03.2012. Made: 27.03.2012. Laid: 27.03.2012. Coming into force: 01.04.2012. Effect: S.I. 2001/838 amended. Territorial extent & classification: E/W/S/NI. General. - 4p.: 30 cm. - 978-0-11-152293-6 £4.00

Coast protection, England

The Designation of Features (Appeals) (England) Regulations 2012 No. 2012/1945. - Enabling power: Flood and Water Management Act 2010, ss. 30, 48 (2), sch. 1, para. 15. - Issued: 26.07.2012. Made: 23.07.2012. Coming into force: In accord. with reg. 1 (b). Effect: None. Territorial extent & classification: E. General. - 4p.: 30 cm. - 978-0-11-152770-2 £4.00

The Designation of Features (Notices) (England) Regulations 2012 No. 2012/1693. - Enabling power: Flood and Water Management Act 2010, ss. 30, 48 (2), sch. 1, para. 16. - Issued: 03.07.2012. Made: 27.06.2012. Laid: 29.06.2012. Coming into force: 25.07.2012. Effect: None. Territorial extent & classification: E. General. - 4p.: 30 cm. - 978-0-11-152609-5 £4.00

Coast protection, England and Wales

The Flood and Water Management Act 2010 (Commencement No. 6 and Transitional Provisions) Order 2012 No. 2012/879 (C.25). - Enabling power: Flood and Water Management Act 2010, ss. 48 (2), 49 (3) (h) (i) (6). Bringing into operation various provisions of this Act on 06.04.2012, in accord. with art. 3. - Issued: 22.03.2012. Made: 19.03.2012. Effect: None. Territorial extent & classification: E/W. General. - 8p.: 30 cm. - 978-0-11-152259-2 £5.75

The Flood and Water Management Act 2010 (Commencement No. 7) Order 2012 No. 2012/2000 (C.79). - Enabling power: Flood and Water Management Act 2010, s. 49 (3) (h) (i). Bringing into operation various provisions of this Act on 01.08.2012, in accord. with art. 2. - Issued: 01.08.2012. Made: 30.07.2012. Effect: None. Territorial extent & classification: E/W. General. - 8p.: 30 cm. - 978-0-11-152791-7 £5.75

Coast protection, Wales

The Designation of Features (Appeals) (Wales) Regulations 2012 No. 2012/1819 (W.228). - Enabling power: Flood and Water Management Act 2010, ss. 30, 48 (2), sch. 1, para. 15. - Issued: 02.08.2012. Made: 10.07.2012. Coming into force: 11.07.2012, in accord. with reg. 1 (1). Effect: None. Territorial extent & classification: W. General. - In English and Welsh. Welsh title: Rheoliadau Dynodi Nodweddion (Apelau) (Cymru) 2012. - 8p.: 30 cm. - 978-0-348-10642-8 £4.00

The Designation of Features (Notices) (Wales) Regulations 2012 No. 2012/1692 (W.218). - Enabling power: Flood and Water Management Act 2010, ss. 30, 48 (2), sch. 1, para. 16. - Issued: 19.07.2012. Made: 28.06.2012. Laid before the National Assembly for Wales: 29.06.2012. Coming into force: 20.07.2012. Effect: None. Territorial extent & classification: W. General. - In English and Welsh. Welsh title: Rheoliadau Dynodi Nodweddion (Hysbysiadau) (Cymru) 2012. - 4p.: 30 cm. - 978-0-348-10635-0 £4.00

Coinage

The Trial of the Pyx (Amendment) Order 2012 No. 2012/2746. - Enabling power: Coinage Act 1971, s. 8 (2) (3). - Issued: 12.11.2012. Made: 07.11.2012. Coming into force: 08.11.2012. Effect: S.I. 1998/1764 amended. Territorial extent & classification: E/W/S/NI. General. - 4p.: 30 cm. - 978-0-11-153060-3 £4.00

Commons, Wales

The Commons Act 2006 (Commencement No. 2, Transitional Provisions and Savings) (Wales) Order 2012 No. 2012/739 (W.99) (C.19). - Enabling power: Commons Act 2006, ss. 56 (1), 59 (1). Bringing into operation various provisions of this Act on 01.04.2012, in accord. with arts. 2, 3. - Issued: 30.03.2012. Made: 07.03.2012. Effect: None. Territorial extent & classification: W. General. - In English & Welsh. Welsh title: Gorchymyn Deddf Tiroedd Comin 2006 (Cychwyn Rhif 2, Darpariaethau Trosiannol ac Arbedion) (Cymru) 2012. - 12p.: 30 cm. - 978-0-348-10573-5 £5.75

The Commons Act 2006 (Commencement No. 3) (Wales) Order 2012 No. 2012/806 (W.113) (C.21). - Enabling power: Commons Act 2006, s. 56 (1). Bringing into operation various provisions of this Act on 01.04.2012, in accord. with art. 2. - Issued: 05.04.2012. Made: 09.03.2012. Effect: None. Territorial extent & classification: W. General. - In English & Welsh. Welsh title: Gorchymyn Deddf Tiroedd Comin 2006 (Cychwyn Rhif 2) (Cymru) 2012. - 4p.: 30 cm. - 978-0-348-10587-2 £4.00

The Commons (Deregistration and Exchange Orders) (Interim Arrangements) (Wales) Regulations 2012 No. 2012/740 (W.100). - Enabling power: Commons Act 2006, ss. 17 (3), 24 (1) (2) (m), 59 (1). - Issued: 30.03.2012. Made: 07.03.2012. Laid before the National Assembly for Wales: 08.03.2012. Coming into force: 01.04.2012. Effect: None. Territorial extent & classification: W. General. - In English & Welsh. Welsh title: Rheoliadau Tiroedd Comin (Gorchmynion Dadgofrestru a Chyfnewid) (Trefniadau Interim) (Cymru) 2012. - 12p.: 30 cm. - 978-0-348-10574-2 £5.75

The Deregistration and Exchange of Common Land and Greens (Procedure) (Wales) Regulations 2012 No. 2012/738 (W.98). - Enabling power: Commons Act 2006, s. 17 (10), 24 (1) (2) (5), 59 (1). - Issued: 30.03.2012. Made: 07.03.2012. Laid before the National Assembly for Wales: 08.03.2012. Coming into force: 01.04.2012. Effect: None. Territorial extent & classification: W. General. - In English & Welsh. Welsh title: Rheoliadau Dadgofrestru a Chyfnewid Tir Comin a Meysydd Tref neu Bentref (Gweithdrefn) (Cymru) 2012. - 16p.: 30 cm. - 978-0-348-10575-9 £5.75

The Works on Common Land, etc. (Procedure) (Wales) Regulations 2012 No. 2012/737 (W.97). - Enabling power: Commons Act 2006, ss. 39 (6), 40, 59 (1). - Issued: 28.03.2012. Made: 07.03.2012. Laid before the National Assembly for Wales: 08.03.2012. Coming into force: 01.04.2012. Effect: None. Territorial extent & classification: W. General. - In English and Welsh. Welsh language title: Rheoliadau Gwaith ar Diroedd Comin, etc. (Gweithdrefn) (Cymru) 2012. - 16p.: 30 cm. - 978-0-348-10566-7 £5.75

Community infrastructure levy, England and Wales

The Community Infrastructure Levy (Amendment) Regulations 2012 No. 2012/2975. - Enabling power: Planning Act 2008, ss. 205 (1) (2), 209 (5), 211 (5) (6), 214 (2), 216 (1) (4) (a) (7) (d) (f), 217 (1) to (3), 220 (1) (2) (a) (d) (e) (j) (3), 222 (1). - Issued: 30.11.2012. Made: 28.11.2012. Coming into force: In accord. with reg. 1. Effect: S.I. 2010/948 amended. Territorial extent & classification: E/W. General. - Supersedes draft SI (ISBN 9780111529270) issued on 15.10.2012. - 12p.: 30 cm. - 978-0-11-153134-1 £5.75

The Localism Act 2011 (Commencement No. 2 and Transitional and Saving Provision) Order 2012 No. 2012/57 (C. 2). - Enabling power: Localism Act 2011, ss. 37, 240 (2) (7) (8). Bringing into operation various provisions of the 2011 Act on 15.01.2012; 31.01.2012. - Issued: 16.01.2012. Made: 11.01.2012. Effect: None. Territorial extent & classification: E/W and S in part. General. - 12p.: 30 cm. - 978-0-11-151911-0 £5.75

Companies

The Accounting Standards (Prescribed Bodies) (United States of America and Japan) Regulations 2012 No. 2012/2405. - Enabling power: Companies Act 2006, ss. 464 (1) (3), 1292 (1) (a). - Issued: 20.09.2012. Made: 17.09.2012. Coming into force: 01.10.2012. Effect: None. Territorial extent & classification: E/W/S/NI. General. - 2p.: 30 cm. - 978-0-11-152892-1 £4.00

The Community Interest Company (Amendment) Regulations 2012 No. 2012/2335. - Enabling power: Companies (Audit, Investigations and Community Enterprise) Act 2004, ss. 34 (2) (3) (c), 62 (2). - Issued: 14.09.2012. Made: 10.09.2012. Coming into force: 01.10.2012. Effect: S.I. 2005/1788 amended. Territorial extent & classification: E/W/S/NI. General. - Supersedes draft SI (ISBN 9780111525494) issued 18.06.2012. - 4p.: 30 cm. - 978-0-11-152875-4 £4.00

The Companies Act 2006 (Amendment of Part 23) (Investment Companies) Regulations 2012 No. 2012/952. - Enabling power: European Communities Act 1972, s. 2 (2). - Issued: 02.04.2012. Made: 27.03.2012. Coming into force: 06.04.2012. Effect: 2006 c. 46 amended & 2009 c. 10; 2010 c. 4 partially repealed. Territorial extent & classification: E/W/S/NI. General. - Supersedes draft S.I. (ISBN 9780111519981) issued 10.02.2012. - 4p.: 30 cm. - 978-0-11-152317-9 £4.00

The Companies and Limited Liability Partnerships (Accounts and Audit Exemptions and Change of Accounting Framework) Regulations 2012 No. 2012/2301. - Enabling power: European Communities Act 1972, s. 2 (2) & Limited Liability Partnerships Act 2000, ss. 15, 17 & Companies Act 2006, ss. 468, 473, 484, 1043, 1104 (2) (a), 1105 (2) (d), 1108 (2) (b), 1292 (1) (c). - Issued: 11.09.2012. Made: 06.09.2012. Laid: 07.09.2012. Coming into force: 01.10.2012. Effect: 2006 c. 46; S.I. 2008/1911; 2009/1803, 1804, 2436 amended. Territorial extent & classification: E/W/S/NI. General. - With correction slip dated September 2012. - 16p.: 30 cm. - 978-0-11-152872-3 £5.75

The Statutory Auditors (Amendment of Companies Act 2006 and Delegation of Functions etc) Order 2012 No. 2012/1741. - Enabling power: European Communities Act 1972, s. 2 (2) (a) (b) & Companies Act 2006, ss. 464 (1) (3), 504 (1) (b) (ii), 525 (1) (a) (ii), 1228 (1) (2) (6), 1231 (4), 1239, 1252 (1) (2) (b) (4) (a) (5) (6) (7) (8), 1253 (4), 1292 (1) (b) (c) (2), sch. 13, paras 7 (3), 11 (2) (3) (a). - Issued: 06.07.2012. Made: 02.07.2012. Coming into force: 02.07.2012. Effect: 2006 c.46 amended & S.I. 1996/1975; 2005/590, 672; 2007/865, 3494; 2008/629, 1911; 2009/209, 2436; 2011/99 amended & S.I. 2007/3534; 2008/496, 651 revoked. Territorial extent & classification: E/W/S/NI. General. - Supersedes draft (ISBN 97801111524404) issued 17.05.2012. EC note: Part 2 of the Order amends the 2006 Act, it re-implements obligations in Directive 2006/43/EC on statutory audits of annual accounts and consolidated accounts and makes provision for matters which arise out of or relate to these obligations. - 20p.: 30 cm. - 978-0-11-152631-6 £5.75

The Supervision of Accounts and Reports (Prescribed Body) and Companies (Defective Accounts and Directors' Reports) (Authorised Persons) Order 2012 No. 2012/1439. - Enabling power: Companies (Audit, Investigations and Community Enterprise) Act 2004, ss. 14 (1) (5) (8), 15E & Companies Act 2006, ss. 457 (1) (2) (5) (6), 462, 1292 (1) (b) (c). - Issued: 12.06.2012. Made: 31.05.2012. Laid: 11.06.2012. Coming into force: 02.07.2012. Effect: 2004 c.27; 2006 c. 46 amended & S.I. 2007/2583 so far as unrevoked (revoked with savings by SI 2008/623); 2008/623 revoked. Territorial extent & classification: E/W/S/NI. General. - 8p.: 30 cm. - 978-0-11-152504-3 £4.00

Competition

The Competition Act 1998 (Public Policy Exclusion) Order 2012 No. 2012/710. - Enabling power: Competition Act 1998, sch. 3, paras. 7 (1) (2). - Issued: 08.03.2012. Made: 06.03.2012. Laid: 07.03.2012. Coming into force: 28.03.2012. Effect: None. Territorial extent & classification: E/W/S/NI. General. - 4p.: 30 cm. - 978-0-11-152154-0 £4.00

The Enterprise Act 2002 (Merger Fees) (Amendment and Revocation) Order 2012 No. 2012/1878. - Enabling power: Enterprise Act 2002, ss. 121, 124 (2). - Issued: 20.07.2012. Made: 17.07.2012. Laid: 18.07.2012. Coming into force: 01.10.2012. Effect: S.I. 2003/1370 amended & S.I. 2005/3558 revoked. Territorial extent & classification: E/W/S/NI. General. - 4p.: 30 cm. - 978-0-11-152737-5 £4.00

Constitutional law

The Forestry Commissioners (Climate Change Functions) (Scotland) Order 2012 (Consequential Modifications) Order 2012 No. 2012/2855 (S.1). - Enabling power: Scotland Act 1998, ss. 104, 112 (1), 113 (2) (4) (5) (7). - Issued: 14.11.2012. Made: 07.11.2012. Coming into force: 08.11.2012. In accord. with art. 1 (2). Effect: 1967 c.10 modified. Territorial extent & classification: S. General. - Supersedes draft SI (ISBN 9780111526705) issued on 16.07.2012. - 4p.: 30 cm. - 978-0-11-153079-5 £4.00

The Glasgow Commonwealth Games Act 2008 (Ticket Touting Offence) (England and Wales and Northern Ireland) Order 2012 No. 2012/1852. - Enabling power: Scotland Act 1998, ss. 104, 112 (1), 113 (1) (2) (3). - Issued: 26.07.2012. Made: 16.07.2012. Laid: 18.07.2012. Coming into force: 29.11.2012. Effect: None. Territorial extent & classification: E/W/S/NI. General. - 8p.: 30 cm. - 978-0-11-152722-1 £4.00

The Housing (Scotland) Act 2010 (Consequential Provisions and Modifications) Order 2012 No. 2012/700. - Enabling power: Scotland Act 1998, ss. 104, 112 (1), 113 (2) (5), 114 (1). - Issued: 13.03.2012. Made: 05.03.2012. Coming into force: 01.04.2012. Effect: 1975 c. 24; 1985 c. 69; 1986 c. 45; 1992 c. 12; 1994 c. 23; 2002 c. 40; 2003 c. 14; 2007 c. 3; 2010 c. 4 & S.I. 1987/1968; 1999/584; 2001/1201; 2004/692; 2005/1379; 2006/213, 214, 264; 2008/346; 2009/214, 1801 amended & S.I. 2008/948; 2009/1941 partially revoked. Territorial extent & classification: UK. General. - Supersedes draft S.I. (ISBN 9780111519080) issued 18.01.2012. - 8p.: 30 cm. - 978-0-11-152166-3 £5.75

The Northern Ireland Act 1998 (Devolution of Policing and Justice Functions) Order 2012 No. 2012/2595. - Enabling power: Northern Ireland Act 1998, ss. 86 (1), (3A) (4). - Issued: 24.10.2012. Made: 17.10.2012. Coming into force: In accord. with art. 1 (2). Effect: 1954 c.33 (NI),1993 c.8; 1999 c.33; 2003 c.6; 2006 c.48; 2007 c.30; 2009 c.26; 2010 c.4, 17, 23, 25 & S.I. 1981/228 (NI. 8); 1994/426 (NI.1); 1996/3159 (NI.23); 2000/1787; 2005/2078; 2007/912 (NI.6); 2009/2615 amended. Territorial extent & classification: NI. General. - Supersedes draft SI (ISBN 9780111525203) issued 14.06.2012. - 16p.: 30 cm. - 978-0-11-152970-6 £5.75

The Partnership Council for Wales (Local Health Boards and National Health Service Trusts) Order 2012 No. 2012/746 (W.101). - Enabling power: Government of Wales Act 2006, s. 72 (5) (e). - Issued: 28.03.2012. Made: 07.03.2012. Laid before the National Assembly for Wales: 09.03.2012. Coming into force: 03.04.2012. Effect: None. Territorial extent & classification: W. General. - In English and Welsh. Welsh title: Gorchymyn Cyngor Partneriaeth Cymru (Byrddau Iechyd Lleol ac Ymddiriedolaethau Gwasanaeth Iechyd Gwladol) 2012. - 4p.: 30 cm. - 978-0-348-10569-8 £4.00

The Scotland Act 2012 (Commencement No. 1) Order 2012 No. 2012/1710 (C.67). - Enabling power: Scotland Act 2012, s. 44 (5). Bringing into operation various provisions of the 2012 Act on 03.07.2012; 15.10.2012. - Issued: 09.07.2012. Made: 29.06.2012. Effect: None. Territorial extent & classification: E/W/S/NI. General. - 4p.: 30 cm. - 978-0-11-152639-2 £4.00

The Scotland Act 2012 (Commencement No. 2) Order 2012 No. 2012/2516 (C.99). - Enabling power: Scotland Act 2012, s. 44 (5). Bringing into operation various provisions of the 2012 Act on 31.10.2012, 01.08.2013. - Issued: 10.10.2012. Made: 03.10.2012. Effect: None. Territorial extent & classification: E/W/S/NI. General. - 4p.: 30 cm. - 978-0-11-152910-2 £4.00

The Scottish Administration (Offices) Order 2005 No. 2012/3073. - Enabling power: Scotland Act 1998, s. 126 (8) (b). - Issued: 19.12.2012. Made: 12.12.2012. Laid before Parliament: 19.12.2012. Laid before the Scottish Parliament: 19.12.2012. Coming into force: In accord. with art. 1 (2) to (4). Effect: S.I. 1999/1127 partially revoked & S.I. 2005/1467 revoked. Territorial extent & classification: E/W/S/NI. General. - 4p.: 30 cm. - 978-0-11-153245-4 £4.00

Consumer credit

The Consumer Credit (Green Deal) Regulations 2012 No. 2012/2798. - Enabling power: Consumer Credit Act 1974, ss. 55 (1), 60 (1), 77A (2), 95 (1), 95B (1) (b) (3) (c), 182 (2), 189 (1). - Issued: 16.11.2012. Made: 07.11.2012. Laid: 09.11.2012. Coming into force: 28.01.2013. Effect: S.I. 1983/1553, 1564; 2004/1483; 2007/1167; 2010/1013, 1014 amended. Territorial extent & classification: E/W/S. General. - 8p.: 30 cm. - 978-0-11-153058-0 £5.75

The Consumer Credit (Total Charge for Credit) (Amendment) Regulations 2012 No. 2012/1745. - Enabling power: Consumer Credit Act 1974, ss. 20, 182 (2). - Issued: 09.07.2012. Made: 05.07.2012. Laid: 06.07.2012. Coming into force: 01.01.2013. Effect: S.I. 2010/1011 amended. Territorial extent & classification: E/W/S/NI. General. - EC note: These Regulations implement Directive 2011/90/EU amending Part II of Annex I to Directive 2008/48/EC. - 8p.: 30 cm. - 978-0-11-152636-1 £4.00

Consumer protection

The Consumer Rights (Payment Surcharges) Regulations 2012 No. 2012/3110. - Enabling power: European Communities Act 1972, s. 2 (2). - Issued: 21.12.2012. Made: 18.12.2012. Laid: 19.12.2012. Coming into force: 06.04.2013. Effect: None. Territorial extent & classification: E/W/S/NI. General. - 8p.: 30 cm. - 978-0-11-153276-8 £5.75

The Cosmetic Products (Safety) (Amendment) Regulations 2012 No. 2012/2263. - Enabling power: Consumer Protection Act 1987, s. 11. - Issued: 07.09.2012. Made: 02.09.2012. Laid: 05.09.2012. Coming into force: 31.10.2012. Effect: S.I. 2008/1284 amended. Territorial extent & classification: E/W/S/NI. General. - EC note: These Regs amend S.I. 2008/1284 (the Principal Regulations) to give effect to Council Directive 2011/84/EU amending Directive 76/768/EEC concerning cosmetic products for the purpose of adapting Annex III thereto to technical progress. The Principal Regulations implemented Council Directive 76/768/EEC on the approximation of the laws of the Member States relating to cosmetic products. - 4p.: 30 cm. - 978-0-11-152847-1 £4.00

The Customs Disclosure of Information and Miscellaneous Amendments Regulations 2012 No. 2012/1848. - Enabling power: European Communities Act 1972, s. 2 (2). - Issued: 17.07.2012. Made: 12.07.2012. Laid: 16.07.2012. Coming into force: 10.08.2012. Effect: S.I. 2002/1144; 2005/1803; 2006/3418; 2010/1554 amended. Territorial extent & classification: E/W/S/NI. General. - EC note: These Regulations creates an offence of the unauthorised disclosure of customs information which has been disclosed by a specified person listed in reg. 3 (2) to a market surveillance authority under art. 27 (2) of Regulation 765/2008 setting out the requirements for accreditation and market surveillance relating to the marketing of products and repealing Regulation 339/93/EEC. - 8p.: 30 cm. - 978-0-11-152712-2 £4.00

The Medical Devices (Amendment) Regulations 2012 No. 2012/1426. - Enabling power: European Communities Act 1972, s. 2 (2), sch. 2, para 1A & Consumer Protection 1987, s. 11. - Issued: 21.06.2012. Made: 29.05.2012. Laid: 11.06.2012. Coming into force: 01.07.2012. Effect: S.I. 2002/618 amended. Territorial extent & classification: E/W/S/NI. General. - EC note: These Regulations amend the Medical Devices Regulations 2002 to allow references to Council Directives 90/385/EEC & 93/42/EEC to include amendments by Directive 2007/47/EC. They also implement Commission Directive 2011/100/EU, which amends Council Directive 98/79/EC. - 4p.: 30 cm. - 978-0-11-152527-2 £4.00

The Product Safety Amendment and Revocation Regulations 2012 No. 2012/2963. - Enabling power: Consumer Protection Act 1987, s. 11. - Issued: 30.11.2012. Made: 24.11.2012. Laid: 28.11.2012. Coming into force: 06.04.2013. Effect: S.I. 2010/1554 amended & S.I. 1998/2406 revoked. Territorial extent & classification: E/W/S/NI. General. - 2p.: 30 cm. - 978-0-11-153130-3 £4.00

The Product Safety (Revocation) Regulations 2012 No. 2012/1815. - Enabling power: European Communities Act 1972, s. 2 (2) & Consumer Protection Act 1987, s. 11. - Issued: 13.07.2012. Made: 11.07.2012. Laid: 12.07.2012. Coming into force: 01.10.2012. Effect: S.I. 1987/1979; 1995/1629 revoked in part & S.I. 1972/1957; 1976/2; 1984/1802; 1987/1337; 1989/149, 2288; 1991/2693; 1992/2620, 2923 ; 1996/2756; 1997/2866; 2009/1347 revoked. Territorial extent & classification: E/W/S/NI. General. - 4p.: 30 cm. - 978-0-11-152679-8 £4.00

The Textile Products (Labelling and Fibre Composition) Regulations 2012 No. 2012/1102. - Enabling power: European Communities Act 1972, s. 2 (2), sch. 2, para. 1A. - Issued: 20.04.2012. Made: 17.04.2012. Laid: 18.04.2012. Coming into force: 08.05.2012. Effect: S.I. 1986/26; 1988/1350; 1994/450; 1998/1169; 2005/1401; 2008/6, 15; 2009/1034 revoked. Territorial extent & classification: E/W/S/NI. General. - EC note: These Regulations set out the enforcement provisions including the sanctions that will apply to Regulation (EU) no. 1007/2011 on textile fibres, related labelling and marking of fibre composition of textile products and repealing Council Directive 73/44/EEC & Directive 96/73/EC & 2008/121/EC. - 12p.: 30 cm. - 978-0-11-152363-6 £5.75

Contracting out, England

The Contracting Out (Local Authorities Social Services Functions) (England) (Amendment) Order 2012 No. 2012/3003. - Enabling power: Deregulation and Contracting Out Act 1994, ss. 69 (4), 70 (2) (4), 77 (1). - Issued: 06.12.2012. Made: 03.12.2012. Coming into force: 13.12.2012. Effect: S.I. 2011/1568 amended. Territorial extent & classification: E. General. - Supersedes draft SI (ISBN 9780111529331) issued 15.10.2012. - 2p.: 30 cm. - 978-0-11-153169-3 £4.00

Control of fuel and electricity

The Oil Stocking Order 2012 No. 2012/2862. - Enabling power: Energy Act 1976, s. 17 (2) (3) & European Communities Act 1972, s. 2 (2). - Issued: 23.11.2012. Made: 12.11.2012. Laid: 16.11.2012. Coming into force: 31.12.2012. Effect: S.I. 1976/2162; 1982/968; 1983/909 revoked with saving. Territorial extent & classification: E/W/S/NI. General. - 16p.: 30 cm. - 978-0-11-153082-5 £5.75

Copyright

The Copyright and Performances (Application to Other Countries) (Amendment) Order 2012 No. 2012/1754. - Enabling power: Copyright, Designs and Patents Act 1988, ss. 159. - Issued: 17.07.2012. Made: 10.07.2012. Laid: 17.07.2012. Coming into force: In accord. with art. 1. Effect: S.I. 2012/799 amended. Territorial extent & classification: E/W/S/NI. General. - 4p.: 30 cm. - 978-0-11-152689-7 £4.00

The Copyright and Performances (Application to Other Countries) Order 2012 No. 2012/799. - Enabling power: Copyright, Designs and Patents Act 1988, ss. 159, 208 & European Communities Act 1972, s. 2 (2). - Issued: 15.03.2012. Made: 14.03.2012. Laid: 15.03.2012. Coming into force: 06.04.2012. Effect: S.I. 2008/677; 2009/2745 revoked. Territorial extent & classification: E/W/S/NI. General. - 16p.: 30 cm. - 978-0-11-152228-8 £5.75

The Copyright (Repeal of the Copyright Act 2911) (Jersey) Order 2012 No. 2012/1753. - Enabling power: Copyright, Designs and Patents Act 1988, s. 170, sch. 1, para. 36 (3). - Issued: 17.07.2012. Made: 10.07.2012. Coming into force: In accord. with art. 1. Effect: 1911 c.46 repealed to the extent that it has effect in the Bailiwick of Jersey. Territorial extent & classification: E/W/S/NI. General. - 2p.: 30 cm. - 978-0-11-152690-3 £4.00

Coroners, England and Wales

The Coroners and Justice Act 2009 (Commencement No. 10) Order 2012 No. 2012/2374 (C.92). - Enabling power: Coroners and Justice Act 2009, ss. 176 (3), 182 (4) (5). Bringing into operation various provisions of the 2009 Act on 24.09.2012 & 08.10.2012, in accord. with arts. 2, 3. - Issued: 17.09.2012. Made: 13.09.2012. Effect: None. Territorial extent & classification: E/W/S. General. - 8p.: 30 cm. - 978-0-11-152880-8 £4.00

The Lincolnshire (Coroners' Districts) Order 2012 No. 2012/574. - Enabling power: Coroners Act 1988, s. 4 (2). - Issued: 01.03.2012. Made: 27.02.2012. Laid: 01.03.2012 Coming into force: 01.04.2012 in respect of art. 3 & 01.06.2012 in respect of art. 4, in accord. with art. 2 (1). Effect: S.I. 2003/2753 revoked. Territorial extent & classification: E/W (but applies to England only). General. - 2p.: 30 cm. - 978-0-11-152096-3 £4.00

Coroners, Wales

The North Wales (East and Central) (Coroners' District) Order 2012 No. 2012/2605. - Enabling power: Coroners Act 1988, s. 4A (1) (7) & Welsh Language Act 1993, s. 25. - Issued: 17.10.2012. Made: 15.10.2012. Laid: 17.10.2012. Coming into force: 01.01.2013. Effect: S.I. 1996/661, 662 amended. Territorial extent & classification: W. General. - 2p.: 30 cm. - 978-0-11-152951-5 £4.00

Corporation tax

The Authorised Investment Funds (Tax) (Amendment No. 3) Regulations 2012 No. 2012/3043. - Enabling power: Finance (No. 2) Act 2005, ss. 17 (3), 18 (1) (h). - Issued: 07.12.2012. Made: 06.12.2012. Laid: 07.12.2012. Coming into force: 01.01.2013. Effect: S.I. 2006/964 amended. Territorial extent & classification: E/W/S/NI. General. - With correction slip dated December 2012. - 4p.: 30 cm. - 978-0-11-153194-5 *£4.00*

The Authorised Investment Funds (Tax) (Amendment No. 2) Regulations 2012 No. 2012/1783. - Enabling power: Finance (No. 2) Act 2005, ss. 17 (3), 18 (5). - Issued: 10.07.2012. Made: 09.07.2012. Laid: 10.07.2012. Coming into force: 01.08.2012. Effect: S.I. 2006/964 amended. Territorial extent & classification: E/W/S/NI. General. - With correction slip dated November 2012 correcting the title to 'Amendment no. 2'. - 4p.: 30 cm. - 978-0-11-152648-4 *£4.00*

The Authorised Investment Funds (Tax) (Amendment) Regulations 2012 No. 2012/519. - Enabling power: Finance (No. 2) Act 2005, ss. 17 (3), 18. - Issued: 28.02.2012. Made: 27.02.2012 at 10.00am. Laid: 27.02.2012 at 1.00pm. Coming into force: 27.02.2012 at 1.30pm. Effect: S.I. 2006/964; 2008/3159 amended. Territorial extent & classification: E/W/S/NI. General. - 4p.: 30 cm. - 978-0-11-152071-0 *£4.00*

The British Waterways Board (Tax Consequences) Order 2012 No. 2012/1709. - Enabling power: Public Bodies Act 2011, s. 25. - Issued: 03.07.2012. Made: 02.07.2012 at 12 noon. Laid: 02.07.2012 at 3 p.m. Coming into force: 02.07.2012 at 3.30 p.m. Effect: None. Territorial extent and classification: E/W/S/NI. General. - 8p.: 30 cm. - 978-0-11-152617-0 *£4.00*

The Business Premises Renovation Allowances (Amendment) Regulations 2012 No. 2012/868. - Enabling power: Capital Allowances Act 2001, ss. 360B (2) (b) (5), 360D (4). - Issued: 20.03.2012. Made: 19.03.2012. Laid: 20.03.2012. Coming into force: 11.04.2012. Effect: S.I. 2007/945 amended. Territorial extent & classification: E/W/S/NI. General. - 4p.: 30 cm. - 978-0-11-152249-3 *£4.00*

The Capital Allowances (Energy-saving Plant and Machinery) (Amendment) Order 2012 No. 2012/1832. - Enabling power: Capital Allowances Act 2001, ss. 45A (3) (4). - Issued: 16.07.2012. Made: 12.07.2012. Laid: 13.07.2012. Coming into force: 02.08.2012. Effect: S.I. 2001/2541 amended. Territorial extent & classification: E/W/S/NI. General. - 2p.: 30 cm. - 978-0-11-152700-9 *£4.00*

The Capital Allowances (Environmentally Beneficial Plant and Machinery) (Amendment No. 2) Order 2012 No. 2012/2602. - Enabling power: Capital Allowances Act 2001, s. 45H (3) to (5). - Issued: 16.10.2012. Made: 15.10.2012. Laid: 16.10.2012. Coming into force: 07.11.2012. Effect: S.I. 2003/2076 amended. Territorial extent & classification: E/W/S/NI. General. - 2p.: 30 cm. - 978-0-11-152949-2 *£4.00*

The Capital Allowances (Environmentally Beneficial Plant and Machinery) (Amendment) Order 2012 No. 2012/1838. - Enabling power: Capital Allowances Act 2001, s. 45H (3) to (5). - Issued: 13.07.2012. Made: 12.07.2012. Laid: 13.07.2012. Coming into force: 02.08.2012. Effect: S.I. 2003/2076 amended. Territorial extent & classification: E/W/S/NI. General. - 2p.: 30 cm. - 978-0-11-152705-4 *£4.00*

The Controlled Foreign Companies (Excluded Banking Business Profits) Regulations 2012 No. 2012/3041. - Enabling power: Taxation (International and Other Provisions) Act 2010, s. 371FD. - Issued: 10.12.2012. Made: 05.12.2012. Laid: 07.12.2012. Coming into force: 01.01.2013. Effect: None. Territorial extent & classification: E/W/S/NI. General. - 4p.: 30 cm. - 978-0-11-153191-4 *£4.00*

The Controlled Foreign Companies (Excluded Territories) Regulations 2012 No. 2012/3024. - Enabling power: Taxation (International and Other Provisions) Act 2010, s. 371KB (2) (3). - Issued: 06.12.2012. Made: 03.12.2012. Laid: 05.12.2012. Coming into force: 01.01.2013. Effect: 2010 c. 8 modified. Territorial extent & classification: E/W/S/NI. General. - 8p.: 30 cm. - 978-0-11-153172-3 *£4.00*

The Double Taxation Relief and International Tax Enforcement (Bahrain) Order 2012 No. 2012/3075. - Enabling power: Taxation (International and Other Provisions) Act 2010, s. 2 & Finance Act 2006, s. 173 (1) to (3). - Issued: 17.12.2012. Made: 12.12.2012. Effect: None. Territorial extent & classification: E/W/S/NI. General. - Supersedes draft SI (ISBN 9780111527078) issued 17.07.2012. - 24p.: 30 cm. - 978-0-11-153244-7 *£5.75*

The Double Taxation Relief and International Tax Enforcement (Barbados) Order 2012 No. 2012/3076. - Enabling power: Taxation (International and Other Provisions) Act 2010, s. 2 & Finance Act 2006, s. 173 (1) to (3). - Issued: 17.12.2012. Made: 12.12.2012. Effect: None. Territorial extent & classification: E/W/S/NI. General. - Supersedes draft SI (ISBN 9780111527160) issued 17.07.2012. - 20p.: 30 cm. - 978-0-11-153242-3 *£5.75*

The Double Taxation Relief and International Tax Enforcement (Liechtenstein) Order 2012 No. 2012/3077. - Enabling power: Taxation (International and Other Provisions) Act 2010, s. 2 & Finance Act 2006, s. 173 (1) to (3). - Issued: 17.12.2012. Made: 12.12.2012. Effect: None. Territorial extent & classification: E/W/S/NI. General. - Supersedes draft SI (ISBN 9780111527092) issued 17.07.2012. - 24p.: 30 cm. - 978-0-11-153241-6 *£5.75*

The Double Taxation Relief and International Tax Enforcement (Singapore) Order 2012 No. 2012/3078. - Enabling power: Taxation (International and Other Provisions) Act 2010, s. 2 & Finance Act 2006, s. 173 (1) to (3). - Issued: 17.07.2012. Made: 12.12.2012. Effect: None. Territorial extent & classification: E/W/S/NI. General. - Supersedes draft SI (ISBN 9780111527153) issued 17.07.2012. - 12p.: 30 cm. - 978-0-11-153240-9 £5.75

The Enactment of Extra-Statutory Concessions Order 2012 No. 2012/266. - Enabling power: Finance Act 2008, s. 160. - Issued: 06.02.2012. Made: 02.02.2012. Coming into force: 01.03.2012. Effect: 1992 c. 12; 1994 c. 9; 2003 c. 1; 2005 c. 5; 2009 c. 4; 2010 c. 4 amended. Territorial extent & classification: E/W/S/NI. General. - Supersedes draft SI (ISBN 9780111519134) issued on 12.01.2012. - 20p.: 30 cm. - 978-0-11-151984-4 £5.75

The Finance Act 2010, Schedule 6, Part 1 (Further Consequential and Incidental Provision etc) Order 2012 No. 2012/735. - Enabling power: Finance Act 2010, sch. 6, para. 29 (1) (2). - Issued: 12.03.2012. Made: 08.03.2012. Laid: 09.03.2012. Coming into force: 01.04.2012. Effect: 2009 c.4 amended. Territorial extent & classification: E/W/S/NI. General. - 4p.: 30 cm. - 978-0-11-152181-6 £4.00

The Finance Act 2010, Schedule 6, Part 2 (Commencement) Order 2012 No. 2012/736 (C.18). - Enabling power: Finance Act 2010, sch. 6, para. 34 (1) (b) (2) (3). Bringing into operation various provisions of this Act on 01.04.2012. - Issued: 12.03.2012. Made: 08.03.2012. Effect: None. Territorial extent & classification: E/W/S/NI. General. - 8p.: 30 cm. - 978-0-11-152189-2 £5.75

The Friendly Societies (Modification of the Tax Acts) Regulations 2012 No. 2012/3008. - Enabling power: Finance Act 2012, ss. 151 (3) (4) (6), 158 (5) (7), 166 (6) (8), 167 (4) (6). - Issued: 05.12.2012. Made: 03.12.2012. Laid: 04.12.2012. Coming into force: 31.12.2012. Effect: 2001 c. 2; 2012 c.14 modified & S.I. 2005/2014; 2007/2134, 2145; 2008/1937, 1942 revoked. Territorial extent & classification: E/W/S/NI. General. - 8p.: 30 cm. - 978-0-11-153164-8 £5.75

The Income Tax (Construction Industry Scheme) (Amendment) Regulations 2012 No. 2012/820. - Enabling power: Taxes Management Act 1970, s. 113 (1) & Finance Act 2002, s. 136 & Finance Act 2003, s. 205 & Finance Act 2004, ss. 62 (3) (6) (7), 71, 73, 75, sch. 11, paras. 4 (3), 8 (2), 12 (2). - Issued: 16.03.2012. Made: 14.03.2012. Laid: 15.03.2012. Coming into force: 06.04.2012. Effect: S.I. 2005/2045 amended. Territorial extent & classification: E/W/S/NI. General. - 4p.: 30 cm. - 978-0-11-152229-5 £4.00

The Insurance Companies and CFCs (Avoidance of Double Charge) Regulations 2012 No. 2012/3044. - Enabling power: Taxation of Chargeable Gains Act 1992, s. 213A. - Issued: 07.12.2012. Made: 06.12.2012. Laid: 07.12.2012. Coming into force: 31.12.2012. Effect: 1992 c.12 modified. Territorial extent & classification: E/W/S/NI. General. - 4p.: 30 cm. - 978-0-11-153195-2 £4.00

The Insurance Companies (Transitional Provisions) Regulations 2012 No. 2012/3009. - Enabling power: Finance Act 2012, sch. 17 (Part 2), paras 6 (3), 7 (2) (e), 8 (2), 37. - Issued: 05.12.2012. Made: 03.12.2012. Laid: 04.12.2012. Coming into force: 31.12.2012. Effect: 2012 c.14 amended. Territorial extent & classification: E/W/S/NI. General. - 12p.: 30 cm. - 978-0-11-153160-0 £5.75

The London Legacy Development Corporation (Tax Consequences) Regulations 2012 No. 2012/701. - Enabling power: Localism Act 2011, sch. 24, part 3. - Issued: 07.03.2012. Made: 06.03.2012. Laid: 07.03.2012. Coming into force: 31.03.2012. Effect: None. Territorial extent & classification: UK. General. - 4p.: 30 cm. - 978-0-11-152152-6 £4.00

The Postal Services Act 2011 (Taxation) Regulations 2012 No. 2012/764. - Enabling power: Postal Services Act 2011, ss. 23, 89 (2). - Issued: 12.03.2012. Made: 08.03.2012. Laid: 09.03.2012. Coming into force: In accord. with reg. 1 (1). Effect: None. Territorial extent & classification: E/W/S/NI. General. - 16p.: 30 cm. - 978-0-11-152180-9 £5.75

The Research and Development (Qualifying Bodies) (Tax) Order 2012 No. 2012/286. - Enabling power: Corporation Tax Act 2009, s. 1142 (1) (e) (3) (4). - Issued: 08.02.2012. Made: 06.02.2012. Laid: 07.02.2012. Coming into force: 28.02.2012. Effect: S.I. 2009/1343 revoked. Territorial extent & classification: E/W/S/NI. General. - 8p.: 30 cm. - 978-0-11-151992-9 £4.00

The Taxation (International and Other Provisions) Act 2010 (Part 7) (Amendment) Regulations 2012 No. 2012/3045. - Enabling power: Taxation (International and Other Provisions) Act 2010, ss. 298A (1) (4) (5). - Issued: 10.12.2012. Made: 05.12.2012. Laid: 07.12.2012. Coming into force: 01.01.2013. Effect: 2010 c.8 amended. Territorial extent & classification: E/W/S/NI. General. - 4p.: 30 cm. - 978-0-11-153196-9 £4.00

The Taxation of Chargeable Gains (Gilt-edged Securities) Order 2012 No. 2012/1843. - Enabling power: Taxation of Chargeable Gains Act 1992, sch. 9, para. 1. - Issued: 16.07.2012. Made: 12.07.2012. Effect: None. Territorial extent & classification: E/W/S/NI. General. - 2p.: 30 cm. - 978-0-11-152706-1 £4.00

The Tax Treatment of Financing Costs and Income (Correction of Mismatches: Partnerships and Pensions) Regulations 2012 No. 2012/3111. - Enabling power: Taxation (International and Other Provisions) Act 2010, s. 336A. - Issued: 18.12.2012. Made: 14.12.2012. Laid: 17.12.2012. Coming into force: 07.01.2013. Effect: 2010 c.8 & S.I. 2010/3025 amended. Territorial extent & classification: E/W/S/NI. General. - 8p.: 30 cm. - 978-0-11-153258-4 £4.00

Council tax, England

The Council Tax (Administration and Enforcement) (Amendment) (England) Regulations 2012 No. 2012/672. - Enabling power: Local Government Finance Act 1992, s. 113 (1) (2), sch. 2, paras. 1 (1), 2 (4) (a), sch. 4, paras. 1 (1), 2 (1), 3. - Issued: 07.03.2012. Made: 02.03.2012. Laid: 07.03.2012. Coming into force: 01.04.2012. Effect: S.I. 1992/613 amended in relation to England. Territorial extent & classification: E. General. - 4p.: 30 cm. - 978-0-11-152135-9 *£4.00*

The Council Tax (Administration and Enforcement) (Amendment) (No. 2) (England) Regulations 2012 No. 2012/3086. - Enabling power: Local Government Finance Act 1992, s. 113 (1) (2), sch. 2, paras. 1 (1), 2 (2) (4) (a) (ia) (j), 4 to 6, 8 to 10, 16. - Issued: 18.12.2012. Made: 11.12.2012. Laid: 18.12.2012. Coming into force: 10.01.2013 for reg. 2 (4) and 2 (1) insofar as its relates to reg. 2 (4) & 01.04.2013 for remaining purposes. Effect: S.I. 1992/613 amended in relation to England. Territorial extent & classification: E. General. - 8p.: 30 cm. - 978-0-11-153223-2 *£5.75*

The Council Tax (Demand Notices) (England) (Amendment) Regulations 2012 No. 2012/3087. - Enabling power: Local Government Finance Act 1992, ss. 113 (1) (2), sch. 2, paras. 1 (1), 2 (4) (e). - Issued: 18.12.2012. Made: 11.12.2012. Laid: 18.12.2012. Coming into force: 31.01.2013. Effect: SI 2011/3038 amended. Territorial extent & classification: E. General. - 4p.: 30 cm. - 978-0-11-153224-9 *£4.00*

The Council Tax (Exempt Dwellings) (England) (Amendment) Order 2012 No. 2012/2965. - Enabling power: Local Government Finance Act 1992, s. 4. - Issued: 30.11.2012. Made: 26.11.2012. Laid: 30.11.2012. Coming into force: 01.04.2013. Effect: S.I. 1992/558 amended in relation to England. Territorial extent & classification: E. General. - 2p.: 30 cm. - 978-0-11-153132-7 *£4.00*

The Council Tax (Prescribed Classes of Dwellings) (England) (Amendment) Regulations 2012 No. 2012/2964. - Enabling power: Local Government Finance Act 1992, s. 11A (1) (2) (4) (4A), 11B (2) (3). - Issued: 30.11.2012. Made: 26.11.2012. Laid: 30.11.2012. Coming into force: 01.04.2013. Effect: S.I. 2003/3011 amended. Territorial extent & classification: E. General. - 4p.: 30 cm. - 978-0-11-153131-0 *£4.00*

The Council Tax Reduction Schemes (Default Scheme) (England) Regulations 2012 No. 2012/2886. - Enabling power: Local Government Finance Act 1992, s. 113 (1) (2), sch. 1A, para. 4. - Issued: 26.11.2012. Made: 16.11.2012. Laid: 22.11.2012. Coming into force: 18.12.2012. Effect: None. Territorial extent & classification: E. General. - 162p.: 30 cm. - 978-0-11-153098-6 *£22.50*

The Council Tax Reduction Schemes (Prescribed Requirements and Default Scheme) (England) (Amendment) Regulations 2012 No. 2012/3085. - Enabling power: Local Government Finance Act 1992, s. 113 (1), sch. 1A, paras 2, 4. - Issued: 17.12.2012. Made: 11.12.2012. Laid: 17.12.2012. Coming into force: 10.01.2013. Effect: SI 2012/2885, 2886 amended. Territorial extent & classification: E. General. - 4p.: 30 cm. - 978-0-11-153222-5 *£4.00*

The Council Tax Reduction Schemes (Prescribed Requirements) (England) Regulations 2012 No. 2012/2885. - Enabling power: Local Government Finance Act 1992, s. 113 (1) (2), sch. 1A, para. 2. - Issued: 26.11.2012. Made: 16.11.2012. Laid: 22.11.2012. Coming into force: 27.11.2012. Effect: None. Territorial extent & classification: E. General. - 93p.: 30 cm. - 978-0-11-153096-2 *£15.50*

The Local Authorities (Calculation of Council Tax Base) (England) Regulations 2012 No. 2012/2914. - Enabling power: Local Government Finance Act 1992, ss. 31B (1) (3) (4) (5), 34 (4), 42B (1) (3) (4) (5), 45 (3) (4) (5), 45 (3) (4) (5), 48 (3) to (6), 52ZX (5) (7) (8), 113 (1) (2). - Issued: 26.11.2012. Made: 20.11.2012. Laid: 26.11.2012. Coming into force: 30.11.2012. Effect: S.I. 1992/2789, 2903, 2904; 1994/2826; 2003/2613; 2008/3022; 2009/3193; 2011/696 amended & S.I. 1992/612, 1742, 2943; 1999/3123,3437; 2003/3012, 3181 revoked. Territorial extent & classification: E. General. - 12p.: 30 cm. - 978-0-11-153110-5 *£5.75*

The Local Authorities (Conduct of Referendums) (Council Tax Increases) (England) Regulations 2012 No. 2012/444. - Enabling power: Local Government Finance Act 1992, ss. 52ZQ, 113. - Issued: 23.02.2012. Made: 17.02.2012. Coming into force: In accord. with reg. 1. Effect: 5 Acts & 8 SIs modified. Territorial extent & classification: E. General. - Supersedes draft S.I. (ISBN 9780111519035) issued 11.01.2012. - 128p.: 30 cm. - 978-0-11-152046-8 *£18.50*

The Local Authorities (Referendums Relating to Council Tax Increases) Regulations 2012 No. 2012/460. - Enabling power: Local Government Finance Act 1992, ss. 31 (6), 52ZK (8), 52ZM (4), 52ZN (8), 52ZX (5) (7) (8), 113 (1) & Localism Act 2011, ss. 235 (2), 236 (1). - Issued: 24.02.2012. Made: 21.02.2012. Laid: 24.02.2012. Coming into force: 16.03.2012. Effect: S.I. 1992/612, 2789, 2903; 1996/263, 2794; 2001/3384; 2008/626; 2009/5; 2011/696 amended. Territorial extent & classification: E. General. - 8p.: 30 cm. - 978-0-11-152051-2 *£5.75*

Council tax, England and Wales

The Health and Social Care Act 2008 (Consequential Amendments) (Council Tax) Order 2012 No. 2012/1915. - Enabling power: Health and Social Care Act 2008, s. 167 (1) (b) (3). - Issued: 24.07.2012. Made: 18.07.2012. Laid: 24.07.2012. Coming into force: 23.08.2012. Effect: S.I. 1992/549, 551 amended. Territorial extent & classification: E. General. - 2p.: 30 cm. - 978-0-11-152759-7 *£4.00*

Council tax, Wales

The Council Tax Reduction Schemes and Prescribed Requirements (Wales) Regulations 2012 No. 2012/3144 (W.316). - Enabling power: Local Government Finance Act 1992, s. 113A (4), sch. 1B, paras 2 to 7. - Issued: 31.12.2012. Made: 19.12.2012. Coming into force: 20.12.2012 in accord. with reg. 1 (2). Effect: None. Territorial extent & classification: W. General. - 164p.: 30 cm. - 978-0-348-10674-9 £22.50

The Council Tax Reduction Schemes (Default Scheme) (Wales) Regulations 2012 No. 2012/3145 (W.317). - Enabling power: Local Government Finance Act 1992, s. 13A (4) (c) (5), sch. 1B, para. 6. - Issued: 31.12.2012. Made: 19.12.2012. Coming into force: 20.12.2012 in accord. with reg. 1 (2). Effect: None. Territorial extent & classification: W. General. - 152p.: 30 cm. - 978-0-10-545648-3 £22.50

Countryside

The Conservation of Habitats and Species (Amendment) Regulations 2012 No. 2012/1927. - Enabling power: European Communities Act 1972, s. 2 (2). - Issued: 25.07.2012. Made: 20.07.2012. Laid before Parliament & the National Assembly for Wales: 25.07.2012. Coming into force: 16.08.2012. Effect: 1949 c.97; S.I. 2010/490 amended. Territorial extent & classification: E/W/S/NI. General. - EC note: These Regulations amend the S.I. 2010/490 Regulations and transpose certain aspects of Directive 2009/147/EC on the conservation of wild birds. - 16p.: 30 cm. - 978-0-11-152765-8 £5.75

Countryside, England

The Access to the Countryside (Appeals against Works Notices) (England) (Amendment) Regulations 2012 No. 2012/67. - Enabling power: Countryside and Rights of Way Act 2000, ss. 38 (6), 44 (2), 45 (1) & Marine and Coastal Access Act 2009, s. 316 (1), sch. 20, para. 4 (5). - Issued: 16.01.2012. Made: 12.01.2012. Laid: 16.01.2012. Coming into force: 15.02.2012. Effect: S.I. 2011/2019 amended. Territorial extent & classification: E. General. - This Statutory Instrument has been made in consequence of defects in S.I. 2011/2019 (ISBN 9780111514658) and is being issued free of charge to all known recipients of that Statutory Instrument. - 4p.: 30 cm. - 978-0-11-151921-9 £4.00

The Access to the Countryside (Coastal Margin) (Weymouth Bay) Order 2012 No. 2012/1559. - Enabling power: Countryside and Rights of Way Act 2000, s. 3A (10). - Issued: 21.06.2012. Made: 18.06.2012. Effect: None. Territorial extent & classification: E. General. - 2p.: 30 cm. - 978-0-11-152560-9 £4.00

County courts, England and Wales

The Allocation and Transfer of Proceedings (Amendment) (No. 2) Order 2012 No. 2012/1955. - Enabling power: Children Act 1989, s. 92 (6), sch. 11, Part 1. - Issued: 27.07.2012. Made: 18.07.2012. Laid: 26.07.2012. Coming into force: 10.09.2012. Effect: S.I. 2008/2836 amended. Territorial extent & classification: E/W. General. - 2p.: 30 cm. - 978-0-11-152771-9 £4.00

The Allocation and Transfer of Proceedings (Amendment) Order 2012 No. 2012/642. - Enabling power: Children Act 1989, s. 92 (6), sch. 11, Part 1. - Issued: 05.03.2012. Made: 28.02.2012. Laid: 05.03.2012. Coming into force: 02.04.2012. Effect: S.I. 2008/2836 amended. Territorial extent & classification: E/W. General. - 2p.: 30 cm. - 978-0-11-152112-0 £4.00

The Civil Courts (Amendment) (No. 2) Order 2012 No. 2012/1954. - Enabling power: County Courts Act 1984, s. 2 (1) & Matrimonial and Family Proceedings Act 1984, s. 33 (1) & Senior Courts Act 1981, s. 99 (1). - Issued: 27.07.2012. Made: 23.07.2012. Laid: 26.07.2012. Coming into force: 10.09.2012. Effect: S.I. 1983/713 amended. Territorial extent & classification: E/W. General. - 2p.: 30 cm. - 978-0-11-152773-3 £4.00

The Civil Courts (Amendment) Order 2012 No. 2012/643. - Enabling power: County Courts Act 1984, s. 2 (1) & Matrimonial and Family Proceedings Act 1984, s. 33 (1) & Senior Courts Act 1981, s. 99 (1). - Issued: 05.03.2012. Made: 01.03.2012. Laid: 05.03.2012. Coming into force: 02.04.2012. Effect: S.I. 1983/713 amended. Territorial extent & classification: E/W. General. - 4p.: 30 cm. - 978-0-11-152111-3 £4.00

The Civil Procedure (Amendment No. 2) Rules 2012 No. 2012/2208 (L.8). - Enabling power: Civil Procedure Act 1997, s. 2. - Issued: 30.08.2012. Made: 07.08.2012. Laid: 29.08.2012. Coming into force: 01.10.2012, in accord. with rule 1. Effect: S.I. 1998/3132 amended. Territorial extent & classification: E/W. General. - 24p.: 30 cm. - 978-0-11-152839-6 £5.75

The Civil Procedure (Amendment) Rules 2011 No. 2012/505 (L.2). - Enabling power: Civil Procedure Act 1997, s. 2. - Issued: 02.03.2012. Made: 23.02.2012. Laid: 27.02.2012. Coming into force: 19.03.2012. Effect: S.I. 1998/3132 amended. Territorial extent & classification: E/W. General. - 4p.: 30 cm. - 978-0-11-152066-6 £4.00

The Family Procedure (Amendment) (No. 2) Rules 2012 No. 2012/1462. - Enabling power: Courts Act 2003, s. 75. - Issued: 11.06.2012. Made: 31.05.2012. Laid: 07.06.2012. Coming into force: 01.07.2012. Effect: S.I. 2010/2955 amended. Territorial extent & classification: E/W. General. - 2p.: 30 cm. - 978-0-11-152508-1 £4.00

The Family Procedure (Amendment No. 3) Rules 2012 No. 2012/2046 (L.7). - Enabling power: Courts Act 2003, ss. 75, 76. - Issued: 08.08.2012. Made: 31.07.2012. Laid: 07.08.2012. Coming into force: 30.009.2012. Effect: S.I. 2010/2955 amended. Territorial extent & classification: E/W. General. - 4p.: 30 cm. - 978-0-11-152799-3 £4.00

The Family Procedure (Amendment No. 4) Rules 2012 No. 2012/2806 (L.10). - Enabling power: Courts Act 2003, ss. 75, 76 & Civil Jurisdiction and Judgments Act 1982, ss. 12, 48. - Issued: 12.11.2012. Made: 06.11.2012. Laid: 09.11.2012. Coming into force: 20.12.2012. Effect: S.I. 2010/2955 amended. Territorial extent & classification: E/W. General. - 12p.: 30 cm. - 978-0-11-153059-7 £5.75

The Family Procedure (Amendment No. 5) Rules 2012 No. 2012/3061. - Enabling power: Courts Act 2003, ss. 75, 76. - Issued: 13.12.2013. Made: 10.12.2012. Laid: 13.12.2012. Coming into force: 31.01.2013. Effect: S.I. 2010/2955 amended. Territorial extent & classification: E/W. General. - 12p.: 30 cm. - 978-0-11-153210-2 £5.75

The Family Procedure (Amendment) Rules 2012 No. 2012/679 (L.3). - Enabling power: Civil Jurisdiction and Judgements Act 1982, ss. 12, 48 & Adoption and Children Act 2002, ss. 102, 141 (1) & Courts Act 2003, ss. 75, 76. - Issued: 07.03.2012. Made: 01.03.2012. Laid: 06.03.2012. Coming into force: 06.04.2012. Effect: S.I. 2010/2955 amended. Territorial extent & classification: E/W. General. - 8p.: 30 cm. - 978-0-11-152133-5 £5.75

Court martial (appeals), England and Wales

The Costs in the Court Martial Appeal Court Regulations 2012 No. 2012/1805. - Enabling power: Court Martial Appeals Act 1968, ss. 31 (5) (b), 33B (1) (e). - Issued: 13.07.2012. Made: 09.07.2012. Laid: 12.07.2012. Coming into force: 01.10.2012. Effect: None. Territorial extent & classification: E/W. General. - [8]p.: 30 cm. - 978-0-11-152667-5 £4.00

Criminal law

The Belarus (Asset-Freezing) Regulations 2012 No. 2012/1509. - Enabling power: European Communities Act 1972, s. 2 (2), sch. 2, para. 1A. - Issued: 14.06.2012. Made: 12.06.2012. Laid: 13.06.2012. Coming into force: 04.07.2012. Effect: None. Territorial extent & classification: E/W/S/NI. General. - Revoked by SI 2013/164 (ISBN 9780111533932). EC note: These regs make provision relating to the enforcement of Council Regulation 765/2006 concerning restrictive measures in respect of Belarus. - 12p.: 30 cm. - 978-0-11-152533-3 £5.75

The Burma/Myanmar (Financial Restrictions) (Suspension) Regulations 2012 No. 2012/1302. - Enabling power: European Communities Act 1972, s. 2 (2). - Issued: 17.05.2012. Made: 16.05.2012. Laid: 16.05.2012. Coming into force: 17.05.2012. Effect: S.I. 2009/1495 parts 3 and 5 suspended until 30.04.2013. Territorial extent & classification: E/W/S/NI. General. - EC note: Various sanctions measures contained in Council Regulation 194/2008 including the financial sanctions measures have been suspended until 30 April 2013 by Council Regulation 409/2012 with effect from 16 May 2012. - 2p.: 30 cm. - 978-0-11-152452-7 £4.00

The Criminal Justice Act 2003 (Commencement No. 29 and Saving Provisions) (Amendment) Order 2012 No. 2012/2761. - Enabling power: Criminal Justice Act 2003, s. 336 (3) (4). - Issued: 07.11.2012. Made: 04.11.2012. Coming into force: 04.11.2012. Effect: S.I. 2012/2574 (C.103) amended. Territorial extent & classification: E/W/S. General. - 2p.: 30 cm. - 978-0-11-153042-9 £4.00

The Criminal Justice Act 2003 (Commencement No. 29 and Saving Provisions) Order 2012 No. 2012/2574 (C.103). - Enabling power: Criminal Justice Act 2003, ss. 330 (4), 336 (3) (4). Bringing into operation various provisions of the 2003 Act on 05.11.2012 & 01.01.2013. in accord. with arts. 2, 3, 4. - Issued: 16.10.2012. Made: 06.10.2012. Effect: None. Territorial extent & classification: E/W/S. General. - 12p.: 30 cm. - 978-0-11-152937-9 £5.75

The Democratic Republic of the Congo (Asset-Freezing) Regulations 2012 No. 2012/1511. - Enabling power: European Communities Act 1972, s. 2 (2), sch. 2, para. 1A. - Issued: 14.06.2012. Made: 12.06.2012. Laid: 14.06.2012. Coming into force: 05.07.2012. Effect: S.I. 2005/1517 revoked. Territorial extent & classification: E/W/S/NI. General. - EC note: These regs make provision relating to the enforcement of Council Regulation 1183/2005 concerning restrictive measures in respect of the Democratic Republic of the Congo. - 12p.: 30 cm. - 978-0-11-152535-7 £5.75

The Domestic Violence, Crime and Victims Act (Amendment) 2012 (Commencement) Order 2012 No. 2012/1432 (C.54). - Enabling power: Domestic Violence, Crime and Victims (Amendment) Act 2012, s. 4 (2). Bringing into operation provisions of the 2012 Act on 02.07.2012 in accord. with art. 2. - Issued: 06.06.2012. Made: 28.05.2012. Effect: None. Territorial extent & classification: E/W/S/NI. General. - 2p.: 30 cm. - 978-0-11-152499-2 £4.00

The Eritrea (Asset-Freezing) Regulations 2012 No. 2012/1515. - Enabling power: European Communities Act 1972, s. 2 (2), sch. 2, para. 1A. - Issued: 14.06.2012. Made: 12.06.2012. Laid: 14.06.2012. Coming into force: 05.07.2012. Effect: None. Territorial extent & classification: E/W/S/NI. General. - EC note: These regs make provision relating to the enforcement of Council Regulation 667/2010 concerning restrictive measures in respect of Eritrea. - 12p.: 30 cm. - 978-0-11-152537-1 £5.75

The Guinea-Bissau (Asset-Freezing) Regulations 2012 No. 2012/1301. - Enabling power: European Communities Act 1972, s. 2 (2), sch. 2, para. 1A. - Issued: 17.05.2012. Made: 16.05.2012. Laid: 16.05.2012. Coming into force: 06.06.2012. Effect: None. Territorial extent & classification: E/W/S/NI. General. - EC note: These regs make provision relating to the enforcement of Council Regulation 377/2012 restrictive measures directed against certain persons, entities and bodies threatening the peace, security or stability of the Republic of Guinea-Bissau. - 12p.: 30 cm. - 978-0-11-152451-0 £5.75

The International Criminal Tribunal for the former Yugoslavia (Financial Sanctions Against Indictees) (Revocation) Regulations 2012 No. 2012/1510. - Enabling power: European Communities Act 1972, s. 2 (2). - Issued: 14.06.2012. Made: 12.06.2012. Laid: 13.06.2012. Coming into force: 04.07.2012. Effect: S.I. 2005/1527 revoked. Territorial extent & classification: E/W/S/NI. General. - EC note: The revoked 2005 Regulations provided for criminal penalties for breach of the financial sanctions provisions of Council Regulation 1763/2004. Council Regulation 1763/2004 has been repealed by Council Regulation 1048/2011, therefore these regulations accordingly revoke the criminal penalties for breach of the financial sanctions provisions. - 2p.: 30 cm. - 978-0-11-152534-0 £4.00

The Iran (European Union Financial Sanctions) (Amendment No. 2) Regulations 2012 No. 2012/2909. - Enabling power: European Communities Act 1972, s. 2 (2), sch. 2, para. 1A. - Issued: 21.11.2012. Made: 20.11.2012. Laid: 21.11.2012. Coming into force: 22.11.2012. Effect: S.I. 2012/925 amended. Territorial extent & classification: E/W/S/NI. General. - EC note: These Regs amend the 2012 regulations (SI 2012/925 ISBN 9780111522882) which made provision relating to the enforcement of Council Reg (EU) 267/2012 concerning restrictive measures against Iran and repealing Reg no. 961/2010. Council Implementing Regulation 1067/2012 amends the 1st Council Regulation by adding derogations from the asset freezing measures in certain circumstances. The derogations permit certain transactions relating to a production sharing agreement, and relating to certain contracts for the supply of Iranian crude oil and petroleum products. - 2p.: 30 cm. - 978-0-11-153106-8 £4.00

The Iran (European Union Financial Sanctions) (Amendment) Regulations 2012 No. 2012/190. - Enabling power: European Communities Act 1972, s. 2 (2). - Issued: 27.01.2012. Made: 26.01.2012. Laid: 27.01.2012. Coming into force: 28.01.2012. Effect: S.I. 2010/2937 amended. Territorial extent & classification: E/W/S/NI. General. - Revoked by S.I. 2012/925 (ISBN 9780111522882). EC note: These Regs make provision relating to the enforcement of Council Reg (EU) no. 961/2010 on restrictive measures against Iran and repealing Reg no. 423/2007. - 2p.: 30 cm. - 978-0-11-151954-7 £4.00

The Iran (European Union Financial Sanctions) Regulations 2012 No. 2012/925. - Enabling power: European Communities Act 1972, s. 2 (2), sch. 2, para. 1A. - Issued: 27.03.2012. Made: 26.03.2012 at 11.00 am. Laid: 26.03.2012 at 2.00 pm. Coming into force: 26.03.2012 at 3.00 pm. Effect: 2008 c.28 amended & partially repealed & S.I. 2010/2937; 2012/190 revoked. Territorial extent & classification: E/W/S/NI. General. - EC note: These Regs make provision relating to the enforcement of Council Reg (EU) 267/2012 concerning restrictive measures against Iran and repealing Reg no. 961/2010. - This Statutory Instrument has been printed in substitution of the SI of the same number and is being issued free of charge to all known recipients of that Statutory Instrument. - 16p.: 30 cm. - 978-0-11-152288-2 £5.75

The Iraq (Asset-Freezing) Regulations 2012 No. 2012/1489. - Enabling power: European Communities Act 1972, s. 2 (2), sch. 2, para. 1A. - Issued: 12.06.2012. Made: 11.06.2012. Laid: 11.06.2012. Coming into force: 02.07.2012. Effect: S.I. 2001/3649; 2003/1519 amended & S.I. 2000/3241; 2004/1498, 1660, 1779 revoked. Territorial extent & classification: E/W/S/NI. General. - EC note: These Regulations make provision relating to the enforcement of Council Regulation 1210/2003 concerning restrictive measures in respect of Iraq. - With correction slip dated January 2013. - 12p.: 30 cm. - 978-0-11-152521-0 £5.75

The Lebanon and Syria (Asset-Freezing) Regulations 2012 No. 2012/1517. - Enabling power: European Communities Act 1972, s. 2 (2), sch. 2, para. 1A. - Issued: 14.06.2012. Made: 12.06.2012. Laid: 14.06.2012. Coming into force: 05.07.2012. Effect: S.I. 2005/3432 revoked. Territorial extent & classification: E/W/S/NI. General. - EC note: These regs make provision relating to the enforcement of Council Regulation 305/2006 imposing restrictive measures against certain persons suspected of involvement in the assassination of former Lebanese Prime Minister Rafiq Hariri. - 12p.: 30 cm. - 978-0-11-152539-5 £5.75

The Legal Aid, Sentencing and Punishment of Offenders Act 2012 (Commencement No. 3 and Saving Provision) Order 2012 No. 2012/2770 (C.110). - Enabling power: Legal Aid, Sentencing and Punishment of Offenders Act 2012, s. 15 (1) (5). Bringing into operation various provisions of the 2012 Act on 03.12.2012 in accord. with art 2. - Issued: 07.11.2012. Made: 01.11.2012. Effect: None. Territorial extent & classification: E/W/S. General. - 4p.: 30 cm. - 978-0-11-153045-0 £4.00

The Liberia (Asset-Freezing) Regulations 2012 No. 2012/1516. - Enabling power: European Communities Act 1972, s. 2 (2), sch. 2, para. 1A. - Issued: 14.06.2012. Made: 12.06.2012. Laid: 14.06.2012. Coming into force: 05.07.2012. Effect: S.I. 2004/1264, 2574 revoked. Territorial extent & classification: E/W/S/NI. General. - EC note: These regs make provision relating to the enforcement of Council Regulation 872/2004 concerning further restrictive measures in relation to Liberia. - 12p.: 30 cm. - 978-0-11-152538-8 £5.75

The Libya (Asset-Freezing) (Amendment) Regulations 2012 No. 2012/56. - Enabling power: European Communities Act 1972, s. 2 (2). - Issued: 12.01.2012. Made: 11.01.2012 at 11.00 am. Laid: 11.01.2012 at 3.30 pm. Coming into force: 11.01.2012 at 4.30 pm. Effect: S.I. 2011/605 amended. Territorial extent & classification: E/W/S/NI. General. - EC note: These Regulations make provision effect to Council Regulation 1360/2011 amending Council Regulation EU) 204/2011 concerning restrictive measures in view of the situation in Libya. - 2p.: 30 cm. - 978-0-11-151910-3 £4.00

Criminal law

The Republic of Guinea (Asset-Freezing) Regulations 2012 No. 2012/1508. - Enabling power: European Communities Act 1972, s. 2 (2), sch. 2, para. 1A. - Issued: 14.06.2012. Made: 12.06.2012. Laid: 13.06.2012. Coming into force: 04.07.2012. Effect: None. Territorial extent & classification: E/W/S/NI. General. - EC note: These regs make provision relating to the enforcement of Council Regulation 1284/2009 imposing certain specific restrictive measures in respect of the Republic of Guinea. - 12p.: 30 cm. - 978-0-11-152532-6 £5.75

The Sudan (Asset-Freezing) Regulations 2012 No. 2012/1507. - Enabling power: European Communities Act 1972, s. 2 (2), sch. 2, para. 1A. - Issued: 14.06.2012. Made: 12.06.2012. Laid: 13.06.2012. Coming into force: 04.07.2012. Effect: S.I. 2006/1454 revoked. Territorial extent & classification: E/W/S/NI. General. - EC note: These regs make provision relating to the enforcement of Council Regulation 1184/2005 imposing certain specific restrictive measures directed against certain persons impeding the peace process and breaking international law in the conflict in the Darfur region of Sudan. - 12p.: 30 cm. - 978-0-11-152531-9 £5.75

The Syria (European Union Financial Sanctions) (Amendment No. 2) Regulations 2012 No. 2012/2524. - Enabling power: European Communities Act 1972, s. 2 (2), sch. 2, para. 1A. - Issued: 05.10.2012. Made: 04.10.2012. Laid: 05.10.2012. Coming into force: 26.10.2012. Effect: S.I. 2011/129 amended & S.I. 2012/639 revoked. Territorial extent & classification: E/W/S/NI. General. - EC note: These Regulations implement Council Regulation (EU) 867/2012 amending derogations contained in Council Regulation (EU) 36/2012. - 2p.: 30 cm. - 978-0-11-152914-0 £4.00

The Syria (European Union Financial Sanctions) (Amendment) Regulations 2012 No. 2012/639. - Enabling power: European Communities Act 1972, s. 2 (2), sch. 2, para. 1A. - Issued: 05.03.2012. Made: 01.03.2012. Laid: 02.03.2012. Coming into force: 03.03.2012. Effect: S.I. 2011/129 amended. Territorial extent & classification: E/W/S/NI. General. - Revoked by SI 2012/2524 (ISBN 9780111529140). EC note: These Regulations amend the 2012 Regs by making provision for limited exceptions to the asset freeze reflecting the new derogations. - 2p.: 30 cm. - 978-0-11-152110-6 £4.00

The Syria (European Union Financial Sanctions) Regulations 2012 No. 2012/129. - Enabling power: European Communities Act 1972, s. 2 (2), sch. 2, para. 1A. - Issued: 20.01.2012. Made: 19.01.2012 at 11.00 am. Laid: 19.01.2012 at 2.30 pm. Coming into force: 19.01.2012 at 3.00 pm. Effect: S.I. 2011/1244, 2479 revoked. Territorial extent & classification: E/W/S/NI. General. - Ec note: Makes provision relating to the enforcement of Council Regulation (EU) no. 36/2012 of 18 January 2012 concerning restrictive measures in view of the situation in Syria and repealing Council Regulation no. 442/2009. - 16p.: 30 cm. - 978-0-11-151934-9 £5.75

The United Nations Personnel (Isle of Man) Order 2012 No. 2012/2594. - Enabling power: United Nations Personnel Act 1997, s. 9 (2). - Issued: 22.10.2012. Made: 17.10.2012. Coming into force: 18.10.2012 in accord. with art. 1. Effect: None. Territorial extent & classification: IoM. General. - 2p.: 30 cm. - 978-0-11-152975-1 £4.00

Criminal law, England

The Crime and Disorder (Formulation and Implementation of Strategy) (Amendment) Regulations 2012 No. 2012/2660. - Enabling power: Crime and Disorder Act 1998, s. 6 (2) (3) (4) (4A). - Issued: 26.10.2012. Made: 22.10.2012. Laid: 25.10.2012. Coming into force: 22.11.2012. Effect: S.I. 2007/1830 amended. Territorial extent & classification: E. General. - 4p.: 30 cm. - 978-0-11-152992-8 £4.00

Criminal law, England and Wales

The Costs in Criminal Cases (General) (Amendment) Regulations 2012 No. 2012/1804. - Enabling power: Prosecution of Offences Act 1985, ss. 20, 29 (2). - Issued: 13.07.2012. Made: 09.07.2012. Laid: 12.07.2012. Coming into force: 01.10.2012. Effect: S.I. 1986/1335 amended. Territorial extent & classification: E/W. General. - 4p.: 30 cm. - 978-0-11-152666-8 £4.00

The Crime and Disorder Act 1998 (Service of Prosecution Evidence) (Amendment) Regulations 2012 No. 2012/1345. - Enabling power: Crime and Disorder Act 1998, sch. 3, para 1. - Issued: 24.05.2012. Made: 18.05.2012. Laid: 22.05.2012. Coming into force: 18.06.2012. Effect: S.I. 2005/902 amended. Territorial extent & classification: E/W. General. - 2p.: 30 cm. - 978-0-11-152466-4 £4.00

The Crime (International Co-operation) Act 2003 (Designation of Prosecuting Authorities) (Amendment) Order 2012 No. 2012/146. - Enabling power: Crime (International Co-operation) Act 2003, s. 7 (5). - Issued: 26.01.2012. Made: 22.01.2012. Laid: 25.01.2012. Coming into force: 20.02.2012. Effect: S.I. 2004/1034 amended. Territorial extent & classification: E/W/NI. General. - 2p.: 30 cm. - 978-0-11-151941-7 £4.00

The Crime (Sentences) Act 1997 (Commencement No. 5) Order 2012 No. 2012/2901 (C.112). - Enabling power: Crime (Sentences) Act 1997, s. 57 (2). Bringing into operation various provisions of the 1997 Act on 03.12.2012. - Issued: 22.11.2012. Made: 17.11.2012. Effect: None. Territorial extent & classification: E/W. General. - 2p.: 30 cm. - 978-0-11-153093-1 £4.00

The Criminal Justice Act 1988 (Reviews of Sentencing) (Amendment) Order 2012 No. 2012/1833. - Enabling power: Criminal Justice Act 1988, s. 35 (4). - Issued: 16.07.2012. Made: 09.07.2012. Laid: 16.07.2012. Coming into force: 06.08.2012. Effect: S.I. 2006/1116 amended. Territorial extent & classification: E/W. General. - 4p.: 30 cm. - 978-0-11-152701-6 £4.00

The Criminal Justice Act 2003 (Commencement No. 27) Order 2012 No. 2012/825 (C.22). - Enabling power: Criminal Justice Act 2003, s. 336 (3) (4). Bringing into operation various provisions of the 2003 Act on 19.03.2012. in accord. with art. 2. - Issued: 16.03.2012. Made: 13.03.2012. Effect: None. Territorial extent & classification: E/W. General. - 8p.: 30 cm. - 978-0-11-152218-9 £5.75

The Criminal Justice Act 2003 (Commencement No. 28 and Saving Provisions) Order 2012 No. 2012/1320 (C.48). - Enabling power: Criminal Justice Act 2003, ss. 330 (4), 336 (3) (4). Bringing into operation various provisions of the 2003 Act on 18.05.2012 & 18.06.2012. in accord. with arts. 2, 3, 4. - Issued: 24.05.2012. Made: 17.05.2012. Effect: None. Territorial extent & classification: E/W. General. - 12p.: 30 cm. - 978-0-11-152464-0 £5.75

The Criminal Justice Act 2003 (Commencement No. 30 and Consequential Amendment) Order 2012 No. 2012/2905 (C.113). - Enabling power: Criminal Justice Act 2003, s. 336 (3). Bringing into operation various provisions of the 2003 Act in accord. with arts 2 & 3. - Issued: 22.11.2012. Made: 17.11.2012. Effect: S.I. 2005/950 amended. Territorial extent & classification: E/W. General. - 8p.: 30 cm. - 978-0-11-153099-3 £5.75

The Criminal Justice Act 2003 (Surcharge) Order 2012 No. 2012/1696. - Enabling power: Criminal Justice Act 2003, ss. 161A (2), 161B, 330 (4). - Issued: 03.07.2012. Made: 28.06.2012. Laid: 02.07.2012. Coming into force: 01.10.2012. Effect: None. Territorial extent & classification: E/W. General. - 8p.: 30 cm. - 978-0-11-152611-8 £4.00

The Criminal Justice and Police Act 2001 (Amendment) Order 2012 No. 2012/1430. - Enabling power: Criminal Justice and Police Act 2001, s. 1 (2). - Issued: 08.06.2012. Made: 30.05.2012. Coming into force: In accord. with art. 1 (2). Effect: 2001 c. 16 amended. Territorial extent & classification: E/W. General. - Supersedes draft S.I. (ISBN 9780111522738) issued 26.03.2011. - 2p.: 30 cm. - 978-0-11-152500-5 £4.00

The Domestic Violence, Crime and Victims Act 2004 (Commencement No. 15) Order 2012 No. 2012/1697 (C.66). - Enabling power: Domestic Violence, Crime and Victims Act 2004, s. 60. Bringing into operation various provisions of the 2004 Act on 01.10.2012 in accord. with art. 2. - Issued: 03.07.2012. Made: 28.06.2012. Effect: None. Territorial extent & classification: E/W. General. - 4p.: 30 cm. - 978-0-11-152610-1 £4.00

The Legal Aid, Sentencing and Punishment of Offenders Act 2012 (Commencement No. 1) Order 2012 No. 2012/1956 (C.77). - Enabling power: Legal Aid, Sentencing and Punishment of Offenders Act 2012, s. 151 (1). Bringing into operation various provisions of the 2012 Act on 01.09.2012. - Issued: 30.07.2012. Made: 24.07.2012. Coming into force: 30.07.2012. Effect: None. Territorial extent & classification: E/W. General. - 2p.: 30 cm. - 978-0-11-152772-6 £4.00

The Legal Aid, Sentencing and Punishment of Offenders Act 2012 (Commencement No. 2 and Specification of Commencement Date) Order 2012 No. 2012/2412 (C.94). - Enabling power: Legal Aid, Sentencing and Punishment of Offenders Act 2012, ss. 141 (12), 151 (1). Bringing into operation various provisions of the 2012 Act on 01.10.2012 in accordance with arts 2, 3. - Issued: 24.09.2012. Made: 18.09.2012. Effect: None. Territorial extent & classification: E/W/S/NI. General. - 4p.: 30 cm. - 978-0-11-152897-6 £4.00

The Legal Aid, Sentencing and Punishment of Offenders Act 2012 (Commencement No. 4 and Saving Provisions) Order 2012 No. 2012/2906 (C.114). - Enabling power: Legal Aid, Sentencing and Punishment of Offenders Act 2012, s. 151 (1) (5) (b). Bringing into operation various provisions of the 2012 Act on 03.12.2012 in accord. with art. 2. - Issued: 22.11.2012. Made: 17.11.2012. Effect: None. Territorial extent & classification: E/W/S/NI/IoM/British Overseas Territories. General. - 8p.: 30 cm. - 978-0-11-153100-6 £4.00

The Legal Aid, Sentencing and Punishment of Offenders Act 2012 (Consequential and Saving Provisions) Regulations 2012 No. 2012/2824. - Enabling power: Legal Aid, Sentencing and Punishment of Offenders Act 2012, ss. 149 (1) (2). - Issued: 14.11.2012. Made: 08.11.2012. Laid: 12.11.2012. Coming into force: 03.12.2012. Effect: S.I. 1991/1505 amended. Territorial extent & classification: E/W but these Regs make provision in relation to the Armed Forces Act 2006 which extends to the UK. General. - 4p.: 30 cm. - 978-0-11-153076-4 £4.00

The Licensing Act 2003 (Persistent Selling of Alcohol to Children) (Prescribed Form of Closure Notice) Regulations 2012 No. 2012/963. - Enabling power: Licensing Act 2003, s. 169A (3). - Issued: 04.04.2012. Made: 24.03.2012. Laid: 30.03.2012. Coming into force: 25.04.2012. Effect: S.I. 2007/1183 revoked. Territorial extent & classification: E/W. General. - 4p.: 30 cm. - 978-0-11-152333-9 £4.00

The Penalties for Disorderly Behaviour (Amount of Penalty) (Amendment) Order 2012 No. 2012/1431. - Enabling power: Criminal Justice and Police Act 2001, s. 3 (1) (1A). - Issued: 08.06.2012. Made: 30.05.2012. Laid: 01.06.2012. Coming into force: 30.06.2012. Effect: S.I. 2002/1837 amended. Territorial extent & classification: E/W. General. - 2p.: 30 cm. - 978-0-11-152501-2 £4.00

The Prosecution of Offences Act 1985 (Specified Proceedings) (Amendment No. 2) Order 2012 No. 2012/2067. - Enabling power: Prosecution of Offences Act 1985, s. 3 (3). - Issued: 10.08.2012. Made: 08.08.2012. Laid: 10.08.2012. Coming into force: 03.09.2012. Effect: S.I. 1999/904 amended. Territorial extent & classification: E/W. General. - This Statutory Instrument has been made in consequence of a defect in SI 2012/1635 (ISBN 9780111525777) and is being issued free of charge to all known recipients of that Statutory instrument. - 2p.: 30 cm. - 978-0-11-152804-4 £4.00

The Prosecution of Offences Act 1985 (Specified Proceedings) (Amendment No. 3) Order 2012 No. 2012/2681. - Enabling power: Prosecution of Offences Act 1985, s. 3 (3). - Issued: 29.10.2012. Made: 25.10.2012. Laid: 26.10.2012. Coming into force: 19.11.2012. Effect: S.I. 1999/904 amended. Territorial extent & classification: E/W. General. - 4p.: 30 cm. - 978-0-11-153009-2 £4.00

The Prosecution of Offences Act 1985 (Specified Proceedings) (Amendment) Order 2012 No. 2012/1635. - Enabling power: Prosecution of Offences Act 1985, s. 3 (3). - Issued: 26.06.2012. Made: 21.06.2012. Laid: 26.06.2012. Coming into force: 17.07.2012. Effect: S.I. 1999/904 amended. Territorial extent & classification:E/W. General. - This SI has been corrected by SI 2012/2067 (ISBN 9780111528044) which is being issued free of charge to all known recipients of SI 2012/1635. - 2p.: 30 cm. - 978-0-11-152577-7 £4.00

The Prosecution of Offences (Custody Time Limits) (Amendment) Regulations 2012 No. 2012/1344. - Enabling power: Prosecution of Offences Act 1985, ss. 22 (1) (2), 29 (2). - Issued: 24.05.2012. Made: 17.05.2012. Laid: 22.05.2012. Coming into force: 18.06.2012. Effect: S.I. 1987/299 amended. Territorial extent & classification: E/W. General. - 2p.: 30 cm. - 978-0-11-152465-7 £4.00

The Protection of Freedoms Act 2012 (Commencement No. 2) Order 2012 No. 2012/2075 (C.82). - Enabling power: Protection of Freedoms Act 2012, ss. 116 (1), 120 (1). Bringing into operation various provisions of the 2012 Act on 10.08.2012, 01.10.2012 & 01.11.2012, 25.11.2012, in accord. with arts 2 to 5. - Issued: 10.08.2012. Made: 07.08.2012. Effect: None. Territorial extent & classification: E/W/S/NI. General. - 4p.: 30 cm. - 978-0-11-152805-1 £4.00

The Recovery of Costs (Remand to Youth Detention Accommodation) (England and Wales) Regulations 2012 No. 2012/2822. - Enabling power: Legal Aid, Sentencing and Punishment of Offenders Act 2012, s. 103 (2). - Issued: 14.11.2012. Made: 08.11.2012. Laid: 12.11.2012. Coming into force: 03.12.2012. Effect: None. Territorial extent & classification: E/W. General. - 4p.: 30 cm. - 978-0-11-153075-7 £4.00

The Serious Organised Crime and Police Act 2005 (Designated Sites under Section 128) (Amendment No. 2) Order 2012 No. 2012/2709. - Enabling power: Serious Organised Crime and Police Act 2005, s. 128 (2). - Issued: 01.11.2012. Made: 26.10.2012. Laid: 31.10.2012. Coming into force: 01.11.2012 in accord. with art. 1 (1). Effect: S.I. 2007/930 amended. Territorial extent & classification: E/W. General. - This Statutory Instrument has been made in consequence of an omission in SI 2012/1769 (ISBN 9780111526521) and is being issued free of charge to all known recipients of that Statutory instrument. - 2p.: 30 cm. - 978-0-11-153020-7 £4.00

The Serious Organised Crime and Police Act 2005 (Designated Sites under Section 128) (Amendment) Order 2012 No. 2012/1769. - Enabling power: Serious Organised Crime and Police Act 2005, s. 128 (2). - Issued: 11.07.2012. Made: 05.07.2012. Laid: 10.07.2012. Coming into force: 01.10.2012. Effect: S.I. 2007/930 amended. Territorial extent & classification: E/W. General. - This SI has been corrected by SI 2012/2709 (ISBN 9780111530207) which is being sent free of charge to all known recipients of 2012/1769. - 4p.: 30 cm. - 978-0-11-152652-1 £4.00

The Sexual Offences Act 2003 (Notification Requirements) (England and Wales) Regulations 2012 No. 2012/1876. - Enabling power: Sexual Offences Act 2003, ss. 83 (5) (5A), 84 (1) (5A), 85 (5), 86, 138 (4). - Issued: 20.07.2012. Made: 16.07.2012. Coming into force: In accord. with reg. 1 (2). Effect: S.I. 2004/1220 amended. Territorial extent & classification: E/W. General. - Supersedes draft S.I. (ISBN 9780111521410) issued 07.03.2012. - 8p.: 30 cm. - 978-0-11-152736-8 £5.75

The Sexual Offences Act 2003 (Remedial) Order 2012 No. 2012/1883. - Enabling power: Human Rights Act 1998, s. 10 (2), sch. 2, para 1 (1) (a) (c) (d) (2) (3). - Issued: 20.07.2012. Made: 16.07.2012. Coming into force: 30.07.2012. Effect: 2003 c. 42 amended. Territorial extent & classification: E/W. General. - Supersedes draft S.I. (ISBN 9780111521403) issued 07.03.2012. - 8p.: 30 cm. - 978-0-11-152738-2 £5.75

Criminal law, Northern Ireland

The Crime (International Co-operation) Act 2003 (Designation of Prosecuting Authorities) (Amendment) Order 2012 No. 2012/146. - Enabling power: Crime (International Co-operation) Act 2003, s. 7 (5). - Issued: 26.01.2012. Made: 22.01.2012. Laid: 25.01.2012. Coming into force: 20.02.2012. Effect: S.I. 2004/1034 amended. Territorial extent & classification: E/W/NI. General. - 2p.: 30 cm. - 978-0-11-151941-7 £4.00

Criminal procedure, England and Wales

The Coroners and Justice Act 2009 (Commencement No. 10) Order 2012 No. 2012/2374 (C.92). - Enabling power: Coroners and Justice Act 2009, ss. 176 (3), 182 (4) (5). Bringing into operation various provisions of the 2009 Act on 24.09.2012 & 08.10.2012, in accord. with arts. 2, 3. - Issued: 17.09.2012. Made: 13.09.2012. Effect: None. Territorial extent & classification: E/W/S. General. - 8p.: 30 cm. - 978-0-11-152880-8 £4.00

The Police and Justice Act 2006 (Commencement No. 15) Order 2012 No. 2012/2373 (C.91). - Enabling power: Police and Justice Act 2006, ss. 49 (3), 53 (1). Bringing into operation various provisions of the 2006 Act on 08.10.2012, in accord. with art. 2. - Issued: 17.09.2012. Made: 13.09.2012. Effect: None. Territorial extent & classification: E/W. General. - 4p.: 30 cm. - 978-0-11-152879-2 £4.00

Customs

The Export Control (Amendment) (No. 2) Order 2012 No. 2012/1910. - Enabling power: European Communities Act 1972, s. 2 (2) & Export Control Act 2002, ss. 1, 2, 3, 4, 5, 7. - Issued: 23.07.2012. Made: 18.07.2012. Laid: 20.07.2012. Coming into force: 10.08.2012. Effect: S.I. 2008/3231 amended. Territorial extent & classification: E/W/S/NI. General. - 12p.: 30 cm. - 978-0-11-152757-3 £5.75

The Export Control (Amendment) Order 2012 No. 2012/929. - Enabling power: Export Control Act 2002, ss. 1, 5. - Issued: 27.03.2012. Made: 23.03.2012. Laid: 26.03.2012. Coming into force: 16.04.2012. Effect: S.I. 2008/3231 amended & S.I. 2010/1127 revoked. Territorial extent & classification: E/W/S/NI. General. - With correction slip dated August 2012. - 4p.: 30 cm. - 978-0-11-152287-5 £4.00

The Export Control (Iran Sanctions) Order 2012 No. 2012/1243. - Enabling power: European Communities Act 1972, s. 2 (2), sch. 2, para. 1A & Export Control Act 2002, ss. 1, 2, 3, 4, 5, 7. - Issued: 10.05.2012. Made: 03.05.2012. Laid: 10.05.2012. Coming into force: 01.06.2012. Effect: S.I. 2011/1297 revoked. Territorial extent & classification: E/W/S/NI. General. - EC note: Makes provision relating to the enforcement of certain restrictive measures against Iran set out in Council Regulation (EU) 267/2012 repealing Council Regulation (EU) 961/2010 and Council Regulation (EU) 264/2012 amending Regulation (EU) 359/2011. - 12p.: 30 cm. - 978-0-11-152412-1 £5.75

The Export Control (Syria and Burma Sanctions Amendment) and Miscellaneous Revocations Order 2012 No. 2012/2125. - Enabling power: European Communities Act 1972, s. 2 (2) & Export Control Act 2002, ss. 1, 2, 3, 4, 5, 7. - Issued: 20.08.2012. Made: 15.08.2012. Laid: 16.08.2012. Coming into force: 06.09.2012. Effect: S.I. 2012/810, 1098 amended & S.I. 1993/1200, 2232; 2002/315 revoked. Territorial extent & classification: E/W/S/NI. General. - EC note: This Order makes provision for the enforcement of certain new trade sanctions against Syria specified in Council Regulation (EU) no. 509/2012 and Council Regulation (EU) no. 545/2012 both of which amend Council Regulation (EU) no. 36/2012 concerning restrictive measures in view of the situation in Syria. In addition Council Regulation 409/2012 temporary suspends certain trade restrictions against Burma specified by Council Regulation 194/2008. This Order makes consequential amendments to the Export Control (Burma) Order 2008 to provide for the enforcement provisions in relation to the trade measures which have been temporarily suspended by the Burma Amendment Regulations to cease to have effect until the date specified in that Regulations. - 8p.: 30 cm. - 978-0-11-152826-6 £4.00

The Export Control (Syria Sanctions) and (Miscellaneous Amendments) Order 2012 No. 2012/810. - Enabling power: European Communities Act 1972, s. 2 (2), sch. 2, para. 1A & Export Control Act 2002, ss. 1, 2, 3, 4, 5, 7. - Issued: 15.03.2012. Made: 08.03.2012. Laid: 14.03.2012. Coming into force: 05.04.2012. Effect: S.I. 2011/1304, 2010 partially revoked & S.I. 2009/1174 revoked. Territorial extent & classification: E/W/S/NI. General. - EC note: This Order makes provision for the enforcement of certain restrictive measures specified in Council Regulation 36/2012 (as last amended by Council Regulation 168/2012 concerning restrictive measures in view of the situation in Syria and repealing Council Regulation 442/2011 (the Syria Regulation). - 8p.: 30 cm. - 978-0-11-152208-0 £5.75

The Forest Law Enforcement, Governance and Trade Regulations 2012 No. 2012/178. - Enabling power: European Communities Act 1972, s. 2 (2), sch. 2, para. 1A. - Issued: 30.01.2012. Made: 25.01.2012. Laid: 30.01.2012. Coming into force: 20.02.2012. Effect: 1979 c. 2 modified. Territorial extent & classification: E/W/S/NI. General. - EC note: These Regulations enforce Council Regulation 2173/2005 on the establishment of a FLEGT licensing scheme for imports of timber into the European Community and Community Regulation 1024/2008 which lays down detailed measures for the implementation of the FLEGT Regulation. - 8p.: 30 cm. - 978-0-11-151952-3 £5.75

Dangerous drugs

The Misuse of Drugs Act 1971 (Amendment) Order 2012 No. 2012/1390. - Enabling power: Misuse of Drugs Act 1971, s. 2 (2). - Issued: 06.06.2012. Made: 30.05.2012. Coming into force: In accord. with art. 1. Effect: 1971 c. 38 amended. Territorial extent & classification: E/W/S/NI. General. - Supersedes draft SI (ISBN 9780111520857) issued on 01.03.2012. - 4p.: 30 cm. - 978-0-11-152497-8 £4.00

The Misuse of Drugs Act 1971 (Temporary Class Drug) Order 2012 No. 2012/980. - Enabling power: Misuse of Drugs Act 1971, ss. 2A (1) (5), 7A (2) (3) (6), 31 (1). - Issued: 25.05.2012. Made: 29.03.2012. Laid: 03.04.2012. Coming into force: 05.04.2012. Effect: None. Territorial extent & classification: E/W/S/NI. General. - Approved by both Houses of Parliament. Supersedes previously published SI of same number (ISBN 9780111523223) issued on 04.04.2012. - 4p.: 30 cm. - 978-0-11-152479-4 £4.00

The Misuse of Drugs Act 1971 (Temporary Class Drug) Order 2012 No. 2012/980. - Enabling power: Misuse of Drugs Act 1971, ss. 2A (1) (5), 7A (2) (3) (6), 31 (1). - Issued: 04.04.2012. Made: 29.03.2012. Laid: 03.04.2012. Coming into force: 05.04.2012. Effect: None. Territorial extent & classification: E/W/S/NI. General. - Superseded by Affirmed SI of same number but different ISBN (9780111524794) issued on 25.05.2012. For approval for resolution of each House of Parliament within forty days beginning with the day on which the Order was made, subject to extension for periods of dissolution, prorogation and adjournment of both Houses for more than four days. - 2p.: 30 cm. - 978-0-11-152322-3 £4.00

Misuse of Drugs (Amendment) (England, Wales and Scotland) Order 2012 No. 2012/277 *NOT PUBLISHED - Revoked by S.I. 2012/385 before issuing*

The Misuse of Drugs (Amendment) (England, Wales and Scotland) (Revocation) Regulations 2012 No. 2012/385. - Enabling power: Misuse of Drugs Act 1971, ss. 7, 10, 22, 31. - Issued: 17.02.2012. Made: 15.02.2012. Laid: 17.02.2012. Coming into force: 12.03.2012. Effect: S.I. 2012/277 (which was not published) revoked. Territorial extent & classification: E/W/S. General. - 2p.: 30 cm. - 978-0-11-152028-4 £4.00

The Misuse of Drugs (Amendment No. 2) (England, Wales and Scotland) Regulations 2012 No. 2012/973. - Enabling power: Misuse of Drugs Act 1971, ss. 7, 10, 22, 31. - Issued: 02.04.2012. Made: 27.03.2012. Laid: 30.03.2012. Coming into force: 23.04.2012. Effect: S.I. 2001/3998 amended. Territorial extent & classification: E/W/S. General. - 8p.: 30 cm. - 978-0-11-152316-2 £5.75

The Misuse of Drugs (Amendment No. 3) (England, Wales and Scotland) Regulations 2012 No. 2012/1311. - Enabling power: Misuse of Drugs Act 1971, ss. 7, 10, 22, 31. - Issued: 22.05.2012. Made: 16.05.2012. Laid: 21.05.2012. Coming into force: 13.06.2012. Effect: S.I. 2001/3998 amended. Territorial extent & classification: E/W/S. General. - 2p.: 30 cm. - 978-0-11-152457-2 £4.00

Misuse of Drugs (Designation) (Amendment) (England, Wales and Scotland) Order 2012 No. 2012/276 *NOT PUBLISHED Revoked by S.I. 2012/384 before issuing*

The Misuse of Drugs (Designation) (Amendment) (England, Wales and Scotland) (Revocation) Order 2012 No. 2012/384. - Enabling power: Misuse of Drugs Act 1971, s. 7 (4). - Issued: 17.02.2012. Made: 15.02.2012. Laid: 17.02.2012. Coming into force: 12.03.2012. Effect: S.I. 2012/276 (which was not published) revoked. Territorial extent & classification: E/W/S. General. - 2p.: 30 cm. - 978-0-11-152027-7 £4.00

The Misuse of Drugs (Designation) (Amendment No. 2) (England, Wales and Scotland) Order 2012 No. 2012/1310. - Enabling power: Misuse of Drugs Act 1971, s. 7 (4). - Issued: 22.05.2012. Made: 16.05.2012. Laid: 21.05.2012. Coming into force: 13.06.2012. Effect: S.I. 2001/3997 amended. Territorial extent & classification: E/W/S. General. - 2p.: 30 cm. - 978-0-11-152456-5 £4.00

Dangerous drugs, England and Wales

The Misuse of Drugs (Supply to Addicts) (Amendment) Regulations 2012 No. 2012/2394. - Enabling power: Misuse of Drugs Act 1971, ss. 10 (1) (2) (i) (2A), 31. - Issued: 20.09.2012. Made: 16.09.2012. Laid: 19.09.2012. Coming into force: 31.10.2012. Effect: S.I. 1997/1001 amended. Territorial extent & classification: E/W/S. General. - 2p.: 30 cm. - 978-0-11-152885-3 £4.00

Dangerous drugs, Scotland

The Misuse of Drugs (Supply to Addicts) (Amendment) Regulations 2012 No. 2012/2394. - Enabling power: Misuse of Drugs Act 1971, ss. 10 (1) (2) (i) (2A), 31. - Issued: 20.09.2012. Made: 16.09.2012. Laid: 19.09.2012. Coming into force: 31.10.2012. Effect: S.I. 1997/1001 amended. Territorial extent & classification: E/W/S. General. - 2p.: 30 cm. - 978-0-11-152885-3 £4.00

Data protection

The Data Protection (Processing of Sensitive Personal Data) Order 2012 No. 2012/1978. - Enabling power: Data Protection Act 1998, s. 67 (2), sch. 3, para. 10. - Issued: 31.07.2012. Made: 25.07.2012. Coming into force: In accord. with art. 1. Effect: None. Territorial extent & classification: E/W/S/NI. General. - Supersedes draft S.I. (ISBN 9780111524299) issued 15.05.2012. - 2p.: 30 cm. - 978-0-11-152784-9 £4.00

Debt management and relief: Debt relief orders

The Tribunals, Courts and Enforcement Act 2007 (Consequential Amendments) Order 2012 No. 2012/2404. - Enabling power: Tribunals, Courts and Enforcement Act 2007, s. 145 (1) (2) (b). - Issued: 19.09.2012. Made: 15.09.2012. Coming into force: 01.10.2012. Effect: 63 acts & 56 SIs amended. Territorial extent & classification: E/W/S/NI. General. - Supersedes draft S.I. (ISBN 9780111525807) issued 27.06.2012. - 32p.: 30 cm. - 978-0-11-152893-8 £9.75

Defence

The Armed Forces Act 2011 (Commencement No. 1, Transitional and Transitory Provisions) Order 2012 No. 2012/669 (C. 15). - Enabling power: Armed Forces Act 2011, s. 32 (3) to (5). Bringing into operation various provisions of the 2011 Act on 08.03.2012, 02.04.2012. - Issued: 08.05.2009. Made: 01.03.2012. Effect: None. Territorial extent & classification: E/W/S/NI. General. - 4p.: 30 cm. - 978-0-11-152125-0 £4.00

The Armed Forces Act 2011 (Commencement No. 2) Order 2012 No. 2012/2921 (C. 116). - Enabling power: Armed Forces Act 2011, s. 32 (3). Bringing into operation various provisions of the 2011 Act on 14.12.2012. - Issued: 26.11.2012. Made: 16.11.2012. Effect: None. Territorial extent & classification: E/W/S/NI. General. - 2p.: 30 cm. - 978-0-11-153114-3 £4.00

The Armed Forces Act (Continuation) Order 2012 No. 2012/1750. - Enabling power: Armed Forces Act 2006, s. 382 (2). - Issued: 17.07.2012. Made: 10.07.2012. Coming into force: 10.07.2012. Effect: The Armed Forces Act 2006 shall, instead of expiring on 03.11.2012, continue in force until 03.11.2013. Territorial extent & classification: E/W/S/NI, IoM & British Overseas Territories. General. - Supersedes draft S.I. (ISBN 9780111524756) issued 25.05.2012. - 2p.: 30 cm. - 978-0-11-152686-6 £4.00

The Armed Forces (Powers of Stop and Search, Search, Seizure and Retention) (Amendment) Order 2012 No. 2012/2919. - Enabling power: Armed Forces Act 2006, ss. 85, 86, 323, 380 (1). - Issued: 26.11.2012. Made: 16.11.2012. Laid: 23.11.2012. Coming into force: 14.12.2012. Effect: S.I. 2009/2056 amended. Territorial extent & classification: E/W/S/NI. General. - 8p.: 30 cm. - 978-0-11-153113-6 £4.00

The Coroners and Justice Act 2009 (Commencement No. 10) Order 2012 No. 2012/2374 (C.92). - Enabling power: Coroners and Justice Act 2009, ss. 176 (3), 182 (4) (5). Bringing into operation various provisions of the 2009 Act on 24.09.2012 & 08.10.2012, in accord. with arts. 2, 3. - Issued: 17.09.2012. Made: 13.09.2012. Effect: None. Territorial extent & classification: E/W/S. General. - 8p.: 30 cm. - 978-0-11-152880-8 £4.00

The Legal Aid, Sentencing and Punishment of Offenders Act 2012 (Commencement No. 4 and Saving Provisions) Order 2012 No. 2012/2906 (C.114). - Enabling power: Legal Aid, Sentencing and Punishment of Offenders Act 2012, s. 151 (1) (5) (b). Bringing into operation various provisions of the 2012 Act on 03.12.2012 in accord. with art. 2. - Issued: 22.11.2012. Made: 17.11.2012. Effect: None. Territorial extent & classification: E/W/S/NI/IoM/British Overseas Territories. General. - 8p.: 30 cm. - 978-0-11-153100-6 £4.00

The Legal Aid, Sentencing and Punishment of Offenders Act 2012 (Consequential and Saving Provisions) Regulations 2012 No. 2012/2824. - Enabling power: Legal Aid, Sentencing and Punishment of Offenders Act 2012, ss. 149 (1) (2). - Issued: 14.11.2012. Made: 08.11.2012. Laid: 12.11.2012. Coming into force: 03.12.2012. Effect: S.I. 1991/1505 amended. Territorial extent & classification: E/W but these Regs make provision in relation to the Armed Forces Act 2006 which extends to the UK. General. - 4p.: 30 cm. - 978-0-11-153076-4 £4.00

The Ot Moor Range Byelaws 2012 No. 2012/1478. - Enabling power: Military Lands Act 1892, ss. 14 (1), 15. - Issued: 19.06.2012. Made: 30.05.2012. Coming into force: 30.09.2012. Effect: S.I. 1980/39 revoked. Territorial extent & classification: E. General. - This Statutory Instrument has been printed in substitution of the SI of the same number and ISBN (issued 15.06.2012) and is being issued free of charge to all known recipients that Statutory Instrument. - 16p., col. maps: 30 cm. - 978-0-11-152517-3 £8.25

The Police and Criminal Evidence Act 1984 (Armed Forces) (Amendment) Order 2012 No. 2012/2505. - Enabling power: Police and Criminal Evidence Act 1984, s. 113 (1). - Issued: 04.10.2012. Made: 01.10.2012. Laid: 04.10.2012. Coming into force: 30.10.2012. Effect: S.I. 2009/1922 amended. Territorial extent & classification: E/W/S/NI/IoM/British Overseas Territories. General. - 2p.: 30 cm. - 978-0-11-152909-6 £4.00

The Protection of Military Remains Act 1986 (Designation of Vessels and Controlled Sites) Order 2012 No. 2012/1110. - Enabling power: Protection of Military Remains Act 1986, s. 1 (2). - Issued: 08.05.2012. Made: 16.04.2012. Coming into force: 01.06.2012. Effect: S.I. 2009/3380 revoked. Territorial extent & classification: E/W/S/NI. General. - This statutory instrument has been issued in consequence of an error in the version issued on 20.04.2012 (same ISBN) and is being issued free of charge to all known recipients of the original. - 8p.: 30 cm. - 978-0-11-152367-4 £4.00

The Visiting Forces and International Military Headquarters (EU SOFA) (Tax Designation) Order 2012 No. 2012/3070. - Enabling power: Income Tax (Earnings and Pensions) Act 2003, s. 303 & Income Tax Act 2007, s. 833 & Inheritance Tax Act 1984, s.155. - Issued: 17.12.2012. Made: 12.12.2012. Coming into force: In accord. with art. 1 (2). Effect: None. Territorial extent & classification: E/W/S/NI. General. - 4p.: 30 cm. - 978-0-11-153237-9 £4.00

The Visiting Forces and International Military Headquarters (NATO and PfP) (Tax Designation) Order 2012 No. 2012/3071. - Enabling power: Finance Act 1960, s. 74A & Inheritance Tax Act 1984, s.155 & Income Tax (Earnings and Pensions) Act 2003, s. 303 & Income Tax Act 2007, s. 833. - Issued: 17.12.2012. Made: 12.12.2012. Coming into force: In accord. with art. 1 (2). Effect: S.I. 1961/580; 1960/581; 1998/1513, 1514, 1515, 1516, 1517, 1518 revoked (13.12.2012). Territorial extent & classification: E/W/S/NI. General. - [8]p.: 30 cm. - 978-0-11-153238-6 £4.00

Defence, England

The Caversfield Service Family Accommodation Byelaws 2012 No. 2012/3088. - Enabling power: Military Lands Act 1892, s. 14 (1). - Issued: 17.12.2012. Made: 11.12.2012. Coming into force: 11.04.2013. Effect: None. Territorial extent & classification: E. General. - With correction slip dated January 2013. - 12p., col. maps: 30 cm. - 978-0-11-153217-1 £8.25

Destructive animals

The Mink Keeping (Prohibition) (Wales) Order 2012 No. 2012/1427 (W. 177). - Enabling power: Destructive Imported Animals Act 1932, s. 10 (1). - Issued: 08.06.2012. Made: 08.05.2012. Laid before the National Assembly for Wales: 08.05.2012. Coming into force: 01.06.2012. Effect: None. Territorial extent & classification: W. General. - Approved by the National Assembly for Wales. Supersedes Unnumbered WSI (ISBN 9780348106053) issued 17.05.2012. With correction slip dated July 2012. - 4p.: 30 cm. - 978-0-348-10619-0 £4.00

Destructive animals, Wales

The Mink Keeping (Prohibition) (Wales) Order 2012 No. 2012/Unnumbered (W.). - Enabling power: Destructive Imported Animals Act 1932, s. 10 (1). - Issued: 17.05.2012. Made: 08.05.2012. Laid before the National Assembly for Wales: 08.05.2012. Coming into force: 01.06.2012. Effect: None. Territorial extent & classification: W. General. - For approval by resolution of the National Assembly for Wales. Superseded by WSI 2012/1427 (W.177) (ISBN 9780348106190) issued 08.06.2012. - 4p.: 30 cm. - 978-0-348-10605-3 £4.00

Devolution, Scotland

The Forestry Commissioners (Climate Change Functions) (Scotland) Order 2012 (Consequential Modifications) Order 2012 No. 2012/2855 (S.1). - Enabling power: Scotland Act 1998, ss. 104, 112 (1), 113 (2) (4) (5) (7). - Issued: 14.11.2012. Made: 07.11.2012. Coming into force: 08.11.2012. In accord. with art. 1 (2). Effect: 1967 c.10 modified. Territorial extent & classification: S. General. - Supersedes draft SI (ISBN 9780111526705) issued on 16.07.2012. - 4p.: 30 cm. - 978-0-11-153079-5 £4.00

The Glasgow Commonwealth Games Act 2008 (Ticket Touting Offence) (England and Wales and Northern Ireland) Order 2012 No. 2012/1852. - Enabling power: Scotland Act 1998, ss. 104, 112 (1), 113 (1) (2) (3). - Issued: 26.07.2012. Made: 16.07.2012. Laid: 18.07.2012. Coming into force: 29.11.2012. Effect: None. Territorial extent & classification: E/W/S/NI. General. - 8p.: 30 cm. - 978-0-11-152722-1 £4.00

The Housing (Scotland) Act 2010 (Consequential Provisions and Modifications) Order 2012 No. 2012/700. - Enabling power: Scotland Act 1998, ss. 104, 112 (1), 113 (2) (5), 114 (1). - Issued: 13.03.2012. Made: 05.03.2012. Coming into force: 01.04.2012. Effect: 1975 c. 24; 1985 c. 69; 1986 c. 45; 1992 c. 12; 1994 c. 23; 2002 c. 40; 2003 c. 14; 2007 c. 3; 2010 c. 4 & S.I. 1987/1968; 1999/584; 2001/1201; 2004/692; 2005/1379; 2006/213, 214, 264; 2008/346; 2009/214, 1801 amended & S.I. 2008/948; 2009/1941 partially revoked. Territorial extent & classification: UK. General. - Supersedes draft S.I. (ISBN 9780111519080) issued 18.01.2012. - 8p.: 30 cm. - 978-0-11-152166-3 £5.75

The Scotland Act 2012 (Commencement No. 1) Order 2012 No. 2012/1710 (C.67). - Enabling power: Scotland Act 2012, s. 44 (5). Bringing into operation various provisions of the 2012 Act on 03.07.2012; 15.10.2012. - Issued: 09.07.2012. Made: 29.06.2012. Effect: None. Territorial extent & classification: E/W/S/NI. General. - 4p.: 30 cm. - 978-0-11-152639-2 £4.00

The Scotland Act 2012 (Commencement No. 2) Order 2012 No. 2012/2516 (C.99). - Enabling power: Scotland Act 2012, s. 44 (5). Bringing into operation various provisions of the 2012 Act on 31.10.2012, 01.08.2013. - Issued: 10.10.2012. Made: 03.10.2012. Effect: None. Territorial extent & classification: E/W/S/NI. General. - 4p.: 30 cm. - 978-0-11-152910-2 £4.00

The Scottish Administration (Offices) Order 2005 No. 2012/3073. - Enabling power: Scotland Act 1998, s. 126 (8) (b). - Issued: 19.12.2012. Made: 12.12.2012. Laid before Parliament: 19.12.2012. Laid before the Scottish Parliament: 19.12.2012. Coming into force: In accord. with art. 1 (2) to (4). Effect: S.I. 1999/1127 partially revoked & S.I. 2005/1467 revoked. Territorial extent & classification: E/W/S/NI. General. - 4p.: 30 cm. - 978-0-11-153245-4 £4.00

Diplomatic Service

The Consular Fees (Amendment) Order 2012 No. 2012/1752. - Enabling power: Consular Fees Act 1980, s. 1 (1) (4A) (4B). - Issued: 16.07.2012. Made: 10.07.2012. Coming into force: 03.09.2012. Effect: S.I. 2012/798 amended. Territorial extent & classification: E/W/S/NI. General. - 4p.: 30 cm. - 978-0-11-152672-9 £4.00

The Consular Fees Order 2012 No. 2012/798. - Enabling power: Consular Fees Act 1980, s. 1 (1). - Issued: 16.03.2012. Made: 14.03.2012. Coming into force: 06.04.2012. Effect: S.I. 2011/738, 1691 revoked. Territorial extent & classification: E/W/S/NI. General. - 8p.: 30 cm. - 978-0-11-152233-2 £5.75

Disabled persons

The Rail Vehicle Accessibility (Non-Interoperable Rail System) (London Underground Circle, District and Hammersmith & City Lines S7 Vehicles) Exemption Order 2012 No. 2012/105. - Enabling power: Equality Act 2010, ss. 183 (1) (2) (4) (b) (5), 207 (1) (4). - Issued: 23.01.2012. Made: 12.01.2012. Laid: 18.01.2012. Coming into force: 13.02.2012. Effect: None. Territorial extent & classification: E/W/S. General. - 12p.: 30 cm. - 978-0-11-151930-1 £5.75

Disabled persons, England

The Disabled People's Right to Control (Pilot Scheme) (England) (Amendment) Regulations 2012 No. 2012/3048. - Enabling power: Welfare Reform Act 2009, ss. 41, 44, 45 (2), 46, 50. - Issued: 10.12.2012. Made: 06.12.2012. Coming into force: 12.12.2012. Effect: S.I. 2010/2862 amended. Territorial extent & classification: E. General. - Supersedes draft SI (ISBN 9780111529935) issued on 24.10.2012. - 4p.: 30 cm. - 978-0-11-153203-4 £4.00

Dogs, England: Control of dogs

The Controls on Dogs (Designation of the Common Council of the City of London as a Secondary Authority) Order 2012 No. 2012/1223. - Enabling power: Clean Neighbourhoods and Environment Act 2005, s. 58 (3). - Issued: 10.05.2012. Made: 01.05.2012. Laid: 10.05.2012. Coming into force: 31.05.2012. Effect: None. Territorial extent & classification: E. General. - 4p.: 30 cm. - 978-0-11-152410-7 £4.00

Ecclesiastical law, England

The Ecclesiastical Judges, Legal Officers and Others (Fees) Order 2012 No. 2012/1846. - Enabling power: Ecclesiastical Fees Measure 1986, s. 6 (1) (1A) (2). - Issued: 26.07.2012. Made 06.07.2012. Laid: 19.07.2012. Coming into force: 01.01.2013. Effect: S.I. 2011/1731 revoked. Territorial extent & classification: E. General. - 12p.: 30 cm. - 978-0-11-152724-5 £5.75

The Ecclesiastical Offices (Terms of Service) (Consequential Provisions) Order 2012 No. 2012/992. - Enabling power: Ecclesiastical Offices (Terms of Service) Measure 2009 no. 1, s. 11 (1). - Issued: 12.04.2012. Made (sealed by the Archbishops' Council): 29.03.2012. Laid: 12.04.2012. Coming into force: 01.07.2012. Effect: Mission and Pastoral Measure 2011 amended. Territorial extent & classification: E. General. - 4p.: 30 cm. - 978-0-11-152334-6 £4.00

The Legal Officers (Annual Fees) Order 2012 No. 2012/1847. - Enabling power: Ecclesiastical Fees Measure 1986, s. 5 (1) (2). - Issued: 26.07.2012. Made: 06.07.2012. Laid: 19.07.2012. Coming into force: 01.01.2013. Effect: S.I. 2011/1735 revoked. Territorial extent & classification: E. General. - 12p.: 30 cm. - 978-0-11-152723-8 £5.75

The Parochial Fees and Scheduled Matters Amending Order 2012 No. 2012/993. - Enabling power: Ecclesiastical Fees Measure 1986, ss. 1 (1) (6), 2. - Issued: 12.04.2012. Made: 29.03.2012. Laid before Parliament: 12.04.2012. Coming into force: 01.01.2013. Effect: Ecclesiastical Fees Measure 1986 amended & S.I. 2010/1924 revoked. Territorial extent & classification: E. General. - 8p.: 30 cm. - 978-0-11-152335-3 £5.75

Education

The Education (Student Loans) (Repayment) (Amendment) (No. 2) Regulations 2012 No. 2012/1309. - Enabling power: Education Act 2011, ss. 76, 78 & Teaching and Higher Education Act 1998, ss. 22, 42. - Issued: 22.05.2012. Made: 16.05.2012. Laid before Parliament and the National Assembly for Wales: 21.05.2012. Coming into force: 18.06.2012. Effect: S.I. 2009/470 amended. Territorial extent & classification: E/WS/NI. General. - 12p.: 30 cm. - 978-0-11-152455-8 £5.75

The Education (Student Loans) (Repayment) (Amendment) Regulations 2012 No. 2012/836. - Enabling power: Teaching and Higher Education Act 1998, ss. 22 (5), 42 (6) & Education (Scotland) Act 1980, ss. 73 (f), 73B (3). - Issued: 19.03.2012. Made: 13.03.2012. Laid: 16.03.2012. Coming into force: 06.04.2012. Effect: S.I. 2009/470 amended. Territorial extent & classification: This instrument has the same territorial extent and application as the provisions it amends in the 2009 Regulations. The 2009 Regulations extend to England and Wales but they also extend to all of the United Kingdom in so far as they impose any obligation or confer any power on HMRC, an employer or a borrower in relation to repayment under Parts 3 or 4 of those Regulations. General. - 8p.: 30 cm. - 978-0-11-152234-9 £5.75

Education, England

The Academies (Land Transfer Schemes) Regulations 2012 No. 2012/1829. - Enabling power: Academies Act 2010, sch. 1, para. 21 & Education Act 1996, s. 569 (4). - Issued: 16.07.2012. Made: 12.07.2012. Laid: 13.07.2012. Coming into force: 03.08.2012. Effect: None. Territorial extent & classification: E. General. - 4p.: 30 cm. - 978-0-11-152702-3 £4.00

The Alternative Provision Academies and 16 to 19 Academies (Consequential Amendments to Subordinate Legislation) (England) Order 2012 No. 2012/979. - Enabling power: Education Act 2011, ss. 54 (2) (b), 78 (2) (c). - Issued: 04.04.2012. Made: 29.03.2012. Laid: 04.04.2012. Coming into force: 01.05.2012. Effect: S.I. 1975/193, 1023; 1992/42; 1998/2876; 1999/584; 2001/1403, 2891, 2894, 3455, 3967; 2002/233, 2086, 2978, 3177; 2003/523, 1917; 2004/118; 2005/1437; 2006/3199; 2007/463, 1065; 2008/1729, 3080, 3089; 2009/1563, 2680; 2010/781, 990, 1997, 2571, 2919; 2011/1627 amended. Territorial extent & classification: E. General. - 12p.: 30 cm. - 978-0-11-152318-6 £5.75

The Alternative Provision Academies (Consequential Amendments to Acts) (England) Order 2012 No. 2012/976. - Enabling power: Education Act 2011, ss. 54 (2), 78 (2). - Issued: 04.04.2012. Made: 29.03.2012. Coming into force: 01.04.2012 in accord. with reg. 1. Effect: 1989 c. 41; 1996 c.56; 1998 c. 31, 39; 2002 c. 32; 2004 c. 31; 2005 c. 5; 2006 c. 21, 47; 2008 c. 25; 2009 c. 4; 2010 c. 15 amended. Territorial extent & classification: E. General. - Supersedes draft S.I. (ISBN 9780111519707) issued 01.02.2012. - 8p.: 30 cm. - 978-0-11-152319-3 £4.00

The Apprenticeships (Alternative English Completion Conditions) Regulations 2012 No. 2012/1199. - Enabling power: Apprenticeships, Skills, Children and Learning Act 2009, ss. 1 (5), 262 (3). - Issued: 04.05.2012. Made: 30.04.2012. Coming into force: 01.05.2012. Effect: None. Territorial extent & classification: E. General. - Supersedes draft S.I. (ISBN 9780111520994) issued 05.03.2012. - 8p.: 30 cm. - 978-0-11-152397-1 £4.00

The Consistent Financial Reporting (England) (Amendment) Regulations 2012 No. 2012/674. - Enabling power: Education Act 2002, s. 44. - Issued: 08.02.2012. Made: 02.03.2012. Laid: 08.03.2012. Coming into force: 31.03.2012. Effect: S.I. 2003/373; 2004/393; 2006/437; 2007/599; 2008/46 revoked. Territorial extent & classification: E. General. - 4p.: 30 cm. - 978-0-11-152143-4 £4.00

The Designation of Rural Primary Schools (England) Order 2012 No. 2012/1197. - Enabling power: Education and Inspections Act 2006, s. 15. - Issued: 08.05.2012. Made: 01.05.2012. Coming into force: 03.05.2012. Effect: S.I. 2009/3346 revoked. Territorial extent & classification: E. General. - 2p.: 30 cm. - 978-0-11-152396-4 £4.00

The Designation of Schools Having a Religious Character (Independent Schools) (England) (No. 1) Order 2012 No. 2012/967. - Enabling power: School Standards and Framework Act 1998, s. 69 (3). - Issued: 03.04.2012. Made: 28.03.2012. Coming into force: 28.03.2012. Effect: None. Territorial extent & classification: E. General. - 2p.: 30 cm. - 978-0-11-152312-4 £4.00

The Designation of Schools Having a Religious Character (Independent Schools) (England) (No. 2) Order 2012 No. 2012/2265. - Enabling power: School Standards and Framework Act 1998, s. 69 (3). - Issued: 07.09.2012. Made: 31.08.2012. Coming into force: 31.08.2012. Effect: None. Territorial extent & classification: E. General. - 4p.: 30 cm. - 978-0-11-152866-2 £4.00

The Designation of Schools Having a Religious Character (Independent Schools) (England) (No. 3) Order 2012 No. 2012/3174. - Enabling power: School Standards and Framework Act 1998, s. 69 (3). - Issued: 28.12.2012. Made: 21.12.2012. Coming into force: 21.12.2012. Effect: S.I. 2003/3328; 2004/577, 1378, 2089, 2986; 2006/1533; 2008/2340; 2010/3031 partially revoked. Territorial extent & classification: E. General. - 6p.: 30 cm. - 978-0-11-153292-8 £4.00

The Diocese of Leicester (Educational Endowments) (Old School Thurcaston) Order 2012 No. 2012/987. - Enabling power: Education Act 1996, ss. 554, 556. - Issued: 04.04.2012. Made: 30.03.2012. Coming into force: 21.04.2012. Effect: None. Territorial extent & classification: E. Local. - Available at http://www.legislation.gov.uk/uksi/2012/987/contents/made *Non-print*

The Diocese of St. Albans (Educational Endowments) (No. 2) Order 1998 (Amendment) Order 2012 No. 2012/986. - Enabling power: Education Act 1996, ss. 554, 556. - Issued: 04.04.2012. Made: 30.03.2012. Coming into force: 21.04.2012. Effect: S.I. 1998/2331 amended. Territorial extent & classification: E. Local. - Available at http://www.legislation.gov.uk/uksi/2012/986/contents/made *Non-print*

The Diocese of St. Albans (Educational Endowments) (Radlett Church of England School) Order 2012 No. 2012/2008. - Enabling power: Education Act 1996, ss. 554, 556. - Issued: 02.08.2012. Made: 25.07.2012. Coming into force: 16.08.2012. Effect: None. Territorial extent & classification: E. Local. - Available at http://www.legislation.gov.uk/uksi/2012/2008/contents/made *Non-print*

The Dissolution of Further Education Corporations and Sixth Form College Corporations (Prescribed Bodies) (England) Regulations 2012 No. 2012/1167. - Enabling power: Further and Higher Education Act 1992, ss. 27B (1), 33P (1). - Issued: 01.05.2012. Made: 21.04.2012. Laid: 30.04.2012. Coming into force: 21.05.2012. Effect: None. Territorial extent & classification: E. General. - 4p.: 30 cm. - 978-0-11-152391-9 £4.00

The Easton and Otley College (Government) Regulations 2012 No. 2012/1749. - Enabling power: Further and Higher Education Act 1992, ss. 20 (2), 21 (1), sch. 4. - Issued: 10.07.2012. Made: 04.07.2012. Laid: 06.07.2012. Coming into force: 31.07.2012. Effect: None. Territorial extent & classification: E. General. - 20p.: 30 cm. - 978-0-11-152635-4 £5.75

The Easton and Otley College (Incorporation) Order 2012 No. 2012/1748. - Enabling power: Further and Higher Education Act 1992, ss. 16 (1) (a) (5), 17 (2) (b). - Issued: 09.07.2012. Made: 04.07.2012. Laid: 06.07.2012. Coming into force: 31.07.2012. Effect: None. Territorial extent & classification: E. General. - 2p.: 30 cm. - 978-0-11-152634-7 £4.00

The Education Act 2011 (Commencement No. 2 and Transitional and Savings Provisions) Order 2012 No. 2012/84 (C.4). - Enabling power: Education Act 2011, s. 82 (3) (7). Bringing into operation various provisions of the 2011 Act on 15.01.2012, 01.02.2012, in accord. with art. 2. - Issued: 18.01.2012. Made: 12.01.2012. Effect: None. Territorial extent & classification: E. General. - 4p.: 30 cm. - 978-0-11-151924-0 £4.00

The Education (Amendment of the Curriculum Requirements for Fourth Key Stage) (England) Order 2012 No. 2012/2056. - Enabling power: Education Act 2002, s. 86. - Issued: 10.08.2012. Made: 06.08.2012. Coming into force: 01.09.2012. Effect: 2002 c. 32 amended in relation to England. Territorial extent & classification: E. General. - Supersedes draft SI (ISBN 9780111525067) issued 11.06.2012. - 2p.: 30 cm. - 978-0-11-152801-3 £4.00

The Education (Charges for Early Years Provision) Regulations 2012 No. 2012/962. - Enabling power: Education Act 1996, s. 451 (2A). - Issued: 03.04.2012. Made: 27.03.2012. Laid: 03.04.2012. Coming into force: 01.09.2012. Effect: None. Territorial extent & classification: E. General. - 2p.: 30 cm. - 978-0-11-152311-7 £4.00

The Education (Educational Provision for Improving Behaviour) (Amendment) Regulations 2012 No. 2012/2532. - Enabling power: Education Act 2002, ss. 29A (3) (b) (4), 210 (7). - Issued: 11.10.2012. Made: 04.10.2012. Laid: 11.10.2012. Coming into force: 01.01.2013. Effect: S.I. 2010/1156 amended. Territorial extent & classification: E. General. - 2p.: 30 cm. - 978-0-11-152916-4 £4.00

The Education (Exemption from School Inspection) (England) Regulations 2012 No. 2012/1293. - Enabling power: Education Act 2005, ss. 5 (4A), 120 (2) (a). - Issued: 21.05.2012. Made: 15.05.2012. Laid: 18.05.2012. Coming into force: 08.06.2012. Effect: None. Territorial extent & classification: E. General. - 4p.: 30 cm. - 978-0-11-152443-5 £4.00

The Education (Head Teachers' Qualifications) (England) (Revocation) Regulations 2012 No. 2012/18. - Enabling power: Education Act 2002, s. 135. - Issued: 12.01.2012. Made: 05.01.2012. Laid: 12.01.2012. Coming into force: 08.02.2012. Effect: S.I. 2003/3111; 2005/875, 3322; 2011/602 revoked. Territorial extent & classification: E. General. - 2p.: 30 cm. - 978-0-11-151898-4 £4.00

The Education (Independent School Standards) (England) (Amendment) Regulations 2012 No. 2012/2962. - Enabling power: Education Act 2002, ss. 157, 210 (7). - Issued: 04.12.2012. Made: 26.11.2012. Laid: 04.12.2012. Coming into force: 01.01.2013. Effect: S.I. 2010/1997 amended. Territorial extent & classification: E. General. - 8p.: 30 cm. - 978-0-11-153129-7 £5.75

The Education (Induction Arrangements for School Teachers) (England) (Amendment) Regulations 2012 No. 2012/513. - Enabling power: Education Act 2002, ss. 135A, 135B, 141C (1) (b), 214 (1). - Issued: 05.03.2012. Made: 28.02.2012. Laid: 05.03.2012. Coming into force: 01.04.2012. Effect: S.I. 2008/657 amended. Territorial extent & classification: E. General. - 8p.: 30 cm. - 978-0-11-152089-5 £4.00

The Education (Induction Arrangements for School Teachers) (England) Regulations 2012 No. 2012/1115. - Enabling power: Education Act 2002, ss. 135A, 135B, 141C (1) (b), 210 (4) (7), 214 (1) (2) (b). - Issued: 23.04.2012. Made: 18.04.2012. Laid: 20.04.2012. Coming into force: In accord. with reg. 1. Effect: S.I. 2008/657 revoked with savings. Territorial extent & classification: E. General. - 16p.: 30 cm. - 978-0-11-152368-1 £5.75

The Education (Information About Individual Pupils) (England) (Amendment) Regulations 2012 No. 2012/1919. - Enabling power: Education Act 1996, ss. 537A (1) (2), 569 (4). - Issued: 30.07.2012. Made: 19.07.2012. Laid: 30.07.2012. Coming into force: 01.01.2013. Effect: S.I. 2006/2601 amended. Territorial extent & classification: E. General. - 2p.: 30 cm. - 978-0-11-152761-0 £4.00

The Education (National Curriculum) (Key Stage 2 Assessment Arrangements) (England) (Amendment) Order 2012 No. 2012/838. - Enabling power: Education Act 2002, s. 87 (6A) (a). - Issued: 21.06.2012. Made: 14.03.2012. Coming into force: 15.03.2012 in accord. with reg. 1. Effect: S.I. 2003/1038 amended. Territorial extent & classification: E. General. - This Statutory Instrument has been printed in substitution of the SI of the same number (and ISBN, issued on 21.03.2012) and is being issued free of charge to all known recipients of that SI. - 4p.: 30 cm. - 978-0-11-152246-2 £4.00

The Education (Penalty Notices) (England) (Amendment) Regulations 2012 No. 2012/1046. - Enabling power: Education Act 1996, ss. 444B (1) (2) (4), 569 & Education and Inspections Act 2006, ss. 106 (1) (2) (4), 181. - Issued: 16.04.2012. Made: 02.04.2012. Laid: 16.04.2012. Coming into force: 01.09.2012. Effect: S.I. 2007/1867 amended. Territorial extent & classification: E. General. - 2p.: 30 cm. - 978-0-11-152354-4 £4.00

The Education (Pupil Referral Units) (Application of Enactments) (England) (Amendment) Regulations 2012 No. 2012/1201. - Enabling power: Education Act 1996, ss. 569 (4), sch. 1, para. 3 & Academies Act 2010, s. 1D (2). - Issued: 29.05.2012. Made: 01.05.2012. Laid: 08.05.2012. Coming into force: 31.05.2012 for regs 1, 2, 4 & 01.09.2012 for all other purposes. Effect: S.I. 2007/ 2979 amended. Territorial extent & classification: E. General. - This Statutory Instrument has been printed in substitution of the SI of the same number and ISBN (issued on 08.05.2012) and is being issued free of charge to all known recipients of that Statutory Instrument. - 4p.: 30 cm. - 978-0-11-152398-8 £4.00

The Education (School Government) (Terms of Reference) (England) (Amendment) Regulations 2012 No. 2012/1845. - Enabling power: Education Act 2002, ss. 21 (3). - Issued: 17.07.2012. Made: 12.07.2012. Laid: 17.07.2012. Coming into force: 01.09.2012. Effect: S.I. 2000/2122 amended. Territorial extent & classification: E. General. - 2p.: 30 cm. - 978-0-11-152713-9 £4.00

The Education (School Performance Information) (England) (Amendment) Regulations 2012 No. 2012/1274. - Enabling power: Education Act 1996, ss. 537A (1) (2), 569 (4). - Issued: 18.05.2012. Made: 14.05.2012. Laid: 18.05.2012. Coming into force: 08.06.2012. Effect: S.I. 2007/2324 amended. Territorial extent & classification: E. General. - 4p.: 30 cm. - 978-0-11-152434-3 £4.00

The Education (School Teachers' Appraisal) (England) (Amendment) Regulations 2012 No. 2012/2055. - Enabling power: Education Act 2002, ss. 131 (1), 210 (7). - Issued: 10.08.2012. Made: 06.08.2012. Laid: 10.08.2012. Coming into force: 01.09.2012. Effect: S.I. 2012/115 amended. Territorial extent & classification: E. General. - 2p.: 30 cm. - 978-0-11-152800-6 £4.00

The Education (School Teachers' Appraisal) (England) Regulations 2012 No. 2012/115. - Enabling power: Education Act 2002, ss. 131 (1) (2) (3), 210 (7). - Issued: 24.01.2012. Made: 17.01.2012. Laid: 24.01.2012. Coming into force: 01.09.2012. Effect: S.I. 2006/2661 revoked with saving. Territorial extent & classification: E. General. - 8p.: 30 cm. - 978-0-11-151932-5 £4.00

The Education (School Teachers) (Qualifications and Appraisal) (Miscellaneous Amendments) (England) Regulations 2012 No. 2012/431. - Enabling power: Education Act 2002, ss. 131 (3), 132 (1) (2), 145 (1), 210 (7). - Issued: 13.03.2012. Made: 08.03.2012. Laid: 09.03.2012. Coming into force: 01.04.2012. Effect: S.I. 2003/1662; 2012/115 amended. Territorial extent & classification: E. General. - 4p.: 30 cm. - 978-0-11-152184-7 £4.00

The Education (School Teachers) (Qualifications and Specified Work) (Miscellaneous Amendments) (England) Regulations 2012 No. 2012/1736. - Enabling power: Education Act 2002, ss. 132 (1) (2), 133 (1) (4) (5), 145 (1), 210 (7). - Issued: 09.07.2012. Made: 03.07.2012. Laid: 09.07.2012. Coming into force: 01.09.2012. Effect: S.I. 2003/1662; 2012/762 amended. Territorial extent & classification: E. General. - 2p.: 30 cm. - 978-0-11-152637-8 £4.00

The Education (Specified Work) (England) Regulations 2012 No. 2012/762. - Enabling power: Education Act 2002, ss. 133, 134, 145, 210 (7). - Issued: 13.03.2012. Made: 08.03.2012. Laid: 09.03.2012. Coming into force: 01.04.2012. Effect: S.I. 2003/1663 revoked with savings & S.I. 2007/2117; 2008/1883 revoked. Territorial extent & classification: E. General. - 8p.: 30 cm. - 978-0-11-152176-2 £5.75

The Education (Student Fees, Awards and Support) (Amendment) Regulations 2012 No. 2012/1653. - Enabling power: Education (Fees and Awards) Act 1983, ss. 1, 2 & Teaching and Higher Education Act 1998, ss. 22, 42 (6) & Higher Education Act 2004, ss. 24, 47. - Issued: 03.07.2012. Made: 26.06.2012. Laid: 26.06.2012. Coming into force: In accord. with reg. 1. Effect: S.I. 2007/778, 779; 2011/1986 amended Territorial extent & classification: E. General. - 20p.: 30 cm. - 978-0-11-152590-6 £5.75

The Education (Student Support) (European University Institute) Regulations 2010 (Amendment) Regulations 2012 No. 2012/3059. - Enabling power: Teaching and Higher Education Act 1998, ss. 22, 42 (6), 43 (1). - Issued: 12.12.2012. Made: 06.12.2012. Laid: 10.12.2012. Coming into force: 31.12.2012. Effect: S.I. 2010/447 amended. Territorial extent & classification: E. General. - 4p.: 30 cm. - 978-0-11-153204-1 £4.00

The Filton College and Stroud College of Further Education (Dissolution) Order 2012 No. 2012/52. - Enabling power: Further and Higher Education Act 1992, s. 27. - Issued: 17.01.2012. Made: 07.01.2012. Laid: 12.01.2012. Coming into force: 01.02.2012. Effect: None. Territorial extent & classification: E. General. - 2p.: 30 cm. - 978-0-11-151907-3 £4.00

The Further Education Corporations (Publication of Proposals) (England) Regulations 2012 No. 2012/1157. - Enabling power: Further and Higher Education Act 1992, ss. 16A (1), 27 (2) (3), 89 (4). - Issued: 01.05.2012. Made: 21.04.2012. Laid: 30.04.2012. Coming into force: 21.05.2012. Effect: None. Territorial extent & classification: E. General. - 4p.: 30 cm. - 978-0-11-152390-2 £4.00

The Further Education Institutions and 16 to 19 Academies (Specification and Disposal of Articles) Regulations 2012 No. 2012/1925. - Enabling power: Further and Higher Education Act 1992, ss. 85AA (3) (f), 85AC (7), 89 (4). - Issued: 25.07.2012. Made: 18.07.2012. Coming into force: 01.09.2012. Effect: None. Territorial extent & classification: E. General. - 4.: 30 cm. - 978-0-11-152763-4 £4.00

The Further Education Institutions (Exemption from Inspection) (England) Regulations 2012 No. 2012/2576. - Enabling power: Education and Inspections Act 2006, s. 125 (1A). - Issued: 17.10.2012. Made: 10.10.2012. Laid: 15.10.2012. Coming into force: 05.11.2012. Effect: None. Territorial extent & classification: E. General. - 2p.: 30 cm. - 978-0-11-152939-3 £4.00

The Further Education Loans Regulations 2012 No. 2012/1818. - Enabling power: Teaching and Higher Education Act 1998, ss. 22, 42 (6). - Issued: 13.07.2012. Made: 11.07.2012. Laid: 12.07.2012. Coming into force: 01.09.2012. Effect: None. Territorial extent & classification: E. General. - 20p.: 30 cm. - 978-0-11-152693-4 £5.75

The Further Education Teachers' Continuing Professional Development and Registration (England) (Revocation) Regulations 2012 No. 2012/2165. - Enabling power: Education Act 2002, ss. 136 (c), 210 (7). - Issued: 24.08.2012. Made: 20.08.2012. Laid: 22.08.2012. Coming into force: 30.09.2012. Effect: S.I. 2012/747 partially revoked & 2007/2116 revoked. Territorial extent & classification: E. General. - 2p.: 30 cm. - 978-0-11-152831-0 £4.00

The Further Education Teachers' Qualifications, Continuing Professional Development and Registration (England) (Amendment) Regulations 2012 No. 2012/747. - Enabling power: Education Act 2002, ss. 136 (a) (c), 145, 210 (7). - Issued: 12.03.2012. Made: 07.03.2012. Laid: 09.03.2012. Coming into force: 01.04.2012. Effect: S.I. 2007/2116, 2264 amended. Territorial extent & classification: E. General. - Partially revoked by SI 2012/2165 (ISBN 9780111528310). - 4p.: 30 cm. - 978-0-11-152178-6 £4.00

The Further Education Teachers' Qualifications (England) (Amendment) Regulations 2012 No. 2012/2166. - Enabling power: Education Act 2002, ss. 136 (a) (c), 145, 210 (7). - Issued: 24.08.2012. Made: 20.08.2012. Laid: 22.08.2012. Coming into force: 30.09.2012. Effect: S.I. 2007/2264 amended. Territorial extent & classification: E. General. - 4p.: 30 cm. - 978-0-11-152832-7 £4.00

The Information as to Provision of Education (England) (Amendment) Regulations 2012 No. 2012/1554. - Enabling power: Education Act 1996, ss. 29 (3), 569 (4). - Issued: 22.06.2012. Made: 18.06.2012. Laid: 22.06.2012. Coming into force: 16.06.2012. Effect: S.I. 2008/4 amended. Territorial extent & classification: E. General. - 4p.: 30 cm. - 978-0-11-152557-9 £4.00

The Inspectors of Education, Children's Services and Skills Order 2012 No. 2012/2597. - Enabling power: Education and Inspections Act 2006, s. 114 (1). - Issued: 25.10.2012. Made: 17.10.2012. Coming into force: 18.10.2012. Effect: None. Territorial extent & classification: E. General. - 2p.: 30 cm. - 978-0-11-152973-7 £4.00

The Legislative Reform (Annual Review of Local Authorities) Order 2012 No. 2012/1879. - Enabling power: Legislative and Regulatory Reform Act 2006, s. 1. - Issued: 30.07.2012. Made: 17.07.2012. Coming into force: 18.07.2012 in accord. with art. 1. Effect: 2006 c. 40 amended. Territorial extent & classification: E. General. - Supersedes draft S.I. (ISBN 9780111524091) issued 10.05.2012. - 4p.: 30 cm. - 978-0-11-152739-9 £4.00

The National Curriculum (Exceptions for First, Second, Third and Fourth Key Stages) (England) Regulations 2012 No. 2012/1926. - Enabling power: Education Act 2002, s. 91. - Issued: 30.07.2012. Made: 23.07.2012. Laid: 30.07.2012. Coming into force: 01.09.2012. Effect: None. Territorial extent & classification: E. General. - 4p.: 30 cm. - 978-0-11-152764-1 £4.00

The Office of Qualifications and Examinations Regulation (Determination of Turnover for Monetary Penalties) Order 2012 No. 2012/1768. - Enabling power: Apprenticeships, Skills, Children and Learning Act 2009, s. 151B (2). - Issued: 11.07.2012. Made: 05.07.2012. Coming into force: 06.07.2012. In accord. with reg. 1. Effect: None. Territorial extent & classification: E/NI. General. - Supersedes draft SI (ISBN 9780111524398) issued on 18.05.2012. - 4p.: 30 cm. - 978-0-11-152651-4 £4.00

The Pupil Referral Units (Miscellaneous Amendments) (England) Regulations 2012 No. 2012/1825. - Enabling power: Education Act 1996, s. 569 (4), sch. 1, paras 3, 3A, 15. - Issued: 16.07.2012. Made: 10.07.2012. Laid: 13.07.2012. Coming into force: In accord. with reg. 1. Effect: S.I. 2007/ 2978, 2979; 2010/1071 amended & S.I. 2010/1920 revoked (01.09.2012). Territorial extent & classification: E. General. - 12p.: 30 cm. - 978-0-11-152697-2 £5.75

The Pupil Referral Units (Miscellaneous Amendments) (No. 2) (England) Regulations 2012 No. 2012/3158. - Enabling power: Education Act 1996, s. 569 (4), sch. 1, paras 3, 6 (2), 15 (1) (b) (2) (d) (2) (e) (2) (h). - Issued: 28.12.2012. Made: 19.12.2012. Laid: 28.12.2012. Coming into force: 01.04.2013. Effect: S.I. 2007/ 2978, 2979; 2009/2680 amended. Territorial extent & classification: E. General. - 8p.: 30 cm. - 978-0-11-153282-9 £5.75

The School Admission (Appeals Arrangements) (England) Regulations 2012 No. 2012/9. - Enabling power: School Standards and Framework Act 1998, ss. 94 (5) (5A) (5C), 95 (3) (3A) (3B), 138 (7). - Issued: 10.01.2012. Made: 03.01.2012. Laid: 10.01.2012. Coming into force: 01.02.2012. Effect: S.I. 2002/2899; 2007/3206; 2008/3092 revoked with saving. Territorial extent & classification: E. General. - 8p.: 30 cm. - 978-0-11-151890-8 £4.00

The School Admissions (Admission Arrangements and Co-ordination of Admission Arrangements) (England) Regulations 2012 No. 2012/8. - Enabling power: School Standards and Framework Act 1998, ss. 88B, 88C, 88E, 88F, 88H, 88K, 88M, 88N, 88O, 88Q, 92, 100, 102, 138 (7) & Education Act 1996, s. 29 (5). - Issued: 10.01.2012. Made: 03.01.2012. Laid: 10.01.2012. Coming into force: 01.02.2012. Effect: S.I. 2008/3093 amended & S.I. 2008/3089, 3090, 3091 revoked with saving. Territorial extent & classification: E. General. - 20p.: 30 cm. - 978-0-11-151891-5 £5.75

The School Admissions Code and School Admission Appeals Code (Appointed Day) (England) Order 2012 No. 2012/216. - Enabling power: School Standards and Framework Act 1998, s. 85 (5). Appointing 01.02.2012 for the coming into force of the School Admissions Code and School Admission Appeals Code (copies of drafts of which were laid before each House of Parliament on 01.12.2011). - Issued: 03.02.2012. Made: 30.01.2012. Effect: None. Territorial extent & classification: E. General. - 4p.: 30 cm. - 978-0-11-151974-5 £4.00

The School Admissions (Infant Class Sizes) (England) Regulations 2012 No. 2012/10. - Enabling power: School Standards and Framework Act 1998, ss. 1, 138 (7). - Issued: 10.01.2012. Made: 03.01.2012. Laid: 10.01.2012. Coming into force: 01.02.2012. Effect: S.I. 1998/1973; 2006/3409 revoked. Territorial extent & classification: E. General. - 8p.: 30 cm. - 978-0-11-151894-6 £4.00

The School and Early Years Finance (England) Regulations 2012 No. 2012/2991. - Enabling power: School Standards and Framework Act 1998, ss. 45A, 45AA, 47, 47ZA, 47A (4), 48 (1) (2), 49 (2) (2A), 138 (7), sch. 14, para. 2B & Education Act 2002, s. 24 (3). - Issued: 07.12.2012. Made: 27.11.2012. Laid: 07.12.2012. Coming into force: 01.01.2013. Effect: None. Territorial extent & classification: E. General. - 32p.: 30 cm. - 978-0-11-153148-8 £9.75

The School Behaviour (Determination and Publicising of Measures in Academies) Regulations 2012 No. 2012/619. - Enabling power: Education Act 1996, ss. 550Z (4B) (b), 569 (4). - Issued: 07.03.2012. Made: 29.02.2012. Laid: 07.03.2012. Coming into force: 01.04.2012. Effect: None. Territorial extent & classification: E. General. - 2p.: 30 cm. - 978-0-11-152124-3 £4.00

The School Discipline (Pupil Exclusions and Reviews) (England) Regulations 2012 No. 2012/1033. - Enabling power: Education Act 1996, ss. 19 (3B), 494 (5), 569 (4) & Education Act 2002, ss. 51A (3) (5) (6) (7) (8) (9) (10) (12), 210 (7), 214 & Education and Inspections Act 2006, ss. 100, 102, 104, 181 (2). - Issued: 13.04.2012. Made: 03.04.2012. Laid: 13.04.2012. Coming into force: 01.09.2012. Effect: 2002 c. 32 modified & S.I. 1999/495; 2003/1021, 1377; 2006/1751, 2601;2007/958, 1869, 1870; 2012/335 amended & S.I. 2004/402; 2006/2189; 2008/2683 partially revoked (with saving) & S.I. 2002/3178; 2007/1868; 2008/532 revoked (with saving). Territorial extent & classification: E. General. - 28p.: 30 cm. - 978-0-11-152353-7 £5.75

The School Finance (England) (Amendment) Regulations 2012 No. 2012/335. - Enabling power: School Standards and Framework Act 1998, ss. 45A, 45AA, 47, 47ZA, 47A (4), 48 (1) (2), 49 (2) (2A), 138 (7), sch. 14, para. 2B, sch. 14. - Issued: 16.02.2012. Made: 08.02.2012. Laid: 16.02.2012. Coming into force: 15.02.2012. Effect: S.I. 2008/228; 2010/210 revoked. Territorial extent & classification: E. General. - 36p.: 30 cm. - 978-0-11-152018-5 £9.75

The School Governance (Constitution) (England) Regulations 2012 No. 2012/1034. - Enabling power: Education Act 2002, ss. 19 (1A) (2) (3) (4A) (4B), 20 (2) (3), 210 (7). - Issued: 19.04.2012. Made: 14.04.2012. Laid: 19.04.2012. Coming into force: 01.09.2012. Effect: S.I. 2007/958 amended & S.I. 2007/957 revoked with savings. Territorial extent & classification: E. General. - 20p.: 30 cm. - 978-0-11-152357-5 £5.75

The School Governance (England) (Amendment) Regulations 2012 No. 2012/421. - Enabling power: Education Act 2002, ss. 19 (2) (3), 20 (2). - Issued: 24.02.2012. Made: 17.02.2012. Laid: 24.02.2012. Coming into force: 17.03.2012. Effect: S.I. 2007/957, 960 amended. Territorial extent & classification: E. General. - 4p.: 30 cm. - 978-0-11-152041-3 £4.00

The School Governance (Federations) (England) Regulations 2012 No. 2012/1035. - Enabling power: Education Act 2002, ss. 19 (1A) (2) (3) (4A) (4B) (8), 20 (2) (3) (4), 24, 25, 34 (5), 35 (4) (5), 36 (4) (5), 210 (7) & Academies Act 2010, s. 3 (6). - Issued: 19.04.2012. Made: 14.04.2012. Laid: 19.04.2012. Coming into force: 01.09.2012. Effect: 1998 c. 31; S.I. 2003/1377; 2009/2680; 2012/1034 modified & S.I. 2007/960 revoked with savings. Territorial extent & classification: E. General. - 28p.: 30 cm. - 978-0-11-152358-2 £5.75

The School Information (England) (Amendment) Regulations 2012 No. 2012/1124. - Enabling power: Education Act 1996, ss. 537, 569 (4). - Issued: 25.04.2012. Made: 19.04.2012. Laid: 20.04.2012. Coming into force: 01.09.2012. Effect: S.I. 2008/3093 amended. Territorial extent & classification: E. General. - 8p.: 30 cm. - 978-0-11-152371-1 £4.00

The Schools Forums (England) Regulations 2012 No. 2012/2261. - Enabling power: School Standards and Framework Act 1998, ss. 47A, 138 (7). - Issued: 07.09.2012. Made: 03.09.2012. Laid: 07.09.2012. Coming into force: 01.10.2012. Effect: S.I. 2010/344 revoked. Territorial extent & classification: E. General. - 8p.: 30 cm. - 978-0-11-152845-7 £5.75

The Schools (Specification and Disposal of Articles) Regulations 2012 No. 2012/951. - Enabling power: Education Act 1996, ss. 550ZA (3) (f), 550ZC (7). - Issued: 03.04.2012. Made: 27.03.2012. Coming into force: 01.04.2012. Effect: None. Territorial extent & classification: E. General. - Supersedes draft SI (ISBN 9780111519356) issued on 24.02.2012. - 4p.: 30 cm. - 978-0-11-152314-8 £4.00

The School Staffing (England) (Amendment) Regulations 2012 No. 2012/1740. - Enabling power: Education Act 2002, ss. 35 (4) (5) (a) (b) (d), 36 (4) (5) (a) (b) (e). - Issued: 10.07.2012. Made: 03.07.2012. Laid: 10.07.2012. Coming into force: 01.09.2012. Effect: S.I. 2009/2680 amended. Territorial extent & classification: E. General. - 2p.: 30 cm. - 978-0-11-152646-0 £4.00

The School Teachers' Incentive Payments (England) Order 2012 No. 2012/878. - Enabling power: Education Act 2002, s. 123 (4) (a). - Issued: 26.03.2012. Made: 19.03.2012. Laid: 26.03.2012. Coming into force: 01.09.2012. Effect: None. Territorial extent & classification: E. General. - 2p.: 30 cm. - 978-0-11-152258-5 £4.00

The Sixth Form College Corporations (Publication of Proposals) (England) Regulations 2012 No. 2012/1158. - Enabling power: Further and Higher Education Act 1992, ss. 33C (3), 33N (2) (3), 89 (4). - Issued: 04.05.2012. Made: 30.04.2012. Laid: 01.05.2012. Coming into force: 22.05.2012. Effect: S.I. 2010/2609 revoked (with saving). Territorial extent & classification: E. General. - 8p.: 30 cm. - 978-0-11-152393-3 £4.00

The Special Educational Needs (Direct Payments) (Pilot Scheme) Order 2012 No. 2012/206. - Enabling power: Education Act 1996, ss. 532B (1), 532C (1). - Issued: 03.02.2012. Made: 29.01.2012. Coming into force: 30.01.2012. Effect: None. Territorial extent & classification: E. General. - With correction slip dated February 2012. Supersedes draft SI (ISBN 9780111517741) issued 12.12.2011. - 16p.: 30 cm. - 978-0-11-151963-9 £5.75

The Student Fees (Basic and Higher Amounts) (Approved Plans) (England) (Amendment) Regulations 2012 No. 2012/433. - Enabling power: Education Act 2011, ss. 24 (6), 36, 47. - Issued: 23.02.2012. Made: 14.02.2012. Laid: 22.02.2012. Coming into force: In accord. with art. 1, 15.03.2012; 01.08.2012; 01.09.2012. Effect: S.I. 2004/1932, 2473; 2010/3020, 3021 amended. Territorial extent & classification: E. General. - 8p.: 30 cm. - 978-0-11-152042-0 £5.75

The Teachers' Disciplinary (England) Regulations 2012 No. 2012/560. - Enabling power: Education Act 2002, ss. 141A (2), 141D (3), 141E (3), 210 (7), sch. 11A. - Issued: 05.03.2012. Made: 28.02.2012. Laid: 05.03.2012. Coming into force: 01.04.2012. Effect: None. Territorial extent & classification: E. General. - 8p.: 30 cm. - 978-0-11-152091-8 £5.75

The Wiltshire Council (Arrangements for the Provision of Suitable Education) Order 2012 No. 2012/1107. - Enabling power: Education Act 2002, ss. 2 (1), 210. - Issued: 23.04.2012. Made: 18.04.2012. Laid: 23.04.2012. Coming into force: 18.05.2012. Effect: 1996 c.56; 2006 c.40; 2010 c.32 modified & S.I. 1999/495; 2006/1751; 2007/1065, 1870; 2012/335 modified. Territorial extent & classification: E. General. - 8p.: 30 cm. - 978-0-11-152364-3 £5.75

The Young People's Learning Agency Abolition (Consequential Amendments to Subordinate Legislation) (England) Order 2012 No. 2012/956. - Enabling power: Education Act 2011, ss. 67 (2), 78 (2) (c). - Issued: 04.04.2012. Made: 26.03.2012. Laid: 03.04.2012. Coming into force: 01.05.2012. Effect: S.I. 1979/597; 1987/1967; 1992/548; 1996/207, 2890; 1999/584; 2001/2857; 2003/1917; 2005/2038; 2006/213, 214, 215, 216; 2007/779, 1065, 1288, 1289, 1355, 2260, 3475; 2008/794; 2009/1563; 2010/1941 amended. Territorial extent & classification: E/W. General. - 8p.: 30 cm. - 978-0-11-152320-9 £5.75

Education, England and Wales

The Education Act 2011 (Abolition of the GTCE Consequential Amendments and Revocations) Order 2012 No. 2012/1153. - Enabling power: Education Act 2011, ss.11 (2), 78 (2) (a) (c). - Issued: 03.05.2012. Made: 25.04.2012. Laid: 03.05.2012. Coming into force: 25.05.2012. Effect: S.I. 2009/2610 amended; S.I. 2003/2039; 2007/2602, 3224; 2009/1924; 2010/1836 partially revoked; S.I. 2009/3200 revoked in so far as it applied in relation to England; and S.I. 1999/1726, 2019; 2000/1447, 2175, 2176; 2001/23, 1267, 1268, 1270, 3993; 2003/985, 1186; 2004/1886, 1935; 2007/1883; 2008/1884, 3256; 2011/2785 revoked. Territorial extent & classification: E/W. General. - 4p.: 30 cm. - 978-0-11-152384-1 £4.00

The Education Act 2011 (Commencement No. 3 and Transitional and Savings Provisions) Order 2012 No. 2012/924 (C.30). - Enabling power: Education Act 2011, s. 82 (3) (7). Bringing into operation various provisions of the 2011 Act on 01.04.2012, 01.05.2012, in accord. with arts 2 & 3. - Issued: 28.03.2012. Made: 22.03.2012. Effect: None. Territorial extent & classification: E/W. General. - 8p.: 30 cm. - 978-0-11-152286-8 £4.00

The Education Act 2011 (Commencement No. 4 and Transitional and Savings Provisions) Order 2012 No. 2012/1087 (C.33). - Enabling power: Education Act 2011, s. 82 (3) (7). Bringing into operation various provisions of the 2011 Act on 01.08.2012, 01.09.2012, in accord. with arts 2 & 3. - Issued: 19.04.2012. Made: 12.04.2012. Effect: None. Territorial extent & classification: E/W. General. - 4p.: 30 cm. - 978-0-11-152359-9 £4.00

The Education Act 2011 (Commencement No. 5) Order 2012 No. 2012/2213 (C.87). - Enabling power: Education Act 2011, s. 82 (3) (7). Bringing into operation various provisions of the 2011 Act in accord. with arts 2, 3, 4, 5. - Issued: 31.08.2012. Made: 28.08.2012. Effect: None. Territorial extent & classification: E/W. General. - 4p.: 30 cm. - 978-0-11-152840-2 £4.00

The Education Act 2011 (Consequential Amendments to Subordinate Legislation) Order 2012 No. 2012/765. - Enabling power: Education Act 2011, ss.11 (2), 16 (2), 26 (2), 78 (2) (c). - Issued: 13.03.2012. Made: 08.03.2012. Laid: 09.03.2012. Coming into force: 01.04.2012. Effect: 17 instruments amended. Territorial extent & classification: Amendments and revokes have the same extent as the provisions to which they relate. General. - 4p.: 30 cm. - 978-0-11-152191-5 £4.00

The Education and Skills Act 2008 (Commencement No. 8) Order 2012 No. 2012/2197 (C.86). - Enabling power: Education and Skills Act 2008, s. 173 (4) (8). Bringing into operation various provisions of the 2008 Act on 03.09.2012, in accord. with art. 2. - Issued: 30.08.2012. Made: 23.08.2012. Effect: None. Territorial extent & classification: E/W. General. - 4p.: 30 cm. - 978-0-11-152838-9 £4.00

The Education (School Teachers' Prescribed Qualifications etc) (Amendment) Order 2012 No. 2012/694. - Enabling power: Education Act 2002, ss. 122 (5), 210 (7). - Issued: 08.03.2012. Made: 05.03.2012. Laid: 08.03.2012. Coming into force: 01.04.2012. Effect: S.I. 2003/1709 amended. Territorial extent & classification: E/W. General. - 2p.: 30 cm. - 978-0-11-152148-9 *£4.00*

The Education (Teacher Student Loans) (Repayment etc) (Amendment) Regulations 2012 No. 2012/555. - Enabling power: Education Act 2002, s. 186. - Issued: 05.03.2012. Made: 28.02.2012. Laid: 05.03.2012. Coming into force: 01.04.2012. Effect: S.I. 2003/1917 amended & S.I. 2002/2086 revoked. Territorial extent & classification: E/W. General. - 2p.: 30 cm. - 978-0-11-152090-1 *£4.00*

The School Premises (England) Regulations 2012 No. 2012/1943. - Enabling power: Education Act 1996, ss. 542 (1), 569 (4). - Issued: 30.07.2012. Made: 19.07.2012. Laid: 30.07.2012. Coming into force: 31.10.2012. Effect: S.I. 1999/2 amended. Territorial extent & classification: E/W. General. - 4p.: 30 cm. - 978-0-11-152768-9 *£4.00*

The School Teachers' Pay and Conditions Order 2012 No. 2012/2051. - Enabling power: Education Act 2002, ss. 122 (1), 123, 124. - Issued: 14.08.2012. Made: 09.08.2012. Laid: 10.08.2012. Coming into force: 01.09.2012. Effect: S.I. 2011/1917 revoked. Territorial extent & classification: E/W. General. - 2p.: 30 cm. - 978-0-11-152809-9 *£4.00*

The Teachers' Pensions (Amendment) (No. 2) Regulations 2012 No. 2012/2270. - Enabling power: Superannuation Act 1972, ss. 9, 12, sch. 3. - Issued: 07.09.2012. Made: 03.09.2012. Laid: 07.09.2012. Coming into force: 01.10.2012. Effect: S.I. 2010/990 amended. Territorial extent & classification: E/W. General. - 4p.: 30 cm. - 978-0-11-152852-5 *£4.00*

The Teachers' Pensions (Amendment) Regulations 2012 No. 2012/673. - Enabling power: Superannuation Act 1972, ss. 9, 12, sch. 3. - Issued: 09.03.2012. Made: 02.03.2012. Laid: 08.03.2012. Coming into force: 01.04.2012. Effect: S.I. 2010/990 amended. Territorial extent & classification: E/W. General. - 4p.: 30 cm. - 978-0-11-152153-3 *£4.00*

Education, Northern Ireland

The Office of Qualifications and Examinations Regulation (Determination of Turnover for Monetary Penalties) Order 2012 No. 2012/1768. - Enabling power: Apprenticeships, Skills, Children and Learning Act 2009, s. 151B (2). - Issued: 11.07.2012. Made: 05.07.2012. Coming into force: 06.07.2012. In accord. with reg. 1. Effect: None. Territorial extent & classification: E/NI. General. - Supersedes draft SI (ISBN 9780111524398) issued on 18.05.2012. - 4p.: 30 cm. - 978-0-11-152651-4 *£4.00*

Education, Wales

The Assembly Learning Grants and Loans (Higher Education) (Wales) (No. 2) (Amendment) (No. 2) Regulations 2012 No. 2012/1156 (W.139). - Enabling power: Teaching and Higher Education Act 1998, ss. 22, 42 (6). - Issued: 17.05.2012. Made: 26.04.2012. Laid before the National Assembly for Wales: 27.04.2012. Coming into force: 18.05.2012. Effect: S.I. 2011/886 (W.130) amended. Territorial extent & classification: W. General. - In English and Welsh. Welsh title: Rheoliadau Grantiau a Benthyciadau Dysgu'r Cynulliad (Addysg Uwch) (Cymru) (Rhif 2) (Diwygio) (Rhif 2) 2012. - 8p.: 30 cm. - 978-0-348-10607-7 *£5.75*

The Assembly Learning Grants and Loans (Higher Education) (Wales) (No. 2) (Amendment) Regulations 2012 No. 2012/14 (W.5). - Enabling power: Teaching and Higher Education Act 1998, ss. 22, 42 (6). - Issued: 27.01.2012. Made: 04.01.2012. Laid before the National Assembly for Wales: 06.01.2012. Coming into force: 01.02.2012. Effect: S.I. 2011/886 (W.130) amended. Territorial extent & classification: W. General. - In English and Welsh. Welsh title: Rheoliadau Grantiau a Benthyciadau Dysgu'r Cynulliad (Addysg Uwch) (Cymru) (Rhif 2) (Diwygio) 2012. - 12p.: 30 cm. - 978-0-348-10541-4 *£5.75*

The Cancellation of Student Loans for Living Costs Liability (Wales) Regulations 2012 No. 2012/1518 (W.201). - Enabling power: Teaching and Higher Education Act 1998, ss. 22, 42 (6). - Issued: 27.06.2012. Made: 12.06.2012. Laid before the National Assembly for Wales: 15.06.2012. Coming into force: 01.08.2012. Effect: None. Territorial extent & classification: W. General. - In English and Welsh. Welsh title: Rheoliadau Dileu Atebolrwydd dros Fenthyciadau i Fyfyrwyr at Gostau Byw (Cymru) 2012. - 8p.: 30 cm. - 978-0-348-10628-2 *£4.00*

The Coleg Menai Further Education Corporation (Dissolution) Order 2012 No. 2012/631 (W.88). - Enabling power: Further and Higher Education Act 1992, s. 27. - Issued: 23.03.2012. Made: 29.02.2012. Laid before the National Assembly for Wales: 02.03.2012. Coming into force: 01.04.2012. Effect: None. Territorial extent & classification: W. General. - In English and Welsh. Welsh title: Gorchymyn Corfforaeth Addysg Bellach Coleg Menai (Diddymu) 2012. - 4p.: 30 cm. - 978-0-348-10563-6 *£4.00*

The Collaboration Between Education Bodies (Wales) Regulations 2012 No. 2012/2655 (W.287). - Enabling power: Education (Wales) Measure 2011, ss. 6 (1) (2), 32. - Issued: 05.11.2012. Made: 22.10.2012. Laid before the National Assembly for Wales: 23.10.2012. Coming into force: 16.11.2012. Effect: S.I. 2008/168 (W.21), 3082 (W.271) revoked. Territorial extent & classification: W. General. - In English and Welsh. Welsh title: Rheoliadau Cydlafurio Rhwng Chyrff Addysg (Cymru) 2012. - 16p.: 30 cm. - 978-0-348-10662-6 *£5.75*

The Diocese of Swansea & Brecon (Educational Endowments) (Llandegley) (Wales) Order 2012 No. 2012/1703 (W.221). - Enabling power: Education Act 1996, ss. 554, 556 (2). - Issued: 19.07.2012. Made: 27.06.2012. Coming into force: 01.08.2012. Effect: None. Territorial extent & classification: W. General. - In English and Welsh. Welsh language title: Gorchymyn Esgobaeth Abertawe ac Aberhonddu (Gwaddolion Addysgol) (Llandegley) (Cymru) 2012. - 8p.: 30 cm. - 978-0-348-10632-9 £4.00

The Education (Induction Arrangements for School Teachers) (Wales) (Amendment) Regulations 2012 No. 2012/1675 (W.216). - Enabling power: Teaching and Higher Education Act 1998, ss. 19, 42 (6) (7). - Issued: 19.07.2012. Made: 26.06.2012. Laid before the National Assembly for Wales: 28.06.2012. Coming into force: 01.09.2012. Effect: S.I. 2005/1818 (W.146) amended. Territorial extent & classification: W. General. - In English and Welsh. Welsh language title: Rheoliadau Addysg (Trefniadau Ymsefydlu ar gyfer Athrawon Ysgol) (Cymru) (Diwygio) 2012. - 8p.: 30 cm. - 978-0-348-10634-3 £5.75

The Education (Listed Bodies) (Wales) Order 2012 No. 2012/1259 (W.154). - Enabling power: Education Reform Act 1988, ss. 216 (2), 232 (5). - Issued: 20.06.2012. Made: 09.05.2012. Coming into force: 04.06.2012. Effect: S.I. 2007/2794 (W.234); 2009/710 (W.62) revoked. Territorial extent & classification: W. General. - In English and Welsh. Welsh title: Gorchymyn Addysg (Cyrff sy'n Cael eu Rhestru) (Cymru) 2012. - 28p.: 30 cm. - 978-0-348-10625-1 £5.75

The Education (Middle Schools) (Wales) Regulations 2012 No. 2012/1797 (W.227). - Enabling power: Education Act 1996, ss. 5 (4), 569 (4) (5). - Issued: 25.07.2012. Made: 06.06.2012. Laid before the National Assembly for Wales: 10.06.2012. Coming into force: 01.09.2012. Effect: S.I. 1980/918; 1994/581 revoked with savings. Territorial extent & classification: W. General. - In English and Welsh. Welsh title: Rheoliadau Addysg (Ysgolion Canol) (Cymru) 2012. - 8p.: 30 cm. - 978-0-348-10640-4 £5.75

The Education (Recognised Bodies) (Wales) Order 2012 No. 2012/1260 (W.155). - Enabling power: Education Reform Act 1988, s. 216 (1). - Issued: 30.05.2012. Made: 09.05.2012. Coming into force: 04.06.2012. Effect: S.I. 2007/2795 (W.235); 2009/667 (W.59) revoked. Territorial extent & classification: W. General. - In English and Welsh. Welsh title: Gorchymyn Addysg (Cyrff sy'n Cael eu Cydnabod) (Cymru) 2012. - 12p.: 30 cm. - 978-0-348-10614-5 £5.75

The Education (School Day and School Year) (Wales) (Amendment) Regulations 2012 No. 2012/248 (W.41). - Enabling power: Education Act 1996, ss. 551, 569 (4) (5). - Issued: 23.02.2012. Made: 01.02.2012. Laid before the National Assembly for Wales: 02.02.2012. Coming into force: 24.02.2012. Effect: S.I. 2003/3231 (W.311) amended. Territorial extent & classification: W. General. - In English and Welsh. Welsh title: Rheoliadau Addysg (Y Diwrnod Ysgol a'r Flwyddyn Ysgol) (Cymru) (Diwygio) 2012. - 4p.: 30 cm. - 978-0-348-10694-7 £4.00

The Education (Student Support) (Wales) Regulations 2012 No. 2012/3097 (W.313). - Enabling power: Teaching and Higher Education Act 1998, ss. 22, 42 (6). - Issued: 16.01.2013. Made: 12.12.2012. Laid before the National Assembly for Wales: 14.12.2012. Coming into force: 04.01.2013. Effect: S.I. 2011/886 (W.130) amended and then revoked with savings in relation to Wales on 01.09.2013. Territorial extent & classification: W. General. - With correction slip dated February 2013. - In English and Welsh. Welsh title: Rheoliadau Addysg (Cymorth i Fyfyrwyr) (Cymru) 2012. - 224p.: 30 cm. - 978-0-348-10675-6 £28.75

The Education (Wales) Measure 2009 (Commencement No. 3 and Transitional Provisions) Order 2012 No. 2012/320 (W.51) (C.10). - Enabling power: Education (Wales) Measure 2009, ss. 24 (2), 26 (3). Bringing into force various provisions of the 2009 Measure on 10.02.2012, 06.03.2012, in accord. with arts 2, 3. - Issued: 23.02.2012. Made: 08.02.2012. Effect: None. Territorial extent & classification: W. General. - In English and Welsh. Welsh title: Gorchymyn Mesur Addysg (Cymru) 2009 (Cychwyn Rhif 3 a Darpariaethau Trosiannol) 2012. - 8p.: 30 cm. - 978-0-348-10693-0 £5.75

The Education (Wales) Measure 2009 (Pilot) Regulations 2012 No. 2012/321 (W.52). - Enabling power: Education (Wales) Measure 2009, s. 17 (1) (2). - Issued: 23.02.2012. Made: 08.02.2012. Laid before the National Assembly for Wales: 13.02.2012. Coming into force: 06.03.2012. Effect: None. Territorial extent & classification: W. General. - In English and Welsh. Welsh title: Rheoliadau Mesur Addysg (Cymru) 2009 (Treialu) 2012. - 8p.: 30 cm. - 978-0-348-10692-3 £5.75

The Education (Wales) Measure 2011 (Commencement No. 1) Order 2012 No. 2012/2656 (W.288) (C.106). - Enabling power: Education (Wales) Measure 2011, ss. 32. Bringing into force various provisions of the 2011 Measure on 16.11.2012, in accord. with art 2. - Issued: 05.11.2012. Made: 22.10.2012. Effect: None. Territorial extent & classification: W. General. - In English and Welsh. Welsh title: Gorchymyn Mesur Addysg (Cymru) 2011 (Cychwyn Rhif 1) 2012. - 4p.: 30 cm. - 978-0-348-10663-3 £4.00

The General Teaching Council for Wales (Additional Functions) (Amendment) Order 2012 No. 2012/167 (W.26). - Enabling power: Teaching and Higher Education Act 1998, ss. 7 (1) (4), 42 (6) (7). - Issued: 10.02.2012. Made: 20.01.2012. Laid before the National Assembly for Wales: 26.01.2012. Coming into force: In accord. with reg. 1 (2). Effect: S.I. 2000/1941 (W.139) amended. Territorial extent & classification: W. General. - In English and Welsh. Welsh language title: Gorchymyn Cyngor Addysgu Cyffredinol Cymru (Swyddogaethau Ychwanegol) (Diwygio) 2012. - 4p.: 30 cm. - 978-0-348-10551-3 £4.00

The General Teaching Council for Wales (Amendment) Order 2012 No. 2012/168 (W.27). - Enabling power: Teaching and Higher Education Act 1998, s. 8 (1) (2). - Issued: 10.02.2012. Made: 20.01.2012. Laid before the National Assembly for Wales: 26.01.2012. Coming into force: In accord. with reg 1 (2). Effect: S.I. 1998/2911 amended. Territorial extent & classification: W. General. - In English and Welsh. Welsh title: Gorchymyn Cyngor Addysgu Cyffredinol Cymru (Diwygio) 2012. - 4p.: 30 cm. - 978-0-348-10553-7 £4.00

The General Teaching Council for Wales (Constitution) (Amendment) Regulations 2012 No. 2012/169 (W.28). - Enabling power: Teaching and Higher Education Act 1998, ss. 1 (5) (7), 42 (6) (7), sch. 1, para. 3. - Issued: 10.02.2012. Made: 20.01.2012. Laid before the National Assembly for Wales: 26.01.2012. Coming into force: In accord. with reg. 1(2). Effect: S.I. 1999/1619 amended. Territorial extent & classification: W. General. - In English and Welsh. Welsh language title: Rheoliadau Cyngor Addysgu Cyffredinol Cymru (Cyfansoddiad) (Diwygio) 2012. - 4p.: 30 cm. - 978-0-348-10552-0 £4.00

The General Teaching Council for Wales (Disciplinary Functions) (Amendment) Regulations 2012 No. 2012/170 (W.29). - Enabling power: Teaching and Higher Education Act 1998, ss. 6, 42 (6) (7), sch. 2, paras. 1 (1) (4). - Issued: 10.02.2012. Made: 20.01.2012. Laid before the National Assembly for Wales: 26.01.2012. Coming into force: In accord. with reg. 1 (2). Effect: S.I. 2001/1424 (W.99) amended. Territorial extent & classification: W. General. - In English and Welsh. Welsh language title: Rheoliadau Cyngor Addysgu Cyffredinol Cymru (Swyddogaethau Disgyblu) (Diwygio) 2012. - 8p.: 30 cm. - 978-0-348-10547-6 £4.00

The General Teaching Council for Wales (Functions) (Amendment) Regulations 2012 No. 2012/166 (W.25). - Enabling power: Teaching and Higher Education Act 1998, ss. 3 (3D), 4 (2), 42 (6) (7). - Issued: 10.02.2012. Made: 20.01.2012. Laid before the National Assembly for Wales: 26.01.2012. Coming into force: In accord. with reg. 1 (2). Effect: S.I. 2000/1979 (W.140) amended. Territorial extent & classification: W. General. - In English and Welsh. Welsh language title: Rheoliadau Cyngor Addysgu Cyffredinol Cymru (Swyddogaethau Disgyblu) (Diwygio) 2012. - 8p.: 30 cm. - 978-0-348-10548-3 £4.00

The Higher Education Funding Council for Wales (Supplementary Functions and Revocation) Order 2012 No. 2012/1904 (W.231). - Enabling power: Further and Higher Education Act 1992, ss. 69 (5), 89 (4). - Issued: 02.08.2012. Made: 18.07.2012. Laid before the National Assembly for Wales: 19.07.2012. Coming into force: 31.08.2012. Effect: S.I. 2011/965 (W.139) revoked. Territorial extent & classification: W. General. - In English and Welsh. Welsh title: Gorchymyn Cyngor Cyllido Addysg Uwch Cymru (Swyddogaethau Atodol a Dirymu) 2012. - 4p.: 30 cm. - 978-0-348-10644-2 £4.00

The National Curriculum (Assessment Arrangements on Entry to the Foundation Phase) (Wales) (Revocation) Order 2012 No. 2012/935 (W.121). - Enabling power: Education Act 2002, ss. 108 (2) (b) (iii) (5) (6) (9) (11), 210. - Issued: 11.04.2012. Made: 23.03.2012. Laid before the National Assembly for Wales: 27.03.2012. Coming into force: 18.04.2012. Effect: S.I. 2011/1947 (W.213) revoked. Territorial extent & classification: W. General. - In English and Welsh. Welsh title: Gorchymyn y Cwricwlwm Cenedlaethol (Trefniadau Asesu wrth Dderbyn i'r Cyfnod Sylfaenol) (Cymru) (Dirymu) 2012. - 4p.: 30 cm. - 978-0-348-10592-6 £4.00

The Recognised Persons (Monetary Penalties) (Determination of Turnover) (Wales) Order 2012 No. 2012/1248 (W.153). - Enabling power: Education Act 1997, s. 32AB (2). - Issued: 30.05.2012. Made: 09.05.2012. Coming into force: 09.05.2012. Effect: None. Territorial extent & classification: W. General. - In English and Welsh. Welsh title: Gorchymyn Personau Cydnabyddedig (Cosbau Ariannol) (Penderfynu Trosiant) (Cymru) 2012. - 4p.: 30 cm. - 978-0-348-10613-8 £4.00

The School Governance (Transition from an Interim Executive Board) (Wales) Regulations 2012 No. 2012/1643 (W.212). - Enabling power: School Standards and Framework Act 1998, sch. 1A, para 19 (2) (3) & Education Act 2002, s. 19. - Issued: 19.07.2012. Made: 22.06.2012. Laid before the National Assembly for Wales: 26.06.2012. Coming into force: 01.09.2012. Effect: S.I. 2005/2914 (W.211) modified. Territorial extent & classification: W. General. - In English and Welsh. Welsh language title: Rheoliadau Llywodraethu Ysgolion (Trosi o fod yn Fwrdd Gweithredol Interim) (Cymru) 2012. - 8p.: 30 cm. - 978-0-348-10637-4 £5.75

The School Teachers' Qualifications (Wales) Regulations 2012 No. 2012/724 (W.96). - Enabling power: Education Act 2002, ss. 132, 145, 210 (7) & Teaching and Higher Education Act 1998, ss. 19, 42 (6) (7). - Issued: 28.03.2012. Made: 06.03.2012. Laid before the National Assembly for Wales: 08.03.2012. Coming into force: 01.04.2012. Effect: S.I. 1999/2817 (W.18); 2002/1663 (W.158); 2005/1818 (W.146) amended & S.I. 2004/1729 (W. 173) revoked with saving. Territorial extent & classification: W. General. - In English and Welsh. Welsh language title: Rheoliadau Cymwysterau Athrawon Ysgol (Cymru) 2012. - 16p.: 30 cm. - 978-0-348-10568-1 £5.75

The Special Educational Needs Tribunal for Wales (Amendment) Regulations 2012 No. 2012/1418 (W.174). - Enabling power: Education Act 1996, ss. 336 (1) (2), 569 (4) (5). - Issued: 13.06.2012. Made: 25.05.2012. Laid before the National Assembly for Wales: 30.05.2012. Coming into force: 21.06.2012. Effect: S.I. 2012/322 (W.53) amended. Territorial extent & classification: W. General. - In English and Welsh. Welsh title: Rheoliadau Tribiwnlys Anghenion Addysgol Arbennig Cymru (Diwygio) 2012. - 4p.: 30 cm. - 978-0-348-10622-0 £4.00

The Special Educational Needs Tribunal for Wales Regulations 2012 No. 2012/322 (W.53). - Enabling power: Education Act 1996, ss. 326A (4) (6), 332ZC (1) (3), 333 (5), 334 (2), 336 (1) (2) (2A) (4A), 336A, 569 (4) (5) & Equality Act 2010, s. 207 (4), sch. 17, paras 6A, 6 (1) (2) (3) (4) (5) (7). - Issued: 08.02.2012. Made: 08.02.2012. Laid before the National Assembly for Wales: 13.02.2012. Coming into force: 06.03.2012. Effect: S.I. 2001/600, 3982; 2002/1985, 2787 revoked with savings. Territorial extent & classification: W. General. - In English and Welsh. Welsh title: Rheoliadau Tribiwnlys Anghenion Addysgol Arbennig Cymru 2012. - 64p.: 30 cm. - 978-0-348-10558-2 £10.75

The Student Fees (Qualifying Courses and Persons) (Wales) (Amendment) Regulations 2012 No. 2012/1630 (W.209). - Enabling power: Higher Education Act 2004, ss. 28 (6), 47 (5). - Issued: 12.07.2012. Made: 20.06.2012. Laid before the National Assembly for Wales: 22.06.2012. Coming into force: 01.09.2012. Effect: S.I. 2011/691 (W.103) amended. Territorial extent & classification: W. General. - In English and Welsh. Welsh title: Rheoliadau Ffioedd Myfyrwyr (Cyrsiau a Phersonau Cymhwysol) (Cymru) (Diwygio) 2012. - 4p.: 30 cm. - 978-0-348-10631-2 £4.00

Electricity

The Electricity and Gas (Competitive Tenders for Smart Meter Communication Licences) Regulations 2012 No. 2012/2414. - Enabling power: Electricity Act 1989, ss. 56FC, 60 & Gas Act 1986, ss. 41HC, 47. - Issued: 27.09.2012. Made: 19.09.2012. Laid: 21.09.2012. Coming into force: 12.10.2012. Effect: None. Territorial extent & classification: E/W/S. General. - 20p.: 30 cm. - 978-0-11-152899-0 £5.75

The Electricity and Gas (Energy Companies Obligation) Order 2012 No. 2012/3018. - Enabling power: Gas Act 1986, ss. 33BC, 33BD & Electricity Act 1989, ss. 41A, 41B & Utilities Act 2000, ss. 103, 103A. - Issued: 06.12.2012. Made: 04.12.2012. Coming into force: 05.12.2012, in accord. with art. 1. Effect: None. Territorial extent & classification: E/W/S. General. - Supersedes draft SI (ISBN 9780111530276) issued 02.11.2012. - 24p.: 30 cm. - 978-0-11-153166-2 £5.75

The Electricity and Gas (Smart Meters Licensable Activity) Order 2012 No. 2012/2400. - Enabling power: Electricity Act 1989, ss. 56FA (1) (5) (6), 60 & Gas Act 1986, ss. 41HA (1) (5) (6), 47. - Issued: 25.09.2012. Made: 18.09.2012. Coming into force: In accord. with art. 1. Effect: 1986 c. 44, c. 45; 1989 c. 29; 2000 c. 27; 2002 c. 40; 2007 c. 17; 2008 c. 32 & S.I. 1999/1549; 2002/2665 amended. Territorial extent & classification: E/W/S. General. - Supersedes draft SI (ISBN 9780111527412) issued 20.07.2012. - 16p.: 30 cm. - 978-0-11-152894-5 £5.75

The Feed-in Tariffs Order 2012 No. 2012/2782. - Enabling power: Energy Act 2008, ss. 41 (4), 43 (3) (a), 104 (2). - Issued: 15.11.2012. Made: 06.11.2012. Laid: 08.11.2012. Coming into force: 01.12.2012. Effect: S.I. 2010/678; 2011/1181, 1655, 2364; 2012/671, 1393, 2268 revoked. Territorial extent & classification: E/W/S. General. - 28p.: 30 cm. - 978-0-11-153048-1 £5.75

The Feed-in Tariffs (Specified Maximum Capacity and Functions) (Amendment No. 2) Order 2012 No. 2012/1393. - Enabling power: Energy Act 2008, ss. 43 (3) (a), 104 (2). - Issued: 01.06.2012. Made: 24.05.2012. Laid: 29.05.2012. Coming into force: 01.08.2012. Effect: S.I. 2010/678 amended. Territorial extent & classification: E/W/S. General. - Revoked by SI 2012/2782 (ISBN 9780111530481). - 4p.: 30 cm. - 978-0-11-152486-2 £4.00

The Feed-in Tariffs (Specified Maximum Capacity and Functions) (Amendment No. 3) Order 2012 No. 2012/2268. - Enabling power: Energy Act 2008, ss. 43 (3) (a), 104 (2). - Issued: 12.09.2012. Made: 03.09.2012. Laid: 07.09.2012. Coming into force: 01.10.2012. Effect: S.I. 2010/678 amended. Territorial extent & classification: E/W/S. General. - Revoked by SI 2012/2782 (ISBN 9780111530481). - 2p.: 30 cm. - 978-0-11-152850-1 £4.00

The Feed-in Tariffs (Specified Maximum Capacity and Functions) (Amendment) Order 2012 No. 2012/671. - Enabling power: Energy Act 2008, ss. 43 (3) (a), 104 (2). - Issued: 15.03.2012. Made: 05.03.2012. Laid: 08.03.2012. Coming into force: 01.04.2012. Effect: S.I. 2010/678 amended. Territorial extent & classification: E/W/S. General. - Revoked by SI 2012/2782 (ISBN 9780111530481). - 2p.: 30 cm. - 978-0-11-152171-7 £4.00

Electricity, England and Wales

The Electricity (Exemption from the Requirement for a Generation Licence) (Covanta Ince Parl Limited) (England and Wales) Order 2012 No. 2012/2911. - Enabling power: Electricity Act 1989, s. 5. - Issued: 29.11.2012. Made: 19.11.2012. Laid: 22.11.2012. Coming into force: 28.12.2012. Effect: None. Territorial extent & classification: E/W. General. - 2p.: 30 cm. - 978-0-11-153109-9 £4.00

The Electricity (Exemption from the Requirement for a Generation Licence) (Curen) (England and Wales) Order 2012 No. 2012/2740. - Enabling power: Electricity Act 1989, s. 5. - Issued: 08.11.2012. Made: 31.10.2012. Laid: 05.11.2012. Coming into force: 06.12.2012. Effect: None. Territorial extent & classification: E/W. General. - 2p.: 30 cm. - 978-0-11-153034-4 £4.00

The Electricity (Exemption from the Requirement for a Supply Licence) (MVV Environment Devonport Limited) (England and Wales) Order 2012 No. 2012/1646. - Enabling power: Electricity Act 1989, s. 5. - Issued: 05.07.2012. Made: 26.06.2012. Laid: 28.06.2012. Coming into force: 27.07.2012. Effect: None. Territorial extent & classification: E/W. General. - 2p.: 30 cm. - 978-0-11-152588-3 £4.00

Electromagnetic compatibility

The Wireless Telegraphy (Control of Interference from Apparatus) (The London Olympic Games and Paralympic Games) Regulations 2012 No. 2012/1519. - Enabling power: Wireless Telegraphy Act 2006, ss. 54 (1), 122 (7). - Issued: 15.06.2012. Made: 11.06.2012. Laid: 14.06.2012. Coming into force: 23.07.2012. Effect: None. Territorial extent & classification: E/W/S/NI. General. - With correction slip dated February 2013. - 4p.: 30 cm. - 978-0-11-152542-5 £4.00

Electronic communications

The Broadcasting (Local Digital Television Programme Services and Independent Productions) (Amendment) Order 2012 No. 2012/1842. - Enabling power: Communications Act 2003, ss. 244 (1), 277 (2), 309 (2), 402 (3), sch. 12, paras. 1 (2), 7 (2). - Issued: 23.07.2012. Made: 11.07.2012. Coming into force: In accord. with art. 1. Effect: S.I. 1991/1408; 2012/292 amended. Territorial extent & classification: E/W/S/NI. General. - Supersedes draft SI (ISBN 9780111524695) issued on 24.05.2012. - 4p.: 30 cm. - 978-0-11-152714-6 £4.00

The Communications (Bailiwick of Guernsey) (Amendment) Order 2012 No. 2012/2688. - Enabling power: Communications Act 2003, ss. 402 (3) (c), 411 (6) (8). - Issued: 12.11.2012. Made: 07.11.2012. Coming into force: 05.12.2012. Effect: S.I. 2003/3195 amended. Territorial extent & classification: Guernsey. General. - 2p.: 30 cm. - 978-0-11-153072-6 £4.00

The Wireless Telegraphy Act 2006 (Directions to OFCOM) Order 2012 No. 2012/293. - Enabling power: Wireless Telegraphy Act 2006, ss. 5, 121 (3). - Issued: 17.02.2012. Made: 13.02.2012. Coming into force: 14.02.2012. Effect: None. Territorial extent & classification: E/W/S/NI. General. - Supersedes draft SI (ISBN 9780111518229) issued on 16.12.2011. - 4p.: 30 cm. - 978-0-11-152026-0 £4.00

The Wireless Telegraphy (Licence Award) (Amendment) Regulations 2012 No. 2012/2970. - Enabling power: Wireless Telegraphy Act 2006, ss. 14 (1) (2) (3) (4) (6) (7), 122 (7). - Issued: 30.11.2012. Made: 27.11.2012. Coming into force: 30.11.2012. Effect: S.I. 2012/2817 amended. Territorial extent & classification: E/W/S/NI. General. - This Statutory Instrument has been made in consequence of defects in SI 2012/2817 (ISBN 9780111530740) and is being issued free of charge to all known recipients of that Statutory Instruments. - 2p.: 30 cm. - 978-0-11-153133-4 £4.00

The Wireless Telegraphy (Licence Award) Regulations 2012 No. 2012/2817. - Enabling power: Wireless Telegraphy Act 2006, ss. 14 (1) (2) (3) (4) (6) (7), 122 (7). - Issued: 14.11.2012. Made: 09.11.2012. Coming into force: 23.11.2012. Effect: None. Territorial extent & classification: E/W/S/NI/IoM/Ch.Is. General. - This SI has been corrected by SI 2012/2970 (ISBN 9780111531334) which is being sent free of charge to all known recipients of 2012/2817. - 72p.: 30 cm. - 978-0-11-153074-0 £10.75

The Wireless Telegraphy (Licence Charges) (Amendment) Regulations 2012 No. 2012/1075. - Enabling power: Wireless Telegraphy Act 2006, ss. 12, 13 (2), 122 (7). - Issued: 19.04.2012. Made: 12.04.2012. Coming into force: 03.05.2012. Effect: S.I. 2011/1128 amended. Territorial extent & classification: E/W/S/NI/IoM/Ch.Is. General. - 16p.: 30 cm. - 978-0-11-152356-8 £5.75

The Wireless Telegraphy (Limitation on Number of Licences) Order 2012 No. 2012/3138. - Enabling power: Wireless Telegraphy Act 2006, s. 29 (1) to (3). - Issued: 24.12.2012. Made: 19.12.2012. Coming into force: 04.01.2013. Effect: None. Territorial extent & classification: E/W/S/NI. General. - 2p.: 30 cm. - 978-0-11-153278-2 £4.00

The Wireless Telegraphy (Register) Regulations 2012 No. 2012/2186. - Enabling power: Wireless Telegraphy Act 2006, ss. 31 (1) (2), 122 (7). - Issued: 30.08.2012. Made: 23.08.2012. Coming into force: 13.09.2012. Effect: S.I. 2004/3155; 2006/340, 1808; 2007/381, 3389; 2008/689, 2104, 3193; 2009/14; 2011/439, 1508, 2756 revoked. Territorial extent & classification: E/W/S/NI (not CI or IoM). General. - With correction slip dated February 2013. - 8p.: 30 cm. - 978-0-11-152836-5 £5.75

The Wireless Telegraphy (Spectrum Trading) Regulations 2012 No. 2012/2187. - Enabling power: Wireless Telegraphy Act 2006, ss. 30 (1) (3), 122 (7). - Issued: 30.08.2012. Made: 23.08.2012. Coming into force: 13.09.2012. Effect: S.I. 2004/3154; 2006/339, 1807; 2007/380, 3387; 2008/688, 2105, 3192 revoked. Territorial extent & classification: E/W/S/NI [not CI or IoM]. General. - With correction slip dated February 2013. - 12p.: 30 cm. - 978-0-11-152837-2 £5.75

Employment and training

The Industrial Training Levy (Construction Industry Training Board) Order 2012 No. 2012/958. - Enabling power: Industrial Training Act 1982, ss. 11 (2), 12 (3) (4). - Issued: 29.03.2012. Made: 27.03.2012. Coming into force: On the day after it was made. Effect: None. Territorial extent & classification: E/W/S. General. - Supersedes draft S.I. (ISBN 9780111520215) issued 13.02.2012. - 8p.: 30 cm. - 978-0-11-152302-5 £5.75

The Industrial Training Levy (Engineering Construction Industry Training Board) Order 2012 No. 2012/959. - Enabling power: Industrial Training Act 1982, ss. 11 (2) (2C), 12 (3) (4). - Issued: 29.03.2012. Made: 27.03.2012. Coming into force: On the day after the day it is made. Effect: None. Territorial extent & classification: E/W/S. General. - Supersedes draft S.I. (ISBN 9780111521014) issued 29.03.2012. - 8p.: 30 cm. - 978-0-11-152303-2 £5.75

Employment and training, England

The Apprenticeships (Form of Apprenticeship Agreement) Regulations 2012 No. 2012/844. - Enabling power: Apprenticeships, Skills, Children and Learning Act 2009, ss. 32 (2) (b), 36 (4), 262 (1). - Issued: 19.03.2012. Made: 15.03.2012. Laid: 16.03.2012. Coming into force: 06.04.2012. Effect: None. Territorial extent & classification: E. General. - 4p.: 30 cm. - 978-0-11-152238-7 *£4.00*

Employment and training, England and Wales

The Apprenticeships, Skills, Children and Learning Act 2009 (Consequential Amendments to Subordinate Legislation) (England and Wales) Order 2012 No. 2012/3112. - Enabling power: Apprenticeships, Skills, Children and Learning Act 2009, s. 265 (1) (2). - Issued: 19.12.2012. Made: 12.12.2012. Laid: 18.12.2012. Coming into force: 09.01.2013. Effect: S.I. 1999/584; 2002/2034 amended. Territorial extent & classification: E. General. - 4p.: 30 cm. - 978-0-11-153263-8 *£4.00*

Employment tribunals

The Employment Tribunals Act 1996 (Tribunal Composition) Order 2012 No. 2012/988. - Enabling power: Employment Tribunals Act 1996, s. 41 (2). - Issued: 03.04.2012. Made: 30.03.2012. Coming into force: 06.04.2012. Effect: 1996 c. 17 amended. Territorial extent & classification: E/W/S. General. - Supersedes draft S.I. (ISBN 9780111519967) issued 10.02.2012. With correction slip dated June 2012. - 2p.: 30 cm. - 978-0-11-152327-8 *£4.00*

The Employment Tribunals (Constitution and Rules of Procedure) (Amendment) Regulations 2012 No. 2012/468. - Enabling power: Employment Tribunals Act 1996, ss. 7 (1) (5), 9 (2) (a), 13 (1) (a), 41 (4). - Issued: 27.02.2012. Made: 21.02.2012. Laid: 24.02.2012. Coming into force: 06.04.2012. Effect: S.I. 2004/1861 amended. Territorial extent & classification: E/W/S. General. - 4p.: 30 cm. - 978-0-11-152054-3 *£4.00*

The Employment Tribunals (Increase of Maximum Deposit) Order 2012 No. 2012/149. - Enabling power: Employment Tribunals Act 1996, s. 9 (3). - Issued: 27.01.2012. Made: 23.01.2012. Laid: 24.01.2012. Coming into force: 15.02.2012. Effect: 1996 c.17 amended & S.I. 2001/237 revoked. Territorial extent & classification: E/W/S. General. - 2p.: 30 cm. - 978-0-11-151944-8 *£4.00*

Energy

The Energy Act 2010 (Commencement) Order 2012 No. 2012/1841(C.72). - Enabling power: Energy Act 2010, s. 38 (2). Bringing into operation various provisions of the 2010 Act on 16.07.2012, in accord. with art. 2. - Issued: 19.07.2012. Made: 12.07.2012. Effect: None. Territorial extent & classification: E/W/S. General. - 2p.: 30 cm. - 978-0-11-152731-3 *£4.00*

The Energy Act 2011 (Commencement No. 1 and Saving) Order 2012 No. 2012/873 (C.24). - Enabling power: Energy Act 2011, s. 121 (1) (6). Bringing into operation various provisions of the 2011 Act on 21.03.2012, in accord. with art. 2. - Issued: 27.03.2012. Made: 20.03.2012. Effect: None. Territorial extent & classification: E/W/S. General. - 4p.: 30 cm. - 978-0-11-152254-7 *£4.00*

The Renewable Heat Incentive Scheme (Amendment) Regulations 2012 No. 2012/1999. - Enabling power: Energy Act 2008, ss. 100, 104. - Issued: 06.08.2012. Made: 30.07.2012. Coming into force: 31.07.2012, in accord. with reg. 1. Effect: S.I. 2011/2860 amended. Territorial extent & classification: E/W/S. General. - Supersedes draft S.I. (ISBN 9780111525296) issued 15.06.2012. - 8p.: 30 cm. - 978-0-11-152790-0 *£5.75*

Energy: Sustainable and renewable fuels

The Energy Act 2004 (Amendment) Regulations 2012 No. 2012/2723. - Enabling power: European Communities Act 1972, s. 2 (2). - Issued: 05.11.2012. Made: 29.10.2012. Laid: 01.11.2012. Coming into force: 04.12.2012. Effect: 2004 c.20 amended. Territorial extent & classification: E/W/S/NI. General. - EC note: These Regulations enable effect to be given to certain requirements contained in Directive 98/707/EC. - 4p.: 30 cm. - 978-0-11-153024-5 *£4.00*

Energy conservation

The Ecodesign for Energy-Related Products and Energy Information (Amendment) Regulations 2012 No. 2012/3005. - Enabling power: European Communities Act 1972, s. 2 (2). - Issued: 05.12.2012. Made: 03.12.2012. Laid: 05.12.2012. Coming into force: In accord. with reg. 1. Effect: S.I. 2010/2617; 2011/1524 amended. Territorial extent & classification: UK. General. - 4p.: 30 cm. - 978-0-11-153159-4 *£4.00*

The Energy Act 2011 (Amendment) (Energy Performance of Buildings) Regulations 2012 No. 2012/3170. - Enabling power: European Communities Act 1972, s. 2 (2). - Issued: 02.01.2013. Made: 20.12.2012. Laid: 02.01.2012. Coming into force: 25.01.2013. Effect: 2011 c.16 amended. Territorial extent & classification: E/W/S. General. - EC note: The amendments made by this instrument ensure that section 11 of the 2011 Act is consistent with recent changes to the implementation in England and Wales and Scotland of article 7 of Directive 2002/91/EC on the energy performance of buildings. - 4p.: 30 cm. - 978-0-11-153287-4 £4.00

The Green Deal (Acknowledgment) Regulations 2012 No. 2012/1661. - Enabling power: Energy Act 2011, ss. 14 (4) (5), 15 (3), 40 (1). - Issued: 05.07.2012. Made: 27.06.2012. Laid: 28.06.2012. Coming into force: 28.01.2013. Effect: None. Territorial extent & classification: E/W. General. - 4p.: 30 cm. - 978-0-11-152596-8 £4.00

The Green Deal (Disclosure) Regulations 2012 No. 2012/1660. - Enabling power: Energy Act 2011, ss. 12 (2) (b) (5) (c) (6), 40 (1). - Issued: 05.07.2012. Made: 27.06.2012. Laid: 28.06.2012. Coming into force: 28.01.2013. Effect: None. Territorial extent & classification: E/W/S. General. - 8p.: 30 cm. - 978-0-11-152597-5 £4.00

The Green Deal (Energy Efficiency Improvements) Order 2012 No. 2012/2106. - Enabling power: Energy Act 2011, s. 2 (4) (a) (5) (b). - Issued: 20.08.2012. Made: 06.08.2012. Coming into force: In accord. with art. 1. Effect: None. Territorial extent & classification: E/W/S. General. - Supersedes draft SI (ISBN 9780111525289) issued on 15.06.2012. - 4p.: 30 cm. - 978-0-11-152816-7 £4.00

The Green Deal Framework (Disclosure, Acknowledgment, Redress etc.) (Amendment) Regulations 2012 No. 2012/3021. - Enabling power: Energy Act 2011, ss. 8 (4), 40 (1). - Issued: 06.12.2012. Made: 04.12.2012. Coming into force: 05.12.2012, in accord. with reg. 1. Effect: S.I. 2012/2079 amended. Territorial extent & classification: E/W/S. General. - Supersedes draft SI (ISBN 9780111530283) issued on 02.11.2012. - 2p.: 30 cm. - 978-0-11-153171-6 £4.00

The Green Deal Framework (Disclosure, Acknowledgment, Redress etc.) Regulations 2012 No. 2012/2079. - Enabling power: European Communities Act 1972, s. 2 (2) & Energy Act 2011, ss. 2 (9) (10), 3 (1) (3) (5) to (9), 4 (1) (4) (5) (8) (9), 5 (1) (3) (5), 6 (1) (2) (4) (5), 8 (3) (4), 13 (1) (2), 15 (1) (2), 16 (1) (2), 34 (1) (2), 35 (2) to (4), 40 (1). - Issued: 13.08.2012. Made: 06.08.2012. Coming into force: In accord. with reg. 1. Effect: None. Territorial extent & classification: E/W/S. General. - Supersedes draft S.I. (ISBN 9780111525227) issued 20.06.2012. - 44p.: 30 cm. - 978-0-11-152808-2 £9.75

The Green Deal (Qualifying Energy Improvements) Order 2012 No. 2012/2105. - Enabling power: Energy Act 2011, s. 1 (4) (b). - Issued: 20.08.2012. Made: 06.08.2012. Coming into force: 28.01.2013. Effect: None. Territorial extent & classification: E/W/S. General. - Supersedes draft SI (ISBN 9780111525234) issued on 15.06.2012. - 4p.: 30 cm. - 978-0-11-152815-0 £4.00

Energy conservation, England

The Home Energy Efficiency Scheme (England) (Amendment) Regulations 2012 No. 2012/2140. - Enabling power: Social Security Act 1990, s. 15. - Issued: 23.08.2012. Made: 16.08.2012. Laid: 21.08.2012. Coming into force: 12.09.2012. Effect: S.I. 2005/1530 amended. Territorial extent & classification: E. General. - With correction slip dated September 2012. - 4p.: 30 cm. - 978-0-11-152828-0 £4.00

Enforcement of civil penalties, England

The Penalty Charges Enforcement (London) Regulations 2012 No. 2012/1234. - Enabling power: London Local Authorities Act 2007, ss. 64 (1) (2), 82 (1). - Issued: 10.05.2012. Made: 03.05.2012. Laid: 10.05.2012. Coming into force: 18.06.2012. Effect: None. Territorial extent & classification: Greater London/E. General. - 4p.: 30 cm. - 978-0-11-152411-4 £4.00

Environmental protection

The Advisory Committee on Hazardous Substances (Abolition) Order 2012 No. 2012/1923. - Enabling power: Public Bodies Act 2011, ss. 1 (1), 6 (1) (5), 35 (2). - Issued: 25.07.2012. Made: 21.07.2012. Coming into force: In accord. with art. 1. Effect: 1967 c. 13; 1975 c. 24; 1990 c. 43; 2000 c. 36; 2011 c. 24 partially repealed & S.I. 1993/1572; 1999/1319 partially revoked & S.I. 1991/1487, 1488 revoked. Territorial extent & classification: E/W/S/NI. General. - Supersedes draft S.I. (ISBN 9780111520741) issued 29.02.2012. For approval by resolution of each House of Parliament after the expiry of the 40-day period specified in section 11 (4) of the Public Bodies Act 2011. - 4p.: 30 cm. - 978-0-11-152762-7 £4.00

The Batteries and Accumulators (Placing on the Market) (Amendment) Regulations 2012 No. 2012/1139. - Enabling power: European Communities Act 1972, s. 2 (2). - Issued: 27.04.2012. Made: 24.04.2012. Laid: 25.04.2012. Coming into force: 31.05.2012. Effect: S.I. 2008/2164 amended. Territorial extent & classification: E/W/S/NI. General. - EC note: These Regulations give effect to article 21(2) of Directive 2066/66/EC to provide for the capacity labelling of portable secondary (rechargeable) and automotive batteries and accumulators. - 4p.: 30 cm. - 978-0-11-152380-3 £4.00

The INSPIRE (Amendment) Regulations 2012 No. 2012/1672. - Enabling power: European Communities Act 1972, s 2 (2). - Issued: 11.07.2012. Made: 01.07.2012. Laid: 05.07.2012. Coming into force: 01.08.2012. Effect: S.I. 2009/3157 amended. Territorial extent & classification: E/W/S/NI but has no application to S. General. - INSPIRE = Infrastructure for Spatial Information in the European Community. EC note: These Regulations amend the INSPIRE Regulations which implemented Directive 2007/2/EC to transpose requirements not previously transposed in accordance with Reg (EU) 1089/2010. - 8p.: 30 cm. - 978-0-11-152626-2 £4.00

The Marine and Coastal Access Act 2009 (Transitional Provisions) Order 2012 No. 2012/698. - Enabling power: Marine and Coastal Access Act 2009. s. 320. - Issued: 09.03.2012. Made: 03.03.2012. Laid: 09.03.2012. Coming into force: 06.04.2012. Effect: None. Territorial extent & classification: E. General. - 4p.: 30 cm. - 978-0-11-152160-1 £4.00

The Producer Responsibility Obligations (Packaging Waste) (Amendment) Regulations 2012 No. 2012/3082. - Enabling power: European Communities Act 1972, s. 2 (2), sch. 2, para. 1A & Environment Act 1995, ss. 93 to 95. - Issued: 14.12.2012. Made: 10.12.2012. Coming into force: In accord.with reg. 1 (1) (b). Effect: S.I. 2007/871; 2010/2849 amended. Territorial extent & classification: E/W/S. General. - Supersedes draft SI (ISBN 9780111529652) issued 19.10.2012. - 8p.: 30 cm. - 978-0-11-153215-7 £4.00

The Public Bodies (Abolition of Environment Protection Advisory Committees) Order 2012 No. 2012/2407. - Enabling power: Public Bodies Act 2011, ss. 1 (1), 6 (1) (5), 35 (2). - Issued: 21.09.2012. Made: 18.09.2012. Coming into force: In accord. with art. 1. Effect: 2011 c. 24 partially repealed (20.09.2012). Territorial extent & classification: E/W. General. - Supersedes draft S.I. (ISBN 9780111524671) issued 24.05.2012. - 2p.: 30 cm. - 978-0-11-152895-2 £4.00

The Public Bodies (Abolition of Regional and Local Fisheries Advisory Committees) Order 2012 No. 2012/2406. - Enabling power: Public Bodies Act 2011, ss. 1 (1), 6 (1) (5), 35 (2). - Issued: 21.09.2012. Made: 18.09.2012. Coming into force: In accord. with art. 1. Effect: 2011 c. 24 partially repealed (20.09.2012). Territorial extent & classification: E/W. General. - Supersedes draft S.I. (ISBN 9780111524725) issued 24.05.2012. - 2p.: 30 cm. - 978-0-11-152896-9 £4.00

The Restriction of the Use of Certain Hazardous Substances in Electrical and Electronic Equipment Regulations 2012 No. 2012/3032. - Enabling power: European Communities Act 1972, s. 2 (2), sch. 2, para. 1A. - Issued: 10.12.2012. Made: 04.12.2012. Laid: 07.12.2012. Coming into force: 02.01.2013. Effect: SI 2004/693; 2007/3544 amended & SI 2008/37; 2009/581 revoked. Territorial extent & classification: E/W/S/NI. General. - 28p.: 30 cm. - 978-0-11-153185-3 £5.75

The Storage of Carbon Dioxide (Inspections etc.) Regulations 2012 No. 2012/461. - Enabling power: European Communities Act 1972, s. 2 (2) & Energy Act 2008, ss. 19, 21, 27, 104 (2). - Issued: 29.02.2012. Made: 22.02.2012. Coming into force: 23.02.2012, in accord. with reg. 1. Effect: S.I. 2010/2221 amended. Territorial extent & classification: UK territorial sea (except adjacent to Scotland) and the area extending beyond the territorial sea designated as a Gas Importation and Storage Zone. General. - Supersedes draft S.I. (ISBN 9780111516904) issued 21.11.2011. - EC note: These Regulations form part of the implementation by the United Kingdom of Directive 2009/31/EC on geological storage of carbon dioxide. In particular they implement art. 15 on the inspection of carbon dioxide storage complexes. - 8p.: 30 cm. - 978-0-11-152053-6 £5.75

The Volatile Organic Compounds in Paints, Varnishes and Vehicle Refinishing Products Regulations 2012 No. 2012/1715. - Enabling power: European Communities Act 1972, s. 2 (2). - Issued: 05.07.2012. Made: 27.06.2012. Laid: 05.07.2012. Coming into force: 27.07.2012. Effect: S.I. 2005/2773; 2009/3145; 2010/783 revoked. Territorial extent & classification: E/W/S/NI. General. - EC note: These Regulations implement Directive 2004/42/EC on the limitation of emissions of volatile organic compounds due to use of organic solvents in certain paints, varnishes and vehicle refinishing products. - 12p.: 30 cm. - 978-0-11-152627-9 £5.75

Environmental protection: Emissions trading

The Community Emissions Trading Scheme (Allocation of Allowances for Payment) Regulations 2012 No. 2012/2661. - Enabling power: Finance Act 2007, s. 16 (2) (4) & European Communities Act 1972, s. 2 (2). - Issued: 24.10.2012. Made: 23.10.2012. Laid: 24.10.2012. Coming into force: 14.11.2012. Effect: 2007 c.11 partially repealed with saving & S.I. 2008/1825 revoked with saving. Territorial extent & classification: E/W/S/NI. General. - 4p.: 30 cm. - 978-0-11-152994-2 £4.00

Environmental protection, England

The Contaminated Land (England) (Amendment) Regulations 2012 No. 2012/263. - Enabling power: Environmental Protection Act 1990, ss. 78C (8) (9) (10), 78G (5) (6), 78L (4) (5). - Issued: 07.02.2012. Made: 02.02.2012. Laid: 07.02.2012. Coming into force: 06.04.2012. Effect: S.I. 2006/1380 amended. Territorial extent & classification: E. General. - EC note: These Regulations amend SI 2006/1380 so as to take account of protected areas under Directive 2000/60/EC establishing a framework for Community action in the field of water policy. - 4p.: 30 cm. - 978-0-11-151981-3 £4.00

The Controlled Waste (England and Wales) (Amendment) Regulations 2012 No. 2012/2320. - Enabling power: Environmental Protection Act 1990, s. 75 (7) (d) (8). - Issued: 13.09.2012. Made: 07.09.2012. Laid before Parliament: 12.09.2012. Coming into force: 09.10.2012. Effect: S.I. 2012/811 amended. Territorial extent & classification: E/W but applies to England only. General. - This Statutory instrument has been made in consequence of defects in SI 2012/811 (ISBN 9780111522097) and is being issued free of charge to all known recipients of that statutory instrument. - 4p.: 30 cm. - 978-0-11-152874-7 £4.00

The Designation of Features (Appeals) (England) Regulations 2012 No. 2012/1945. - Enabling power: Flood and Water Management Act 2010, ss. 30, 48 (2), sch. 1, para. 15. - Issued: 26.07.2012. Made: 23.07.2012. Coming into force: In accord. with reg. 1 (b). Effect: None. Territorial extent & classification: E. General. - 4p.: 30 cm. - 978-0-11-152770-2 £4.00

The Designation of Features (Notices) (England) Regulations 2012 No. 2012/1693. - Enabling power: Flood and Water Management Act 2010, ss. 30, 48 (2), sch. 1, para. 16. - Issued: 03.07.2012. Made: 27.06.2012. Laid: 29.06.2012. Coming into force: 25.07.2012. Effect: None. Territorial extent & classification: E. General. - 4p.: 30 cm. - 978-0-11-152609-5 £4.00

The Environmental Offences (Fixed Penalties) (Miscellaneous Provisions) (Amendment) Regulations 2012 No. 2012/1151. - Enabling power: Environmental Protection Act 1990, s. 47ZB (4) (5). - Issued: 10.05.2012. Made: 21.04.2012. Laid: 10.05.2012. Coming into force: 30.05.2012. Effect: S. I. 2007/175 amended. Territorial extent & classification: E. General. - 2p.: 30 cm. - 978-0-11-152383-4 £4.00

The Environmental Protection Act 1990 (Amendment of Fixed Penalty Amount) (England) Order 2012 No. 2012/1150. - Enabling power: Environmental Protection Act 1990, s. 47ZB (6). - Issued: 10.05.2012. Made: 21.04.2012. Laid: 10.05.2012. Coming into force: 30.05.2012. Effect: 1990 c.43 amended. Territorial extent & classification: E. General. - 2p.: 30 cm. - 978-0-11-152381-0 £4.00

Environmental protection, England and Wales

The Commission for Architecture and the Built Environment (Dissolution) Order 2012 No. 2012/147. - Enabling power: Clean Neighbourhoods and Environment Act 2005, ss. 90, 95 (2). - Issued: 25.01.2012. Made: 20.01.2012. Coming into force: 21.01.2012 in accord. with art. 1. Effect: 1999 c. 29; 2005 c. 16 & S.I. 2006/1466 partially repealed/revoked. Territorial extent & classification: E/W. General. - Supersedes draft S.I. (ISBN 9780111517413) issued 01.12.2011. - 4p.: 30 cm. - 978-0-11-151942-4 £4.00

The Controlled Waste (England and Wales) Regulations 2012 No. 2012/811. - Enabling power: European Communities Act 1972, s. 2 (2) & Environmental Protection Act 1990, ss. 45 (3), 75 (7) (d) (8), 96 (2) (b). - Issued: 15.03.2012. Made: 12.03.2012. Laid before Parliament & National Assembly for Wales: 15.03.2012. Coming into force: 06.04.2012. Effect: S.I. 2005/2900; 2006/123 (W.16), 937; 2007/3538; 2010/675; 2011/881 amended & S.I. 1992/588; 1995/288 revoked in relation to England and Wales. Territorial extent & classification: E/W. General. - With correction slip dated May 2012. EC note: Regulation 3 provides that certain waste is not to be classified as household, industrial or commercial waste, in particular waste which falls outside the scope of Directive 2008/98/EC on waste. - 16p.: 30 cm. - 978-0-11-152209-7 £5.75

The Environmental Permitting (England and Wales) (Amendment) Regulations 2012 No. 2012/630. - Enabling power: Pollution Prevention and Control Act 1999, ss. 2, 7 (9), sch. 1. - Issued: 05.03.2012. Made: 28.02.2012. Laid before Parliament and the National Assembly for Wales: 05.03.2012. Coming into force: 06.04.2012. Effect: S.I. 2008/314; 2009/153, 995 (W.81); 2010/105, 265, 490, 675 amended. Territorial extent & classification: E/W. General. - 16p.: 30 cm. - 978-0-11-152107-6 £5.75

The Environmental Protection Act 1990 (Commencement No. 19) Order 2012 No. 2012/898 (C. 28). - Enabling power: Environmental Protection Act 1990, s. 164 (3). Bringing into operation various provisions of the 1990 Act on 01.04.2012 in accord. with art. 2. - Issued: 23.03.2012. Made: 20.03.2012. Effect: None. Territorial extent & classification: E/W. General. - 8p.: 30 cm. - 978-0-11-152267-7 £5.75

The Flood and Water Management Act 2010 (Commencement No. 6 and Transitional Provisions) Order 2012 No. 2012/879 (C.25). - Enabling power: Flood and Water Management Act 2010, ss. 48 (2), 49 (3) (h) (i) (6). Bringing into operation various provisions of this Act on 06.04.2012, in accord. with art. 3. - Issued: 22.03.2012. Made: 19.03.2012. Effect: None. Territorial extent & classification: E/W. General. - 8p.: 30 cm. - 978-0-11-152259-2 £5.75

The Flood and Water Management Act 2010 (Commencement No. 7) Order 2012 No. 2012/2000 (C.79). - Enabling power: Flood and Water Management Act 2010, s. 49 (3) (h) (i). Bringing into operation various provisions of this Act on 01.08.2012, in accord. with art. 2. - Issued: 01.08.2012. Made: 30.07.2012. Effect: None. Territorial extent & classification: E/W. General. - 8p.: 30 cm. - 978-0-11-152791-7 £5.75

The Waste (England and Wales) (Amendment) Regulations 2012 No. 2012/1889. - Enabling power: European Communities Act 1972, s. 2 (2). - Issued: 20.07.2012. Made: 17.07.2012. Laid: 19.07.2012. Coming into force: 01.10.2012. Effect: S.I. 2011/988 amended. Territorial extent & classification: E/W. General. - This Statutory Instrument has been made in consequence of a defects in S.I. 2011/988 (ISBN 9780111509890) and is being issued free of charge to all known recipients of that Statutory Instrument. EC note: These Regulations amend S.I. 2011/988 to ensure proper transposition of Directive 2008/98/EC of the European Parliament and of the Council on waste. - 4p.: 30 cm. - 978-0-11-152743-6 £4.00

Environmental protection, Wales

The Contaminated Land (Wales) (Amendment) Regulations 2012 No. 2012/283 (W.47). - Enabling power: Environmental Protection Act 1990, ss. 78C (8) (9) (10), 78G (5) (6), 78L (4) (5). - Issued: 23.02.2012. Made: 03.02.2012. Laid before the National Assembly for Wales: 07.02.2012. Coming into force: 06.04.2012. Effect: S.I. 2006/2989 (W.278) amended. Territorial extent & classification: W. General. - In English and Welsh. Welsh title: Rheoliadau Tir Halogedig (Cymru) (Diwygio) 2012. - 8p.: 30 cm. - 978-0-348-10696-1 £4.00

The Designation of Features (Appeals) (Wales) Regulations 2012 No. 2012/1819 (W.228). - Enabling power: Flood and Water Management Act 2010, ss. 30, 48 (2), sch. 1, para. 15. - Issued: 02.08.2012. Made: 10.07.2012. Coming into force: 11.07.2012, in accord. with reg. 1 (1). Effect: None. Territorial extent & classification: W. General. - In English and Welsh. Welsh title: Rheoliadau Dynodi Nodweddion (Apelau) (Cymru) 2012. - 8p.: 30 cm. - 978-0-348-10642-8 £4.00

The Designation of Features (Notices) (Wales) Regulations 2012 No. 2012/1692 (W.218). - Enabling power: Flood and Water Management Act 2010, ss. 30, 48 (2), sch. 1, para. 16. - Issued: 19.07.2012. Made: 28.06.2012. Laid before the National Assembly for Wales: 29.06.2012. Coming into force: 20.07.2012. Effect: None. Territorial extent & classification: W. General. - In English and Welsh. Welsh title: Rheoliadau Dynodi Nodweddion (Hysbysiadau) (Cymru) 2012. - 4p.: 30 cm. - 978-0-348-10635-0 £4.00

The Landfill Allowances Scheme (Wales) (Amendment) Regulations 2012 No. 2012/65 (W.16). - Enabling power: Waste and Emissions Trading Act 2003, ss. 11 (1) (2) (b) (d) (f) (3), 12(1) (2) (4), 24 (1) (c), 26 (3). - Issued: 27.01.2012. Made: 10.01.2012. Laid before the National Assembly for Wales: 12.01.2012. Coming into force: 15.01.2012 at 12.01am for Regs 2, 3 and the remainder of these Regulations immediately after that. Effect: S.I. 2004/1490 (W.155) amended & S.I. 2011/2555 (W.279), 3042 (W.320) revoked. Territorial extent & classification: W. General. - This Welsh Statutory Instrument has been made in consequence of a defect in WSI 2011/3042 (W.320) (ISBN 9780348105384) and is being issued free of charge to all known recipients of that instrument. - In English and Welsh. Welsh title: Rheoliadau'r Cynllun Lwfansau Tirlenwi (Cymru) (Diwygio) 2012. - 8p.: 30 cm. - 978-0-348-10544-5 £4.00

The Natural Resources Body for Wales (Establishment) Order 2012 No. 2012/1903 (W.230). - Enabling power: Public Bodies Act 2011, ss. 13 (7), 15 (1). - Issued: 02.08.2012. Made: 18.07.2012. Coming into force: 19.07.2012, in accord. with art. 1. Effect: None. Territorial extent & classification: W. General. - In English and Welsh. Welsh title: Gorchymyn Corff Adnoddau Naturiol Cymru (Sefydlu) 2012. - 16p.: 30 cm. - 978-0-348-10647-3 £5.75

Equality

The Equality Act 2010 (Age Exceptions) Order 2012 No. 2012/2466. - Enabling power: Equality Act 2010, ss. 197 (1), 207 (4) (6). - Issued: 28.09.2012. Made: 19.09.2012. Coming into force: 01.10.2012. Effect: 2010 c.15 amended. Territorial extent & classification: E/W/S. General. - Supersedes draft SI (ISBN 9780111525692) issued on 26.06.2012. - 8p.: 30 cm. - 978-0-11-152903-4 £5.75

The Equality Act 2010 (Amendment) Order 2012 No. 2012/334. - Enabling power: European Communities Act 1972, s. 2 (2). - Issued: 15.02.2012. Made: 08.02.2012. Laid: 13.02.2012. Coming into force: 06.04.2012. Effect: 2010 c.15 amended. Territorial extent & classification: E/W/S. General. - 2p.: 30 cm. - 978-0-11-152016-1 £4.00

The Equality Act 2010 (Amendment) Regulations 2012 No. 2012/2992. - Enabling power: European Communities Act 1972, s. 2 (2). - Issued: 03.12.2012. Made: 29.11.2012. Laid: 30.11.2012. Coming into force: 21.12.2012. Effect: 2010 c.15 amended. Territorial extent & classification: E/W/S. General. - 2p.: 30 cm. - 978-0-11-153146-4 £4.00

The Equality Act 2010 (Commencement No. 9) Order 2012 No. 2012/1569 (C.59). - Enabling power: Equality Act 2010, s. 216 (3). Bringing into operation various provisions of the 2010 Act on 01.10.2012. - Issued: 21.06.2012. Made: 18.06.2012. Effect: None. Territorial extent & classification: E/W/S. General. - 8p.: 30 cm. - 978-0-11-152562-3 £5.75

The Equality Act 2010 (Commencement No. 10) Order 2012 No. 2012/2184 (C.85). - Enabling power: Equality Act 2010, s. 216 (3). Bringing into operation various provisions of the 2010 Act on 01.09.2012. - Issued: 30.08.2012. Made: 22.08.2012. Effect: None. Territorial extent & classification: E/W/S. General. - 8p.: 30 cm. - 978-0-11-152835-8 £5.75

European Union

The European Communities (Designation) (No. 2) Order 2012 No. 2012/2752. - Enabling power: European Communities Act 1972, s. 2 (2). - Issued: 14.11.2012. Made: 07.11.2012. Laid: 14.11.2012. Coming into force: 05.12.2012. Effect: None. Territorial extent & classification: E/W/S/NI. General. - 4p.: 30 cm. - 978-0-11-153062-7 £4.00

The European Communities (Designation) Order 2012 No. 2012/1759. - Enabling power: European Communities Act 1972, s. 2 (2). - Issued: 17.07.2012. Made: 10.07.2012. Laid: 17.07.2012. Coming into force: 07.08.2012. Effect: S.I. 1992/1315; 1993/2661; 2000/3057; 2002/2840; 2004/1283, 2642, 3328 partially revoked. Territorial extent & classification: E/W/S/NI. General. - 4p.: 30 cm. - 978-0-11-152685-9 £4.00

The European Union (Definition of Treaties) (Republic of Korea Framework Agreement) Order 2012 No. 2012/358. - Enabling power: European Communities Act 1972, s. 1 (3). - Issued: 17.02.2012. Made: 15.02.2012. Coming into force: In accord with art. 2. Effect: None. Territorial extent & classification: E/W/S/NI. General. - Supersedes draft SI (ISBN 9780111517864) issued on 12.12.2011. - 2p.: 30 cm. - 978-0-11-152032-1 £4.00

The European Union (Definition of Treaties) (Republic of Korea Free Trade Agreement) Order 2012 No. 2012/357. - Enabling power: European Communities Act 1972, s. 1 (3). - Issued: 17.02.2012. Made: 15.02.2012. Coming into force: In accord with art. 2. Effect: None. Territorial extent & classification: E/W/S/NI. General. - Supersedes draft SI (ISBN 9780111517789) issued on 14.12.2011. - 2p.: 30 cm. - 978-0-11-152031-4 £4.00

The European Union (Definition of Treaties) (Second Agreement amending the Cotonou Agreement) Order 2012 No. 2012/797. - Enabling power: European Communities Act 1972, s. 1 (3). - Issued: 16.03.2012. Made: 14.03.2012. Coming into force: In accord with art. 2. Effect: None. Territorial extent & classification: E/W/S/NI. General. - Supersedes draft SI (ISBN 9780111514191) issued 26.07.2011. - 2p.: 30 cm. - 978-0-11-152232-5 £4.00

The Treaty of Lisbon (Changes in Terminology or Numbering) Order 2012 No. 2012/1809. - Enabling power: European Union (Amendment) Act 2008, s. 3 (4) (5) & European Communities Act 1972, s. 2 (2). - Issued: 12.07.2012. Made: 11.07.2012. Laid: 11.07.2012. Coming into force: 01.08.2012. Effect: Broadly amends definitions in i) Acts of Parliament ii) Acts of the Scottish Parliament and iii) instruments made under an Act of Parliament or an Act of the Scottish Parliament (or both) and specifically amends 34 Acts, 53 SIs & 8 SSIs. Territorial extent & classification: E/W/S/NI. General. - 28p.: 30 cm. - 978-0-11-152665-1 £5.75

Excise

The Aircraft Operators (Accounts and Records) (Amendment) Regulations 2012 No. 2012/3020. - Enabling power: Customs and Excise Management Act 1979, s. 118A (1) (2) & Finance Act 1994, sch. 6, para. 1 (1). - Issued: 06.12.2012. Made: 03.12.2012. Laid: 05.12.2012. Coming into force: 01.04.2013 for reg. 4 & 01.01.2013 for all other purposes. Effect: S.I. 1994/1737 amended. Territorial extent & classification: E/W/S/NI. General. - 2p.: 30 cm. - 978-0-11-153170-9 £4.00

The Air Passenger Duty (Amendment) Regulations 2012 No. 2012/3017. - Enabling power: Finance Act 1994, ss. 33 (7), 33A (4), 43 (1). - Issued: 06.12.2012. Made: 03.12.2012. Laid: 05.12.2012. Coming into force: 01.04.2013 for reg. 5, 01.01.2013 for all other purposes. Effect: S.I. 1994/1738 amended. Territorial extent & classification: E/W/S/NI. General. - 2p.: 30 cm. - 978-0-11-153165-5 £4.00

The Excise Duties (Road Fuel Gas) (Reliefs) Regulations 2012 No. 2012/3056. - Enabling power: Hydrocarbon Oil Duties Act 1979, s. 20AA (1) (a) (2) (a) (b) (c) (h). - Issued: 12.12.2012. Made: 07.12.2012. Laid: 11.12.2012. Coming into force: 01.01.2013. Effect: None. Territorial extent & classification: E/W/S/NI. General. - 2p.: 30 cm. - 978-0-11-153211-9 £4.00

The Excise Duties (Surcharges or Rebates) (Hydrocarbon Oils etc.) Order 2012 No. 2012/3055. - Enabling power: Excise Duties (Surcharges or Rebates) Act 1979, ss. 1 (2), 2 (3). - Issued: 11.12.2012. Made: 10.12.2012. Laid: 11.12.2012. Coming into force: 01.01.2013. Effect: None. Territorial extent & classification: E/W/S/NI. General. - 4p.: 30 cm. - 978-0-11-153209-6 £4.00

The Excise Goods (Holding, Movement and Duty Point) (Amendment) Regulations 2012 No. 2012/2786. - Enabling power: Customs and Excise Management Act 1979, s. 93 (1) (d) (2) (a) (e) (fa) (3) & Alcoholic Liquor Duties Act 1979, s. 41A (7) & European Communities Act 1972, s. 2 (2). - Issued: 09.11.2012. Made: 06.11.2012. Laid: 08.11.2012. Coming into force: 01.12.2012. Effect: S.I. 2010/593 amended. Territorial extent & classification: E/W/S/NI. General. - These Regulations have been made in consequence of a defect in S.I. 2011/2225 (ISBN 9780111515280) and are being issued free of charge to all known recipients of that statutory instrument. - 2p.: 30 cm. - 978-0-11-153051-1 £4.00

The Finance Act 1994, Section 30A (Appointed Day) Order 2012 No. 2012/3015 (C.121). - Enabling power: Finance Act 1994, s. 30A (9). Bringing into operation various provisions of the 1994 Act on 01.01.2013. - Issued: 05.12.2012. Made: 03.12.2012. Effect: None. Territorial extent & classification: E/W/S/NI. General. - 2p.: 30 cm. - 978-0-11-153162-4 £4.00

The Gaming Duty (Amendment) Regulations 2012 No. 2012/1897. - Enabling power: Finance Act 1997, ss. 12 (4). - Issued: 20.07.2012. Made: 18.07.2012. Laid: 19.07.2012. Coming into force: 01.10.2012. Effect: S.I. 1997/2196 amended & S.I. 2010/1677 revoked. Territorial extent & classification: E/W/S/NI. General. - 2p.: 30 cm. - 978-0-11-152746-7 £4.00

The Machine Games Duty (Exemptions) Order 2012 No. 2012/2898. - Enabling power: Finance Act 2012, sch. 24, paras. 8 (1) (b) (2), 39 (2). - Issued: 20.11.2012. Made: 19.11.2012. Laid: 19.11.2012. Coming into force: 01.02.2013. Effect: None. Territorial extent & classification: E/W/S/NI. General. - Superseded by later version of same number but different ISBN (9780111532331) issued on 14.12.2012. For approval by resolution of that House within 28 days, subject to extension for periods of dissolution, prorogation or adjournment for more than 4 days. - 4p.: 30 cm. - 978-0-11-153090-0 £4.00

The Machine Games Duty (Exemptions) Order 2012 No. 2012/2898. - Enabling power: Finance Act 2012, sch. 24, paras. 8 (1) (b) (2), 39 (2). - Issued: 14.12.2012. Made: 19.11.2012. Laid: 19.11.2012. Coming into force: 01.02.2013. Effect: None. Territorial extent & classification: E/W/S/NI. General. - Approved by the House of Commons. Supersedes previous version of same number but different ISBN (9780111530900) issued on 20.11.2012. - 4p.: 30 cm. - 978-0-11-153233-1 £4.00

The Machine Games Duty Regulations 2012 No. 2012/2500. - Enabling power: Finance Act 2012, sch. 24, paras. 18, 19, 24, 39. - Issued: 04.10.2012. Made: 01.10.2012. Laid: 03.10.2012. Coming into force: 01.11.2012, for the purposes of parts 1, 2, 4, 5 and sch. 1; 01.02.2013, for the purposes of part 3 and sch. 2. Effect: None. Territorial extent & classification: E/W/S/NI. General. - 16p.: 30 cm. - 978-0-11-152907-2 £5.75

The Remote Gambling (Double Taxation Relief) Regulations 2012 No. 2012/1900. - Enabling power: Betting and Gaming Duties Act 1981, s. 261C, sch. 1, paras 2 (5), 2A (4). - Issued: 20.07.2012. Made: 18.07.2012. Laid: 19.07.2012. Coming into force: 09.08.2012. Effect: None. Territorial extent & classification: E/W/S/NI. General. - 4p.: 30 cm. - 978-0-11-152750-4 £4.00

Family law: Child support

The Child Maintenance and Other Payments Act 2008 (Commencement No. 8) Order 2012 No. 2012/1649 (C.61). - Enabling power: Child Maintenance and Other Payments Act 2008, s. 62 (3). Bringing into operation various provisions of the 2008 Act on 27.06.2012, in accord. with art. 2. - Issued: 27.06.2012. Made: 25.06.2012. Effect: None. Territorial extent & classification: E/W/S. General. - 4p.: 30 cm. - 978-0-11-152587-6 £4.00

The Child Maintenance and Other Payments Act 2008 (Commencement No. 9) and the Welfare Reform Act 2009 (Commencement No. 9) Order 2012 No. 2012/2523 (C.101). - Enabling power: Child Maintenance and Other Payments Act 2008, s. 62 (3) & Welfare Reform Act 2009, s. 61 (3). Bringing into operation various provisions of the 2008 and 2009 Acts on 08.10.2012, in accord. with art. 2. - Issued: 05.10.2012. Made: 04.10.2012. Effect: None. Territorial extent & classification: E/W/S. General. - 8p.: 30 cm. - 978-0-11-152913-3 £4.00

The Child Maintenance and Other Payments Act 2008 (Commencement No. 10 and Transitional Provisions) Order 2012 No. 2012/3042 (C.122). - Enabling power: Child Maintenance and Other Payments Act 2008, s. 62 (3) (4). Bringing into operation various provisions of the 2008 Act on 10.12.2012, in accord. with art. 4. - Issued: 07.12.2012. Made: 05.12.2012. Effect: None. Territorial extent & classification: E/W/S. General. - 8p.: 30 cm. - 978-0-11-153190-7 £5.75

The Child Support Maintenance Calculation Regulations 2012 No. 2012/2677 . - Enabling power: Child Support Act 1991, ss. 3 (3), 5 (3), 12 (4) (5), 14 (1) (1A), 16 (1) (4) (6), 17 (2) (3) (5), 20 (4) (5), 28ZA (2) (b) (4) (c), 28ZB (6) (c) (8), 28A (5), 28B (2) (c), 28C (2) (b) (5), 28F (2) (b) (3) (b) (5), 28G (2) (3), 42, 51 (1) (2), 52 (4), 54, 55 (1) (b), sch. 1, paras 3 (2) (3), 4 (1) (2), 5, 5A (6) (b), 7 (3), 8 (2), 9, 10 (1) (2), 10C (2) (b), 11, sch. 4A, paras 2, 4, 5, sch. 4B, paras 2 (2) to (5), 4, 5, 6. - Issued: 26.10.2012. Made: 20.10.2012. Coming into force: In accord. with reg. 1. Effect: None. Territorial extent & classification: E/W/S. General. - Supersedes draft SI (ISBN 9780111526132) issued 02.07.2012. - 48p.: 30 cm. - 978-0-11-153006-1 £9.75

The Child Support Maintenance (Changes to Basic Rate Calculation and Minimum Amount of Liability) Regulations 2012 No. 2012/2678. - Enabling power: Child Support Act 1991, s. 52 (4), sch. 1, para. 10A (1). - Issued: 26.10.2012. Made: 23.10.2012. Coming into force: In accord. with reg. 1. Effect: 1991 c.48 modified. Territorial extent & classification: E/W/S. General. - Supersedes draft SI (ISBN 9780111526156) issued 02.04.2012. - 4p.: 30 cm. - 978-0-11-153005-4 £4.00

The Child Support Management of Payments and Arrears (Amendment) Regulations 2012 No. 2012/3002. - Enabling power: Child Support Act 1991, ss. 14 (3), 41D (2) (3), 41E, 51 (1), 52 (4). - Issued: 04.12.2012. Made: 28.11.2012. Coming into force: In accord. with reg. 1. Effect: S.I. 2008/2551; 2009/3151 amended. Territorial extent & classification: E/W/S. General. - Supersedes draft SI (ISBN 9780111529300) issued 15.10.2012. - 8p.: 30 cm. - 978-0-11-153150-1 £5.75

The Child Support (Meaning of Child and New Calculation Rules) (Consequential and Miscellaneous Amendment) Regulations 2012 No. 2012/2785. - Enabling power: Child Support Act 1991, ss. 14 (1), 29 (3) (3A), 51 (1) (2), 52 (4), 54, 55 (1) & Child Maintenance and Other Payments Act 2008, ss. 55 (4), 57 (2). - Issued: 08.11.2012. Made: 02.11.2012. Laid: 08.11.2012. Coming into force: In accord. with reg. 1. Effect: S.I. 1992/1813, 2001/157 amended and then revoked in accord. with reg. 1; S.I. 1992/1989, 2645; 1999/991; 2000/3177; 2001/157; 2008/2551; 2008/2685 (L.13) amended & S.I. 1992/1815; 1993/925; 1996/2907; 2001/155, 156 revoked. Territorial extent & classification: E/W/S. General. - 12p.: 30 cm. - 978-0-11-153050-4 £5.75

The Child Support (Miscellaneous Amendments) Regulations 2012 No. 2012/712. - Enabling power: Child Support Act 1991, ss. 17 (3) (5), 29 (2) (3), 51 (1) (2) (i), 52 (4), 54, sch. 1, para.10 (1) (2). - Issued: 08.03.2012. Made: 05.03.2012. Laid: 08.03.2012. Coming into force: 30.04.2012. Effect: S.I. 1992/1813, 1815, 1989; 2001/155; 2009/3151 amended. Territorial extent & classification: E/W/S. General. - 8p.: 30 cm. - 978-0-11-152155-7 £4.00

The Child Support (Northern Ireland Reciprocal Arrangements) Amendment Regulations 2012 No. 2012/2380. - Enabling power: Northern Ireland Act 1998, s. 87 (4) (9). - Issued: 08.10.2012. Made: 17.09.2012. Laid: 17.09.2012. Coming into force: 29.10.2012. Effect: S.I. 1993/584 amended. Territorial extent & classification: E/W/S. General. - 8p.: 30 cm. - 978-0-11-152883-9 £4.00

The Public Bodies (Child Maintenance and Enforcement Commission: Abolition and Transfer of Functions) Order 2012 No. 2012/2007. - Enabling power: Public Bodies Act 2011, ss. 1 (1) (2), 6 (1) (5), 23 (1) (a), 35 (2). - Issued: 01.08.2012. Made: 31.07.2012. Coming into force: In accord. with art. 1. Effect: 1967 c.13; 1975 c.24, c.25; 1991 c.48; 1998 c.14; 2000 c.23, c.36; 2002 c.22; 2003 c.42; 2008 c.6; 2009 c.24; 2010 c.15; 2011 c.24; 2012 c.5; S.I. 1992/1815, 1989; 1996/2907; 1999/991; 2001/155, 156; 2008/2551, 2685, 2698; 2009/2615, 2982, 3151; 2010/480, 521, 912, 2955 amended. Territorial extent & classification: E/W/S. General. - Supersedes draft S.I. (ISBN 9780111523728) issued 23.04.2012. - 28p.: 30 cm. - 978-0-11-152792-4 £5.75

Family proceedings

The Family Procedure (Amendment) (No. 2) Rules 2012 No. 2012/1462. - Enabling power: Courts Act 2003, s. 75. - Issued: 11.06.2012. Made: 31.05.2012. Laid: 07.06.2012. Coming into force: 01.07.2012. Effect: S.I. 2010/2955 amended. Territorial extent & classification: E/W. General. - 2p.: 30 cm. - 978-0-11-152508-1 £4.00

The Family Procedure (Amendment No. 3) Rules 2012 No. 2012/2046 (L.7). - Enabling power: Courts Act 2003, ss. 75, 76. - Issued: 08.08.2012. Made: 31.07.2012. Laid: 07.08.2012. Coming into force: 30.009.2012. Effect: S.I. 2010/2955 amended. Territorial extent & classification: E/W. General. - 4p.: 30 cm. - 978-0-11-152799-3 £4.00

The Family Procedure (Amendment No. 4) Rules 2012 No. 2012/2806 (L.10). - Enabling power: Courts Act 2003, ss. 75, 76 & Civil Jurisdiction and Judgments Act 1982, ss. 12, 48. - Issued: 12.11.2012. Made: 06.11.2012. Laid: 09.11.2012. Coming into force: 20.12.2012. Effect: S.I. 2010/2955 amended. Territorial extent & classification: E/W. General. - 12p.: 30 cm. - 978-0-11-153059-7 £5.75

The Family Procedure (Amendment No. 5) Rules 2012 No. 2012/3061. - Enabling power: Courts Act 2003, ss. 75, 76. - Issued: 13.12.2013. Made: 10.12.2012. Laid: 13.12.2012. Coming into force: 31.01.2013. Effect: S.I. 2010/2955 amended. Territorial extent & classification: E/W. General. - 12p.: 30 cm. - 978-0-11-153210-2 £5.75

The Family Procedure (Amendment) Rules 2012 No. 2012/679 (L.3). - Enabling power: Civil Jurisdiction and Judgements Act 1982, ss. 12, 48 & Adoption and Children Act 2002, ss. 102, 141 (1) & Courts Act 2003, ss. 75, 76. - Issued: 07.03.2012. Made: 01.03.2012. Laid: 06.03.2012. Coming into force: 06.04.2012. Effect: S.I. 2010/2955 amended. Territorial extent & classification: E/W. General. - 8p.: 30 cm. - 978-0-11-152133-5 £5.75

Fees and charges

The European Economic Interest Grouping and European Public Limited-Liability Company (Fees) Revocation Regulations 2012 No. 2012/2300. - Enabling power: Finance Act 1973, s. 56 (1) (2). - Issued: 11.09.2012. Made: 06.09.2012. Laid: 07.09.2012. Coming into force: 01.10.2012. Effect: S.I. 2009/2492 revoked. Territorial extent & classification: E/W/S. General. - 2p.: 30 cm. - 978-0-11-152871-6 £4.00

The Local Policing Bodies (Consequential Amendments) Regulations 2012 No. 2012/61. - Enabling power: Police and Criminal Evidence Act 1984, s. 63B (6) & Animal Welfare Act 2006, ss. 6 (4) (5) (6) (8) (14) & Violent Crime Reduction Act 2006, ss. 15, 16 (7), 17 (6), 20 (5). - Issued: 17.01.2012. Made: 10.01.2012. Coming into force: 16.01.2012. Effect: S.I. 2001/2645; 2007/1120; 2008/1430 amended. Territorial extent & classification: E/W. General. - Supersedes draft SI (ISBN 9780111517130) issued on 22.11.2011. - 4p.: 30 cm. - 978-0-11-151915-8 £4.00

The Measuring Instruments (EEC Requirements) (Fees) (Amendment) Regulations 2012 No. 2012/751. - Enabling power: Finance Act 1973, s. 56 (1) (2). - Issued: 12.03.2012. Made: 07.03.2012. Laid: 09.03.2012. Coming into force: 06.04.2012. Effect: S.I. 2004/1300 amended & S.I. 2008/732; 2010/728 partially revoked. Territorial extent & classification: E/W/S/NI. General. - 4p.: 30 cm. - 978-0-11-152179-3 £4.00

The Medicines (Products for Human Use) (Fees) (Amendment) Regulations 2012 No. 2012/2546. - Enabling power: Medicines Act 1971, s. 1 (1) & European Communities Act 1972, s. 2 (2) & Finance Act 1973, s. 56 (1) (2). - Issued: 10.10.2012. Made: 04.10.2012. Laid: 10.10.2012. Coming into force: 02.11.2012. Effect: S.I. 2012/504 amended. Territorial extent & classification: E/W/S/NI. General. - 4p.: 30 cm. - 978-0-11-152917-1 £4.00

The Medicines (Products for Human Use) (Fees) Regulations 2012 No. 2012/504. - Enabling power: Medicines Act 1971, s. 1 (1) (2) & European Communities Act 1972, s. 2 (2) & Finance Act 1973, s. 56 (1) (2). - Issued: 29.02.2012. Made: 23.02.2012. Laid: 29.02.2012. Coming into force: 01.04.2012. Effect: S.I. 2004/1031 amended & S.I. 1994/105 amended & partially revoked with savings & S.I. 2010/551 revoked with savings. Territorial extent & classification: E/W/S/NI. General. - 77p.: 30 cm. - 978-0-11-152069-7 £13.75

The Registrar of Companies (Fees) (Companies, Overseas Companies and Limited Liability Partnerships) Regulations 2012 No. 2012/1907. - Enabling power: Companies Act 2006, ss. 243 (3), 1063 (1) to (3), 1292 (1). - Issued: 25.07.2012. Made: 18.07.2012. Laid: 23.07.2012. Coming into force: 01.10.2012. Effect: S.I. 2009/2101, 2439; 2011/309 revoked. Territorial extent & classification: E/W/S/NI. General. - 28p.: 30 cm. - 978-0-11-152755-9 £5.75

The Registrar of Companies (Fees) (European Economic Interest Grouping and European Public Liability Company) Regulations 2012 No. 2012/1908. - Enabling power: Companies Act 2006, ss. 1063 (1) to (3), 1292 (1). - Issued: 25.07.2012. Made: 18.07.2012. Laid: 23.07.2012. Coming into force: 01.10.2012. Effect: S.I. 2009/2403; 2011/324 revoked. Territorial extent & classification: E/W/S/NI. General. - 12p.: 30 cm. - 978-0-11-152753-5 £5.75

Fees and charges, England and Wales

The Public Bodies (Water Supply and Water Quality) (Inspection Fees) Order 2012 No. 2012/3101 (W.314). - Enabling power: Public Bodies Act 2011, ss. 14 (3), 15 (1). - Issued: 17.01.2013. Made: 12.12.2012. Coming into force: 13.12.2012 in accord. with art. 1. Effect: None. Territorial extent & classification: E/W. General. - In English and Welsh. Welsh title: Gorchymyn Cyrff Cyhoeddus (Cyflenwad Dwr ac Ansawdd Dwr) (Ffioedd Arolygu) 2012. - 8p.: 30 cm. - 978-0-348-10677-0 £5.75

Financial services

The Financial Services and Markets Act 2000 (Regulated Activities) (Amendment) Order 2012 No. 2012/1906. - Enabling power: Financial Services and Markets Act 2000, ss. 22 (1) (5), 426, 428 (3), sch. 2, para. 25 & European Communities Act 1972, s. 2 (2). - Issued: 20.07.2012. Made: 19.07.2012. Coming into force: 20.07.2012 in accord. with art .1. Effect: 2000 c. 8 & S.I. 2001/544; 2001/1217, 1227; 2007/2157; 2011/2699 amended. Territorial extent & classification: E/W/S/NI. General. - Supersedes draft S.I. (ISBN 9780111525654) issued 21.06.2012. EC note: This Order implements the requirement in art. 18 of Commission Regulation 1031/2010 on the timing, administration and other aspects of auctioning of greenhouse gas allowances for the UK to have enacted legislation enabling the Financial Services Authority to authorise certain categories of people to make them eligible to bid in auctions of emissions allowances on their own account or on behalf of clients and implements related provisions in arts 6 (5) and 59 of that Regulation. - 12p.: 30 cm. - 978-0-11-152754-2 £5.75

The Money Laundering (Amendment) Regulations 2012 No. 2012/2298. - Enabling power: European Communities Act 1972, s. 2 (2). - Issued: 10.09.2012. Made: 06.09.2012. Laid: 10.09.2012. Coming into force: 01.10.2012. Effect: S.I. 2007/2157 amended. Territorial extent & classification: E/W/S/NI. General. - These regs amend the Money Laundering Regulations 2007 (S.I. 2007/2157) which implemented in part Dir 2005/60/EC. - 8p.: 30 cm. - 978-0-11-152869-3 £5.75

Financial services and markets

The Capital Requirements (Amendment) Regulations 2012 No. 2012/917. - Enabling power: European Communities Act 1972, s. 2 (2). - Issued: 26.03.2012. Made: 22.03.2012. Laid: 23.03.2012. Coming into force: 16.04.2012. Effect: 1986 c.53; 2000 c.8; 2008 c.2; 2009 c.1; S.I. 1998/1130; 2001/2188, 3755; 2004/1862; 2005/590; 2006/3221; 2007/126; 2008/346 amended. Territorial extent & classification: E/W/S/NI. General. - EC note: These Regulations implement, in part, Directives 2010/78/EU; 2010/76/EU. - 8p.: 30 cm. - 978-0-11-152280-6 £5.75

The Financial Services and Markets Act 2000 (Disclosure of Confidential Information) (Amendment) Regulations 2012 No. 2012/3019. - Enabling power: Financial Services and Markets Act 2000, ss. 349 (1) (b) (2) (3), 417 (1). - Issued: 05.12.2012. Made: 04.12.2012. Laid: 05.12.2012. Coming into force: 26.12.2012. Effect: S.I. 2001/2188 amended. Territorial extent & classification: E/W/S/NI. General. - This Statutory instrument has been made in consequence of a defect in SI 2012/916 (ISBN 9780111522820) and is being issued free of charge to all known recipients of that Statutory Instrument. - 2p.: 30 cm. - 978-0-11-153168-6 £4.00

The Financial Services and Markets Act 2000 (Exemption) (Amendment) Order 2012 No. 2012/763. - Enabling power: Financial Services and Markets Act 2000, s. 38. - Issued: 12.03.2012. Made: 08.03.2012. Laid: 09.03.2012. Coming into force: In accord. with art. 1 (2). Effect: S.I. 2001/1201 amended. Territorial extent & classification: E/W/S/NI. General. - 2p.: 30 cm. - 978-0-11-152177-9 £4.00

The Financial Services and Markets Act 2000 (Gibraltar) (Amendment) Order 2012 No. 2012/2017. - Enabling power: Financial Services and Markets Act 2000, ss. 409 (1) (a) (b) (d) (5), 428 (3). - Issued: 03.08.2012. Made: 27.07.2012. Laid: 02.08.2012. Coming into force: 24.08.2012. Effect: S.I. 2001/3084 amended. Territorial extent & classification: E/W/S/NI. General. - EC note: This Order amends SI 2001/3084 to enable management companies as defined in art. 6 of Directive 2009/65/EC on the coordination of laws, regulations and administrative provisions relating to undertakings for collective investment in transferable securities which are based in Gibraltar to exercise certain rights to establish branches and provide services in the UK. - 4p.: 30 cm. - 978-0-11-152794-8 £4.00

The Financial Services and Markets Act 2000 (Short Selling) Regulations 2012 No. 2012/2554. - Enabling power: European Communities Act 1972. s. 2 (2). - Issued: 09.10.2012. Made: 04.10.2012. Laid: 09.10.2012. Coming into force: 01.11.2012. Effect: 2000 c.8; S.I. 2001/2188 amended. Territorial extent & classification: E/W/S/NI. General. - EC note: Implements certain articles of regulation (EU) 236/2012 on short selling and certain aspects of credit default swaps. - 8p.: 30 cm. - 978-0-11-152926-3 £5.75

The Financial Services (Omnibus 1 Directive) Regulations 2012 No. 2012/916. - Enabling power: European Communities Act 1972, s. 2 (2). - Issued: 27.03.2012. Made: 22.03.2012. Laid: 23.03.2012. Coming into force: 16.04.2012. Effect: 2000 c.8; S.I. 2001/2188; 2004/1862 amended. Territorial extent & classification: E/W/S/NI. General. - A defect in this SI has been corrected by SI 2012/3019 (ISBN 9780111531686) which is being issued free of charge to all known recipients of 2012/916. - 12p.: 30 cm. - 978-0-11-152282-0 £5.75

The Payment Services Regulations 2012 No. 2012/1791. - Enabling power: European Communities Act 1972, s. 2 (2). - Issued: 11.07.2012. Made: 09.07.2012. Laid: 10.07.2012. Coming into force: In accord. with art. 1 (2). Effect: S.I. 2007/2157; 2009/209; 2011/99 amended. Territorial extent & classification: E/W/S/NI. General. - 4p.: 30 cm. - 978-0-11-152653-8 £4.00

The Payments in Euro (Credit Transfers and Direct Debits) Regulations 2012 No. 2012/3122. - Enabling power: European Communities Act 1972, s. 2 (2). - Issued: 19.12.2012. Made: 17.12.2012. Laid: 18.12.2012. Coming into force: 15.01.2013. Effect: 2000 c.8 & S.I. 2001/1420, 2188 modified & SI 2010/89 revoked with savings. Territorial extent & classification: E/W/S/NI. General. - EC note: These Regulations are made pursuant to the UK's obligations under Regulation 924/2009. - 16p.: 30 cm. - 978-0-11-153259-1 £5.75

The Prospectus Regulations 2012 No. 2012/1538. - Enabling power: European Communities Act 1972, s. 2 (2). - Issued: 18.06.2012. Made: 14.06.2012. Laid: 15.06.2012. Coming into force: 01.07.2012. Effect: 2000 c.8 amended. Territorial extent & classification: E/W/S/NI. General. - EC note: These Regs amend provisions of the Financial Services and Markets Act 2000 to implement in part Directive 2010/73/EU which amends Directive 2003/71/EC on the prospectus to be published when securities are offered to the public or admitted to trading and also amends Directive 2004/109/EC on the harmonisation of transparency requirements in relation to information about issuers whose securities are admitted to trading on a regulated market. - 8p.: 30 cm. - 978-0-11-152551-7 £5.75

The Regulated Covered Bonds (Amendment) Regulations 2012 No. 2012/2977. - Enabling power: European Communities Act 1972, s. 2 (2). - Issued: 29.11.2012. Made: 28.11.2012. Laid: 29.11.2012. Coming into force: 01.01.2013. Effect: S.I. 2011/2859 amended. Territorial extent & classification: E/W/S/NI. General. - 2p.: 30 cm. - 978-0-11-153136-5 £4.00

The Undertakings for Collective Investment in Transferable Securities (Amendment) Regulations 2012 No. 2012/2015. - Enabling power: European Communities Act 1972, s. 2 (2). - Issued: 02.08.2012. Made: 27.07.2012. Laid: 02.08.2012. Coming into force: 24.08.2012. Effect: 2000 c. 8 & S.I. 2011/1613 amended. Territorial extent & classification: E/W/S/NI. General. - This Statutory Instrument has been made in consequence of defects in S.I. 2011/1613 (ISBN 9780111513064) and is being issued free of charge to all known recipients of that Statutory Instrument. EC note: These Regulations further implement Directive 2009/65/EC. - 2p.: 30 cm. - 978-0-11-152793-1 £4.00

Fire and rescue services, England

The Bedfordshire Fire Services (Combined Scheme) (Variation) Order 2012 No. 2012/2879. - Enabling power: Fire and Rescue Services Act 2004, s. 4 (4). - Issued: 20.11.2012. Made: 15.11.2012. Laid: 20.11.2012. Coming into force: 17.12.2012. Effect: S.I. 1996/2918 amended. Territorial extent and classification: E. General. - 2p.: 30 cm. - 978-0-11-153083-2 £4.00

The Fire and Rescue Authorities (National Framework) (England) Order 2012 No. 2012/1886. - Enabling power: Fire and Rescue Services Act 2004, s. 21 (6). - Issued: 19.07.2012. Made: 13.07.2012. Laid: 19.07.2012. Coming into force: 17.08.2012. Effect: None. Territorial extent and classification: E. General. - 2p.: 30 cm. - 978-0-11-152740-5 £4.00

The Firefighters' Pension Scheme (Amendment) (England) Order 2012 No. 2012/953. - Enabling power: Fire Services Act 1947, s. 26 (1) to (5). - Issued: 29.03.2012. Made: 27.03.2012. Laid: 29.03.2012. Coming into force: 01.04.2012. Effect: S.I. 1992/129 amended in relation to England. Territorial extent & classification: E. General. - 4p.: 30 cm. - 978-0-11-152300-1 £4.00

The Firefighters' Pension Scheme (England) (Amendment) (No. 2) Order 2012 No. 2012/2988. - Enabling power: Fire and Rescue Services Act 2004, ss. 34, 60. - Issued: 05.12.2012. Made: 29.11.2012. Laid: 05.12.2012. Coming into force: 31.12.2012. Effect: S.I. 2006/3432 amended in relation to England. Territorial extent & classification: E. General. - 4p.: 30 cm. - 978-0-11-153143-3 £4.00

The Firefighters' Pension Scheme (England) (Amendment) Order 2012 No. 2012/954. - Enabling power: Fire and Rescue Services Act 2004, ss. 34, 60. - Issued: 29.03.2012. Made: 27.03.2012. Laid: 29.03.2012. Coming into force: 01.04.2012. Effect: S.I. 2006/3432 amended in relation to England. Territorial extent & classification: E. General. - 4p.: 30 cm. - 978-0-11-152301-8 £4.00

The Localism Act 2011 (Commencement No. 3) Order 2012 No. 2012/411 (C. 11). - Enabling power: Localism Act 2011, s. 240 (2) (7). Bringing into operation various provisions of the 2011 Act on 18.02.2012, in accord. with art. 2. - Issued: 20.02.2012. Made: 17.02.2012. Effect: None. Territorial extent & classification: E/W. General. - 4p.: 30 cm. - 978-0-11-152038-3 £4.00

Fire and rescue services, England and Wales

The Localism Act 2011 (Commencement No. 2 and Saving Provision) (Wales) Order 2012 No. 2012/887 (W.118) (C.26). - Enabling power: Localism Act 2011, s. 240 (3) (4) (7). Bringing into operation various provisions of the Act on 01.04.2012, in accord. with art. 2. - Issued: 03.04.2012. Made: 14.03.2012. Coming into force: 01.04.2012. Effect: None. Territorial extent & classification: W. General. - In English and Welsh. Welsh language title: Gorchymyn Deddf Lleoliaeth 2011 (Cychwyn Rhif 2 a Darpariaeth Arbed) (Cymru) 2012. - 8p.: 30 cm. - 978-0-348-10579-7 £5.75

Fire and rescue services, Wales

The Fire and Rescue Services (National Framework) (Wales) Order 2012 No. 2012/934 (W.120). - Enabling power: Fire and Rescue Services Act 2004, ss. 21 (6), 62. - Issued: 11.04.2012. Made: 24.03.2012. Laid before the National Assembly for Wales: 27.03.2012. Coming into force: 20.04.2012. Effect: The Fire and Rescue National Framework for Wales 2008-2011 is replaced by the Fire and Rescue National Framework for Wales 2012, published by the Welsh Ministers on 27.03.2012. Territorial extent & classification: W. General. - In English and Welsh. Welsh title: Gorchymyn y Gwasanaethau Tân ac Achub (Fframwaith Cenedlaethol) (Cymru) 2012. - 4p.: 30 cm. - 978-0-348-10590-2 £4.00

The Firefighters' Pension Scheme (Wales) (Contributions) (Amendment) Order 2012 No. 2012/972 (W.127). - Enabling power: Fire and Rescue Services Act 2004, ss. 34, 60, 62. - Issued: 17.04.2012. Made: 28.03.2012. Laid: 29.04.2012. Coming into force: 01.04.2012. Effect: S.I. 2007/1072 (W.110) amended. Territorial extent & classification: W. General. - In English and Welsh. Welsh language title: Gorchymyn Cynllun Pensiwn y Diffoddwyr Tân (Cymru) (Cyfraniadau) (Diwygio) 2012. - 4p.: 30 cm. - 978-0-348-10596-4 £4.00

The Firefighters' Pension (Wales) Scheme (Contributions) (Amendment) Order 2012 No. 2012/974 (W.128). - Enabling power: Fire Services Act 1947, s. 26 (1). - Issued: 17.04.2012. Made: 28.03.2012. Laid before the National Assembly for Wales: 29.03.2012. Coming into force: 01.04.2012. Effect: S.I. 1992/129 amended. Territorial extent & classification: W. General. - In English and Welsh. Welsh title: Gorchymyn Cynllun Pensiwn y Dynion Tân (Cymru) (Cyfraniadau) (Diwygio) 2012. - 8p.: 30 cm. - 978-0-348-10593-3 £4.00

Fire precautions, Wales

The Fire Safety (Employees' Capabilities) (Wales) Regulations 2012 No. 2012/1085 (W.133). - Enabling power: S.I. 2005/1541, art. 24. - Issued: 01.05.2012. Made: 08.04.2012. Laid before the National Assembly for Wales: 16.04.2012. Coming into force: 12.05.2012. Effect: None. Territorial extent & classification: W. General. - EC note: These Regulations implement article 6 (3) (b) of Council Directive 89/391/EEC on the introduction of measures to encourage improvements in the safety and health of worker at work and mirror regulation 13 (1) of S.I. 1999/3242 (ISBN 9780110856254). - In English and Welsh. Welsh title: Rheoliadau Diogelwch Tân (Galluoedd Cyflogeion) (Cymru) 2012. - 4p.: 30 cm. - 978-0-348-10599-5 £4.00

Flood risk management, England

The Designation of Features (Appeals) (England) Regulations 2012 No. 2012/1945. - Enabling power: Flood and Water Management Act 2010, ss. 30, 48 (2), sch. 1, para. 15. - Issued: 26.07.2012. Made: 23.07.2012. Coming into force: In accord. with reg. 1 (b). Effect: None. Territorial extent & classification: E. General. - 4p.: 30 cm. - 978-0-11-152770-2 £4.00

The Designation of Features (Notices) (England) Regulations 2012 No. 2012/1693. - Enabling power: Flood and Water Management Act 2010, ss. 30, 48 (2), sch. 1, para. 16. - Issued: 03.07.2012. Made: 27.06.2012. Laid: 29.06.2012. Coming into force: 25.07.2012. Effect: None. Territorial extent & classification: E. General. - 4p.: 30 cm. - 978-0-11-152609-5 £4.00

Flood risk management, England and Wales

The Flood and Water Management Act 2010 (Commencement No. 6 and Transitional Provisions) Order 2012 No. 2012/879 (C.25). - Enabling power: Flood and Water Management Act 2010, ss. 48 (2), 49 (3) (h) (i) (6). Bringing into operation various provisions of this Act on 06.04.2012, in accord. with art. 3. - Issued: 22.03.2012. Made: 19.03.2012. Effect: None. Territorial extent & classification: E/W. General. - 8p.: 30 cm. - 978-0-11-152259-2 £5.75

The Flood and Water Management Act 2010 (Commencement No. 7) Order 2012 No. 2012/2000 (C.79). - Enabling power: Flood and Water Management Act 2010, s. 49 (3) (h) (i). Bringing into operation various provisions of this Act on 01.08.2012, in accord. with art. 2. - Issued: 01.08.2012. Made: 30.07.2012. Effect: None. Territorial extent & classification: E/W. General. - 8p.: 30 cm. - 978-0-11-152791-7 £5.75

Flood risk management, Wales

The Designation of Features (Appeals) (Wales) Regulations 2012 No. 2012/1819 (W.228). - Enabling power: Flood and Water Management Act 2010, ss. 30, 48 (2), sch. 1, para. 15. - Issued: 02.08.2012. Made: 10.07.2012. Coming into force: 11.07.2012, in accord. with reg. 1 (1). Effect: None. Territorial extent & classification: W. General. - In English and Welsh. Welsh title: Rheoliadau Dynodi Nodweddion (Apelau) (Cymru) 2012. - 8p.: 30 cm. - 978-0-348-10642-8 £4.00

The Designation of Features (Notices) (Wales) Regulations 2012 No. 2012/1692 (W.218). - Enabling power: Flood and Water Management Act 2010, ss. 30, 48 (2), sch. 1, para. 16. - Issued: 19.07.2012. Made: 28.06.2012. Laid before the National Assembly for Wales: 29.06.2012. Coming into force: 20.07.2012. Effect: None. Territorial extent & classification: W. General. - In English and Welsh. Welsh title: Rheoliadau Dynodi Nodweddion (Hysbysiadau) (Cymru) 2012. - 4p.: 30 cm. - 978-0-348-10635-0 £4.00

Food contamination

The Food Protection (Emergency Prohibitions) (Radioactivity in Sheep) (Wales) (Revocation) Order 2012 No. 2012/2978 (W.304). - Enabling power: Animal Health Act 1981, s. 11 & Food and Environment Protection Act 1985, ss. 1 (1) (2) (10), 24 (1) (3). - Issued: 14.12.2012. Made: 28.11.2012. Coming into force: 29.11.2012. In accord. with art. 1. Effect: S.I. 1991/5, 58, 2780; 1994/63; 1995/46; 1998/72; 2011/2759 revoked in relation to Wales(29.11.2012). Territorial extent & classification: W. General. - In English and Welsh. Welsh title: Gorchymyn Diogelu Bwyd (Gwaharddiadau Brys) (Ymbelydredd mewn Defaid) (Cymru) (Dirymu) 2012. - 4p.: 30 cm. - 978-0-348-10668-8 £4.00

Food, England

The Food Additives (England) (Amendment) and the Extraction of Solvents in Food (Amendment) (England) Regulations 2012 No. 2012/1155. - Enabling power: Food Safety Act 1990, ss. 16 (1) (a) (c) (f), 17(1) (2), 48 (1). - Issued: 30.04.2012. Made: 25.04.2012. Laid: 30.04.2012. Coming into force: 23.05.2012. Effect: S.I. 1993/1658; 2009/3238 amended. Territorial extent & classification: E. General. - EC note: These Regulations implement in England: Commission Regulation (EU) no. 1129/2011; no. 1130/2011; 1131/2011; 231/2012. - 8p.: 30 cm. - 978-0-11-152386-5 £4.00

The Food Hygiene (England) (Amendment) Regulations 2012 No. 2012/1742. - Enabling power: European Communities Act 1972, s. 2 (2), sch. 2, para. 1A & Food Safety Act 1990, s. 48 (1). - Issued: 06.07.2012. Made: 02.07.2012. Laid: 06.07.2012. Coming into force: 30.07.2012. Effect: S.I. 2006/14 amended. Territorial extent & classification: E. General. - EC note: These Regulations amend the Food Hygiene (England) Regulations 2006 (S.I. 2006/14, as already amended) by updating the definitions of certain EU instruments that are referred to in those Regulations. In addition these Regulation specify the form and size of the special health mark to be applied to meat derived from animals that have undergone emergency slaughter outside the slaughterhouse. - 8p.: 30 cm. - 978-0-11-152632-3 £5.75

The Materials and Articles in Contact with Food (England) Regulations 2012 No. 2012/2619. - Enabling power: Food Safety Act 1990, ss. 16 (2), 17 (1) (2), 26 (1) (a) (2) (a) (3), 31, 48 (1). - Issued: 22.10.2012. Made: 17.10.2012. Laid: 22.10.2012. Coming into force: 20.11.2012. Effect: S.I. 1990/2463; 1996/1499 amended & S.I. 2006/1179; 2009/205; 2010/2225; 2011/231 revoked. Territorial extent & classification: E. General. - EC note: These regulations provide for the implementation of the following Directives and the enforcement of the following EU regulations. Council Directive 78/142/EEC; 84/500/EEC; 2007/42/EC. Regulation (EC) 1935/2004 and Commission Regulations (EC) 1895/2005; 2023/2006; 450/2009; 10/2011. - 20p.: 30 cm. - 978-0-11-152964-5 £5.75

The Specified Products from China (Restriction on First Placing on the Market) (England) (Amendment) Regulations 2012 No. 2012/47. - Enabling power: European Communities Act 1972 , s. 2 (2). - Issued: 12.01.2012. Made: 09.01.2012. Laid: 11.01.2012. Coming into force: 12.01.2012. Effect: S.I. 2008/1079 amended. Territorial extent & classification: E. General. - EC note: These Regulations implement, in England, Commission Implementing Decision 2011/884/EU on emergency measures regarding the unauthorised genetically modified rice in rice products originating from China and repealing Decision 2008/289/EC. The Commission Implementing Decision provides for import restrictions that previously applied to Bt 63 genetically modified rice to apply, with modifications, to all unauthorised GM rice. - 4p.: 30 cm. - 978-0-11-151905-9 £4.00

Food, Wales

The Authorised Officers (Meat Inspection) (Revocation) (England) Regulations 2012 No. 2012/690. - Enabling power: Food Safety Act 1990, s. 5 (6). - Issued: 08.03.2012. Made: 04.03.2012. Laid: 08.03.2012. Coming into force: 06.04.2012. Effect: S.I. 1987/133 revoked. Territorial extent & classification: E. General. - 2p.: 30 cm. - 978-0-11-152145-8 £4.00

The Authorised Officers (Meat Inspection) (Revocation) (Wales) Regulations 2012 No. 2012/826 (W.114). - Enabling power: Food Safety Act 1990, s. 5 (6). - Issued: 05.04.2012. Made: 13.03.2012. Laid before the National Assembly for Wales: 15.03.2012. Coming into force: 06.04.2012. Effect: S.I. 1987/133 revoked. Territorial extent & classification: W. General. - In English and Welsh: Welsh title: Rheoliadau Swyddogion Awdurdodedig (Archwilio Cig) (Dirymu) (Cymru) 2012. - 4p.: 30 cm. - 978-0-348-10585-8 £4.00

The Food Additives (Wales) (Amendment) and the Extraction Solvents in Food (Amendment) (Wales) Regulations 2012 No. 2012/1198 (W.148). - Enabling power: Food Safety Act 1990, ss. 16 (1) (a) (c) (f), 17 (1) (2), 48 (1). - Issued: 17.05.2012. Made: 27.04.2012. Laid before the National Assembly for Wales: 02.05.2012. Coming into force: 23.05.2012. Effect: S.I. 1993/1658; 2009/3378 (W.300) amended. Territorial extent & classification: W. General. - EC note: These Regulations implement in Wales Commission Directive (EU) no. 1129/2011; 1130/2011; 231/2012. - In English and Welsh. Welsh title: Rheoliadau Ychwanegion Bwyd (Cymru) (Diwygio) a Thoddyddion Echdynnu mewn Bwyd (Diwygio) (Cymru) 2012. - 8p.: 30 cm. - 978-0-348-10608-4 £5.75

The Food Hygiene (Wales) (Amendment) (No. 2) Regulations 2012 No. 2012/1765 (W.225). - Enabling power: European Communities Act 1972, s. 2 (2), sch. 2, para 1A & Food Safety Act 1990, ss. 16 (1) (e), 48 (1). - Issued: 25.07.2012. Made: 04.07.2012. Laid before the National Assembly for Wales: 06.07.2012. Coming into force: 30.07.2012. Effect: S.I. 2006/31 (W.5) amended. Territorial extent & classification: W. General. - In English and Welsh. Welsh title: Rheoliadau Hylendid Bwyd (Cymru) (Diwygio) (Rhif 2) 2012. - 12p.: 30 cm. - 978-0-348-10641-1 £5.75

The Food Hygiene (Wales) (Amendment) Regulations 2012 No. 2012/975 (W.129). - Enabling power: European Communities Act 1972, s. 2 (2). - Issued: 17.04.2012. Made: 28.03.2012. Laid before the National Assembly for Wales: 30.03.2012. Coming into force: 01.05.2012. Effect: S.I. 2006/31 (W.5) amended. Territorial extent & classification: W. General. - In English and Welsh. Welsh title: Rheoliadau Hylendid Bwyd (Cymru) (Diwygio) 2012. - 4p.: 30 cm. - 978-0-348-10594-0 £4.00

The Materials and Articles in Contact with Food (Wales) Regulations 2012 No. 2012/2705 (W.291). - Enabling power: Food Safety Act 1990, ss. 16 (2), 17 (1) (2), 26 (1) (a) (2) (a) (3), 31, 48 (1) & European Communities Act 1972, sch. 2, para. 1A. - Issued: 19.11.2012. Made: 27.10.2012. Laid before the National Assembly for Wales: 30.10.2012. Coming into force: 20.11.2012. Effect: S.I. 1990/2463; 1996/1499 amended in relation to Wales & S.I. 2006/1704 (W.166); 2009/481 (W.49); 2010/2288 (W.200); 2011/233 (W.45) revoked. Territorial extent & classification: W. General. - EC note: These Regulations provide for the implementation of the following Directives and the enforcement of the following EU Regulations: Council Directives 78/142/EEC, 84/500/EEC; Commission Directive 2007/42/EC; Regulations (EC) 1935/2004, 1895/2005, 2023/2006, 450/2009, 10/2011. - In English and Welsh. Welsh language title: Rheoliadau Deunyddiau ac Eitemau mewn Cysylltiad â Bwyd (Cymru) 2012. - 24p.: 30 cm. - 978-0-348-10666-4 £5.75

The Specified Products from China (Restriction on First Placing on the Market) (Wales) (Amendment) Regulations 2012 No. 2012/64 (W.15). - Enabling power: European Communities Act 1972, s. 2 (2). - Issued: 27.01.2012. Made: 11.01.2012. Laid before the National Assembly for Wales: 12.01.2012. Coming into force: 12.01.2012. Effect: S.I. 2008/1080 (W.114) amended. Territorial extent & classification: W. General. - EC note: These Regulations amend SI 2008/1080 (W.114) in order to implement Commission Implementing Decision 2011/884/EU on emergency measures regarding unauthorised genetically modified rice in rice products originating from China and repealing Decision 2008/289/EC. The Commission Decision provides for import restrictions that previously applied to Bt 63 genetically modified rice to apply, with modifications, to all unauthorised GM rice. - In English and Welsh: Welsh title: Rheoliadau Cynhyrchion Penodedig o Tsieina (Cyfyngiad ar eu Rhoi Gyntaf ar y Farchnad) (Cymru) (Diwygio) 2012. - 8p.: 30 cm. - 978-0-348-10545-2 £5.75

Forestry

The Forestry Commissioners (Climate Change Functions) (Scotland) Order 2012 (Consequential Modifications) Order 2012 No. 2012/2855 (S.1). - Enabling power: Scotland Act 1998, ss. 104, 112 (1), 113 (2) (4) (5) (7). - Issued: 14.11.2012. Made: 07.11.2012. Coming into force: 08.11.2012. In accord. with art. 1 (2). Effect: 1967 c.10 modified. Territorial extent & classification: S. General. - Supersedes draft SI (ISBN 9780111526705) issued on 16.07.2012. - 4p.: 30 cm. - 978-0-11-153079-5 £4.00

Freedom of information

The Constitutional Reform and Governance Act 2010 (Commencement No. 7) Order 2012 No. 2012/3001 (C.119). - Enabling power: Constitutional Reform and Governance Act 2010, s. 52 (2). Bringing into operation various provisions of the 2010 Act on 30.11.2012 & 01.01.2013. - Issued: 04.12.2012. Made: 29.11.2012. Effect: None. Territorial extent & classification: E/W/S/NI. General. - 4p.: 30 cm. - 978-0-11-153149-5 £4.00

The Freedom of Information (Definition of Historical Records) (Transitional and Saving Provisions) Order 2012 No. 2012/3029. - Enabling power: Constitutional Reform and Governance Act 2010, s. 46 (2) (3). - Issued: 07.12.2012. Made: 05.12.2012. Laid: 06.12.2012. Coming into force: 01.01.2013. Effect: None. Territorial extent & classification: E/W/NI. General. - 4p.: 30 cm. - 978-0-11-153178-5 £4.00

Freedom of information, England and Wales

The Protection of Freedoms Act 2012 (Commencement No. 1) Order 2012 No. 2012/1205 (C.41). - Enabling power: Protection of Freedoms Act 2012, s. 120 (1). Bringing into operation various provisions of the 2012 Act on 09.05.2012, 01.07.2012 & 10.07.2012. - Issued: 08.05.2012. Made: 02.05.2012. Effect: None. Territorial extent & classification: E/W/S/NI. General. - 4p.: 30 cm. - 978-0-11-152402-2 £4.00

Freedom of information, Northern Ireland

The Protection of Freedoms Act 2012 (Commencement No. 1) Order 2012 No. 2012/1205 (C.41). - Enabling power: Protection of Freedoms Act 2012, s. 120 (1). Bringing into operation various provisions of the 2012 Act on 09.05.2012, 01.07.2012 & 10.07.2012. - Issued: 08.05.2012. Made: 02.05.2012. Effect: None. Territorial extent & classification: E/W/S/NI. General. - 4p.: 30 cm. - 978-0-11-152402-2 £4.00

Gas

The Electricity and Gas (Competitive Tenders for Smart Meter Communication Licences) Regulations 2012 No. 2012/2414. - Enabling power: Electricity Act 1989, ss. 56FC, 60 & Gas Act 1986, ss. 41HC, 47. - Issued: 27.09.2012. Made: 19.09.2012. Laid: 21.09.2012. Coming into force: 12.10.2012. Effect: None. Territorial extent & classification: E/W/S. General. - 20p.: 30 cm. - 978-0-11-152899-0 £5.75

The Electricity and Gas (Energy Companies Obligation) Order 2012 No. 2012/3018. - Enabling power: Gas Act 1986, ss. 33BC, 33BD & Electricity Act 1989, ss. 41A, 41B & Utilities Act 2000, ss. 103, 103A. - Issued: 06.12.2012. Made: 04.12.2012. Coming into force: 05.12.2012, in accord. with art. 1. Effect: None. Territorial extent & classification: E/W/S. General. - Supersedes draft SI (ISBN 9780111530276) issued 02.11.2012. - 24p.: 30 cm. - 978-0-11-153166-2 £5.75

The Electricity and Gas (Smart Meters Licensable Activity) Order 2012 No. 2012/2400. - Enabling power: Electricity Act 1989, ss. 56FA (1) (5) (6), 60 & Gas Act 1986, ss. 41HA (1) (5) (6), 47. - Issued: 25.09.2012. Made: 18.09.2012. Coming into force: In accord. with art. 1. Effect: 1986 c. 44, c. 45; 1989 c. 29; 2000 c. 27; 2002 c. 40; 2007 c. 17; 2008 c. 32 & S.I. 1999/1549; 2002/2665 amended. Territorial extent & classification: E/W/S. General. - Supersedes draft SI (ISBN 9780111527412) issued 20.07.2012. - 16p.: 30 cm. - 978-0-11-152894-5 £5.75

Gender recognition

The Gender Recognition Register (Application Fees) (Amendment) Order 2012 No. 2012/920. - Enabling power: Gender Recognition Act 2004, ss. 7 (2), 24 (1). - Issued: 26.03.2012. Made: 22.03.2012. Laid: 26.03.2012. Coming into force: 16.04.2012. Effect: S.I. 2006/758 amended. Territorial extent & classification: E/W/S/NI. General. - 2p.: 30 cm. - 978-0-11-152279-0 £4.00

Geneva conventions

The Geneva Conventions Act (Jersey) Order 2010 No. 2012/2589. - Enabling power: Geneva Conventions Act 1957, s. 8 (2). - Issued: 22.10.2012. Made: 17.10.2012. Coming into force: In accord. with art. 1. Effect: None. Territorial extent & classification: Jersey. General. - 2p.: 30 cm. - 978-0-11-152974-4 £4.00

Government resources and accounts

The Government Resources and Accounts Act 2000 (Audit of Public Bodies) Order 2012 No. 2012/854. - Enabling power: Government Resources and Accounts Act 2000, s. 25 (6) (7). - Issued: 19.03.2012. Made: 14.03.2012. Coming into force: In accord. with art. 1. Effect: 1993 c.18; 2007 c.21; S.I. 2003/1326; 2009/476; 2011/817 amended. Territorial extent & classification: E/W/S/NI. General. - 8p.: 30 cm. - 978-0-11-152243-1 £4.00

The Government Resources and Accounts Act 2000 (Estimates and Accounts) (Amendment) Order 2012 No. 2012/3135. - Enabling power: Government Resources and Accounts Act 2000, s. 4A (3) (4). - Issued: 19.12.2012. Made: 18.12.2012. Laid: 19.12.2012. Coming into force: 29.01.2013. Effect: SI 2012/717 amended. Territorial extent & classification: E/W/S/NI. General. - 8p.: 30 cm. - 978-0-11-153270-6 £5.75

The Government Resources and Accounts Act 2000 (Estimates and Accounts) Order 2012 No. 2012/717. - Enabling power: Government Resources and Accounts Act 2000, s. 4A (3) (4). - Issued: 08.03.2012. Made: 07.03.2012. Laid: 08.03.2012. Coming into force: 01.04.2012. Effect: None. Territorial extent & classification: E/W/S/NI. General. - 16p.: 30 cm. - 978-0-11-152162-5 £5.75

The National Health Service Bodies (Summarised Accounts) Order 2012 No. 2012/2789. - Enabling power: Government Resources and Accounts Act 2000, s. 14 (1). - Issued: 08.11.2012. Made: 06.11.2012. Laid: 07.11.2012. Coming into force: 29.11.2012. Effect: None. Territorial extent & classification: E. General. - 12p.: 30 cm. - 978-0-11-153054-2 £5.75

The Whole of Government Accounts (Designation of Bodies) Order 2012 No. 2012/1803. - Enabling power: Government Resources and Accounts Act 2000, s. 10 (1). - Issued: 12.07.2012. Made: 10.07.2012. Laid: 11.07.2012. Coming into force: 01.08.2012. Effect: None. Territorial extent & classification: E/W/S/NI. General. - 72p.: 30 cm. - 978-0-11-152663-7 £13.75

Harbours, docks, piers and ferries

The Caernarfon Harbour Trust (Constitution) Harbour Revision Order 2012 No. 2012/1984. - Enabling power: Harbours Act 1964, s. 14 (1) (3). - Issued: 03.08.2012. Made: 27.07.2012. Laid: 02.08.2012. Coming into force: 25.08.2012. Effect: S.I. 1989/2493 partially revoked. Territorial extent & classification: W. Local. - 12p.: 30 cm. - 978-0-11-152786-3 £5.75

The Cowes Harbour Revision Order 2012 No. 2012/3080. - Enabling power: Harbours Act 1964, s. 14 (2) (a). - Issued: 17.12.2012. Made: 10.12.2012. Laid: 13.12.2012. Coming into force: 07.01.2013. Effect: None. Territorial extent & classification: E. Local. - 16p.: 30 cm. - 978-0-11-153220-1 £5.75

The Dover Harbour Revision Order 2012 No. 2012/416. - Enabling power: Harbours Act 1964, s. 14 (7). - Issued: 23.12.2012. Made: 16.02.2012. Coming into force: 16.03.2012. Effect: None. Territorial extent & classification: E. Local. - 16p.: 30 cm. - 978-0-11-152040-6 £5.75

The Hinkley Point Harbour Empowerment Order 2012 No. 2012/1914. - Enabling power: Harbours Act 1964, s. 16. - Issued: 27.07.2012. Made: 19.07.2012. Laid: 24.07.2012. Coming into force: 16.08.2012. Effect: None. Territorial extent & classification: E. Local. - 40p., 6 maps: 30 cm. - 978-0-11-152758-0 £9.75

The Milford Haven Port Authority (Constitution) Harbour Revision Order 2012 No. 2012/1154. - Enabling power: Harbours Act 1964, s. 14 (1) (3). - Issued: 03.05.2012. Made: 25.04.2012. Laid: 30.04.2012. Coming into force: 24.05.2012. Effect: 2002 c. v. amended. Territorial extent & classification: W. Local. - 8p.: 30 cm. - 978-0-11-152385-8 £4.00

The Poole Harbour Revision Order 2012 No. 2012/1777. - Enabling power: Harbours Act 1964, s. 14 (7). - Issued: 16.07.2012. Made: 05.07.2012. Coming into force: 23.07.2012. Effect: Poole Harbour Act 1756; 1895 c. lxx; 1925 c. vi revoked & 1891 c. clix; 1894 c. cxii; 1914 c. clv; 1923 c. vi; S.I. 2001/2820 partially revoked. Territorial extent & classification: E. Local. - 34p.: 30 cm. - 978-0-11-152669-9 £9.75

The Port of Ipswich Harbour Revision Order 2012 No. 2012/3129. - Enabling power: Harbours Act 1964, s. 14 (1). - Issued: 27.12.2012. Made: 18.12.2012. Laid: 20.12.2012. Coming into force: 15.01.2013. Effect: None. Territorial extent & classification: E. Local. - 8p., 1 fig: 30 cm. - 978-0-11-153273-7 £4.00

Health and personal social services, Northern Ireland

The Health Service Branded Medicines (Control of Prices and Supply of Information) Amendment Regulations 2012 No. 2012/2791. - Enabling power: National Health Service Act 2006, ss. 262 (1), 263 (1), 266 (1) (a), 272 (7). - Issued: 09.11.2012. Made: 06.11.2012. Laid: 09.11.2012. Coming into force: 01.01.2013. Effect: S.I. 2008/3258 amended & S.I. 2011/2955 revoked. Territorial extent & classification: E/W/S/NI. General. - 2p.: 30 cm. - 978-0-11-153053-5 £4.00

Health and safety

The Advisory Committee on Hazardous Substances (Abolition) Order 2012 No. 2012/1923. - Enabling power: Public Bodies Act 2011, ss. 1 (1), 6 (1) (5), 35 (2). - Issued: 25.07.2012. Made: 21.07.2012. Coming into force: In accord. with art. 1. Effect: 1967 c. 13; 1975 c. 24; 1990 c. 43; 2000 c. 36; 2011 c. 24 partially repealed & S.I. 1993/1572; 1999/1319 partially revoked & S.I. 1991/1487, 1488 revoked. Territorial extent & classification: E/W/S/NI. General. - Supersedes draft S.I. (ISBN 9780111520741) issued 29.02.2012. For approval by resolution of each House of Parliament after the expiry of the 40-day period specified in section 11 (4) of the Public Bodies Act 2011. - 4p.: 30 cm. - 978-0-11-152762-7 £4.00

The Control of Asbestos Regulations 2012 No. 2012/632. - Enabling power: Health and Safety at Work etc. Act 1974, ss. 15 (1) (2) (3) (4) (5) (6) (b) (9), 18 (2), 80 (1), 82 (3), sch. 3, paras. 1 (1) to (4), 3 (2), 4, 6, 8 to 11, 13 (1) (3), 14, 15 (1), 16, 20 & European Communities Act 1972, s. 2 (2). - Issued: 05.03.2012. Made: 27.02.2012. Laid: 05.03.2012. Coming into force: 06.04.2012. Effect: S.I. 1992/2966; 1998/494, 2306; 2002/2677; 2004/1964; 2006/557; 2007/320; 2008/2852; 2010/2984 amended & S.I. 2006/2739 revoked & replaced. Territorial extent & classification: E/W/S. General. - EC note: These Regulations implement in Great Britain - Council Directive 2009/148/EC (which repealed and replaced Council Directive 83/477/EEC (as amended)); Council Directive 90/394/EEC; Council Directive 98/24/EC. - 28p.: 30 cm. - 978-0-11-152108-3 £5.75

The Customs Disclosure of Information and Miscellaneous Amendments Regulations 2012 No. 2012/1848. - Enabling power: European Communities Act 1972, s. 2 (2). - Issued: 17.07.2012. Made: 12.07.2012. Laid: 16.07.2012. Coming into force: 10.08.2012. Effect: S.I. 2002/1144; 2005/1803; 2006/3418; 2010/1554 amended. Territorial extent & classification: E/W/S/NI. General. - EC note: These Regulations creates an offence of the unauthorised disclosure of customs information which has been disclosed by a specified person listed in reg. 3 (2) to a market surveillance authority under art. 27 (2) of Regulation 765/2008 setting out the requirements for accreditation and market surveillance relating to the marketing of products and repealing Regulation 339/93/EEC. - 8p.: 30 cm. - 978-0-11-152712-2 £4.00

The Health and Safety (Fees) Regulations 2012 No. 2012/1652. - Enabling power: European Communities Act 1972, s. 2 (2) & Health and Safety at Work etc. Act 1974, ss. 43 (2) (4) (5) (6), 82 (3) (a). - Issued: 28.06.2012. Made: 25.06.2012. Laid: 28.06.2012. Coming into force: 01.10.2012. Effect: S.I. 2010/579 revoked. Territorial extent and classification: E/W/S. General. - 40p.: 30 cm. - 978-0-11-152591-3 £9.75

The Health and Safety (Miscellaneous Revocations) Regulations 2012 No. 2012/1537. - Enabling power: Health and Safety at Work etc. Act 1974, ss. 15 (1) (3) (a), 49 (1) (4). - Issued: 18.06.2012. Made: 13.06.2012. Laid: 18.06.2012. Coming into force: 01.10.2012. Effect: S.R.& O. 1906/679 & S.I. 1950/65; 1962/1667; 1973/36; 1981/1332; 1982/877; 2005/228 revoked. Territorial extent & classification: E/W/S. General. - 2p.: 30 cm. - 978-0-11-152550-0 £4.00

The Identification and Traceability of Explosives (Amendment) Regulations 2012 No. 2012/638. - Enabling power: Health and Safety at Work etc. Act 1974, ss. 15 (1) (9), 82 (3) (a). - Issued: 06.03.2012. Made: 01.03.2012. Laid: 06.03.2012. Coming into force: 05.04.2012. Effect: S.I. 2010/1004 amended. Territorial extent & classification: E/W/S. General. - EC note: These Regulations amend the 2010 Regulations (SI 2010/1004) which implement Directive 2008/43. The amendment to the commencement date is in partial implementation of arts 1.4 and 2.1 of Commission Directive 2012/4/EU which amends the 2008 Directive. - 4p.: 30 cm. - 978-0-11-152120-5 £4.00

The Reporting of Injuries, Diseases and Dangerous Occurrences (Amendment) Regulations 2012 No. 2012/199. - Enabling power: Health and Safety at Work etc. Act 1974, s. 15 (1) (2) (3) (a) (4) (a) (9), sch. 3, paras 15 (1), 16 , 20. - Issued: 31.01.2012. Made: 26.01.2012. Laid: 31.01.2012. Coming into force: 06.04.2012. Effect: S.I. 1977/500; 1989/971; 1995/3163 amended. Territorial extent & classification: Applies to GB and extends to premises and activities specified in the Health and Safety at Work etc Act 1974 (Application Outside Great Britain) Order 2001. General. - 8p.: 30 cm. - 978-0-11-151962-2 £4.00

Health care and associated professions

The Health and Social Care Act 2012 (Commencement No. 1 and Transitory Provision) Order 2012 No. 2012/1319 (C.47). - Enabling power: Health and Social Care Act 2012, ss. 304 (10), 306. Bringing into operation various provisions of this Act on 01.06.2012, 01.07.2012, 01.08.2012 in accord. with art. 2. - Issued: 22.05.2012. Made: 17.05.2012. Coming into force: .- Effect: S.I. 2010/781 amended. Territorial extent & classification: E/W. General. - 8p.: 30 cm. - 978-0-11-152461-9 £4.00

The Health and Social Care Act 2012 (Commencement No. 2 and Transitional, Savings and Transitory Provisions) Order 2012 No. 2012/1831 (C.71). - Enabling power: Health and Social Care Act 2012, ss. 304 (10), 306. Bringing into operation various provisions of the 2012 Act in accord. with art. 2. - Issued: 16.07.2012. Made: 11.07.2012. Coming into force: .- Effect: None. Territorial extent & classification: E/W. General. - 16p.: 30 cm. - 978-0-11-152699-6 £5.75

The Health and Social Care Act 2012 (Commencement No. 3, Transitional, Savings and Transitory Provisions and Amendment) Order 2012 No. 2012/2657 (C.107). - Enabling power: Health and Social Care Act 2012, ss. 304 (10), 306. Bringing into operation various provisions of the 2012 Act on 01.11.2012 in accord. with art. 2. - Issued: 25.10.2012. Made: 22.10.2012. Effect: 2012 c.7; S.I. 2912/1831 (C.71) amended. Territorial extent & classification: E. General. - 12p.: 30 cm. - 978-0-11-152990-4 £5.75

The Health and Social Care Act 2012 (Consequential Amendments - the Professional Standards Authority for Health and Social Care) Order 2012 No. 2012/2672. - Enabling power: Health and Social Care Act 2012, s. 303. - Issued: 29.10.2012. Made: 24.10.2012. Laid: 29.10.2012. Coming into force: In accord. with art. 1 (2). Effect: S.I. 2002/254; 2008/2927; 2010/231, 1000, 1616, 2476, 2969 amended. Territorial extent & classification: E. General. - 4p.: 30 cm. - 978-0-11-153002-3 £4.00

Health care and associated professions: Dentists

The General Dental Council (Constitution) (Amendment) Order 2012 No. 2012/1655. - Enabling power: Dentists Act 1984, s. 1 (2A), sch. 1, para. 1B. - Issued: 29.06.2012. Made: 26.06.2012. Laid: 29.06.2012. Coming into force: 01.10.2013. Effect: S.I. 2009/1808 amended. Territorial extent & classification: E/W/S/NI. General. - 2p.: 30 cm. - 978-0-11-152593-7 £4.00

Health care and associated professions: Doctors

The General Medical Council (Constitution) (Amendment) Order 2012 No. 2012/1654. - Enabling power: Medical Act 1983, s. 1 (2), sch. 1, para. 1B. - Issued: 29.06.2012. Made: 26.06.2012. Laid: 29.06.2012. Coming into force: 01.01.2013. Effect: S.I. 2008/2554 amended. Territorial extent & classification: E/W/S/NI. General. - 2p.: 30 cm. - 978-0-11-152595-1 £4.00

The General Medical Council (Licence to Practise and Revalidation) Regulations Order of Council 2012 No. 2012/2685. - Enabling power: Medical Act 1983, ss. 29A (2) to (4), 29B (1) (2) (3), 29D (1) (1A) (2), 29E (1) to (2A), 29J (1) (3), 41 (7). - Issued: 29.10.2012. Made: 20.10.2012. Laid: 29.10.2012. Coming into force: 03.12.2012. Effect: S.I. 2009/2739 revoked. Territorial extent & classification: E/W/S/NI. General. - 16p: 30 cm. - 978-0-11-153015-3 £5.75

The Medical Profession (Miscellaneous Amendments) Order 2008 (Commencement No. 4) Order of Council 2012 No. 2012/2686 (C.109). - Enabling power: S.I. 2008/3131, art. 1 (4). Bringing into operation various provisions of the 2008 Order on 03.12.2012, in accord. with art. 1. - Issued: 29.10.2012. Made: 20.10.2012. Effect: None. Territorial extent & classification: E/W/S/NI. General. - With correction slip dated January 2013. - 4p.: 30 cm. - 978-0-11-153011-5 £4.00

The Postgraduate Medical Education and Training (Amendment) Order of Council 2012 No. 2012/344. - Enabling power: Medical Act 1983, s. 34D (3). - Issued: 16.02.2012. Made: 07.02.2012. Laid: 16.02.2012. Coming into force: 16.03.2012. Effect: S.I. 2010/473 amended. Territorial extent & classification: E/W/S/NI. General. - 8p.: 30 cm. - 978-0-11-152024-6 £4.00

Health care and associated professions: Nurses and midwives

The Nursing and Midwifery Council (Education, Registration and Registration Appeals) (Amendment) Rules Order of Council 2012 No. 2012/2754. - Enabling power: S.I. 2002/253, arts 7 (2), 12 (1), 32, 47 (2). - Issued: 06.11.2012. Made: 26.10.2012. Laid: 05.11.2012. Coming into force: 14.01.2013. Effect: S.I. 2004/1767 amended. Territorial extent & classification: E/W/S/NI. General. - 8p.: 30 cm. - 978-0-11-153037-5 £4.00

The Nursing and Midwifery Council (Fees) (Amendment) Rules Order of Council 2012 No. 2012/3026. - Enabling power: S.I. 2002/253, arts 7 (1) (2), 33 (7) (a), 47 (2). - Issued: 06.12.2012. Made: 04.12.2012. Laid: 06.12.2012. Coming into force: 01.02.2013. Effect: S.I. 2002/253 amended. Territorial extent & classification: E/W/S/NI. General. - 4p.: 30 cm. - 978-0-11-153176-1 £4.00

The Nursing and Midwifery Council (Constitution) (Amendment) Order 2012 No. 2012/2745. - Enabling power: S.I. 2002/253, art. 3 (7A), sch. 1, para. 1A, 1B. - Issued: 05.11.2012. Made: 02.11.2012. Laid: 05.11.2012. Coming into force: 01.05.2013. Effect: S.I. 2008/2553 amended. Territorial extent & classification: E/W/S/NI. General. - 2p.: 30 cm. - 978-0-11-153036-8 £4.00

The Nursing and Midwifery Council (Fitness to Practise) (Amendment) Rules 2011 Order of Council 2012 No. 2012/17. - Enabling power: S.I. 2002/253, arts 26 (3), 30 (9), 32 (1) (2), 47 (2). - Issued: 09.01.2012. Made: 05.01.2012. Laid: 09.01.2012. Coming into force: 06.02.2012. Effect: S.I. 2004/1761 amended. Territorial extent & classification: E/W/S/NI. General. - With correction slip dated February 2012. - 8p.: 30 cm. - 978-0-11-151899-1 £5.75

The Nursing and Midwifery Council (Midwives) Rules Order of Council 2012 No. 2012/3025. - Enabling power: S.I. 2002/253, arts 42, 43, 47 (2). - Issued: 06.12.2012. Made: 04.12.2012. Laid: 06.12.2012. Coming into force: 01.01.2013. Effect: S.I. 2004/1764 revoked. Territorial extent & classification: E/W/S/NI. General. - 12p.: 30 cm. - 978-0-11-153175-4 £5.75

Health care and associated professions: Opticians

The General Optical Council (Continuing Education and Training Rules) (Amendment) Order of Council 2012 No. 2012/2882. - Enabling power: Opticians Act 1989, ss. 11A, 11B (6), 23 (A) (2), 31A. - Issued: 19.11.2012. Made: 11.11.2012. Laid: 19.11.2012. Coming into force: 01.01.2013. Effect: S.I. 2005/1473 amended. Territorial extent & classification: E/W/S/NI. General. - 12p.: 30 cm. - 978-0-11-153084-9 £5.75

Healthcare and associated professions: Osteopaths

The General Osteopathic Council (Application for Registration and Fees) (Amendment) Rules Order of Council 2012 No. 2012/1101. - Enabling power: Osteopaths Act 1993, ss. 6 (2), 35 (2). - Issued: 19.04.2012. Made: 16.04.2012. Coming into force: 09.05.2012. Effect: S.I. 2000/1038 amended. Territorial extent & classification: E/W/S/NI. General. - 4p.: 30 cm. - 978-0-11-152362-9 £4.00

Health care and associated professions: Pharmacy

The General Pharmaceutical Council (Amendment of Miscellaneous Provisions) Rules Order of Council 2012 No. 2012/3171. - Enabling power: S.I. 2010/231, arts. 18 (2), 23 (1) (a) (c), 61 (1) (2) (c), 63 (4), 66 (1), sch. 1, para. 5. - Issued: 07.01.2012. Made: 20.12.2012. Laid before Westminster & Scottish Parliaments: 07.01.2012. Coming into force: 05.02.2012. Effect: S.I. 2010/1615, 1616, 1617 amended Territorial extent & classification: E/W/S. General. - 16p.: 30 cm. - 978-0-11-153290-4 £5.75

Health care and associated professions: Professions complementary to dentistry

The General Dental Council (Constitution) (Amendment) Order 2012 No. 2012/1655. - Enabling power: Dentists Act 1984, s. 1 (2A), sch. 1, para. 1B. - Issued: 29.06.2012. Made: 26.06.2012. Laid: 29.06.2012. Coming into force: 01.10.2013. Effect: S.I. 2009/1808 amended. Territorial extent & classification: E/W/S/NI. General. - 2p.: 30 cm. - 978-0-11-152593-7 £4.00

Health care and associated professions: Social workers

The General Social Care Council (Transfer of Register and Abolition - Transitional and Saving Provision) Order of Council 2012 No. 2012/1480. - Enabling power: Health and Social Care Act 2012, ss. 230 (2), 304 (10) (a). - Issued: 20.06.2012. Made: 18.06.2012. Laid: 20.06.2012. Coming into force: In accord. with art. 1 (2). Effect: None. Territorial extent & classification: E/W/S/NI. General. - With correction slip dated August 2012. - 8p.: 30 cm. - 978-0-11-152556-2 £5.75

The Health and Social Care Act 2012 (Consequential Provision - Social Workers) Order 2012 No. 2012/1479. - Enabling power: Health and Social Care Act 2012, ss. 303 (1) (2). - Issued: 20.06.2012. Made: 18.06.2012. Laid: 20.06.2012. Coming into force: In accord. with art. 1 (2). Effect: 105 statutory instruments/rules amended. Territorial extent & classification: E/W/S/NI. General. - With correction slip dated January 2013. - 25p.: 30 cm. - 978-0-11-152559-3 £5.75

Highways, England

The A1 Trunk Road (Elkesley Junctions Improvement) Order 2012 No. 2012/839. - Enabling power: Highways Act 1980, ss. 10, 41. - Issued: 28.03.2012. Made: 12.03.2012. Coming into force: 16.05.2012. Effect: None. Territorial extent & classification: E. Local. - 8p., plan: 30 cm. - 978-0-11-152237-0 £4.00

The A30 Trunk Road (Turks Head Link) (Trunking) Order 2012 No. 2012/2856. - Enabling power: Highways Act 1980, s. 10. - Issued: 15.11.2012. Made: 13.11.2012. Coming into force: 27.11.2012. Effect: None. Territorial extent & classification: E. General. - 4p., map: 30 cm. - 978-0-11-153080-1 £4.00

The A282 Trunk Road (Dartford - Thurrock Crossing Charging Scheme) Order 2012 No. 2012/2387. - Enabling power: Transport Act 2000, ss. 167, 168, 171, 172 (2). - Issued: 20.09.2012. Made: 14.09.2012. Coming into force: 01.10.2012. Effect: S.I. 2008/1951 revoked. Territorial extent & classification: E. General. - 8p.: 30 cm. - 978-0-11-152882-2 £5.75

The A453 Birmingham to Nottingham Trunk Road (M1 Junction 24 to A52 Nottingham Improvement and Slip Roads) Order 2012 No. 2012/1219. - Enabling power: Highways Act 1980, ss. 10, 41, 106. - Issued: 15.05.2012. Made: 02.05.2012. Coming into force: 24.05.2012. Effect: None. Territorial extent & classification: E. Local. - 8p.: 30 cm. - 978-0-11-152406-0 £5.75

The A453 Birmingham to Nottingham Trunk Road (M1 Junction 24 to A52 Nottingham Improvement) (Detrunking) Order 2012 No. 2012/1218. - Enabling power: Highways Act 1980, s. 10. - Issued: 15.05.2012. Made: 02.05.2012. Coming into force: 24.05.2012. Effect: None. Territorial extent & classification: E. Local. - 4p.: 30 cm. - 978-0-11-152405-3 £4.00

The Dunham Bridge (Revision of Tolls) Order 2012 No. 2012/852. - Enabling power: Transport Charges &c. (Miscellaneous Provisions) Act 1954, s. 6. - Issued: 20.03.2012. Made: 15.03.2012. Coming into force: 30.03.2012. Effect: S.I. 2007/1455 revoked. Territorial extent & classification: E. Local. - Available at http://www.legislation.gov.uk/uksi/2012/852/contents/made *Non-print*

The Humber Bridge Board (Membership) Order 2012 No. 2012/1392. - Enabling power: Humber Bridge Act 1959, s. 97. - Issued: 30.05.2012. Made: 24.05.2012. Coming into force: 31.05.2012. Effect: None. Territorial extent & classification: E. General. - 2p.: 30 cm. - 978-0-11-152482-4 £4.00

The Humber Bridge (Debts) Order 2012 No. 2012/716. - Enabling power: Humber Bridge (Debts) Act 1996, s. 1 (1). - Issued: 14.03.2012. Made: 05.03.2012. Laid: 08.03.2012. Coming into force: 31.03.2012 & 01.04.2012, in accord. with art. 1. Effect: S.I. 2011/1718 revoked (01.04.2012). Territorial extent & classification: E. Local. - 4p.: 30 cm. - 978-0-11-152170-0 £4.00

The M54 Motorway (Junction 2 Improvements i54 Strategic Employment Area) (Connecting Roads) Order 2012 No. 2012/1385. - Enabling power: Highways Act 1980, ss. 16, 17, 19. - Issued: 21.08.2012. Made: 17.05.2012. Coming into force: 07.06.2012. Effect: None. Territorial extent & classification: E. Local. - 4p., plan: 30 cm. - 978-0-11-152807-5 £4.00

The M54 Motorway (Junction 2 Improvements i54 Strategic Employment Area) (Trunk Roads) Order 2012 No. 2012/1384. - Enabling power: Highways Act 1980, ss. 10, 41, 106. - Issued: 21.08.2012. Made: 17.05.2012. Coming into force: 07.06.2012. Effect: None. Territorial extent & classification: E. Local. - 8p., plan: 30 cm. - 978-0-11-152806-8 £5.75

The Portsmouth City Council Access to Portsmouth (1) - Tipner Interchange, M275 Motorway Slip Roads Scheme 2009 Confirmation Instrument 2012 No. 2012/463. - Enabling power: Highways Act 1980, ss. 16, 17. - Issued: 29.02.2012. Made: 09.02.2012. Coming into force: In accord. with art. 1. Effect: None. Territorial extent classification: E. Local. - This Statutory Instrument has been printed in substitution of the SI of the same number and is being issued free of charge to all known recipients of that Statutory Instrument. Supersedes previous S.I. (ISBN 9780111520505) issued 29.02.2012. - 4p., plan: 30 cm. - 978-0-11-152137-3 £4.00

The Portsmouth City Council Access to Portsmouth (1) - Tipner Interchange, M275 Motorway Slip Roads Scheme 2009 Confirmation Instrument 2012 No. 2012/463. - Enabling power: Highways Act 1980, ss. 16, 17. - Issued: 29.02.2012. Made: 09.02.2012. Coming into force: In accord. with art. 1. Effect: None. Territorial extent classification: E. Local. - Superseded by S.I. 2012/463 (same number) (ISBN 9780111521373) issued on 07.03.2012. - 4p., plan: 30 cm. - 978-0-11-152050-5 £4.00

The River Tyne (Tunnels) (Revision of Tolls) Order 2012 No. 2012/3053. - Enabling power: Tyne and Wear Act 1976, s. 13 & SI 2005/2222, sch. 14. - Issued: 11.12.2012. Made: 04.12.2012. Coming into force: 01.01.2013. Effect: S.I. 2011/2922 revoked. Territorial extent & classification: E. Local. - Available at http://www.legislation.gov.uk/uksi/2012/3053/contents/made *Non-print*

The Severn Bridges Tolls Order 2012 No. 2012/3136. - Enabling power: Severn Bridges Act 1992, s. 9 (1) (2) (b) (3) (b) (4) (6). - Issued: 28.12.2012. Made: 18.12.2012. Coming into force: 01.01.2013. Effect: S.I. 2011/3060 revoked. Territorial extent & classification: E. Local. - 2p.: 30 cm. - 978-0-11-153279-9 £4.00

The Street Works (Charges for Occupation of the Highway) (England) Regulations 2012 No. 2012/425. - Enabling power: New Roads and Street Works Act 1991, ss. 74A, 104. - Issued: 27.02.2012. Made: 20.02.2012. Laid: 21.02.2012. Coming into force: 14.03.2012. Effect: S.I. 2001/4060 revoked. Territorial extent & classification: E. General. - 8p.: 30 cm. - 978-0-11-152043-7 £4.00

The Street Works (Charges for Occupation of the Highway) (Transport for London) Order 2012 No. 2012/1322. - Enabling power: New Roads and Street Works Act 1991, ss. 74A (2). - Issued: 25.05.2012. Made: 18.05.2012. Coming into force: 11.06.2012. Effect: None. Territorial extent & classification: E. General. - 2p.: 30 cm. - 978-0-11-152462-6 £4.00

The Street Works (Charges for Unreasonably Prolonged Occupation of the Highway) (England) (Amendment) Regulations 2012 No. 2012/2272. - Enabling power: New Roads and Street Works Act 1991, ss. 74, 104 (1). - Issued: 11.09.2012. Made: 02.09.2012. Laid: 06.09.2012. Coming into force: 01.10.2012. Effect: S.I. 2009/303 amended. Territorial extent & classification: E. General. - 8p.: 30 cm. - 978-0-11-152854-9 £4.00

The Sunderland City Council (Sunderland Strategic Transport Corridor - New Wear Bridge) Scheme 2009 Confirmation Instrument 2012 No. 2012/2706. - Enabling power: Highways Act 1980, s. 106 (3). - Issued: 05.11.2012. Made: 18.10.2012. Coming into force: In accord. with art. 1. Effect: None. Territorial extent & classification: E. Local. - 8p., plans: 30 cm. - 978-0-11-153019-1 £5.75

The Sunderland City Council (Sunderland Strategic Transport Corridor - Temporary Works New Wear Bridge) Scheme 2009 Confirmation Instrument 2012 No. 2012/2710. - Enabling power: Highways Act 1980, s. 106 (3). - Issued: 05.11.2012. Made: 18.10.2012. Coming into force: In accord. with art. 1. Effect: None. Territorial extent & classification: E. Local. - 8p., plans: 30 cm. - 978-0-11-153018-4 £5.75

The Traffic Management (Barnsley Metropolitan Borough Council) Permit Scheme Order 2012 No. 2012/1289. - Enabling power: Traffic Management Act 2004, ss. 34 (4) (5), 39 (2). - Issued: 22.05.2012. Made: 10.05.2012. Coming into force: 12.06.2012. Effect: None. Territorial extent & classification: E. General. - 122p.: 30 cm. - 978-0-11-152447-3 £18.50

The Traffic Management (Bedford Borough Council) Permit Scheme Order 2012 No. 2012/2541. - Enabling power: Traffic Management Act 2004, ss. 34 (4) (5), 39 (2). - Issued: 12.10.2012. Made: 03.10.2012. Coming into force: 05.11.2012. Effect: None. Territorial extent & classification: E. General. - 116p.: 30 cm. - 978-0-11-152918-8 £18.50

The Traffic Management (Doncaster Borough Council) Permit Scheme Order 2012 No. 2012/1282. - Enabling power: Traffic Management Act 2004, ss. 34 (4) (5), 39 (2). - Issued: 22.05.2012. Made: 10.05.2012. Coming into force: 12.06.2012. Effect: None. Territorial extent & classification: E. General. - 122p.: 30 cm. - 978-0-11-152444-2 £18.50

The Traffic Management (Hertfordshire County Council) Permit Scheme Order 2012 No. 2012/2549. - Enabling power: Traffic Management Act 2004, ss. 34 (4) (5), 39 (2). - Issued: 12.10.2012. Made: 03.10.2012. Coming into force: 05.11.2012. Effect: None. Territorial extent & classification: E. General. - 117p.: 30 cm. - 978-0-11-152921-8 £18.50

The Traffic Management (Leeds City Council) Permit Scheme Order 2012 No. 2012/1295. - Enabling power: Traffic Management Act 2004, ss. 34 (4) (5), 39 (2). - Issued: 07.06.2012. Made: 10.05.2012. Coming into force: 12.06.2012. Effect: None. Territorial extent & classification: E. General. - 122p., ill.: 30 cm. - 978-0-11-152450-3 £18.50

The Traffic Management (London Borough of Bexley) Permit Scheme Order 2012 No. 2012/3102. - Enabling power: Traffic Management Act 2004, ss. 34 (4) (5), 39 (2). - Issued: 20.12.2012. Made: 10.12.2012. Coming into force: 18.02.2013. Effect: None. Territorial extent & classification: E. General. - 116p.: 30 cm. - 978-0-11-153256-0 £18.50

The Traffic Management (London Borough of Havering) Permit Scheme Order 2012 No. 2012/3103. - Enabling power: Traffic Management Act 2004, ss. 34 (4) (5), 39 (2). - Issued: 20.12.2012. Made: 10.12.2012. Coming into force: 01.04.2013. Effect: None. Territorial extent & classification: E. General. - 116p.: 30 cm. - 978-0-11-153255-3 £18.50

The Traffic Management (London Borough of Merton) Permit Scheme Order 2012 No. 2012/3105. - Enabling power: Traffic Management Act 2004, ss. 34 (4) (5), 39 (2). - Issued: 20.12.2012. Made: 10.12.2012. Coming into force: 14.01.2013. Effect: None. Territorial extent & classification: E. General. - 116p.: 30 cm. - 978-0-11-153253-9 £18.50

The Traffic Management (London Borough of Sutton) Permit Scheme Order 2012 No. 2012/3106. - Enabling power: Traffic Management Act 2004, ss. 34 (4) (5), 39 (2). - Issued: 20.12.2012. Made: 10.12.2012. Coming into force: 14.01.2013. Effect: None. Territorial extent & classification: E. General. - 115p.: 30 cm. - 978-0-11-153252-2 £18.50

The Traffic Management (London Borough of Tower Hamlets) Permit Scheme Order 2012 No. 2012/3107. - Enabling power: Traffic Management Act 2004, ss. 34 (4) (5), 39 (2). - Issued: 20.12.2012. Made: 10.12.2012. Coming into force: 14.01.2013. Effect: None. Territorial extent & classification: E. General. - 116p.: 30 cm. - 978-0-11-153251-5 £18.50

The Traffic Management (Luton Borough Council) Permit Scheme Order 2012 No. 2012/2547. - Enabling power: Traffic Management Act 2004, ss. 34 (4) (5), 39 (2). - Issued: 12.10.2012. Made: 03.10.2012. Coming into force: 05.11.2012. Effect: None. Territorial extent & classification: E. General. - 117p.: 30 cm. - 978-0-11-152919-5 £18.50

The Traffic Management (Rotherham Borough Council) Permit Scheme Order 2012 No. 2012/1284. - Enabling power: Traffic Management Act 2004, ss. 34 (4) (5), 39 (2). - Issued: 22.05.2012. Made: 10.05.2012. Coming into force: 12.06.2012. Effect: None. Territorial extent & classification: E. General. - 122p.: 30 cm. - 978-0-11-152445-9 £18.50

The Traffic Management (Royal Borough of Kingston upon Thames) Permit Scheme Order 2012 No. 2012/3104. - Enabling power: Traffic Management Act 2004, ss. 34 (4) (5), 39 (2). - Issued: 20.12.2012. Made: 10.12.2012. Coming into force: 01.03.2012. Effect: None. Territorial extent & classification: E. General. - 117p.: 30 cm. - 978-0-11-153254-6 £18.50

The Traffic Management (Sheffield City Council) Permit Scheme Order 2012 No. 2012/1294. - Enabling power: Traffic Management Act 2004, ss. 34 (4) (5), 39 (2). - Issued: 07.06.2012. Made: 10.05.2012. Coming into force: 12.06.2012. Effect: None. Territorial extent & classification: E. General. - 122p., ill.: 30 cm. - 978-0-11-152449-7 £18.50

The Traffic Management (Southend-On-Sea Borough Council) Permit Scheme Order 2012 No. 2012/2548. - Enabling power: Traffic Management Act 2004, ss. 34 (4) (5), 39 (2). - Issued: 12.10.2012. Made: 03.10.2012. Coming into force: 05.11.2012. Effect: None. Territorial extent & classification: E. General. - 117p.: 30 cm. - 978-0-11-152920-1 £18.50

The Traffic Management (St Helens Borough Council) Permit Scheme Order 2012 No. 2012/785. - Enabling power: Traffic Management Act 2004, ss. 34 (4) (5), 39 (2). - Issued: 19.03.2012. Made: 07.03.2012. Coming into force: 10.04.2012. Effect: None. Territorial extent & classification: E. General. - 52p.: 30 cm. - 978-0-11-152199-1 £9.75

The Traffic Management (The Council of the Borough of Kirklees) Permit Scheme Order 2012 No. 2012/1286. - Enabling power: Traffic Management Act 2004, ss. 34 (4) (5), 39 (2). - Issued: 22.05.2012. Made: 10.05.2012. Coming into force: 12.06.2012. Effect: None. Territorial extent & classification: E. General. - 122p.: 30 cm. - 978-0-11-152446-6 £18.50

Highways, Wales

The Cardiff to Glan Conwy Trunk Road (A470) (Maes Yr Helmau to Cross Foxes Improvement and De-Trunking) Order 2012 No. 2012/157 (W.21). - Enabling power: Highways Act 1980, ss. 10, 12. - Issued: 27.01.2012. Made: 23.01.2012. Coming into force: 06.02.2012. Effect: None. Territorial extent & classification: W. Local. - Available at http://www.legislation.gov.uk/wsi/2012/157/contents/made . - In English and Welsh. Welsh title: Gorchymyn Cefnffordd Caerdydd I Lan Conwy (Yr A470) (Gwelliant Maes yr Helmau I Cross Foxes a Thynnu Statws Cefnffordd) 2012 *Non-print*

The Denbighshire County Council (Construction of Foryd Harbour Walking and Cycling Bridge) Scheme 2011 Confirmation Instrument 2012 No. 2012/870 (W.117). - Enabling power: Highways Act 1980, s. 106 (3). - Issued: 23.03.2012. Made: 15.03.2012. Coming into force: 28.03.2012. Effect: None. Territorial extent & classification: W. Local. - Available at http://www.legislation.gov.uk/wsi/2012/870/contents/made . - In English and Welsh. Welsh title: Offeryn Cadarnhau Cynllun Cyngor Sir Ddinbych (Adeiladu Pont Cerdded a Beicio Harbwr y Foryd) 2011 2012 *Non-print*

The Neath to Abergavenny Trunk Road (A465) (Abergavenny to Hirwaun Dualling and Slip Roads) and East of Abercynon to East of Dowlais Trunk Road (A4060) and Cardiff to Glan Conwy Trunk Road (A470) (Connecting Roads) Order 1999 (Brynmawr to Tredegar) (Amendment) Order 2012 No. 2012/2092 (W.242). - Enabling power: Highways Act 1980, s. 10. - Issued: 16.08.2012. Made: 10.08.2012. Coming into force: 23.08.2012. Effect: S.I. 1999/2720 (W.9) amended. Territorial extent & classification: W. Local. - Available at http://www.legislation.gov.uk/wsi/2012/2092/contents/made. - In English and Welsh. Welsh title: Gorchymyn Cefnffordd Castell-nedd - Y Fenni (A465) (Deuoli o'r Fenni i Hirwaun a'r Ffyrdd Ymuno ac Ymadael) a Ffordd Man i'r Dwyrain o Abercynon -Man i'r Dwyrain o Ddowlais (A4060) a Chefnffordd Caerdydd - Glanconwy (A470) (Ffyrdd Cysylltu) 1999 (Bryn-mawr i Dredegar) (Diwygio) 2012 *Non-print*

The St Clears to Pembroke Dock Trunk Road (A477) (St Clears - Red Roses Improvement and De-trunking) Order 2012 No. 2012/48 (W.11). - Enabling power: Highways Act 1980, ss. 10, 12. - Issued: 13.01.2012. Made: 05.01.2012. Coming into force: 18.01.2012. Effect: None. Territorial extent & classification: W. Local. - Available at http://www.legislation.gov.uk/wsi/2012/48/contents/made. - In English and Welsh. Welsh title: Gorchymyn Cefnffordd Sanclêr i Ddoc Penfro (Yr A477) (Gwelliant Sanclêr - Rhos-Goch a Thynnu Statws Cefnffordd) 2012 *Non-print*

Horticulture, England and Wales

The Quality Standards for Green Bananas (England and Wales) Regulations 2012 No. 2012/947. - Enabling power: European Communities Act 1972, s. 2 (2), sch. 2, para. 1A. - Issued: 29.03.2012. Made: 21.03.2012. Laid: 29.03.2012. Coming into force: 11.05.2012. Effect: 1928 c. 19; 1931 c. 40; 1958 c. 47; 1964 c. 28; 1986 c. 20 disapplied in E/W in respect of bananas. Territorial extent & classification: E/W. General. - EC note: These Regulations provide for the enforcement in England & Wales of EU marketing standards for bananas set out in Commission Implementing Regulation (EU) 1333/2011. - 16p.: 30 cm. - 978-0-11-152297-4 *£5.75*

Housing

The Housing (Scotland) Act 2010 (Consequential Provisions and Modifications) Order 2012 No. 2012/700. - Enabling power: Scotland Act 1998, ss. 104, 112 (1), 113 (2) (5), 114 (1). - Issued: 13.03.2012. Made: 05.03.2012. Coming into force: 01.04.2012. Effect: 1975 c. 24; 1985 c. 69; 1986 c. 45; 1992 c. 12; 1994 c. 23; 2002 c. 40; 2003 c. 14; 2007 c. 3; 2010 c. 4 & S.I. 1987/1968; 1999/584; 2001/1201; 2004/692; 2005/1379; 2006/213, 214, 264; 2008/346; 2009/214, 1801 amended & S.I. 2008/948; 2009/1941 partially revoked. Territorial extent & classification: UK. General. - Supersedes draft S.I. (ISBN 9780111519080) issued 18.01.2012. - 8p.: 30 cm. - 978-0-11-152166-3 *£5.75*

The Rent Officers (Housing Benefit Functions) (Amendment) Order 2012 No. 2012/646. - Enabling power: Housing Act 1996, s. 122 (1) (6). - Issued: 06.03.2012. Made: 29.02.2012. Laid: 06.03.2012. Coming into force: 02.04.2012. Effect: S.I. 1997/1984, 1995 amended. Territorial extent & classification: E/W/S. General. - 8p.: 30 cm. - 978-0-11-152116-8 *£4.00*

Housing, England

The Allocation of Housing and Homelessness (Eligibility) (England) (Amendment) Regulations 2012 No. 2012/2588. - Enabling power: Housing Act 1996, ss. 160ZA (4), 172 (4), 185 (3), 215 (2). - Issued: 17.10.2012. Made: 11.10.2012. Laid: 17.10.2012. Coming into force: 08.11.2012. Effect: S.I. 2006/1294 amended. Territorial extent & classification: E. General. - 4p.: 30 cm. - 978-0-11-152945-4 *£4.00*

The Allocation of Housing (Qualification Criteria for Armed Forces) (England) Regulations 2012 No. 2012/1869. - Enabling power: Housing Act 1996, s. 160ZA (8) (b). - Issued: 19.07.2012. Made: 16.07.2012. Laid: 19.07.2012. Coming into force: 24.08.2012. Effect: None. Territorial extent & classification: E. General. - 2p.: 30 cm. - 978-0-11-152720-7 *£4.00*

The Flexible Tenancies (Review Procedures) Regulations 2012 No. 2012/695. - Enabling power: Housing Act 1985, ss. 107B (6), 107E (4). - Issued: 08.03.2012. Made: 05.03.2012. Laid: 08.03.2012. Coming into force: 01.04.2012. Effect: None. Territorial extent & classification: E. General. - 4p.: 30 cm. - 978-0-11-152149-6 *£4.00*

The Homelessness (Suitability of Accommodation) (England) Order 2012 No. 2012/2601. - Enabling power: Housing Act 1996, ss. 210 (2) (a) (b), 215 (2). - Issued: 17.10.2123. Made: 11.10.2012. Laid: 17.10.2012. Coming into force: 09.11.2012. Effect: None. Territorial extent & classification: E. General. - 4p.: 30 cm. - 978-0-11-152948-5 *£4.00*

The Houses in Multiple Occupation (Specified Educational Establishments) (England) Regulations 2012 No. 2012/249. - Enabling power: Housing Act 2004, sch. 14, para. 4 (2). - Issued: 08.02.2012. Made: 02.02.2012. Laid: 08.02.2012. Coming into force: 14.03.2012. Effect: S.I. 2010/2616 revoked. Territorial extent & classification: E. General. - 8p.: 30 cm. - 978-0-11-151978-3 £5.75

The Housing Act 1996 (Additional Preference for Armed Forces) (England) Regulations 2012 No. 2012/2989. - Enabling power: Housing Act 1996, s. 166A (7). - Issued: 30.11.2012. Made: 29.11.2012. Coming into force: In accord. with reg. 1. Effect: 1996 c.52 amended. Territorial extent & classification: E. General. - Supersedes draft SI (ISBN 9780111529508) issued on 18.10.2012. - 2p.: 30 cm. - 978-0-11-153144-0 £4.00

The Housing and Regeneration Act 2008 (Consequential Provisions) Order 2012 No. 2012/2552. - Enabling power: Housing and Regeneration Act 2008, s. 321. - Issued: 11.10.2012. Made: 08.10.2012. Laid: 11.10.2012. Coming into force: 05.11.2012. Effect: S.I. 1972/853 amended. Territorial extent & classification: E. General. - 2p.: 30 cm. - 978-0-11-152924-9 £4.00

The Housing (Empty Dwelling Management Orders) (Prescribed Period of Time and Additional Prescribed Requirements) (England) (Amendment) Order 2012 No. 2012/2625. - Enabling power: Housing Act 2004, ss. 134 (5) (b) (c), 250. - Issued: 23.10.2012. Made: 17.10.2012. Laid: 23.10.201.2 Coming into force: 15.11.2012. Effect: S.I. 2006/367 amended. Territorial extent & classification: E. General. - 4p.: 30 cm. - 978-0-11-152969-0 £4.00

The Housing (Right to Buy) (Limit on Discount) (England) Order 2012 No. 2012/734. - Enabling power: Housing Act 1985, s. 131. - Issued: 12.03.2012. Made: 07.03.2012. Laid: 12.03.2012. Coming into force: 02.04.2012. Effect: S.I. 1998/2997 revoked. Territorial extent & classification: E. General. - 4p.: 30 cm. - 978-0-11-152165-6 £4.00

The Housing (Right to Manage) (England) Regulations 2012 No. 2012/1821. - Enabling power: Housing Act 1985, ss. 27 (4) (17), 27AB. - Issued: 13.07.2012. Made: 10.07.2012. Laid: 13.07.2012. Coming into force: 06.08.2012. Effect: S.I. 2008/2361 revoked with saving. Territorial extent & classification: E. General. - 12p.: 30 cm. - 978-0-11-152692-7 £5.75

The Licensing and Management of Houses in Multiple Occupation and Other Houses (Miscellaneous Provisions) (Amendment) (England) Regulations 2012 No. 2012/2111. - Enabling power: Housing Act 2004, ss. 63 (5) (6), 87 (5) (6), 250 (2). - Issued: 17.08.2012. Made: 11.08.2012. Laid: 17.08.2012. Coming into force: 10.09.2012. Effect: S.I. 2006/373 amended. Territorial extent & classification: E. General. - 4p.: 30 cm. - 978-0-11-152821-1 £4.00

The Localism Act 2011 (Commencement No. 2 and Transitional Provisions) (England) Order 2012 No. 2012/2599 (C.104). - Enabling power: Localism Act 2011, s. 240 (2) (7). Bringing into operation various provisions of the 2011 Act, for England only, on 09.11.2012. - Issued: 18.10.2012. Made: 11.10.2012. Effect: None. Territorial extent & classification: E. General. - 4p.: 30 cm. - 978-0-11-152946-1 £4.00

The Localism Act 2011 (Commencement No. 7 and Transitional, Savings and Transitory Provisions) Order 2012 No. 2012/2029 (C.80). - Enabling power: Localism Act 2011, s. 240 (2) (7). Bringing into operation various provisions of the 2011 Act on 03.08.2012, in accord. with art. 2. - Issued: 07.08.2012. Made: 02.08.2012. Effect: S.I. 2012/628 partially revoked (03.08.2012). Territorial extent & classification: E/W. General. - 8p.: 30 cm. - 978-0-11-152796-2 £4.00

The Localism Act 2011 (Housing and Regeneration Functions in Greater London) (Consequential, Transitional and Saving Provisions) (No. 2) Order 2012 No. 2012/702. - Enabling power: Localism Act 2011, s. 194 (1). - Issued: 08.03.2012. Made: 05.03.2012. Coming into force: 01.04.2012. Effect: 2011 c.20; S.I. 1989/869; 2010/948; 1986/2194; 1992/1708; 1980/1697; 1987/1968 amended. Territorial extent & classification: E. General. - 4p.: 30 cm. - 978-0-11-152151-9 £4.00

The Transfer of Tenancies and Right to Acquire (Exclusion) Regulations 2012 No. 2012/696. - Enabling power: Localism Act 2011, s. 158 (10) & Housing and Regeneration Act 2008, s. 180 (2A). - Issued: 08.03.2012. Made: 05.03.2012. Laid: 08.03.2012. Coming into force: 01.04.2012. Effect: None. Territorial extent & classification: E. General. - 4p.: 30 cm. - 978-0-11-152150-2 £4.00

Housing, England and Wales

The Localism Act 2011 (Commencement No. 2 and Transitional and Saving Provision) Order 2012 No. 2012/57 (C. 2). - Enabling power: Localism Act 2011, ss. 37, 240 (2) (7) (8). Bringing into operation various provisions of the 2011 Act on 15.01.2012; 31.01.2012. - Issued: 16.01.2012. Made: 11.01.2012. Effect: None. Territorial extent & classification: E/W and S in part. General. - 12p.: 30 cm. - 978-0-11-151911-0 £5.75

The Localism Act 2011 (Commencement No. 4 and Transitional, Transitory and Saving Provisions) Order 2012 No. 2012/628 (C.14). - Enabling power: Localism Act 2011, s. 240 (2) (7). Bringing into operation various provisions of the 2011 Act in accord. with arts. 2 to 8. - Issued: 07.03.2012. Made: 01.03.2012. Effect: None. Territorial extent & classification: E/W. General. - Partially revoked by S.I. 2012/2029 (C.80) (ISBN 9780111527962). - 12p.: 30 cm. - 978-0-11-152126-7 £5.75

The Localism Act 2011 (Commencement No. 5 and Transitional, Saving and Transitory Provisions) Order 2012 No. 2012/1008 (C.32). - Enabling power: Localism Act 2011, s. 240 (2) (7). Bringing into operation various provisions of the 2011 Act in accord. with arts. 2 to 6. - Issued: 05.04.2012. Made: 03.04.2012. Effect: None. Territorial extent & classification: E/W. General. - 8p.: 30 cm. - 978-0-11-152337-7 £5.75

The Localism Act 2011 (Commencement No. 6 and Transitional, Savings and Transitory Provisions) Order 2012 No. 2012/1463 (C.56). - Enabling power: Localism Act 2011, s. 240 (2) (7). Bringing into operation various provisions of the 2011 Act in accord. with arts. 2 to 5. - Issued: 11.06.2012. Made: 06.06.2012. Effect: None. Territorial extent & classification: E/W. General. - 8p.: 30 cm. - 978-0-11-152509-8 £5.75

The Localism Act 2011 (Regulation of Social Housing) (Consequential Provisions) Order 2012 No. 2012/641. - Enabling power: Localism Act 2011, s. 236 (1). - Issued: 07.03.2012. Made: 01.03.2012. Laid: 07.03.2012. Coming into force: 01.04.2012 in accord. with art. 1 (2). Effect: S.I. 1980/1697; 1981/15; 1987/1968; 1999/2277; 2001/1201; 2007/3544; 2011/2260 amended. Territorial extent & classification: E/W. General. - 4p.: 30 cm. - 978-0-11-152127-4 £4.00

Housing, Wales

The Housing (Wales) Measure 2011 (Commencement No. 2) Order 2012 No. 2012/2091 (W.241) (C.83). - Enabling power: Housing (Wales) Measure 2011, s. 90 (2). Bringing into operation various provisions of the 2011 Measure on 03.09.2012 in accord. with art. 1. - Issued: 06.09.2012. Made: 09.08.2012. Effect: None. Territorial extent & classification: W. General. - In English and Welsh: Welsh title: Gorchymyn Mesur Tai (Cymru) 2011 (Cychwyn Rhif 2) 2012. - 4p.: 30 cm. - 978-0-348-10649-7 £4.00

The Housing (Wales) Measure 2011 (Consequential Amendments to Subordinate Legislation) Order 2012 No. 2012/2090 (W.240). - Enabling power: Housing (Wales) Measure 2011, ss. 34 (1) (2) (3) (b), 89 (1) (2). - Issued: 10.09.2012. Made: 09.08.2012. Laid before the National Assembly for Wales: 13.08.2012. Coming into force: 03.09.2012. Effect: S.I. 1993/2240, 2241; 1997/619; 2005/2681 (W.187) amended. Territorial extent & classification: W. General. - In English and Welsh: Welsh title: Gorchymyn Mesur Tai (Cymru) 2011 (Diwygiadau Canlyniadol i Is-ddeddfwriaeth) 2012. - 12p.: 30 cm. - 978-0-348-10650-3 £5.75

The Localism Act 2011 (Commencement No. 2 and Saving Provision) (Wales) Order 2012 No. 2012/887 (W.118) (C.26). - Enabling power: Localism Act 2011, s. 240 (3) (4) (7). Bringing into operation various provisions of the Act on 01.04.2012, in accord. with art. 2. - Issued: 03.04.2012. Made: 14.03.2012. Coming into force: 01.04.2012. Effect: None. Territorial extent & classification: W. General. - In English and Welsh. Welsh language title: Gorchymyn Deddf Lleoliaeth 2011 (Cychwyn Rhif 2 a Darpariaeth Arbed) (Cymru) 2012. - 8p.: 30 cm. - 978-0-348-10579-7 £5.75

The Residential Property Tribunal Procedures and Fees (Wales) Regulations 2012 No. 2012/531 (W.83). - Enabling power: Housing Act 2004, s. 250 (2), sch. 13. - Issued: 02.04.2012. Made: 23.02.2012. Laid before the National Assembly for Wales: 28.02.2012. Coming into force: 21.03.2012. Effect: S.I. 2006/1641 (W. 156), 1642 (W. 157) revoked. Territorial extent & classification: W. General. - In English and Welsh. Welsh title: Rheoliadau Gweithdrefnau a Ffioedd Tribiwnlys Eiddo Preswyl (Cymru) 2012. - 62p.: 30 cm. - 978-0-348-10576-6 £10.75

Human tissue

The Quality and Safety of Organs Intended for Transplantation Regulations 2012 No. 2012/1501. - Enabling power: European Communities Act 1972, s. 2 (2), sch. 2, para. 1A. - Issued: 14.06.2012. Made: 11.06.2012. Laid: 14.06.2012. Coming into force: 12.07.2012 & 27.08.2012. In accord. with reg. 1 (2) (3). Effect: 2004 c.30; S.I. 2006/1260, 1659; 2007/1523; S.S.I. 2006/390 amended. Territorial extent & classification: E/W/S/NI. General (except for reg. 25 (2) (3) (4) (7) which applies to E/W/NI and part 7 which applies to S. only). - 20p.: 30 cm. - 978-0-11-152524-1 £5.75

Immigration

The Immigration and Asylum (Jersey) Order 2012 No. 2012/2593. - Enabling power: Immigration Act 1971, s. 36 & Asylum and Immigration Act 1996, s. 13 (5) & Immigration and Asylum Act 1999, s. 170 (7). - Issued: 22.10.2012. Made: 17.10.2012. Coming into force: In accord. with art. 1. Effect: S.I. 1993/1797; 1998/1070; 2003/1252 amended. Territorial extent & classification: Jersey. General. - 2p.: 30 cm. - 978-0-11-152972-0 £4.00

The Immigration and Nationality (Cost Recovery Fees) (Amendment) Regulations 2012 No. 2012/2276. - Enabling power: Immigration, Asylum and Nationality Act 2006, ss. 51 (3), 52 (1) (3) (6). - Issued: 07.09.2012. Made: 04.09.2012. Laid: 06.09.2012. Coming into force: 01.10.2012. Effect: S.I. 2012/813 amended. Territorial extent & classification: E/W/S/NI. General. - 4p.: 30 cm. - 978-0-11-152858-7 £4.00

The Immigration and Nationality (Cost Recovery Fees) Regulations 2012 No. 2012/813. - Enabling power: Immigration, Asylum and Nationality Act 2006, ss. 51 (3), 52 (1) (3) (6). - Issued: 16.03.2012. Made: 13.03.2012. Laid: 15.03.2012. Coming into force: 06.04.2012. Effect: S.I. 2011/790 revoked. Territorial extent & classification: E/W/S/NI. General. - 20p.: 30 cm. - 978-0-11-152217-2 £5.75

The Immigration and Nationality (Fees) Regulations 2012 No. 2012/971. - Enabling power: Immigration, Asylum and Nationality Act 2006, ss. 51 (3), 52 (1) (3) (6). - Issued: 03.04.2012. Made: 27.03.2012. Coming into force: 06.04.2012. Effect: S.I. 2011/1055 revoked. Territorial extent & classification: E/W/S/NI. General. - Supersedes draft S.I. (ISBN 9780111520154) issued 14.02.2012. With correction slip dated May 2012. - 20p.: 30 cm. - 978-0-11-152313-1 £5.75

The Immigration Appeals (Family Visitor) Regulations 2012 No. 2012/1532. - Enabling power: Nationality, Immigration and Asylum Act 2002, ss. 88A (1) (a) (2) (a) (c), 112 (1) (3). - Issued: 19.06.2012. Made: 13.06.2012. Laid: 18.06.2012. Coming into force: 09.07.2012. Effect: None. Territorial extent & classification: E/W/S/NI. General. - 4p.: 30 cm. - 978-0-11-152547-0 £4.00

The Immigration, Asylum and Nationality Act 2006 (Commencement No. 8 and Transitional and Saving Provisions) (Amendment) Order 2012 No. 2012/1531 (C.57). - Enabling power: Immigration, Asylum and Nationality Act 2006, s. 62. Bringing into operation various provisions of the 2006 Act on 09.07.2012. - Issued: 18.06.2012. Made: 13.06.2012. Effect: S.I. 2008/310 amended. Territorial extent & classification: E/W/S/NI. General. - 2p.: 30 cm. - 978-0-11-152546-3 £4.00

The Immigration (Biometric Registration) (Amendment) Regulations 2012 No. 2012/594. - Enabling power: UK Borders Act 2007, ss. 5, 6 (6), 7. - Issued: 01.03.2012. Made: 28.02.2012. Coming into force: In accord. with reg. 1 (2). Effect: S.I. 2008/3048 amended. Territorial extent & classification: E/W/S/NI. General. - Supersedes draft SI (ISBN 9780111517727) issued on 08.12.2011. - 8p.: 30 cm. - 978-0-11-152095-6 £4.00

The Immigration (Designation of Travel Bans) (Amendment No. 2) Order 2012 No. 2012/2058. - Enabling power: Immigration Act 1971, s. 8B (5). - Issued: 17.08.2012. Made: 13.08.2012. Laid: 15.08.2012. Coming into force: 17.08.2012. Effect: S.I. 2000/2724 amended. Territorial extent & classification: E/W/S/NI. General. - EC note: This Order amends SI 2000/2724, Part 2 of the schedule to list Council Implementing Decision 2012/393/CFSP(Afghanistan), Council Implementing Decision 2012/454/CFSP (Afghanistan), Council Decision 2012/457/cfsp (Iran), Council Decision 2012/388/CFSP (Somalia) and Council Implementing Decision 2012/424/CFSP (Syria). - 2p.: 30 cm. - 978-0-11-152818-1 £4.00

The Immigration (Designation of Travel Bans) (Amendment No. 3) Order 2012 No. 2012/3010. - Enabling power: Immigration Act 1971, s. 8B (5). - Issued: 07.12.2012. Made: 05.12.2012. Laid: 06.12.2012. Coming into force: 07.12.2012. Effect: S.I. 2000/2724 amended. Territorial extent & classification: E/W/S/NI. General. - EC note: This Order amends SI 2000/2724, Part 2 of the schedule to list Council Implementing Decision 2012/642/CFSP (Belarus), Council Implementing Decision 2012/516/CFSP (Guinea-Bissau), Council Decision 2012/635/CFSP (Iran), Council Decision 2012/527/CFSP (Moldova), Council Decision 2012/633/CFSP (Somalia), and Council Implementing Decision 2012/739/CFSP (Syria). - 2p.: 30 cm. - 978-0-11-153179-2 £4.00

The Immigration (Designation of Travel Bans) (Amendment) Order 2012 No. 2012/1663. - Enabling power: Immigration Act 1971, s. 8B (5). - Issued: 02.07.2012. Made: 28.06.2012. Laid: 29.06.2012. Coming into force: 03.07.2012. Effect: S.I. 2000/2724 amended & S.I. 2011/2489, 2930 revoked. Territorial extent & classification: E/W/S/NI. General. - 12p.: 30 cm. - 978-0-11-152608-8 £5.75

The Immigration (European Economic Area) (Amendment) (No. 2) Regulations 2012 No. 2012/2560. - Enabling power: European Communities Act 1972, s. 2 (2) & Nationality, Immigration and Asylum Act 2002, s. 109. - Issued: 18.10.2012. Made: 11.10.2012. Laid: 17.10.2012. Coming into force: 08.11.2012. Effect: S.I. 2006/1003 amended. Territorial extent & classification: E/W/S/NI. General. - 8p.: 30 cm. - 978-0-11-152952-2 £4.00

The Immigration (European Economic Area) (Amendment) Regulations 2012 No. 2012/1547. - Enabling power: European Communities Act 1972, s. 2 (2) & Nationality, Immigration and Asylum Act 2002, s. 109. - Issued: 25.06.2012. Made: 19.06.2012. Laid: 22.06.2012. Coming into force: 16.07.2012; 16.10.2012 in accord. with reg. 2. Effect: S.I. 1993/1813; 2003/658, 2818; 2006/1003; 2007/3290 amended. Territorial extent & classification: E/W/S/NI. General. - With correction slip dated July 2012. - 16p.: 30 cm. - 978-0-11-152570-8 £5.75

The Immigration (Jersey) Order 2012 No. 2012/1763. - Enabling power: Immigration, Asylum and Nationality Act 2006, s. 63 (3) & Immigration and Asylum Act 1999, s. 170 (7). - Issued: 16.07.2012. Made: 10.07.2012. Coming into force: In accord. with art. 1. Effect: 1999 c. 33; 2006 c. 13 modified. Territorial extent & classification: Jersey. General. - 8p.: 30 cm. - 978-0-11-152674-3 £4.00

The Immigration (Passenger Transit Visa) (Amendment) (No. 2) Order 2012 No. 2012/771. - Enabling power: Immigration and Asylum Act 1999, s. 41. - Issued: 14.03.2012. Made: 08.03.2012. Laid: 13.03.2012. Coming into force: 03.04.2012. Effect: S.I. 2003/1185 amended. Territorial extent & classification: E/W/S/NI. General. - With correction slip dated March 2012. - 2p.: 30 cm. - 978-0-11-152193-9 £4.00

The Immigration (Passenger Transit Visa) (Amendment) Order 2012 No. 2012/116. - Enabling power: Immigration and Asylum Act 1999, s. 41. - Issued: 23.01.2012. Made: 14.01.2012. Laid: 20.01.2012. Coming into force: 10.02.2012. Effect: S.I. 2003/1185 amended. Territorial extent & classification: E/W/S/NI. General. - 2p.: 30 cm. - 978-0-11-151933-2 £4.00

The Nationality, Immigration and Asylum Act 2002 (Authority to Carry) Regulations 2012 No. 2012/1894. - Enabling power: Nationality, Immigration and Asylum Act 2002, s. 124. - Issued: 23.07.2012. Made: 18.07.2012. Coming into force: 25.07.2012. Effect: None. Territorial extent & classification: E/W/S/NI. General. - Supersedes draft S.I. (ISBN 9780111523896) issued 01.05.2012. - 4p.: 30 cm. - 978-0-11-152744-3 £4.00

The Nationality, Immigration and Asylum Act 2002 (Commencement No. 13) Order 2012 No. 2012/1263 (C.44). - Enabling power: Nationality, Immigration and Asylum Act 2002, s. 162 (1) (6). Bringing into operation various provisions of the 2002 Act on 11.05.2012. - Issued: 15.05.2012. Made: 10.05.2012. Effect: None. Territorial extent & classification: E/W/S/NI. General. - 4p.: 30 cm. - 978-0-11-152425-1 £4.00

The Nationality, Immigration and Asylum Act 2002 (Commencement No. 14) Order 2012 No. 2012/1887 (C.73). - Enabling power: Nationality, Immigration and Asylum Act 2002, s. 162 (1). Bringing into operation various provisions of the 2002 Act on 18.07.2012. - Issued: 23.07.2012. Made: 17.07.2012. Effect: None. Territorial extent & classification: E/W/S/NI. General. - 4p.: 30 cm. - 978-0-11-152742-9 £4.00

The UK Borders Act 2007 (Border and Immigration Inspectorate) (Joint Working etc.) Order 2012 No. 2012/2876. - Enabling power: UK Borders Act 2007, ss. 52 (2) (3), 55 (1). - Issued: 21.11.2012. Made: 19.11.2012. Laid: 19.11.2012. Coming into force: 11.12.2012. Effect: None. Territorial extent & classification: E/W/S/NI. General. - 2p.: 30 cm. - 978-0-11-153091-7 £4.00

Income tax

The Authorised Investment Funds (Tax) (Amendment) Regulations 2012 No. 2012/519. - Enabling power: Finance (No. 2) Act 2005, ss. 17 (3), 18. - Issued: 28.02.2012. Made: 27.02.2012 at 10.00am. Laid: 27.02.2012 at 1.00pm. Coming into force: 27.02.2012 at 1.30pm. Effect: S.I. 2006/964; 2008/3159 amended. Territorial extent & classification: E/W/S/NI. General. - 4p.: 30 cm. - 978-0-11-152071-0 £4.00

The Business Investment Relief Regulations 2012 No. 2012/1898. - Enabling power: Income Tax Act 2007, ss. 809VJ (4) (5). - Issued: 20.07.2012. Made: 18.07.2012. Laid: 19.07.2012. Coming into force: 10.08.2012. Effect: None. Territorial extent & classification: E/W/S/NI. General. - 4p.: 30 cm. - 978-0-11-152748-1 £4.00

The Business Premises Renovation Allowances (Amendment) Regulations 2012 No. 2012/868. - Enabling power: Capital Allowances Act 2001, ss. 360B (2) (b) (5), 360D (4). - Issued: 20.03.2012. Made: 19.03.2012. Laid: 20.03.2012. Coming into force: 11.04.2012. Effect: S.I. 2007/945 amended. Territorial extent & classification: E/W/S/NI. General. - 4p.: 30 cm. - 978-0-11-152249-3 £4.00

The Capital Allowances (Energy-saving Plant and Machinery) (Amendment) Order 2012 No. 2012/1832. - Enabling power: Capital Allowances Act 2001, ss. 45A (3) (4). - Issued: 16.07.2012. Made: 12.07.2012. Laid: 13.07.2012. Coming into force: 02.08.2012. Effect: S.I. 2001/2541 amended. Territorial extent & classification: E/W/S/NI. General. - 2p.: 30 cm. - 978-0-11-152700-9 £4.00

The Capital Allowances (Environmentally Beneficial Plant and Machinery) (Amendment No. 2) Order 2012 No. 2012/2602. - Enabling power: Capital Allowances Act 2001, s. 45H (3) to (5). - Issued: 16.10.2012. Made: 15.10.2012. Laid: 16.10.2012. Coming into force: 07.11.2012. Effect: S.I. 2003/2076 amended. Territorial extent & classification: E/W/S/NI. General. - 2p.: 30 cm. - 978-0-11-152949-2 £4.00

The Capital Allowances (Environmentally Beneficial Plant and Machinery) (Amendment) Order 2012 No. 2012/1838. - Enabling power: Capital Allowances Act 2001, s. 45H (3) to (5). - Issued: 13.07.2012. Made: 12.07.2012. Laid: 13.07.2012. Coming into force: 02.08.2012. Effect: S.I. 2003/2076 amended. Territorial extent & classification: E/W/S/NI. General. - 2p.: 30 cm. - 978-0-11-152705-4 £4.00

The Car and Van Fuel Benefit Order 2012 No. 2012/3037. - Enabling power: Income Tax (Earnings and Pensions) Act 2003, s. 170 (5) (6). - Issued: 07.12.2012. Made: 06.12.2012. Laid: 07.12.2012. Coming into force: 31.12.2012. Effect: 2003 c. 1 amended. Territorial extent & classification: E/W/S/NI. General. - 2p.: 30 cm. - 978-0-11-153182-2 £4.00

The Car Fuel Benefit Order 2012 No. 2012/915. - Enabling power: Income Tax (Earnings and Pensions) Act 2003, s. 170 (5) (6). - Issued: 26.03.2012. Made: 22.03.2012. Laid: 23.03.2012. Coming into force: 02.04.2012. Effect: 2003 c. 1 amended. Territorial extent & classification: E/W/S/NI. General. - 2p.: 30 cm. - 978-0-11-152274-5 £4.00

The Child Trust Funds, Registered Pension Schemes and Stamp Duty Reserve Tax (Consequential Amendments) Regulations 2012 No. 2012/886. - Enabling power: Child Trust Funds Act 2004, ss. 13, 28 (1) (2) & Finance Act 1986, s. 98 & Finance Act 2004, ss. ss. 267 (10), 268 (10). - Issued: 21.03.2012. Made: 21.03.2012. Laid: 21.03.2012. Coming into force: 06.04.2012. Effect: S.I. 1986/1711; 2004/1450; 2005/3452 amended. Territorial extent & classification: E/W/S/NI. General. - 4p.: 30 cm. - 978-0-11-152265-3 £4.00

The Double Taxation Relief and International Tax Enforcement (Bahrain) Order 2012 No. 2012/3075. - Enabling power: Taxation (International and Other Provisions) Act 2010, s. 2 & Finance Act 2006, s. 173 (1) to (3). - Issued: 17.12.2012. Made: 12.12.2012. Effect: None. Territorial extent & classification: E/W/S/NI. General. - Supersedes draft SI (ISBN 9780111527078) issued 17.07.2012. - 24p.: 30 cm. - 978-0-11-153244-7 £5.75

The Double Taxation Relief and International Tax Enforcement (Barbados) Order 2012 No. 2012/3076. - Enabling power: Taxation (International and Other Provisions) Act 2010, s. 2 & Finance Act 2006, s. 173 (1) to (3). - Issued: 17.12.2012. Made: 12.12.2012. Effect: None. Territorial extent & classification: E/W/S/NI. General. - Supersedes draft SI (ISBN 9780111527160) issued 17.07.2012. - 20p.: 30 cm. - 978-0-11-153242-3 £5.75

The Double Taxation Relief and International Tax Enforcement (Liechtenstein) Order 2012 No. 2012/3077. - Enabling power: Taxation (International and Other Provisions) Act 2010, s. 2 & Finance Act 2006, s. 173 (1) to (3). - Issued: 17.12.2012. Made: 12.12.2012. Effect: None. Territorial extent & classification: E/W/S/NI. General. - Supersedes draft SI (ISBN 9780111527092) issued 17.07.2012. - 24p.: 30 cm. - 978-0-11-153241-6 £5.75

The Double Taxation Relief and International Tax Enforcement (Singapore) Order 2012 No. 2012/3078. - Enabling power: Taxation (International and Other Provisions) Act 2010, s. 2 & Finance Act 2006, s. 173 (1) to (3). - Issued: 17.07.2012. Made: 12.12.2012. Effect: None. Territorial extent & classification: E/W/S/NI. General. - Supersedes draft SI (ISBN 9780111527153) issued 17.07.2012. - 12p.: 30 cm. - 978-0-11-153240-9 £5.75

The Enactment of Extra-Statutory Concessions Order 2012 No. 2012/266. - Enabling power: Finance Act 2008, s. 160. - Issued: 06.02.2012. Made: 02.02.2012. Coming into force: 01.03.2012. Effect: 1992 c. 12; 1994 c. 9; 2003 c. 1; 2005 c. 5; 2009 c. 4; 2010 c. 4 amended. Territorial extent & classification: E/W/S/NI. General. - Supersedes draft SI (ISBN 9780111519134) issued on 12.01.2012. - 20p.: 30 cm. - 978-0-11-151984-4 £5.75

The Finance Act 2004, Section 180 (5) (Modification) Regulations 2012 No. 2012/1258. - Enabling power: Finance Act 2011, s.70. - Issued: 14.05.2012. Made: 10.05.2012. Laid: 11.05.2012. Coming into force: 01.06.2012. Effect: 2004 c.12 modified. Territorial extent & classification: E/W/S/NI. General. - 2p.: 30 cm. - 978-0-11-152421-3 £4.00

The Finance Act 2010, Schedule 6, Part 1 (Further Consequential and Incidental Provision etc) Order 2012 No. 2012/735. - Enabling power: Finance Act 2010, sch. 6, para. 29 (1) (2). - Issued: 12.03.2012. Made: 08.03.2012. Laid: 09.03.2012. Coming into force: 01.04.2012. Effect: 2009 c.4 amended. Territorial extent & classification: E/W/S/NI. General. - 4p.: 30 cm. - 978-0-11-152181-6 £4.00

The Finance Act 2010, Schedule 6, Part 2 (Commencement) Order 2012 No. 2012/736 (C.18). - Enabling power: Finance Act 2010, sch. 6, para. 34 (1) (b) (2) (3). Bringing into operation various provisions of this Act on 01.04.2012. - Issued: 12.03.2012. Made: 08.03.2012. Effect: None. Territorial extent & classification: E/W/S/NI. General. - 8p.: 30 cm. - 978-0-11-152189-2 £5.75

The Finance Act 2012 (Enterprise Investment Scheme) (Appointed Day) Order 2012 No. 2012/1896 (C. 74). - Enabling power: Finance Act 2012, sch. 7, paras. 23 (1), 33 (1). Bringing into operation various provisions of the 2012 Act on 19th July 2012, in accord. with art. 2. - Issued: 20.07.2012. Made: 18.07.2012. Effect: None. Territorial extent & classification: E/W/S/NI. General. - 2p.: 30 cm. - 978-0-11-152747-4 £4.00

The Finance Act 2012 (Venture Capital Trusts) (Appointed Day) Order 2012 No. 2012/1901 (C.75). - Enabling power: Finance Act 2012, sch. 8, para. 20 (1). Bringing into operation various provisions of the 2012 Act on 19.07.2012. - Issued: 20.07.2012. Made: 18.07.2012. Effect: None. Territorial extent & classification: E/W/S/NI. General. - 2p.: 30 cm. - 978-0-11-152751-1 £4.00

The Income Tax (Construction Industry Scheme) (Amendment) Regulations 2012 No. 2012/820. - Enabling power: Taxes Management Act 1970, s. 113 (1) & Finance Act 2002, s. 136 & Finance Act 2003, s. 205 & Finance Act 2004, ss. 62 (3) (6) (7), 71, 73, 75, sch. 11, paras. 4 (3), 8 (2), 12 (2). - Issued: 16.03.2012. Made: 14.03.2012. Laid: 15.03.2012. Coming into force: 06.04.2012. Effect: S.I. 2005/2045 amended. Territorial extent & classification: E/W/S/NI. General. - 4p.: 30 cm. - 978-0-11-152229-5 £4.00

The Income Tax (Entertainers and Sportsmen) (Amendment) Regulations 2012 No. 2012/1359. - Enabling power: Income Tax Act 2007, ss. 967 (1), 969 (2), 970 (5). - Issued: 24.05.2012. Made: 22.05.2012. Laid: 23.05.2012. Coming into force: 01.07.2012. Effect: S.I. 1987/530 amended. Territorial extent & classification: E/W/S/NI. General. - 2p.: 30 cm. - 978-0-11-152474-9 £4.00

The Income Tax (Exemption of Minor Benefits) (Amendment) Regulations 2012 No. 2012/1808. - Enabling power: Income Tax (Earnings and Pensions) Act 2003, s. 210. - Issued: 12.07.2012. Made: 10.07.2012. Laid: 11.07.2012. Coming into force: 06.04.2013. Effect: S.I. 2002/205; 2003/1434 amended. Territorial extent & classification: E/W/S/NI. General. - 2p.: 30 cm. - 978-0-11-152662-0 £4.00

The Income Tax (Indexation) Order 2012 No. 2012/3047. - Enabling power: Income Tax Act 2007, ss. 21 (5), 57 (6). - Issued: 10.12.2012. Made: 06.12.2012. Effect: None. Territorial extent & classification: E/W/S/NI. General. - 2p.: 30 cm. - 978-0-11-153198-3 £4.00

The Income Tax (Limits for Enterprise Management Incentives) Order 2012 No. 2012/1360. - Enabling power: Income Tax (Earnings and Pensions) Act 2003, sch. 5, para. 54 (1) (b) (i) (2). - Issued: 24.05.2012. Made: 22.05.2012. Laid: 23.05.2012. Coming into force: 16.06.2012. Effect: 2003 c.1 amended. Territorial extent & classification: E/W/S/NI. General. - 2p.: 30 cm. - 978-0-11-152476-3 £4.00

The Income Tax (Pay As You Earn) (Amendment No. 2) Regulations 2012 No. 2012/1895. - Enabling power: Finance Act 2002, s. 136 & Income Tax (Earnings and Pensions) Act 2003, s. 684. - Issued: 20.07.2012. Made: 18.07.2012. Laid: 19.07.2012. Coming into force: 09.08.2012. Effect: S.I. 2003/2682 amended. Territorial extent & classification: E/W/S/NI. General. - 2p.: 30 cm. - 978-0-11-152745-0 £4.00

The Income Tax (Pay As You Earn) (Amendment) Regulations 2012 No. 2012/822. - Enabling power: Taxes Management Act 1970, ss. 59A (10), 59B (8), 98A, 113 (1) & Finance Act 1999, s. 133 & Finance Act 2002, s. 136 & Income Tax (Earnings and Pensions) Act 2003, ss. 684, 706, 707, 710. - Issued: 16.03.2012. Made: 14.03.2012. Laid: 15.03.2012. Coming into force: 06.04.2012. Effect: S.I. 2003/2682 amended. Territorial extent & classification: E/W/S/NI. General. - 30p.: 30 cm. - 978-0-11-152231-8 £5.75

The Income Tax (Professional Fees) Order 2012 No. 2012/3004. - Enabling power: Income Tax (Earnings and Pensions) Act 2003, s. 343 (3) (4). - Issued: 04.12.2012. Made: 30.11.2012. Coming into force: 01.12.2012. Effect: 2003 c.1 amended. Territorial extent & classification: E/W/S/NI. General. - 2p.: 30 cm. - 978-0-11-153156-3 £4.00

The Income Tax (Purchased Life Annuities) (Amendment) Regulations 2012 No. 2012/2902. - Enabling power: Income Tax (Trading and Other Income) Act 2005, s. 724 (1) (c). - Issued: 22.11.2012. Made: 19.11.2012. Laid: 21.11.2012. Coming into force: 21.12.2012. Effect: S.I. 2008/562 amended. Territorial extent & classification: E/W/S/NI. General. - 4p.: 30 cm. - 978-0-11-153094-8 £4.00

The Individual Savings Account (Amendment) (No. 2) Regulations 2012 No. 2012/1871. - Enabling power: Income Tax (Trading and Other Income) Act 2005, ss. 694 to 699, 701 & Taxation of Chargeable Gains Act 1992, s. 151. - Issued: 18.07.2012. Made: 16.07.2012. Laid: 17.07.2012. Coming into force: 08.08.2012. Effect: S.I. 1998/1870 amended. Territorial extent & classification: E/W/S/NI. General. - 16p.: 30 cm. - 978-0-11-152719-1 £5.75

The Individual Savings Account (Amendment) Regulations 2012 No. 2012/705. - Enabling power: Income Tax (Trading and Other Income) Act 2005, s. 694 & Taxation of Chargeable Gains Act 1992, s. 151. - Issued: 08.03.2012. Made: 06.03.2012. Laid: 07.02.2012. Coming into force: 06.04.2012. Effect: S.I. 1998/1870 amended. Territorial extent & classification: E/W/S/NI. General. - 2p.: 30 cm. - 978-0-11-152156-4 £4.00

The London Legacy Development Corporation (Tax Consequences) Regulations 2012 No. 2012/701. - Enabling power: Localism Act 2011, sch. 24, part 3. - Issued: 07.03.2012. Made: 06.03.2012. Laid: 07.03.2012. Coming into force: 31.03.2012. Effect: None. Territorial extent & classification: UK. General. - 4p.: 30 cm. - 978-0-11-152152-6 £4.00

The Pension Schemes (Application of UK Provisions to Relevant Non-UK Schemes) (Amendment) Regulations 2012 No. 2012/1795. - Enabling power: Finance Act 2004, sch. 34, para. 7 (1) (2) (a). - Issued: 12.07.2012. Made: 10.07.2012. Laid: 11.07.2012. Coming into force: 01.08.2012. Effect: S.I. 2006/207 amended. Territorial extent & classification: E/W/S/NI. General. - 8p.: 30 cm. - 978-0-11-152656-9 £4.00

The Pension Schemes (Categories of Country and Requirements for Overseas Pension Schemes and Recognised Overseas Pension Schemes) (Amendment) Regulations 2012 No. 2012/1221. - Enabling power: Finance Act 2004, s. 150 (8). - Issued: 08.05.2012. Made: 03.05.2012. Laid: 04.05.2012. Coming into force: 25.05.2012. Effect: S.I. 2006/206 amended. Territorial extent & classification: E/W/S/NI. General. - 2p.: 30 cm. - 978-0-11-152408-4 £4.00

The Postal Services Act 2011 (Taxation) Regulations 2012 No. 2012/764. - Enabling power: Postal Services Act 2011, ss. 23, 89 (2). - Issued: 12.03.2012. Made: 08.03.2012. Laid: 09.03.2012. Coming into force: In accord. with reg. 1 (1). Effect: None. Territorial extent & classification: E/W/S/NI. General. - 16p.: 30 cm. - 978-0-11-152180-9 £5.75

The Qualifying Care Relief (Specified Social Care Schemes) (Amendment) Order 2012 No. 2012/794. - Enabling power: Income Tax (Trading and other Income) Act 2005, s. 806A (4) (5). - Issued: 14.03.2012. Made: 12.03.2012. Laid: 13.03.2012. Coming into force: 05.04.2012. Effect: S.I. 2011/1712 amended. Territorial extent & classification: E/W/S/NI. General. - 4p.: 30 cm. - 978-0-11-152200-4 £4.00

The Registered Pension Schemes and Overseas Pension Schemes (Miscellaneous Amendments) Regulations 2012 No. 2012/884. - Enabling power: Finance Act 1999, ss. 132, 133 (2); Finance Act 2002, ss. 135, 136 & Finance Act 2004, ss. 150 (7) (8), 169 (4), 251 (1) (4), sch. 33, para. 5 (2); sch. 36, para. 51 (4). - Issued: 21.03.2012. Made: 20.03.2012. Laid: 21.03.2012. Coming into force: 06.04.2012. Effect: S.I. 2006/206, 208, 567, 570 amended. Territorial extent & classification: E/W/S/NI. General. - 8p.: 30 cm. - 978-0-11-152263-9 £5.75

The Registered Pension Schemes (Authorised Payments) (Amendment) (No. 2) Regulations 2012 No. 2012/1881. - Enabling power: Finance Act 2004, s. 164 (1) (f) (2). - Issued: 19.07.2012. Made: 17.07.2012. Laid: 18.02.2012. Coming into force: 08.08.2012. Effect: S.I. 2009/1171 amended. Territorial extent & classification: E/W/S/NI. General. - 4p.: 30 cm. - 978-0-11-152734-4 £4.00

The Registered Pension Schemes (Authorised Payments) (Amendment) Regulations 2012 No. 2012/522. - Enabling power: Finance Act 2012, s. 164 (1) (f) (2). - Issued: 29.02.2012. Made: 27.02.2012. Laid: 28.02.2012. Coming into force: 06.04.2012. Effect: S.I. 2009/1171 amended. Territorial extent & classification: E/W/S/NI. General. - 2p.: 30 cm. - 978-0-11-152078-9 £4.00

The Registered Pension Schemes (Relevant Annuities) (Amendment) Regulations 2012 No. 2012/2940. - Enabling power: Finance Act 2004, s. 282 (A1), sch. 28, para. 14 (2) (3). - Issued: 28.11.2012. Made: 23.11.2012. Laid: 27.11.2012. Coming into force: 21.12.2012. Effect: S.I. 2006/129 amended. Territorial extent & classification: E/W/S/NI. General. - 2p.: 30 cm. - 978-0-11-153121-1 £4.00

The Skipton Fund Limited (Application of Sections 731, 733 and 734 of the Income Tax (Trading and Other Income) Act 2005) (Amendment) Order 2012 No. 2012/1188. - Enabling power: Income Tax (Trading and other Income) Act 2005, 732 (2). - Issued: 03.05.2012. Made: 30.04.2012. Laid: 01.05.2012. Coming into force: 23.05.2012. Effect: S.I. 2011/1157 amended. Territorial extent & classification: E/W/S/NI. General. - 2p.: 30 cm. - 978-0-11-152395-7 £4.00

The Visiting Forces and International Military Headquarters (NATO and PfP) (Tax Designation) Order 2012 No. 2012/3071. - Enabling power: Finance Act 1960, s. 74A & Inheritance Tax Act 1984, s.155 & Income Tax (Earnings and Pensions) Act 2003, s. 303 & Income Tax Act 2007, s. 833. - Issued: 17.12.2012. Made: 12.12.2012. Coming into force: In accord. with art. 1 (2). Effect: S.I. 1961/580; 1960/581; 1998/1513, 1514, 1515, 1516, 1517, 1518 revoked (13.12.2012). Territorial extent & classification: E/W/S/NI. General. - [8]p.: 30 cm. - 978-0-11-153238-6 £4.00

Infrastructure planning

The Infrastructure Planning (Environmental Impact Assessment) (Amendment) Regulations 2012 No. 2012/787. - Enabling power: European Communities Act 1972, s. 2 (2). - Issued: 15.03.2012. Made: 12.03.2012. Laid: 15.03.2012. Coming into force: 13.04.2012. Effect: S.I. 2009/2263 amended. Territorial extent & classification: E/W/S. General. - EC note: These Regs amend the 2009 Regulations which implemented Directive 2011/92/EU on the assessment of the effects of certain public and private projects on the environment. - 8p.: 30 cm. - 978-0-11-152196-0 £4.00

The Localism Act 2011 (Commencement No. 2 and Transitional and Saving Provision) Order 2012 No. 2012/57 (C. 2). - Enabling power: Localism Act 2011, ss. 37, 240 (2) (7) (8). Bringing into operation various provisions of the 2011 Act on 15.01.2012; 31.01.2012. - Issued: 16.01.2012. Made: 11.01.2012. Effect: None. Territorial extent & classification: E/W and S in part. General. - 12p.: 30 cm. - 978-0-11-151911-0 £5.75

The Localism Act 2011 (Commencement No. 4 and Transitional, Transitory and Saving Provisions) Order 2012 No. 2012/628 (C.14). - Enabling power: Localism Act 2011, s. 240 (2) (7). Bringing into operation various provisions of the 2011 Act in accord. with arts. 2 to 8. - Issued: 07.03.2012. Made: 01.03.2012. Effect: None. Territorial extent & classification: E/W. General. - Partially revoked by S.I. 2012/2029 (C.80) (ISBN 9780111527962). - 12p.: 30 cm. - 978-0-11-152126-7 £5.75

The Localism Act 2011 (Infrastructure Planning) (Consequential Amendments) Regulations 2012 No. 2012/635. - Enabling power: Localism Act 2011, s. 236. - Issued: 06.03.2012. Made: 01.03.2012. Laid: 06.03.2012. Coming into force: 01.04.2012. Effect: S.I. 2009/2263, 2264; 2010/102, 103, 104, 106, 305, 490, 948; 2011/2055 amended. Territorial extent & classification: E/W/S. General. - 12p.: 30 cm. - 978-0-11-152123-6 £5.75

The Local Policing Bodies (Consequential Amendments No. 2) Regulations 2012 No. 2012/2732. - Enabling power: Police Reform Act 2002, ss. 43, 105 (4) & Planning Act 2008, ss. 4, 7, 37, 42, 48, 51, 56, 58, 59, 127 (7), 232, sch. 6, paras 2, 4, 6. - Issued: 05.11.2012. Made: 30.10.2012. Laid: 01.11.2012. Coming into force: 22.11.2012. Effect: S.I. 2004/915; 2009/1302, 2264; 2010/102, 104; 2011/2055 amended. Territorial extent & classification: E/W. General. - 4p.: 30 cm. - 978-0-11-153032-0 £4.00

The Network Rail (Ipswich Chord) Order 2012 No. 2012/2284. - Enabling power: Planning Act 2008. ss. 114, 115, 120, 122. sch. 5, pt 1, paras 1 to 3, 10 to 17, 24, 26, 36, 37. - Issued: 12.09.2012. Made: 05.09.2012. Coming into force: 26.09.2012. Effect: 1965 c. 56; 1973 c.26 modified. Territorial extent & classification: E. General. - 48p.: 30 cm. - 978-0-11-152868-6 £9.75

The Network Rail (North Doncaster Chord) Order 2012 No. 2012/2635. - Enabling power: Planning Act 2008. ss. 114, 115, 120, 122. sch. 5, pt 1, paras 1 to 3, 10 to 17, 24, 26, 36, 37. - Issued: 25.10.2012. Made: 16.10.2012. Coming into force: 06.11.2012. Effect: None. Territorial extent & classification: E. General. - 54p.: 30 cm. - 978-0-11-152980-5 £9.75

Infrastructure planning, England

The Infrastructure Planning (Waste Water Transfer and Storage) Order 2012 No. 2012/1645. - Enabling power: Planning Act 2008, ss. 14 (3) (4), 232 (3) (b). - Issued: 28.06.2012. Made: 22.06.2012. Coming into force: 23.06.2012. Effect: 2008 c.29 amended. Territorial extent & classification: E. General. - Supersedes draft S.I. (ISBN 9780111522899) issued 29.03.2012. - 4p.: 30 cm. - 978-0-11-152585-2 £4.00

Inheritance tax

The Finance Act 2010, Schedule 6, Part 2 (Commencement) Order 2012 No. 2012/736 (C.18). - Enabling power: Finance Act 2010, sch. 6, para. 34 (1) (b) (2) (3). Bringing into operation various provisions of this Act on 01.04.2012. - Issued: 12.03.2012. Made: 08.03.2012. Effect: None. Territorial extent & classification: E/W/S/NI. General. - 8p.: 30 cm. - 978-0-11-152189-2 £5.75

The Inheritance Tax (Market Makers and Discount Houses) Regulations 2012 No. 2012/2903. - Enabling power: Finance Act 1986. ss. 106 (5), 107 (5). - Issued: 22.11.2012. Made: 19.11.2012. Laid: 21.11.2012. Coming into force: 31.12.2012. Effect: 1984 c. 51 amended. Territorial extent & classification: E/W/S/NI. General. - 4p.: 30 cm. - 978-0-11-153095-5 £4.00

The Visiting Forces and International Military Headquarters (NATO and PfP) (Tax Designation) Order 2012 No. 2012/3071. - Enabling power: Finance Act 1960, s. 74A & Inheritance Tax Act 1984, s.155 & Income Tax (Earnings and Pensions) Act 2003, s. 303 & Income Tax Act 2007, s. 833. - Issued: 17.12.2012. Made: 12.12.2012. Coming into force: In accord. with art. 1 (2). Effect: S.I. 1961/580; 1960/581; 1998/1513, 1514, 1515, 1516, 1517, 1518 revoked (13.12.2012). Territorial extent & classification: E/W/S/NI. General. - [8]p.: 30 cm. - 978-0-11-153238-6 £4.00

Insolvency

The Insolvency Act 1986 (Disqualification from Parliament) Order 2012 No. 2012/1544. - Enabling power: Enterprise Act 2002, s. 266 (3). - Issued: 19.05.2012. Made: 13.06.2012. Coming into force: 14.06.2012 in accord. with art. 1. Effect: 1986 c. 45 amended. Territorial extent & classification: E/W/S/NI. General. - 4p.: 30 cm. - 978-0-11-152554-8 £4.00

Insolvency, England and Wales

The Insolvency (Amendment) Rules 2012 No. 2012/469. - Enabling power: Insolvency Act 1986, ss. 412. - Issued: 28.02.2012. Made: 21.02.2012. Laid: 27.02.2012. Coming into force: 19.03.2012. Effect: S.I. 1986/1925 amended. Territorial extent & classification: E/W. General. - 2p.: 30 cm. - 978-0-11-152057-4 £4.00

The Insolvency Practitioners and Insolvency Services Account (Fees) (Amendment) Order 2012 No. 2012/2264. - Enabling power: Insolvency Act 1986, s. 415A. - Issued: 07.09.2012. Made: 02.09.2012. Laid: 05.09.2012. Coming into force: 01.10.2012. Effect: S.I. 2003/3363 amended. Territorial extent & classification: E/W. General. - 2p.: 30 cm. - 978-0-11-152848-8 £4.00

Insurance premium tax

The Enactment of Extra-Statutory Concessions Order 2012 No. 2012/266. - Enabling power: Finance Act 2008, s. 160. - Issued: 06.02.2012. Made: 02.02.2012. Coming into force: 01.03.2012. Effect: 1992 c. 12; 1994 c. 9; 2003 c. 1; 2005 c. 5; 2009 c. 4; 2010 c. 4 amended. Territorial extent & classification: E/W/S/NI. General. - Supersedes draft SI (ISBN 9780111519134) issued on 12.01.2012. - 20p.: 30 cm. - 978-0-11-151984-4 £5.75

International development

The International Bank for Reconstruction and Development (General Capital Increase) Order 2011 No. 2012/517. - Enabling power: International Development Act 2002, s. 11. - Issued: 29.02.2012. Made: 12.12.2011. Coming into force: 13.12.2011 in accord. with art. 1. Effect: None. Territorial extent & classification: E/W/S/NI. General. - Supersedes draft S.I. (ISBN 9780111515242) issued 12.09.2011. - 4p.: 30 cm. - 978-0-11-152072-7 £4.00

The International Bank for Reconstruction and Development (Selective Capital Increase) Order 2011 No. 2012/518. - Enabling power: International Development Act 2002, s. 11. - Issued: 29.02.2012. Made: 12.12.2011. Coming into force: 13.12.2011, in accord. with art. 1. Effect: None. Territorial extent & classification: E/W/S/NI. General. - Supersedes draft S.I. (ISBN 9780111515235) issued 12.09.2011. - 4p.: 30 cm. - 978-0-11-152077-2 £4.00

The International Development Association (Multilateral Debt Relief Initiative) (Amendment) Order 2011 No. 2012/520. - Enabling power: International Development Act 2002, s. 11. - Issued: 29.02.2012. Made: 12.12.2012. Coming into force: 13.12.2011, in accord. with art. 1. Effect: S.I. 2006/2323 amended. Territorial extent & classification: E/W/S/NI. General. - Supersedes draft S.I. (ISBN 9780111515259) issued 12.09.2011. - 2p.: 30 cm. - 978-0-11-152076-5 £4.00

The International Development Association (Sixteenth Replenishment) Order 2011 No. 2012/492. - Enabling power: International Development Act 2002, s. 11. - Issued: 28.02.2012. Made: 12.12.2011. Coming into force: 13.12.2011. in accord. with art. 1. Effect: None. Territorial extent & classification: E/W/S/NI. General. - Supersedes draft S.I. (ISBN 9780111515266) issued 12.09.2011. - 4p.: 30 cm. - 978-0-11-152065-9 £4.00

The International Fund for Agricultural Development (Eighth Replenishment) Order 2012 No. 2012/2790. - Enabling power: International Development Act 2002, s. 11. - Issued: 08.11.2012. Made: 22.08.2012. Coming into force: 23.08.2012 in accord. with art. 1. Effect: None. Territorial extent & classification: E/W/S/NI. General. - Supersedes draft SI (ISBN 9780111522165) issued on 16.03.2012. - 4p.: 30 cm. - 978-0-11-153055-9 £4.00

Investigatory powers

The Protection of Freedoms Act 2012 (Commencement No. 2) Order 2012 No. 2012/2075 (C.82). - Enabling power: Protection of Freedoms Act 2012, ss. 116 (1), 120 (1). Bringing into operation various provisions of the 2012 Act on 10.08.2012, 01.10.2012 & 01.11.2012, 25.11.2012, in accord. with arts 2 to 5. - Issued: 10.08.2012. Made: 07.08.2012. Effect: None. Territorial extent & classification: E/W/S/NI. General. - 4p.: 30 cm. - 978-0-11-152805-1 £4.00

Investigatory powers, England and Wales

The Regulation of Investigatory Powers (Directed Surveillance and Covert Human Intelligence Sources) (Amendment) Order 2012 No. 2012/1500. - Enabling power: Regulation of Investigatory Powers Act 2000, ss. 30 (3) (6), 78 (5). - Issued: 15.06.2012. Made: 11.06.2012. Laid: 14.06.2012. Coming into force: 01.11.2012. Effect: S.I. 2010/521 amended. Territorial extent & classification: E/W. General. - 4p.: 30 cm. - 978-0-11-152526-5 £4.00

Iron and steel

The European Communities (Iron and Steel Employees Re-adaption Benefits Scheme) (No. 2) (Revocation) Regulations 2012 No. 2012/2262. - Enabling power: European Communities Act 1972, s. 2 (2). - Issued: 07.09.2012. Made: 02.09.2012. Laid: 05.09.2012. Coming into force: 01.10.2012. Effect: S.I. 1988/538; 1994/141; 1996/3182 revoked. Territorial extent & classification: E/W/S/NI. General. - 2p.: 30 cm. - 978-0-11-152846-4 £4.00

Judgments

The International Recovery of Maintenance (Hague Convention 2007 etc) Regulations 2012 No. 2012/2814. - Enabling power: European Communities Act 1972, s. 2 (2). - Issued: 12.11.2012. Made: 07.11.2012. Laid: 09.11.2012. Coming into force: In accord. with reg. 1. Effect: 1920 c.33; 1958 c.39; 1970 c.31; 1971 c.32; 1972 c.18; 1980 c.43; 1982 c.27; 1989 c.41; 1992 c.5; S.I. 1975/423, 2187; 1993/593; 1995/2709; 2007/2005; 2009/1109; 2011/1484 amended. Territorial extent & classification: E/W/S/NI. General. - 28p.: 30 cm. - 978-0-11-153073-3 £5.75

The International Recovery of Maintenance (Hague Convention 2007) (Rules of Court) Regulations 2012 No. 2012/1770. - Enabling power: European Communities Act 1972, s. 2 (2). - Issued: 10.07.2012. Made: 04.07.2012. Laid: 09.07.2012. Coming into force: 31.07.2012. Effect: 1980 c.43; 1982 c.27 amended. Territorial extent & classification: E/W/S/NI. General. - 4p.: 30 cm. - 978-0-11-152642-2 £4.00

Juries, England and Wales

The Juror's Allowances (Amendment) Regulations 2012 No. 2012/1826. - Enabling power: Juries Act 1974, s. 19 (1). - Issued: 16.07.2012. Made: 11.07.2012. Coming into force: 30.07.2012. Effect: S.I. 1978/1579 amended. Territorial extent & classification: E/W. General. - 2p.: 30 cm. - 978-0-11-152698-9 £4.00

Justices of the Peace, England and Wales

The Local Justice Areas (No. 2) Order 2012 No. 2012/1555. - Enabling power: Courts Act 2003, ss. 8 (4), 108 (6). - Issued: 21.06.2012. Made: 16.06.2012. Laid: 21.06.2012. Coming into force: In accord. with art. 1. Effect: S.I. 2005/554 amended. Territorial extent & classification: E/W. General. - With correction slip dated February 2013. - 4p.: 30 cm. - 978-0-11-152558-6 £4.00

The Local Justice Areas (No. 3) Order 2012 No. 2012/3128. - Enabling power: Courts Act 2003, ss. 8 (4), 108 (6). - Issued: 20.12.2012. Made: 17.12.2012. Laid: 19.12.2012. Coming into force: In accord. with art. 1. Effect: S.I. 2005/554 amended. Territorial extent & classification: E/W. General. - 4p.: 30 cm. - 978-0-11-153269-0 £4.00

The Local Justice Areas Order 2012 No. 2012/1277. - Enabling power: Courts Act 2003, ss. 8 (4), 108 (6). - Issued: 17.05.2012. Made: 14.05.2012. Laid: 17.05.2012. Coming into force: In accord. with art. 1. Effect: S.I. 2005/554 amended. Territorial extent & classification: E/W. General. - 4p.: 30 cm. - 978-0-11-152436-7 £4.00

Land charges, England and Wales

The Land Charges (Amendment) Rules 2012 No. 2012/2884. - Enabling power: Land Charges Act 1972, s. ss. 16 (1), 17 (1) (2). - Issued: 22.11.2012. Made: 12.11.2012. Coming into force: 17.12.2012. Effect: S.I. 1974/1286 amended. Territorial extent & classification: E/W. General. - 12p.: 30 cm. - 978-0-11-153107-5 £5.75

The Land Charges Fees (Amendment) Rules 2012 No. 2012/2910. - Enabling power: Land Charges Act 1972, ss. 9 (1), 10 (2), 16 (1), 17 (1). - Issued: 22.11.2012. Made: 20.11.2012. Coming into force: 17.12.2012. Effect: S.I. 1990/327 amended. Territorial extent & classification: E/W. General. - 4p.: 30 cm. - 978-0-11-153108-2 £4.00

Land drainage, England

The Axe Brue Internal Drainage Board Order 2012 No. 2012/1024. - Enabling power: Land Drainage Act 1991, s. 3 (5) (7). - Issued: 12.04.2012. Made: 10.01.2012. Coming into force: In accord. with art. 1. Effect: None. Territorial extent & classification: E. Local. - 4p.: 30 cm. - 978-0-11-152343-8 £4.00

The Cowick and Snaith Internal Drainage Board Order 2012 No. 2012/1025. - Enabling power: Land Drainage Act 1991, s. 3 (5) (7). - Issued: 12.04.2012. Made: 10.02.2012. Coming into force: In accord. with art. 1. Effect: None. Territorial extent & classification: E. Local. - 4p.: 30 cm. - 978-0-11-152344-5 £4.00

The Danvm Drainage Commissioners Order 2012 No. 2012/1026. - Enabling power: Land Drainage Act 1991, s. 3 (5) (7). - Issued: 10.04.2012. Made: 10.01.2012. Coming into force: In accord with art. 1. Effect: None. Territorial extent & classification: E. Local. - 4p.: 30 cm. - 978-0-11-152345-2 £4.00

The Doncaster East Internal Drainage Board Order 2012 No. 2012/1027. - Enabling power: Land Drainage Act 1991, s. 3 (5) (7). - Issued: 10.04.2012. Made: 10.02.2012. Coming into force: In accord with art. 1. Effect: None. Territorial extent & classification: E. Local. - 4p.: 30 cm. - 978-0-11-152346-9 £4.00

The Needham and Laddus Internal Drainage Board Order 2012 No. 2012/1028. - Enabling power: Land Drainage Act 1991, s. 3 (5) (7). - Issued: 12.04.2012. Made: 24.02.2012. Coming into force: In accord. with art. 1. Effect: None. Territorial extent & classification: E. Local. - 4p.: 30 cm. - 978-0-11-152347-6 £4.00

The North Level District (2010) Internal Drainage Board Order 2012 No. 2012/1029. - Enabling power: Land Drainage Act 1991, s. 3 (5) (7). - Issued: 10.04.2012. Made: 10.01.2012. Coming into force: In accord with art. 1. Effect: None. Territorial extent & classification: E. Local. - 4p.: 30 cm. - 978-0-11-152348-3 £4.00

The Ouse and Humber Drainage Board Order 2012 No. 2012/1030. - Enabling power: Land Drainage Act 1991, s. 3 (5) (7). - Issued: 12.04.2012. Made: 10.02.2012. Coming into force: In accord. with art. 1. Effect: None. Territorial extent & classification: E. Local. - 4p.: 30 cm. - 978-0-11-152349-0 £4.00

The Swale & Ure Drainage Board Order 2012 No. 2012/1031. - Enabling power: Land Drainage Act 1991, s. 3 (5) (7). - Issued: 10.04.2012. Made: 13.01.2012. Coming into force: In accord with art. 1. Effect: None. Territorial extent & classification: E. Local. - 4p.: 30 cm. - 978-0-11-152350-6 £4.00

The Trent Valley Internal Drainage Board Order 2012 No. 2012/1032. - Enabling power: Land Drainage Act 1991, s. 3 (5) (7). - Issued: 10.04.2012. Made: 10.02.2012. Coming into force: In accord with art. 1. Effect: None. Territorial extent & classification: E. Local. - 4p.: 30 cm. - 978-0-11-152351-3 £4.00

Landfill tax

The Landfill Tax (Amendment) Regulations 2012 No. 2012/885. - Enabling power: Finance Act 1996, ss. 51 (1), 53 (1), 53 (4) (a). - Issued: 21.03.2012. Made: 20.03.2012. Laid: 21.03.2012. Coming into force: 01.04.2012. Effect: S.I. 1996/1527 amended. Territorial extent & classification: E/W/S/NI. General. - 2p.: 30 cm. - 978-0-11-152264-6 £4.00

The Landfill Tax (Qualifying Material) (Amendment) Order 2012 No. 2012/940. - Enabling power: Finance Act 1996, ss. 42 (3), 63 (5). - Issued: 28.03.2012. Made: 26.03.2012. Laid: 27.03.2012. Coming into force: 01.04.2012. Effect: S.I. 2011/1017 amended. Territorial extent & classification: E/W/S/NI. General. - For approval by resolution of the House of Commons within twenty eight days beginning with the day on which the Order was made. - 2p.: 30 cm. - 978-0-11-152292-9 £4.00

Landlord and tenant, England

The Agricultural Holdings (Units of Production) (England) Order 2012 No. 2012/2573. - Enabling power: Agricultural Holdings Act 1986, sch. 6, para. 4. - Issued: 16.10.2012. Made: 08.10.2012. Laid: 12.10.2012. Coming into force: 07.11.2012. Effect: S.I. 2011/2451 revoked. Territorial extent & classification: E. General. - 8p.: 30 cm. - 978-0-11-152936-2 £4.00

Landlord and tenant, Wales

The Agricultural Holdings (Units of Production) (Wales) Order 2012 No. 2012/3022 (W.306). - Enabling power: Agricultural Holdings Act 1986, sch. 6, para. 4. - Issued: 20.12.2012. Made: 04.12.2012. Laid before the National Assembly for Wales: 05.12.2012. Coming into force: 26.12.2012. Effect: W.S.I. 2011/2831 (W.304) revoked. Territorial extent & classification: W. General. - In English and Welsh: Welsh title: Gorchymyn Daliadau Amaethyddol (Unedau Cynhyrchu) (Cymru) 2012. - 12p.: 30 cm. - 978-0-348-10671-8 £5.75

Land registration, England and Wales

The Land Registration Fee Order 2012 No. 2012/1969. - Enabling power: Land Registration Act 2002, ss. 102, 128 (1). - Issued: 30.07.2012. Made: 24.07.2012. Laid: 27.07.2012. Coming into force: 22.10.2012. Effect: S.I. 2009/845 revoked. Territorial extent & classification: E/W. General. - 16p.: 30 cm. - 978-0-11-152781-8 £5.75

Legal aid and advice, England and Wales

The Civil Legal Aid (Family Relationship) Regulations 2012 No. 2012/2684. - Enabling power: Legal Aid, Sentencing and Punishment of Offenders Act 2012, part 1, sch. 1, para. 12 (8) (b), 14 (8) (b). - Issued: 30.10.2012. Made: 25.10.2012. Laid: 29.10.2012. Coming into force: 01.04.201.2 Effect: None. Territorial extent & classification: E/W. General. - 2p.: 30 cm. - 978-0-11-153010-8 £4.00

The Civil Legal Aid (Immigration Interviews) (Exceptions) Regulations 2012 No. 2012/2683. - Enabling power: Legal Aid, Sentencing and Punishment of Offenders Act 2012, s. 4 (1) (2), part 1, sch. 1, para. 30 (3). - Issued: 30.10.2012. Made: 25.10.2012. Laid: 29.10.2012. Coming into force: 01.04.2012. Effect: None. Territorial extent & classification: E/W. General. - 2p.: 30 cm. - 978-0-11-153012-2 £4.00

The Civil Legal Aid (Prescribed Types of Pollution of the Environment) Regulations 2012 No. 2012/2687. - Enabling power: Legal Aid, Sentencing and Punishment of Offenders Act 2012, sch. 1, part 1, para. 42 (1). - Issued: 30.10.2012. Made: 25.10.2012. Laid: 29.10.2012. Coming into force: 01.04.2012. Effect: None. Territorial extent & classification: E/W. General. - 2p.: 30 cm. - 978-0-11-153013-9 £4.00

The Civil Legal Aid (Procedure) Regulations 2012 No. 2012/3098. - Enabling power: Legal Aid, Sentencing and Punishment of Offenders Act 2012, ss. 5 (2) (4), 12 (2) to (6), 28 (1) (3), 41 (1) (a) (b) (2) (3) (a) (b), sch. 3, para. 3 (3) (4). - Issued: 18.12.2012. Made: 12.12.2012. Laid: 17.12.2012. Coming into force: 01.04.2013 Effect: None. Territorial extent & classification: E/W. General. - 36p.: 30 cm. - 978-0-11-153249-2 £9.75

Legal profession, England and Wales

The Solicitors' (Non-Contentious Business) Remuneration (Amendment) Order 2012 No. 2012/171. - Enabling power: Solicitors Act 1974, s. 56. - Issued: 27.01.2012. Made: 25.01.2012. Laid: 27.01.2012. Coming into force: 20.02.2012. Effect: S.I. 2009/1931 amended. Territorial extent & classification: E/W. General. - 2p.: 30 cm. - 978-0-11-151951-6 £4.00

Legal Services Commission, England and Wales

The Criminal Defence Service (Funding) (Amendment No.2) Order 2012 No. 2012/1343. - Enabling power: Access to Justice Act 1999, ss. 14 (3), 25 (8A). - Issued: 24.05.2012. Made: 17.05.2012. Laid: 22.05.2012. Coming into force: 18.06.2012. Effect: S.I. 2007/1174 amended. Territorial extent & classification: E/W. General. - With correction slips dated November 2012 and February 2013. - 4p.: 30 cm. - 978-0-11-152468-8 £4.00

The Criminal Defence Service (Funding) (Amendment) Order 2012 No. 2012/750. - Enabling power: Access to Justice Act 1999, ss. 14 (3), 25 (8A). - Issued: 09.03.2012. Made: 07.03.2012. Laid: 09.03.2012. Coming into force: 01.04.2012. Effect: S.I. 2007/1174 amended. Territorial extent & classification: E/W. General. - With correction slip dated March 2012. - 8p.: 30 cm. - 978-0-11-152172-4 £5.75

Legal services, England and Wales

The Legal Aid, Sentencing and Punishment of Offenders Act 2012 (Commencement No. 2 and Specification of Commencement Date) Order 2012 No. 2012/2412 (C.94). - Enabling power: Legal Aid, Sentencing and Punishment of Offenders Act 2012, ss. 141 (12), 151 (1). Bringing into operation various provisions of the 2012 Act on 01.10.2012 in accordance with arts 2, 3. - Issued: 24.09.2012. Made: 18.09.2012. Effect: None. Territorial extent & classification: E/W/S/NI. General. - 4p.: 30 cm. - 978-0-11-152897-6 £4.00

The Legal Services Act 2007 (Alteration of Limit) Order 2012 No. 2012/3091. - Enabling power: Legal Services Act 2007, s. 139 (1). - Issued: 17.12.2012. Made: 11.12.2012. Laid: 17.12.2012. Coming into force: 01.02.2013. Effect: None. Territorial extent & classification: E/W. General. - 2p.: 30 cm. - 978-0-11-153225-6 £4.00

The Legal Services Act 2007 (Legal Complaints) (Parties) Order 2012 No. 2012/3092. - Enabling power: Legal Services Act 2007, s. 128 (4) (d). - Issued: 17.12.2012. Made: 11.12.2012. Laid: 17.12.2012. Coming into force: 01.02.2013. Effect: None. Territorial extent & classification: E/W. General. - 2p.: 30 cm. - 978-0-11-153226-3 £4.00

The Legal Services Act 2007 (The Law Society) (Modification of Functions) (Amendment) Order 2012 No. 2012/2987. - Enabling power: Legal Services Act 2007, ss. 69 (1) (4) (6) (7). - Issued: 03.12.2012. Made: 29.11.2012. Coming into force: 30.11.2012 in accord. with art. 2. Effect: S.I. 2011/1716 amended. Territorial extent & classification: E/W. General. - Supersedes draft SI (ISBN 9780111529287) issued 15.10.2012. - 2p.: 30 cm. - 978-0-11-153142-6 £4.00

Libraries

The Public Lending Right Scheme 1982 (Commencement of Variation) (No. 2) Order 2012 No. 2012/3123. - Enabling power: Public Lending Right Act 1979, s. 3 (7). - Issued: 19.12.2012. Made: 17.12.2012. Laid: 18.12.2012. Coming into force: 09.01.2013. Effect: None. Territorial extent & classification: E/W/S/NI. General. - 2p.: 30 cm. - 978-0-11-153262-1 £4.00

The Public Lending Right Scheme 1982 (Commencement of Variation) Order 2012 No. 2012/63. - Enabling power: Public Lending Right Act 1979, s. 3 (7). - Issued: 16.01.2012. Made: 10.01.2012. Laid: 12.01.2012. Coming into force: 03.02.2012. Effect: None. Territorial extent & classification: E/W/S/NI. General. - 2p.: 30 cm. - 978-0-11-151919-6 £4.00

Licences and licensing, England and Wales

The Late Night Levy (Application and Administration) Regulations 2012 No. 2012/2730. - Enabling power: Police Reform and Social Responsibility Act 2011, ss. 126, 128, 129, 131, 134, 136. - Issued: 02.11.2012. Made: 29.10.2012. Coming into force: 31.10.2012. Effect: None. Territorial extent & classification: E/W. General. - Supersedes draft SI (ISBN 9780111526309) issued 05.07.2012. - 8p.: 30 cm. - 978-0-11-153026-9 £5.75

The Late Night Levy (Expenses, Exemptions and Reductions) Regulations 2012 No. 2012/2550. - Enabling power: Police Reform and Social Responsibility Act 2011, ss. 130, 135, 136. - Issued: 11.10.2012. Made: 04.10.2012. Laid: 09.10.2012. Coming into force: 31.10.2012. Effect: None. Territorial extent & classification: E/W. General. - With correction slips dated November 2012 & January 2013. - 8p.: 30 cm. - 978-0-11-152923-2 £4.00

The Licensing Act 2003 (Diamond Jubilee Licensing Hours) Order 2012 No. 2012/828. - Enabling power: Licensing Act 2003, ss. 172 (1) (3), 197 (2). - Issued: 16.03.2012. Made: 09.03.2012. Coming into force: 16.03.2012. Effect: None. Territorial extent & classification: E/W. General. - Supersedes draft S.I. (ISBN 9780111519141) issued on 17.01.2012. - 2p.: 30 cm. - 978-0-11-152221-9 £4.00

The Licensing Act 2003 (Early Morning Alcohol Restriction Orders) Regulations 2012 No. 2012/2551. - Enabling power: Licensing Act 2003, ss. 9 (2), 172A to 172C, 172E, 183, 193. - Issued: 11.10.2012. Made: 03.10.2012. Laid: 09.10.2012. Coming into force: 31.10.2012. Effect: S.I. 2005/44 amended. Territorial extent & classification: E/W. General. - 8p.: 30 cm. - 978-0-11-152922-5 £5.75

The Licensing Act 2003 (Forms and Notices) (Amendment) Regulations 2012 No. 2012/2290. - Enabling power: Licensing Act 2003, ss. 17 (2) to (4), 29 (4) (6), 34 (2), 41A (2), 54, 71 (3) to (5), 84 (2), 86A (2), 91, 100 (4) (5), 193. - Issued: 24.09.2012. Made: 05.09.2012. Laid: 10.09.2012. Coming into force: 01.10.2012. Effect: S.I. 2005/42, 2918 amended. Territorial extent & classification: E/W. General. - 116p.: 30 cm. - 978-0-11-152867-9 £18.50

The Licensing Act 2003 (Permitted Temporary Activities) (Notices) (Amendment) Regulations 2012 No. 2012/960. - Enabling power: Licensing Act 2003, ss. 100 (4) (5), 104A (2), 106A (4), 107 (7), 193. - Issued: 04.04.2012. Made: 24.03.2012. Laid: 30.03.2012. Coming into force: 25.04.2012. Effect: S.I. 2005/2918 amended. Territorial extent & classification: E/W. General. - 20p.: 30 cm. - 978-0-11-152332-2 £5.75

The Licensing Act 2003 (Persistent Selling of Alcohol to Children) (Prescribed Form of Closure Notice) Regulations 2012 No. 2012/963. - Enabling power: Licensing Act 2003, s. 169A (3). - Issued: 04.04.2012. Made: 24.03.2012. Laid: 30.03.2012. Coming into force: 25.04.2012. Effect: S.I. 2007/1183 revoked. Territorial extent & classification: E/W. General. - 4p.: 30 cm. - 978-0-11-152333-9 £4.00

The Licensing Act 2003 (Personal Licences) (Amendment) Regulations 2012 No. 2012/946. - Enabling power: Licensing Act 2003, ss. 133 (1), 193. - Issued: 02.04.2012. Made: 24.03.2012. Laid: 30.03.2012. Coming into force: 25.04.2012. Effect: S.I. 2005/41 amended. Territorial extent & classification: E/W. General. - 12p.: 30 cm. - 978-0-11-152309-4 £5.75

The Licensing Act 2003 (Premises Licences and Club Premises Certificates) (Amendment) Regulations 2012 No. 2012/955. - Enabling power: Licensing Act 2003, ss. 17 (5) (aa), 30 (2), 34 (5), 41A (4), 51 (3), 53A (3), 54, 71 (6) (aa), 84 (4), 86A (4), 87 (3), 91, 167 (4), 193. - Issued: 03.04.2012. Made: 24.03.2012. Laid: 30.03.2012. Coming into force: 25.04.2012. Effect: None. Territorial extent & classification: E/W. General. - 20p.: 30 cm. - 978-0-11-152324-7 £5.75

The Live Music Act 2012 (Commencement) Order 2012 No. 2012/2115 (C.84). - Enabling power: Live Music Act 2012, s. 4 (2). Bringing into operation all the provisions of the 2012 Act on 01.10.2012. - Issued: 17.08.2012. Made: 14.08.2012. Effect: None. Territorial extent & classification: E/W. General. - 2p.: 30 cm. - 978-0-11-152825-9 £4.00

The Police Reform and Social Responsibility Act 2011 (Commencement No. 4) Order 2012 No. 2012/896 (C.27). - Enabling power: Police Reform and Social Responsibility Act 2011, s. 157 (1). Bringing into operation various provisions of the 2011 Act on 22.03.2012 in accord. with art. 2. - Issued: 23.03.2012. Made: 20.03.2012. Effect: None. Territorial extent & classification: E/W. General. - 4p.: 30 cm. - 978-0-11-152266-0 £4.00

The Police Reform and Social Responsibility Act 2011 (Commencement No. 5) Order 2012 No. 2012/1129 (C.38). - Enabling power: Police Reform and Social Responsibility Act 2011, s. 157 (1). Bringing into operation various provisions of the 2011 Act on 25.04.2012 in accord. with art. 2. - Issued: 25.04.2012. Made: 23.04.2012. Effect: None. Territorial extent & classification: E/W. General. - 4p.: 30 cm. - 978-0-11-152375-9 £4.00

The Police Reform and Social Responsibility Act 2011 (Commencement No. 6) Order 2012 No. 2012/2670 (C.108). - Enabling power: Police Reform and Social Responsibility Act 2011, s. 157 (1). Bringing into operation various provisions of the 2011 Act on 31.10.2012 in accord. with art. 2. - Issued: 26.10.2012. Made: 23.10.2012. Effect: None. Territorial extent & classification: E/W. General. - 8p.: 30 cm. - 978-0-11-153000-9 £4.00

Licensing (liquor)

The Health and Social Care Act 2012 (Commencement No. 1 and Transitory Provision) Order 2012 No. 2012/1319 (C.47). - Enabling power: Health and Social Care Act 2012, ss. 304 (10), 306. Bringing into operation various provisions of this Act on 01.06.2012, 01.07.2012, 01.08.2012 in accord. with art. 2. - Issued: 22.05.2012. Made: 17.05.2012. Coming into force: .- Effect: S.I. 2010/781 amended. Territorial extent & classification: E/W. General. - 8p.: 30 cm. - 978-0-11-152461-9 £4.00

Licensing (marine)

The Marine and Coastal Access Act 2009 (Transitional Provisions) Order 2012 No. 2012/698. - Enabling power: Marine and Coastal Access Act 2009. s. 320. - Issued: 09.03.2012. Made: 03.03.2012. Laid: 09.03.2012. Coming into force: 06.04.2012. Effect: None. Territorial extent & classification: E. General. - 4p.: 30 cm. - 978-0-11-152160-1 £4.00

Limited liability partnerships

The Companies and Limited Liability Partnerships (Accounts and Audit Exemptions and Change of Accounting Framework) Regulations 2012 No. 2012/2301. - Enabling power: European Communities Act 1972, s. 2 (2) & Limited Liability Partnerships Act 2000, ss. 15, 17 & Companies Act 2006, ss. 468, 473, 484, 1043, 1104 (2) (a), 1105 (2) (d), 1108 (2) (b), 1292 (1) (c). - Issued: 11.09.2012. Made: 06.09.2012. Laid: 07.09.2012. Coming into force: 01.10.2012. Effect: 2006 c. 46; S.I. 2008/1911; 2009/1803, 1804, 2436 amended. Territorial extent & classification: E/W/S/NI. General. - With correction slip dated September 2012. - 16p.: 30 cm. - 978-0-11-152872-3 £5.75

Local government, England

The Assets of Community Value (England) Regulations 2012 No. 2012/2421. - Enabling power: Localism Act 2011, ss. 87 (5), 88 (3), 89 (4) (5), 91 (2) (d), 92 (5), 95 (5) (e) (j) (6), 99 (1), 101 (1). - Issued: 21.09.2012. Made: 20.09.2012. Coming into force: 21.09.2012, in accord. with reg. 1 (1). Effect: S.I. 2003/1417 amended. Territorial extent & classification: E. General. - Supersedes draft S.I. (ISBN 9780111526293) issued 04.07.2012. - 16p.: 30 cm. - 978-0-11-152901-0 £5.75

The Broxbourne (Electoral Changes) Order 2012 No. 2012/159. - Enabling power: Local Democracy, Economic Development and Construction Act 2009, s. 59 (1). - Issued: 27.01.2012. Made: 24.01.2012. Coming into force: In accord. with art. 1 (2). Effect: None. Territorial extent & classification: E. General. - Supersedes draft SI (ISBN 9780111516881) issued 17.11.2011. - 8p.: 30 cm. - 978-0-11-151945-5 £4.00

The Buckinghamshire (Electoral Changes) Order 2012 No. 2012/1396. - Enabling power: Local Democracy, Economic Development and Construction Act 2009, s. 59 (1). - Issued: 30.05.2012. Made: 25.05.2012. Coming into force: In accord. with art. 2. Effect: None. Territorial extent & classification: E. General. - Supersedes draft SI (ISBN 9780111522523) issued on 22.03.2012. - 12p.: 30 cm. - 978-0-11-152487-9 £5.75

The Bus Lane Contraventions (Approved Local Authorities) (England) (Amendment) and Civil Enforcement of Parking Contraventions Designation (No. 2) Order 2012 No. 2012/2659. - Enabling power: Traffic Management Act 2004, s. 89 (3), sch. 8, para. 8 (1), sch. 10, para. 3 (1) & Transport Act 2000, s. 144 (3) (b). - Issued: 06.11.2012. Made: 30.10.2012. Laid: 02.11.2012. Coming into force: 30.11.2012. Effect: S.I. 2005/2755 amended & S.I. 2001/894 revoked. Territorial extent & classification: E. General. - 20p., 10 maps: 30 cm. - 978-0-11-153033-7 £5.75

The Bus Lane Contraventions (Approved Local Authorities) (England) (Amendment) and Civil Enforcement of Parking Contraventions Designation Order 2012 No. 2012/846. - Enabling power: Traffic Management Act 2004, s. 89 (3), sch. 8, para. 8 (1), sch. 10, para. 3 (1) & Transport Act 2000, s. 144 (3) (b). - Issued: 29.03.2012. Made: 21.03.2012. Laid: 23.03.2012. Coming into force: 16.04.2012, arts. 1 to 3, and 5; 11.06.2012, art. 4. Effect: S.I. 2005/2755 amended & S.I. 2006/1445; 2007/2535 revoked. Territorial extent & classification: E. General. - 16p., 6 maps: 30 cm. - 978-0-11-152271-4 £5.75

The City of Birmingham (Mayoral Referendum) Order 2012 No. 2012/324. - Enabling power: Local Government Act 2000, ss. 9N, 105. - Issued: 13.02.2012. Made: 08.02.2012. Coming into force: In accord. with art. 1. Effect: None. Territorial extent & classification: E. General. - Supersedes draft SI (ISBN 9780111517581) issued 05.12.2011. - 2p.: 30 cm. - 978-0-11-152005-5 £4.00

The City of Bradford (Mayoral Referendum) Order 2012 No. 2012/325. - Enabling power: Local Government Act 2000, ss. 9N, 105. - Issued: 13.02.2012. Made: 08.02.2012. Coming into force: In accord. with art. 1. Effect: None. Territorial extent & classification: E. General. - Supersedes draft SI (ISBN 9780111517567) issued 05.12.2011. - 2p.: 30 cm. - 978-0-11-152006-2 £4.00

The City of Bristol (Mayoral Referendum) Order 2012 No. 2012/326. - Enabling power: Local Government Act 2000, ss. 9N, 105. - Issued: 13.02.2012. Made: 08.02.2012. Coming into force: In accord. with art. 1. Effect: None. Territorial extent & classification: E. General. - Supersedes draft SI (ISBN 9780111517598) issued 05.12.2011. - 2p.: 30 cm. - 978-0-11-152007-9 £4.00

The City of Coventry (Mayoral Referendum) Order 2012 No. 2012/327. - Enabling power: Local Government Act 2000, ss. 9N, 105. - Issued: 13.02.2012. Made: 08.02.2012. Coming into force: In accord. with art. 1. Effect: None. Territorial extent & classification: E. General. - Supersedes draft SI (ISBN 9780111517574) issued 05.12.2011. - 2p.: 30 cm. - 978-0-11-152008-6 £4.00

The City of Leeds (Mayoral Referendum) Order 2012 No. 2012/328. - Enabling power: Local Government Act 2000, ss. 9N, 105. - Issued: 13.02.2012. Made: 08.02.2012. Coming into force: In accord. with art. 1. Effect: None. Territorial extent & classification: E. General. - Supersedes draft SI (ISBN 9780111517611) issued 05.12.2011. - 2p.: 30 cm. - 978-0-11-152009-3 £4.00

The City of Manchester (Mayoral Referendum) Order 2012 No. 2012/329. - Enabling power: Local Government Act 2000, ss. 9N, 105. - Issued: 13.02.2012. Made: 08.02.2012. Coming into force: In accord. with art. 1. Effect: None. Territorial extent & classification: E. General. - Supersedes draft SI (ISBN 9780111517529) issued 05.12.2011. - 2p.: 30 cm. - 978-0-11-152010-9 £4.00

The City of Newcastle-upon-Tyne (Mayoral Referendum) Order 2012 No. 2012/330. - Enabling power: Local Government Act 2000, ss. 9N, 105. - Issued: 13.02.2012. Made: 08.02.2012. Coming into force: In accord. with art. 1. Effect: None. Territorial extent & classification: E. General. - Supersedes draft SI (ISBN 9780111517499) issued 05.12.2012. - 2p.: 30 cm. - 978-0-11-152011-6 £4.00

The City of Nottingham (Mayoral Referendum) Order 2012 No. 2012/331. - Enabling power: Local Government Act 2000, ss. 9N, 105. - Issued: 13.02.2012. Made: 08.02.2012. Coming into force: In accord. with art. 1. Effect: None. Territorial extent & classification: E. General. - Supersedes draft SI (ISBN 9780111517512) issued 05.12.2011. - 2p.: 30 cm. - 978-0-11-152012-3 £4.00

The City of Sheffield (Mayoral Referendum) Order 2012 No. 2012/332. - Enabling power: Local Government Act 2000, ss. 9N, 105. - Issued: 13.02.2012. Made: 08.02.2012. Coming into force: In accord. with art. 1. Effect: None. Territorial extent & classification: E. General. - Supersedes draft SI (ISBN 9780111517543) issued 13.02.2012. - 2p.: 30 cm. - 978-0-11-152013-0 £4.00

The City of Wakefield (Mayoral Referendum) Order 2012 No. 2012/333. - Enabling power: Local Government Act 2000, ss. 9N, 105. - Issued: 13.02.2012. Made: 08.02.2012. Coming into force: In accord. with art. 1. Effect: None. Territorial extent & classification: E. General. - Supersedes draft SI (ISBN 9780111517505) issued 05.12.2012. - 2p.: 30 cm. - 978-0-11-152014-7 £4.00

The Community Right to Challenge (Expressions of Interest and Excluded Services) (England) Regulations 2012 No. 2012/1313. - Enabling power: Localism Act 2011, ss. 81 (1) (b) (5), 235 (2) (a). - Issued: 21.05.2012. Made: 17.05.2012. Laid: 21.05.2012. Coming into force: 27.06.2012. Effect: None. Territorial extent and classification: E. General. - 4p.: 30 cm. - 978-0-11-152460-2 £4.00

The Community Right to Challenge (Fire and Rescue Authorities and Rejection of Expressions of Interest) (England) Regulations 2012 No. 2012/1647. - Enabling power: Localism Act 2011, ss. 81 (2) (d), 83 (11), 235 (2) (a). - Issued: 27.06.2012. Made: 26.06.2012. Coming into force: In accord. with reg. 1. Effect: None. Territorial extent and classification: E. General. - Supersedes draft S.I. (ISBN 9780111523872) issued 30.04.2012. - 4p.: 30 cm. - 978-0-11-152584-5 £4.00

The County of Shropshire (Electoral Changes) Order 2012 No. 2012/2935. - Enabling power: Local Government and Public Involvement in Health Act 2007, s. 92 (3). - Issued: 28.11.2012. Made: 23.11.2012. Coming into force: In accord. with art. 1 (2). Effect: None. Territorial extent & classification: E. Local. - Available at http://www.legislation.gov.uk/uksi/2012/2935/contents/made *Non-print*

The Cumbria (Electoral Changes) Order 2012 No. 2012/3113. - Enabling power: Local Democracy, Economic Development and Construction Act 2009, s. 59 (1). - Issued: 20.12.2012. Made: 17.12.2012. Coming into force: In accord. with art. 2. Effect: None. Territorial extent & classification: E. General. - Supersedes draft SI (ISBN 9780111529478) issued 20.12.2012. With correction slip dated February 2013. - 12p.: 30 cm. - 978-0-11-153267-6 £5.75

The Daventry (Electoral Changes) Order 2012 No. 2012/160. - Enabling power: Local Democracy, Economic Development and Construction Act 2009, s. 59 (1). - Issued: 27.01.2012. Made: 24.01.2012. Coming into force: In accord. with arts. 1 (2) (3) (4). Effect: None. Territorial extent & classification: E. General. - Supersedes draft SI (ISBN 9780111516553) issued 07.11.2011. - 8p.: 30 cm. - 978-0-11-151946-2 £5.75

The Derbyshire (Electoral Changes) Order 2012 No. 2012/2986. - Enabling power: Local Democracy, Economic Development and Construction Act 2009, s. 59 (1). - Issued: 04.12.2012. Made: 29.11.2012. Coming into force: In accord. with art. 1 (2) (3). Effect: None. Territorial extent & classification: E. General. - Supersedes draft SI (ISBN 9780111529539) issued 18.10.2012. - 12p.: 30 cm. - 978-0-11-153141-9 £5.75

The District of Blaby (Electoral Changes) Order 2012 No. 2012/2854. - Enabling power: Local Government and Public Involvement in Health Act 2007, s. 92 (3). - Issued: 16.11.2012. Made: 12.11.2012. Coming into force: In accord. with art. 1, 2, 3. Effect: None. Territorial extent & classification: E. Local. - Available at http://www.legislation.gov.uk/uksi/2012/2854/contents/made *Non-print*

The District of Craven (Electoral Changes) Order 2012 No. 2012/3150. - Enabling power: Local Government and Public Involvement in Health Act 2007, s. 92 (3). - Issued: 27.12.2012. Made: 20.12.2012. Coming into force: In accord. with art. 1 (2) to (4). Effect: None. Territorial extent & classification: E. Local. - Available at http://www.legislation.gov.uk/uksi/2012/3150/contents/made *Non-print*

The District of West Oxfordshire (Electoral Changes) Order 2012 No. 2012/2993. - Enabling power: Local Government and Public Involvement in Health Act 2007, s. 92 (3). - Issued: 05.12.2012. Made: 29.11.2012. Coming into force: In accord. with art. 1 (2) (3). Effect: None. Territorial extent & classification: E. Local. - Available at http://www.legislation.gov.uk/uksi/2012/2993/contents/made *Non-print*

The Durham (Electoral Changes) Order 2012 No. 2012/1394. - Enabling power: Local Democracy, Economic Development and Construction Act 2009, s. 59 (1). - Issued: 30.05.2012. Made: 25.05.2012. Coming into force: In accord. with art. 2. Effect: None. Territorial extent & classification: E. General. - Supersedes draft SI (ISBN 9780111522516) issued 22.03.2012. - 12p.: 30 cm. - 978-0-11-152484-8 £5.75

The Gloucestershire (Electoral Changes) Order 2012 No. 2012/877. - Enabling power: Local Democracy, Economic Development and Construction Act 2009, s. 59 (1). - Issued: 23.03.2012. Made: 20.03.2012. Coming into force: In accord. with art. 2. Effect: None. Territorial extent & classification: E. General. - Supersedes draft S.I. (ISBN 9780111519714) issued 02.02.2012. - 8p.: 30 cm. - 978-0-11-152257-8 £5.75

The Hart (Electoral Changes) Order 2012 No. 2012/1395. - Enabling power: Local Democracy, Economic Development and Construction Act 2009, s. 59 (1). - Issued: 30.05.2012. Made: 25.05.2012. Coming into force: In accord. with art. 2. Effect: None. Territorial extent & classification: E. General. - Supersedes draft SI (ISBN 9780111522509) issued on 22.03.2012. - 8p.: 30 cm. - 978-0-11-152485-5 £5.75

The Hartlepool (Electoral Changes) Order 2012 No. 2012/3. - Enabling power: Local Democracy, Economic Development and Construction Act 2009, s. 59 (1). - Issued: 06.01.2012. Made: 03.01.2012. Coming into force: In accord. with arts. 1 (2) (3). Effect: None. Territorial extent & classification: E. General. - Supersedes draft SI (ISBN 9780111516539) issued on 07.11.2011. - 8p.: 30 cm. - 978-0-11-151888-5 £4.00

The Huntingdonshire (Electoral Changes) Order 2012 No. 2012/51. - Enabling power: Local Government and Public Involvement in Health Act 2007, s. 92 (3). - Issued: 13.01.2012. Made: 10.01.2012. Coming into force: In accord. with art. 1 (2). Effect: None. Territorial extent & classification: E. Local. - Available at http://www.legislation.gov.uk/uksi/2012/51/contents/made *Non-print*

The King's Lynn and West Norfolk (Electoral Changes) Order 2012 No. 2012/3260. - Enabling power: Local Government and Public Involvement in Health Act 2007, s. 92 (3). - Issued: 14.01.2013. Made: 20.12.2012. Coming into force: In accord. with art. 1 (2) (3). Effect: None. Territorial extent & classification: E. Local. - Revoked by SI 2013/220 (Non-print). - Available at http://www.legislation.gov.uk/uksi/2012/3260/contents/made *Non-print*

The Local Authorities (Armorial Bearings) Order 2012 No. 2012/1760. - Enabling power: Local Government Act 1972, s. 247. - Issued: 13.07.2012. Made: 10.07.2012. Coming into force: 11.07.2012. Effect: None. Territorial extent & classification: E. General. - 2p.: 30 cm. - 978-0-11-152671-2 £4.00

The Local Authorities (Arrangements for the Discharge of Functions) (England) Regulations 2012 No. 2012/1019. - Enabling power: Local Government Act 2000, ss. 9EA, 9EB, 105. - Issued: 10.04.2012. Made: 30.03.2012. Laid: 10.04.2012. Coming into force: 04.05.2012. Effect: S.I. 2000/2851; 2001/3961 revoked. Territorial extent & classification: E. General. - 8p.: 30 cm. - 978-0-11-152338-4 £5.75

The Local Authorities (Capital Finance and Accounting) (England) (Amendment) (No. 2) Regulations 2012 No. 2012/711. - Enabling power: Local Government Act 2003, ss. 9 (3), 11, 123. - Issued: 09.03.2012. Made: 07.03.2012. Laid: 09.03.2012. Coming into force: 31.03.2012 for regs 1 to 3 & 01.04.2012 for remainder. Effect: S.I. 2003/3146 amended. Territorial extent & classification: E. General. - 16p.: 30 cm. - 978-0-11-152168-7 £5.75

The Local Authorities (Capital Finance and Accounting) (England) (Amendment) (No. 3) Regulations 2012 No. 2012/1324. - Enabling power: Local Government Act 2003, ss. 9 (3), 11, 123. - Issued: 22.05.2012. Made: 18.05.2012. Laid: 22.05.2012. Coming into force: 14.06.2012. Effect: S.I. 2003/3146 amended. Territorial extent & classification: E. General. - This Statutory Instrument has been printed to correct errors in S.I. 2012/711 (ISBN 9780111521687) and is being issued free of charge to all known recipients of that Statutory Instrument. - 8p.: 30 cm. - 978-0-11-152463-3 £5.75

The Local Authorities (Capital Finance and Accounting) (England) (Amendment) (No. 4) Regulations 2012 No. 2012/2269. - Enabling power: Local Government Act 2003, ss. 9 (3), 11, 123. - Issued: 06.09.2012. Made: 04.09.2012. Laid: 06.09.2012. Coming into force: 30.09.2012. Effect: S.I. 2003/3146 amended. Territorial extent & classification: E. General. - 4p.: 30 cm. - 978-0-11-152851-8 £4.00

Local government, England

The Local Authorities (Capital Finance and Accounting) (England) (Amendment) Regulations 2012 No. 2012/265. - Enabling power: Local Government Act 2003, ss. 7 (2) (b) (3) (c), 8 (3), 9 (3) (b), 16 (2) (a), 21 (2) (b). - Issued: 08.02.2012. Made: 02.02.2012. Laid: 08.02.2012. Coming into force: 31.03.2012 for regs 1 to 3 (a), 4 (2), 7 (b), 8 & 01.04.2012 for regs 3 (b) (c), 4 (1) (3), 5, 6 and remainder of reg. 7, in accord. with reg. 1. Effect: S.I. 2003/3146 amended. Territorial extent & classification: E. General. - With correction slips dated April 2012 and July 2012. - 4p.: 30 cm. - 978-0-11-151983-7 £4.00

The Local Authorities (Committee System) (England) Regulations 2012 No. 2012/1020. - Enabling power: Local Government Act 2000, ss. 9J, 9JA, 105. - Issued: 10.04.2012. Made: 30.03.2012. Laid: 10.04.2012. Coming into force: 04.05.2012. Effect: S.I. 2001/1299 revoked. Territorial extent & classification: E. General. - 16p.: 30 cm. - 978-0-11-152339-1 £5.75

The Local Authorities (Conduct of Referendums) (England) Regulations 2012 No. 2012/323. - Enabling power: Local Government Act 2000, ss. 9MG, 105. - Issued: 13.02.2012. Made: 08.02.2012. Coming into force: In accord. with reg. 1. Effect: 1983 c. 2; 1985 c. 50; 2000 c. 2, c. 22, c. 41; 2006 c. 22 & S.I. 1960/543; 2001/341 modified & S.I. 2007/2089 revoked. Territorial extent & classification: E. General. - Supersedes draft SI (ISBN 9780111517604) issued on 05.12.2011. - 128p.: 30 cm. - 978-0-11-152004-8 £18.50

The Local Authorities (Elected Mayors) (Elections, Terms of Office and Casual Vacancies) (England) Regulations 2012 No. 2012/336. - Enabling power: Local Government Act 2000, ss. 9HB, 105. - Issued: 15.02.2012. Made: 08.02.2012. Laid: 15.02.2012. Coming into force: 09.03.2012. Effect: S.I. 2001/2544 revoked. Territorial extent & classification: E. General. - 8p.: 30 cm. - 978-0-11-152017-8 £5.75

The Local Authorities (Executive Arrangements) (Meetings and Access to Information) (England) Regulations 2012 No. 2012/2089. - Enabling power: Local Government Act 2000, ss. 9G, 9GA, 105. - Issued: 15.08.2012. Made: 10.08.2012. Laid: 15.08.2012. Coming into force: 10.09.2012. Effect: S.I. 2000/3272; 2002/716; 2006/69 revoked. Territorial extent and classification: E. General. - 16p.: 30 cm. - 978-0-11-152814-3 £5.75

The Local Authorities (Exemption from Political Restrictions) (Designation) Regulations 2012 No. 2012/1644. - Enabling power: Local Government and Housing Act 1989, ss. 3A (7B) (7C), 190. - Issued: 28.06.2012. Made: 25.06.2012. Laid: 28.06.2012. Coming into force: 26.07.2012. Effect: None. Territorial extent & classification: E. General. - 4p.: 30 cm. - 978-0-11-152586-9 £4.00

The Local Authorities (Overview and Scrutiny Committees) (England) Regulations 2012 No. 2012/1021. - Enabling power: Local Government Act 2000, ss. 9FI, 9GA (8), 105. - Issued: 10.04.2012. Made: 30.03.2012. Laid: 10.04.2012. Coming into force: 04.05.2012. Effect: S.I. 2009/1919 revoked. Territorial extent & classification: E. General. - 4p.: 30 cm. - 978-0-11-152340-7 £4.00

The Local Elections (Declaration of Acceptance of Office) Order 2012 No. 2012/1465. - Enabling power: Local Government Act 1972, s. 83 (1) (4). - Issued: 13.06.2012. Made: 06.06.2012. Laid: 13.06.2012. Coming into force: 09.07.2012. Effect: S.I. 2001/3941 revoked. Territorial extent & classification: E. General. - 4p.: 30 cm. - 978-0-11-152511-1 £4.00

The Local Government Officers (Political Restrictions) (Amendment) (England) Regulations 2012 No. 2012/1772. - Enabling power: Local Government and Housing Act 1989, ss. 1 (5) (6), 190 (1). - Issued: 11.07.2012. Made: 05.07.2012. Laid: 11.07.2012. Coming into force: 06.08.2012. Effect: S.I. 1990/851 amended. Territorial extent & classification: E. General. - 2p.: 30 cm. - 978-0-11-152650-7 £4.00

The Localism Act 2011 (Commencement No. 1) (England) Order 2012 No. 2012/2420 (C.95). - Enabling power: Localism Act 2011, s. 240 (2). Bringing into operation various provisions of the 2011 Act on 21.09.2012, in accord. with art. 2. - Issued: 21.09.2012. Made: 20.09.2012. Effect: None. Territorial extent & classification: E. General. - 4p.: 30 cm. - 978-0-11-152900-3 £4.00

The Localism Act 2011 (Commencement No. 3) Order 2012 No. 2012/411 (C. 11). - Enabling power: Localism Act 2011, s. 240 (2) (7). Bringing into operation various provisions of the 2011 Act on 18.02.2012, in accord. with art. 2. - Issued: 20.02.2012. Made: 17.02.2012. Effect: None. Territorial extent & classification: E/W. General. - 4p.: 30 cm. - 978-0-11-152038-3 £4.00

The Localism Act 2011 (Local Authority Governance Transitional Provisions) (England) Order 2012 No. 2012/1023. - Enabling power: Localism Act 2011, s. 23. - Issued: 10.04.2012. Made: 30.03.2012. Laid: 10.04.2012. Coming into force: 04.05.2012. Effect: None. Territorial extent & classification: E. General. - 4p.: 30 cm. - 978-0-11-152342-1 £4.00

Local government, England

The NHS Bodies and Local Authorities (Partnership Arrangements, Care Trusts, Public Health and Local Healthwatch) Regulations 2012 No. 2012/3094. - Enabling power: National Health Service Act 2006, ss. ss. 73A (1) (f), 73B (2) (e), 73C (1) (2), 75 (1) to (4), 76 (1), 77 (1) (1A) (1B) (5A) to (5C) (8), 111 (1), 272 (7) (8) & Health and Social Care (Community Health and Standards) Act 2003, s. 115 (1) (2) (4) to (6) & Local Government and Public Involvement in Health Act 2007, ss. 222 (2) (b) (8) (b) (9) (10), 223, 224 (1), 226 (6), 229 (2), 240 (10). - Issued: 17.02.2012. Made: 12.12.2012. Laid: 17.12.2012. Coming into force: In accord. with reg. 1 (2). Effect: S.I. 2000/617; 2010/1743 amended & S.I. 2006/185 revoked with saving & S.I. 2001/3788; 2008/528 revoked. Territorial extent & classification: E. General. - 32p.: 30 cm. - 978-0-11-153247-8 £5.75

The North Devon (Electoral Changes) Order 2012 No. 2012/1013. - Enabling power: Local Government and Public Involvement in Health Act 2007, s. 92 (3). - Issued: 12.04.2012. Made: 04.04.2012. Coming into force: In accord. with art. 2. Effect: None. Territorial extent & classification: E. Local. - Available at http://www.legislation.gov.uk/uksi/2012/1013/contents/made *Non-print*

The Overview and Scrutiny (Reference by Councillors) (Excluded Matters) (England) Order 2012 No. 2012/1022. - Enabling power: Local Government Act 2000, ss. 9FC (5), 105. - Issued: 10.04.2012. Made: 30.03.2012. Laid before Parliament: 10.04.2012. Coming into force: 04.05.2012. Effect: S.I. 2008/3261 revoked. Territorial extent & classification: E. General. - 4p.: 30 cm. - 978-0-11-152341-4 £4.00

The Oxfordshire (Electoral Changes) Order 2012 No. 2012/1812. - Enabling power: Local Democracy, Economic Development and Construction Act 2009, s. 59 (1). - Issued: 13.07.2012. Made: 10.07.2012. Coming into force: In accord. with art. 2. Effect: None. Territorial extent & classification: E. General. - Supersedes draft SI (ISBN 9780111524329) issued 17.05.2012. - 12p.: 30 cm. - 978-0-11-152677-4 £5.75

The Parish Councils (General Power of Competence) (Prescribed Conditions) Order 2012 No. 2012/965. - Enabling power: Localism Act 2011, ss. 8 (2), 235 (2). - Issued: 30.03.2012. Made: 27.03.2012. Coming into force: 28.03.2012 in accord. with art. 1 (1). Effect: None. Territorial extent & classification: E. General. - Supersedes draft S.I. (ISBN 9780111519868) issued 09.02.2012. - 4p.: 30 cm. - 978-0-11-152307-0 £4.00

The Relevant Authorities (Disclosable Pecuniary Interests) Regulations 2012 No. 2012/1464. - Enabling power: Localism Act 2011, ss. 30 (3), 235 (2). - Issued: 08.06.2012. Made: 06.06.2012. Laid: 08.06.2012. Coming into force: 01.07.2012. Effect: None. Territorial extent & classification: E. General. - With correction slip dated July 2012. - 4p.: 30 cm. - 978-0-11-152510-4 £4.00

The Rugby (Electoral Changes) Order 2012 No. 2012/4. - Enabling power: Local Democracy, Economic Development and Construction Act 2009, s. 59 (1). - Issued: 06.01.2012. Made: 03.01.2012. Coming into force: In accord. with arts. 1 (2) (3) (4). Effect: None. Territorial extent & classification: E. General. - Supersedes draft SI (ISBN 9780111516560) issued on 07.11.2011. - 8p.: 30 cm. - 978-0-11-151889-2 £5.75

The Rushmoor (Electoral Changes) Order 2012 No. 2012/161. - Enabling power: Local Democracy, Economic Development and Construction Act 2009, s. 59 (1). - Issued: 27.01.2012. Made: 24.01.2012. Coming into force: In accord. with art. 1 (2). Effect: None. Territorial extent & classification: E. General. - Supersedes draft SI (ISBN 9780111516898) issued 17.11. 2011. - 4p.: 30 cm. - 978-0-11-151947-9 £4.00

The Slough (Electoral Changes) Order 2012 No. 2012/2769. - Enabling power: Local Democracy, Economic Development and Construction Act 2009, s. 59 (1). - Issued: 08.11.2012. Made: 05.11.2012. Coming into force: In accord. with art. 2. Effect: None. Territorial extent & classification: E. General. - Supersedes draft SI (ISBN 9780111527283) issued 19.07.2012. - 8p.: 30 cm. - 978-0-11-153046-7 £5.75

The Somerset (Electoral Changes) Order 2012 No. 2012/2984. - Enabling power: Local Democracy, Economic Development and Construction Act 2009, s. 59 (1). - Issued: 18.01.2013. Made: 29.11.2012. Coming into force: In accord. with art. 1 (2) (3). Effect: None. Territorial extent & classification: E. General. - This Statutory Instrument has been printed in substitution of the SI of the same number and is being issued free of charge to all known recipients of that SI, issued 04.12.2012. Supersedes draft SI (ISBN 9780111529546) issued 18.10.2012. - 12p.: 30 cm. - 978-0-11-153139-6 £5.75

The Staffordshire (Electoral Changes) Order 2012 No. 2012/875. - Enabling power: Local Democracy, Economic Development and Construction Act 2009, s. 59 (1). - Issued: 23.03.2012. Made: 20.03.2012. Coming into force: In accord. with art. 2. Effect: None. Territorial extent & classification: E. General. - Supersedes draft S.I. (ISBN 9780111519660) issued 02.02.2012. - 8p.: 30 cm. - 978-0-11-152255-4 £5.75

The St Albans and Welwyn Hatfield (Boundary Change) Order 2012 No. 2012/667. - Enabling power: Local Government and Public Involvement in Health Act 2007, ss. 10, 11, 12, 13, 15. - Issued: 07.03.2012. Made: 02.03.2012. Coming into force: In accord. with art. 1. Effect: None. Territorial extent & classification: E. General. - Supersedes draft S.I. (ISBN 9780111519172) issued 16.01.2012. - 8p., maps: 30 cm. - 978-0-11-152136-6 £4.00

Local government, England

The Surrey (Electoral Changes) Order 2012 No. 2012/1872. - Enabling power: Local Democracy, Economic Development and Construction Act 2009, s. 59 (1). - Issued: 19.07.2012. Made: 10.07.2012. Coming into force: In accord. with art. 2. Effect: None. Territorial extent & classification: E. General. - Supersedes draft SI (ISBN 9780111524312) issued 17.05.2012. - 8p.: 30 cm. - 978-0-11-152727-6 £5.75

The Sustainable Communities Regulations 2012 No. 2012/1523. - Enabling power: Sustainable Communities Act 2007, ss. 5B, 5D (1). - Issued: 18.06.2012. Made: 13.06.2012. Laid: 18.06.2012. Coming into force: 26.07.2012. Effect: None. Territorial extent & classification: E. General. - 4p.: 30 cm. - 978-0-11-152543-2 £4.00

The Swale (Electoral Changes) Order 2012 No. 2012/2985. - Enabling power: Local Democracy, Economic Development and Construction Act 2009, s. 59 (1). - Issued: 04.12.2012. Made: 29.11.2012. Coming into force: In accord. with art. 1 (2). Effect: None. Territorial extent & classification: E. General. - Supersedes draft SI (ISBN 9780111529553) issued 18.10.2012. - 8p.: 30 cm. - 978-0-11-153140-2 £4.00

The Swindon (Electoral Changes) Order 2012 No. 2012/2. - Enabling power: Local Democracy, Economic Development and Construction Act 2009, s. 59 (1). - Issued: 06.01.2012. Made: 03.01.2012. Coming into force: In accord. with arts. 1 (2) (3) (4). Effect: None. Territorial extent & classification: E. General. - Supersedes draft SI (ISBN 9780111516577) issued on 07.11.2011. - 8p.: 30 cm. - 978-0-11-151887-8 £5.75

The West Lindsey (Electoral Changes) Order 2012 No. 2012/1. - Enabling power: Local Democracy, Economic Development and Construction Act 2009, s. 59 (1). - Issued: 06.01.2012. Made: 03.01.2012. Coming into force: In accord. with art. 1 (2). Effect: None. Territorial extent & classification: E. General. - Supersedes draft SI (ISBN 9780111516546) issued on 07.11.2011. - 4p.: 30 cm. - 978-0-11-151886-1 £4.00

Local government, England: Finance

The Local Government (Structural Changes) (Finance) (Amendment) Regulations 2012 No. 2012/20. - Enabling power: Local Government and Public Involvement in Health Act 2007, ss. 14, 240 (10). - Issued: 10.01.2012. Made: 06.01.2012. Laid: 10.01.2012. Coming into force: 25.01.2012. Effect: 1992 c.14 & S.I. 1992/612, 2904; 2008/3022 amended. Territorial extent & classification: E. General. - 16p.: 30 cm. - 978-0-11-151900-4 £5.75

The Transport Levying Bodies (Amendment) Regulations 2012 No. 2012/213. - Enabling power: Local Government Finance Act 1988, ss. 74, 143 (1) (2). - Issued: 06.02.2012. Made: 30.01.2012. Laid: 02.02.2012. Coming into force: 24.02.2012. Effect: S.I. 1992/2789 amended. Territorial extent & classification: E. General. - 4p.: 30 cm. - 978-0-11-151973-8 £4.00

Local government, England and Wales

The Local Authorities (Mayoral Elections) (England and Wales) (Amendment) Regulations 2012 No. 2012/2059. - Enabling power: Local Government Act 2000, ss. 44, 105. - Issued: 10.08.2012. Made: 06.08.2012. Coming into force: 07.08.2012, in accord. with reg. 1. Effect: S.I. 2007/1024 amended. Territorial extent & classification: E/W. General. - Supersedes draft SI (ISBN 9780111525197) issued 12.06.2012. - 20p.: 30 cm. - 978-0-11-152802-0 £5.75

The Local Government Act 2000 (Commencement No. 9) Order 2012 No. 2012/1358 (C.51). - Enabling power: Local Government Act 2000, s. 108 (3) (7). Bringing into operation various provisions of the 2000 Act on 22.05.2012. - Issued: 24.05.2012. Made: 21.05.2012. Effect: None. Territorial extent and classification: E/W. General. - 4p.: 30 cm. - 978-0-11-152473-2 £4.00

The Localism Act 2011 (Commencement No. 2 and Transitional and Saving Provision) Order 2012 No. 2012/57 (C. 2). - Enabling power: Localism Act 2011, ss. 37, 240 (2) (7) (8). Bringing into operation various provisions of the 2011 Act on 15.01.2012; 31.01.2012. - Issued: 16.01.2012. Made: 11.01.2012. Effect: None. Territorial extent & classification: E/W and S in part. General. - 12p.: 30 cm. - 978-0-11-151911-0 £5.75

The Localism Act 2011 (Commencement No. 4 and Transitional, Transitory and Saving Provisions) Order 2012 No. 2012/628 (C.14). - Enabling power: Localism Act 2011, s. 240 (2) (7). Bringing into operation various provisions of the 2011 Act in accord. with arts. 2 to 8. - Issued: 07.03.2012. Made: 01.03.2012. Effect: None. Territorial extent & classification: E/W. General. - Partially revoked by S.I. 2012/2029 (C.80) (ISBN 9780111527962). - 12p.: 30 cm. - 978-0-11-152126-7 £5.75

The Localism Act 2011 (Commencement No. 5 and Transitional, Saving and Transitory Provisions) Order 2012 No. 2012/1008 (C.32). - Enabling power: Localism Act 2011, s. 240 (2) (7). Bringing into operation various provisions of the 2011 Act in accord. with arts. 2 to 6. - Issued: 05.04.2012. Made: 03.04.2012. Effect: None. Territorial extent & classification: E/W. General. - 8p.: 30 cm. - 978-0-11-152337-7 £5.75

The Localism Act 2011 (Commencement No. 6 and Transitional, Savings and Transitory Provisions) (Amendment) Order 2012 No. 2012/1714. - Enabling power: Localism Act 2011, s. 240 (2) (7). - Issued: 04.07.2012. Made: 02.07.2012. Coming into force: 03.07.2012 in accord. with art. 1 (1). Effect: S.I. 2012/1463 (C.56) amended. Territorial extent & classification: E/W. General. - 2p.: 30 cm. - 978-0-11-152623-1 £4.00

The Localism Act 2011 (Commencement No. 6 and Transitional, Savings and Transitory Provisions) Order 2012 No. 2012/1463 (C.56). - Enabling power: Localism Act 2011, s. 240 (2) (7). Bringing into operation various provisions of the 2011 Act in accord. with arts. 2 to 5. - Issued: 11.06.2012. Made: 06.06.2012. Effect: None. Territorial extent & classification: E/W. General. - 8p.: 30 cm. - 978-0-11-152509-8 £5.75

The Localism Act 2011 (Commencement No. 8 and Transitional, Transitory and Savings Provisions) Order 2012 No. 2012/2913 (C.115). - Enabling power: Localism Act 2011, s. 240 (2) (7). Bringing into operation various provisions of the 2011 Act, in relation to England and Wales, on 22.11.2012, in accord. with art. 2, 3, 4, 5, 6. - Issued: 22.11.2012. Made: 20.11.2012. Effect: None. Territorial extent & classification: E/W. General. - 8p.: 30 cm. - 978-0-11-153111-2 £5.75

The Localism Act 2011 (Consequential Amendments) Order 2012 No. 2012/961. - Enabling power: Localism Act 2011, s. 236. - Issued: 30.03.2012. Made: 27.03.2012. Coming into force: 28.03.2012 except fort art. 3, sch. 2; 06.04.2012 for art. 3, sch. 2 in accord. with art. 1 (2). Effect: 1961 c.33; 1965 c.12; 1972 c.70; 1980 c.66; 2002 c.41; 2003 c.43; 2004 c.5; 2006 c.40; 2008 c.14; S.I. 2002/522; 2003/1987; 2008/239 amended. Territorial extent & classification: E/W. General. - Supersedes draft S.I. (ISBN 9780111519912) issued 09.02.2012. - 8p.: 30 cm. - 978-0-11-152306-3 £4.00

The Local Policing Bodies (Consequential Amendments) Regulations 2012 No. 2012/61. - Enabling power: Police and Criminal Evidence Act 1984, s. 63B (6) & Animal Welfare Act 2006, ss. 6 (4) (5) (6) (8) (14) & Violent Crime Reduction Act 2006, ss. 15, 16 (7), 17 (6), 20 (5). - Issued: 17.01.2012. Made: 10.01.2012. Coming into force: 16.01.2012. Effect: S.I. 2001/2645; 2007/1120; 2008/1430 amended. Territorial extent & classification: E/W. General. - Supersedes draft SI (ISBN 9780111517130) issued on 22.11.2011. - 4p.: 30 cm. - 978-0-11-151915-8 £4.00

The Standards Board for England (Abolition) Order 2012 No. 2012/668. - Enabling power: Localism Act 2011, sch. 4, para. 57. - Issued: 07.03.2012. Made: 02.03.2012. Laid: 07.03.2012. Coming into force: 01.04.2012. Effect: None. Territorial extent & classification: E/W. General. - 2p.: 30 cm. - 978-0-11-152134-2 £4.00

Local government, Wales

The Abergavenny Improvement Act 1854 (Repeal) Order 2012 No. 2012/629 (W.87). - Enabling power: Local Government (Wales) Act 1994, s. 58. - Issued: 23.03.2012. Made: 28.02.2012. Laid before the National Assembly for Wales: 02.03.2012. Coming into force: 26.03.2012. Effect: 1854 c. 49 partially repealed. Territorial extent & classification: W. General. - In English and Welsh. Welsh language title: Gorchymyn Deddf Gwella'r Fenni 1854 (Diddymu) 2012. - 4p.: 30 cm. - 978-0-348-10564-3 £4.00

The Fire and Rescue Authorities (Improvement Plans) (Wales) Order 2012 No. 2012/1143 (W.137). - Enabling power: Local Government (Wales) Measure 2009, ss. 15 (7) (b), 50 (2) (a). - Issued: 09.05.2012. Made: 21.04.2012. Laid before the National Assembly for Wales: 25.04.2012. Coming into force: 21.05.2012. Effect: S.I. 2010/481 (W.50) revoked. Territorial extent & classification: W. General. - In English and Welsh. Welsh title: Gorchymyn Awdurdodau Tân ac Achub (Cynlluniau Gwella) (Cymru) 2012. - 4p.: 30 cm. - 978-0-348-10600-8 £4.00

The Isle of Anglesey (Electoral Arrangements) Order 2012 No. 2012/2676 (W.290). - Enabling power: Local Government Act 2000, s. 58 (2). - Issued: 13.02.2013. Made: 24.10.2012. Coming into force: In accord. with art. 1 (2). Effect: S.I. 1992/2923 revoked. Territorial extent & classification: W. General. - This SI has been printed in substitution of the SI of the same number (ISBN 9780348106640) issued 09.11.2012 and is being issued free of charge to all known recipients of that SI. - In English and Welsh. Welsh title: Gorchymyn Ynys Môn (Trefniadau Etholiadol) 2012. - 8p.: 30 cm. - 978-0-348-10700-5 £5.75

The Isle of Anglesey (Electoral Arrangements) Order 2012 No. 2012/2676 (W.290). - Enabling power: Local Government Act 2000, s. 58 (2). - Issued: 09.11.2012. Made: 24.10.2012. Coming into force: In accord. with art. 1 (2). Effect: S.I. 1992/2923 revoked. Territorial extent & classification: W. General. - Superseded by SI of the same number (ISBN 9780348107005) which is being sent free of charge to all known recipients of this SI. - In English and Welsh. Welsh title: Gorchymyn Ynys Môn (Trefniadau Etholiadol) 2012. - 8p.: 30 cm. - 978-0-348-10664-0 £5.75

The Isle of Anglesey Local Authorities (Change to the Years of Ordinary Elections) Order 2012 No. 2012/686 (W.94). - Enabling power: Local Government Act 2000, ss. 87, 105 (2), 106 (1) (b) (c). - Issued: 30.03.2012. Made: 06.03.2012. Laid before the National Assembly for Wales: 08.03.2012. Coming into force: 27.03.2012. Effect: None. Territorial extent & classification: W. General. - In English and Welsh. Welsh title: Gorchymyn Awdurdodau Lleol Ynys Môn (Newid Blynyddoedd Etholiadau Cyffredin) 2012. - 8p.: 30 cm. - 978-0-348-10572-8 £4.00

The Local Election Survey (Wales) Regulation 2012 No. 2012/685 (W.93). - Enabling power: Local Government (Wales) Measure 2011, ss. 1 (3) (a), 1 (3) (b), 2 (2), 175. - Issued: 30.03.2012. Made: 04.03.2012. Laid before the National Assembly for Wales: 06.03.2012. Coming into force: 31.03.2012. Effect: None. Territorial extent & classification: W. General. - In English and Welsh: Welsh title: Rheoliadau Arolygon Etholiadau Lleol (Cymru) 2012. - 16p.: 30 cm. - 978-0-348-10571-1 £5.75

The Local Government (Performance Indicators) (Wales) Order 2012 No. 2012/2539 (W.278). - Enabling power: Local Government (Wales) Measure 2009, ss. 8 (1) (a) (2), 50 (2). - Issued: 22.10.2012. Made: 02.10.2012. Laid before the National Assembly for Wales: 08.10.2012. Coming into force: 01.11.2012. In accord. with art. 1 (3) in relation to the financial year beginning 1 April 2013 and subsequent financial years. Effect: S.I. 2010/482 (W.51) revoked but continues to have effect in so far as it applies to Performance Indicators and Standards for the financial year beginning on 1 April 2012. Territorial extent & classification: W. General. - In English and Welsh. Welsh title: Gorchymyn Llywodraeth Leol (Dangosyddion Perfformiad) (Cymru) 2012. - 12p.: 30 cm. - 978-0-348-10658-9 £5.75

The Local Government (Wales) Measure 2011 (Commencement No. 2 and Saving Provisions) Order 2012 No. 2012/1187 (W.145) (C.40). - Enabling power: Local Government (Wales) Measure 2011 (nawm 4), s. 178 (3). Bringing various provisions of the 2011 Measure into operation on 30.04.2012. - Issued: 17.05.2012. Made: 29.04.2012. Effect: None. Territorial extent & classification: W. General. - In English and Welsh. Welsh title: Gorchymyn Mesur Llywodraeth Leol (Cymru) 2011 (Cychwyn Rhif 2 a Darpariaethau Arbed) 2012. - 12p.: 30 cm. - 978-0-348-10604-6 £5.75

The Localism Act 2011 (Commencement No. 1) (Wales) Order 2012 No. 2012/193 (W.31) (C.6). - Enabling power: Localism Act 2011, s. 240 (3). Bringing into operation various provisions of the Act on 31.01.2012, in accord. with art. 2. - Issued: 10.02.2012. Made: 25.01.2012. Coming into force: 31.01.2012. Effect: None. Territorial extent & classification: W. General. - In English and Welsh. Welsh language title: Gorchymyn Deddf Lleoliaeth 2011 (Cychwyn Rhif 1) (Cymru) 2012. - 4p.: 30 cm. - 978-0-348-10550-6 £4.00

The Localism Act 2011 (Commencement No. 2 and Saving Provision) (Wales) Order 2012 No. 2012/887 (W.118) (C.26). - Enabling power: Localism Act 2011, s. 240 (3) (4) (7). Bringing into operation various provisions of the Act on 01.04.2012, in accord. with art. 2. - Issued: 03.04.2012. Made: 14.03.2012. Coming into force: 01.04.2012. Effect: None. Territorial extent & classification: W. General. - In English and Welsh. Welsh language title: Gorchymyn Deddf Lleoliaeth 2011 (Cychwyn Rhif 2 a Darpariaeth Arbed) (Cymru) 2012. - 8p.: 30 cm. - 978-0-348-10579-7 £5.75

The Partnership Council for Wales (Local Health Boards and National Health Service Trusts) Order 2012 No. 2012/746 (W.101). - Enabling power: Government of Wales Act 2006, s. 72 (5) (e). - Issued: 28.03.2012. Made: 07.03.2012. Laid before the National Assembly for Wales: 09.03.2012. Coming into force: 03.04.2012. Effect: None. Territorial extent & classification: W. General. - In English and Welsh. Welsh title: Gorchymyn Cyngor Partneriaeth Cymru (Byrddau Iechyd Lleol ac Ymddiriedolaethau Gwasanaeth Iechyd Gwladol) 2012. - 4p.: 30 cm. - 978-0-348-10569-8 £4.00

The Pembrokeshire (St. Mary Out Liberty and Tenby Communities) Order 2012 No. 2012/805 (W.112). - Enabling power: Local Government Act 1972, s. 58 (2). - Issued: 05.04.2012. Made: 10.03.2012. Coming into force: 01.04.2012. Effect: None. Territorial extent & classification: W. General. - In English and Welsh. Welsh title: Gorchymyn Sir Benfro (Cymunedau Llanfair Dinbych-ypysgod a Dinbych-y-pysgod) 2012. - 8p., col. maps: 30 cm. - 978-0-348-10586-5 £8.25

Local government, Wales: Finance

The Local Authorities (Alteration of Requisite Calculations) (Wales) Regulations 2012 No. 2012/521 (W.82). - Enabling power: Local Government Finance Act 1992, ss. 32 (9), 33 (4), 43 (7), 44 (4), 113 (2). - Issued: 23.03.2012. Made: 22.02.2012. Laid before the National Assembly for Wales: 27.02.2012. Coming into force: 28.02.2012. Effect: 1992 c. 14 modified. Territorial extent & classification: W. General. - In English and Welsh. Welsh title: Rheoliadau Awdurdodau Lleol (Addasu Cyfrifiadau Angenrheidiol) (Cymru) 2012. - 8p.: 30 cm. - 978-0-348-10562-9 £5.75

London government

The Greater London Authority Act 1999 (Amendment) Order 2012 No. 2012/1530. - Enabling power: Greater London Authority Act 1999, ss. 31 (9), 420 (1). - Issued: 19.06.2012. Made: 13.06.2012. Laid: -. Coming into force: 01.07.2012. Effect: 1999 c.29 amended. Territorial extent & classification: E. General. - Supersedes draft SI (ISBN 9780111522196) issued on 19.03.2012. - 2p.: 30 cm. - 978-0-11-152544-9 £4.00

The Greater London Authority (Consolidated Council Tax Requirement Procedure) (No. 2) Regulations 2012 No. 2012/3125. - Enabling power: Greater London Authority Act 1999, sch. 6, para. 10. - Issued: 20.12.2012. Made: 18.12.2012. Laid: 20.12.2012. Coming into force: 14.01.2013. Effect: 1999 c. 29 amended. Territorial extent & classification: E. General. - 2p.: 30 cm. - 978-0-11-153268-3 £4.00

The Greater London Authority (Consolidated Council Tax Requirement Procedure) Regulations 2012 No. 2012/15. - Enabling power: Greater London Authority Act 1999, sch. 6, para. 10. - Issued: 09.01.2012. Made: 05.01.2012. Laid: 09.01.2012. Coming into force: 31.01.2021. Effect: 1999 c. 29 amended. Territorial extent & classification: E. General. - 2p.: 30 cm. - 978-0-11-151897-7 £4.00

The Greater London Authority Elections (Amendment) Rules 2012 No. 2012/198. - Enabling power: Representation of the People Act 1983, s. 36 (2A) (2B). - Issued: 31.01.2012. Made: 26.01.2012. Laid: 31.01.2012. Coming into force: 01.03.2012. Effect: S.I. 2007/3541 amended. Territorial extent & classification: E. General. - 12p.: 30 cm. - 978-0-11-151961-5 £5.75

The Greater London Authority (Limitation of Salaries) (Amendment) Order 2012 No. 2012/234. - Enabling power: Greater London Authority Act 1999, s. 25. - Issued: 07.02.2012. Made: 01.02.2012. Laid: 07.02.2012. Coming into force: 03.05.2012. Effect: S.I. 2000/1032 amended. Territorial extent & classification: E. General. - 2p.: 30 cm. - 978-0-11-151975-2 £4.00

The Localism Act 2011 (Commencement No. 4 and Transitional, Transitory and Saving Provisions) Order 2012 No. 2012/628 (C.14). - Enabling power: Localism Act 2011, s. 240 (2) (7). Bringing into operation various provisions of the 2011 Act in accord. with arts. 2 to 8. - Issued: 07.03.2012. Made: 01.03.2012. Effect: None. Territorial extent & classification: E/W. General. - Partially revoked by S.I. 2012/2029 (C.80) (ISBN 9780111527962). - 12p.: 30 cm. - 978-0-11-152126-7 £5.75

The Localism Act 2011 (Commencement No. 5 and Transitional, Saving and Transitory Provisions) Order 2012 No. 2012/1008 (C.32). - Enabling power: Localism Act 2011, s. 240 (2) (7). Bringing into operation various provisions of the 2011 Act in accord. with arts. 2 to 6. - Issued: 05.04.2012. Made: 03.04.2012. Effect: None. Territorial extent & classification: E/W. General. - 8p.: 30 cm. - 978-0-11-152337-7 £5.75

The Localism Act 2011 (Commencement No. 6 and Transitional, Savings and Transitory Provisions) Order 2012 No. 2012/1463 (C.56). - Enabling power: Localism Act 2011, s. 240 (2) (7). Bringing into operation various provisions of the 2011 Act in accord. with arts. 2 to 5. - Issued: 11.06.2012. Made: 06.06.2012. Effect: None. Territorial extent & classification: E/W. General. - 8p.: 30 cm. - 978-0-11-152509-8 £5.75

The Localism Act 2011 (Housing and Regeneration Functions in Greater London) (Consequential, Transitory, Transitional and Saving Provisions) Order 2012 No. 2012/666. - Enabling power: Localism Act 2011, ss. 194 (1), 236 (1). - Issued: 07.03.2012. Made: 02.03.2012. Laid: 07.03.2012. Coming into force: In accord. with art. 1 (2). Effect: S.I. 2008/1342; 1999/2277 amended & S.I. 1997/2862; 2003/1907; 2007/75; 2009/1360; 2010/948 partially revoked (31.03.2012). Territorial extent & classification: E/W. General. - 4p.: 30 cm. - 978-0-11-152130-4 £4.00

The Penalty Charges Enforcement (London) Regulations 2012 No. 2012/1234. - Enabling power: London Local Authorities Act 2007, ss. 64 (1) (2), 82 (1). - Issued: 10.05.2012. Made: 03.05.2012. Laid: 10.05.2012. Coming into force: 18.06.2012. Effect: None. Territorial extent & classification: Greater London/E. General. - 4p.: 30 cm. - 978-0-11-152411-4 £4.00

London Olympic Games and Paralympic Games, Wales

The London Olympic Games and Paralympic Games (Advertising and Trading) (Wales) Regulations 2012 No. 2012/60 (W.14). - Enabling power: London Olympic Games and Paralympic Games Act 2006, ss. 19, 20 (1),22 (8), 25, 26 (1), 28 (6). - Issued: 30.01.2012. Made: 10.01.2012. Coming into force: 11.01.2012 in accord. with reg. 1 (2). Effect: None. Territorial extent & classification: W. General. - In English and Welsh: Welsh title: Rheoliadau Gemau Olympaidd a Gemau Paralympaidd Llundain (Hysbysebu a Masnachu) (Cymru) 2012. - 24p.: 30 cm. - 978-0-348-10546-9 £5.75

Magistrates' courts, England and Wales

The Criminal Procedure (Amendment) Rules 2012 No. 2012/3089 (L.12). - Enabling power: Courts Act 2003, s. 69 & Criminal Justice Act 2003, s. 174 (4). - Issued: 17.12.2012. Made: 11.12.2012. Laid: 13.12.2012. Coming into force: 01.04.2013. Effect: S.I. 2012/1726 amended. Territorial extent and classification: E/W. General. - 12p.: 30 cm. - 978-0-11-153218-8 £5.75

The Criminal Procedure Rules 2012 No. 2012/1726 (L.6). - Enabling power: Senior Courts Act 1981, ss. 52, 73 (2), 74 (2) (3) (4), 87 (4); Police and Criminal Evidence Act 1984, s. 81; Criminal Procedure and Investigations Act 1996, ss. 19, 20 (3), sch. 2, para. 4; Powers of Criminal Courts (Sentencing) Act 2000, s. 155 (7); Terrorism Act 2000, sch. 5, para. 10, sch. 6, para. 4, sch. 6A, para. 5; Proceeds of Crime Act 2002, ss. 91, 351 (2), 362 (2), 369 (2), 375 (1); Courts Act 2003, s. 69; & Criminal Justice Act 2003, s. 132 (4). - Issued: 16.07.2012. Made: 02.07.2012. Laid: 12.07.2012. Coming into force: 01.10.2012. Effect: S.I. 2011/1709 revoked. Territorial extent and classification: E/W. General. - 331p.: 30 cm. - 978-0-11-152633-0 £38.00

The Family Procedure (Amendment) (No. 2) Rules 2012 No. 2012/1462. - Enabling power: Courts Act 2003, s. 75. - Issued: 11.06.2012. Made: 31.05.2012. Laid: 07.06.2012. Coming into force: 01.07.2012. Effect: S.I. 2010/2955 amended. Territorial extent & classification: E/W. General. - 2p.: 30 cm. - 978-0-11-152508-1 £4.00

The Family Procedure (Amendment No. 3) Rules 2012 No. 2012/2046 (L.7). - Enabling power: Courts Act 2003, ss. 75, 76. - Issued: 08.08.2012. Made: 31.07.2012. Laid: 07.08.2012. Coming into force: 30.009.2012. Effect: S.I. 2010/2955 amended. Territorial extent & classification: E/W. General. - 4p.: 30 cm. - 978-0-11-152799-3 £4.00

The Family Procedure (Amendment No. 4) Rules 2012 No. 2012/2806 (L.10). - Enabling power: Courts Act 2003, ss. 75, 76 & Civil Jurisdiction and Judgments Act 1982, ss. 12, 48. - Issued: 12.11.2012. Made: 06.11.2012. Laid: 09.11.2012. Coming into force: 20.12.2012. Effect: S.I. 2010/2955 amended. Territorial extent & classification: E/W. General. - 12p.: 30 cm. - 978-0-11-153059-7 £5.75

The Family Procedure (Amendment No. 5) Rules 2012 No. 2012/3061. - Enabling power: Courts Act 2003, ss. 75, 76. - Issued: 13.12.2013. Made: 10.12.2012. Laid: 13.12.2012. Coming into force: 31.01.2013. Effect: S.I. 2010/2955 amended. Territorial extent & classification: E/W. General. - 12p.: 30 cm. - 978-0-11-153210-2 £5.75

The Family Procedure (Amendment) Rules 2012 No. 2012/679 (L.3). - Enabling power: Civil Jurisdiction and Judgements Act 1982, ss. 12, 48 & Adoption and Children Act 2002, ss. 102, 141 (1) & Courts Act 2003, ss. 75, 76. - Issued: 07.03.2012. Made: 01.03.2012. Laid: 06.03.2012. Coming into force: 06.04.2012. Effect: S.I. 2010/2955 amended. Territorial extent & classification: E/W. General. - 8p.: 30 cm. - 978-0-11-152133-5 £5.75

The Magistrates' Courts (Detention and Forfeiture of Cash) (Amendment) Rules 2012 No. 2012/1275 (L.4). - Enabling power: Magistrates' Courts Act 1980, s. 144. - Issued: 17.05.2012. Made: 13.05.2012. Laid: 17.05.2012. Coming into force: 02.07.2012. Effect: S.I. 2002/2998 (L.17) amended. Territorial extent & classification: E/W. General. - 2p.: 30 cm. - 978-0-11-152433-6 £4.00

The Magistrates' Courts (Regulation of Investigatory Powers) Rules 2012 No. 2012/2563 (L.19). - Enabling power: Magistrates' Courts Act 1980, s. 144 (1), 145 (1). - Issued: 12.10.2012. Made: 06.10.2012. Laid: 11.10.2012. Coming into force: 01.11.2012. Effect: None. Territorial extent & classification: E/W. General. - 4p.: 30 cm. - 978-0-11-152929-4 £4.00

Magistrates' courts, England and Wales: Procedure

The Magistrates' Courts (Sexual Offences Act 2003) (Miscellaneous Amendments) Rules 2012 No. 2012/2018. - Enabling power: Magistrates' Courts Act 1980, ss. 144 (1), 145 (1). - Issued: 03.08.2012. Made: 31.07.2012. Laid: 03.08.2012. Coming into force: 03.09.2012. Effect: S.I. 2004/1051, 1052, 1053, 1054 amended. Territorial extent & classification: E/W. General. - 4p.: 30 cm. - 978-0-11-152795-5 £4.00

Marine management

The Conservation of Habitats and Species (Amendment) Regulations 2012 No. 2012/1927. - Enabling power: European Communities Act 1972, s. 2 (2). - Issued: 25.07.2012. Made: 20.07.2012. Laid before Parliament & the National Assembly for Wales: 25.07.2012. Coming into force: 16.08.2012. Effect: 1949 c.97; S.I. 2010/490 amended. Territorial extent & classification: E/W/S/NI. General. - EC note: These Regulations amend the S.I. 2010/490 Regulations and transpose certain aspects of Directive 2009/147/EC on the conservation of wild birds. - 16p.: 30 cm. - 978-0-11-152765-8 £5.75

Marine pollution

The Merchant Shipping (Ship-to-Ship Transfers) (Amendment) Regulations 2012 No. 2012/742. - Enabling power: Merchant Shipping Act 1995, s. 130. - Issued: 15.03.2012. Made: 05.03.2012. Laid: 09.03.2012. Coming into force: 31.03.2012. Effect: S.I. 2010/1228 amended. Territorial extent & classification: E/W/S/NI. General. - 8p.: 30 cm. - 978-0-11-152167-0 £4.00

Medicines

The Human Use Medicines Regulations 2012 No. 2012/1916. - Enabling power: European Communities Act 1972, s. 2 (2) (5) & Medicines Act 1968, ss. 87 (1), 88 (1) (2), 91 (2), 129 (1) (2) (5). - Issued: 24.07.2012. Made: 19.07.2012. Laid: 24.07.2012. Coming into force: 14.08.2012. Effect: 1968 c.29, c.67; 1971 c.69; 1975 c.25; 1987 c.43; 1990 c.43; 1994 c.23; 1999 c.8; 2003 c.21; 2007 asp 113 & S.I. 1972/1265 (NI. 14); 1976/1213 (N.I. 22), 1214 (N.I. 23); 1978/1006; 1980/14; 1981/1115 (N.I. 22); 1986/1700, 1761; 1989/684; 1995/449; 1997/1830, 1997/2778 (N.I. 19), 2779 (N.I. 20); 2000/620; 2001/880, 1841, 3998; 2002/3170; 2003/1076, 1374, 1376, 1571, 1680; 2004/291, 478, 627, 1022, 1031, 1975; 2005/1478; 2007/121, 1523, 3544; 2008/548, 944, 1270, 3258 & S.S.I. 2004/115, 116; 2009/45, 183, 669; 2010/2880 & S.R. 1987/414; 1995/8; 1996/81; 1997/381; 1998/28, 45; 1999/433; 2001/422, 2002/1; 2003/34, 493; 2004/140; 2005/160, 161, 176; 2006/478; 2007/68, 234, 236 amended & S.I. 1973/367; 1976/968; 1978/40; 1983/1724; 1999/1129; 1992/605; 1993/834; 1994/105, 899, 1932, 1933, 3144; 1995/2321; 1996/482; 1997/1830; 1998/3105; 1999/267, 784; 2002/236; 2003/1618, 2317; 2004/480; 2005/765, 768, 1094, 1520, 1710, 2750, 2754, 2787, 2589; 2006/395, 1952; 2008/1692, 3097; 2009/1164, 3062; 2010/1882 revoked. Territorial extent & classification: E/W/S/NI. General. - With correction slip dated November 2012. - 318p.: 30 cm. - 978-0-11-152760-3 £38.00

The Medicines (Products for Human Use) (Fees) (Amendment) Regulations 2012 No. 2012/2546. - Enabling power: Medicines Act 1971, s. 1 (1) & European Communities Act 1972, s. 2 (2) & Finance Act 1973, s. 56 (1) (2). - Issued: 10.10.2012. Made: 04.10.2012. Laid: 10.10.2012. Coming into force: 02.11.2012. Effect: S.I. 2012/504 amended. Territorial extent & classification: E/W/S/NI. General. - 4p.: 30 cm. - 978-0-11-152917-1 £4.00

The Medicines (Products for Human Use) (Fees) Regulations 2012 No. 2012/504. - Enabling power: Medicines Act 1971, s. 1 (1) (2) & European Communities Act 1972, s. 2 (2) & Finance Act 1973, s. 56 (1) (2). - Issued: 29.02.2012. Made: 23.02.2012. Laid: 29.02.2012. Coming into force: 01.04.2012. Effect: S.I. 2004/1031 amended & S.I. 1994/105 amended & partially revoked with savings & S.I. 2010/551 revoked with savings. Territorial extent & classification: E/W/S/NI. General. - 77p.: 30 cm. - 978-0-11-152069-7 £13.75

The Veterinary Medicines (Amendment) Regulations 2012 No. 2012/2711. - Enabling power: European Communities Act 1972, s. 2 (2). - Issued: 02.11.2012. Made: 26.10.2012. Laid: 02.11.2012. Coming into force: 01.12.2012. Effect: S. I. 2011/2159 amended. Territorial extent & classification: E/W/S/NI. General. - 4p.: 30 cm. - 978-0-11-153021-4 £4.00

Mental health, England

The Mental Health (Hospital, Guardianship and Treatment) (England) (Amendment) Regulations 2012 No. 2012/1118. - Enabling power: Mental Health Act 1983, s. 64H (2). - Issued: 23.04.2012. Made: 18.04.2012. Laid: 23.04.2012. Coming into force: In accord. with reg. 1 (2). Effect: S.I. 2008/1184 amended. Territorial extent & classification: E. General. - 2p.: 30 cm. - 978-0-11-152369-8 £4.00

The National Health Service Commissioning Board and Clinical Commissioning Groups (Responsibilities and Standing Rules) Regulations 2012 No. 2012/2996. - Enabling power: Mental Health Act 1983, ss. 117 (2E) (2G) & National Health Service Act 2006, ss. 3 (1B), 3A (3), 3B (1), 6E, 223E (3), 223J (3), 272 (7) & Health and Social Care Act 2012, s. 75. - Issued: 05.12.2012. Made: 03.12.2012. Laid: 05.12.2012. Coming into force: In accord. with reg. 1. Effect: None. Territorial extent & classification: E. General. - 52p.: 30 cm. - 978-0-11-153158-7 £9.75

Mental health, England and Wales

The Health and Social Care Act 2012 (Commencement No. 1 and Transitory Provision) Order 2012 No. 2012/1319 (C.47). - Enabling power: Health and Social Care Act 2012, ss. 304 (10), 306. Bringing into operation various provisions of this Act on 01.06.2012, 01.07.2012, 01.08.2012 in accord. with art. 2. - Issued: 22.05.2012. Made: 17.05.2012. Coming into force: .- Effect: S.I. 2010/781 amended. Territorial extent & classification: E/W. General. - 8p.: 30 cm. - 978-0-11-152461-9 £4.00

The Mental Health (Wales) Measure 2010 (Commencement No. 2) Order 2012 No. 2012/1397 (W.169) (C.52). - Enabling power: Mental Health (Wales) Measure 2010, ss. 52 (2), 55 (3). Bringing into operation various provisions of this Measure on 06.06.2012 in accord. with art. 2. - Issued: 13.06.2012. Made: 28.05.2012. Effect: None. Territorial extent & classification: W. General. - In English and Welsh. Welsh title: Gorchymyn Mesur Iechyd Meddwl (Cymru) 2010 (Cychwyn Rhif 2) 2012. - 8p.: 30 cm. - 978-0-348-10621-3 £4.00

The Mental Health (Wales) Measure 2010 (Commencement No. 3) Order 2012 No. 2012/2411 (W.261) (C.93). - Enabling power: Mental Health (Wales) Measure 2010, ss. 52 (2), 55 (3). Bringing into operation various provisions of this Measure on 01.10.2012 in accord. with art. 2. - Issued: 15.10.2012. Made: 15.09.2012. Effect: None. Territorial extent & classification: W. General. - In English and Welsh. Welsh title: Gorchymyn Mesur Iechyd Meddwl (Cymru) 2010 (Cychwyn Rhif 3) 2012. - 8p.: 30 cm. - 978-0-348-10654-1 £5.75

Mental health, Wales

The Mental Health (Hospital, Guardianship, Community Treatment and Consent to Treatment) (Wales) (Amendment) Regulations 2012 No. 2012/1265 (W.158). - Enabling power: Mental Health Act 1983, s. 64H (2). - Issued: 08.06.2012. Made: 09.05.2012. Laid before the National Assembly for Wales: 11.05.2012. Coming into force: 02.06.2012. Effect: S.I. 2008/2439 (W.212) amended. Territorial extent & classification: W. General. - In English and Welsh. Welsh title: Rheoliadau Iechyd Meddwl (Ysbyty, Gwarcheidiaeth, Triniaeth Gymunedol a Chydsynio i Driniaeth) (Cymru) (Diwygio) 2012. - 4p.: 30 cm. - 978-0-348-10620-6 £4.00

The Mental Health (Primary Care Referrals and Eligibility to Conduct Primary Mental Health Assessments) (Wales) Regulations 2012 No. 2012/1305 (W.166). - Enabling power: Mental Health (Wales) Measure 2010, ss. 7 (6) (a), 47 (1) (a) (2), 52 (2). - Issued: 08.06.2012. Made: 15.05.2012. Coming into force: 01.10.2012. Effect: None. Territorial extent & classification: W. General. - In English and Welsh. Welsh title: Rheoliadau Iechyd Meddwl (Atgyfeiriadau Gofal Sylfaenol a Chymhwystra i Gynnal Asesiadau Iechyd Meddwl Sylfaenol) (Cymru) 2012. - 8p.: 30 cm. - 978-0-348-10618-3 £5.75

The Mental Health (Regional Provision) (Wales) Regulations 2012 No. 2012/1244 (W.152). - Enabling power: Mental Health (Wales) Measure 2010, ss. 45, 46, 52 (2). - Issued: 06.06.2012. Made: 08.05.2012. Coming into force: In accord. with reg. 1 (2). Effect: None. Territorial extent & classification: W. General. - In English and Welsh. Welsh title: Rheoliadau Iechyd Meddwl (Darpariaeth Ranbarthol) (Cymru) 2012. - 8p.: 30 cm. - 978-0-348-10615-2 £5.75

The Mental Health (Secondary Mental Health Services) (Wales) Order 2012 No. 2012/1428 (W.178). - Enabling power: Mental Health (Wales) Measure 2010, ss. 49 (4), 52 (2). - Issued: 13.06.2012. Made: 29.05.2012. Coming into force: 06.06.2012. Effect: None. Territorial extent & classification: W. General. - In English and Welsh. Welsh title: Gorchymyn Iechyd Meddwl (Gwasanaethau Iechyd Meddwl Eilaidd) (Cymru) 2012. - 4p.: 30 cm. - 978-0-348-10623-7 £4.00

Merchant shipping

The Merchant Shipping (Accident Reporting and Investigation) Regulations 2012 No. 2012/1743. - Enabling power: Merchant Shipping Act 1995, s. 267. - Issued: 11.07.2012. Made: 04.07.2012. Laid: 04.07.2012. Coming into force: 31.07.2012. Effect: None. Territorial extent & classification: E/W/S/NI. General. - These Regulations replace The Merchant Shipping (Accident Reporting and Investigation) Regulations 2005 (S.I.2005/881) and implement the provisions of Directive 2009/18/EC establishing the fundamental principles governing the investigation of accidents in the maritime transport sector and amending Council Directive 1999/35/EC and Directive 2002/59/EC. - 20p.: 30 cm. - 978-0-11-152649-1 £5.75

The Merchant Shipping and Fishing Vessels (Health and Safety at Work) (Chemical Agents) (Amendment) Regulations 2012 No. 2012/1844. - Enabling power: European Communities Act 1972, s. 2 (2) & Merchant Shipping Act 1995, ss. 85 (1) (a) (b) (3), 86 (1). - Issued: 23.07.2012. Made: 12.07.2012. Laid: 17.07.2012. Coming into force: 10.08.2012. Effect: S.I. 2010/330 amended. Territorial extent & classification: E/W/S/NI. General. - EC note: These Regulations implement Commission Directive 2009/161/EU which establishes a third list of indicative occupational exposure limit values for exposure to chemical agents at work. They do so by amending the definition of national occupational exposure limit value in the Merchant Shipping and Fishing Vessels (Health and Safety at Work) (Chemical Agents) Regulations 2010 so that it includes a reference to the list of values in the Annex to that Directive. - 4p.: 30 cm. - 978-0-11-152726-9 £4.00

The Merchant Shipping (Carriage of Passengers by Sea) Regulations 2012 No. 2012/3152. - Enabling power: European Communities Act 1972, s. 2 (2). - Issued: 27.12.2012. Made: 19.12.2012. Laid: 21.12.2012. Coming into force: 31.12.2012 for regs 2, 4 & 12.01.2013 for remaining regs. Effect: 1995 c. 21 amended. Territorial extent & classification: E/W/S/NI. General. - EC note: These Regs. are made to support the operation of Regulation 392/2009 on the liability of carriers of passengers by sea in the event of accidents which comes into effect on 31 December 2012. - 8p.: 30 cm. - 978-0-11-153280-5 £5.75

The Merchant Shipping (Compulsory Insurance of Shipowners for Maritime Claims) Regulations 2012 No. 2012/2267. - Enabling power: European Communities Act 1972, s. 2 (2) & Merchant Shipping Act 1995, s. 192A. - Issued: 11.09.2012. Made: 03.09.2012. Laid: 06.09.2012. Coming into force: In accord. with reg. 1 (2). Effect: None. Territorial extent & classification: E/W/S/NI. General. - EC note: These Regulations transpose Directive 2009/20/EC on the insurance of shipowners for maritime claims. - 8p.: 30 cm. - 978-0-11-152849-5 £5.75

Merchant shipping: Maritime security

The Port Security (Port of Aberdeen) Designation Order 2012 No. 2012/2607. - Enabling power: European Communities Act 1972, s. 2 (2). - Issued: 23.10.2012. Made: 15.10.2012. Laid: 18.10.2012. Coming into force: 19.11.2012. Effect: None. Territorial extent & classification: E/W/S/NI. General. - 8p., col. map: 30 cm. - 978-0-11-152957-7 £8.25

The Port Security (Port of Grangemouth) Designation Order 2012 No. 2012/2608. - Enabling power: European Communities Act 1972, s. 2 (2). - Issued: 23.10.2012. Made: 15.10.2012. Laid: 18.10.2012. Coming into force: 19.11.2012. Effect: None. Territorial extent & classification: E/W/S/NI. General. - EC note: This Order is one of a series to implement Directive 2005/65/EC on enhancing port security at individual ports across the UK. The Directive was transposed in relation to the UK as a whole by the Port Security Regulations 2009 (S.I. 2009/2048). - 8p., col. map: 30 cm. - 978-0-11-152960-7 £8.25

The Port Security (Port of Portland) Designation Order 2012 No. 2012/2609. - Enabling power: European Communities Act 1972, s. 2 (2). - Issued: 23.10.2012. Made: 15.10.2012. Laid: 18.10.2012. Coming into force: 19.11.2012. Effect: None. Territorial extent & classification: E/W/S/NI. General. - EC note: This Order is one of a series to implement Directive 2005/65/EC on enhancing port security at individual ports across the UK. The Directive was transposed in relation to the UK as a whole by the Port Security Regulations 2009 (S.I. 2009/2048). - 8p., col. map: 30 cm. - 978-0-11-152962-1 £8.25

The Port Security (Port of Tees and Hartlepool) Designation Order 2012 No. 2012/2610. - Enabling power: European Communities Act 1972, s. 2 (2). - Issued: 23.10.2012. Made: 15.10.2012. Laid: 18.10.2012. Coming into force: 19.11.2012. Effect: None. Territorial extent & classification: E/W/S/NI. General. - 16p., col. maps: 30 cm. - 978-0-11-152958-4 £8.25

The Port Security (Port of Workington) Designation Order 2012 No. 2012/2611. - Enabling power: European Communities Act 1972, s. 2 (2). - Issued: 23.10.2012. Made: 15.10.2012. Laid: 18.10.2012. Coming into force: 19.11.2012. Effect: None. Territorial extent & classification: E/W/S/NI. General. - EC note: This Order is one of a series to implement Directive 2005/65/EC on enhancing port security at individual ports across the UK. The Directive was transposed in relation to the UK as a whole by the Port Security Regulations 2009 (S.I. 2009/2048). - 8p., col. map: 30 cm. - 978-0-11-152963-8 £8.25

Merchant shipping: Safety

The Merchant Shipping (Passenger Ships on Domestic Voyages) (Amendment) Regulations 2012 No. 2012/2636. - Enabling power: Merchant Shipping Act 1995, ss. 85 (1) (a) (b) (3) (7), 86 (1). - Issued: 25.10.2012. Made: 18.10.2012. Laid: 23.10.2012. Coming into force: 16.11.2012. Effect: S.I. 1995/1210; 2000/2687; 2004/302 amended. Territorial extent & classification: E/W/S/NI. General. - EC note: These Regs. implement DIR 2010/36/EU amending DIR 2009/45/EU on safety rules and standards for passenger ships. - 8p.: 30 cm. - 978-0-11-152981-2 £4.00

Ministers of the Crown

The Transfer of Functions (Sea Fisheries) Order 2012 No. 2012/2747. - Enabling power: Ministers of the Crown Act 1975, s. 1. - Issued: 14.11.2012. Made: 07.11.2012. Laid: 14.11.2012. Coming into force: 05.12.2012. Effect: None. Territorial extent & classification: E/W/S/NI. General. - 4p.: 30 cm. - 978-0-11-153061-0 £4.00

The Transfer of Functions (Secretary of State for Culture, Media and Sport) Order 2012 No. 2012/2590. - Enabling power: Ministers of Crown Act 1975, ss. 1, 2. - Issued: 24.10.2012. Made: 17.10.2012. Laid: 24.10.2012. Coming into force: 14.11.2012. Effect: 1920 c. 15; 1996 c. 61; 2008 c. 17, 18; S.I. 1990/1519; 2006/1466; 2010/501 amended. Territorial extent & classification: E/W/S/NI. General. - 8p.: 30 cm. - 978-0-11-152967-6 £4.00

Mobile homes, Wales

The Mobile Homes Act 1983 (Jurisdiction of Residential Property Tribunals) (Wales) Order 2012 No. 2012/899 (W.119). - Enabling power: Housing Act 2004, ss. 229 (3) (4), 250 (2). - Issued: 17.04.2012. Made: 20.03.2012. Coming into force: 21.03.2012. Effect: 1983 c. 34; 2004 c. 34 amended. Territorial extent & classification: W. General. - In English and Welsh. Welsh title: Gorchymyn Deddf Cartrefi Symudol 1983 (Awdurdodaeth Tribiwnlysoedd Eiddo Preswyl) (Cymru) 2012. - 12p.: 30 cm. - 978-0-348-10597-1 £5.75

The Mobile Homes (Written Statement) (Wales) Regulations 2012 No. 2012/2675 (W.289). - Enabling power: Mobile Homes Act 1983, s. 1 (2) (e). - Issued: 09.11.2012. Made: 24.10.2012. Laid before the National Assembly for Wales: 29.10.2012. Coming into force: 19.11.2012. Effect: S.I. 2007/3164 (W.275) revoked. Territorial extent & classification: W. General. - In English and Welsh. Welsh title: Rheoliadau Cartrefi Symudol (Datganiad Ysgrifenedig) (Cymru) 2012. - 12p.: 30 cm. - 978-0-348-10665-7 £5.75

National assistance services, England

The National Assistance (Assessment of Resources) Amendment (England) Regulations 2012 No. 2012/2336. - Enabling power: National Assistance Act 1948, s. 22 (5). - Issued: 17.09.2012. Made: 11.09.2012. Laid: 17.09.2012. Coming into force: 29.10.2012. Effect: S.I. 1992/2977 amended. Territorial extent & classification: E. General. - 2p.: 30 cm. - 978-0-11-152876-1 £4.00

The National Assistance (Sums for Personal Requirements) Amendment (England) Regulations 2012 No. 2012/663. - Enabling power: National Assistance Act 1948, s. 22 (4). - Issued: 08.03.2012. Made: 29.02.2012. Laid: 08.03.2012. Coming into force: 09.04.2012. Effect: S.I. 2003/628 amended. Territorial extent & classification: E. General. - 2p.: 30 cm. - 978-0-11-152128-1 £4.00

National assistance services, Wales

The National Assistance (Sums for Personal Requirements) (Assessment of Resources and Miscellaneous Amendments) (Wales) Regulations 2012 No. 2012/842 (W.115). - Enabling power: National Assistance Act 1948, s. 22 (4) (5). - Issued: 03.04.2012. Made: 14.03.2012. Laid before the National Assembly for Wales: 16.03.2012. Coming into force: 09.04.2012. Effect: S.I. 1992/2977; 2003/931 (W.121) amended & W.S.I. 2011/708 (W.110) partially revoked. Territorial extent & classification: W. General. - In English & Welsh. Welsh title: Rheoliadau Cymorth Gwladol (Symiau at Anghenion Personol) (Asesu Adnoddau a Diwygiadau Amrywiol) (Cymru) 2012. - 8p.: 30 cm. - 978-0-348-10580-3 £4.00

National debt

The National Savings Stock Register (Amendment) Regulations 2012 No. 2012/1877. - Enabling power: National Debt Act 1972, s. 3. - Issued: 19.07.2012. Made: 16.07.2012. Laid: 18.07.2012. Coming into force: 20.09.2012. Effect: S.I. 1976/2012 amended. Territorial extent & classification: E/W/S/NI. General. - 12p.: 30 cm. - 978-0-11-152732-0 £5.75

The Savings Certificates (Amendment) Regulations 2012 No. 2012/1882. - Enabling power: National Debt Act 1972, s. 11. - Issued: 19.07.2012. Made: 16.07.2012. Laid: 18.07.2012. Coming into force: 20.09.2012. Effect: S.I. 1991/1031 amended. Territorial extent and classification: E/W/S/NI. General. - 8p.: 30 cm. - 978-0-11-152735-1 £5.75

The Savings Certificates (Children's Bonus Bonds) (Amendment) Regulations 2012 No. 2012/1880. - Enabling power: National Debt Act 1972, s. 11. - Issued: 19.07.2012. Made: 16.07.2012. Laid: 18.07.2012. Coming into force: 20.09.2012. Effect: S.I. 1991/1407 amended. Territorial extent & classification: E/W/S/NI. General. - 12p.: 30 cm. - 978-0-11-152733-7 £5.75

National Health Service

The Health and Social Care Act 2012 (Commencement No. 1 and Transitory Provision) Order 2012 No. 2012/1319 (C.47). - Enabling power: Health and Social Care Act 2012, ss. 304 (10), 306. Bringing into operation various provisions of this Act on 01.06.2012, 01.07.2012, 01.08.2012 in accord. with art. 2. - Issued: 22.05.2012. Made: 17.05.2012. Coming into force: .- Effect: S.I. 2010/781 amended. Territorial extent & classification: E/W. General. - 8p.: 30 cm. - 978-0-11-152461-9 £4.00

The NHS Commissioning Board Authority (Abolition and Transfer of Staff, Property and Liabilities) and the Health and Social Care Act 2012 (Consequential Amendments) Order 2012 No. 2012/1641. - Enabling power: National Health Service Act 2006, ss. 28 (1) (2), 272 (7) (8), 273 (1) & Health and Social Care Act 2012, s. 303. - Issued: 27.06.2012. Made: 21.06.2012. Laid: 27.06.2012. Coming into force: In accord. with art. 1 (2). Effect: S.I. 1990/260, 2024; 1995/2800, 2801; 1996/251, 686, 707; 1999/260, 873, 874, 1549; 2000/89; 2001/715; 2002/348; 2004/1031, 1861; 2005/408, 500, 1447, 2415, 2531; 2008/2252, 2558; 2009/462, 779 (W.67); 1385 (W.141), 3097 (W.270), 3112; 2010/2841; 2011/2237, 2250, 2260, 2341; 2012/922, 1290 amended. Territorial extent & classification: Same as secondary legislation amended - mostly only E/W. General. - With correction slip dated July 2012. - 24p.: 30 cm. - 978-0-11-152582-1 £5.75

National Health Service, England

The Barts Health National Health Service Trust (Establishment) and the Barts and The London National Health Service Trust, the Newham University Hospital National Health Service Trust and the Whipps Cross University Hospital National Health Service Trust (Dissolution) Order 2012 No. 2012/796. - Enabling power: National Health Service Act 2006, ss. 25 (1), 272 (7) (8), 273 (1), sch. 4, paras 5, 28. - Issued: 15.03.2012. Made: 12.03.2012. Coming into force: 01.04.2012. Effect: S.I. 1994/307, 308; 2000/1414 revoked. Territorial extent & classification: E. General. - 4p.: 30 cm. - 978-0-11-152204-2 £4.00

The Care Quality Commission (Healthwatch England Committee) Regulations 2012 No. 2012/1640. - Enabling power: Health and Social Care Act 2008, s. 161 (3) (4), sch. 1, para. 6 (1A) (5A) to (5D). - Issued: 27.06.2012. Made: 21.06.2012. Laid: 27.06.2012. Coming into force: In accord. with reg. 1. Effect: None. Territorial extent & classification: E. General. - 12p.: 30 cm. - 978-0-11-152581-4 £5.75

The Care Quality Commission (Registration) and (Additional Functions) and Health and Social Care Act 2008 (Regulated Activities) (Amendment) Regulations 2012 No. 2012/921. - Enabling power: Health and Social Care Act 2008, ss. 16 (d), 20, 59 (1), 65 (1) (3), 86 (2), 87 (1) (2), 161 (3) (4). - Issued: 27.03.2012. Made: 22.03.2012. Laid: 27.03.2012. Coming into force: In accord. with reg. 1 (2). Effect: S.I. 2009/3112; 2010/781; 2011/1551 amended & S.I. 2009/3112 partially revoked (18.06.2012) & S.I. 2010/49 revoked (18.06.2012). Territorial extent & classification: E. General. - 8p.: 30 cm. - 978-0-11-152283-7 £5.75

The Care Quality Commission (Registration and Membership) (Amendment) Regulations 2012 No. 2012/1186. - Enabling power: Health and Social Care Act 2008, ss. 20, 161 (3), sch. 1, para. 3 (4). - Issued: 03.05.2012. Made: 30.04.2012. Laid: 03.05.2012. Coming into force: 01.06.2012. Effect: S.I. 2009/3112 amended. Territorial extent & classification: E. General. - 2p.: 30 cm. - 978-0-11-152394-0 £4.00

The Health Act 2009 (Commencement No. 5) Order 2012 No. 2012/1902 (C.76). - Enabling power: Health Act 2009, s. 40 (1). Bringing into operation various provisions of the 2009 Act on 01.09.2012 in accord. with art. 2. - Issued: 23.07.2012. Made: 18.07.2012. Effect: None. Territorial extent & classification: E. General. - 4p.: 30 cm. - 978-0-11-152752-8 £4.00

The Health and Social Care Act 2008 (Regulated Activities) (Amendment) Regulations 2012 No. 2012/1513. - Enabling power: Health and Social Care Act 2008, ss. 8 (1), 20, 35, 161 (3) (4). - Issued: 14.06.2012. Made: 12.06.2012. Coming into force: In accord. with reg. 1 (2). Effect: S.I. 2010/781 amended. Territorial extent & classification: E. General. - Supersedes draft SI (ISBN 9780111522752) issued on 27.03.2012. - 8p.: 30 cm. - 978-0-11-152536-4 £5.75

The Health and Social Care Act 2012 (Commencement No. 2 and Transitional, Savings and Transitory Provisions) Order 2012 No. 2012/1831 (C.71). - Enabling power: Health and Social Care Act 2012, ss. 304 (10), 306. Bringing into operation various provisions of the 2012 Act in accord. with art. 2. - Issued: 16.07.2012. Made: 11.07.2012. Coming into force: .- Effect: None. Territorial extent & classification: E/W. General. - 16p.: 30 cm. - 978-0-11-152699-6 £5.75

The Health and Social Care Act 2012 (Commencement No. 3, Transitional, Savings and Transitory Provisions and Amendment) Order 2012 No. 2012/2657 (C.107). - Enabling power: Health and Social Care Act 2012, ss. 304 (10), 306. Bringing into operation various provisions of the 2012 Act on 01.11.2012 in accord. with art. 2. - Issued: 25.10.2012. Made: 22.10.2012. Effect: 2012 c.7; S.I. 2912/1831 (C.71) amended. Territorial extent & classification: E. General. - 12p.: 30 cm. - 978-0-11-152990-4 £5.75

The Health Education England (Establishment and Constitution) Order 2012 No. 2012/1273. - Enabling power: National Health Service Act 2006, ss. 28 (1) (2) (4), 272 (7) (8). - Issued: 18.05.2012. Made: 15.05.2012. Laid: 18.05.2012. Coming into force: 28.06.2012. Effect: None. Territorial extent & classification: E. General. - 4p.: 30 cm. - 978-0-11-152438-1 £4.00

The Health Education England Regulations 2012 No. 2012/1290. - Enabling power: National Health Service Act 2006, ss. 29 (2), 272 (7) (8), sch. 6, paras 5, 13. - Issued: 18.05.2012. Made: 15.05.2012. Laid: 18.05.2012. Coming into force: 28.06.2012. Effect: None. Territorial extent & classification: E. General. - 12p.: 30 cm. - 978-0-11-152448-0 £5.75

The Health Research Authority (Amendment) Regulations 2012 No. 2012/1108. - Enabling power: National Health Service Act 2006, ss. 272 (7) (8), sch. 6, paras 5, 13. - Issued: 23.04.2012. Made: 17.04.2012. Laid: 23.04.2012. Coming into force: 28.05.2012. Effect: S.I. 2011/2341 amended. Territorial extent & classification: E. General. - 12p.: 30 cm. - 978-0-11-152365-0 £5.75

The Health Research Authority (Establishment and Constitution) Amendment Order 2012 No. 2012/1109. - Enabling power: National Health Service Act 2006, ss. 28 (1) (2) (4), 272 (7) (8), 273 (1). - Issued: 23.04.2012. Made: 17.04.2012. Laid: 23.04.2012. Coming into force: 28.05.2012. Effect: S.I. 1990/2024; 2000/89; 2011/2323 amended. Territorial extent & classification: E. General. - 4p.: 30 cm. - 978-0-11-152366-7 £4.00

The Health Service Commissioner for England (Special Health Authorities) Order 2012 No. 2012/3072. - Enabling power: Health Service Commissioners Act 1993, s. 2 (5) (b) (6). - Issued: 19.12.2012. Made: 12.12.2012. Laid: 19.12.2012. Coming into force: 17.01.2013. Effect: None. Territorial extent & classification: E. General. - 2p.: 30 cm. - 978-0-11-153246-1 £4.00

The Imperial College Healthcare National Health Service Trust (Establishment) and the Hammersmith Hospitals National Health Service Trust and the St Mary's National Health Service Trust (Dissolution) (Amendment) Order 2012 No. 2012/755. - Enabling power: National Health Service Act 2006, ss. 25 (1), 273 (1). - Issued: 13.03.2012. Made: 07.03.2012. Coming into force: 01.04.2012. Effect: S.I. 2007/2755 amended. Territorial extent & classification: E. General. - 2p.: 30 cm. - 978-0-11-152183-0 £4.00

The Isle of Wight National Health Service Trust (Establishment) Order 2012 No. 2012/786. - Enabling power: National Health Service Act 2006, ss. 25 (1), 272 (7), sch. 4, para. 5. - Issued: 15.03.2012. Made: 10.03.2012. Coming into force: 01.04.2012. Effect: None. Territorial extent & classification: E. General. - 2p.: 30 cm. - 978-0-11-152197-7 £4.00

The National Health Service (Charges for Drugs and Appliances) Amendment Regulations 2012 No. 2012/470. - Enabling power: National Health Service Act 2006, ss. 172, 272 (7) (8). - Issued: 27.02.2012. Made: 22.02.2012. Laid: 27.02.2012. Coming into force: 01.04.2012. Effect: S.I. 2000/620 amended. Territorial extent & classification: E. General. - 4p.: 30 cm. - 978-0-11-152056-7 £4.00

The National Health Service (Charges to Overseas Visitors) Amendment Regulations 2012 No. 2012/1586. - Enabling power: National Health Service Act 2006, ss. 175, 272 (7) (8). - Issued: 25.06.2012. Made: 19.06.2012. Laid: 25.06.2012. Coming into force: 01.10.2012. Effect: S.I. 2011/1556 amended. Territorial extent & classification: E. General. - 4p.: 30 cm. - 978-0-11-152567-8 £4.00

The National Health Service (Clinical Commissioning Groups) Regulations 2012 No. 2012/1631. - Enabling power: National Health Service Act 2006, ss. 14A (4),14C (3), 14E (3), 14G (4), 14H (2), 14L (6), 14N, 272 (7) (8), sch 1A, para. 2 (2) & Health and Social Care Act 2012, s. 304 (9) (10), sch. 6, para. 8. - Issued: 26.06.2012. Made: 21.06.2012. Laid: 26.06.2012. Coming into force: In accord. with reg. 1 (1). Effect: None. Territorial extent & classification: E. General. - 16p.: 30 cm. - 978-0-11-152574-6 £5.75

The National Health Service Commissioning Board and Clinical Commissioning Groups (Responsibilities and Standing Rules) Regulations 2012 No. 2012/2996. - Enabling power: Mental Health Act 1983, ss. 117 (2E) (2G) & National Health Service Act 2006, ss. 3 (1B), 3A (3), 3B (1), 6E, 223E (3), 223J (3), 272 (7) & Health and Social Care Act 2012, s. 75. - Issued: 05.12.2012. Made: 03.12.2012. Laid: 05.12.2012. Coming into force: In accord. with reg. 1. Effect: None. Territorial extent & classification: E. General. - 52p.: 30 cm. - 978-0-11-153158-7 £9.75

The National Health Service (Functions of Strategic Health Authorities and Primary Care Trusts and Administration Arrangements) (England) (Amendment) Regulations 2012 No. 2012/417. - Enabling power: National Health Service Act 2006, ss. 7 (1), 8, 272 (7), 273 (1) (4). - Issued: 21.02.2012. Made: 16.02.2012. Laid: 21.02.2012. Coming into force: 01.04.2012. Effect: S.I. 2002/2375 amended. Territorial extent & classification: E. General. - 4p.: 30 cm. - 978-0-11-152039-0 £4.00

The National Health Service (Local Pharmaceutical Services) (Amendment) Regulations 2012 No. 2012/1467. - Enabling power: National Health Service Act 2006, s. 272 (7) (8) (a), sch. 12, para. 3. - Issued: 08.06.2012. Made: 07.06.2012. Laid: 08.06.2012. Coming into force: 01.07.2012. Effect: S.I. 2006/552 amended. Territorial extent & classification: E. General. - 2p.: 30 cm. - 978-0-11-152512-8 £4.00

The National Health Service (Optical Charges and Payments) (Amendment) Regulations 2012 No. 2012/515. - Enabling power: National Health Service Act 2006, s. 115 (3) (b), 179, 272 (7) (8). - Issued: 29.02.2012. Made: 23.02.2012. Laid: 29.02.2012. Coming into force: 01.04.2012. Effect: S.I. 1997/818 amended. Territorial extent & classification: E. General. - 4p.: 30 cm. - 978-0-11-152075-8 £4.00

The National Health Service (Pharmaceutical Services) Amendment Regulations 2012 No. 2012/1399. - Enabling power: National Health Service Act 2006, ss. 126, 129, 272 (7) (8). - Issued: 30.05.2012. Made: 28.05.2012. Laid: 30.05.2012. Coming into force: 01.07.2012. Effect: S.I. 2005/641 amended. Territorial extent & classification: E. General. - Revoked by SI 2012/1909 (ISBN 9780111527566). - 2p.: 30 cm. - 978-0-11-152490-9 £4.00

The National Health Service (Pharmaceutical Services) Regulations 2012 No. 2012/1909. - Enabling power: National Health Service Act 2006, ss. 8, 22, 126, 128A, 129, 130, 132, 148, 150A, 151 (5) (7), 154, 159 (9), 160, 162, 163 (3), 164, 172, 182, 272 (7) (8) & Health Act 2009, s. 37 (1). - Issued: 23.07.2012. Made: 18.07.2012. Laid: 23.07.2012. Coming into force: 01.09.2012. Effect: S.I. 1996/707 amended in relation to Eng. & S.I. 1997/908; 2000/618, 620; 2002/888, 2016; 2004/291, 627; 2006/552; 2009/309 amended & S.I. 2002/2469; 2003/1937; 2004/1771; 2005/848; 2006/562; 2007/2951, 3101; 2008/653, 1700, 2683; 2010/231 partially revoked in relation to Eng. & S.I. 2005/1015, 3315, 3491; 2006/552, 562, 913, 1056, 1501, 3373; 2007/674; 2008/1514; 2009/309, 599, 2205; 2010/22, 231, 914 partially revoked & S.I. 1992/664; 1995/3091; 1996/703; 1998/674 revoked in relation to Eng. & S.I. 2005/641, 1501; 2008/683; 2009/3340; 2011/2136; 2012/1399 revoked. Territorial extent & classification: E. General. - This SI has been corrected by SI 2012/2371 (ISBN 9780111528778) which is being sent free of charge to all known recipients of 2009/1909. - 184p.: 30 cm. - 978-0-11-152756-6 £26.75

The National Health Service (Pharmaceutical Services) Regulations 2012 (Amendment) Regulations 2012 No. 2012/2371. - Enabling power: National Health Service Act 2006, ss. 126, 129, 130, 132, 272 (7) (8). - Issued: 17.09.2012. Made: 12.09.2012. Laid: 17.09.2012. Coming into force: 01.11.2012. Effect: S.I. 2012/1909 amended. Territorial extent & classification: E. General. - This Statutory Instrument has been made in consequence of defects in S.I. 2012/1909 (ISBN 9780111527566) and is being issued free of charge to all known recipients of that Statutory Instrument. - 4p.: 30 cm. - 978-0-11-152877-8 £4.00

The National Health Service (Primary Dental Services) (Amendments Related to Units of Dental Activity) Regulations 2012 No. 2012/2273. - Enabling power: National Health Service Act 2006, ss. 104, 109, 272 (7). - Issued: 07.09.2012. Made: 03.09.2012. Laid: 07.09.2012. Coming into force: 01.11.2012. Effect: S.I. 2005/3361, 3373 amended. Territorial extent & classification: E. General. - 2p.: 30 cm. - 978-0-11-152855-6 £4.00

The National Health Service (Primary Dental Services) (Miscellaneous Amendments) Regulations 2012 No. 2012/502. - Enabling power: National Health Service Act 2006, ss. 14 (2) (b), 19 (2) (b), 104, 109, 176, 272 (7) (8). - Issued: 28.02.2012. Made: 23.02.2012. Laid: 28.02.2012. Coming into force: 01.04.2012. Effect: S.I. 2005/3361, 3373, 3477; 2006/596 amended. Territorial extent & classification: E. General. - This Statutory instrument rectifies a defect in S.I. 2011/1182 (ISBN 9780111510940) and is being issued free of charge to all known recipients of that Statutory Instrument. - 8p.: 30 cm. - 978-0-11-152063-5 £4.00

The National Health Service (Primary Medical Services) (Miscellaneous Amendments) Regulations 2012 No. 2012/970. - Enabling power: National Health Service Act 2006, ss. 85, 89, 94, 272 (7) (8). - Issued: 02.04.2012. Made: 28.03.2012. Laid: 02.04.2012. Coming into force: 30.04.2010. Effect: S.I. 2004/291, 627 amended. Territorial extent & classification: E. General. - 20p.: 30 cm. - 978-0-11-152310-0 £5.75

The National Health Service (Quality Accounts) Amendment Regulations 2012 No. 2012/3081. - Enabling power: Health Act 2009, ss. 8, 9 (5), 10 (3). - Issued: 14.12.2012. Made: 10.12.2012. Laid: 14.12.2012. Coming into force: In accord. with reg. 1 (2). Effect: S.I. 2010/279 amended. Territorial extent & classification: E. General. - 8p.: 30 cm. - 978-0-11-153214-0 £5.75

The National Health Service (Travel Expenses and Remission of Charges) Amendment Regulations 2012 No. 2012/1650. - Enabling power: National Health Service Act 2006, ss. 182, 183, 184, 272 (7). - Issued: 28.06.2012. Made: 25.06.2012. Laid: 28.06.2012. Coming into force: 01.08.2012. Effect: S.I. 2003/2382 amended. Territorial extent & classification: E. General. - 2p.: 30 cm. - 978-0-11-152589-0 £4.00

The National Health Service Trust Development Authority (Establishment and Constitution) Order 2012 No. 2012/901. - Enabling power: National Health Service Act 2006, ss. 28 (1) (2) (4), 272 (7) (8). - Issued: 27.03.2012. Made: 22.03.2012. Laid: 27.03.2012. Coming into force: 01.06.2012. Effect: None. Territorial extent & classification: E. General. - 4p.: 30 cm. - 978-0-11-152281-3 £4.00

The National Health Service Trust Development Authority Regulations 2012 No. 2012/922. - Enabling power: National Health Service Act 2006, ss. 29 (2), 272 (7) (8), sch. 6, paras 5, 13. - Issued: 27.03.2012. Made: 22.03.2012. Laid: 27.03.2012. Coming into force: 01.06.2012. Effect: None. Territorial extent & classification: E. General. - 12p.: 30 cm. - 978-0-11-152284-4 £5.75

The National Health Service Trusts (Originating Capital) Order 2012 No. 2012/779. - Enabling power: National Health Service Act 2006, ss. 272 (7), sch. 5, para. 1 (1). - Issued: 15.03.2012. Made: 08.03.2012. Coming into force: 31.03.2012. Effect: None. Territorial extent & classification: E. General. - 2p.: 30 cm. - 978-0-11-152195-3 £4.00

The National Patient Safety Agency (Amendment) Regulations 2012 No. 2012/1425. - Enabling power: National Health Service Act 2006, ss. 272 (7) (8), 273 (1), sch. 6, para. 5. - Issued: 07.06.2012. Made: 29.05.2012. Laid: 07.06.2012. Coming into force: 09.07.2012. Effect: S.I. 2001/1742 amended. Territorial extent & classification: E. General. - 4p.: 30 cm. - 978-0-11-152494-7 £4.00

The National Patient Safety Agency (Establishment and Constitution) (Amendment) Order 2012 No. 2012/1424. - Enabling power: National Health Service Act 2006, ss. 28 (1) (2) (4), 272 (7) (8), 273 (1). - Issued: 07.06.2012. Made: 29.05.2012. Laid: 07.06.2012. Coming into force: 09.07.2012. Effect: S.I. 2001/1743 amended. Territorial extent & classification: E. General. - 2p.: 30 cm. - 978-0-11-152493-0 £4.00

The NHS Bodies and Local Authorities (Partnership Arrangements, Care Trusts, Public Health and Local Healthwatch) Regulations 2012 No. 2012/3094. - Enabling power: National Health Service Act 2006, ss. 73A (1) (f), 73B (2) (e), 73C (1) (2), 75 (1) to (4), 76 (1), 77 (1) (1A) (1B) (5A) to (5C) (8), 111 (1), 272 (7) (8) & Health and Social Care (Community Health and Standards) Act 2003, s. 115 (1) (2) (4) to (6) & Local Government and Public Involvement in Health Act 2007, ss. 222 (2) (b) (8) (b) (9) (10), 223, 224 (1), 226 (6), 229 (2), 240 (10). - Issued: 17.02.2012. Made: 12.12.2012. Laid: 17.12.2012. Coming into force: In accord. with reg. 1 (2). Effect: S.I. 2000/617; 2010/1743 amended & S.I. 2006/185 revoked with saving & S.I. 2001/3788; 2008/528 revoked. Territorial extent & classification: E. General. - 32p.: 30 cm. - 978-0-11-153247-8 £5.75

The NHS Bodies (Transfer of Trust Property) Order 2012 No. 2012/1512. - Enabling power: National Health Service Act 2006, ss. 213, 217 (2), 272 (7) (8). - Issued: 15.06.2012. Made: 11.06.2012. Laid: 15.06.2012. Coming into force: 16.07.2012. Effect: None. Territorial extent & classification: E. General. - 4p.: 30 cm. - 978-0-11-152540-1 £4.00

The NHS Bodies (Transfer of Trust Property) Order (No. 2) 2012 No. 2012/2755. - Enabling power: National Health Service Act 2006, ss. 213, 217 (2), 272 (7) (8). - Issued: 06.11.2012. Made: 01.11.2012. Laid: 06.11.2012. Coming into force: 17.12.2012. Effect: None. Territorial extent & classification: E. General. - 4p.: 30 cm. - 978-0-11-153038-2 £4.00

The NHS Foundation Trusts (Trust Funds: Appointment of Trustees) Amendment (No. 2) Order 2012 No. 2012/2950. - Enabling power: National Health Service Act 2006, ss. 51 (1) (2), 64 (5) (6), 273 (1). - Issued: 29.11.2012. Made: 26.11.2012. Coming into force: 01.12.2012. Effect: S.I. 2007/1766 amended & S.I. 2012/2891 revoked. Territorial extent & classification: E. General. - This Order supersedes SI 2012/2891 (ISBN 9780111530863) published on 21 November and is being issued free of charge to all known recipients of that statutory instrument. - 4p.: 30 cm. - 978-0-11-153124-2 £4.00

The NHS Foundation Trusts (Trust Funds: Appointment of Trustees) Amendment Order 2012 No. 2012/2891. - Enabling power: National Health Service Act 2006, ss. 51 (1) (2), 64 (5) (6), 273 (1). - Issued: 21.11.2012. Made: 15.11.2012. Coming into force: 01.12.2012. Effect: S.I. 2007/1766 amended. Territorial extent & classification: E. General. - Superseded by S.I. 2012/2950 (ISBN 9780111531242) issued 29.11.2012. - 2p.: 30 cm. - 978-0-11-153086-3 £4.00

The Oxfordshire Learning Disability National Health Service Trust (Dissolution) Order 2012 No. 2012/2570. - Enabling power: National Health Service Act 2006, ss. 25 (1), 272 (7), 273 (1), sch. 4, para. 28 (1). - Issued: 16.10.2012. Made: 09.10.2012. Coming into force: 01.11.2012. Effect: S.I. 1992/2574 revoked. Territorial extent & classification: E. General. - 2p.: 30 cm. - 978-0-11-152934-8 £4.00

The Royal Brompton and Harefield NHS Foundation Trust (Transfer of Trust Property) Order 2012 No. 2012/950. - Enabling power: National Health Service Act 2006, ss. 51 (3), 64 (5) (b). - Issued: 29.03.2012. Made: 27.03.2012. Coming into force: 01.04.2012. Effect: None. Territorial extent & classification: E. General. - 2p.: 30 cm. - 978-0-11-152298-1 £4.00

The Royal Wolverhampton Hospitals National Health Service Trust (Establishment) Amendment Order 2012 No. 2012/1837. - Enabling power: National Health Service Act 2006, ss. 25 (1), 272 (7) (8), 273 (1). - Issued: 17.07.2012. Made: 11.07.2012. Coming into force: 15.08.2012. Effect: S.I. 1993/2574 amended/partially revoked. Territorial extent & classification: E. General. - 2p.: 30 cm. - 978-0-11-152704-7 £4.00

The Scarborough and North East Yorkshire Health Care National Health Service Trust (Dissolution) Order 2012 No. 2012/1514. - Enabling power: National Health Service Act 2006, ss. 25 (1), 272 (7), 273 (1), sch. 4, para. 28. - Issued: 15.06.2012. Made: 10.06.2012. Coming into force: 01.07.2012. Effect: S.I. 1991/2398 revoked. Territorial extent & classification: E. General. - 2p.: 30 cm. - 978-0-11-152541-8 £4.00

The Shropshire Community National Health Service Trust (Establishment) Amendment Order 2012 No. 2012/2317. - Enabling power: National Health Service Act 2006, ss. 25 (1), 272 (7), 273 (1). - Issued: 13.09.2012. Made: 08.09.2012. Coming into force: 17.09.2012. Effect: S.I. 2011/1519 amended. Territorial extent & classification: E. General. - 2p.: 30 cm. - 978-0-11-152873-0 £4.00

The South London Healthcare National Health Service Trust (Appointment of Trust Special Administrator) Order 2012 No. 2012/1806. - Enabling power: National Health Service Act 2006, ss. 65B (1) (3), 272 (7). - Issued: 13.07.2012. Made: 11.07.2012. Laid: 13.07.2012. Coming into force: 16.07.2012. Effect: None. Territorial extent & classification: E. General. - 2p.: 30 cm. - 978-0-11-152695-8 £4.00

The South London Healthcare National Health Service Trust (Extension of Time for Trust Special Administrator to Provide a Draft Report) Order 2012 No. 2012/1824. - Enabling power: National Health Service Act 2006, ss. 65J (2), 272 (7). - Issued: 13.07.2012. Made: 11.07.2012. Laid: 13.07.2012. Coming into force: 16.07.2012. Effect: None. Territorial extent & classification: E. General. - 2p.: 30 cm. - 978-0-11-152694-1 £4.00

The Special Health Authorities (Establishment and Constitution Orders) Amendment Order 2012 No. 2012/476. - Enabling power: National Health Service Act 2006, ss. 28 (1) (2) (4), 272 (7) (8), 273 (1). - Issued: 27.02.2012. Made: 22.02.2012. Laid: 27.02.2012. Coming into force: 01.04.2012. Effect: S.I. 1999/220; 2001/1743; 2004/585; 2010/2841 amended. Territorial extent & classification: E. General. - 4p.: 30 cm. - 978-0-11-152058-1 £4.00

The Torbay and Southern Devon Health and Care National Health Service Trust (Establishment) Order 2012 No. 2012/788. - Enabling power: National Health Service Act 2006, ss. 25 (1), 272 (7), sch. 4, para. 5. - Issued: 15.03.2012. Made: 10.03.2012. Coming into force: 01.04.2012. Effect: None. Territorial extent & classification: E. General. - 2p.: 30 cm. - 978-0-11-152198-4 £4.00

The Trafford Healthcare National Health Service Trust (Dissolution) Order 2012 No. 2012/803. - Enabling power: National Health Service Act 2006, ss. 25 (1), 272 (7), 273 (1), sch. 4, para. 28 (1). - Issued: 15.03.2012. Made: 12.03.2012. Coming into force: 01.04.2012. Effect: S.I. 1994/180 amended. Territorial extent & classification: E. General. - 2p.: 30 cm. - 978-0-11-152205-9 £4.00

National Health Service, England and Wales

The Health Service Branded Medicines (Control of Prices and Supply of Information) Amendment Regulations 2012 No. 2012/2791. - Enabling power: National Health Service Act 2006, ss. 262 (1), 263 (1), 266 (1) (a), 272 (7). - Issued: 09.11.2012. Made: 06.11.2012. Laid: 09.11.2012. Coming into force: 01.01.2013. Effect: S.I. 2008/3258 amended & S.I. 2011/2955 revoked. Territorial extent & classification: E/W/S/NI. General. - 2p.: 30 cm. - 978-0-11-153053-5 £4.00

The National Health Service Pension Scheme and Injury Benefits (Amendment) Regulations 2012 No. 2012/610. - Enabling power: Superannuation Act 1972, ss. 10 (1) (2), 12 (1) (2) (4), sch. 3. - Issued: 05.03.2012. Made: 28.02.2012. Laid: 05.03.2012. Coming into force: 01.04.2012. Effect: S.I. 1995/300, 866; 2000/619; 2008/653 amended. Territorial extent & classification: E/W. General. - 12p.: 30 cm. - 978-0-11-152105-2 £5.75

The Personal Injuries (NHS Charges) (Amounts) Amendment Regulations 2012 No. 2012/387. - Enabling power: Health and Social Care (Community Health and Standards) Act 2003, ss. 153 (2) (5), 195 (1) (2). - Issued: 20.02.2012. Made: 15.02.2012. Laid: 20.02.2012. Coming into force: 01.04.2012. Effect: S.I. 2007/115 amended (with saving). Territorial extent & classification: E/W. General. - 2p.: 30 cm. - 978-0-11-152033-8 £4.00

National Health Service, Scotland

The Health Service Branded Medicines (Control of Prices and Supply of Information) Amendment Regulations 2012 No. 2012/2791. - Enabling power: National Health Service Act 2006, ss. 262 (1), 263 (1), 266 (1) (a), 272 (7). - Issued: 09.11.2012. Made: 06.11.2012. Laid: 09.11.2012. Coming into force: 01.01.2013. Effect: S.I. 2008/3258 amended & S.I. 2011/2955 revoked. Territorial extent & classification: E/W/S/NI. General. - 2p.: 30 cm. - 978-0-11-153053-5 £4.00

National Health Service, Wales

The Carers Strategies (Wales) (Amendment) Regulations 2012 No. 2012/282 (W.46). - Enabling power: Carers Strategies (Wales) Measure 2010, ss. 5 (1) (2), 10 (2). - Issued: 23.02.2012. Made: 03.02.2012. Laid before the National Assembly for Wales: 07.02.2012. Coming into force: 29.02.2012. Effect: S.I. 2011/2939 (W.315) amended/partially revoked. Territorial extent & classification: W. General. - In English and Welsh. Welsh title: Rheoliadau Strategaethau ar gyfer Gofalwyr (Cymru) (Diwygio) 2012. - 4p.: 30 cm. - 978-0-348-10687-9 £4.00

The Children and Families (Wales) Measure 2010 (Commencement No. 4) Order 2012 No. 2012/191 (W.30) (C.5). - Enabling power: Children and Families (Wales) Measure 2010, ss. 74 (2), 75 (3). Bringing into operation various provisions of the 2010 Measure on 27.01.2012, 31.01.2012, 28.02.2012, 31.03.2012 in accord. with arts. 2, 3, 4, 5. - Issued: 10.02.2012. Made: 26.01.2012. Effect: None. Territorial extent & classification: W. General. - In English and Welsh. Welsh title: Gorchymyn Mesur Plant a Theuluoedd (Cymru) 2010 (Cychwyn Rhif 4) 2012. - 8p.: 30 cm. - 978-0-348-10549-0 £5.75

The Health Act 2009 (Commencement No. 3) (Wales) Order 2012 No. 2012/1288 (W.165)(C.45). - Enabling power: Health Act 2009, ss. 40 (2) (b). Bringing into operation various provisions of the 2009 Act on 01.06.2012; 03.12.2012; 06.04.2015 in accord. with art 2. - Issued: 31.05.2012. Made: 14.05.2012. Effect: None. Territorial extent & classification: W. General. - In English and Welsh. Welsh title: Gorchymyn Deddf Iechyd 2009 (Cychwyn Rhif 3) (Cymru) 2012. - 8p.: 30 cm. - 978-0-348-10610-7 £5.75

The Integrated Family Support Teams (Composition of Teams and Board Functions) (Wales) Regulations 2012 No. 2012/202 (W.33). - Enabling power: Children and Families (Wales) Measure 2010, ss. 60 (1), 62 (2). - Issued: 23.02.2012. Made: 30.01.2012. Laid before the National Assembly for Wales: 31.01.2012. Coming into force: 28.02.2012. Effect: S.I. 2010/1690 (W.159) revoked. Territorial extent & classification: W. General. - In English & Welsh. Welsh title: Rheoliadau Timau Integredig Cymorth i Deuluoedd (Cyfansoddiad Timau a Swyddogaethau Byrddau) (Cymru) 2012. - 8p.: 30 cm. - 978-0-348-10690-9 £5.75

The Integrated Family Support Teams (Family Support Functions) (Wales) Regulations 2012 No. 2012/204 (W.34). - Enabling power: Children and Families (Wales) Measure 2010, s. 58 (2). - Issued: 16.02.2012. Made: 30.01.2012. Laid before the National Assembly for Wales: 31.01.2012. Coming into force: 28.02.2012. Effect: S.I. 2010/1701 (W.162); 2011/191 (W. 36) revoked. Territorial extent & classification: W. General. - In English & Welsh. Welsh title: Rheoliadau Timau Integredig Cymorth i Deuluoedd (Swyddogaethau Cymorth i Deuluoedd) (Cymru) 2012. - 8p.: 30 cm. - 978-0-348-10554-4 £5.75

The Integrated Family Support Teams (Review of Cases) (Wales) Regulations 2012 No. 2012/205 (W.35). - Enabling power: Children and Families (Wales) Measure 2010, ss. 63 (a), 74 (2) & Children Act 1989, ss. 26 (1) (2), 104 (4), 104A (1) (2). - Issued: 23.02.2012. Made: 30.01.2012. Laid before the National Assembly for Wales: 31.01.2012. Coming into force: 28.02.2012. Effect: S.I. 2010/1700 (W.161) partially revoked. Territorial extent & classification: W. General. - In English & Welsh. Welsh title: Rheoliadau Timau Integredig Cymorth i Deuluoedd (Adolygu Achosion) (Cymru) 2012. - 8p.: 30 cm. - 978-0-348-10691-6 £5.75

The National Health Service (Dental Charges) (Wales) (Amendment) Regulations 2012 No. 2012/1893 (W.229). - Enabling power: National Health Service (Wales) Act 2006, ss. 125, 203 (9) (10). - Issued: 02.08.2012. Made: 17.07.2012. Laid before the National Assembly for Wales: 19.07.2012. Coming into force: 01.09.2012. Effect: S.I. 2006/491 (W.60) amended. Territorial extent & classification: W. General. - In English and Welsh: Rheoliadau'r Gwasanaeth Iechyd Gwladol (Ffioedd Deintyddol) (Cymru) (Diwygio) 2012. - 4p.: 30 cm. - 978-0-348-10643-5 £4.00

The National Health Service (Optical Charges and Payments) (Amendment) (Wales) Regulations 2012 No. 2012/684 (W.92). - Enabling power: National Health Service (Wales) Act 2006, ss. 128, 129, 203 (9) (10). - Issued: 28.03.2012. Made: 04.03.2012. Laid before the National Assembly for Wales: 06.03.2012. Coming into force: 01.04.2012. Effect: S.I. 1997/818 amended in relation to Wales. Territorial extent & classification: W. General. - In English and Welsh. Welsh title: Rheoliadau'r Gwasanaeth Iechyd Gwladol (Ffioedd a Thaliadau Optegol)(Diwygio)(Cymru) 2012. - 8p.: 30 cm. - 978-0-348-10567-4 £5.75

The National Health Service (Primary Dental Services) (Amendments Related to Units of Dental Activity) (Wales) Regulations 2012 No. 2012/2572 (W.283). - Enabling power: National Health Service (Wales) Act 2006, ss. 61, 66, 203 (9). - Issued: 29.10.2012. Made: 09.10.2012. Laid before the National Assembly for Wales: 11.10.2012. Coming into force: 01.11.2012. Effect: S.I. 2006/490 (W.59) amended. Territorial extent & classification: W. General. - In English and Welsh: Rheoliadau'r Gwasanaeth Iechyd Gwladol (Gwasanaethau Deintyddol Sylfaenol) (Diwygiadau sy'n Ymwneud ag Unedau o Weithgaredd Deintyddol) (Cymru) 2012. - 4p.: 30 cm. - 978-0-348-10661-9 £4.00

The National Health Service (Travelling Expenses and Remission of Charges) (Wales) (Amendment) Regulations 2012 No. 2012/800 (W.109). - Enabling power: National Health Service (Wales) Act 2006, ss. 130, 131, 132 & 203 (9) (10). - Issued: 05.04.2012. Made: 09.03.2012. Laid before the National Assembly for Wales: 14.03.2012. Coming into force: 09.04.2012. Effect: S.I. 2007/1104 (W.116) amended. Territorial extent & classification: W. General. - In English and Welsh. Welsh title: Rheoliadau'r Gwasanaeth Iechyd Gwladol (Treuliau Teithio a Pheidio â Chodi Tâl) (Cymru) (Diwygio) 2012. - 4p.: 30 cm. - 978-0-348-10588-9 £4.00

The Velindre National Health Service Trust (Establishment) Amendment Order 2012 No. 2012/1262 (W.157). - Enabling power: National Health Service (Wales) Act 2006, ss. 18 (1), 204 (1), sch. 3, para. 5. - Issued: 17.05.2012. Made: 08.05.2012. Coming into force: 01.06.2012. Effect: S.I. 1993/2328 amended. Territorial extent & classification: W. General. - 4p.: 30 cm. - 978-0-348-10602-2 £4.00

The Velindre National Health Service Trust Shared Services Committee (Wales) Regulations 2012 No. 2012/1261 (W.156). - Enabling power: National Health Service (Wales) Act 2006, ss. 19 (1), 203 (9) (10), sch. 3, para. 4 (1) (f). - Issued: 17.05.2012. Made: 08.05.2012. Laid before the National Assembly for Wales: 11.05.2012. Coming into force: 01.06.2012. Effect: None. Territorial extent & classification: W. General. - In English and Welsh. Welsh title: Rheoliadau Pwyllgor Cydwasanaethau Ymddiriedolaeth Gwasanaeth Iechyd Gwladol Felindre (Cymru) 2012. - 12p.: 30 cm. - 978-0-348-10603-9 £5.75

The Welsh Ministers and Local Health Boards (Transfer of Property, Rights and Liabilities) (Wales) Order 2012 No. 2012/1429 (W.179). - Enabling power: National Health Service (Wales) Act 2006, ss. 203 (9) (10), sch. 3, para. 9. - Issued: 19.06.2012. Made: 29.05.2012. Coming into force: 01.06.2012. Effect: None. Territorial extent & classification: W. General. - In English and Welsh. Welsh title: Gorchymyn Gweinidogion Cymru a Byrddau Iechyd Lleol (Trosglwyddo Eiddo, Hawliau a Rhwymedigaethau) (Cymru) 2012. - 8p.: 30 cm. - 978-0-348-10626-8 £5.75

Nationality

The Immigration and Nationality (Cost Recovery Fees) Regulations 2012 No. 2012/813. - Enabling power: Immigration, Asylum and Nationality Act 2006, ss. 51 (3), 52 (1) (3) (6). - Issued: 16.03.2012. Made: 13.03.2012. Laid: 15.03.2012. Coming into force: 06.04.2012. Effect: S.I. 2011/790 revoked. Territorial extent & classification: E/W/S/NI. General. - 20p.: 30 cm. - 978-0-11-152217-2 £5.75

The Immigration and Nationality (Cost Recovery Fees) Regulations 2012 No. 2012/2276. - Enabling power: Immigration, Asylum and Nationality Act 2006, ss. 51 (3), 52 (1) (3) (6). - Issued: 07.09.2012. Made: 04.09.2012. Laid: 06.09.2012. Coming into force: 01.10.2012. Effect: S.I. 2012/813 amended. Territorial extent & classification: E/W/S/NI. General. - 4p.: 30 cm. - 978-0-11-152858-7 £4.00

The Immigration and Nationality (Fees) Regulations 2012 No. 2012/971. - Enabling power: Immigration, Asylum and Nationality Act 2006, ss. 51 (3), 52 (1) (3) (6). - Issued: 03.04.2012. Made: 27.03.2012. Coming into force: 06.04.2012. Effect: S.I. 2011/1055 revoked. Territorial extent & classification: E/W/S/NI. General. - Supersedes draft S.I. (ISBN 9780111520154) issued 14.02.2012. With correction slip dated May 2012. - 20p.: 30 cm. - 978-0-11-152313-1 £5.75

Northern Ireland

The District Electoral Areas Commissioner (Northern Ireland) Order 2012 No. 2012/3074. - Enabling power: Northern Ireland Act 1998, s. 84 (1) (3). - Issued: 19.12.2012. Made: 12.12.2012. Coming into force: In accord. with art. 1 (2). Effect: S.I. 1984/360 amended. Territorial extent & classification: NI. General. - Supersedes draft SI (ISBN 9780111529430) issued 17.07.2012. - 4p.: 30 cm. - 978-0-11-153243-0 £4.00

The Jobseeker's Allowance (Members of the Forces) (Northern Ireland) (Amendment) Regulations 2012 No. 2012/2569. - Enabling power: S.I. 1995/2705 (NI. 15), arts 2 (2), 24 (1) (3), 36 (2). - Issued: 15.10.2012. Made: 10.10.2012. Laid: 15.10.2012. Coming into force: 05.11.2012. Effect: S.I. 1997/932 amended. Territorial extent & classification: NI. General. - 2p.: 30 cm. - 978-0-11-152935-5 £4.00

The Northern Ireland Act 1998 (Devolution of Policing and Justice Functions) Order 2012 No. 2012/2595. - Enabling power: Northern Ireland Act 1998, ss. 86 (1), (3A) (4). - Issued: 24.10.2012. Made: 17.10.2012. Coming into force: In accord. with art. 1 (2). Effect: 1954 c.33 (NI),1993 c.8; 1999 c.33; 2003 c.6; 2006 c.48; 2007 c.30; 2009 c.26; 2010 c.4, 17, 23, 25 & S.I. 1981/228 (NI. 8); 1994/426 (NI.1); 1996/3159 (NI.23); 2000/1787; 2005/2078; 2007/912 (NI.6); 2009/2615 amended. Territorial extent & classification: NI. General. - Supersedes draft SI (ISBN 9780111525203) issued 14.06.2012. - 16p.: 30 cm. - 978-0-11-152970-6 £5.75

Official secrets

The Official Secrets Act 1989 (Prescription) (Amendment) Order 2012 No. 2012/2900. - Enabling power: Official Secrets Act 1989, s. 12 (1) (g), 13 (1). - Issued: 22.11.2012. Made: 14.11.2012. Coming into force: 22.11.2012. Effect: S.I. 1990/200 amended. Territorial extent & classification: E/W/NI (However, the Act provides that the offences (except those under section 8(1), (4) and (5)) can be committed by a Crown servant or British citizen anywhere in the UK). - Supersedes draft SI (ISBN 9780111526071) issued on 02.07.2012. - 2p.: 30 cm. - 978-0-11-153092-4 £4.00

Offshore installations

The Offshore Installations (Safety Zones) (No. 2) Order 2012 No. 2012/941. - Enabling power: Petroleum Act 1987, s. 22 (1) (2). - Issued: 29.03.2012. Made: 20.03.2012. Coming into force: 01.05.2012. Effect: None. Territorial extent & classification: E/W/S. General. - 2p.: 30 cm. - 978-0-11-152294-3 £4.00

The Offshore Installations (Safety Zones) (No. 3) Order 2012 No. 2012/1574. - Enabling power: Petroleum Act 1987, s. 22 (1) (2). - Issued: 21.06.2012. Made: 18.06.2012. Coming into force: 13.07.2012. Effect: None. Territorial extent & classification: E/W/S. General. - 2p.: 30 cm. - 978-0-11-152564-7 £4.00

The Offshore Installations (Safety Zones) (No. 4) Order 2012 No. 2012/3159. - Enabling power: Petroleum Act 1987, s. 22 (1) (2). - Issued: 28.12.2012. Made: 20.12.2012. Coming into force: 10.01.2013. Effect: S.I. 2005/3227; 2012/1574 amended. Territorial extent & classification: E/W/S. General. - 4p.: 30 cm. - 978-0-11-153283-6 £4.00

The Offshore Installations (Safety Zones) Order 2012 No. 2012/503. - Enabling power: Petroleum Act 1987, s. 22 (1) (2). - Issued: 29.02.2012. Made: 23.02.2012. Coming into force: 23.03.2012. Effect: None. Territorial extent & classification: E/W/S. General. - 2p.: 30 cm. - 978-0-11-152068-0 £4.00

The Offshore (Oil and Gas) Installation and Pipeline Abandonment Fees Regulations 2012 No. 2012/949. - Enabling power: Petroleum Act 1987, s. 22 (1) (2). - Issued: 04.04.2012. Made: 26.03.2012. Laid: 29.03.2012. Coming into force: 20.04.2012. Effect: None. Territorial extent & classification: E/W/S/NI. General. - 4p.: 30 cm. - 978-0-11-152315-5 £4.00

Oil tax

The Qualifying Oil Fields Order 2012 No. 2012/3153. - Enabling power: Corporation Tax Act 2010, s. 349. - Issued: 21.12.2012. Made: 20.12.2012. Coming into force: 21.12.2012. In accord. with art. 1. Effect: 2010 c.4 amended & S.I. 2010/610 revoked. Territorial extent & classification: E/W/S/NI. General. - Approved by Parliament. Supersedes draft SI (ISBN 9780111530788) issued on 14.11.2012. - 8p.: 30 cm. - 978-0-11-153277-5 £5.75

Open spaces

The Royal Parks and Other Open Spaces (Amendment) (No. 2) Regulations 2012 No. 2012/957. - Enabling power: Parks Regulation (Amendment) Act 1926, s. 2 (1) (1A). - Issued: 30.03.2012. Made: 27.03.2012. Coming into force: 28.03.2012 in accord. with reg. 1. Effect: S.I. 1997/1639 amended. Territorial extent and classification: All of the UK but there is no effect anywhere other than England. General. - Supersedes draft S.I. (ISBN 9780111519936) issued 09.02.2012. - 4p.: 30 cm. - 978-0-11-152308-7 £4.00

The Royal Parks and Other Open Spaces (Amendment) Regulations 2012 No. 2012/98. - Enabling power: Parks Regulation (Amendment) Act 1926, s. 2 (1). - Issued: 18.01.2012. Made: 13.01.2012. Coming into force: 14.01.2012 in accord. with reg. 1. Effect: S.I. 1997/1639 amended. Territorial extent and classification: Extends to UK but applies only to E. General. - Supersedes draft S.I. (ISBN 9780111516867) issued 16.11.2011. - 2p.: 30 cm. - 978-0-11-151925-7 £4.00

Overseas territories

The Afghanistan (United Nations Measures) (Overseas Territories) Order 2012 No. 2012/1758. - Enabling power: United Nations Act 1946, s. 1; Saint Helena Act 1833, s. 112 & British Settlements Acts 1887 and 1945. - Issued: 17.07.2012. Made: 10.07.2012. Laid: 17.07.2012. Coming into force: 07.08.2012. Effect: None. Territorial extent & classification: Anguilla, British Antarctic Territory, British Indian Ocean Territory, Cayman Islands, Falkland Islands, Montserrat, Pitcairn (including Henderson, Ducie and Oeno Islands), St. Helena, Ascension and Tristan da Cunha, South Georgia & South Sandwich Islands, The Sovereign Base Areas of Akrotiri & Dhekelia in the Island of Cyprus, Turks & Caicos Islands, Virgin Islands. General. - 20p.: 30 cm. - 978-0-11-152687-3 £5.75

The Al-Qaida (United Nations Measures) (Overseas Territories) (Amendment) Order 2012 No. 2012/3064. - Enabling power: United Nations Act 1946, s. 1 & Saint Helena Act 1833, s. 112 & British Settlements Acts 1887 and 1945. - Issued: 19.12.2012. Made: 12.12.2012. Laid: 19.12.2012. Coming into force: 09.01.2013. Effect: S.I. 2012/1757 amended. Territorial extent & classification: Anguilla, British Antarctic Territory, British Indian Ocean Territory, Cayman Islands, Falkland Islands, Montserrat, Pitcairn (including Henderson, Ducie and Oeno Islands), St. Helena, Ascension and Tristan da Cunha, South Georgia & South Sandwich Islands, The Sovereign Base Areas of Akrotiri & Dhekelia in the Island of Cyprus, Turks & Caicos Islands, Virgin Islands. General. - 2p.: 30 cm. - 978-0-11-153230-0 £4.00

The Al-Qaida (United Nations Measures) (Overseas Territories) Order 2012 No. 2012/1757. - Enabling power: United Nations Act 1946, s. 1; Saint Helena Act 1833, s. 112 & British Settlements Acts 1887 and 1945. - Issued: 17.07.2012. Made: 10.07.2012. Laid: 17.07.2012. Coming into force: 07.08.2012. Effect: S.I. 2002/112, 266 revoked. Territorial extent & classification: Anguilla, British Antarctic Territory, British Indian Ocean Territory, Cayman Islands, Falkland Islands, Montserrat, Pitcairn (including Henderson, Ducie and Oeno Islands), St. Helena, Ascension and Tristan da Cunha, South Georgia & South Sandwich Islands, The Sovereign Base Areas of Akrotiri & Dhekelia in the Island of Cyprus, Turks & Caicos Islands, Virgin Islands. General. - 20p.: 30 cm. - 978-0-11-152683-5 £5.75

The Burma (Restrictive Measures) (Overseas Territories) (Suspension) Order 2012 No. 2012/2596. - Enabling power: Saint Helena Act 1833, s. 112 & British Settlements Acts 1887 & 1945. - Issued: 22.10.2012. Made: 17.10.2012. Laid: 18.10.2012. Coming into force: 19.10.2012. Effect: S.I. 2009/3008 amended. Territorial extent & classification: Anguilla, British Antarctic Territory, British Indian Ocean Territory, Cayman Islands, Falkland Islands, Montserrat, Pitcairn, Henderson, Ducie and Oeno Islands, St Helena, Ascension and Tristan da Cunha, South Georgia and the South Sandwich Islands, The Sovereign Base Areas of Akrotiri and Dhekelia in the Island of Cyprus, Turks and Caicos Islands, Virgin Islands. General. - 2p.: 30 cm. - 978-0-11-152976-8 £4.00

The Cote d'Ivoire (Sanctions) (Overseas Territories) Order 2012 No. 2012/3067. - Enabling power: United Nations Act 1946, s. 1 & Saint Helena Act 1833, s. 112 & British Settlements Acts 1887, 1945. - Issued: 19.12.2012. Made: 12.12.2012. Laid: 19.12.2012. Coming into force: 09.01.2013. Effect: SI 2005/242; 2006/610 revoked. Territorial extent & classification: Anguilla, British Antarctic Territory, British Indian Ocean Territory, Cayman Islands, Falkland Islands, Montserrat, Pitcairn, Henderson, Ducie and Oeno Islands, St. Helena, Ascension & Tristan da Cunha, South Georgia and South Sandwich Islands, The Sovereign Base Areas of Akrotiri and Dhekelia in the Island of Cyprus, Turks and Caicos Islands, Virgin Islands. General. - 20p.: 30 cm. - 978-0-11-153229-4 £5.75

The Democratic People's Republic of Korea (Sanctions) (Overseas Territories) Order 2012 No. 2012/3066. - Enabling power: United Nations Act 1946, s. 1 & Saint Helena Act 1833, s. 112 & British Settlements Acts 1887, 1945. - Issued: 19.12.2012. Made: 12.12.2012. Laid: 19.12.2012. Coming into force: 09.01.2013. Effect: SI 2006/3327 revoked. Territorial extent & classification: Anguilla, British Antarctic Territory, British Indian Ocean Territory, Cayman Islands, Falkland Islands, Montserrat, Pitcairn, Henderson, Ducie and Oeno Islands, St. Helena, Ascension & Tristan da Cunha, South Georgia and South Sandwich Islands, The Sovereign Base Areas of Akrotiri and Dhekelia in the Island of Cyprus, Turks and Caicos Islands, Virgin Islands. General. - 20p.: 30 cm. - 978-0-11-153235-5 £5.75

The Democratic Republic of the Congo (Restrictive Measures) (Overseas Territories) (Amendment) Order 2012 No. 2012/2750. - Enabling power: United Nations Act 1946, s. 1 & Saint Helena Act 1833, s. 112 & British Settlements Acts 1887 and 1945. - Issued: 14.11.2012. Made: 07.11.2012. Laid: 14.11.2012. Coming into force: 05.11.2012. Effect: S.I. 2003/2627 amended. Territorial extent & classification: E/W/S/NI. General. - 4p.: 30 cm. - 978-0-11-153064-1 £4.00

The Eritrea (Sanctions) (Overseas Territories) Order 2012 No. 2012/2751. - Enabling power: United Nations Act 1946, s. 1 & Saint Helena Act 1833, s. 112 & British Settlements Acts 1887, 1945. - Issued: 14.11.2012. Made: 07.11.2012. Laid: 14.11.2012. Coming into force: 05.12.2012. Effect: None. Territorial extent & classification: Anguilla, Bermuda, British Antarctic Territory, British Indian Ocean Territory, Cayman Islands, Falkland Islands, Montserrat, Pitcairn, Henderson, Ducie and Oeno Islands, St. Helena and Dependencies, South Georgia and South Sandwich Islands, The Sovereign Base Areas of Akrotiri and Dhekelia in the Island of Cyprus, Turks and Caicos Islands, Virgin Islands. General. - 20p.: 30 cm. - 978-0-11-153067-2 £5.75

The Guinea-Bissau (Sanctions) (Overseas Territories) Order 2012 No. 2012/3068. - Enabling power: United Nations Act 1946, s. 1 & Saint Helena Act 1833, s. 112 & British Settlements Acts 1887, 1945. - Issued: 19.12.2012. Made: 12.12.2012. Laid: 19.12.2012. Coming into force: 09.01.2013. Effect: None. Territorial extent & classification: Anguilla, British Antarctic Territory, British Indian Ocean Territory, Cayman Islands, Falkland Islands, Montserrat, Pitcairn, Henderson, Ducie and Oeno Islands, St. Helena, Ascension & Tristan da Cunha, South Georgia and South Sandwich Islands, The Sovereign Base Areas of Akrotiri and Dhekelia in the Island of Cyprus, Turks and Caicos Islands, Virgin Islands. General. - 12p.: 30 cm. - 978-0-11-153234-8 £5.75

The Iran (Restrictive Measures) (Overseas Territories) (Amendment) Order 2012 No. 2012/1389. - Enabling power: Saint Helena Act 1833, s. 112 & British Settlement Acts 1887 and 1945. - Issued: 07.06.2012. Made: 30.05.2012. Laid: 07.06.2012. Coming into force: 28.06.2012. Effect: S.I. 2011/2989 amended. Territorial extent & classification: Anguilla, British Antarctic Territory, British Indian Ocean Territory, Cayman Islands, Falkland Islands, Montserrat, Pitcairn (including Henderson, Ducie and Oeno Islands), St Helena, Ascension and Tristan da Cunha, South Georgia and the South Sandwich Islands, the Sovereign Base Areas of Akrotiri and Dhekelia, the Turks and Caicos Islands and the Virgin Islands. General. - 12p.: 30 cm. - 978-0-11-152496-1 £5.75

The Iran (Restrictive Measures) (Overseas Territories) Order 2012 No. 2012/1756. - Enabling power: United Nations Act 1946, s. 1 & Saint Helena Act 1833, s. 112 & British Settlement Acts 1887 and 1945. - Issued: 11.07.2012. Made: 10.07.2012. Laid: 11.07.2012. Coming into force: 12.07.2012. Effect: S.I. 2007/282, 2132 revoked. Territorial extent & classification: Anguilla, British Antarctic Territory, British Indian Ocean Territory, Cayman Islands, Falkland Islands, Montserrat, Pitcairn (including Henderson, Ducie and Oeno Islands), St Helena, Ascension and Tristan da Cunha, South Georgia and the South Sandwich Islands, the Sovereign Base Areas of Akrotiri and Dhekelia, the Turks and Caicos Islands and the Virgin Islands. General. - 30p.: 30 cm. - 978-0-11-152660-6 £5.75

The Liberia (Restrictive Measures) (Overseas Territories) (Amendment) Order 2012 No. 2012/2749. - Enabling power: United Nations Act 1946, s. 1 & Saint Helena Act 1833, s. 112 & British Settlements Acts 1887 & 1945. - Issued: 14.11.2012. Made: 07.11.2012. Laid: 14.11.2012. Coming into force: 05.12.2012. Effect: S.I. 2004/347 amended. Territorial extent & classification: Anguilla, British Antarctic Territory, British Indian Ocean Territory, Cayman Islands, Falkland Islands, Montserrat, Pitcairn, Henderson, Ducie and Oeno Islands, St. Helena and Dependencies, South Georgia and South Sandwich Islands, The Sovereign Base Areas of Akrotiri and Dhekelia in the Island of Cyprus, Turks and Caicos Islands, Virgin Islands. General. - EC note: This Order gives effect to the modified arms embargo measures provided for in UN Security Council Resolution 1903 (2009) and Council Decision 2010/129/CFSP. - 4p.: 30 cm. - 978-0-11-153066-5 £4.00

The Libya (Restrictive Measures) (Overseas Territories) (Amendment) Order 2012 No. 2012/356. - Enabling power: United Nations Act 1946, s. 1 & Saint Helena Act 1833, s. 112 & British Settlements Acts 1887 & 1945. - Issued: 17.02.2012. Made: 15.02.2012. Laid: 16.02.2012. Coming into force: 17.02.2012. Effect: S.I. 2011/1080 amended. Territorial extent & classification: Overseas Territories/E/W/S/NI. General. - EC note: This Order amends the 2011 Order to give effect to a decision of the UN Sanctions Committee (of 16.12.2011) to remove the Central Bank of Libya and the Libyan Arab Foreign Bank from the scope of the partial asset freeze imposed in UNSCR 2009 (2011) and to reflect Council Regulation 1360/2011 adopted by Council of European Union (on 20.12.2011) giving effect to that decision in the EU. - 2p.: 30 cm. - 978-0-11-152029-1 £4.00

The Pitcairn (Court of Appeal) Order 2012 No. 2012/1761. - Enabling power: British Settlements Acts 1887 & 1945. - Issued: 17.07.2012. Made: 10.07.2012. Laid: 17.07.2012. Coming into force: 10.08.2012. Effect: None. Territorial extent & classification: Pitcairn, Henderson, Ducie and Oeno Island. General. - 2p.: 30 cm. - 978-0-11-152684-2 £4.00

The Restrictive Measures (Amendment) (Overseas Territories) Order 2012 No. 2012/362. - Enabling power: Saint Helena Act 1833, s. 112 & British Settlement Acts 1887 and 1945 & United Nations Act 1946, s. 1 & Export Control Act 2002, s. 16 (5). - Issued: 17.02.2012. Made: 15.02.2012. Laid: 16.02.2012. Coming into force: 08.03.2012. Effect: 47 SI's amended & S.I. 1992/1303; 1993/2808; 1994/1324; 1995/1032 revoked. Territorial extent & classification: Overseas Territories/E/W/S/NI. General. - 4p.: 30 cm. - 978-0-11-152030-7 £4.00

The Somalia (Sanctions) (Overseas Territories) Order 2012 No. 2012/3065. - Enabling power: United Nations Act 1946, s. 1 & Saint Helena Act 1833, s. 112 & British Settlements Acts 1887, 1945. - Issued: 19.12.2012. Made: 12.12.2012. Laid: 19.12.2012. Coming into force: 09.01.2013. Effect: SI 2002/2631 revoked. Territorial extent & classification: Anguilla, British Antarctic Territory, British Indian Ocean Territory, Cayman Islands, Falkland Islands, Montserrat, Pitcairn, Henderson, Ducie and Oeno Islands, St. Helena, Ascension & Tristan da Cunha, South Georgia and South Sandwich Islands, The Sovereign Base Areas of Akrotiri and Dhekelia in the Island of Cyprus, Turks and Caicos Islands, Virgin Islands. General. - 20p.: 30 cm. - 978-0-11-153228-7 £5.75

The Sudan and South Sudan (Restrictive Measures) (Overseas Territories) Order 2012 No. 2012/361. - Enabling power: Saint Helena Act 1833, s. 112 & British Settlements Acts 1887 & 1945. - Issued: 22.02.2012. Made: 15.02.2012. Laid: 22.02.2012. Coming into force: 14.03.2012. Effect: S.I. 2004/349 revoked. Territorial extent & classification: Anguilla, British Antarctic Territory, British Indian Ocean Territory, Cayman Is., Falkland Is., Montserrat, Pitcairn, Henderson, Ducie & Oeno Is., St Helena, Ascension & Tristan da Cunha, South Georgia & the South Sandwich Is., the Sovereign Base Areas of Akrotiri & Dhekelia (Cyprus), Turks & Caicos Is., Virgin Is. General. - 16p.: 30 cm. - 978-0-11-152035-2 £5.75

The Syria (Restrictive Measures) (Overseas Territories) (Amendment) Order 2012 No. 2012/3069. - Enabling power: Saint Helena Act 1833, s. 112 & British Settlements Acts 1887, 1945. - Issued: 19.12.2012. Made: 12.12.2012. Laid: 19.12.2012. Coming into force: 09.01.2013. Effect: SI 2012/1755 amended. Territorial extent & classification: Anguilla, British Antarctic Territory, British Indian Ocean Territory, Cayman Islands, Falkland Islands, Montserrat, Pitcairn, Henderson, Ducie and Oeno Islands, St. Helena, Ascension & Tristan da Cunha, South Georgia and South Sandwich Islands, The Sovereign Base Areas of Akrotiri and Dhekelia in the Island of Cyprus, Turks and Caicos Islands, Virgin Islands. General. - 8p.: 30 cm. - 978-0-11-153236-2 £5.75

The Syria (Restrictive Measures) (Overseas Territories) Order 2012 No. 2012/1755. - Enabling power: Saint Helena Act 1833, s. 112 & British Settlements Acts 1887 & 1945. - Issued: 11.07.2012. Made: 10.07.2012. Laid: 11.07.2012. Coming into force: 12.07.2012. Effect: S.I. 2011/1678 revoked. Territorial extent & classification: Anguilla, British Antarctic Territory, British Indian Ocean Territory, Cayman Is., Falkland Is., Montserrat, Pitcairn, Henderson, Ducie & Oeno Is., St Helena, Ascension Island & Tristan da Cunha, South Georgia & South Sandwich Is., the Sovereign Base Areas of Akrotiri & Dhekelia (Cyprus), Turks & Caicos Is., Virgin Is. General. - EC note: This Order gives effect in the specified overseas territories to measures adopted by the Council Decision 2011/782/CFSP and Council Regulation 36/2012 which repealed and replaced Decision 2011/273/CFSP and Regulation 442/2011. - 28p.: 30 cm. - 978-0-11-152659-0 £5.75

The Zimbabwe (Sanctions) (Overseas Territories) Order 2012 No. 2012/2753. - Enabling power: Saint Helena Act 1833, s. 112 & British Settlements Acts 1887 and 1945. - Issued: 14.11.2012. Made: 07.11.2012. Laid: 14.11.2012. Coming into force: 05.12.2012. Effect: S.I. 2002/1077, 2627; 2004/1111; 2005/3183 revoked. Territorial extent & classification: Anguilla, Bermuda, British Antarctic Territory, British Indian Ocean Territory, Cayman Islands, Falkland Islands, Montserrat, Pitcairn, Henderson, Ducie and Oeno Islands, St. Helena and Dependencies, South Georgia and South Sandwich Islands, The Sovereign Base Areas of Akrotiri and Dhekelia in the Island of Cyprus, Turks and Caicos Islands, Virgin Islands. General. - 20p.: 30 cm. - 978-0-11-153071-9 £5.75

Parliament

House of Commons Members' Fund Resolution 2012 No. 2012/1866. - Enabling power: House of Commons Members' Fund Act 1948, s. 3 & House of Commons Members' Fund and Parliamentary Pensions Act 1981, s. 2. - Issued: 18.07.2012. Made: 13.06.2012. Coming into force: In accordance with the resolution. Effect: S.I. 2005/657 amended. Territorial extent & classification: E/W/S/NI. General. - 2p.: 30 cm. - 978-0-11-152721-4 £4.00

The Insolvency Act 1986 (Disqualification from Parliament) Order 2012 No. 2012/1544. - Enabling power: Enterprise Act 2002, s. 266 (3). - Issued: 19.05.2012. Made: 13.06.2012. Coming into force: 14.06.2012 in accord. with art. 1. Effect: 1986 c. 45 amended. Territorial extent & classification: E/W/S/NI. General. - 4p.: 30 cm. - 978-0-11-152554-8 £4.00

Pensions

The Armed Forces and Reserve Forces (Compensation Scheme) (Amendment) Order 2012 No. 2012/1573. - Enabling power: Armed Forces (Pensions and Compensation) Act 2004, s. 1 (2). - Issued: 21.06.2012. Made: 16.06.2012. Laid: 21.06.2012. Coming into force: 21.07.2012. Effect: S.I. 2011/517 amended. Territorial extent & classification: E/W/S/NI. General. - 4p.: 30 cm. - 978-0-11-152563-0 £4.00

The Armed Forces (Enhanced Learning Credit Scheme and Further and Higher Education Commitment Scheme) Order 2012 No. 2012/1796. - Enabling power: Armed Forces (Pensions and Compensation) Act 2004, s. 1 (1) (3). - Issued: 12.07.2012. Made: 09.07.2012. Laid: 12.07.2012. Coming into force: 02.09.2012. Effect: None. Territorial extent & classification: E/W/S/NI. General. - 12p.: 30 cm. - 978-0-11-152657-6 £5.75

The Automatic Enrolment (Earnings Trigger and Qualifying Earnings Band) Order 2012 No. 2012/1506. - Enabling power: Pensions Act 2008, ss. 3 (1) (c), 5 (1) (c), 13 (1) (a) (b). - Issued: 15.06.2012. Made: 14.06.2012. Coming into force: 15.06.2012. Effect: 2008 c. 30 amended. Territorial extent & classification: E/W/S. General. - 4p.: 30 cm. - 978-0-11-152548-7 £4.00

The Automatic Enrolment (Miscellaneous Amendments) Regulations 2012 No. 2012/215. - Enabling power: Pension Schemes Act 1993, ss. 111A (15) (b), 181,182 (2) (3) & Pensions Act 1995, ss. 49 (8), 124 (1), 174 (2) (3) & Pensions Act 2008, ss. 2 (3), 3 (2) (5) (6), 4 (1) to (3) (5), 5 (4) (6) (8), 6 (1) (b) (2), 7 (5), 10, 11, 12, 15 (1) (2), 16 (2), 22 (4), 23 (1) (b) (c) (3) (6), 24 (1) (a) (b), 29 (2) (4), 30 (5) (7A) (8), 37 (3), 38 (2) (3) (4), 40 (4), 41 (4) (5), 43 (3), 52 (3), 54 (3), 60, 99, 144 (2) (4). - Issued: 01.02.2012. Made: 31.01.2012. Laid: 01.02.2012. Coming into force: 01.06.2012. Effect: S.I. 2010/4, 5 amended & S.I. 2010/772 amended/part revoked. Territorial extent & classification: E/W/S. General. - 20p.: 30 cm. - 978-0-11-151972-1 £5.75

The Automatic Enrolment (Offshore Employment) Order 2012 No. 2012/1388. - Enabling power: Pensions Act 2008, ss. 97 (1) (4) (5), 144 (2). - Issued: 06.06.2012. Made: 30.05.2012. Coming into force: 01.07.2012. Effect: None. Territorial extent & classification: E/W/S. General. - Supersedes draft S.I. (ISBN 9780111519882) issued 07.02.2012. - 4p.: 30 cm. - 978-0-11-152498-5 £4.00

The Compromise Agreements (Description of Person) (Automatic Enrolment) Order 2012 No. 2012/212. - Enabling power: Pensions Act 2008, ss. 58 (6) (d), 99. - Issued: 01.02.2012. Made: 31.01.2012. Laid: 01.02.2012. Coming into force: 01.07.2012. Effect: None. Territorial extent & classification: E/W/S. General. - 2p.: 30 cm. - 978-0-11-151967-7 £4.00

The Employers' Duties (Implementation) (Amendment) Regulations 2012 No. 2012/1813. - Enabling power: Pensions Act 2008, ss. 12, 29 (2), 30 (8), 99, 144 (2) (4). - Issued: 12.07.2012. Made: 10.07.2012. Laid: 12.07.2012. Coming into force: 01.10.2012. Effect: S.I. 2010/4 amended. Territorial extent & classification: E/W/S. General. - 8p.: 30 cm. - 978-0-11-152681-1 £5.75

The Guaranteed Minimum Pensions Increase Order 2012 No. 2012/693. - Enabling power: Pension Schemes Act 1993, s. 109 (4). - Issued: 09.03.2012. Made: 03.03.2012. Coming into force: 06.04.2012. Effect: None. Territorial extent & classification: E/W/S. General. - Supersedes draft S.I. (ISBN 9780111519509) issued 30.01.2012. - 2p.: 30 cm. - 978-0-11-152158-8 £4.00

The Judicial Pensions (Contributions) Regulations 2012 No. 2012/516. - Enabling power: District Judges (Magistrates' Courts) Pensions Act (Northern Ireland) 1960, s. 8A (1) (6) (7) & Judicial Pensions Act 1981, s. 33ZA (1) (6) (7) & Judicial Pensions and Retirement Act 1993, ss. 9A (1), 29. - Issued: 08.02.2012. Made: 20.02.2012. Laid: 08.03.2012. Coming into force: 01.04.2012. Effect: S.I. 1995/639 amended. Territorial extent & classification: E/W/S/NI. General. - 4p.: 30 cm. - 978-0-11-152088-8 £4.00

The Judicial Pensions (European Court of Human Rights) (Amendment) Order 2012 No. 2012/489. - Enabling power: Human Rights Act 1998, s. 18. - Issued: 08.03.2012. Made: 20.02.2012. Laid: 08.03.2012. Coming into force: 01.04.2012. Effect: S.I. 1998/2768 amended. Territorial extent & classification: E/W/S/NI. General. - 2p.: 30 cm. - 978-0-11-152060-4 £4.00

The Naval, Military and Air Forces Etc. (Disablement and Death) Service Pensions (Amendment) Order 2012 No. 2012/359. - Enabling power: Social Security (Miscellaneous Provisions) Act 1977, ss. 12 (1), 24 (3). - Issued: 22.02.2012. Made: 15.02.2012. Laid: 22.02.2012. Coming into force: 09.04.2012. Effect: S.I. 2006/606 amended. Territorial extent & classification: E/W/S/NI. General. - 12p.: 30 cm. - 978-0-11-152036-9 £5.75

The Occupational and Personal Pension Schemes (Automatic Enrolment) (Amendment) (No. 2) Regulations 2012 No. 2012/1477. - Enabling power: Pensions Act 2004, ss. 292A (a), 315 (2), 318 (1). - Issued: 11.06.2012. Made: 08.06.2012. Laid: 11.06.2012. Coming into force: 02.07.2012. Effect: S.I. 2010/772 amended. Territorial extent & classification: E/W/S. General. - 2p.: 30 cm. - 978-0-11-152515-9 £4.00

The Occupational and Personal Pension Schemes (Automatic Enrolment) (Amendment No.3) Regulations 2012 No. 2012/2691. - Enabling power: Pensions Act 2008, s. 16 (3) (c), 99, 144 (2) (4). - Issued: 20.10.2012. Made: 25.10.2012. Coming into force: 01.11.2012. Effect: S.I. 2010/772 amended. Territorial extent & classification: E/W/S. General. - Supersedes draft SI (ISBN 9780111526163) issued 02.07.2012. - 2p.: 30 cm. - 978-0-11-153016-0 £4.00

The Occupational and Personal Pension Schemes (Automatic Enrolment) (Amendment) Regulations 2012 No. 2012/1257. - Enabling power: Pension Schemes Act 1993, ss. 111A (15) (b), 181,182 (2) (3); Pensions Act 1995, ss. 49 (8), 124 (1), 174 (2) (3) and Pensions Act 2008, ss. 2 (3), 3 (2) (5) (6), 5 (2) (4) (6) to (8), 6 (1) (b) (2), 7 (4) (5) (6), 8 (2) (b) (3) to (6), 9 (3), 10, 15 (1) (2), 16 (2) (3) (c), 17 (1) (c), 18 (c), 22 (4) to (7), 23 (1) (b) (c) (3) (6), 24 (1) (a) (b), 25, 27, 28 (1) (2) (b) (3A) (4) to (7), 30 (5) (6) (c) (7A), 33 (2), 37 (3), 60, 96 (2), 98, 99, 144 (2) (4). - Issued: 15.05.2012. Made: 08.05.2012. Coming into force: 01.07.2012. Effect: S.I. 2010/772 amended. Territorial extent & classification: E/W/S. General. - Supersedes draft S.I. (ISBN 9780111519875) issued on 07.02.2012. - 16p.: 30 cm. - 978-0-11-152420-6 £5.75

The Occupational and Personal Pension Schemes (Levies - Amendment) Regulations 2012 No. 2012/539. - Enabling power: Pension Schemes Act 1993, ss. 175 (1) to (3), 181 (1), 182 (2) & Pensions Act 2004, ss. 117 (1) (3), 315 (2), 318 (1). - Issued: 01.03.2012. Made: 25.02.2012. Laid: 01.03.2012. Coming into force: 01.04.2012. Effect: S.I. 2005/626, 842 amended. Territorial extent & classification: E/W/S. General. - 4p.: 30 cm. - 978-0-11-152084-0 £4.00

The Occupational and Personal Pension Schemes (Prescribed Bodies) Regulations 2012 No. 2012/1817. - Enabling power: Pension Schemes Act 1993, ss. 12A (4) (5), 113 (1) (3A), 181 (1); Pensions Act 1995, ss. 67D (4) (5), 73B (4) (a), 75 (5), 75A (4) (5), 119, 124 (1) & Pensions Act 2004, ss. 230 (3), 318 (1). - Issued: 12.07.2012. Made: 11.07.2012. Laid: 12.07.2012. Coming into force: 09.08.2012. Effect: S.I. 1987/1110; 1996/1172, 1655, 3126, 3128; 2000/1403; 2005/678, 3377; 2006/759 amended. Territorial extent & classification: E/W/S. General. - 4p.: 30 cm. - 978-0-11-152682-8 £4.00

The Occupational Pension Schemes (Contracting-out and Modification of Schemes) (Amendment) Regulations 2012 No. 2012/542. - Enabling power: Pension Schemes Act 1993, ss. 12A (4), 16 (3), 181 (1), 182 (3) & Pensions Act 1995, s. 68 (2) (e), 124 (1), 174 (3). - Issued: 29.02.2012. Made: 25.02.2012. Laid: 29.02.2012. Coming into force: 06.04.2012. Effect: S.I. 1996/1172; 2006/759 amended. Territorial extent & classification: E/W/S. General. - Regulation 2(3) of this instrument is made in consequence of a defect in S.I. 2011/1294 (ISBN 9780111511558) and this instrument is being issued free of charge to all known recipients of the S.I. 2011/1294. - 4p.: 30 cm. - 978-0-11-152082-6 £4.00

The Occupational Pension Schemes (Disclosure of Information) (Amendment) Regulations 2012 No. 2012/1811. - Enabling power: Pension Schemes Act 1993, s. 113 (1) (2) (e) (3), 181 (1), 182 (2) (3). - Issued: 12.07.2012. Made: 11.07.2012. Laid: 12.07.2012. Coming into force: 01.10.2012. Effect: S.I. 1996/1655 amended. Territorial extent & classification: E/W/S. General. - 2p.: 30 cm. - 978-0-11-152678-1 £4.00

The Occupational Pensions (Revaluation) Order 2012 No. 2012/2952. - Enabling power: Pension Schemes Act 1993, sch. 3, para. 2 (1). - Issued: 29.11.2012. Made: 26.11.2012. Laid: 29.11.2012. Coming into force: 01.01.2013. Effect: None. Territorial extent & classification: E/W/S. General. - 2p.: 30 cm. - 978-0-11-153127-3 £4.00

The Pension Protection Fund and Occupational Pension Schemes (Levy Ceiling and Compensation Cap) Order 2012 No. 2012/528. - Enabling power: Pensions Act 2004, ss. 178 (1) (6), 315 (2) (5), sch. 7, paras. 26 (7), 27 (2) (3). - Issued: 29.02.2012. Made: 25.02.2012. Laid: 29.02.2012. Coming into force: In accord. with art. 1 (2). Effect: S.I. 2006/3105; 2008/217; 2009/200; 2010/1; 2011/169, 840, 841 revoked (on 01.04.2012). Territorial extent & classification: E/W/S. General. - 4p.: 30 cm. - 978-0-11-152079-6 £4.00

The Pension Protection Fund (Miscellaneous Amendments) (No. 2) Regulations 2012 No. 2012/3083. - Enabling power: Pensions Act 2004, ss. 143 (3) (4) (5), 143A (5), 151 (4), 156 (1), 185 (4) (a), 203 (1), 207 (1) (2) (5) (a), 307 (1) (b), 315 (2) (4) (5), 318 (1). - Issued: 13.12.2012. Made: 11.12.2012. Laid: 13.12.2012. Coming into force: 24.01.2012. Effect: S.I. 2005/441, 590, 669, 672, 674, 2184; 2007/865; 2012/1688 amended. Territorial extent & classification: E/W/S. General. - This Statutory Instrument has been made in consequence of a defect in SI 2012/1688 (ISBN 9780111526064) and is being issued free of charge to all known recipients of that Statutory Instrument. - 16p.: 30 cm. - 978-0-11-153216-4 £5.75

The Pension Protection Fund (Miscellaneous Amendments) Regulations 2012 No. 2012/1688. - Enabling power: Pensions Act 2004, ss. 143 (3) (4) (5), 143A (5), 151 (4), 156 (1), 185 (4) (a), 203 (1), 207 (1) (2) (5) (a), 213 (1) (2) (b), 307 (1) (b) (2) (b), 315 (2) (4) (5), 318 (1). - Issued: 02.07.2012. Made: 28.06.2012. Laid: 02.07.2012. Coming into force: 23.07.2012. Effect: S.I. 2005/441, 590, 669, 672, 674, 2024, 2184; 2007/865 amended. Territorial extent & classification: E/W/S. General. - With correction slip dated July 2012. This SI has been corrected by SI 2012/3083 (ISBN 9780111532164) which is being sent free of charge to all known recipients of 2012/1688. - 16p.: 30 cm. - 978-0-11-152606-4 £5.75

The Pensions Act 2004 (Disclosure of Restricted Information by the Pensions Register - Amendment) Order 2012 No. 2012/691. - Enabling power: Pensions Act 2004, s. 86 (2) (a) (iii). - Issued: 08.03.2012. Made: 03.03.2012. Laid: 08.03.2012. Coming into force: 06.04.2012. Effect: 2004 c.27 amended. Territorial extent & classification: E/W/S. General. - 2p.: 30 cm. - 978-0-11-152146-5 £4.00

The Pensions Act 2007 (Commencement No. 4) (Amendment) Order 2012 No. 2012/911 (C.29). - Enabling power: Pensions Act 2007, s. 30 (2) (b). - Issued: 23.03.2012. Made: 20.03.2012. Effect: S.I. 2011/1267 amended. Territorial extent & classification: E/W/S. General. - This Statutory Instrument, in articles 2(a) and (c), corrects a defect in SI 2011/1267 (ISBN 9780111511336) and is being issued free of charge to all known recipients of that Statutory Instrument. - 2p.: 30 cm. - 978-0-11-152270-7 £4.00

The Pensions Act 2008 (Abolition of Protected Rights) (Consequential Amendments) (No. 2) (Amendment) Order 2012 No. 2012/709. - Enabling power: Pensions Act 2008, s. 145 (1) (2). - Issued: 09.03.2012. Made: 03.03.2012. Coming into force: Immediately before 06.04.2012 in accord. with art. 1 (2). Effect: S.I. 2011/1730 amended. Territorial extent & classification: E/W/S. General. - Supersedes draft SI (ISBN 9780111519493) issued on 30.01.2012. - 4p.: 30 cm. - 978-0-11-152161-8 £4.00

The Pensions Act 2008 (Commencement No. 12) Order 2012 No. 2012/683 (C.17). - Enabling power: Pensions Act 2008, s. 149 (1) (6). Bringing into operation various provisions of the 2008 Act on 06.03.2012, 07.03.2012 in accord. with art. 2. - Issued: 06.03.2012. Made: 03.03.2012. Coming to force: -. Effect: None. Territorial extent & classification: E/W/S. General. - 4p.: 30 cm. - 978-0-11-152139-7 £4.00

The Pensions Act 2008 (Commencement No. 13) Order 2012 No. 2012/1682 (C.65). - Enabling power: Pensions Act 2008, ss. 144 (4), 149 (1). Bringing into operation various provisions of the 2008 Act on 30.06.2012 in accord. with art. 2. - Issued: 29.06.2012. Made: 28.06.2012. Coming to force: -. Effect: None. Territorial extent & classification: E/W/S. General. - 8p.: 30 cm. - 978-0-11-152605-7 £4.00

The Pensions Act 2008 (Commencement No. 14 and Supplementary Provisions) Order 2012 No. 2012/2480 (C.97). - Enabling power: Pensions Act 2008, ss. 144 (2) (a), 149 (1). Bringing into operation various provisions of the 2008 Act on 01.10.2012 in accord. with art. 2. - Issued: 28.09.2012. Made: 27.09.2012. Coming to force: -. Effect: None. Territorial extent & classification: E/W/S. General. - 8p.: 30 cm. - 978-0-11-152904-1 £4.00

The Pensions Act 2011 (Commencement No. 2) Order 2012 No. 2012/682 (C.16). - Enabling power: Pensions Act 2011, s. 38 (4). Bringing into operation various provisions of the 2011 Act on 06.03.2012, in accord. with art. 2. - Issued: 06.03.2012. Made: 03.03.2012. Coming to force: -. Effect: None. Territorial extent & classification: E/W/S. General. - 2p.: 30 cm. - 978-0-11-152138-0 £4.00

The Pensions Act 2011 (Commencement No. 3) Order 2012 No. 2012/1681 (C.64). - Enabling power: Pensions Act 2011, s. 38 (4) (5). Bringing into operation various provisions of the 2011 Act on 30.06.2012 & 23.07.2012, in accord. with arts 2 & 3. - Issued: 29.06.2012. Made: 28.06.2012. Coming to force: -. Effect: None. Territorial extent & classification: E/W/S. General. - 4p.: 30 cm. - 978-0-11-152600-2 £4.00

The Pensions Increase (Review) Order 2012 No. 2012/782. - Enabling power: Social Security Pensions Act 1975, s. 59 (1) (2) (5) (5ZA). - Issued: 13.03.2012. Made: 08.03.2012. Laid: 12.03.2012. Coming into force: 09.04.2012. Effect: None. Territorial extent & classification: E/W/S/NI. General. - 8p.: 30 cm. - 978-0-11-152194-6 £4.00

The Pensions (Institute and Faculty of Actuaries and Consultation by Employers - Amendment) Regulations 2012 No. 2012/692. - Enabling power: Pension Schemes Act 1993, ss. 19 (4) (c), 73 (4) (b), 97 (1), 101AF (1), 101D (4) (b), 181 (1), 182 (2) (3), sch. 2, para. 5 (3C) (c) & Pension Schemes (Northern Ireland) Act 1993, s. 177 (2), sch. 1, para. 5 (3C) (c) (4A) & Pensions Act 1995, ss. 37 (3) (a), 47 (5) (b), 67C (7) (a) (ii), 75 (5), 124 (1), 174 (2) (3) & Pensions Act 2004, ss. 23 (10), 143 (11) (a) (ii) (a), 156 (6), 179 (2), 259 (1) (2), 260 (1), 315 (2) (4) (5), 318 (1), sch. 5, para. 22 (4) (a). - Issued: 08.03.2012. Made: 03.03.2012. Laid: 08.03.2012. Coming into force: 06.04.2012. Effect: S.I. 1991/167; 1996/1715, 1847, 3128; 1997/784; 1998/1397; S.R. 1998/208; S.I. 2000/1054; 2005/672, 686; 2006/33, 349, 597, 759, 802; 2007/865 amended. Territorial extent & classification: E/W/S/NI. General. - [8]p.: 30 cm. - 978-0-11-152147-2 £4.00

The Personal Injuries (Civilians) Scheme (Amendment) Order 2012 No. 2012/670. - Enabling power: Personal Injuries (Emergency Provisions) Act 1939, ss. 1, 2. - Issued: 08.03.2012. Made: 29.03.2012. Laid: 07.03.2012. Coming into force: 09.04.2012. Effect: S.I. 1983/686 amended. Territorial extent & classification: E/W/S/NI. General. - 8p.: 30 cm. - 978-0-11-152131-1 £5.75

Pensions, England

The Firefighters' Pension Scheme (Amendment) (England) Order 2012 No. 2012/953. - Enabling power: Fire Services Act 1947, s. 26 (1) to (5). - Issued: 29.03.2012. Made: 27.03.2012. Laid: 29.03.2012. Coming into force: 01.04.2012. Effect: S.I. 1992/129 amended in relation to England. Territorial extent & classification: E. General. - 4p.: 30 cm. - 978-0-11-152300-1 £4.00

The Firefighters' Pension Scheme (England) (Amendment) (No. 2) Order 2012 No. 2012/2988. - Enabling power: Fire and Rescue Services Act 2004, ss. 34, 60. - Issued: 05.12.2012. Made: 29.11.2012. Laid: 05.12.2012. Coming into force: 31.12.2012. Effect: S.I. 2006/3432 amended in relation to England. Territorial extent & classification: E. General. - 4p.: 30 cm. - 978-0-11-153143-3 £4.00

The Firefighters' Pension Scheme (England) (Amendment) Order 2012 No. 2012/954. - Enabling power: Fire and Rescue Services Act 2004, ss. 34, 60. - Issued: 29.03.2012. Made: 27.03.2012. Laid: 29.03.2012. Coming into force: 01.04.2012. Effect: S.I. 2006/3432 amended in relation to England. Territorial extent & classification: E. General. - 4p.: 30 cm. - 978-0-11-152301-8 £4.00

Pensions, England and Wales

The Local Government Pension Scheme (Miscellaneous) Regulations 2012 No. 2012/1989. - Enabling power: Superannuation Act 1972, ss. 7, 12, 24. - Issued: 01.08.2012. Made: 27.08.2012. Laid: 01.08.2012. Coming into force: 01.10.2012. Effect: S.I. 2006/2914; 2007/1166; 2008/238, 239 amended. Territorial extent & classification: E/W. General. - 20p.: 30 cm. - 978-0-11-152787-0 £5.75

The Police Pensions (Amendment No. 2) Regulations 2012 No. 2012/2811. - Enabling power: Police Pensions Act 1976, s. 1. - Issued: 13.11.2012. Made: 06.11.2012. Laid: 12.11.2012. Coming into force: 03.12.2012. Effect: S.I. 1987/257; 2006/3415 amended. Territorial extent & classification: E/W. General. - 4p.: 30 cm. - 978-0-11-153063-4 £4.00

The Police Pensions (Amendment No. 3) Regulations 2012 No. 2012/3057. - Enabling power: Police Pensions Act 1976, s. 1. - Issued: 11.12.2012. Made: 05.12.2012. Laid: 10.12.2012. Coming into force: 01.01.2013. Effect: S.I. 1987/257; 2006/3415 amended. Territorial extent & classification: E/W. General. - 8p.: 30 cm. - 978-0-11-153206-5 £4.00

The Police Pensions (Amendment) Regulations 2012 No. 2012/640. - Enabling power: Police Pensions Act 1976, ss. 1 to 7. - Issued: 06.03.2012. Made: 28.02.2012. Laid: 05.03.2012. Coming into force: 01.04.2012. Effect: S.I. 1987/257, 2215; 2006/3415 amended. Territorial extent & classification: E/W. General. - 4p.: 30 cm. - 978-0-11-152118-2 £4.00

The Police Pensions (Descriptions of Service) Order 2012 No. 2012/2954. - Enabling power: Police Pensions Act 1976, s. 11A (1) & Police Act 1996, s. 97A (1). - Issued: 29.11.2012. Made: 26.11.2012. Laid: 28.11.2012. Coming into force: 21.12.2012. Effect: 1976 c.35; 1996 c.16; S.I. 1987/257 amended. Territorial extent & classification: E/W. General. - 4p.: 30 cm. - 978-0-11-153128-0 £4.00

Pensions, Wales

The Firefighters' Pension Scheme (Wales) (Contributions) (Amendment) Order 2012 No. 2012/972 (W.127). - Enabling power: Fire and Rescue Services Act 2004, ss. 34, 60, 62. - Issued: 17.04.2012. Made: 28.03.2012. Laid: 29.04.2012. Coming into force: 01.04.2012. Effect: S.I. 2007/1072 (W.110) amended. Territorial extent & classification: W. General. - In English and Welsh. Welsh language title: Gorchymyn Cynllun Pensiwn y Diffoddwyr Tân (Cymru) (Cyfraniadau) (Diwygio) 2012. - 4p.: 30 cm. - 978-0-348-10596-4 £4.00

The Firefighters' Pension (Wales) Scheme (Contributions) (Amendment) Order 2012 No. 2012/974 (W.128). - Enabling power: Fire Services Act 1947, s. 26 (1). - Issued: 17.04.2012. Made: 28.03.2012. Laid before the National Assembly for Wales: 29.03.2012. Coming into force: 01.04.2012. Effect: S.I. 1992/129 amended. Territorial extent & classification: W. General. - In English and Welsh. Welsh title: Gorchymyn Cynllun Pensiwn y Dynion Tân (Cymru) (Cyfraniadau) (Diwygio) 2012. - 8p.: 30 cm. - 978-0-348-10593-3 £4.00

Pesticides

The Plant Protection Products (Sustainable Use) Regulations 2012 No. 2012/1657. - Enabling power: European Communities Act 1972, s. 2 (2). - Issued: 29.06.2012. Made: 20.06.2012. Laid: 27.06.2012. Coming into force: In accord. with reg. 1. Effect: S.I. 2011/2131; S.R. 2011/295 amended & S.I. 1997/189; S.R. 1997/470 revoked (18.07.2012). Territorial extent & classification: E/W/S/NI. General. - EC note: These Regulations transpose Directive 2009/128/EC establishing a framework for Community action to achieve the sustainable use of pesticides and provide enforcement provisions. - 36p.: 30 cm. - 978-0-11-152598-2 £9.75

Plant health

The Plant Health (Forestry) (Amendment) Order 2012 No. 2012/2707. - Enabling power: Plant Health Act 1967, ss. 2 (1), 3 (1) & European Communities Act 1972, sch. 2, para. 1A. - Issued: 30.10.2012. Made: 29.10.2012 at 1pm. Laid: 29.10.2012. Coming into force: 29.10.2012 & 21.11.2012. In accord. with art .1 (2). Effect: S.I. 2005/2517 amended. Territorial extent & classification: E/W/S. General. - EC note: This Order amends S.I. 2005/2517 to introduce emergency measures to prevent the introduction and spread of Chalara fraxinea T. Kowalski, including its teleomorph Hymenoscyphus pseudoalbidus, a cause of ash dieback. This Order also implements Commission Directive 2008/61/EC which replaced Commission Directive 95/44/EC. - 8p.: 30 cm. - 978-0-11-153017-7 £4.00

Plant health, England

The Plant Health (England) (Amendment) (No. 2) Order 2012 No. 2012/3033. - Enabling power: Plant Health Act 1967, ss. 2 (1), 3 (1). - Issued: 10.12.2012. Made: 05.12.2012. Laid: 06.12.2012. Coming into force: 07.12.2012. Effect: S.I. 2005/2530 amended. Territorial extent & classification: E. General. - 4p.: 30 cm. - 978-0-11-153180-8 £4.00

The Plant Health (England) (Amendment) Order 2012 No. 2012/2922. - Enabling power: Plant Health Act 1967, ss. 2 (1), 3 (1). - Issued: 26.11.2012. Made: 21.11.2012. Laid: 22.11.2012. Coming into force: 14.12.2012. Effect: S.I. 2005/2530 amended. Territorial extent & classification: E. General. - 4p.: 30 cm. - 978-0-11-153115-0 £4.00

The Plant Health (Fees) (England) Regulations 2012 No. 2012/745. - Enabling power: Finance Act 1973, s. 56 (1) (2) & European Communities Act 1972, s. 2 (2). - Issued: 12.03.2012. Made: 06.03.2012. Laid: 12.03.2012. Coming into force: 06.04.2012. Effect: S.I. 1996/26 revoked in relation to England & S.I. 2004/1165 partially revoked & S.I. 2006/1160; 2007/720; 2010/2693; 2012/103 revoked. Territorial extent & classification: E. General. - 12p.: 30 cm. - 978-0-11-152188-5 £5.75

The Plant Health (Import Inspection Fees) (England) (Amendment) Regulations 2012 No. 2012/103. - Enabling power: Finance Act 1973, s. 56 (1) (2). - Issued: 19.01.2012. Made: 12.01.2012. Laid: 19.01.2012. Coming into force: 13.02.2012. Effect: S.I. 2010/2693 amended. Territorial extent & classification: E. General. - Revoked by S.I. 2012/745 (ISBN 9780111521885). - 8p.: 30 cm. - 978-0-11-151927-1 £4.00

The Plant Health (Miscellaneous Amendments) (England) Regulations 2012 No. 2012/697. - Enabling power: European Communities Act 1972, s. 2 (2). - Issued: 09.03.2012. Made: 03.03.2012. Laid: 09.03.2012. Coming into force: 01.04.2012. Effect: S.I. 2004/1165; 2005/2530 amended. Territorial extent & classification: E. General. - EC note: These Regulations enforce Commission Implementing Decision 2011/87/EU as regards potatoes originating in Egypt and Decision 1/2010 of the Joint Committee on Agriculture relating to plant health controls on trade in plant material with Switzerland. - 4p.: 30 cm. - 978-0-11-152159-5 £4.00

Plant health, Wales

The Plant Health (Fees) (Wales) Regulations 2012 No. 2012/1493 (W.191). - Enabling power: European Communities Act 1972, s. 2 (2) & Finance Act 1973, s. 56 (1) (2). - Issued: 22.06.2012. Made: 05.06.2012. Laid before the National Assembly for Wales: 12.06.2012. Coming into force: 06.07.2012. Effect: S.I. 1996/26; 2004/2245 (W.209); 2006/2961 (W.267); 2007/1765 (W.154); 2010/2917 (W.242); 2012/285 (W.49) revoked. Territorial extent & classification: W. General. - EC note: Relates to the implementation of article 13d of Council Directive 2000/29/EC. - In English & Welsh. Welsh title: Rheoliadau Iechyd Planhigion (Ffioedd) (Cymru) 2012. - 24p.: 30 cm. - 978-0-348-10627-5 £5.75

The Plant Health (Import Inspection Fees) (Wales) (Amendment) Regulations 2012 No. 2012/285 (W.49). - Enabling power: Finance Act 1973, s. 56 (1) (2). - Issued: 23.02.2012. Made: 02.02.2012. Laid before the National Assembly for Wales: 07.02.2012. Coming into force: 29.02.2012. Effect: W.S.I. 2010/2917 (W.242) amended. Territorial extent & classification: W. General. - Revoked by W.S.I. 2012/1493 (W.191) (ISBN 9780348106275). EC note: Relate to the implementation of article 13d of Council Directive 2000/29/EC. - In English & Welsh. Welsh title: Rheoliadau Iechyd Planhigion (Ffioedd Arolygu Mewnforio) (Cymru) (Diwygio) 2012. - 12p.: 30 cm. - 978-0-348-10686-2 £5.75

The Plant Health (Wales) (Amendment) Order 2012 No. 2012/3143 (W.315). - Enabling power: Plant Health Act 1967, s. 2 (1), 3 (1). - Issued: 17.01.2013. Made: 19.12.2012. Laid before the National Assembly for Wales: 20.12.2012. Coming into force: 11.01.2013. Effect: S.I. 2006/1643 (W.158) amended. Territorial extent & classification: W. General. - In English & Welsh. Welsh title: Gorchymyn Iechyd Planhigion (Cymru) (Diwygio) 2012. - 4p.: 30 cm. - 978-0-348-10679-4 £4.00

Police

The Ministry of Defence Police (Performance) Regulations 2012 No. 2012/808. - Enabling power: Ministry of Defence Police Act 1987, ss. 3A, 4. - Issued: 16.03.2012. Made: 13.03.2012. Laid: 15.03.2012. Coming into force: 06.04.2012. Effect: S.I. 2009/3069, 3070 amended. Territorial extent & classification: E/W/S/NI. General. - 32p.: 30 cm. - 978-0-11-152206-6 £9.75

The Police Act 1997 (Criminal Records and Registration) (Guernsey) (Amendment No. 2) Regulations 2012 No. 2012/2666. - Enabling power: Police Act 1997, ss. 113A (6), 125. - Issued: 26.10.2012. Made: 23.10.2012. Coming into force: 19.11.2012. Effect: S.I. 2009/3297 amended. Territorial extent & classification: Guernsey. General. - 2p.: 30 cm. - 978-0-11-152995-9 £4.00

The Police Act 1997 (Criminal Records and Registration) (Guernsey) (Amendment) Regulations 2012 No. 2012/2107. - Enabling power: Police Act 1997, ss. 113B (9), 125. - Issued: 20.08.2012. Made: 14.08.2012. Coming into force: 10.09.2012. Effect: S.I. 2009/3297 amended. Territorial extent & classification: Guernsey. General. - 2p.: 30 cm. - 978-0-11-152817-4 £4.00

The Police Act 1997 (Criminal Records and Registration) (Isle of Man) (Amendment No. 2) Regulations 2012 No. 2012/2667. - Enabling power: Police Act 1997, ss. 113A (6), 125. - Issued: 26.10.2012. Made: 23.10.2012. Coming into force: 19.11.2012. Effect: S.I. 2011/2296 amended. Territorial extent & classification: Isle of Man. General. - 2p.: 30 cm. - 978-0-11-152997-3 £4.00

The Police Act 1997 (Criminal Records and Registration) (Isle of Man) (Amendment) Regulations 2012 No. 2012/2109. - Enabling power: Police Act 1997, ss. 113B (9), 125. - Issued: 20.08.2012. Made: 14.08.2012. Coming into force: 10.09.2012. Effect: S.I. 2011/2296 amended. Territorial extent & classification: Isle of Man. General. - 2p.: 30 cm. - 978-0-11-152819-8 £4.00

The Police Act 1997 (Criminal Records and Registration) (Jersey) (Amendment No. 2) Regulations 2012 No. 2012/2668. - Enabling power: Police Act 1997, ss. 113A (6), 125. - Issued: 26.10.2012. Made: 23.10.2012. Coming into force: 19.11.2012. Effect: S.I. 2010/1087 amended. Territorial extent & classification: Jersey. General. - 2p.: 30 cm. - 978-0-11-152998-0 £4.00

The Police Act 1997 (Criminal Records and Registration) (Jersey) (Amendment) Regulations 2012 No. 2012/2108. - Enabling power: Police Act 1997, ss. 113B (9), 125. - Issued: 20.08.2012. Made: 14.08.2012. Coming into force: 10.09.2012. Effect: S.I. 2010/1087 amended. Territorial extent & classification: Jersey. General. - 2p.: 30 cm. - 978-0-11-152820-4 £4.00

The Police Act 1997 (Criminal Records) (Guernsey) (Amendment) Order 2012 No. 2012/1762. - Enabling power: Serious Organised Crime and Police Act 2005, s. 168 & Safeguarding Vulnerable Groups Act 2006, s. 66 (4) & Protection of Freedoms Act 2012, s. 118. - Issued: 16.07.2012. Made: 10.07.2012. Coming into force: In accord. with art 1 (2) to (3) (b). Effect: 2012 c. 9 modified & S.I. 2009/3215 amended. Territorial extent & classification: Guernsey. General. - 8p.: 30 cm. - 978-0-11-152673-6 £5.75

The Police Act 1997 (Criminal Records) (Isle of Man) (Amendment) Order 2012 No. 2012/2598. - Enabling power: Serious Organised Crime and Police Act 2005, s. 168 & Safeguarding Vulnerable Groups Act 2006, s. 66 (4) & Protection of Freedoms Act 2012, s. 118. - Issued: 22.10.2012. Made: 17.10.2012. Coming into force: In accord. with art. 1 (2) (3). Effect: 2012 c.9; S.I. 2012/764 amended. Territorial extent & classification: Isle of Man. General. - 8p.: 30 cm. - 978-0-11-152977-5 £5.75

The Police Act 1997 (Criminal Records) (Jersey) (Amendment) Order 2012 No. 2012/2591. - Enabling power: Serious Organised Crime and Police Act 2005, s. 168 & Safeguarding Vulnerable Groups Act 2006, s. 66 (4) & Safeguarding Vulnerable Groups Act 2006, s. 66 (4) & Protection of Freedoms Act 2012, s. 118. - Issued: 22.10.2012. Made: 17.10.2012. Coming into force: In accord. with art. 1 (2) to (3) (b). Effect: 2012 c.9; S.I. 2010/765 amended. Territorial extent & classification: Jersey. General. - With correction slip dated November 2012. - 8p.: 30 cm. - 978-0-11-152971-3 £5.75

Police, England and Wales

The Crime and Security Act 2010 (Commencement No. 5) Order 2012 No. 2012/584 (C.12). - Enabling power: Crime and Security Act 2010, s. 59 (1). Bringing various provisions of the 2010 Act into operation on 26.03.2012. - Issued: 01.03.2012. Made: 28.02.2012. Effect: None. Territorial extent & classification: E/W. General. - 2p.: 30 cm. - 978-0-11-152094-9 £4.00

The Crime and Security Act 2010 (Commencement No. 6) Order 2012 No. 2012/1615 (C.60). - Enabling power: Crime and Security Act 2010, s. 59 (1) (4). Bringing various provisions of the 2010 Act into operation on 30.06.2012. - Issued: 25.06.2012. Made: 20.06.2012. Effect: None. Territorial extent & classification: E/W. General. - 2p.: 30 cm. - 978-0-11-152571-5 £4.00

The Criminal Justice and Police Act 2001 (Amendment) Order 2012 No. 2012/1430. - Enabling power: Criminal Justice and Police Act 2001, s. 1 (2). - Issued: 08.06.2012. Made: 30.05.2012. Coming into force: In accord. with art. 1 (2). Effect: 2001 c. 16 amended. Territorial extent & classification: E/W. General. - Supersedes draft S.I. (ISBN 9780111522738) issued 26.03.2011. - 2p.: 30 cm. - 978-0-11-152500-5 £4.00

The Elected Local Policing Bodies (Complaints and Misconduct) Regulations 2012 No. 2012/62. - Enabling power: Police Reform and Social Responsibility Act 2011, ss. 31, 154 (5), sch. 7. - Issued: 17.01.2012. Made: 10.01.2012. Coming into force: 16.01.2012. Effect: None. Territorial extent & classification: E/W. General. - Supersedes draft SI (ISBN 9780111516843) issued on 16.11.2011. - 28p.: 30 cm. - 978-0-11-151916-5 £5.75

The Elected Local Policing Bodies (Specified Information) (Amendment) Order 2012 No. 2012/2479. - Enabling power: Police Reform and Social Responsibility Act 2011, s. 11 (2). - Issued: 03.10.2012. Made: 27.09.2012. Laid: 02.10.2012. Coming into force: 22.11.2012. Effect: S.I. 2011/3050 amended. Territorial extent & classification: E/W. General. - 4p.: 30 cm. - 978-0-11-152905-8 £4.00

The Local Policing Bodies (Consequential Amendments and Transitional Provision) Order 2012 No. 2012/2733. - Enabling power: Employment Rights Act 1996, ss. 209 (1) (b), 236 & Police Act 1996, sch. 4A, para. 3 (4) & Police Reform and Social Responsibility Act 2011, sch. 15, para. 24. - Issued: 05.11.2012. Made: 30.10.2012. Laid: 01.11.2012. Coming into force: 22.11.2012. Effect: S.I. 1999/2277; 2007/1170 amended. Territorial extent & classification: E/W. General. - 4p.: 30 cm. - 978-0-11-153029-0 £4.00

The Local Policing Bodies (Consequential Amendments No. 2) Regulations 2012 No. 2012/2732. - Enabling power: Police Reform Act 2002, ss. 43, 105 (4) & Planning Act 2008, ss. 4, 7, 37, 42, 48, 51, 56, 58, 59, 127 (7), 232, sch. 6, paras 2, 4, 6. - Issued: 05.11.2012. Made: 30.10.2012. Laid: 01.11.2012. Coming into force: 22.11.2012. Effect: S.I. 2004/915; 2009/1302, 2264; 2010/102, 104; 2011/2055 amended. Territorial extent & classification: E/W. General. - 4p.: 30 cm. - 978-0-11-153032-0 £4.00

The Local Policing Bodies (Consequential Amendments) Regulations 2012 No. 2012/61. - Enabling power: Police and Criminal Evidence Act 1984, s. 63B (6) & Animal Welfare Act 2006, ss. 6 (4) (5) (6) (8) (14) & Violent Crime Reduction Act 2006, ss. 15, 16 (7), 17 (6), 20 (5). - Issued: 17.01.2012. Made: 10.01.2012. Coming into force: 16.01.2012. Effect: S.I. 2001/2645; 2007/1120; 2008/1430 amended. Territorial extent & classification: E/W. General. - Supersedes draft SI (ISBN 9780111517130) issued on 22.11.2011. - 4p.: 30 cm. - 978-0-11-151915-8 £4.00

The National Police Records (Recordable Offences) (Amendment) Regulations 2012 No. 2012/1713. - Enabling power: Police and Criminal Evidence Act 1984, s. 27 (4). - Issued: 05.07.2012. Made: 02.07.2012. Laid: 04.07.2012. Coming into force: 30.07.2012. Effect: S.I. 2000/1139 amended. Territorial extent & classification: E/W. General. - With correction slip dated July 2012. - 2p.: 30 cm. - 978-0-11-152619-4 £4.00

The Penalties for Disorderly Behaviour (Amount of Penalty) (Amendment) Order 2012 No. 2012/1431. - Enabling power: Criminal Justice and Police Act 2001, s. 3 (1) (1A). - Issued: 08.06.2012. Made: 30.05.2012. Laid: 01.06.2012. Coming into force: 30.06.2012. Effect: S.I. 2002/1837 amended. Territorial extent & classification: E/W. General. - 2p.: 30 cm. - 978-0-11-152501-2 £4.00

The Police Act 1997 (Criminal Records) (Amendment No. 2) Regulations 2012 No. 2012/2114. - Enabling power: Police Act 1997, ss. 113B (2) (b) (9), 113BA (1), 113BB (1), 125 (1) (2). - Issued: 20.08.2012. Made: 14.08.2012. Laid: 16.08.2012. Coming into force: 10.09.2012. Effect: S.I. 2002/233; 2009/1882 amended & S.I. 2002/233 partially revoked. Territorial extent & classification: E/W. General. - 8p.: 30 cm. - 978-0-11-152824-2 £4.00

The Police Act 1997 (Criminal Records) (Amendment No. 3) Regulations 2012 No. 2012/2669. - Enabling power: Police Act 1997, ss. 113A (6), 125 (1) (2). - Issued: 26.10.2012. Made: 23.10.2012. Laid: 25.10.2012. Coming into force: 19.11.2012. Effect: S.I. 2002/233 amended. Territorial extent & classification: E/W. General. - 2p.: 30 cm. - 978-0-11-152999-7 £4.00

The Police Act 1997 (Criminal Records) (Amendment No. 4) Regulations 2012 No. 2012/3016. - Enabling power: Police Act 1997, ss. 113B (2) (b), 125. - Issued: 06.12.2012. Made: 30.11.2012. Laid: 05.12.2012. Coming into force: 31.12.2012. Effect: S.I. 2002/233 amended. Territorial extent & classification: E/W. General. - 2p.: 30 cm. - 978-0-11-153163-1 £4.00

The Police Act 1997 (Criminal Records) (Amendment) Regulations 2012 No. 2012/523. - Enabling power: Police Act 1997, ss. 113B (2) (b), 113BA (1), 113BB (1). - Issued: 01.03.2012. Made: 23.02.2012. Laid: 29.02.2012. Coming into force: 26.02.2012. Effect: S.I. 2002/233; 2009/1882 amended. Territorial extent & classification: E/W. General. - 2p.: 30 cm. - 978-0-11-152081-9 £4.00

The Police (Amendment No. 2) Regulations 2012 No. 2012/680. - Enabling power: Police Act 1996, s. 50. - Issued: 08.03.2012. Made: 02.03.2012. Laid: 07.03.2012. Coming into force: 01.04.2012. Effect: S.I. 2003/527 amended. Territorial extent & classification: E/W. General- 2p.: 30 cm. - 978-0-11-152144-1 £4.00

The Police (Amendment No. 3) Regulations 2012 No. 2012/1960. - Enabling power: Police Act 1996, s. 50. - Issued: 31.07.2012. Made: 24.07.2012. Laid: 27.07.2012. Coming into force: 20.08.2012. Effect: S.I. 2003/527 amended. Territorial extent & classification: E/W. General. - 8p.: 30 cm. - 978-0-11-152775-7 £5.75

The Police (Amendment No. 4) Regulations 2012 No. 2012/2712. - Enabling power: Police Act 1996, s. 50. - Issued: 01.11.2012. Made: 29.10.2012. Laid: 31.10.2012. Coming into force: 22.11.2012. Effect: S.I. 2003/527 amended. Territorial extent & classification: E/W. General. - 4p.: 30 cm. - 978-0-11-153022-1 £4.00

The Police (Amendment No. 5) Regulations 2012 No. 2012/3058. - Enabling power: Police Act 1996, s. 50. - Issued: 11.12.2012. Made: 04.12.2012. Laid: 10.12.2012. Coming into force: 01.01.2013. Effect: S.I. 2003/527 amended. Territorial extent & classification: E/W. General. - 2p.: 30 cm. - 978-0-11-153205-8 £4.00

Police, England and Wales

The Police (Amendment) Regulations 2012 No. 2012/192. - Enabling power: Police Act 1996, s. 50. - Issued: 31.01.2012. Made: 26.01.2012 Laid: 30.01.2012. Coming into force: 23.02.2012. Effect: S.I. 2003/527 amended. Territorial extent & classification: E/W. General- 4p.: 30 cm. - 978-0-11-151958-5 £4.00

The Police and Crime Commissioner (Disqualification) (Supplementary Provisions) Regulations 2012 No. 2012/2087. - Enabling power: Police Reform and Social Responsibility Act 2011, ss. 65 (3), 66 (8), 154 (5) (a). - Issued: 14.08.2012. Made: 09.08.2012. Laid: 13.08.2012. Coming into force: 15.09.2012. Effect: None. Territorial extent & classification: E/W. General. - 4p.: 30 cm. - 978-0-11-152812-9 £4.00

The Police and Crime Commissioner Elections (Declaration of Acceptance of Office) Order 2012 No. 2012/2553. - Enabling power: Police Reform and Social Responsibility Act 2011, ss. 70 (1) (a), 154 (5) (a) (c), as extended by section 26 (3) of the Welsh Language Act 1993. - Issued: 11.10.2012. Made: 08.10.2012. Laid: 10.10.2012. Coming into force: 15.11.2012. Effect: None. Territorial extent & classification: E/W. General. - With correction slip dated November 2012. - 4p.: 30 cm. - 978-0-11-152925-6 £4.00

The Police and Crime Commissioner Elections (Designation of Local Authorities) (No. 2) Order 2012 No. 2012/2084. - Enabling power: Police Reform and Social Responsibility Act 2011, s. 75 (1). - Issued: 10.08.2012. Made: 09.08.2012. Coming into force: 10.08.2012, in accord. with art. 1 (2). Effect: S.I. 2012/1963 revoked. Territorial extent & classification: E/W. General. - 4p.: 30 cm. - 978-0-11-152810-5 £4.00

The Police and Crime Commissioner Elections (Designation of Local Authorities) Order 2012 No. 2012/1963. - Enabling power: Police Reform and Social Responsibility Act 2011, ss. 75 (1). - Issued: 31.07.2012. Made: 24.07.2012. Coming into force: In accord. with art. 1 (2). Effect: None. Territorial extent & classification: E/W. General. - Revoked by SI 2012/2084 (ISBN 9780111528105). - 4p.: 30 cm. - 978-0-11-152778-8 £4.00

The Police and Crime Commissioner Elections (Designation of Police Area Returning Officers) (No. 2) Order 2012 No. 2012/2085. - Enabling power: Police Reform and Social Responsibility Act 2011, ss. 54 (1) (b). - Issued: 10.08.2012. Made: 09.08.2102. Coming into force: 10.08.2012. In accord. with reg. 1 (2). Effect: S.I. 2012/1965 revoked. Territorial extent & classification: E/W. General. - 4p.: 30 cm. - 978-0-11-152811-2 £4.00

The Police and Crime Commissioner Elections (Designation of Police Area Returning Officers) Order 2012 No. 2012/1965. - Enabling power: Police Reform and Social Responsibility Act 2011, s. 54 (1) (b). - Issued: 31.07.2012. Made: 24.07.2012. Coming into force: In accord. with reg. 1 (2). Effect: None. Territorial extent & classification: E/W. General. - Revoked by SI 2012/2085 (ISBN 9780111528112). - 4p.: 30 cm. - 978-0-11-152779-5 £4.00

The Police and Crime Commissioner Elections (Functions of Returning Officers) Regulations 2012 No. 2012/1918. - Enabling power: Police Reform and Social Responsibility Act 2011, ss. 54 (2), 154 (5) (a) (c). - Issued: 31.07.2012. Made: 24.07.2102. Coming into force: In accord. with reg. 1 (2). Effect: None. Territorial extent & classification: E/W. General. - Supersedes draft S.I. (ISBN 9780111524534) issued 22.05.2012. - 8p.: 30 cm. - 978-0-11-152777-1 £4.00

The Police and Crime Commissioner Elections (Local Returning Officers' and Police Area Returning Officers' Charges) Order 2012 No. 2012/2378. - Enabling power: Police Reform and Social Responsibility Act 2011, ss. 55 (1), 154 (5). - Issued: 18.09.2012. Made: 12.09.2012. Coming into force: 13.09.2012, in accord. with art. 1. Effect: None. Territorial extent & classification: E/W. General. - 16p.: 30 cm. - 978-0-11-152881-5 £5.75

The Police and Crime Commissioner Elections Order 2012 No. 2012/1917. - Enabling power: Police Reform and Social Responsibility Act 2011, ss. 58 (1) (5), 154 (5). - Issued: 08.08.2012. Made: 24.07.2012. Coming into force: 25.07.2012 in accord. with art. 1 (2). Effect: 2000 c. 22; 2006 c. 22 & S.I. 2004/293, 294; 2006/3304, 3305; 2007/1024 amended. Territorial extent & classification: E/W. General. - Supersedes draft S.I. (ISBN 9780111525302) issued 15.06.2012. - 204p.: 30 cm. - 978-0-11-152803-7 £26.75

The Police and Crime Commissioner Elections (Returning Officers' Accounts) Regulations 2012 No. 2012/2088. - Enabling power: Police Reform and Social Responsibility Act 2011, ss. 55 (10), 154 (5) (a) (c). - Issued: 14.08.2012. Made: 09.08.2012. Laid: 13.08.2012. Coming into force: 15.09.2012. Effect: None. Territorial extent & classification: E/W. General. - 4p.: 30 cm. - 978-0-11-152813-6 £4.00

The Police and Crime Commissioner Elections (Welsh Forms) Order 2012 No. 2012/2768. - Enabling power: Police Reform and Social Responsibility Act 2011, ss. 58 (1), 154 (5). - Issued: 16.10.2012. Made: 30.10.2012. Coming into force: In accord. with art. 1 (2). Effect: None. Territorial extent & classification: E/W. General. - Supersedes draft S.I. (ISBN 9780111529416) issued 16.10.2012. - 8p.: 30 cm. - 978-0-11-153044-3 £5.75

The Police and Crime Panels (Application of Local Authority Enactments) Regulations 2012 No. 2012/2734. - Enabling power: Police Reform and Social Responsibility Act 2011, sch. 6, para. 36 (1). - Issued: 05.11.2012. Made: 30.10.2012. Laid: 01.11.2012. Coming into force: 22.11.2012. Effect: None. Territorial extent & classification: E/W. General. - 8p.: 30 cm. - 978-0-11-153030-6 £5.75

The Police and Crime Panels (Modification of Functions) Regulations 2012 No. 2012/2504. - Enabling power: Police Reform and Social Responsibility Act 2011, sch. 6, para. 40. - Issued: 04.10.2012. Made: 02.10.2012. Coming into force: 03.10.2012 in accord. with reg. 1. Effect: 2011 c.13 modified. Territorial extent & classification: E/W. General. - Supersedes draft S.I. (ISBN 9780111525074) issued 15.06.2012. - 2p.: 30 cm. - 978-0-11-152908-9 £4.00

The Police and Crime Panels (Nominations, Appointments and Notifications) Regulations 2012 No. 2012/1433. - Enabling power: Police Reform and Social Responsibility Act 2011, sch. 6, paras 37, 38, 39. - Issued: 08.06.2012. Made: 31.05.2012. Laid: 07.06.2012. Coming into force: 02.07.2012. Effect: None. Territorial extent & classification: E/W. General. - 4p.: 30 cm. - 978-0-11-152502-9 £4.00

The Police and Crime Panels (Precepts and Chief Constable Appointments) Regulations 2012 No. 2012/2271. - Enabling power: Police Reform and Social Responsibility Act 2011, sch. 5, paras 7, 8; sch. 8, paras 9, 10. - Issued: 07.09.2012. Made: 03.09.2012. Laid: 06.09.2012. Coming into force: 22.11.2012. Effect: None. Territorial extent & classification: E/W. General. - 8p.: 30 cm. - 978-0-11-152853-2 £4.00

The Police and Criminal Evidence Act 1984 (Codes of Practice) (Revision of Codes C, G and H) Order 2012 No. 2012/1798. - Enabling power: Police and Criminal Evidence Act 1984, s. 67 (5). - Issued: 12.07.2012. Made: 09.07.2012. Coming into force: 10.7.2012 in accord. with art. 1 (1). Effect: None. Territorial extent & classification: E/W. General. - Supersedes draft SI (ISBN 9780111524183) issued on 11.05.2012. - 2p.: 30 cm. - 978-0-11-152658-3 £4.00

The Police Appeals Tribunals Rules 2012 No. 2012/2630. - Enabling power: Police Act 1996, s. 85. - Issued: 25.10.2012. Made: 18.10.2012. Laid: 23.10.2012. Coming into force: 22.11.2012. Effect: S.I. 2008/2863; 2011/3029 revoked with saving. Territorial extent & classification: E/W. General. - 12p.: 30 cm. - 978-0-11-152984-3 £5.75

The Police Authority (Amendment) Regulations 2012 No. 2012/536. - Enabling power: Police Act 1996, sch. 2, para. 1. - Issued: 01.03.2012. Made: 27.02.2012. Laid: 29.02.2012. Coming into force: 01.04.2012. Effect: S.I. 2008/630 amended. Territorial extent & classification: E/W. General. - 2p.: 30 cm. - 978-0-11-152083-3 £4.00

The Police (Collaboration: Specified Function) Order 2012 No. 2012/1690. - Enabling power: Police Act 1996, s. 23FA (1) (2) (6). - Issued: 02.07.2012. Made: 28.06.2012. Coming into force: 29.06.2012 in accord. with art. 1. Effect: None. Territorial extent & classification: E/W. General. - Supersedes draft S.I. (ISBN 9780111522691) issued 28.03.2012. - 2p.: 30 cm. - 978-0-11-152612-5 £4.00

The Police (Complaints and Misconduct) Regulations 2012 No. 2012/1204. - Enabling power: Police Reform Act 2002, ss. 13, 20 (5), 21 (10) (12), 23, 29 (1), 39 (9), 105 (4) (5), sch. 3, paras 2 (8), 3 (7), 4 (1) (b) (4), 7 (1) (1A) (3), 8 (2), 11 (2) (c), 13 (4), 14C (2), 17 (7), 19B (7) (10), 19C (2) (b), 19D, 21 (1) (1A) (2) (4) (6), 22 (7), 23 (11), 24 (9), 25 (13), 29. - Issued: 08.05.2012. Made: 01.05.2012. Laid: 03.05.2012. Coming into force: 22.11.2012. Effect: S.I. 2004/643; 2006/1406; 2008/2866; 2011/3028 revoked (with saving). Territorial extent & classification: E/W. General. - 28p.: 30 cm. - 978-0-11-152401-5 £5.75

The Police (Conduct) Regulations 2012 No. 2012/2632. - Enabling power: Police Act 1996, ss. 50, 51, 84. - Issued: 25.10.2012. Made: 18.10.2012. Laid: 23.10.2012. Coming into force: 22.11.2012. Effect: S.I. 2004/645; 2008/2864 revoked with saving. Territorial extent & classification: E/W. General. - 40p.: 30 cm. - 978-0-11-152985-0 £9.75

The Police Pensions (Amendment No. 2) Regulations 2012 No. 2012/2811. - Enabling power: Police Pensions Act 1976, s. 1. - Issued: 13.11.2012. Made: 06.11.2012. Laid: 12.11.2012. Coming into force: 03.12.2012. Effect: S.I. 1987/257; 2006/3415 amended. Territorial extent & classification: E/W. General. - 4p.: 30 cm. - 978-0-11-153063-4 £4.00

The Police Pensions (Amendment No. 3) Regulations 2012 No. 2012/3057. - Enabling power: Police Pensions Act 1976, s. 1. - Issued: 11.12.2012. Made: 05.12.2012. Laid: 10.12.2012. Coming into force: 01.01.2013. Effect: S.I. 1987/257; 2006/3415 amended. Territorial extent & classification: E/W. General. - 8p.: 30 cm. - 978-0-11-153206-5 £4.00

The Police Pensions (Amendment) Regulations 2012 No. 2012/640. - Enabling power: Police Pensions Act 1976, ss. 1 to 7. - Issued: 06.03.2012. Made: 28.02.2012. Laid: 05.03.2012. Coming into force: 01.04.2012. Effect: S.I. 1987/257, 2215; 2006/3415 amended. Territorial extent & classification: E/W. General. - 4p.: 30 cm. - 978-0-11-152118-2 £4.00

The Police Pensions (Descriptions of Service) Order 2012 No. 2012/2954. - Enabling power: Police Pensions Act 1976, s. 11A (1) & Police Act 1996, s. 97A (1). - Issued: 29.11.2012. Made: 26.11.2012. Laid: 28.11.2012. Coming into force: 21.12.2012. Effect: 1976 c.35; 1996 c.16; S.I. 1987/257 amended. Territorial extent & classification: E/W. General. - 4p.: 30 cm. - 978-0-11-153128-0 £4.00

The Police (Performance) Regulations 2012 No. 2012/2631. - Enabling power: Police Act 1996, ss. 50, 51, 84. - Issued: 25.10.2012. Made: 18.10.2012. Laid: 23.10.2012. Coming into force: 22.11.2012. Effect: S.I. 2008/2862; 2011/3027 revoked with savings. Territorial extent & classification: E/W. General. - 36p.: 30 cm. - 978-0-11-152986-7 £9.75

The Police Reform and Social Responsibility Act 2011 (Commencement No. 3 and Transitional Provisions) (Amendment) Order 2012 No. 2012/75. - Enabling power: Police Reform and Social Responsibility Act 2011, ss. 154 (5), 157 (1). - Issued: 18.01.2012. Made: 12.01.2012. Effect: S.I. 2011/3019 (C.110) amended. Territorial extent & classification: E/W. General. - This Statutory Instrument has been made in consequence of defects in S.I. 2011/3019 (C.110) and is being issued free of charge to all known recipients of that Statutory instrument. - 2p.: 30 cm. - 978-0-11-151922-6 £4.00

The Police Reform and Social Responsibility Act 2011 (Commencement No. 5) Order 2012 No. 2012/1129 (C.38). - Enabling power: Police Reform and Social Responsibility Act 2011, s. 157 (1). Bringing into operation various provisions of the 2011 Act on 25.04.2012 in accord. with art. 2. - Issued: 25.04.2012. Made: 23.04.2012. Effect: None. Territorial extent & classification: E/W. General. - 4p.: 30 cm. - 978-0-11-152375-9 £4.00

The Police Reform and Social Responsibility Act 2011 (Commencement No. 7 and Transitional Provisions and Commencement No. 3 and Transitional Provisions (Amendment)) Order 2012 No. 2012/2892 (C.111). - Enabling power: Police Reform and Social Responsibility Act 2011, ss. 154 (5), 157 (1). Bringing into operation various provisions of the 2011 Act on 22.11.2012 in accord. with art. 2. - Issued: 21.11.2012. Made: 14.11.2012. Effect: S.I. 2011/3019 amended. Territorial extent & classification: E/W. General. - 8p.: 30 cm. - 978-0-11-153085-6 £5.75

The Policing and Crime Act 2009 (Commencement No. 8) Order 2012 No. 2012/2235 (C.90). - Enabling power: Policing and Crime Act 2009, s. 116 (1). Bringing into operation various provisions of the 2009 Act on 10.09.2012. - Issued: 04.09.2012. Made: 28.08.2012. Effect: None. Territorial extent & classification: E/W/NI. General. - 4p.: 30 cm. - 978-0-11-152843-3 £4.00

The Protection of Freedoms Act 2012 (Commencement No. 1) Order 2012 No. 2012/1205 (C.41). - Enabling power: Protection of Freedoms Act 2012, s. 120 (1). Bringing into operation various provisions of the 2012 Act on 09.05.2012, 01.07.2012 & 10.07.2012. - Issued: 08.05.2012. Made: 02.05.2012. Effect: None. Territorial extent & classification: E/W/S/NI. General. - 4p.: 30 cm. - 978-0-11-152402-2 £4.00

The Protection of Freedoms Act 2012 (Disclosure and Barring Service Transfer of Functions) Order 2012 No. 2012/3006. - Enabling power: Protection of Freedoms Act 2012, ss. 88, 89. - Issued: 05.12.2012. Made: 29.11.2012. Coming into force: 01.12.2012. Effect: 13 Acts amended & 46 SI's and SR's amended & 1998 c.29 & SI 2007/1351 (NI.11) partially revoked. Territorial extent & classification: E/W/NI. General. - Supersedes draft SI (ISBN 9780111529409) issued 16.10.2012. - 24p.: 30 cm. - 978-0-11-153157-0 £5.75

The Special Constables (Amendment) Regulations 2012 No. 2012/1961. - Enabling power: Police Act 1996, ss. 50 (7), 51. - Issued: 31.07.2012. Made: 24.07.2012. Laid: 27.07.2012. Coming into force: 20.08.2012. Effect: S.I. 1965/536 amended. Territorial extent & classification: E/W. General. - 8p.: 30 cm. - 978-0-11-152776-4 £5.75

The Welsh Language (Police Names) Order 2012 No. 2012/2606. - Enabling power: Welsh Language Act 1993, s. 25 (1). - Issued: 19.10.2012. Made: 12.10.2012. Laid: 17.10.2012. Coming into force: 22.11.20112. Effect: None. Territorial extent & classification: E/W. General. - 2p.: 30 cm. - 978-0-11-152956-0 £4.00

Police, Northern Ireland

The Policing and Crime Act 2009 (Commencement No. 8) Order 2012 No. 2012/2235 (C.90). - Enabling power: Policing and Crime Act 2009, s. 116 (1). Bringing into operation various provisions of the 2009 Act on 10.09.2012. - Issued: 04.09.2012. Made: 28.08.2012. Effect: None. Territorial extent & classification: E/W/NI. General. - 4p.: 30 cm. - 978-0-11-152843-3 £4.00

Postal services

The Postal Services Act 2011 (Commencement No. 3 and Saving Provisions) Order 2012 No. 2012/1095 (C.34). - Enabling power: Postal Services Act 2011, s. 93 (3). Bringing into operation various provisions of the 2011 Act on 23.04.2012, in accord. with art. 3. - Issued: 18.04.2012. Made: 16.04.2012. Effect: None. Territorial extent & classification: E/W/S/NI. General. - 4p.: 30 cm. - 978-0-11-152360-5 £4.00

The Postal Services Act 2011 (Disclosure of Information) Order 2012 No. 2012/1128. - Enabling power: Postal Services Act 2011, s. 56 (2) (3). - Issued: 23.04.2012. Made: 19.04.2012. Coming into force: 20.04.2012 in accord. with art. 1. Effect: None. Territorial extent & classification: E/W/S/NI. General. - Supersedes draft S.I. (ISBN 9780111521021) issued 02.03.2012. - 8p.: 30 cm. - 978-0-11-152374-2 £5.75

The Postal Services Act 2011 (Penalties) (Rules for Calculation of Turnover) Order 2012 No. 2012/1127. - Enabling power: Postal Services Act 2011, sch. 7, para. 7 (2). - Issued: 23.04.2012. Made: 19.04.2012. Coming into force: 20.04.2012 in accord. with art. 1. Effect: None. Territorial extent & classification: E/W/S/NI. General. - Supersedes draft S.I. (ISBN 9780111520239) issued 13.02.2012. - 2p.: 30 cm. - 978-0-11-152373-5 £4.00

The Postal Services Act 2011 (Specified Day) Order 2012 No. 2012/966. - Enabling power: Postal Services Act 2011, s. 25. - Issued: 29.03.2012. Made: 27.03.2012. Coming into force: 01.04.2012, in accord. with art. 2. Effect: None. Territorial extent & classification: E/W/S/NI. General. - 2p.: 30 cm. - 978-0-11-152305-6 £4.00

The Postal Services Act 2011 (Transfer of Accrued Pension Rights) Order 2012 No. 2012/687. - Enabling power: Postal Services Act 2011, ss. 17, 18, 19, 20 (6), 25, 26, 89 (2). - Issued: 12.03.2012. Made: 08.03.2012. Laid: 09.03.2012. Coming into force: In accord. with art. 1 (2) to (4). Effect: None. Territorial extent & classification: E/W/S/NI. General. - 104p.: 30 cm. - 978-0-11-152187-8 *16.00*

The Postal Services Act 2011 (Transfer of Assets) Order 2012 No. 2012/688. - Enabling power: Postal Services Act 2011, ss. 21, 22, 25, 26 (1), 89 (2). - Issued: 12.03.2012. Made: 08.03.2012. Laid: 09.03.2012. Coming into force: In accord. with art. 1 (2). Effect: None. Territorial extent & classification: E/W/S/NI. General. - 24p.: 30 cm. - 978-0-11-152182-3 *£5.75*

The Postal Services (Universal Postal Service) Order 2012 No. 2012/936. - Enabling power: Postal Services Act 2011, ss. 30 (1). - Issued: 29.03.2012. Made: 26.03.2012. Coming into force: 01.04.2012. Effect: None. Territorial extent & classification: E/W/S/NI. General. - With correction slip dated February 2013. - 16p.: 30 cm. - 978-0-11-152291-2 *£5.75*

Prevention and suppression of terrorism

The Coroners and Justice Act 2009 (Commencement No. 9) Order 2012 No. 2012/1810 (C.70). - Enabling power: Coroners and Justice Act 2009, s. 182 (5). Bringing into operation various provisions of the 2009 Act on 07.08.2012. - Issued: 13.07.2012. Made: 04.07.2012. Effect: None. Territorial extent & classification: E/W/S/NI. General. - 4p.: 30 cm. - 978-0-11-152676-7 *£4.00*

The Counter-Terrorism Act 2008 (Code of Practice for the Video Recording with Sound of Post-Charge Questioning) Order 2012 No. 2012/1793. - Enabling power: Counter-Terrorism Act 2008, s. 26 (4). - Issued: 12.07.2012. Made: 09.07.2012. Coming into force: 10.07.2012. Effect: None. Territorial extent & classification: E/W/S/NI. General. - Supersedes draft SI (ISBN 9780111524145) issued on 11.05.2012. - 2p.: 30 cm. - 978-0-11-152664-4 *£4.00*

The Counter-Terrorism Act 2008 (Commencement No. 5) Order 2012 No. 2012/1121 (C.37). - Enabling power: Counter-Terrorism Act 2008, s. 100 (5). Bringing into operation various provisions of the 2008 Act on 30.04.2012. - Issued: 20.04.2012. Made: 19.04.2012. Effect: None. Territorial extent & classification: E/W/S/NI. General. - 2p.: 30 cm. - 978-0-11-152370-4 *£4.00*

The Counter-Terrorism Act 2008 (Commencement No. 6) Order 2012 No. 2012/1724 (C.68). - Enabling power: Counter-Terrorism Act 2008, s. 100 (5). Bringing into operation various provisions of the 2008 Act on 10.07.2012. - Issued: 05.07.2012. Made: 03.07.2012. Effect: None. Territorial extent & classification: E/W/S/NI. General. - 2p.: 30 cm. - 978-0-11-152628-6 *£4.00*

The Counter-Terrorism Act 2008 (Commencement No. 7) Order 2012 No. 2012/1966 (C.78). - Enabling power: Counter-Terrorism Act 2008, s. 100 (5). Bringing into operation various provisions of the 2008 Act on 26.07.2012. - Issued: 27.07.2012. Made: 25.07.2012. Effect: None. Territorial extent & classification: E/W/S. General. - 2p.: 30 cm. - 978-0-11-152780-1 *£4.00*

The Protection of Freedoms Act 2012 (Commencement No. 1) Order 2012 No. 2012/1205 (C.41). - Enabling power: Protection of Freedoms Act 2012, s. 120 (1). Bringing into operation various provisions of the 2012 Act on 09.05.2012, 01.07.2012 & 10.07.2012. - Issued: 08.05.2012. Made: 02.05.2012. Effect: None. Territorial extent & classification: E/W/S/NI. General. - 4p.: 30 cm. - 978-0-11-152402-2 *£4.00*

The Protection of Freedoms Act 2012 (Commencement No. 3) Order 2012 No. 2012/2234 (C.89). - Enabling power: Protection of Freedoms Act 2012, ss. 116 (1), 120 (1). Bringing into operation various provisions of the 2012 Act on 10.09.2012 & 01.10.2012 in accord. with arts 2 to 3. - Issued: 04.09.2012. Made: 28.08.2012. Effect: None. Territorial extent & classification: E/W/S/NI. General. - 8p.: 30 cm. - 978-0-11-152842-6 *£5.75*

The Schedule 5 to the Anti-terrorism, Crime and Security Act 2001 (Modification) Order 2012 No. 2012/1466. - Enabling power: Anti-terrorism, Crime and Security Act 2001, s. 58 (2). - Issued: 12.06.2012. Made: 07.06.2012. Coming into force: 01.10.2012. Effect: 2001 c.24 amended. Territorial extent & classification: E/W/S/NI. General. - Supersedes draft SI (ISBN 9780111521069) issued on 14.03.2012. - 4p.: 30 cm. - 978-0-11-152513-5 *£4.00*

The Terrorism Act 2000 and Proceeds of Crime Act 2002 (Business in the Regulated Sector) (No. 2) Order 2012 No. 2012/2299. - Enabling power: Terrorism Act 2000, sch. 3A, para. 5 & Proceeds of Crime Act 2002, sch. 9, para. 5. - Issued: 10.09.2012. Made: 06.09.2012. Laid: 10.09.2012. Coming into force: 01.10.2012. Effect: 2000 c. 11; 2002 c. 29 amended. Territorial extent & classification: E/W/S/NI. General. - 4p.: 30 cm. - 978-0-11-152870-9 *£4.00*

The Terrorism Act 2000 and Proceeds of Crime Act 2002 (Business in the Regulated Sector) Order 2012 No. 2012/1534. - Enabling power: Terrorism Act 2000, sch. 3A, para. 5 & Proceeds of Crime Act 2002, sch. 9, para. 5. - Issued: 18.06.2012. Made: 14.06.2012. Laid: 15.06.2012. Coming into force: 07.07.2012. Effect: 2000 c. 11; 2002 c. 29 amended. Territorial extent & classification: E/W/S/NI. General. - 4p.: 30 cm. - 978-0-11-152552-4 *£4.00*

The Terrorism Act 2000 (Codes of Practice for the Exercise of Stop and Search Powers) Order 2012 No. 2012/1794. - Enabling power: Terrorism Act 2000, s. 47AB (2). - Issued: 12.07.2012. Made: 09.07.2012. Coming into force: 10.07.2012. Effect: None. Territorial extent & classification: E/W/S/NI. General. - Supersedes draft SI (ISBN 9780111524176) issued on 11.05.2012. - 2p.: 30 cm. - 978-0-11-152655-2 *£4.00*

The Terrorism Act 2000 (Proscribed Organisations) (Amendment) (No. 2) Order 2012 No. 2012/2937. - Enabling power: Terrorism Act 2000, s. 3 (3) (a). - Issued: 26.11.2012. Made: 22.11.2012. Coming into force: 23.11.2012. Effect: 2000 c. 11 amended. Territorial extent & classification: E/W/S/NI. General. - Supersedes draft SI (ISBN 9780111530887) issued on 20.11.2012. - 2p.: 30 cm. - 978-0-11-153119-8 £4.00

The Terrorism Act 2000 (Proscribed Organisations) (Amendment) Order 2012 No. 2012/1771. - Enabling power: Terrorism Act 2000, s. 3 (3) (a). - Issued: 09.07.2012. Made: 05.07.2012. Coming into force: 06.07.2012. Effect: 2011 c.11 amended. Territorial extent & classification: E/W/S/NI. General. - Supersedes draft SI (ISBN 9780111526187) issued on 04.07.2012. - 2p.: 30 cm. - 978-0-11-152641-5 £4.00

The Terrorism Act 2000 (Video Recording with Sound of Interviews and Associated Code of Practice) Order 2012 No. 2012/1792. - Enabling power: Terrorism Act 2000, sch. 8, para. 3 (2) (b) (3) (4) (b), 4 (4). - Issued: 12.07.2012. Made: 09.07.2012. Coming into force: 10.07.2012. Effect: None. Territorial extent & classification: E/W/S. General. - Supersedes draft SI (ISBN 9780111524152) issued 11.05.2012. - 2p.: 30 cm. - 978-0-11-152661-3 £4.00

Prevention of nuclear proliferation: Terrorist financing and money laundering

The Financial Restrictions (Iran) Order 2012 No. 2012/2904. - Enabling power: Counter-Terrorism Act 2008, sch. 7, paras. 1, 3, 9, 13, 14. - Issued: 08.01.2013. Made: 20.11.2012. Laid: 20.11.2012. Coming into force: 21.11.2012. Effect: None. Territorial extent & classification: E/W/S/NI. General. - Revoked by SI 2013/162 (ISBN 9780111533918). Approved by Parliament and supersedes pre approval version (ISBN 9780111530979) issued on 21.11.2012. This Order replaces SI 2011/2775 (ISBN 9780111518601) which ceased to have effect after one year. - 4p.: 30 cm. - 978-0-11-153299-7 £4.00

The Financial Restrictions (Iran) Order 2012 No. 2012/2904. - Enabling power: Counter-Terrorism Act 2008, sch. 7, paras. 1, 3, 9, 13, 14. - Issued: 21.11.2012. Made: 20.11.2012. Laid: 20.11.2012. Coming into force: 21.11.2012. Effect: None. Territorial extent & classification: E/W/S/NI. General. - Superseded by Approved SI of same number but different ISBN (9780111532997) issued on 08.01.2013. For approval by resolution of each House of Parliament within twenty-eight days beginning with the day on which the Order was made, subject to extension for periods of dissolution or prorogation, or adjournment of both House for more than four days. This Order replaces SI 2011/2775 (ISBN 9780111518601) which ceased to have effect after one year. - 4p.: 30 cm. - 978-0-11-153097-9 £4.00

Prices

The Indication of Prices (Beds) (Revocation) Order 2012 No. 2012/1816. - Enabling power: Prices Act 1974, 4 (3). - Issued: 13.07.2012. Made: 11.07.2012. Laid: 12.07.2012. Coming into force: 01.10.2012. Effect: S.I. 1978/1716 revoked. Territorial extent & classification: E/W/S/NI. General. - 2p.: 30 cm. - 978-0-11-152691-0 £4.00

Prisons, England

The Closure of Prisons (H.M. Prison Latchmere House) Order 2012 No. 2012/681. - Enabling power: Prison Act 1952, s. 37. - Issued: 09.03.2012. Made: 05.03.2012. Laid: 09.03.2012. Coming into force: 01.04.2012. Effect: None. Territorial extent & classification: E. General. - 2p.: 30 cm. - 978-0-11-152157-1 £4.00

The Closure of Prisons (H.M. Prison Wellingborough) Order 2012 No. 2012/2990. - Enabling power: Prison Act 1952, s. 37 (1). - Issued: 03.12.2012. Made: 29.11.2012. Laid: 30.11.2012. Coming into force: 21.12.2012. Effect: None. Territorial extent & classification: E. General. - 2p.: 30 cm. - 978-0-11-153145-7 £4.00

The Closure of Prisons Order 2012 No. 2012/50. - Enabling power: Prison Act 1952, s. 37. - Issued: 11.01.2012. Made: 10.01.2012. Laid: 11.01.2012. Coming into force: 08.02.2012. Effect: None. Territorial extent & classification: E. General. - 2p.: 30 cm. - 978-0-11-151906-6 £4.00

Probation, England and Wales

The Offender Management Act 2007 (Establishment of Probation Trusts) (Amendment) Order 2012 No. 2012/1215. - Enabling power: Offender Management Act 2007, s. 5 (1), sch. 1, para. 13 (6). - Issued: 04.05.2012. Made: 03.05.2012. Laid: 04.05.2012. Coming into force: 30.05.2012. Effect: S.I. 2010/195 amended. Territorial extent & classification: E/W. General. - 2p.: 30 cm. - 978-0-11-152404-6 £4.00

Proceeds of crime

The Terrorism Act 2000 and Proceeds of Crime Act 2002 (Business in the Regulated Sector) (No. 2) Order 2012 No. 2012/2299. - Enabling power: Terrorism Act 2000, sch. 3A, para. 5 & Proceeds of Crime Act 2002, sch. 9, para. 5. - Issued: 10.09.2012. Made: 06.09.2012. Laid: 10.09.2012. Coming into force: 01.10.2012. Effect: 2000 c. 11; 2002 c. 29 amended. Territorial extent & classification: E/W/S/NI. General. - 4p.: 30 cm. - 978-0-11-152870-9 £4.00

The Terrorism Act 2000 and Proceeds of Crime Act 2002 (Business in the Regulated Sector) Order 2012 No. 2012/1534. - Enabling power: Terrorism Act 2000, sch. 3A, para. 5 & Proceeds of Crime Act 2002, sch. 9, para. 5. - Issued: 18.06.2012. Made: 14.06.2012. Laid: 15.06.2012. Coming into force: 07.07.2012. Effect: 2000 c. 11; 2002 c. 29 amended. Territorial extent & classification: E/W/S/NI. General. - 4p.: 30 cm. - 978-0-11-152552-4 £4.00

Proceeds of crime, England and Wales

The Proceeds of Crime Act 2002 (External Requests and Orders) Order 2005 (England and Wales) (Appeals under Part 2) (Amendment) Order 2012 No. 2012/138. - Enabling power: S.I. 2005/3181 arts. 5, 47 (3), 48 (2). - Issued: 25.01.2012. Made: 19.01.2012. Laid: 24.01.2012. Coming into force: 29.02.2012. Effect: None. Territorial extent & classification: E/W. General. - 12p.: 30 cm. - 978-0-11-151938-7 £5.75

Protection of vulnerable adults, England and Wales

The Disclosure and Barring Service (Core Functions) Order 2012 No. 2012/2522. - Enabling power: Protection of Freedoms Act 2012, sch. 8, para. 8 (1) (d). - Issued: 09.10.2012. Made: 03.10.2012. Laid: 05.10.2012. Coming into force: 01.12.2012. Effect: None. Territorial extent & classification: E/W. General. - 4p.: 30 cm. - 978-0-11-152912-6 £4.00

The Protection of Freedoms Act 2012 (Commencement No. 3) Order 2012 No. 2012/2234 (C.89). - Enabling power: Protection of Freedoms Act 2012, ss. 116 (1), 120 (1). Bringing into operation various provisions of the 2012 Act on 10.09.2012 & 01.10.2012 in accord. with arts 2 to 3. - Issued: 04.09.2012. Made: 28.08.2012. Effect: None. Territorial extent & classification: E/W/S/NI. General. - 8p.: 30 cm. - 978-0-11-152842-6 £5.75

The Protection of Freedoms Act 2012 (Commencement No. 4) Order 2012 No. 2012/2521 (C.100). - Enabling power: Protection of Freedoms Act 2012, s. 120 (1). Bringing into operation various provisions of the 2012 Act on 15.10.2012 & 01.12.2012 in accord. with arts 2 and 3. - Issued: 08.10.2012. Made: 03.10.2012. Effect: None. Territorial extent & classification: E/W/NI. General. - 4p.: 30 cm. - 978-0-11-152911-9 £4.00

The Protection of Freedoms Act 2012 (Disclosure and Barring Service Transfer of Functions) Order 2012 No. 2012/3006. - Enabling power: Protection of Freedoms Act 2012, ss. 88, 89. - Issued: 05.12.2012. Made: 29.11.2012. Coming into force: 01.12.2012. Effect: 13 Acts amended & 46 SI's and SR's amended & 1998 c.29 & SI 2007/1351 (NI.11) partially revoked. Territorial extent & classification: E/W/NI. General. - Supersedes draft SI (ISBN 9780111529409) issued 16.10.2012. - 24p.: 30 cm. - 978-0-11-153157-0 £5.75

The Safeguarding Vulnerable Groups Act 2006 (Commencement No. 8 and Saving) Order 2012 No. 2012/2231 (C.88). - Enabling power: Safeguarding Vulnerable Groups Act 2006, ss. 64 (1) (b) (2) (b), 65. Bringing into operation various provisions of the 2006 Act on the dates specified in the Order. - Issued: 04.09.2012. Made: 28.08.2012. Effect: None. Territorial extent & classification: E/W. General. - 8p.: 30 cm. - 978-0-11-152841-9 £5.75

The Safeguarding Vulnerable Groups Act 2006 (Controlled Activity and Prescribed Criteria) Regulations 2012 No. 2012/2160. - Enabling power: Safeguarding Vulnerable Groups Act 2006, ss. 23 (1), 61 (5), 64 (1) (a) (3), sch. 3, paras 1 (1), 2 (1), 7 (1), 8 (1), 24 (1) (2). - Issued: 21.08.2012. Made: 20.08.2012. Coming into force: In accord. with reg 1. Effect: S.I. 2009/37 amended & S.I. 2010/1146 partially revoked (03.09.2012). Territorial extent & classification: E/W. General. - Supersedes draft S.I. (ISBN 9780111524275) issued 16.05.2012. - 8p.: 30 cm. - 978-0-11-152830-3 £5.75

The Safeguarding Vulnerable Groups Act 2006 (Miscellaneous Provisions) Order 2012 No. 2012/2113. - Enabling power: Safeguarding Vulnerable Groups Act 2006, ss. 43 (7), 48 (6), 49 (6), sch. 4, para. 9, sch. 7, para. 2. - Issued: 20.08.2012. Made: 14.08.2012. Laid: 16.08.2012. Coming into force: 10.09.2012, in accord. art. 1. Effect: 2006 c. 47 amended. Territorial extent & classification: E/W. General. - 4p.: 30 cm. - 978-0-11-152823-5 £4.00

The Safeguarding Vulnerable Groups Act 2006 (Miscellaneous Provisions) Regulations 2012 No. 2012/2112. - Enabling power: Safeguarding Vulnerable Groups Act 2006, ss. 2 (5), 35 (1), 36 (1), 37 (2), 39 (1) (5), 41 (1), 42 (2), 45 (1) (5), 46 (1) (2), 50A (1) (d), 60 (1) (5), sch. 3, para. 15, sch. 4, para. 7 (1) (f) (g). - Issued: 20.08.2012. Made: 14.08.2012. Laid: 16.08.2012. Coming into force: 10.09.2012, in accord. with reg. 1 (2) (3). Effect: S.I. 2008/16, 474, 3265; 2009/1548 amended. Territorial extent & classification: E/W. General. - 8p.: 30 cm. - 978-0-11-152822-8 £5.75

The Safeguarding Vulnerable Groups (Miscellaneous Amendments) Order 2012 No. 2012/2157. - Enabling power: Safeguarding Vulnerable Groups Act 2006, ss. 59 (11), 64 (1) (2) (3), sch. 4, paras 6, 9. - Issued: 21.08.2012. Made: 20.08.2012. Coming into force: In accord. with art. 1. Effect: S.I. 2009/1797, 2610 amended & partially revoked (10.09.2012) & 1997 c. 50 modified. Territorial extent & classification: E/W. General. - Supersedes draft S.I. (ISBN 9780111524190) issued 16.05.2012. - 4p.: 30 cm. - 978-0-11-152829-7 £4.00

Protection of vulnerable adults, Northern Ireland

The Protection of Freedoms Act 2012 (Commencement No. 2) Order 2012 No. 2012/2075 (C.82). - Enabling power: Protection of Freedoms Act 2012, ss. 116 (1), 120 (1). Bringing into operation various provisions of the 2012 Act on 10.08.2012, 01.10.2012 & 01.11.2012, 25.11.2012, in accord. with arts 2 to 5. - Issued: 10.08.2012. Made: 07.08.2012. Effect: None. Territorial extent & classification: E/W/S/NI. General. - 4p.: 30 cm. - 978-0-11-152805-1 £4.00

The Protection of Freedoms Act 2012 (Commencement No. 3) Order 2012 No. 2012/2234 (C.89). - Enabling power: Protection of Freedoms Act 2012, ss. 116 (1), 120 (1). Bringing into operation various provisions of the 2012 Act on 10.09.2012 & 01.10.2012 in accord. with arts 2 to 3. - Issued: 04.09.2012. Made: 28.08.2012. Effect: None. Territorial extent & classification: E/W/S/NI. General. - 8p.: 30 cm. - 978-0-11-152842-6 £5.75

The Protection of Freedoms Act 2012 (Commencement No. 4) Order 2012 No. 2012/2521 (C.100). - Enabling power: Protection of Freedoms Act 2012, s. 120 (1). Bringing into operation various provisions of the 2012 Act on 15.10.2012 & 01.12.2012 in accord. with arts 2 and 3. - Issued: 08.10.2012. Made: 03.10.2012. Effect: None. Territorial extent & classification: E/W/NI. General. - 4p.: 30 cm. - 978-0-11-152911-9 £4.00

The Protection of Freedoms Act 2012 (Disclosure and Barring Service Transfer of Functions) Order 2012 No. 2012/3006. - Enabling power: Protection of Freedoms Act 2012, ss. 88, 89. - Issued: 05.12.2012. Made: 29.11.2012. Coming into force: 01.12.2012. Effect: 13 Acts amended & 46 SI's and SR's amended & 1998 c.29 & SI 2007/1351 (NI.11) partially revoked. Territorial extent & classification: E/W/NI. General. - Supersedes draft SI (ISBN 9780111529409) issued 16.10.2012. - 24p.: 30 cm. - 978-0-11-153157-0 £5.75

Protection of wrecks, England

The Protection of Wrecks (Designation) (England) (No. 2) Order 2012 No. 2012/1807. - Enabling power: Protection of Wrecks Act 1973, s. 1 (1) (2). - Issued: 13.07.2012. Made: 10.07.2012. Laid: 11.07.2012. Coming into force: 03.08.2012. Effect: None. Territorial extent & classification: E. General. - 2p.: 30 cm. - 978-0-11-152668-2 £4.00

The Protection of Wrecks (Designation) (England) Order 2012 No. 2012/1773. - Enabling power: Protection of Wrecks Act 1973, s. 1 (1) (2), 3 (2). - Issued: 10.07.2012. Made: 04.07.2012. Laid: 09.07.2012. Coming into force: 31.07.2012. Effect: S.I. 2008/2775 revoked. Territorial extent & classification: E. General. - 2p.: 30 cm. - 978-0-11-152643-9 £4.00

Public bodies

The Advisory Committee on Hazardous Substances (Abolition) Order 2012 No. 2012/1923. - Enabling power: Public Bodies Act 2011, ss. 1 (1), 6 (1) (5), 35 (2). - Issued: 25.07.2012. Made: 21.07.2012. Coming into force: In accord. with art. 1. Effect: 1967 c. 13; 1975 c. 24; 1990 c. 43; 2000 c. 36; 2011 c. 24 partially repealed & S.I. 1993/1572; 1999/1319 partially revoked & S.I. 1991/1487, 1488 revoked. Territorial extent & classification: E/W/S/NI. General. - Supersedes draft S.I. (ISBN 9780111520741) issued 29.02.2012. For approval by resolution of each House of Parliament after the expiry of the 40-day period specified in section 11 (4) of the Public Bodies Act 2011. - 4p.: 30 cm. - 978-0-11-152762-7 £4.00

The British Waterways Board (Transfer of Functions) Order 2011 No. 2012/1659. - Enabling power: Public Bodies Act 2011, ss. 5 (1), 6 (1) to (3), 35 (2). - Issued: 04.07.2012. Made: 01.07.2012. Coming into force: 02.07.2012 in accord. with art. 1. Effect: 29 Acts and 9 statutory instruments amended & S.I. 2003/1545 revoked. Territorial extent & classification: E/W/S/NI. General. - Supersedes draft S.I. (ISBN 9780111521045) issued 02.03.2012. - 32p.: 30 cm. - 978-0-11-152621-7 £5.75

The Inland Waterways Advisory Council (Abolition) Order 2012 No. 2012/1658. - Enabling power: Public Bodies Act 2011, ss. 1 (1), 6 (1), 35 (2). - Issued: 04.07.2012. Made: 01.07.2012. Coming into force: 02.07.2012 in accord. with art. 1. Effect: 1995 c. i amended & partially revoked & 1968 c. 73; 1974 c. 24; 1983 c. ii; 2000 c. 36; 2006 c. 16 partially repealed & S.I. 1993/1119; 1999/1319; 2000/3251; 2006/1466; 2007/570 partially revoked. Territorial extent & classification: E/W/S. - Supersedes draft S.I. (ISBN 9780111521038) issued 02.03.2012. - 4p.: 30 cm. - 978-0-11-152620-0 £4.00

The Localism Act 2011 (Commencement No. 5 and Transitional, Saving and Transitory Provisions) Order 2012 No. 2012/1008 (C.32). - Enabling power: Localism Act 2011, s. 240 (2) (7). Bringing into operation various provisions of the 2011 Act in accord. with arts. 2 to 6. - Issued: 05.04.2012. Made: 03.04.2012. Effect: None. Territorial extent & classification: E/W. General. - 8p.: 30 cm. - 978-0-11-152337-7 £5.75

The Public Bodies (Abolition of Courts Boards) Order 2012 No. 2012/1206. - Enabling power: Public Bodies Act 2011, ss. 1 (1), 6 (1) (5), 35 (2). - Issued: 04.05.2012. Made: 01.05.2012. Coming into force: 02.05.2012, 03.05.2012 in accord. with art. 1. Effect: 2000 c.36; 2003 c. 39; 2005 c. 4; 2011 c. 24 partially repealed & S.I. 2005/2593; 2007/1609 amended & S.I. 2006/1016 partially revoked & S.I. 2004/1192, 1193; 2007/1022; 2009/3184 revoked. Territorial extent & classification: E/W/S/NI. General. - Supersedes draft S.I. (ISBN 9780111519592) issued 01.02.2012. - 8p.: 30 cm. - 978-0-11-152403-9 £5.75

The Public Bodies (Abolition of Crown Court Rule Committee and Magistrates' Courts Rule Committee) Order 2012 No. 2012/2398. - Enabling power: Public Bodies Act 2011, ss. 1, 6 (1) (5), 35 (2). - Issued: 20.09.2012. Made: 17.09.2012. Coming into force: In accord. with art. 1(2). Effect: 1980 c. 43; 1981 c. 54, 2003 c. 39 amended & partially repealed & 1990 c. 41; 2000 c. 36; 2005 c. 4; 2007 c. 29 partially repealed. Territorial extent & classification: UK (E/W in principle and the same extent as provisions they amend). General. - Supersedes draft SI (ISBN 9780111524541) issued on 18.05.2012. - 8p.: 30 cm. - 978-0-11-152889-1 £4.00

The Public Bodies (Abolition of Environment Protection Advisory Committees) Order 2012 No. 2012/2407. - Enabling power: Public Bodies Act 2011, ss. 1 (1), 6 (1) (5), 35 (2). - Issued: 21.09.2012. Made: 18.09.2012. Coming into force: In accord. with art. 1. Effect: 2011 c. 24 partially repealed (20.09.2012). Territorial extent & classification: E/W. General. - Supersedes draft S.I. (ISBN 9780111524671) issued 24.05.2012. - 2p.: 30 cm. - 978-0-11-152895-2 £4.00

The Public Bodies (Abolition of Her Majesty's Inspectorate of Courts Administration and the Public Guardian Board) Order 2012 No. 2012/2401. - Enabling power: Public Bodies Act 2011, ss. 1, 6 (1) (2) (a) (5), 35 (2). - Issued: 11.05.2012. Made: 17.09.2012. Coming into force: In accord. with art. 1. Effect: 1952 c. 52; 1996 c. 16; 1998 c. 18; 2000 c. 10, 43; 2003 c. 39; 2004 c. 23, 31; 2005 c. 9; 2006 c. 40, 48; 2007 c. 28; 2008 c. 14; 2009 c. 25; 2011 c. 24 amended/partially repealed & S.I. 2005/1973; 2006/1016; 2007/603; 2008/912 partially revoked & S.I. 2007/1176, 1770 revoked. Territorial extent & classification: E/W/S/NI. General. - Supersedes draft S.I. (ISBN 9780111524169) issued 11.05.2012. - 12p.: 30 cm. - 978-0-11-152891-4 £5.75

The Public Bodies (Abolition of Regional and Local Fisheries Advisory Committees) Order 2012 No. 2012/2406. - Enabling power: Public Bodies Act 2011, ss. 1 (1), 6 (1) (5), 35 (2). - Issued: 21.09.2012. Made: 18.09.2012. Coming into force: In accord. with art. 1. Effect: 2011 c. 24 partially repealed (20.09.2012). Territorial extent & classification: E/W. General. - Supersedes draft S.I. (ISBN 9780111524725) issued 24.05.2012. - 2p.: 30 cm. - 978-0-11-152896-9 £4.00

The Public Bodies (Abolition of the Commission for Rural Communities) Order 2012 No. 2012/2654. - Enabling power: Public Bodies Act 2011, ss. 1 (1), 6 (1) (5), 35 (2). - Issued: 25.10.2012. Made: 18.10.2012. Coming into force: In accord. with art. 1. Effect: 1947 c. 40; 1972 c. 11; 1975 c. 24; 1984 c. 51; 2000 c. 36; 2006 c. 16; 2011 c. 24 (This Act only partially repealed on 02.04.2013) partially repealed (01.01.2013) & S.I. 2009/1302, 2264; 2010/102, 104, 601; 2011/2055 partially revoked (01.04.2013). Territorial extent & classification: E/W. General. - Supersedes draft SI (ISBN 9780111524596) issued 21.05.2012. - 4p.: 30 cm. - 978-0-11-152987-4 £4.00

The Public Bodies (Abolition of the National Endowment for Science, Technology and the Arts) Order 2012 No. 2012/964. - Enabling power: Public Bodies Act 2011, ss. 1 (1), 6 (1) (5), 35 (2). - Issued: 29.03.2012. Made: 27.03.2012. Coming into force: 01.04.2012. Effect: 2011 c.24 & 15 other acts amended and S.I. 2006/396 revoked. Territorial extent & classification: E/W/S/NI. - Supersedes draft S.I. (ISBN 9780111519394) issued 26.01.2012. - 8p.: 30 cm. - 978-0-11-152304-9 £4.00

The Public Bodies Act 2011 (Commencement No. 2) Order 2012 No. 2012/1662 (C.63). - Enabling power: Public Bodies Act 2011, s. 38 (3). Bringing into operation various provisions of the 2011 Act on 01.07.2012, in accord. with art. 2. - Issued: 29.06.2012. Made: 27.06.2012. Effect: None. Territorial extent & classification: E. General. - 2p.: 30 cm. - 978-0-11-152599-9 £4.00

The Public Bodies Act 2011 (Transitional Provision) Order 2012 No. 2012/1471. - Enabling power: Public Bodies Act 2011, s. 30 (7). - Issued: 11.06.2012. Made: 07.06.2012. Laid: 08.06.2012. Coming into force: 01.07.2012. Effect: None. Territorial extent & classification: E. General. - 2p.: 30 cm. - 978-0-11-152516-6 £4.00

The Public Bodies (Child Maintenance and Enforcement Commission: Abolition and Transfer of Functions) Order 2012 No. 2012/2007. - Enabling power: Public Bodies Act 2011, ss. 1 (1) (2), 6 (1) (5), 23 (1) (a), 35 (2). - Issued: 01.08.2012. Made: 31.07.2012. Coming into force: In accord. with art. 1. Effect: 1967 c.13; 1975 c.24, c.25; 1991 c.48; 1998 c.14; 2000 c.23, c.36; 2002 c.22; 2003 c.42; 2008 c.6; 2009 c.24; 2010 c.15; 2011 c.24; 2012 c.5; S.I. 1992/1815, 1989; 1996/2907; 1999/991; 2001/155, 156; 2008/2551, 2685, 2698; 2009/2615, 2982, 3151; 2010/480, 521, 912, 2955 amended. Territorial extent & classification: E/W/S. General. - Supersedes draft S.I. (ISBN 9780111523728) issued 23.04.2012. - 28p.: 30 cm. - 978-0-11-152792-4 £5.75

Public bodies, England and Wales

The Public Bodies (Water Supply and Water Quality) (Inspection Fees) Order 2012 No. 2012/3101 (W.314). - Enabling power: Public Bodies Act 2011, ss. 14 (3), 15 (1). - Issued: 17.01.2013. Made: 12.12.2012. Coming into force: 13.12.2012 in accord. with art. 1. Effect: None. Territorial extent & classification: E/W. General. - In English and Welsh. Welsh title: Gorchymyn Cyrff Cyhoeddus (Cyflenwad Dwr ac Ansawdd Dwr) (Ffioedd Arolygu) 2012. - 8p.: 30 cm. - 978-0-348-10677-0 £5.75

Public bodies, Wales

The Natural Resources Body for Wales (Establishment) Order 2012 No. 2012/1903 (W.230). - Enabling power: Public Bodies Act 2011, ss. 13 (7), 15 (1). - Issued: 02.08.2012. Made: 18.07.2012. Coming into force: 19.07.2012, in accord. with art. 1. Effect: None. Territorial extent & classification: W. General. - In English and Welsh. Welsh title: Gorchymyn Corff Adnoddau Naturiol Cymru (Sefydlu) 2012. - 16p.: 30 cm. - 978-0-348-10647-3 £5.75

Public health

The Health and Social Care Act 2012 (Commencement No. 2 and Transitional, Savings and Transitory Provisions) Order 2012 No. 2012/1831 (C.71). - Enabling power: Health and Social Care Act 2012, ss. 304 (10), 306. Bringing into operation various provisions of the 2012 Act in accord. with art. 2. - Issued: 16.07.2012. Made: 11.07.2012. Coming into force: .- Effect: None. Territorial extent & classification: E/W. General. - 16p.: 30 cm. - 978-0-11-152699-6 £5.75

The Motor Fuel (Composition and Content) (Amendment) Regulations 2012 No. 2012/2567. - Enabling power: Clean Air Act 1993, ss. 30, 31, 32 (1), 63 (1) & European Communities Act 1972, s. 2 (2). - Issued: 17.10.2012. Made: 10.10.2012. Laid: 12.10.2012. Coming into force: 07.11.2012. Effect: S.I. 1999/3107 amended. Territorial extent & classification: E/W/S/NI. General. - EC note: The 1999 Regulations are amended as these Regulations transpose the changes to Annexes I and II of Directive 98/70/EC relating to the quality of petrol and diesel fuels made by Commission Directive 2011/63/EU. The 2011 Directive updates footnotes in Annexes I and II of Directive 98/70/EC so as to reference the latest versions of the industry fuel standards EN228 and EN590. These standards are referenced to define the methods used for testing whether fuels comply with the specifications listed in the respective annexes. - 4p.: 30 cm. - 978-0-11-152931-7 £4.00

Public health, England

The Care Quality Commission (Healthwatch England Committee) Regulations 2012 No. 2012/1640. - Enabling power: Health and Social Care Act 2008, s. 161 (3) (4), sch. 1, para. 6 (1A) (5A) to (5D). - Issued: 27.06.2012. Made: 21.06.2012. Laid: 27.06.2012. Coming into force: In accord. with reg. 1. Effect: None. Territorial extent & classification: E. General. - 12p.: 30 cm. - 978-0-11-152581-4 £5.75

The Care Quality Commission (Registration) and (Additional Functions) and Health and Social Care Act 2008 (Regulated Activities) (Amendment) Regulations 2012 No. 2012/921. - Enabling power: Health and Social Care Act 2008, ss. 16 (d), 20, 59 (1), 65 (1) (3), 86 (2), 87 (1) (2), 161 (3) (4). - Issued: 27.03.2012. Made: 22.03.2012. Laid: 27.03.2012. Coming into force: In accord. with reg. 1 (2). Effect: S.I. 2009/3112; 2010/781; 2011/1551 amended & S.I. 2009/3112 partially revoked (18.06.2012) & S.I. 2010/49 revoked (18.06.2012). Territorial extent & classification: E. General. - 8p.: 30 cm. - 978-0-11-152283-7 £5.75

The Care Quality Commission (Registration and Membership) (Amendment) Regulations 2012 No. 2012/1186. - Enabling power: Health and Social Care Act 2008, ss. 20, 161 (3), sch. 1, para. 3 (4). - Issued: 03.05.2012. Made: 30.04.2012. Laid: 03.05.2012. Coming into force: 01.06.2012. Effect: S.I. 2009/3112 amended. Territorial extent & classification: E. General. - 2p.: 30 cm. - 978-0-11-152394-0 £4.00

The Health Act 2009 (Commencement No. 6) Order 2012 No. 2012/2647 (C.105). - Enabling power: Health Act 2009, s. 40 (1) (4). Bringing into operation various provisions of the 2009 Act on 31.10.2012, in accord. with art. 2. - Issued: 24.10.2012. Made: 19.10.2012. Effect: None. Territorial extent & classification: E. General. - 4p.: 30 cm. - 978-0-11-152983-6 £4.00

The Health and Social Care Act 2008 (Regulated Activities) (Amendment) Regulations 2012 No. 2012/1513. - Enabling power: Health and Social Care Act 2008, ss. 8 (1), 20, 35, 161 (3) (4). - Issued: 14.06.2012. Made: 12.06.2012. Coming into force: In accord. with reg. 1 (2). Effect: S.I. 2010/781 amended. Territorial extent & classification: E. General. - Supersedes draft SI (ISBN 9780111522752) issued on 27.03.2012. - 8p.: 30 cm. - 978-0-11-152536-4 £5.75

The Smoke-free (Signs) Regulations 2012 No. 2012/1536. - Enabling power: Health Act 2006, s. 6 (2) (3) (4). - Issued: 19.06.2012. Made: 11.06.2012. Laid: 19.06.2012. Coming into force: 01.10.2012. Effect: S.I. 2007/923 revoked. Territorial extent & classification: E. General. - 2p.: 30 cm. - 978-0-11-152553-1 £4.00

The Tobacco Advertising and Promotion (Display and Specialist Tobacconists) (England) (Amendment) Regulations 2012 No. 2012/677. - Enabling power: Tobacco Advertising and Promotion Act 2002, ss. 4 (3), 6 (A1), 7B (3), 19 (2). - Issued: 07.03.2012. Made: 04.03.2012. Laid: 07.03.2012. Coming into force: 06.04.2012, for the purpose of the amendments of the Display Regulations for the purpose of large shops other than bulk tobacconists & 06.04.2015, for the purpose of amendments of the Specialist Tobacconist Regulations, and for all other purposes. Effect: S.I. 2010/445, 446 amended. Territorial extent & classification: E. General. - 4p.: 30 cm. - 978-0-11-152132-8 £4.00

Public health, England: Contamination of food

The Food Protection (Emergency Prohibitions) (Radioactivity in Sheep) (England) (Revocation) Order 2012 No. 2012/2658. - Enabling power: Food and Environment Protection Act 1985, ss. 1 (1) (2) (10), 24 (1) (3). - Issued: 26.10.2012. Made: 21.10.2012. Laid: 26.10.2012. Coming into force: 30.11.2012. Effect: S.I. 1991/6, 2776; 1993/33; 1994/65; 1995/39; 1996/62 revoked. Territorial extent & classification: E. General. - 2p.: 30 cm. - 978-0-11-152989-8 £4.00

Public health, England and Wales

The Health and Social Care Act 2008 (Consequential Amendments) (Council Tax) Order 2012 No. 2012/1915. - Enabling power: Health and Social Care Act 2008, s. 167 (1) (b) (3). - Issued: 24.07.2012. Made: 18.07.2012. Laid: 24.07.2012. Coming into force: 23.08.2012. Effect: S.I. 1992/549, 551 amended. Territorial extent & classification: E. General. - 2p.: 30 cm. - 978-0-11-152759-7 £4.00

Public health, Wales

The Food Protection (Emergency Prohibitions) (Radioactivity in Sheep) (Wales) (Revocation) Order 2012 No. 2012/2978 (W.304). - Enabling power: Animal Health Act 1981, s. 11 & Food and Environment Protection Act 1985, ss. 1 (1) (2) (10), 24 (1) (3). - Issued: 14.12.2012. Made: 28.11.2012. Coming into force: 29.11.2012. In accord. with art. 1. Effect: S.I. 1991/5, 58, 2780; 1994/63; 1995/46; 1998/72; 2011/2759 revoked in relation to Wales(29.11.2012). Territorial extent & classification: W. General. - In English and Welsh. Welsh title: Gorchymyn Diogelu Bwyd (Gwaharddiadau Brys) (Ymbelydredd mewn Defaid) (Cymru) (Dirymu) 2012. - 4p.: 30 cm. - 978-0-348-10668-8 £4.00

The Tobacco Advertising and Promotion (Display of Prices) (Wales) Regulations 2012 No. 2012/1911 (W.233). - Enabling power: Tobacco Advertising and Promotion Act 2002, ss. 7C, 19 (2) & Welsh Language Act 1993, s. 26 (3). - Issued: 02.08.2012. Made: 18.07.2015. Coming into force: 03.12.2012, for large shops & 06.04.2015 for all other purposes, in accord. with reg. 1 (1). Effect: None. Territorial extent & classification: W. General. - In English and Welsh. Welsh title: Rheoliadau Hysbysebu a Hyrwyddo Tybaco (Arddangos Prisiau) (Cymru) 2012. - 12p.: 30 cm. - 978-0-348-10645-9 £5.75

The Tobacco Advertising and Promotion (Display) (Wales) Regulations 2012 No. 2012/1285 (W.163). - Enabling power: Tobacco Advertising and Promotion Act 2002, ss. 4 (3), 7A (2), 7B (3), 19 (2) & Welsh Language Act 1993, s. 26 (3). - Issued: 30.05.2012. Made: 14.05.2015. Laid before the National Assembly for Wales: 16.05.2015. Coming into force: 03.12.2012, for large shops other than bulk tobacconists & 06.04.2015, for all other purposes in accord. with reg. 1 (1). Effect: S.I. 2004/765 revoked in relation to Wales. Territorial extent & classification: W. General. - In English and Welsh. Welsh title: Rheoliadau Hysbysebu a Hyrwyddo Tybaco (Arddangos) (Cymru) 2012. - 12p.: 30 cm. - 978-0-348-10612-1 £5.75

The Tobacco Advertising and Promotion (Specialist Tobacconists) (Wales) Regulations 2012 No. 2012/1287 (W.164). - Enabling power: Tobacco Advertising and Promotion Act 2002, ss. 6 (A1), 7B (3), 19 (2). - Issued: 31.05.2012. Made: 14.05.2012. Laid before the National Assembly for Wales: 16.05.2012. Coming into force: 06.04.2015. Effect: S.I. 2004/1277 revoked. Territorial extent & classification: W. General. - In English and Welsh. Welsh title: Rheoliadau Hysbysebu a Hyrwyddo Tybaco (Gwerthwyr Tybaco Arbenigol) (Cymru) 2012. - 8p.: 30 cm. - 978-0-348-10611-4 £4.00

Public passenger transport

The Public Service Vehicles (Operators' Licences) (Fees) (Amendment) Regulations 2012 No. 2012/306. - Enabling power: Public Passenger Vehicles Act 1981, ss. 52 (1) (a), 60 (1) (e). - Issued: 13.02.2012. Made: 07.02.2012. Laid: 13.02.2012. Coming into force: 01.04.2012. Effect: S.I. 1995/2909 amended. Territorial extent & classification: E/W/S. General. - 2p.: 30 cm. - 978-0-11-152001-7 £4.00

Public passenger transport, England

The Localism Act 2011 (Commencement No. 3) Order 2012 No. 2012/411 (C. 11). - Enabling power: Localism Act 2011, s. 240 (2) (7). Bringing into operation various provisions of the 2011 Act on 18.02.2012, in accord. with art. 2. - Issued: 20.02.2012. Made: 17.02.2012. Effect: None. Territorial extent & classification: E/W. General. - 4p.: 30 cm. - 978-0-11-152038-3 £4.00

Public procurement, England and Wales

The Public Services Reform (Social Value) Act 2012 (Commencement) Order 2012 No. 2012/3173 (C. 124). - Enabling power: Public Services (Social Value) Act 2012, s. 4 (3). Bringing into operation various provisions of the 2012 Act on 31.01.2013, in accord. with s. 2. - Issued: 27.12.2012. Made: 20.12.2012. Effect: None. Territorial extent & classification: E/W. General. - 2p.: 30 cm. - 978-0-11-153286-7 £4.00

Public records

The Constitutional Reform and Governance Act 2010 (Commencement No. 7) Order 2012 No. 2012/3001 (C.119). - Enabling power: Constitutional Reform and Governance Act 2010, s. 52 (2). Bringing into operation various provisions of the 2010 Act on 30.11.2012 & 01.01.2013. - Issued: 04.12.2012. Made: 29.11.2012. Effect: None. Territorial extent & classification: E/W/S/NI. General. - 4p.: 30 cm. - 978-0-11-153149-5 £4.00

The Public Record Office (Fees) Regulations 2012 No. 2012/1665. - Enabling power: Public Records Act 1958, s. 2 (5). - Issued: 29.06.2012. Made: 20.06.2012. Coming into force: 30.07.2012. Effect: S.I. 2005/471 revoked. Territorial extent & classification: E/W/S/NI. General. - 4p.: 30 cm. - 978-0-11-152601-9 £4.00

The Public Records (Transfer to the Public Record Office) (Transitional and Saving Provisions) Order 2012 No. 2012/3028. - Enabling power: Constitutional Reform and Governance act 2010, s. 45 (2) (3). - Issued: 07.12.2012. Made: 05.12.2012. Laid: 06.12.2012. Coming into force: 01.01.2013. Effect: None. Territorial extent & classification: E/W. General. - 4p.: 30 cm. - 978-0-11-153177-8 £4.00

Public sector information

The INSPIRE (Amendment) Regulations 2012 No. 2012/1672. - Enabling power: European Communities Act 1972, s 2 (2). - Issued: 11.07.2012. Made: 01.07.2012. Laid: 05.07.2012. Coming into force: 01.08.2012. Effect: S.I. 2009/3157 amended. Territorial extent & classification: E/W/S/NI but has no application to S. General. - INSPIRE = Infrastructure for Spatial Information in the European Community. EC note: These Regulations amend the INSPIRE Regulations which implemented Directive 2007/2/EC to transpose requirements not previously transposed in accordance with Reg (EU) 1089/2010. - 8p.: 30 cm. - 978-0-11-152626-2 £4.00

Rating and valuation, England

The Central Rating List (England) (Amendment) Regulations 2012 No. 2012/1292. - Enabling power: Local Government Finance Act 1988, ss. 53 (1) (2) (4), 143 (1) (2). - Issued: 21.05.2012. Made: 15.05.2012. Laid: 21.05.2012. Coming into force: In accord. with reg. 1. Effect: S.I. 2005/551 amended. Territorial extent & classification: E. General. - 2p.: 30 cm. - 978-0-11-152441-1 £4.00

The Council Tax and Non-Domestic Rating (Demand Notices) (England) (Amendment) Regulations 2012 No. 2012/538. - Enabling power: Local Government Finance Act 1988, ss. 143 (1) (2), sch. 9, paras 1, 2 (2) (ga) (h). - Issued: 05.03.2012. Made: 27.02.2012. Laid: 05.03.2012. Coming into force: 31.03.2012. Effect: S.I. 2003/2613 amended. Territorial extent & classification: E. General. - With correction slip dated March 2012. - 8p.: 30 cm. - 978-0-11-152087-1 £5.75

The Localism Act 2011 (Commencement No. 4 and Transitional, Transitory and Saving Provisions) Order 2012 No. 2012/628 (C.14). - Enabling power: Localism Act 2011, s. 240 (2) (7). Bringing into operation various provisions of the 2011 Act in accord. with arts. 2 to 8. - Issued: 07.03.2012. Made: 01.03.2012. Effect: None. Territorial extent & classification: E/W. General. - Partially revoked by S.I. 2012/2029 (C.80) (ISBN 9780111527962). - 12p.: 30 cm. - 978-0-11-152126-7 £5.75

The Non-Domestic Rating and Business Rate Supplements (Deferred Payments) (England) Regulations 2012 No. 2012/994. - Enabling power: Local Government Finance Act 1988, ss. 143 (1) (2), 146 (6), sch. 8, para. 6 (5) (6), sch. 9, paras 1 to 4 & Business Rate Supplements Act 2009, ss. 21, 29 (3). - Issued: 05.04.2012. Made: 02.04.2012. Laid: 05.04.2012. Coming into force: 30.04.2012. Effect: S.I. 1989/1058, 2260; 1992/3082; 2003/2613 amended. Territorial extent & classification: E. General. - With correction slip dated June 2012. - 20p.: 30 cm. - 978-0-11-152330-8 £5.75

The Non-Domestic Rating (Cancellation of Backdated Liabilities) Regulations 2012 No. 2012/537. - Enabling power: Local Government Finance Act 1988, ss. 49A (1), 143 (1). - Issued: 05.03.2012. Made: 27.02.2012. Laid: 05.03.2012. Coming into force: 31.03.2012. Effect: None. Territorial extent & classification: E. General. - 4p.: 30 cm. - 978-0-11-152093-2 £4.00

The Non-Domestic Rating (Collection and Enforcement) (Amendment) (England) Regulations 2012 No. 2012/24. - Enabling power: Local Government Finance Act 1988, s. 143 (2), sch. 9, paras 1 - 4. - Issued: 12.01.2012. Made: 06.01.2012. Laid: 12.01.2012. Coming into force: 15.02.2012. Effect: S.I. 1989/1058, 2260 amended. Territorial extent & classification: E. General. - 4p.: 30 cm. - 978-0-11-151901-1 £4.00

The Non-Domestic Rating Contributions (England) (Amendment) Regulations 2012 No. 2012/664. - Enabling power: Local Government Finance Act 1988, s. 143 (1) (2), sch. 8, paras. 4, 6. - Issued: 07.03.2012. Made: 02.03.2012. Laid: 07.03.2012. Coming into force: 31.03.2012. Effect: S.I. 1992/3082 amended. Territorial extent & classification: E. General. - 4p.: 30 cm. - 978-0-11-152129-8 £4.00

The Non-Domestic Rating (Electronic Communications) (England) Order 2012 No. 2012/25. - Enabling power: Electronic Communications Act 2000, s. 8. - Issued: 12.01.2012. Made: 06.01.2012. Laid: 12.01.2012. Coming into force: 15.02.2012. Effect: S.I. 1989/1058 amended in relation to England. Territorial extent & classification: E. General. - 2p.: 30 cm. - 978-0-11-151902-8 £4.00

The Non-Domestic Rating (Small Business Rate Relief) (England) Order 2012 No. 2012/148. - Enabling power: Local Government Finance Act 1988, ss. 43 (4B) (a), 44 (9) (a), 143 (1) (2). - Issued: 26.01.2012. Made: 23.01.2012. Laid: 26.01.2012. Coming into force: 25.02.2012. Effect: S.I. 2004/3351 revoked in respect of chargeable days falling after 31 March 2012. Territorial extent & classification: E. General. - 4p.: 30 cm. - 978-0-11-151943-1 £4.00

The Non-Domestic Rating (Waterways) (England) Regulations 2012 No. 2012/1291. - Enabling power: Local Government Finance Act 1988, ss. 63 (3), 65 (4), 143 (1) (2). - Issued: 21.05.2012. Made: 15.05.2012. Laid: 21.05.2012. Coming into force: 15.06.2012. Effect: None. Territorial extent & classification: E. General. - 4p.: 30 cm. - 978-0-11-152442-8 £4.00

Rating and valuation, Wales

The Non-Domestic Rating Contributions (Wales) (Amendment) Regulations 2012 No. 2012/3036 (W.310). - Enabling power: Local Government Finance Act 1988, ss. 60, 140 (4), 143 (1), sch. 8, paras 4, 6. - Issued: 20.12.2012. Made: 04.12.2012. Laid before the National Assembly for Wales: 07.12.2012. Coming into force: 31.12.2012. Effect: S.I. 1992/3238 amended. Territorial extent & classification: W. General. - In English and Welsh: Welsh title: Rheoliadau Cyfraniadau Ardrethu Annomestig (Cymru) (Diwygio) 2012. - 4p.: 30 cm. - 978-0-348-10672-5 £4.00

The Non-Domestic Rating (Deferred Payments) (Wales) Regulations 2012 No. 2012/466 (W.77). - Enabling power: Local Government Finance Act 1988, ss. 60, 62, 143 (1) (2), 146 (6), sch. 8, para 6 (5) (6), sch. 9, paras 1 to 4. - Issued: 09.03.2012. Made: 20.02.2012. Laid before the National Assembly for Wales: 23.02.2012. Coming into force: 16.03.2012 Effect: S.I. 1989/1058; 2260 amended in relation to Wales & S.I. 1992/3238; 1993/252 modified & S.I. 2009/2154 (W.179) partially revoked. Territorial extent & classification: W. General. - In English and Welsh: Rheoliadau Ardrethu Annomestig (Taliadau Gohiriedig) (Cymru) 2012. - 12p.: 30 cm. - 978-0-348-10560-5 £5.75

The Non-Domestic Rating (Demand Notices) (Wales) (Amendment) Regulations 2012 No. 2012/467 (W.78). - Enabling power: Local Government Finance Act 1988, ss. 62, 146 (6), sch. 9, paras 1, 2 (2) & Welsh Language Act 1993, s. 26 (3). - Issued: 09.03.2012. Made: 20.02.2012. Laid before the National Assembly for Wales: 23.02.2012. Coming into force: 16.03.2012. Effect: S.I. 1993/252 amended. Territorial extent & classification: W. General. - In English and Welsh: Welsh title: Rheoliadau Ardrethu Annomestig (Hysbysiadau Galw am Dalu) (Cymru) (Diwygio) 2012. - 4p.: 30 cm. - 978-0-348-10559-9 £4.00

The Non-Domestic Rating (Small Business Relief) (Wales) (Amendment) Order 2012 No. 2012/465 (W.76). - Enabling power: Local Government Finance Act 1988, ss. 43 (4B) (b), 44 (9), 143 (1), 146 (6). - Issued: 09.03.2012. Made: 20.02.2012. Laid before the National Assembly for Wales: 23.02.2012. Coming into force: 16.03.2012. Effect: S.I. 2008/2770 (W.246) amended. Territorial extent & classification: W. General. - With correction slip dated February 2013. - In English and Welsh: Welsh title: Gorchymyn Ardrethu Annomestig (Rhyddhad Ardrethi i Fusnesau Bach) (Cymru) (Diwygio) 2012. - 4p.: 30 cm. - 978-0-348-10561-2 £4.00

Recovery of taxes

The European Administrative Co-operation (Taxation) Regulations 2012 No. 2012/3062. - Enabling power: European Communities Act 1972, s. 2 (2), sch. 2, para. 1A. - Issued: 12.12.2012. Made: 10.12.2012. Laid: 11.12.2012. Coming into force: 01.01.2013. Effect: 2003 c.14; 2005 c.22 partially repealed. Territorial extent & classification: E/W/S/NI. General. - 4p.: 30 cm. - 978-0-11-153213-3 £4.00

Registration of births, deaths, marriages, etc., England and Wales

The Registration of Births, Deaths and Marriages (Fees) (Amendment) Order 2012 No. 2012/760. - Enabling power: Public Expenditure and Receipts Act 1968, s. 5 (1) (2), sch. 3, paras 1, 2. - Issued: 13.03.2012. Made: 08.03.2012. Laid: 09.03.2012. Coming into force: 01.04.2012. Effect: S.I. 2010/441 amended. Territorial extent & classification: E/W. General. - 8p.: 30 cm. - 978-0-11-152175-5 £5.75

The Registration of Births and Deaths Regulations 1987 (Amendment) Regulations 2012 No. 2012/1203. - Enabling power: Welfare Reform Act 2009, s. 57 (1) (2). - Issued: 08.05.2012. Made: 02.05.2012. Laid: 03.05.2012. Coming into force: 28.05.2012. Effect: S.I. 1987/2088, 2089 amended. Territorial extent & classification: E/W. General. - 8p.: 30 cm. - 978-0-11-152400-8 £5.75

The Welfare Reform Act 2009 (Commencement No. 8) Order 2012 No. 2012/1256 (C.43). - Enabling power: Welfare Reform Act 2009, s. 61 (5). Bringing into operation various provisions of the 2009 Act on 21.05.2012 & 28.05.2012, in accord. with art 2. - Issued: 14.05.2012. Made: 10.05.2012. Effect: None. Territorial extent & classification: E/W/S. General. - 4p.: 30 cm. - 978-0-11-152422-0 £4.00

Regulatory reform

The Legislative Reform (Annual Review of Local Authorities) Order 2012 No. 2012/1879. - Enabling power: Legislative and Regulatory Reform Act 2006, s. 1. - Issued: 30.07.2012. Made: 17.07.2012. Coming into force: 18.07.2012 in accord. with art. 1. Effect: 2006 c. 40 amended. Territorial extent & classification: E. General. - Supersedes draft S.I. (ISBN 9780111524091) issued 10.05.2012. - 4p.: 30 cm. - 978-0-11-152739-9 £4.00

The Legislative Reform (Civil Partnership) Order 2012 No. 2012/3100. - Enabling power: Legislative and Regulatory Reform Act 2006, s. 1. - Issued: 19.12.2012. Made: 04.12.2012. Coming into force: 05.12.2012. Effect: 2004 c.33 amended. Territorial extent & classification: E/W/S/NI. General. - 2p.: 30 cm. - 978-0-11-153257-7 £4.00

The Local Better Regulation Office (Dissolution and Transfer of Functions, Etc.) Order 2012 No. 2012/246. - Enabling power: Regulatory Enforcement and Sanctions Act 2008, s. 18. - Issued: 03.02.2012. Made: 01.02.2012. Coming into force: 02.02.2012 in accord. with art. 1. Effect: 1967 c. 13; 1972 c. 11; 1975 c. 24; 2000 c. 36 partially repealed & 2008 c. 13 amended & partially repealed. Territorial extent & classification: E/W/S/NI. General. - Supersedes draft S.I. (ISBN 9780111517772) issued 09.12.2011. - 8p.: 30 cm. - 978-0-11-151977-6 £5.75

Rehabilitation of offenders

The Legal Aid, Sentencing and Punishment of Offenders Act 2012 (Commencement No. 2 and Specification of Commencement Date) Order 2012 No. 2012/2412 (C.94). - Enabling power: Legal Aid, Sentencing and Punishment of Offenders Act 2012, ss. 141 (12), 151 (1). Bringing into operation various provisions of the 2012 Act on 01.10.2012 in accordance with arts 2, 3. - Issued: 24.09.2012. Made: 18.09.2012. Effect: None. Territorial extent & classification: E/W/S/NI. General. - 4p.: 30 cm. - 978-0-11-152897-6 £4.00

Rehabilitation of offenders, England and Wales

The Rehabilitation of Offenders Act 1974 (Exceptions) (Amendment) (England and Wales) Order 2012 No. 2012/1957. - Enabling power: Rehabilitation of Offenders Act 1974, ss. 4 (4), 10 (1), sch. 2, para. 4. - Issued: 27.07.2012. Made: 24.07.2012. Coming into force: In accord. with art. 1. Effect: S.I. 1975/1023 amended. Territorial extent & classification: E/W. General. - Supersedes draft SI (ISBN 9780111524237) issued on 14.05.2012. - 4p.: 30 cm. - 978-0-11-152774-0 £4.00

Representation of the people

The Electoral Registration Data Schemes (No. 2) Order 2012 No. 2012/3232. - Enabling power: Political Parties and Elections Act 2009, ss. 35, 36. - Issued: 07.01.2013. Made: 19.12.2012. Coming into force: 20.12.2012, in accord. with art 1. Effect: None. Territorial extent & classification: E/W/S/NI. General. - Supersedes draft SI (ISBN 9780111530078) issued 30.10.2012. - 8p.: 30 cm. - 978-0-11-153294-2 £5.75

The Electoral Registration Data Schemes Order 2012 No. 2012/1944. - Enabling power: Political Parties and Elections Act 2009, ss. 35, 36. - Issued: 26.07.2012. Made: 17.07.2012. Coming into force: In accord. with art 1. Effect: S.I. 2011/1466 revoked. Territorial extent & classification: E/W/S/NI. General. - Supersedes draft S.I. (ISBN 9780111524077) issued 11.05.2012. - 8p.: 30 cm. - 978-0-11-152769-6 £4.00

Representation of the people, England

The Greater London Authority Elections (Amendment) Rules 2012 No. 2012/198. - Enabling power: Representation of the People Act 1983, s. 36 (2A) (2B). - Issued: 31.01.2012. Made: 26.01.2012. Laid: 31.01.2012. Coming into force: 01.03.2012. Effect: S.I. 2007/3541 amended. Territorial extent & classification: E. General. - 12p.: 30 cm. - 978-0-11-151961-5 £5.75

Representation of the people, Wales

The National Assembly for Wales (Returning Officers' Charges) (Amendment) Order 2012 No. 2012/2478 (W.270). - Enabling power: S.I. 2007/236, art. 23. - Issued: 15.10.2012. Made: 25.09.2012. Coming into force: 01.10.2012. Effect: S.I. 2011/632 (W.92) amended. Territorial extent & classification: W. General. - In English & Welsh. Welsh title: Gorchymyn Cynulliad Cenedlaethol Cymru (Taliadau Swyddogion Canlyniadau) (Diwygio) 2012. - 12p.: 30 cm. - 978-0-348-10656-5 £5.75

Revenue and customs

The Customs (Inspections by Her Majesty's Inspectors of Constabulary and the Scottish Inspectors) Regulations 2012 No. 2012/2840. - Enabling power: Borders Citizenship and Immigration Act 2009, ss. 29, 37 (2). - Issued: 15.11.2012. Made: 12.11.2012. Laid: 14.11.2012. Coming into force: 10.12.2012. Effect: None. Territorial extent & classification: E/W/S/NI - but there is no provision for Northern Ireland as there are no detention centres there. General. - 8p.: 30 cm. - 978-0-11-153077-1 £5.75

The Taxes, etc. (Fees for Payment by Telephone) Regulations 2012 No. 2012/689. - Enabling power: Finance Act 2008, s. 136. - Issued: 07.03.2012. Made: 05.03.2012. Laid: 06.03.2012. Coming into force: 02.04.2012. Effect: S.I. 2009/3073 revoked. Territorial extent & classification: E/W/S/NI. General. - 2p.: 30 cm. - 978-0-11-152142-7 £4.00

Rights in performances

The Copyright and Performances (Application to Other Countries) Order 2012 No. 2012/799. - Enabling power: Copyright, Designs and Patents Act 1988, ss. 159, 208 & European Communities Act 1972, s. 2 (2). - Issued: 15.03.2012. Made: 14.03.2012. Laid: 15.03.2012. Coming into force: 06.04.2012. Effect: S.I. 2008/677; 2009/2745 revoked. Territorial extent & classification: E/W/S/NI. General. - 16p.: 30 cm. - 978-0-11-152228-8 £5.75

Rights of the subject, England and Wales

The Protection of Freedoms Act 2012 (Commencement No. 3) Order 2012 No. 2012/2234 (C.89). - Enabling power: Protection of Freedoms Act 2012, ss. 116 (1), 120 (1). Bringing into operation various provisions of the 2012 Act on 10.09.2012 & 01.10.2012 in accord. with arts 2 to 3. - Issued: 04.09.2012. Made: 28.08.2012. Effect: None. Territorial extent & classification: E/W/S/NI. General. - 8p.: 30 cm. - 978-0-11-152842-6 £5.75

The Protection of Freedoms Act 2012 (Relevant Official Records) Order 2012 No. 2012/2279. - Enabling power: Protection of Freedoms Act 2012, s. 95 (5) (6). - Issued: 07.09.2012. Made: 04.09.2012. Laid: 06.09.2012. Coming into force: 01.10.2012. Effect: None. Territorial extent & classification: E/W. General. - 4p.: 30 cm. - 978-0-11-152861-7 £4.00

Rights of the subject, England and Wales: Powers of entry

The Protection of Freedoms Act 2012 (Commencement No. 1) Order 2012 No. 2012/1205 (C.41). - Enabling power: Protection of Freedoms Act 2012, s. 120 (1). Bringing into operation various provisions of the 2012 Act on 09.05.2012, 01.07.2012 & 10.07.2012. - Issued: 08.05.2012. Made: 02.05.2012. Effect: None. Territorial extent & classification: E/W/S/NI. General. - 4p.: 30 cm. - 978-0-11-152402-2 £4.00

Rights of the subject, England and Wales: Surveillance cameras

The Protection of Freedoms Act 2012 (Commencement No. 1) Order 2012 No. 2012/1205 (C.41). - Enabling power: Protection of Freedoms Act 2012, s. 120 (1). Bringing into operation various provisions of the 2012 Act on 09.05.2012, 01.07.2012 & 10.07.2012. - Issued: 08.05.2012. Made: 02.05.2012. Effect: None. Territorial extent & classification: E/W/S/NI. General. - 4p.: 30 cm. - 978-0-11-152402-2 £4.00

Road traffic

The Community Drivers' Hours and Recording Equipment Regulations 2012 No. 2012/1502. - Enabling power: Transport Act 1968, s. 96 (10) & European Communities Act 1972, s. 2 (2). - Issued: 19.06.2012. Made: 11.06.2012. Laid: 14.06.2012. Coming into force: 16.07.2012. Effect: 1986/2128 amended & S.I. 2007/2370 revoked. Territorial extent & classification: E/W/S/NI. General. - 8p.: 30 cm. - 978-0-11-152525-8 £4.00

The Driving Instruction (Compensation Scheme) Regulations 2012 No. 2012/1548. - Enabling power: Road Traffic Act 1988, ss. 131A, 141. - Issued: 25.06.2012. Made: 18.06.2012. Laid: 20.06.2012. Coming into force: 13.06.2012. Effect: None. Territorial extent & classification: E/W/S. General. - 12p.: 30 cm. - 978-0-11-152555-5 £5.75

The Driving Instruction (Suspension and Exemption Powers) Act 2009 (Commencement No. 1) Order 2012 No. 2012/1356 (C.49). - Enabling power: Driving Instruction (Suspension and Exemption Powers) Act 2009, s. 7 (3). Bringing into operation various provisions of the 2009 Act on 08.06.2012 & 06.07.2012. - Issued: 29.05.2012. Made: 22.05.2012. Effect: None. Territorial extent & classification: E/W/S. General. - 2p.: 30 cm. - 978-0-11-152471-8 £4.00

The Goods Vehicles (Licensing of Operators) (Fees) (Amendment) Regulations 2012 No. 2012/308. - Enabling power: Goods Vehicles (Licensing of Operators) Act 1995, ss. 45 (1), 57 (1) (7). - Issued: 13.02.2012. Made: 07.02.2012. Laid: 13.02.2012. Coming into force: 01.04.2012. Effect: S.I. 1995/3000 amended. Territorial extent & classification: E/W/S. General. - 2p.: 30 cm. - 978-0-11-152003-1 £4.00

The Goods Vehicles (Plating and Testing) (Amendment) Regulations 2012 No. 2012/305. - Enabling power: Road Traffic Act 1988, ss. 49, 51 (1), 63A. - Issued: 13.02.2012. Made: 07.02.2012. Laid: 13.02.2012. Coming into force: 01.04.2012. Effect: S.I. 1988/1478 amended. Territorial extent & classification: E/W/S. General. - 8p.: 30 cm. - 978-0-11-152000-0 £4.00

The Motor Vehicles (Driving Licences) (Amendment) Regulations 2012 No. 2012/977. - Enabling power: European Communities Act 1972, s. 2 (2) & Road Traffic Act 1988, ss. 89 (3) (a) (c) (4) (a) (5), 97 (3), 98 (4), 99 (7ZA), 99A (6), 101 (2) (3), 105 (1) (2) (a) (ee) (f) (g) (3). - Issued: 04.04.2012. Made: 27.03.2012. Laid: 30.03.2012. Coming into force: 19.01.2013, for regs 2 & 4; 20.04.2012, for remainder. Effect: 1988 c. 52; 2006 c. 49; S.I. 1999/2864 amended. Territorial extent & classification: E/W/S. General. - EC note: Implement Directive 2006/126/EC. - 30p.: 30 cm. - 978-0-11-152321-6 £5.75

The Motor Vehicles (Tests) (Amendment) (No. 2) Regulations 2012 No. 2012/2652. - Enabling power: Road Traffic Act 1988, s. 47 (5). - Issued: 25.10.2012. Made: 21.10.2012. Laid: 25.10.2012. Coming into force: 18.11.2012. Effect: S.I. 1981/1694 amended. Territorial extent & classification: E/W/S. General. - 2p.: 30 cm. - 978-0-11-152982-9 £4.00

The Motor Vehicles (Tests) (Amendment) Regulations 2012 No. 2012/307. - Enabling power: Road Traffic Act 1988, ss. 45 (7), 46 (1) (f) (7). - Issued: 13.02.2012. Made: 07.02.2012. Laid: 13.02.2012. Coming into force: 01.04.2012. Effect: S.I. 1981/1694 amended. Territorial extent & classification: E/W/S. General. - 4p.: 30 cm. - 978-0-11-152002-4 £4.00

The Rehabilitation Courses (Relevant Drink Offences) Regulations 2012 No. 2012/2939. - Enabling power: Road Traffic Offenders Act 1988, ss. 34B (3) (10), 34BA (5), 34C (4). - Issued: 30.11.2012. Made: 22.11.2012. Laid: 27.11.2012. Coming into force: 21.12.2012 for regs 1-4, 5 (1) (2), 7 (1) (4) (a), 12 (insofar as it relates to reg.3) & 24.06.2013 for all other regs and reg. 12 for remaining purposes, in accord. with reg. 1. Effect: S.I. 1992/3013 revoked (24.06.2013). Territorial extent & classification: E/W/S. General. - 12p.: 30 cm. - 978-0-11-153122-8 £5.75

The Road Safety Act 2006 (Commencement No. 8) Order 2012 No. 2012/1357 (C.50). - Enabling power: Road Safety Act 2006, s. 61. Bringing into operation various provisions of the 2006 Act on 21.05.2012 in accord. with art. 2. - Issued: 29.05.2012. Made: 10.05.2012. Effect: None. Territorial extent & classification: E/W/S. General. - 4p.: 30 cm. - 978-0-11-152470-1 £4.00

The Road Safety Act 2006 (Commencement No. 9 and Transitional Provisions) Order 2012 No. 2012/2938 (C.117). - Enabling power: Road Safety Act 2006, s. 61 (1) (2) (6). Bringing into operation various provisions of the 2006 Act in accord. with art. 2. - Issued: 30.11.2012. Made: 22.11.2012. Effect: None. Territorial extent & classification: E/W/S. General. - 4p.: 30 cm. - 978-0-11-153120-4 £4.00

The Road Vehicles (Construction and Use) (Amendment) Regulations 2012 No. 2012/1404. - Enabling power: Road Traffic Act 1988, s. 41 (1) (2) (5). - Issued: 06.06.2012. Made: 28.05.2012. Laid: 30.05.2012. Coming into force: 25.06.2012. Effect: S.I. 1986/1078 amended & S.I. 1996/2085; 1997/1544; 1998/1563; 2000/1434; 2001/1825; 2002/1474; 2003/1690; 2010/2060 partially revoked & S.I. 1999/1521, 1959; 2004/1706; 2005/1641; 2006/1756; 2007/1817; 2008/1702; 2009/1806 revoked. Territorial extent & classification: E/W/S. General. - 4p.: 30 cm. - 978-0-11-152491-6 £4.00

The Road Vehicles (Individual Approval) (Fees) (Amendment) Regulations 2012 No. 2012/1271. - Enabling power: Finance Act 1973, s. 56 (1) (2) & Finance Act 1990, s. 128. - Issued: 21.05.2012. Made: 10.05.2012. Laid: 16.05.2012. Coming into force: 20.06.2012. Effect: S.I. 2009/718 amended. Territorial extent & classification: E/W/S. General. - 2p.: 30 cm. - 978-0-11-152435-0 £4.00

The Road Vehicles (Registration and Licensing) (Amendment) (No. 2) Regulations 2012 No. 2012/443. - Enabling power: Vehicle Excise and Registration Act 1994, ss. 57 (1) (2) (3), 61B. - Issued: 24.02.2012. Made: 20.02.2012. Laid: 23.02.2012. Coming into force: 23.03.2012. Effect: S.I. 2002/2742 amended. Territorial extent & classification: E/W/S/NI. General. - 4p.: 30 cm. - 978-0-11-152045-1 £4.00

The Road Vehicles (Registration and Licensing) (Amendment) Regulations 2012 No. 2012/304. - Enabling power: Vehicle Excise and Registration Act 1994, s. 57 (1) to (3), 61B (1) (d). - Issued: 13.02.2012. Made: 07.02.2012. Laid: 13.02.2012. Coming into force: 01.04.2012. Effect: S.I. 2002/2742 amended. Territorial extent & classification: E/W/S/NI. General. - 4p.: 30 cm. - 978-0-11-151999-8 £4.00

Road traffic: Speed limits

The A3 Trunk Road (Hindhead) (Derestriction and Variable Speed Limit) Order 2012 No. 2012/2138. - Enabling power: Road Traffic Regulation Act 1984, ss. 84 (1) (c) (1A) (2), 82 (2), 83 (1), sch. 9, para. 27 (1). - Issued: 21.08.2012. Made: 13.08.2012. Coming into force: 27.08.2012. Effect: S.I. 2011/1534 revoked. Territorial extent & classification: E. Local. - Available at http://www.legislation.gov.uk/uksi/2012/2138/contents/made *Non-print*

The A5 and A38 Trunk Roads (Weeford Roundabout, Staffordshire) (Derestriction) Order 2012 No. 2012/2033. - Enabling power: Road Traffic Regulation Act 1984, ss. 82 (2), 83 (1), sch. 9. para. 27 (1). - Issued: 07.08.2012. Made: 12.07.2012. Coming into force: 26.07.2012. Effect: None. Territorial extent & classification: E. Local. - Available at http://www.legislation.gov.uk/uksi/2012/2033/contents/made *Non-print*

The A5 Trunk Road (A5148/A5127 Junction, Shenstone, Staffordshire) (50 Miles Per Hour Speed Limit and Derestriction) Order 2012 No. 2012/1097. - Enabling power: Road Traffic Regulation Act 1984, ss. 82 (2), 83 (1), 84 (1) (a) (2), sch. 9, para. 27 (1). - Issued: 19.04.2012. Made: 15.03.2012. Coming into force: 29.03.2012. Effect: S.I. 2004/1212 revoked. Territorial extent & classification: E. Local. - Available at http://www.legislation.gov.uk/uksi/2012/1097/contents/made *Non-print*

The A5 Trunk Road (Brownhills to Muckley Corner) (40 Miles Per Hour, 50 Miles Per Hour Speed Limit and Derestriction) Order 2012 No. 2012/2735. - Enabling power: Road Traffic Regulation Act 1984, ss. 82 (2), 83 (1), 84 (1) (a) (2), sch. 9, para.27 (1). - Issued: 06.11.2012. Made: 11.10.2012. Coming into force: 25.10.2012. Effect: S.I. 1976/1186; 1986/1654 revoked. Territorial extent & classification: E. Local. - Available at http://www.legislation.gov.uk/uksi/2012/2735/contents/made *Non-print*

The A5 Trunk Road (Churchillbridge to Brownhills) (Derestriction) Order 2012 No. 2012/2974. - Enabling power: Road Traffic Regulation Act 1984, ss. 82 (2), 83 (1). - Issued: 05.12.2012. Made: 25.10.2012. Coming into force: 08.11.2012. Effect: None. Territorial extent & classification: E. Local. - Available at http://www.legislation.gov.uk/uksi/2012/2974/contents/made *Non-print*

The A5 Trunk Road (West of Bonehill to East of the M42 Junction 10 Roundabout) (Derestriction) Order 2012 No. 2012/1125. - Enabling power: Road Traffic Regulation Act 1984, ss. 82 (2), 83 (1), sch. 9, para. 27 (1). - Issued: 25.04.2012. Made: 22.03.2012. Coming into force: 05.04.2012. Effect: S.I. 1996/2464 varied & S.I. 1986/603 revoked. Territorial extent & classification: E. Local. - Available at http://www.legislation.gov.uk/uksi/2012/1125/contents/made *Non-print*

The A31 Trunk Road (Canford Bottom Roundabout) (40 Miles Per Hour Speed Limit) Order 2012 No. 2012/1382. - Enabling power: Road Traffic Regulation Act 1984, s. 84 (1) (a) (2), sch. 9, para. 27 (1). - Issued: 28.05.2012. Made: 21.05.2012. Coming into force: 01.06.2012. Effect: S.I. 1999/924 revoked. Territorial extent & classification: E. Local. - Available at http://www.legislation.gov.uk/uksi/2012/1382/contents/made *Non-print*

The A35 Trunk Road (Dorchester Bypass) (Derestriction) Order 2000 (Variation) Order 2012 No. 2012/2150. - Enabling power: Road Traffic Regulation Act 1984, s. 84 (1) (a) (2), sch. 9, para. 27 (1). - Issued: 22.08.2012. Made: 14.08.2012. Coming into force: 24.08.2012. Effect: S.I. 2000/839 varied. Territorial extent & classification: E. Local. - Available at http://www.legislation.gov.uk/uksi/2012/2150/contents/made *Non-print*

The A38 Trunk Road (A5121/Clay Mills Interchange to Egginton) (Derestriction) Order 2012 No. 2012/2027. - Enabling power: Road Traffic Regulation Act 1984, s. 82 (2), 83 (1), sch. 9. para. 27 (1). - Issued: 06.08.2012. Made: 12.07.2012. Coming into force: 26.07.2012. Effect: None. Territorial extent & classification: E. Local. - Available at http://www.legislation.gov.uk/uksi/2012/2027/contents/made *Non-print*

The A38 Trunk Road (A5148/A5206 Roundabout, Lichfield, Staffordshire) (Derestriction) Order 2012 No. 2012/2028. - Enabling power: Road Traffic Regulation Act 1984, ss. 82 (2), 83 (1), sch. 9. para. 27 (1). - Issued: 07.08.2012. Made: 12.07.2012. Coming into force: 26.07.2012. Effect: None. Territorial extent & classification: E. Local. - Available at http://www.legislation.gov.uk/uksi/2012/2028/contents/made *Non-print*

The A38 Trunk Road (Dobwalls to Carminow Cross, Bodmin) (40 & 50 mph Speed Limit) Order 2003 (Variation) and (Twelvewoods Roundabout, Dobwalls) (De-Restriction) Order 2010 (Revocation) Order 2012 No. 2012/1863. - Enabling power: Road Traffic Regulation Act 1984, ss. 84 (1) (a) (2), sch. 9, para. 27 (1). - Issued: 20.07.2012. Made: 10.07.2012. Coming into force: 23.07.2012. Effect: S.I. 2010/347 revoked. Territorial extent & classification: E. Local. - Available at http://www.legislation.gov.uk/uksi/2012/1863/contents/made *Non-print*

The A38 Trunk Road (Hilliard's Cross to Branston Interchange, Staffordshire) (30 Miles Per Hour Speed Limit and Derestriction) Order 2012 No. 2012/2034. - Enabling power: Road Traffic Regulation Act 1984, ss. 82 (2), 83 (1), 84 (1) (a) (2), sch. 9. para. 27 (1). - Issued: 07.08.2012. Made: 12.07.2012. Coming into force: 26.07.2012. Effect: None. Territorial extent & classification: E. Local. - Available at http://www.legislation.gov.uk/uksi/2012/2034/contents/made *Non-print*

The A38 Trunk Road (M5 Junction 4, Worcestershire) (Derestriction) Order 2012 No. 2012/1802. - Enabling power: Road Traffic Regulation Act 1984, ss. 82 (2), 83 (1), sch. 9, para. 27 (1). - Issued: 19.07.2012. Made: 28.06.2012. Coming into force: 12.07.2012. Effect: None. Territorial extent & classification: E. Local. - Available at http://www.legislation.gov.uk/uksi/2012/1802/contents/made *Non-print*

The A38 Trunk Road (M5 Junction 5, Worcestershire) (Derestriction) Order 2012 No. 2012/1884. - Enabling power: Road Traffic Regulation Act 1984, ss. 82 (2), 83 (1), sch. 9, para. 27 (1). - Issued: 23.07.2012. Made: 28.06.2012. Coming into force: 12.07.2012. Effect: None. Territorial extent & classification: E. Local. - Available at http://www.legislation.gov.uk/uksi/2012/1884/contents/made *Non-print*

The A38 Trunk Road (M50 Junction 1, Gloucestershire) (50 Miles Per Hour Speed Limit and Derestriction) Order 2012 No. 2012/1113. - Enabling power: Road Traffic Regulation Act 1984, ss. 82 (2), 83 (1), 84 (1) (a) (2), sch. 9, para. 27 (1). - Issued: 23.04.2012. Made: 29.03.2012. Coming into force: 12.04.2012. Effect: The Gloucestershire County Council and Worcestershire County Council (Various Parishes) (Various Speed Limits on the A38) Order 2004 amended. Territorial extent & classification: E. Local. - Available at http://www.legislation.gov.uk/uksi/2012/1113/contents/made *Non-print*

The A38 Trunk Road (Twelvewoods Roundabout, Dobwalls, Cornwall) (40 mph Speed Limit and De-Restriction) Order 2012 No. 2012/1864. - Enabling power: Road Traffic Regulation Act 1984, ss. 82 (2), 83 (1), 84 (1) (a) (2). - Issued: 20.07.2012. Made: 10.07.2012. Coming into force: 23.07.2012. Effect: None. Territorial extent & classification: E. Local. - Available at http://www.legislation.gov.uk/uksi/2012/1864/contents/made *Non-print*

The A45 Trunk Road (M42 Junction 6 to East of Stonebridge Roundabout) (60 Miles Per Hour Speed Limit) Order 2012 No. 2012/1126. - Enabling power: Road Traffic Regulation Act 1984, s. 84 (1) (a) (2), sch. 9, para. 27 (1). - Issued: 25.04.2012. Made: 22.03.2012. Coming into force: 05.04.2012. Effect: The 70 Miles Per Hour, 60 Miles Per Hour and 50 Miles Per Hour (Temporary Speed Limit) Order 1977 amended. Territorial extent & classification: E. Local. - Available at http://www.legislation.gov.uk/uksi/2012/1126/contents/made *Non-print*

The A45 Trunk Road (Ryton on Dunsmore, Warwickshire) (50 Miles Per Hour Speed Limit) Order 2012 No. 2012/2144. - Enabling power: Road Traffic Regulation Act 1984, s. 84 (1) (a) (2), sch. 9, para. 27 (1). - Issued: 22.08.2012. Made: 02.08.2012. Coming into force: 16.08.2012. Effect: S.I. The 70 miles per hour, 60 miles per hour and 50 miles per hour (Temporary Speed Limit) Order 1977 amended & S.I. 2001/1007 revoked. Territorial extent & classification: E. Local. - Available at http://www.legislation.gov.uk/uksi/2012/2144/contents/made *Non-print*

The A46 Trunk Road (A45 Interchange, Coventry, Warwickshire) (Derestriction) Order 2012 No. 2012/1875. - Enabling power: Road Traffic Regulation Act 1984, ss. 82 (2), 83 (1), sch. 9, para. 27 (1). - Issued: 23.07.2012. Made: 28.06.2012. Coming into force: 12.07.2012. Effect: None. Territorial extent & classification: E. Local. - Available at http://www.legislation.gov.uk/uksi/2012/1875/contents/made *Non-print*

The A46 Trunk Road (Widmerpool to Farndon, Nottinghamshire) (Derestriction) Order 2012 No. 2012/1123. - Enabling power: Road Traffic Regulation Act 1984, ss. 82 (2), 83 (1), 122A, sch. 9, para. 27 (1). - Issued: 24.04.2012. Made: 08.03.2012. Coming into force: 22.03.2012. Effect: S.I. 1991/2440 varied. Territorial extent & classification: E. Local. - Available at http://www.legislation.gov.uk/uksi/2012/1123/contents/made *Non-print*

The A49 Trunk Road (South of Hereford) (Restriction and Derestriction) Order 2012 No. 2012/1098. - Enabling power: Road Traffic Regulation Act 1984, ss. 82 (2), 83 (1), 84 (1) (a) (2), sch. 9, para. 27 (1). - Issued: 19.04.2012. Made: 02.03.2012. Coming into force: 16.03.2012. Effect: S.I. 2004/1420 revoked. Territorial extent & classification: E. Local. - Available at http://www.legislation.gov.uk/uksi/2012/1098/contents/made *Non-print*

The A52 Trunk Road (Radcliffe on Trent to Bingham, Nottinghamshire) (Derestriction) Order 2012 No. 2012/1099. - Enabling power: Road Traffic Regulation Act 1984, ss. 82 (2), 83 (1), 122A, sch. 9, para. 27 (1). - Issued: 19.04.2012. Made: 08.03.2012. Coming into force: 22.03.2012. Effect: S.I. 1987/767; 2000/3012 revoked. Territorial extent & classification: E. Local. - Available at http://www.legislation.gov.uk/uksi/2012/1099/contents/made *Non-print*

The A120 Trunk Road (Coggeshall Bypass, Essex) (50 Miles Per Hour Speed Limit) Order 2012 No. 2012/2850. - Enabling power: Road Traffic Regulation Act 1984, s. 84 (1) (a) (2). - Issued: 16.11.2012. Made: 05.11.2012. Coming into force: 17.11.2012. Effect: None. Territorial extent & classification: E. Local. - Available at http://www.legislation.gov.uk/uksi/2012/2850/contents/made *Non-print*

The A259 Trunk Road (Bexhill) (50 Miles Per Hour Speed Limit) Order 2012 No. 2012/2312. - Enabling power: Road Traffic Regulation Act 1984, s. 84 (1) (a) (2). - Issued: 12.09.2012. Made: 03.09.2012. Coming into force: 14.09.2012. Effect: None. Territorial extent & classification: E. Local. - Available at http://www.legislation.gov.uk/uksi/2012/2312/contents/made *Non-print*

The A259 Trunk Road (Guestling Green - Guestling Thorn) (Speed Limits) Order 2012 No. 2012/2306. - Enabling power: Road Traffic Regulation Act 1984, s. 84 (1) (a) (2). - Issued: 11.09.2012. Made: 03.09.2012. Coming into force: 14.09.2012. Effect: None. Territorial extent & classification: E. Local. - Available at http://www.legislation.gov.uk/uksi/2012/2306/contents/made *Non-print*

The A259 Trunk Road (Main Road, Icklesham) (40 Miles Per Hour Speed Limit) Order 2012 No. 2012/2307. - Enabling power: Road Traffic Regulation Act 1984, s. 84 (1) (a) (2). - Issued: 11.09.2012. Made: 03.09.2012. Coming into force: 14.09.2012. Effect: None. Territorial extent & classification: E. Local. - Available at http://www.legislation.gov.uk/uksi/2012/2307/contents/made *Non-print*

The A259 Trunk Road (Rye) (30 Miles Per Hour Speed Limit) Order 2012 No. 2012/2313. - Enabling power: Road Traffic Regulation Act 1984, ss. 82 (2), 83 (1), 84 (1) (a) (2), sch. 9, para. 27 (1). - Issued: 12.09.2012. Made: 03.09.2012. Coming into force: 14.09.2012. Effect: None. Territorial extent & classification: E. Local. - Available at http://www.legislation.gov.uk/uksi/2012/2313/contents/made *Non-print*

The A303 Trunk Road (Hayes End Roundabout, South Petherton) (40mph Speed Limit and Derestriction) Order 2011 (Variation) Order 2012 No. 2012/1378. - Enabling power: Road Traffic Regulation Act 1984, s. 84 (1) (a) (2), sch. 9, para. 27 (1). - Issued: 28.05.2012. Made: 16.05.2012. Coming into force: 28.05.2012. Effect: None. Territorial extent & classification: E. Local. - Available at http://www.legislation.gov.uk/uksi/2012/1378/contents/made *Non-print*

The A446 Trunk Road (A452 to M6 Junction 4, Warwickshire) (Derestriction) Order 2012 No. 2012/1874. - Enabling power: Road Traffic Regulation Act 1984, ss. 82 (2), 83 (1), sch. 9, para. 27 (1). - Issued: 23.07.2012. Made: 28.06.2012. Coming into force: 12.07.2012. Effect: None. Territorial extent & classification: E. Local. - Available at http://www.legislation.gov.uk/uksi/2012/1874/contents/made *Non-print*

The A456 Trunk Road (M5 Junction 3) (Derestriction) Order 2012 No. 2012/2025. - Enabling power: Road Traffic Regulation Act 1984, s. 82 (2), 83 (1), sch. 9. para. 27 (1). - Issued: 06.08.2012. Made: 12.07.2012. Coming into force: 26.07.2012. Effect: None. Territorial extent & classification: E. Local. - Available at http://www.legislation.gov.uk/uksi/2012/2025/contents/made *Non-print*

The A483 Trunk Road (Maesbury Road Junction, Oswestry, Shropshire) (50 Miles Per Hour Speed Limit) Order 2012 No. 2012/3186. - Enabling power: Road Traffic Regulation Act 1984, s. 84 (1) (a) (2), sch. 9, para. 27 (1). - Issued: 02.01.2013. Made: 30.11.2012. Coming into force: 14.12.2012. Effect: S.I. 1995/1096 revoked. Territorial extent & classification: E. Local. - Available at http://www.legislation.gov.uk/uksi/2012/3186/contents/made *Non-print*

Road traffic: Traffic regulation

The A1(M) Motorway, A194(M) Motorway and the A184 Trunk Road (Junction 64 to Testos Roundabout) (Temporary Restriction and Prohibition of Traffic) Order 2012 No. 2012/482. - Enabling power: Road Traffic Regulation Act 1984, s. 14 (1) (a). - Issued: 29.02.2012. Made: 16.02.2012. Coming into force: 26.02.2012. Effect: None. Territorial extent & classification: E. Local. - Available at http://www.legislation.gov.uk/uksi/2012/482/contents/made *Non-print*

The A1(M) Motorway and the A1 Trunk Road (Barton Interchange to Scotch Corner Interchange) (Temporary Restriction and Prohibition of Traffic) Order 2012 No. 2012/2339. - Enabling power: Road Traffic Regulation Act 1984, s. 14 (1) (a) (7). - Issued: 14.09.2012. Made: 06.09.2012. Coming into force: 16.09.2012. Effect: None. Territorial extent & classification: E. Local. - Available at http://www.legislation.gov.uk/uksi/2012/2339/contents/made *Non-print*

The A1(M) Motorway and the A1 Trunk Road (Catterick to Junction 56) (Temporary Restriction and Prohibition of Traffic) Order 2012 No. 2012/1220. - Enabling power: Road Traffic Regulation Act 1984, s. 14 (1) (a) (7). - Issued: 10.05.2012. Made: 26.04.2012. Coming into force: 06.05.2012. Effect: None. Territorial extent & classification: E. Local. - Available at http://www.legislation.gov.uk/uksi/2012/1220/contents/made *Non-print*

The A1(M) Motorway and the A1 Trunk Road (Junction 64 to Eighton Lodge Interchange) (Temporary Restriction and Prohibition of Traffic) Order 2012 No. 2012/2153. - Enabling power: Road Traffic Regulation Act 1984, s. 14 (1) (a) (7) & S.I. 1982/1163, reg. 16 (2). - Issued: 22.08.2012. Made: 16.08.2012. Coming into force: 27.08.2012. Effect: None. Territorial extent & classification: E. Local. - Available at http://www.legislation.gov.uk/uksi/2012/2153/contents/made *Non-print*

The A1(M) Motorway (Great Yorkshire Show) (Temporary Restriction and Prohibition of Traffic) Order 2012 No. 2012/1789. - Enabling power: Road Traffic Regulation Act 1984, s. 16A (2) (a). - Issued: 19.07.2012. Made: 28.06.2012. Coming into force: 09.07.2012. Effect: None. Territorial extent & classification: E. Local. - Available at http://www.legislation.gov.uk/uksi/2012/1789/contents/made *Non-print*

The A1(M) Motorway (Hatfield Tunnel) (Temporary Prohibition of Traffic) Order 2012 No. 2012/1252. - Enabling power: Road Traffic Regulation Act 1984, s. 14 (1) (a). - Issued: 18.05.2012. Made: 08.05.2012. Coming into force: 01.06.2012. Effect: None. Territorial extent & classification: E. Local. - Available at http://www.legislation.gov.uk/uksi/2012/1252/contents/made *Non-print*

The A1(M) Motorway (Junction 1, Northbound Carriageway) (Temporary Prohibition of Traffic) Order 2012 No. 2012/272. - Enabling power: Road Traffic Regulation Act 1984, s. 14 (1) (a). - Issued: 10.02.2012. Made: 30.01.2012. Coming into force: 18.02.2012. Effect: None. Territorial extent & classification: E. Local. - Available at http://www.legislation.gov.uk/uksi/2012/272/contents/made *Non-print*

The A1(M) Motorway (Junction 6, Northbound Exit Slip Road) (Temporary Prohibition of Traffic) Order 2012 No. 2012/89. - Enabling power: Road Traffic Regulation Act 1984, s. 14 (1) (a). - Issued: 18.01.2012. Made: 09.01.2012. Coming into force: 28.01.2012. Effect: None. Territorial extent & classification: E. Local. - Available at http://www.legislation.gov.uk/uksi/2012/89/contents/made *Non-print*

The A1(M) Motorway (Junction 6 to Junction 10) (Temporary Prohibition of Traffic) Order 2012 No. 2012/2621. - Enabling power: Road Traffic Regulation Act 1984, s. 14 (1) (a). - Issued: 22.10.2012. Made: 08.10.2012. Coming into force: 15.10.2012. Effect: None. Territorial extent & classification: E. Local. - Available at http://www.legislation.gov.uk/uksi/2012/2621/contents/made *Non-print*

The A1(M) Motorway (Junction 7 Stevenage, Hertfordshire) Slip Roads (Temporary Prohibition of Traffic) Order 2012 No. 2012/1590. - Enabling power: Road Traffic Regulation Act 1984, s. 14 (1) (b). - Issued: 26.06.2012. Made: 11.06.2012. Coming into force: 18.06.2012. Effect: None. Territorial extent & classification: E. Local. - Available at http://www.legislation.gov.uk/uksi/2012/1590/contents/made *Non-print*

The A1(M) Motorway (Junction 14 to Junction 15, Cambridgeshire) Northbound (Temporary Restriction and Prohibition of Traffic) Order 2012 No. 2012/2170. - Enabling power: Road Traffic Regulation Act 1984, s. 14 (1) (a). - Issued: 24.08.2012. Made: 20.08.2012. Coming into force: 27.08.2012. Effect: None. Territorial extent & classification: E. Local. - Available at http://www.legislation.gov.uk/uksi/2012/2170/contents/made *Non-print*

The A1(M) Motorway (Junction 16 Norman Cross, City of Peterborough) Southbound (Temporary Restriction and Prohibition of Traffic) Order 2012 No. 2012/1255. - Enabling power: Road Traffic Regulation Act 1984, s. 14 (1) (a) (7). - Issued: 18.05.2012. Made: 08.05.2012. Coming into force: 15.05.2012. Effect: None. Territorial extent & classification: E. Local. - Available at http://www.legislation.gov.uk/uksi/2012/1255/contents/made *Non-print*

The A1(M) Motorway (Junction 17), and the A1 Trunk Road (Fletton Parkway to North of Wansford) and the A47 Trunk Road (Wansford) (Temporary Restriction and Prohibition of Traffic) Order 2012 No. 2012/2243. - Enabling power: Road Traffic Regulation Act 1984, s. 14 (1) (a). - Issued: 04.09.2012. Made: 28.08.2012. Coming into force: 04.09.2012. Effect: None. Territorial extent & classification: E. Local. - Available at http://www.legislation.gov.uk/uksi/2012/2243/contents/made *Non-print*

The A1(M) Motorway (Junction 17) and the A1 Trunk Road (Fletton Parkway to North of Wansford, Peterborough) (Temporary Restriction and Prohibition of Traffic) Order 2012 No. 2012/354. - Enabling power: Road Traffic Regulation Act 1984, s. 14 (1) (a). - Issued: 15.02.2012. Made: 06.02.2012. Coming into force: 13.02.2012. Effect: None. Territorial extent & classification: E. Local. - Available at http://www.legislation.gov.uk/uksi/2012/354/contents/made *Non-print*

The A1(M) Motorway (Junction 34, Blyth) (Temporary Prohibition of Traffic) Order 2012 No. 2012/1374. - Enabling power: Road Traffic Regulation Act 1984, s. 14 (1) (a). - Issued: 28.05.2012. Made: 17.05.2012. Coming into force: 27.05.2012. Effect: None. Territorial extent & classification: E. Local. - Available at http://www.legislation.gov.uk/uksi/2012/1374/contents/made *Non-print*

The A1(M) Motorway (Junction 35, Wadworth) (Temporary Prohibition of Traffic) Order 2012 No. 2012/1565. - Enabling power: Road Traffic Regulation Act 1984, s. 14 (1) (a). - Issued: 22.06.2012. Made: 07.06.2012. Coming into force: 17.06.2012. Effect: None. Territorial extent & classification: E. Local. - Available at http://www.legislation.gov.uk/uksi/2012/1565/contents/made *Non-print*

The A1(M) Motorway (Junction 36, Olympic Torch Relay) (Temporary Prohibition of Traffic) Order 2012 No. 2012/1613. - Enabling power: Road Traffic Regulation Act 1984, s. 16A (2) (a). - Issued: 28.06.2012. Made: 14.06.2012. Coming into force: 25.06.2012. Effect: None. Territorial extent & classification: E. Local. - Available at http://www.legislation.gov.uk/uksi/2012/1613/contents/made *Non-print*

The A1(M) Motorway (Junction 36 to Junction 37) (Temporary Prohibition of Traffic) Order 2012 No. 2012/2358. - Enabling power: Road Traffic Regulation Act 1984, s. 14 (1) (a). - Issued: 17.09.2012. Made: 06.09.2012. Coming into force: 16.09.2012. Effect: None. Territorial extent & classification: E. Local. - Available at http://www.legislation.gov.uk/uksi/2012/2358/contents/made *Non-print*

The A1(M) Motorway (Junction 36, Warmsworth) (Temporary Prohibition of Traffic) (No. 2) Order 2012 No. 2012/261. - Enabling power: Road Traffic Regulation Act 1984, s. 14 (1) (a). - Issued: 07.02.2012. Made: 26.01.2012. Coming into force: 05.02.2012. Effect: None. Territorial extent & classification: E. Local. - Available at http://www.legislation.gov.uk/uksi/2012/261/contents/made *Non-print*

The A1(M) Motorway (Junction 36, Warmsworth) (Temporary Prohibition of Traffic) Order 2012 No. 2012/82. - Enabling power: Road Traffic Regulation Act 1984, s. 14 (1) (a). - Issued: 18.01.2012. Made: 05.01.2012. Coming into force: 15.01.2012. Effect: None. Territorial extent & classification: E. Local. - Available at http://www.legislation.gov.uk/uksi/2012/82/contents/made *Non-print*

The A1(M) Motorway (Junction 37, Marr) (Temporary Prohibition of Traffic) (No. 2) Order 2012 No. 2012/2011. - Enabling power: Road Traffic Regulation Act 1984, s. 14 (1) (a). - Issued: 02.08.2012. Made: 19.07.2012. Coming into force: 29.07.2012. Effect: None. Territorial extent & classification: E. Local. - Available at http://www.legislation.gov.uk/uksi/2012/2011/contents/made *Non-print*

The A1(M) Motorway (Junction 37, Marr) (Temporary Prohibition of Traffic) Order 2012 No. 2012/565. - Enabling power: Road Traffic Regulation Act 1984, s. 14 (1) (a). - Issued: 01.03.2012. Made: 23.02.2012. Coming into force: 04.03.2012. Effect: None. Territorial extent & classification: E. Local. - Available at http://www.legislation.gov.uk/uksi/2012/565/contents/made *Non-print*

The A1(M) Motorway (Junction 37 to Junction 38) (Temporary Prohibition of Traffic) Order 2012 No. 2012/1067. - Enabling power: Road Traffic Regulation Act 1984, s. 14 (1) (a). - Issued: 16.04.2012. Made: 05.04.2012. Coming into force: 15.04.2012. Effect: None. Territorial extent & classification: E. Local. - Available at http://www.legislation.gov.uk/uksi/2012/1067/contents/made *Non-print*

The A1(M) Motorway (Junction 38, Redhouse) (Temporary Prohibition of Traffic) (No. 2) Order 2012 No. 2012/2245. - Enabling power: Road Traffic Regulation Act 1984, s. 14 (1) (a). - Issued: 04.09.2012. Made: 09.08.2012. Coming into force: 19.08.2012. Effect: None. Territorial extent & classification: E. Local. - Available at http://www.legislation.gov.uk/uksi/2012/2245/contents/made *Non-print*

The A1(M) Motorway (Junction 38, Redhouse) (Temporary Prohibition of Traffic) Order 2012 No. 2012/1716. - Enabling power: Road Traffic Regulation Act 1984, s. 14 (1) (a). - Issued: 12.07.2012. Made: 21.06.2012. Coming into force: 01.07.2012. Effect: None. Territorial extent & classification: E. Local. - Available at http://www.legislation.gov.uk/uksi/2012/1716/contents/made *Non-print*

The A1(M) Motorway (Junction 42, Selby Fork) (Temporary Prohibition of Traffic) Order 2012 No. 2012/1835. - Enabling power: Road Traffic Regulation Act 1984, s. 14 (1) (a). - Issued: 19.07.2012. Made: 05.07.2012. Coming into force: 15.07.2012. Effect: None. Territorial extent & classification: E. Local. - Available at http://www.legislation.gov.uk/uksi/2012/1835/contents/made *Non-print*

The A1(M) Motorway (Junction 42 to Junction 44) (Temporary Restriction and Prohibition of Traffic) Order 2012 No. 2012/855. - Enabling power: Road Traffic Regulation Act 1984, s. 14 (1) (a) (7). - Issued: 23.03.2012. Made: 15.03.2012. Coming into force: 24.03.2012. Effect: None. Territorial extent & classification: E. Local. - Available at http://www.legislation.gov.uk/uksi/2012/855/contents/made *Non-print*

The A1(M) Motorway (Junction 44) and the A64 Trunk Road (Bramham Interchange to Headley Bar Interchange) (Temporary Restriction and Prohibition of Traffic) Order 2012 No. 2012/2014. - Enabling power: Road Traffic Regulation Act 1984, s. 14 (1) (a). - Issued: 06.08.2012. Made: 19.07.2012. Coming into force: 29.07.2012. Effect: None. Territorial extent & classification: E. Local. - Available at http://www.legislation.gov.uk/uksi/2012/2014/contents/made *Non-print*

The A1(M) Motorway (Junction 44, Bramham) (Temporary Prohibition of Traffic) Order 2012 No. 2012/2062. - Enabling power: Road Traffic Regulation Act 1984, s. 14 (1) (a). - Issued: 10.08.2012. Made: 26.07.2012. Coming into force: 07.08.2012. Effect: None. Territorial extent & classification: E. Local. - Available at http://www.legislation.gov.uk/uksi/2012/2062/contents/made *Non-print*

The A1(M) Motorway (Junction 44 to Junction 42) (Temporary Prohibition of Traffic) Order 2012 No. 2012/2566. - Enabling power: Road Traffic Regulation Act 1984, s. 14 (1) (a). - Issued: 12.10.2012. Made: 04.10.2012. Coming into force: 14.10.2012. Effect: None. Territorial extent & classification: E. Local. - Available at http://www.legislation.gov.uk/uksi/2012/2566/contents/made *Non-print*

The A1(M) Motorway (Junction 45 to Junction 42) (Temporary Prohibition of Traffic) Order 2012 No. 2012/1606. - Enabling power: Road Traffic Regulation Act 1984, s. 14 (1) (a). - Issued: 27.06.2012. Made: 14.06.2012. Coming into force: 24.06.2012. Effect: None. Territorial extent & classification: E. Local. - Available at http://www.legislation.gov.uk/uksi/2012/1606/contents/made *Non-print*

The A1(M) Motorway (Junction 45 to Junction 46) (Temporary Restriction and Prohibition of Traffic) Order 2012 No. 2012/1247. - Enabling power: Road Traffic Regulation Act 1984, s. 14 (1) (a) (7). - Issued: 18.05.2012. Made: 03.05.2012. Coming into force: 13.05.2012. Effect: None. Territorial extent & classification: E. Local. - Available at http://www.legislation.gov.uk/uksi/2012/1247/contents/made *Non-print*

The A1(M) Motorway (Junction 46 to Junction 48) (Temporary Restriction and Prohibition of Traffic) Order 2012 No. 2012/1068. - Enabling power: Road Traffic Regulation Act 1984, s. 14 (1) (a) (7). - Issued: 16.04.2012. Made: 05.04.2012. Coming into force: 15.04.2012. Effect: None. Territorial extent & classification: E. Local. - Available at http://www.legislation.gov.uk/uksi/2012/1068/contents/made *Non-print*

The A1(M) Motorway (Junction 47, Allerton Moor) (Temporary Restriction and Prohibition of Traffic) Order 2012 No. 2012/1541. - Enabling power: Road Traffic Regulation Act 1984, s. 14 (1) (a). - Issued: 20.06.2012. Made: 31.05.2012. Coming into force: 10.06.2012. Effect: None. Territorial extent & classification: E. Local. - Available at http://www.legislation.gov.uk/uksi/2012/1541/contents/made *Non-print*

The A1(M) Motorway (Junction 50, Baldersby) (Temporary 50 Miles Per Hour Speed Restriction) Order 2012 No. 2012/3277. - Enabling power: Road Traffic Regulation Act 1984, s. 14 (1) (a). - Issued: 15.01.2013. Made: 27.12.2012. Coming into force: 06.01.2013. Effect: None. Territorial extent & classification: E. Local. - Available at http://www.legislation.gov.uk/uksi/2012/3277/contents/made *Non-print*

The A1(M) Motorway (Junction 56, Barton) (Temporary Restriction and Prohibition of Traffic) Order 2012 No. 2012/530. - Enabling power: Road Traffic Regulation Act 1984, s. 14 (1) (a) (7). - Issued: 01.03.2012. Made: 21.02.2012. Coming into force: 04.03.2012. Effect: None. Territorial extent & classification: E. Local. - Available at http://www.legislation.gov.uk/uksi/2012/530/contents/made *Non-print*

The A1(M) Motorway (Junction 56 to Junction 58) (Temporary Restriction of Traffic) Order 2012 No. 2012/1078. - Enabling power: Road Traffic Regulation Act 1984, s. 14 (1) (a). - Issued: 17.04.2012. Made: 05.04.2012. Coming into force: 15.04.2012. Effect: None. Territorial extent & classification: E. Local. - Available at http://www.legislation.gov.uk/uksi/2012/1078/contents/made *Non-print*

The A1(M) Motorway (Junction 57 to Junction 58) (Temporary Restriction and Prohibition of Traffic) Order 2012 No. 2012/2847. - Enabling power: Road Traffic Regulation Act 1984, s. 14 (1) (a). - Issued: 16.11.2012. Made: 01.11.2012. Coming into force: 11.11.2012. Effect: None. Territorial extent & classification: E. Local. - Available at http://www.legislation.gov.uk/uksi/2012/2847/contents/made *Non-print*

The A1(M) Motorway (Junction 57 to Junction 58) (Temporary Restriction of Traffic) Order 2012 No. 2012/1786. - Enabling power: Road Traffic Regulation Act 1984, s. 14 (1) (a). - Issued: 18.07.2012. Made: 28.06.2012. Coming into force: 06.07.2012. Effect: None. Territorial extent & classification: E. Local. - Available at http://www.legislation.gov.uk/uksi/2012/1786/contents/made *Non-print*

The A1(M) Motorway (Junction 58, Burtree) (Temporary 30 Miles Per Hour Speed Restriction) Order 2012 No. 2012/1535. - Enabling power: Road Traffic Regulation Act 1984, s. 14 (1) (a). - Issued: 19.06.2012. Made: 31.05.2012. Coming into force: 10.06.2012. Effect: None. Territorial extent & classification: E. Local. - Available at http://www.legislation.gov.uk/uksi/2012/1535/contents/made *Non-print*

The A1(M) Motorway (Junction 58, Burtree) (Temporary Restriction and Prohibition of Traffic) Order 2012 No. 2012/2041. - Enabling power: Road Traffic Regulation Act 1984, s. 14 (1) (a). - Issued: 08.08.2012. Made: 25.07.2012. Coming into force: 05.08.2012. Effect: None. Territorial extent & classification: E. Local. - Available at http://www.legislation.gov.uk/uksi/2012/2041/contents/made *Non-print*

The A1(M) Motorway (Junction 58 to Junction 59 and Junction 60) (Temporary Restriction of Traffic) Order 2012 No. 2012/2135. - Enabling power: Road Traffic Regulation Act 1984, s. 14 (1) (a). - Issued: 21.08.2012. Made: 09.08.2012. Coming into force: 17.08.2012. Effect: None. Territorial extent & classification: E. Local. - Available at http://www.legislation.gov.uk/uksi/2012/2135/contents/made *Non-print*

The A1(M) Motorway (Junction 58 to Junction 59) (Temporary Restriction and Prohibition of Traffic) Order 2012 No. 2012/1114. - Enabling power: Road Traffic Regulation Act 1984, s. 14 (1) (a). - Issued: 23.04.2012. Made: 12.04.2012. Coming into force: 25.04.2012. Effect: None. Territorial extent & classification: E. Local. - Available at http://www.legislation.gov.uk/uksi/2012/1114/contents/made *Non-print*

The A1(M) Motorway (Junction 59) (Temporary Restriction and Prohibition of Traffic) Order 2012 No. 2012/87. - Enabling power: Road Traffic Regulation Act 1984, s. 14 (1) (a). - Issued: 18.01.2012. Made: 06.01.2012. Coming into force: 15.01.2012. Effect: None. Territorial extent & classification: E. Local. - Available at http://www.legislation.gov.uk/uksi/2012/87/contents/made *Non-print*

The A1(M) Motorway (Junction 59 to Junction 58) (Temporary Restriction and Prohibition of Traffic) Order 2012 No. 2012/475. - Enabling power: Road Traffic Regulation Act 1984, s. 14 (1) (a). - Issued: 29.02.2012. Made: 16.02.2012. Coming into force: 26.02.2012. Effect: None. Territorial extent & classification: E. Local. - Available at http://www.legislation.gov.uk/uksi/2012/475/contents/made *Non-print*

Road traffic: Traffic regulation

The A1(M) Motorway (Junction 59 to Junction 60) (Temporary Restriction and Prohibition of Traffic) (No. 2) Order 2012 No. 2012/2936. - Enabling power: Road Traffic Regulation Act 1984, s. 14 (1) (a) & S.I. 1982/1163, reg. 16 (2). - Issued: 28.11.2012. Made: 14.11.2012. Coming into force: 18.11.2012. Effect: None. Territorial extent & classification: E. Local. - Available at http://www.legislation.gov.uk/uksi/2012/2936/contents/made *Non-print*

The A1(M) Motorway (Junction 59 to Junction 60) (Temporary Restriction and Prohibition of Traffic) Order 2012 No. 2012/1822. - Enabling power: Road Traffic Regulation Act 1984, s. 14 (1) (a) (7). - Issued: 19.07.2012. Made: 28.06.2012. Coming into force: 08.07.2012. Effect: None. Territorial extent & classification: E. Local. - Available at http://www.legislation.gov.uk/uksi/2012/1822/contents/made *Non-print*

The A1(M) Motorway (Junction 60 to Junction 61) (Temporary Restriction and Prohibition of Traffic) (No. 2) Order 2012 No. 2012/2428. - Enabling power: Road Traffic Regulation Act 1984, s. 14 (1) (a) & S.I. 1982/1163, reg. 16 (2). - Issued: 25.09.2012. Made: 11.09.2012. Coming into force: 16.09.2012. Effect: None. Territorial extent & classification: E. Local. - Available at http://www.legislation.gov.uk/uksi/2012/2428/contents/made *Non-print*

The A1(M) Motorway (Junction 60 to Junction 61) (Temporary Restriction and Prohibition of Traffic) Order 2012 No. 2012/778. - Enabling power: Road Traffic Regulation Act 1984, s. 14 (1) (a) (7). - Issued: 20.03.2012. Made: 08.03.2012. Coming into force: 18.03.2012. Effect: None. Territorial extent & classification: E. Local. - Available at http://www.legislation.gov.uk/uksi/2012/778/contents/made *Non-print*

The A1(M) Motorway (Junction 61, Bowburn) (Temporary Restriction and Prohibition of Traffic) Order 2012 No. 2012/2212. - Enabling power: Road Traffic Regulation Act 1984, s. 14 (1) (a). - Issued: 31.08.2012. Made: 23.08.2012. Coming into force: 04.09.2012. Effect: None. Territorial extent & classification: E. Local. - Available at http://www.legislation.gov.uk/uksi/2012/2212/contents/made *Non-print*

The A1(M) Motorway (Junction 61 to Junction 60) (Temporary Restriction and Prohibition of Traffic) (No. 2) Order 2012 No. 2012/1361. - Enabling power: Road Traffic Regulation Act 1984, s. 14 (1) (a). - Issued: 28.05.2012. Made: 10.05.2012. Coming into force: 20.05.2012. Effect: None. Territorial extent & classification: E. Local. - Available at http://www.legislation.gov.uk/uksi/2012/1361/contents/made *Non-print*

The A1(M) Motorway (Junction 61 to Junction 60) (Temporary Restriction and Prohibition of Traffic) Order 2012 No. 2012/656. - Enabling power: Road Traffic Regulation Act 1984, s. 14 (1) (a). - Issued: 14.03.2012. Made: 01.03.2012. Coming into force: 11.03.2012. Effect: None. Territorial extent & classification: E. Local. - Available at http://www.legislation.gov.uk/uksi/2012/656/contents/made *Non-print*

The A1(M) Motorway (Junction 61 to Junction 63) (Temporary Restriction and Prohibition of Traffic) Order 2012 No. 2012/3108. - Enabling power: Road Traffic Regulation Act 1984, s. 14 (1) (a) & S.I. 1982/1163, reg. 16 (2). - Issued: 20.12.2012. Made: 22.11.2012. Coming into force: 02.12.2012. Effect: None. Territorial extent & classification: E. Local. - Available at http://www.legislation.gov.uk/uksi/2012/3108/contents/made *Non-print*

The A1(M) Motorway (Junction 62, Carrville) (Temporary Restriction and Prohibition of Traffic) Order 2012 No. 2012/2136. - Enabling power: Road Traffic Regulation Act 1984, s. 14 (1) (a). - Issued: 21.08.2012. Made: 09.08.2012. Coming into force: 19.08.2012. Effect: None. Territorial extent & classification: E. Local. - Available at http://www.legislation.gov.uk/uksi/2012/2136/contents/made *Non-print*

The A1(M) Motorway (Junction 62, Carville) (Temporary 50 Miles Per Hour and 40 Miles Per Hour Speed Restriction) Order 2012 No. 2012/2738. - Enabling power: Road Traffic Regulation Act 1984, s. 14 (1) (a). - Issued: 06.11.2012. Made: 18.10.2012. Coming into force: 28.10.2012. Effect: None. Territorial extent & classification: E. Local. - Available at http://www.legislation.gov.uk/uksi/2012/2738/contents/made *Non-print*

The A1(M) Motorway (Junction 63, Blind Lane Interchange) (Temporary Restriction and Prohibition of Traffic) (No. 2) Order 2012 No. 2012/1539. - Enabling power: Road Traffic Regulation Act 1984, s. 14 (1) (a). - Issued: 20.06.2012. Made: 31.05.2012. Coming into force: 10.06.2012. Effect: None. Territorial extent & classification: E. Local. - Available at http://www.legislation.gov.uk/uksi/2012/1539/contents/made *Non-print*

The A1(M) Motorway (Junction 63, Blind Lane Interchange) (Temporary Restriction and Prohibition of Traffic) (No. 3) Order 2012 No. 2012/1611. - Enabling power: Road Traffic Regulation Act 1984, s. 14 (1) (a). - Issued: 28.06.2012. Made: 14.06.2012. Coming into force: 24.06.2012. Effect: None. Territorial extent & classification: E. Local. - Available at http://www.legislation.gov.uk/uksi/2012/1611/contents/made *Non-print*

The A1(M) Motorway (Junction 63, Blind Lane Interchange) (Temporary Restriction and Prohibition of Traffic) Order 2012 No. 2012/540. - Enabling power: Road Traffic Regulation Act 1984, s. 14 (1) (a). - Issued: 01.03.2012. Made: 21.02.2012. Coming into force: 04.03.2012. Effect: None. Territorial extent & classification: E. Local. - Available at http://www.legislation.gov.uk/uksi/2012/540/contents/made *Non-print*

The A1(M) Motorway (Junction 63 to Junction 61) (Temporary Restriction and Prohibition of Traffic) Order 2012 No. 2012/2042. - Enabling power: Road Traffic Regulation Act 1984, s. 14 (1) (a). - Issued: 08.08.2012. Made: 25.07.2012. Coming into force: 05.08.2012. Effect: None. Territorial extent & classification: E. Local. - Available at http://www.legislation.gov.uk/uksi/2012/2042/contents/made *Non-print*

The A1(M) Motorway (Junctions 2 - 6) (Temporary Restriction and Prohibition of Traffic) Order 2012 No. 2012/91. - Enabling power: Road Traffic Regulation Act 1984, s. 14 (1) (a) (7). - Issued: 18.01.2012. Made: 09.01.2012. Coming into force: 28.01.2012. Effect: None. Territorial extent & classification: E. Local. - Available at http://www.legislation.gov.uk/uksi/2012/91/contents/made *Non-print*

The A1(M) Motorway (Junctions 4 - 1, Southbound) (Temporary Prohibition of Traffic) Order 2012 No. 2012/1668. - Enabling power: Road Traffic Regulation Act 1984, s. 14 (1) (a). - Issued: 03.07.2012. Made: 18.06.2012. Coming into force: 07.07.2012. Effect: None. Territorial extent & classification: E. Local. - Available at http://www.legislation.gov.uk/uksi/2012/1668/contents/made *Non-print*

The A1(M) Motorway (Junctions 15 to 17) and the A1(M) Spur Motorway (Alconbury) (Slip Roads) (Temporary Prohibition of Traffic) Order 2012 No. 2012/2073. - Enabling power: Road Traffic Regulation Act 1984, s. 14 (1) (a). - Issued: 13.08.2012. Made: 30.07.2012. Coming into force: 06.08.2012. Effect: None. Territorial extent & classification: E. Local. - Available at http://www.legislation.gov.uk/uksi/2012/2073/contents/made *Non-print*

The A1 Trunk Road (A1(M) Junction 1, Northbound Exit Slip Road) (Temporary Prohibition of Traffic) Order 2012 No. 2012/1578. - Enabling power: Road Traffic Regulation Act 1984, s. 14 (1) (a). - Issued: 26.06.2012. Made: 11.06.2012. Coming into force: 30.06.2012. Effect: None. Territorial extent & classification: E. Local. - Available at http://www.legislation.gov.uk/uksi/2012/1578/contents/made *Non-print*

The A1 Trunk Road (Adderstone to Middleton) (Temporary Restriction and Prohibition of Traffic) Order 2012 No. 2012/2348. - Enabling power: Road Traffic Regulation Act 1984, s. 14 (1) (a). - Issued: 14.09.2012. Made: 06.09.2012. Coming into force: 16.09.2012. Effect: None. Territorial extent & classification: E. Local. - Available at http://www.legislation.gov.uk/uksi/2012/2348/contents/made *Non-print*

The A1 Trunk Road (Alnwick Bypass) (Temporary Restriction and Prohibition of Traffic) Order 2012 No. 2012/120. - Enabling power: Road Traffic Regulation Act 1984, s. 14 (1) (a) (7). - Issued: 23.01.2012. Made: 12.01.2012. Coming into force: 21.01.2012. Effect: None. Territorial extent & classification: E. Local. - Available at http://www.legislation.gov.uk/uksi/2012/120/contents/made *Non-print*

The A1 Trunk Road (Alwalton to Wothorpe, Peterborough) Northbound (Temporary Restriction and Prohibition of Traffic) Order 2012 No. 2012/447. - Enabling power: Road Traffic Regulation Act 1984, s. 14 (1) (a). - Issued: 24.02.2012. Made: 13.02.2012. Coming into force: 20.02.2012. Effect: None. Territorial extent & classification: E. Local. - Available at http://www.legislation.gov.uk/uksi/2012/447/contents/made *Non-print*

The A1 Trunk Road and the A1(M) Motorway (A5135 Junction - Junction 6) (Temporary Prohibition of Traffic) Order 2012 No. 2012/2465. - Enabling power: Road Traffic Regulation Act 1984, s. 14 (1) (a). - Issued: 01.10.2012. Made: 24.09.2012. Coming into force: 14.10.2012. Effect: None. Territorial extent & classification: E. Local. - Available at http://www.legislation.gov.uk/uksi/2012/2465/contents/made *Non-print*

The A1 Trunk Road and the A1(M) Motorway (Barnsdale Bar Interchange to Junction 41) (Temporary Restriction and Prohibition of Traffic) Order 2012 No. 2012/1542. - Enabling power: Road Traffic Regulation Act 1984, s. 14 (1) (a). - Issued: 20.06.2012. Made: 31.05.2012. Coming into force: 08.06.2012. Effect: None. Territorial extent & classification: E. Local. - Available at http://www.legislation.gov.uk/uksi/2012/1542/contents/made *Non-print*

The A1 Trunk Road and the A1(M) Motorway (Junctions 1, 3 and 4, Northbound Slip Roads) (Temporary Prohibition of Traffic) Order 2012 No. 2012/1037. - Enabling power: Road Traffic Regulation Act 1984, s. 14 (1) (a). - Issued: 12.04.2012. Made: 26.03.2012. Coming into force: 16.04.2012. Effect: None. Territorial extent & classification: E. Local. - Available at http://www.legislation.gov.uk/uksi/2012/1037/contents/made *Non-print*

Road traffic: Traffic regulation

The A1 Trunk Road and the A66 Trunk Road (Scotch Corner Interchange) (Temporary Restriction and Prohibition of Traffic) Order 2012 No. 2012/1451. - Enabling power: Road Traffic Regulation Act 1984, s. 14 (1) (a) (7). - Issued: 12.06.2012. Made: 24.05.2012. Coming into force: 06.06.2012. Effect: None. Territorial extent & classification: E. Local. - Available at http://www.legislation.gov.uk/uksi/2012/1451/contents/made *Non-print*

The A1 Trunk Road and the A69 Trunk Road (Denton Burn Interchange) (Temporary Restriction and Prohibition of Traffic) Order 2012 No. 2012/2825. - Enabling power: Road Traffic Regulation Act 1984, s. 14 (1) (a). - Issued: 14.11.2012. Made: 23.10.2012. Coming into force: 28.10.2012. Effect: None. Territorial extent & classification: E. Local. - Available at http://www.legislation.gov.uk/uksi/2012/2825/contents/made *Non-print*

The A1 Trunk Road (Apleyhead, Nottinghamshire) (Temporary Prohibition of Traffic) Order 2012 No. 2012/1444. - Enabling power: Road Traffic Regulation Act 1984, s. 14 (1) (a). - Issued: 12.06.2012. Made: 14.05.2012. Coming into force: 21.05.2012. Effect: None. Territorial extent & classification: E. Local. - Available at http://www.legislation.gov.uk/uksi/2012/1444/contents/made *Non-print*

The A1 Trunk Road (Apleyhead to Blyth, Nottinghamshire) (Temporary Prohibition of Traffic) Order 2012 No. 2012/392. - Enabling power: Road Traffic Regulation Act 1984, s. 14 (1) (a). - Issued: 21.02.2012. Made: 30.01.2012. Coming into force: 06.02.2012. Effect: None. Territorial extent & classification: E. Local. - Available at http://www.legislation.gov.uk/uksi/2012/392/contents/made *Non-print*

The A1 Trunk Road (Apleyhead to Ranby, Nottinghamshire) (Temporary Restriction and Prohibition of Traffic) Order 2012 No. 2012/254. - Enabling power: Road Traffic Regulation Act 1984, s. 14 (1) (a). - Issued: 06.02.2012. Made: 23.01.2012. Coming into force: 30.01.2012. Effect: None. Territorial extent & classification: E. Local. - Available at http://www.legislation.gov.uk/uksi/2012/254/contents/made *Non-print*

The A1 Trunk Road (Astwick and Sandy, Central Bedfordshire) Northbound (Temporary Prohibition of Traffic) Order 2012 No. 2012/831. - Enabling power: Road Traffic Regulation Act 1984, s. 14 (1) (a). - Issued: 20.03.2012. Made: 12.03.2012. Coming into force: 19.03.2012. Effect: None. Territorial extent & classification: E. Local. - Available at http://www.legislation.gov.uk/uksi/2012/831/contents/made *Non-print*

The A1 Trunk Road (Astwick, Central Bedfordshire to Hinxworth, Hertfordshire) Southbound (Temporary Restriction and Prohibition of Traffic) Order 2012 No. 2012/1589. - Enabling power: Road Traffic Regulation Act 1984, s. 14 (1) (a). - Issued: 26.06.2012. Made: 11.06.2012. Coming into force: 18.06.2012. Effect: None. Territorial extent & classification: E. Local. - Available at http://www.legislation.gov.uk/uksi/2012/1589/contents/made *Non-print*

The A1 Trunk Road (Barnsdale Bar Interchange) (Temporary Prohibition of Traffic) Order 2012 No. 2012/2757. - Enabling power: Road Traffic Regulation Act 1984, s. 14 (1) (a). - Issued: 07.11.2012. Made: 18.10.2012. Coming into force: 30.10.2012. Effect: None. Territorial extent & classification: E. Local. - Available at http://www.legislation.gov.uk/uksi/2012/2757/contents/made *Non-print*

The A1 Trunk Road (Barrowby to Gonerby Moor, Lincolnshire) (Temporary Prohibition of Traffic) Order 2012 No. 2012/2381. - Enabling power: Road Traffic Regulation Act 1984, s. 14 (1) (a). - Issued: 18.09.2012. Made: 28.08.2012. Coming into force: 04.09.2012. Effect: None. Territorial extent & classification: E. Local. - Available at http://www.legislation.gov.uk/uksi/2012/2381/contents/made *Non-print*

The A1 Trunk Road (Beeston, Central Bedfordshire) (Temporary Restriction and Prohibition of Traffic and Pedestrians) Order 2012 No. 2012/2239. - Enabling power: Road Traffic Regulation Act 1984, s. 14 (1) (a). - Issued: 04.09.2012. Made: 28.08.2012. Coming into force: 04.09.2012. Effect: None. Territorial extent & classification: E. Local. - Available at http://www.legislation.gov.uk/uksi/2012/2239/contents/made *Non-print*

The A1 Trunk Road (Biggleswade South Roundabout to Black Cat Roundabout, Bedfordshire) (Temporary Prohibition of Traffic) Order 2012 No. 2012/2324. - Enabling power: Road Traffic Regulation Act 1984, s. 14 (1) (a). - Issued: 13.09.2012. Made: 03.09.2012. Coming into force: 10.09.2012. Effect: None. Territorial extent & classification: E. Local. - Available at http://www.legislation.gov.uk/uksi/2012/2324/contents/made *Non-print*

The A1 Trunk Road (Brampton Hut Interchange, Cambridgeshire) Slip Roads (Temporary Prohibition of Traffic) Order 2012 No. 2012/2072. - Enabling power: Road Traffic Regulation Act 1984, s. 14 (1) (a). - Issued: 13.08.2012. Made: 30.07.2012. Coming into force: 06.08.2012. Effect: None. Territorial extent & classification: E. Local. - Available at http://www.legislation.gov.uk/uksi/2012/2072/contents/made *Non-print*

The A1 Trunk Road (Brampton Hut to Buckden, Cambridgeshire) Southbound (Temporary Prohibition of Traffic) Order 2012 No. 2012/2172. - Enabling power: Road Traffic Regulation Act 1984, s. 14 (1) (a). - Issued: 24.08.2012. Made: 20.08.2012. Coming into force: 24.08.2012. Effect: None. Territorial extent & classification: E. Local. - Available at http://www.legislation.gov.uk/uksi/2012/2172/contents/made *Non-print*

The A1 Trunk Road (Carlton on Trent to Markham Moor, Nottinghamshire) (Temporary Prohibition of Traffic) Order 2012 No. 2012/888. - Enabling power: Road Traffic Regulation Act 1984, s. 14 (1) (a). - Issued: 26.03.2012. Made: 12.03.2012. Coming into force: 19.03.2012. Effect: None. Territorial extent & classification: E. Local. - Available at http://www.legislation.gov.uk/uksi/2012/888/contents/made *Non-print*

The A1 Trunk Road (Carpenter's Lodge to Stamford) (Temporary Restriction and Prohibition of Traffic) Order 2012 No. 2012/2169. - Enabling power: Road Traffic Regulation Act 1984, s. 14 (1) (b). - Issued: 24.08.2012. Made: 20.08.2012. Coming into force: 27.08.2012. Effect: None. Territorial extent & classification: E. Local. - Available at http://www.legislation.gov.uk/uksi/2012/2169/contents/made *Non-print*

The A1 Trunk Road (Catterick North Interchange) (Temporary Prohibition of Traffic) Order 2012 No. 2012/1938. - Enabling power: Road Traffic Regulation Act 1984, s. 14 (1) (a). - Issued: 30.07.2012. Made: 12.07.2012. Coming into force: 19.07.2012. Effect: None. Territorial extent & classification: E. Local. - Available at http://www.legislation.gov.uk/uksi/2012/1938/contents/made *Non-print*

The A1 Trunk Road (Catterick South Interchange) (Temporary Restriction and Prohibition of Traffic) Order 2012 No. 2012/2639. - Enabling power: Road Traffic Regulation Act 1984, s. 14 (1) (a). - Issued: 23.10.2012. Made: 11.10.2012. Coming into force: 21.10.2012. Effect: None. Territorial extent & classification: E. Local. - Available at http://www.legislation.gov.uk/uksi/2012/2639/contents/made *Non-print*

The A1 Trunk Road (Catterick to Barton) (Temporary Restriction and Prohibition of Traffic) Order 2012 No. 2012/2436. - Enabling power: Road Traffic Regulation Act 1984, s. 14 (1) (a) (7). - Issued: 26.09.2012. Made: 13.09.2012. Coming into force: 23.09.2012. Effect: None. Territorial extent & classification: E. Local. - Available at http://www.legislation.gov.uk/uksi/2012/2436/contents/made *Non-print*

The A1 Trunk Road (Charlton Mires to North Charlton) (Temporary Restriction and Prohibition of Traffic) Order 2012 No. 2012/2484. - Enabling power: Road Traffic Regulation Act 1984, s. 14 (1) (a). - Issued: 02.10.2012. Made: 27.09.2012. Coming into force: 07.10.2012. Effect: None. Territorial extent & classification: E. Local. - Available at http://www.legislation.gov.uk/uksi/2012/2484/contents/made *Non-print*

The A1 Trunk Road (Clifton Interchange to Fairmoor Interchange) (Temporary Restriction and Prohibition of Traffic) Order 2012 No. 2012/527. - Enabling power: Road Traffic Regulation Act 1984, s. 14 (1) (a). - Issued: 01.03.2012. Made: 21.02.2012. Coming into force: 04.03.2012. Effect: None. Territorial extent & classification: E. Local. - Available at http://www.legislation.gov.uk/uksi/2012/527/contents/made *Non-print*

The A1 Trunk Road (Colsterworth, Lincolnshire) (Temporary Restriction and Prohibition of Traffic) Order 2012 No. 2012/380. - Enabling power: Road Traffic Regulation Act 1984, s. 14 (1) (a). - Issued: 17.02.2012. Made: 06.02.2012. Coming into force: 13.02.2012. Effect: None. Territorial extent & classification: E. Local. - Available at http://www.legislation.gov.uk/uksi/2012/380/contents/made *Non-print*

The A1 Trunk Road (Darrington Interchange) (Temporary Prohibition of Traffic) (No.2) Order 2012 No. 2012/2640. - Enabling power: Road Traffic Regulation Act 1984, s. 14 (1) (a). - Issued: 23.10.2012. Made: 11.10.2012. Coming into force: 21.10.2012. Effect: None. Territorial extent & classification: E. Local. - Available at http://www.legislation.gov.uk/uksi/2012/2640/contents/made *Non-print*

The A1 Trunk Road (Darrington Interchange) (Temporary Prohibition of Traffic) Order 2012 No. 2012/774. - Enabling power: Road Traffic Regulation Act 1984, s. 14 (1) (a). - Issued: 20.03.2012. Made: 08.03.2012. Coming into force: 18.03.2012. Effect: None. Territorial extent & classification: E. Local. - Available at http://www.legislation.gov.uk/uksi/2012/774/contents/made *Non-print*

The A1 Trunk Road (Denwick Interchange) (Temporary Prohibition of Traffic) Order 2012 No. 2012/118. - Enabling power: Road Traffic Regulation Act 1984, s. 14 (1) (a). - Issued: 23.01.2012. Made: 10.01.2012. Coming into force: 18.01.2012. Effect: None. Territorial extent & classification: E. Local. - Available at http://www.legislation.gov.uk/uksi/2012/118/contents/made *Non-print*

The A1 Trunk Road (Denwick Interchange) (Temporary Restriction and Prohibition of Traffic) Order 2012 No. 2012/996. - Enabling power: Road Traffic Regulation Act 1984, s. 14 (1) (a). - Issued: 05.04.2012. Made: 22.03.2012. Coming into force: 01.04.2012. Effect: None. Territorial extent & classification: E. Local. - Available at http://www.legislation.gov.uk/uksi/2012/996/contents/made *Non-print*

The A1 Trunk Road (Denwick to Charlton Mires) (Temporary Restriction and Prohibition of Traffic) Order 2012 No. 2012/41. - Enabling power: Road Traffic Regulation Act 1984, s. 14 (1) (a). - Issued: 11.01.2012. Made: 03.01.2012. Coming into force: 08.01.2012. Effect: None. Territorial extent & classification: E. Local. - Available at http://www.legislation.gov.uk/uksi/2012/41/contents/made *Non-print*

The A1 Trunk Road (Denwick to North Charlton) (Temporary Restriction and Prohibition of Traffic) Order 2012 No. 2012/1533. - Enabling power: Road Traffic Regulation Act 1984, s. 14 (1) (a). - Issued: 19.06.2012. Made: 31.05.2012. Coming into force: 10.06.2012. Effect: None. Territorial extent & classification: E. Local. - Available at http://www.legislation.gov.uk/uksi/2012/1533/contents/made *Non-print*

The A1 Trunk Road (Denwick to Wandylaw) (Temporary Restriction and Prohibition of Traffic) Order 2012 No. 2012/529. - Enabling power: Road Traffic Regulation Act 1984, s. 14 (1) (a). - Issued: 01.03.2012. Made: 21.02.2012. Coming into force: 04.03.2012. Effect: None. Territorial extent & classification: E. Local. - Available at http://www.legislation.gov.uk/uksi/2012/529/contents/made *Non-print*

The A1 Trunk Road (Duns Road Junction) (Temporary 50 Miles Per Hour Speed Restriction) Order 2012 No. 2012/2341. - Enabling power: Road Traffic Regulation Act 1984, s. 14 (1) (a). - Issued: 14.09.2012. Made: 06.09.2012. Coming into force: 16.09.2012. Effect: None. Territorial extent & classification: E. Local. - Available at http://www.legislation.gov.uk/uksi/2012/2341/contents/made *Non-print*

The A1 Trunk Road (Dunston Interchange to Metro Centre Interchange) (Temporary Prohibition of Traffic) Order 2012 No. 2012/1784. - Enabling power: Road Traffic Regulation Act 1984, s. 14 (1) (a). - Issued: 18.07.2012. Made: 25.06.2012. Coming into force: 29.06.2012. Effect: None. Territorial extent & classification: E. Local. - Available at http://www.legislation.gov.uk/uksi/2012/1784/contents/made *Non-print*

The A1 Trunk Road (Dunston Interchange to Metro Centre Interchange) (Temporary Restriction and Prohibition of Traffic) Order 2012 No. 2012/1727. - Enabling power: Road Traffic Regulation Act 1984, s. 14 (1) (a). - Issued: 13.07.2012. Made: 21.06.2012. Coming into force: 01.07.2012. Effect: None. Territorial extent & classification: E. Local. - Available at http://www.legislation.gov.uk/uksi/2012/1727/contents/made *Non-print*

The A1 Trunk Road (Eighton Lodge Interchange) (Temporary Restriction and Prohibition of Traffic) Order 2012 No. 2012/770. - Enabling power: Road Traffic Regulation Act 1984, s. 14 (1) (a). - Issued: 20.03.2012. Made: 08.03.2012. Coming into force: 19.03.2012. Effect: None. Territorial extent & classification: E. Local. - Available at http://www.legislation.gov.uk/uksi/2012/770/contents/made *Non-print*

The A1 Trunk Road (Eighton Lodge Interchange to Coalhouse Interchange) (Temporary Restriction and Prohibition of Traffic) (No. 2) Order 2012 No. 2012/2739. - Enabling power: Road Traffic Regulation Act 1984, s. 14 (1) (a). - Issued: 06.11.2012. Made: 18.10.2012. Coming into force: 28.10.2012. Effect: None. Territorial extent & classification: E. Local. - Available at http://www.legislation.gov.uk/uksi/2012/2739/contents/made *Non-print*

The A1 Trunk Road (Eighton Lodge Interchange to Coalhouse Interchange) (Temporary Restriction and Prohibition of Traffic) Order 2012 No. 2012/259. - Enabling power: Road Traffic Regulation Act 1984, s. 14 (1) (a). - Issued: 06.02.2012. Made: 26.01.2012. Coming into force: 04.02.2012. Effect: None. Territorial extent & classification: E. Local. - Available at http://www.legislation.gov.uk/uksi/2012/259/contents/made *Non-print*

The A1 Trunk Road (Eighton Lodge Interchange to Lobley Hill Interchange) (Temporary Prohibition of Traffic) Order 2012 No. 2012/2047. - Enabling power: Road Traffic Regulation Act 1984, s. 14 (1) (a). - Issued: 09.08.2012. Made: 25.07.2012. Coming into force: 02.08.2012. Effect: None. Territorial extent & classification: E. Local. - Available at http://www.legislation.gov.uk/uksi/2012/2047/contents/made *Non-print*

The A1 Trunk Road (Elkesley, Nottinghamshire) (Temporary Restriction and Prohibition of Traffic) Order 2012 No. 2012/2881. - Enabling power: Road Traffic Regulation Act 1984, s. 14 (1) (a). - Issued: 20.11.2012. Made: 05.11.2012. Coming into force: 12.11.2012. Effect: None. Territorial extent & classification: E. Local. - Available at http://www.legislation.gov.uk/uksi/2012/2881/contents/made *Non-print*

The A1 Trunk Road (Fawdon Interchange to Kenton Bar Interchange) (Temporary Restriction and Prohibition of Traffic) Order 2012 No. 2012/772. - Enabling power: Road Traffic Regulation Act 1984, s. 14 (1) (a). - Issued: 20.03.2012. Made: 08.03.2012. Coming into force: 14.03.2012. Effect: None. Territorial extent & classification: E. Local. - Available at http://www.legislation.gov.uk/uksi/2012/772/contents/made *Non-print*

The A1 Trunk Road (Felton and Charlton Mires) (Temporary 40 Miles Per Hour and 10 Miles Per Hour Speed Restriction) Order 2012 No. 2012/477. - Enabling power: Road Traffic Regulation Act 1984, s. 14 (1) (a). - Issued: 29.02.2012. Made: 16.02.2012. Coming into force: 26.02.2012. Effect: None. Territorial extent & classification: E. Local. - Available at http://www.legislation.gov.uk/uksi/2012/477/contents/made *Non-print*

The A1 Trunk Road (Felton) (Temporary Restriction and Prohibition of Traffic) Order 2012 No. 2012/2133. - Enabling power: Road Traffic Regulation Act 1984, s. 14 (1) (a). - Issued: 20.08.2012. Made: 09.08.2012. Coming into force: 19.08.2012. Effect: None. Territorial extent & classification: E. Local. - Available at http://www.legislation.gov.uk/uksi/2012/2133/contents/made *Non-print*

The A1 Trunk Road (Felton to Guyzance) (Temporary Restriction and Prohibition of Traffic) Order 2012 No. 2012/2151. - Enabling power: Road Traffic Regulation Act 1984, s. 14 (1) (a). - Issued: 22.08.2012. Made: 16.08.2012. Coming into force: 28.08.2012. Effect: None. Territorial extent & classification: E. Local. - Available at http://www.legislation.gov.uk/uksi/2012/2151/contents/made *Non-print*

The A1 Trunk Road (Fenwick Junction to Haggerston Junction) (Temporary Restriction and Prohibition of Traffic) Order 2012 No. 2012/2437. - Enabling power: Road Traffic Regulation Act 1984, s. 14 (1) (a). - Issued: 27.09.2012. Made: 13.09.2012. Coming into force: 22.09.2012. Effect: None. Territorial extent & classification: E. Local. - Available at http://www.legislation.gov.uk/uksi/2012/2437/contents/made *Non-print*

The A1 Trunk Road (Gateshead Quays Interchange) (Temporary Prohibition of Traffic) Order 2012 No. 2012/2638. - Enabling power: Road Traffic Regulation Act 1984, s. 14 (1) (a). - Issued: 23.10.2012. Made: 11.10.2012. Coming into force: 21.10.2012. Effect: None. Territorial extent & classification: E. Local. - Available at http://www.legislation.gov.uk/uksi/2012/2638/contents/made *Non-print*

The A1 Trunk Road (Gonerby Moor, Lincolnshire) (Temporary Restriction and Prohibition of Traffic) Order 2012 No. 2012/379. - Enabling power: Road Traffic Regulation Act 1984, s. 14 (1) (a). - Issued: 17.02.2012. Made: 06.02.2012. Coming into force: 13.02.2012. Effect: None. Territorial extent & classification: E. Local. - Available at http://www.legislation.gov.uk/uksi/2012/379/contents/made *Non-print*

The A1 Trunk Road (Gosforth Park Interchange to Seaton Burn Interchange) (Temporary Restriction and Prohibition of Traffic) (No. 2) Order 2012 No. 2012/1785. - Enabling power: Road Traffic Regulation Act 1984, s. 14 (1) (a). - Issued: 18.07.2012. Made: 28.06.2012. Coming into force: 05.07.2012. Effect: None. Territorial extent & classification: E. Local. - Available at http://www.legislation.gov.uk/uksi/2012/1785/contents/made *Non-print*

The A1 Trunk Road (Gosforth Park Interchange to Seaton Burn Interchange) (Temporary Restriction and Prohibition of Traffic) Order 2012 No. 2012/258. - Enabling power: Road Traffic Regulation Act 1984, s. 14 (1) (a). - Issued: 06.02.2012. Made: 26.01.2012. Coming into force: 05.02.2012. Effect: None. Territorial extent & classification: E. Local. - Available at http://www.legislation.gov.uk/uksi/2012/258/contents/made *Non-print*

The A1 Trunk Road (Grantham, Lincolnshire) (Temporary Prohibition of Traffic) Order 2012 No. 2012/3233. - Enabling power: Road Traffic Regulation Act 1984, s. 14 (1) (a). - Issued: 08.01.2013. Made: 03.12.2012. Coming into force: 10.12.2012. Effect: None. Territorial extent & classification: E. Local. - Available at http://www.legislation.gov.uk/uksi/2012/3233/contents/made *Non-print*

The A1 Trunk Road (Grantham, Lincolnshire) (Temporary Restriction and Prohibition of Traffic) Order 2012 No. 2012/2895. - Enabling power: Road Traffic Regulation Act 1984, s. 14 (1) (a). - Issued: 22.11.2012. Made: 02.11.2012. Coming into force: 09.11.2012. Effect: None. Territorial extent & classification: E. Local. - Available at http://www.legislation.gov.uk/uksi/2012/2895/contents/made *Non-print*

The A1 Trunk Road (Grantham to North Muskham) (Temporary Restriction and Prohibition of Traffic) Order 2012 No. 2012/2800. - Enabling power: Road Traffic Regulation Act 1984, s. 14 (1) (a). - Issued: 09.11.2012. Made: 19.10.2012. Coming into force: 26.10.2012. Effect: None. Territorial extent & classification: E. Local. - Available at http://www.legislation.gov.uk/uksi/2012/2800/contents/made *Non-print*

The A1 Trunk Road (Grantham to Stamford, Lincolnshire) (Temporary Prohibition of Traffic) Order 2012 No. 2012/1983. - Enabling power: Road Traffic Regulation Act 1984, s. 14 (1) (a). - Issued: 31.07.2012. Made: 16.07.2012. Coming into force: 23.07.2012. Effect: None. Territorial extent & classification: E. Local. - Available at http://www.legislation.gov.uk/uksi/2012/1983/contents/made *Non-print*

The A1 Trunk Road (Hail Weston to Buckden, Cambridgeshire) (Temporary Prohibition of Traffic) Order 2012 No. 2012/1603. - Enabling power: Road Traffic Regulation Act 1984, s. 14 (1) (a). - Issued: 25.06.2012. Made: 28.05.2012. Coming into force: 04.06.2012. Effect: None. Territorial extent & classification: E. Local. - Available at http://www.legislation.gov.uk/uksi/2012/1603/contents/made *Non-print*

The A1 Trunk Road (Hebron to Tritlington) (Temporary Restriction and Prohibition of Traffic) Order 2012 No. 2012/406. - Enabling power: Road Traffic Regulation Act 1984, s. 14 (1) (a). - Issued: 21.02.2012. Made: 09.02.2012. Coming into force: 18.02.2012. Effect: None. Territorial extent & classification: E. Local. - Available at http://www.legislation.gov.uk/uksi/2012/406/contents/made *Non-print*

The A1 Trunk Road (Highfields Roundabout to Folly Farm) (Temporary Restriction and Prohibition of Traffic) Order 2012 No. 2012/2848. - Enabling power: Road Traffic Regulation Act 1984, s. 14 (1) (a) (7). - Issued: 16.11.2012. Made: 01.11.2012. Coming into force: 11.11.2012. Effect: None. Territorial extent & classification: E. Local. - Available at http://www.legislation.gov.uk/uksi/2012/2848/contents/made *Non-print*

The A1 Trunk Road (Langford, Bedfordshire) Northbound Entry Slip Road (Temporary Prohibition of Traffic) Order 2012 No. 2012/2102. - Enabling power: Road Traffic Regulation Act 1984, s. 14 (1) (a). - Issued: 16.08.2012. Made: 06.08.2012. Coming into force: 13.08.2012. Effect: None. Territorial extent & classification: E. Local. - Available at http://www.legislation.gov.uk/uksi/2012/2102/contents/made *Non-print*

The A1 Trunk Road (Layby at Brownieside) (Temporary Prohibition of Traffic) Order 2012 No. 2012/121. - Enabling power: Road Traffic Regulation Act 1984, s. 14 (1) (a). - Issued: 23.01.2012. Made: 12.01.2012. Coming into force: 22.01.2012. Effect: None. Territorial extent & classification: E. Local. - Available at http://www.legislation.gov.uk/uksi/2012/121/contents/made *Non-print*

The A1 Trunk Road (Layby at Lobley Hill Interchange) (Temporary Prohibition of Traffic) Order 2012 No. 2012/2485. - Enabling power: Road Traffic Regulation Act 1984, s. 14 (1) (a). - Issued: 02.10.2012. Made: 27.09.2012. Coming into force: 07.10.2012. Effect: None. Territorial extent & classification: E. Local. - Available at http://www.legislation.gov.uk/uksi/2012/2485/contents/made *Non-print*

The A1 Trunk Road (Layby at Skellow) (Temporary Prohibition of Traffic) Order 2012 No. 2012/3290. - Enabling power: Road Traffic Regulation Act 1984, s. 14 (1) (a). - Issued: 15.01.2013. Made: 27.12.2012. Coming into force: 06.01.2013. Effect: None. Territorial extent & classification: E. Local. - Available at http://www.legislation.gov.uk/uksi/2012/3290/contents/made *Non-print*

The A1 Trunk Road (Layby at Wentedge Road Junction) (Temporary Prohibition of Traffic) Order 2012 No. 2012/1066. - Enabling power: Road Traffic Regulation Act 1984, s. 14 (1) (a). - Issued: 16.04.2012. Made: 05.04.2012. Coming into force: 15.04.2012. Effect: None. Territorial extent & classification: E. Local. - Available at http://www.legislation.gov.uk/uksi/2012/1066/contents/made *Non-print*

The A1 Trunk Road (Leeming to Catterick) (Temporary Restriction and Prohibition of Traffic) (No. 2) Order 2012 No. 2012/2206. - Enabling power: Road Traffic Regulation Act 1984, s. 14 (1) (a) (7). - Issued: 30.08.2012. Made: 23.08.2012. Coming into force: 30.08.2012. Effect: None. Territorial extent & classification: E. Local. - Available at http://www.legislation.gov.uk/uksi/2012/2206/contents/made *Non-print*

The A1 Trunk Road (Leeming to Catterick) (Temporary Restriction and Prohibition of Traffic) Order 2012 No. 2012/69. - Enabling power: Road Traffic Regulation Act 1984, s. 14 (1) (a). - Issued: 17.01.2012. Made: 04.01.2012. Coming into force: 15.01.2012. Effect: None. Territorial extent & classification: E. Local. - Available at http://www.legislation.gov.uk/uksi/2012/69/contents/made *Non-print*

The A1 Trunk Road (Lobley Hill Interchange to Eighton Lodge Interchange) (Temporary Prohibition of Traffic) Order 2012 No. 2012/1850. - Enabling power: Road Traffic Regulation Act 1984, s. 14 (1) (a). - Issued: 19.07.2012. Made: 05.07.2012. Coming into force: 16.07.2012. Effect: None. Territorial extent & classification: E. Local. - Available at http://www.legislation.gov.uk/uksi/2012/1850/contents/made *Non-print*

The A1 Trunk Road (Markham Moor, Nottinghamshire) (Temporary Prohibition of Traffic) Order 2012 No. 2012/1443. - Enabling power: Road Traffic Regulation Act 1984, s. 14 (1) (a). - Issued: 12.06.2012. Made: 14.05.2012. Coming into force: 21.05.2012. Effect: None. Territorial extent & classification: E. Local. - Available at http://www.legislation.gov.uk/uksi/2012/1443/contents/made *Non-print*

The A1 Trunk Road (near Grantham, Lincolnshire) (Temporary Restriction and Prohibition of Traffic) Order 2012 No. 2012/1202. - Enabling power: Road Traffic Regulation Act 1984, s. 14 (1) (a). - Issued: 08.05.2012. Made: 24.04.2012. Coming into force: 01.05.2012. Effect: None. Territorial extent & classification: E. Local. - Available at http://www.legislation.gov.uk/uksi/2012/1202/contents/made *Non-print*

The A1 Trunk Road (Newton-on-the-Moor to Alnwick Bypass) (Temporary Restriction and Prohibition of Traffic) Order 2012 No. 2012/1991. - Enabling power: Road Traffic Regulation Act 1984, s. 14 (1) (a) (7). - Issued: 01.08.2012. Made: 19.07.2012. Coming into force: 31.07.2012. Effect: None. Territorial extent & classification: E. Local. - Available at http://www.legislation.gov.uk/uksi/2012/1991/contents/made *Non-print*

The A1 Trunk Road (North Charlton) (Temporary Restriction and Prohibition of Traffic) Order 2012 No. 2012/81. - Enabling power: Road Traffic Regulation Act 1984, s. 14 (1) (a). - Issued: 18.01.2012. Made: 05.01.2012. Coming into force: 16.01.2012. Effect: None. Territorial extent & classification: E. Local. - Available at http://www.legislation.gov.uk/uksi/2012/81/contents/made *Non-print*

The A1 Trunk Road (North Muskham, Nottinghamshire) (Temporary Prohibition of Traffic in Layby) Order 2012 No. 2012/2195. - Enabling power: Road Traffic Regulation Act 1984, s. 14 (1) (a). - Issued: 29.08.2012. Made: 21.08.2012. Coming into force: 28.08.2012. Effect: None. Territorial extent & classification: E. Local. - Available at http://www.legislation.gov.uk/uksi/2012/2195/contents/made *Non-print*

The A1 Trunk Road (Scremerston Roundabout to East Ord Roundabout) (Temporary Restriction and Prohibition of Traffic) Order 2012 No. 2012/3114. - Enabling power: Road Traffic Regulation Act 1984, s. 14 (1) (a). - Issued: 20.12.2012. Made: 22.11.2012. Coming into force: 01.12.2012. Effect: None. Territorial extent & classification: E. Local. - Available at http://www.legislation.gov.uk/uksi/2012/3114/contents/made *Non-print*

The A1 Trunk Road (Scremeston Roundabout to Paxton Junction) (Temporary Restriction and Prohibition of Traffic) Order 2012 No. 2012/1452. - Enabling power: Road Traffic Regulation Act 1984, s. 14 (1) (a). - Issued: 12.06.2012. Made: 24.05.2012. Coming into force: 05.06.2012. Effect: None. Territorial extent & classification: E. Local. - Available at http://www.legislation.gov.uk/uksi/2012/1452/contents/made *Non-print*

The A1 Trunk Road (Shotton Lane Interchange) (Temporary Restriction and Prohibition of Traffic) Order 2012 No. 2012/1939. - Enabling power: Road Traffic Regulation Act 1984, s. 14 (1) (a). - Issued: 30.07.2012. Made: 12.07.2012. Coming into force: 22.07.2012. Effect: None. Territorial extent & classification: E. Local. - Available at http://www.legislation.gov.uk/uksi/2012/1939/contents/made *Non-print*

The A1 Trunk Road (Stannington Interchange) (Temporary Restriction and Prohibition of Traffic) Order 2012 No. 2012/1992. - Enabling power: Road Traffic Regulation Act 1984, s. 14 (1) (a). - Issued: 01.08.2012. Made: 19.07.2012. Coming into force: 26.07.2012. Effect: None. Territorial extent & classification: E. Local. - Available at http://www.legislation.gov.uk/uksi/2012/1992/contents/made *Non-print*

The A1 Trunk Road (Stannington Interchange to Warreners House Interchange) (Temporary Restriction and Prohibition of Traffic) Order 2012 No. 2012/43. - Enabling power: Road Traffic Regulation Act 1984, s. 14 (1) (a) (7). - Issued: 11.01.2012. Made: 03.01.2012. Coming into force: 08.01.2012. Effect: None. Territorial extent & classification: E. Local. - Available at http://www.legislation.gov.uk/uksi/2012/43/contents/made *Non-print*

The A1 Trunk Road (Swalwell Interchange) (Temporary Prohibition of Traffic) Order 2012 No. 2012/1610. - Enabling power: Road Traffic Regulation Act 1984, s. 14 (1) (a). - Issued: 27.06.2012. Made: 14.06.2012. Coming into force: 21.06.2012. Effect: None. Territorial extent & classification: E. Local. - Available at http://www.legislation.gov.uk/uksi/2012/1610/contents/made *Non-print*

The A1 Trunk Road (Tempsford, Bedfordshire) (Temporary Prohibition of Traffic) Order 2012 No. 2012/2103. - Enabling power: Road Traffic Regulation Act 1984, s. 14 (1) (a). - Issued: 16.08.2012. Made: 06.08.2012. Coming into force: 13.08.2012. Effect: None. Territorial extent & classification: E. Local. - Available at http://www.legislation.gov.uk/uksi/2012/2103/contents/made *Non-print*

The A1 Trunk Road (Tempsford to Black Cat Roundabout, Bedfordshire) Northbound (Temporary Restriction and Prohibition of Pedestrians) Order 2012 No. 2012/1596. - Enabling power: Road Traffic Regulation Act 1984, s. 14 (1) (a). - Issued: 27.06.2012. Made: 11.06.2012. Coming into force: 18.06.2012. Effect: None. Territorial extent & classification: E. Local. - Available at http://www.legislation.gov.uk/uksi/2012/1596/contents/made *Non-print*

The A1 Trunk Road (Thornhaugh, Peterborough) (Closure of Gap in the Central Reservation) Order 2012 No. 2012/841. - Enabling power: Road Traffic Regulation Act 1984, ss. 1 (1), 2 (1) (2). - Issued: 20.03.2012. Made: 14.03.2012. Coming into force: 28.03.2012. Effect: None. Territorial extent & classification: E. Local. - Available at http://www.legislation.gov.uk/uksi/2012/841/contents/made *Non-print*

The A1 Trunk Road (Thornhaugh, Peterborough) (Temporary Restriction and Prohibition of Traffic) Order 2012 No. 2012/665. - Enabling power: Road Traffic Regulation Act 1984, s. 14 (1) (a). - Issued: 14.03.2012. Made: 02.03.2012. Coming into force: 09.03.2012. Effect: None. Territorial extent & classification: E. Local. - Available at http://www.legislation.gov.uk/uksi/2012/665/contents/made *Non-print*

The A1 Trunk Road (Tinwell, Rutland) (Temporary Prohibition of Traffic) Order 2012 No. 2012/1140. - Enabling power: Road Traffic Regulation Act 1984, s. 14 (1) (b). - Issued: 12.04.2012. Made: 10.04.2012. Coming into force: 17.04.2012. Effect: None. Territorial extent & classification: E. Local. - Available at http://www.legislation.gov.uk/uksi/2012/1140/contents/made *Non-print*

The A1 Trunk Road (Various Locations) (Temporary Restriction and Prohibition of Traffic) Order 2012 No. 2012/316. - Enabling power: Road Traffic Regulation Act 1984, s. 14 (1) (a). - Issued: 15.02.2012. Made: 02.02.2012. Coming into force: 11.02.2012. Effect: None. Territorial extent & classification: E. Local. - Available at http://www.legislation.gov.uk/uksi/2012/316/contents/made *Non-print*

The A1 Trunk Road (Wandylaw) (Temporary 40 Miles Per Hour Speed Restriction) Order 2012 No. 2012/257. - Enabling power: Road Traffic Regulation Act 1984, s. 14 (1) (a). - Issued: 06.02.2012. Made: 26.01.2012. Coming into force: 31.01.2012. Effect: None. Territorial extent & classification: E. Local. - Available at http://www.legislation.gov.uk/uksi/2012/257/contents/made *Non-print*

The A1 Trunk Road (Wandylaw to Adderstone) (Temporary Restriction and Prohibition of Traffic) Order 2012 No. 2012/2207. - Enabling power: Road Traffic Regulation Act 1984, s. 14 (1) (a). - Issued: 30.08.2012. Made: 23.08.2012. Coming into force: 02.09.2012. Effect: None. Territorial extent & classification: E. Local. - Available at http://www.legislation.gov.uk/uksi/2012/2207/contents/made *Non-print*

The A1 Trunk Road (Warenford to Adderstone) (Temporary Restriction and Prohibition of Traffic) Order 2012 No. 2012/1612. - Enabling power: Road Traffic Regulation Act 1984, s. 14 (1) (a). - Issued: 28.06.2012. Made: 14.06.2012. Coming into force: 24.06.2012. Effect: None. Territorial extent & classification: E. Local. - Available at http://www.legislation.gov.uk/uksi/2012/1612/contents/made *Non-print*

The A1 Trunk Road (Warenford to Hemphole) (Temporary Restriction and Prohibition of Traffic) Order 2012 No. 2012/2873. - Enabling power: Road Traffic Regulation Act 1984, s. 14 (1) (a). - Issued: 19.11.2012. Made: 08.11.2012. Coming into force: 18.11.2012. Effect: None. Territorial extent & classification: E. Local. - Available at http://www.legislation.gov.uk/uksi/2012/2873/contents/made *Non-print*

The A1 Trunk Road (West Cawledge to Alnwick) (Temporary 50 Miles Per Hour Speed Restriction) Order 2012 No. 2012/3191. - Enabling power: Road Traffic Regulation Act 1984, s. 14 (1) (a). - Issued: 02.01.2013. Made: 04.12.2012. Coming into force: 09.12.2012. Effect: None. Territorial extent & classification: E. Local. - Available at http://www.legislation.gov.uk/uksi/2012/3191/contents/made *Non-print*

The A1 Trunk Road (West Mains to Haggerston) (Temporary Restriction and Prohibition of Traffic) Order 2012 No. 2012/2637. - Enabling power: Road Traffic Regulation Act 1984, s. 14 (1) (a). - Issued: 23.10.2012. Made: 11.10.2012. Coming into force: 23.10.2012. Effect: None. Territorial extent & classification: E. Local. - Available at http://www.legislation.gov.uk/uksi/2012/2637/contents/made *Non-print*

The A1 Trunk Road (Wyboston, Bedfordshire) (Temporary Prohibition of Traffic) Order 2012 No. 2012/2142. - Enabling power: Road Traffic Regulation Act 1984, s. 14 (1) (a). - Issued: 21.08.2012. Made: 13.08.2012. Coming into force: 20.08.2012. Effect: None. Territorial extent & classification: E. Local. - Available at http://www.legislation.gov.uk/uksi/2012/2142/contents/made *Non-print*

The A1 Trunk Road (Wyboston, Bedfordshire to Alconbury, Cambridgeshire) and the A428 Trunk Road (Easton Socon to Madingley, Cambridgeshire) Lay-bys (Temporary Prohibition of Traffic) Order 2012 No. 2012/2853. - Enabling power: Road Traffic Regulation Act 1984, s. 14 (1) (a). - Issued: 16.11.2012. Made: 05.11.2012. Coming into force: 12.11.2012. Effect: None. Territorial extent & classification: E. Local. - Available at http://www.legislation.gov.uk/uksi/2012/2853/contents/made *Non-print*

The A2 Trunk Road and the M2 Motorway (Junction 1, Coastbound) (Temporary Restriction and Prohibition of Traffic) Order 2012 No. 2012/912. - Enabling power: Road Traffic Regulation Act 1984, s. 14 (1) (a). - Issued: 26.03.2012. Made: 19.03.2012. Coming into force: 07.04.2012. Effect: None. Territorial extent & classification: E. Local. - Available at http://www.legislation.gov.uk/uksi/2012/912/contents/made *Non-print*

The A2 Trunk Road (Brenley Corner, Coastbound) (Temporary 40 Miles Per Hour Speed Restriction) Order 2012 No. 2012/1411. - Enabling power: Road Traffic Regulation Act 1984, s. 14 (1) (a). - Issued: 01.06.2012. Made: 21.05.2012. Coming into force: 09.06.2012. Effect: None. Territorial extent & classification: E. Local. - Available at http://www.legislation.gov.uk/uksi/2012/1411/contents/made *Non-print*

The A2 Trunk Road (Brenley Corner - New Dover Road Interchange) (Temporary Restriction and Prohibition of Traffic) Order 2012 No. 2012/1453. - Enabling power: Road Traffic Regulation Act 1984, s. 14 (1) (a). - Issued: 12.06.2012. Made: 28.05.2012. Coming into force: 16.06.2012. Effect: None. Territorial extent & classification: E. Local. - Available at http://www.legislation.gov.uk/uksi/2012/1453/contents/made *Non-print*

The A2 Trunk Road (Brenley Corner - Thanington Road Interchange) (Temporary Prohibition of Traffic) Order 2012 No. 2012/2305. - Enabling power: Road Traffic Regulation Act 1984, s. 14 (1) (a). - Issued: 11.09.2012. Made: 03.09.2012. Coming into force: 22.09.2012. Effect: None. Territorial extent & classification: E. Local. - Available at http://www.legislation.gov.uk/uksi/2012/2305/contents/made *Non-print*

The A2 Trunk Road (Darenth Interchange and Bean Interchange) (Temporary Prohibition of Traffic) Order 2012 No. 2012/3148. - Enabling power: Road Traffic Regulation Act 1984, s. 14 (1) (a). - Issued: 27.12.2012. Made: 26.11.2012. Coming into force: 09.01.2013. Effect: None. Territorial extent & classification: E. Local. - Available at http://www.legislation.gov.uk/uksi/2012/3148/contents/made *Non-print*

The A2 Trunk Road (Dartford Heath, Slip Roads) (Temporary Prohibition of Traffic) Order 2012 No. 2012/1557. - Enabling power: Road Traffic Regulation Act 1984, s. 14 (1) (a). - Issued: 22.06.2012. Made: 06.06.2012. Coming into force: 30.06.2012. Effect: None. Territorial extent & classification: E. Local. - Available at http://www.legislation.gov.uk/uksi/2012/1557/contents/made *Non-print*

The A2 Trunk Road (Dover - Lydden) (Temporary Restriction and Prohibition of Traffic) Order 2012 No. 2012/1226. - Enabling power: Road Traffic Regulation Act 1984, s. 14 (1) (a). - Issued: 10.05.2012. Made: 30.04.2012. Coming into force: 19.05.2012. Effect: None. Territorial extent & classification: E. Local. - Available at http://www.legislation.gov.uk/uksi/2012/1226/contents/made *Non-print*

The A2 Trunk Road (Dover Road, Barham) (Temporary Restriction and Prohibition of Traffic) Order 2012 No. 2012/598. - Enabling power: Road Traffic Regulation Act 1984, s. 14 (1) (a). - Issued: 06.03.2012. Made: 27.02.2012. Coming into force: 17.03.2012. Effect: None. Territorial extent & classification: E. Local. - Available at http://www.legislation.gov.uk/uksi/2012/598/contents/made *Non-print*

The A2 Trunk Road (Dunkirk, Eastbound) (Temporary Prohibition of Traffic) Order 2012 No. 2012/3202. - Enabling power: Road Traffic Regulation Act 1984, s. 14 (1) (a). - Issued: 02.01.2013. Made: 10.12.2012. Coming into force: 02.01.2013. Effect: None. Territorial extent & classification: E. Local. - Available at http://www.legislation.gov.uk/uksi/2012/3202/contents/made *Non-print*

The A2 Trunk Road (Guston Roundabout - Dover Eastern Docks Roundabout) (Temporary Prohibition of Traffic) Order 2012 No. 2012/3223. - Enabling power: Road Traffic Regulation Act 1984, s. 14 (1) (a). - Issued: 07.01.2013. Made: 10.12.2012. Coming into force: 12.01.2013. Effect: None. Territorial extent & classification: E. Local. - Available at http://www.legislation.gov.uk/uksi/2012/3223/contents/made *Non-print*

The A2 Trunk Road (Halfway Street - Whitfield Roundabout) (Temporary Restriction and Prohibition of Traffic) Order 2012 No. 2012/2961. - Enabling power: Road Traffic Regulation Act 1984, s. 14 (1) (a). - Issued: 30.11.2012. Made: 19.11.2012. Coming into force: 08.12.2012. Effect: None. Territorial extent & classification: E. Local. - Available at http://www.legislation.gov.uk/uksi/2012/2961/contents/made *Non-print*

The A2 Trunk Road (Jubilee Way, Coastbound Carriageway) (Temporary Prohibition of Traffic) Order 2012 No. 2012/2361. - Enabling power: Road Traffic Regulation Act 1984, s. 14 (1) (a). - Issued: 17.09.2012. Made: 10.09.2012. Coming into force: 01.10.2012. Effect: None. Territorial extent & classification: E. Local. - Available at http://www.legislation.gov.uk/uksi/2012/2361/contents/made *Non-print*

Road traffic: Traffic regulation

The A2 Trunk Road (Liss to Ham Barn Roundabout) (Temporary Prohibition of Pedestrians and Cyclists) Order 2012 No. 2012/2365. - Enabling power: Road Traffic Regulation Act 1984, s. 14 (1) (a). - Issued: 18.09.2012. Made: 10.09.2012. Coming into force: 01.10.2012. Effect: None. Territorial extent & classification: E. Local. - Available at http://www.legislation.gov.uk/uksi/2012/2365/contents/made *Non-print*

The A2 Trunk Road (Littledale Viaduct) (Temporary Restriction and Prohibition of Traffic) Order 2012 No. 2012/2509. - Enabling power: Road Traffic Regulation Act 1984, s. 14 (1) (a). - Issued: 05.10.2012. Made: 01.10.2012. Coming into force: 20.10.2012. Effect: None. Territorial extent & classification: E. Local. - Available at http://www.legislation.gov.uk/uksi/2012/2509/contents/made *Non-print*

The A2 Trunk Road (Lydden - Bonny Bush) (Temporary Restriction and Prohibition of Traffic) Order 2012 No. 2012/1575. - Enabling power: Road Traffic Regulation Act 1984, s. 14 (1) (a). - Issued: 25.06.2012. Made: 11.06.2012. Coming into force: 30.06.2012. Effect: None. Territorial extent & classification: E. Local. - Available at http://www.legislation.gov.uk/uksi/2012/1575/contents/made *Non-print*

The A2 Trunk Road (Lydden Hill Junction) (Temporary Restriction and Prohibition of Traffic) Order 2012 No. 2012/2227. - Enabling power: Road Traffic Regulation Act 1984, s. 14 (1) (a). - Issued: 03.09.2012. Made: 28.08.2012. Coming into force: 15.09.2012. Effect: None. Territorial extent & classification: E. Local. - Available at http://www.legislation.gov.uk/uksi/2012/2227/contents/made *Non-print*

The A2 Trunk Road (Lydden Hill - Whitfield Roundabout) (Temporary Restriction and Prohibition of Traffic) Order 2012 No. 2012/549. - Enabling power: Road Traffic Regulation Act 1984, s. 14 (1) (a). - Issued: 01.03.2012. Made: 20.02.2012. Coming into force: 10.03.2012. Effect: None. Territorial extent & classification: E. Local. - Available at http://www.legislation.gov.uk/uksi/2012/549/contents/made *Non-print*

The A2 Trunk Road (M25 Junction 2, Slip/Link Roads) (Temporary Prohibition of Traffic) Order 2012 No. 2012/1192. - Enabling power: Road Traffic Regulation Act 1984, s. 14 (1) (a). - Issued: 04.05.2012. Made: 23.04.2012. Coming into force: 12.05.2012. Effect: None. Territorial extent & classification: E. Local. - Available at http://www.legislation.gov.uk/uksi/2012/1192/contents/made *Non-print*

The A2 Trunk Road (Pepper Hill Junction) (Temporary Restriction and Prohibition of Traffic) Order 2012 No. 2012/2308. - Enabling power: Road Traffic Regulation Act 1984, s. 14 (1) (a). - Issued: 11.09.2012. Made: 03.09.2012. Coming into force: 15.09.2012. Effect: None. Territorial extent & classification: E. Local. - Available at http://www.legislation.gov.uk/uksi/2012/2308/contents/made *Non-print*

The A2 Trunk Road (Upper Harbledown - Bridge, Coastbound) (Temporary Restriction and Prohibition of Traffic) Order 2012 No. 2012/1045. - Enabling power: Road Traffic Regulation Act 1984, s. 14 (1) (a). - Issued: 13.04.2012. Made: 26.03.2012. Coming into force: 14.04.2012. Effect: None. Territorial extent & classification: E. Local. - Available at http://www.legislation.gov.uk/uksi/2012/1045/contents/made *Non-print*

The A2 Trunk Road (Upper Harbledown - Whitfield, Slip Roads) (Temporary Prohibition of Traffic) Order 2012 No. 2012/3137. - Enabling power: Road Traffic Regulation Act 1984, s. 14 (1) (a). - Issued: 27.12.2012. Made: 26.11.2012. Coming into force: 17.12.2012. Effect: None. Territorial extent & classification: E. Local. - Available at http://www.legislation.gov.uk/uksi/2012/3137/contents/made *Non-print*

The A3(M) Motorway and A3 Trunk Road (A3(M) Junction 2 - Clanfield) (Temporary Restriction and Prohibition of Traffic) Order 2012 No. 2012/2780. - Enabling power: Road Traffic Regulation Act 1984, s. 14 (1) (a). - Issued: 08.11.2012. Made: 22.10.2012. Coming into force: 10.11.2012. Effect: None. Territorial extent & classification: E. Local. - Available at http://www.legislation.gov.uk/uksi/2012/2780/contents/made *Non-print*

The A3(M) Motorway and the A3 Trunk Road (Clanfield - New Barn Farm Lane) (Temporary Restriction and Prohibition of Traffic) Order 2012 No. 2012/2443. - Enabling power: Road Traffic Regulation Act 1984, s. 14 (1) (a). - Issued: 27.09.2012. Made: 17.09.2012. Coming into force: 06.10.2012. Effect: None. Territorial extent & classification: E. Local. - Available at http://www.legislation.gov.uk/uksi/2012/2443/contents/made *Non-print*

The A3(M) Motorway and the A3 Trunk Road (Junctions 2 - 1, Northbound) (Temporary Prohibition of Traffic) Order 2012 No. 2012/597. - Enabling power: Road Traffic Regulation Act 1984, s. 14 (1) (a). - Issued: 06.03.2012. Made: 27.02.2012. Coming into force: 17.03.2012. Effect: None. Territorial extent & classification: E. Local. - Available at http://www.legislation.gov.uk/uksi/2012/597/contents/made *Non-print*

The A3(M) Motorway (Junction 5, Southbound Carriageway) (Temporary Prohibition of Traffic) Order 2012 No. 2012/2229. - Enabling power: Road Traffic Regulation Act 1984, s. 14 (1) (a). - Issued: 03.09.2012. Made: 28.08.2012. Coming into force: 15.09.2012. Effect: None. Territorial extent & classification: E. Local. - Available at http://www.legislation.gov.uk/uksi/2012/2229/contents/made *Non-print*

The A3(M) Motorway (Junctions 1 - 2, Southbound Carriageway) (Temporary Prohibition of Traffic) Order 2012 No. 2012/3200. - Enabling power: Road Traffic Regulation Act 1984, s. 14 (1) (a). - Issued: 02.01.2013. Made: 10.12.2012. Coming into force: 05.01.2013. Effect: None. Territorial extent & classification: E. Local. - Available at http://www.legislation.gov.uk/uksi/2012/3200/contents/made *Non-print*

The A3(M) Motorway (Junctions 2 - 3, Southbound) (Temporary Prohibition of Traffic) Order 2012 No. 2012/1182. - Enabling power: Road Traffic Regulation Act 1984, s. 14 (1) (a). - Issued: 02.05.2012. Made: 23.04.2012. Coming into force: 12.05.2012. Effect: None. Territorial extent & classification: E. Local. - Available at http://www.legislation.gov.uk/uksi/2012/1182/contents/made *Non-print*

The A3(M) Motorway (Junctions 3 - 5, Southbound) (Temporary Prohibition of Traffic) Order 2012 No. 2012/2069. - Enabling power: Road Traffic Regulation Act 1984, s. 14 (1) (a). - Issued: 13.08.2012. Made: 30.07.2012. Coming into force: 18.08.2012. Effect: None. Territorial extent & classification: E. Local. - Available at http://www.legislation.gov.uk/uksi/2012/2069/contents/made *Non-print*

The A3(M) Motorway (Junctions 5 - 3, Northbound) (Temporary Prohibition of Traffic) (No. 2) Order 2012 No. 2012/3142. - Enabling power: Road Traffic Regulation Act 1984, s. 14 (1) (a). - Issued: 27.12.2012. Made: 26.11.2012. Coming into force: 15.12.2012. Effect: None. Territorial extent & classification: E. Local. - Available at http://www.legislation.gov.uk/uksi/2012/3142/contents/made *Non-print*

The A3 Trunk Road (Berelands Interchange, Carriageways) (Temporary Prohibition of Traffic) Order 2012 No. 2012/2224. - Enabling power: Road Traffic Regulation Act 1984, s. 14 (1) (a). - Issued: 03.09.2012. Made: 28.08.2012. Coming into force: 15.09.2012. Effect: None. Territorial extent & classification: E. Local. - Available at http://www.legislation.gov.uk/uksi/2012/2224/contents/made *Non-print*

The A3 Trunk Road (Dennis Interchange - Burpham Interchange) (Temporary Prohibition of Traffic) Order 2012 No. 2012/1524. - Enabling power: Road Traffic Regulation Act 1984, s. 14 (1) (a). - Issued: 19.06.2012. Made: 06.06.2012. Coming into force: 23.06.2012. Effect: None. Territorial extent & classification: E. Local. - Available at http://www.legislation.gov.uk/uksi/2012/1524/contents/made *Non-print*

The A3 Trunk Road (Esher - Ockham) (Temporary Prohibition of Traffic) Order 2012 No. 2012/3184. - Enabling power: Road Traffic Regulation Act 1984, s. 14 (1) (a). - Issued: 31.12.2012. Made: 03.12.2012. Coming into force: 15.01.2013. Effect: None. Territorial extent & classification: E. Local. - Available at http://www.legislation.gov.uk/uksi/2012/3184/contents/made *Non-print*

The A3 Trunk Road (Hammer Lane Junction - A3(M) Junction 1) (Temporary Restriction and Prohibition of Traffic) Order 2012 No. 2012/1952. - Enabling power: Road Traffic Regulation Act 1984, s. 14 (1) (a). - Issued: 30.07.2012. Made: 16.07.2012. Coming into force: 08.08.2012. Effect: None. Territorial extent & classification: E. Local. - Available at http://www.legislation.gov.uk/uksi/2012/1952/contents/made *Non-print*

The A3 Trunk Road (Hindhead Tunnel) (Temporary Restriction and Prohibition of Traffic) Order 2012 No. 2012/2159. - Enabling power: Road Traffic Regulation Act 1984, s. 14 (1) (a). - Issued: 23.08.2012. Made: 20.08.2012. Coming into force: 12.09.2012. Effect: None. Territorial extent & classification: E. Local. - Available at http://www.legislation.gov.uk/uksi/2012/2159/contents/made *Non-print*

The A3 Trunk Road (Hook Rise Junction - Esher Common Junction) (Temporary Prohibition of Traffic) Order 2012 No. 2012/3141. - Enabling power: Road Traffic Regulation Act 1984, s. 14 (1) (a). - Issued: 27.12.2012. Made: 26.11.2012. Coming into force: 15.12.2012. Effect: None. Territorial extent & classification: E. Local. - Available at http://www.legislation.gov.uk/uksi/2012/3141/contents/made *Non-print*

The A3 Trunk Road (M25 Junction 10 - Hammer Lane Junction) (Temporary Restriction and Prohibition of Traffic) Order 2012 No. 2012/1854. - Enabling power: Road Traffic Regulation Act 1984, s. 14 (1) (a). - Issued: 20.07.2012. Made: 09.07.2012. Coming into force: 01.08.2012. Effect: None. Territorial extent & classification: E. Local. - Available at http://www.legislation.gov.uk/uksi/2012/1854/contents/made *Non-print*

The A3 Trunk Road (North of Painshill Interchange - North of Wisley Interchange) (Temporary 50/40 Miles Per Hour Speed Restriction) Order 2012 No. 2012/1365. - Enabling power: Road Traffic Regulation Act 1984, s. 14 (1) (a). - Issued: 28.05.2012. Made: 14.05.2012. Coming into force: 02.06.2012. Effect: None. Territorial extent & classification: E. Local. - Available at http://www.legislation.gov.uk/uksi/2012/1365/contents/made *Non-print*

The A3 Trunk Road (North of Painshill Interchange - North of Wisley Interchange) (Temporary 50 Miles Per Hour Speed Restriction) (No. 2) Order 2012 No. 2012/2863. - Enabling power: Road Traffic Regulation Act 1984, s. 14 (1) (a), sch. 9, para. 27 (1). - Issued: 16.11.2012. Made: 05.11.2012. Coming into force: 24.11.2012. Effect: S.I. 2012/1365 revoked. Territorial extent & classification: E. Local. - Available at http://www.legislation.gov.uk/uksi/2012/2863/contents/made *Non-print*

The A3 Trunk Road (Stoke Interchange - Hog's Back Interchange) (Temporary Prohibition of Traffic) Order 2012 No. 2012/2162. - Enabling power: Road Traffic Regulation Act 1984, s. 14 (1) (a). - Issued: 23.08.2012. Made: 20.08.2012. Coming into force: 08.09.2012. Effect: None. Territorial extent & classification: E. Local. - Available at http://www.legislation.gov.uk/uksi/2012/2162/contents/made *Non-print*

The A3 Trunk Road (Surrey, Olympic Cycle Races - Esher Common Junction) (Temporary Prohibition of Traffic) Order 2012 No. 2012/1799. - Enabling power: London Olympic and Paralympic Games Act 2006, s. 16 (1) & Road Traffic Regulation Act 1984, s. 16A. - Issued: 19.07.2012. Made: 02.07.2012. Coming into force: 28.07.2012. Effect: None. Territorial extent & classification: E. Local. - Available at http://www.legislation.gov.uk/uksi/2012/1799/contents/made *Non-print*

The A3 Trunk Road (Surrey, Olympic Cycle Time Trial - Painshill Junction) (Temporary Prohibition of Traffic) Order 2012 No. 2012/1790. - Enabling power: London Olympic and Paralympic Games Act 2006, s. 16 (1) & Road Traffic Regulation Act 1984, s. 16A. - Issued: 19.07.2012. Made: 02.07.2012. Coming into force: 01.08.2012. Effect: None. Territorial extent & classification: E. Local. - Available at http://www.legislation.gov.uk/uksi/2012/1790/contents/made *Non-print*

The A3 Trunk Road (Woolmer Road Junction - Milford Junction) (Temporary Prohibition of Traffic) Order 2012 No. 2012/414. - Enabling power: Road Traffic Regulation Act 1984, s. 14 (1) (a). - Issued: 21.02.2012. Made: 13.02.2012. Coming into force: 03.03.2012. Effect: None. Territorial extent & classification: E. Local. - Available at http://www.legislation.gov.uk/uksi/2012/414/contents/made *Non-print*

The A3 Trunk Road (Woolmer Road Junction, Southbound Slip Roads) (Temporary Prohibition of Traffic) Order 2012 No. 2012/1525. - Enabling power: Road Traffic Regulation Act 1984, s. 14 (1) (a). - Issued: 19.06.2012. Made: 06.06.2012. Coming into force: 23.06.2012. Effect: None. Territorial extent & classification: E. Local. - Available at http://www.legislation.gov.uk/uksi/2012/1525/contents/made *Non-print*

The A4 Trunk Road and A46 Trunk Road (London Road Junction, Bath) (Temporary Prohibition of Traffic) Order 2012 No. 2012/927. - Enabling power: Road Traffic Regulation Act 1984, s. 14 (1) (a). - Issued: 28.03.2012. Made: 21.03.2012. Coming into force: 30.03.2012. Effect: None. Territorial extent & classification: E. Local. - Available at http://www.legislation.gov.uk/uksi/2012/927/contents/made *Non-print*

The A4 Trunk Road (Crowley Way, Avonmouth) (Temporary Prohibition of Traffic) Order 2012 No. 2012/1161. - Enabling power: Road Traffic Regulation Act 1984, s. 14 (1) (a). - Issued: 01.05.2012. Made: 19.04.2012. Coming into force: 28.04.2012. Effect: None. Territorial extent & classification: E. Local. - Available at http://www.legislation.gov.uk/uksi/2012/1161/contents/made *Non-print*

The A5 and A49 Trunk Roads (Shropshire) (Temporary Prohibition of Traffic) Order 2012 No. 2012/2721. - Enabling power: Road Traffic Regulation Act 1984, s. 14 (1) (a). - Issued: 02.11.2012. Made: 01.10.2012. Coming into force: 08.10.2012. Effect: None. Territorial extent & classification: E. Local. - Available at http://www.legislation.gov.uk/uksi/2012/2721/contents/made *Non-print*

The A5 and A483 Trunk Roads (Mile End Roundabout, Shropshire) (Temporary Prohibition of Traffic) Order 2012 No. 2012/1687. - Enabling power: Road Traffic Regulation Act 1984, s. 14 (1) (a). - Issued: 03.07.2012. Made: 11.06.2012. Coming into force: 18.06.2012. Effect: None. Territorial extent & classification: E. Local. - Available at http://www.legislation.gov.uk/uksi/2012/1687/contents/made *Non-print*

The A5 Trunk Road (A4146 Kelly's Kitchen Roundabout, Milton Keynes) (Temporary 50 Miles Per Hour Speed Restriction) (No. 2) Order 2012 No. 2012/3276. - Enabling power: Road Traffic Regulation Act 1984, s. 14 (1) (a). - Issued: 14.01.2013. Made: 24.12.2012. Coming into force: 04.01.2013. Effect: None. Territorial extent & classification: E. Local. - Available at http://www.legislation.gov.uk/uksi/2012/3276/contents/made *Non-print*

Road traffic: Traffic regulation

The A5 Trunk Road (A4146 Kelly's Kitchen Roundabout, Milton Keynes) (Temporary 50 Miles Per Hour Speed Restriction) Order 2012 No. 2012/499. - Enabling power: Road Traffic Regulation Act 1984, s. 14 (2) (a). - Issued: 01.03.2012. Made: 20.02.2012. Coming into force: 27.02.2012. Effect: None. Territorial extent & classification: E. Local. - Available at http://www.legislation.gov.uk/uksi/2012/499/contents/made *Non-print*

The A5 Trunk Road (Abbey Hill, Redmoor and Caldecotte, Milton Keynes) Slip Roads (Temporary Prohibition of Traffic) Order 2012 No. 2012/2469. - Enabling power: Road Traffic Regulation Act 1984, s. 14 (1) (a). - Issued: 01.10.2012. Made: 24.09.2012. Coming into force: 01.10.2012. Effect: None. Territorial extent & classification: E. Local. - Available at http://www.legislation.gov.uk/uksi/2012/2469/contents/made *Non-print*

The A5 Trunk Road and M6 Toll Motorway (Churchbridge, Staffordshire) (Temporary Prohibition of Traffic) Order 2012 No. 2012/741. - Enabling power: Road Traffic Regulation Act 1984, s. 14 (1) (a). - Issued: 19.03.2012. Made: 02.03.2012. Coming into force: 09.03.2012. Effect: None. Territorial extent & classification: E. Local. - Available at http://www.legislation.gov.uk/uksi/2012/741/contents/made *Non-print*

The A5 Trunk Road (Atherstone, Warwickshire) (Temporary Prohibition of Traffic) Order 2012 No. 2012/3121. - Enabling power: Road Traffic Regulation Act 1984, s. 14 (1) (a). - Issued: 20.12.2012. Made: 19.11.2012. Coming into force: 26.11.2012. Effect: None. Territorial extent & classification: E. Local. - Available at http://www.legislation.gov.uk/uksi/2012/3121/contents/made *Non-print*

The A5 Trunk Road (Bayston Hill Roundabout to Woodcote Roundabout, Shropshire) (Temporary Prohibition of Traffic) Order 2012 No. 2012/1146. - Enabling power: Road Traffic Regulation Act 1984, s. 14 (1) (a). - Issued: 27.04.2012. Made: 16.04.2012. Coming into force: 23.04.2012. Effect: None. Territorial extent & classification: E. Local. - Available at http://www.legislation.gov.uk/uksi/2012/1146/contents/made *Non-print*

The A5 Trunk Road (Bayston Hill to Emstrey, Shropshire) (Temporary Prohibition of Traffic) Order 2012 No. 2012/2386. - Enabling power: Road Traffic Regulation Act 1984, s. 14 (1) (a). - Issued: 18.09.2012. Made: 28.08.2012. Coming into force: 04.09.2012. Effect: None. Territorial extent & classification: E. Local. - Available at http://www.legislation.gov.uk/uksi/2012/2386/contents/made *Non-print*

The A5 Trunk Road (Brownhills to Wall) (Temporary Prohibition of Traffic) Order 2012 No. 2012/2009. - Enabling power: Road Traffic Regulation Act 1984, s. 14 (1) (a). - Issued: 02.08.2012. Made: 16.07.2012. Coming into force: 23.07.2012. Effect: None. Territorial extent & classification: E. Local. - Available at http://www.legislation.gov.uk/uksi/2012/2009/contents/made *Non-print*

The A5 Trunk Road (Brownhills West and Churchbridge, Staffordshire) (Temporary Prohibition of Traffic) Order 2012 No. 2012/2117. - Enabling power: Road Traffic Regulation Act 1984, s. 14 (1) (a). - Issued: 17.08.2012. Made: 27.07.2012. Coming into force: 03.08.2012. Effect: None. Territorial extent & classification: E. Local. - Available at http://www.legislation.gov.uk/uksi/2012/2117/contents/made *Non-print*

The A5 Trunk Road (Cannock, Staffordshire) (Temporary Prohibition of Traffic) Order 2012 No. 2012/2888. - Enabling power: Road Traffic Regulation Act 1984, s. 14 (1) (a). - Issued: 20.11.2012. Made: 06.11.2012. Coming into force: 13.11.2012. Effect: None. Territorial extent & classification: E. Local. - Available at http://www.legislation.gov.uk/uksi/2012/2888/contents/made *Non-print*

The A5 Trunk Road (Churncote Roundabout to Edgebold Roundabout, Shrewsbury) (Temporary Prohibition of Traffic) Order 2012 No. 2012/583. - Enabling power: Road Traffic Regulation Act 1984, s. 14 (1) (a). - Issued: 06.03.2012. Made: 17.02.2012. Coming into force: 24.02.2012. Effect: None. Territorial extent & classification: E. Local. - Available at http://www.legislation.gov.uk/uksi/2012/583/contents/made *Non-print*

The A5 Trunk Road (Churncote to Shottaton, Shropshire) (Temporary Prohibition of Traffic) Order 2012 No. 2012/3117. - Enabling power: Road Traffic Regulation Act 1984, s. 14 (1) (a). - Issued: 20.12.2012. Made: 19.11.2012. Coming into force: 26.11.2012. Effect: None. Territorial extent & classification: E. Local. - Available at http://www.legislation.gov.uk/uksi/2012/3117/contents/made *Non-print*

The A5 Trunk Road (Dordon to Atherstone, Warwickshire) (Temporary Prohibition of Traffic) Order 2012 No. 2012/1592. - Enabling power: Road Traffic Regulation Act 1984, s. 14 (1) (a). - Issued: 26.06.2012. Made: 30.05.2012. Coming into force: 06.06.2012. Effect: None. Territorial extent & classification: E. Local. - Available at http://www.legislation.gov.uk/uksi/2012/1592/contents/made *Non-print*

The A5 Trunk Road (Dordon, Warwickshire) (Temporary Prohibition of Traffic) Order 2012 No. 2012/1988. - Enabling power: Road Traffic Regulation Act 1984, s. 14 (1) (a). - Issued: 01.08.2012. Made: 06.07.2012. Coming into force: 13.07.2012. Effect: None. Territorial extent & classification: E. Local. - Available at http://www.legislation.gov.uk/uksi/2012/1988/contents/made *Non-print*

The A5 Trunk Road (Dunstable, B4540 Kensworth Turn and A505 Junction, Central Bedfordshire) (Temporary Prohibition of Traffic) Order 2012 No. 2012/1728. - Enabling power: Road Traffic Regulation Act 1984, s. 16A (2) (a). - Issued: 13.07.2012. Made: 25.06.2012. Coming into force: 09.07.2012. Effect: None. Territorial extent & classification: E. Local. - Available at http://www.legislation.gov.uk/uksi/2012/1728/contents/made *Non-print*

The A5 Trunk Road (East of Rugby) (Temporary Restriction and Prohibition of Traffic) Order 2012 No. 2012/2542. - Enabling power: Road Traffic Regulation Act 1984, s. 14 (1) (a). - Issued: 10.10.2012. Made: 17.09.2012. Coming into force: 24.09.2012. Effect: None. Territorial extent & classification: E. Local. - Available at http://www.legislation.gov.uk/uksi/2012/2542/contents/made *Non-print*

The A5 Trunk Road (Emstrey to Meole Brace, Shropshire) (Temporary Prohibition of Traffic) Order 2012 No. 2012/2003. - Enabling power: Road Traffic Regulation Act 1984, s. 14 (1) (a). - Issued: 02.08.2012. Made: 09.07.2012. Coming into force: 16.07.2012. Effect: None. Territorial extent & classification: E. Local. - Available at http://www.legislation.gov.uk/uksi/2012/2003/contents/made *Non-print*

The A5 Trunk Road (Felton Butler to Ensdon, Shropshire) (Temporary Restriction and Prohibition of Traffic) Order 2012 No. 2012/1583. - Enabling power: Road Traffic Regulation Act 1984, s. 14 (1) (a). - Issued: 26.06.2012. Made: 18.05.2012. Coming into force: 25.05.2012. Effect: None. Territorial extent & classification: E. Local. - Available at http://www.legislation.gov.uk/uksi/2012/1583/contents/made *Non-print*

The A5 Trunk Road (Gibbett Hill Roundabout, Warwickshire) (Temporary Restriction and Prohibition of Traffic) Order 2012 No. 2012/390. - Enabling power: Road Traffic Regulation Act 1984, s. 14 (1) (a). - Issued: 21.02.2012. Made: 30.01.2012. Coming into force: 06.02.2012. Effect: None. Territorial extent & classification: E. Local. - Available at http://www.legislation.gov.uk/uksi/2012/390/contents/made *Non-print*

The A5 Trunk Road (Gobowen, Shropshire) (Temporary Restriction and Prohibition of Traffic) Order 2012 No. 2012/2123. - Enabling power: Road Traffic Regulation Act 1984, s. 14 (1) (a). - Issued: 17.08.2012. Made: 30.07.2012. Coming into force: 06.08.2012. Effect: None. Territorial extent & classification: E. Local. - Available at http://www.legislation.gov.uk/uksi/2012/2123/contents/made *Non-print*

The A5 Trunk Road (Hinckley, Leicestershire) (Temporary Restriction and Prohibition of Traffic) (No.2) Order 2012 No. 2012/2538. - Enabling power: Road Traffic Regulation Act 1984, s. 14 (1) (a). - Issued: 09.10.2012. Made: 14.09.2012. Coming into force: 21.09.2012. Effect: None. Territorial extent & classification: E. Local. - Available at http://www.legislation.gov.uk/uksi/2012/2538/contents/made *Non-print*

The A5 Trunk Road (Hinckley, Leicestershire) (Temporary Restriction and Prohibition of Traffic) Order 2012 No. 2012/2180. - Enabling power: Road Traffic Regulation Act 1984, s. 14 (1) (a). - Issued: 28.08.2012. Made: 10.08.2012. Coming into force: 17.08.2012. Effect: None. Territorial extent & classification: E. Local. - Available at http://www.legislation.gov.uk/uksi/2012/2180/contents/made *Non-print*

The A5 Trunk Road (Hockliffe, Bedfordshire) (Temporary Prohibition of Pedestrians) Order 2012 No. 2012/2777. - Enabling power: Road Traffic Regulation Act 1984, s. 14 (1) (a). - Issued: 08.11.2012. Made: 22.10.2012. Coming into force: 29.10.2012. Effect: None. Territorial extent & classification: E. Local. - Available at http://www.legislation.gov.uk/uksi/2012/2777/contents/made *Non-print*

The A5 Trunk Road (Kilsby, Northamptonshire) (Temporary Prohibition of Traffic) Order 2012 No. 2012/577. - Enabling power: Road Traffic Regulation Act 1984, s. 14 (1) (a). - Issued: 06.03.2012. Made: 13.02.2012. Coming into force: 20.02.2012. Effect: None. Territorial extent & classification: E. Local. - Available at http://www.legislation.gov.uk/uksi/2012/577/contents/made *Non-print*

The A5 Trunk Road (Kilsby, Northamptonshire) (Temporary Restriction and Prohibition of Traffic) Order 2012 No. 2012/3126. - Enabling power: Road Traffic Regulation Act 1984, s. 14 (1) (a). - Issued: 20.12.2012. Made: 19.11.2012. Coming into force: 26.11.2012. Effect: None. Territorial extent & classification: E. Local. - Available at http://www.legislation.gov.uk/uksi/2012/3126/contents/made *Non-print*

The A5 Trunk Road (Mancetter Roundabout, Atherstone, Warwickshire) (Temporary Prohibition of Traffic) (No.2) Order 2012 No. 2012/866. - Enabling power: Road Traffic Regulation Act 1984, s. 14 (1) (a). - Issued: 23.03.2012. Made: 12.03.2012. Coming into force: 19.03.2012. Effect: None. Territorial extent & classification: E. Local. - Available at http://www.legislation.gov.uk/uksi/2012/866/contents/made *Non-print*

The A5 Trunk Road (Mancetter Roundabout, Atherstone, Warwickshire) (Temporary Restriction of Traffic) Order 2012 No. 2012/655. - Enabling power: Road Traffic Regulation Act 1984, s. 14 (1) (a). - Issued: 14.03.2012. Made: 28.02.2012. Coming into force: 06.03.2012. Effect: None. Territorial extent & classification: E. Local. - Available at http://www.legislation.gov.uk/uksi/2012/655/contents/made *Non-print*

The A5 Trunk Road (Markyate, Hertfordshire to Dunstable, Central Bedfordshire) (Temporary 10 Miles Per Hour and 30 Miles Per Hour Speed Restriction) Order 2012 No. 2012/600. - Enabling power: Road Traffic Regulation Act 1984, s. 14 (1) (a). - Issued: 06.03.2012. Made: 27.02.2012. Coming into force: 05.03.2012. Effect: None. Territorial extent & classification: E. Local. - Available at http://www.legislation.gov.uk/uksi/2012/600/contents/made *Non-print*

The A5 Trunk Road (Mile Oak, Tamworth, Staffordshire) (Slip Road) (Temporary Prohibition of Traffic) Order 2012 No. 2012/2889. - Enabling power: Road Traffic Regulation Act 1984, s. 14 (1) (a). - Issued: 20.11.2012. Made: 06.11.2012. Coming into force: 13.11.2012. Effect: None. Territorial extent & classification: E. Local. - Available at http://www.legislation.gov.uk/uksi/2012/2889/contents/made *Non-print*

The A5 Trunk Road (Near Towcester Northamptonshire) (Temporary 40 Miles Per Hour Speed Limit) Order 2012 No. 2012/1599. - Enabling power: Road Traffic Regulation Act 1984, s. 14 (1) (a). - Issued: 25.06.2012. Made: 28.05.2012. Coming into force: 04.06.2012. Effect: None. Territorial extent & classification: E. Local. - Available at http://www.legislation.gov.uk/uksi/2012/1599/contents/made *Non-print*

The A5 Trunk Road (North of Brownhills) (Temporary Prohibition of Traffic) Order 2012 No. 2012/317. - Enabling power: Road Traffic Regulation Act 1984, s. 14 (1) (a). - Issued: 15.02.2012. Made: 20.01.2012. Coming into force: 27.01.2012. Effect: None. Territorial extent & classification: E. Local. - Available at http://www.legislation.gov.uk/uksi/2012/317/contents/made *Non-print*

The A5 Trunk Road (North of Weedon, Northamptonshire) (Temporary Restriction and Prohibition of Traffic) Order 2012 No. 2012/2561. - Enabling power: Road Traffic Regulation Act 1984, s. 14 (1) (a). - Issued: 12.10.2012. Made: 19.09.2012. Coming into force: 26.09.2012. Effect: None. Territorial extent & classification: E. Local. - Available at http://www.legislation.gov.uk/uksi/2012/2561/contents/made *Non-print*

The A5 Trunk Road (Preston to Emstrey, Shropshire) (Temporary Prohibition of Traffic) Order 2012 No. 2012/2536. - Enabling power: Road Traffic Regulation Act 1984, s. 14 (1) (a). - Issued: 09.10.2012. Made: 12.09.2012. Coming into force: 19.09.2012. Effect: None. Territorial extent & classification: E. Local. - Available at http://www.legislation.gov.uk/uksi/2012/2536/contents/made *Non-print*

The A5 Trunk Road (Preston to M54, Shropshire) (Temporary Prohibition of Traffic) Order 2012 No. 2012/2369. - Enabling power: Road Traffic Regulation Act 1984, s. 14 (1) (a). - Issued: 18.09.2012. Made: 28.08.2012. Coming into force: 04.09.2012. Effect: None. Territorial extent & classification: E. Local. - Available at http://www.legislation.gov.uk/uksi/2012/2369/contents/made *Non-print*

The A5 Trunk Road (Redmoor Roundabout, Milton Keynes) Westbound Entry Slip Road (Temporary Prohibition of Traffic) Order 2012 No. 2012/2519. - Enabling power: Road Traffic Regulation Act 1984, s. 14 (1) (a). - Issued: 08.10.2012. Made: 01.10.2012. Coming into force: 08.10.2012. Effect: None. Territorial extent & classification: E. Local. - Available at http://www.legislation.gov.uk/uksi/2012/2519/contents/made *Non-print*

The A5 Trunk Road (Sheep Lane Roundabout, Central Bedfordshire to A421 Redmoor Roundabout, Milton Keynes) (Temporary Prohibition of Traffic) Order 2012 No. 2012/2915. - Enabling power: Road Traffic Regulation Act 1984, s. 14 (1) (a). - Issued: 23.11.2012. Made: 12.11.2012. Coming into force: 19.11.2012. Effect: None. Territorial extent & classification: E. Local. - Available at http://www.legislation.gov.uk/uksi/2012/2915/contents/made *Non-print*

The A5 Trunk Road (Sheep Lane Roundabout, Central Bedfordshire to A4146 Kelly's Kitchen Roundabout, Milton Keynes) (Temporary Prohibition of Traffic) Order 2012 No. 2012/2366. - Enabling power: Road Traffic Regulation Act 1984, s. 14 (1) (a). - Issued: 18.09.2012. Made: 10.09.2012. Coming into force: 17.09.2012. Effect: None. Territorial extent & classification: E. Local. - Available at http://www.legislation.gov.uk/uksi/2012/2366/contents/made *Non-print*

Road traffic: Traffic regulation

The A5 Trunk Road (Sheep Lane to Dunstable, Central Bedfordshire) (Temporary Prohibition of Traffic) Order 2012 No. 2012/508. - Enabling power: Road Traffic Regulation Act 1984, s. 14 (1) (a). - Issued: 01.03.2012. Made: 20.02.2012. Coming into force: 27.02.2012. Effect: None. Territorial extent & classification: E. Local. - Available at http://www.legislation.gov.uk/uksi/2012/508/contents/made *Non-print*

The A5 Trunk Road (Shrewsbury, Shropshire) (Temporary Prohibition of Traffic) Order 2012 No. 2012/2893. - Enabling power: Road Traffic Regulation Act 1984, s. 14 (1) (a). - Issued: 22.11.2012. Made: 06.11.2012. Coming into force: 13.11.2012. Effect: None. Territorial extent & classification: E. Local. - Available at http://www.legislation.gov.uk/uksi/2012/2893/contents/made *Non-print*

The A5 Trunk Road (Shrewsbury, Shropshire) (Temporary Restriction and Prohibition of Traffic) Order 2012 No. 2012/1981. - Enabling power: Road Traffic Regulation Act 1984, s. 14 (1) (a). - Issued: 31.07.2012. Made: 02.07.2012. Coming into force: 09.07.2012. Effect: None. Territorial extent & classification: E. Local. - Available at http://www.legislation.gov.uk/uksi/2012/1981/contents/made *Non-print*

The A5 Trunk Road (Smockington, Leicestershire) (Temporary Restriction and Prohibition of Traffic) Order 2012 No. 2012/2720. - Enabling power: Road Traffic Regulation Act 1984, s. 14 (1) (a). - Issued: 02.11.2012. Made: 01.10.2012. Coming into force: 08.10.2012. Effect: None. Territorial extent & classification: E. Local. - Available at http://www.legislation.gov.uk/uksi/2012/2720/contents/made *Non-print*

The A5 Trunk Road (South East of Atherstone, Warwickshire) (Temporary Prohibition of Traffic) Order 2012 No. 2012/3120. - Enabling power: Road Traffic Regulation Act 1984, s. 14 (1) (a). - Issued: 20.12.2012. Made: 19.11.2012. Coming into force: 26.11.2012. Effect: None. Territorial extent & classification: E. Local. - Available at http://www.legislation.gov.uk/uksi/2012/3120/contents/made *Non-print*

The A5 Trunk Road (Tamworth, Staffordshire) (Eastbound Entry Slip Road) (Temporary Prohibition of Traffic) Order 2012 No. 2012/2804. - Enabling power: Road Traffic Regulation Act 1984, s. 14 (1) (a). - Issued: 09.11.2012. Made: 22.10.2012. Coming into force: 29.10.2012. Effect: None. Territorial extent & classification: E. Local. - Available at http://www.legislation.gov.uk/uksi/2012/2804/contents/made *Non-print*

The A5 Trunk Road (Tamworth, Staffordshire) (Slip Roads) (Temporary Prohibition of Traffic) Order 2012 No. 2012/3304. - Enabling power: Road Traffic Regulation Act 1984, s. 14 (1) (a). - Issued: 17.01.2013. Made: 24.12.2012. Coming into force: 31.12.2012. Effect: None. Territorial extent & classification: E. Local. - Available at http://www.legislation.gov.uk/uksi/2012/3304/contents/made *Non-print*

The A5 Trunk Road (Tamworth, Staffordshire) (Temporary Prohibition of Traffic) Order 2012 No. 2012/2967. - Enabling power: Road Traffic Regulation Act 1984, s. 14 (1) (a). - Issued: 30.11.2012. Made: 09.11.2012. Coming into force: 16.11.2012. Effect: None. Territorial extent & classification: E. Local. - Available at http://www.legislation.gov.uk/uksi/2012/2967/contents/made *Non-print*

The A5 Trunk Road (Tamworth, Staffordshire) (Westbound Exit Slip Road) (Temporary Prohibition of Traffic) Order 2012 No. 2012/1987. - Enabling power: Road Traffic Regulation Act 1984, s. 14 (1) (a). - Issued: 01.08.2012. Made: 06.07.2012. Coming into force: 13.07.2012. Effect: None. Territorial extent & classification: E. Local. - Available at http://www.legislation.gov.uk/uksi/2012/1987/contents/made *Non-print*

The A5 Trunk Road (Towcester, Northamptonshire) (Temporary Restriction and Prohibition of Traffic) Order 2012 No. 2012/255. - Enabling power: Road Traffic Regulation Act 1984, s. 14 (1) (a). - Issued: 06.02.2012. Made: 23.01.2012. Coming into force: 30.01.2012. Effect: None. Territorial extent & classification: E. Local. - Available at http://www.legislation.gov.uk/uksi/2012/255/contents/made *Non-print*

The A5 Trunk Road (Wall to Muckley Corner, Staffordshire) (Temporary Prohibition of Traffic) Order 2012 No. 2012/2390. - Enabling power: Road Traffic Regulation Act 1984, s. 14 (1) (a). - Issued: 20.09.2012. Made: 29.08.2012. Coming into force: 05.09.2012. Effect: None. Territorial extent & classification: E. Local. - Available at http://www.legislation.gov.uk/uksi/2012/2390/contents/made *Non-print*

The A5 Trunk Road (Watford Gap, Northamptonshire) (Temporary Prohibition of Traffic in Layby) Order 2012 No. 2012/2004. - Enabling power: Road Traffic Regulation Act 1984, s. 14 (1) (a). - Issued: 02.08.2012. Made: 13.07.2012. Coming into force: 20.07.2012. Effect: None. Territorial extent & classification: E. Local. - Available at http://www.legislation.gov.uk/uksi/2012/2004/contents/made *Non-print*

Road traffic: Traffic regulation

The A5 Trunk Road (Watling Street, Staffordshire) (Temporary 30 Miles Per Hour Speed Restriction) Order 2012 No. 2012/2894. - Enabling power: Road Traffic Regulation Act 1984, s. 14 (1) (a). - Issued: 22.11.2012. Made: 02.11.2012. Coming into force: 09.11.2012. Effect: None. Territorial extent & classification: E. Local. - Available at http://www.legislation.gov.uk/uksi/2012/2894/contents/ma de *Non-print*

The A5 Trunk Road (Weedon, Northamptonshire) (Temporary Prohibition of Traffic) Order 2012 No. 2012/3317. - Enabling power: Road Traffic Regulation Act 1984, s. 14 (1) (a). - Issued: 17.01.2013. Made: 31.12.2012. Coming into force: 07.01.2013. Effect: None. Territorial extent & classification: E. Local. - Available at http://www.legislation.gov.uk/uksi/2012/3317/contents/ma de *Non-print*

The A5 Trunk Road (Weedon to Kilsby, Northamptonshire) (Temporary Restriction and Prohibition of Traffic) Order 2012 No. 2012/123. - Enabling power: Road Traffic Regulation Act 1984, s. 14 (1) (a). - Issued: 23.01.2012. Made: 06.01.2012. Coming into force: 13.01.2012. Effect: None. Territorial extent & classification: E. Local. - Available at http://www.legislation.gov.uk/uksi/2012/123/contents/mad e *Non-print*

The A5 Trunk Road (Woodcote to Churncote, Shropshire) (Temporary Prohibition of Traffic) Order 2012 No. 2012/2002. - Enabling power: Road Traffic Regulation Act 1984, s. 14 (1) (a). - Issued: 02.08.2012. Made: 09.07.2012. Coming into force: 16.07.2012. Effect: None. Territorial extent & classification: E. Local. - Available at http://www.legislation.gov.uk/uksi/2012/2002/contents/ma de *Non-print*

The A6 Trunk Road (Derbyshire) (Temporary Prohibition of Traffic) Order 2012 No. 2012/3329. - Enabling power: Road Traffic Regulation Act 1984, s. 14 (1) (a). - Issued: 05.02.2013. Made: 31.12.2012. Coming into force: 07.01.2013. Effect: None. Territorial extent & classification: E. Local. - Available at http://www.legislation.gov.uk/uksi/2012/3329/contents/ma de *Non-print*

The A11 Trunk Road (B1085 Red Lodge Interchange to A1101/A1065 Five Ways Roundabout Barton Mills, Suffolk) (Temporary Restriction and Prohibition of Traffic) Order 2012 No. 2012/3298. - Enabling power: Road Traffic Regulation Act 1984, s. 14 (1) (a). - Issued: 16.01.2013. Made: 31.12.2012. Coming into force: 07.01.2013. Effect: None. Territorial extent & classification: E. Local. - Available at http://www.legislation.gov.uk/uksi/2012/3298/contents/ma de *Non-print*

The A11 Trunk Road (Balsham, Cambridge) (Temporary Prohibition of Traffic) Order 2012 No. 2012/2614. - Enabling power: Road Traffic Regulation Act 1984, s. 14 (1) (a). - Issued: 22.10.2012. Made: 08.10.2012. Coming into force: 15.10.2012. Effect: None. Territorial extent & classification: E. Local. - Available at http://www.legislation.gov.uk/uksi/2012/2614/contents/ma de *Non-print*

The A11 Trunk Road (Besthorpe, Norfolk) Lay-by (Temporary Prohibition of Traffic) Order 2012 No. 2012/506. - Enabling power: Road Traffic Regulation Act 1984, s. 14 (1) (b). - Issued: 01.03.2012. Made: 20.02.2012. Coming into force: 27.02.2012. Effect: None. Territorial extent & classification: E. Local. - Available at http://www.legislation.gov.uk/uksi/2012/506/contents/mad e *Non-print*

The A11 Trunk Road (Besthorpe, Norfolk) (Prohibition of Entry) Order 2012 No. 2012/1857. - Enabling power: Road Traffic Regulation Act 1984, s. 1 (1), 2 (1) (2). - Issued: 20.07.2012. Made: 09.07.2012. Coming into force: 23.07.2012. Effect: None. Territorial extent & classification: E. Local. - Available at http://www.legislation.gov.uk/uksi/2012/1857/contents/ma de *Non-print*

The A11 Trunk Road (Brandon Road to London Road, Thetford, Norfolk) (Temporary Restriction and Prohibition of Traffic) Order 2012 No. 2012/2515. - Enabling power: Road Traffic Regulation Act 1984, s. 14 (1) (a), 5 (b) (7). - Issued: 08.10.2012. Made: 01.10.2012. Coming into force: 08.10.2012. Effect: None. Territorial extent & classification: E. Local. - Available at http://www.legislation.gov.uk/uksi/2012/2515/contents/ma de *Non-print*

The A11 Trunk Road (Fiveways to Thetford Improvement) (Temporary Restriction and Prohibition of Traffic) Order 2012 No. 2012/3140. - Enabling power: Road Traffic Regulation Act 1984, s. 14 (1) (a). - Issued: 27.12.2012. Made: 26.10.2012. Coming into force: 02.11.2012. Effect: None. Territorial extent & classification: E. Local. - Available at http://www.legislation.gov.uk/uksi/2012/3140/contents/ma de *Non-print*

The A11 Trunk Road (Nine Mile Hill to Six Mile Bottom, Cambridgeshire) (Temporary Restriction and Prohibition of Traffic) Order 2012 No. 2012/2328. - Enabling power: Road Traffic Regulation Act 1984, s. 14 (1) (a). - Issued: 13.09.2012. Made: 03.09.2012. Coming into force: 10.09.2012. Effect: None. Territorial extent & classification: E. Local. - Available at http://www.legislation.gov.uk/uksi/2012/2328/contents/ma de *Non-print*

The A11 Trunk Road (Red Lodge Bypass, Suffolk) Northbound (Temporary Restriction and Prohibition of Traffic) Order 2012 No. 2012/452. - Enabling power: Road Traffic Regulation Act 1984, s. 14 (1) (a). - Issued: 24.02.2012. Made: 13.02.2012. Coming into force: 20.02.2012. Effect: None. Territorial extent & classification: E. Local. - Available at http://www.legislation.gov.uk/uksi/2012/452/contents/made *Non-print*

The A11 Trunk Road (Red Lodge Interchange to Waterhall Interchange, Suffolk) Southbound (Temporary Restriction and Prohibition of Traffic) Order 2012 No. 2012/2145. - Enabling power: Road Traffic Regulation Act 1984, s. 14 (1) (a). - Issued: 22.08.2012. Made: 13.08.2012. Coming into force: 20.08.2012. Effect: None. Territorial extent & classification: E. Local. - Available at http://www.legislation.gov.uk/uksi/2012/2145/contents/made *Non-print*

The A11 Trunk Road (Six Mile Bottomm, Fulbourn/Balsham and Abingdon, Cambridgeshire) (Temporary Prohibition of Traffic) Order 2012 No. 2012/349. - Enabling power: Road Traffic Regulation Act 1984, s. 14 (1) (a). - Issued: 15.02.2012. Made: 06.02.2012. Coming into force: 13.02.2012. Effect: None. Territorial extent & classification: E. Local. - Available at http://www.legislation.gov.uk/uksi/2012/349/contents/made *Non-print*

The A11 Trunk Road (Snetterton to Roudham Heath, Norfolk) Southbound (Temporary Restriction and Prohibition of Traffic) Order 2012 No. 2012/2071. - Enabling power: Road Traffic Regulation Act 1984, s. 14 (1) (a). - Issued: 13.08.2012. Made: 30.07.2012. Coming into force: 06.08.2012. Effect: None. Territorial extent & classification: E. Local. - Available at http://www.legislation.gov.uk/uksi/2012/2071/contents/made *Non-print*

The A11 Trunk Road (South of Nine Mile Hill) and the A14 Trunk Road (Between Junction 35 and Junction 37) (Cambridgeshire) Lay-bys (Temporary Prohibition of Traffic) Order 2012 No. 2012/2481. - Enabling power: Road Traffic Regulation Act 1984, s. 14 (1) (a). - Issued: 02.10.2012. Made: 24.09.2012. Coming into force: 01.10.2012. Effect: None. Territorial extent & classification: E. Local. - Available at http://www.legislation.gov.uk/uksi/2012/2481/contents/made *Non-print*

The A11 Trunk Road (Waterhall Interchange, Newmarket, Suffolk) (Temporary Prohibition of Traffic) Order 2012 No. 2012/2023. - Enabling power: Road Traffic Regulation Act 1984, s. 14 (1) (a). - Issued: 06.08.2012. Made: 23.07.2012. Coming into force: 30.07.2012. Effect: None. Territorial extent & classification: E. Local. - Available at http://www.legislation.gov.uk/uksi/2012/2023/contents/made *Non-print*

The A11 Trunk Road (Wymondham Bypass, B1172 Spooner Row to B1135 Tuttles Lane, Norfolk) (Temporary Restriction and Prohibition of Traffic) Order 2012 No. 2012/1626. - Enabling power: Road Traffic Regulation Act 1984, s. 14 (1) (a). - Issued: 28.06.2012. Made: 18.06.2012. Coming into force: 25.06.2012. Effect: None. Territorial extent & classification: E. Local. - Available at http://www.legislation.gov.uk/uksi/2012/1626/contents/made *Non-print*

The A12 and A120 Trunk Roads (Colchester Northern Bypass, Essex) (Temporary Restriction and Prohibition of Traffic) Order 2012 No. 2012/289. - Enabling power: Road Traffic Regulation Act 1984, s. 14 (1) (a). - Issued: 10.02.2012. Made: 30.01.2012. Coming into force: 06.02.2012. Effect: None. Territorial extent & classification: E. Local. - Available at http://www.legislation.gov.uk/uksi/2012/289/contents/made *Non-print*

The A12 Trunk Road (Bascule Bridge, Lowestoft, Suffolk) (Temporary Prohibition of Traffic and Pedestrians) (No. 2) Order 2012 No. 2012/2852. - Enabling power: Road Traffic Regulation Act 1984, s. 14 (1) (a). - Issued: 16.11.2012. Made: 05.11.2012. Coming into force: 12.11.2012. Effect: None. Territorial extent & classification: E. Local. - Available at http://www.legislation.gov.uk/uksi/2012/2852/contents/made *Non-print*

The A12 Trunk Road (Bascule Bridge, Lowestoft, Suffolk) (Temporary Prohibition of Traffic and Pedestrians) Order 2012 No. 2012/1136. - Enabling power: Road Traffic Regulation Act 1984, s. 14 (1) (a). - Issued: 26.04.2012. Made: 16.04.2012. Coming into force: 23.04.2012. Effect: None. Territorial extent & classification: E. Local. - Available at http://www.legislation.gov.uk/uksi/2012/1136/contents/made *Non-print*

The A12 Trunk Road (Bentley Drive to Rackham's Corner, Lowestoft, Suffolk) (Temporary Prohibition of Traffic) Order 2012 No. 2012/288. - Enabling power: Road Traffic Regulation Act 1984, s. 14 (1) (a). - Issued: 10.02.2012. Made: 30.01.2012. Coming into force: 06.02.2012. Effect: None. Territorial extent & classification: E. Local. - Available at http://www.legislation.gov.uk/uksi/2012/288/contents/made *Non-print*

The A12 Trunk Road (Breydon Bridge, Great Yarmouth, Norfolk) (Temporary Prohibition of Traffic and Pedestrians) (No. 2) Order 2012 No. 2012/2775. - Enabling power: Road Traffic Regulation Act 1984, s. 14 (1) (a) (7). - Issued: 08.11.2012. Made: 22.10.2012. Coming into force: 29.10.2012. Effect: None. Territorial extent & classification: E. Local. - Available at http://www.legislation.gov.uk/uksi/2012/2775/contents/made *Non-print*

The A12 Trunk Road (Breydon Bridge, Great Yarmouth, Norfolk) (Temporary Prohibition of Traffic and Pedestrians) Order 2012 No. 2012/1296. - Enabling power: Road Traffic Regulation Act 1984, s. 14 (1) (a) (7). - Issued: 21.05.2012. Made: 08.05.2012. Coming into force: 15.05.2012. Effect: None. Territorial extent & classification: E. Local. - Available at http://www.legislation.gov.uk/uksi/2012/1296/contents/made *Non-print*

The A12 Trunk Road (Colchester Road to Nayland Road, Colchester, Essex) Northbound (Temporary Restriction and Prohibition of Traffic) Order 2012 No. 2012/100. - Enabling power: Road Traffic Regulation Act 1984, s. 14 (1) (a). - Issued: 19.01.2012. Made: 09.01.2012. Coming into force: 16.01.2012. Effect: None. Territorial extent & classification: E. Local. - Available at http://www.legislation.gov.uk/uksi/2012/100/contents/made *Non-print*

The A12 Trunk Road (Copdeck Mill Interchange, Ipswich, Suffolk) (Temporary Prohibition of Traffic) Order 2012 No. 2012/1625. - Enabling power: Road Traffic Regulation Act 1984, s. 14 (1) (a). - Issued: 28.06.2012. Made: 18.06.2012. Coming into force: 25.06.2012. Effect: None. Territorial extent & classification: E. Local. - Available at http://www.legislation.gov.uk/uksi/2012/1625/contents/made *Non-print*

The A12 Trunk Road (Harfrey's Roundabout, Great Yarmouth to Victoria Road Roundabout, Gorleston, Norfolk) Southbound (Temporary Prohibition of Traffic) Order 2012 No. 2012/1297. - Enabling power: Road Traffic Regulation Act 1984, s. 14 (1) (a). - Issued: 21.05.2012. Made: 08.05.2012. Coming into force: 15.05.2012. Effect: None. Territorial extent & classification: E. Local. - Available at http://www.legislation.gov.uk/uksi/2012/1297/contents/made *Non-print*

The A12 Trunk Road (Ingatestone Bypass, Junction 12 to North of Junction 13, Essex) (Temporary Prohibition of Traffic) Order 2012 No. 2012/351. - Enabling power: Road Traffic Regulation Act 1984, s. 14 (1) (a). - Issued: 15.02.2012. Made: 06.02.2012. Coming into force: 13.02.2012. Effect: None. Territorial extent & classification: E. Local. - Available at http://www.legislation.gov.uk/uksi/2012/351/contents/made *Non-print*

The A12 Trunk Road (Junction 12 Marylands Interchange to Junction 15 Webb's Farm Interchange, Essex) (Temporary Restriction and Prohibition of Traffic) Order 2012 No. 2012/620. - Enabling power: Road Traffic Regulation Act 1984, s. 14 (1) (a). - Issued: 07.03.2012. Made: 27.02.2012. Coming into force: 05.03.2012. Effect: None. Territorial extent & classification: E. Local. - Available at http://www.legislation.gov.uk/uksi/2012/620/contents/made *Non-print*

The A12 Trunk Road (Junction 13 Trueloves Interchange to Junction 19 Boreham Interchange, Chelmsford, Essex) (Temporary Restriction and Prohibition of Traffic) Order 2012 No. 2012/2586. - Enabling power: Road Traffic Regulation Act 1984, s. 14 (1) (a). - Issued: 16.10.2012. Made: 08.10.2012. Coming into force: 15.10.2012. Effect: None. Territorial extent & classification: E. Local. - Available at http://www.legislation.gov.uk/uksi/2012/2586/contents/made *Non-print*

The A12 Trunk Road (Junction 15 Webbs Farm Interchange, Chelmsford, Essex) Northbound (Temporary Prohibition of Traffic) Order 2012 No. 2012/2912. - Enabling power: Road Traffic Regulation Act 1984, s. 14 (1) (a). - Issued: 23.11.2012. Made: 12.11.2012. Coming into force: 19.11.2012. Effect: None. Territorial extent & classification: E. Local. - Available at http://www.legislation.gov.uk/uksi/2012/2912/contents/made *Non-print*

The A12 Trunk Road (Junction 18 Sandon to Junction 20B Hatfield Peverel North, Essex) (Temporary Restriction and Prohibition of Traffic) Order 2012 No. 2012/350. - Enabling power: Road Traffic Regulation Act 1984, s. 14 (1) (a). - Issued: 15.02.2012. Made: 06.02.2012. Coming into force: 13.02.2012. Effect: None. Territorial extent & classification: E. Local. - Available at http://www.legislation.gov.uk/uksi/2012/350/contents/made *Non-print*

The A12 Trunk Road (Junction 19 Boreham Interchange to Junction 21 Witham South Interchange, Essex) (Temporary Restriction and Prohibition of Traffic) Order 2012 No. 2012/2325. - Enabling power: Road Traffic Regulation Act 1984, s. 14 (1) (a). - Issued: 13.09.2012. Made: 03.09.2012. Coming into force: 10.09.2012. Effect: None. Territorial extent & classification: E. Local. - Available at http://www.legislation.gov.uk/uksi/2012/2325/contents/made *Non-print*

The A12 Trunk Road (Junction 19 Boreham Interchange to Junction 24 Kelvedon North Interchange, Essex) Northbound (Temporary Restriction and Prohibition of Traffic) Order 2012 No. 2012/2616. - Enabling power: Road Traffic Regulation Act 1984, s. 14 (1) (a). - Issued: 22.10.2012. Made: 08.10.2012. Coming into force: 15.10.2012. Effect: None. Territorial extent & classification: E. Local. - Available at http://www.legislation.gov.uk/uksi/2012/2616/contents/made *Non-print*

The A12 Trunk Road (Junction 20a Hatfield Peverel Interchange to Junction 19 Boreham Interchange, Essex) Southbound (Temporary Restriction and Prohibition of Traffic) Order 2012 No. 2012/3327. - Enabling power: Road Traffic Regulation Act 1984, s. 14 (1) (a). - Issued: 18.01.2013. Made: 31.12.2012. Coming into force: 07.01.2013. Effect: None. Territorial extent & classification: E. Local. - Available at http://www.legislation.gov.uk/uksi/2012/3327/contents/made *Non-print*

The A12 Trunk Road (Junction 25 Marks Tey Interchange to Junction 26 Eight Ash Green Interchange, Essex) (Temporary Restriction and Prohibition of Traffic) Order 2012 No. 2012/2327. - Enabling power: Road Traffic Regulation Act 1984, s. 14 (1) (a). - Issued: 13.09.2012. Made: 03.09.2012. Coming into force: 10.09.2012. Effect: None. Territorial extent & classification: E. Local. - Available at http://www.legislation.gov.uk/uksi/2012/2327/contents/made *Non-print*

The A12 Trunk Road (Junction 26 Eight Ash Green Interchange, Colchester, Essex) Slip Roads (Temporary Prohibition of Traffic) Order 2012 No. 2012/2175. - Enabling power: Road Traffic Regulation Act 1984, s. 14 (1) (a). - Issued: 28.08.2012. Made: 20.08.2012. Coming into force: 27.08.2012. Effect: None. Territorial extent & classification: E. Local. - Available at http://www.legislation.gov.uk/uksi/2012/2175/contents/made *Non-print*

The A12 Trunk Road (Junction 26 Eight Ash Green Interchange to Junction 28 Severalls Interchange, Essex) Northbound (Temporary Restriction and Prohibition of Traffic) Order 2012 No. 2012/1737. - Enabling power: Road Traffic Regulation Act 1984, s. 14 (1) (a). - Issued: 17.07.2012. Made: 25.06.2012. Coming into force: 02.07.2012. Effect: None. Territorial extent & classification: E. Local. - Available at http://www.legislation.gov.uk/uksi/2012/1737/contents/made *Non-print*

The A12 Trunk Road (Junction 29 Crown Interchange, Colchester, Essex) Southbound (Temporary Prohibition of Traffic) Order 2012 No. 2012/3296. - Enabling power: Road Traffic Regulation Act 1984, s. 14 (1) (a). - Issued: 16.01.2013. Made: 31.12.2012. Coming into force: 07.01.2013. Effect: None. Territorial extent & classification: E. Local. - Available at http://www.legislation.gov.uk/uksi/2012/3296/contents/made *Non-print*

The A12 Trunk Road (Kelvedon Bypass, Essex) (Temporary Restriction and Prohibition of Traffic) Order 2012 No. 2012/208. - Enabling power: Road Traffic Regulation Act 1984, s. 14 (1) (a). - Issued: 01.02.2012. Made: 23.01.2012. Coming into force: 30.01.2012. Effect: None. Territorial extent & classification: E. Local. - Available at http://www.legislation.gov.uk/uksi/2012/208/contents/made *Non-print*

The A12 Trunk Road (Kelvedon Bypass, Junction 23 Kelvedon (South) Interchange to Junction 24 Kelvedon (North) Interchange, Essex) (Temporary Restriction and Prohibition of Traffic) Order 2012 No. 2012/455. - Enabling power: Road Traffic Regulation Act 1984, s. 14 (1) (a). - Issued: 24.02.2012. Made: 13.02.2012. Coming into force: 20.02.2012. Effect: None. Territorial extent & classification: E. Local. - Available at http://www.legislation.gov.uk/uksi/2012/455/contents/made *Non-print*

The A12 Trunk Road (Lowestoft, Suffolk) (Temporary Prohibition of Traffic) Order 2012 No. 2012/106. - Enabling power: Road Traffic Regulation Act 1984, s. 14 (1) (a). - Issued: 20.01.2012. Made: 09.01.2012. Coming into force: 16.01.2012. Effect: None. Territorial extent & classification: E. Local. - Available at http://www.legislation.gov.uk/uksi/2012/106/contents/made *Non-print*

The A12 Trunk Road (Ongar Road Bridge, Brentwood, Essex) (Temporary Restriction and Prohibition of Traffic) Order 2012 No. 2012/2247. - Enabling power: Road Traffic Regulation Act 1984, s. 14 (1) (a). - Issued: 04.09.2012. Made: 28.08.2012. Coming into force: 04.09.2012. Effect: None. Territorial extent & classification: E. Local. - Available at http://www.legislation.gov.uk/uksi/2012/2247/contents/made *Non-print*

The A12 Trunk Road (Rackhams Corner Roundabout Corton to Links Road Roundabout Gorleston, Norfolk) (Temporary Prohibition of Traffic) Order 2012 No. 2012/1227. - Enabling power: Road Traffic Regulation Act 1984, s. 14 (1) (a). - Issued: 10.05.2012. Made: 30.04.2012. Coming into force: 07.05.2012. Effect: None. Territorial extent & classification: E. Local. - Available at http://www.legislation.gov.uk/uksi/2012/1227/contents/made *Non-print*

The A12 Trunk Road (South of Coles Oak Lane, Dedham, Essex to North of Four Sisters Interchange Junction 31, Suffolk) (Temporary Restriction and Prohibition of Traffic) Order 2012 No. 2012/2323. - Enabling power: Road Traffic Regulation Act 1984, s. 14 (1) (a). - Issued: 13.09.2012. Made: 03.09.2012. Coming into force: 10.09.2012. Effect: None. Territorial extent & classification: E. Local. - Available at http://www.legislation.gov.uk/uksi/2012/2323/contents/made *Non-print*

The A13 and A1089 Trunk Roads (Wennington Interchange - Marshfoot Interchange) (Temporary Prohibition of Traffic) Order 2012 No. 2012/2771. - Enabling power: Road Traffic Regulation Act 1984, s. 14 (1) (a). - Issued: 08.11.2012. Made: 22.10.2012. Coming into force: 14.11.2012. Effect: None. Territorial extent & classification: E. Local. - Available at http://www.legislation.gov.uk/uksi/2012/2771/contents/made *Non-print*

The A13 Trunk Road (A126 Lakeside Junction) (No Entry) Order 2012 No. 2012/2918. - Enabling power: Road Traffic Regulation Act 1984, ss. 1 (1), 2 (1) (2). - Issued: 23.11.2012. Made: 12.11.2012. Coming into force: 23.11.2012. Effect: None. Territorial extent & classification: E. Local. - Available at http://www.legislation.gov.uk/uksi/2012/2918/contents/made *Non-print*

The A13 Trunk Road (Lakeside Junction, Exit Slip Road) (Temporary Prohibition of Traffic) Order 2012 No. 2012/1251. - Enabling power: Road Traffic Regulation Act 1984, s. 14 (1) (a). - Issued: 18.05.2012. Made: 08.05.2012. Coming into force: 26.05.2012. Effect: None. Territorial extent & classification: E. Local. - Available at http://www.legislation.gov.uk/uksi/2012/1251/contents/made *Non-print*

The A13 Trunk Road (Mardyke Interchange) (Temporary Prohibition of Traffic) Order 2012 No. 2012/3208. - Enabling power: Road Traffic Regulation Act 1984, s. 14 (1) (a). - Issued: 02.01.2013. Made: 10.12.2012. Coming into force: 05.01.2013. Effect: None. Territorial extent & classification: E. Local. - Available at http://www.legislation.gov.uk/uksi/2012/3208/contents/made *Non-print*

The A14 and A11 Trunk Roads (Junction 37 Exning to Junction 39 Kentford, Suffolk) Eastbound (Temporary Restriction and Prohibition of Traffic) Order 2012 No. 2012/1627. - Enabling power: Road Traffic Regulation Act 1984, s. 14 (1) (a). - Issued: 28.06.2012. Made: 18.06.2012. Coming into force: 25.06.2012. Effect: None. Territorial extent & classification: E. Local. - Available at http://www.legislation.gov.uk/uksi/2012/1627/contents/made *Non-print*

The A14 and A11 Trunk Roads (Junction 38 Waterhall Interchange, Newmarket, Suffolk) (Temporary Restriction and Prohibition of Traffic) Order 2012 No. 2012/493. - Enabling power: Road Traffic Regulation Act 1984, s. 14 (1) (a). - Issued: 29.02.2012. Made: 20.02.2012. Coming into force: 27.02.2012. Effect: None. Territorial extent & classification: E. Local. - Available at http://www.legislation.gov.uk/uksi/2012/493/contents/made *Non-print*

The A14 and A428 Trunk Roads (Junction 31 Girton Interchange, Cambridgeshire) (Temporary Prohibition of Traffic) Order 2012 No. 2012/546. - Enabling power: Road Traffic Regulation Act 1984, s. 14 (1) (a). - Issued: 01.03.2012. Made: 20.02.2012. Coming into force: 27.02.2012. Effect: None. Territorial extent & classification: E. Local. - Available at http://www.legislation.gov.uk/uksi/2012/546/contents/made *Non-print*

The A14 Trunk Road (Brington Overbridge, Junction 16 Catworth, Cambridgeshire) (Temporary Prohibition of Traffic) Order 2012 No. 2012/2316. - Enabling power: Road Traffic Regulation Act 1984, s. 14 (1) (a). - Issued: 12.09.2012. Made: 03.09.2012. Coming into force: 10.09.2012. Effect: None. Territorial extent & classification: E. Local. - Available at http://www.legislation.gov.uk/uksi/2012/2316/contents/made *Non-print*

The A14 Trunk Road (Cranford to Burton Latimer, Northamptonshire) (Temporary Prohibition of Traffic) Order 2012 No. 2012/3316. - Enabling power: Road Traffic Regulation Act 1984, s. 14 (1) (a). - Issued: 17.01.2013. Made: 28.12.2012. Coming into force: 04.01.2013. Effect: None. Territorial extent & classification: E. Local. - Available at http://www.legislation.gov.uk/uksi/2012/3316/contents/made *Non-print*

The A14 Trunk Road (East of Junction 13, Thrapston, Northamptonshire) Westbound (Temporary Prohibition of Traffic) Order 2012 No. 2012/2503. - Enabling power: Road Traffic Regulation Act 1984, s. 14 (1) (a). - Issued: 05.10.2012. Made: 24.09.2012. Coming into force: 01.10.2012. Effect: None. Territorial extent & classification: E. Local. - Available at http://www.legislation.gov.uk/uksi/2012/2503/contents/made *Non-print*

The A14 Trunk Road (East of Junction 58 Levington Interchange to Junction 56 Wherstead Interchange, Ipswich, Suffolk) Westbound (Temporary Restriction and Prohibition of Traffic) Order 2012 No. 2012/3295. - Enabling power: Road Traffic Regulation Act 1984, s. 14 (1) (a). - Issued: 15.01.2013. Made: 31.12.2012. Coming into force: 07.01.2013. Effect: None. Territorial extent & classification: E. Local. - Available at http://www.legislation.gov.uk/uksi/2012/3295/contents/made *Non-print*

The A14 Trunk Road (Ipswich Southern Bypass, Junction 54 Sproughton Interchange to Junction 57 Nacton Interchange) (Temporary Restriction and Prohibition of Traffic) Order 2012 No. 2012/2615. - Enabling power: Road Traffic Regulation Act 1984, s. 14 (1) (a). - Issued: 22.10.2012. Made: 08.10.2012. Coming into force: 15.10.2012. Effect: None. Territorial extent & classification: E. Local. - Available at http://www.legislation.gov.uk/uksi/2012/2615/contents/made *Non-print*

A14 Trunk Road (Junction 4)) (Rothwell, Northamptonshire) (Temporary Prohibition of Traffic) Order 2012 No. 2012/1323. - Enabling power: Road Traffic Regulation Act 1984, s. 14 (1) (a). - Issued: 23.05.2012. Made: 30.04.2012. Coming into force: 07.05.2012. Effect: None. Territorial extent & classification: E. Local. - Available at http://www.legislation.gov.uk/uksi/2012/1323/contents/made *Non-print*

The A14 Trunk Road Junction 7 (Northamptonshire) (Temporary Prohibition of Traffic) Order 2012 No. 2012/1986. - Enabling power: Road Traffic Regulation Act 1984, s. 14 (1) (a). - Issued: 01.08.2012. Made: 04.07.2012. Coming into force: 11.07.2012. Effect: None. Territorial extent & classification: E. Local. - Available at http://www.legislation.gov.uk/uksi/2012/1986/contents/made *Non-print*

The A14 Trunk Road (Junction 12) (Thrapston, Northamptonshire) (Slip Road) (Temporary Prohibition of Traffic) Order 2012 No. 2012/35. - Enabling power: Road Traffic Regulation Act 1984, s. 14 (1) (a). - Issued: 11.01.2012. Made: 03.01.2012. Coming into force: 10.01.2012. Effect: None. Territorial extent & classification: E. Local. - Available at http://www.legislation.gov.uk/uksi/2012/35/contents/made *Non-print*

The A14 Trunk Road (Junction 13 Thrapston, Northamptonshire and Junction 20 Ellington to Junction 21 Brampton Hut, Cambridgeshire) (Temporary Prohibition of Traffic) Order 2012 No. 2012/1556. - Enabling power: Road Traffic Regulation Act 1984, s. 14 (1) (a). - Issued: 22.06.2012. Made: 06.06.2012. Coming into force: 13.06.2012. Effect: None. Territorial extent & classification: E. Local. - Available at http://www.legislation.gov.uk/uksi/2012/1556/contents/made *Non-print*

The A14 Trunk Road (Junction 21 Brampton Hut Interchange to Junction 23 Spittals Interchange) Eastbound (Cambridgeshire) (Temporary Prohibition of Traffic) Order 2012 No. 2012/2617. - Enabling power: Road Traffic Regulation Act 1984, s. 14 (1) (a). - Issued: 22.10.2012. Made: 08.10.2012. Coming into force: 15.10.2012. Effect: None. Territorial extent & classification: E. Local. - Available at http://www.legislation.gov.uk/uksi/2012/2617/contents/made *Non-print*

The A14 Trunk Road (Junction 22 Brampton Interchange and Junction 24 Godmanchester Interchange) Slip Roads (Cambridgeshire) (Temporary Prohibition of Traffic) Order 2012 No. 2012/1458. - Enabling power: Road Traffic Regulation Act 1984, s. 14 (1) (a). - Issued: 12.06.2012. Made: 28.05.2012. Coming into force: 06.06.2012. Effect: None. Territorial extent & classification: E. Local. - Available at http://www.legislation.gov.uk/uksi/2012/1458/contents/made *Non-print*

The A14 Trunk Road (Junction 23 Spittals Interchange, Cambridgeshire) Eastbound Exit Slip Road (Temporary Prohibition of Traffic) Order 2012 No. 2012/2143. - Enabling power: Road Traffic Regulation Act 1984, s. 14 (1) (a). - Issued: 21.08.2012. Made: 14.08.2012. Coming into force: 21.08.2012. Effect: None. Territorial extent & classification: E. Local. - Available at http://www.legislation.gov.uk/uksi/2012/2143/contents/made *Non-print*

The A14 Trunk Road (Junction 23 Spittals Interchange, Cambridgeshire) (Temporary Prohibition of Traffic) Order 2012 No. 2012/1623. - Enabling power: Road Traffic Regulation Act 1984, s. 14 (1) (a). - Issued: 28.06.2012. Made: 18.06.2012. Coming into force: 25.06.2012. Effect: None. Territorial extent & classification: E. Local. - Available at http://www.legislation.gov.uk/uksi/2012/1623/contents/made *Non-print*

The A14 Trunk Road (Junction 23 Spittals Interchange to Junction 24 Godmanchester Interchange, Cambridgeshire) (Temporary Prohibition of Traffic) Order 2012 No. 2012/3328. - Enabling power: Road Traffic Regulation Act 1984, s. 14 (1) (a). - Issued: 28.01.2013. Made: 26.11.2012. Coming into force: 03.12.2012. Effect: None. Territorial extent & classification: E. Local. - Available at http://www.legislation.gov.uk/uksi/2012/3328/contents/made *Non-print*

The A14 Trunk Road (Junction 23 Spittals Interchange to Junction 24 Godmanchester Interchange, Cambridgeshire) (Temporary Restriction and Prohibition of Traffic) Order 2012 No. 2012/2163. - Enabling power: Road Traffic Regulation Act 1984, s. 14 (1) (a). - Issued: 23.08.2012. Made: 20.08.2012. Coming into force: 27.08.2012. Effect: None. Territorial extent & classification: E. Local. - Available at http://www.legislation.gov.uk/uksi/2012/2163/contents/made *Non-print*

The A14 Trunk Road (Junction 23 Spittals Interchange to Junction 24 Godmanchester Interchange, Cambridgeshire) (Temporary Restriction and Prohibition of Traffic) Order 2012 No. 2012/29. - Enabling power: Road Traffic Regulation Act 1984, s. 14 (1) (a). - Issued: 11.01.2012. Made: 03.01.2012. Coming into force: 10.01.2012. Effect: None. Territorial extent & classification: E. Local. - Available at http://www.legislation.gov.uk/uksi/2012/29/contents/made *Non-print*

The A14 Trunk Road (Junction 23 Spittals Interchange to Junction 31 Girton Interchange, Cambridgeshire) and M11 Motorway (Junction 13 to A14) (Temporary Prohibition of Traffic) Order 2012 No. 2012/1827. - Enabling power: Road Traffic Regulation Act 1984, s. 14 (1) (a). - Issued: 19.07.2012. Made: 02.07.2012. Coming into force: 09.07.2012. Effect: None. Territorial extent & classification: E. Local. - Available at http://www.legislation.gov.uk/uksi/2012/1827/contents/made *Non-print*

The A14 Trunk Road (Junction 25 Hemingford Abbots Interchange, Cambridgeshire) Westbound Exit Slip Road (Temporary Prohibition of Traffic) Order 2012 No. 2012/3154. - Enabling power: Road Traffic Regulation Act 1984, s. 14 (1) (a). - Issued: 28.12.2012. Made: 26.11.2012. Coming into force: 03.12.2012. Effect: None. Territorial extent & classification: E. Local. - Available at http://www.legislation.gov.uk/uksi/2012/3154/contents/made *Non-print*

The A14 Trunk Road (Junction 29 Bar Hill to Junctino 33 Milton, Cambridgeshire) (Temporary Prohibition of Traffic) Order 2012 No. 2012/209. - Enabling power: Road Traffic Regulation Act 1984, s. 14 (1) (a). - Issued: 01.02.2012. Made: 23.01.2012. Coming into force: 30.01.2012. Effect: None. Territorial extent & classification: E. Local. - Available at http://www.legislation.gov.uk/uksi/2012/209/contents/made *Non-print*

Road traffic: Traffic regulation

The A14 Trunk Road (Junction 33 Milton to Junction 32 Histon, Cambridge) Westbound (Temporary Prohibition of Traffic) Order 2012 No. 2012/2440. - Enabling power: Road Traffic Regulation Act 1984, s. 14 (1) (a). - Issued: 27.09.2012. Made: 17.09.2012. Coming into force: 24.09.2012. Effect: None. Territorial extent & classification: E. Local. - Available at http://www.legislation.gov.uk/uksi/2012/2440/contents/made *Non-print*

The A14 Trunk Road (Junction 35 Stow-Cum-Quy Interchange, Cambridgeshire) Westbound (Temporary Prohibition of Traffic) Order 2012 No. 2012/453. - Enabling power: Road Traffic Regulation Act 1984, s. 14 (1) (a). - Issued: 24.02.2012. Made: 13.02.2012. Coming into force: 20.02.2012. Effect: None. Territorial extent & classification: E. Local. - Available at http://www.legislation.gov.uk/uksi/2012/453/contents/made *Non-print*

The A14 Trunk Road (Junction 38 Waterhall Interchange to Junction 42 Westley Interchange, Suffolk) (Temporary Restriction and Prohibition of Traffic) Order 2012 No. 2012/2331. - Enabling power: Road Traffic Regulation Act 1984, s. 14 (1) (a). - Issued: 13.09.2012. Made: 03.09.2012. Coming into force: 10.09.2012. Effect: None. Territorial extent & classification: E. Local. - Available at http://www.legislation.gov.uk/uksi/2012/2331/contents/made *Non-print*

The A14 Trunk Road (Junction 40 Higham Interchange to Junction 41 Risby Interchange, Suffolk) (Temporary Restriction and Prohibition of Traffic) (No. 2) Order 2012 No. 2012/1459. - Enabling power: Road Traffic Regulation Act 1984, s. 14 (1) (a), sch. 9, para. 27 (1). - Issued: 12.06.2012. Made: 28.05.2012. Coming into force: 04.06.2012. Effect: S.I. 2012/509 revoked. Territorial extent & classification: E. Local. - Available at http://www.legislation.gov.uk/uksi/2012/1459/contents/made *Non-print*

The A14 Trunk Road (Junction 40 Higham Interchange to Junction 41 Risby Interchange, Suffolk) (Temporary Restriction and Prohibition of Traffic) Order 2012 No. 2012/509. - Enabling power: Road Traffic Regulation Act 1984, s. 14 (1) (a). - Issued: 01.03.2012. Made: 20.02.2012. Coming into force: 27.02.2012. Effect: None. Territorial extent & classification: E. Local. - Revoked by SI 2012/1459 (Non-print). - Available at http://www.legislation.gov.uk/uksi/2012/509/contents/made *Non-print*

The A14 Trunk Road (Junction 46 Thurston, Suffolk) Eastbound (Temporary Restriction and Prohibition of Traffic) Order 2012 No. 2012/1062. - Enabling power: Road Traffic Regulation Act 1984, s. 14 (1) (a). - Issued: 16.04.2012. Made: 02.04.2012. Coming into force: 09.04.2012. Effect: None. Territorial extent & classification: E. Local. - Available at http://www.legislation.gov.uk/uksi/2012/1062/contents/made *Non-print*

The A14 Trunk Road (Junction 48 Crossways Interchange to Junction 51 Beacon Hill Interchange, Stowmarket, Suffolk) Northbound (Temporary Restriction and Prohibition of Traffic) Order 2012 No. 2012/101. - Enabling power: Road Traffic Regulation Act 1984, s. 14 (1) (a). - Issued: 20.01.2012. Made: 09.01.2012. Coming into force: 16.01.2012. Effect: None. Territorial extent & classification: E. Local. - Available at http://www.legislation.gov.uk/uksi/2012/101/contents/made *Non-print*

The A14 Trunk Road (Junction 49 Tot Hill Interchange to Junction 50 Cedars Interchange, Stowmarket, Suffolk) Eastbound (Temporary Restriction and Prohibition of Traffic) Order 2012 No. 2012/2470. - Enabling power: Road Traffic Regulation Act 1984, s. 14 (1) (a). - Issued: 01.10.2012. Made: 24.09.2012. Coming into force: 01.10.2012. Effect: None. Territorial extent & classification: E. Local. - Available at http://www.legislation.gov.uk/uksi/2012/2470/contents/made *Non-print*

The A14 Trunk Road (Junction 49 Tot Hill Interchange to Junction 51 Beacon Hill Interchange, Suffolk) (Temporary Restriction and Prohibition of Traffic) Order 2012 No. 2012/2368. - Enabling power: Road Traffic Regulation Act 1984, s. 14 (1) (a). - Issued: 18.09.2012. Made: 10.09.2012. Coming into force: 17.09.2012. Effect: None. Territorial extent & classification: E. Local. - Available at http://www.legislation.gov.uk/uksi/2012/2368/contents/made *Non-print*

The A14 Trunk Road (Junction 51 Beacon Hill Interchange and Junction 52 Claydon Interchange, Suffolk) Westbound (Temporary Restriction and Prohibition of Traffic) Order 2012 No. 2012/2851. - Enabling power: Road Traffic Regulation Act 1984, s. 14 (1) (a). - Issued: 16.11.2012. Made: 05.11.2012. Coming into force: 12.11.2012. Effect: None. Territorial extent & classification: E. Local. - Available at http://www.legislation.gov.uk/uksi/2012/2851/contents/made *Non-print*

The A14 Trunk Road (Junction 52 Claydon Interchange, Ipswich, Suffolk) Westbound (Temporary Prohibition of Traffic) Order 2012 No. 2012/3299. - Enabling power: Road Traffic Regulation Act 1984, s. 14 (1) (a). - Issued: 16.01.2013. Made: 31.12.2012. Coming into force: 07.01.2013. Effect: None. Territorial extent & classification: E. Local. - Available at http://www.legislation.gov.uk/uksi/2012/3299/contents/made *Non-print*

The A14 Trunk Road (Junction 57 Nacton and Junction 56 Wherstead, Ipswich, Suffolk) Westbound (Temporary Restriction and Prohibition of Traffic) Order 2012 No. 2012/30. - Enabling power: Road Traffic Regulation Act 1984, s. 14 (1) (a). - Issued: 11.01.2012. Made: 03.01.2012. Coming into force: 10.01.2012. Effect: None. Territorial extent & classification: E. Local. - Available at http://www.legislation.gov.uk/uksi/2012/30/contents/made *Non-print*

Road traffic: Traffic regulation

The A14 Trunk Road (Junction 58 Levington Interchange to Junction 55 Copdock Interchange, Suffolk) (Temporary Restriction and Prohibition of Traffic) Order 2012 No. 2012/1550. - Enabling power: Road Traffic Regulation Act 1984, s. 14 (1) (a). - Issued: 20.06.2012. Made: 06.06.2012. Coming into force: 13.06.2012. Effect: None. Territorial extent & classification: E. Local. - Available at http://www.legislation.gov.uk/uksi/2012/1550/contents/made *Non-print*

The A14 Trunk Road (Junction 58 Levington Interchange to Junction 62 Dock Gate 1 Roundabout, Felixstowe, Suffolk) (Temporary Restriction and Prohibition of Traffic) Order 2012 No. 2012/2074. - Enabling power: Road Traffic Regulation Act 1984, s. 14 (1) (a) 5 (b) (7). - Issued: 13.08.2012. Made: 30.07.2012. Coming into force: 06.08.2012. Effect: None. Territorial extent & classification: E. Local. - Available at http://www.legislation.gov.uk/uksi/2012/2074/contents/made *Non-print*

The A14 Trunk Road (Junction 58 Seven Hills Interchange, Ipswich, Suffolk) (Temporary Restriction and Prohibition of Traffic) Order 2012 No. 2012/510. - Enabling power: Road Traffic Regulation Act 1984, s. 14 (1) (a). - Issued: 01.03.2012. Made: 20.02.2012. Coming into force: 27.02.2012. Effect: None. Territorial extent & classification: E. Local. - Available at http://www.legislation.gov.uk/uksi/2012/510/contents/made *Non-print*

The A14 Trunk Road (Junction 61 Port of Felixstowe to Junction 62 Dock Gate 1, Suffolk) (Temporary Restriction and Prohibition of Traffic) Order 2012 No. 2012/451. - Enabling power: Road Traffic Regulation Act 1984, s. 14 (1) (a). - Issued: 24.02.2012. Made: 13.02.2012. Coming into force: 20.02.2012. Effect: None. Territorial extent & classification: E. Local. - Available at http://www.legislation.gov.uk/uksi/2012/451/contents/made *Non-print*

The A14 Trunk Road (Kemarsh to Rothwell, Northamptonshire) (Temporary Prohibition of Traffic) Order 2012 No. 2012/3131. - Enabling power: Road Traffic Regulation Act 1984, s. 14 (1) (a). - Issued: 20.12.2012. Made: 19.11.2012. Coming into force: 26.11.2012. Effect: None. Territorial extent & classification: E. Local. - Available at http://www.legislation.gov.uk/uksi/2012/3131/contents/made *Non-print*

The A14 Trunk Road (Kettering, Northamptonshire) (Temporary 50 Miles Per Hour Speed Restriction) Order 2012 No. 2012/2383. - Enabling power: Road Traffic Regulation Act 1984, s. 14 (1) (a). - Issued: 18.09.2012. Made: 28.08.2012. Coming into force: 04.09.2012. Effect: None. Territorial extent & classification: E. Local. - Available at http://www.legislation.gov.uk/uksi/2012/2383/contents/made *Non-print*

The A14 Trunk Road (Kettering, Northamptonshire) (Temporary Prohibition of Traffic) Order 2012 No. 2012/2703. - Enabling power: Road Traffic Regulation Act 1984, s. 14 (1) (a). - Issued: 01.11.2012. Made: 24.09.2012. Coming into force: 01.10.2012. Effect: None. Territorial extent & classification: E. Local. - Available at http://www.legislation.gov.uk/uksi/2012/2703/contents/made *Non-print*

The A14 Trunk Road (Leighton Bromswold and Woolley, Cambridgeshire) (Temporary Prohibition of Traffic) Order 2012 No. 2012/207. - Enabling power: Road Traffic Regulation Act 1984, s. 14 (1) (a). - Issued: 01.02.2012. Made: 23.01.2012. Coming into force: 30.01.2012. Effect: None. Territorial extent & classification: E. Local. - Available at http://www.legislation.gov.uk/uksi/2012/207/contents/made *Non-print*

The A14 Trunk Road (Naseby, Northamptonshire) (Temporary Prohibition of Traffic) Order 2012 No. 2012/2972. - Enabling power: Road Traffic Regulation Act 1984, s. 14 (1) (a). - Issued: 05.12.2012. Made: 13.11.2012. Coming into force: 20.11.2012. Effect: None. Territorial extent & classification: E. Local. - Available at http://www.legislation.gov.uk/uksi/2012/2972/contents/made *Non-print*

The A14 Trunk Road (South of Junction 47A Elmswell Interchange to Junction 50 Cedars Interchange, Suffolk) Eastbound (Temporary Restriction and Prohibition of Traffic) Order 2012 No. 2012/2321. - Enabling power: Road Traffic Regulation Act 1984, s. 14 (1) (a). - Issued: 14.09.2012. Made: 03.09.2012. Coming into force: 10.09.2012. Effect: None. Territorial extent & classification: E. Local. - Available at http://www.legislation.gov.uk/uksi/2012/2321/contents/made *Non-print*

The A14 Trunk Road (Stowupland, Suffolk) (Prohibition of Entry) Order 2012 No. 2012/2696. - Enabling power: Road Traffic Regulation Act 1984, ss. 1 (1), 2 (1) (2). - Issued: 30.10.2012. Made: 17.10.2012. Coming into force: 31.10.2012. Effect: None. Territorial extent & classification: E. Local. - Available at http://www.legislation.gov.uk/uksi/2012/2696/contents/made *Non-print*

The A14 Trunk Road (Thrapston, Northamptonshire) (Temporary Restriction and Prohibition of Traffic) Order 2012 No. 2012/2722. - Enabling power: Road Traffic Regulation Act 1984, s. 14 (1) (a). - Issued: 02.11.2012. Made: 05.10.2012. Coming into force: 12.10.2012. Effect: None. Territorial extent & classification: E. Local. - Available at http://www.legislation.gov.uk/uksi/2012/2722/contents/made *Non-print*

Road traffic: Traffic regulation

The A14 Trunk Road (Trimley Bypass, Suffolk) Westbound (Temporary Restriction and Prohibition of Traffic) Order 2012 No. 2012/604. - Enabling power: Road Traffic Regulation Act 1984, s. 14 (1) (a), 5 (b) (7). - Issued: 06.03.2012. Made: 27.02.2012. Coming into force: 05.03.2012. Effect: None. Territorial extent & classification: E. Local. - Available at http://www.legislation.gov.uk/uksi/2012/604/contents/made *Non-print*

The A14 Trunk Road (West of Junction 47 Woolpit/Elmswell Interchange to Junction 49 Tot Hill Interchange, Suffolk) (Temporary Restriction and Prohibition of Traffic) Order 2012 No. 2012/1063. - Enabling power: Road Traffic Regulation Act 1984, s. 14 (1) (a) 5 (b) (6). - Issued: 16.04.2012. Made: 02.04.2012. Coming into force: 09.04.2012. Effect: None. Territorial extent & classification: E. Local. - Available at http://www.legislation.gov.uk/uksi/2012/1063/contents/made *Non-print*

The A19 Trunk Road and the A66 Trunk Road (Olympic Torch Relay) (Temporary Prohibition of Traffic) Order 2012 No. 2012/1562. - Enabling power: Road Traffic Regulation Act 1984, s. 16A (2) (a). - Issued: 22.06.2012. Made: 07.06.2012. Coming into force: 16.06.2012. Effect: None. Territorial extent & classification: E. Local. - Available at http://www.legislation.gov.uk/uksi/2012/1562/contents/made *Non-print*

The A19 Trunk Road and the A66 Trunk Road (Stockton Road Interchange) (Temporary Prohibition of Traffic) Order 2012 No. 2012/217. - Enabling power: Road Traffic Regulation Act 1984, s. 14 (1) (a). - Issued: 03.02.2012. Made: 23.01.2012. Coming into force: 29.01.2012. Effect: None. Territorial extent & classification: E. Local. - Available at http://www.legislation.gov.uk/uksi/2012/217/contents/made *Non-print*

The A19 Trunk Road (Castle Eden) (Temporary Restriction and Prohibition of Traffic) Order 2012 No. 2012/2214. - Enabling power: Road Traffic Regulation Act 1984, s. 14 (1) (a). - Issued: 31.08.2012. Made: 23.08.2012. Coming into force: 03.09.2012. Effect: None. Territorial extent & classification: E. Local. - Available at http://www.legislation.gov.uk/uksi/2012/2214/contents/made *Non-print*

The A19 Trunk Road (Crathorne Junction to Parkway Interchange) (Temporary Restriction and Prohibition of Traffic) Order 2012 No. 2012/2459. - Enabling power: Road Traffic Regulation Act 1984, s. 14 (1) (a). - Issued: 28.09.2012. Made: 20.09.2012. Coming into force: 27.09.2012. Effect: None. Territorial extent & classification: E. Local. - Available at http://www.legislation.gov.uk/uksi/2012/2459/contents/made *Non-print*

The A19 Trunk Road (Dudley Lane Interchange) (Temporary Prohibition of Traffic) Order 2012 No. 2012/1173. - Enabling power: Road Traffic Regulation Act 1984, s. 14 (1) (a). - Issued: 02.05.2012. Made: 20.04.2012. Coming into force: 27.04.2012. Effect: None. Territorial extent & classification: E. Local. - Available at http://www.legislation.gov.uk/uksi/2012/1173/contents/made *Non-print*

The A19 Trunk Road (Easington Interchange to Ryhope Interchange) (Temporary Restriction and Prohibition of Traffic) Order 2012 No. 2012/1076. - Enabling power: Road Traffic Regulation Act 1984, s. 14 (1) (a). - Issued: 17.04.2012. Made: 05.04.2012. Coming into force: 14.04.2012. Effect: None. Territorial extent & classification: E. Local. - Available at http://www.legislation.gov.uk/uksi/2012/1076/contents/made *Non-print*

The A19 Trunk Road (Great North Run) (Temporary Prohibition of Traffic) Order 2012 No. 2012/2353. - Enabling power: Road Traffic Regulation Act 1984, s. 16A (2) (a). - Issued: 17.09.2012. Made: 06.09.2012. Coming into force: 15.09.2012. Effect: None. Territorial extent & classification: E. Local. - Available at http://www.legislation.gov.uk/uksi/2012/2353/contents/made *Non-print*

The A19 Trunk Road (Herrington Interchange to Seaton Interchange) (Temporary Restriction and Prohibition of Traffic) Order 2012 No. 2012/1216. - Enabling power: Road Traffic Regulation Act 1984, s. 14 (1) (a). - Issued: 10.05.2012. Made: 26.04.2012. Coming into force: 07.05.2012. Effect: None. Territorial extent & classification: E. Local. - Available at http://www.legislation.gov.uk/uksi/2012/1216/contents/made *Non-print*

The A19 Trunk Road (Holystone Interchange to Silverlink Interchange) (Temporary Restriction and Prohibition of Traffic) Order 2012 No. 2012/1112. - Enabling power: Road Traffic Regulation Act 1984, s. 14 (1) (a). - Issued: 23.04.2012. Made: 12.04.2012. Coming into force: 22.04.2012. Effect: None. Territorial extent & classification: E. Local. - Available at http://www.legislation.gov.uk/uksi/2012/1112/contents/made *Non-print*

The A19 Trunk Road (Howdon Interchange to Holystone Interchange) (Temporary Restriction and Prohibition of Traffic) Order 2012 No. 2012/556. - Enabling power: Road Traffic Regulation Act 1984, s. 14 (1) (a). - Issued: 01.03.2012. Made: 21.02.2012. Coming into force: 04.03.2012. Effect: None. Territorial extent & classification: E. Local. - Available at http://www.legislation.gov.uk/uksi/2012/556/contents/made *Non-print*

The A19 Trunk Road (Howdon Interchange to Silverlink Interchange) (Temporary Prohibition of Traffic) (No. 2) Order 2012 No. 2012/2297. - Enabling power: Road Traffic Regulation Act 1984, s. 14 (1) (a). - Issued: 11.09.2012. Made: 30.08.2012. Coming into force: 09.09.2012. Effect: None. Territorial extent & classification: E. Local. - Available at http://www.legislation.gov.uk/uksi/2012/2297/contents/made *Non-print*

The A19 Trunk Road (Howdon Interchange to Silverlink Interchange) (Temporary Prohibition of Traffic) Order 2012 No. 2012/1077. - Enabling power: Road Traffic Regulation Act 1984, s. 14 (1) (a). - Issued: 17.04.2012. Made: 05.04.2012. Coming into force: 15.04.2012. Effect: None. Territorial extent & classification: E. Local. - Available at http://www.legislation.gov.uk/uksi/2012/1077/contents/made *Non-print*

The A19 Trunk Road (Killingworth Interchange) (Temporary 50 Miles Per Hour Speed Restriction) Order 2012 No. 2012/3192. - Enabling power: Road Traffic Regulation Act 1984, s. 14 (1) (a). - Issued: 02.01.2013. Made: 06.12.2012. Coming into force: 16.12.2012. Effect: None. Territorial extent & classification: E. Local. - Available at http://www.legislation.gov.uk/uksi/2012/3192/contents/made *Non-print*

The A19 Trunk Road (Laybys at Howdon) (Temporary Prohibition of Traffic) Order 2012 No. 2012/2846. - Enabling power: Road Traffic Regulation Act 1984, s. 14 (1) (a). - Issued: 16.11.2012. Made: 01.11.2012. Coming into force: 11.11.2012. Effect: None. Territorial extent & classification: E. Local. - Available at http://www.legislation.gov.uk/uksi/2012/2846/contents/made *Non-print*

The A19 Trunk Road (Lindisfarne Roundabout to Silverlink Roundabout) (Temporary Restriction and Prohibition of Traffic) Order 2008 (Revocation) Order 2012 No. 2012/1122. - Enabling power: Road Traffic Regulation Act 1984, ss. 14 (1) (a), 15 (2). - Issued: 24.04.2012. Made: 12.04.2012. Coming into force: 23.04.2012. Effect: S.I. 2008/1388 revoked. Territorial extent & classification: E. Local. - Available at http://www.legislation.gov.uk/uksi/2012/1122/contents/made *Non-print*

The A19 Trunk Road (Moor Farm Roundabout to Holystone Interchange) (Temporary Restriction and Prohibition of Traffic) Order 2012 No. 2012/2628. - Enabling power: Road Traffic Regulation Act 1984, s. 14 (1) (a). - Issued: 23.10.2012. Made: 11.10.2012. Coming into force: 21.10.2012. Effect: None. Territorial extent & classification: E. Local. - Available at http://www.legislation.gov.uk/uksi/2012/2628/contents/made *Non-print*

The A19 Trunk Road (Moor Farm Roundabout to Killingworth Interchange) (Temporary Prohibition of Traffic) Order 2012 No. 2012/1853. - Enabling power: Road Traffic Regulation Act 1984, s. 14 (1) (a). - Issued: 20.07.2012. Made: 05.07.2012. Coming into force: 16.07.2012. Effect: None. Territorial extent & classification: E. Local. - Available at http://www.legislation.gov.uk/uksi/2012/1853/contents/made *Non-print*

The A19 Trunk Road (Moor Farm Roundabout to Seaton Burn Interchange) (Temporary Prohibition of Traffic) (No. 2) Order 2012 No. 2012/2821. - Enabling power: Road Traffic Regulation Act 1984, s. 14 (1) (a). - Issued: 13.11.2012. Made: 25.10.2012. Coming into force: 04.11.2012. Effect: None. Territorial extent & classification: E. Local. - Available at http://www.legislation.gov.uk/uksi/2012/2821/contents/made *Non-print*

The A19 Trunk Road (Moor Farm Roundabout to Seaton Burn Interchange) (Temporary Prohibition of Traffic) Order 2012 No. 2012/2024. - Enabling power: Road Traffic Regulation Act 1984, s. 14 (1) (a). - Issued: 06.08.2012. Made: 23.07.2012. Coming into force: 27.07.2012. Effect: None. Territorial extent & classification: E. Local. - Available at http://www.legislation.gov.uk/uksi/2012/2024/contents/made *Non-print*

The A19 Trunk Road (Moor Farm to Seaton Burn) (Temporary Restriction and Prohibition of Traffic) (No. 2) Order 2012 No. 2012/2137. - Enabling power: Road Traffic Regulation Act 1984, s. 14 (1) (a). - Issued: 21.08.2012. Made: 09.08.2012. Coming into force: 19.08.2012. Effect: None. Territorial extent & classification: E. Local. - Available at http://www.legislation.gov.uk/uksi/2012/2137/contents/made *Non-print*

The A19 Trunk Road (Moor Farm to Seaton Burn) (Temporary Restriction and Prohibition of Traffic) Order 2012 No. 2012/1609. - Enabling power: Road Traffic Regulation Act 1984, s. 14 (1) (a). - Issued: 27.06.2012. Made: 14.06.2012. Coming into force: 24.06.2012. Effect: None. Territorial extent & classification: E. Local. - Available at http://www.legislation.gov.uk/uksi/2012/1609/contents/made *Non-print*

The A19 Trunk Road (Osmotherley Interchange to Tontine Interchange) (Temporary Prohibition of Traffic) Order 2012 No. 2012/2497. - Enabling power: Road Traffic Regulation Act 1984, s. 14 (1) (a). - Issued: 03.10.2012. Made: 27.09.2012. Coming into force: 07.10.2012. Effect: None. Territorial extent & classification: E. Local. - Available at http://www.legislation.gov.uk/uksi/2012/2497/contents/made *Non-print*

The A19 Trunk Road (Parkway Interchange to Trenholme Bar) (Temporary Restriction and Prohibition of Traffic) Order 2012 No. 2012/2296. - Enabling power: Road Traffic Regulation Act 1984, s. 14 (1) (a). - Issued: 10.09.2012. Made: 30.08.2012. Coming into force: 08.09.2012. Effect: None. Territorial extent & classification: E. Local. - Available at http://www.legislation.gov.uk/uksi/2012/2296/contents/made *Non-print*

The A19 Trunk Road (Portrack Interchange to Parkway Interchange) (Temporary Restriction and Prohibition of Traffic) Order 2012 No. 2012/1608. - Enabling power: Road Traffic Regulation Act 1984, s. 14 (1) (a). - Issued: 27.06.2012. Made: 14.06.2012. Coming into force: 23.06.2012. Effect: None. Territorial extent & classification: E. Local. - Available at http://www.legislation.gov.uk/uksi/2012/1608/contents/made *Non-print*

The A19 Trunk Road (Seaton Burn Interchange) (Temporary 50 Miles Per Hour Speed Restriction) Order 2012 No. 2012/44. - Enabling power: Road Traffic Regulation Act 1984, s. 14 (1) (a). - Issued: 11.01.2012. Made: 03.01.2012. Coming into force: 08.01.2012. Effect: None. Territorial extent & classification: E. Local. - Available at http://www.legislation.gov.uk/uksi/2012/44/contents/made *Non-print*

The A19 Trunk Road (Sheraton Interchange to Castle Eden Interchange) (Temporary Prohibition of Traffic) Order 2012 No. 2012/2874. - Enabling power: Road Traffic Regulation Act 1984, s. 14 (1) (a). - Issued: 19.11.2012. Made: 08.11.2012. Coming into force: 16.11.2012. Effect: None. Territorial extent & classification: E. Local. - Available at http://www.legislation.gov.uk/uksi/2012/2874/contents/made *Non-print*

The A19 Trunk Road (Sheraton Interchange to Wolviston Interchange) (Temporary Restriction and Prohibition of Traffic) Order 2012 No. 2012/1383. - Enabling power: Road Traffic Regulation Act 1984, s. 14 (1) (a). - Issued: 01.06.2012. Made: 17.05.2012. Coming into force: 26.05.2012. Effect: None. Territorial extent & classification: E. Local. - Available at http://www.legislation.gov.uk/uksi/2012/1383/contents/made *Non-print*

The A19 Trunk Road (Silverlink Interchange to Killingworth Interchange) (Temporary Restriction and Prohibition of Traffic) Order 2012 No. 2012/2343. - Enabling power: Road Traffic Regulation Act 1984, s. 14 (1) (a). - Issued: 14.09.2012. Made: 06.09.2012. Coming into force: 16.09.2012. Effect: None. Territorial extent & classification: E. Local. - Available at http://www.legislation.gov.uk/uksi/2012/2343/contents/made *Non-print*

The A19 Trunk Road (Silverlink to Seaton Burn) (Temporary Restriction and Prohibition of Traffic) Order 2012 No. 2012/474. - Enabling power: Road Traffic Regulation Act 1984, s. 14 (1) (a). - Issued: 29.02.2012. Made: 16.02.2012. Coming into force: 26.02.2012. Effect: None. Territorial extent & classification: E. Local. - Available at http://www.legislation.gov.uk/uksi/2012/474/contents/made *Non-print*

The A19 Trunk Road (Stockton Ring Road to Wolviston Interchange) (Temporary Prohibition of Traffic) Order 2012 No. 2012/2154. - Enabling power: Road Traffic Regulation Act 1984, s. 14 (1) (a). - Issued: 23.08.2012. Made: 16.08.2012. Coming into force: 27.08.2012. Effect: None. Territorial extent & classification: E. Local. - Available at http://www.legislation.gov.uk/uksi/2012/2154/contents/made *Non-print*

The A19 Trunk Road (Stockton Road Interchange to Portrack Interchange) (Temporary Prohibition of Traffic) Order 2012 No. 2012/85. - Enabling power: Road Traffic Regulation Act 1984, s. 14 (1) (a). - Issued: 18.01.2012. Made: 05.01.2012. Coming into force: 15.01.2012. Effect: None. Territorial extent & classification: E. Local. - Available at http://www.legislation.gov.uk/uksi/2012/85/contents/made *Non-print*

The A19 Trunk Road (Testos Roundabout to Lindisfarne Interchange) (Temporary Restriction and Prohibition of Traffic) Order 2012 No. 2012/1476. - Enabling power: Road Traffic Regulation Act 1984, s. 14 (1) (a). - Issued: 12.06.2012. Made: 30.05.2012. Coming into force: 08.06.2012. Effect: None. Territorial extent & classification: E. Local. - Available at http://www.legislation.gov.uk/uksi/2012/1476/contents/made *Non-print*

The A19 Trunk Road (Tontine Interchange) (Temporary Prohibition of Traffic) Order 2012 No. 2012/773. - Enabling power: Road Traffic Regulation Act 1984, s. 14 (1) (a). - Issued: 20.03.2012. Made: 08.03.2012. Coming into force: 13.03.2012. Effect: None. Territorial extent & classification: E. Local. - Available at http://www.legislation.gov.uk/uksi/2012/773/contents/made *Non-print*

The A19 Trunk Road (York Road Interchange to Osmotherley Interchange) (Temporary Restriction and Prohibition of Traffic) Order 2012 No. 2012/2483. - Enabling power: Road Traffic Regulation Act 1984, s. 14 (1) (a). - Issued: 02.10.2012. Made: 20.09.2012. Coming into force: 30.09.2012. Effect: None. Territorial extent & classification: E. Local. - Available at http://www.legislation.gov.uk/uksi/2012/2483/contents/made *Non-print*

Road traffic: Traffic regulation

The A20 Trunk Road (Alkham Valley Interchange and Courtwood Interchange, Slip Roads) (Temporary Prohibition of Traffic) Order 2012 No. 2012/3180. - Enabling power: Road Traffic Regulation Act 1984, s. 14 (1) (a). - Issued: 31.12.2012. Made: 03.12.2012. Coming into force: 21.01.2013. Effect: None. Territorial extent & classification: E. Local. - Available at http://www.legislation.gov.uk/uksi/2012/3180/contents/made *Non-print*

The A20 Trunk Road (Alkham Valley Interchange - Western Heights Roundabout, Coastbound) (Temporary Prohibition of Traffic) Order 2012 No. 2012/1044. - Enabling power: Road Traffic Regulation Act 1984, s. 14 (1) (a). - Issued: 13.04.2012. Made: 26.03.2012. Coming into force: 14.04.2012. Effect: None. Territorial extent & classification: E. Local. - Available at http://www.legislation.gov.uk/uksi/2012/1044/contents/made *Non-print*

The A20 Trunk Road and the M20 Motorway (Alkham Valley Interchange - M20 Junction 13) (Temporary Restriction and Prohibition of Traffic) Order 2012 No. 2012/3201. - Enabling power: Road Traffic Regulation Act 1984, s. 14 (1) (a). - Issued: 02.01.2013. Made: 10.12.2012. Coming into force: 26.01.2013. Effect: None. Territorial extent & classification: E. Local. - Available at http://www.legislation.gov.uk/uksi/2012/3201/contents/made *Non-print*

The A20 Trunk Road (East of Cauldham Lane - Courtwood) (Temporary Restriction and Prohibition of Traffic) Order 2012 No. 2012/434. - Enabling power: Road Traffic Regulation Act 1984, s. 14 (1) (a). - Issued: 22.02.2012. Made: 13.02.2012. Coming into force: 03.03.2012. Effect: None. Territorial extent & classification: E. Local. - Available at http://www.legislation.gov.uk/uksi/2012/434/contents/made *Non-print*

The A20 Trunk Road (M20 Junction 13 - Dover Eastern Docks Roundabout) (Temporary Restriction and Prohibition of Traffic) Order 2012 No. 2012/1733. - Enabling power: London Olympic and Paralympic Games Act 2006, s. 16 (1) & Road Traffic Regulation Act 1984, s. 16A. - Issued: 17.07.2012. Made: 25.06.2012. Coming into force: 14.07.2012. Effect: None. Territorial extent & classification: E. Local. - Available at http://www.legislation.gov.uk/uksi/2012/1733/contents/made *Non-print*

The A20 Trunk Road (Petham Court Bridge, Lay-by) (Temporary Prohibition of Traffic) Order 2012 No. 2012/1619. - Enabling power: Road Traffic Regulation Act 1984, s. 14 (1) (a). - Issued: 28.06.2012. Made: 18.06.2012. Coming into force: 09.07.2012. Effect: None. Territorial extent & classification: E. Local. - Available at http://www.legislation.gov.uk/uksi/2012/1619/contents/made *Non-print*

The A20 Trunk Road (Townwall Street, Gap Closure) (Temporary Prohibition of Traffic) Order 2012 No. 2012/2510. - Enabling power: Road Traffic Regulation Act 1984, s. 14 (1) (a). - Issued: 05.10.2012. Made: 01.10.2012. Coming into force: 20.10.2012. Effect: None. Territorial extent & classification: E. Local. - Available at http://www.legislation.gov.uk/uksi/2012/2510/contents/made *Non-print*

The A21 and the A26 Trunk Roads (Morley's Interchange - Flimwell Close) (Temporary Prohibition of Traffic) Order 2012 No. 2012/3250. - Enabling power: Road Traffic Regulation Act 1984, s. 14 (1) (a). - Issued: 09.01.2013. Made: 17.12.2012. Coming into force: 02.02.2013. Effect: None. Territorial extent & classification: E. Local. - Available at http://www.legislation.gov.uk/uksi/2012/3250/contents/made *Non-print*

The A21 Trunk Road and the M25 Motorway (M25 Junction 5 - Morley's Interchange) (Temporary Restriction and Prohibition of Traffic) Order 2012 No. 2012/142. - Enabling power: Road Traffic Regulation Act 1984, s. 14 (1) (a). - Issued: 25.01.2012. Made: 16.01.2012. Coming into force: 04.02.2012. Effect: None. Territorial extent & classification: E. Local. - Available at http://www.legislation.gov.uk/uksi/2012/142/contents/made *Non-print*

The A21 Trunk Road (Bluemans Lane Junction) (Temporary Speed Restrictions) Order 2012 No. 2012/3264. - Enabling power: Road Traffic Regulation Act 1984, s. 14 (1) (a). - Issued: 14.01.2013. Made: 17.12.2012. Coming into force: 02.02.2013. Effect: None. Territorial extent & classification: E. Local. - Available at http://www.legislation.gov.uk/uksi/2012/3264/contents/made *Non-print*

The A21 Trunk Road (Castle Hill - Kipping's Cross) (Temporary Restriction and Prohibition of Traffic) Order 2012 No. 2012/1951. - Enabling power: Road Traffic Regulation Act 1984, s. 14 (1) (a). - Issued: 30.07.2012. Made: 16.07.2012. Coming into force: 04.08.2012. Effect: None. Territorial extent & classification: E. Local. - Available at http://www.legislation.gov.uk/uksi/2012/1951/contents/made *Non-print*

The A21 Trunk Road (Flimwell)(Temporary 50 Miles Per Hour Speed Restriction) Order 2012 No. 2012/3199. - Enabling power: Road Traffic Regulation Act 1984, s. 14 (1) (a). - Issued: 02.01.2013. Made: 10.12.2012. Coming into force: 29.12.2012. Effect: None. Territorial extent & classification: E. Local. - Available at http://www.legislation.gov.uk/uksi/2012/3199/contents/made *Non-print*

The A21 Trunk Road (Forstal Farm Roundabout, Lamberhurst) (Temporary 40 Miles Per Hour Speed Restriction) Order 2012 No. 2012/2860. - Enabling power: Road Traffic Regulation Act 1984, s. 14 (1) (a). - Issued: 16.11.2012. Made: 05.11.2012. Coming into force: 24.11.2012. Effect: None. Territorial extent & classification: E. Local. - Available at http://www.legislation.gov.uk/uksi/2012/2860/contents/made *Non-print*

The A21 Trunk Road (John's Cross - Baldslow) (Temporary Prohibition of Traffic) Order 2012 No. 2012/131. - Enabling power: Road Traffic Regulation Act 1984, s. 14 (1) (a). - Issued: 24.01.2012. Made: 16.01.2012. Coming into force: 04.02.2012. Effect: None. Territorial extent & classification: E. Local. - Available at http://www.legislation.gov.uk/uksi/2012/131/contents/made *Non-print*

The A21 Trunk Road (John's Cross - Robertsbridge) (Temporary Restriction and Prohibition of Traffic) Order 2012 No. 2012/3248. - Enabling power: Road Traffic Regulation Act 1984, s. 14 (1) (a). - Issued: 08.01.2013. Made: 17.12.2012. Coming into force: 02.02.2013. Effect: None. Territorial extent & classification: E. Local. - Available at http://www.legislation.gov.uk/uksi/2012/3248/contents/made *Non-print*

The A21 Trunk Road (Kent Street/Whydown Hill) (Temporary Speed Restrictions) Order 2012 No. 2012/2927. - Enabling power: Road Traffic Regulation Act 1984, s. 14 (1) (a). - Issued: 26.11.2012. Made: 12.11.2012. Coming into force: 01.12.2012. Effect: None. Territorial extent & classification: E. Local. - Available at http://www.legislation.gov.uk/uksi/2012/2927/contents/made *Non-print*

The A21 Trunk Road (Middle Lodge Roundabout, Near Pembury) (Temporary 30 Miles Per Hour Speed Restriction) Order 2012 No. 2012/905. - Enabling power: Road Traffic Regulation Act 1984, s. 14 (1) (a). - Issued: 26.03.2012. Made: 19.03.2012. Coming into force: 07.04.2012. Effect: None. Territorial extent & classification: E. Local. - Available at http://www.legislation.gov.uk/uksi/2012/905/contents/made *Non-print*

The A21 Trunk Road (Morley's Interchange - Pembury Road Interchange, Slip Roads) (Temporary Prohibition of Traffic) (No. 2) Order 2012 No. 2012/3263. - Enabling power: Road Traffic Regulation Act 1984, s. 14 (1) (a). - Issued: 14.01.2013. Made: 17.12.2012. Coming into force: 04.02.2013. Effect: None. Territorial extent & classification: E. Local. - Available at http://www.legislation.gov.uk/uksi/2012/3263/contents/made *Non-print*

The A21 Trunk Road (Morley's Interchange - Pembury Road Interchange, Slip Roads) (Temporary Prohibition of Traffic) Order 2012 No. 2012/134. - Enabling power: Road Traffic Regulation Act 1984, s. 14 (1) (a). - Issued: 24.01.2012. Made: 16.01.2012. Coming into force: 04.02.2012. Effect: None. Territorial extent & classification: E. Local. - Available at http://www.legislation.gov.uk/uksi/2012/134/contents/made *Non-print*

The A21 Trunk Road (Morley's Interchange - Vauxhall Lane Junction) (Temporary Restriction and Prohibition of Traffic) (No. 2) Order 2012 No. 2012/2161. - Enabling power: Road Traffic Regulation Act 1984, s. 14 (1) (a). - Issued: 23.08.2012. Made: 20.08.2012. Coming into force: 08.09.2012. Effect: None. Territorial extent & classification: E. Local. - Available at http://www.legislation.gov.uk/uksi/2012/2161/contents/made *Non-print*

The A21 Trunk Road (Morley's Interchange - Vauxhall Lane Junction) (Temporary Restriction and Prohibition of Traffic) Order 2012 No. 2012/95. - Enabling power: Road Traffic Regulation Act 1984, s. 14 (1) (a). - Issued: 19.01.2012. Made: 09.01.2012. Coming into force: 28.01.2012. Effect: None. Territorial extent & classification: E. Local. - Available at http://www.legislation.gov.uk/uksi/2012/95/contents/made *Non-print*

The A21 Trunk Road (Morley's Interchange - Westerham Road Overbridge) (Temporary Restriction and Prohibition of Traffic) Order 2012 No. 2012/410. - Enabling power: Road Traffic Regulation Act 1984, s. 14 (1) (a). - Issued: 21.02.2012. Made: 13.02.2012. Coming into force: 01.03.2012. Effect: None. Territorial extent & classification: E. Local. - Available at http://www.legislation.gov.uk/uksi/2012/410/contents/made *Non-print*

The A21 Trunk Road (Northbridge Street Roundabout) (Temporary Prohibition of Traffic) Order 2012 No. 2012/2650. - Enabling power: Road Traffic Regulation Act 1984, s. 16A (2) (a). - Issued: 25.10.2012. Made: 15.10.2012. Coming into force: 03.11.2012. Effect: None. Territorial extent & classification: E. Local. - Available at http://www.legislation.gov.uk/uksi/2012/2650/contents/made *Non-print*

The A21 Trunk Road (Quarry Hill Interchange - Longfield Roundabout) (Temporary Restriction and Prohibition of Traffic) Order 2012 No. 2012/3239. - Enabling power: Road Traffic Regulation Act 1984, s. 14 (1) (a). - Issued: 08.01.2013. Made: 17.12.2012. Coming into force: 26.01.2013. Effect: None. Territorial extent & classification: E. Local. - Available at http://www.legislation.gov.uk/uksi/2012/3239/contents/made *Non-print*

Road traffic: Traffic regulation

The A21 Trunk Road (Riccards Lane and Stream Lane) (Temporary Restriction and Prohibition of Traffic) Order 2012 No. 2012/3247. - Enabling power: Road Traffic Regulation Act 1984, s. 14 (1) (a). - Issued: 08.01.2013. Made: 17.12.2012. Coming into force: 02.02.2013. Effect: None. Territorial extent & classification: E. Local. - Available at http://www.legislation.gov.uk/uksi/2012/3247/contents/made *Non-print*

The A21 Trunk Road (South of Flimwell) (Temporary Speed Restrictions) Order 2012 No. 2012/3207. - Enabling power: Road Traffic Regulation Act 1984, s. 14 (1) (a). - Issued: 02.01.2013. Made: 10.12.2012. Coming into force: 19.01.2013. Effect: None. Territorial extent & classification: E. Local. - Available at http://www.legislation.gov.uk/uksi/2012/3207/contents/made *Non-print*

The A21 Trunk Road (Tonbridge By-Pass, Stocks Green) (Temporary Restriction and Prohibition of Traffic) Order 2012 No. 2012/341. - Enabling power: Road Traffic Regulation Act 1984, s. 14 (1) (a). - Issued: 15.02.2012. Made: 06.02.2012. Coming into force: 25.02.2012. Effect: None. Territorial extent & classification: E. Local. - Available at http://www.legislation.gov.uk/uksi/2012/341/contents/made *Non-print*

The A23 Trunk Road (Albourne - Patcham Interchange) (Temporary Restriction and Prohibition of Traffic) Order 2012 No. 2012/1180. - Enabling power: Road Traffic Regulation Act 1984, s. 14 (1) (a). - Issued: 02.05.2012. Made: 23.04.2012. Coming into force: 12.05.2012. Effect: None. Territorial extent & classification: E. Local. - Available at http://www.legislation.gov.uk/uksi/2012/1180/contents/made *Non-print*

The A23 Trunk Road and the A27 Trunk Road (Patcham Junction, Link Roads) (Temporary Prohibition of Traffic) Order 2012 No. 2012/3187. - Enabling power: Road Traffic Regulation Act 1984, s. 14 (1) (a). - Issued: 02.01.2013. Made: 03.12.2012. Coming into force: 21.01.2013. Effect: None. Territorial extent & classification: E. Local. - Available at http://www.legislation.gov.uk/uksi/2012/3187/contents/made *Non-print*

The A23 Trunk Road and the M23 Motorway (Junctions 9 - 11, Slip Roads) (Temporary Prohibition of Traffic) Order 2012 No. 2012/3181. - Enabling power: Road Traffic Regulation Act 1984, s. 14 (1) (a). - Issued: 31.12.2012. Made: 03.12.2012. Coming into force: 28.01.2013. Effect: None. Territorial extent & classification: E. Local. - Available at http://www.legislation.gov.uk/uksi/2012/3181/contents/made *Non-print*

The A23 Trunk Road (Bolney Interchange - South of Albourne) (Temporary Restriction and Prohibition of Traffic) Order 2012 No. 2012/182. - Enabling power: Road Traffic Regulation Act 1984, s. 14 (1) (a). - Issued: 31.01.2012. Made: 23.01.2012. Coming into force: 11.02.2012. Effect: None. Territorial extent & classification: E. Local. - Available at http://www.legislation.gov.uk/uksi/2012/182/contents/made *Non-print*

The A23 Trunk Road (Dale Hill and Mill Road Roundabout) (Temporary Restriction and Prohibition of Traffic) Order 2012 No. 2012/200. - Enabling power: Road Traffic Regulation Act 1984, s. 14 (1) (a). - Issued: 01.02.2012. Made: 23.01.2012. Coming into force: 11.02.2012. Effect: None. Territorial extent & classification: E. Local. - Available at http://www.legislation.gov.uk/uksi/2012/200/contents/made *Non-print*

The A23 Trunk Road (Handcross - Warninglid) (Temporary Restriction and Prohibition of Traffic) Order 2012 No. 2012/1472. - Enabling power: Road Traffic Regulation Act 1984, s. 14 (1) (a). - Issued: 12.06.2012. Made: 28.05.2012. Coming into force: 16.06.2012. Effect: None. Territorial extent & classification: E. Local. - Available at http://www.legislation.gov.uk/uksi/2012/1472/contents/made *Non-print*

The A23 Trunk Road (Stalkers Copse - Patcham Interchange) (Temporary Restriction and Prohibition of Traffic) Order 2012 No. 2012/2518. - Enabling power: Road Traffic Regulation Act 1984, s. 14 (1) (a). - Issued: 08.10.2012. Made: 01.10.2012. Coming into force: 20.10.2012. Effect: None. Territorial extent & classification: E. Local. - Available at http://www.legislation.gov.uk/uksi/2012/2518/contents/made *Non-print*

The A23 Trunk Road (Warninglid Interchange - Hickstead Interchange, Slip Roads) (Temporary Prohibition of Traffic) Order 2012 No. 2012/3183. - Enabling power: Road Traffic Regulation Act 1984, s. 14 (1) (a). - Issued: 31.12.2012. Made: 03.12.2012. Coming into force: 21.01.2013. Effect: None. Territorial extent & classification: E. Local. - Available at http://www.legislation.gov.uk/uksi/2012/3183/contents/made *Non-print*

The A23 Trunk Road (Warninglid Junction - Pease Pottage Interchange) (Temporary Prohibition of Cyclists and Pedestrians) Order 2012 No. 2012/2360. - Enabling power: Road Traffic Regulation Act 1984, s. 14 (1) (b). - Issued: 17.09.2012. Made: 10.09.2012. Coming into force: 11.09.2012. Effect: None. Territorial extent & classification: E. Local. - Available at http://www.legislation.gov.uk/uksi/2012/2360/contents/made *Non-print*

Road traffic: Traffic regulation

The A24 and the A27 Trunk Roads (Goodwood Road, Hill Barn Lane and Broadwater Street West) (Temporary Prohibition of Traffic) Order 2012 No. 2012/319. - Enabling power: Road Traffic Regulation Act 1984, s. 14 (1) (a). - Issued: 15.02.2012. Made: 06.02.2012. Coming into force: 11.02.2012. Effect: None. Territorial extent & classification: E. Local. - Available at http://www.legislation.gov.uk/uksi/2012/319/contents/made *Non-print*

The A26 Trunk Road (Beddingham Roundabout - South of The Lay) (Temporary 40 Miles Per Hour Speed Restriction) Order 2012 No. 2012/2646. - Enabling power: Road Traffic Regulation Act 1984, s. 14 (1) (a). - Issued: 25.10.2012. Made: 15.10.2012. Coming into force: 03.11.2012. Effect: None. Territorial extent & classification: E. Local. - Available at http://www.legislation.gov.uk/uksi/2012/2646/contents/made *Non-print*

The A26 Trunk Road (New Road) (Temporary Speed Restriction) Order 2012 No. 2012/2508. - Enabling power: Road Traffic Regulation Act 1984, s. 14 (1) (a). - Issued: 05.10.2012. Made: 01.10.2012. Coming into force: 20.10.2012. Effect: None. Territorial extent & classification: E. Local. - Available at http://www.legislation.gov.uk/uksi/2012/2508/contents/made *Non-print*

The A26 Trunk Road (Southease - South Heighton) (Temporary Restriction and Prohibition of Traffic) Order 2012 No. 2012/2924. - Enabling power: Road Traffic Regulation Act 1984, s. 14 (1) (a). - Issued: 26.11.2012. Made: 12.11.2012. Coming into force: 01.12.2012. Effect: None. Territorial extent & classification: E. Local. - Available at http://www.legislation.gov.uk/uksi/2012/2924/contents/made *Non-print*

The A27 Trunk Road and the A23 Trunk Road (Patcham Interchange) (Temporary Restriction and Prohibition of Traffic) Order 2012 No. 2012/27. - Enabling power: Road Traffic Regulation Act 1984, s. 14 (1) (a). - Issued: 11.01.2012. Made: 03.01.2012. Coming into force: 14.01.2012. Effect: None. Territorial extent & classification: E. Local. - Available at http://www.legislation.gov.uk/uksi/2012/27/contents/made *Non-print*

The A27 Trunk Road and the M27, M275 and A3(M) Motorways (M27 Junction 12-Langstone Interchange) (Temporary Restriction and Prohibition of Traffic) (Amendment) Order 2012 No. 2012/2916. - Enabling power: Road Traffic Regulation Act 1984, s. 14 (1) (a). - Issued: 23.11.2012. Made: 09.11.2012. Coming into force: 12.11.2012. Effect: S.I. 2012/2779 amended. Territorial extent & classification: E. Local. - Available at http://www.legislation.gov.uk/uksi/2012/2916/contents/made *Non-print*

The A27 Trunk Road and the M27, M275 and A3(M) Motorways (M27 Junction 12 - Langstone Interchange) (Temporary Restriction and Prohibition of Traffic) Order 2012 No. 2012/2779. - Enabling power: Road Traffic Regulation Act 1984, s. 14 (1) (a). - Issued: 08.11.2012. Made: 22.10.2012. Coming into force: 10.11.2012. Effect: None. Territorial extent & classification: E. Local. - Available at http://www.legislation.gov.uk/uksi/2012/2779/contents/made *Non-print*

The A27 Trunk Road and the M27 Motorway (Eastern Road Interchange - M27 Junction 12, Westbound) (Temporary Prohibition of Traffic) Order 2012 No. 2012/494. - Enabling power: Road Traffic Regulation Act 1984, s. 14 (1) (a). - Issued: 01.03.2012. Made: 20.02.2012. Coming into force: 10.03.2012. Effect: None. Territorial extent & classification: E. Local. - Available at http://www.legislation.gov.uk/uksi/2012/494/contents/made *Non-print*

The A27 Trunk Road (Arundel Road, Worthing) (Temporary Restriction and Prohibition of Traffic) Order 2012 No. 2012/3243. - Enabling power: Road Traffic Regulation Act 1984, s. 14 (1) (a). - Issued: 08.01.2013. Made: 17.12.2012. Coming into force: 26.01.2013. Effect: None. Territorial extent & classification: E. Local. - Available at http://www.legislation.gov.uk/uksi/2012/3243/contents/made *Non-print*

The A27 Trunk Road (Ashcombe Roundabout - Beddingham Roundabout) (Temporary Restriction and Prohibition of Traffic) Order 2012 No. 2012/1183. - Enabling power: Road Traffic Regulation Act 1984, s. 14 (1) (a). - Issued: 02.05.2012. Made: 23.04.2012. Coming into force: 12.05.2012. Effect: None. Territorial extent & classification: E. Local. - Available at http://www.legislation.gov.uk/uksi/2012/1183/contents/made *Non-print*

The A27 Trunk Road (Clapham - Broadwater) (Temporary Speed Restriction) Order 2012 No. 2012/3252. - Enabling power: Road Traffic Regulation Act 1984, s. 14 (1) (a). - Issued: 09.01.2013. Made: 17.12.2012. Coming into force: 05.01.2013. Effect: None. Territorial extent & classification: E. Local. - Available at http://www.legislation.gov.uk/uksi/2012/3252/contents/made *Non-print*

The A27 Trunk Road (Cop Hall Roundabout, Dedicated Link Road) (Temporary Prohibition of Traffic) Order 2012 No. 2012/3212. - Enabling power: Road Traffic Regulation Act 1984, s. 14 (1) (a). - Issued: 04.01.2013. Made: 10.12.2012. Coming into force: 28.01.2013. Effect: None. Territorial extent & classification: E. Local. - Available at http://www.legislation.gov.uk/uksi/2012/3212/contents/made *Non-print*

Road traffic: Traffic regulation

The A27 Trunk Road (Crossbush Interchange) (Temporary Restriction and Prohibition of Traffic) Order 2012 No. 2012/437. - Enabling power: Road Traffic Regulation Act 1984, s. 14 (1) (a). - Issued: 22.02.2012. Made: 13.02.2012. Coming into force: 03.03.2012. Effect: None. Territorial extent & classification: E. Local. - Available at http://www.legislation.gov.uk/uksi/2012/437/contents/made *Non-print*

The A27 Trunk Road (Crossbush Interchange - Worthing) (Temporary Restriction and Prohibition of Traffic) Order 2012 No. 2012/2357. - Enabling power: Road Traffic Regulation Act 1984, s. 14 (1) (a). - Issued: 17.09.2012. Made: 10.09.2012. Coming into force: 29.09.2012. Effect: None. Territorial extent & classification: E. Local. - Available at http://www.legislation.gov.uk/uksi/2012/2357/contents/made *Non-print*

The A27 Trunk Road (Drusilla's Roundabout) (Temporary Restriction and Prohibition of Traffic) Order 2012 No. 2012/3257. - Enabling power: Road Traffic Regulation Act 1984, s. 14 (1) (a). - Issued: 09.01.2013. Made: 17.12.2012. Coming into force: 26.01.2013. Effect: None. Territorial extent & classification: E. Local. - Available at http://www.legislation.gov.uk/uksi/2012/3257/contents/made *Non-print*

The A27 Trunk Road (Eastern Road Interchange - Warblington Interchange) (Temporary Speed Restrictions) Order 2012 No. 2012/3147. - Enabling power: Road Traffic Regulation Act 1984, s. 14 (1) (a). - Issued: 27.12.2012. Made: 26.11.2012. Coming into force: 15.12.2012. Effect: None. Territorial extent & classification: E. Local. - Available at http://www.legislation.gov.uk/uksi/2012/3147/contents/made *Non-print*

The A27 Trunk Road (East of Grove Lodge Roundabout - East of Adur Interchange) (Temporary Restriction and Prohibition of Traffic) Order 2012 No. 2012/2237. - Enabling power: Road Traffic Regulation Act 1984, s. 14 (1) (a). - Issued: 04.09.2012. Made: 28.08.2012. Coming into force: 15.09.2012. Effect: None. Territorial extent & classification: E. Local. - Available at http://www.legislation.gov.uk/uksi/2012/2237/contents/made *Non-print*

The A27 Trunk Road (East of Thornwell Road - East of Berwick Roundabout) (Temporary Restriction and Prohibition of Traffic) Order 2012 No. 2012/294. - Enabling power: Road Traffic Regulation Act 1984, s. 14 (1) (a). - Issued: 10.02.2012. Made: 30.01.2012. Coming into force: 18.02.2012. Effect: None. Territorial extent & classification: E. Local. - Available at http://www.legislation.gov.uk/uksi/2012/294/contents/made *Non-print*

The A27 Trunk Road (Falmer Interchange, Eastbound) (Temporary Prohibition of Traffic) Order 2012 No. 2012/3216. - Enabling power: Road Traffic Regulation Act 1984, s. 14 (1) (a). - Issued: 04.01.2013. Made: 10.12.2012. Coming into force: 05.01.2013. Effect: None. Territorial extent & classification: E. Local. - Available at http://www.legislation.gov.uk/uksi/2012/3216/contents/made *Non-print*

The A27 Trunk Road (Falmer Interchange - West of Southwick Tunnel) (Temporary Restriction and Prohibition of Traffic) Order 2012 No. 2012/2364. - Enabling power: Road Traffic Regulation Act 1984, s. 14 (1) (a). - Issued: 17.09.2012. Made: 10.09.2012. Coming into force: 29.09.2012. Effect: None. Territorial extent & classification: E. Local. - Available at http://www.legislation.gov.uk/uksi/2012/2364/contents/made *Non-print*

The A27 Trunk Road (Fishbourne Roundabout - Portfield Roundabout) (Temporary Restriction and Prohibition of Traffic) Order 2012 No. 2012/2859. - Enabling power: Road Traffic Regulation Act 1984, s. 14 (1) (a). - Issued: 16.11.2012. Made: 05.11.2012. Coming into force: 24.11.2012. Effect: None. Territorial extent & classification: E. Local. - Available at http://www.legislation.gov.uk/uksi/2012/2859/contents/made *Non-print*

The A27 Trunk Road (Hangleton Interchange and Carden Avenue, Slip Roads) (Temporary Prohibition of Traffic) Order 2012 No. 2012/2502. - Enabling power: Road Traffic Regulation Act 1984, s. 14 (1) (a). - Issued: 05.10.2012. Made: 01.10.2012. Coming into force: 20.10.2012. Effect: None. Territorial extent & classification: E. Local. - Available at http://www.legislation.gov.uk/uksi/2012/2502/contents/made *Non-print*

The A27 Trunk Road (Hilsea, Eastbound Entry Slip Road) (Temporary Prohibition of Traffic) Order 2012 No. 2012/1407. - Enabling power: Road Traffic Regulation Act 1984, s. 14 (1) (a). - Issued: 01.06.2012. Made: 21.05.2012. Coming into force: 09.06.2012. Effect: None. Territorial extent & classification: E. Local. - Available at http://www.legislation.gov.uk/uksi/2012/1407/contents/made *Non-print*

The A27 Trunk Road (Holmbush Interchange to Hangleton) (Temporary Prohibition of Traffic) Order 2012 No. 2012/732. - Enabling power: Road Traffic Regulation Act 1984, s. 14 (1) (a). - Issued: 19.03.2012. Made: 05.03.2012. Coming into force: 01.04.2012. Effect: None. Territorial extent & classification: E. Local. - Available at http://www.legislation.gov.uk/uksi/2012/732/contents/made *Non-print*

Road traffic: Traffic regulation

The A27 Trunk Road (Langstone Interchange, Slip Roads) (Temporary Prohibition of Traffic) Order 2012 No. 2012/2778. - Enabling power: Road Traffic Regulation Act 1984, s. 14 (1) (a). - Issued: 08.11.2012. Made: 22.10.2012. Coming into force: 15.11.2012. Effect: None. Territorial extent & classification: E. Local. - Available at http://www.legislation.gov.uk/uksi/2012/2778/contents/made *Non-print*

The A27 Trunk Road (Lewes Road, Near Eastbourne) (Temporary Speed Restrictions) Order 2012 No. 2012/164. - Enabling power: Road Traffic Regulation Act 1984, s. 14 (1) (a). - Issued: 30.01.2012. Made: 16.01.2012. Coming into force: 04.02.2012. Effect: None. Territorial extent & classification: E. Local. - Available at http://www.legislation.gov.uk/uksi/2012/164/contents/made *Non-print*

The A27 Trunk Road (Old Shoreham Road and Shoreham Bypass) (Temporary Restriction and Prohibition of Traffic) Order 2012 No. 2012/2101. - Enabling power: Road Traffic Regulation Act 1984, s. 14 (1) (b). - Issued: 16.08.2012. Made: 06.08.2012. Coming into force: 25.08.2012. Effect: None. Territorial extent & classification: E. Local. - Available at http://www.legislation.gov.uk/uksi/2012/2101/contents/made *Non-print*

The A27 Trunk Road (Oving Road) (Temporary Prohibition of Traffic) Order 2012 No. 2012/894. - Enabling power: Road Traffic Regulation Act 1984, s. 14 (1) (a). - Issued: 26.03.2012. Made: 19.03.2012. Coming into force: 07.04.2012. Effect: None. Territorial extent & classification: E. Local. - Available at http://www.legislation.gov.uk/uksi/2012/894/contents/made *Non-print*

The A27 Trunk Road (Polegate - Pevensey Roundabout) (Temporary Restriction and Prohibition of Traffic) Order 2012 No. 2012/3205. - Enabling power: Road Traffic Regulation Act 1984, s. 14 (1) (a). - Issued: 02.01.2013. Made: 10.12.2012. Coming into force: 26.01.2013. Effect: None. Territorial extent & classification: E. Local. - Available at http://www.legislation.gov.uk/uksi/2012/3205/contents/made *Non-print*

The A27 Trunk Road (Polegate - Wilmington) (Temporary Speed Restrictions) Order 2012 No. 2012/1527. - Enabling power: Road Traffic Regulation Act 1984, s. 14 (1) (a). - Issued: 19.06.2012. Made: 06.06.2012. Coming into force: 23.06.2012. Effect: None. Territorial extent & classification: E. Local. - Available at http://www.legislation.gov.uk/uksi/2012/1527/contents/made *Non-print*

The A27 Trunk Road (Portfield Roundabout - Ford Roundabout) (Temporary Restriction and Prohibition of Traffic) Order 2012 No. 2012/3266. - Enabling power: Road Traffic Regulation Act 1984, s. 14 (1) (a). - Issued: 14.01.2013. Made: 17.12.2012. Coming into force: 19.01.2013. Effect: None. Territorial extent & classification: E. Local. - Available at http://www.legislation.gov.uk/uksi/2012/3266/contents/made *Non-print*

The A27 Trunk Road (Ripe Lane - The Street) (Temporary Prohibition of Traffic) (No. 2) Order 2012 No. 2012/3253. - Enabling power: Road Traffic Regulation Act 1984, s. 14 (1) (a), sch. 9, para. 27 (1). - Issued: 09.01.2013. Made: 17.12.2012. Coming into force: 19.01.2013. Effect: S.I. 2012/2439 revoked. Territorial extent & classification: E. Local. - Available at http://www.legislation.gov.uk/uksi/2012/3253/contents/made *Non-print*

The A27 Trunk Road (Ripe Lane - The Street) (Temporary Prohibition of Traffic) Order 2012 No. 2012/2439. - Enabling power: Road Traffic Regulation Act 1984, s. 14 (1) (a). - Issued: 27.09.2012. Made: 17.09.2012. Coming into force: 06.10.2012. Effect: None. Territorial extent & classification: E. Local. - Revoked by S.I. 2012/3253 (Non-print). - Available at http://www.legislation.gov.uk/uksi/2012/2439/contents/made *Non-print*

The A27 Trunk Road (Selmeston - Berwick) (Temporary Restriction and Prohibition of Traffic) Order 2012 No. 2012/2526. - Enabling power: Road Traffic Regulation Act 1984, s. 14 (1) (a). - Issued: 10.10.2012. Made: 01.10.2012. Coming into force: 20.10.2012. Effect: None. Territorial extent & classification: E. Local. - Available at http://www.legislation.gov.uk/uksi/2012/2526/contents/made *Non-print*

The A27 Trunk Road (Selmeston - Firle) (Temporary Restriction and Prohibition of Traffic) Order 2011 Variation Order 2012 No. 2012/26. - Enabling power: Road Traffic Regulation Act 1984, s. 14 (1) (a), sch. 9, para. 27 (1). - Issued: 11.01.2012. Made: 03.01.2012. Coming into force: 14.01.2012. Effect: S.I. 2011/2771 varied. Territorial extent & classification: E. Local. - Available at http://www.legislation.gov.uk/uksi/2012/26/contents/made *Non-print*

The A27 Trunk Road (Stockbridge Roundabout - Nyton Road) (Temporary Restriction and Prohibition of Traffic) Order 2012 No. 2012/1041. - Enabling power: Road Traffic Regulation Act 1984, s. 14 (1) (a). - Issued: 12.04.2012. Made: 26.03.2012. Coming into force: 14.04.2012. Effect: None. Territorial extent & classification: E. Local. - Available at http://www.legislation.gov.uk/uksi/2012/1041/contents/made *Non-print*

The A27 Trunk Road (Tear Drop Roundabout, Eastbound Entry Slip Road) (Temporary Prohibition of Traffic) Order 2012 No. 2012/1551. - Enabling power: Road Traffic Regulation Act 1984, s. 14 (1) (a). - Issued: 20.06.2012. Made: 06.06.2012. Coming into force: 23.06.2012. Effect: None. Territorial extent & classification: E. Local. - Available at http://www.legislation.gov.uk/uksi/2012/1551/contents/made *Non-print*

The A27 Trunk Road (Upper Brighton Road, Lancing) (Temporary Restriction and Prohibition of Traffic) Order 2012 No. 2012/271. - Enabling power: Road Traffic Regulation Act 1984, s. 14 (1) (a). - Issued: 10.02.2012. Made: 30.01.2012. Coming into force: 18.02.2012. Effect: None. Territorial extent & classification: E. Local. - Available at http://www.legislation.gov.uk/uksi/2012/271/contents/made *Non-print*

The A27 Trunk Road (Upper Brighton Road, Worthing) (Temporary Restriction and Prohibition of Traffic) Order 2012 No. 2012/2835. - Enabling power: Road Traffic Regulation Act 1984, s. 14 (1) (a). - Issued: 15.11.2012. Made: 22.10.2012. Coming into force: 10.11.2012. Effect: None. Territorial extent & classification: E. Local. - Available at http://www.legislation.gov.uk/uksi/2012/2835/contents/made *Non-print*

The A27 Trunk Road (Warblington Interchange - Broad Marsh/Bedhampton Interchange, Carriageways) (Temporary Speed Restrictions) Order 2012 No. 2012/723. - Enabling power: Road Traffic Regulation Act 1984, s. 14 (1) (a). - Issued: 19.03.2012. Made: 05.03.2012. Coming into force: 24.03.2012. Effect: None. Territorial extent & classification: E. Local. - Available at http://www.legislation.gov.uk/uksi/2012/723/contents/made *Non-print*

The A27 Trunk Road (Warblington Interchange - Falmer Interchange, Slip Roads) (Temporary Prohibition of Traffic) Order 2012 No. 2012/3182. - Enabling power: Road Traffic Regulation Act 1984, s. 14 (1) (a). - Issued: 31.12.2012. Made: 03.12.2012. Coming into force: 28.01.2013. Effect: None. Territorial extent & classification: E. Local. - Available at http://www.legislation.gov.uk/uksi/2012/3182/contents/made *Non-print*

The A27 Trunk Road (Warblington Interchange - Fishbourne Roundabout) (Temporary Prohibition of Traffic) Order 2012 No. 2012/606. - Enabling power: Road Traffic Regulation Act 1984, s. 14 (1) (a). - Issued: 06.03.2012. Made: 27.02.2012. Coming into force: 17.03.2012. Effect: None. Territorial extent & classification: E. Local. - Available at http://www.legislation.gov.uk/uksi/2012/606/contents/made *Non-print*

The A27 Trunk Road (West of Ford Road Roundabout) (Temporary Prohibition of Traffic) Order 2012 No. 2012/3222. - Enabling power: Road Traffic Regulation Act 1984, s. 14 (1) (a). - Issued: 07.01.2013. Made: 10.12.2012. Coming into force: 05.01.2013. Effect: None. Territorial extent & classification: E. Local. - Available at http://www.legislation.gov.uk/uksi/2012/3222/contents/made *Non-print*

The A27 Trunk Road (West of Glynde Junction - East of Lower Tilton Farm) (Temporary Restriction and Prohibition of Traffic) Order 2012 No. 2012/413. - Enabling power: Road Traffic Regulation Act 1984, s. 14 (1) (a). - Issued: 21.02.2012. Made: 13.02.2012. Coming into force: 03.03.2012. Effect: None. Territorial extent & classification: E. Local. - Available at http://www.legislation.gov.uk/uksi/2012/413/contents/made *Non-print*

The A30 Trunk Road & A38 Trunk Road (Various Laybys) (Temporary Prohibition of Traffic) Order 2012 No. 2012/2931. - Enabling power: Road Traffic Regulation Act 1984, s. 14 (1) (a). - Issued: 26.11.2012. Made: 14.11.2012. Coming into force: 17.11.2012. Effect: None. Territorial extent & classification: E. Local. - Available at http://www.legislation.gov.uk/uksi/2012/2931/contents/made *Non-print*

The A30 Trunk Road (Avers Junction, Redruth, and Treswithian Junction, Camborne) (Temporary Restriction and Prohibition of Traffic) Order 2012 No. 2012/3270. - Enabling power: Road Traffic Regulation Act 1984, s. 14 (1) (a). - Issued: 14.01.2013. Made: 21.12.2012. Coming into force: 29.12.2012. Effect: None. Territorial extent & classification: E. Local. - Available at http://www.legislation.gov.uk/uksi/2012/3270/contents/made *Non-print*

The A30 Trunk Road (Avers Roundabout to Scorrier Interchange, Redruth, Cornwall) (Temporary Prohibition and Restriction of Traffic) Order 2012 No. 2012/175. - Enabling power: Road Traffic Regulation Act 1984, s. 14 (1) (a). - Issued: 31.01.2012. Made: 19.01.2012. Coming into force: 28.01.2012. Effect: None. Territorial extent & classification: E. Local. - Available at http://www.legislation.gov.uk/uksi/2012/175/contents/made *Non-print*

The A30 Trunk Road (Bodmin Bypass) (Temporary Restriction of Traffic) Order 2012 No. 2012/2078. - Enabling power: Road Traffic Regulation Act 1984, s. 14 (1) (a). - Issued: 13.08.2012. Made: 01.08.2012. Coming into force: 04.08.2012. Effect: None. Territorial extent & classification: E. Local. - Available at http://www.legislation.gov.uk/uksi/2012/2078/contents/made *Non-print*

The A30 Trunk Road (Bolventor to Temple, Near Bodmin) (Temporary Restriction and Prohibition of Traffic) Order 2012 No. 2012/2450. - Enabling power: Road Traffic Regulation Act 1984, s. 14 (1) (a). - Issued: 27.09.2012. Made: 19.09.2012. Coming into force: 22.09.2012. Effect: None. Territorial extent & classification: E. Local. - Available at http://www.legislation.gov.uk/uksi/2012/2450/contents/made *Non-print*

Road traffic: Traffic regulation

The A30 Trunk Road (Carland Cross to Chiverton Cross, Cornwall) (Temporary Prohibition of Traffic) Order 2012 No. 2012/544. - Enabling power: Road Traffic Regulation Act 1984, s. 14 (1) (a). - Issued: 01.03.2012. Made: 22.02.2012. Coming into force: 25.02.2012. Effect: None. Territorial extent & classification: E. Local. - Available at http://www.legislation.gov.uk/uksi/2012/544/contents/made *Non-print*

The A30 Trunk Road (Chiverton Cross to Carland Cross, Cornwall) (Temporary Restriction and Prohibition of Traffic) Order 2012 No. 2012/2620. - Enabling power: Road Traffic Regulation Act 1984, s. 14 (1) (a). - Issued: 22.10.2012. Made: 09.10.2012. Coming into force: 13.10.2012. Effect: None. Territorial extent & classification: E. Local. - Available at http://www.legislation.gov.uk/uksi/2012/2620/contents/made *Non-print*

The A30 Trunk Road (Crooked Billet - Greater London Boundary) (Temporary Prohibition of Traffic) Order 2012 No. 2012/1549. - Enabling power: Road Traffic Regulation Act 1984, s. 14 (1) (a). - Issued: 20.06.2012. Made: 06.06.2012. Coming into force: 23.06.2012. Effect: None. Territorial extent & classification: E. Local. - Available at http://www.legislation.gov.uk/uksi/2012/1549/contents/made *Non-print*

The A30 Trunk Road (Daisymount Junction to Moor Lane Roundabout, Exeter) (Temporary Prohibition of Traffic) Order 2012 No. 2012/1012. - Enabling power: Road Traffic Regulation Act 1984, s. 14 (1) (a). - Issued: 12.04.2012. Made: 27.03.2012. Coming into force: 31.03.2012. Effect: None. Territorial extent & classification: E. Local. - Available at http://www.legislation.gov.uk/uksi/2012/1012/contents/made *Non-print*

The A30 Trunk Road (Fingle Glen Junction, Devon) (Temporary Prohibition of Traffic) Order 2012 No. 2012/419. - Enabling power: Road Traffic Regulation Act 1984, s. 14 (1) (a). - Issued: 22.02.2012. Made: 14.02.2012. Coming into force: 18.02.2012. Effect: None. Territorial extent & classification: E. Local. - Available at http://www.legislation.gov.uk/uksi/2012/419/contents/made *Non-print*

The A30 Trunk Road (Five Lanes Junction to Kennards House Junction, Near Launceston) (Temporary Restriction and Prohibition of Traffic) Order 2012 No. 2012/2342. - Enabling power: Road Traffic Regulation Act 1984, s. 14 (1) (a). - Issued: 14.09.2012. Made: 05.09.2012. Coming into force: 14.09.2012. Effect: None. Territorial extent & classification: E. Local. - Available at http://www.legislation.gov.uk/uksi/2012/2342/contents/made *Non-print*

The A30 Trunk Road (Highgate Junction to Carland Cross, Cornwall) (Temporary Restriction and Prohibition of Traffic) Order 2012 No. 2012/2120. - Enabling power: Road Traffic Regulation Act 1984, s. 14 (1) (a). - Issued: 17.08.2012. Made: 08.08.2012. Coming into force: 11.08.2012. Effect: None. Territorial extent & classification: E. Local. - Available at http://www.legislation.gov.uk/uksi/2012/2120/contents/made *Non-print*

The A30 Trunk Road (Honiton to Daisymount Junction) (Temporary Prohibition of Traffic) Order 2012 No. 2012/1090. - Enabling power: Road Traffic Regulation Act 1984, s. 14 (1) (a). - Issued: 19.04.2012. Made: 10.04.2012. Coming into force: 13.04.2012. Effect: None. Territorial extent & classification: E. Local. - Available at http://www.legislation.gov.uk/uksi/2012/1090/contents/made *Non-print*

The A30 Trunk Road (Innis Downs to Indian Queens, Cornwall) (24 Hour Clearway) Order 2012 No. 2012/1705. - Enabling power: Road Traffic Regulation Act 1984, ss. 1 (1), 2 (1) (2), 3 (2), 4 (1). - Issued: 12.07.2012. Made: 19.06.2012. Coming into force: 02.07.2012. Effect: None. Territorial extent & classification: E. Local. - Available at http://www.legislation.gov.uk/uksi/2012/1705/contents/made *Non-print*

The A30 Trunk Road (Innis Downs to Pounds Conce, Near Bodmin) (Temporary Restriction and Prohibition of Traffic) Order 2012 No. 2012/2286. - Enabling power: Road Traffic Regulation Act 1984, s. 14 (1) (a). - Issued: 10.09.2012. Made: 29.08.2012. Coming into force: 08.09.2012. Effect: None. Territorial extent & classification: E. Local. - Available at http://www.legislation.gov.uk/uksi/2012/2286/contents/made *Non-print*

The A30 Trunk Road (Launceston to Okehampton) (Temporary Prohibition of Traffic) Order 2012 No. 2012/832. - Enabling power: Road Traffic Regulation Act 1984, s. 14 (1) (a). - Issued: 20.03.2012. Made: 13.03.2012. Coming into force: 17.03.2012. Effect: None. Territorial extent & classification: E. Local. - Available at http://www.legislation.gov.uk/uksi/2012/832/contents/made *Non-print*

The A30 Trunk Road (Liftondown to Launceston, Cornwall) (Temporary Restriction and Prohibition of Traffic) Order 2012 No. 2012/2426. - Enabling power: Road Traffic Regulation Act 1984, s. 14 (1) (a). - Issued: 25.09.2012. Made: 12.09.2012. Coming into force: 21.09.2012. Effect: None. Territorial extent & classification: E. Local. - Available at http://www.legislation.gov.uk/uksi/2012/2426/contents/made *Non-print*

The A30 Trunk Road (Llongrock to Redruth, Cornwall) (Temporary Restriction and Prohibition of Traffic) Order 2012 No. 2012/2035. - Enabling power: Road Traffic Regulation Act 1984, s. 14 (1) (a). - Issued: 07.08.2012. Made: 24.07.2012. Coming into force: 28.07.2012. Effect: None. Territorial extent & classification: E. Local. - Available at http://www.legislation.gov.uk/uksi/2012/2035/contents/made *Non-print*

The A30 Trunk Road (M5 Junction 29 Interchange) (Temporary Restriction of Traffic) Order 2012 No. 2012/3157. - Enabling power: Road Traffic Regulation Act 1984, s. 14 (1) (b). - Issued: 28.12.2012. Made: 28.11.2012. Coming into force: 01.12.2012. Effect: None. Territorial extent & classification: E. Local. - Available at http://www.legislation.gov.uk/uksi/2012/3157/contents/made *Non-print*

The A30 Trunk Road (M25 Junction 13, Link Road) (Temporary Prohibition of Traffic) Order 2012 No. 2012/830. - Enabling power: Road Traffic Regulation Act 1984, s. 14 (1) (a). - Issued: 20.03.2012. Made: 12.03.2012. Coming into force: 02.04.2012. Effect: None. Territorial extent & classification: E. Local. - Available at http://www.legislation.gov.uk/uksi/2012/830/contents/made *Non-print*

The A30 Trunk Road (Okehampton Laybys) (Temporary Prohibition of Traffic) Order 2012 No. 2012/2202. - Enabling power: Road Traffic Regulation Act 1984, s. 14 (1) (a). - Issued: 30.08.2012. Made: 23.08.2012. Coming into force: 31.08.2012. Effect: None. Territorial extent & classification: E. Local. - Available at http://www.legislation.gov.uk/uksi/2012/2202/contents/made *Non-print*

The A30 Trunk Road (Okehampton) (Temporary Prohibition of Traffic) Order 2012 No. 2012/28. - Enabling power: Road Traffic Regulation Act 1984, s. 14 (1) (a). - Issued: 11.01.2012. Made: 03.01.2012. Coming into force: 11.01.2012. Effect: None. Territorial extent & classification: E. Local. - Available at http://www.legislation.gov.uk/uksi/2012/28/contents/made *Non-print*

The A30 Trunk Road (Okehampton to Launceston) (Temporary Restriction and Prohibition of Traffic) (Number 2) Order 2012 No. 2012/2580. - Enabling power: Road Traffic Regulation Act 1984, s. 14 (1) (a). - Issued: 16.10.2012. Made: 05.10.2012. Coming into force: 12.10.2012. Effect: None. Territorial extent & classification: E. Local. - Available at http://www.legislation.gov.uk/uksi/2012/2580/contents/made *Non-print*

The A30 Trunk Road (Okehampton to Launceston) (Temporary Restriction and Prohibition of Traffic) Order 2012 No. 2012/543. - Enabling power: Road Traffic Regulation Act 1984, s. 14 (1) (a). - Issued: 01.03.2012. Made: 22.02.2012. Coming into force: 02.03.2012. Effect: None. Territorial extent & classification: E. Local. - Available at http://www.legislation.gov.uk/uksi/2012/543/contents/made *Non-print*

The A30 Trunk Road (Penzance to Bodmin) (Temporary Prohibition of Traffic) Order 2012 No. 2012/442. - Enabling power: Road Traffic Regulation Act 1984, s. 14 (1) (a). - Issued: 24.02.2012. Made: 15.02.2012. Coming into force: 18.02.2012. Effect: None. Territorial extent & classification: E. Local. - Available at http://www.legislation.gov.uk/uksi/2012/442/contents/made *Non-print*

The A30 Trunk Road (Scorrier Junction, Redruth) (Temporary Restriction and Prohibition of Traffic) Order 2012 No. 2012/3269. - Enabling power: Road Traffic Regulation Act 1984, s. 14 (1) (a). - Issued: 14.01.2013. Made: 19.12.2012. Coming into force: 31.12.2012. Effect: None. Territorial extent & classification: E. Local. - Available at http://www.legislation.gov.uk/uksi/2012/3269/contents/made *Non-print*

The A30 Trunk Road (Sourton Cross Junction, Near Okehampton) (Temporary Prohibition of Traffic) Order 2012 No. 2012/2332. - Enabling power: Road Traffic Regulation Act 1984, s. 14 (1) (b). - Issued: 13.09.2012. Made: 03.09.2012. Coming into force: 13.09.2012. Effect: None. Territorial extent & classification: E. Local. - Available at http://www.legislation.gov.uk/uksi/2012/2332/contents/made *Non-print*

The A30 Trunk Road (Sourton Cross to Okehampton) (Temporary Restriction and Prohibition of Traffic) Order 2012 No. 2012/3274. - Enabling power: Road Traffic Regulation Act 1984, s. 14 (1) (a). - Issued: 14.01.2013. Made: 21.12.2012. Coming into force: 31.12.2012. Effect: None. Territorial extent & classification: E. Local. - Available at http://www.legislation.gov.uk/uksi/2012/3274/contents/made *Non-print*

The A30 Trunk Road (Staines By-Pass, Lay-By) (Temporary Prohibition of Traffic) Order 2012 No. 2012/3255. - Enabling power: Road Traffic Regulation Act 1984, s. 14 (1) (a). - Issued: 09.01.2013. Made: 17.12.2012. Coming into force: 26.01.2013. Effect: None. Territorial extent & classification: E. Local. - Available at http://www.legislation.gov.uk/uksi/2012/3255/contents/made *Non-print*

The A30 Trunk Road (Tedburn St Mary to Whiddon Down, Devon) (Temporary Restriction and Prohibition of Traffic) Order 2012 No. 2012/2836. - Enabling power: Road Traffic Regulation Act 1984, s. 14 (1) (a). - Issued: 15.11.2012. Made: 31.10.2012. Coming into force: 03.11.2012. Effect: None. Territorial extent & classification: E. Local. - Available at http://www.legislation.gov.uk/uksi/2012/2836/contents/made *Non-print*

The A30 Trunk Road (Temple, Near Bodmin) (Temporary Restriction and Prohibition of Traffic) Order 2012 No. 2012/1800. - Enabling power: Road Traffic Regulation Act 1984, s. 14 (1) (a). - Issued: 19.07.2012. Made: 03.07.2012. Coming into force: 11.07.2012. Effect: None. Territorial extent & classification: E. Local. - Available at http://www.legislation.gov.uk/uksi/2012/1800/contents/made *Non-print*

The A30 Trunk Road (Treswithian Westbound Entry Slip Road, Camborne) (Temporary Restriction and Prohibition of Traffic) Order 2012 No. 2012/418. - Enabling power: Road Traffic Regulation Act 1984, s. 14 (1) (a). - Issued: 22.02.2012. Made: 14.02.2012. Coming into force: 18.02.2012. Effect: None. Territorial extent & classification: E. Local. - Available at http://www.legislation.gov.uk/uksi/2012/418/contents/made *Non-print*

The A30 Trunk Road (Upottery to Monkton, Near Honiton) (Temporary Prohibition of Traffic) Order 2012 No. 2012/225. - Enabling power: Road Traffic Regulation Act 1984, s. 14 (1) (a). - Issued: 03.02.2012. Made: 24.01.2012. Coming into force: 30.01.2012. Effect: None. Territorial extent & classification: E. Local. - Available at http://www.legislation.gov.uk/uksi/2012/225/contents/made *Non-print*

The A30 Trunk Road (Whiddon Down Junction, Devon) (Temporary Prohibition of Traffic) Order 2012 No. 2012/2529. - Enabling power: Road Traffic Regulation Act 1984, s. 14 (1) (a). - Issued: 09.10.2012. Made: 03.10.2012. Coming into force: 06.10.2012. Effect: None. Territorial extent & classification: E. Local. - Available at http://www.legislation.gov.uk/uksi/2012/2529/contents/made *Non-print*

The A31 Trunk Road (Bere Regis Roundabout - Roundhouse Roundabout) (Temporary Prohibition of Traffic) Order 2012 No. 2012/2233. - Enabling power: Road Traffic Regulation Act 1984, s. 14 (1) (a). - Issued: 04.09.2012. Made: 28.08.2012. Coming into force: 15.09.2012. Effect: None. Territorial extent & classification: E. Local. - Available at http://www.legislation.gov.uk/uksi/2012/2233/contents/made *Non-print*

The A31 Trunk Road (Cadnam Interchange - West Moors Interchange) (Temporary Prohibition of Traffic) (No.2) Order 2012 No. 2012/3197. - Enabling power: Road Traffic Regulation Act 1984, s. 14 (1) (a), sch. 9, para. 27 (1). - Issued: 02.01.2013. Made: 10.12.2012. Coming into force: 02.02.2013. Effect: None. Territorial extent & classification: E. Local. - Available at http://www.legislation.gov.uk/uksi/2012/3197/contents/made *Non-print*

The A31 Trunk Road (Cadnam Interchange - West Moors Interchange) (Temporary Prohibition of Traffic) Order 2012 No. 2012/1080. - Enabling power: Road Traffic Regulation Act 1984, s. 14 (1) (a). - Issued: 17.04.2012. Made: 10.04.2012. Coming into force: 28.04.2012. Effect: None. Territorial extent & classification: E. Local. - Available at http://www.legislation.gov.uk/uksi/2012/1080/contents/made *Non-print*

The A31 Trunk Road (Cadnam - Verwood Interchange) (Temporary Restriction and Prohibition of Traffic) Order 2012 No. 2012/420. - Enabling power: Road Traffic Regulation Act 1984, s. 14 (1) (a). - Issued: 22.02.2012. Made: 13.02.2012. Coming into force: 05.03.2012. Effect: None. Territorial extent & classification: E. Local. - Available at http://www.legislation.gov.uk/uksi/2012/420/contents/made *Non-print*

The A31 Trunk Road (Merley Roundabout) (No Entry) Order 2012 No. 2012/1159. - Enabling power: London Olympic Games and Paralympic Games Act 2006, s. 14 (4) & Road Traffic Regulation Act 1984, s. 1. - Issued: 01.05.2012. Made: 16.04.2012. Coming into force: 29.06.2012. Effect: Ceases to have effect on 14.09.2012. Territorial extent & classification: E. Local. - Available at http://www.legislation.gov.uk/uksi/2012/1159/contents/made, Includes map *Non-print*

The A31 Trunk Road (Picket Post Interchange & Ringwood Interchange, Slip Roads) (Temporary Prohibition of Traffic) Order 2012 No. 2012/480. - Enabling power: Road Traffic Regulation Act 1984, s. 14 (1) (a). - Issued: 29.02.2012. Made: 20.02.2012. Coming into force: 10.03.2012. Effect: None. Territorial extent & classification: E. Local. - Available at http://www.legislation.gov.uk/uksi/2012/480/contents/made *Non-print*

The A31 Trunk Road (Poulner Hill Interchange, Eastbound Exit Slip Road) (Temporary Prohibition of Traffic) Order 2012 No. 2012/3254. - Enabling power: Road Traffic Regulation Act 1984, s. 14 (1) (a). - Issued: 09.01.2013. Made: 17.12.2012. Coming into force: 02.02.2013. Effect: None. Territorial extent & classification: E. Local. - Available at http://www.legislation.gov.uk/uksi/2012/3254/contents/made *Non-print*

The A31 Trunk Road (Ringwood Interchange and Ashley Heath Interchange) (Temporary Prohibition of Traffic) Order 2012 No. 2012/2226. - Enabling power: Road Traffic Regulation Act 1984, s. 14 (1) (a). - Issued: 03.09.2012. Made: 28.08.2012. Coming into force: 15.09.2012. Effect: None. Territorial extent & classification: E. Local. - Available at http://www.legislation.gov.uk/uksi/2012/2226/contents/made *Non-print*

Road traffic: Traffic regulation

The A31 Trunk Road (Ringwood Interchange, Carriageways) (Temporary Prohibition of Traffic) Order 2012 No. 2012/181. - Enabling power: Road Traffic Regulation Act 1984, s. 14 (1) (a). - Issued: 31.01.2012. Made: 23.01.2012. Coming into force: 11.02.2012. Effect: None. Territorial extent & classification: E. Local. - Available at http://www.legislation.gov.uk/uksi/2012/181/contents/made *Non-print*

The A31 Trunk Road (Rufus Stone) (Temporary Prohibition of Traffic) Order 2012 No. 2012/2582. - Enabling power: Road Traffic Regulation Act 1984, s. 14 (1) (a). - Issued: 16.10.2012. Made: 08.10.2012. Coming into force: 27.10.2012. Effect: None. Territorial extent & classification: E. Local. - Available at http://www.legislation.gov.uk/uksi/2012/2582/contents/made *Non-print*

The A31 Trunk Road (Verwood Interchange - Bere Regis Roundabout) (Temporary Restriction and Prohibition of Traffic) Order 2012 No. 2012/496. - Enabling power: Road Traffic Regulation Act 1984, s. 14 (1) (a). - Issued: 01.03.2012. Made: 20.02.2012. Coming into force: 12.03.2012. Effect: None. Territorial extent & classification: E. Local. - Available at http://www.legislation.gov.uk/uksi/2012/496/contents/made *Non-print*

The A31 Trunk Road (Verwood Interchange, Westbound Exit Slip Road) (Temporary Prohibition of Traffic) Order 2012 No. 2012/2311. - Enabling power: Road Traffic Regulation Act 1984, s. 14 (1) (a). - Issued: 12.09.2012. Made: 03.09.2012. Coming into force: 22.09.2012. Effect: None. Territorial extent & classification: E. Local. - Available at http://www.legislation.gov.uk/uksi/2012/2311/contents/made *Non-print*

The A31 Trunk Road (West Street, Near Ringwood) (Temporary Prohibition of Traffic) Order 2012 No. 2012/2584. - Enabling power: Road Traffic Regulation Act 1984, s. 14 (1) (a). - Issued: 16.10.2012. Made: 08.10.2012. Coming into force: 27.10.2012. Effect: None. Territorial extent & classification: E. Local. - Available at http://www.legislation.gov.uk/uksi/2012/2584/contents/made *Non-print*

The A34 Trunk Road (Abingdon - South Hinksey) (Temporary Restriction and Prohibition of Traffic) Order 2012 No. 2012/2139. - Enabling power: Road Traffic Regulation Act 1984, s. 14 (1) (a). - Issued: 21.08.2012. Made: 13.08.2012. Coming into force: 01.09.2012. Effect: None. Territorial extent & classification: E. Local. - Available at http://www.legislation.gov.uk/uksi/2012/2139/contents/made *Non-print*

The A34 Trunk Road and the M3 Motorway (M3 Junction 9) (Temporary Prohibition of Traffic) (No. 2) Order 2012 No. 2012/2350. - Enabling power: Road Traffic Regulation Act 1984, s. 14 (1) (a), sch. 9, para. 27 (1). - Issued: 14.09.2012. Made: 03.09.2012. Coming into force: 22.09.2012. Effect: S.I. 2012/607 revoked. Territorial extent & classification: E. Local. - Available at http://www.legislation.gov.uk/uksi/2012/2350/contents/made *Non-print*

The A34 Trunk Road and the M3 Motorway (M3 Junction 9) (Temporary Prohibition of Traffic) Order 2012 No. 2012/607. - Enabling power: Road Traffic Regulation Act 1984, s. 14 (1) (a). - Issued: 06.03.2012. Made: 27.02.2012. Coming into force: 17.03.2012. Effect: None. Territorial extent & classification: E. Local. - Revoked by SI 2012/2350 (non-print). - Available at http://www.legislation.gov.uk/uksi/2012/607/contents/made *Non-print*

The A34 Trunk Road (Bullington Cross - A343 Junction, near Enborne Row) (Temporary Prohibition of Traffic) Order 2012 No. 2012/3242. - Enabling power: Road Traffic Regulation Act 1984, s. 14 (1) (a). - Issued: 08.01.2013. Made: 17.12.2012. Coming into force: 02.02.2013. Effect: None. Territorial extent & classification: E. Local. - Available at http://www.legislation.gov.uk/uksi/2012/3242/contents/made *Non-print*

The A34 Trunk Road (Bullington Cross - Kings Worthy) (Temporary Prohibition of Traffic) Order 2012 No. 2012/2236. - Enabling power: Road Traffic Regulation Act 1984, s. 14 (1) (a). - Issued: 04.09.2012. Made: 28.08.2012. Coming into force: 15.09.2012. Effect: None. Territorial extent & classification: E. Local. - Available at http://www.legislation.gov.uk/uksi/2012/2236/contents/made *Non-print*

The A34 Trunk Road (Chieveley Interchange - Beedon Interchange) (Temporary Restriction and Prohibition of Traffic) Order 2012 No. 2012/3246. - Enabling power: Road Traffic Regulation Act 1984, s. 14 (1) (a). - Issued: 08.01.2013. Made: 17.12.2012. Coming into force: 05.01.2013. Effect: None. Territorial extent & classification: E. Local. - Available at http://www.legislation.gov.uk/uksi/2012/3246/contents/made *Non-print*

The A34 Trunk Road (Chieveley Interchange, Carriageways) (Temporary Prohibition of Traffic) Order 2012 No. 2012/1935. - Enabling power: Road Traffic Regulation Act 1984, s. 14 (1) (a). - Issued: 26.07.2012. Made: 18.06.2012. Coming into force: 07.07.2012. Effect: None. Territorial extent & classification: E. Local. - Available at http://www.legislation.gov.uk/uksi/2012/1935/contents/made *Non-print*

The A34 Trunk Road (Chieveley Services, Slip Roads) (Temporary Prohibition of Traffic) Order 2012 No. 2012/343. - Enabling power: Road Traffic Regulation Act 1984, s. 14 (1) (a). - Issued: 15.02.2012. Made: 06.02.2012. Coming into force: 25.02.2012. Effect: None. Territorial extent & classification: E. Local. - Available at http://www.legislation.gov.uk/uksi/2012/343/contents/made *Non-print*

The A34 Trunk Road (Chilton Interchange, Northbound Exit Slip Road) (Temporary Prohibition of Traffic) Order 2012 No. 2012/1639. - Enabling power: Road Traffic Regulation Act 1984, s. 14 (1) (a). - Issued: 29.06.2012. Made: 18.06.2012. Coming into force: 07.07.2012. Effect: None. Territorial extent & classification: E. Local. - Available at http://www.legislation.gov.uk/uksi/2012/1639/contents/made *Non-print*

The A34 Trunk Road (Chilton Interchange, Southbound Entry Slip Road) (Temporary Prohibition of Traffic) Order 2012 No. 2012/1581. - Enabling power: Road Traffic Regulation Act 1984, s. 14 (1) (a). - Issued: 25.06.2012. Made: 11.06.2012. Coming into force: 30.06.2012. Effect: None. Territorial extent & classification: E. Local. - Available at http://www.legislation.gov.uk/uksi/2012/1581/contents/made *Non-print*

The A34 Trunk Road (Hinksey Hill Interchange, Northbound Exit Slip Road) (Temporary Prohibition of Traffic) Order 2012 No. 2012/1552. - Enabling power: Road Traffic Regulation Act 1984, s. 14 (1) (a). - Issued: 20.06.2012. Made: 06.06.2012. Coming into force: 23.06.2012. Effect: None. Territorial extent & classification: E. Local. - Available at http://www.legislation.gov.uk/uksi/2012/1552/contents/made *Non-print*

The A34 Trunk Road (Hinksey Hill Interchange - North of Peartree Interchange) (Temporary Restriction and Prohibition of Traffic) Order 2012 No. 2012/2449. - Enabling power: Road Traffic Regulation Act 1984, s. 14 (1) (a). - Issued: 27.09.2012. Made: 17.09.2012. Coming into force: 06.10.2012. Effect: None. Territorial extent & classification: E. Local. - Available at http://www.legislation.gov.uk/uksi/2012/2449/contents/made *Non-print*

The A34 Trunk Road (Islip Interchange, Slip Roads) (Temporary Prohibition of Traffic) Order 2012 No. 2012/1618. - Enabling power: Road Traffic Regulation Act 1984, s. 14 (1) (a). - Issued: 28.06.2012. Made: 18.06.2012. Coming into force: 07.07.2012. Effect: None. Territorial extent & classification: E. Local. - Available at http://www.legislation.gov.uk/uksi/2012/1618/contents/made *Non-print*

The A34 Trunk Road (M3 Junction 9 - Andover Road Interchange) (Temporary Prohibition of Traffic) Order 2012 No. 2012/1670. - Enabling power: Road Traffic Regulation Act 1984, s. 14 (1) (a). - Issued: 03.07.2012. Made: 25.06.2012. Coming into force: 20.07.2012. Effect: None. Territorial extent & classification: E. Local. - Available at http://www.legislation.gov.uk/uksi/2012/1670/contents/made *Non-print*

The A34 Trunk Road (M3 Junction 9 - M40 Junction 9, Lay-bys) (Temporary Prohibition of Traffic) Order 2012 No. 2012/3149. - Enabling power: Road Traffic Regulation Act 1984, s. 14 (1) (a). - Issued: 27.12.2012. Made: 26.11.2012. Coming into force: 20.12.2012. Effect: None. Territorial extent & classification: E. Local. - Available at http://www.legislation.gov.uk/uksi/2012/3149/contents/made *Non-print*

The A34 Trunk Road (M3 Junction 9 - Tot Hill Interchange) (Temporary Speed Restrictions) Order 2012 No. 2012/2849. - Enabling power: Road Traffic Regulation Act 1984, s. 14 (1) (a). - Issued: 16.11.2012. Made: 05.11.2012. Coming into force: 29.11.2012. Effect: None. Territorial extent & classification: E. Local. - Available at http://www.legislation.gov.uk/uksi/2012/2849/contents/made *Non-print*

The A34 Trunk Road (M40 Junction 9 - West Ilsley) (Temporary Restriction and Prohibition of Traffic) Order 2012 No. 2012/1010. - Enabling power: Road Traffic Regulation Act 1984, s. 14 (1) (a). - Issued: 12.04.2012. Made: 26.03.2012. Coming into force: 16.04.2012. Effect: None. Territorial extent & classification: E. Local. - Available at http://www.legislation.gov.uk/uksi/2012/1010/contents/made *Non-print*

The A34 Trunk Road (Marcham Interchange) (Temporary Prohibition of Traffic) Order 2012 No. 2012/3261. - Enabling power: Road Traffic Regulation Act 1984, s. 14 (1) (a). - Issued: 14.01.2013. Made: 17.12.2012. Coming into force: 02.02.2013. Effect: None. Territorial extent & classification: E. Local. - Available at http://www.legislation.gov.uk/uksi/2012/3261/contents/made *Non-print*

The A34 Trunk Road (Milton Interchange - Chieveley Interchange) (Temporary Restriction and Prohibition of Traffic) Order 2012 No. 2012/1707. - Enabling power: Road Traffic Regulation Act 1984, s. 14 (1) (a). - Issued: 19.07.2012. Made: 02.07.2012. Coming into force: 21.07.2012. Effect: None. Territorial extent & classification: E. Local. - Available at http://www.legislation.gov.uk/uksi/2012/1707/contents/made *Non-print*

The A34 Trunk Road (Milton Interchange - Cow Lane) (Temporary Restriction and Prohibition of Traffic) Order 2012 No. 2012/3224. - Enabling power: Road Traffic Regulation Act 1984, s. 14 (1) (a). - Issued: 07.01.2013. Made: 10.12.2012. Coming into force: 05.01.2013. Effect: None. Territorial extent & classification: E. Local. - Available at http://www.legislation.gov.uk/uksi/2012/3224/contents/made *Non-print*

The A34 Trunk Road (Speen - East Ilsley, Slip Roads) (Temporary Prohibition of Traffic) Order 2012 No. 2012/1621. - Enabling power: Road Traffic Regulation Act 1984, s. 14 (1) (a). - Issued: 28.06.2012. Made: 18.06.2012. Coming into force: 14.07.2012. Effect: None. Territorial extent & classification: E. Local. - Available at http://www.legislation.gov.uk/uksi/2012/1621/contents/made *Non-print*

The A34 Trunk Road (Three Maids Hill Interchange, Slip Roads) (Temporary Prohibition of Traffic) Order 2012 No. 2012/1622. - Enabling power: Road Traffic Regulation Act 1984, s. 14 (1) (a). - Issued: 28.06.2012. Made: 18.06.2012. Coming into force: 07.07.2012. Effect: None. Territorial extent & classification: E. Local. - Available at http://www.legislation.gov.uk/uksi/2012/1622/contents/made *Non-print*

The A34 Trunk Road (Tot Hill Interchange - West Ilsley Interchange) (Temporary Restriction of Traffic) Order 2012 No. 2012/1366. - Enabling power: Road Traffic Regulation Act 1984, s. 14 (1) (a). - Issued: 28.05.2012. Made: 14.05.2012. Coming into force: 02.06.2012. Effect: None. Territorial extent & classification: E. Local. - Available at http://www.legislation.gov.uk/uksi/2012/1366/contents/made *Non-print*

The A35 Trunk Road (Axminster Bypass Laybys) (Temporary Prohibition of Traffic) Order 2012 No. 2012/1089. - Enabling power: Road Traffic Regulation Act 1984, s. 14 (1) (a). - Issued: 19.04.2012. Made: 10.04.2012. Coming into force: 13.04.2012. Effect: None. Territorial extent & classification: E. Local. - Available at http://www.legislation.gov.uk/uksi/2012/1089/contents/made *Non-print*

The A35 Trunk Road (Fulvens Bends, Morcombelake) (Temporary Restriction of Traffic) Order 2012 No. 2012/2482. - Enabling power: Road Traffic Regulation Act 1984, s. 14 (1) (b). - Issued: 02.10.2012. Made: 25.09.2012. Coming into force: 01.10.2012. Effect: None. Territorial extent & classification: E. Local. - Available at http://www.legislation.gov.uk/uksi/2012/2482/contents/made *Non-print*

The A35 Trunk Road (Honiton to Axminster) (Temporary Prohibition of Traffic) Order 2012 No. 2012/1276. - Enabling power: Road Traffic Regulation Act 1984, s. 14 (1) (a). - Issued: 18.05.2012. Made: 08.05.2012. Coming into force: 11.05.2012. Effect: None. Territorial extent & classification: E. Local. - Available at http://www.legislation.gov.uk/uksi/2012/1276/contents/made *Non-print*

The A35 Trunk Road (Honiton to Axminster) (Temporary Restriction and Prohibition of Traffic) Order 2012 No. 2012/1149. - Enabling power: Road Traffic Regulation Act 1984, s. 14 (1) (a). - Issued: 27.04.2012. Made: 17.04.2012. Coming into force: 24.04.2012. Effect: None. Territorial extent & classification: E. Local. - Available at http://www.legislation.gov.uk/uksi/2012/1149/contents/made *Non-print*

The A35 Trunk Road (Kingston Ponds Layby, Dorchester) (Temporary Prohibition of Traffic) Order 2012 No. 2012/1280. - Enabling power: Road Traffic Regulation Act 1984, s. 14 (1) (a). - Issued: 18.05.2012. Made: 08.05.2012. Coming into force: 12.05.2012. Effect: None. Territorial extent & classification: E. Local. - Available at http://www.legislation.gov.uk/uksi/2012/1280/contents/made *Non-print*

The A35 Trunk Road (Monkton Road, Honiton) (Temporary Prohibition of Traffic) Order 2012 No. 2012/2781. - Enabling power: Road Traffic Regulation Act 1984, s. 14 (1) (a). - Issued: 08.11.2012. Made: 23.10.2012. Coming into force: 27.10.2012. Effect: None. Territorial extent & classification: E. Local. - Available at http://www.legislation.gov.uk/uksi/2012/2781/contents/made *Non-print*

The A35 Trunk Road (Puddletown to Bere Regis) (Temporary Prohibition of Traffic) Order 2012 No. 2012/1680. - Enabling power: Road Traffic Regulation Act 1984, s. 14 (1) (a). - Issued: 03.07.2012. Made: 19.06.2012. Coming into force: 23.06.2012. Effect: None. Territorial extent & classification: E. Local. - Available at http://www.legislation.gov.uk/uksi/2012/1680/contents/made *Non-print*

The A36 Trunk Road (Beckington Roundabout North) (Temporary Prohibition of Traffic) Order 2012 No. 2012/1229. - Enabling power: Road Traffic Regulation Act 1984, s. 14 (1) (a). - Issued: 10.05.2012. Made: 01.05.2012. Coming into force: 05.05.2012. Effect: None. Territorial extent & classification: E. Local. - Available at http://www.legislation.gov.uk/uksi/2012/1229/contents/made *Non-print*

The A36 Trunk Road (Beckington, Somerset) (Temporary Restriction of Traffic) Order 2012 No. 2012/552. - Enabling power: Road Traffic Regulation Act 1984, s. 14 (1) (a). - Issued: 01.03.2012. Made: 22.02.2012. Coming into force: 28.02.2012. Effect: None. Territorial extent & classification: E. Local. - Available at http://www.legislation.gov.uk/uksi/2012/552/contents/made *Non-print*

The A36 Trunk Road (Beckington to Warminster) (Temporary Prohibition of Traffic) Order 2012 No. 2012/119. - Enabling power: Road Traffic Regulation Act 1984, s. 14 (1) (a). - Issued: 23.01.2012. Made: 12.01.2012. Coming into force: 21.01.2012. Effect: None. Territorial extent & classification: E. Local. - Available at http://www.legislation.gov.uk/uksi/2012/119/contents/made *Non-print*

The A36 Trunk Road (Churchill Way, Salisbury) (Temporary Prohibition of Traffic) Order 2012 No. 2012/1373. - Enabling power: Road Traffic Regulation Act 1984, s. 14 (1) (a). - Issued: 28.05.2012. Made: 15.05.2012. Coming into force: 19.05.2012. Effect: None. Territorial extent & classification: E. Local. - Available at http://www.legislation.gov.uk/uksi/2012/1373/contents/made *Non-print*

The A36 Trunk Road (Hinton Charterhouse, Near Bath, and Black Dog Hill, Near Frome) (Temporary Restriction of Traffic) Order 2012 No. 2012/301. - Enabling power: Road Traffic Regulation Act 1984, s. 14 (1) (a). - Issued: 10.02.2012. Made: 01.02.2012. Coming into force: 11.02.2012. Effect: None. Territorial extent & classification: E. Local. - Available at http://www.legislation.gov.uk/uksi/2012/301/contents/made *Non-print*

The A36 Trunk Road (Near Ower, Hampshire) (Temporary Restriction of Traffic) Order 2012 No. 2012/1371. - Enabling power: Road Traffic Regulation Act 1984, s. 14 (1) (a). - Issued: 28.05.2012. Made: 17.05.2012. Coming into force: 23.05.2012. Effect: None. Territorial extent & classification: E. Local. - Available at http://www.legislation.gov.uk/uksi/2012/1371/contents/made *Non-print*

The A36 Trunk Road (Salisbury to Alderbury) (Temporary Prohibition of Traffic) Order 2012 No. 2012/1283. - Enabling power: Road Traffic Regulation Act 1984, s. 14 (1) (a). - Issued: 18.05.2012. Made: 08.05.2012. Coming into force: 14.05.2012. Effect: None. Territorial extent & classification: E. Local. - Available at http://www.legislation.gov.uk/uksi/2012/1283/contents/made *Non-print*

The A36 Trunk Road (Salisbury to Whaddon) (Temporary Prohibition of Traffic) Order 2012 No. 2012/45. - Enabling power: Road Traffic Regulation Act 1984, s. 14 (1) (a). - Issued: 11.01.2012. Made: 04.01.2012. Coming into force: 13.01.2012. Effect: None. Territorial extent & classification: E. Local. - Available at http://www.legislation.gov.uk/uksi/2012/45/contents/made *Non-print*

The A36 Trunk Road (Warminster) (Temporary Restriction of Traffic) Order 2012 No. 2012/440. - Enabling power: Road Traffic Regulation Act 1984, s. 14 (1) (a). - Issued: 22.02.2012. Made: 15.02.2012. Coming into force: 28.02.2012. Effect: None. Territorial extent & classification: E. Local. - Available at http://www.legislation.gov.uk/uksi/2012/440/contents/made *Non-print*

The A36 Trunk Road (Woolverton to Beckington) (Temporary Prohibition of Traffic) Order 2012 No. 2012/1281. - Enabling power: Road Traffic Regulation Act 1984, s. 14 (1) (a). - Issued: 18.05.2012. Made: 08.05.2012. Coming into force: 12.05.2012. Effect: None. Territorial extent & classification: E. Local. - Available at http://www.legislation.gov.uk/uksi/2012/1281/contents/made *Non-print*

The A38 and A5148 Trunk Roads (Lichfield, Staffordshire) (Temporary Prohibition of Traffic) Order 2012 No. 2012/1922. - Enabling power: Road Traffic Regulation Act 1984, s. 14 (1) (b). - Issued: 25.07.2012. Made: 22.06.2012. Coming into force: 29.06.2012. Effect: None. Territorial extent & classification: E. Local. - Available at http://www.legislation.gov.uk/uksi/2012/1922/contents/made *Non-print*

The A38 and A5148 Trunk Roads (Swinfen to Streethay, Staffordshire) (Temporary Prohibition of Traffic) Order 2012 No. 2012/1355. - Enabling power: Road Traffic Regulation Act 1984, s. 14 (1) (a). - Issued: 24.05.2012. Made: 07.05.2012. Coming into force: 14.05.2012. Effect: None. Territorial extent & classification: E. Local. - Available at http://www.legislation.gov.uk/uksi/2012/1355/contents/made *Non-print*

The A38 Trunk Road (Allestree, Derby) (Temporary Restriction and Prohibition of Traffic) (No. 2) Order 2012 No. 2012/3169. - Enabling power: Road Traffic Regulation Act 1984, s. 14 (1) (a). - Issued: 28.12.2012. Made: 26.11.2012. Coming into force: 03.12.2012. Effect: None. Territorial extent & classification: E. Local. - Available at http://www.legislation.gov.uk/uksi/2012/3169/contents/made *Non-print*

The A38 Trunk Road (Allestree, Derby) (Temporary Restriction and Prohibition of Traffic) Order 2012 No. 2012/1326. - Enabling power: Road Traffic Regulation Act 1984, s. 14 (1) (a). - Issued: 23.05.2012. Made: 07.05.2012. Coming into force: 14.05.2012. Effect: None. Territorial extent & classification: E. Local. - Available at http://www.legislation.gov.uk/uksi/2012/1326/contents/made *Non-print*

The A38 Trunk Road (Alrewas, Staffordshire) (Southbound Exit Slip Road) (Temporary Prohibition of Traffic) Order 2012 No. 2012/1052. - Enabling power: Road Traffic Regulation Act 1984, s. 14 (1) (a). - Issued: 13.04.2012. Made: 27.03.2012. Coming into force: 03.04.2012. Effect: None. Territorial extent & classification: E. Local. - Available at http://www.legislation.gov.uk/uksi/2012/1052/contents/made *Non-print*

The A38 Trunk Road (Alrewas, Staffordshire) (Temporary Prohibition of Traffic) Order 2012 No. 2012/179. - Enabling power: Road Traffic Regulation Act 1984, s. 14 (1) (a). - Issued: 31.01.2012. Made: 16.01.2012. Coming into force: 23.01.2012. Effect: None. Territorial extent & classification: E. Local. - Available at http://www.legislation.gov.uk/uksi/2012/179/contents/made *Non-print*

The A38 Trunk Road (Alrewas to Barton Turn, Staffordshire) (Temporary Prohibition of Traffic) Order 2012 No. 2012/1584. - Enabling power: Road Traffic Regulation Act 1984, s. 14 (1) (a). - Issued: 26.06.2012. Made: 28.05.2012. Coming into force: 04.06.2012. Effect: None. Territorial extent & classification: E. Local. - Available at http://www.legislation.gov.uk/uksi/2012/1584/contents/made *Non-print*

The A38 Trunk Road (Alrewas to Lichfield) (Temporary Prohibition of Traffic) Order 2012 No. 2012/382. - Enabling power: Road Traffic Regulation Act 1984, s. 14 (1) (a). - Issued: 17.02.2012. Made: 07.02.2012. Coming into force: 14.02.2012. Effect: None. Territorial extent & classification: E. Local. - Available at http://www.legislation.gov.uk/uksi/2012/382/contents/made *Non-print*

The A38 Trunk Road (Alrewas to Streethay, Staffordshire) (Temporary Prohibition of Traffic) Order 2012 No. 2012/1685. - Enabling power: Road Traffic Regulation Act 1984, s. 14 (1) (a). - Issued: 03.07.2012. Made: 06.06.2012. Coming into force: 13.06.2012. Effect: None. Territorial extent & classification: E. Local. - Available at http://www.legislation.gov.uk/uksi/2012/1685/contents/made *Non-print*

The A38 Trunk Road (Ashburton to Buckfastleigh, Devon) (Temporary Restriction and Prohibition of Traffic) Order 2012 No. 2012/2198. - Enabling power: Road Traffic Regulation Act 1984, s. 14 (1) (a). - Issued: 29.08.2012. Made: 22.08.2012. Coming into force: 01.09.2012. Effect: None. Territorial extent & classification: E. Local. - Available at http://www.legislation.gov.uk/uksi/2012/2198/contents/made *Non-print*

The A38 Trunk Road (Ashburton to Lower Dean, Devon) (Temporary Restriction and Prohibition of Traffic) Order 2012 No. 2012/1780. - Enabling power: Road Traffic Regulation Act 1984, s. 14 (1) (a). - Issued: 18.07.2012. Made: 27.06.2012. Coming into force: 04.07.2012. Effect: None. Territorial extent & classification: E. Local. - Available at http://www.legislation.gov.uk/uksi/2012/1780/contents/made *Non-print*

The A38 Trunk Road (Barton-under-Needwood, Staffordshire) (Footway) (Temporary Prohibition of Traffic) (No. 4) Order 2012 No. 2012/2122. - Enabling power: Road Traffic Regulation Act 1984, s. 14 (1) (a). - Issued: 17.08.2012. Made: 06.08.2012. Coming into force: 13.08.2012. Effect: None. Territorial extent & classification: E. Local. - Available at http://www.legislation.gov.uk/uksi/2012/2122/contents/made *Non-print*

The A38 Trunk Road (Barton - under - Needwood, Staffordshire) (Temporary Prohibition of Traffic) (No. 2) Order 2012 No. 2012/377. - Enabling power: Road Traffic Regulation Act 1984, s. 14 (1) (a). - Issued: 17.02.2012. Made: 06.02.2012. Coming into force: 13.02.2012. Effect: None. Territorial extent & classification: E. Local. - Available at http://www.legislation.gov.uk/uksi/2012/377/contents/made *Non-print*

The A38 Trunk Road (Barton-under-Needwood, Staffordshire) (Temporary Prohibition of Traffic) (No. 3) Order 2012 No. 2012/2121. - Enabling power: Road Traffic Regulation Act 1984, s. 14 (1) (a). - Issued: 17.08.2012. Made: 30.07.2012. Coming into force: 06.08.2012. Effect: None. Territorial extent & classification: E. Local. - Available at http://www.legislation.gov.uk/uksi/2012/2121/contents/made *Non-print*

The A38 Trunk Road (Barton under Needwood, Staffordshire) (Temporary Prohibition of Traffic) Order 2012 No. 2012/363. - Enabling power: Road Traffic Regulation Act 1984, s. 14 (1) (a). - Issued: 16.02.2012. Made: 30.01.2012. Coming into force: 06.02.2012. Effect: None. Territorial extent & classification: E. Local. - Available at http://www.legislation.gov.uk/uksi/2012/363/contents/made *Non-print*

The A38 Trunk Road (Barton-under-Needwood to Lichfield, Staffordshire) (Temporary Prohibition of Traffic) Order 2012 No. 2012/1776. - Enabling power: Road Traffic Regulation Act 1984, s. 14 (1) (a). - Issued: 18.07.2012. Made: 18.06.2012. Coming into force: 25.06.2012. Effect: None. Territorial extent & classification: E. Local. - Available at http://www.legislation.gov.uk/uksi/2012/1776/contents/made *Non-print*

The A38 Trunk Road (Burton-on-Trent, Staffordshire) (Slip Roads) (Temporary Prohibition of Traffic) Order 2012 No. 2012/2843. - Enabling power: Road Traffic Regulation Act 1984, s. 14 (1) (a). - Issued: 16.11.2012. Made: 29.10.2012. Coming into force: 05.11.2012. Effect: None. Territorial extent & classification: E. Local. - Available at http://www.legislation.gov.uk/uksi/2012/2843/contents/made *Non-print*

The A38 Trunk Road (Burton upon Trent, Staffordshire) (Temporary Prohibition of Traffic) Order 2012 No. 2012/2728. - Enabling power: Road Traffic Regulation Act 1984, s. 14 (1) (b). - Issued: 02.11.2012. Made: 01.10.2012. Coming into force: 08.10.2012. Effect: None. Territorial extent & classification: E. Local. - Available at http://www.legislation.gov.uk/uksi/2012/2728/contents/made *Non-print*

Road traffic: Traffic regulation

The A38 Trunk Road (Chudleigh Knighton to Exeter Racecourse) (Temporary Restriction and Prohibition of Traffic) Order 2012 No. 2012/2116. - Enabling power: Road Traffic Regulation Act 1984, s. 14 (1) (a). - Issued: 17.08.2012. Made: 07.08.2012. Coming into force: 11.08.2012. Effect: None. Territorial extent & classification: E. Local. - Available at http://www.legislation.gov.uk/uksi/2012/2116/contents/made *Non-print*

The A38 Trunk Road (Chudleigh, Near Newton Abbot) (Temporary Prohibition of Traffic) Order 2012 No. 2012/113. - Enabling power: Road Traffic Regulation Act 1984, s. 14 (1) (a), sch. 9, para. 27 (1). - Issued: 20.01.2012. Made: 11.01.2012. Coming into force: 14.01.2012. Effect: S.I. 2011/2251 revoked. Territorial extent & classification: E. Local. - Available at http://www.legislation.gov.uk/uksi/2012/113/contents/made *Non-print*

The A38 Trunk Road (Clay Lane Junction to Drumbridges Junction, Devon) (Temporary Restriction and Prohibition of Traffic) Order 2012 No. 2012/2783. - Enabling power: Road Traffic Regulation Act 1984, s. 14 (1) (a). - Issued: 09.11.2012. Made: 24.10.2012. Coming into force: 27.10.2012. Effect: None. Territorial extent & classification: E. Local. - Available at http://www.legislation.gov.uk/uksi/2012/2783/contents/made *Non-print*

The A38 Trunk Road (Clay Mills, Staffordshire) (Slip Road) (Temporary Prohibition of Traffic) Order 2012 No. 2012/1744. - Enabling power: Road Traffic Regulation Act 1984, s. 14 (1) (b). - Issued: 17.07.2012. Made: 18.06.2012. Coming into force: 25.06.2012. Effect: None. Territorial extent & classification: E. Local. - Available at http://www.legislation.gov.uk/uksi/2012/1744/contents/made *Non-print*

The A38 Trunk Road (Clay Mills to South of Findern) (Temporary Prohibition of Traffic) Order 2012 No. 2012/616. - Enabling power: Road Traffic Regulation Act 1984, s. 14 (1) (a). - Issued: 07.03.2012. Made: 24.02.2012. Coming into force: 02.03.2012. Effect: None. Territorial extent & classification: E. Local. - Available at http://www.legislation.gov.uk/uksi/2012/616/contents/made *Non-print*

The A38 Trunk Road (Clay Mills to Toyota Interchange) (Temporary Prohibition of Traffic) Order 2012 No. 2012/1702. - Enabling power: Road Traffic Regulation Act 1984, s. 14 (1) (a). - Issued: 12.07.2012. Made: 11.06.2012. Coming into force: 18.06.2012. Effect: None. Territorial extent & classification: E. Local. - Available at http://www.legislation.gov.uk/uksi/2012/1702/contents/made *Non-print*

The A38 Trunk Road (Deep Lane Junction, Plympton to Ivybridge) (Temporary Restriction and Prohibition of Traffic) Order 2012 No. 2012/2744. - Enabling power: Road Traffic Regulation Act 1984, s. 14 (1) (a). - Issued: 06.11.2012. Made: 19.10.2012. Coming into force: 24.10.2012. Effect: None. Territorial extent & classification: E. Local. - Available at http://www.legislation.gov.uk/uksi/2012/2744/contents/made *Non-print*

The A38 Trunk Road (Dobwalls Bypass, Cornwall) (24 Hours Clearway) Order 2012 No. 2012/1376. - Enabling power: Road Traffic Regulation Act 1984, ss. 1 (1), 2 (1) (2). - Issued: 28.05.2012. Made: 16.05.2012. Coming into force: 28.05.2012. Effect: None. Territorial extent & classification: E. Local. - Available at http://www.legislation.gov.uk/uksi/2012/1376/contents/made *Non-print*

The A38 Trunk Road (Dobwalls Bypass, Cornwall) (Temporary Prohibition of Traffic) Order 2012 No. 2012/3156. - Enabling power: Road Traffic Regulation Act 1984, s. 14 (1) (a). - Issued: 28.12.2012. Made: 28.11.2012. Coming into force: 01.12.2012. Effect: None. Territorial extent & classification: E. Local. - Available at http://www.legislation.gov.uk/uksi/2012/3156/contents/made *Non-print*

The A38 Trunk Road (Drybridge Junction to Marley Head Junction, Near South Brent) (Temporary Prohibition and Restriction of Traffic) (Number 2) Order 2011 Variation Order 2012 No. 2012/242. - Enabling power: Road Traffic Regulation Act 1984, s. 14 (1) (a), sch. 9, para. 27 (1). - Issued: 06.02.2012. Made: 26.01.2012. Coming into force: 28.01.2012. Effect: S.I. 2011/3087 varied. Territorial extent & classification: E. Local. - Available at http://www.legislation.gov.uk/uksi/2012/242/contents/made *Non-print*

The A38 Trunk Road (Findern, Derbyshire) (Temporary Prohibition of Traffic) Order 2012 No. 2012/2794. - Enabling power: Road Traffic Regulation Act 1984, s. 14 (1) (a). - Issued: 09.11.2012. Made: 15.10.2012. Coming into force: 22.10.2012. Effect: None. Territorial extent & classification: E. Local. - Available at http://www.legislation.gov.uk/uksi/2012/2794/contents/made *Non-print*

The A38 Trunk Road (Findern Interchange, Derbyshire) (Temporary Prohibition of Traffic) Order 2012 No. 2012/3177. - Enabling power: Road Traffic Regulation Act 1984, s. 14 (1) (a). - Issued: 31.12.2012. Made: 26.11.2012. Coming into force: 03.12.2012. Effect: None. Territorial extent & classification: E. Local. - Available at http://www.legislation.gov.uk/uksi/2012/3177/contents/made *Non-print*

Road traffic: Traffic regulation

The A38 Trunk Road (Forder Valley Junction to Marsh Mills Junction, Plymouth) (Temporary Prohibition of Traffic) Order 2012 No. 2012/557. - Enabling power: Road Traffic Regulation Act 1984, s. 14 (1) (a). - Issued: 01.03.2012. Made: 23.02.2012. Coming into force: 03.03.2012. Effect: None. Territorial extent & classification: E. Local. - Available at http://www.legislation.gov.uk/uksi/2012/557/contents/made *Non-print*

The A38 Trunk Road (Fradley - Alrewas, Staffordshire) (Temporary Prohibition of Traffic) Order 2012 No. 2012/621. - Enabling power: Road Traffic Regulation Act 1984, s. 14 (1) (a). - Issued: 07.03.2012. Made: 24.02.2012. Coming into force: 02.03.2012. Effect: None. Territorial extent & classification: E. Local. - Available at http://www.legislation.gov.uk/uksi/2012/621/contents/made *Non-print*

The A38 Trunk Road (Glynn Valley, Near Bodmin) (Temporary Prohibition of Traffic) Order 2012 No. 2012/2287. - Enabling power: Road Traffic Regulation Act 1984, s. 14 (1) (a). - Issued: 10.09.2012. Made: 29.08.2012. Coming into force: 01.09.2012. Effect: None. Territorial extent & classification: E. Local. - Available at http://www.legislation.gov.uk/uksi/2012/2287/contents/made *Non-print*

The A38 Trunk Road (Harcombe Bends to Haldon Hill) (Temporary Restriction and Prohibition of Traffic) Order 2012 No. 2012/302. - Enabling power: Road Traffic Regulation Act 1984, s. 14 (1) (a). - Issued: 10.02.2012. Made: 01.02.2012. Coming into force: 08.02.2012. Effect: None. Territorial extent & classification: E. Local. - Available at http://www.legislation.gov.uk/uksi/2012/302/contents/made *Non-print*

The A38 Trunk Road (Harcombe to Chudleigh) (Temporary Restriction and Prohibition of Traffic) Order 2012 No. 2012/3155. - Enabling power: Road Traffic Regulation Act 1984, s. 14 (1) (a). - Issued: 28.12.2012. Made: 27.11.2012. Coming into force: 30.11.2012. Effect: None. Territorial extent & classification: E. Local. - Available at http://www.legislation.gov.uk/uksi/2012/3155/contents/made *Non-print*

The A38 Trunk Road (Ivybridge Eastbound Entry Slip Road) (Temporary Prohibition of Traffic) Order 2012 No. 2012/441. - Enabling power: Road Traffic Regulation Act 1984, s. 14 (1) (a). - Issued: 22.02.2012. Made: 15.02.2012. Coming into force: 18.02.2012. Effect: None. Territorial extent & classification: E. Local. - Available at http://www.legislation.gov.uk/uksi/2012/441/contents/made *Non-print*

The A38 Trunk Road (Lichfield Cross to Branston) (Temporary Restriction and Prohibition of Traffic) Order 2012 No. 2012/3175. - Enabling power: Road Traffic Regulation Act 1984, s. 14 (1) (a). - Issued: 31.12.2102. Made: 26.11.2012. Coming into force: 03.12.2012. Effect: None. Territorial extent & classification: E. Local. - Available at http://www.legislation.gov.uk/uksi/2012/3175/contents/made *Non-print*

The A38 Trunk Road (Liskeard, Cornwall) (Temporary Prohibition of Traffic) Order 2012 No. 2012/311. - Enabling power: Road Traffic Regulation Act 1984, s. 14 (1) (a). - Issued: 15.02.2012. Made: 01.02.2012. Coming into force: 04.02.2012. Effect: None. Territorial extent & classification: E. Local. - Available at http://www.legislation.gov.uk/uksi/2012/311/contents/made *Non-print*

The A38 Trunk Road (Liskeard, Cornwall) (Temporary Restriction and Prohibition of Traffic) Order 2012 No. 2012/383. - Enabling power: Road Traffic Regulation Act 1984, s. 14 (1) (a). - Issued: 17.02.2012. Made: 08.02.2012. Coming into force: 18.02.2012. Effect: None. Territorial extent & classification: E. Local. - Available at http://www.legislation.gov.uk/uksi/2012/383/contents/made *Non-print*

The A38 Trunk Road (Liskeard to Trerulefoot) (Temporary Restriction and Prohibition of Traffic) Order 2012 No. 2012/2528. - Enabling power: Road Traffic Regulation Act 1984, s. 14 (1) (a). - Issued: 09.10.2012. Made: 03.10.2012. Coming into force: 06.10.2012. Effect: None. Territorial extent & classification: E. Local. - Available at http://www.legislation.gov.uk/uksi/2012/2528/contents/made *Non-print*

The A38 Trunk Road (Little Eaton and Holbrook, Derbyshire) (Temporary Restriction and Prohibition of Traffic) Order 2012 No. 2012/2388. - Enabling power: Road Traffic Regulation Act 1984, s. 14 (1) (a). - Issued: 20.09.2012. Made: 28.08.2012. Coming into force: 04.09.2012. Effect: None. Territorial extent & classification: E. Local. - Available at http://www.legislation.gov.uk/uksi/2012/2388/contents/made *Non-print*

The A38 Trunk Road (M5 Junction 31 to Haldon Hill) (Temporary Restriction and Prohibition of Traffic) Order 2012 No. 2012/2784. - Enabling power: Road Traffic Regulation Act 1984, s. 14 (1) (a). - Issued: 09.11.2012. Made: 24.10.2012. Coming into force: 27.10.2012. Effect: None. Territorial extent & classification: E. Local. - Available at http://www.legislation.gov.uk/uksi/2012/2784/contents/made *Non-print*

The A38 Trunk Road (March Mills to Forder Valley, Plymouth) (Temporary Restriction and Prohibition of Traffic) Order 2012 No. 2012/1236. - Enabling power: Road Traffic Regulation Act 1984, s. 14 (1) (a). - Issued: 11.05.2012. Made: 02.05.2012. Coming into force: 05.05.2012. Effect: None. Territorial extent & classification: E. Local. - Revoked by S.I. 2012/1862 (Non-print). - Available at http://www.legislation.gov.uk/uksi/2012/1236/contents/made *Non-print*

The A38 Trunk Road (Moorswater Junction, Liskeard) (Temporary Restriction of Traffic) Order 2012 No. 2012/2200. - Enabling power: Road Traffic Regulation Act 1984, s. 14 (1) (a). - Issued: 30.08.2012. Made: 22.08.2012. Coming into force: 25.08.2012. Effect: None. Territorial extent & classification: E. Local. - Available at http://www.legislation.gov.uk/uksi/2012/2200/contents/made *Non-print*

The A38 Trunk Road (Near Ashburton and Newton Abbot) (Temporary Restriction of Traffic) Order 2012 No. 2012/2981. - Enabling power: Road Traffic Regulation Act 1984, s. 14 (1) (a). - Issued: 05.12.2012. Made: 21.11.2012. Coming into force: 24.11.2012. Effect: None. Territorial extent & classification: E. Local. - Available at http://www.legislation.gov.uk/uksi/2012/2981/contents/made *Non-print*

The A38 Trunk Road (Plymouth) (Temporary Restriction and Prohibition of Traffic) Order 2012 No. 2012/1862. - Enabling power: Road Traffic Regulation Act 1984, s. 14 (1) (a), sch. 9, para. 27 (1). - Issued: 20.07.2012. Made: 10.07.2012. Coming into force: 14.07.2012. Effect: S.I. 2012/1236 revoked. Territorial extent & classification: E. Local. - Available at http://www.legislation.gov.uk/uksi/2012/1862/contents/made *Non-print*

The A38 Trunk Road (Pridhamsleigh to Lower Dean, Buckfastleigh, Devon) (Temporary Restriction and Prohibition of Traffic) Order 2012 No. 2012/227. - Enabling power: Road Traffic Regulation Act 1984, s. 14 (1) (a). - Issued: 03.02.2012. Made: 24.01.2012. Coming into force: 27.01.2012. Effect: None. Territorial extent & classification: E. Local. - Available at http://www.legislation.gov.uk/uksi/2012/227/contents/made *Non-print*

The A38 Trunk Road (Saltash Tunnel) (Temporary Prohibition of Traffic) Order 2012 No. 2012/76. - Enabling power: Road Traffic Regulation Act 1984, s. 14 (1) (a). - Issued: 17.01.2012. Made: 05.01.2012. Coming into force: 10.01.2012. Effect: None. Territorial extent & classification: E. Local. - Available at http://www.legislation.gov.uk/uksi/2012/76/contents/made *Non-print*

The A38 Trunk Road (Smithaleigh Junction, Plympton Bypass) (Temporary Prohibition of Traffic) Order 2012 No. 2012/110. - Enabling power: Road Traffic Regulation Act 1984, s. 14 (1) (a), sch. 9, para. 27 (1). - Issued: 20.01.2012. Made: 11.01.2012. Coming into force: 14.01.2012. Effect: S.I. 2011/1916 revoked. Territorial extent & classification: E. Local. - Available at http://www.legislation.gov.uk/uksi/2012/110/contents/made *Non-print*

The A38 Trunk Road (South Brent, Devon) (Temporary Prohibition and Restriction of Traffic) Order 2012 No. 2012/77. - Enabling power: Road Traffic Regulation Act 1984, s. 14 (1) (a). - Issued: 17.01.2012. Made: 05.01.2012. Coming into force: 14.01.2012. Effect: None. Territorial extent & classification: E. Local. - Available at http://www.legislation.gov.uk/uksi/2012/77/contents/made *Non-print*

The A38 Trunk Road (Staffordshire) (Temporary Prohibition of Traffic) Order 2012 No. 2012/1147. - Enabling power: Road Traffic Regulation Act 1984, s. 14 (1) (a). - Issued: 27.04.2012. Made: 16.04.2012. Coming into force: 23.04.2012. Effect: None. Territorial extent & classification: E. Local. - Available at http://www.legislation.gov.uk/uksi/2012/1147/contents/made *Non-print*

The A38 Trunk Road (Streethay, Staffordshire) (Temporary Prohibition of Traffic) Order 2012 No. 2012/1953. - Enabling power: Road Traffic Regulation Act 1984, s. 14 (1) (b). - Issued: 30.07.2012. Made: 22.06.2012. Coming into force: 29.06.2012. Effect: None. Territorial extent & classification: E. Local. - Available at http://www.legislation.gov.uk/uksi/2012/1953/contents/made *Non-print*

The A38 Trunk Road (Swinfen to Weeford, Staffordshire) (Temporary Prohibition of Traffic) Order 2012 No. 2012/2392. - Enabling power: Road Traffic Regulation Act 1984, s. 14 (1) (a). - Issued: 20.09.2012. Made: 03.09.2012. Coming into force: 10.09.2012. Effect: None. Territorial extent & classification: E. Local. - Available at http://www.legislation.gov.uk/uksi/2012/2392/contents/made *Non-print*

The A38 Trunk Road (Tideford, Cornwall) (Temporary Restriction and Prohibition of Traffic) Order 2012 No. 2012/545. - Enabling power: Road Traffic Regulation Act 1984, s. 14 (1) (a). - Issued: 01.03.2012. Made: 22.02.2012. Coming into force: 25.02.2012. Effect: None. Territorial extent & classification: E. Local. - Available at http://www.legislation.gov.uk/uksi/2012/545/contents/made *Non-print*

Road traffic: Traffic regulation

The A38 Trunk Road (Toyota Interchange to Clay Mills) (Temporary Prohibition of Traffic) Order 2012 No. 2012/1676. - Enabling power: Road Traffic Regulation Act 1984, s. 14 (1) (a). - Issued: 03.07.2012. Made: 06.06.2012. Coming into force: 13.07.2012. Effect: None. Territorial extent & classification: E. Local. - Available at http://www.legislation.gov.uk/uksi/2012/1676/contents/made *Non-print*

The A38 Trunk Road (Trerulefoot Roundabout to Stoketon Cross, Near Saltash) (Temporary Prohibition and Restriction of Traffic) Order 2012 No. 2012/54. - Enabling power: Road Traffic Regulation Act 1984, s. 14 (1) (a). - Issued: 13.01.2012. Made: 04.01.2012. Coming into force: 07.01.2012. Effect: None. Territorial extent & classification: E. Local. - Available at http://www.legislation.gov.uk/uksi/2012/54/contents/made *Non-print*

The A38 Trunk Road (Weeford to Branston, Staffordshire) (Slip Roads) (Temporary Prohibition of Traffic) Order 2012 No. 2012/218. - Enabling power: Road Traffic Regulation Act 1984, s. 14 (1) (a). - Issued: 03.02.2012. Made: 20.01.2012. Coming into force: 27.01.2012. Effect: None. Territorial extent & classification: E. Local. - Available at http://www.legislation.gov.uk/uksi/2012/218/contents/made *Non-print*

The A38 Trunk Road (Woodpecker Junction, Near South Brent) (Temporary Prohibition of Traffic) Order 2012 No. 2012/2333. - Enabling power: Road Traffic Regulation Act 1984, s. 14 (1) (b). - Issued: 13.09.2012. Made: 03.09.2012. Coming into force: 13.09.2012. Effect: None. Territorial extent & classification: E. Local. - Available at http://www.legislation.gov.uk/uksi/2012/2333/contents/made *Non-print*

The A38 Trunk Road (Woodpecker Junction, South Brent) (Temporary Restriction and Prohibition of Traffic) Order 2012 No. 2012/932. - Enabling power: Road Traffic Regulation Act 1984, s. 14 (1) (a). - Issued: 28.03.2012. Made: 22.03.2012. Coming into force: 31.03.2012. Effect: None. Territorial extent & classification: E. Local. - Available at http://www.legislation.gov.uk/uksi/2012/932/contents/made *Non-print*

The A40 Trunk Road (Denham Court Drive, Denham) (Temporary Prohibition of Traffic) Order 2012 No. 2012/715. - Enabling power: Road Traffic Regulation Act 1984, s. 14 (1) (b). - Issued: 19.03.2012. Made: 05.03.2012. Coming into force: 24.03.2012. Effect: None. Territorial extent & classification: E. Local. - Available at http://www.legislation.gov.uk/uksi/2012/715/contents/made *Non-print*

The A40 Trunk Road (Denham Roundabout) (Temporary Prohibition of Traffic) Order 2012 No. 2012/1856. - Enabling power: Road Traffic Regulation Act 1984, s. 14 (1) (a). - Issued: 20.07.2012. Made: 09.07.2012. Coming into force: 01.08.2012. Effect: None. Territorial extent & classification: E. Local. - Available at http://www.legislation.gov.uk/uksi/2012/1856/contents/made *Non-print*

The A40 Trunk Road (Glewstone, Herefordshire) (Temporary Restriction and Prohibition of Traffic) Order 2012 No. 2012/3307. - Enabling power: Road Traffic Regulation Act 1984, s. 14 (1) (a). - Issued: 17.01.2013. Made: 24.12.2012. Coming into force: 31.12.2012. Effect: None. Territorial extent & classification: E. Local. - Available at http://www.legislation.gov.uk/uksi/2012/3307/contents/made *Non-print*

The A40 Trunk Road (Golden Valley Bypass, Gloucestershire) (Temporary Prohibition of Traffic) Order 2012 No. 2012/398. - Enabling power: Road Traffic Regulation Act 1984, s. 14 (1) (a). - Issued: 21.02.2012. Made: 07.02.2012. Coming into force: 11.02.2012. Effect: None. Territorial extent & classification: E. Local. - Available at http://www.legislation.gov.uk/uksi/2012/398/contents/made *Non-print*

The A40 Trunk Road (M5 Junction 11 to Elmbridge Court Roundabout, Gloucester) (Temporary Prohibition of Traffic) Order 2012 No. 2012/491. - Enabling power: Road Traffic Regulation Act 1984, s. 14 (1) (a). - Issued: 29.02.2012. Made: 20.02.2012. Coming into force: 28.02.2012. Effect: None. Territorial extent & classification: E. Local. - Available at http://www.legislation.gov.uk/uksi/2012/491/contents/made *Non-print*

The A40 Trunk Road (Over Roundabout to Longford Roundabout, Gloucester) (Temporary Prohibition of Traffic) Order 2012 No. 2012/1055. - Enabling power: Road Traffic Regulation Act 1984, s. 14 (1) (a). - Issued: 13.04.2012. Made: 29.03.2012. Coming into force: 10.04.2012. Effect: None. Territorial extent & classification: E. Local. - Available at http://www.legislation.gov.uk/uksi/2012/1055/contents/made *Non-print*

The A40 Trunk Road (Ross - on - Wye, Herefordshire) (Temporary Restriction and Prohibition of Traffic) (No. 2) Order 2012 No. 2012/2005. - Enabling power: Road Traffic Regulation Act 1984, s. 14 (1) (a). - Issued: 02.08.2012. Made: 22.06.2012. Coming into force: 29.06.2012. Effect: None. Territorial extent & classification: E. Local. - Available at http://www.legislation.gov.uk/uksi/2012/2005/contents/made *Non-print*

Road traffic: Traffic regulation

The A40 Trunk Road (Ross - on - Wye, Herefordshire) (Temporary Restriction and Prohibition of Traffic) Order 2012 No. 2012/611. - Enabling power: Road Traffic Regulation Act 1984, s. 14 (1) (a). - Issued: 07.03.2012. Made: 20.02.2012. Coming into force: 27.02.2012. Effect: None. Territorial extent & classification: E. Local. - Available at http://www.legislation.gov.uk/uksi/2012/611/contents/made *Non-print*

The A40 Trunk Road (Whitchurch to Ross-on-Wye, Herefordshire) (Temporary Restriction and Prohibition of Traffic) (No. 2) Order 2012 No. 2012/2049. - Enabling power: Road Traffic Regulation Act 1984, s. 14 (1) (a). - Issued: 09.08.2012. Made: 20.07.2012. Coming into force: 27.07.2012. Effect: S.I. 2012/1318 revoked. Territorial extent & classification: E. Local. - Available at http://www.legislation.gov.uk/uksi/2012/2049/contents/made *Non-print*

The A40 Trunk Road (Whitchurch to Ross-on-Wye, Herefordshire) (Temporary Restriction and Prohibition of Traffic) Order 2012 No. 2012/1318. - Enabling power: Road Traffic Regulation Act 1984, s. 14 (1) (a). - Issued: 22.05.2012. Made: 30.04.2012. Coming into force: 07.05.2012. Effect: None. Territorial extent & classification: E. Local. - Revoked by SI 2012/2049 (Non-print). - Available at http://www.legislation.gov.uk/uksi/2012/1318/contents/made. Revoked by S.I. 2012/2049 [non print] *Non-print*

The A40 Trunk Road (Whitchurch to Ross on Wye) (Temporary Prohibition of Traffic) Order 2012 No. 2012/3306. - Enabling power: Road Traffic Regulation Act 1984, s. 14 (1) (a). - Issued: 17.01.2013. Made: 24.12.2012. Coming into force: 31.12.2012. Effect: None. Territorial extent & classification: E. Local. - Available at http://www.legislation.gov.uk/uksi/2012/3306/contents/made *Non-print*

The A42 Trunk Road (Ashby-de-la-Zouch, Leicestershire) (Temporary Restriction and Prohibition of Traffic) Order 2012 No. 2012/2399. - Enabling power: Road Traffic Regulation Act 1984, s. 14 (1) (a). - Issued: 24.09.2012. Made: 03.09.2012. Coming into force: 10.09.2012. Effect: None. Territorial extent & classification: E. Local. - Available at http://www.legislation.gov.uk/uksi/2012/2399/contents/made *Non-print*

The A42 Trunk Road (Ashby-de-la- Zouch to M1 Junction 23a) (Temporary Prohibition of Traffic) Order 2012 No. 2012/1315. - Enabling power: Road Traffic Regulation Act 1984, s. 14 (1) (a). - Issued: 22.05.2012. Made: 30.04.2012. Coming into force: 07.05.2012. Effect: None. Territorial extent & classification: E. Local. - Available at http://www.legislation.gov.uk/uksi/2012/1315/contents/made *Non-print*

The A43 Trunk Road (Brackley to Towcester, Northamptonshire) (Silverstone British Grand Prix) (Temporary Restriction and Prohibition of Traffic) Order 2012 No. 2012/1739. - Enabling power: Road Traffic Regulation Act 1984, s. 14 (1) (b). - Issued: 17.07.2012. Made: 18.06.2012. Coming into force: 25.06.2012. Effect: None. Territorial extent & classification: E. Local. - Available at http://www.legislation.gov.uk/uksi/2012/1739/contents/made *Non-print*

The A43 Trunk Road (Northamptonshire and Oxfordshire) (Temporary Prohibition of Traffic) Order 2012 No. 2012/2422. - Enabling power: Road Traffic Regulation Act 1984, s. 14 (1) (a). - Issued: 25.09.2012. Made: 10.09.2012. Coming into force: 17.09.2012. Effect: None. Territorial extent & classification: E. Local. - Available at http://www.legislation.gov.uk/uksi/2012/2422/contents/made *Non-print*

The A43 Trunk Road (Towcester to Brackley, Northamptonshire) (Temporary Prohibition of Traffic) Order 2012 No. 2012/1936. - Enabling power: Road Traffic Regulation Act 1984, s. 14 (1) (a). - Issued: 30.07.2012. Made: 26.06.2012. Coming into force: 03.07.2012. Effect: None. Territorial extent & classification: E. Local. - Available at http://www.legislation.gov.uk/uksi/2012/1936/contents/made *Non-print*

The A43 Trunk Road (Towcester to M1 Junction 15a, Northamptonshire) (Temporary Restriction and Prohibition of Traffic) Order 2012 No. 2012/2053. - Enabling power: Road Traffic Regulation Act 1984, s. 14 (1) (a). - Issued: 09.08.2012. Made: 23.07.2012. Coming into force: 30.07.2012. Effect: None. Territorial extent & classification: E. Local. - Available at http://www.legislation.gov.uk/uksi/2012/2053/contents/made *Non-print*

The A43 Trunk Road (Towcester to Silverstone, Northamptonshire) (Temporary Prohibition of Traffic) Order 2012 No. 2012/1141. - Enabling power: Road Traffic Regulation Act 1984, s. 14 (1) (a). - Issued: 27.04.2012. Made: 10.04.2012. Coming into force: 17.04.2012. Effect: None. Territorial extent & classification: E. Local. - Available at http://www.legislation.gov.uk/uksi/2012/1141/contents/made *Non-print*

The A43 Trunk Road (Towcester to Silverstone, Northamptonshire) (Temporary Restriction and Prohibition of Traffic) Order 2012 No. 2012/2718. - Enabling power: Road Traffic Regulation Act 1984, s. 14 (1) (a). - Issued: 02.11.2012. Made: 01.10.2012. Coming into force: 08.10.2012. Effect: None. Territorial extent & classification: E. Local. - Available at http://www.legislation.gov.uk/uksi/2012/2718/contents/made *Non-print*

Road traffic: Traffic regulation

The A45 Trunk Road and the M42 Motorway (M42 Junction 6) (Temporary Prohibition of Traffic) Order 2012 No. 2012/1325. - Enabling power: Road Traffic Regulation Act 1984, s. 14 (1) (a). - Issued: 23.05.2012. Made: 07.05.2012. Coming into force: 14.05.2012. Effect: None. Territorial extent & classification: E. Local. - Available at http://www.legislation.gov.uk/uksi/2012/1325/contents/made *Non-print*

The A45 Trunk Road (Brackmills to Earls Barton, Northampton) (Temporary Prohibition of Traffic) Order 2012 No. 2012/2727. - Enabling power: Road Traffic Regulation Act 1984, s. 14 (1) (a). - Issued: 02.11.2012. Made: 08.10.2012. Coming into force: 15.10.2012. Effect: None. Territorial extent & classification: E. Local. - Available at http://www.legislation.gov.uk/uksi/2012/2727/contents/made *Non-print*

The A45 Trunk Road (Earls Barton, Northamptonshire) (Temporary Prohibition of Traffic) Order 2012 No. 2012/2797. - Enabling power: Road Traffic Regulation Act 1984, s. 14 (1) (a). - Issued: 09.11.2012. Made: 15.10.2012. Coming into force: 22.10.2012. Effect: None. Territorial extent & classification: E. Local. - Available at http://www.legislation.gov.uk/uksi/2012/2797/contents/made *Non-print*

The A45 Trunk Road (Festival Island, Coventry) (Temporary Prohibition of Traffic) Order 2012 No. 2012/1746. - Enabling power: Road Traffic Regulation Act 1984, s. 14 (1) (a). - Issued: 17.07.2012. Made: 18.06.2012. Coming into force: 25.06.2012. Effect: None. Territorial extent & classification: E. Local. - Available at http://www.legislation.gov.uk/uksi/2012/1746/contents/made *Non-print*

The A45 Trunk Road (Festival Roundabout, Coventry) (Temporary Prohibition of Traffic) Order 2012 No. 2012/744. - Enabling power: Road Traffic Regulation Act 1984, s. 14 (1) (a). - Issued: 19.03.2012. Made: 02.03.2012. Coming into force: 09.03.2012. Effect: None. Territorial extent & classification: E. Local. - Available at http://www.legislation.gov.uk/uksi/2012/744/contents/made *Non-print*

The A45 Trunk Road (Hardingstone, Northamptonshire) (Temporary Restriction and Prohibition of Traffic) Order 2012 No. 2012/3166. - Enabling power: Road Traffic Regulation Act 1984, s. 14 (1) (a). - Issued: 28.12.2012. Made: 23.11.2012. Coming into force: 30.11.2012. Effect: None. Territorial extent & classification: E. Local. - Available at http://www.legislation.gov.uk/uksi/2012/3166/contents/made *Non-print*

The A45 Trunk Road (Higham Ferrers and Wellingborough, Northamptonshire) (Temporary Restriction and Prohibition of Traffic) Order 2012 No. 2012/2829. - Enabling power: Road Traffic Regulation Act 1984, s. 14 (1) (a). - Issued: 15.11.2012. Made: 22.10.2012. Coming into force: 29.10.2012. Effect: None. Territorial extent & classification: E. Local. - Available at http://www.legislation.gov.uk/uksi/2012/2829/contents/made *Non-print*

The A45 Trunk Road (Northampton) (Temporary Prohibition and Restriction of Traffic) Order 2012 No. 2012/2899. - Enabling power: Road Traffic Regulation Act 1984, s. 14 (1) (a). - Issued: 22.11.2012. Made: 02.11.2012. Coming into force: 09.11.2012. Effect: None. Territorial extent & classification: E. Local. - Available at http://www.legislation.gov.uk/uksi/2012/2899/contents/made *Non-print*

The A45 Trunk Road (Northampton) (Temporary Prohibition of Traffic) (No. 2) Order 2012 No. 2012/1442. - Enabling power: Road Traffic Regulation Act 1984, s. 14 (1) (a). - Issued: 12.06.2012. Made: 14.05.2012. Coming into force: 21.05.2012. Effect: None. Territorial extent & classification: E. Local. - Available at http://www.legislation.gov.uk/uksi/2012/1442/contents/made *Non-print*

The A45 Trunk Road (Northampton) (Temporary Prohibition of Traffic) Order 2012 No. 2012/108. - Enabling power: Road Traffic Regulation Act 1984, s. 14 (1) (a). - Issued: 20.01.2012. Made: 06.01.2012. Coming into force: 13.01.2012. Effect: None. Territorial extent & classification: E. Local. - Available at http://www.legislation.gov.uk/uksi/2012/108/contents/made *Non-print*

The A45 Trunk Road (North of Thurlaston to Memorial Island, Warwickshire) (Temporary 40 Miles Per Hour Speed Restriction) Order 2012 No. 2012/591. - Enabling power: Road Traffic Regulation Act 1984, s. 14 (1) (a). - Issued: 06.03.2012. Made: 17.02.2012. Coming into force: 24.02.2012. Effect: None. Territorial extent & classification: E. Local. - Available at http://www.legislation.gov.uk/uksi/2012/591/contents/made *Non-print*

The A45 Trunk Road (Ryton-on-Dunsmore to Blue Boar, Warwickshire) (Temporary Prohibition of Traffic) Order 2012 No. 2012/648. - Enabling power: Road Traffic Regulation Act 1984, s. 14 (1) (a). - Issued: 14.03.2012. Made: 24.02.2012. Coming into force: 02.03.2012. Effect: None. Territorial extent & classification: E. Local. - Available at http://www.legislation.gov.uk/uksi/2012/648/contents/made *Non-print*

The A45 Trunk Road (Ryton-on-Dunsmore, Warwickshire) (Temporary Prohibition of Traffic) (No.2) Order 2012 No. 2012/2183. - Enabling power: Road Traffic Regulation Act 1984, s. 14 (1) (a). - Issued: 28.08.2012. Made: 15.08.2012. Coming into force: 22.08.2012. Effect: None. Territorial extent & classification: E. Local. - Available at http://www.legislation.gov.uk/uksi/2012/2183/contents/made *Non-print*

The A45 Trunk Road (Ryton-on-Dunsmore, Warwickshire) (Temporary Prohibition of Traffic) (No. 3) Order 2012 No. 2012/2425. - Enabling power: Road Traffic Regulation Act 1984, s. 14 (1) (a). - Issued: 25.09.2012. Made: 07.09.2012. Coming into force: 14.09.2012. Effect: None. Territorial extent & classification: E. Local. - Available at http://www.legislation.gov.uk/uksi/2012/2425/contents/made *Non-print*

The A45 Trunk Road (Ryton on Dunsmore, Warwickshire) (Temporary Prohibition of Traffic) Order 2012 No. 2012/2124. - Enabling power: Road Traffic Regulation Act 1984, s. 14 (1) (a). - Issued: 17.08.2012. Made: 06.08.2012. Coming into force: 13.08.2012. Effect: None. Territorial extent & classification: E. Local. - Available at http://www.legislation.gov.uk/uksi/2012/2124/contents/made *Non-print*

The A45 Trunk Road (South of Coventry) (Temporary Prohibition of Traffic) Order 2012 No. 2012/3176. - Enabling power: Road Traffic Regulation Act 1984, s. 14 (1) (a). - Issued: 31.12.2012. Made: 26.11.2012. Coming into force: 03.12.2012. Effect: None. Territorial extent & classification: E. Local. - Available at http://www.legislation.gov.uk/uksi/2012/3176/contents/made *Non-print*

The A45 Trunk Road (Thurlaston Roundabout, Warwickshire) (Temporary Prohibition of Traffic) Order 2012 No. 2012/370. - Enabling power: Road Traffic Regulation Act 1984, s. 14 (1) (a). - Issued: 17.02.2012. Made: 30.01.2012. Coming into force: 06.02.2012. Effect: None. Territorial extent & classification: E. Local. - Available at http://www.legislation.gov.uk/uksi/2012/370/contents/made *Non-print*

The A45 Trunk Road (Tollbar End to Ryton-on-Dunsmore, Warwickshire) (Temporary Prohibition of Traffic) Order 2012 No. 2012/229. - Enabling power: Road Traffic Regulation Act 1984, s. 14 (1) (a). - Issued: 03.02.2012. Made: 23.01.2012. Coming into force: 30.01.2012. Effect: None. Territorial extent & classification: E. Local. - Available at http://www.legislation.gov.uk/uksi/2012/229/contents/made *Non-print*

The A45 Trunk Road (Wellingborough, Northamptonshire) (Slip Road) (Temporary Prohibition of Traffic) Order 2012 No. 2012/2001. - Enabling power: Road Traffic Regulation Act 1984, s. 14 (1) (a). - Issued: 02.08.2012. Made: 09.07.2012. Coming into force: 16.07.2012. Effect: None. Territorial extent & classification: E. Local. - Available at http://www.legislation.gov.uk/uksi/2012/2001/contents/made *Non-print*

The A45 Trunk Road (Wellingborough, Northamptonshire) (Temporary Prohibition and Restriction of Traffic) (No. 2) Order 2012 No. 2012/2799. - Enabling power: Road Traffic Regulation Act 1984, s. 14 (1) (a). - Issued: 09.11.2012. Made: 15.10.2012. Coming into force: 22.10.2012. Effect: None. Territorial extent & classification: E. Local. - Available at http://www.legislation.gov.uk/uksi/2012/2799/contents/made *Non-print*

The A45 Trunk Road (Wellingborough, Northamptonshire) (Temporary Prohibition and Restriction of Traffic) Order 2012 No. 2012/252. - Enabling power: Road Traffic Regulation Act 1984, s. 14 (1) (a). - Issued: 06.02.2012. Made: 20.01.2012. Coming into force: 27.01.2012. Effect: None. Territorial extent & classification: E. Local. - Available at http://www.legislation.gov.uk/uksi/2012/252/contents/made *Non-print*

The A45 Trunk Road (Wellingborough, Northamptonshire) (Temporary Prohibition of Traffic) Order 2012 No. 2012/2385. - Enabling power: Road Traffic Regulation Act 1984, s. 14 (1) (a). - Issued: 18.09.2012. Made: 28.08.2012. Coming into force: 04.09.2012. Effect: None. Territorial extent & classification: E. Local. - Available at http://www.legislation.gov.uk/uksi/2012/2385/contents/made *Non-print*

The A45 Trunk Road (Wootton to Brackmills, Northamptonshire) (Temporary Prohibition of Traffic) Order 2012 No. 2012/1701. - Enabling power: Road Traffic Regulation Act 1984, s. 14 (1) (a). - Issued: 12.07.2012. Made: 11.06.2012. Coming into force: 18.06.2012. Effect: None. Territorial extent & classification: E. Local. - Available at http://www.legislation.gov.uk/uksi/2012/1701/contents/made *Non-print*

The A46 Trunk Road (A607 Hobby Horse Roundabout, Syston, to A1133 Winthorpe Roundabout, Newark-on-Trent) (24 Hours Clearway and Prohibition of Waiting) Order 2012 No. 2012/1082. - Enabling power: Road Traffic Regulation Act 1984, ss. 1 (1), 2 (1) (2), 4 (1), 122A, sch. 9, para. 27 (1). - Issued: 17.04.2012. Made: 08.03.2012. Coming into force: 22.03.2012. Effect: S.I. 1963/1172; 1991/1635 varied & S.I. 1969/1421 revoked. Territorial extent & classification: E. Local. - Available at http://www.legislation.gov.uk/uksi/2012/1082/contents/made *Non-print*

Road traffic: Traffic regulation

The A46 Trunk Road (Ashchurch, Gloucestershire) (Temporary Restriction and Prohibition of Traffic) Order 2012 No. 2012/2973. - Enabling power: Road Traffic Regulation Act 1984, s. 14 (1) (a). - Issued: 05.12.2012. Made: 12.11.2012. Coming into force: 19.11.2012. Effect: None. Territorial extent & classification: E. Local. - Available at http://www.legislation.gov.uk/uksi/2012/2973/contents/made *Non-print*

The A46 Trunk Road (Aston Cross - Teddington Hands, Gloucestershire) (Temporary Restriction and Prohibition of Traffic) Order 2012 No. 2012/859. - Enabling power: Road Traffic Regulation Act 1984, s. 14 (1) (a). - Issued: 23.03.2012. Made: 09.03.2012. Coming into force: 16.03.2012. Effect: None. Territorial extent & classification: E. Local. - Available at http://www.legislation.gov.uk/uksi/2012/859/contents/made *Non-print*

The A46 Trunk Road (Bidford-on-Avon, Worcestershire) (Temporary Prohibition of Traffic) Order 2012 No. 2012/1930. - Enabling power: Road Traffic Regulation Act 1984, s. 14 (1) (a). - Issued: 26.07.2012. Made: 25.06.2012. Coming into force: 02.07.2012. Effect: None. Territorial extent & classification: E. Local. - Available at http://www.legislation.gov.uk/uksi/2012/1930/contents/made *Non-print*

The A46 Trunk Road (Binley, Coventry) (Temporary Restriction and Prohibition of Traffic) Order 2012 No. 2012/1103. - Enabling power: Road Traffic Regulation Act 1984, s. 14 (1) (a). - Issued: 20.04.2012. Made: 04.04.2012. Coming into force: 11.04.2012. Effect: None. Territorial extent & classification: E. Local. - Available at http://www.legislation.gov.uk/uksi/2012/1103/contents/made *Non-print*

The A46 Trunk Road (Cold Ashton Roundabout to London Road Junction, Bath) (Temporary Restriction and Prohibition of Traffic) Order 2012 No. 2012/3291. - Enabling power: Road Traffic Regulation Act 1984, s. 14 (1) (a). - Issued: 15.01.2013. Made: 31.12.2012. Coming into force: 09.01.2013. Effect: None. Territorial extent & classification: E. Local. - Available at http://www.legislation.gov.uk/uksi/2012/3291/contents/made *Non-print*

The A46 Trunk Road (Coventry Eastern Bypass) (Temporary Prohibition of Traffic) Order 2012 No. 2012/2424. - Enabling power: Road Traffic Regulation Act 1984, s. 14 (1) (a). - Issued: 25.09.2012. Made: 10.09.2012. Coming into force: 17.09.2012. Effect: None. Territorial extent & classification: E. Local. - Available at http://www.legislation.gov.uk/uksi/2012/2424/contents/made *Non-print*

The A46 Trunk Road (Evesham Bypass) (Temporary Restriction and Prohibition of Traffic) Order 2012 No. 2012/876. - Enabling power: Road Traffic Regulation Act 1984, s. 14 (1) (a). - Issued: 26.03.2012. Made: 12.03.2012. Coming into force: 19.03.2012. Effect: None. Territorial extent & classification: E. Local. - Available at http://www.legislation.gov.uk/uksi/2012/876/contents/made *Non-print*

The A46 Trunk Road (Evesham, Worcestershire) (Temporary Restriction and Prohibition of Traffic) (No. 2) Order 2012 No. 2012/3313. - Enabling power: Road Traffic Regulation Act 1984, s. 14 (1) (a). - Issued: 17.01.2013. Made: 24.12.2012. Coming into force: 31.12.2012. Effect: None. Territorial extent & classification: E. Local. - Available at http://www.legislation.gov.uk/uksi/2012/3313/contents/made *Non-print*

The A46 Trunk Road (Evesham, Worcestershire) (Temporary Restriction and Prohibition of Traffic) Order 2012 No. 2012/571. - Enabling power: Road Traffic Regulation Act 1984, s. 14 (1) (a). - Issued: 02.03.2012. Made: 13.02.2012. Coming into force: 20.02.2012. Effect: None. Territorial extent & classification: E. Local. - Available at http://www.legislation.gov.uk/uksi/2012/571/contents/made *Non-print*

The A46 Trunk Road (Evesham, Worcestershire) (Temporary Restriction of Traffic) Order 2012 No. 2012/733. - Enabling power: Road Traffic Regulation Act 1984, s. 14 (1) (a). - Issued: 19.03.2012. Made: 02.03.2012. Coming into force: 09.03.2012. Effect: None. Territorial extent & classification: E. Local. - Available at http://www.legislation.gov.uk/uksi/2012/733/contents/made *Non-print*

The A46 Trunk Road (Fosse Way, Nottinghamshire and Lincolnshire) (Temporary Prohibition of Traffic) Order 2012 No. 2012/391. - Enabling power: Road Traffic Regulation Act 1984, s. 14 (1) (a). - Issued: 21.02.2012. Made: 30.01.2012. Coming into force: 06.02.2012. Effect: None. Territorial extent & classification: E. Local. - Available at http://www.legislation.gov.uk/uksi/2012/391/contents/made *Non-print*

The A46 Trunk Road (Fosse Way, Nottinghamshire) (Temporary Prohibition of Traffic) Order 2012 No. 2012/2805. - Enabling power: Road Traffic Regulation Act 1984, s. 14 (1) (a). - Issued: 09.11.2012. Made: 22.10.2012. Coming into force: 29.10.2012. Effect: None. Territorial extent & classification: E. Local. - Available at http://www.legislation.gov.uk/uksi/2012/2805/contents/made *Non-print*

The A46 Trunk Road (Groby to Anstey, Leicestershire) (Temporary Prohibition of Traffic) Order 2012 No. 2012/2178. - Enabling power: Road Traffic Regulation Act 1984, s. 14 (1) (a). - Issued: 28.08.2012. Made: 10.08.2012. Coming into force: 17.08.2012. Effect: None. Territorial extent & classification: E. Local. - Available at http://www.legislation.gov.uk/uksi/2012/2178/contents/made *Non-print*

Road traffic: Traffic regulation

The A46 Trunk Road (Hinton Cross, Worcestershire) (Temporary Restriction of Traffic) Order 2012 No. 2012/1921. - Enabling power: Road Traffic Regulation Act 1984, s. 14 (1) (a). - Issued: 25.07.2012. Made: 18.06.2012. Coming into force: 25.06.2012. Effect: None. Territorial extent & classification: E. Local. - Available at http://www.legislation.gov.uk/uksi/2012/1921/contents/made *Non-print*

The A46 Trunk Road (Junction with the A452, near Kenilworth, Warwickshire) (Temporary Prohibition of Traffic) Order 2012 No. 2012/1441. - Enabling power: Road Traffic Regulation Act 1984, s. 14 (1) (a). - Issued: 12.06.2012. Made: 15.05.2012. Coming into force: 22.05.2012. Effect: None. Territorial extent & classification: E. Local. - Available at http://www.legislation.gov.uk/uksi/2012/1441/contents/made *Non-print*

The A46 Trunk Road (London Road Junction, Bath) (Temporary Prohibition of Traffic) Order 2012 No. 2012/1421. - Enabling power: Road Traffic Regulation Act 1984, s. 14 (1) (a). - Issued: 01.06.2012. Made: 22.05.2012. Coming into force: 26.05.2012. Effect: None. Territorial extent & classification: E. Local. - Available at http://www.legislation.gov.uk/uksi/2012/1421/contents/made *Non-print*

The A46 Trunk Road (M1 Junction 21a to Dalby, Leicestershire) (Temporary Prohibition of Traffic) Order 2012 No. 2012/3303. - Enabling power: Road Traffic Regulation Act 1984, s. 14 (1) (a). - Issued: 16.01.2013. Made: 24.12.2012. Coming into force: 31.12.2012. Effect: None. Territorial extent & classification: E. Local. - Available at http://www.legislation.gov.uk/uksi/2012/3303/contents/made *Non-print*

The A46 Trunk Road (Newark-on-Trent, Nottinghamshire) (Temporary Prohibition of Traffic) Order 2012 No. 2012/378. - Enabling power: Road Traffic Regulation Act 1984, s. 14 (1) (a). - Issued: 17.02.2012. Made: 06.02.2012. Coming into force: 13.02.2012. Effect: None. Territorial extent & classification: E. Local. - Available at http://www.legislation.gov.uk/uksi/2012/378/contents/made *Non-print*

The A46 Trunk Road (Sedgeberrow, Worcestershire) (Temporary Prohibition of Traffic) Order 2012 No. 2012/3229. - Enabling power: Road Traffic Regulation Act 1984, s. 14 (1) (b). - Issued: 07.01.2013. Made: 04.12.2012. Coming into force: 11.12.2012. Effect: None. Territorial extent & classification: E. Local. - Available at http://www.legislation.gov.uk/uksi/2012/3229/contents/made *Non-print*

The A46 Trunk Road (Shottery to Red Hill) (Temporary Restriction and Prohibition of Traffic) Order 2012 No. 2012/1678. - Enabling power: Road Traffic Regulation Act 1984, s. 14 (1) (a). - Issued: 03.07.2012. Made: 06.06.2012. Coming into force: 13.06.2012. Effect: None. Territorial extent & classification: E. Local. - Available at http://www.legislation.gov.uk/uksi/2012/1678/contents/made *Non-print*

The A46 Trunk Road (Stratford-upon-Avon, Warwickshire) (Temporary Restriction and Prohibition of Traffic) Order 2012 No. 2012/1932. - Enabling power: Road Traffic Regulation Act 1984, s. 14 (1) (a). - Issued: 26.07.2012. Made: 25.06.2012. Coming into force: 02.07.2012. Effect: None. Territorial extent & classification: E. Local. - Available at http://www.legislation.gov.uk/uksi/2012/1932/contents/made *Non-print*

The A46 Trunk Road (Teddington Hands to Sedgeberrow) (Temporary Prohibition of Traffic) Order 2012 No. 2012/1686. - Enabling power: Road Traffic Regulation Act 1984, s. 14 (1) (a). - Issued: 03.07.2012. Made: 06.06.2012. Coming into force: 13.06.2012. Effect: None. Territorial extent & classification: E. Local. - Available at http://www.legislation.gov.uk/uksi/2012/1686/contents/made *Non-print*

The A46 Trunk Road (Wanlip and Syston, Leicestershire) (Temporary Prohibition of Traffic) Order 2012 No. 2012/2402. - Enabling power: Road Traffic Regulation Act 1984, s. 14 (1) (a). - Issued: 24.09.2012. Made: 03.09.2012. Coming into force: 10.09.2012. Effect: None. Territorial extent & classification: E. Local. - Available at http://www.legislation.gov.uk/uksi/2012/2402/contents/made *Non-print*

The A46 Trunk Road (Wanlip, Leicestershire) (Temporary Prohibition of Traffic) Order 2012 No. 2012/3133. - Enabling power: Road Traffic Regulation Act 1984, s. 14 (1) (a). - Issued: 20.12.2012. Made: 16.11.2012. Coming into force: 23.11.2012. Effect: None. Territorial extent & classification: E. Local. - Available at http://www.legislation.gov.uk/uksi/2012/3133/contents/made *Non-print*

The A46 Trunk Road (Warwick Bypass) (Temporary Prohibition of Traffic) Order 2012 No. 2012/1594. - Enabling power: Road Traffic Regulation Act 1984, s. 14 (1) (b). - Issued: 27.06.2012. Made: 28.05.2012. Coming into force: 04.06.2012. Effect: None. Territorial extent & classification: E. Local. - Available at http://www.legislation.gov.uk/uksi/2012/1594/contents/made *Non-print*

The A46 Trunk Road (Warwick to Coventry) (Temporary Prohibition of Traffic in Laybys) Order 2012 No. 2012/2725. - Enabling power: Road Traffic Regulation Act 1984, s. 14 (1) (a). - Issued: 02.11.2012. Made: 08.10.2012. Coming into force: 15.10.2012. Effect: None. Territorial extent & classification: E. Local. - Available at http://www.legislation.gov.uk/uksi/2012/2725/contents/made *Non-print*

The A47 Trunk Road (Acle, Norfolk) Eastbound Exit Slip Road (Temporary Prohibition of Traffic) Order 2012 No. 2012/599. - Enabling power: Road Traffic Regulation Act 1984, s. 14 (1) (a). - Issued: 06.03.2012. Made: 27.02.2012. Coming into force: 05.03.2012. Effect: None. Territorial extent & classification: E. Local. - Available at http://www.legislation.gov.uk/uksi/2012/599/contents/made *Non-print*

The A47 Trunk Road (Acle Straight, Norfolk) (Temporary Prohibition of Traffic) Order 2012 No. 2012/1624. - Enabling power: Road Traffic Regulation Act 1984, s. 14 (1) (a). - Issued: 29.06.2012. Made: 18.06.2012. Coming into force: 25.06.2012. Effect: None. Territorial extent & classification: E. Local. - Available at http://www.legislation.gov.uk/uksi/2012/1624/contents/made *Non-print*

The A47 Trunk Road (Blofield Bypass, Postwick Interchange to Yarmouth Road Junction, Norfolk) (Temporary Restriction and Prohibition of Traffic) Order 2012 No. 2012/2827. - Enabling power: Road Traffic Regulation Act 1984, s. 14 (1) (a). - Issued: 14.11.2012. Made: 29.10.2012. Coming into force: 05.11.2012. Effect: None. Territorial extent & classification: E. Local. - Available at http://www.legislation.gov.uk/uksi/2012/2827/contents/made *Non-print*

The A47 Trunk Road (Dereham, Norfolk) (Temporary Restriction and Prohibition of Traffic) Order 2012 No. 2012/722. - Enabling power: Road Traffic Regulation Act 1984, s. 14 (1) (a). - Issued: 19.03.2012. Made: 05.03.2012. Coming into force: 12.03.2012. Effect: None. Territorial extent & classification: E. Local. - Available at http://www.legislation.gov.uk/uksi/2012/722/contents/made *Non-print*

The A47 Trunk Road (Dogsthorpe to Thorney, City of Peterborough) (Temporary Prohibition of Traffic) Order 2012 No. 2012/2217. - Enabling power: Road Traffic Regulation Act 1984, s. 14 (1) (a). - Issued: 31.08.2012. Made: 24.08.2012. Coming into force: 31.08.2012. Effect: None. Territorial extent & classification: E. Local. - Available at http://www.legislation.gov.uk/uksi/2012/2217/contents/made *Non-print*

The A47 Trunk Road (Guyhirn Roundabout to Redmoor Lane Roundabout, Wisbech, Cambridgeshire) (Temporary Prohibition of Traffic) Order 2012 No. 2012/2326. - Enabling power: Road Traffic Regulation Act 1984, s. 14 (1) (a). - Issued: 13.09.2012. Made: 03.09.2012. Coming into force: 10.09.2012. Effect: None. Territorial extent & classification: E. Local. - Available at http://www.legislation.gov.uk/uksi/2012/2326/contents/made *Non-print*

The A47 Trunk Road (Hardwick Interchange, Kings Lynn, Norfolk) Westbound Entry Slip Road (Temporary Prohibition of Traffic) Order 2012 No. 2012/3193. - Enabling power: Road Traffic Regulation Act 1984, s. 14 (1) (a). - Issued: 02.01.2013. Made: 10.12.2012. Coming into force: 17.12.2012. Effect: None. Territorial extent & classification: E. Local. - Available at http://www.legislation.gov.uk/uksi/2012/3193/contents/made *Non-print*

The A47 Trunk Road (Ipswich Road Interchange to Trowse Interchange, Norwich, Norfolk) Eastbound (Temporary Restriction and Prohibition of Traffic) Order 2012 No. 2012/3294. - Enabling power: Road Traffic Regulation Act 1984, s. 14 (1) (a). - Issued: 15.01.2013. Made: 31.12.2012. Coming into force: 07.01.2013. Effect: None. Territorial extent & classification: E. Local. - Available at http://www.legislation.gov.uk/uksi/2012/3294/contents/made *Non-print*

The A47 Trunk Road (Kings Lynn to Swaffham, Norfolk) (Temporary Prohibition of Traffic) Order 2012 No. 2012/1469. - Enabling power: Road Traffic Regulation Act 1984, s. 14 (1) (a). - Issued: 12.06.2012. Made: 28.05.2012. Coming into force: 04.06.2012. Effect: None. Territorial extent & classification: E. Local. - Available at http://www.legislation.gov.uk/uksi/2012/1469/contents/made *Non-print*

The A47 Trunk Road (Longwater Interchange to Watton Road Interchange, Norwich, Norfolk) (Temporary Restriction and Prohibition of Traffic) Order 2012 No. 2012/498. - Enabling power: Road Traffic Regulation Act 1984, s. 14 (1) (a). - Issued: 01.03.2012. Made: 20.02.2012. Coming into force: 27.02.2012. Effect: None. Territorial extent & classification: E. Local. - Available at http://www.legislation.gov.uk/uksi/2012/498/contents/made *Non-print*

The A47 Trunk Road (Longwater to Easton, Costessey, Norfolk) (Westbound) (Temporary Restriction and Prohibition of Traffic) Order 2012 No. 2012/2774. - Enabling power: Road Traffic Regulation Act 1984, s. 14 (1) (a). - Issued: 08.11.2012. Made: 22.10.2012. Coming into force: 29.10.2012. Effect: None. Territorial extent & classification: E. Local. - Available at http://www.legislation.gov.uk/uksi/2012/2774/contents/made *Non-print*

The A47 Trunk Road (Pullover Roundabout to Hardwick Interchange, Kings Lynn, Norfolk) (Temporary Prohibition of Traffic) Order 2012 No. 2012/2828. - Enabling power: Road Traffic Regulation Act 1984, s. 14 (1) (a). - Issued: 14.11.2012. Made: 29.10.2012. Coming into force: 05.11.2012. Effect: None. Territorial extent & classification: E. Local. - Available at http://www.legislation.gov.uk/uksi/2012/2828/contents/made *Non-print*

The A47 Trunk Road (Soke Parkway, Bretton Gate Interchange to A1260 Thorpe Wood Interchange, City of Peterborough) Westbound (Temporary Restriction and Prohibition of Traffic) Order 2012 No. 2012/1735. - Enabling power: Road Traffic Regulation Act 1984, s. 14 (1) (a). - Issued: 17.07.2012. Made: 25.07.2012. Coming into force: 02.07.2012. Effect: None. Territorial extent & classification: E. Local. - Available at http://www.legislation.gov.uk/uksi/2012/1735/contents/made *Non-print*

The A47 Trunk Road (Soke Parkway, Nene Parkway Interchange Junction 15 to Paston Parkway Interchange Junction 20, City of Peterborough) (Temporary Prohibition of Traffic) Order 2012 No. 2012/2776. - Enabling power: Road Traffic Regulation Act 1984, s. 14 (1) (a). - Issued: 08.11.2012. Made: 22.10.2012. Coming into force: 29.10.2012. Effect: None. Territorial extent & classification: E. Local. - Available at http://www.legislation.gov.uk/uksi/2012/2776/contents/made *Non-print*

The A47 Trunk Road (Swaffham Bypass, Norwich Road to Castleacre Road, Norfolk) Westbound (Temporary Prohibition of Traffic) Order 2012 No. 2012/2966. - Enabling power: Road Traffic Regulation Act 1984, s. 14 (1) (a). - Issued: 30.11.2012. Made: 19.11.2012. Coming into force: 26.11.2012. Effect: None. Territorial extent & classification: E. Local. - Available at http://www.legislation.gov.uk/uksi/2012/2966/contents/made *Non-print*

The A47 Trunk Road (Terrington St John to King's Lynn, Norfolk) (Temporary Restriction and Prohibition of Traffic) Order 2012 No. 2012/1546. - Enabling power: Road Traffic Regulation Act 1984, s. 14 (1) (a). - Issued: 20.06.2012. Made: 06.06.2012. Coming into force: 13.06.2012. Effect: None. Territorial extent & classification: E. Local. - Available at http://www.legislation.gov.uk/uksi/2012/1546/contents/made *Non-print*

The A47 Trunk Road (Thorney, City of Peterborough and Wisbech, Cambridgeshire) (Temporary Restriction and Prohibition of Traffic) Order 2012 No. 2012/348. - Enabling power: Road Traffic Regulation Act 1984, s. 14 (1) (a). - Issued: 15.02.2012. Made: 06.02.2012. Coming into force: 13.02.2012. Effect: None. Territorial extent & classification: E. Local. - Available at http://www.legislation.gov.uk/uksi/2012/348/contents/made *Non-print*

The A47 Trunk Road (Thorney to Dogsthorpe, City of Peterborough) (Temporary Prohibition of Traffic) (No. 2) Order 2012 No. 2012/3314. - Enabling power: Road Traffic Regulation Act 1984, s. 14 (1) (a). - Issued: 17.01.2013. Made: 26.11.2012. Coming into force: 03.12.2012. Effect: None. Territorial extent & classification: E. Local. - Available at http://www.legislation.gov.uk/uksi/2012/3314/contents/made *Non-print*

The A47 Trunk Road (Toftwood Interchange, Dereham, Norfolk) Westbound Slip Roads (Temporary Prohibition of Traffic) Order 2012 No. 2012/1460. - Enabling power: Road Traffic Regulation Act 1984, s. 14 (1) (a). - Issued: 12.06.2012. Made: 28.05.2012. Coming into force: 04.06.2012. Effect: None. Territorial extent & classification: E. Local. - Available at http://www.legislation.gov.uk/uksi/2012/1460/contents/made *Non-print*

The A47 Trunk Road (Trowse Interchange to Cucumber Lane Roundabout, Norwich, Norfolk) (Temporary Restriction and Prohibition of Traffic) Order 2012 No. 2012/2441. - Enabling power: Road Traffic Regulation Act 1984, s. 14 (1) (a). - Issued: 27.09.2012. Made: 17.09.2012. Coming into force: 24.09.2012. Effect: None. Territorial extent & classification: E. Local. - Available at http://www.legislation.gov.uk/uksi/2012/2441/contents/made *Non-print*

The A47 Trunk Road (West of Wendling to Dereham, Norfolk) (Temporary Restriction and Prohibition of Traffic) Order 2012 No. 2012/2472. - Enabling power: Road Traffic Regulation Act 1984, s. 14 (1) (a). - Issued: 01.10.2012. Made: 24.09.2012. Coming into force: 01.10.2012. Effect: None. Territorial extent & classification: E. Local. - Available at http://www.legislation.gov.uk/uksi/2012/2472/contents/made *Non-print*

The A49 Trunk Road (Bayston Hill, Shropshire) (Temporary Prohibition of Traffic) Order 2012 No. 2012/3227. - Enabling power: Road Traffic Regulation Act 1984, s. 14 (1) (a). - Issued: 07.01.2013. Made: 05.12.2012. Coming into force: 12.12.2012. Effect: None. Territorial extent & classification: E. Local. - Available at http://www.legislation.gov.uk/uksi/2012/3227/contents/made *Non-print*

The A49 Trunk Road (Brimfield to Stockton Cross, Herefordshire) (Temporary Prohibition of Traffic) Order 2012 No. 2012/3228. - Enabling power: Road Traffic Regulation Act 1984, s. 14 (1) (a). - Issued: 07.01.2013. Made: 05.12.2012. Coming into force: 12.12.2012. Effect: None. Territorial extent & classification: E. Local. - Available at http://www.legislation.gov.uk/uksi/2012/3228/contents/made *Non-print*

The A49 Trunk Road (Bromfield to Craven Arms) (Temporary Prohibition of Traffic) Order 2012 No. 2012/582. - Enabling power: Road Traffic Regulation Act 1984, s. 14 (1) (a). - Issued: 06.03.2012. Made: 17.02.2012. Coming into force: 24.02.2012. Effect: None. Territorial extent & classification: E. Local. - Available at http://www.legislation.gov.uk/uksi/2012/582/contents/made *Non-print*

The A49 Trunk Road (Church Stretton to Craven Arms, Shropshire) (Temporary Prohibition of Traffic) Order 2012 No. 2012/581. - Enabling power: Road Traffic Regulation Act 1984, s. 14 (1) (a). - Issued: 06.03.2012. Made: 17.02.2012. Coming into force: 24.02.2012. Effect: None. Territorial extent & classification: E. Local. - Available at http://www.legislation.gov.uk/uksi/2012/581/contents/made *Non-print*

The A49 Trunk Road (Craven Arms to Church Stretton, Shropshire) (Temporary Restriction and Prohibition of Traffic) (No. 2) Order 2012 No. 2012/2803. - Enabling power: Road Traffic Regulation Act 1984, s. 14 (1) (a). - Issued: 09.11.2012. Made: 22.10.2012. Coming into force: 29.10.2012. Effect: None. Territorial extent & classification: E. Local. - Available at http://www.legislation.gov.uk/uksi/2012/2803/contents/made *Non-print*

The A49 Trunk Road (Craven Arms to Church Stretton, Shropshire) (Temporary Restriction and Prohibition of Traffic) Order 2012 No. 2012/1684. - Enabling power: Road Traffic Regulation Act 1984, s. 14 (1) (a). - Issued: 03.07.2012. Made: 06.06.2012. Coming into force: 13.06.2012. Effect: None. Territorial extent & classification: E. Local. - Available at http://www.legislation.gov.uk/uksi/2012/1684/contents/made *Non-print*

The A49 Trunk Road (Hereford) (Temporary Prohibition of Traffic) Order 2012 No. 2012/219. - Enabling power: Road Traffic Regulation Act 1984, s. 14 (1) (a). - Issued: 03.02.2012. Made: 20.01.2012. Coming into force: 27.01.2012. Effect: None. Territorial extent & classification: E. Local. - Available at http://www.legislation.gov.uk/uksi/2012/219/contents/made *Non-print*

The A49 Trunk Road (Hereford to Hope under Dismore) (Temporary Prohibition of Traffic) Order 2012 No. 2012/1774. - Enabling power: Road Traffic Regulation Act 1984, s. 14 (1) (a). - Issued: 17.07.2012. Made: 18.06.2012. Coming into force: 25.06.2012. Effect: None. Territorial extent & classification: E. Local. - Available at http://www.legislation.gov.uk/uksi/2012/1774/contents/made *Non-print*

The A49 Trunk Road (Hereford to Llandinabo, Herefordshire) (Temporary Prohibition of Traffic) Order 2012 No. 2012/3308. - Enabling power: Road Traffic Regulation Act 1984, s. 14 (1) (a). - Issued: 17.01.2013. Made: 24.12.2012. Coming into force: 31.12.2012. Effect: None. Territorial extent & classification: E. Local. - Available at http://www.legislation.gov.uk/uksi/2012/3308/contents/made *Non-print*

The A49 Trunk Road (Hereford to Ross-on-Wye, Herefordshire) (Temporary Restriction and Prohibition of Traffic) Order 2012 No. 2012/126. - Enabling power: Road Traffic Regulation Act 1984, s. 14 (1) (a). - Issued: 23.01.2012. Made: 06.01.2012. Coming into force: 13.01.2012. Effect: None. Territorial extent & classification: E. Local. - Available at http://www.legislation.gov.uk/uksi/2012/126/contents/made *Non-print*

The A49 Trunk Road (Hertford) (Temporary Prohibition of Traffic) (No. 2) Order 2012 No. 2012/1436. - Enabling power: Road Traffic Regulation Act 1984, s. 14 (1) (b). - Issued: 06.06.2012. Made: 14.05.2012. Coming into force: 21.05.2012. Effect: None. Territorial extent & classification: E. Local. - Available at http://www.legislation.gov.uk/uksi/2012/1436/contents/made *Non-print*

The A49 Trunk Road (Leominster to Kimbolton, Herefordshire) (Temporary Restriction and Prohibition of Traffic) Order 2012 No. 2012/2182. - Enabling power: Road Traffic Regulation Act 1984, s. 14 (1) (a). - Issued: 28.08.2012. Made: 15.08.2012. Coming into force: 22.08.2012. Effect: None. Territorial extent & classification: E. Local. - Available at http://www.legislation.gov.uk/uksi/2012/2182/contents/made *Non-print*

The A49 Trunk Road (Leominster to Ludlow) (Temporary Prohibition of Traffic) Order 2012 No. 2012/769. - Enabling power: Road Traffic Regulation Act 1984, s. 14 (1) (a). - Issued: 20.03.2012. Made: 02.03.2012. Coming into force: 09.03.2012. Effect: None. Territorial extent & classification: E. Local. - Available at http://www.legislation.gov.uk/uksi/2012/769/contents/made *Non-print*

The A49 Trunk Road (Ludlow, Shropshire) (Temporary Restriction of Traffic) Order 2012 No. 2012/243. - Enabling power: Road Traffic Regulation Act 1984, s. 14 (1) (a). - Issued: 06.02.2012. Made: 23.01.2012. Coming into force: 30.01.2012. Effect: None. Territorial extent & classification: E. Local. - Available at http://www.legislation.gov.uk/uksi/2012/243/contents/made *Non-print*

The A49 Trunk Road (South of Hereford) (Temporary Prohibition of Traffic) Order 2012 No. 2012/754. - Enabling power: Road Traffic Regulation Act 1984, s. 14 (1) (a). - Issued: 19.03.2012. Made: 02.03.2012. Coming into force: 09.03.2012. Effect: None. Territorial extent & classification: E. Local. - Available at http://www.legislation.gov.uk/uksi/2012/754/contents/made *Non-print*

Road traffic: Traffic regulation

The A49 Trunk Road (Victoria Street, Hereford) (Temporary Prohibition of Traffic) (No. 2) Order 2012 No. 2012/2880. - Enabling power: Road Traffic Regulation Act 1984, s. 14 (1) (a). - Issued: 20.11.2012. Made: 02.11.2012. Coming into force: 09.11.2012. Effect: None. Territorial extent & classification: E. Local. - Available at http://www.legislation.gov.uk/uksi/2012/2880/contents/made *Non-print*

The A49 Trunk Road (Victoria Street, Hereford) (Temporary Prohibition of Traffic) Order 2012 No. 2012/2540. - Enabling power: Road Traffic Regulation Act 1984, s. 14 (1) (a). - Issued: 09.10.2012. Made: 17.09.2012. Coming into force: 24.09.2012. Effect: None. Territorial extent & classification: E. Local. - Available at http://www.legislation.gov.uk/uksi/2012/2540/contents/made *Non-print*

The A49 Trunk Road (Wilton to South of Harewood End, Herefordshire) (Temporary Prohibition of Traffic) Order 2012 No. 2012/2534. - Enabling power: Road Traffic Regulation Act 1984, s. 14 (1) (a). - Issued: 09.10.2012. Made: 17.09.2012. Coming into force: 24.09.2012. Effect: None. Territorial extent & classification: E. Local. - Available at http://www.legislation.gov.uk/uksi/2012/2534/contents/made *Non-print*

The A49 Trunk Road (Wistantow, Shropshire) (Temporary Prohibition of Traffic) Order 2012 No. 2012/3168. - Enabling power: Road Traffic Regulation Act 1984, s. 14 (1) (a). - Issued: 28.12.2012. Made: 26.11.2012. Coming into force: 03.12.2012. Effect: None. Territorial extent & classification: E. Local. - Available at http://www.legislation.gov.uk/uksi/2012/3168/contents/made *Non-print*

The A50 and A500 Trunk Roads (Stoke-on-Trent, Staffordshire) (Temporary Prohibition of Traffic) Order 2012 No. 2012/625. - Enabling power: Road Traffic Regulation Act 1984, s. 14 (1) (a). - Issued: 07.03.2012. Made: 24.02.2012. Coming into force: 02.03.2012. Effect: None. Territorial extent & classification: E. Local. - Available at http://www.legislation.gov.uk/uksi/2012/625/contents/made *Non-print*

The A50 Trunk Road (Aston on Trent) (Temporary Prohibition of Traffic) Order 2012 No. 2012/2418. - Enabling power: Road Traffic Regulation Act 1984, s. 14 (1) (a). - Issued: 24.09.2012. Made: 07.09.2012. Coming into force: 14.09.2012. Effect: None. Territorial extent & classification: E. Local. - Available at http://www.legislation.gov.uk/uksi/2012/2418/contents/made *Non-print*

The A50 Trunk Road (Blythe Bridge, Staffordshire and Hilton, Derbyshire) (Temporary Restriction and Prohibition of Traffic) Order 2012 No. 2012/651. - Enabling power: Road Traffic Regulation Act 1984, s. 14 (1) (a). - Issued: 14.03.2012. Made: 24.02.2012. Coming into force: 02.03.2012. Effect: None. Territorial extent & classification: E. Local. - Available at http://www.legislation.gov.uk/uksi/2012/651/contents/made *Non-print*

The A50 Trunk Road (Blythe Bridge to Chellaston, Staffordshire and Derbyshire) (Temporary Prohibition of Traffic in Laybys) Order 2012 No. 2012/3237. - Enabling power: Road Traffic Regulation Act 1984, s. 14 (1) (a). - Issued: 08.01.2013. Made: 16.11.2012. Coming into force: 23.11.2012. Effect: None. Territorial extent & classification: E. Local. - Available at http://www.legislation.gov.uk/uksi/2012/3237/contents/made *Non-print*

The A50 Trunk Road (Chellaston Interchange) (Slip Road) (Temporary Prohibition of Traffic) Order 2012 No. 2012/3231. - Enabling power: Road Traffic Regulation Act 1984, s. 14 (1) (a). - Issued: 08.01.2013. Made: 03.12.2012. Coming into force: 10.12.2012. Effect: None. Territorial extent & classification: E. Local. - Available at http://www.legislation.gov.uk/uksi/2012/3231/contents/made *Non-print*

The A50 Trunk Road (Derbyshire and Staffordshire) (Temporary Prohibition of Traffic) Order 2012 No. 2012/1595. - Enabling power: Road Traffic Regulation Act 1984, s. 14 (1) (a). - Issued: 27.06.2012. Made: 25.05.2012. Coming into force: 01.06.2012. Effect: None. Territorial extent & classification: E. Local. - Available at http://www.legislation.gov.uk/uksi/2012/1595/contents/made *Non-print*

The A50 Trunk Road (Derbyshire) (Temporary Prohibition of Traffic) Order 2012 No. 2012/1997. - Enabling power: Road Traffic Regulation Act 1984, s. 14 (1) (a). - Issued: 02.08.2012. Made: 09.07.2012. Coming into force: 16.07.2012. Effect: None. Territorial extent & classification: E. Local. - Available at http://www.legislation.gov.uk/uksi/2012/1997/contents/made *Non-print*

The A50 Trunk Road (Hatton to Sudbury, Derbyshire) (Temporary Restriction and Prohibition of Traffic) Order 2012 No. 2012/1892. - Enabling power: Road Traffic Regulation Act 1984, s. 14 (1) (a). - Issued: 23.07.2012. Made: 25.06.2012. Coming into force: 02.07.2012. Effect: None. Territorial extent & classification: E. Local. - Available at http://www.legislation.gov.uk/uksi/2012/1892/contents/made *Non-print*

The A50 Trunk Road (Heron Cross, Stoke-on-Trent) (Temporary Prohibition of Traffic) Order 2012 No. 2012/3320. - Enabling power: Road Traffic Regulation Act 1984, s. 14 (1) (a). - Issued: 16.01.2013. Made: 31.12.2012. Coming into force: 07.01.2013. Effect: None. Territorial extent & classification: E. Local. - Available at http://www.legislation.gov.uk/uksi/2012/3320/contents/made *Non-print*

The A50 Trunk Road (Junction with the A6, Aston-on-Trent, Derbyshire) (Temporary Prohibition of Traffic) Order 2012 No. 2012/1314. - Enabling power: Road Traffic Regulation Act 1984, s. 14 (1) (a). - Issued: 22.05.2012. Made: 27.04.2012. Coming into force: 04.05.2012. Effect: None. Territorial extent & classification: E. Local. - Available at http://www.legislation.gov.uk/uksi/2012/1314/contents/made *Non-print*

Road traffic: Traffic regulation

The A50 Trunk Road (M1 Junction 24a, Leicestershire) (Temporary Prohibition of Traffic) Order 2012 No. 2012/55. - Enabling power: Road Traffic Regulation Act 1984, s. 14 (1) (a). - Issued: 16.01.2012. Made: 04.01.2012. Coming into force: 11.01.2012. Effect: None. Territorial extent & classification: E. Local. - Available at http://www.legislation.gov.uk/uksi/2012/55/contents/made *Non-print*

The A50 Trunk Road (Meir Tunnel, Staffordshire) (Temporary Prohibition of Traffic) Order 2012 No. 2012/2127. - Enabling power: Road Traffic Regulation Act 1984, s. 14 (1) (a). - Issued: 17.08.2012. Made: 06.08.2012. Coming into force: 13.08.2012. Effect: None. Territorial extent & classification: E. Local. - Available at http://www.legislation.gov.uk/uksi/2012/2127/contents/made *Non-print*

The A50 Trunk Road (Meir Tunnel, Stoke on Trent, Staffordshire) (Temporary Prohibition of Traffic) Order 2012 No. 2012/2203. - Enabling power: Road Traffic Regulation Act 1984, s. 14 (1) (a). - Issued: 30.08.2012. Made: 22.08.2012. Coming into force: 29.08.2012. Effect: None. Territorial extent & classification: E. Local. - Available at http://www.legislation.gov.uk/uksi/2012/2203/contents/made *Non-print*

The A50 Trunk Road (Normacot, Stoke on Trent) (Slip Road) (Temporary Prohibition of Traffic) Order 2012 No. 2012/1051. - Enabling power: Road Traffic Regulation Act 1984, s. 14 (1) (a). - Issued: 13.04.2012. Made: 26.03.2012. Coming into force: 02.04.2012. Effect: None. Territorial extent & classification: E. Local. - Available at http://www.legislation.gov.uk/uksi/2012/1051/contents/made *Non-print*

The A50 Trunk Road (Shardlow, Derbyshire) (Temporary Prohibition of Traffic) Order 2012 No. 2012/2968. - Enabling power: Road Traffic Regulation Act 1984, s. 14 (1) (a). - Issued: 30.11.2012. Made: 12.11.2012. Coming into force: 19.11.2012. Effect: None. Territorial extent & classification: E. Local. - Available at http://www.legislation.gov.uk/uksi/2012/2968/contents/made *Non-print*

The A50 Trunk Road (South of Derby) (Temporary Prohibition of Traffic) Order 2012 No. 2012/2043. - Enabling power: Road Traffic Regulation Act 1984, s. 14 (1) (a). - Issued: 08.08.2012. Made: 20.07.2012. Coming into force: 27.07.2012. Effect: None. Territorial extent & classification: E. Local. - Available at http://www.legislation.gov.uk/uksi/2012/2043/contents/made *Non-print*

The A50 Trunk Road (Staffordshire) (Temporary Prohibition of Traffic in Laybys) Order 2012 No. 2012/864. - Enabling power: Road Traffic Regulation Act 1984, s. 14 (1) (a). - Issued: 23.03.2012. Made: 09.03.2012. Coming into force: 16.03.2012. Effect: None. Territorial extent & classification: E. Local. - Available at http://www.legislation.gov.uk/uksi/2012/864/contents/made *Non-print*

The A50 Trunk Road (Sudbury - Derby, Derbyshire) (Temporary Prohibition of Traffic in Laybys) Order 2012 No. 2012/856. - Enabling power: Road Traffic Regulation Act 1984, s. 14 (1) (a). - Issued: 23.03.2012. Made: 08.03.2012. Coming into force: 15.03.2012. Effect: None. Territorial extent & classification: E. Local. - Available at http://www.legislation.gov.uk/uksi/2012/856/contents/made *Non-print*

The A50 Trunk Road (Sudbury to Aston on Trent) (Temporary Prohibition of Traffic) Order 2012 No. 2012/2040. - Enabling power: Road Traffic Regulation Act 1984, s. 14 (1) (a). - Issued: 08.08.2012. Made: 20.07.2012. Coming into force: 27.07.2012. Effect: None. Territorial extent & classification: E. Local. - Available at http://www.legislation.gov.uk/uksi/2012/2040/contents/made *Non-print*

The A50 Trunk Road (Uttoxeter - Derby) (Temporary Prohibition of Traffic in Laybys) Order 2012 No. 2012/857. - Enabling power: Road Traffic Regulation Act 1984, s. 14 (1) (a). - Issued: 23.03.2012. Made: 08.03.2012. Coming into force: 15.03.2012. Effect: None. Territorial extent & classification: E. Local. - Available at http://www.legislation.gov.uk/uksi/2012/857/contents/made *Non-print*

The A50 Trunk Road (Uttoxeter to Sudbury, Derbyshire and Staffordshire) (Temporary Prohibition of Traffic) Order 2012 No. 2012/3312. - Enabling power: Road Traffic Regulation Act 1984, s. 14 (1) (a). - Issued: 17.01.2013. Made: 28.12.2012. Coming into force: 04.01.2013. Effect: None. Territorial extent & classification: E. Local. - Available at http://www.legislation.gov.uk/uksi/2012/3312/contents/made *Non-print*

The A50 Trunk Road (Uttoxeter to Sudbury) (Temporary Prohibition of Traffic) Order 2012 No. 2012/1929. - Enabling power: Road Traffic Regulation Act 1984, s. 14 (1) (a). - Issued: 26.07.2012. Made: 25.06.2012. Coming into force: 02.07.2012. Effect: None. Territorial extent & classification: E. Local. - Available at http://www.legislation.gov.uk/uksi/2012/1929/contents/made *Non-print*

The A52 and A5111 Trunk Roads (Derby) (Temporary Prohibition of Traffic) Order 2012 No. 2012/3288. - Enabling power: Road Traffic Regulation Act 1984, s. 14 (1) (a). - Issued: 15.01.2013. Made: 29.10.2012. Coming into force: 05.11.2012. Effect: None. Territorial extent & classification: E. Local. - Available at http://www.legislation.gov.uk/uksi/2012/3288/contents/made *Non-print*

The A52 and A5111 Trunk Roads (Spondon, Derbyshire) (Temporary Prohibition of Traffic) Order 2012 No. 2012/612. - Enabling power: Road Traffic Regulation Act 1984, s. 14 (1) (a). - Issued: 07.03.2012. Made: 20.02.2012. Coming into force: 27.02.2012. Effect: None. Territorial extent & classification: E. Local. - Available at http://www.legislation.gov.uk/uksi/2012/612/contents/made *Non-print*

Road traffic: Traffic regulation

The A52 and A5111 Trunk Roads (Spondon Interchange, Derby) (Temporary Prohibition of Traffic) Order 2012 No. 2012/1196. - Enabling power: Road Traffic Regulation Act 1984, s. 14 (1) (a). - Issued: 04.05.2012. Made: 24.04.2012. Coming into force: 01.05.2012. Effect: None. Territorial extent & classification: E. Local. - Available at http://www.legislation.gov.uk/uksi/2012/1196/contents/made, Includes map *Non-print*

The A52 Trunk Road (Gamston to Grantham) (24 Hours Clearway) Order 2012 No. 2012/1093. - Enabling power: Road Traffic Regulation Act 1984, ss. 1 (1), 2 (1) (2), 4 1), 122A, sch. 9, para. 27 (1). - Issued: 19.04.2012. Made: 08.03.2012. Coming into force: 22.03.2012. Effect: Nottinghamshire County Council (Prohibition of Waiting) (Clearways) Order 1963 varied & S.I. 1987/768; 1990/174 revoked. Territorial extent & classification: E. Local. - Available at http://www.legislation.gov.uk/uksi/2012/1093/contents/made *Non-print*

The A55 Trunk Road (Junction 37 Northbound and Southbound Exit and Entry Slip Roads) (Temporary Prohibition of Traffic) Order 2012 No. 2012/2285. - Enabling power: Road Traffic Regulation Act 1984, s. 14 (1) (a). - Issued: 10.09.2012. Made: 28.08.2012. Coming into force: 16.09.2012. Effect: None. Territorial extent & classification: E. Local. - Available at http://www.legislation.gov.uk/uksi/2012/2285/contents/made *Non-print*

The A55 Trunk Road (Junctions 38-40 Northbound Carriageway and Slip Roads) (Temporary Prohibition of Traffic) Order 2012 No. 2012/2456. - Enabling power: Road Traffic Regulation Act 1984, s. 14 (1) (a). - Issued: 28.09.2012. Made: 18.09.2012. Coming into force: 25.09.2012. Effect: None. Territorial extent & classification: E. Local. - Available at http://www.legislation.gov.uk/uksi/2012/2456/contents/made *Non-print*

The A55 Trunk Road (Junctions 39-40) and the M53 Motorway (Junction 12) Northbound and Southbound Carriageways and Slip Roads (Temporary Prohibition of Traffic) Order 2012 No. 2012/1602. - Enabling power: Road Traffic Regulation Act 1984, s. 14 (1) (a). - Issued: 25.06.2012. Made: 12.06.2012. Coming into force: 17.06.2012. Effect: None. Territorial extent & classification: E. Local. - Available at http://www.legislation.gov.uk/uksi/2012/1602/contents/made *Non-print*

The A56 Trunk Road (Northbound and Southbound), the M66 Motorway (Southbound) and the M65 (Junction 8 Westbound Dedicated Left Turn) (Temporary Prohibition and Restriction of Traffic) Order 2012 No. 2012/2022. - Enabling power: Road Traffic Regulation Act 1984, s. 14 (1) (a). - Issued: 06.08.2012. Made: 19.07.2012. Coming into force: 23.07.2012. Effect: None. Territorial extent & classification: E. Local. - Available at http://www.legislation.gov.uk/uksi/2012/2022/contents/made *Non-print*

The A56 Trunk Road (Northbound Carriageway at the Junction with the A682 Northbound) (Temporary Prohibition of Traffic) Order 2012 No. 2012/2473. - Enabling power: Road Traffic Regulation Act 1984, s. 14 (1) (a). - Issued: 01.10.2012. Made: 19.09.2012. Coming into force: 22.09.2012. Effect: None. Territorial extent & classification: E. Local. - Available at http://www.legislation.gov.uk/uksi/2012/2473/contents/made *Non-print*

The A56 Trunk Road (Southbound Carriageway between the A681 (Haslingden Road) and the A682 (St Mary's Way) and Slip Road) (Temporary Prohibition of Traffic) Order 2012 No. 2012/2334. - Enabling power: Road Traffic Regulation Act 1984, s. 14 (1) (a). - Issued: 13.09.2012. Made: 30.08.2012. Coming into force: 16.09.2012. Effect: None. Territorial extent & classification: E. Local. - Available at http://www.legislation.gov.uk/uksi/2012/2334/contents/made *Non-print*

The A57 Trunk Road (Mottram Roundabout to Market Street) (Temporary Prohibition of Traffic) Order 2012 No. 2012/3162. - Enabling power: Road Traffic Regulation Act 1984, s. 14 (1) (a). - Issued: 28.12.2012. Made: 29.11.2012. Coming into force: 09.12.2012. Effect: None. Territorial extent & classification: E. Local. - Available at http://www.legislation.gov.uk/uksi/2012/3162/contents/made *Non-print*

The A63 Trunk Road (Brighton Street Interchange to Mytongate Gyratory) (Temporary Prohibition of Traffic) Order 2012 No. 2012/2758. - Enabling power: Road Traffic Regulation Act 1984, s. 14 (1) (a). - Issued: 07.11.2012. Made: 17.10.2012. Coming into force: 24.10.2012. Effect: None. Territorial extent & classification: E. Local. - Available at http://www.legislation.gov.uk/uksi/2012/2758/contents/made *Non-print*

The A63 Trunk Road (Brighton Street Interchange to Priory Way Interchange) (Temporary Restriction and Prohibition of Traffic) Order 2012 No. 2012/3289. - Enabling power: Road Traffic Regulation Act 1984, s. 14 (1) (a). - Issued: 15.01.2013. Made: 27.12.2012. Coming into force: 06.01.2013. Effect: None. Territorial extent & classification: E. Local. - Available at http://www.legislation.gov.uk/uksi/2012/3289/contents/made *Non-print*

The A63 Trunk Road (Daltry Street Interchange) (Temporary Prohibition of Traffic) (No. 2) Order 2012 No. 2012/2945. - Enabling power: Road Traffic Regulation Act 1984, s. 14 (1) (a). - Issued: 28.11.2012. Made: 15.11.2012. Coming into force: 25.11.2012. Effect: None. Territorial extent & classification: E. Local. - Available at http://www.legislation.gov.uk/uksi/2012/2945/contents/made *Non-print*

The A63 Trunk Road (Daltry Street Interchange) (Temporary Prohibition of Traffic) Order 2012 No. 2012/1719. - Enabling power: Road Traffic Regulation Act 1984, s. 14 (1) (a). - Issued: 12.06.2012. Made: 21.06.2012. Coming into force: 01.07.2012. Effect: None. Territorial extent & classification: E. Local. - Available at http://www.legislation.gov.uk/uksi/2012/1719/contents/made *Non-print*

The A63 Trunk Road (Daltry Street Interchange to Garrison Road Roundabout) (Temporary Prohibition of Traffic) Order 2012 No. 2012/2349. - Enabling power: Road Traffic Regulation Act 1984, s. 14 (1) (a). - Issued: 14.09.2012. Made: 06.09.2012. Coming into force: 17.09.2012. Effect: None. Territorial extent & classification: E. Local. - Available at http://www.legislation.gov.uk/uksi/2012/2349/contents/made *Non-print*

The A63 Trunk Road (Market Place to Garrison Road Roundabout) (Temporary Prohibition of Traffic and Pedestrians) Order 2012 No. 2012/1070. - Enabling power: Road Traffic Regulation Act 1984, s. 14 (1) (a). - Issued: 16.04.2012. Made: 05.04.2012. Coming into force: 14.04.2012. Effect: None. Territorial extent & classification: E. Local. - Available at http://www.legislation.gov.uk/uksi/2012/1070/contents/made *Non-print*

The A63 Trunk Road (Melton Interchange to Western Interchange) (Temporary Prohibition of Traffic) Order 2012 No. 2012/1069. - Enabling power: Road Traffic Regulation Act 1984, s. 14 (1) (a). - Issued: 16.04.2012. Made: 05.04.2012. Coming into force: 15.04.2012. Effect: None. Territorial extent & classification: E. Local. - Available at http://www.legislation.gov.uk/uksi/2012/1069/contents/made *Non-print*

The A63 Trunk Road (Priory Way Interchange to Melton Interchange) (Temporary Prohibition of Traffic) Order 2012 No. 2012/2158. - Enabling power: Road Traffic Regulation Act 1984, s. 14 (1) (a). - Issued: 23.08.2012. Made: 16.08.2012. Coming into force: 26.08.2012. Effect: None. Territorial extent & classification: E. Local. - Available at http://www.legislation.gov.uk/uksi/2012/2158/contents/made *Non-print*

The A63 Trunk Road (Priory Way Interchange to Western Interchange) (Temporary Prohibition of Traffic) Order 2012 No. 2012/3161. - Enabling power: Road Traffic Regulation Act 1984, s. 14 (1) (a). - Issued: 28.12.2012. Made: 29.11.2012. Coming into force: 07.12.2012. Effect: None. Territorial extent & classification: E. Local. - Available at http://www.legislation.gov.uk/uksi/2012/3161/contents/made *Non-print*

The A63 Trunk Road (South Cave Interchange) (Temporary Prohibition of Traffic) Order 2012 No. 2012/2068. - Enabling power: Road Traffic Regulation Act 1984, s. 14 (1) (a). - Issued: 13.08.2012. Made: 26.07.2012. Coming into force: 05.08.2012. Effect: None. Territorial extent & classification: E. Local. - Available at http://www.legislation.gov.uk/uksi/2012/2068/contents/made *Non-print*

The A63 Trunk Road (Welton Interchange) (Temporary Prohibition of Traffic) Order 2012 No. 2012/2204. - Enabling power: Road Traffic Regulation Act 1984, s. 14 (1) (a). - Issued: 30.08.2012. Made: 23.08.2012. Coming into force: 02.09.2012. Effect: None. Territorial extent & classification: E. Local. - Available at http://www.legislation.gov.uk/uksi/2012/2204/contents/made *Non-print*

The A63 Trunk Road (Welton Interchange to Melton Interchange) (Temporary Prohibition of Traffic) Order 2012 No. 2012/3287. - Enabling power: Road Traffic Regulation Act 1984, s. 14 (1) (a). - Issued: 15.01.2013. Made: 27.12.2012. Coming into force: 06.01.2013. Effect: None. Territorial extent & classification: E. Local. - Available at http://www.legislation.gov.uk/uksi/2012/3287/contents/made *Non-print*

The A63 Trunk Road (Western Interchange) (Temporary Prohibition of Traffic) Order 2012 No. 2012/660. - Enabling power: Road Traffic Regulation Act 1984, s. 14 (1) (a). - Issued: 14.03.2012. Made: 01.03.2012. Coming into force: 11.03.2012. Effect: None. Territorial extent & classification: E. Local. - Available at http://www.legislation.gov.uk/uksi/2012/660/contents/made *Non-print*

The A64 Trunk Road (Askham Bar Interchange to Headley Bar Interchange) (Temporary Prohibition of Traffic) Order 2012 No. 2012/2295. - Enabling power: Road Traffic Regulation Act 1984, s. 14 (1) (a). - Issued: 11.09.2012. Made: 30.08.2012. Coming into force: 09.09.2012. Effect: None. Territorial extent & classification: E. Local. - Available at http://www.legislation.gov.uk/uksi/2012/2295/contents/made *Non-print*

The A64 Trunk Road (Askham Bryan Interchange) (Temporary Prohibition of Traffic) Order 2012 No. 2012/2875. - Enabling power: Road Traffic Regulation Act 1984, s. 14 (1) (a). - Issued: 19.11.2012. Made: 08.11.2012. Coming into force: 15.11.2012. Effect: None. Territorial extent & classification: E. Local. - Available at http://www.legislation.gov.uk/uksi/2012/2875/contents/made *Non-print*

The A64 Trunk Road (Barton Hill) (Temporary Prohibition of Traffic) Order 2012 No. 2012/456. - Enabling power: Road Traffic Regulation Act 1984, s. 14 (1) (a). - Issued: 24.02.2012. Made: 16.02.2012. Coming into force: 26.02.2012. Effect: None. Territorial extent & classification: E. Local. - Available at http://www.legislation.gov.uk/uksi/2012/456/contents/made *Non-print*

Road traffic: Traffic regulation

The A64 Trunk Road (Barton Hill to Scotchman Lane) (Temporary Restriction and Prohibition of Traffic) Order 2012 No. 2012/262. - Enabling power: Road Traffic Regulation Act 1984, s. 14 (1) (a). - Issued: 07.02.2012. Made: 26.01.2012. Coming into force: 05.02.2012. Effect: None. Territorial extent & classification: E. Local. - Available at http://www.legislation.gov.uk/uksi/2012/262/contents/made *Non-print*

The A64 Trunk Road (Bond Hill Interchange to Grimston Bar Interchange) (Temporary Prohibition of Traffic) Order 2012 No. 2012/269. - Enabling power: Road Traffic Regulation Act 1984, s. 14 (1) (a). - Issued: 10.02.2012. Made: 27.01.2012. Coming into force: 05.02.2012. Effect: None. Territorial extent & classification: E. Local. - Available at http://www.legislation.gov.uk/uksi/2012/269/contents/made *Non-print*

The A64 Trunk Road (Brambling Fields Interchange) (Temporary Prohibition of Traffic) Order 2012 No. 2012/2807. - Enabling power: Road Traffic Regulation Act 1984, s. 14 (1) (a). - Issued: 12.11.2012. Made: 25.10.2012. Coming into force: 04.11.2012. Effect: None. Territorial extent & classification: E. Local. - Available at http://www.legislation.gov.uk/uksi/2012/2807/contents/made *Non-print*

The A64 Trunk Road (Brambling Fields Interchange) (Temporary Restriction and Prohibition of Traffic) Order 2012 No. 2012/39. - Enabling power: Road Traffic Regulation Act 1984, s. 14 (1) (a). - Issued: 11.01.2012. Made: 03.01.2012. Coming into force: 08.01.2012. Effect: None. Territorial extent & classification: E. Local. - Available at http://www.legislation.gov.uk/uksi/2012/39/contents/made *Non-print*

The A64 Trunk Road (Bus Stop Laybys at Huttons Ambo) (Temporary Prohibition of Traffic) Order 2012 No. 2012/2956. - Enabling power: Road Traffic Regulation Act 1984, s. 14 (1) (a). - Issued: 30.11.2012. Made: 15.11.2012. Coming into force: 25.11.2012. Effect: None. Territorial extent & classification: E. Local. - Available at http://www.legislation.gov.uk/uksi/2012/2956/contents/made *Non-print*

The A64 Trunk Road (East and West Heslerton) (Temporary Restriction and Prohibition of Traffic) Order 2012 No. 2012/2759. - Enabling power: Road Traffic Regulation Act 1984, s. 14 (1) (a). - Issued: 07.11.2012. Made: 18.10.2012. Coming into force: 28.10.2012. Effect: None. Territorial extent & classification: E. Local. - Available at http://www.legislation.gov.uk/uksi/2012/2759/contents/made *Non-print*

The A64 Trunk Road (Flaxton to Whitwell) (Temporary Restriction and Prohibition of Traffic) Order 2012 No. 2012/1178. - Enabling power: Road Traffic Regulation Act 1984, s. 14 (1) (a). - Issued: 02.05.2012. Made: 20.04.2012. Coming into force: 29.04.2012. Effect: None. Territorial extent & classification: E. Local. - Available at http://www.legislation.gov.uk/uksi/2012/1178/contents/made *Non-print*

The A64 Trunk Road (Fulford Interchange to Askham Bar Interchange) (Temporary Restriction and Prohibition of Traffic) Order 2012 No. 2012/2578. - Enabling power: Road Traffic Regulation Act 1984, s. 14 (1) (a). - Issued: 16.10.2012. Made: 04.10.2012. Coming into force: 14.10.2012. Effect: None. Territorial extent & classification: E. Local. - Available at http://www.legislation.gov.uk/uksi/2012/2578/contents/made *Non-print*

The A64 Trunk Road (Fulford Interchange to Bond Hill Interchange) (Temporary Prohibition of Traffic) Order 2012 No. 2012/122. - Enabling power: Road Traffic Regulation Act 1984, s. 14 (1) (a). - Issued: 23.01.2012. Made: 12.01.2012. Coming into force: 22.01.2012. Effect: None. Territorial extent & classification: E. Local. - Available at http://www.legislation.gov.uk/uksi/2012/122/contents/made *Non-print*

The A64 Trunk Road (Grimston Bar Interchange) (Temporary Prohibition of Traffic) Order 2012 No. 2012/1617. - Enabling power: Road Traffic Regulation Act 1984, s. 14 (1) (a). - Issued: 28.06.2012. Made: 14.06.2012. Coming into force: 24.06.2012. Effect: None. Territorial extent & classification: E. Local. - Available at http://www.legislation.gov.uk/uksi/2012/1617/contents/made *Non-print*

The A64 Trunk Road (Grimston Bar Interchange) (Temporary Restriction and Prohibition of Traffic) Order 2012 No. 2012/3286. - Enabling power: Road Traffic Regulation Act 1984, s. 14 (1) (a). - Issued: 15.01.2013. Made: 27.12.2012. Coming into force: 06.01.2013. Effect: None. Territorial extent & classification: E. Local. - Available at http://www.legislation.gov.uk/uksi/2012/3286/contents/made *Non-print*

The A64 Trunk Road (Headley Bar Interchange) (Temporary Prohibition of Traffic) Order 2012 No. 2012/124. - Enabling power: Road Traffic Regulation Act 1984, s. 14 (1) (a). - Issued: 23.01.2012. Made: 12.01.2012. Coming into force: 22.01.2012. Effect: None. Territorial extent & classification: E. Local. - Available at http://www.legislation.gov.uk/uksi/2012/124/contents/made *Non-print*

Road traffic: Traffic regulation

The A64 Trunk Road (Hopgrove Roundabout to Grimston Bar Interchange) (Temporary Restriction and Prohibition of Traffic) Order 2012 No. 2012/2205. - Enabling power: Road Traffic Regulation Act 1984, s. 14 (1) (a). - Issued: 30.08.2012. Made: 23.08.2012. Coming into force: 02.09.2012. Effect: None. Territorial extent & classification: E. Local. - Available at http://www.legislation.gov.uk/uksi/2012/2205/contents/made *Non-print*

The A64 Trunk Road (Hopgrove Roundabout to Whitwell) (Temporary 40 Miles Per Hour Speed Restriction) Order 2012 No. 2012/37. - Enabling power: Road Traffic Regulation Act 1984, s. 14 (1) (a). - Issued: 11.01.2012. Made: 03.01.2012. Coming into force: 08.01.2012. Effect: None. Territorial extent & classification: E. Local. - Available at http://www.legislation.gov.uk/uksi/2012/37/contents/made *Non-print*

The A64 Trunk Road (Malton to Rillington) (Temporary Restriction and Prohibition of Traffic) Order 2012 No. 2012/1250. - Enabling power: Road Traffic Regulation Act 1984, s. 14 (1) (a). - Issued: 18.05.2012. Made: 03.05.2012. Coming into force: 13.05.2012. Effect: None. Territorial extent & classification: E. Local. - Available at http://www.legislation.gov.uk/uksi/2012/1250/contents/made *Non-print*

The A64 Trunk Road (Musley Bank Interchange) (Temporary Restriction and Prohibition of Traffic) Order 2012 No. 2012/2351. - Enabling power: Road Traffic Regulation Act 1984, s. 14 (1) (a). - Issued: 14.09.2012. Made: 06.09.2012. Coming into force: 16.09.2012. Effect: None. Territorial extent & classification: E. Local. - Available at http://www.legislation.gov.uk/uksi/2012/2351/contents/made *Non-print*

The A64 Trunk Road (Pickering Interchange) (Temporary Restriction and Prohibition of Traffic) Order 2012 No. 2012/314. - Enabling power: Road Traffic Regulation Act 1984, s. 14 (1) (a). - Issued: 15.02.2012. Made: 02.02.2012. Coming into force: 12.02.2012. Effect: None. Territorial extent & classification: E. Local. - Available at http://www.legislation.gov.uk/uksi/2012/314/contents/made *Non-print*

The A64 Trunk Road (Rillington) (Temporary Prohibition of Traffic) Order 2012 No. 2012/405. - Enabling power: Road Traffic Regulation Act 1984, s. 14 (1) (a). - Issued: 21.02.2012. Made: 09.02.2012. Coming into force: 19.02.2012. Effect: None. Territorial extent & classification: E. Local. - Available at http://www.legislation.gov.uk/uksi/2012/405/contents/made *Non-print*

The A64 Trunk Road (Sherburn to Ganton) (Temporary Restriction and Prohibition of Traffic) Order 2012 No. 2012/2955. - Enabling power: Road Traffic Regulation Act 1984, s. 14 (1) (a). - Issued: 30.11.2012. Made: 15.11.2012. Coming into force: 25.11.2012. Effect: None. Territorial extent & classification: E. Local. - Available at http://www.legislation.gov.uk/uksi/2012/2955/contents/made *Non-print*

The A64 Trunk Road (Staxton) (Temporary Restriction and Prohibition of Traffic) Order 2012 No. 2012/1214. - Enabling power: Road Traffic Regulation Act 1984, s. 14 (1) (a). - Issued: 10.05.2012. Made: 26.04.2012. Coming into force: 06.05.2012. Effect: None. Territorial extent & classification: E. Local. - Available at http://www.legislation.gov.uk/uksi/2012/1214/contents/made *Non-print*

The A64 Trunk Road (Staxton to Seamer Roundabout) (Temporary Restriction and Prohibition of Traffic) Order 2012 No. 2012/2760. - Enabling power: Road Traffic Regulation Act 1984, s. 14 (1) (a). - Issued: 07.11.2012. Made: 18.10.2012. Coming into force: 28.10.2012. Effect: None. Territorial extent & classification: E. Local. - Available at http://www.legislation.gov.uk/uksi/2012/2760/contents/made *Non-print*

The A64 Trunk Road (Tadcaster Bar Interchange to Headley Bar Interchange) (Temporary Prohibition of Traffic) Order 2012 No. 2012/1073. - Enabling power: Road Traffic Regulation Act 1984, s. 14 (1) (a). - Issued: 17.04.2012. Made: 05.04.2012. Coming into force: 15.04.2012. Effect: None. Territorial extent & classification: E. Local. - Available at http://www.legislation.gov.uk/uksi/2012/1073/contents/made *Non-print*

The A64 Trunk Road (Tadcaster Bar) (Temporary Prohibition of Traffic) (No. 2) Order 2012 No. 2012/1566. - Enabling power: Road Traffic Regulation Act 1984, s. 14 (1) (a). - Issued: 22.06.2012. Made: 07.06.2012. Coming into force: 17.06.2012. Effect: None. Territorial extent & classification: E. Local. - Available at http://www.legislation.gov.uk/uksi/2012/1566/contents/made *Non-print*

The A64 Trunk Road (Tadcaster Bar) (Temporary Prohibition of Traffic) Order 2012 No. 2012/260. - Enabling power: Road Traffic Regulation Act 1984, s. 14 (1) (a). - Issued: 06.02.2012. Made: 26.01.2012. Coming into force: 05.02.2012. Effect: None. Territorial extent & classification: E. Local. - Available at http://www.legislation.gov.uk/uksi/2012/260/contents/made *Non-print*

The A66(M) Motorway (Blackwell Spur) (Temporary Prohibition of Traffic) (No. 2) Order 2012 No. 2012/2626. - Enabling power: Road Traffic Regulation Act 1984, s. 14 (1) (a). - Issued: 23.10.2012. Made: 11.10.2012. Coming into force: 21.10.2012. Effect: None. Territorial extent & classification: E. Local. - Available at http://www.legislation.gov.uk/uksi/2012/2626/contents/made *Non-print*

The A66(M) Motorway (Blackwell Spur) (Temporary Prohibition of Traffic) Order 2012 No. 2012/1731. - Enabling power: Road Traffic Regulation Act 1984, s. 14 (1) (a). - Issued: 13.07.2012. Made: 21.06.2012. Coming into force: 01.07.2012. Effect: None. Territorial extent & classification: E. Local. - Available at http://www.legislation.gov.uk/uksi/2012/1731/contents/made *Non-print*

The A66 Trunk Road (Acklam Road Interchange) (Temporary Prohibition of Traffic) Order 2012 No. 2012/1628. - Enabling power: Road Traffic Regulation Act 1984, s. 14 (1) (a). - Issued: 28.06.2012. Made: 31.05.2012. Coming into force: 10.06.2012. Effect: None. Territorial extent & classification: E. Local. - Available at http://www.legislation.gov.uk/uksi/2012/1628/contents/made *Non-print*

The A66 Trunk Road (Appleby Junction Layby Closure) (Temporary Prohibition of Traffic) Order 2012 No. 2012/2737. - Enabling power: Road Traffic Regulation Act 1984, s. 14 (1) (a). - Issued: 06.11.2012. Made: 18.10.2012. Coming into force: 04.11.2012. Effect: None. Territorial extent & classification: E. Local. - Available at http://www.legislation.gov.uk/uksi/2012/2737/contents/made *Non-print*

The A66 Trunk Road (Banks Gate Junction to Barras Junction) (Temporary Prohibition and Restriction of Traffic) Order 2012 No. 2012/2959. - Enabling power: Road Traffic Regulation Act 1984, s. 14 (1) (a). - Issued: 30.11.2012. Made: 15.11.2012. Coming into force: 02.12.2012. Effect: None. Territorial extent & classification: E. Local. - Available at http://www.legislation.gov.uk/uksi/2012/2959/contents/made *Non-print*

The A66 Trunk Road (Bassenthwaite Lake) (Temporary Prohibition and Restriction of Traffic) (No. 2) Order 2012 No. 2012/2359. - Enabling power: Road Traffic Regulation Act 1984, s. 14 (1) (a). - Issued: 17.09.2012. Made: 07.09.2012. Coming into force: 21.09.2012. Effect: None. Territorial extent & classification: E. Local. - Available at http://www.legislation.gov.uk/uksi/2012/2359/contents/made *Non-print*

The A66 Trunk Road (Bassenthwaite Lake) (Temporary Prohibition and Restriction of Traffic) Order 2012 No. 2012/1092. - Enabling power: Road Traffic Regulation Act 1984, s. 14 (1) (a). - Issued: 19.04.2012. Made: 05.04.2012. Coming into force: 13.04.2012. Effect: None. Territorial extent & classification: E. Local. - Available at http://www.legislation.gov.uk/uksi/2012/1092/contents/made *Non-print*

The A66 Trunk Road (Beckes Junction to Highgate) (Temporary Prohibition and Restriction of Traffic) Order 2012 No. 2012/2983. - Enabling power: Road Traffic Regulation Act 1984, s. 14 (1) (a). - Issued: 05.12.2012. Made: 22.11.2012. Coming into force: 08.12.2012. Effect: None. Territorial extent & classification: E. Local. - Available at http://www.legislation.gov.uk/uksi/2012/2983/contents/made *Non-print*

The A66 Trunk Road (Beck Wythop to Hursthole) (Temporary Prohibition and Restriction of Traffic) Order 2012 No. 2012/128. - Enabling power: Road Traffic Regulation Act 1984, s. 14 (1) (a). - Issued: 23.01.2012. Made: 12.01.2012. Coming into force: 29.01.2012. Effect: None. Territorial extent & classification: E. Local. - Available at http://www.legislation.gov.uk/uksi/2012/128/contents/made *Non-print*

The A66 Trunk Road (Blackwell Roundabout to Blands Corner Roundabout) (Temporary Prohibition of Traffic) Order 2012 No. 2012/1241. - Enabling power: Road Traffic Regulation Act 1984, s. 14 (1) (a). - Issued: 11.05.2012. Made: 03.05.2012. Coming into force: 13.05.2012. Effect: None. Territorial extent & classification: E. Local. - Available at http://www.legislation.gov.uk/uksi/2012/1241/contents/made *Non-print*

The A66 Trunk Road (Bowes Interchange to Cross Lanes Junction) (Temporary Restriction and Prohibition of Traffic) Order 2012 No. 2012/1708. - Enabling power: Road Traffic Regulation Act 1984, s. 14 (1) (a) (7). - Issued: 12.07.2012. Made: 20.06.2012. Coming into force: 24.06.2012. Effect: None. Territorial extent & classification: E. Local. - Available at http://www.legislation.gov.uk/uksi/2012/1708/contents/made *Non-print*

The A66 Trunk Road (Bowes to the Cumbrian Border) (Temporary Restriction and Prohibition of Traffic) Order 2012 No. 2012/2347. - Enabling power: Road Traffic Regulation Act 1984, s. 14 (1) (a) (7). - Issued: 14.09.2012. Made: 06.09.2012. Coming into force: 16.09.2012. Effect: None. Territorial extent & classification: E. Local. - Available at http://www.legislation.gov.uk/uksi/2012/2347/contents/made *Non-print*

The A66 Trunk Road (Brougham Bridges, Penrith) (Temporary Prohibition and Restriction of Traffic) Order 2012 No. 2012/2220. - Enabling power: Road Traffic Regulation Act 1984, s. 14 (1) (a). - Issued: 31.08.2012. Made: 23.08.2012. Coming into force: 31.08.2012. Effect: None. Territorial extent & classification: E. Local. - Available at http://www.legislation.gov.uk/uksi/2012/2220/contents/made *Non-print*

Road traffic: Traffic regulation

The A66 Trunk Road (Brough Bypass) (Temporary Prohibition and Restriction of Traffic) Order 2012 No. 2012/1949. - Enabling power: Road Traffic Regulation Act 1984, s. 14 (1) (a). - Issued: 30.07.2012. Made: 12.07.2012. Coming into force: 28.07.2012. Effect: None. Territorial extent & classification: E. Local. - Available at http://www.legislation.gov.uk/uksi/2012/1949/contents/made *Non-print*

The A66 Trunk Road (Brough to North Stainmore) (Temporary Prohibition and Restriction of Traffic) Order 2012 No. 2012/2340. - Enabling power: Road Traffic Regulation Act 1984, s. 14 (1) (a). - Issued: 14.09.2012. Made: 31.08.2012. Coming into force: 02.09.2012. Effect: None. Territorial extent & classification: E. Local. - Available at http://www.legislation.gov.uk/uksi/2012/2340/contents/made *Non-print*

The A66 Trunk Road (Carkin Moor to West Layton) (Temporary Restriction and Prohibition of Traffic) Order 2012 No. 2012/3116. - Enabling power: Road Traffic Regulation Act 1984, s. 14 (1) (a). - Issued: 20.12.2012. Made: 22.11.2012. Coming into force: 23.11.2012. Effect: None. Territorial extent & classification: E. Local. - Available at http://www.legislation.gov.uk/uksi/2012/3116/contents/made *Non-print*

The A66 Trunk Road (Coltsford Bridge, Brough) (Temporary Prohibition and Restriction of Traffic) Order 2012 No. 2012/409. - Enabling power: Road Traffic Regulation Act 1984, s. 14 (1) (a). - Issued: 21.02.2012. Made: 09.02.2012. Coming into force: 12.02.2012. Effect: None. Territorial extent & classification: E. Local. - Available at http://www.legislation.gov.uk/uksi/2012/409/contents/made *Non-print*

The A66 Trunk Road (Crosthwaite Roundabout, Keswick) (Temporary Prohibition and Restriction of Traffic) Order 2012 No. 2012/2871. - Enabling power: Road Traffic Regulation Act 1984, s. 14 (1) (a). - Issued: 19.11.2012. Made: 08.11.2012. Coming into force: 25.11.2012. Effect: None. Territorial extent & classification: E. Local. - Available at http://www.legislation.gov.uk/uksi/2012/2871/contents/made *Non-print*

The A66 Trunk Road (Dacre Junction to Newbiggin Junction) (Temporary Restriction and Prohibition of Traffic) Order 2012 No. 2012/2816. - Enabling power: Road Traffic Regulation Act 1984, s. 14 (1) (a). - Issued: 13.11.2012. Made: 25.10.2012. Coming into force: 03.11.2012. Effect: None. Territorial extent & classification: E. Local. - Available at http://www.legislation.gov.uk/uksi/2012/2816/contents/made *Non-print*

The A66 Trunk Road (Elton Interchange to Yarm Road Interchange) (Temporary Restriction and Prohibition of Traffic) Order 2012 No. 2012/1729. - Enabling power: Road Traffic Regulation Act 1984, s. 14 (1) (a). - Issued: 13.07.2012. Made: 21.06.2012. Coming into force: 01.07.2012. Effect: None. Territorial extent & classification: E. Local. - Available at http://www.legislation.gov.uk/uksi/2012/1729/contents/made *Non-print*

The A66 Trunk Road (Embleton Junction Improvements) (Temporary Prohibition and Restriction of Traffic) Order 2012 No. 2012/1717. - Enabling power: Road Traffic Regulation Act 1984, s. 14 (1) (a). - Issued: 12.07.2012. Made: 21.06.2012. Coming into force: 08.07.2012. Effect: None. Territorial extent & classification: E. Local. - Available at http://www.legislation.gov.uk/uksi/2012/1717/contents/made *Non-print*

The A66 Trunk Road (Greta Bridge) (Temporary Restriction and Prohibition of Traffic) Order 2012 No. 2012/1787. - Enabling power: Road Traffic Regulation Act 1984, s. 14 (1) (a) (7). - Issued: 18.07.2012. Made: 28.06.2012. Coming into force: 08.07.2012. Effect: None. Territorial extent & classification: E. Local. - Available at http://www.legislation.gov.uk/uksi/2012/1787/contents/made *Non-print*

The A66 Trunk Road (Greta, Keswick) (Temporary Restriction of Traffic) Order 2012 No. 2012/2772. - Enabling power: Road Traffic Regulation Act 1984, s. 14 (1) (a). - Issued: 08.11.2012. Made: 11.10.2012. Coming into force: 28.10.2012. Effect: None. Territorial extent & classification: E. Local. - Available at http://www.legislation.gov.uk/uksi/2012/2772/contents/made *Non-print*

The A66 Trunk Road (Highbarn to Whinfell) (Temporary Prohibition and Restriction of Traffic) Order 2012 No. 2012/2823. - Enabling power: Road Traffic Regulation Act 1984, s. 14 (1) (a). - Issued: 14.11.2012. Made: 19.10.2012. Coming into force: 21.10.2012. Effect: None. Territorial extent & classification: E. Local. - Available at http://www.legislation.gov.uk/uksi/2012/2823/contents/made *Non-print*

The A66 Trunk Road (Hutton Moor to Lowside) (Temporary Prohibition and Restriction of Traffic) Order 2012 No. 2012/2998. - Enabling power: Road Traffic Regulation Act 1984, s. 14 (1) (a). - Issued: 05.12.2012. Made: 22.11.2012. Coming into force: 08.12.2012. Effect: None. Territorial extent & classification: E. Local. - Available at http://www.legislation.gov.uk/uksi/2012/2998/contents/made *Non-print*

Road traffic: Traffic regulation

The A66 Trunk Road (Morton Palms Roundabout to Elton Interchange) (Temporary Restriction and Prohibition of Traffic) Order 2012 No. 2012/88. - Enabling power: Road Traffic Regulation Act 1984, s. 14 (1) (a) (7). - Issued: 18.01.2012. Made: 06.01.2012. Coming into force: 15.01.2012. Effect: None. Territorial extent & classification: E. Local. - Available at http://www.legislation.gov.uk/uksi/2012/88/contents/made *Non-print*

The A66 Trunk Road (Morton Palms Roundabout to Little Burdon Roundabout) (Temporary Prohibition of Traffic) Order 2012 No. 2012/2152. - Enabling power: Road Traffic Regulation Act 1984, s. 14 (1) (a). - Issued: 22.08.2012. Made: 16.08.2012. Coming into force: 27.08.2012. Effect: None. Territorial extent & classification: E. Local. - Available at http://www.legislation.gov.uk/uksi/2012/2152/contents/made *Non-print*

The A66 Trunk Road (Naddle Beck Layby Closure) (Temporary Prohibition of Traffic) Order 2012 No. 2012/183. - Enabling power: Road Traffic Regulation Act 1984, s. 14 (1) (a). - Issued: 31.01.2012. Made: 19.01.2012. Coming into force: 05.02.2012. Effect: None. Territorial extent & classification: E. Local. - Available at http://www.legislation.gov.uk/uksi/2012/183/contents/made *Non-print*

The A66 Trunk Road (Newlands Beck Bridge) (Temporary Restriction of Traffic) Order 2012 No. 2012/563. - Enabling power: Road Traffic Regulation Act 1984, s. 14 (1) (a). - Issued: 01.03.2012. Made: 22.02.2012. Coming into force: 26.02.2012. Effect: None. Territorial extent & classification: E. Local. - Available at http://www.legislation.gov.uk/uksi/2012/563/contents/made *Non-print*

The A66 Trunk Road (Palliard to Light Trees, Stainmore) (Temporary Restriction and Prohibition of Traffic) Order 2012 No. 2012/2020. - Enabling power: Road Traffic Regulation Act 1984, s. 14 (1) (a). - Issued: 06.08.2012. Made: 19.07.2012. Coming into force: 04.08.2012. Effect: None. Territorial extent & classification: E. Local. - Available at http://www.legislation.gov.uk/uksi/2012/2020/contents/made *Non-print*

The A66 Trunk Road (Rheged to Brougham) (Temporary Prohibition and Restriction of Traffic) Order 2012 No. 2012/721. - Enabling power: Road Traffic Regulation Act 1984, s. 14 (1) (a). - Issued: 19.03.2012. Made: 01.03.2012. Coming into force: 18.03.2012. Effect: None. Territorial extent & classification: E. Local. - Available at http://www.legislation.gov.uk/uksi/2012/721/contents/made *Non-print*

The A66 Trunk Road (Rokeby Grange to Smallways) (Temporary Restriction and Prohibition of Traffic) Order 2012 No. 2012/657. - Enabling power: Road Traffic Regulation Act 1984, s. 14 (1) (a). - Issued: 14.03.2012. Made: 01.03.2012. Coming into force: 11.03.2012. Effect: None. Territorial extent & classification: E. Local. - Available at http://www.legislation.gov.uk/uksi/2012/657/contents/made *Non-print*

The A66 Trunk Road (Rokeby Park to Thorpe Grange) (Temporary Restriction and Prohibition of Traffic) Order 2012 No. 2012/2083. - Enabling power: Road Traffic Regulation Act 1984, s. 14 (1) (a). - Issued: 14.08.2012. Made: 02.08.2012. Coming into force: 12.08.2012. Effect: None. Territorial extent & classification: E. Local. - Available at http://www.legislation.gov.uk/uksi/2012/2083/contents/made *Non-print*

The A66 Trunk Road (Sandford Thorn Bridge, Coupland) (Temporary Restriction of Traffic) Order 2012 No. 2012/299. - Enabling power: Road Traffic Regulation Act 1984, s. 14 (1) (a). - Issued: 10.02.2012. Made: 01.02.2012. Coming into force: 17.02.2012. Effect: None. Territorial extent & classification: E. Local. - Available at http://www.legislation.gov.uk/uksi/2012/299/contents/made *Non-print*

The A66 Trunk Road (Sandford to Warcop) (Temporary Prohibition and Restriction of Traffic) Order 2012 No. 2012/2673. - Enabling power: Road Traffic Regulation Act 1984, s. 14 (1) (a). - Issued: 29.10.2012. Made: 12.10.2012. Coming into force: 27.10.2012. Effect: None. Territorial extent & classification: E. Local. - Available at http://www.legislation.gov.uk/uksi/2012/2673/contents/made *Non-print*

The A66 Trunk Road (Scotch Corner to Carkin Moor) (Temporary Restriction and Prohibition of Traffic) Order 2012 No. 2012/1730. - Enabling power: Road Traffic Regulation Act 1984, s. 14 (1) (a) (7). - Issued: 16.07.2012. Made: 21.06.2012. Coming into force: 01.07.2012. Effect: None. Territorial extent & classification: E. Local. - Available at http://www.legislation.gov.uk/uksi/2012/1730/contents/made *Non-print*

The A66 Trunk Road (Scotch Corner to Winston Crossroads) (Temporary Restriction and Prohibition of Traffic) Order 2012 No. 2012/658. - Enabling power: Road Traffic Regulation Act 1984, s. 14 (1) (a). - Issued: 14.03.2012. Made: 01.03.2012. Coming into force: 11.03.2012. Effect: None. Territorial extent & classification: E. Local. - Available at http://www.legislation.gov.uk/uksi/2012/658/contents/made *Non-print*

Road traffic: Traffic regulation

The A66 Trunk Road (Slapestones Roundabout to Baron's Cross Resurfacing) (Temporary Restriction and Prohibition of Traffic) Order 2012 No. 2012/2496. - Enabling power: Road Traffic Regulation Act 1984, s. 14 (1) (a). - Issued: 03.10.2012. Made: 27.09.2012. Coming into force: 14.10.2012. Effect: None. Territorial extent & classification: E. Local. - Available at http://www.legislation.gov.uk/uksi/2012/2496/contents/made *Non-print*

The A66 Trunk Road (Smallways to Ravenworth) (Temporary Restriction and Prohibition of Traffic) Order 2012 No. 2012/2486. - Enabling power: Road Traffic Regulation Act 1984, s. 14 (1) (a) (7). - Issued: 02.10.2012. Made: 27.09.2012. Coming into force: 07.10.2012. Effect: None. Territorial extent & classification: E. Local. - Available at http://www.legislation.gov.uk/uksi/2012/2486/contents/made *Non-print*

The A66 Trunk Road (Teesside Park Interchange) (Temporary Prohibition of Traffic) Order 2012 No. 2012/2627. - Enabling power: Road Traffic Regulation Act 1984, s. 14 (1) (a). - Issued: 23.10.2012. Made: 11.10.2012. Coming into force: 21.10.2012. Effect: None. Territorial extent & classification: E. Local. - Available at http://www.legislation.gov.uk/uksi/2012/2627/contents/made *Non-print*

The A69 Trunk Road (Denton Burn Interchange to West Denton Interchange) (Temporary Prohibition of Traffic) Order 2012 No. 2012/1941. - Enabling power: Road Traffic Regulation Act 1984, s. 14 (1) (a). - Issued: 30.07.2012. Made: 12.07.2012. Coming into force: 20.07.2012. Effect: None. Territorial extent & classification: E. Local. - Available at http://www.legislation.gov.uk/uksi/2012/1941/contents/made *Non-print*

The A69 Trunk Road (Lemington Interchange and Stagshaw Interchange) (Temporary Restriction and Prohibition of Traffic) Order 2012 No. 2012/1217. - Enabling power: Road Traffic Regulation Act 1984, s. 14 (1) (a). - Issued: 10.05.2012. Made: 23.04.2012. Coming into force: 02.05.2012. Effect: None. Territorial extent & classification: E. Local. - Available at http://www.legislation.gov.uk/uksi/2012/1217/contents/made *Non-print*

The A69 Trunk Road (Newcastle upon Tyne to Carlisle) (Temporary Restriction and Prohibition of Traffic) Order 2012 No. 2012/1000. - Enabling power: Road Traffic Regulation Act 1984, s. 14 (1) (a). - Issued: 05.04.2012. Made: 22.03.2012. Coming into force: 31.03.2012. Effect: None. Territorial extent & classification: E. Local. - Available at http://www.legislation.gov.uk/uksi/2012/1000/contents/made *Non-print*

The A69 Trunk Road (Throckley Interchange to West Denton Interchange) (Temporary Prohibition of Traffic) Order 2012 No. 2012/2082. - Enabling power: Road Traffic Regulation Act 1984, s. 14 (1) (a). - Issued: 14.08.2012. Made: 02.08.2012. Coming into force: 10.08.2012. Effect: None. Territorial extent & classification: E. Local. - Available at http://www.legislation.gov.uk/uksi/2012/2082/contents/made *Non-print*

The A120 Trunk Road (Coggeshall Bypass, Braintree, Essex) (Temporary Restriction and Prohibition of Traffic) Order 2012 No. 2012/2460. - Enabling power: Road Traffic Regulation Act 1984, s. 14 (1) (a). - Issued: 28.09.2012. Made: 17.09.2012. Coming into force: 24.09.2012. Effect: None. Territorial extent & classification: E. Local. - Available at http://www.legislation.gov.uk/uksi/2012/2460/contents/made *Non-print*

The A120 Trunk Road (Coggeshall, Essex) (Temporary Restriction and Prohibition of Traffic and Pedestrians) Order 2012 No. 2012/355. - Enabling power: Road Traffic Regulation Act 1984, s. 14 (1) (a). - Issued: 15.02.2012. Made: 06.02.2012. Coming into force: 13.02.2012. Effect: None. Territorial extent & classification: E. Local. - Available at http://www.legislation.gov.uk/uksi/2012/355/contents/made *Non-print*

The A120 Trunk Road (East of Marks Farm Roundabout to Galleys Roundabout, Braintree, Essex) (Temporary Restriction and Prohibition of Traffic) Order 2012 No. 2012/3292. - Enabling power: Road Traffic Regulation Act 1984, s. 14 (1) (a). - Issued: 15.01.2013. Made: 31.12.2012. Coming into force: 07.01.2013. Effect: None. Territorial extent & classification: E. Local. - Available at http://www.legislation.gov.uk/uksi/2012/3292/contents/made *Non-print*

The A120 Trunk Road (Great Dunmow to Stansted, Essex) Westbound (Temporary Prohibition of Traffic) Order 2012 No. 2012/1475. - Enabling power: Road Traffic Regulation Act 1984, s. 14 (1) (a). - Issued: 12.06.2012. Made: 30.05.2012. Coming into force: 06.06.2012. Effect: None. Territorial extent & classification: E. Local. - Available at http://www.legislation.gov.uk/uksi/2012/1475/contents/made *Non-print*

The A120 Trunk Road (Horsley Cross to A12 Crown Interchange, Colchester, Essex) Westbound (Temporary Restriction and Prohibition of Traffic) Order 2012 No. 2012/602. - Enabling power: Road Traffic Regulation Act 1984, s. 14 (1) (a). - Issued: 06.03.2012. Made: 27.02.2012. Coming into force: 05.03.2012. Effect: None. Territorial extent & classification: E. Local. - Available at http://www.legislation.gov.uk/uksi/2012/602/contents/made *Non-print*

The A120 Trunk Road (Horsley Cross to Cansey Lane, Tendring, Essex) (Temporary Restriction and Prohibition of Traffic) Order 2012 No. 2012/1461. - Enabling power: Road Traffic Regulation Act 1984, s. 14 (1) (a). - Issued: 12.06.2012. Made: 28.05.2012. Coming into force: 04.06.2012. Effect: None. Territorial extent & classification: E. Local. - Available at http://www.legislation.gov.uk/uksi/2012/1461/contents/made *Non-print*

The A120 Trunk Road (Horsley Cross to Great Bromley, Essex) (Temporary Restriction and Prohibition of Traffic) Order 2012 No. 2012/454. - Enabling power: Road Traffic Regulation Act 1984, s. 14 (1) (a). - Issued: 24.02.2012. Made: 13.02.2012. Coming into force: 20.02.2012. Effect: None. Territorial extent & classification: E. Local. - Available at http://www.legislation.gov.uk/uksi/2012/454/contents/made *Non-print*

The A120 Trunk Road (Old London Road to Church Lane, Marks Tey, Colchester, Essex) (Temporary Restriction and Prohibition of Traffic and Pedestrians) Order 2012 No. 2012/2475. - Enabling power: Road Traffic Regulation Act 1984, s. 14 (1) (a). - Issued: 01.10.2012. Made: 24.09.2012. Coming into force: 01.10.2012. Effect: None. Territorial extent & classification: E. Local. - Available at http://www.legislation.gov.uk/uksi/2012/2475/contents/made *Non-print*

The A120 Trunk Road (Priory Wood Roundabout to Dunmow, Stansted, Essex) (Temporary Restriction and Prohibition of Traffic) Order 2012 No. 2012/2694. - Enabling power: Road Traffic Regulation Act 1984, s. 14 (1) (a). - Issued: 30.10.2012. Made: 15.10.2012. Coming into force: 22.10.2012. Effect: None. Territorial extent & classification: E. Local. - Available at http://www.legislation.gov.uk/uksi/2012/2694/contents/made *Non-print*

The A120 Trunk Road (Ramsey, Tendring, Essex) (Temporary Restriction and Prohibition of Traffic) Order 2012 No. 2012/2663. - Enabling power: Road Traffic Regulation Act 1984, s. 14 (1) (a). - Issued: 26.10.2012. Made: 15.10.2012. Coming into force: 22.10.2012. Effect: None. Territorial extent & classification: E. Local. - Available at http://www.legislation.gov.uk/uksi/2012/2663/contents/made *Non-print*

The A160 Trunk Road (Eastfield Road to Manby Roundabout) (Temporary Restriction and Prohibition of Traffic) (No. 2) Order 2012 No. 2012/2432. - Enabling power: Road Traffic Regulation Act 1984, s. 14 (1) (a). - Issued: 26.09.2012. Made: 13.09.2012. Coming into force: 23.09.2012. Effect: None. Territorial extent & classification: E. Local. - Available at http://www.legislation.gov.uk/uksi/2012/2432/contents/made *Non-print*

The A160 Trunk Road (Eastfield Road to Manby Roundabout) (Temporary Restriction and Prohibition of Traffic) Order 2012 No. 2012/1119. - Enabling power: Road Traffic Regulation Act 1984, s. 14 (1) (a). - Issued: 24.04.2012. Made: 12.04.2012. Coming into force: 24.04.2012. Effect: None. Territorial extent & classification: E. Local. - Available at http://www.legislation.gov.uk/uksi/2012/1119/contents/made *Non-print*

The A160 Trunk Road (Harbrough Roundabout to Eastfield Road) (Temporary Prohibition of Traffic) Order 2012 No. 2012/2837. - Enabling power: Road Traffic Regulation Act 1984, s. 14 (1) (a). - Issued: 15.11.2012. Made: 31.10.2012. Coming into force: 06.11.2012. Effect: None. Territorial extent & classification: E. Local. - Available at http://www.legislation.gov.uk/uksi/2012/2837/contents/made *Non-print*

The A160 Trunk Road (Manby Roundabout to Town Street) (Temporary Prohibition of Traffic) Order 2012 No. 2012/2562. - Enabling power: Road Traffic Regulation Act 1984, s. 14 (1) (a). - Issued: 12.10.2012. Made: 02.10.2012. Coming into force: 07.10.2012. Effect: None. Territorial extent & classification: E. Local. - Available at http://www.legislation.gov.uk/uksi/2012/2562/contents/made *Non-print*

The A160 Trunk Road (Ulceby Road to Habrough Road Roundabout) (Temporary Prohibition of Traffic) Order 2012 No. 2012/2845. - Enabling power: Road Traffic Regulation Act 1984, s. 14 (1) (a). - Issued: 15.11.2012. Made: 01.11.2012. Coming into force: 08.11.2012. Effect: None. Territorial extent & classification: E. Local. - Available at http://www.legislation.gov.uk/uksi/2012/2845/contents/made *Non-print*

The A174 Trunk Road (Parkway) (Temporary Prohibition of Traffic) Order 2012 No. 2012/1823. - Enabling power: Road Traffic Regulation Act 1984, s. 14 (1) (a). - Issued: 19.07.2012. Made: 25.06.2012. Coming into force: 01.07.2012. Effect: None. Territorial extent & classification: E. Local. - Available at http://www.legislation.gov.uk/uksi/2012/1823/contents/made *Non-print*

The A180 Trunk Road (Brocklesbury Interchange to Stallingborough Interchange) (Temporary Restriction and Prohibition of Traffic) Order 2012 No. 2012/2577. - Enabling power: Road Traffic Regulation Act 1984, s. 14 (1) (a). - Issued: 16.10.2012. Made: 04.10.2012. Coming into force: 14.10.2012. Effect: None. Territorial extent & classification: E. Local. - Available at http://www.legislation.gov.uk/uksi/2012/2577/contents/made *Non-print*

Road traffic: Traffic regulation

The A180 Trunk Road (Brocklesby Interchange) (Temporary Prohibition of Traffic) Order 2012 No. 2012/36. - Enabling power: Road Traffic Regulation Act 1984, s. 14 (1) (a). - Issued: 11.01.2012. Made: 03.01.2012. Coming into force: 08.01.2012. Effect: None. Territorial extent & classification: E. Local. - Available at http://www.legislation.gov.uk/uksi/2012/36/contents/made *Non-print*

The A180 Trunk Road (Brocklesby Interchange to Barnetby Interchange) (Temporary Restriction and Prohibition of Traffic) Order 2012 No. 2012/2131. - Enabling power: Road Traffic Regulation Act 1984, s. 14 (1) (a). - Issued: 20.08.2012. Made: 09.08.2012. Coming into force: 19.08.2012. Effect: None. Territorial extent & classification: E. Local. - Available at http://www.legislation.gov.uk/uksi/2012/2131/contents/made *Non-print*

The A180 Trunk Road (Great Coates Interchange) (Temporary Prohibition of Traffic) Order 2012 No. 2012/2944. - Enabling power: Road Traffic Regulation Act 1984, s. 14 (1) (a). - Issued: 28.11.2012. Made: 15.11.2012. Coming into force: 25.11.2012. Effect: None. Territorial extent & classification: E. Local. - Available at http://www.legislation.gov.uk/uksi/2012/2944/contents/made *Non-print*

The A180 Trunk Road (Great Coates Interchange to Pyewipe Roundabout) (Temporary Prohibition of Traffic) Order 2012 No. 2012/659. - Enabling power: Road Traffic Regulation Act 1984, s. 14 (1) (a). - Issued: 14.03.2012. Made: 01.03.2012. Coming into force: 11.03.2012. Effect: None. Territorial extent & classification: E. Local. - Available at http://www.legislation.gov.uk/uksi/2012/659/contents/made *Non-print*

The A180 Trunk Road (Pyewipe Roundabout to Great Coates Interchange) (Temporary Prohibition of Traffic) Order 2012 No. 2012/2492. - Enabling power: Road Traffic Regulation Act 1984, s. 14 (1) (a). - Issued: 03.10.2012. Made: 27.09.2012. Coming into force: 07.10.2012. Effect: None. Territorial extent & classification: E. Local. - Available at http://www.legislation.gov.uk/uksi/2012/2492/contents/made *Non-print*

The A180 Trunk Road (Stallingborough Interchange to Great Coates Interchange) (Temporary Prohibition of Traffic) Order 2012 No. 2012/228. - Enabling power: Road Traffic Regulation Act 1984, s. 14 (1) (a). - Issued: 03.02.2012. Made: 19.01.2012. Coming into force: 26.01.2012. Effect: None. Territorial extent & classification: E. Local. - Available at http://www.legislation.gov.uk/uksi/2012/228/contents/made *Non-print*

The A184 Trunk Road (Whitemare Pool Interchange) (Temporary Prohibition of Traffic) Order 2012 No. 2012/42. - Enabling power: Road Traffic Regulation Act 1984, s. 14 (1) (a). - Issued: 11.01.2012. Made: 03.01.2012. Coming into force: 08.01.2012. Effect: None. Territorial extent & classification: E. Local. - Available at http://www.legislation.gov.uk/uksi/2012/42/contents/made *Non-print*

The A194(M) Motorway (Birtley Interchange to Follingsby Interchange) (Temporary Restriction and Prohibition of Traffic) Order 2012 No. 2012/3115. - Enabling power: Road Traffic Regulation Act 1984, s. 14 (1) (a). - Issued: 20.12.2012. Made: 22.11.2012. Coming into force: 02.12.2012. Effect: None. Territorial extent & classification: E. Local. - Available at http://www.legislation.gov.uk/uksi/2012/3115/contents/made *Non-print*

The A249 Trunk Road (Grovehurst Road Junction - Bobbing Junction) (Temporary Prohibition of Traffic) Order 2012 No. 2012/893. - Enabling power: Road Traffic Regulation Act 1984, s. 14 (1) (a). - Issued: 26.03.2012. Made: 19.03.2012. Coming into force: 07.04.2012. Effect: None. Territorial extent & classification: E. Local. - Available at http://www.legislation.gov.uk/uksi/2012/893/contents/made *Non-print*

The A249 Trunk Road (Key Street - Cowstead Roundabout) (Temporary Prohibition of Traffic) Order 2012 No. 2012/3179. - Enabling power: Road Traffic Regulation Act 1984, s. 14 (1) (a). - Issued: 31.12.2012. Made: 03.12.2012. Coming into force: 21.01.2013. Effect: None. Territorial extent & classification: E. Local. - Available at http://www.legislation.gov.uk/uksi/2012/3179/contents/made *Non-print*

The A259 Trunk Road (East Guldeford and Star Level Crossings) (Temporary Prohibition of Traffic) Order 2012 No. 2012/3195. - Enabling power: Road Traffic Regulation Act 1984, s. 14 (1) (a). - Issued: 02.01.2013. Made: 10.12.2012. Coming into force: 19.01.2013. Effect: None. Territorial extent & classification: E. Local. - Available at http://www.legislation.gov.uk/uksi/2012/3195/contents/made *Non-print*

The A259 Trunk Road (Green Lane - Pevensey Levels) (Temporary Restriction and Prohibition of Traffic) Order 2012 No. 2012/1057. - Enabling power: Road Traffic Regulation Act 1984, s. 14 (1) (a). - Issued: 13.04.2012. Made: 02.04.2012. Coming into force: 21.04.2012. Effect: None. Territorial extent & classification: E. Local. - Available at http://www.legislation.gov.uk/uksi/2012/1057/contents/made *Non-print*

The A259 Trunk Road (Guestling House - North of The White Hart) (Temporary 40 Miles Per Hour Speed Restriction) Order 2012 No. 2012/2692. - Enabling power: Road Traffic Regulation Act 1984, s. 14 (1) (a). - Issued: 30.10.2012. Made: 15.10.2012. Coming into force: 03.11.2012. Effect: None. Territorial extent & classification: E. Local. - Available at http://www.legislation.gov.uk/uksi/2012/2692/contents/made *Non-print*

The A259 Trunk Road (Icklesham) (Temporary 40 Miles Per Hour Speed Restriction) Order 2012 No. 2012/2858. - Enabling power: Road Traffic Regulation Act 1984, s. 14 (1) (a). - Issued: 16.11.2012. Made: 05.11.2012. Coming into force: 24.11.2012. Effect: None. Territorial extent & classification: E. Local. - Available at http://www.legislation.gov.uk/uksi/2012/2858/contents/made *Non-print*

The A259 Trunk Road (Little Common Road, Bexhill) (No. 2) (Temporary Prohibition of Traffic) Order 2012 No. 2012/2700. - Enabling power: Road Traffic Regulation Act 1984, s. 16A (2) (a). - Issued: 01.11.2012. Made: 15.10.2012. Coming into force: 03.11.2012. Effect: None. Territorial extent & classification: E. Local. - Available at http://www.legislation.gov.uk/uksi/2012/2700/contents/made *Non-print*

The A259 Trunk Road (Little Common Road, Bexhill) (Temporary Prohibition of Traffic) Order 2012 No. 2012/547. - Enabling power: Road Traffic Regulation Act 1984, s. 16A (2) (a). - Issued: 01.03.2012. Made: 20.02.2012. Coming into force: 10.03.2012. Effect: None. Territorial extent & classification: E. Local. - Available at http://www.legislation.gov.uk/uksi/2012/547/contents/made *Non-print*

The A259 Trunk Road (Pevensey Roundabout) (Temporary 40 Miles Per Hour Speed Restriction) Order 2012 No. 2012/2438. - Enabling power: Road Traffic Regulation Act 1984, s. 14 (1) (a). - Issued: 27.09.2012. Made: 17.09.2012. Coming into force: 06.10.2012. Effect: None. Territorial extent & classification: E. Local. - Available at http://www.legislation.gov.uk/uksi/2012/2438/contents/made *Non-print*

The A259 Trunk Road (Rye) (Temporary Restriction and Prohibition of Traffic) Order 2012 No. 2012/3196. - Enabling power: Road Traffic Regulation Act 1984, s. 14 (1) (a). - Issued: 02.01.2013. Made: 10.12.2012. Coming into force: 05.01.2013. Effect: None. Territorial extent & classification: E. Local. - Available at http://www.legislation.gov.uk/uksi/2012/3196/contents/made *Non-print*

The A259 Trunk Road (Various Roads, Rye) (Temporary Restriction and Prohibition of Traffic) Order 2012 No. 2012/2651. - Enabling power: Road Traffic Regulation Act 1984, s. 16A (2) (a). - Issued: 25.10.2012. Made: 15.10.2012. Coming into force: 03.11.2012. Effect: None. Territorial extent & classification: E. Local. - Available at http://www.legislation.gov.uk/uksi/2012/2651/contents/made *Non-print*

The A259 Trunk Road (Winchelsea - Rye) (Temporary 30 Miles Per Hour Speed Restriction) Order 2012 No. 2012/483. - Enabling power: Road Traffic Regulation Act 1984, s. 14 (1) (a). - Issued: 29.02.2012. Made: 20.02.2012. Coming into force: 10.03.2012. Effect: None. Territorial extent & classification: E. Local. - Available at http://www.legislation.gov.uk/uksi/2012/483/contents/made *Non-print*

The A259 Trunk Road (Winchelsea) (Temporary Restriction and Prohibition of Traffic) Order 2012 No. 2012/2960. - Enabling power: Road Traffic Regulation Act 1984, s. 14 (1) (a). - Issued: 30.11.2012. Made: 19.11.2012. Coming into force: 08.12.2012. Effect: None. Territorial extent & classification: E. Local. - Available at http://www.legislation.gov.uk/uksi/2012/2960/contents/made *Non-print*

The A282 Trunk Road (Junctions 1A - 2) (Temporary Prohibition of Traffic) Order 2012 No. 2012/2100. - Enabling power: Road Traffic Regulation Act 1984, s. 14 (1) (a). - Issued: 16.08.2012. Made: 06.08.2012. Coming into force: 01.09.2012. Effect: None. Territorial extent & classification: E. Local. - Available at http://www.legislation.gov.uk/uksi/2012/2100/contents/made *Non-print*

The A282 Trunk Road (M25 Junctions 31 - 30, Link/Slip Roads) (Temporary Prohibition of Traffic) Order 2012 No. 2012/2242. - Enabling power: Road Traffic Regulation Act 1984, s. 14 (1) (a). - Issued: 04.09.2012. Made: 28.08.2012. Coming into force: 15.09.2012. Effect: None. Territorial extent & classification: E. Local. - Available at http://www.legislation.gov.uk/uksi/2012/2242/contents/made *Non-print*

The A303 Trunk Road (A30 Junction to Marsh, Devon) (Temporary Restriction of Traffic) Order 2012 No. 2012/512. - Enabling power: Road Traffic Regulation Act 1984, s. 14 (1) (a). - Issued: 01.03.2012. Made: 21.02.2012. Coming into force: 28.02.2012. Effect: None. Territorial extent & classification: E. Local. - Available at http://www.legislation.gov.uk/uksi/2012/512/contents/made *Non-print*

The A303 Trunk Road (Amesbury, Wiltshire) (Temporary Prohibition of Traffic) Order 2012 No. 2012/1406. - Enabling power: Road Traffic Regulation Act 1984, s. 14 (1) (a). - Issued: 01.06.2012. Made: 22.05.2012. Coming into force: 28.05.2012. Effect: None. Territorial extent & classification: E. Local. - Available at http://www.legislation.gov.uk/uksi/2012/1406/contents/made *Non-print*

The A303 Trunk Road (Amesbury, Wiltshire) (Temporary Restriction and Prohibition of Traffic) (Number 2) Order 2012 No. 2012/1801. - Enabling power: Road Traffic Regulation Act 1984, s. 14 (1) (b). - Issued: 19.07.2012. Made: 03.07.2012. Coming into force: 07.07.2012. Effect: None. Territorial extent & classification: E. Local. - Available at http://www.legislation.gov.uk/uksi/2012/1801/contents/made *Non-print*

Road traffic: Traffic regulation

The A303 Trunk Road (Amesbury, Wiltshire) (Temporary Restriction and Prohibition of Traffic) Order 2012 No. 2012/551. - Enabling power: Road Traffic Regulation Act 1984, s. 14 (1) (a). - Issued: 01.03.2012. Made: 22.02.2012. Coming into force: 28.02.2012. Effect: None. Territorial extent & classification: E. Local. - Available at http://www.legislation.gov.uk/uksi/2012/551/contents/made *Non-print*

The A303 Trunk Road (Ham Hill, Somerset) (Temporary Prohibition of Traffic) Order 2012 No. 2012/318. - Enabling power: Road Traffic Regulation Act 1984, s. 14 (1) (a). - Issued: 15.02.2012. Made: 06.02.2012. Coming into force: 13.02.2012. Effect: None. Territorial extent & classification: E. Local. - Available at http://www.legislation.gov.uk/uksi/2012/318/contents/made *Non-print*

The A303 Trunk Road (Horton to Marsh) (Temporary Prohibition and Restriction of Traffic) Order 2012 No. 2012/484. - Enabling power: Road Traffic Regulation Act 1984, s. 14 (1) (a). - Issued: 29.02.2012. Made: 20.02.2012. Coming into force: 28.02.2012. Effect: None. Territorial extent & classification: E. Local. - Available at http://www.legislation.gov.uk/uksi/2012/484/contents/made *Non-print*

The A303 Trunk Road (Hundred Acre Interchange, Westbound Entry Slip Road) (Temporary Prohibition of Traffic) Order 2012 No. 2012/203. - Enabling power: Road Traffic Regulation Act 1984, s. 14 (1) (a). - Issued: 01.02.2012. Made: 23.01.2012. Coming into force: 11.02.2012. Effect: None. Territorial extent & classification: E. Local. - Available at http://www.legislation.gov.uk/uksi/2012/203/contents/made *Non-print*

The A303 Trunk Road (Ilchester Mead to Podimore, Somerset) (Temporary Prohibition of Traffic) Order 2012 No. 2012/550. - Enabling power: Road Traffic Regulation Act 1984, s. 14 (1) (a). - Issued: 01.03.2012. Made: 22.02.2012. Coming into force: 28.02.2012. Effect: None. Territorial extent & classification: E. Local. - Available at http://www.legislation.gov.uk/uksi/2012/550/contents/made *Non-print*

The A303 Trunk Road (Ilminster to South Petherton, Somerset) (Temporary Prohibition of Traffic) Order 2012 No. 2012/1683. - Enabling power: Road Traffic Regulation Act 1984, s. 14 (1) (a). - Issued: 03.07.2012. Made: 19.06.2012. Coming into force: 22.06.2012. Effect: None. Territorial extent & classification: E. Local. - Available at http://www.legislation.gov.uk/uksi/2012/1683/contents/made *Non-print*

The A303 Trunk Road (Longbarrow Roundabout, Wiltshire) (Temporary Restriction of Traffic) Order 2012 No. 2012/2199. - Enabling power: Road Traffic Regulation Act 1984, s. 14 (1) (a). - Issued: 30.08.2012. Made: 22.08.2012. Coming into force: 01.09.2012. Effect: None. Territorial extent & classification: E. Local. - Available at http://www.legislation.gov.uk/uksi/2012/2199/contents/made *Non-print*

The A303 Trunk Road (M3 Junction 8 - Parkhouse Interchange) (Temporary Restriction and Prohibition of Traffic) Order 2012 No. 2012/1455. - Enabling power: Road Traffic Regulation Act 1984, s. 14 (1) (a). - Issued: 12.06.2012. Made: 28.05.2012. Coming into force: 20.06.2012. Effect: None. Territorial extent & classification: E. Local. - Available at http://www.legislation.gov.uk/uksi/2012/1455/contents/made *Non-print*

The A303 Trunk Road (Parkhouse Interchange, Eastbound Slip Roads) (Temporary Prohibition of Traffic) Order 2012 No. 2012/1081. - Enabling power: Road Traffic Regulation Act 1984, s. 14 (1) (a). - Issued: 17.04.2012. Made: 10.04.2012. Coming into force: 28.04.2012. Effect: None. Territorial extent & classification: E. Local. - Available at http://www.legislation.gov.uk/uksi/2012/1081/contents/made *Non-print*

The A303 Trunk Road (Picket Twenty Interchange - Parkhouse Interchange) (Temporary Restriction and Prohibition of Traffic) Order 2012 No. 2012/2363. - Enabling power: Road Traffic Regulation Act 1984, s. 14 (1) (a). - Issued: 17.09.2012. Made: 10.09.2012. Coming into force: 29.09.2012. Effect: None. Territorial extent & classification: E. Local. - Available at http://www.legislation.gov.uk/uksi/2012/2363/contents/made *Non-print*

The A303 Trunk Road (Picket Twenty Interchange - Salisbury Road Interchange) (Temporary Prohibition of Traffic) Order 2012 No. 2012/728. - Enabling power: Road Traffic Regulation Act 1984, s. 14 (1) (a). - Issued: 19.03.2012. Made: 05.03.2012. Coming into force: 24.03.2012. Effect: None. Territorial extent & classification: E. Local. - Available at http://www.legislation.gov.uk/uksi/2012/728/contents/made *Non-print*

The A303 Trunk Road (Salisbury Road Interchange, Slip Roads) (Temporary Prohibition of Traffic) Order 2012 No. 2012/1184. - Enabling power: Road Traffic Regulation Act 1984, s. 14 (1) (a). - Issued: 02.05.2012. Made: 23.04.2012. Coming into force: 12.05.2012. Effect: None. Territorial extent & classification: E. Local. - Available at http://www.legislation.gov.uk/uksi/2012/1184/contents/made *Non-print*

The A303 Trunk Road (Stonehenge Summer Solstice, Wiltshire) (Temporary Restriction and Prohibition of Traffic) Order 2012 No. 2012/1414. - Enabling power: Road Traffic Regulation Act 1984, s. 14 (1) (b). - Issued: 01.06.2012. Made: 23.05.2012. Coming into force: 30.05.2012. Effect: None. Territorial extent & classification: E. Local. - Available at http://www.legislation.gov.uk/uksi/2012/1414/contents/made *Non-print*

The A303 Trunk Road (Stonehenge Winter Solstice, Wiltshire) (Temporary Restriction and Prohibition of Traffic) Order 2012 No. 2012/3225. - Enabling power: Road Traffic Regulation Act 1984, s. 14 (1) (b). - Issued: 07.01.2013. Made: 12.12.2012. Coming into force: 18.12.2012. Effect: None. Territorial extent & classification: E. Local. - Available at http://www.legislation.gov.uk/uksi/2012/3225/contents/made *Non-print*

The A303 Trunk Road (Winchester Road and Picket Twenty) (Temporary Prohibition of Traffic) Order 2012 No. 2012/2230. - Enabling power: Road Traffic Regulation Act 1984, s. 14 (1) (a). - Issued: 04.09.2012. Made: 28.08.2012. Coming into force: 15.09.2012. Effect: None. Territorial extent & classification: E. Local. - Available at http://www.legislation.gov.uk/uksi/2012/2230/contents/made *Non-print*

The A303 Trunk Road (Wiremead Lane, Thruxton) (Temporary Prohibition of Traffic) Order 2012 No. 2012/342. - Enabling power: Road Traffic Regulation Act 1984, s. 14 (1) (a). - Issued: 15.02.2012. Made: 06.02.2012. Coming into force: 25.02.2012. Effect: None. Territorial extent & classification: E. Local. - Available at http://www.legislation.gov.uk/uksi/2012/342/contents/made *Non-print*

The A404(M) Motorway (Junction 9a - M4 Junction 8/9) (Temporary Prohibition of Traffic) Order 2012 No. 2012/1577. - Enabling power: Road Traffic Regulation Act 1984, s. 14 (1) (a). - Issued: 27.06.2012. Made: 11.06.2012. Coming into force: 30.06.2012. Effect: None. Territorial extent & classification: E. Local. - Available at http://www.legislation.gov.uk/uksi/2012/1577/contents/made *Non-print*

The A404(M) Motorway (Junction 9B - M4 Junction 8/9) (Temporary Restriction and Prohibition of Traffic) Order 2012 No. 2012/2467. - Enabling power: Road Traffic Regulation Act 1984, s. 14 (1) (a). - Issued: 01.10.2012. Made: 24.09.2012. Coming into force: 19.10.2012. Effect: None. Territorial extent & classification: E. Local. - Available at http://www.legislation.gov.uk/uksi/2012/2467/contents/made *Non-print*

The A404(M) Motorway (M4 Junction 8/9 - A404(M) Junction 9b) (Temporary Restriction and Prohibition of Traffic) Order 2012 No. 2012/3194. - Enabling power: Road Traffic Regulation Act 1984, s. 14 (1) (a). - Issued: 02.01.2013. Made: 10.12.2012. Coming into force: 05.01.2013. Effect: None. Territorial extent & classification: E. Local. - Available at http://www.legislation.gov.uk/uksi/2012/3194/contents/made *Non-print*

The A404 Trunk Road and the A404(M) Motorway (A404(M) Junction 9B - M40 Junction 4) (Temporary Restriction and Prohibition of Traffic) Order 2012 No. 2012/2442. - Enabling power: Road Traffic Regulation Act 1984, s. 14 (1) (a). - Issued: 27.09.2012. Made: 17.09.2012. Coming into force: 08.10.2012. Effect: None. Territorial extent & classification: E. Local. - Available at http://www.legislation.gov.uk/uksi/2012/2442/contents/made *Non-print*

The A405 Trunk Road (M1 Junction 6) (Temporary Prohibition of Traffic) Order 2012 No. 2012/1079. - Enabling power: Road Traffic Regulation Act 1984, s. 14 (1) (a). - Issued: 17.04.2012. Made: 10.04.2012. Coming into force: 04.05.2012. Effect: None. Territorial extent & classification: E. Local. - Available at http://www.legislation.gov.uk/uksi/2012/1079/contents/made *Non-print*

The A417 Trunk Road (Air Balloon Roundabout to Burford Road Junction, Gloucestershire) (Temporary Prohibition of Traffic) Order 2012 No. 2012/2119. - Enabling power: Road Traffic Regulation Act 1984, s. 14 (1) (a). - Issued: 17.08.2012. Made: 08.08.2012. Coming into force: 11.08.2012. Effect: None. Territorial extent & classification: E. Local. - Available at http://www.legislation.gov.uk/uksi/2012/2119/contents/made *Non-print*

The A417 Trunk Road (Brockworth to Air Balloon Roundabout, Crickley Hill, Gloucestershire) (Temporary Prohibition of Traffic) Order 2012 No. 2012/1560. - Enabling power: Road Traffic Regulation Act 1984, s. 14 (1) (a). - Issued: 22.06.2012. Made: 06.06.2012. Coming into force: 09.06.2012. Effect: None. Territorial extent & classification: E. Local. - Available at http://www.legislation.gov.uk/uksi/2012/1560/contents/made *Non-print*

The A419 Trunk Road (Blundsdon to Calcutt, Wiltshire) (Prohibition of U Turns) (Experimental) Order 2012 No. 2012/80. - Enabling power: Road Traffic Regulation Act 1984, ss. 9 (1) (a) (3), 10 (1) (2). - Issued: 18.01.2012. Made: 03.01.2012. Coming into force: 16.01.2012. Effect: None. Territorial extent & classification: E. Local. - Available at http://www.legislation.gov.uk/uksi/2012/80/contents/made *Non-print*

Road traffic: Traffic regulation

The A419 Trunk Road (Castle Eaton, Kingshill and Lower Widhill Farm Junctions, Near Cricklade, Wiltshire) (Temporary Prohibition of Traffic) Order 2012 No. 2012/1781. - Enabling power: Road Traffic Regulation Act 1984, s. 14 (1) (b). - Issued: 18.07.2012. Made: 27.06.2012. Coming into force: 05.07.2012. Effect: None. Territorial extent & classification: E. Local. - Available at http://www.legislation.gov.uk/uksi/2012/1781/contents/made *Non-print*

The A419 Trunk Road (Cirencester) (Temporary Prohibition of Traffic) Order 2012 No. 2012/1420. - Enabling power: Road Traffic Regulation Act 1984, s. 14 (1) (a). - Issued: 01.06.2012. Made: 22.05.2012. Coming into force: 26.05.2012. Effect: None. Territorial extent & classification: E. Local. - Available at http://www.legislation.gov.uk/uksi/2012/1420/contents/made *Non-print*

The A419 Trunk Road (Commonhead Roundabout, Swindon) (Temporary Prohibition of Traffic) Order 2012 No. 2012/2930. - Enabling power: Road Traffic Regulation Act 1984, s. 14 (1) (a). - Issued: 26.11.2012. Made: 14.11.2012. Coming into force: 17.11.2012. Effect: None. Territorial extent & classification: E. Local. - Available at http://www.legislation.gov.uk/uksi/2012/2930/contents/made *Non-print*

The A419 Trunk Road (Commonhead to Cricklade) (Temporary Prohibition of Traffic) Order 2012 No. 2012/2736. - Enabling power: Road Traffic Regulation Act 1984, s. 14 (1) (a). - Issued: 06.11.2012. Made: 18.10.2012. Coming into force: 26.10.2012. Effect: None. Territorial extent & classification: E. Local. - Available at http://www.legislation.gov.uk/uksi/2012/2736/contents/made *Non-print*

The A419 Trunk Road (Cricklade to South Cerney) (Temporary Prohibition of Traffic) Order 2012 No. 2012/2146. - Enabling power: Road Traffic Regulation Act 1984, s. 14 (1) (a). - Issued: 22.08.2012. Made: 15.08.2012. Coming into force: 18.08.2012. Effect: None. Territorial extent & classification: E. Local. - Available at http://www.legislation.gov.uk/uksi/2012/2146/contents/made *Non-print*

The A419 Trunk Road (Highworth (Rat-trap) Junction, Swindon) (Temporary Prohibition of Traffic) Order 2012 No. 2012/1369. - Enabling power: Road Traffic Regulation Act 1984, s. 14 (1) (a). - Issued: 28.05.2012. Made: 17.05.2012. Coming into force: 26.05.2012. Effect: None. Territorial extent & classification: E. Local. - Available at http://www.legislation.gov.uk/uksi/2012/1369/contents/made *Non-print*

The A419 Trunk Road (White Hart Junction to Lady Lane Junction, Swindon) (Temporary Prohibition of Traffic) Order 2012 No. 2012/930. - Enabling power: Road Traffic Regulation Act 1984, s. 14 (1) (a). - Issued: 28.03.2012. Made: 22.03.2012. Coming into force: 31.03.2012. Effect: None. Territorial extent & classification: E. Local. - Available at http://www.legislation.gov.uk/uksi/2012/930/contents/made *Non-print*

The A419 Trunk Road (White Hart Junction to Turnpike Junction, Swindon) (Temporary Restriction and Prohibition of Traffic) Order 2012 No. 2012/2866. - Enabling power: Road Traffic Regulation Act 1984, s. 14 (1) (a). - Issued: 19.11.2012. Made: 06.11.2012. Coming into force: 10.11.2012. Effect: None. Territorial extent & classification: E. Local. - Available at http://www.legislation.gov.uk/uksi/2012/2866/contents/made *Non-print*

The A421 Trunk Road (Bedford Southern Bypass, Elstow to Renhold) (Temporary Prohibition of Traffic) Order 2012 No. 2012/2164. - Enabling power: Road Traffic Regulation Act 1984, s. 14 (1) (a). - Issued: 23.08.2012. Made: 20.08.2012. Coming into force: 27.08.2012. Effect: None. Territorial extent & classification: E. Local. - Available at http://www.legislation.gov.uk/uksi/2012/2164/contents/made *Non-print*

The A421 Trunk Road (Bedford Southern Bypass, Elstow) Westbound (Temporary Prohibition of Traffic) Order 2012 No. 2012/2104. - Enabling power: Road Traffic Regulation Act 1984, s. 14 (1) (a). - Issued: 16.08.2012. Made: 06.08.2012. Coming into force: 13.08.2012. Effect: None. Territorial extent & classification: E. Local. - Available at http://www.legislation.gov.uk/uksi/2012/2104/contents/made *Non-print*

The A421 Trunk Road (Bedford Southern Bypass) (Temporary Prohibition of Traffic) Order 2012 No. 2012/603. - Enabling power: Road Traffic Regulation Act 1984, s. 14 (1) (a). - Issued: 06.03.2012. Made: 27.02.2012. Coming into force: 05.03.2012. Effect: None. Territorial extent & classification: E. Local. - Available at http://www.legislation.gov.uk/uksi/2012/603/contents/made *Non-print*

The A428 Trunk Road (Croxton to Cambourne, Cambridgeshire) (Temporary Restriction and Prohibition of Traffic) Order 2012 No. 2012/2517. - Enabling power: Road Traffic Regulation Act 1984, s. 14 (1) (a). - Issued: 08.10.2012. Made: 01.10.2012. Coming into force: 08.10.2012. Effect: None. Territorial extent & classification: E. Local. - Available at http://www.legislation.gov.uk/uksi/2012/2517/contents/made *Non-print*

Road traffic: Traffic regulation

The A446 and A452 Trunk Roads (Temporary Restriction and Prohibition of Traffic) Order 2012 No. 2012/2037. - Enabling power: Road Traffic Regulation Act 1984, s. 14 (1) (a). - Issued: 08.08.2012. Made: 11.07.2012. Coming into force: 18.07.2012. Effect: None. Territorial extent & classification: E. Local. - Available at http://www.legislation.gov.uk/uksi/2012/2037/contents/made *Non-print*

The A446 Trunk Road (A452 Chester Road to M6 Junction 4) (Temporary Prohibition of Traffic) Order 2012 No. 2012/2099. - Enabling power: Road Traffic Regulation Act 1984, s. 14 (1) (a). - Issued: 16.08.2012. Made: 20.07.2012. Coming into force: 27.07.2012. Effect: None. Territorial extent & classification: E. Local. - Available at http://www.legislation.gov.uk/uksi/2012/2099/contents/made *Non-print*

The A449 and A5 Trunk Roads (Gailey, Shropshire) (Temporary Restriction and Prohibition of Traffic) Order 2012 No. 2012/2724. - Enabling power: Road Traffic Regulation Act 1984, s. 14 (1) (a). - Issued: 02.11.2012. Made: 08.10.2012. Coming into force: 15.10.2012. Effect: None. Territorial extent & classification: E. Local. - Available at http://www.legislation.gov.uk/uksi/2012/2724/contents/made *Non-print*

The A449 Trunk Road (Four Ashes to M54 Junction 2) (Temporary Restriction and Prohibition of Traffic) Order 2012 No. 2012/388. - Enabling power: Road Traffic Regulation Act 1984, s. 14 (1) (a). - Issued: 21.02.2012. Made: 27.01.2012. Coming into force: 03.02.2012. Effect: None. Territorial extent & classification: E. Local. - Available at http://www.legislation.gov.uk/uksi/2012/388/contents/made *Non-print*

The A449 Trunk Road (Gailey to Four Ashes, Staffordshire) (Temporary Prohibition of Traffic) Order 2012 No. 2012/3132. - Enabling power: Road Traffic Regulation Act 1984, s. 14 (1) (a). - Issued: 20.12.2012. Made: 19.11.2012. Coming into force: 26.11.2012. Effect: None. Territorial extent & classification: E. Local. - Available at http://www.legislation.gov.uk/uksi/2012/3132/contents/made *Non-print*

The A449 Trunk Road (M54 Junction 2, Coven Heath to Gailey) (Temporary Prohibition of Traffic) Order 2012 No. 2012/617. - Enabling power: Road Traffic Regulation Act 1984, s. 14 (1) (a). - Issued: 07.03.2012. Made: 24.02.2012. Coming into force: 02.03.2012. Effect: None. Territorial extent & classification: E. Local. - Available at http://www.legislation.gov.uk/uksi/2012/617/contents/made *Non-print*

The A449 Trunk Road (Ross on Wye, Herefordshire) (Temporary Restriction of Traffic) Order 2012 No. 2012/3230. - Enabling power: Road Traffic Regulation Act 1984, s. 14 (1) (a). - Issued: 08.01.2013. Made: 03.12.2012. Coming into force: 10.12.2012. Effect: None. Territorial extent & classification: E. Local. - Available at http://www.legislation.gov.uk/uksi/2012/3230/contents/made *Non-print*

The A452 and the A446 Trunk Roads (Coleshill, Warwickshire) (Temporary Prohibition of Traffic) Order 2012 No. 2012/1920. - Enabling power: Road Traffic Regulation Act 1984, s. 14 (1) (a). - Issued: 25.07.2012. Made: 25.06.2012. Coming into force: 02.07.2012. Effect: None. Territorial extent & classification: E. Local. - Available at http://www.legislation.gov.uk/uksi/2012/1920/contents/made *Non-print*

The A452 Trunk Road (Warwickshire) (Temporary Prohibition of Traffic) Order 2012 No. 2012/2719. - Enabling power: Road Traffic Regulation Act 1984, s. 14 (1) (a). - Issued: 02.11.2012. Made: 01.10.2012. Coming into force: 08.10.2012. Effect: None. Territorial extent & classification: E. Local. - Available at http://www.legislation.gov.uk/uksi/2012/2719/contents/made *Non-print*

The A453 and A52 Trunk Roads (Nottingham) (Temporary Prohibition of Traffic) Order 2012 No. 2012/858. - Enabling power: Road Traffic Regulation Act 1984, s. 14 (1) (a). - Issued: 23.03.2012. Made: 09.03.2012. Coming into force: 16.03.2012. Effect: None. Territorial extent & classification: E. Local. - Available at http://www.legislation.gov.uk/uksi/2012/858/contents/made *Non-print*

The A453 Trunk Road (Clifton, Nottingham) (Temporary Prohibition of Traffic) (No.2) Order 2012 No. 2012/2537. - Enabling power: Road Traffic Regulation Act 1984, s. 14 (1) (a). - Issued: 09.10.2012. Made: 14.09.2012. Coming into force: 21.09.2012. Effect: None. Territorial extent & classification: E. Local. - Available at http://www.legislation.gov.uk/uksi/2012/2537/contents/made *Non-print*

The A453 Trunk Road (Clifton, Nottingham) (Temporary Prohibition of Traffic) Order 2012 No. 2012/615. - Enabling power: Road Traffic Regulation Act 1984, s. 14 (1) (a). - Issued: 07.03.2012. Made: 20.02.2012. Coming into force: 27.02.2012. Effect: None. Territorial extent & classification: E. Local. - Available at http://www.legislation.gov.uk/uksi/2012/615/contents/made *Non-print*

The A453 Trunk Road (M1 Junction 24 to Crusader Roundabout, Nottingham) (Temporary Restriction and Prohibition of Traffic) Order 2012 No. 2012/107. - Enabling power: Road Traffic Regulation Act 1984, s. 14 (1) (a). - Issued: 20.01.2012. Made: 09.01.2012. Coming into force: 16.01.2012. Effect: None. Territorial extent & classification: E. Local. - Available at http://www.legislation.gov.uk/uksi/2012/107/contents/made *Non-print*

Road traffic: Traffic regulation

The A458 Trunk Road (Cardeston to Colcott, Shropshire) (Temporary Restriction and Prohibition of Traffic) Order 2012 No. 2012/1582. - Enabling power: Road Traffic Regulation Act 1984, s. 14 (1) (a). - Issued: 25.06.2012. Made: 01.06.2012. Coming into force: 08.06.2012. Effect: None. Territorial extent & classification: E. Local. - Available at http://www.legislation.gov.uk/uksi/2012/1582/contents/made *Non-print*

The A458 Trunk Road (Rowton to Wollaston, Shropshire) (Temporary Prohibition of Traffic) Order 2012 No. 2012/2192. - Enabling power: Road Traffic Regulation Act 1984, s. 14 (1) (a). - Issued: 29.08.2012. Made: 20.08.2012. Coming into force: 27.08.2012. Effect: None. Territorial extent & classification: E. Local. - Available at http://www.legislation.gov.uk/uksi/2012/2192/contents/made *Non-print*

The A483 Trunk Road (Llanymynech and Pant, Shropshire) (Temporary Prohibition of Traffic) Order 2012 No. 2012/1450. - Enabling power: Road Traffic Regulation Act 1984, s. 14 (1) (b). - Issued: 12.06.2012. Made: 16.05.2012. Coming into force: 23.05.2012. Effect: None. Territorial extent & classification: E. Local. - Available at http://www.legislation.gov.uk/uksi/2012/1450/contents/made *Non-print*

The A483 Trunk Road (Llynclys to South of Oswestry, Shropshire) (Temporary Restriction and Prohibition of Traffic) Order 2012 No. 2012/613. - Enabling power: Road Traffic Regulation Act 1984, s. 14 (1) (a). - Issued: 07.03.2012. Made: 24.02.2012. Coming into force: 02.03.2012. Effect: None. Territorial extent & classification: E. Local. - Available at http://www.legislation.gov.uk/uksi/2012/613/contents/made *Non-print*

The A483 Trunk Road (South East of Oswestry, Shropshire) (Temporary Restriction and Prohibition of Traffic) Order 2012 No. 2012/3325. - Enabling power: Road Traffic Regulation Act 1984, s. 14 (1) (a). - Issued: 18.01.2013. Made: 31.12.2012. Coming into force: 07.01.2013. Effect: None. Territorial extent & classification: E. Local. - Available at http://www.legislation.gov.uk/uksi/2012/3325/contents/made *Non-print*

The A494 Trunk Road (Chester Half Marathon) (Temporary Prohibition of Traffic) Order 2012 No. 2012/1211. - Enabling power: Road Traffic Regulation Act 1984, s. 16A (2) (a). - Issued: 08.05.2012. Made: 25.04.2012. Coming into force: 12.05.2012. Effect: None. Territorial extent & classification: E. Local. - Available at http://www.legislation.gov.uk/uksi/2012/1211/contents/made *Non-print*

The A494 Trunk Road (Deeside Park) (Westbound Entry Slip Road from the A540 Parkgate Road) (Temporary Prohibition of Traffic) Order 2012 No. 2012/1307. - Enabling power: Road Traffic Regulation Act 1984, s. 14 (1) (a). - Issued: 22.05.2012. Made: 09.05.2012. Coming into force: 22.05.2012. Effect: None. Territorial extent & classification: E. Local. - Available at http://www.legislation.gov.uk/uksi/2012/1307/contents/made *Non-print*

The A500 Trunk Road (Between M6 Junction 15 and Junction 16, Staffordshire) (Temporary Prohibition of Traffic) Order 2012 No. 2012/569. - Enabling power: Road Traffic Regulation Act 1984, s. 14 (1) (a). - Issued: 02.03.2012. Made: 13.02.2012. Coming into force: 20.02.2012. Effect: None. Territorial extent & classification: E. Local. - Available at http://www.legislation.gov.uk/uksi/2012/569/contents/made *Non-print*

The A500 Trunk Road (Hanchurch to Barthomley) (24 Hour Clearway, Prohibition of Waiting and Right Turn Ban) Order 2012 No. 2012/3267. - Enabling power: Road Traffic Regulation Act 1984, ss. 1 (1), 2 (1) (2), 4 (1), sch. 9, para. 27 (1). - Issued: 14.01.2013. Made: 13.12.2012. Coming into force: 27.12.2012. Effect: S.I. 1997/2019 varied & S.I. 1999/1584 revoked. Territorial extent & classification: E. Local. - Available at http://www.legislation.gov.uk/uksi/2012/3267/contents/made *Non-print*

The A500 Trunk Road (Hanford to Northwood, Staffordshire) (Temporary Prohibition of Traffic) Order 2012 No. 2012/2006. - Enabling power: Road Traffic Regulation Act 1984, s. 14 (1) (a). - Issued: 02.08.2012. Made: 16.07.2012. Coming into force: 23.07.2012. Effect: None. Territorial extent & classification: E. Local. - Available at http://www.legislation.gov.uk/uksi/2012/2006/contents/made *Non-print*

The A500 Trunk Road (M6 Junction 16- Talke Pits, Staffordshire) (Temporary Restriction and Prohibition of Traffic) Order 2012 No. 2012/3315. - Enabling power: Road Traffic Regulation Act 1984, s. 14 (1) (a). - Issued: 17.01.2013. Made: 24.12.2012. Coming into force: 31.12.2012. Effect: None. Territorial extent & classification: E. Local. - Available at http://www.legislation.gov.uk/uksi/2012/3315/contents/made *Non-print*

The A500 Trunk Road (Porthill, Newcastle-under-Lyme, Staffordshire) (Temporary Prohibition of Traffic in Layby) Order 2012 No. 2012/2188. - Enabling power: Road Traffic Regulation Act 1984, s. 14 (1) (a). - Issued: 29.08.2012. Made: 20.08.2012. Coming into force: 27.08.2012. Effect: None. Territorial extent & classification: E. Local. - Available at http://www.legislation.gov.uk/uksi/2012/2188/contents/made *Non-print*

The A500 Trunk Road (Stoke on Trent) (Slip Road) (Temporary Prohibition of Traffic) Order 2012 No. 2012/2419. - Enabling power: Road Traffic Regulation Act 1984, s. 14 (1) (a). - Issued: 25.09.2012. Made: 10.09.2012. Coming into force: 17.09.2012. Effect: None. Territorial extent & classification: E. Local. - Available at http://www.legislation.gov.uk/uksi/2012/2419/contents/made *Non-print*

The A500 Trunk Road (Stoke-on-Trent, Staffordshire) (Temporary Prohibition of Traffic) (No. 2) Order 2012 No. 2012/3326. - Enabling power: Road Traffic Regulation Act 1984, s. 14 (1) (a). - Issued: 18.01.2013. Made: 31.12.2012. Coming into force: 07.01.2013. Effect: None. Territorial extent & classification: E. Local. - Available at http://www.legislation.gov.uk/uksi/2012/3326/contents/made *Non-print*

The A500 Trunk Road (Stoke-on-Trent, Staffordshire) (Temporary Prohibition of Traffic) Order 2012 No. 2012/231. - Enabling power: Road Traffic Regulation Act 1984, s. 14 (1) (a). - Issued: 03.02.2012. Made: 23.01.2012. Coming into force: 30.01.2012. Effect: None. Territorial extent & classification: E. Local. - Available at http://www.legislation.gov.uk/uksi/2012/231/contents/made *Non-print*

The A500 Trunk Road (Tunstall Northern Bypass to M6 Junction 16, Staffordshire) (Temporary Prohibition of Traffic) Order 2012 No. 2012/2126. - Enabling power: Road Traffic Regulation Act 1984, s. 14 (1) (a). - Issued: 17.08.2012. Made: 06.08.2012. Coming into force: 13.08.2012. Effect: None. Territorial extent & classification: E. Local. - Available at http://www.legislation.gov.uk/uksi/2012/2126/contents/made *Non-print*

The A550, A5117 and A494 Trunk Roads (Dunkirk Junction to Deeside Park Junction) (24 Hour Clearway) Order 2012 No. 2012/1571. - Enabling power: Road Traffic Regulation Act 1984, ss. 1 (1), 2 (1) (2), sch. 9, para. 27. - Issued: 22.06.2012. Made: 07.06.2012. Coming into force: 15.06.2012. Effect: S.I. 1963/1172 varied. Territorial extent & classification: E. Local. - Available at http://www.legislation.gov.uk/uksi/2012/1571/contents/made *Non-print*

The A550 Trunk Road (Woodbank Junction with A494 to Junction with A41 Chester Road) (Temporary Prohibition and Restriction of Traffic) Order 2012 No. 2012/2664. - Enabling power: Road Traffic Regulation Act 1984, s. 14 (1) (a). - Issued: 26.10.2012. Made: 10.10.2012. Coming into force: 14.10.2012. Effect: None. Territorial extent & classification: E. Local. - Available at http://www.legislation.gov.uk/uksi/2012/2664/contents/made *Non-print*

The A556 Trunk Road (Northbound and Southbound Carriageways between the A5034 and the A556/A56/M56 Roundabout) and the M56 (Temporary Prohibition of Traffic) Order 2012 No. 2012/402. - Enabling power: Road Traffic Regulation Act 1984, s. 14 (1) (a). - Issued: 21.02.2012. Made: 07.02.2012. Coming into force: 14.02.2012. Effect: None. Territorial extent & classification: E. Local. - Available at http://www.legislation.gov.uk/uksi/2012/402/contents/made *Non-print*

The A556 Trunk Road (RHS Flower Show) (Temporary Prohibition of Right Turns) Order 2012 No. 2012/1891. - Enabling power: Road Traffic Regulation Act 1984, s. 16A (2) (a). - Issued: 23.07.2012. Made: 10.07.2012. Coming into force: 16.07.2012. Effect: None. Territorial extent & classification: E. Local. - Available at http://www.legislation.gov.uk/uksi/2012/1891/contents/made *Non-print*

The A556 Trunk Road (Southbound Carriageway between Bucklow Hill and the A50) (Temporary Prohibition of Traffic) Order 2012 No. 2012/2565. - Enabling power: Road Traffic Regulation Act 1984, s. 14 (1) (a). - Issued: 12.10.2012. Made: 02.10.2012. Coming into force: 21.10.2012. Effect: None. Territorial extent & classification: E. Local. - Available at http://www.legislation.gov.uk/uksi/2012/2565/contents/made *Non-print*

The A585 Trunk Road (Fleetwood Road Northbound Carriageway and Cycle Track) (Temporary Prohibition of Traffic and Cyclists) Order 2012 No. 2012/3234. - Enabling power: Road Traffic Regulation Act 1984, s. 14 (1) (a). - Issued: 08.01.2013. Made: 10.12.2012. Coming into force: 12.12.2012. Effect: None. Territorial extent & classification: E. Local. - Available at http://www.legislation.gov.uk/uksi/2012/3234/contents/made *Non-print*

The A585 Trunk Road (Norcross Junction Resurfacing) (Temporary Restriction and Prohibition of Traffic) Order 2012 No. 2012/436. - Enabling power: Road Traffic Regulation Act 1984, s. 14 (1) (a). - Issued: 22.02.2012. Made: 14.02.2012. Coming into force: 17.02.2012. Effect: None. Territorial extent & classification: E. Local. - Available at http://www.legislation.gov.uk/uksi/2012/436/contents/made *Non-print*

The A590 Trunk Road (A590/M6 Junction 36 Roundabout to Brettargh Holt Roundabout) and the M6 Motorway (Junction 36 Northbound Exit Slip Road) (Temporary Prohibition and Restriction of Traffic) (No 2) Order 2012 No. 2012/1447. - Enabling power: Road Traffic Regulation Act 1984, s. 14 (1) (a). - Issued: 12.06.2012. Made: 23.05.2012. Coming into force: 09.06.2012. Effect: None. Territorial extent & classification: E. Local. - Available at http://www.legislation.gov.uk/uksi/2012/1447/contents/made *Non-print*

Road traffic: Traffic regulation

The A590 Trunk Road (A590/M6 Junction 36 Roundabout to Brettarg Holt Roundabout) and the M6 Motorway (Junction 36 Northbound Exit Slip Road) (Temporary Prohibition and Restriction of Traffic) Order 2012 No. 2012/1117. - Enabling power: Road Traffic Regulation Act 1984, s. 14 (1) (a). - Issued: 23.04.2012. Made: 11.04.2012. Coming into force: 15.04.2012. Effect: None. Territorial extent & classification: E. Local. - Available at http://www.legislation.gov.uk/uksi/2012/1117/contents/made *Non-print*

The A590 Trunk Road (Barr End, Greenodd) (Temporary Prohibition of Traffic) Order 2012 No. 2012/256. - Enabling power: Road Traffic Regulation Act 1984, s. 14 (1) (b). - Issued: 06.02.2012. Made: 24.01.2012. Coming into force: 26.01.2012. Effect: None. Territorial extent & classification: E. Local. - Available at http://www.legislation.gov.uk/uksi/2012/256/contents/made *Non-print*

The A590 Trunk Road (Barr End Rockface, Greenodd) (Temporary Prohibition and Restriction of Traffic) Order 2012 No. 2012/130. - Enabling power: Road Traffic Regulation Act 1984, s. 14 (1) (a). - Issued: 23.01.2012. Made: 12.01.2012. Coming into force: 16.01.2012. Effect: None. Territorial extent & classification: E. Local. - Available at http://www.legislation.gov.uk/uksi/2012/130/contents/made *Non-print*

The A590 Trunk Road (Dykelands Bridge, Ulverston) (Temporary Prohibition of Traffic) Order 2012 No. 2012/2258. - Enabling power: Road Traffic Regulation Act 1984, s. 14 (1) (a). - Issued: 05.09.2012. Made: 29.08.2012. Coming into force: 14.09.2012. Effect: None. Territorial extent & classification: E. Local. - Available at http://www.legislation.gov.uk/uksi/2012/2258/contents/made *Non-print*

The A590 Trunk Road Eastbound (A590/M6 Junction 36 Roundabout to Brettargh Holt Roundabout) and Eastbound Entry Slip Road (Temporary Restriction of Traffic) Order 2012 No. 2012/2431. - Enabling power: Road Traffic Regulation Act 1984, s. 14 (1) (a). - Issued: 26.09.2012. Made: 12.09.2012. Coming into force: 30.09.2012. Effect: None. Territorial extent & classification: E. Local. - Available at http://www.legislation.gov.uk/uksi/2012/2431/contents/made *Non-print*

The A590 Trunk Road (Lightburn Road, Ulverston) (Temporary Prohibition and Restriction of Traffic) Order 2012 No. 2012/407. - Enabling power: Road Traffic Regulation Act 1984, s. 14 (1) (a). - Issued: 21.02.2012. Made: 08.02.2012. Coming into force: 26.02.2012. Effect: None. Territorial extent & classification: E. Local. - Available at http://www.legislation.gov.uk/uksi/2012/407/contents/made *Non-print*

The A590 Trunk Road (Lindale Hill Resurfacing) (Temporary Prohibition and Restriction of Traffic) Order 2012 No. 2012/300. - Enabling power: Road Traffic Regulation Act 1984, s. 14 (1) (a). - Issued: 10.02.2012. Made: 01.02.2012. Coming into force: 19.02.2012. Effect: None. Territorial extent & classification: E. Local. - Available at http://www.legislation.gov.uk/uksi/2012/300/contents/made *Non-print*

The A590 Trunk Road (Mill Side Junction, Witherslack) (Temporary Prohibition and Restriction of Traffic) Order 2012 No. 2012/2344. - Enabling power: Road Traffic Regulation Act 1984, s. 14 (1) (a). - Issued: 14.09.2012. Made: 05.09.2012. Coming into force: 21.09.2012. Effect: None. Territorial extent & classification: E. Local. - Available at http://www.legislation.gov.uk/uksi/2012/2344/contents/made *Non-print*

The A590 Trunk Road (Rusland Pool, Haverthwaite, Resufacing) (Temporary Restriction and Prohibition of Traffic) Order 2012 No. 2012/997. - Enabling power: Road Traffic Regulation Act 1984, s. 14 (1) (a). - Issued: 05.04.2012. Made: 21.03.2012. Coming into force: 25.03.2012. Effect: None. Territorial extent & classification: E. Local. - Available at http://www.legislation.gov.uk/uksi/2012/997/contents/made *Non-print*

The A590 Trunk Road (Swan Street to Booths Roundabout, Ulverston) (Temporary Prohibition and Restriction of Traffic) Order 2012 No. 2012/2346. - Enabling power: Road Traffic Regulation Act 1984, s. 14 (1) (a). - Issued: 14.09.2012. Made: 05.09.2012. Coming into force: 25.09.2012. Effect: None. Territorial extent & classification: E. Local. - Available at http://www.legislation.gov.uk/uksi/2012/2346/contents/made *Non-print*

The A595 Trunk Road (Layby Closures) (Temporary Prohibition of Traffic) Order 2012 No. 2012/312. - Enabling power: Road Traffic Regulation Act 1984, s. 14 (1) (a). - Issued: 15.02.2012. Made: 25.01.2012. Coming into force: 12.02.2012. Effect: None. Territorial extent & classification: E. Local. - Available at http://www.legislation.gov.uk/uksi/2012/312/contents/made *Non-print*

The A595 Trunk Road (Westlakes to Biggrigg) (Temporary Prohibition and Restriction of Traffic) Order 2012 No. 2012/3300. - Enabling power: Road Traffic Regulation Act 1984, s. 14 (1) (a). - Issued: 16.01.2013. Made: 24.12.2012. Coming into force: 13.01.2013. Effect: None. Territorial extent & classification: E. Local. - Available at http://www.legislation.gov.uk/uksi/2012/3300/contents/made *Non-print*

The A616 Trunk Road (Manchester Road to Flouch Roundabout) (Temporary Restriction and Prohibition of Traffic) Order 2012 No. 2012/2792. - Enabling power: Road Traffic Regulation Act 1984, s. 14 (1) (a). - Issued: 09.11.2012. Made: 23.10.2012. Coming into force: 28.10.2012. Effect: None. Territorial extent & classification: E. Local. - Available at http://www.legislation.gov.uk/uksi/2012/2792/contents/made *Non-print*

The A616 Trunk Road (Westwood Roundabout to Newton Chambers Roundabout) (Temporary Prohibition of Traffic) Order 2012 No. 2012/2066. - Enabling power: Road Traffic Regulation Act 1984, s. 14 (1) (a). - Issued: 13.08.2012. Made: 26.07.2012. Coming into force: 07.08.2012. Effect: None. Territorial extent & classification: E. Local. - Available at http://www.legislation.gov.uk/uksi/2012/2066/contents/made *Non-print*

The A616 Trunk Road (Wortley Junction) (Temporary Prohibition of Traffic) Order 2012 No. 2012/1839. - Enabling power: Road Traffic Regulation Act 1984, s. 14 (1) (a). - Issued: 19.07.2012. Made: 05.07.2012. Coming into force: 15.07.2012. Effect: None. Territorial extent & classification: E. Local. - Available at http://www.legislation.gov.uk/uksi/2012/1839/contents/made *Non-print*

The A627(M) Motorway (Junction 1 - 4 Northbound and Southbound Carriageways, Slip Roads and Circulatory Carriageway) (Temporary Prohibition and Restriction of Traffic) Order 2012 No. 2012/1601. - Enabling power: Road Traffic Regulation Act 1984, s. 14 (1) (a) (7). - Issued: 25.06.2012. Made: 12.06.2012. Coming into force: 30.06.2012. Effect: None. Territorial extent & classification: E. Local. - Available at http://www.legislation.gov.uk/uksi/2012/1601/contents/made *Non-print*

The A628 Trunk Road (Crowden Brook Bridge) (Temporary Restriction and Prohibition of Traffic) Order 2012 No. 2012/313. - Enabling power: Road Traffic Regulation Act 1984, s. 14 (1) (a). - Issued: 15.02.2012. Made: 02.02.2012. Coming into force: 11.02.2012. Effect: None. Territorial extent & classification: E. Local. - Available at http://www.legislation.gov.uk/uksi/2012/313/contents/made *Non-print*

The A628 Trunk Road (Flouch Roundabout to Gun Inn Junction) (Temporary Prohibition of Traffic) Order 2012 No. 2012/2294. - Enabling power: Road Traffic Regulation Act 1984, s. 14 (1) (a). - Issued: 10.09.2012. Made: 30.08.2012. Coming into force: 09.09.2012. Effect: None. Territorial extent & classification: E. Local. - Available at http://www.legislation.gov.uk/uksi/2012/2294/contents/made *Non-print*

The A628 Trunk Road (Pemberton Layby) (Temporary Prohibition of Traffic) Order 2012 No. 2012/1181. - Enabling power: Road Traffic Regulation Act 1984, s. 14 (1) (a). - Issued: 02.05.2012. Made: 20.04.2012. Coming into force: 29.04.2012. Effect: None. Territorial extent & classification: E. Local. - Available at http://www.legislation.gov.uk/uksi/2012/1181/contents/made *Non-print*

The A631 Trunk Road (Tinsley Viaduct) (Temporary Restriction and Prohibition of Traffic) Order 2012 No. 2012/2065. - Enabling power: Road Traffic Regulation Act 1984, s. 14 (1) (a). - Issued: 13.08.2012. Made: 26.07.2012. Coming into force: 05.08.2012. Effect: None. Territorial extent & classification: E. Local. - Available at http://www.legislation.gov.uk/uksi/2012/2065/contents/made *Non-print*

The A631 Trunk Road (Tinsley Viaduct) (Temporary Restriction and Prohibition of Traffic) Order 2012 No. 2012/564. - Enabling power: Road Traffic Regulation Act 1984, s. 14 (1) (a). - Issued: 01.03.2012. Made: 23.02.2012. Coming into force: 04.03.2012. Effect: None. Territorial extent & classification: E. Local. - Available at http://www.legislation.gov.uk/uksi/2012/564/contents/made *Non-print*

The A663 Trunk Road (Broadway, Chadderton) (Temporary Restriction of Traffic) Order 2012 No. 2012/1049. - Enabling power: Road Traffic Regulation Act 1984, s. 14 (1) (a). - Issued: 13.04.2012. Made: 28.03.2012. Coming into force: 01.04.2012. Effect: None. Territorial extent & classification: E. Local. - Available at http://www.legislation.gov.uk/uksi/2012/1049/contents/made *Non-print*

The A663 Trunk Road (Burnley Lane Subway, Chadderton) (Temporary Prohibition of Pedestrians and Cyclists) (No 2) Order 2012 No. 2012/1828. - Enabling power: Road Traffic Regulation Act 1984, s. 14 (1) (a). - Issued: 19.07.2012. Made: 04.07.2012. Coming into force: 22.07.2012. Effect: None. Territorial extent & classification: E. Local. - Available at http://www.legislation.gov.uk/uksi/2012/1828/contents/made *Non-print*

The A663 Trunk Road (Burnley Lane Subway, Chadderton) (Temporary Prohibition of Pedestrians and Cyclists) Order 2012 No. 2012/840. - Enabling power: Road Traffic Regulation Act 1984, s. 14 (1) (a). - Issued: 20.03.2012. Made: 14.03.2012. Coming into force: 30.03.2012. Effect: None. Territorial extent & classification: E. Local. - Available at http://www.legislation.gov.uk/uksi/2012/840/contents/made *Non-print*

The A663 Trunk Road (Southbound Entry Slip Road from the A627) (Temporary Prohibition of Traffic) Order 2012 No. 2012/1979. - Enabling power: Road Traffic Regulation Act 1984, s. 14 (1) (a). - Issued: 31.07.2012. Made: 18.07.2012. Coming into force: 26.07.2012. Effect: None. Territorial extent & classification: E. Local. - Available at http://www.legislation.gov.uk/uksi/2012/1979/contents/made *Non-print*

The A663 Trunk Road (Whitegate Lane to Jardine Way) (Temporary Prohibition of Traffic) Order 2012 No. 2012/2514. - Enabling power: Road Traffic Regulation Act 1984, s. 14 (1) (a). - Issued: 05.10.2012. Made: 01.10.2012. Coming into force: 16.10.2012. Effect: None. Territorial extent & classification: E. Local. - Available at http://www.legislation.gov.uk/uksi/2012/2514/contents/made *Non-print*

The A696 Trunk Road (Kenton Bar Interchange to Airport Roundabout) (Temporary Restriction and Prohibition of Traffic) Order 2012 No. 2012/541. - Enabling power: Road Traffic Regulation Act 1984, s. 14 (1) (a). - Issued: 01.03.2012. Made: 21.02.2012. Coming into force: 04.03.2012. Effect: None. Territorial extent & classification: E. Local. - Available at http://www.legislation.gov.uk/uksi/2012/541/contents/made *Non-print*

The A696 Trunk Road (Kenton Bar Interchange to Prestwick Road End Roundabout) (Temporary Restriction and Prohibition of Traffic) Order 2012 No. 2012/2622. - Enabling power: Road Traffic Regulation Act 1984, s. 14 (1) (a). - Issued: 22.10.2012. Made: 10.10.2012. Coming into force: 14.10.2012. Effect: None. Territorial extent & classification: E. Local. - Available at http://www.legislation.gov.uk/uksi/2012/2622/contents/made *Non-print*

The A1033 Trunk Road (Marfleet Roundabout to Northern Gateway Roundabout) (Temporary Prohibition of Traffic) Order 2012 No. 2012/2215. - Enabling power: Road Traffic Regulation Act 1984, s. 14 (1) (a). - Issued: 31.08.2012. Made: 23.08.2012. Coming into force: 02.09.2012. Effect: None. Territorial extent & classification: E. Local. - Available at http://www.legislation.gov.uk/uksi/2012/2215/contents/made *Non-print*

The A1033 Trunk Road (Southcoates Roundabout to Northern Gateway Roundabout) (Temporary Prohibition of Traffic) Order 2012 No. 2012/3160. - Enabling power: Road Traffic Regulation Act 1984, s. 14 (1) (a). - Issued: 28.12.2012. Made: 29.11.2012. Coming into force: 11.12.2012. Effect: None. Territorial extent & classification: E. Local. - Available at http://www.legislation.gov.uk/uksi/2012/3160/contents/made *Non-print*

The A1053 Trunk Road (Greystone Road) (Temporary Prohibition of Traffic) Order 2012 No. 2012/1120. - Enabling power: Road Traffic Regulation Act 1984, s. 14 (1) (b). - Issued: 24.04.2012. Made: 12.04.2012. Coming into force: 21.04.2012. Effect: None. Territorial extent & classification: E. Local. - Available at http://www.legislation.gov.uk/uksi/2012/1120/contents/made *Non-print*

The A2070 Trunk Road (A2042 Junction, Slip Roads) (Temporary Prohibition of Traffic) Order 2012 No. 2012/3146. - Enabling power: Road Traffic Regulation Act 1984, s. 14 (1) (a). - Issued: 27.12.2012. Made: 26.11.2012. Coming into force: 17.12.2012. Effect: None. Territorial extent & classification: E. Local. - Available at http://www.legislation.gov.uk/uksi/2012/3146/contents/made *Non-print*

The A2070 Trunk Road (Bad Munstereifel Road) (Temporary 40 Miles Per Hour Speed Restriction) Order 2012 No. 2012/3206. - Enabling power: Road Traffic Regulation Act 1984, s. 14 (1) (a). - Issued: 02.01.2013. Made: 10.12.2012. Coming into force: 05.01.2013. Effect: None. Territorial extent & classification: E. Local. - Available at http://www.legislation.gov.uk/uksi/2012/3206/contents/made *Non-print*

The A5006 Trunk Road (Stoke on Trent, Staffordshire) (Temporary Prohibition of Traffic) Order 2012 No. 2012/2802. - Enabling power: Road Traffic Regulation Act 1984, s. 14 (1) (a). - Issued: 09.11.2012. Made: 22.10.2012. Coming into force: 29.10.2012. Effect: None. Territorial extent & classification: E. Local. - Available at http://www.legislation.gov.uk/uksi/2012/2802/contents/made *Non-print*

The A5036 Trunk Road (Atlantic Park Junction) (Temporary Prohibition of Traffic) Order 2012 No. 2012/649. - Enabling power: Road Traffic Regulation Act 1984, s. 14 (1) (a). - Issued: 14.03.2012. Made: 28.02.2012. Coming into force: 15.03.2012. Effect: None. Territorial extent & classification: E. Local. - Available at http://www.legislation.gov.uk/uksi/2012/649/contents/made *Non-print*

The A5036 Trunk Road (Junctions with the A5038 Netherton Way and the A567 Bridge Road, Litherland) (Temporary Prohibition of Traffic) Order 2012 No. 2012/1980. - Enabling power: Road Traffic Regulation Act 1984, s. 14 (1) (a). - Issued: 31.07.2012. Made: 18.07.2012. Coming into force: 02.08.2012. Effect: None. Territorial extent & classification: E. Local. - Available at http://www.legislation.gov.uk/uksi/2012/1980/contents/made *Non-print*

The A5036 Trunk Road (Junctions with the A5038 Netherton Way and the B5194 Copy Lane, Litherland) (Temporary Prohibition of Traffic) Order 2012 No. 2012/783. - Enabling power: Road Traffic Regulation Act 1984, s. 14 (1) (a). - Issued: 20.03.2012. Made: 07.03.2012. Coming into force: 23.03.2012. Effect: None. Territorial extent & classification: E. Local. - Available at http://www.legislation.gov.uk/uksi/2012/783/contents/made *Non-print*

The A5103 Trunk Road (Southbound Exit Slip Road to the A560 and the Northbound Entry Slip Road from the B5167) (Temporary Prohibition of Traffic) Order 2012 No. 2012/295. - Enabling power: Road Traffic Regulation Act 1984, s. 14 (1) (a). - Issued: 10.02.2012. Made: 31.01.2012. Coming into force: 05.02.2012. Effect: None. Territorial extent & classification: E. Local. - Available at http://www.legislation.gov.uk/uksi/2012/295/contents/made *Non-print*

The A5111 and A52 Trunk Roads (Derby) (Temporary Prohibition of Traffic) Order 2012 No. 2012/1968. - Enabling power: Road Traffic Regulation Act 1984, s. 14 (1) (a). - Issued: 30.07.2012. Made: 10.07.2012. Coming into force: 17.07.2012. Effect: None. Territorial extent & classification: E. Local. - Available at http://www.legislation.gov.uk/uksi/2012/1968/contents/made *Non-print*

The A5148 Trunk Road (A38/A5148 Interchange, Swinfen, Staffordshire) (Temporary Prohibition of Traffic) Order 2012 No. 2012/1435. - Enabling power: Road Traffic Regulation Act 1984, s. 14 (1) (a). - Issued: 06.06.2012. Made: 11.05.2012. Coming into force: 18.05.2012. Effect: None. Territorial extent & classification: E. Local. - Available at http://www.legislation.gov.uk/uksi/2012/1435/contents/made *Non-print*

The London - Penzance Trunk Road (A38) (Dobwalls to Trerulefoot Roundabout) (Prohibition of Waiting) (Clearways) Order 1978 (Variation) Order 2009 (Revocation) Order 2012 No. 2012/1377. - Enabling power: Road Traffic Regulation Act 1984, ss. 1 (1), 2 (1) (2), sch. 9, para. 27 (1). - Issued: 28.05.2012. Made: 16.05.2012. Coming into force: 28.05.2012. Effect: S.I. 2009/3350 revoked. Territorial extent & classification: E. Local. - Available at http://www.legislation.gov.uk/uksi/2012/1377/contents/made *Non-print*

The M1 and M6 Motorways (M1 Junctions 19 to 20) (Temporary Restriction and Prohibition of Traffic) Order 2012 No. 2012/253. - Enabling power: Road Traffic Regulation Act 1984, s. 14 (1) (a) (7). - Issued: 06.02.2012. Made: 20.01.2012. Coming into force: 27.01.2012. Effect: S.I. 2010/2260; 2011/2023 revoked. Territorial extent & classification: E. Local. - Available at http://www.legislation.gov.uk/uksi/2012/253/contents/made *Non-print*

The M1 and M6 Motorways (M6 Junction 1 and M1 Junctions 19 to 20) (Temporary Restriction and Prohibition of Traffic) Order 2012 No. 2012/576. - Enabling power: Road Traffic Regulation Act 1984, s. 14 (1) (a) (7). - Issued: 06.03.2012. Made: 13.02.2012. Coming into force: 20.02.2012. Effect: None. Territorial extent & classification: E. Local. - Available at http://www.legislation.gov.uk/uksi/2012/576/contents/made *Non-print*

The M1 and M69 Motorways (M1 Junctions 21 and 21a) and A46 Trunk Road (Temporary Prohibition and Restriction of Traffic) Order 2012 No. 2012/633. - Enabling power: Road Traffic Regulation Act 1984, s. 14 (1) (a). - Issued: 07.03.2012. Made: 28.02.2012. Coming into force: 06.03.2012. Effect: None. Territorial extent & classification: E. Local. - Available at http://www.legislation.gov.uk/uksi/2012/633/contents/made *Non-print*

The M1 Motorway, A50 and A453 Trunk Roads (M1 Junction 24, Leicestershire) (Temporary Restriction and Prohibition of Traffic) (No. 2) Order 2012 No. 2012/3262. - Enabling power: Road Traffic Regulation Act 1984, s. 14 (1) (a). - Issued: 14.01.2013. Made: 05.11.2012. Coming into force: 12.11.2012. Effect: None. Territorial extent & classification: E. Local. - Available at http://www.legislation.gov.uk/uksi/2012/3262/contents/made *Non-print*

The M1 Motorway and A43 Trunk Road (M1 Junction 15a, Northamptonshire) (Temporary Prohibition of Traffic) Order 2012 No. 2012/2545. - Enabling power: Road Traffic Regulation Act 1984, s. 14 (1) (a). - Issued: 10.10.2012. Made: 17.09.2012. Coming into force: 24.09.2012. Effect: None. Territorial extent & classification: E. Local. - Available at http://www.legislation.gov.uk/uksi/2012/2545/contents/made *Non-print*

The M1 Motorway and A50 and A453 Trunk Roads (M1 Junction 24, Leicestershire) (Temporary Restriction and Prohibition of Traffic) Order 2012 No. 2012/2384. - Enabling power: Road Traffic Regulation Act 1984, s. 14 (1) (a). - Issued: 18.09.2012. Made: 28.08.2012. Coming into force: 04.09.2012. Effect: None. Territorial extent & classification: E. Local. - Available at http://www.legislation.gov.uk/uksi/2012/2384/contents/made *Non-print*

The M1 Motorway and M45 Motorway (M1 Junction 17 to M45 Junction 1) (Temporary Restriction and Prohibition of Traffic) Order 2012 No. 2012/2838. - Enabling power: Road Traffic Regulation Act 1984, s. 14 (1) (a). - Issued: 15.11.2012. Made: 22.10.2012. Coming into force: 29.10.2012. Effect: None. Territorial extent & classification: E. Local. - Available at http://www.legislation.gov.uk/uksi/2012/2838/contents/made *Non-print*

The M1 Motorway and the A42 Trunk Road (M1 Junction 23a to A42 Junction 13) (Temporary Prohibition of Traffic) Order 2012 No. 2012/2173. - Enabling power: Road Traffic Regulation Act 1984, s. 14 (1) (a). - Issued: 24.08.2012. Made: 20.08.2012. Coming into force: 27.08.2012. Effect: None. Territorial extent & classification: E. Local. - Available at http://www.legislation.gov.uk/uksi/2012/2173/contents/made *Non-print*

The M1 Motorway and the A453 Trunk Road (M1 Junction 24 to West Bridgford) (Temporary Restriction and Prohibition of Traffic) Order 2012 No. 2012/3311. - Enabling power: Road Traffic Regulation Act 1984, s. 14 (1) (a) & S.I. 1982/1163, reg. 16 (2). - Issued: 16.01.2013. Made: 28.12.2012. Coming into force: 04.01.2013. Effect: None. Territorial extent & classification: E. Local. - Available at http://www.legislation.gov.uk/uksi/2012/3311/contents/made *Non-print*

The M1 Motorway and the M18 Motorway (Thurcroft Interchange) (Temporary Prohibition of Traffic) Order 2012 No. 2012/125. - Enabling power: Road Traffic Regulation Act 1984, s. 14 (1) (a). - Issued: 23.01.2012. Made: 12.01.2012. Coming into force: 22.01.2012. Effect: None. Territorial extent & classification: E. Local. - Available at http://www.legislation.gov.uk/uksi/2012/125/contents/made *Non-print*

The M1 Motorway and the M18 Motorway (Thurcroft Interchange to Bramley Interchange) (Temporary Restriction and Prohibition of Traffic) Order 2012 No. 2012/2642. - Enabling power: Road Traffic Regulation Act 1984, s. 14 (1) (a) & S.I. 1982/1163, s.16 (2). - Issued: 23.10.2012. Made: 11.10.2012. Coming into force: 21.10.2012. Effect: None. Territorial extent & classification: E. Local. - Available at http://www.legislation.gov.uk/uksi/2012/2642/contents/made *Non-print*

The M1 Motorway and the M25 Motorway (M1 Junctions 6 - 1 and M25 Junctions 17 - 20) (Temporary Restriction and Prohibition of Traffic) Order 2012 No. 2012/2098. - Enabling power: Road Traffic Regulation Act 1984, s. 14 (1) (a). - Issued: 16.08.2012. Made: 06.08.2012. Coming into force: 25.08.2012. Effect: None. Territorial extent & classification: E. Local. - Available at http://www.legislation.gov.uk/uksi/2012/2098/contents/made *Non-print*

The M1 Motorway and the M62 Motorway (Lofthouse Interchange) (Temporary Prohibition of Traffic) Order 2012 No. 2012/2012. - Enabling power: Road Traffic Regulation Act 1984, s. 14 (1) (a). - Issued: 02.08.2012. Made: 19.07.2012. Coming into force: 29.07.2012. Effect: None. Territorial extent & classification: E. Local. - Available at http://www.legislation.gov.uk/uksi/2012/2012/contents/made *Non-print*

The M1 Motorway (Between Junction 14 and Junction 15, Buckinghamshire) (Temporary Restriction and Prohibition of Traffic) Order 2012 No. 2012/2471. - Enabling power: Road Traffic Regulation Act 1984, s. 14 (1) (a). - Issued: 01.10.2012. Made: 24.09.2012. Coming into force: 01.10.2012. Effect: None. Territorial extent & classification: E. Local. - Available at http://www.legislation.gov.uk/uksi/2012/2471/contents/made *Non-print*

The M1 Motorway (Between Junctions 20 and 21, Leicestershire) (Temporary Restriction and Prohibition of Traffic) Order 2012 No. 2012/758. - Enabling power: Road Traffic Regulation Act 1984, s. 14 (1) (a) (7). - Issued: 19.03.2012. Made: 05.03.2012. Coming into force: 12.03.2012. Effect: None. Territorial extent & classification: E. Local. - Available at http://www.legislation.gov.uk/uksi/2012/758/contents/made *Non-print*

The M1 Motorway (Hartwell to Whilton Locks, Northamptonshire) (Temporary Restriction and Prohibition of Traffic) Order 2012 No. 2012/3302. - Enabling power: Road Traffic Regulation Act 1984, s. 14 (1) (a) & S.I. 1982/1163, reg. 16 (2). - Issued: 16.01.2013. Made: 24.12.2012. Coming into force: 31.12.2012. Effect: None. Territorial extent & classification: E. Local. - Available at http://www.legislation.gov.uk/uksi/2012/3302/contents/made *Non-print*

The M1 Motorway (Junction 6A) Southbound Exit Slip Road (Temporary Prohibition of Traffic) Order 2012 No. 2012/2367. - Enabling power: Road Traffic Regulation Act 1984, s. 14 (1) (a). - Issued: 18.09.2012. Made: 10.09.2012. Coming into force: 17.09.2012. Effect: None. Territorial extent & classification: E. Local. - Available at http://www.legislation.gov.uk/uksi/2012/2367/contents/made *Non-print*

The M1 Motorway (Junction 6, Southbound Exit Slip Road) (Temporary Prohibition of Traffic) Order 2012 No. 2012/412. - Enabling power: Road Traffic Regulation Act 1984, s. 14 (1) (a). - Issued: 21.02.2012. Made: 13.02.2012. Coming into force: 03.03.2012. Effect: None. Territorial extent & classification: E. Local. - Available at http://www.legislation.gov.uk/uksi/2012/412/contents/made *Non-print*

The M1 Motorway (Junction 11, Bedfordshire) Exit Slip Roads (Temporary Prohibition of Traffic) Order 2012 No. 2012/1820. - Enabling power: Road Traffic Regulation Act 1984, s. 16A (2) (a). - Issued: 19.07.2012. Made: 25.06.2012. Coming into force: 09.07.2012. Effect: None. Territorial extent & classification: E. Local. - Available at http://www.legislation.gov.uk/uksi/2012/1820/contents/made *Non-print*

The M1 Motorway (Junction 13 to Junction 15, Milton Keynes) (Temporary Restriction and Prohibition of Traffic) Order 2012 No. 2012/2693. - Enabling power: Road Traffic Regulation Act 1984, s. 14 (1) (a) & S.I. 1982/1163, s. 16 (2). - Issued: 30.10.2012. Made: 15.10.2012. Coming into force: 22.10.2012. Effect: None. Territorial extent & classification: E. Local. - Available at http://www.legislation.gov.uk/uksi/2012/2693/contents/made *Non-print*

Road traffic: Traffic regulation

The M1 Motorway (Junction 13 to Junction 15) (Temporary Restriction and Prohibition of Traffic) Order 2012 No. 2012/2076. - Enabling power: Road Traffic Regulation Act 1984, s. 14 (1) (a) (7). - Issued: 13.08.2012. Made: 30.07.2012. Coming into force: 06.08.2012. Effect: None. Territorial extent & classification: E. Local. - Available at http://www.legislation.gov.uk/uksi/2012/2076/contents/made *Non-print*

The M1 Motorway (Junction 14 Milton Keynes and Newport Pagnell Service Area Buckinghamshire) (Temporary Restriction and Prohibition of Traffic) Order 2012 No. 2012/1298. - Enabling power: Road Traffic Regulation Act 1984, s. 14 (1) (a). - Issued: 21.05.2012. Made: 08.05.2012. Coming into force: 15.05.2012. Effect: None. Territorial extent & classification: E. Local. - Available at http://www.legislation.gov.uk/uksi/2012/1298/contents/made *Non-print*

The M1 Motorway (Junction 15a) (Northbound Exit Slip Road) (Temporary Prohibition of Traffic) Order 2012 No. 2012/251. - Enabling power: Road Traffic Regulation Act 1984, s. 14 (1) (a). - Issued: 06.02.2012. Made: 16.01.2012. Coming into force: 23.01.2012. Effect: None. Territorial extent & classification: E. Local. - Available at http://www.legislation.gov.uk/uksi/2012/251/contents/made *Non-print*

The M1 Motorway (Junction 15a) (Slip Road) (Temporary Prohibition of Traffic) Order 2012 No. 2012/2971. - Enabling power: Road Traffic Regulation Act 1984, s. 14 (1) (a). - Issued: 30.11.2012. Made: 14.11.2012. Coming into force: 21.11.2012. Effect: None. Territorial extent & classification: E. Local. - Available at http://www.legislation.gov.uk/uksi/2012/2971/contents/made *Non-print*

The M1 Motorway (Junction 15a to Junction 16) (Temporary 50 Miles Per Hour Speed Restriction) Order 2012 No. 2012/2832. - Enabling power: Road Traffic Regulation Act 1984, s. 14 (1) (a). - Issued: 15.11.2012. Made: 24.10.2012. Coming into force: 31.10.2012. Effect: None. Territorial extent & classification: E. Local. - Available at http://www.legislation.gov.uk/uksi/2012/2832/contents/made *Non-print*

The M1 Motorway (Junction 15) (Southbound Entry Slip Road) (Temporary Prohibition of Traffic) Order 2012 No. 2012/2097. - Enabling power: Road Traffic Regulation Act 1984, s. 14 (1) (a). - Issued: 16.08.2012. Made: 09.07.2012. Coming into force: 16.07.2012. Effect: None. Territorial extent & classification: E. Local. - Available at http://www.legislation.gov.uk/uksi/2012/2097/contents/made *Non-print*

The M1 Motorway (Junction 15) (Temporary Prohibition of Traffic) Order 2012 No. 2012/1679. - Enabling power: Road Traffic Regulation Act 1984, s. 14 (1) (a). - Issued: 03.07.2012. Made: 06.06.2012. Coming into force: 13.06.2012. Effect: None. Territorial extent & classification: E. Local. - Available at http://www.legislation.gov.uk/uksi/2012/1679/contents/made *Non-print*

The M1 Motorway (Junction 15) (Temporary Restriction and Prohibition of Traffic) (No. 2) Order 2012 No. 2012/2211. - Enabling power: Road Traffic Regulation Act 1984, s. 14 (1) (a) (7) & S.I. 1982/1163, reg. 16 (2). - Issued: 31.08.2012. Made: 10.08.2012. Coming into force: 17.08.2012. Effect: None. Territorial extent & classification: E. Local. - Available at http://www.legislation.gov.uk/uksi/2012/2211/contents/made *Non-print*

The M1 Motorway (Junction 18 to Junction 15) (Temporary 50 Miles Per Hour Speed Restriction) Order 2012 No. 2012/2391. - Enabling power: Road Traffic Regulation Act 1984, s. 14 (1) (a). - Issued: 20.09.2012. Made: 03.09.2012. Coming into force: 10.09.2012. Effect: None. Territorial extent & classification: E. Local. - Available at http://www.legislation.gov.uk/uksi/2012/2391/contents/made *Non-print*

The M1 Motorway (Junction 19 to Junction 18) (Temporary Restriction and Prohibition of Traffic) Order 2012 No. 2012/1434. - Enabling power: Road Traffic Regulation Act 1984, s. 14 (1) (a) (7). - Issued: 06.06.2012. Made: 14.05.2012. Coming into force: 21.05.2012. Effect: None. Territorial extent & classification: E. Local. - Available at http://www.legislation.gov.uk/uksi/2012/1434/contents/made *Non-print*

The M1 Motorway (Junction 20 to Junction 21a) (Temporary 50 Miles Per Hour Speed Restriction) Order 2012 No. 2012/2201. - Enabling power: Road Traffic Regulation Act 1984, s. 14 (1) (a). - Issued: 30.08.2012. Made: 21.08.2012. Coming into force: 28.08.2012. Effect: None. Territorial extent & classification: E. Local. - Available at http://www.legislation.gov.uk/uksi/2012/2201/contents/made *Non-print*

The M1 Motorway (Junction 21, Leicestershire) (Temporary Prohibition of Traffic) Order 2012 No. 2012/889. - Enabling power: Road Traffic Regulation Act 1984, s. 14 (1) (a). - Issued: 26.03.2012. Made: 12.03.2012. Coming into force: 19.03.2012. Effect: None. Territorial extent & classification: E. Local. - Available at http://www.legislation.gov.uk/uksi/2012/889/contents/made *Non-print*

The M1 Motorway (Junction 22) (Slip Roads) (Temporary Prohibition of Traffic) Order 2012 No. 2012/1327. - Enabling power: Road Traffic Regulation Act 1984, s. 14 (1) (a). - Issued: 23.05.2012. Made: 07.05.2012. Coming into force: 14.05.2012. Effect: None. Territorial extent & classification: E. Local. - Available at http://www.legislation.gov.uk/uksi/2012/1327/contents/made *Non-print*

The M1 Motorway (Junction 22 to Junction 23) (Temporary Restriction and Prohibition of Traffic) Order 2012 No. 2012/3215. - Enabling power: Road Traffic Regulation Act 1984, s. 14 (1) (a) & S.I. 1982/1163, reg. 16 (2). - Issued: 04.01.2013. Made: 19.11.2012. Coming into force: 26.11.2012. Effect: None. Territorial extent & classification: E. Local. - Available at http://www.legislation.gov.uk/uksi/2012/3215/contents/made *Non-print*

The M1 Motorway (Junction 23) (Slip Road) (Temporary Prohibition of Traffic) Order 2012 No. 2012/3167. - Enabling power: Road Traffic Regulation Act 1984, s. 14 (1) (a). - Issued: 28.12.2012. Made: 26.11.2012. Coming into force: 03.12.2012. Effect: None. Territorial extent & classification: E. Local. - Available at http://www.legislation.gov.uk/uksi/2012/3167/contents/made *Non-print*

The M1 Motorway (Junction 23) (Temporary Restriction and Prohibition of Traffic) Order 2012 No. 2012/1200. - Enabling power: Road Traffic Regulation Act 1984, s. 14 (1) (a) (7). - Issued: 08.05.2012. Made: 24.04.2012. Coming into force: 01.05.2012. Effect: None. Territorial extent & classification: E. Local. - Available at http://www.legislation.gov.uk/uksi/2012/1200/contents/made *Non-print*

The M1 Motorway (Junction 24 and Junction 24a) (Temporary Prohibition of Traffic) Order 2012 No. 2012/2842. - Enabling power: Road Traffic Regulation Act 1984, s. 14 (1) (a). - Issued: 16.11.2012. Made: 29.10.2012. Coming into force: 05.11.2012. Effect: None. Territorial extent & classification: E. Local. - Available at http://www.legislation.gov.uk/uksi/2012/2842/contents/made *Non-print*

The M1 Motorway (Junction 24a) (Northbound Entry Slip Road) (Temporary Prohibition of Traffic) Order 2012 No. 2012/759. - Enabling power: Road Traffic Regulation Act 1984, s. 14 (1) (a). - Issued: 20.03.2012. Made: 05.03.2012. Coming into force: 12.03.2012. Effect: None. Territorial extent & classification: E. Local. - Available at http://www.legislation.gov.uk/uksi/2012/759/contents/made *Non-print*

The M1 Motorway (Junction 24a) (Southbound Exit Slip Road) (Temporary Prohibition of Traffic) Order 2012 No. 2012/3163. - Enabling power: Road Traffic Regulation Act 1984, s. 14 (1) (a). - Issued: .12.2012. Made: 26.11.2012. Coming into force: 03.12.2012. Effect: None. Territorial extent & classification: E. Local. - Available at http://www.legislation.gov.uk/uksi/2012/3163/contents/made *Non-print*

The M1 Motorway (Junction 24) (Southbound Entry Slip Road) (Temporary Prohibition of Traffic) Order 2012 No. 2012/3127. - Enabling power: Road Traffic Regulation Act 1984, s. 14 (1) (a). - Issued: 20.12.2012. Made: 19.11.2012. Coming into force: 26.11.2012. Effect: None. Territorial extent & classification: E. Local. - Available at http://www.legislation.gov.uk/uksi/2012/3127/contents/made *Non-print*

The M1 Motorway (Junction 26) (Southbound Exit Slip Road) (Temporary Prohibition of Traffic) Order 2012 No. 2012/393. - Enabling power: Road Traffic Regulation Act 1984, s. 14 (1) (a). - Issued: 21.02.2012. Made: 30.01.2012. Coming into force: 06.02.2012. Effect: None. Territorial extent & classification: E. Local. - Available at http://www.legislation.gov.uk/uksi/2012/393/contents/made *Non-print*

The M1 Motorway (Junction 27) (Slip Road) (Temporary Prohibition of Traffic) Order 2012 No. 2012/2716. - Enabling power: Road Traffic Regulation Act 1984, s. 14 (1) (a). - Issued: 02.11.2012. Made: 02.10.2012. Coming into force: 09.10.2012. Effect: None. Territorial extent & classification: E. Local. - Available at http://www.legislation.gov.uk/uksi/2012/2716/contents/made *Non-print*

The M1 Motorway (Junction 31 to Junction 32 and Woodall Services) (Temporary Restriction and Prohibition of Traffic) Order 2012 No. 2012/3000. - Enabling power: Road Traffic Regulation Act 1984, s. 14 (1) (a). - Issued: 05.12.2012. Made: 22.11.2012. Coming into force: 02.12.2012. Effect: None. Territorial extent & classification: E. Local. - Available at http://www.legislation.gov.uk/uksi/2012/3000/contents/made *Non-print*

The M1 Motorway (Junction 31 to Junction 32) (Temporary Restriction and Prohibition of Traffic) Order 2012 No. 2012/3285. - Enabling power: Road Traffic Regulation Act 1984, s. 14 (1) (a) & S.I. 1982/1163, reg. 16 (2). - Issued: 15.01.2013. Made: 27.12.2012. Coming into force: 06.01.2013. Effect: None. Territorial extent & classification: E. Local. - Available at http://www.legislation.gov.uk/uksi/2012/3285/contents/made *Non-print*

The M1 Motorway (Junction 32 to Junction 33) and the M18 Motorway (Thurcroft Interchange to Junction 1) (Temporary Restriction and Prohibition of Traffic) Order 2012 No. 2012/2641. - Enabling power: Road Traffic Regulation Act 1984, s. 14 (1) (a) & S.I. 1982/1163, s.16 (2). - Issued: 23.10.2012. Made: 11.10.2012. Coming into force: 19.10.2012. Effect: None. Territorial extent & classification: E. Local. - Available at http://www.legislation.gov.uk/uksi/2012/2641/contents/made *Non-print*

Road traffic: Traffic regulation

The M1 Motorway (Junction 33, Catcliffe) (Temporary Prohibition of Traffic) Order 2012 No. 2012/2094. - Enabling power: Road Traffic Regulation Act 1984, s. 14 (1) (a). - Issued: 15.08.2012. Made: 02.08.2012. Coming into force: 13.08.2012. Effect: None. Territorial extent & classification: E. Local. - Available at http://www.legislation.gov.uk/uksi/2012/2094/contents/made *Non-print*

The M1 Motorway (Junction 33) (Temporary Restriction and Prohibition of Traffic) Order 2012 No. 2012/3284. - Enabling power: Road Traffic Regulation Act 1984, s. 14 (1) (a). - Issued: 15.01.2013. Made: 27.12.2012. Coming into force: 06.01.2013. Effect: None. Territorial extent & classification: E. Local. - Available at http://www.legislation.gov.uk/uksi/2012/3284/contents/made *Non-print*

The M1 Motorway (Junction 34) and the A631 Trunk Road (Tinsley Viaduct) (Temporary Prohibition of Traffic) (No. 2) Order 2012 No. 2012/526. - Enabling power: Road Traffic Regulation Act 1984, s. 14 (1) (a). - Issued: 01.03.2012. Made: 21.02.2012. Coming into force: 26.02.2012. Effect: None. Territorial extent & classification: E. Local. - Available at http://www.legislation.gov.uk/uksi/2012/526/contents/made *Non-print*

The M1 Motorway (Junction 34) and the A631 Trunk Road (Tinsley Viaduct) (Temporary Prohibition of Traffic) Order 2012 No. 2012/40. - Enabling power: Road Traffic Regulation Act 1984, s. 14 (1) (a). - Issued: 11.01.2012. Made: 03.01.2012. Coming into force: 08.01.2012. Effect: None. Territorial extent & classification: E. Local. - Available at http://www.legislation.gov.uk/uksi/2012/40/contents/made *Non-print*

The M1 Motorway (Junction 34, Tinsley Viaduct) (Temporary Prohibition of Traffic) Order 2012 No. 2012/2095. - Enabling power: Road Traffic Regulation Act 1984, s. 14 (1) (a). - Issued: 15.08.2012. Made: 02.08.2012. Coming into force: 12.08.2012. Effect: None. Territorial extent & classification: E. Local. - Available at http://www.legislation.gov.uk/uksi/2012/2095/contents/made *Non-print*

The M1 Motorway (Junction 34 to Junction 35) (Temporary Restriction and Prohibition of Traffic) Order 2012 No. 2012/268. - Enabling power: Road Traffic Regulation Act 1984, s. 14 (1) (a) (7). - Issued: 10.02.2012. Made: 27.01.2012. Coming into force: 06.02.2012. Effect: None. Territorial extent & classification: E. Local. - Available at http://www.legislation.gov.uk/uksi/2012/268/contents/made *Non-print*

The M1 Motorway (Junction 35A, Stocksbridge) (Temporary Restriction and Prohibition of Traffic) Order 2012 No. 2012/2491. - Enabling power: Road Traffic Regulation Act 1984, s. 14 (1) (a) & S.I. 1982/1163, reg. 16 (2). - Issued: 03.10.2012. Made: 27.09.2012. Coming into force: 08.10.2012. Effect: None. Territorial extent & classification: E. Local. - Available at http://www.legislation.gov.uk/uksi/2012/2491/contents/made *Non-print*

The M1 Motorway (Junction 35A to Junction 36) (Temporary Prohibition of Traffic) Order 2012 No. 2012/2132. - Enabling power: Road Traffic Regulation Act 1984, s. 14 (1) (a). - Issued: 20.08.2012. Made: 09.08.2012. Coming into force: 18.08.2012. Effect: None. Territorial extent & classification: E. Local. - Available at http://www.legislation.gov.uk/uksi/2012/2132/contents/made *Non-print*

The M1 Motorway (Junction 35) (Temporary Restriction and Prohibition of Traffic) Order 2012 No. 2012/1071. - Enabling power: Road Traffic Regulation Act 1984, s. 14 (1) (a) (7). - Issued: 16.04.2012. Made: 05.04.2012. Coming into force: 15.04.2012. Effect: None. Territorial extent & classification: E. Local. - Available at http://www.legislation.gov.uk/uksi/2012/1071/contents/made *Non-print*

The M1 Motorway (Junction 36, Tankersley) (Temporary Prohibition of Traffic) Order 2012 No. 2012/2877. - Enabling power: Road Traffic Regulation Act 1984, s. 14 (1) (a). - Issued: 19.11.2012. Made: 08.11.2012. Coming into force: 18.11.2012. Effect: None. Territorial extent & classification: E. Local. - Available at http://www.legislation.gov.uk/uksi/2012/2877/contents/made *Non-print*

The M1 Motorway (Junction 36 to Junction 35A) (Temporary Prohibition of Traffic) Order 2012 No. 2012/403. - Enabling power: Road Traffic Regulation Act 1984, s. 14 (1) (a). - Issued: 21.02.2012. Made: 08.02.2012. Coming into force: 19.02.2012. Effect: None. Territorial extent & classification: E. Local. - Available at http://www.legislation.gov.uk/uksi/2012/403/contents/made *Non-print*

The M1 Motorway (Junction 37 to Junction 38) (Temporary Restriction of Traffic) (No. 2) Order 2012 No. 2012/2958. - Enabling power: Road Traffic Regulation Act 1984, s. 14 (1) (a) & S.I. 1982/1163, reg. 16 (2). - Issued: 30.11.2012. Made: 07.11.2012. Coming into force: 08.11.2012. Effect: None. Territorial extent & classification: E. Local. - Available at http://www.legislation.gov.uk/uksi/2012/2958/contents/made *Non-print*

The M1 Motorway (Junction 37 to Junction 38) (Temporary Restriction of Traffic) Order 2012 No. 2012/2454. - Enabling power: Road Traffic Regulation Act 1984, s. 14 (1) (a) & S.I. 1982/1163, reg. 16 (2). - Issued: 28.09.2012. Made: 20.09.2012. Coming into force: 30.09.2012. Effect: None. Territorial extent & classification: E. Local. - Available at http://www.legislation.gov.uk/uksi/2012/2454/contents/made *Non-print*

The M1 Motorway (Junction 40 and Junction 41) (Temporary Prohibition of Traffic) Order 2012 No. 2012/38. - Enabling power: Road Traffic Regulation Act 1984, s. 14 (1) (a). - Issued: 11.01.2012. Made: 03.01.2012. Coming into force: 08.01.2012. Effect: None. Territorial extent & classification: E. Local. - Available at http://www.legislation.gov.uk/uksi/2012/38/contents/made *Non-print*

The M1 Motorway (Junction 40, Ossett) (Temporary Prohibition of Traffic) Order 2012 No. 2012/2354. - Enabling power: Road Traffic Regulation Act 1984, s. 14 (1) (a). - Issued: 17.09.2012. Made: 06.09.2012. Coming into force: 16.09.2012. Effect: None. Territorial extent & classification: E. Local. - Available at http://www.legislation.gov.uk/uksi/2012/2354/contents/made *Non-print*

The M1 Motorway (Junction 41, Carr Gate) (Temporary Restriction and Prohibition of Traffic) (No. 2) Order 2012 No. 2012/2433. - Enabling power: Road Traffic Regulation Act 1984, s. 14 (1) (a) & S.I. 1982/1163, reg. 16 (2). - Issued: 26.09.2012. Made: 13.09.2012. Coming into force: 23.09.2012. Effect: None. Territorial extent & classification: E. Local. - Available at http://www.legislation.gov.uk/uksi/2012/2433/contents/made *Non-print*

The M1 Motorway (Junction 41, Carr Gate) (Temporary Restriction and Prohibition of Traffic) Order 2012 No. 2012/1445. - Enabling power: Road Traffic Regulation Act 1984, s. 14 (1) (a) (7). - Issued: 12.06.2012. Made: 24.05.2012. Coming into force: 05.06.2012. Effect: None. Territorial extent & classification: E. Local. - Available at http://www.legislation.gov.uk/uksi/2012/1445/contents/made *Non-print*

The M1 Motorway (Junction 42, Junction 44 and Junction 45) and the A1(M) Motorway (Junction 44) (Temporary Restriction and Prohibition of Traffic) Order 2012 No. 2012/473. - Enabling power: Road Traffic Regulation Act 1984, s. 14 (1) (a) (7). - Issued: 29.02.2012. Made: 16.02.2012. Coming into force: 27.02.2012. Effect: None. Territorial extent & classification: E. Local. - Available at http://www.legislation.gov.uk/uksi/2012/473/contents/made *Non-print*

The M1 Motorway (Junction 42, Lofthouse) (Temporary Prohibition of Traffic) Order 2012 No. 2012/2216. - Enabling power: Road Traffic Regulation Act 1984, s. 14 (1) (a). - Issued: 31.08.2012. Made: 23.08.2012. Coming into force: 02.09.2012. Effect: None. Territorial extent & classification: E. Local. - Available at http://www.legislation.gov.uk/uksi/2012/2216/contents/made *Non-print*

The M1 Motorway (Junction 42 to Junction 47), the M62 Motorway (Junction 29) and the M621 Motorway (Temporary Prohibition of Traffic) Order 2012 No. 2012/1540. - Enabling power: Road Traffic Regulation Act 1984, s. 14 (1) (a). - Issued: 20.06.2012. Made: 31.05.2012. Coming into force: 10.06.2012. Effect: None. Territorial extent & classification: E. Local. - Available at http://www.legislation.gov.uk/uksi/2012/1540/contents/made *Non-print*

The M1 Motorway (Junction 44 to Junction 42) (Temporary Prohibition of Traffic) Order 2012 No. 2012/562. - Enabling power: Road Traffic Regulation Act 1984, s. 14 (1) (a). - Issued: 01.03.2012. Made: 23.02.2012. Coming into force: 04.03.2012. Effect: None. Territorial extent & classification: E. Local. - Available at http://www.legislation.gov.uk/uksi/2012/562/contents/made *Non-print*

The M1 Motorway (Junction 46 to Junction 47) (Temporary Prohibition of Traffic) Order 2012 No. 2012/1607. - Enabling power: Road Traffic Regulation Act 1984, s. 14 (1) (a). - Issued: 27.06.2012. Made: 14.06.2012. Coming into force: 24.06.2012. Effect: None. Territorial extent & classification: E. Local. - Available at http://www.legislation.gov.uk/uksi/2012/1607/contents/made *Non-print*

The M1 Motorway (Junctions 1 - 4, Slip Roads) (Temporary Prohibition of Traffic) Order 2012 No. 2012/714. - Enabling power: Road Traffic Regulation Act 1984, s. 14 (1) (a). - Issued: 19.03.2012. Made: 05.03.2012. Coming into force: 01.04.2012. Effect: None. Territorial extent & classification: E. Local. - Available at http://www.legislation.gov.uk/uksi/2012/714/contents/made *Non-print*

The M1 Motorway (Junctions 1 - 5, Northbound) (Temporary Prohibition of Traffic) Order 2012 No. 2012/2240. - Enabling power: Road Traffic Regulation Act 1984, s. 14 (1) (a). - Issued: 04.09.2012. Made: 28.08.2012. Coming into force: 15.09.2012. Effect: None. Territorial extent & classification: E. Local. - Available at http://www.legislation.gov.uk/uksi/2012/2240/contents/made *Non-print*

The M1 Motorway (Junctions 2 and 4, Slip Roads) (Temporary Prohibition of Traffic) Order 2012 No. 2012/1408. - Enabling power: Road Traffic Regulation Act 1984, s. 14 (1) (a). - Issued: 01.06.2012. Made: 21.05.2012. Coming into force: 09.06.2012. Effect: None. Territorial extent & classification: E. Local. - Available at http://www.legislation.gov.uk/uksi/2012/1408/contents/made *Non-print*

The M1 Motorway (Junctions 3, 4 and 6, Slip Roads) (Temporary Prohibition of Traffic) Order 2012 No. 2012/109. - Enabling power: Road Traffic Regulation Act 1984, s. 14 (1) (a). - Issued: 20.01.2012. Made: 09.01.2012. Coming into force: 28.01.2012. Effect: None. Territorial extent & classification: E. Local. - Available at http://www.legislation.gov.uk/uksi/2012/109/contents/made *Non-print*

Road traffic: Traffic regulation

The M1 Motorway (Junctions 5 - 6a, Link/Slip Roads) (Temporary Prohibition of Traffic) Order 2012 No. 2012/1860. - Enabling power: Road Traffic Regulation Act 1984, s. 14 (1) (a). - Issued: 20.07.2012. Made: 09.07.2012. Coming into force: 01.08.2012. Effect: None. Territorial extent & classification: E. Local. - Available at http://www.legislation.gov.uk/uksi/2012/1860/contents/made *Non-print*

The M1 Motorway (Junctions 8 and 9) Slip Roads (Temporary Prohibition of Traffic) Order 2012 No. 2012/720. - Enabling power: Road Traffic Regulation Act 1984, s. 14 (1) (a). - Issued: 19.03.2012. Made: 05.03.2012. Coming into force: 12.03.2012. Effect: None. Territorial extent & classification: E. Local. - Available at http://www.legislation.gov.uk/uksi/2012/720/contents/made *Non-print*

The M1 Motorway (Junctions 10 to 13) (Temporary Prohibition of Traffic) Order 2012 No. 2012/3236. - Enabling power: Road Traffic Regulation Act 1984, s. 14 (1) (a), sch. 9, para. 27 (1). - Issued: 08.01.2013. Made: 17.12.2012. Coming into force: 31.12.2012. Effect: S.I. 2009/2594; 2011/1928 revoked. Territorial extent & classification: E. Local. - Available at http://www.legislation.gov.uk/uksi/2012/3236/contents/made *Non-print*

The M1 Motorway (Junctions 16 to 21) (Temporary Restriction and Prohibition of Traffic) Order 2012 No. 2012/449. - Enabling power: Road Traffic Regulation Act 1984, s. 14 (1) (a) (7). - Issued: 24.02.2012. Made: 03.02.2012. Coming into force: 10.02.2012. Effect: None. Territorial extent & classification: E. Local. - Available at http://www.legislation.gov.uk/uksi/2012/449/contents/made *Non-print*

The M1 Motorway (Junctions 18 to 19) (Temporary Restriction and Prohibition of Traffic) Order 2012 No. 2012/2194. - Enabling power: Road Traffic Regulation Act 1984, s. 14 (1) (a) & S. I. 1982/1163, reg. 16 (2). - Issued: 29.08.2012. Made: 21.08.2012. Coming into force: 28.08.2012. Effect: None. Territorial extent & classification: E. Local. - Available at http://www.legislation.gov.uk/uksi/2012/2194/contents/made *Non-print*

The M1 Motorway (Junctions 20 to19, Leicestershire) (Temporary Prohibition of Traffic) Order 2012 No. 2012/2844. - Enabling power: Road Traffic Regulation Act 1984, s. 14 (1) (a). - Issued: 16.11.2012. Made: 29.10.2012. Coming into force: 05.11.2012. Effect: None. Territorial extent & classification: E. Local. - Available at http://www.legislation.gov.uk/uksi/2012/2844/contents/made *Non-print*

The M1 Motorway (Junctions 20 to 19) (Temporary Prohibition of Traffic) Order 2012 No. 2012/1317. - Enabling power: Road Traffic Regulation Act 1984, s. 14 (1) (a). - Issued: 22.05.2012. Made: 30.04.2012. Coming into force: 07.05.2012. Effect: None. Territorial extent & classification: E. Local. - Available at http://www.legislation.gov.uk/uksi/2012/1317/contents/made *Non-print*

The M1 Motorway (Junctions 21a to 22) (Temporary Prohibition of Traffic) Order 2012 No. 2012/3130. - Enabling power: Road Traffic Regulation Act 1984, s. 14 (1) (a). - Issued: 20.12.2012. Made: 19.11.2012. Coming into force: 26.11.2012. Effect: None. Territorial extent & classification: E. Local. - Available at http://www.legislation.gov.uk/uksi/2012/3130/contents/made *Non-print*

The M1 Motorway (Junctions 21 to 21a) (Temporary 50 Miles Per Hour Speed Restriction) Order 2012 No. 2012/386. - Enabling power: Road Traffic Regulation Act 1984, s. 14 (1) (a). - Issued: 21.02.2012. Made: 27.01.2012. Coming into force: 03.02.2012. Effect: None. Territorial extent & classification: E. Local. - Available at http://www.legislation.gov.uk/uksi/2012/386/contents/made *Non-print*

The M1 Motorway (Junctions 21 to 22) and the A46 Trunk Road (Temporary Prohibition of Traffic) Order 2012 No. 2012/890. - Enabling power: Road Traffic Regulation Act 1984, s. 14 (1) (a). - Issued: 26.03.2012. Made: 19.03.2012. Coming into force: 26.03.2012. Effect: None. Territorial extent & classification: E. Local. - Available at http://www.legislation.gov.uk/uksi/2012/890/contents/made *Non-print*

The M1 Motorway (Junctions 22 to 21a) (Temporary Prohibition of Traffic) Order 2012 No. 2012/2801. - Enabling power: Road Traffic Regulation Act 1984, s. 14 (1) (a). - Issued: 09.11.2012. Made: 19.10.2012. Coming into force: 26.10.2012. Effect: None. Territorial extent & classification: E. Local. - Available at http://www.legislation.gov.uk/uksi/2012/2801/contents/made *Non-print*

The M1 Motorway (Junctions 24 - 25) (Temporary Restriction and Prohibition of Traffic) Order 2012 No. 2012/3318. - Enabling power: Road Traffic Regulation Act 1984, s. 14 (1) (a) & S.I. 1982/1163, reg. 16 (2). - Issued: 17.01.2013. Made: 31.12.2012. Coming into force: 07.01.2013. Effect: None. Territorial extent & classification: E. Local. - Available at http://www.legislation.gov.uk/uksi/2012/3318/contents/made *Non-print*

The M1 Motorway (Lilbourne to Gilmorton, Northamptonshire) (Temporary 50 Miles Per Hour Speed Restriction) Order 2012 No. 2012/3165. - Enabling power: Road Traffic Regulation Act 1984, s. 14 (1) (a). - Issued: 28.12.2012. Made: 23.11.2012. Coming into force: 30.11.2012. Effect: None. Territorial extent & classification: E. Local. - Available at http://www.legislation.gov.uk/uksi/2012/3165/contents/made *Non-print*

The M1 Motorway (Long Eaton, Derbyshire) (Temporary Restriction and Prohibition of Traffic) Order 2012 No. 2012/1937. - Enabling power: Road Traffic Regulation Act 1984, s. 14 (1) (a) (7). - Issued: 30.07.2012. Made: 29.06.2012. Coming into force: 06.07.2012. Effect: None. Territorial extent & classification: E. Local. - Available at http://www.legislation.gov.uk/uksi/2012/1937/contents/made *Non-print*

The M1 Motorway (South of Junction 15 to Junction 13) Southbound (Temporary 50 Miles Per Hour Speed Restriction) Order 2012 No. 2012/32. - Enabling power: Road Traffic Regulation Act 1984, s. 14 (1) (a) (7). - Issued: 11.01.2012. Made: 03.01.2012. Coming into force: 10.01.2012. Effect: None. Territorial extent & classification: E. Local. - Available at http://www.legislation.gov.uk/uksi/2012/32/contents/made *Non-print*

The M1 Motorway (Tibshelf to Junction 28) (Temporary 50 Miles Per Hour Speed Restriction) Order 2012 No. 2012/3319. - Enabling power: Road Traffic Regulation Act 1984, s. 14 (1) (a) & S.I. 1982/1163, reg. 16 (2). - Issued: 16.01.2013. Made: 31.12.2012. Coming into force: 07.01.2013. Effect: None. Territorial extent & classification: E. Local. - Available at http://www.legislation.gov.uk/uksi/2012/3319/contents/made *Non-print*

The M1 Motorway (Woolley Edge Services to Junction 36) (Temporary Restriction and Prohibition of Traffic) Order 2012 No. 2012/3283. - Enabling power: Road Traffic Regulation Act 1984, s. 14 (1) (a) & S.I. 1982/1163, reg. 16 (2). - Issued: 15.01.2013. Made: 27.12.2012. Coming into force: 06.01.2013. Effect: None. Territorial extent & classification: E. Local. - Available at http://www.legislation.gov.uk/uksi/2012/3283/contents/made *Non-print*

The M2 Motorway and the A2 Trunk Road (Junctions 1 - 4, Slip Roads) (Temporary Prohibition of Traffic) Order 2012 No. 2012/1011. - Enabling power: Road Traffic Regulation Act 1984, s. 14 (1) (a). - Issued: 12.04.2012. Made: 26.03.2012. Coming into force: 16.04.2012. Effect: None. Territorial extent & classification: E. Local. - Available at http://www.legislation.gov.uk/uksi/2012/1011/contents/made *Non-print*

The M2 Motorway (Junction 5) (Temporary Restriction and Prohibition of Traffic) Order 2012 No. 2012/2177. - Enabling power: Road Traffic Regulation Act 1984, s. 14 (1) (a). - Issued: 28.08.2012. Made: 20.08.2012. Coming into force: 08.09.2012. Effect: None. Territorial extent & classification: E. Local. - Available at http://www.legislation.gov.uk/uksi/2012/2177/contents/made *Non-print*

The M2 Motorway (Junctions 3 - 2, Londonbound) (Temporary 50 Miles Per Hour Speed Restriction) Order 2012 No. 2012/2362. - Enabling power: Road Traffic Regulation Act 1984, s. 14 (1) (b). - Issued: 17.09.2012. Made: 10.09.2012. Coming into force: 14.09.2012. Effect: None. Territorial extent & classification: E. Local. - Available at http://www.legislation.gov.uk/uksi/2012/2362/contents/made *Non-print*

The M2 Motorway (Junctions 4 - 5) (Temporary Restriction of Traffic) Order 2012 No. 2012/94. - Enabling power: Road Traffic Regulation Act 1984, s. 14 (1) (a) (7). - Issued: 19.01.2012. Made: 09.01.2012. Coming into force: 28.01.2012. Effect: None. Territorial extent & classification: E. Local. - Available at http://www.legislation.gov.uk/uksi/2012/94/contents/made *Non-print*

The M2 Motorway (Junctions 5 - 4, Westbound) (Temporary Restriction and Prohibition of Traffic) Order 2012 No. 2012/3265. - Enabling power: Road Traffic Regulation Act 1984, s. 14 (1) (a). - Issued: 14.01.2013. Made: 17.12.2012. Coming into force: 02.02.2013. Effect: None. Territorial extent & classification: E. Local. - Available at http://www.legislation.gov.uk/uksi/2012/3265/contents/made *Non-print*

The M2 Motorway (Junctions 5 - 7, Slip Roads) (Temporary Prohibition of Traffic) Order 2012 No. 2012/1043. - Enabling power: Road Traffic Regulation Act 1984, s. 14 (1) (a). - Issued: 12.04.2012. Made: 26.03.2012. Coming into force: 16.04.2012. Effect: None. Territorial extent & classification: E. Local. - Available at http://www.legislation.gov.uk/uksi/2012/1043/contents/made *Non-print*

The M2 Motorway (Junctions 6 - 5) (Temporary Prohibition of Traffic) Order 2012 No. 2012/1446. - Enabling power: Road Traffic Regulation Act 1984, s. 14 (1) (a). - Issued: 12.06.2012. Made: 14.05.2012. Coming into force: 02.06.2012. Effect: None. Territorial extent & classification: E. Local. - Available at http://www.legislation.gov.uk/uksi/2012/1446/contents/made *Non-print*

The M2 Motorway (Medway Services, Slip Roads) (Temporary Restriction and Prohibition of Traffic) Order 2012 No. 2012/596. - Enabling power: Road Traffic Regulation Act 1984, s. 14 (1) (a) (7). - Issued: 06.03.2012. Made: 27.02.2012. Coming into force: 17.03.2012. Effect: None. Territorial extent & classification: E. Local. - Available at http://www.legislation.gov.uk/uksi/2012/596/contents/made *Non-print*

The M2 Motorway (Stiff Street and St Catherine's Farm) (Temporary Restriction of Traffic) Order 2012 No. 2012/2464. - Enabling power: Road Traffic Regulation Act 1984, s. 14 (1) (a). - Issued: 28.09.2012. Made: 24.09.2012. Coming into force: 13.10.2012. Effect: None. Territorial extent & classification: E. Local. - Available at http://www.legislation.gov.uk/uksi/2012/2464/contents/made *Non-print*

The M3 Motorway and the A316 Trunk Road (Junction 1, Slip Roads) (Temporary Prohibition of Traffic) Order 2012 No. 2012/3151. - Enabling power: Road Traffic Regulation Act 1984, s. 14 (1) (a). - Issued: 27.12.2012. Made: 26.11.2012. Coming into force: 15.01.2013. Effect: None. Territorial extent & classification: E. Local. - Available at http://www.legislation.gov.uk/uksi/2012/3151/contents/made *Non-print*

The M3 Motorway and the M27 Motorway (Chilworth Interchange - M3 Junction 14, Northbound) (Temporary Prohibition of Traffic) Order 2012 No. 2012/1138. - Enabling power: Road Traffic Regulation Act 1984, s. 14 (1) (a). - Issued: 26.04.2012. Made: 10.04.2012. Coming into force: 01.05.2012. Effect: None. Territorial extent & classification: E. Local. - Available at http://www.legislation.gov.uk/uksi/2012/1138/contents/made *Non-print*

The M3 Motorway (Junction 2, Link Roads) (Temporary Prohibition of Traffic) Order 2012 No. 2012/287. - Enabling power: Road Traffic Regulation Act 1984, s. 14 (1) (a). - Issued: 10.02.2012. Made: 30.01.2012. Coming into force: 18.02.2012. Effect: None. Territorial extent & classification: E. Local. - Available at http://www.legislation.gov.uk/uksi/2012/287/contents/made *Non-print*

The M3 Motorway (Junction 2, Westbound Carriageway) (No. 2) (Temporary Prohibition of Traffic) Order 2012 No. 2012/2708. - Enabling power: Road Traffic Regulation Act 1984, s. 14 (1) (a). - Issued: 01.11.2012. Made: 08.10.2012. Coming into force: 01.11.2012. Effect: None. Territorial extent & classification: E. Local. - Available at http://www.legislation.gov.uk/uksi/2012/2708/contents/made *Non-print*

The M3 Motorway (Junction 2, Westbound Carriageway) (Temporary Prohibition of Traffic) Order 2012 No. 2012/703. - Enabling power: Road Traffic Regulation Act 1984, s. 14 (1) (a). - Issued: 14.03.2012. Made: 05.03.2012. Coming into force: 24.03.2012. Effect: None. Territorial extent & classification: E. Local. - Available at http://www.legislation.gov.uk/uksi/2012/703/contents/made *Non-print*

The M3 Motorway (Junction 4, Eastbound Entry Slip Road) (Temporary Prohibition of Traffic) Order 2012 No. 2012/479. - Enabling power: Road Traffic Regulation Act 1984, s. 14 (1) (a). - Issued: 29.02.2012. Made: 20.02.2012. Coming into force: 10.03.2012. Effect: None. Territorial extent & classification: E. Local. - Available at http://www.legislation.gov.uk/uksi/2012/479/contents/made *Non-print*

The M3 Motorway (Junction 4 - Kitsmead Lane, Carriageways) (Temporary Restriction of Traffic) Order 2012 No. 2012/201. - Enabling power: Road Traffic Regulation Act 1984, s. 14 (1) (a) (7). - Issued: 01.02.2012. Made: 23.01.2012. Coming into force: 15.02.2012. Effect: None. Territorial extent & classification: E. Local. - Available at http://www.legislation.gov.uk/uksi/2012/201/contents/made *Non-print*

The M3 Motorway (Junction 4, Northbound Exit Slip Road) (Temporary Prohibition of Traffic) Order 2012 No. 2012/1526. - Enabling power: Road Traffic Regulation Act 1984, s. 14 (1) (a). - Issued: 19.06.2012. Made: 06.06.2012. Coming into force: 23.06.2012. Effect: None. Territorial extent & classification: E. Local. - Available at http://www.legislation.gov.uk/uksi/2012/1526/contents/made *Non-print*

The M3 Motorway (Junction 4) (Temporary Restriction and Prohibition of Traffic) Order 2012 No. 2012/2232. - Enabling power: Road Traffic Regulation Act 1984, s. 14 (1) (a). - Issued: 04.09.2012. Made: 23.08.2012. Coming into force: 15.09.2012. Effect: None. Territorial extent & classification: E. Local. - Available at http://www.legislation.gov.uk/uksi/2012/2232/contents/made *Non-print*

The M3 Motorway (Junction 10, Southbound Entry Slip Road) (Temporary Prohibition of Traffic) Order 2012 No. 2012/158. - Enabling power: Road Traffic Regulation Act 1984, s. 14 (1) (a). - Issued: 30.01.2012. Made: 16.01.2012. Coming into force: 04.02.2012. Effect: None. Territorial extent & classification: E. Local. - Available at http://www.legislation.gov.uk/uksi/2012/158/contents/made *Non-print*

The M3 Motorway (Junction 13, Southbound Entry Slip Road) (Temporary Prohibition of Traffic) Order 2012 No. 2012/3204. - Enabling power: Road Traffic Regulation Act 1984, s. 14 (1) (a). - Issued: 02.01.2013. Made: 10.12.2012. Coming into force: 05.01.2013. Effect: None. Territorial extent & classification: E. Local. - Available at http://www.legislation.gov.uk/uksi/2012/3204/contents/made *Non-print*

The M3 Motorway (Junction 14, Link Roads) (Temporary Prohibition of Traffic) Order 2012 No. 2012/3258. - Enabling power: Road Traffic Regulation Act 1984, s. 14 (1) (a). - Issued: 09.01.2013. Made: 17.12.2012. Coming into force: 26.01.2013. Effect: None. Territorial extent & classification: E. Local. - Available at http://www.legislation.gov.uk/uksi/2012/3258/contents/made *Non-print*

The M3 Motorway (Junctions 3 - 4) (Temporary Restriction and Prohibition of Traffic) Order 2012 No. 2012/3256. - Enabling power: Road Traffic Regulation Act 1984, s. 14 (1) (a). - Issued: 09.01.2013. Made: 17.11.2012. Coming into force: 26.01.2013. Effect: None. Territorial extent & classification: E. Local. - Available at http://www.legislation.gov.uk/uksi/2012/3256/contents/made *Non-print*

Road traffic: Traffic regulation

The M3 Motorway (Junctions 3 - 12) (Temporary Prohibition of Traffic) Order 2012 No. 2012/92. - Enabling power: Road Traffic Regulation Act 1984, s. 14 (1) (a). - Issued: 18.01.2012. Made: 09.01.2012. Coming into force: 28.01.2012. Effect: None. Territorial extent & classification: E. Local. - Available at http://www.legislation.gov.uk/uksi/2012/92/contents/made *Non-print*

The M3 Motorway (Junctions 3 - 13, Slip Roads) (Temporary Prohibition of Traffic) Order 2012 No. 2012/1088. - Enabling power: Road Traffic Regulation Act 1984, s. 14 (1) (a). - Issued: 18.04.2012. Made: 10.04.2012. Coming into force: 28.04.2012. Effect: None. Territorial extent & classification: E. Local. - Available at http://www.legislation.gov.uk/uksi/2012/1088/contents/made *Non-print*

The M3 Motorway (Junctions 7 - 9) (Temporary Prohibition of Traffic) Order 2012 No. 2012/2238. - Enabling power: Road Traffic Regulation Act 1984, s. 14 (1) (a). - Issued: 04.09.2012. Made: 28.08.2012. Coming into force: 15.09.2012. Effect: None. Territorial extent & classification: E. Local. - Available at http://www.legislation.gov.uk/uksi/2012/2238/contents/made *Non-print*

The M3 Motorway (Junctions 9 - 8) (Temporary Prohibition of Traffic) Order 2012 No. 2012/1131. - Enabling power: Road Traffic Regulation Act 1984, s. 14 (1) (a). - Issued: 26.04.2012. Made: 16.04.2012. Coming into force: 07.05.2012. Effect: None. Territorial extent & classification: E. Local. - Available at http://www.legislation.gov.uk/uksi/2012/1131/contents/made *Non-print*

The M3 Motorway (Junctions 13 and 14, Slip/Link Roads) (Temporary Prohibition of Traffic) Order 2012 No. 2012/1368. - Enabling power: Road Traffic Regulation Act 1984, s. 14 (1) (a). - Issued: 28.05.2012. Made: 14.05.2012. Coming into force: 05.06.2012. Effect: None. Territorial extent & classification: E. Local. - Available at http://www.legislation.gov.uk/uksi/2012/1368/contents/made *Non-print*

The M3 Motorway (Junctions 14 - 4, Carriageways) (Temporary Restriction of Traffic) Order 2012 No. 2012/2861. - Enabling power: Road Traffic Regulation Act 1984, s. 14 (1) (a). - Issued: 16.11.2012. Made: 05.11.2012. Coming into force: 30.11.2012. Effect: None. Territorial extent & classification: E. Local. - Available at http://www.legislation.gov.uk/uksi/2012/2861/contents/made *Non-print*

The M4 and the A404(M) Motorways (M4 Junction 8/9 and A404(M) Junction 9A, Slip Roads) (Temporary Prohibition of Traffic) Order 2012 No. 2012/548. - Enabling power: Road Traffic Regulation Act 1984, s. 14 (1) (a). - Issued: 01.03.2012. Made: 20.02.2012. Coming into force: 07.03.2012. Effect: None. Territorial extent & classification: E. Local. - Available at http://www.legislation.gov.uk/uksi/2012/548/contents/made *Non-print*

The M4 Motorway and the A419 Trunk Road (M4 Junction 15 - Commonhead Roundabout) (Temporary Prohibition of Traffic) Order 2012 No. 2012/96. - Enabling power: Road Traffic Regulation Act 1984, s. 14 (1) (a). - Issued: 19.01.2012. Made: 09.01.2012. Coming into force: 28.01.2012. Effect: None. Territorial extent & classification: E. Local. - Available at http://www.legislation.gov.uk/uksi/2012/96/contents/made *Non-print*

The M4 Motorway (East and West of Junction 14) (Temporary Restriction and Prohibition of Traffic) Order 2012 No. 2012/132. - Enabling power: Road Traffic Regulation Act 1984, s. 14 (1) (a) (7). - Issued: 24.01.2012. Made: 16.01.2012. Coming into force: 04.02.2012. Effect: None. Territorial extent & classification: E. Local. - Available at http://www.legislation.gov.uk/uksi/2012/132/contents/made *Non-print*

The M4 Motorway (East of Junction 15) (Temporary Restriction and Prohibition of Traffic) Order 2012 No. 2012/2908. - Enabling power: Road Traffic Regulation Act 1984, s. 14 (1) (a). - Issued: 23.11.2012. Made: 12.11.2012. Coming into force: 01.12.2012. Effect: None. Territorial extent & classification: E. Local. - Available at http://www.legislation.gov.uk/uksi/2012/2908/contents/made *Non-print*

The M4 Motorway (Junction 4B, Link Road) (Temporary Restriction and Prohibition of Traffic) Order 2012 No. 2012/1364. - Enabling power: Road Traffic Regulation Act 1984, s. 14 (1) (a) (7). - Issued: 28.05.2012. Made: 14.05.2012. Coming into force: 02.06.2012. Effect: None. Territorial extent & classification: E. Local. - Available at http://www.legislation.gov.uk/uksi/2012/1364/contents/made *Non-print*

The M4 Motorway (Junction 4, Eastbound Exit Slip Road) (Temporary Prohibition of Traffic) Order 2012 No. 2012/2648. - Enabling power: Road Traffic Regulation Act 1984, s. 14 (1) (a). - Issued: 26.10.2012. Made: 15.10.2012. Coming into force: 03.11.2012. Effect: None. Territorial extent & classification: E. Local. - Available at http://www.legislation.gov.uk/uksi/2012/2648/contents/made *Non-print*

The M4 Motorway (Junction 5 - West of Junction 14, Carriageways) (Temporary Restriction of Traffic) Order 2012 No. 2012/2310. - Enabling power: Road Traffic Regulation Act 1984, s. 14 (1) (a). - Issued: 12.09.2012. Made: 03.09.2012. Coming into force: 22.09.2012. Effect: None. Territorial extent & classification: E. Local. - Available at http://www.legislation.gov.uk/uksi/2012/2310/contents/made *Non-print*

Road traffic: Traffic regulation

The M4 Motorway (Junction 6, Slip Roads) (Temporary Prohibition of Traffic) Order 2012 No. 2012/2923. - Enabling power: Road Traffic Regulation Act 1984, s. 14 (1) (a). - Issued: 26.11.2012. Made: 12.11.2012. Coming into force: 01.12.2012. Effect: None. Territorial extent & classification: E. Local. - Available at http://www.legislation.gov.uk/uksi/2012/2923/contents/made *Non-print*

The M4 Motorway (Junction 7, Slip and Spur Roads) (Temporary Prohibition of Traffic) Order 2012 No. 2012/2865. - Enabling power: Road Traffic Regulation Act 1984, s. 14 (1) (a). - Issued: 19.11.2012. Made: 05.11.2012. Coming into force: 24.11.2012. Effect: None. Territorial extent & classification: E. Local. - Available at http://www.legislation.gov.uk/uksi/2012/2865/contents/made *Non-print*

The M4 Motorway (Junction 7, Slip Road Closures) (Temporary Prohibition of Traffic) Order 2012 No. 2012/1732. - Enabling power: London Olympic and Paralympic Games Act 2006, 16 (1) & Road Traffic Regulation Act 1984, s. 16A. - Issued: 13.07.2012. Made: 25.06.2012. Coming into force: 07.07.2012. Effect: None. Territorial extent & classification: E. Local. - Available at http://www.legislation.gov.uk/uksi/2012/1732/contents/made *Non-print*

The M4 Motorway (Junction 8/9) (Temporary Restriction and Prohibition of Traffic) Order 2012 No. 2012/2228. - Enabling power: Road Traffic Regulation Act 1984, s. 14 (1) (a). - Issued: 03.09.2012. Made: 28.08.2012. Coming into force: 15.09.2012. Effect: None. Territorial extent & classification: E. Local. - Available at http://www.legislation.gov.uk/uksi/2012/2228/contents/made *Non-print*

The M4 Motorway (Junction 8/9 - West of Junction 7) (Temporary Restriction of Traffic) Order 2012 No. 2012/270. - Enabling power: Road Traffic Regulation Act 1984, s. 14 (1) (a) (7). - Issued: 10.02.2012. Made: 30.01.2012. Coming into force: 18.02.2012. Effect: None. Territorial extent & classification: E. Local. - Available at http://www.legislation.gov.uk/uksi/2012/270/contents/made *Non-print*

The M4 Motorway (Junction 10, Link Roads) (Temporary Prohibition of Traffic) (No. 2) Order 2012 No. 2012/1669. - Enabling power: Road Traffic Regulation Act 1984, s. 14 (1) (a). - Issued: 03.07.2012. Made: 18.06.2012. Coming into force: 07.07.2012. Effect: None. Territorial extent & classification: E. Local. - Available at http://www.legislation.gov.uk/uksi/2012/1669/contents/made *Non-print*

The M4 Motorway (Junction 10, Link Roads) (Temporary Prohibition of Traffic) (No.3) Order 2012 No. 2012/2649. - Enabling power: Road Traffic Regulation Act 1984, s. 14 (1) (a). - Issued: 25.10.2012. Made: 15.10.2012. Coming into force: 03.11.2012. Effect: None. Territorial extent & classification: E. Local. - Available at http://www.legislation.gov.uk/uksi/2012/2649/contents/made *Non-print*

The M4 Motorway (Junction 10, Link Roads) (Temporary Prohibition of Traffic) (No. 4) Order 2012 No. 2012/3297. - Enabling power: Road Traffic Regulation Act 1984, s. 14 (1) (a). - Issued: 16.01.2013. Made: 17.12.2012. Coming into force: 01.02.2013. Effect: None. Territorial extent & classification: E. Local. - Available at http://www.legislation.gov.uk/uksi/2012/3297/contents/made *Non-print*

The M4 Motorway (Junction 10, Link Roads) (Temporary Prohibition of Traffic) Order 2012 No. 2012/97. - Enabling power: Road Traffic Regulation Act 1984, s. 14 (1) (a). - Issued: 19.01.2012. Made: 09.01.2012. Coming into force: 28.01.2012. Effect: None. Territorial extent & classification: E. Local. - Available at http://www.legislation.gov.uk/uksi/2012/97/contents/made *Non-print*

The M4 Motorway (Junction 11, Eastbound Entry Slip Road) (Temporary Prohibition of Traffic) Order 2012 No. 2012/2926. - Enabling power: Road Traffic Regulation Act 1984, s. 14 (1) (a). - Issued: 26.11.2012. Made: 12.11.2012. Coming into force: 01.12.2012. Effect: None. Territorial extent & classification: E. Local. - Available at http://www.legislation.gov.uk/uksi/2012/2926/contents/made *Non-print*

The M4 Motorway (Junction 11, Westbound Entry Slip Road) (Temporary Prohibition of Traffic) Order 2012 No. 2012/3210. - Enabling power: Road Traffic Regulation Act 1984, s. 14 (1) (a). - Issued: 04.01.2013. Made: 10.12.2012. Coming into force: 12.01.2013. Effect: None. Territorial extent & classification: E. Local. - Available at http://www.legislation.gov.uk/uksi/2012/3210/contents/made *Non-print*

The M4 Motorway (Junction 12) (Temporary Restriction and Prohibition of Traffic) Order 2012 No. 2012/2288. - Enabling power: Road Traffic Regulation Act 1984, s. 14 (1) (a). - Issued: 10.09.2012. Made: 28.08.2012. Coming into force: 15.09.2012. Effect: None. Territorial extent & classification: E. Local. - Available at http://www.legislation.gov.uk/uksi/2012/2288/contents/made *Non-print*

The M4 Motorway (Junction 13, Chieveley Interchange) (Temporary Prohibition of Traffic) Order 2012 No. 2012/278. - Enabling power: Road Traffic Regulation Act 1984, s. 14 (1) (a). - Issued: 10.02.2012. Made: 30.01.2012. Coming into force: 18.02.2012. Effect: None. Territorial extent & classification: E. Local. - Available at http://www.legislation.gov.uk/uksi/2012/278/contents/made *Non-print*

The M4 Motorway (Junction 13, Slip Roads) (Temporary Prohibition of Traffic) Order 2012 No. 2012/2309. - Enabling power: Road Traffic Regulation Act 1984, s. 14 (1) (a). - Issued: 11.09.2012. Made: 03.09.2012. Coming into force: 22.09.2012. Effect: None. Territorial extent & classification: E. Local. - Available at http://www.legislation.gov.uk/uksi/2012/2309/contents/made *Non-print*

Road traffic: Traffic regulation

The M4 Motorway (Junction 13) (Temporary Restriction and Prohibition of Traffic) Order 2012 No. 2012/3209. - Enabling power: Road Traffic Regulation Act 1984, s. 14 (1) (a). - Issued: 02.01.2013. Made: 10.12.2012. Coming into force: 29.12.2012. Effect: None. Territorial extent & classification: E. Local. - Available at http://www.legislation.gov.uk/uksi/2012/3209/contents/made *Non-print*

The M4 Motorway (Junction 14, Carriageways) (Temporary Prohibition of Traffic) Order 2012 No. 2012/1454. - Enabling power: Road Traffic Regulation Act 1984, s. 14 (1) (a). - Issued: 12.06.2012. Made: 28.05.2012. Coming into force: 16.06.2012. Effect: None. Territorial extent & classification: E. Local. - Available at http://www.legislation.gov.uk/uksi/2012/1454/contents/made *Non-print*

The M4 Motorway (Junction 14, Slip Roads) (Temporary Prohibition of Traffic) Order 2012 No. 2012/93. - Enabling power: Road Traffic Regulation Act 1984, s. 14 (1) (a). - Issued: 18.01.2012. Made: 09.01.2012. Coming into force: 28.01.2012. Effect: None. Territorial extent & classification: E. Local. - Available at http://www.legislation.gov.uk/uksi/2012/93/contents/made *Non-print*

The M4 Motorway (Junction 15 Eastbound Exit Slip Road) (Temporary Prohibition of Traffic) Order 2012 No. 2012/1304. - Enabling power: Road Traffic Regulation Act 1984, s. 14 (1) (a). - Issued: 21.05.2012. Made: 09.05.2012. Coming into force: 14.05.2012. Effect: None. Territorial extent & classification: E. Local. - Available at http://www.legislation.gov.uk/uksi/2012/1304/contents/made *Non-print*

The M4 Motorway (Junction 15 - West of Junction 14) (Temporary Restriction and Prohibition of Traffic) Order 2012 No. 2012/2355. - Enabling power: Road Traffic Regulation Act 1984, s. 14 (1) (a). - Issued: 17.09.2012. Made: 10.09.2012. Coming into force: 03.10.2012. Effect: None. Territorial extent & classification: E. Local. - Available at http://www.legislation.gov.uk/uksi/2012/2355/contents/made *Non-print*

The M4 Motorway (Junction 16 Slip Roads) (Temporary Prohibition of Traffic) Order 2012 No. 2012/2982. - Enabling power: Road Traffic Regulation Act 1984, s. 14 (1) (a). - Issued: 05.12.2012. Made: 21.11.2012. Coming into force: 24.11.2012. Effect: None. Territorial extent & classification: E. Local. - Available at http://www.legislation.gov.uk/uksi/2012/2982/contents/made *Non-print*

The M4 Motorway (Junction 16) (Temporary Restriction and Prohibition of Traffic) Order 2012 No. 2012/3293. - Enabling power: Road Traffic Regulation Act 1984, s. 14 (1) (a) & S.I. 1982/1163, reg. 16 (2). - Issued: 15.01.2013. Made: 31.12.2012. Coming into force: 04.01.2013. Effect: None. Territorial extent & classification: E. Local. - Available at http://www.legislation.gov.uk/uksi/2012/3293/contents/made *Non-print*

The M4 Motorway (Junction 17 Eastbound) (Temporary Restriction and Prohibition of Traffic) Order 2012 No. 2012/112. - Enabling power: Road Traffic Regulation Act 1984, s. 14 (1) (a) (7). - Issued: 20.01.2012. Made: 11.01.2012. Coming into force: 14.01.2012. Effect: None. Territorial extent & classification: E. Local. - Available at http://www.legislation.gov.uk/uksi/2012/112/contents/made *Non-print*

The M4 Motorway (Junction 19) (Temporary Prohibition of Traffic) (Number 2) Order 2012 No. 2012/1591. - Enabling power: Road Traffic Regulation Act 1984, s. 14 (1) (a). - Issued: 26.06.2012. Made: 23.05.2012. Coming into force: 26.05.2012. Effect: None. Territorial extent & classification: E. Local. - Available at http://www.legislation.gov.uk/uksi/2012/1591/contents/made *Non-print*

The M4 Motorway (Junction 19) (Temporary Prohibition of Traffic) Order 2012 No. 2012/79. - Enabling power: Road Traffic Regulation Act 1984, s. 14 (1) (a). - Issued: 18.01.2012. Made: 05.01.2012. Coming into force: 14.01.2012. Effect: None. Territorial extent & classification: E. Local. - Available at http://www.legislation.gov.uk/uksi/2012/79/contents/made *Non-print*

The M4 Motorway (Junction 19 Westbound Entry Slip Road) (Temporary Prohibition of Traffic) Order 2012 No. 2012/1007. - Enabling power: Road Traffic Regulation Act 1984, s. 14 (1) (a). - Issued: 12.04.2012. Made: 22.03.2012. Coming into force: 30.03.2012. Effect: None. Territorial extent & classification: E. Local. - Available at http://www.legislation.gov.uk/uksi/2012/1007/contents/made *Non-print*

The M4 Motorway (Junction 22 Slip Roads) (Temporary Prohibition of Traffic) Order 2012 No. 2012/931. - Enabling power: Road Traffic Regulation Act 1984, s. 14 (1) (a). - Issued: 28.03.2012. Made: 22.03.2012. Coming into force: 30.03.2012. Effect: None. Territorial extent & classification: E. Local. - Available at http://www.legislation.gov.uk/uksi/2012/931/contents/made *Non-print*

The M4 Motorway (Junction 22) (Temporary Prohibition of Traffic) Order 2012 No. 2012/2531. - Enabling power: Road Traffic Regulation Act 1984, s. 14 (1) (a). - Issued: 09.10.2012. Made: 03.10.2012. Coming into force: 11.10.2012. Effect: None. Territorial extent & classification: E. Local. - Available at http://www.legislation.gov.uk/uksi/2012/2531/contents/made *Non-print*

The M4 Motorway (Junctions 1 - 3, Carriageway/Slip Roads) (Temporary Prohibition of Traffic) Order 2012 No. 2012/2457. - Enabling power: Road Traffic Regulation Act 1984, s. 14 (1) (a). - Issued: 28.09.2012. Made: 21.09.2012. Coming into force: 22.09.2012. Effect: None. Territorial extent & classification: E. Local. - Available at http://www.legislation.gov.uk/uksi/2012/2457/contents/made *Non-print*

The M4 Motorway (Junctions 1 - 3) (Temporary Prohibition of Traffic) Order 2012 No. 2012/731. - Enabling power: Road Traffic Regulation Act 1984, s. 14 (1) (a). - Issued: 19.03.2012. Made: 05.03.2012. Coming into force: 01.04.2012. Effect: None. Territorial extent & classification: E. Local. - Available at http://www.legislation.gov.uk/uksi/2012/731/contents/made *Non-print*

The M4 Motorway (Junctions 1 - 3) (Temporary Restriction of Traffic) (No.2) Order 2012 No. 2012/2070. - Enabling power: Road Traffic Regulation Act 1984, s. 14 (1) (b). - Issued: 13.08.2012. Made: 30.07.2012. Coming into force: 06.08.2012. Effect: None. Territorial extent & classification: E. Local. - Available at http://www.legislation.gov.uk/uksi/2012/2070/contents/made *Non-print*

The M4 Motorway (Junctions 1 - 3) (Temporary Restriction of Traffic) Order 2012 No. 2012/1137. - Enabling power: Road Traffic Regulation Act 1984, s. 14 (1) (b). - Issued: 26.04.2012. Made: 16.04.2012. Coming into force: 19.04.2012. Effect: None. Territorial extent & classification: E. Local. - Available at http://www.legislation.gov.uk/uksi/2012/1137/contents/made *Non-print*

The M4 Motorway (Junctions 1 - 4A) (Temporary Restriction and Prohibition of Traffic) Order 2012 No. 2012/904. - Enabling power: Road Traffic Regulation Act 1984, s. 14 (1) & London Olympic Games and Paralympic Games Act 2006, s. 14 (4) (5A). - Issued: 26.03.2012. Made: 19.03.2012. Coming into force: 10.04.2012. Effect: None. Territorial extent & classification: E. Local. - Available at http://www.legislation.gov.uk/uksi/2012/904/contents/made *Non-print*

The M4 Motorway (Junctions 2 - 1, Eastbound) (Temporary Prohibition of Traffic) Order 2012 No. 2012/99. - Enabling power: Road Traffic Regulation Act 1984, s. 14 (1) (a). - Issued: 19.01.2012. Made: 09.01.2012. Coming into force: 28.01.2012. Effect: None. Territorial extent & classification: E. Local. - Available at http://www.legislation.gov.uk/uksi/2012/99/contents/made *Non-print*

The M4 Motorway (Junctions 2 - 6) (Temporary Prohibition of Traffic) Order 2012 No. 2012/1191. - Enabling power: Road Traffic Regulation Act 1984, s. 14 (1) (a). - Issued: 04.05.2012. Made: 23.04.2012. Coming into force: 12.05.2012. Effect: None. Territorial extent & classification: E. Local. - Available at http://www.legislation.gov.uk/uksi/2012/1191/contents/made *Non-print*

The M4 Motorway (Junctions 3 - 4B) (Temporary Prohibition of Traffic) Order 2012 No. 2012/1132. - Enabling power: Road Traffic Regulation Act 1984, s. 14 (1) (a). - Issued: 03.05.2012. Made: 16.04.2012. Coming into force: 05.05.2012. Effect: None. Territorial extent & classification: E. Local. - Available at http://www.legislation.gov.uk/uksi/2012/1132/contents/made *Non-print*

The M4 Motorway (Junctions 3 - 5, Link and Slip Roads) (Temporary Prohibition of Traffic) Order 2012 No. 2012/1858. - Enabling power: Road Traffic Regulation Act 1984, s. 14 (1) (a). - Issued: 20.07.2012. Made: 09.07.2012. Coming into force: 02.08.2012. Effect: None. Territorial extent & classification: E. Local. - Available at http://www.legislation.gov.uk/uksi/2012/1858/contents/made *Non-print*

The M4 Motorway (Junctions 6 - 8/9) (Temporary Restriction and Prohibition of Traffic) Order 2012 No. 2012/3198. - Enabling power: Road Traffic Regulation Act 1984, s. 14 (1) (a). - Issued: 02.01.2013. Made: 10.12.2012. Coming into force: 12.01.2013. Effect: None. Territorial extent & classification: E. Local. - Available at http://www.legislation.gov.uk/uksi/2012/3198/contents/made *Non-print*

The M4 Motorway (Junctions 6 - 8/9, Westbound) (Temporary Prohibition of Traffic) Order 2012 No. 2012/3203. - Enabling power: Road Traffic Regulation Act 1984, s. 14 (1) (a). - Issued: 02.01.2013. Made: 10.12.2012. Coming into force: 05.01.2013. Effect: None. Territorial extent & classification: E. Local. - Available at http://www.legislation.gov.uk/uksi/2012/3203/contents/made *Non-print*

The M4 Motorway (Junctions 8/9 - 7, Eastbound) (Temporary Prohibition of Traffic) Order 2012 No. 2012/2304. - Enabling power: Road Traffic Regulation Act 1984, s. 14 (1) (a). - Issued: 11.09.2012. Made: 03.09.2012. Coming into force: 22.09.2012. Effect: None. Territorial extent & classification: E. Local. - Available at http://www.legislation.gov.uk/uksi/2012/2304/contents/made *Non-print*

The M4 Motorway (Junctions 10 - 11) (Temporary Restriction and Prohibition of Traffic) (No. 2) Order 2012 No. 2012/3279. - Enabling power: Road Traffic Regulation Act 1984, s. 14 (1) (a). - Issued: 15.01.2013. Made: 17.12.2012. Coming into force: 26.01.2013. Effect: None. Territorial extent & classification: E. Local. - Available at http://www.legislation.gov.uk/uksi/2012/3279/contents/made *Non-print*

The M4 Motorway (Junctions 10 - 11) (Temporary Restriction and Prohibition of Traffic) Order 2012 No. 2012/2581. - Enabling power: Road Traffic Regulation Act 1984, s. 14 (1) (a). - Issued: 16.10.2012. Made: 08.10.2012. Coming into force: 27.10.2012. Effect: None. Territorial extent & classification: E. Local. - Available at http://www.legislation.gov.uk/uksi/2012/2581/contents/made *Non-print*

The M4 Motorway (Junctions 12 and 13, Slip Roads) (Temporary Prohibition of Traffic) Order 2012 No. 2012/400. - Enabling power: Road Traffic Regulation Act 1984, s. 14 (1) (a). - Issued: 21.02.2012. Made: 06.02.2012. Coming into force: 25.02.2012. Effect: None. Territorial extent & classification: E. Local. - Available at http://www.legislation.gov.uk/uksi/2012/400/contents/made *Non-print*

Road traffic: Traffic regulation

The M4 Motorway (Junctions 13 - 14, Carriageways) (Temporary Restriction of Traffic) Order 2012 No. 2012/2585. - Enabling power: Road Traffic Regulation Act 1984, s. 14 (1) (a). - Issued: 16.10.2012. Made: 08.10.2012. Coming into force: 27.10.2012. Effect: None. Territorial extent & classification: E. Local. - Available at http://www.legislation.gov.uk/uksi/2012/2585/contents/made *Non-print*

The M4 Motorway (Junctions 15-16) (Temporary Restriction of Traffic) (Number 2) Order 2012 No. 2012/1558. - Enabling power: Road Traffic Regulation Act 1984, s. 14 (1) (a) (7). - Issued: 22.06.2012. Made: 06.06.2012. Coming into force: 09.06.2012. Effect: None. Territorial extent & classification: E. Local. - Available at http://www.legislation.gov.uk/uksi/2012/1558/contents/made *Non-print*

The M4 Motorway (Junctions 15-16) (Temporary Restriction of Traffic) Order 2012 No. 2012/240. - Enabling power: Road Traffic Regulation Act 1984, s. 14 (1) (a) (7). - Issued: 06.02.2012. Made: 25.01.2012. Coming into force: 01.02.2012. Effect: None. Territorial extent & classification: E. Local. - Available at http://www.legislation.gov.uk/uksi/2012/240/contents/made *Non-print*

The M4 Motorway (Junctions 16 - 17) (Temporary Restriction and Prohibition of Traffic) Order 2012 No. 2012/173. - Enabling power: Road Traffic Regulation Act 1984, s. 14 (1) (a) (7). - Issued: 30.01.2012. Made: 18.01.2012. Coming into force: 24.01.2012. Effect: None. Territorial extent & classification: E. Local. - Available at http://www.legislation.gov.uk/uksi/2012/173/contents/made *Non-print*

The M4 Motorway (Junctions 16 - 17) (Temporary Restriction of Traffic) (Number 2) Order 2012 No. 2012/1152. - Enabling power: Road Traffic Regulation Act 1984, s. 14 (1) (a) (7). - Issued: 01.05.2012. Made: 17.04.2012. Coming into force: 25.04.2012. Effect: None. Territorial extent & classification: E. Local. - Available at http://www.legislation.gov.uk/uksi/2012/1152/contents/made *Non-print*

The M4 Motorway (Junctions 16-17) (Temporary Restriction of Traffic) (Number 3) Order 2012 No. 2012/1473. - Enabling power: Road Traffic Regulation Act 1984, s. 14 (1) (a) (7). - Issued: 12.06.2012. Made: 30.05.2012. Coming into force: 09.06.2012. Effect: None. Territorial extent & classification: E. Local. - Available at http://www.legislation.gov.uk/uksi/2012/1473/contents/made *Non-print*

The M4 Motorway (Junctions 16-17) (Temporary Restriction of Traffic) (Number 4) Order 2012 No. 2012/3190. - Enabling power: Road Traffic Regulation Act 1984, s. 14 (1) (a) & S.I. 1982/1163, reg. 16 (2). - Issued: 02.01.2013. Made: 04.12.2012. Coming into force: 08.12.2012. Effect: None. Territorial extent & classification: E. Local. - Available at http://www.legislation.gov.uk/uksi/2012/3190/contents/made *Non-print*

The M4 Motorway (Junctions 16-17) (Temporary Restriction of Traffic) Order 2012 No. 2012/850. - Enabling power: Road Traffic Regulation Act 1984, s. 14 (1) (a) (7). - Issued: 20.03.2012. Made: 14.03.2012. Coming into force: 19.03.2012. Effect: None. Territorial extent & classification: E. Local. - Available at http://www.legislation.gov.uk/uksi/2012/850/contents/made *Non-print*

The M4 Motorway (Junctions 17-16) (Temporary Restriction of Traffic) (Number 2) Order 2012 No. 2012/1279. - Enabling power: Road Traffic Regulation Act 1984, s. 14 (1) (a) (7). - Issued: 18.05.2012. Made: 08.05.2012. Coming into force: 15.05.2012. Effect: None. Territorial extent & classification: E. Local. - Available at http://www.legislation.gov.uk/uksi/2012/1279/contents/made *Non-print*

The M4 Motorway (Junctions 17-16) (Temporary Restriction of Traffic) Order 2012 No. 2012/1091. - Enabling power: Road Traffic Regulation Act 1984, s. 14 (1) (a) (7). - Issued: 19.04.2012. Made: 10.04.2012. Coming into force: 14.04.2012. Effect: None. Territorial extent & classification: E. Local. - Available at http://www.legislation.gov.uk/uksi/2012/1091/contents/made *Non-print*

The M4 Motorway (Junctions 17-18) (Temporary Restriction and Prohibition of Traffic) Order 2012 No. 2012/1561. - Enabling power: Road Traffic Regulation Act 1984, s. 14 (1) (a). - Issued: 22.06.2012. Made: 06.06.2012. Coming into force: 14.06.2012. Effect: None. Territorial extent & classification: E. Local. - Available at http://www.legislation.gov.uk/uksi/2012/1561/contents/made *Non-print*

The M4 Motorway (Junctions 17-18) (Temporary Restriction of Traffic) Order 2012 No. 2012/2868. - Enabling power: Road Traffic Regulation Act 1984, s. 14 (1) (a) & S.I. 1982/1163, reg. 16 (2). - Issued: 19.11.2012. Made: 06.11.2012. Coming into force: 10.11.2012. Effect: None. Territorial extent & classification: E. Local. - Available at http://www.legislation.gov.uk/uksi/2012/2868/contents/made *Non-print*

The M4 Motorway (Junctions 18-17) (Temporary Prohibition of Traffic) Order 2012 No. 2012/237. - Enabling power: Road Traffic Regulation Act 1984, s. 14 (1) (a). - Issued: 06.02.2012. Made: 25.01.2012. Coming into force: 04.02.2012. Effect: None. Territorial extent & classification: E. Local. - Available at http://www.legislation.gov.uk/uksi/2012/237/contents/made *Non-print*

The M4 Motorway (Junctions 18-17) (Temporary Restriction of Traffic) Order 2012 No. 2012/928. - Enabling power: Road Traffic Regulation Act 1984, s. 14 (1) (a) (7). - Issued: 28.03.2012. Made: 21.03.2012. Coming into force: 30.03.2012. Effect: None. Territorial extent & classification: E. Local. - Available at http://www.legislation.gov.uk/uksi/2012/928/contents/made *Non-print*

Road traffic: Traffic regulation

The M4 Motorway (Junctions 18-19) (Temporary Prohibition of Traffic) Order 2012 No. 2012/291. - Enabling power: Road Traffic Regulation Act 1984, s. 14 (1) (a). - Issued: 10.02.2012. Made: 31.01.2012. Coming into force: 04.02.2012. Effect: None. Territorial extent & classification: E. Local. - Available at http://www.legislation.gov.uk/uksi/2012/291/contents/made *Non-print*

The M4 Motorway (Junctions 19-17) (Temporary Restriction of Traffic) Order 2012 No. 2012/1237. - Enabling power: Road Traffic Regulation Act 1984, s. 14 (1) (a) (7). - Issued: 11.05.2012. Made: 02.05.2012. Coming into force: 05.05.2012. Effect: None. Territorial extent & classification: E. Local. - Available at http://www.legislation.gov.uk/uksi/2012/1237/contents/made *Non-print*

The M4 Motorway, the M5 Motorway, the M48 Motorway and the M32 Motorway (Temporary Restriction of Traffic) Order 2012 No. 2012/1381. - Enabling power: Road Traffic Regulation Act 1984, s. 14 (1) (a). - Issued: 28.05.2012. Made: 18.05.2012. Coming into force: 21.05.2012. Effect: None. Territorial extent & classification: E. Local. - Available at http://www.legislation.gov.uk/uksi/2012/1381/contents/made *Non-print*

The M5 and M6 Motorways (M5 Junction 2 to M6 Junction 9) (Temporary Restriction and Prohibition of Traffic) Order 2012 No. 2012/224. - Enabling power: Road Traffic Regulation Act 1984, s. 14 (1) (a) (7). - Issued: 03.02.2012. Made: 20.01.2012. Coming into force: 27.01.2012. Effect: S.I. 2011/2368 revoked. Territorial extent & classification: E. Local. - Available at http://www.legislation.gov.uk/uksi/2012/224/contents/made *Non-print*

The M5 and M6 Motorways (M6 Junction 8) (Link Road) (Temporary Prohibition of Traffic) Order 2012 No. 2012/2714. - Enabling power: Road Traffic Regulation Act 1984, s. 14 (1) (a). - Issued: 02.11.2012. Made: 01.10.2012. Coming into force: 08.10.2012. Effect: None. Territorial extent & classification: E. Local. - Available at http://www.legislation.gov.uk/uksi/2012/2714/contents/made *Non-print*

The M5 and M42 Motorways (M5 Junction 4a to Junction 5) (Temporary Prohibition of Traffic) Order 2012 No. 2012/2834. - Enabling power: Road Traffic Regulation Act 1984, s. 14 (1) (a). - Issued: 15.11.2012. Made: 24.10.2012. Coming into force: 05.11.2012. Effect: None. Territorial extent & classification: E. Local. - Available at http://www.legislation.gov.uk/uksi/2012/2834/contents/made *Non-print*

The M5 and M42 Motorways (M5 Junctions 4a to 4) (Temporary Prohibition of Traffic) Order 2012 No. 2012/2118. - Enabling power: Road Traffic Regulation Act 1984, s. 14 (1) (a). - Issued: 17.08.2012. Made: 30.07.2012. Coming into force: 06.08.2012. Effect: None. Territorial extent & classification: E. Local. - Available at http://www.legislation.gov.uk/uksi/2012/2118/contents/made *Non-print*

The M5, M6 and M42 Motorways (M6 Junctions 4 to 10) (Temporary Restriction and Prohibition of Traffic) Order 2012 No. 2012/222. - Enabling power: Road Traffic Regulation Act 1984, s. 14 (1) (a) (7). - Issued: 03.02.2012. Made: 20.01.2012. Coming into force: 27.01.2012. Effect: None. Territorial extent & classification: E. Local. - Available at http://www.legislation.gov.uk/uksi/2012/222/contents/made *Non-print*

The M5 Motorway and M42 Motorway (M5 Junction 4a) (Link Roads) (Temporary Prohibition of Traffic) Order 2012 No. 2012/3226. - Enabling power: Road Traffic Regulation Act 1984, s. 14 (1) (a). - Issued: 07.01.2013. Made: 03.12.2012. Coming into force: 10.12.2012. Effect: None. Territorial extent & classification: E. Local. - Available at http://www.legislation.gov.uk/uksi/2012/3226/contents/made *Non-print*

The M5 Motorway (Junction 1 - M6 Junction 8) (Temporary Prohibition of Traffic) Order 2012 No. 2012/2052. - Enabling power: Road Traffic Regulation Act 1984, s. 14 (1) (a). - Issued: 10.08.2012. Made: 23.07.2012. Coming into force: 30.07.2012. Effect: None. Territorial extent & classification: E. Local. - Available at http://www.legislation.gov.uk/uksi/2012/2052/contents/made *Non-print*

The M5 Motorway (Junction 2) (Slip Road) (Temporary Prohibition of Traffic) (No. 2) Order 2012 No. 2012/2841. - Enabling power: Road Traffic Regulation Act 1984, s. 14 (1) (a). - Issued: 15.11.2012. Made: 24.10.2012. Coming into force: 05.11.2012. Effect: None. Territorial extent & classification: E. Local. - Available at http://www.legislation.gov.uk/uksi/2012/2841/contents/made *Non-print*

The M5 Motorway (Junction 2) (Slip Road) (Temporary Prohibition of Traffic) Order 2012 No. 2012/2416. - Enabling power: Road Traffic Regulation Act 1984, s. 14 (1) (a). - Issued: 24.09.2012. Made: 04.09.2012. Coming into force: 11.09.2012. Effect: None. Territorial extent & classification: E. Local. - Available at http://www.legislation.gov.uk/uksi/2012/2416/contents/made *Non-print*

The M5 Motorway (Junction 2) (Southbound Entry Slip Road) (Temporary Prohibition of Traffic) Order 2012 No. 2012/586. - Enabling power: Road Traffic Regulation Act 1984, s. 14 (1) (a). - Issued: 06.03.2012. Made: 17.02.2012. Coming into force: 24.02.2012. Effect: None. Territorial extent & classification: E. Local. - Available at http://www.legislation.gov.uk/uksi/2012/586/contents/made *Non-print*

The M5 Motorway (Junction 2) (Southbound Exit Slip Road) (Temporary Prohibition of Traffic) Order 2012 No. 2012/1148. - Enabling power: Road Traffic Regulation Act 1984, s. 14 (1) (a). - Issued: 27.04.2012. Made: 16.04.2012. Coming into force: 23.04.2012. Effect: None. Territorial extent & classification: E. Local. - Available at http://www.legislation.gov.uk/uksi/2012/1148/contents/made *Non-print*

Road traffic: Traffic regulation

The M5 Motorway (Junction 3) (Northbound Exit Slip Road) (Temporary Prohibition of Traffic) Order 2012 No. 2012/1438. - Enabling power: Road Traffic Regulation Act 1984, s. 14 (1) (a). - Issued: 06.06.2012. Made: 11.05.2012. Coming into force: 18.05.2012. Effect: None. Territorial extent & classification: E. Local. - Available at http://www.legislation.gov.uk/uksi/2012/1438/contents/made *Non-print*

The M5 Motorway (Junction 4a) (Temporary Restriction and Prohibition of Traffic) Order 2012 No. 2012/1998. - Enabling power: Road Traffic Regulation Act 1984, s. 14 (1) (a) (7). - Issued: 02.08.2012. Made: 09.07.2012. Coming into force: 16.07.2012. Effect: None. Territorial extent & classification: E. Local. - Available at http://www.legislation.gov.uk/uksi/2012/1998/contents/made *Non-print*

The M5 Motorway (Junction 5 Northbound Exit Slip Road) (Temporary Prohibition of Traffic) Order 2012 No. 2012/1580. - Enabling power: Road Traffic Regulation Act 1984, s. 14 (1) (a). - Issued: 26.06.2012. Made: 01.06.2012. Coming into force: 08.06.2012. Effect: None. Territorial extent & classification: E. Local. - Available at http://www.legislation.gov.uk/uksi/2012/1580/contents/made *Non-print*

The M5 Motorway (Junction 5 Slip Roads) (Temporary Prohibition of Traffic) Order 2012 No. 2012/3321. - Enabling power: Road Traffic Regulation Act 1984, s. 14 (1) (a). - Issued: 18.01.2013. Made: 31.12.2012. Coming into force: 07.01.2013. Effect: None. Territorial extent & classification: E. Local. - Available at http://www.legislation.gov.uk/uksi/2012/3321/contents/made *Non-print*

The M5 Motorway (Junction 5) (Temporary Prohibition of Traffic) Order 2012 No. 2012/743. - Enabling power: Road Traffic Regulation Act 1984, s. 14 (1) (a). - Issued: 19.03.2012. Made: 02.03.2012. Coming into force: 09.03.2012. Effect: None. Territorial extent & classification: E. Local. - Available at http://www.legislation.gov.uk/uksi/2012/743/contents/made *Non-print*

The M5 Motorway (Junction 5) (Temporary Restriction and Prohibition of Traffic) Order 2012 No. 2012/230. - Enabling power: Road Traffic Regulation Act 1984, s. 14 (1) (a). - Issued: 03.02.2012. Made: 23.01.2012. Coming into force: 30.01.2012. Effect: None. Territorial extent & classification: E. Local. - Available at http://www.legislation.gov.uk/uksi/2012/230/contents/made *Non-print*

The M5 Motorway (Junction 6) (Southbound Entry Slip Road) (Temporary Prohibition of Traffic) Order 2012 No. 2012/2190. - Enabling power: Road Traffic Regulation Act 1984, s. 14 (1) (a). - Issued: 29.08.2012. Made: 20.08.2012. Coming into force: 27.08.2012. Effect: None. Territorial extent & classification: E. Local. - Available at http://www.legislation.gov.uk/uksi/2012/2190/contents/made *Non-print*

The M5 Motorway (Junction 7 to Junction 5) (Temporary Prohibition of Traffic) Order 2012 No. 2012/1142. - Enabling power: Road Traffic Regulation Act 1984, s. 14 (1) (a). - Issued: 27.04.2012. Made: 11.04.2012. Coming into force: 18.04.2012. Effect: None. Territorial extent & classification: E. Local. - Available at http://www.legislation.gov.uk/uksi/2012/1142/contents/made *Non-print*

The M5 Motorway (Junction 8, Strensham Service Area) (Temporary Prohibition of Traffic) Order 2012 No. 2012/2704. - Enabling power: Road Traffic Regulation Act 1984, s. 14 (1) (a). - Issued: 01.11.2012. Made: 25.09.2012. Coming into force: 02.10.2012. Effect: None. Territorial extent & classification: E. Local. - Available at http://www.legislation.gov.uk/uksi/2012/2704/contents/made *Non-print*

The M5 Motorway (Junction 8 to Junction 7) (Temporary Prohibition of Traffic) Order 2012 No. 2012/2795. - Enabling power: Road Traffic Regulation Act 1984, s. 14 (1) (a). - Issued: 09.11.2012. Made: 15.10.2012. Coming into force: 22.11.2012. Effect: None. Territorial extent & classification: E. Local. - Available at http://www.legislation.gov.uk/uksi/2012/2795/contents/made *Non-print*

The M5 Motorway (Junction 10 Slip Roads) (Temporary Prohibition of Traffic) Order 2012 No. 2012/1005. - Enabling power: Road Traffic Regulation Act 1984, s. 14 (1) (a). - Issued: 05.04.2012. Made: 22.03.2012. Coming into force: 30.03.2012. Effect: None. Territorial extent & classification: E. Local. - Available at http://www.legislation.gov.uk/uksi/2012/1005/contents/made *Non-print*

The M5 Motorway (Junction 11A) (Temporary Restriction and Prohibition of Traffic) Order 2012 No. 2012/303. - Enabling power: Road Traffic Regulation Act 1984, s. 14 (1) (a). - Issued: 10.02.2012. Made: 01.02.2012. Coming into force: 11.02.2012. Effect: None. Territorial extent & classification: E. Local. - Available at http://www.legislation.gov.uk/uksi/2012/303/contents/made *Non-print*

The M5 Motorway (Junction 11 Southbound Entry Slip Road) (Temporary Prohibition of Traffic) Order 2012 No. 2012/514. - Enabling power: Road Traffic Regulation Act 1984, s. 14 (1) (a). - Issued: 01.03.2012. Made: 21.02.2012. Coming into force: 25.02.2012. Effect: None. Territorial extent & classification: E. Local. - Available at http://www.legislation.gov.uk/uksi/2012/514/contents/made *Non-print*

The M5 Motorway (Junction 15) and M4 Motorway (Junction 20) (Almondsbury Interchange Slip Roads) (Temporary Prohibition of Traffic) Order 2012 No. 2012/998. - Enabling power: Road Traffic Regulation Act 1984, s. 14 (1) (a). - Issued: 05.04.2012. Made: 22.03.2012. Coming into force: 30.03.2012. Effect: None. Territorial extent & classification: E. Local. - Available at http://www.legislation.gov.uk/uksi/2012/998/contents/made *Non-print*

The M5 Motorway (Junction 17 Northbound Exit Slip Road) (Temporary Prohibition of Traffic) Order 2012 No. 2012/1300. - Enabling power: Road Traffic Regulation Act 1984, s. 14 (1) (a). - Issued: 21.05.2012. Made: 09.05.2012. Coming into force: 12.05.2012. Effect: None. Territorial extent & classification: E. Local. - Available at http://www.legislation.gov.uk/uksi/2012/1300/contents/made *Non-print*

The M5 Motorway (Junction 18 X and W Loops) (Temporary Restriction and Prohibition of Traffic) Order 2012 No. 2012/176. - Enabling power: Road Traffic Regulation Act 1984, s. 14 (1) (a). - Issued: 31.01.2012. Made: 20.01.2012. Coming into force: 28.01.2012. Effect: None. Territorial extent & classification: E. Local. - Available at http://www.legislation.gov.uk/uksi/2012/176/contents/made *Non-print*

The M5 Motorway (Junction 19 Northbound Exit Slip Road) (Temporary Prohibition of Traffic) Order 2012 No. 2012/1415. - Enabling power: Road Traffic Regulation Act 1984, s. 14 (1) (a). - Issued: 01.06.2012. Made: 23.05.2012. Coming into force: 26.05.2012. Effect: None. Territorial extent & classification: E. Local. - Available at http://www.legislation.gov.uk/uksi/2012/1415/contents/made *Non-print*

The M5 Motorway (Junction 19 Slip Roads) (Temporary Prohibition of Traffic) Order 2012 No. 2012/1054. - Enabling power: Road Traffic Regulation Act 1984, s. 14 (1) (a). - Issued: 13.04.2012. Made: 29.03.2012. Coming into force: 07.04.2012. Effect: None. Territorial extent & classification: E. Local. - Available at http://www.legislation.gov.uk/uksi/2012/1054/contents/made *Non-print*

The M5 Motorway (Junction 19) (Temporary Restriction of Traffic) Order 2012 No. 2012/3275. - Enabling power: Road Traffic Regulation Act 1984, s. 14 (1) (a) & S.I. 1982/1163, reg. 16 (2). - Issued: 14.01.2013. Made: 21.12.2012. Coming into force: 31.12.2012. Effect: None. Territorial extent & classification: E. Local. - Available at http://www.legislation.gov.uk/uksi/2012/3275/contents/made *Non-print*

The M5 Motorway (Junction 20) (Temporary Restriction and Prohibition of Traffic) Order 2012 No. 2012/2872. - Enabling power: Road Traffic Regulation Act 1984, s. 14 (1) (a) & S.I. 1982/1163, reg. 16 (2). - Issued: 19.11.2012. Made: 08.11.2012. Coming into force: 16.11.2012. Effect: None. Territorial extent & classification: E. Local. - Available at http://www.legislation.gov.uk/uksi/2012/2872/contents/made *Non-print*

The M5 Motorway (Junction 21) (Temporary Restriction and Prohibition of Traffic) Order 2012 No. 2012/1416. - Enabling power: Road Traffic Regulation Act 1984, s. 14 (1) (a) (7). - Issued: 01.06.2012. Made: 23.05.2012. Coming into force: 26.05.2012. Effect: None. Territorial extent & classification: E. Local. - Available at http://www.legislation.gov.uk/uksi/2012/1416/contents/made *Non-print*

The M5 Motorway (Junction 23) (Temporary Restriction and Prohibition of Traffic) Order 2012 No. 2012/1239. - Enabling power: Road Traffic Regulation Act 1984, s. 14 (1) (a) (7). - Issued: 11.05.2012. Made: 02.05.2012. Coming into force: 08.05.2012. Effect: None. Territorial extent & classification: E. Local. - Available at http://www.legislation.gov.uk/uksi/2012/1239/contents/made *Non-print*

The M5 Motorway (Junction 25) (Temporary Restriction and Prohibition of Traffic) (Number 2) Order 2012 No. 2012/2697. - Enabling power: Road Traffic Regulation Act 1984, s. 14 (1) (a). - Issued: 30.10.2012. Made: 17.10.2012. Coming into force: 26.10.2012. Effect: None. Territorial extent & classification: E. Local. - Available at http://www.legislation.gov.uk/uksi/2012/2697/contents/made *Non-print*

The M5 Motorway (Junction 25) (Temporary Restriction and Prohibition of Traffic) Order 2012 No. 2012/1370. - Enabling power: Road Traffic Regulation Act 1984, s. 14 (1) (a) (7). - Issued: 28.05.2012. Made: 15.05.2012. Coming into force: 19.05.2012. Effect: None. Territorial extent & classification: E. Local. - Available at http://www.legislation.gov.uk/uksi/2012/1370/contents/made *Non-print*

The M5 Motorway (Junction 27 Southbound Entry Slip Road) (Temporary Prohibition of Traffic) Order 2012 No. 2012/914. - Enabling power: Road Traffic Regulation Act 1984, s. 14 (1) (a). - Issued: 28.03.2012. Made: 19.03.2012. Coming into force: 24.03.2012. Effect: None. Territorial extent & classification: E. Local. - Available at http://www.legislation.gov.uk/uksi/2012/914/contents/made *Non-print*

The M5 Motorway (Junction 28 Northbound Exit Slip Road) (Temporary Prohibition of Traffic) Order 2012 No. 2012/1065. - Enabling power: Road Traffic Regulation Act 1984, s. 14 (1) (a). - Issued: 16.04.2012. Made: 05.04.2012. Coming into force: 14.04.2012. Effect: None. Territorial extent & classification: E. Local. - Available at http://www.legislation.gov.uk/uksi/2012/1065/contents/made *Non-print*

The M5 Motorway (Junction 28) (Temporary Restriction and Prohibition of Traffic) Order 2012 No. 2012/1242. - Enabling power: Road Traffic Regulation Act 1984, s. 14 (1) (a) (7). - Issued: 11.05.2012. Made: 04.05.2012. Coming into force: 15.05.2012. Effect: None. Territorial extent & classification: E. Local. - Available at http://www.legislation.gov.uk/uksi/2012/1242/contents/made *Non-print*

The M5 Motorway (Junction 30 Southbound Entry Slip Road) (Temporary Prohibition of Traffic) Order 2012 No. 2012/235. - Enabling power: Road Traffic Regulation Act 1984, s. 14 (1) (a). - Issued: 06.02.2012. Made: 25.01.2012. Coming into force: 04.02.2012. Effect: None. Territorial extent & classification: E. Local. - Available at http://www.legislation.gov.uk/uksi/2012/235/contents/made *Non-print*

Road traffic: Traffic regulation

The M5 Motorway (Junctions 1 and 2) (Slip Roads) (Temporary Prohibition of Traffic) Order 2012 No. 2012/2382. - Enabling power: Road Traffic Regulation Act 1984, s. 14 (1) (a). - Issued: 18.09.2012. Made: 28.08.2012. Coming into force: 04.09.2012. Effect: None. Territorial extent & classification: E. Local. - Available at http://www.legislation.gov.uk/uksi/2012/2382/contents/made *Non-print*

The M5 Motorway (Junctions 1 to 2) (Temporary Restriction and Prohibition of Traffic) Order 2012 No. 2012/1996. - Enabling power: Road Traffic Regulation Act 1984, s. 14 (1) (a) (7). - Issued: 02.08.2012. Made: 09.07.2012. Coming into force: 16.07.2012. Effect: None. Territorial extent & classification: E. Local. - Available at http://www.legislation.gov.uk/uksi/2012/1996/contents/made *Non-print*

The M5 Motorway (Junctions 1 to 3) (Temporary Restriction and Prohibition of Traffic) Order 2012 No. 2012/1600. - Enabling power: Road Traffic Regulation Act 1984, s. 14 (1) (a) (7). - Issued: 25.06.2012. Made: 28.05.2012. Coming into force: 04.06.2012. Effect: None. Territorial extent & classification: E. Local. - Available at http://www.legislation.gov.uk/uksi/2012/1600/contents/made *Non-print*

The M5 Motorway (Junctions 2 to 3) (Temporary Restriction and Prohibition of Traffic) Order 2012 No. 2012/372. - Enabling power: Road Traffic Regulation Act 1984, s. 14 (1) (a) (7). - Issued: 17.02.2012. Made: 31.01.2012. Coming into force: 07.02.2012. Effect: None. Territorial extent & classification: E. Local. - Available at http://www.legislation.gov.uk/uksi/2012/372/contents/made *Non-print*

The M5 Motorway (Junctions 3 to 4) (Temporary Prohibition of Traffic) Order 2012 No. 2012/2423. - Enabling power: Road Traffic Regulation Act 1984, s. 14 (1) (a). - Issued: 25.09.2012. Made: 10.09.2012. Coming into force: 17.09.2012. Effect: None. Territorial extent & classification: E. Local. - Available at http://www.legislation.gov.uk/uksi/2012/2423/contents/made *Non-print*

The M5 Motorway (Junctions 5 to 4a) (Temporary Prohibition of Traffic) (No. 2) Order 2012 No. 2012/1449. - Enabling power: Road Traffic Regulation Act 1984, s. 14 (1) (a). - Issued: 12.06.2012. Made: 23.05.2012. Coming into force: 30.05.2012. Effect: None. Territorial extent & classification: E. Local. - Available at http://www.legislation.gov.uk/uksi/2012/1449/contents/made *Non-print*

The M5 Motorway (Junctions 5 to 4a) (Temporary Prohibition of Traffic) Order 2012 No. 2012/593. - Enabling power: Road Traffic Regulation Act 1984, s. 14 (1) (a). - Issued: 06.03.2012. Made: 20.02.2012. Coming into force: 27.02.2012. Effect: None. Territorial extent & classification: E. Local. - Available at http://www.legislation.gov.uk/uksi/2012/593/contents/made *Non-print*

The M5 Motorway (Junctions 5 to 6) (Temporary Prohibition of Traffic) Order 2012 No. 2012/590. - Enabling power: Road Traffic Regulation Act 1984, s. 14 (1) (a). - Issued: 06.03.2012. Made: 20.02.2012. Coming into force: 27.02.2012. Effect: None. Territorial extent & classification: E. Local. - Available at http://www.legislation.gov.uk/uksi/2012/590/contents/made *Non-print*

The M5 Motorway (Junctions 5 to 6) (Temporary Restriction and Prohibition of Traffic) Order 2012 No. 2012/2839. - Enabling power: Road Traffic Regulation Act 1984, s. 14 (1) (a) & S.I. 1982/1163, reg. 16 (2). - Issued: 15.11.2012. Made: 29.10.2012. Coming into force: 05.11.2012. Effect: None. Territorial extent & classification: E. Local. - Available at http://www.legislation.gov.uk/uksi/2012/2839/contents/made *Non-print*

The M5 Motorway (Junctions 5 to 6, Worcestershire) (Temporary Restriction and Prohibition of Traffic) (No. 2) Order 2012 No. 2012/2193. - Enabling power: Road Traffic Regulation Act 1984, s. 14 (1) (a) & S.I. 1982/1163, reg. 16 (2). - Issued: 29.08.2012. Made: 20.08.2012. Coming into force: 27.08.2012. Effect: S.I. 2012/2128 revoked. Territorial extent & classification: E. Local. - Available at http://www.legislation.gov.uk/uksi/2012/2193/contents/made *Non-print*

The M5 Motorway (Junctions 5 to 6, Worcestershire) (Temporary Restriction and Prohibition of Traffic) Order 2012 No. 2012/2128. - Enabling power: Road Traffic Regulation Act 1984, s. 14 (1) (a). - Issued: 17.08.2012. Made: 30.07.2012. Coming into force: 06.08.2012. Effect: None. Territorial extent & classification: E. Local. - Revoked by S.I. 2012/2193 (Non-print). - Available at http://www.legislation.gov.uk/uksi/2012/2128/contents/made *Non-print*

The M5 Motorway (Junctions 7 to 6) (Temporary Prohibition of Traffic) Order 2012 No. 2012/580. - Enabling power: Road Traffic Regulation Act 1984, s. 14 (1) (a). - Issued: 06.03.2012. Made: 17.02.2012. Coming into force: 24.02.2012. Effect: None. Territorial extent & classification: E. Local. - Available at http://www.legislation.gov.uk/uksi/2012/580/contents/made *Non-print*

The M5 Motorway (Junctions 7 to 8) (Temporary Prohibition of Traffic) Order 2012 No. 2012/587. - Enabling power: Road Traffic Regulation Act 1984, s. 14 (1) (a). - Issued: 06.03.2012. Made: 17.02.2012. Coming into force: 24.02.2012. Effect: None. Territorial extent & classification: E. Local. - Available at http://www.legislation.gov.uk/uksi/2012/587/contents/made *Non-print*

Road traffic: Traffic regulation

The M5 Motorway (Junctions 8 to 6) (Temporary Prohibition of Traffic) Order 2012 No. 2012/373. - Enabling power: Road Traffic Regulation Act 1984, s. 14 (1) (a). - Issued: 17.02.2012. Made: 03.02.2012. Coming into force: 10.02.2012. Effect: None. Territorial extent & classification: E. Local. - Available at http://www.legislation.gov.uk/uksi/2012/373/contents/made *Non-print*

The M5 Motorway (Junctions 9-13) (Temporary Prohibition of Traffic) Order 2012 No. 2012/239. - Enabling power: Road Traffic Regulation Act 1984, s. 14 (1) (a). - Issued: 06.02.2012. Made: 25.01.2012. Coming into force: 04.02.2012. Effect: None. Territorial extent & classification: E. Local. - Available at http://www.legislation.gov.uk/uksi/2012/239/contents/made *Non-print*

The M5 Motorway (Junctions 11A-12 Slip Roads) (Temporary Prohibition of Traffic) Order 2012 No. 2012/1002. - Enabling power: Road Traffic Regulation Act 1984, s. 14 (1) (a). - Issued: 05.04.2012. Made: 22.03.2012. Coming into force: 30.03.2012. Effect: None. Territorial extent & classification: E. Local. - Available at http://www.legislation.gov.uk/uksi/2012/1002/contents/made *Non-print*

The M5 Motorway (Junctions 11A - 12) (Temporary Prohibition of Traffic) Order 2012 No. 2012/1299. - Enabling power: Road Traffic Regulation Act 1984, s. 14 (1) (a). - Issued: 21.05.2012. Made: 09.05.2012. Coming into force: 16.05.2012. Effect: None. Territorial extent & classification: E. Local. - Available at http://www.legislation.gov.uk/uksi/2012/1299/contents/made *Non-print*

The M5 Motorway (Junctions 11A-12) (Temporary Restriction and Prohibition of Traffic) (Number 2) Order 2012 No. 2012/2928. - Enabling power: Road Traffic Regulation Act 1984, s. 14 (1) (a) & S.I. 1982/1163, reg. 16 (2). - Issued: 26.11.2012. Made: 13.11.2012. Coming into force: 17.11.2012. Effect: None. Territorial extent & classification: E. Local. - Available at http://www.legislation.gov.uk/uksi/2012/2928/contents/made *Non-print*

The M5 Motorway (Junctions 11A-12) (Temporary Restriction and Prohibition of Traffic) Order 2012 No. 2012/2695. - Enabling power: Road Traffic Regulation Act 1984, s. 14 (1) (a) & S.I. 1982/1163, reg. 16 (2). - Issued: 30.10.2012. Made: 16.10.2012. Coming into force: 20.10.2012. Effect: None. Territorial extent & classification: E. Local. - Revoked by SI 2013/20 (Non-print). - Available at http://www.legislation.gov.uk/uksi/2012/2695/contents/made *Non-print*

The M5 Motorway (Junctions 11A-12) (Temporary Restriction of Traffic) Order 2012 No. 2012/3271. - Enabling power: Road Traffic Regulation Act 1984, s. 14 (1) (a) & S.I. 1982/1163, reg. 16 (2). - Issued: 14.01.2013. Made: 21.12.2012. Coming into force: 31.12.2012. Effect: None. Territorial extent & classification: E. Local. - Available at http://www.legislation.gov.uk/uksi/2012/3271/contents/made *Non-print*

The M5 Motorway (Junctions 12-11A) (Temporary Restriction of Traffic) Order 2012 No. 2012/1240. - Enabling power: Road Traffic Regulation Act 1984, s. 14 (1) (a) (7). - Issued: 11.05.2012. Made: 03.05.2012. Coming into force: 12.05.2012. Effect: None. Territorial extent & classification: E. Local. - Available at http://www.legislation.gov.uk/uksi/2012/1240/contents/made *Non-print*

The M5 Motorway (Junctions 13-14, Michaelwood Services) (Temporary Prohibition of Traffic) Order 2012 No. 2012/53. - Enabling power: Road Traffic Regulation Act 1984, s. 14 (1) (a), sch. 9, para. 27 (1). - Issued: 13.01.2012. Made: 04.01.2012. Coming into force: 07.01.2012. Effect: S.I. 2011/2482 revoked. Territorial extent & classification: E. Local. - Available at http://www.legislation.gov.uk/uksi/2012/53/contents/made *Non-print*

The M5 Motorway (Junctions 13 - 14) (Temporary Restriction and Prohibition of Traffic) Order 2012 No. 2012/117. - Enabling power: Road Traffic Regulation Act 1984, s. 14 (1) (a) (7). - Issued: 23.01.2012. Made: 11.01.2012. Coming into force: 14.01.2012. Effect: None. Territorial extent & classification: E. Local. - Available at http://www.legislation.gov.uk/uksi/2012/117/contents/made *Non-print*

The M5 Motorway (Junctions 13-14) (Temporary Restriction of Traffic) (Number 2) Order 2012 No. 2012/1160. - Enabling power: Road Traffic Regulation Act 1984, s. 14 (1) (a). - Issued: 01.05.2012. Made: 18.04.2012. Coming into force: 21.04.2012. Effect: None. Territorial extent & classification: E. Local. - Available at http://www.legislation.gov.uk/uksi/2012/1160/contents/made *Non-print*

The M5 Motorway (Junctions 13-14) (Temporary Restriction of Traffic) (Number 3) Order 2012 No. 2012/3272. - Enabling power: Road Traffic Regulation Act 1984, s. 14 (1) (a) & S.I. 1982/1163, reg. 16 (2). - Issued: 14.01.2013. Made: 21.12.2012. Coming into force: 31.12.2012. Effect: None. Territorial extent & classification: E. Local. - Available at http://www.legislation.gov.uk/uksi/2012/3272/contents/made *Non-print*

The M5 Motorway (Junctions 13-14) (Temporary Restriction of Traffic) Order 2012 No. 2012/1047. - Enabling power: Road Traffic Regulation Act 1984, s. 14 (1) (a) (7). - Issued: 13.04.2012. Made: 28.03.2012. Coming into force: 07.04.2012. Effect: None. Territorial extent & classification: E. Local. - Available at http://www.legislation.gov.uk/uksi/2012/1047/contents/made *Non-print*

The M5 Motorway (Junctions 18 and 18A Slip Roads) (Temporary Restriction and Prohibition of Traffic) Order 2012 No. 2012/1001. - Enabling power: Road Traffic Regulation Act 1984, s. 14 (1) (a) (7). - Issued: 05.04.2012. Made: 22.03.2012. Coming into force: 30.03.2012. Effect: None. Territorial extent & classification: E. Local. - Available at http://www.legislation.gov.uk/uksi/2012/1001/contents/made *Non-print*

The M5 Motorway (Junctions 18 and 18A) (Temporary Prohibition of Traffic) Order 2012 No. 2012/78. - Enabling power: Road Traffic Regulation Act 1984, s. 14 (1) (a). - Issued: 17.01.2012. Made: 05.01.2012. Coming into force: 14.01.2012. Effect: None. Territorial extent & classification: E. Local. - Available at http://www.legislation.gov.uk/uksi/2012/78/contents/made *Non-print*

The M5 Motorway (Junctions 19-20) (Temporary Restriction of Traffic) (Number 2) Order 2012 No. 2012/2427. - Enabling power: Road Traffic Regulation Act 1984, s. 14 (1) (a). - Issued: 25.09.2012. Made: 12.09.2012. Coming into force: 15.09.2012. Effect: None. Territorial extent & classification: E. Local. - Available at http://www.legislation.gov.uk/uksi/2012/2427/contents/made *Non-print*

The M5 Motorway (Junctions 19-20) (Temporary Restriction of Traffic) Order 2012 No. 2012/439. - Enabling power: Road Traffic Regulation Act 1984, s. 14 (1) (a). - Issued: 22.02.2012. Made: 15.02.2012. Coming into force: 21.02.2012. Effect: None. Territorial extent & classification: E. Local. - Available at http://www.legislation.gov.uk/uksi/2012/439/contents/made *Non-print*

The M5 Motorway (Junctions 19 - 21) (Temporary Restriction and Prohibition of Traffic) Order 2012 No. 2012/174. - Enabling power: Road Traffic Regulation Act 1984, s. 14 (1) (a) (7). - Issued: 31.01.2012. Made: 18.01.2012. Coming into force: 21.01.2012. Effect: None. Territorial extent & classification: E. Local. - Available at http://www.legislation.gov.uk/uksi/2012/174/contents/made *Non-print*

The M5 Motorway (Junctions 19 and 20 Slip Roads) (Temporary Prohibition of Traffic) Order 2012 No. 2012/1009. - Enabling power: Road Traffic Regulation Act 1984, s. 14 (1) (a). - Issued: 12.04.2012. Made: 22.03.2012. Coming into force: 30.03.2012. Effect: None. Territorial extent & classification: E. Local. - Available at http://www.legislation.gov.uk/uksi/2012/1009/contents/made *Non-print*

The M5 Motorway (Junctions 20-22) (Temporary Restriction and Prohibition of Traffic) Order 2012 No. 2012/424. - Enabling power: Road Traffic Regulation Act 1984, s. 14 (1) (a) (7). - Issued: 22.02.2012. Made: 14.02.2012. Coming into force: 17.02.2012. Effect: None. Territorial extent & classification: E. Local. - Available at http://www.legislation.gov.uk/uksi/2012/424/contents/made *Non-print*

The M5 Motorway (Junctions 21 & 22 Slip Roads) (Temporary Prohibition of Traffic) Order 2012 No. 2012/1004. - Enabling power: Road Traffic Regulation Act 1984, s. 14 (1) (a). - Issued: 05.04.2012. Made: 22.03.2012. Coming into force: 30.03.2012. Effect: None. Territorial extent & classification: E. Local. - Available at http://www.legislation.gov.uk/uksi/2012/1004/contents/made *Non-print*

The M5 Motorway (Junctions 22-23) (Temporary Restriction of Traffic) Order 2012 No. 2012/2564. - Enabling power: Road Traffic Regulation Act 1984, s. 14 (1) (a) & SI 1982/1163, reg. 16 (2). - Issued: 12.10.2012. Made: 04.10.2012. Coming into force: 13.10.2012. Effect: None. Territorial extent & classification: E. Local. - Available at http://www.legislation.gov.uk/uksi/2012/2564/contents/made *Non-print*

The M5 Motorway (Junctions 24 - 22) (Temporary Prohibition of Traffic) Order 2012 No. 2012/399. - Enabling power: Road Traffic Regulation Act 1984, s. 14 (1) (a). - Issued: 21.02.2012. Made: 07.02.2012. Coming into force: 10.02.2012. Effect: None. Territorial extent & classification: E. Local. - Available at http://www.legislation.gov.uk/uksi/2012/399/contents/made *Non-print*

The M5 Motorway (Junctions 24-26) (Temporary Restriction and Prohibition of Traffic) Order 2012 No. 2012/226. - Enabling power: Road Traffic Regulation Act 1984, s. 14 (1) (a) (7). - Issued: 03.02.2012. Made: 24.01.2012. Coming into force: 28.01.2012. Effect: None. Territorial extent & classification: E. Local. - Available at http://www.legislation.gov.uk/uksi/2012/226/contents/made *Non-print*

The M5 Motorway (Junctions 28 and 29 Slip Roads) (Temporary Restriction and Prohibition of Traffic) Order 2012 No. 2012/926. - Enabling power: Road Traffic Regulation Act 1984, s. 14 (1) (a) (7). - Issued: 28.03.2012. Made: 21.03.2012. Coming into force: 30.03.2012. Effect: None. Territorial extent & classification: E. Local. - Available at http://www.legislation.gov.uk/uksi/2012/926/contents/made *Non-print*

The M5 Motorway (Junctions 29-28) (Temporary Restriction of Traffic) Order 2012 No. 2012/1222. - Enabling power: Road Traffic Regulation Act 1984, s. 14 (1) (a). - Issued: 10.05.2012. Made: 30.04.2012. Coming into force: 02.05.2012. Effect: None. Territorial extent & classification: E. Local. - Available at http://www.legislation.gov.uk/uksi/2012/1222/contents/made *Non-print*

The M5 Motorway (M5 Junction 4a to M42 Link Road) (Temporary Prohibition of Traffic) Order 2012 No. 2012/2833. - Enabling power: Road Traffic Regulation Act 1984, s. 14 (1) (a). - Issued: 15.11.2012. Made: 24.10.2012. Coming into force: 05.11.2012. Effect: None. Territorial extent & classification: E. Local. - Available at http://www.legislation.gov.uk/uksi/2012/2833/contents/made *Non-print*

Road traffic: Traffic regulation

The M5 Motorway (Michaelwood Services) (Temporary Prohibition of Traffic) Order 2012 No. 2012/1474. - Enabling power: Road Traffic Regulation Act 1984, s. 14 (1) (a). - Issued: 12.06.2012. Made: 30.05.2012. Coming into force: 05.06.2012. Effect: None. Territorial extent & classification: E. Local. - Available at http://www.legislation.gov.uk/uksi/2012/1474/contents/made *Non-print*

The M5 Motorway (Ray Hall Interchange, Sandwell) (Temporary Prohibition of Traffic) Order 2012 No. 2012/353. - Enabling power: Road Traffic Regulation Act 1984, s. 14 (1) (a). - Issued: 15.02.2012. Made: 30.01.2012. Coming into force: 06.02.2012. Effect: None. Territorial extent & classification: E. Local. - Available at http://www.legislation.gov.uk/uksi/2012/353/contents/made *Non-print*

The M5 Motorway (Sedgemoor Services) (Temporary Prohibition of Traffic) Order 2012 No. 2012/1303. - Enabling power: Road Traffic Regulation Act 1984, s. 14 (1) (a). - Issued: 21.05.2012. Made: 09.05.2012. Coming into force: 12.05.2012. Effect: None. Territorial extent & classification: E. Local. - Available at http://www.legislation.gov.uk/uksi/2012/1303/contents/made *Non-print*

The M6 and M42 Motorways (M6 Junction 4 and M42 Junction 7a) and the A446 Trunk Road (Temporary Prohibition of Traffic) Order 2012 No. 2012/860. - Enabling power: Road Traffic Regulation Act 1984, s. 14 (1) (a). - Issued: 23.03.2012. Made: 09.03.2012. Coming into force: 16.03.2012. Effect: None. Territorial extent & classification: E. Local. - Available at http://www.legislation.gov.uk/uksi/2012/860/contents/made *Non-print*

The M6 and M69 Motorways (M6 Junction 2 to M69 Junction 1) (Temporary Prohibition of Traffic) Order 2012 No. 2012/1747. - Enabling power: Road Traffic Regulation Act 1984, s. 14 (1) (a). - Issued: 17.07.2012. Made: 18.06.2012. Coming into force: 25.06.2012. Effect: None. Territorial extent & classification: E. Local. - Available at http://www.legislation.gov.uk/uksi/2012/1747/contents/made *Non-print*

The M6 (Junctions 2-3) and M69 Motorways (Temporary Restriction and Prohibition of Traffic) Order 2012 No. 2012/34. - Enabling power: Road Traffic Regulation Act 1984, s. 14 (1) (a). - Issued: 11.01.2012. Made: 03.01.2012. Coming into force: 10.01.2012. Effect: None. Territorial extent & classification: E. Local. - Available at http://www.legislation.gov.uk/uksi/2012/34/contents/made *Non-print*

The M6 Motorway and M6 Toll Motorway (Staffordshire) (Temporary Prohibition of Traffic) Order 2012 No. 2012/2796. - Enabling power: Road Traffic Regulation Act 1984, s. 14 (1) (a). - Issued: 09.11.2012. Made: 15.10.2012. Coming into force: 22.10.2012. Effect: None. Territorial extent & classification: E. Local. - Available at http://www.legislation.gov.uk/uksi/2012/2796/contents/made *Non-print*

The M6 Motorway and M42 Motorway (Junctions 7 to 6) (Temporary Prohibition of Traffic) Order 2012 No. 2012/2701. - Enabling power: Road Traffic Regulation Act 1984, s. 14 (1) (a). - Issued: 01.11.2012. Made: 24.09.2012. Coming into force: 01.10.2012. Effect: None. Territorial extent & classification: E. Local. - Available at http://www.legislation.gov.uk/uksi/2012/2701/contents/made *Non-print*

The M6 Motorway and the A500 Trunk Road (M6 Junction 15 - Hanford, Staffordshire) (Temporary Prohibition of Traffic) Order 2012 No. 2012/622. - Enabling power: Road Traffic Regulation Act 1984, s. 14 (1) (a). - Issued: 07.03.2012. Made: 24.02.2012. Coming into force: 02.03.2012. Effect: None. Territorial extent & classification: E. Local. - Available at http://www.legislation.gov.uk/uksi/2012/622/contents/made *Non-print*

The M6 Motorway (Catthorpe, Leicestershire) (Slip Road) (Temporary Prohibition of Traffic) Order 2012 No. 2012/3238. - Enabling power: Road Traffic Regulation Act 1984, s. 14 (1) (a). - Issued: 08.01.2013. Made: 20.11.2012. Coming into force: 27.11.2012. Effect: None. Territorial extent & classification: E. Local. - Available at http://www.legislation.gov.uk/uksi/2012/3238/contents/made *Non-print*

The M6 Motorway (Junction 1) (Northbound Entry Slip Road) (Temporary Prohibition of Traffic) Order 2012 No. 2012/376. - Enabling power: Road Traffic Regulation Act 1984, s. 14 (1) (a). - Issued: 17.02.2012. Made: 06.02.2012. Coming into force: 13.02.2012. Effect: None. Territorial extent & classification: E. Local. - Available at http://www.legislation.gov.uk/uksi/2012/376/contents/made *Non-print*

The M6 Motorway (Junction 1) (Slip Road) (Temporary Prohibition of Traffic) Order 2012 No. 2012/608. - Enabling power: Road Traffic Regulation Act 1984, s. 14 (1) (a). - Issued: 06.03.2012. Made: 20.02.2012. Coming into force: 27.02.2012. Effect: None. Territorial extent & classification: E. Local. - Available at http://www.legislation.gov.uk/uksi/2012/608/contents/made *Non-print*

Road traffic: Traffic regulation

The M6 Motorway (Junction 1 to Junction 4) (Temporary Restriction and Prohibition of Traffic) Order 2012 No. 2012/1050. - Enabling power: Road Traffic Regulation Act 1984, s. 14 (1) (a) (7). - Issued: 13.04.2012. Made: 27.03.2012. Coming into force: 03.04.2012. Effect: None. Territorial extent & classification: E. Local. - Available at http://www.legislation.gov.uk/uksi/2012/1050/contents/made *Non-print*

The M6 Motorway (Junction 2) (Temporary Prohibition of Traffic) Order 2012 No. 2012/236. - Enabling power: Road Traffic Regulation Act 1984, s. 14 (1) (a). - Issued: 06.02.2012. Made: 23.01.2012. Coming into force: 30.01.2012. Effect: None. Territorial extent & classification: E. Local. - Available at http://www.legislation.gov.uk/uksi/2012/236/contents/made *Non-print*

The M6 Motorway (Junction 3) (Slip Road) (Temporary Prohibition of Traffic) Order 2012 No. 2012/1994. - Enabling power: Road Traffic Regulation Act 1984, s. 14 (1) (a). - Issued: 01.08.2012. Made: 09.07.2012. Coming into force: 16.07.2012. Effect: None. Territorial extent & classification: E. Local. - Available at http://www.legislation.gov.uk/uksi/2012/1994/contents/made *Non-print*

The M6 Motorway (Junction 4) (Slip Roads) (Temporary Prohibition of Traffic) Order 2012 No. 2012/368. - Enabling power: Road Traffic Regulation Act 1984, s. 14 (1) (a). - Issued: 17.02.2012. Made: 30.01.2012. Coming into force: 06.02.2012. Effect: None. Territorial extent & classification: E. Local. - Available at http://www.legislation.gov.uk/uksi/2012/368/contents/made *Non-print*

The M6 Motorway (Junction 5) (Temporary Prohibition of Traffic) Order 2012 No. 2012/1700. - Enabling power: Road Traffic Regulation Act 1984, s. 14 (1) (a). - Issued: 12.07.2012. Made: 11.06.2012. Coming into force: 18.06.2012. Effect: None. Territorial extent & classification: E. Local. - Available at http://www.legislation.gov.uk/uksi/2012/1700/contents/made *Non-print*

The M6 Motorway (Junction 6, Birmingham) (Temporary Prohibition of Traffic) Order 2012 No. 2012/3301. - Enabling power: Road Traffic Regulation Act 1984, s. 14 (1) (a). - Issued: 16.01.2013. Made: 21.12.2012. Coming into force: 28.12.2012. Effect: None. Territorial extent & classification: E. Local. - Available at http://www.legislation.gov.uk/uksi/2012/3301/contents/made *Non-print*

The M6 Motorway (Junction 6, Gravelly Hill) (Slip Roads) (Temporary Prohibition of Traffic) (No.2) Order 2012 No. 2012/2543. - Enabling power: Road Traffic Regulation Act 1984, s. 14 (1) (a). - Issued: 10.10.2012. Made: 17.09.2012. Coming into force: 24.09.2012. Effect: None. Territorial extent & classification: E. Local. - Available at http://www.legislation.gov.uk/uksi/2012/2543/contents/made *Non-print*

The M6 Motorway (Junction 6, Gravelly Hill) (Slip Roads) (Temporary Prohibition of Traffic) Order 2012 No. 2012/572. - Enabling power: Road Traffic Regulation Act 1984, s. 14 (1) (a). - Issued: 02.03.2012. Made: 13.02.2012. Coming into force: 20.02.2012. Effect: None. Territorial extent & classification: E. Local. - Available at http://www.legislation.gov.uk/uksi/2012/572/contents/made *Non-print*

The M6 Motorway (Junction 6) (Slip Roads) (Temporary Prohibition of Traffic) (No. 2) Order 2012 No. 2012/1015. - Enabling power: Road Traffic Regulation Act 1984, s. 14 (1) (a). - Issued: 12.04.2012. Made: 12.03.2012. Coming into force: 19.03.2012. Effect: None. Territorial extent & classification: E. Local. - Available at http://www.legislation.gov.uk/uksi/2012/1015/contents/made *Non-print*

The M6 Motorway (Junction 6) (Slip Roads) (Temporary Prohibition of Traffic) (No. 3) Order 2012 No. 2012/2917. - Enabling power: Road Traffic Regulation Act 1984, s. 14 (1) (a). - Issued: 23.11.2012. Made: 05.11.2012. Coming into force: 12.11.2012. Effect: None. Territorial extent & classification: E. Local. - Available at http://www.legislation.gov.uk/uksi/2012/2917/contents/made *Non-print*

The M6 Motorway (Junction 6) (Slip Road) (Temporary Prohibition of Traffic) Order 2012 No. 2012/609. - Enabling power: Road Traffic Regulation Act 1984, s. 14 (1) (a). - Issued: 06.03.2012. Made: 20.02.2012. Coming into force: 27.02.2012. Effect: None. Territorial extent & classification: E. Local. - Available at http://www.legislation.gov.uk/uksi/2012/609/contents/made *Non-print*

The M6 Motorway (Junction 6) (Temporary Restriction and Prohibition of Traffic) Order 2012 No. 2012/1094. - Enabling power: Road Traffic Regulation Act 1984, s. 14 (1) (a) (7). - Issued: 19.04.2012. Made: 05.03.2012. Coming into force: 12.03.2012. Effect: None. Territorial extent & classification: E. Local. - Available at http://www.legislation.gov.uk/uksi/2012/1094/contents/made *Non-print*

The M6 Motorway (Junction 6 to Junction 7) (Temporary Prohibition of Traffic) Order 2012 No. 2012/626. - Enabling power: Road Traffic Regulation Act 1984, s. 14 (1) (a). - Issued: 07.03.2012. Made: 27.02.2012. Coming into force: 05.03.2012. Effect: None. Territorial extent & classification: E. Local. - Available at http://www.legislation.gov.uk/uksi/2012/626/contents/made *Non-print*

The M6 Motorway (Junction 7 to Junction 8) (Temporary Prohibition of Traffic) Order 2012 No. 2012/880. - Enabling power: Road Traffic Regulation Act 1984, s. 14 (1) (a). - Issued: 26.03.2012. Made: 12.03.2012. Coming into force: 19.03.2012. Effect: None. Territorial extent & classification: E. Local. - Available at http://www.legislation.gov.uk/uksi/2012/880/contents/made *Non-print*

The M6 Motorway (Junction 7 to Junction 9) (Temporary Restriction and Prohibition of Traffic) Order 2012 No. 2012/238. - Enabling power: Road Traffic Regulation Act 1984, s. 14 (1) (a). - Issued: 06.02.2012. Made: 20.01.2012. Coming into force: 27.01.2012. Effect: None. Territorial extent & classification: E. Local. - Available at http://www.legislation.gov.uk/uksi/2012/238/contents/made *Non-print*

The M6 Motorway (Junction 8 to Junction 6) (Temporary Prohibition of Traffic) Order 2012 No. 2012/2883. - Enabling power: Road Traffic Regulation Act 1984, s. 14 (1) (a). - Issued: 20.11.2012. Made: 05.11.2012. Coming into force: 12.11.2012. Effect: None. Territorial extent & classification: E. Local. - Available at http://www.legislation.gov.uk/uksi/2012/2883/contents/made *Non-print*

The M6 Motorway (Junction 10a) (Link Road) (Temporary Prohibition of Traffic) Order 2012 No. 2012/2715. - Enabling power: Road Traffic Regulation Act 1984, s. 14 (1) (a). - Issued: 02.11.2012. Made: 01.10.2012. Coming into force: 08.10.2012. Effect: None. Territorial extent & classification: E. Local. - Available at http://www.legislation.gov.uk/uksi/2012/2715/contents/made *Non-print*

The M6 Motorway (Junction 10a to 11) (Temporary Prohibition of Traffic) Order 2012 No. 2012/2887. - Enabling power: Road Traffic Regulation Act 1984, s. 14 (1) (a). - Issued: 20.11.2012. Made: 05.11.2012. Coming into force: 12.11.2012. Effect: None. Territorial extent & classification: E. Local. - Available at http://www.legislation.gov.uk/uksi/2012/2887/contents/made *Non-print*

The M6 Motorway (Junction 10) (Temporary Prohibition of Traffic) Order 2012 No. 2012/241. - Enabling power: Road Traffic Regulation Act 1984, s. 14 (1) (a). - Issued: 06.02.2012. Made: 24.01.2012. Coming into force: 31.01.2012. Effect: None. Territorial extent & classification: E. Local. - Available at http://www.legislation.gov.uk/uksi/2012/241/contents/made *Non-print*

The M6 Motorway (Junction 11) (Northbound Exit Slip Road) (Temporary Prohibition of Traffic) Order 2012 No. 2012/652. - Enabling power: Road Traffic Regulation Act 1984, s. 14 (1) (a). - Issued: 14.03.2012. Made: 29.02.2012. Coming into force: 07.03.2012. Effect: None. Territorial extent & classification: E. Local. - Available at http://www.legislation.gov.uk/uksi/2012/652/contents/made *Non-print*

The M6 Motorway (Junction 11) (Slip Roads) (Temporary Prohibition of Traffic) Order 2012 No. 2012/2535. - Enabling power: Road Traffic Regulation Act 1984, s. 14 (1) (a). - Issued: 09.10.2012. Made: 17.09.2012. Coming into force: 24.09.2012. Effect: None. Territorial extent & classification: E. Local. - Available at http://www.legislation.gov.uk/uksi/2012/2535/contents/made *Non-print*

The M6 Motorway (Junction 11) (Temporary Prohibition of Traffic) (No. 2) Order 2012 No. 2012/2415. - Enabling power: Road Traffic Regulation Act 1984, s. 14 (1) (a). - Issued: 24.09.2012. Made: 03.09.2012. Coming into force: 10.09.2012. Effect: None. Territorial extent & classification: E. Local. - Available at http://www.legislation.gov.uk/uksi/2012/2415/contents/made *Non-print*

The M6 Motorway (Junction 11) (Temporary Prohibition of Traffic) Order 2012 No. 2012/570. - Enabling power: Road Traffic Regulation Act 1984, s. 14 (1) (a). - Issued: 02.03.2012. Made: 10.02.2012. Coming into force: 17.02.2012. Effect: None. Territorial extent & classification: E. Local. - Available at http://www.legislation.gov.uk/uksi/2012/570/contents/made *Non-print*

The M6 Motorway (Junction 12) (Temporary Restriction of Traffic) Order 2012 No. 2012/1593. - Enabling power: Road Traffic Regulation Act 1984, s. 14 (1) (a) (7). - Issued: 27.06.2012. Made: 28.05.2012. Coming into force: 04.06.2012. Effect: None. Territorial extent & classification: E. Local. - Available at http://www.legislation.gov.uk/uksi/2012/1593/contents/made *Non-print*

The M6 Motorway (Junction 12), the M54 Motorway (Junctions 2 - 4), the A5 Trunk Road and the A449 Trunk Road (Temporary Prohibition of Traffic) Order 2012 No. 2012/2129. - Enabling power: Road Traffic Regulation Act 1984, s. 14 (1) (b) (7). - Issued: 20.08.2012. Made: 06.08.2012. Coming into force: 13.08.2012. Effect: None. Territorial extent & classification: E. Local. - Available at http://www.legislation.gov.uk/uksi/2012/2129/contents/made *Non-print*

The M6 Motorway (Junction 12 to Junction 11) (Temporary Prohibition of Traffic) Order 2012 No. 2012/172. - Enabling power: Road Traffic Regulation Act 1984, s. 14 (1) (a). - Issued: 30.01.2012. Made: 16.01.2012. Coming into force: 23.01.2012. Effect: None. Territorial extent & classification: E. Local. - Available at http://www.legislation.gov.uk/uksi/2012/172/contents/made *Non-print*

The M6 Motorway (Junction 14) (Temporary Restriction and Prohibition of Traffic) Order 2012 No. 2012/2717. - Enabling power: Road Traffic Regulation Act 1984, s. 14 (1) (a) & S.I. 1982/1163, reg. 16 (2). - Issued: 02.11.2012. Made: 01.10.2012. Coming into force: 08.10.2012. Effect: None. Territorial extent & classification: E. Local. - Available at http://www.legislation.gov.uk/uksi/2012/2717/contents/made *Non-print*

The M6 Motorway (Junction 15) (Slip Roads) (Temporary Prohibition of Traffic) Order 2012 No. 2012/653. - Enabling power: Road Traffic Regulation Act 1984, s. 14 (1) (a). - Issued: 14.03.2012. Made: 20.02.2012. Coming into force: 27.02.2012. Effect: None. Territorial extent & classification: E. Local. - Available at http://www.legislation.gov.uk/uksi/2012/653/contents/made *Non-print*

The M6 Motorway (Junction 15) (Southbound Exit Slip Road) (Temporary Prohibition of Traffic) Order 2012 No. 2012/2171. - Enabling power: Road Traffic Regulation Act 1984, s. 14 (1) (a). - Issued: 24.08.2012. Made: 10.08.2012. Coming into force: 17.08.2012. Effect: None. Territorial extent & classification: E. Local. - Available at http://www.legislation.gov.uk/uksi/2012/2171/contents/made *Non-print*

The M6 Motorway (Junction 16) (Slip Roads) (Temporary Prohibition of Traffic) Order 2012 No. 2012/623. - Enabling power: Road Traffic Regulation Act 1984, s. 14 (1) (a). - Issued: 07.03.2012. Made: 24.02.2012. Coming into force: 02.03.2012. Effect: None. Territorial extent & classification: E. Local. - Available at http://www.legislation.gov.uk/uksi/2012/623/contents/made *Non-print*

The M6 Motorway (Junction 18, Southbound Entry Slip Road) (Temporary Prohibition of Traffic) Order 2012 No. 2012/297. - Enabling power: Road Traffic Regulation Act 1984, s. 14 (1) (a). - Issued: 10.02.2012. Made: 31.01.2012. Coming into force: 05.02.2012. Effect: None. Territorial extent & classification: E. Local. - Available at http://www.legislation.gov.uk/uksi/2012/297/contents/made *Non-print*

The M6 Motorway (Junction 20-22 Southbound Carriageway and Slip Road) (Temporary Prohibition and Restriction of Traffic) Order 2012 No. 2012/2645. - Enabling power: Road Traffic Regulation Act 1984, s. 14 (1) (a) & S.I. 1982/1163, s.16 (2). - Issued: 25.10.2012. Made: 10.10.2012. Coming into force: 28.10.2012. Effect: None. Territorial extent & classification: E. Local. - Available at http://www.legislation.gov.uk/uksi/2012/2645/contents/made *Non-print*

The M6 Motorway (Junction 20 Southbound and Northbound Slip Roads) and the M56 (Junction 9 Westbound Exit Slip Road to the A50) (Temporary Prohibition of Traffic) Order 2012 No. 2012/2870. - Enabling power: Road Traffic Regulation Act 1984, s. 14 (1) (a). - Issued: 19.11.2012. Made: 07.11.2012. Coming into force: 11.11.2012. Effect: None. Territorial extent & classification: E. Local. - Available at http://www.legislation.gov.uk/uksi/2012/2870/contents/made *Non-print*

The M6 Motorway (Junction 20, Southbound Exit Slip Road) (Temporary Prohibition of Traffic) Order 2012 No. 2012/2148. - Enabling power: Road Traffic Regulation Act 1984, s. 14 (1) (a). - Issued: 22.08.2012. Made: 15.08.2012. Coming into force: 03.09.2012. Effect: None. Territorial extent & classification: E. Local. - Available at http://www.legislation.gov.uk/uksi/2012/2148/contents/made *Non-print*

The M6 Motorway (Junction 22, Southbound Entry Slip Road) (Temporary Prohibition of Traffic) Order 2012 No. 2012/2057. - Enabling power: Road Traffic Regulation Act 1984, s. 14 (1) (a). - Issued: 10.08.2012. Made: 25.07.2012. Coming into force: 12.08.2012. Effect: None. Territorial extent & classification: E. Local. - Available at http://www.legislation.gov.uk/uksi/2012/2057/contents/made *Non-print*

The M6 Motorway (Junction 24 Northbound Entry and Southbound Exit Slip Roads) (Temporary Prohibition of Traffic) Order 2012 No. 2012/2254. - Enabling power: Road Traffic Regulation Act 1984, s. 14 (1) (a). - Issued: 05.09.2012. Made: 28.08.2012. Coming into force: 16.09.2012. Effect: None. Territorial extent & classification: E. Local. - Available at http://www.legislation.gov.uk/uksi/2012/2254/contents/made *Non-print*

The M6 Motorway (Junction 25, Northbound Exit and Southbound Entry Slip Roads) (Temporary Prohibition of Traffic) Order 2012 No. 2012/1704. - Enabling power: Road Traffic Regulation Act 1984, s. 14 (1) (a). - Issued: 12.07.2012. Made: 18.06.2012. Coming into force: 08.07.2012. Effect: None. Territorial extent & classification: E. Local. - Available at http://www.legislation.gov.uk/uksi/2012/1704/contents/made *Non-print*

The M6 Motorway (Junction 31a, Northbound Exit Slip Road) (Temporary Prohibition of Traffic) Order 2012 No. 2012/2867. - Enabling power: Road Traffic Regulation Act 1984, s. 14 (1) (a). - Issued: 19.11.2012. Made: 31.10.2012. Coming into force: 05.11.2012. Effect: None. Territorial extent & classification: E. Local. - Available at http://www.legislation.gov.uk/uksi/2012/2867/contents/made *Non-print*

The M6 Motorway (Junction 32 Northbound and Southbound Link Roads to the M55 Westbound) and the M55 (Junctions 1-2 Westbound Carriageway and Slip Roads) (Temporary Restriction of Traffic) Order 2012 No. 2012/2130. - Enabling power: Road Traffic Regulation Act 1984, s. 14 (1) (a). - Issued: 20.08.2012. Made: 09.08.2012. Coming into force: 12.08.2012. Effect: None. Territorial extent & classification: E. Local. - Available at http://www.legislation.gov.uk/uksi/2012/2130/contents/made *Non-print*

The M6 Motorway (Junction 32 Southbound Link Road to the M55 Westbound) (Temporary Prohibition of Traffic) Order 2012 No. 2012/1568. - Enabling power: Road Traffic Regulation Act 1984, s. 14 (1) (a). - Issued: 22.06.2012. Made: 06.06.2012. Coming into force: 13.06.2012. Effect: None. Territorial extent & classification: E. Local. - Available at http://www.legislation.gov.uk/uksi/2012/1568/contents/made *Non-print*

Road traffic: Traffic regulation

The M6 Motorway (Junction 34, Northbound Entry Slip Road) (Temporary Prohibition of Traffic) Order 2012 No. 2012/1570. - Enabling power: Road Traffic Regulation Act 1984, s. 14 (1) (a). - Issued: 22.06.2012. Made: 07.06.2012. Coming into force: 24.06.2012. Effect: None. Territorial extent & classification: E. Local. - Available at http://www.legislation.gov.uk/uksi/2012/1570/contents/made *Non-print*

The M6 Motorway (Junction 37 Northbound Carriageway) (Temporary Prohibition and Restriction of Traffic) Order 2012 No. 2012/650. - Enabling power: Road Traffic Regulation Act 1984, s. 14 (1) (a) (7). - Issued: 14.03.2012. Made: 29.02.2012. Coming into force: 04.03.2012. Effect: None. Territorial extent & classification: E. Local. - Available at http://www.legislation.gov.uk/uksi/2012/650/contents/made *Non-print*

The M6 Motorway (Junction 39, Northbound Exit Slip Road) (Temporary Prohibition of Traffic) Order 2012 No. 2012/2512. - Enabling power: Road Traffic Regulation Act 1984, s. 14 (1) (a). - Issued: 05.10.2012. Made: 28.09.2012. Coming into force: 07.10.2012. Effect: None. Territorial extent & classification: E. Local. - Available at http://www.legislation.gov.uk/uksi/2012/2512/contents/made *Non-print*

The M6 Motorway (Junction 40, Southbound Exit Slip Road) (Temporary Prohibition of Traffic) Order 2012 No. 2012/1529. - Enabling power: Road Traffic Regulation Act 1984, s. 14 (1) (a). - Issued: 19.06.2012. Made: 30.05.2012. Coming into force: 14.06.2012. Effect: None. Territorial extent & classification: E. Local. - Available at http://www.legislation.gov.uk/uksi/2012/1529/contents/made *Non-print*

The M6 Motorway (Junctions 1 to 2) (Temporary Prohibition of Traffic) (No.2) Order 2012 No. 2012/1316. - Enabling power: Road Traffic Regulation Act 1984, s. 14 (1) (a). - Issued: 22.05.2012. Made: 30.04.2012. Coming into force: 07.05.2012. Effect: None. Territorial extent & classification: E. Local. - Available at http://www.legislation.gov.uk/uksi/2012/1316/contents/made *Non-print*

The M6 Motorway (Junctions 1 to 2) (Temporary Prohibition of Traffic) (No. 3) Order 2012 No. 2012/2831. - Enabling power: Road Traffic Regulation Act 1984, s. 14 (1) (a). - Issued: 15.11.2012. Made: 22.10.2012. Coming into force: 29.10.2012. Effect: None. Territorial extent & classification: E. Local. - Available at http://www.legislation.gov.uk/uksi/2012/2831/contents/made *Non-print*

The M6 Motorway (Junctions 1 to 2) (Temporary Prohibition of Traffic) Order 2012 No. 2012/233. - Enabling power: Road Traffic Regulation Act 1984, s. 14 (1) (a). - Issued: 03.02.2012. Made: 23.01.2012. Coming into force: 30.01.2012. Effect: None. Territorial extent & classification: E. Local. - Available at http://www.legislation.gov.uk/uksi/2012/233/contents/made *Non-print*

The M6 Motorway (Junctions 3 to 4) (Temporary Restriction and Prohibition of Traffic) (No.2) Order 2012 No. 2012/2185. - Enabling power: Road Traffic Regulation Act 1984, s. 14 (1) (a) & S.I. 1982/1163, reg. 16 (2). - Issued: 28.08.2012. Made: 20.08.2012. Coming into force: 27.08.2012. Effect: None. Territorial extent & classification: E. Local. - Available at http://www.legislation.gov.uk/uksi/2012/2185/contents/made *Non-print*

The M6 Motorway (Junctions 3 to 4) (Temporary Restriction and Prohibition of Traffic) Order 2012 No. 2012/2038. - Enabling power: Road Traffic Regulation Act 1984, s. 14 (1) (a) (7). - Issued: 08.08.2012. Made: 09.07.2012. Coming into force: 16.07.2012. Effect: None. Territorial extent & classification: E. Local. - Available at http://www.legislation.gov.uk/uksi/2012/2038/contents/made *Non-print*

The M6 Motorway (Junctions 4 to 2) (Temporary Prohibition of Traffic) Order 2012 No. 2012/585. - Enabling power: Road Traffic Regulation Act 1984, s. 14 (1) (a). - Issued: 06.03.2012. Made: 17.02.2012. Coming into force: 24.02.2012. Effect: None. Territorial extent & classification: E. Local. - Available at http://www.legislation.gov.uk/uksi/2012/585/contents/made *Non-print*

The M6 Motorway (Junctions 9 to 11) and M54 Motorway (M6 to Junction 1) (Temporary Restriction and Prohibition of Traffic) Order 2012 No. 2012/369. - Enabling power: Road Traffic Regulation Act 1984, s. 14 (1) (a) (7). - Issued: 17.02.2012. Made: 30.01.2012. Coming into force: 06.02.2012. Effect: None. Territorial extent & classification: E. Local. - Available at http://www.legislation.gov.uk/uksi/2012/369/contents/made *Non-print*

The M6 Motorway (Junctions 10 to 8) (Temporary Prohibition of Traffic) Order 2012 No. 2012/865. - Enabling power: Road Traffic Regulation Act 1984, s. 14 (1) (a). - Issued: 23.03.2012. Made: 12.03.2012. Coming into force: 19.03.2012. Effect: None. Territorial extent & classification: E. Local. - Available at http://www.legislation.gov.uk/uksi/2012/865/contents/made *Non-print*

The M6 Motorway (Junctions 12 to 16) (Temporary Prohibition of Traffic) Order 2012 No. 2012/2544. - Enabling power: Road Traffic Regulation Act 1984, s. 14 (1) (a). - Issued: 10.10.2012. Made: 17.09.2012. Coming into force: 24.09.2012. Effect: None. Territorial extent & classification: E. Local. - Available at http://www.legislation.gov.uk/uksi/2012/2544/contents/made *Non-print*

The M6 Motorway (Junctions 13 to 14) (Temporary Prohibition of Traffic) Order 2012 No. 2012/933. - Enabling power: Road Traffic Regulation Act 1984, s. 14 (1) (a). - Issued: 28.03.2012. Made: 19.03.2012. Coming into force: 26.03.2012. Effect: None. Territorial extent & classification: E. Local. - Available at http://www.legislation.gov.uk/uksi/2012/933/contents/made *Non-print*

The M6 Motorway (Junctions 14 to 13) (Temporary Prohibition of Traffic) (No. 2) Order 2012 No. 2012/2096. - Enabling power: Road Traffic Regulation Act 1984, s. 14 (1) (a). - Issued: 15.08.2012. Made: 23.07.2012. Coming into force: 30.07.2012. Effect: None. Territorial extent & classification: E. Local. - Available at http://www.legislation.gov.uk/uksi/2012/2096/contents/made *Non-print*

The M6 Motorway (Junctions 14 to 13) (Temporary Prohibition of Traffic) Order 2012 No. 2012/374. - Enabling power: Road Traffic Regulation Act 1984, s. 14 (1) (a). - Issued: 17.02.2012. Made: 03.02.2012. Coming into force: 10.02.2012. Effect: None. Territorial extent & classification: E. Local. - Available at http://www.legislation.gov.uk/uksi/2012/374/contents/made *Non-print*

The M6 Motorway (Junctions 14 to 15) (Temporary Prohibition of Traffic) Order 2012 No. 2012/588. - Enabling power: Road Traffic Regulation Act 1984, s. 14 (1) (a). - Issued: 06.03.2012. Made: 17.02.2012. Coming into force: 24.02.2012. Effect: None. Territorial extent & classification: E. Local. - Available at http://www.legislation.gov.uk/uksi/2012/588/contents/made *Non-print*

The M6 Motorway (Junctions 15 to 16) (Temporary Prohibition of Traffic) Order 2012 No. 2012/589. - Enabling power: Road Traffic Regulation Act 1984, s. 14 (1) (a). - Issued: 06.03.2012. Made: 17.02.2012. Coming into force: 24.02.2012. Effect: None. Territorial extent & classification: E. Local. - Available at http://www.legislation.gov.uk/uksi/2012/589/contents/made *Non-print*

The M6 Motorway (Junctions 16-19 Northbound and Southbound Carriageways and Slip Roads) (Temporary Prohibition and Restriction of Traffic) Order 2012 No. 2012/1308. - Enabling power: Road Traffic Regulation Act 1984, s. 14 (1) (a) (7). - Issued: 22.05.2012. Made: 08.05.2012. Coming into force: 13.05.2012. Effect: None. Territorial extent & classification: E. Local. - Available at http://www.legislation.gov.uk/uksi/2012/1308/contents/made *Non-print*

The M6 Motorway (Junctions 16 - 20 Northbound Carriageway and Slip Roads) and Sandbach Services (Temporary Prohibition and Restriction of Traffic) Order 2012 No. 2012/2250. - Enabling power: Road Traffic Regulation Act 1984, s. 14 (1) (a) & S.I. 1982/1163, reg. 16 (2). - Issued: 05.09.2012. Made: 21.08.2012. Coming into force: 02.09.2012. Effect: None. Territorial extent & classification: E. Local. - Available at http://www.legislation.gov.uk/uksi/2012/2250/contents/made *Non-print*

The M6 Motorway (Junctions 17-18 Northbound and Southbound Carriageways) (Temporary Prohibition and Restriction of Traffic) Order 2012 No. 2012/2246. - Enabling power: Road Traffic Regulation Act 1984, s. 14 (1) (a) & S.I. 1982/1163, reg. 16 (2). - Issued: 04.09.2012. Made: 21.08.2012. Coming into force: 05.09.2012. Effect: None. Territorial extent & classification: E. Local. - Available at http://www.legislation.gov.uk/uksi/2012/2246/contents/made *Non-print*

The M6 Motorway (Junctions 18-19 Northbound and Southbound Carriageways) (Temporary Prohibition and Restriction of Traffic) Order 2012 No. 2012/1163. - Enabling power: Road Traffic Regulation Act 1984, s. 14 (1) (a) (7). - Issued: 01.05.2012. Made: 17.04.2012. Coming into force: 25.04.2012. Effect: None. Territorial extent & classification: E. Local. - Available at http://www.legislation.gov.uk/uksi/2012/1163/contents/made *Non-print*

The M6 Motorway (Junctions 26-28 Northbound and Southbound Carriageways and Slip Roads) (Temporary Prohibition and Restriction of Traffic) Order 2012 No. 2012/1162. - Enabling power: Road Traffic Regulation Act 1984, s. 14 (1) (a) (7). - Issued: 01.05.2012. Made: 16.04.2012. Coming into force: 30.04.2012. Effect: None. Territorial extent & classification: E. Local. - Available at http://www.legislation.gov.uk/uksi/2012/1162/contents/made *Non-print*

The M6 Motorway (Junctions 26-30 Northbound and Southbound) and the M61 Motorway (Junction 9 Northbound and Southbound) (Temporary Prohibition and Restriction of Traffic and Temporary Suspension of Statutory Provisions) Order 2012 No. 2012/1962. - Enabling power: Road Traffic Regulation Act 1984, s. 14 (1) (a) (7). - Issued: 30.07.2012. Made: 17.07.2012. Coming into force: 24.07.2012. Effect: None. Territorial extent & classification: E. Local. - Available at http://www.legislation.gov.uk/uksi/2012/1962/contents/made *Non-print*

The M6 Motorway (Junctions 28-29 Northbound and Southbound Carriageways and Slip Roads) and (Charnock Richard Services Northbound Entry and Exit Slip Roads) (Temporary Prohibition and Restriction of Traffic) Order 2012 No. 2012/567. - Enabling power: Road Traffic Regulation Act 1984, s. 14 (1) (a) (7). - Issued: 02.03.2012. Made: 22.02.2012. Coming into force: 26.02.2012. Effect: None. Territorial extent & classification: E. Local. - Available at http://www.legislation.gov.uk/uksi/2012/567/contents/made *Non-print*

The M6 Motorway (Junctions 29-31) and the M61 Motorway (Junction 9) Northbound Carriageways (Temporary Restriction of Traffic) Order 2012 No. 2012/1788. - Enabling power: Road Traffic Regulation Act 1984, s. 14 (1) (a). - Issued: 18.07.2012. Made: 27.06.2012. Coming into force: 12.07.2012. Effect: None. Territorial extent & classification: E. Local. - Available at http://www.legislation.gov.uk/uksi/2012/1788/contents/made *Non-print*

Road traffic: Traffic regulation

The M6 Motorway (Junctions 29, Southbound Entry Slip Road) (Temporary Prohibition of Traffic) Order 2012 No. 2012/2251. - Enabling power: Road Traffic Regulation Act 1984, s. 14 (1) (a). - Issued: 05.09.2012. Made: 22.08.2012. Coming into force: 09.09.2012. Effect: None. Territorial extent & classification: E. Local. - Available at http://www.legislation.gov.uk/uksi/2012/2251/contents/made *Non-print*

The M6 Motorway (Junctions 33-34 Southbound Carriageway) (Temporary Restriction of Traffic) Order 2012 No. 2012/554. - Enabling power: Road Traffic Regulation Act 1984, s. 14 (1) (a) (7). - Issued: 01.03.2012. Made: 15.02.2012. Coming into force: 02.03.2012. Effect: None. Territorial extent & classification: E. Local. - Available at http://www.legislation.gov.uk/uksi/2012/554/contents/made *Non-print*

The M6 Motorway (Junctions 34 - 35 Northbound and Southbound Carriageways) (Temporary Restriction of Traffic) Order 2012 No. 2012/1873. - Enabling power: Road Traffic Regulation Act 1984, s. 14 (1) (a). - Issued: 23.07.2012. Made: 03.07.2012. Coming into force: 22.07.2012. Effect: None. Territorial extent & classification: E. Local. - Available at http://www.legislation.gov.uk/uksi/2012/1873/contents/made *Non-print*

The M6 Motorway (Junctions 37-38 Northbound Carriageway and Junction 38 Northbound Entry Slip Road) (Temporary Restriction of Traffic) Order 2012 No. 2012/1572. - Enabling power: Road Traffic Regulation Act 1984, s. 14 (1) (a). - Issued: 22.06.2012. Made: 06.06.2012. Coming into force: 24.06.2012. Effect: None. Territorial extent & classification: E. Local. - Available at http://www.legislation.gov.uk/uksi/2012/1572/contents/made *Non-print*

The M6 Motorway (Junctions 37-38 Northbound Carriageway) (Temporary Restriction of Traffic) Order 2012 No. 2012/2345. - Enabling power: Road Traffic Regulation Act 1984, s. 14 (1) (a). - Issued: 14.09.2012. Made: 05.09.2012. Coming into force: 23.09.2012. Effect: None. Territorial extent & classification: E. Local. - Available at http://www.legislation.gov.uk/uksi/2012/2345/contents/made *Non-print*

The M6 Motorway (Junctions 37-39 Northbound and Southbound Carriageways and Junction 38 Southbound Entry Slip Road) (Temporary Prohibition and Restriction of Traffic) Order 2012 No. 2012/2256. - Enabling power: Road Traffic Regulation Act 1984, s. 14 (1) (a). - Issued: 05.09.2012. Made: 29.08.2012. Coming into force: 16.09.2012. Effect: None. Territorial extent & classification: E. Local. - Available at http://www.legislation.gov.uk/uksi/2012/2256/contents/made *Non-print*

The M6 Motorway (Junctions 38-40 Northbound and Southbound Carriageways) and Junction 39 Northbound Entry Slip Road (Temporary Restriction of Traffic) Order 2012 No. 2012/2513. - Enabling power: Road Traffic Regulation Act 1984, s. 14 (1) (a). - Issued: 05.10.2012. Made: 28.09.2012. Coming into force: 14.10.2012. Effect: None. Territorial extent & classification: E. Local. - Available at http://www.legislation.gov.uk/uksi/2012/2513/contents/made *Non-print*

The M6 Motorway (Junctions 39-40 Northbound and Southbound Carriageways) (Temporary Restriction of Traffic) Order 2012 No. 2012/2429. - Enabling power: Road Traffic Regulation Act 1984, s. 14 (1) (a). - Issued: 25.09.2012. Made: 13.09.2012. Coming into force: 30.09.2012. Effect: None. Territorial extent & classification: E. Local. - Available at http://www.legislation.gov.uk/uksi/2012/2429/contents/made *Non-print*

The M6 Motorway (Junctions 39-41 Northbound and Southbound Carriageways) (Temporary Restriction of Traffic) Order 2012 No. 2012/70. - Enabling power: Road Traffic Regulation Act 1984, s. 14 (1) (a). - Issued: 17.01.2012. Made: 04.01.2012. Coming into force: 20.01.2012. Effect: None. Territorial extent & classification: E. Local. - Available at http://www.legislation.gov.uk/uksi/2012/70/contents/made *Non-print*

The M6 Motorway (Junctions 40 - 42 Northbound and Southbound Carriageways) (Temporary Restriction of Traffic) Order 2012 No. 2012/184. - Enabling power: Road Traffic Regulation Act 1984, s. 14 (1) (a). - Issued: 31.01.2012. Made: 19.01.2012. Coming into force: 03.02.2012. Effect: None. Territorial extent & classification: E. Local. - Available at http://www.legislation.gov.uk/uksi/2012/184/contents/made *Non-print*

The M6 Motorway (Junctions 41-42 Northbound and Southbound Carriageways) (Temporary Restriction of Traffic) Order 2012 No. 2012/2997. - Enabling power: Road Traffic Regulation Act 1984, s. 14 (1) (a). - Issued: 05.12.2012. Made: 22.11.2012. Coming into force: 08.12.2012. Effect: None. Territorial extent & classification: E. Local. - Available at http://www.legislation.gov.uk/uksi/2012/2997/contents/made *Non-print*

The M6 Motorway (Junctions 41-43 Northbound Carriageway and Slip Roads) (Temporary Prohibition and Restriction of Traffic) Order 2012 No. 2012/1948. - Enabling power: Road Traffic Regulation Act 1984, s. 14 (1) (a). - Issued: 30.07.2012. Made: 12.07.2012. Coming into force: 29.07.2012. Effect: None. Territorial extent & classification: E. Local. - Available at http://www.legislation.gov.uk/uksi/2012/1948/contents/made *Non-print*

Road traffic: Traffic regulation

The M6 Motorway (Junctions 44-42 Southbound Carriageway and Junction 42 Southbound Entry Slip Road) (Temporary Prohibition and Restriction of Traffic) Order 2012 No. 2012/2039. - Enabling power: Road Traffic Regulation Act 1984, s. 14 (1) (a). - Issued: 08.08.2012. Made: 19.07.2012. Coming into force: 05.08.2012. Effect: None. Territorial extent & classification: E. Local. - Available at http://www.legislation.gov.uk/uksi/2012/2039/contents/made *Non-print*

The M6 Motorway (Junctions 44 - 45 Northbound and Southbound Carriageways) (Temporary Prohibition and Restriction of Traffic) Order 2012 No. 2012/2019. - Enabling power: Road Traffic Regulation Act 1984, s. 14 (1) (a). - Issued: 06.08.2012. Made: 19.07.2012. Coming into force: 22.07.2012. Effect: None. Territorial extent & classification: E. Local. - Available at http://www.legislation.gov.uk/uksi/2012/2019/contents/made *Non-print*

The M6 Motorway (Junctions 44-45 Northbound and Southbound Carriageways) (Temporary Restriction of Traffic) Order 2012 No. 2012/2149. - Enabling power: Road Traffic Regulation Act 1984, s. 14 (1) (a). - Issued: 22.08.2012. Made: 16.08.2012. Coming into force: 01.09.2012. Effect: None. Territorial extent & classification: E. Local. - Available at http://www.legislation.gov.uk/uksi/2012/2149/contents/made *Non-print*

The M6 Motorway (Junction with M1 Motorway, Catthorpe, Leicestershire) (Temporary 50 Miles Per Hour Speed Restriction) Order 2012 No. 2012/1053. - Enabling power: Road Traffic Regulation Act 1984, s. 14 (1) (b). - Issued: 13.04.2012. Made: 27.03.2012. Coming into force: 03.04.2012. Effect: None. Territorial extent & classification: E. Local. - Available at http://www.legislation.gov.uk/uksi/2012/1053/contents/made *Non-print*

The M6 Motorway (M1 Junction 19 to M6 Junction 1) (Temporary Restriction and Prohibition of Traffic) Order 2012 No. 2012/3310. - Enabling power: Road Traffic Regulation Act 1984, s. 14 (1) (a) & S.I. 1982/1163, reg. 16 (2). - Issued: 17.01.2013. Made: 28.12.2012. Coming into force: 04.01.2013. Effect: None. Territorial extent & classification: E. Local. - Available at http://www.legislation.gov.uk/uksi/2012/3310/contents/made *Non-print*

The M6 Motorway (M6 Junction 9 to Junction 8) (Temporary Restriction and Prohibition of Traffic) Order 2012 No. 2012/1321. - Enabling power: Road Traffic Regulation Act 1984, s. 14 (1) (a). - Issued: 23.05.2012. Made: 30.04.2012. Coming into force: 07.05.2012. Effect: None. Territorial extent & classification: E. Local. - Available at http://www.legislation.gov.uk/uksi/2012/1321/contents/made *Non-print*

The M6 Motorway, M6 Toll, M69 Motorway and M42 Motorway (M6 Junction 2 - Junction 4) (Temporary Prohibition of Traffic) Order 2012 No. 2012/2830. - Enabling power: Road Traffic Regulation Act 1984, s. 14 (1) (a). - Issued: 15.11.2012. Made: 22.10.2012. Coming into force: 29.10.2012. Effect: None. Territorial extent & classification: E. Local. - Available at http://www.legislation.gov.uk/uksi/2012/2830/contents/made *Non-print*

The M6 Motorway (North of Junction 15) (Temporary 50 Miles Per Hour Speed Restriction) Order 2012 No. 2012/2969. - Enabling power: Road Traffic Regulation Act 1984, s. 14 (1) (a). - Issued: 30.11.2012. Made: 12.11.2012. Coming into force: 19.11.2012. Effect: None. Territorial extent & classification: E. Local. - Available at http://www.legislation.gov.uk/uksi/2012/2969/contents/made *Non-print*

The M6 Toll Motorway (Junctions T3 and T4) (Temporary Prohibition of Traffic) Order 2012 No. 2012/2417. - Enabling power: Road Traffic Regulation Act 1984, s. 14 (1) (a) & S.I. 1982/1163, reg. 16 (2). - Issued: 24.09.2012. Made: 05.09.2012. Coming into force: 12.09.2012. Effect: None. Territorial extent & classification: E. Local. - Available at http://www.legislation.gov.uk/uksi/2012/2417/contents/made *Non-print*

The M6 Toll Motorway (Junctions T8 to T6) (Temporary Prohibition of Traffic) Order 2012 No. 2012/1778. - Enabling power: Road Traffic Regulation Act 1984, s. 14 (1) (a) (7). - Issued: 18.07.2012. Made: 19.06.2012. Coming into force: 26.06.2012. Effect: None. Territorial extent & classification: E. Local. - Available at http://www.legislation.gov.uk/uksi/2012/1778/contents/made *Non-print*

The M6 Toll Motorway (M6 Junction 11a - M6 Toll Junction 6) (Temporary Prohibition of Traffic) Order 2012 No. 2012/2010. - Enabling power: Road Traffic Regulation Act 1984, s. 14 (1) (a). - Issued: 02.08.2012. Made: 18.07.2012. Coming into force: 25.07.2012. Effect: None. Territorial extent & classification: E. Local. - Available at http://www.legislation.gov.uk/uksi/2012/2010/contents/made *Non-print*

The M6 Toll (Slip Roads) (Temporary Prohibition of Traffic) Order 2012 No. 2012/1437. - Enabling power: Road Traffic Regulation Act 1984, s. 14 (1) (a) (7). - Issued: 06.06.2012. Made: 14.05.2012. Coming into force: 21.05.2012. Effect: None. Territorial extent & classification: E. Local. - Available at http://www.legislation.gov.uk/uksi/2012/1437/contents/made *Non-print*

The M11 Motorway and the M25 Motorway (M11 Junction 4 - Theydon Interchange) (Temporary Prohibition of Traffic) Order 2012 No. 2012/435. - Enabling power: Road Traffic Regulation Act 1984, s. 14 (1) (a). - Issued: 22.02.2012. Made: 13.02.2012. Coming into force: 03.03.2012. Effect: None. Territorial extent & classification: E. Local. - Available at http://www.legislation.gov.uk/uksi/2012/435/contents/made *Non-print*

Road traffic: Traffic regulation

The M11 Motorway (Junction 6) and M25 Motorway (Junction 27) (Temporary Restriction and Prohibition of Traffic) Order 2012 No. 2012/211. - Enabling power: Road Traffic Regulation Act 1984, s. 14 (1) (a) (7). - Issued: 03.02.2012. Made: 23.01.2012. Coming into force: 30.01.2012. Effect: None. Territorial extent & classification: E. Local. - Available at http://www.legislation.gov.uk/uksi/2012/211/contents/made *Non-print*

The M11 Motorway (Junction 6, Southbound Link Road) (Temporary Prohibition of Traffic) Order 2012 No. 2012/90. - Enabling power: Road Traffic Regulation Act 1984, s. 14 (1) (a). - Issued: 18.01.2012. Made: 09.01.2012. Coming into force: 28.01.2012. Effect: None. Territorial extent & classification: E. Local. - Available at http://www.legislation.gov.uk/uksi/2012/90/contents/made *Non-print*

The M11 Motorway (Junction 7, Essex) (Temporary Restriction and Prohibition of Traffic) Order 2012 No. 2012/214. - Enabling power: Road Traffic Regulation Act 1984, s. 14 (1) (a). - Issued: 03.02.2012. Made: 23.01.2012. Coming into force: 30.01.2012. Effect: None. Territorial extent & classification: E. Local. - Available at http://www.legislation.gov.uk/uksi/2012/214/contents/made *Non-print*

The M11 Motorway (Junction 7 to Junction 8, Essex) (Temporary Restriction and Prohibition of Traffic) Order 2012 No. 2012/2618. - Enabling power: Road Traffic Regulation Act 1984, s. 14 (1) (a) & S.I. 1982/1163, s.16 (2). - Issued: 22.10.2012. Made: 08.10.2012. Coming into force: 15.10.2012. Effect: None. Territorial extent & classification: E. Local. - Available at http://www.legislation.gov.uk/uksi/2012/2618/contents/made *Non-print*

The M11 Motorway (Junction 8) (Temporary Restriction and Prohibition of Traffic) Order 2012 No. 2012/2674. - Enabling power: Road Traffic Regulation Act 1984, s. 14 (1) (a). - Issued: 29.10.2012. Made: 15.10.2012. Coming into force: 22.10.2012. Effect: None. Territorial extent & classification: E. Local. - Available at http://www.legislation.gov.uk/uksi/2012/2674/contents/made *Non-print*

The M11 Motorway (Junction 8 to Junction 9, Essex) (Temporary 50 Miles Per Hour Speed Restriction) Order 2012 No. 2012/2329. - Enabling power: Road Traffic Regulation Act 1984, s. 14 (1) (a). - Issued: 14.09.2012. Made: 03.09.2012. Coming into force: 10.09.2012. Effect: None. Territorial extent & classification: E. Local. - Available at http://www.legislation.gov.uk/uksi/2012/2329/contents/made *Non-print*

The M11 Motorway (Junction 11, Cambridgeshire) Slip Roads (Temporary Restriction and Prohibition of Traffic) Order 2012 No. 2012/2174. - Enabling power: Road Traffic Regulation Act 1984, s. 14 (1) (a). - Issued: 28.08.2012. Made: 20.08.2012. Coming into force: 27.08.2012. Effect: None. Territorial extent & classification: E. Local. - Available at http://www.legislation.gov.uk/uksi/2012/2174/contents/made *Non-print*

The M11 Motorway (Junction 12, Cambridgeshire) Slip Roads (Temporary Prohibition of Traffic) Order 2012 No. 2012/1468. - Enabling power: Road Traffic Regulation Act 1984, s. 14 (1) (a). - Issued: 12.06.2012. Made: 28.05.2012. Coming into force: 04.06.2012. Effect: None. Territorial extent & classification: E. Local. - Available at http://www.legislation.gov.uk/uksi/2012/1468/contents/made *Non-print*

The M11 Motorway (Junction 12) Southbound Entry Slip Road (Temporary Prohibition of Traffic) Order 2012 No. 2012/497. - Enabling power: Road Traffic Regulation Act 1984, s. 14 (1) (a). - Issued: 01.03.2012. Made: 20.02.2012. Coming into force: 27.02.2012. Effect: None. Territorial extent & classification: E. Local. - Available at http://www.legislation.gov.uk/uksi/2012/497/contents/made *Non-print*

The M11 Motorway (Junction 13) Northbound Exit Slip Road (Temporary Prohibition of Traffic) Order 2012 No. 2012/1620. - Enabling power: Road Traffic Regulation Act 1984, s. 14 (1) (a). - Issued: 28.06.2012. Made: 18.06.2012. Coming into force: 25.06.2012. Effect: None. Territorial extent & classification: E. Local. - Available at http://www.legislation.gov.uk/uksi/2012/1620/contents/made *Non-print*

The M11 Motorway (Junction 14, Northbound) and the A14 Trunk Road (Junction 31, Westbound) (Girton Interchange, Cambridgeshire) (Temporary Prohibition of Traffic) Order 2012 No. 2012/2315. - Enabling power: Road Traffic Regulation Act 1984, s. 14 (1) (a). - Issued: 12.09.2012. Made: 03.09.2012. Coming into force: 10.09.2012. Effect: None. Territorial extent & classification: E. Local. - Available at http://www.legislation.gov.uk/uksi/2012/2315/contents/made *Non-print*

The M11 Motorway (Junctions 4 - 6) (Temporary Prohibition of Traffic) Order 2012 No. 2012/2026. - Enabling power: Road Traffic Regulation Act 1984, s. 14 (1) (a). - Issued: 06.08.2012. Made: 23.07.2012. Coming into force: 14.08.2012. Effect: None. Territorial extent & classification: E. Local. - Available at http://www.legislation.gov.uk/uksi/2012/2026/contents/made *Non-print*

The M11 Motorway (Junctions 8 and 8A) and the A120 Trunk Road (Priory Wood Roundabout to Dunmow) (Stansted, Essex) (Temporary Restriction and Prohibition of Traffic) Order 2012 No. 2012/507. - Enabling power: Road Traffic Regulation Act 1984, s. 14 (1) (a). - Issued: 01.03.2012. Made: 20.02.2012. Coming into force: 27.02.2012. Effect: None. Territorial extent & classification: E. Local. - Available at http://www.legislation.gov.uk/uksi/2012/507/contents/made *Non-print*

The M18 Motorway (Junction 1) (Temporary Prohibition of Traffic) Order 2012 No. 2012/86. - Enabling power: Road Traffic Regulation Act 1984, s. 14 (1) (a). - Issued: 18.01.2012. Made: 06.01.2012. Coming into force: 14.01.2012. Effect: None. Territorial extent & classification: E. Local. - Available at http://www.legislation.gov.uk/uksi/2012/86/contents/made *Non-print*

The M18 Motorway (Junction 1 to Junction 2) (Temporary Restriction and Prohibition of Traffic) Order 2012 No. 2012/566. - Enabling power: Road Traffic Regulation Act 1984, s. 14 (1) (a) (7). - Issued: 01.03.2012. Made: 23.02.2012. Coming into force: 26.02.2012. Effect: None. Territorial extent & classification: E. Local. - Available at http://www.legislation.gov.uk/uksi/2012/566/contents/made *Non-print*

The M18 Motorway (Junction 2, Wadworth) (Temporary Restriction and Prohibition of Traffic) Order 2012 No. 2012/2643. - Enabling power: Road Traffic Regulation Act 1984, s. 14 (1) (a) & S.I. 1982/1163, s.16 (2). - Issued: 23.10.2012. Made: 11.10.2012. Coming into force: 20.10.2012. Effect: None. Territorial extent & classification: E. Local. - Available at http://www.legislation.gov.uk/uksi/2012/2643/contents/made *Non-print*

The M18 Motorway (Junction 3, St. Catherines) (Temporary Prohibition of Traffic) (No. 2) Order 2012 No. 2012/2957. - Enabling power: Road Traffic Regulation Act 1984, s. 14 (1) (a). - Issued: 30.11.2012. Made: 15.11.2012. Coming into force: 26.11.2012. Effect: None. Territorial extent & classification: E. Local. - Available at http://www.legislation.gov.uk/uksi/2012/2957/contents/made *Non-print*

The M18 Motorway (Junction 3, St. Catherines) (Temporary Prohibition of Traffic) Order 2012 No. 2012/2878. - Enabling power: Road Traffic Regulation Act 1984, s. 14 (1) (a). - Issued: 19.11.2012. Made: 08.11.2012. Coming into force: 15.11.2012. Effect: None. Territorial extent & classification: E. Local. - Available at http://www.legislation.gov.uk/uksi/2012/2878/contents/made *Non-print*

The M18 Motorway (Junction 3 to Junction 2) (Temporary Restriction and Prohibition of Traffic) Order 2012 No. 2012/553. - Enabling power: Road Traffic Regulation Act 1984, s. 14 (1) (a) (7). - Issued: 01.03.2012. Made: 22.02.2012. Coming into force: 01.03.2012. Effect: None. Territorial extent & classification: E. Local. - Available at http://www.legislation.gov.uk/uksi/2012/553/contents/made *Non-print*

The M18 Motorway (Junction 3 to Junction 4) (Temporary Prohibition of Traffic) (No. 2) Order 2012 No. 2012/2762. - Enabling power: Road Traffic Regulation Act 1984, s. 14 (1) (a). - Issued: 07.11.2012. Made: 18.10.2012. Coming into force: 26.10.2012. Effect: None. Territorial extent & classification: E. Local. - Available at http://www.legislation.gov.uk/uksi/2012/2762/contents/made *Non-print*

The M18 Motorway (Junction 3 to Junction 4) (Temporary Prohibition of Traffic) Order 2012 No. 2012/2093. - Enabling power: Road Traffic Regulation Act 1984, s. 14 (1) (a). - Issued: 15.08.2012. Made: 02.08.2012. Coming into force: 10.08.2012. Effect: None. Territorial extent & classification: E. Local. - Available at http://www.legislation.gov.uk/uksi/2012/2093/contents/made *Non-print*

The M18 Motorway (Junction 4, Armthorpe) (Temporary Prohibition of Traffic) Order 2012 No. 2012/2763. - Enabling power: Road Traffic Regulation Act 1984, s. 14 (1) (a). - Issued: 07.11.2012. Made: 18.10.2012. Coming into force: 30.10.2012. Effect: None. Territorial extent & classification: E. Local. - Available at http://www.legislation.gov.uk/uksi/2012/2763/contents/made *Non-print*

The M18 Motorway (Junction 4 to Junction 6) (Temporary Restriction and Prohibition of Traffic) Order 2012 No. 2012/2815. - Enabling power: Road Traffic Regulation Act 1984, s. 14 (1) (a) & S.I. 1982/1163, reg. 16 (2). - Issued: 13.11.2012. Made: 25.10.2012. Coming into force: 04.11.2012. Effect: None. Territorial extent & classification: E. Local. - Available at http://www.legislation.gov.uk/uksi/2012/2815/contents/made *Non-print*

The M18 Motorway (Junction 5) (Temporary Prohibition of Traffic) Order 2012 No. 2012/3281. - Enabling power: Road Traffic Regulation Act 1984, s. 14 (1) (a). - Issued: 15.01.2013. Made: 27.12.2012. Coming into force: 06.01.2013. Effect: None. Territorial extent & classification: E. Local. - Available at http://www.legislation.gov.uk/uksi/2012/3281/contents/made *Non-print*

The M18 Motorway (Junction 6) (Temporary Restriction and Prohibition of Traffic) Order 2012 No. 2012/851. - Enabling power: Road Traffic Regulation Act 1984, s. 14 (1) (a) (7). - Issued: 20.03.2012. Made: 14.03.2012. Coming into force: 18.03.2012. Effect: None. Territorial extent & classification: E. Local. - Available at http://www.legislation.gov.uk/uksi/2012/851/contents/made *Non-print*

Road traffic: Traffic regulation

The M18 Motorway (Junction 6, Thorne) (Temporary 50 Miles Per Hour Speed Restriction) Order 2012 No. 2012/457. - Enabling power: Road Traffic Regulation Act 1984, s. 14 (1) (a). - Issued: 24.02.2012. Made: 16.02.2012. Coming into force: 26.02.2012. Effect: None. Territorial extent & classification: E. Local. - Available at http://www.legislation.gov.uk/uksi/2012/457/contents/made *Non-print*

The M20 Motorway and the A20 Trunk Road (Greater London Boundary - M20 Junction 3) (Temporary Prohibition of Traffic) Order 2012 No. 2012/415. - Enabling power: Road Traffic Regulation Act 1984, s. 14 (1) (a). - Issued: 21.02.2012. Made: 13.02.2012. Coming into force: 03.03.2012. Effect: None. Territorial extent & classification: E. Local. - Available at http://www.legislation.gov.uk/uksi/2012/415/contents/made *Non-print*

The M20 Motorway and the A20 Trunk Road (Junctions 9 - 13, Slip Roads) (Temporary Prohibition of Traffic) Order 2012 No. 2012/1042. - Enabling power: Road Traffic Regulation Act 1984, s. 14 (1) (a). - Issued: 12.04.2012. Made: 26.03.2012. Coming into force: 16.04.2012. Effect: None. Territorial extent & classification: E. Local. - Available at http://www.legislation.gov.uk/uksi/2012/1042/contents/made *Non-print*

The M20 Motorway and the A20 Trunk Road (Junctions 11a - 13, Slip Roads) (Temporary Restriction and Prohibition of Traffic) Order 2012 No. 2012/719. - Enabling power: Road Traffic Regulation Act 1984, s. 14 (1) (a) (7). - Issued: 19.03.2012. Made: 05.03.2012. Coming into force: 24.03.2012. Effect: None. Territorial extent & classification: E. Local. - Available at http://www.legislation.gov.uk/uksi/2012/719/contents/made *Non-print*

The M20 Motorway and the A20 Trunk Road (M20 Junction 1) (Temporary Prohibition of Traffic) Order 2012 No. 2012/1605. - Enabling power: Road Traffic Regulation Act 1984, s. 14 (1) (a). - Issued: 27.06.2012. Made: 14.06.2012. Coming into force: 25.06.2012. Effect: None. Territorial extent & classification: E. Local. - Available at http://www.legislation.gov.uk/uksi/2012/1605/contents/made *Non-print*

The M20 Motorway and the A20 Trunk Road (Roundhill Tunnels) (Temporary Restriction and Prohibition of Traffic) Order 2012 No. 2012/2925. - Enabling power: Road Traffic Regulation Act 1984, s. 14 (1) (a). - Issued: 26.11.2012. Made: 12.11.2012. Coming into force: 07.12.2012. Effect: None. Territorial extent & classification: E. Local. - Available at http://www.legislation.gov.uk/uksi/2012/2925/contents/made *Non-print*

The M20 Motorway and the A20 Trunk Road (Southeast of Junction 10 - Capel-le-Ferne) (Temporary Restriction and Prohibition of Traffic) Order 2012 No. 2012/2141. - Enabling power: Road Traffic Regulation Act 1984, s. 14 (1) (a) (b). - Issued: 21.08.2012. Made: 13.08.2012. Coming into force: 01.09.2012. Effect: None. Territorial extent & classification: E. Local. - Available at http://www.legislation.gov.uk/uksi/2012/2141/contents/made *Non-print*

The M20 Motorway (Junction 2, Slip Roads) (Temporary Prohibition of Traffic) Order 2012 No. 2012/1859. - Enabling power: Road Traffic Regulation Act 1984, s. 14 (1) (a). - Issued: 20.07.2012. Made: 09.07.2012. Coming into force: 02.08.2012. Effect: None. Territorial extent & classification: E. Local. - Available at http://www.legislation.gov.uk/uksi/2012/1859/contents/made *Non-print*

The M20 Motorway (Junction 9, Londonbound Carriageway) (Temporary Restriction and Prohibition of Traffic) Order 2012 No. 2012/1056. - Enabling power: Road Traffic Regulation Act 1984, s. 14 (1) (a). - Issued: 13.04.2012. Made: 02.04.2012. Coming into force: 21.04.2012. Effect: None. Territorial extent & classification: E. Local. - Available at http://www.legislation.gov.uk/uksi/2012/1056/contents/made *Non-print*

The M20 Motorway (Junctions 1 - 3) (Temporary Restriction and Prohibition of Traffic) Order 2012 No. 2012/2077. - Enabling power: Road Traffic Regulation Act 1984, s. 14 (1) (a). - Issued: 13.08.2012. Made: 30.07.2012. Coming into force: 18.08.2012. Effect: None. Territorial extent & classification: E. Local. - Available at http://www.legislation.gov.uk/uksi/2012/2077/contents/made *Non-print*

The M20 Motorway (Junctions 4 - 5, Coastbound) (Temporary Restriction of Traffic) Order 2012 No. 2012/1040. - Enabling power: Road Traffic Regulation Act 1984, s. 14 (1) (a) (7). - Issued: 12.04.2012. Made: 26.03.2012. Coming into force: 14.04.2012. Effect: None. Territorial extent & classification: E. Local. - Available at http://www.legislation.gov.uk/uksi/2012/1040/contents/made *Non-print*

The M20 Motorway (Junctions 4 - 6) (Temporary Restriction and Prohibition of Traffic) Order 2012 No. 2012/2176. - Enabling power: Road Traffic Regulation Act 1984, s. 14 (1) (a). - Issued: 28.08.2012. Made: 20.08.2012. Coming into force: 12.09.2012. Effect: None. Territorial extent & classification: E. Local. - Available at http://www.legislation.gov.uk/uksi/2012/2176/contents/made *Non-print*

The M20 Motorway (Junctions 4 & 7) (Temporary Prohibition of Traffic) Order 2012 No. 2012/478. - Enabling power: Road Traffic Regulation Act 1984, s. 14 (1) (a). - Issued: 29.02.2012. Made: 20.02.2012. Coming into force: 10.03.2012. Effect: None. Territorial extent & classification: E. Local. - Available at http://www.legislation.gov.uk/uksi/2012/478/contents/made *Non-print*

Road traffic: Traffic regulation

The M20 Motorway (Junctions 4 - 8) (Temporary Prohibition of Traffic) Order 2012 No. 2012/713. - Enabling power: Road Traffic Regulation Act 1984, s. 14 (1) (a). - Issued: 19.03.2012. Made: 05.03.2012. Coming into force: 02.04.2012. Effect: None. Territorial extent & classification: E. Local. - Available at http://www.legislation.gov.uk/uksi/2012/713/contents/made *Non-print*

The M20 Motorway (Junctions 5 - 7) (Temporary Restriction and Prohibition of Traffic) Order 2012 No. 2012/2241. - Enabling power: Road Traffic Regulation Act 1984, s. 14 (1) (a). - Issued: 04.09.2012. Made: 28.08.2012. Coming into force: 15.09.2012. Effect: None. Territorial extent & classification: E. Local. - Available at http://www.legislation.gov.uk/uksi/2012/2241/contents/made *Non-print*

The M20 Motorway (Junctions 6 - 7) (Temporary Restriction and Prohibition of Traffic) Order 2012 No. 2012/2662. - Enabling power: Road Traffic Regulation Act 1984, s. 14 (1) (a). - Issued: 26.10.2012. Made: 15.10.2012. Coming into force: 03.11.2012. Effect: None. Territorial extent & classification: E. Local. - Available at http://www.legislation.gov.uk/uksi/2012/2662/contents/made *Non-print*

The M20 Motorway (Junctions 8 - 7, Londonbound) (Temporary Restriction and Prohibition of Traffic) Order 2012 No. 2012/902. - Enabling power: Road Traffic Regulation Act 1984, s. 14 (1) (a). - Issued: 26.03.2012. Made: 19.03.2012. Coming into force: 07.04.2012. Effect: None. Territorial extent & classification: E. Local. - Available at http://www.legislation.gov.uk/uksi/2012/902/contents/made *Non-print*

The M20 Motorway (Junctions 8 - 7) (Temporary Restriction and Prohibition of Traffic) Order 2012 No. 2012/2520. - Enabling power: Road Traffic Regulation Act 1984, s. 14 (1) (a). - Issued: 08.10.2012. Made: 01.10.2012. Coming into force: 20.10.2012. Effect: None. Territorial extent & classification: E. Local. - Available at http://www.legislation.gov.uk/uksi/2012/2520/contents/made *Non-print*

The M20 Motorway (Junctions 8 - 9) (Temporary 50 Miles Per Hour Speed Restriction) Order 2012 No. 2012/3213. - Enabling power: Road Traffic Regulation Act 1984, s. 14 (1) (a). - Issued: 04.01.2013. Made: 10.12.2012. Coming into force: 05.01.2013. Effect: None. Territorial extent & classification: E. Local. - Available at http://www.legislation.gov.uk/uksi/2012/3213/contents/made *Non-print*

The M20 Motorway (Junctions 8 - 10) (Temporary Restriction and Prohibition of Traffic) Order 2012 No. 2012/1413. - Enabling power: Road Traffic Regulation Act 1984, s. 14 (1) (a). - Issued: 01.06.2012. Made: 21.05.2012. Coming into force: 09.06.2012. Effect: None. Territorial extent & classification: E. Local. - Available at http://www.legislation.gov.uk/uksi/2012/1413/contents/made *Non-print*

The M20 Motorway (Junctions 9 - 10) (Temporary Restriction and Prohibition of Traffic) (No. 2) Order 2012 No. 2012/3251. - Enabling power: Road Traffic Regulation Act 1984, s. 14 (1) (a). - Issued: 09.01.2013. Made: 17.12.2012. Coming into force: 01.02.2013. Effect: None. Territorial extent & classification: E. Local. - Available at http://www.legislation.gov.uk/uksi/2012/3251/contents/made *Non-print*

The M20 Motorway (Junctions 9 and 10) (Temporary Restriction and Prohibition of Traffic) Order 2012 No. 2012/495. - Enabling power: Road Traffic Regulation Act 1984, s. 14 (1) (a) (7). - Issued: 01.03.2012. Made: 20.02.2012. Coming into force: 10.03.2012. Effect: None. Territorial extent & classification: E. Local. - Available at http://www.legislation.gov.uk/uksi/2012/495/contents/made *Non-print*

The M20 Motorway (Northwest of Junction 9) (Temporary 50 Miles Per Hour Speed Restriction) Order 2012 No. 2012/133. - Enabling power: Road Traffic Regulation Act 1984, s. 14 (1) (a). - Issued: 24.01.2012. Made: 16.01.2012. Coming into force: 04.02.2012. Effect: None. Territorial extent & classification: E. Local. - Available at http://www.legislation.gov.uk/uksi/2012/133/contents/made *Non-print*

The M23 Motorway and the A23 Trunk Road (M23 Junction 11 - Hickstead) (Temporary Restriction and Prohibition of Traffic) Order 2012 No. 2012/281. - Enabling power: Road Traffic Regulation Act 1984, s. 14 (1) (a). - Issued: 10.02.2012. Made: 30.01.2012. Coming into force: 18.02.2012. Effect: None. Territorial extent & classification: E. Local. - Available at http://www.legislation.gov.uk/uksi/2012/281/contents/made *Non-print*

The M25 and M20 Motorways and the A20 Trunk Road (Swanley Interchange) (Temporary Prohibition of Traffic) Order 2012 No. 2012/1253. - Enabling power: Road Traffic Regulation Act 1984, s. 14 (1) (a). - Issued: 18.05.2012. Made: 08.05.2012. Coming into force: 01.06.2012. Effect: None. Territorial extent & classification: E. Local. - Available at http://www.legislation.gov.uk/uksi/2012/1253/contents/made *Non-print*

The M25 and M26 Motorways and the A20 Trunk Road (M25 Junctions 3 & 5/M26 Junction 2A) (Temporary Prohibition of Traffic) Order 2012 No. 2012/279. - Enabling power: Road Traffic Regulation Act 1984, s. 14 (1) (a). - Issued: 10.02.2012. Made: 30.01.2012. Coming into force: 18.02.2012. Effect: None. Territorial extent & classification: E. Local. - Available at http://www.legislation.gov.uk/uksi/2012/279/contents/made *Non-print*

Road traffic: Traffic regulation

The M25 and the A1(M) Motorways (M25 Junction 23) (Temporary Prohibition of Traffic) Order 2012 No. 2012/401. - Enabling power: Road Traffic Regulation Act 1984, s. 14 (1) (a). - Issued: 21.02.2012. Made: 06.02.2012. Coming into force: 25.02.2012. Effect: None. Territorial extent & classification: E. Local. - Available at http://www.legislation.gov.uk/uksi/2012/401/contents/made *Non-print*

The M25 and the M26 Motorways (Junctions 4 and 5) (Temporary Prohibition of Traffic) Order 2012 No. 2012/1064. - Enabling power: Road Traffic Regulation Act 1984, s. 14 (1) (a). - Issued: 16.04.2012. Made: 02.04.2012. Coming into force: 23.04.2012. Effect: None. Territorial extent & classification: E. Local. - Available at http://www.legislation.gov.uk/uksi/2012/1064/contents/made *Non-print*

The M25 and the M40 Motorways (M25 Junction 16/M40 Junction 1a, Link Roads) (Temporary Prohibition of Traffic) Order 2012 No. 2012/3240. - Enabling power: Road Traffic Regulation Act 1984, s. 14 (1) (a). - Issued: 08.01.2013. Made: 17.12.2012. Coming into force: 19.01.2013. Effect: None. Territorial extent & classification: E. Local. - Available at http://www.legislation.gov.uk/uksi/2012/3240/contents/made *Non-print*

The M25 Motorway and the A2 and A282 Trunk Roads (Junctions 1B - 5) (Temporary Prohibition of Traffic) Order 2012 No. 2012/592. - Enabling power: Road Traffic Regulation Act 1984, s. 14 (1) (a). - Issued: 06.03.2012. Made: 27.02.2012. Coming into force: 22.03.2012. Effect: None. Territorial extent & classification: E. Local. - Available at http://www.legislation.gov.uk/uksi/2012/592/contents/made *Non-print*

The M25 Motorway and the A2 and the A282 Trunk Roads (Junction 2) (Temporary Prohibition of Traffic) Order 2012 No. 2012/1038. - Enabling power: Road Traffic Regulation Act 1984, s. 14 (1) (a). - Issued: 12.04.2012. Made: 26.03.2012. Coming into force: 21.04.2012. Effect: None. Territorial extent & classification: E. Local. - Available at http://www.legislation.gov.uk/uksi/2012/1038/contents/made *Non-print*

The M25 Motorway and the A3 Trunk Road (M25 Junction 10 and A3 Ockham Junction - Esher Common Junction) (Temporary Prohibition of Traffic) Order 2012 No. 2012/140. - Enabling power: Road Traffic Regulation Act 1984, s. 14 (1) (a). - Issued: 24.01.2012. Made: 16.01.2012. Coming into force: 04.02.2012. Effect: None. Territorial extent & classification: E. Local. - Available at http://www.legislation.gov.uk/uksi/2012/140/contents/made *Non-print*

The M25 Motorway and the A13 and the A282 Trunk Roads (Junction 30) (Temporary 50 Miles Per Hour Speed Restriction) Order 2012 No. 2012/3214. - Enabling power: Road Traffic Regulation Act 1984, s. 14 (1) (a). - Issued: 04.01.2013. Made: 10.12.2012. Coming into force: 29.12.2012. Effect: None. Territorial extent & classification: E. Local. - Available at http://www.legislation.gov.uk/uksi/2012/3214/contents/made *Non-print*

The M25 Motorway and the A30 Trunk Road (M25 Junction 13) (Temporary Prohibition of Traffic) Order 2012 No. 2012/707. - Enabling power: Road Traffic Regulation Act 1984, s. 14 (1) (a). - Issued: 14.03.2012. Made: 05.03.2012. Coming into force: 24.03.2012. Effect: None. Territorial extent & classification: E. Local. - Available at http://www.legislation.gov.uk/uksi/2012/707/contents/made *Non-print*

The M25 Motorway and the A40 Trunk Road (M25 Junctions 19, 22 and 23 and Denham Roundabout) (Temporary Prohibition of Traffic) Order 2012 No. 2012/1083. - Enabling power: Road Traffic Regulation Act 1984, s. 14 (1) (a). - Issued: 18.04.2012. Made: 26.03.2012. Coming into force: 16.04.2012. Effect: None. Territorial extent & classification: E. Local. - Available at http://www.legislation.gov.uk/uksi/2012/1083/contents/made *Non-print*

The M25 Motorway and the A282 Trunk Road (Dartford - Thurrock Crossing) (Temporary Restriction and Prohibition of Traffic) Order 2012 No. 2012/3189. - Enabling power: Road Traffic Regulation Act 1984, s. 14 (1) (a). - Issued: 02.01.2013. Made: 03.12.2012. Coming into force: 04.01.2013. Effect: None. Territorial extent & classification: E. Local. - Available at http://www.legislation.gov.uk/uksi/2012/3189/contents/made *Non-print*

The M25 Motorway and the A282 Trunk Road (Junctions 26 - 31) (Temporary Prohibition of Traffic) Order 2012 No. 2012/2583. - Enabling power: Road Traffic Regulation Act 1984, s. 14 (1) (a). - Issued: 16.10.2012. Made: 08.10.2012. Coming into force: 01.11.2012. Effect: None. Territorial extent & classification: E. Local. - Available at http://www.legislation.gov.uk/uksi/2012/2583/contents/made *Non-print*

The M25 Motorway and the A282 Trunk Road (Junctions 30 - 31) (Temporary Prohibition of Traffic) (No. 2) Order 2012 No. 2012/900. - Enabling power: Road Traffic Regulation Act 1984, s. 14 (1) (a). - Issued: 26.03.2012. Made: 19.03.2012. Coming into force: 24.03.2012. Effect: None. Territorial extent & classification: E. Local. - Available at http://www.legislation.gov.uk/uksi/2012/900/contents/made *Non-print*

Road traffic: Traffic regulation

The M25 Motorway and the A282 Trunk Road (Junctions 30 - 31) (Temporary Prohibition of Traffic) Order 2012 No. 2012/704. - Enabling power: Road Traffic Regulation Act 1984, s. 14 (1) (a). - Issued: 14.03.2012. Made: 05.03.2012. Coming into force: 24.03.2012. Effect: None. Territorial extent & classification: E. Local. - Available at http://www.legislation.gov.uk/uksi/2012/704/contents/made *Non-print*

The M25 Motorway and the M1 Motorway (Junctions 21 and 23) (Temporary Restriction and Prohibition of Traffic) Order 2012 No. 2012/2501. - Enabling power: Road Traffic Regulation Act 1984, s. 14 (1) (a). - Issued: 05.10.2012. Made: 01.10.2012. Coming into force: 20.10.2012. Effect: None. Territorial extent & classification: E. Local. - Available at http://www.legislation.gov.uk/uksi/2012/2501/contents/made *Non-print*

The M25 Motorway and the M3 Motorway and the A316 Trunk Road (Thorpe Interchange and Sunbury Cross) (Temporary Prohibition of Traffic) Order 2012 No. 2012/1225. - Enabling power: Road Traffic Regulation Act 1984, s. 14 (1) (a). - Issued: 10.05.2012. Made: 30.04.2012. Coming into force: 19.05.2012. Effect: None. Territorial extent & classification: E. Local. - Available at http://www.legislation.gov.uk/uksi/2012/1225/contents/made *Non-print*

The M25 Motorway and the M3 Motorway (Thorpe Interchange) (Temporary Prohibition of Traffic) Order 2012 No. 2012/1058. - Enabling power: Road Traffic Regulation Act 1984, s. 14 (1) (a). - Issued: 13.04.2012. Made: 02.04.2012. Coming into force: 21.04.2012. Effect: None. Territorial extent & classification: E. Local. - Available at http://www.legislation.gov.uk/uksi/2012/1058/contents/made *Non-print*

The M25 Motorway and the M11 Motorway (M25 Junctions 23 - 27) (Temporary Restriction and Prohibition of Traffic) Order 2012 No. 2012/2653. - Enabling power: Road Traffic Regulation Act 1984, s. 14 (1) (a). - Issued: 25.10.2012. Made: 15.10.2012. Coming into force: 03.11.2012. Effect: None. Territorial extent & classification: E. Local. - Available at http://www.legislation.gov.uk/uksi/2012/2653/contents/made *Non-print*

The M25 Motorway and the M23 Motorway (Junctions 5 - 8) (Temporary Restriction and Prohibition of Traffic) Order 2012 No. 2012/2462. - Enabling power: Road Traffic Regulation Act 1984, ss. 14 (1) (a), 15 (2). - Issued: 28.09.2012. Made: 24.09.2012. Coming into force: 15.10.2012. Effect: None. Territorial extent & classification: E. Local. - Available at http://www.legislation.gov.uk/uksi/2012/2462/contents/made *Non-print*

The M25 Motorway and the M23 Motorway (Merstham Interchange, Link Roads) (Temporary Prohibition of Traffic) Order 2012 No. 2012/2773. - Enabling power: Road Traffic Regulation Act 1984, s. 14 (1) (a). - Issued: 08.11.2012. Made: 22.10.2012. Coming into force: 10.11.2012. Effect: None. Territorial extent & classification: E. Local. - Available at http://www.legislation.gov.uk/uksi/2012/2773/contents/made *Non-print*

The M25 Motorway and the M26 Motorway (M25 Junction 5 and M26 Junctions 1 - 2a) (Temporary Prohibition of Traffic) Order 2012 No. 2012/1224. - Enabling power: Road Traffic Regulation Act 1984, s. 14 (1) (a). - Issued: 10.05.2012. Made: 30.04.2012. Coming into force: 19.05.2012. Effect: None. Territorial extent & classification: E. Local. - Available at http://www.legislation.gov.uk/uksi/2012/1224/contents/made *Non-print*

The M25 Motorway (Bell Common Tunnel) (Temporary Restriction and Prohibition of Traffic) Order 2012 No. 2012/3185. - Enabling power: Road Traffic Regulation Act 1984, s. 14 (1) (a). - Issued: 31.12.2012. Made: 03.12.2012. Coming into force: 04.01.2013. Effect: None. Territorial extent & classification: E. Local. - Available at http://www.legislation.gov.uk/uksi/2012/3185/contents/made *Non-print*

The M25 Motorway (East of Junction 9) (Temporary Restriction of Traffic) Order 2012 No. 2012/137. - Enabling power: Road Traffic Regulation Act 1984, s. 14 (1) (a). - Issued: 24.01.2012. Made: 16.01.2012. Coming into force: 03.02.2012. Effect: None. Territorial extent & classification: E. Local. - Available at http://www.legislation.gov.uk/uksi/2012/137/contents/made *Non-print*

The M25 Motorway (Holmesdale Tunnel) (Temporary Restriction and Prohibition of Traffic) Order 2012 No. 2012/1855. - Enabling power: Road Traffic Regulation Act 1984, s. 14 (1) (a) (7). - Issued: 20.07.2012. Made: 09.07.2012. Coming into force: 01.08.2012. Effect: None. Territorial extent & classification: E. Local. - Available at http://www.legislation.gov.uk/uksi/2012/1855/contents/made *Non-print*

The M25 Motorway (Junction 7, Clockwise) (Temporary Restriction and Prohibition of Traffic) Order 2012 No. 2012/2864. - Enabling power: Road Traffic Regulation Act 1984, s. 14 (1) (a). - Issued: 19.11.2012. Made: 05.11.2012. Coming into force: 24.11.2012. Effect: None. Territorial extent & classification: E. Local. - Available at http://www.legislation.gov.uk/uksi/2012/2864/contents/made *Non-print*

The M25 Motorway (Junction 10) (Temporary 50 Miles Per Hour Speed Restriction) Order 2012 No. 2012/2857. - Enabling power: Road Traffic Regulation Act 1984, s. 14 (1) (a). - Issued: 16.11.2012. Made: 05.11.2012. Coming into force: 24.11.2012. Effect: None. Territorial extent & classification: E. Local. - Available at http://www.legislation.gov.uk/uksi/2012/2857/contents/made *Non-print*

Road traffic: Traffic regulation

The M25 Motorway (Junction 11, Slip Roads) (Temporary Prohibition of Traffic) Order 2012 No. 2012/136. - Enabling power: Road Traffic Regulation Act 1984, s. 14 (1) (a). - Issued: 24.01.2012. Made: 16.01.2012. Coming into force: 04.02.2012. Effect: None. Territorial extent & classification: E. Local. - Available at http://www.legislation.gov.uk/uksi/2012/136/contents/made *Non-print*

The M25 Motorway (Junction 12, Link Roads) (Temporary Prohibition of Traffic) Order 2012 No. 2012/595. - Enabling power: Road Traffic Regulation Act 1984, s. 14 (1) (a). - Issued: 06.03.2012. Made: 27.02.2012. Coming into force: 17.03.2012. Effect: None. Territorial extent & classification: E. Local. - Available at http://www.legislation.gov.uk/uksi/2012/595/contents/made *Non-print*

The M25 Motorway (Junction 14 and Terminal 5 Spur Roads) (Temporary Prohibition of Traffic) Order 2012 No. 2012/1671. - Enabling power: Road Traffic Regulation Act 1984, s. 14 (1) (a). - Issued: 03.07.2012. Made: 25.06.2012. Coming into force: 17.07.2012. Effect: None. Territorial extent & classification: E. Local. - Available at http://www.legislation.gov.uk/uksi/2012/1671/contents/made *Non-print*

The M25 Motorway (Junction 18, Slip Roads) (Temporary Prohibition of Traffic) Order 2012 No. 2012/903. - Enabling power: Road Traffic Regulation Act 1984, s. 14 (1) (a). - Issued: 26.03.2012. Made: 19.03.2012. Coming into force: 07.04.2012. Effect: None. Territorial extent & classification: E. Local. - Available at http://www.legislation.gov.uk/uksi/2012/903/contents/made *Non-print*

The M25 Motorway (Junction 23, Carriageways) (Temporary Prohibition of Traffic) Order 2012 No. 2012/3245. - Enabling power: Road Traffic Regulation Act 1984, s. 14 (1) (a). - Issued: 08.01.2013. Made: 17.12.2012. Coming into force: 12.01.2013. Effect: None. Territorial extent & classification: E. Local. - Available at http://www.legislation.gov.uk/uksi/2012/3245/contents/made *Non-print*

The M25 Motorway (Junction 26, Exit Slip Road) (Temporary Prohibition of Traffic) Order 2012 No. 2012/1254. - Enabling power: Road Traffic Regulation Act 1984, s. 14 (1) (a). - Issued: 18.05.2012. Made: 08.05.2012. Coming into force: 26.05.2012. Effect: None. Territorial extent & classification: E. Local. - Available at http://www.legislation.gov.uk/uksi/2012/1254/contents/made *Non-print*

The M25 Motorway (Junctions 6 - 10, Slip Roads) (Temporary Prohibition of Traffic) Order 2012 No. 2012/3188. - Enabling power: Road Traffic Regulation Act 1984, s. 14 (1) (a). - Issued: 02.01.2013. Made: 03.12.2012. Coming into force: 15.01.2013. Effect: None. Territorial extent & classification: E. Local. - Available at http://www.legislation.gov.uk/uksi/2012/3188/contents/made *Non-print*

The M25 Motorway (Junctions 8 - 7, Anti-clockwise) (Temporary Prohibition of Traffic) Order 2012 No. 2012/139. - Enabling power: Road Traffic Regulation Act 1984, s. 14 (1) (a). - Issued: 24.01.2012. Made: 16.01.2012. Coming into force: 02.02.2012. Effect: None. Territorial extent & classification: E. Local. - Available at http://www.legislation.gov.uk/uksi/2012/139/contents/made *Non-print*

The M25 Motorway (Junctions 9 - 10) (Temporary Restriction and Prohibition of Traffic) Order 2012 No. 2012/3244. - Enabling power: Road Traffic Regulation Act 1984, s. 14 (1) (a). - Issued: 08.01.2013. Made: 17.12.2012. Coming into force: 05.01.2013. Effect: None. Territorial extent & classification: E. Local. - Available at http://www.legislation.gov.uk/uksi/2012/3244/contents/made *Non-print*

The M25 Motorway (Junctions 10 - 12) (Temporary Restriction and Prohibition of Traffic) Order 2012 No. 2012/3211. - Enabling power: Road Traffic Regulation Act 1984, s. 14 (1) (a). - Issued: 04.01.2013. Made: 10.12.2012. Coming into force: 12.01.2013. Effect: None. Territorial extent & classification: E. Local. - Available at http://www.legislation.gov.uk/uksi/2012/3211/contents/made *Non-print*

The M25 Motorway (Junctions 16 - 18) (Temporary Restriction and Prohibition of Traffic) Order 2012 No. 2012/2511. - Enabling power: Road Traffic Regulation Act 1984, s. 14 (1) (a). - Issued: 05.10.2012. Made: 01.10.2012. Coming into force: 20.10.2012. Effect: None. Territorial extent & classification: E. Local. - Available at http://www.legislation.gov.uk/uksi/2012/2511/contents/made *Non-print*

The M25 Motorway (Junctions 17 - 25) (Temporary Prohibition of Traffic) Order 2012 No. 2012/1861. - Enabling power: Road Traffic Regulation Act 1984, s. 14 (1) (a). - Issued: 20.07.2012. Made: 09.07.2012. Coming into force: 01.08.2012. Effect: None. Territorial extent & classification: E. Local. - Available at http://www.legislation.gov.uk/uksi/2012/1861/contents/made *Non-print*

The M25 Motorway (Junctions 24 - 23) (Temporary Restriction and Prohibition of Traffic) Order 2012 No. 2012/1409. - Enabling power: Road Traffic Regulation Act 1984, s. 14 (1) (a) (7). - Issued: 01.06.2012. Made: 21.05.2012. Coming into force: 09.06.2012. Effect: None. Territorial extent & classification: E. Local. - Available at http://www.legislation.gov.uk/uksi/2012/1409/contents/made *Non-print*

The M25 Motorway (Junctions 25 - 26, Holmesdale Tunnel) (Temporary Restriction of Traffic) Order 2012 No. 2012/2527. - Enabling power: Road Traffic Regulation Act 1984, s. 14 (1) (a). - Issued: 09.10.2012. Made: 01.10.2012. Coming into force: 20.10.2012. Effect: None. Territorial extent & classification: E. Local. - Available at http://www.legislation.gov.uk/uksi/2012/2527/contents/made *Non-print*

Road traffic: Traffic regulation

The M25 Motorway (Junctions 29 - 30) (Temporary Prohibition of Traffic) Order 2012 No. 2012/1190. - Enabling power: Road Traffic Regulation Act 1984, s. 14 (1) (a), sch. 9, para. 27 (1). - Issued: 04.05.2012. Made: 23.04.2012. Coming into force: 12.05.2012. Effect: S.I. 2011/2654 revoked. Territorial extent & classification: E. Local. - Available at http://www.legislation.gov.uk/uksi/2012/1190/contents/made *Non-print*

The M25 Motorway, the M4 Motorway and the M40 Motorway (M25 Junctions 15 and 16) (Temporary Restriction and Prohibition of Traffic) Order 2012 No. 2012/3241. - Enabling power: Road Traffic Regulation Act 1984, s. 14 (1) (a). - Issued: 08.01.2013. Made: 17.12.2012. Coming into force: 07.02.2013. Effect: None. Territorial extent & classification: E. Local. - Available at http://www.legislation.gov.uk/uksi/2012/3241/contents/made *Non-print*

The M25 Motorway, the M4 Motorway and the M40 Motorway (M25 Junctions 15 and 16) (Temporary Restriction and Prohibition of Traffic) Order 2012 No. 2012/135. - Enabling power: Road Traffic Regulation Act 1984, s. 14 (1) (a) (7). - Issued: 24.01.2012. Made: 16.01.2012. Coming into force: 07.02.2012. Effect: None. Territorial extent & classification: E. Local. - Available at http://www.legislation.gov.uk/uksi/2012/135/contents/made *Non-print*

The M25 Motorway, the M23 Motorway and the M3 Motorway (M25 Junctions 7 - 13, Slip/Link Roads) (Temporary Restriction and Prohibition of Traffic) Order 2012 No. 2012/2225. - Enabling power: Road Traffic Regulation Act 1984, s. 14 (1) (a). - Issued: 03.09.2012. Made: 28.08.2012. Coming into force: 22.09.2012. Effect: None. Territorial extent & classification: E. Local. - Available at http://www.legislation.gov.uk/uksi/2012/2225/contents/made *Non-print*

The M25, the M3 and the M23 Motorways (M25 Junctions 7, 10, 11 and 12) (Temporary Restriction and Prohibition of Traffic) Order 2012 No. 2012/186. - Enabling power: Road Traffic Regulation Act 1984, s. 14 (1) (a) (7). - Issued: 31.01.2012. Made: 16.01.2012. Coming into force: 04.02.2012. Effect: None. Territorial extent & classification: E. Local. - Available at http://www.legislation.gov.uk/uksi/2012/186/contents/made *Non-print*

The M25, the M4 and the M40 Motorways (M25 Junctions 15, 16 and 18) (Temporary Prohibition of Traffic) Order 2012 No. 2012/102. - Enabling power: Road Traffic Regulation Act 1984, s. 14 (1) (a). - Issued: 20.01.2012. Made: 09.01.2012. Coming into force: 28.01.2012. Effect: None. Territorial extent & classification: E. Local. - Available at http://www.legislation.gov.uk/uksi/2012/102/contents/made *Non-print*

The M26 Motorway (Junction 2A, Slip Roads) (Temporary Prohibition of Traffic) Order 2012 No. 2012/1585. - Enabling power: Road Traffic Regulation Act 1984, s. 14 (1) (a). - Issued: 25.06.2012. Made: 11.06.2012. Coming into force: 04.07.2012. Effect: None. Territorial extent & classification: E. Local. - Available at http://www.legislation.gov.uk/uksi/2012/1585/contents/made *Non-print*

The M26 Motorway (Junctions 1 - 3) (Temporary Restriction and Prohibition of Traffic) Order 2012 No. 2012/2468. - Enabling power: Road Traffic Regulation Act 1984, ss. 14 (1) (a), 15 (2). - Issued: 01.10.2012. Made: 24.09.2012. Coming into force: 15.10.2012. Effect: None. Territorial extent & classification: E. Local. - Available at http://www.legislation.gov.uk/uksi/2012/2468/contents/made *Non-print*

The M27 Motorway (Junction 1, Westbound Exit Slip Road) (Temporary Prohibition of Traffic) Order 2012 No. 2012/1084. - Enabling power: Road Traffic Regulation Act 1984, s. 14 (1) (a). - Issued: 18.04.2012. Made: 10.04.2012. Coming into force: 01.05.2012. Effect: None. Territorial extent & classification: E. Local. - Available at http://www.legislation.gov.uk/uksi/2012/1084/contents/made *Non-print*

The M27 Motorway (Junction 4, Eastbound) (Temporary Prohibition of Traffic) Order 2012 No. 2012/1185. - Enabling power: Road Traffic Regulation Act 1984, s. 14 (1) (a). - Issued: 02.05.2012. Made: 23.04.2012. Coming into force: 12.05.2012. Effect: None. Territorial extent & classification: E. Local. - Available at http://www.legislation.gov.uk/uksi/2012/1185/contents/made *Non-print*

The M27 Motorway (Junction 5, Eastbound Exit Slip Road) (Temporary Prohibition of Traffic) Order 2012 No. 2012/1576. - Enabling power: Road Traffic Regulation Act 1984, s. 14 (1) (a). - Issued: 26.06.2012. Made: 11.06.2012. Coming into force: 30.06.2012. Effect: None. Territorial extent & classification: E. Local. - Available at http://www.legislation.gov.uk/uksi/2012/1576/contents/made *Non-print*

The M27 Motorway (Junction 7, Eastbound Entry Slip Road) (Temporary Prohibition of Traffic) Order 2012 No. 2012/3139. - Enabling power: Road Traffic Regulation Act 1984, s. 14 (1) (a). - Issued: 27.12.2012. Made: 26.11.2012. Coming into force: 15.12.2012. Effect: None. Territorial extent & classification: E. Local. - Available at http://www.legislation.gov.uk/uksi/2012/3139/contents/made *Non-print*

The M27 Motorway (Junction 11, Westbound Entry Slip Road) (Temporary Prohibition of Traffic) Order 2012 No. 2012/1039. - Enabling power: Road Traffic Regulation Act 1984, s. 14 (1) (a). - Issued: 12.04.2012. Made: 26.03.2012. Coming into force: 14.04.2012. Effect: None. Territorial extent & classification: E. Local. - Available at http://www.legislation.gov.uk/uksi/2012/1039/contents/made *Non-print*

The M27 Motorway (Junctions 1 - 2 and Rownhams Service Area, Slip Roads) (Temporary Prohibition of Traffic) Order 2012 No. 2012/1587. - Enabling power: Road Traffic Regulation Act 1984, s. 14 (1) (a). - Issued: 25.06.2012. Made: 11.06.2012. Coming into force: 30.06.2012. Effect: None. Territorial extent & classification: E. Local. - Available at http://www.legislation.gov.uk/uksi/2012/1587/contents/made *Non-print*

The M27 Motorway (Junctions 1 - 12, Carriageways) (Temporary Restriction of Traffic) Order 2012 No. 2012/280. - Enabling power: Road Traffic Regulation Act 1984, s. 14 (1) (a) (7). - Issued: 10.02.2012. Made: 30.01.2012. Coming into force: 21.02.2012. Effect: None. Territorial extent & classification: E. Local. - Available at http://www.legislation.gov.uk/uksi/2012/280/contents/made *Non-print*

The M27 Motorway (Junctions 7 and 8, Slip Roads) (Temporary Prohibition of Traffic) Order 2012 No. 2012/3259. - Enabling power: Road Traffic Regulation Act 1984, s. 14 (1) (a). - Issued: 09.01.2013. Made: 17.12.2012. Coming into force: 26.01.2013. Effect: None. Territorial extent & classification: E. Local. - Available at http://www.legislation.gov.uk/uksi/2012/3259/contents/made *Non-print*

The M27 Motorway (Junctions 11 - 12) (Temporary Restriction and Prohibition of Traffic) Order 2012 No. 2012/16. - Enabling power: Road Traffic Regulation Act 1984, s. 14 (1) (a), sch. 9, para. 27 (1). - Issued: 10.01.2012. Made: 03.01.2012. Coming into force: 07.01.2012. Effect: None. Territorial extent & classification: E. Local. - Available at http://www.legislation.gov.uk/uksi/2012/16/contents/made *Non-print*

The M27 Motorway (Junctions 11 and 12, Slip/Link Roads) (Temporary Prohibition of Traffic) Order 2012 No. 2012/1228. - Enabling power: Road Traffic Regulation Act 1984, s. 14 (1) (a). - Issued: 10.05.2012. Made: 30.04.2012. Coming into force: 21.05.2012. Effect: None. Territorial extent & classification: E. Local. - Available at http://www.legislation.gov.uk/uksi/2012/1228/contents/made *Non-print*

The M32 Motorway (Junctions 2 and 3 Slip Roads) (Temporary Prohibition of Traffic) (Number 2) Order 2012 No. 2012/2929. - Enabling power: Road Traffic Regulation Act 1984, s. 14 (1) (a). - Issued: 26.11.2012. Made: 14.11.2012. Coming into force: 17.11.2012. Effect: None. Territorial extent & classification: E. Local. - Available at http://www.legislation.gov.uk/uksi/2012/2929/contents/made *Non-print*

The M32 Motorway (Junctions 2 and 3 Slip Roads) (Temporary Prohibition of Traffic) Order 2012 No. 2012/999. - Enabling power: Road Traffic Regulation Act 1984, s. 14 (1) (a). - Issued: 05.04.2012. Made: 22.03.2012. Coming into force: 30.03.2012. Effect: None. Territorial extent & classification: E. Local. - Available at http://www.legislation.gov.uk/uksi/2012/999/contents/made *Non-print*

The M40 Motorway (Junction 1, Buckinghamshire) Northbound (Temporary Prohibition of Traffic) Order 2012 No. 2012/290. - Enabling power: Road Traffic Regulation Act 1984, s. 14 (1) (a). - Issued: 10.02.2012. Made: 30.01.2012. Coming into force: 06.02.2012. Effect: None. Territorial extent & classification: E. Local. - Available at http://www.legislation.gov.uk/uksi/2012/290/contents/made *Non-print*

The M40 Motorway (Junction 2) Southbound Entry Slip Road (Temporary Prohibition of Traffic) Order 2012 No. 2012/2477. - Enabling power: Road Traffic Regulation Act 1984, s. 14 (1) (a). - Issued: 02.10.2012. Made: 24.09.2012. Coming into force: 01.10.2012. Effect: None. Territorial extent & classification: E. Local. - Available at http://www.legislation.gov.uk/uksi/2012/2477/contents/made *Non-print*

The M40 Motorway (Junctions 1 - 15) (Temporary Prohibition of Traffic) Order 2012 No. 2012/1405. - Enabling power: Road Traffic Regulation Act 1984, s. 14 (1) (a). - Issued: 01.06.2012. Made: 21.05.2012. Coming into force: 28.05.2012. Effect: None. Territorial extent & classification: E. Local. - Available at http://www.legislation.gov.uk/uksi/2012/1405/contents/made *Non-print*

The M40 Motorway (Junctions 1 to 15) (Temporary Prohibition of Traffic) (No.2) Order 2012 No. 2012/2476. - Enabling power: Road Traffic Regulation Act 1984, s. 14 (1) (a). - Issued: 02.10.2012. Made: 24.09.2012. Coming into force: 01.10.2012. Effect: None. Territorial extent & classification: E. Local. - Available at http://www.legislation.gov.uk/uksi/2012/2476/contents/made *Non-print*

The M42 and M6 Motorways (M42 Junction 8) (Link Road) (Temporary Prohibition of Traffic) (No. 2) Order 2012 No. 2012/2726. - Enabling power: Road Traffic Regulation Act 1984, s. 14 (1) (a). - Issued: 02.11.2012. Made: 08.10.2012. Coming into force: 15.10.2012. Effect: None. Territorial extent & classification: E. Local. - Available at http://www.legislation.gov.uk/uksi/2012/2726/contents/made *Non-print*

The M42 and M6 Motorways (M42 Junction 8) (Link Road) (Temporary Prohibition of Traffic) Order 2012 No. 2012/618. - Enabling power: Road Traffic Regulation Act 1984, s. 14 (1) (a). - Issued: 07.03.2012. Made: 24.02.2012. Coming into force: 02.03.2012. Effect: None. Territorial extent & classification: E. Local. - Available at http://www.legislation.gov.uk/uksi/2012/618/contents/made *Non-print*

The M42 and M6 Motorways (M42 Junctions 6 to 9) (Temporary Prohibition of Traffic) Order 2012 No. 2012/1982. - Enabling power: Road Traffic Regulation Act 1984, s. 14 (1) (a). - Issued: 31.07.2012. Made: 13.07.2012. Coming into force: 20.07.2012. Effect: None. Territorial extent & classification: E. Local. - Available at http://www.legislation.gov.uk/uksi/2012/1982/contents/made *Non-print*

Road traffic: Traffic regulation

The M42 and M6 Toll Motorways (Coleshill to M6 Toll Junction T4) (Temporary Restriction and Prohibition of Traffic) Order 2012 No. 2012/1738. - Enabling power: Road Traffic Regulation Act 1984, s. 14 (1) (a) (7). - Issued: 17.07.2012. Made: 15.06.2012. Coming into force: 22.06.2012. Effect: None. Territorial extent & classification: E. Local. - Available at http://www.legislation.gov.uk/uksi/2012/1738/contents/made *Non-print*

The M42 and M40 Motorways (M42 Junction 3a) (Temporary Prohibition of Traffic) Order 2012 No. 2012/364. - Enabling power: Road Traffic Regulation Act 1984, s. 14 (1) (a). - Issued: 16.02.2012. Made: 30.01.2012. Coming into force: 06.02.2012. Effect: None. Territorial extent & classification: E. Local. - Available at http://www.legislation.gov.uk/uksi/2012/364/contents/made *Non-print*

The M42, M6 and M6 Toll Motorways (M42 Junctions 8 to 9) (Temporary Restriction and Prohibition of Traffic) Order 2012 No. 2012/2036. - Enabling power: Road Traffic Regulation Act 1984, s. 14 (1) (a) (7). - Issued: 08.08.2012. Made: 09.07.2012. Coming into force: 16.07.2012. Effect: None. Territorial extent & classification: E. Local. - Available at http://www.legislation.gov.uk/uksi/2012/2036/contents/made *Non-print*

The M42 Motorway and M6 Toll Motorway (Junction 7 - Junction 9) (Temporary Prohibition of Traffic) Order 2012 No. 2012/2191. - Enabling power: Road Traffic Regulation Act 1984, s. 14 (1) (a). - Issued: 29.08.2012. Made: 21.08.2012. Coming into force: 28.08.2012. Effect: None. Territorial extent & classification: E. Local. - Available at http://www.legislation.gov.uk/uksi/2012/2191/contents/made *Non-print*

The M42 Motorway (Junction 1) (Northbound Entry Slip Road) (Temporary Prohibition of Traffic) Order 2012 No. 2012/352. - Enabling power: Road Traffic Regulation Act 1984, s. 14 (1) (a). - Issued: 15.02.2012. Made: 30.01.2012. Coming into force: 06.02.2012. Effect: None. Territorial extent & classification: E. Local. - Available at http://www.legislation.gov.uk/uksi/2012/352/contents/made *Non-print*

The M42 Motorway (Junction 1) (Slip Roads) (Temporary Prohibition of Traffic) Order 2012 No. 2012/1985. - Enabling power: Road Traffic Regulation Act 1984, s. 14 (1) (a). - Issued: 01.08.2012. Made: 02.07.2012. Coming into force: 09.07.2012. Effect: None. Territorial extent & classification: E. Local. - Available at http://www.legislation.gov.uk/uksi/2012/1985/contents/made *Non-print*

The M42 Motorway (Junction 2) (Slip Roads) (Temporary Prohibition of Traffic) Order 2012 No. 2012/3322. - Enabling power: Road Traffic Regulation Act 1984, s. 14 (1) (a). - Issued: 18.01.2013. Made: 31.12.2012. Coming into force: 07.01.2013. Effect: None. Territorial extent & classification: E. Local. - Available at http://www.legislation.gov.uk/uksi/2012/3322/contents/made *Non-print*

The M42 Motorway (Junction 3a) (Link Road) (Temporary Prohibition of Traffic) Order 2012 No. 2012/1775. - Enabling power: Road Traffic Regulation Act 1984, s. 14 (1) (a). - Issued: 17.07.2012. Made: 18.06.2012. Coming into force: 25.06.2012. Effect: None. Territorial extent & classification: E. Local. - Available at http://www.legislation.gov.uk/uksi/2012/1775/contents/made *Non-print*

The M42 Motorway (Junction 4) (Slip Roads) (Temporary Prohibition of Traffic) Order 2012 No. 2012/232. - Enabling power: Road Traffic Regulation Act 1984, s. 14 (1) (a). - Issued: 03.02.2012. Made: 23.01.2012. Coming into force: 30.01.2012. Effect: None. Territorial extent & classification: E. Local. - Available at http://www.legislation.gov.uk/uksi/2012/232/contents/made *Non-print*

The M42 Motorway (Junction 4) (Southbound Entry Slip Road) (Temporary Prohibition of Traffic) (No. 2) Order 2012 No. 2012/2698. - Enabling power: Road Traffic Regulation Act 1984, s. 14 (1) (a). - Issued: 30.10.2012. Made: 24.09.2012. Coming into force: 01.10.2012. Effect: None. Territorial extent & classification: E. Local. - Available at http://www.legislation.gov.uk/uksi/2012/2698/contents/made *Non-print*

The M42 Motorway (Junction 4) (Temporary Restriction and Prohibition of Traffic) Order 2012 No. 2012/2896. - Enabling power: Road Traffic Regulation Act 1984, s. 14 (1) (a). - Issued: 22.11.2012. Made: 02.11.2012. Coming into force: 09.11.2012. Effect: None. Territorial extent & classification: E. Local. - Available at http://www.legislation.gov.uk/uksi/2012/2896/contents/made *Non-print*

The M42 Motorway (Junction 5) (Temporary Prohibition of Traffic) Order 2012 No. 2012/861. - Enabling power: Road Traffic Regulation Act 1984, s. 14 (1) (a). - Issued: 23.03.2012. Made: 09.03.2012. Coming into force: 16.03.2012. Effect: None. Territorial extent & classification: E. Local. - Available at http://www.legislation.gov.uk/uksi/2012/861/contents/made *Non-print*

The M42 Motorway (Junction 6 to Junction 7) (Temporary Prohibition of Traffic) Order 2012 No. 2012/862. - Enabling power: Road Traffic Regulation Act 1984, s. 14 (1) (a). - Issued: 23.03.2012. Made: 09.03.2012. Coming into force: 16.03.2012. Effect: None. Territorial extent & classification: E. Local. - Available at http://www.legislation.gov.uk/uksi/2012/862/contents/made *Non-print*

Road traffic: Traffic regulation

The M42 Motorway (Junction 8) (Temporary Prohibition of Traffic) Order 2012 No. 2012/2793. - Enabling power: Road Traffic Regulation Act 1984, s. 14 (1) (a). - Issued: 09.11.2012. Made: 15.10.2012. Coming into force: 22.10.2012. Effect: None. Territorial extent & classification: E. Local. - Available at http://www.legislation.gov.uk/uksi/2012/2793/contents/ma de *Non-print*

The M42 Motorway (Junction 9, Warwickshire) (Temporary Prohibition of Traffic) Order 2012 No. 2012/389. - Enabling power: Road Traffic Regulation Act 1984, s. 14 (1) (a). - Issued: 21.02.2012. Made: 27.01.2012. Coming into force: 03.02.2012. Effect: None. Territorial extent & classification: E. Local. - Available at http://www.legislation.gov.uk/uksi/2012/389/contents/mad e *Non-print*

The M42 Motorway (Junction 11) (Temporary Prohibition of Traffic) Order 2012 No. 2012/1104. - Enabling power: Road Traffic Regulation Act 1984, s. 14 (1) (a). - Issued: 20.04.2012. Made: 03.04.2012. Coming into force: 10.04.2012. Effect: None. Territorial extent & classification: E. Local. - Available at http://www.legislation.gov.uk/uksi/2012/1104/contents/ma de *Non-print*

The M42 Motorway (Junctions 1 - M5 Junction 4a) (Temporary Prohibition of Traffic) Order 2012 No. 2012/180. - Enabling power: Road Traffic Regulation Act 1984, s. 14 (1) (a). - Issued: 31.01.2012. Made: 16.01.2012. Coming into force: 23.01.2012. Effect: None. Territorial extent & classification: E. Local. - Available at http://www.legislation.gov.uk/uksi/2012/180/contents/mad e *Non-print*

The M42 Motorway (Junctions 1 to 7) (Temporary Restriction and Prohibition of Traffic) Order 2012 No. 2012/250. - Enabling power: Road Traffic Regulation Act 1984, s. 14 (1) (a) (7). - Issued: 06.02.2012. Made: 23.01.2012. Coming into force: 30.01.2012. Effect: None. Territorial extent & classification: E. Local. - Available at http://www.legislation.gov.uk/uksi/2012/250/contents/mad e *Non-print*

The M42 Motorway (Junctions 3 to 7) (Temporary Restriction and Prohibition of Traffic) Order 2012 No. 2012/1934. - Enabling power: Road Traffic Regulation Act 1984, s. 14 (1) (a) (7). - Issued: 26.07.2012. Made: 29.06.2012. Coming into force: 06.07.2012. Effect: None. Territorial extent & classification: E. Local. - Available at http://www.legislation.gov.uk/uksi/2012/1934/contents/ma de *Non-print*

The M42 Motorway (Junctions 4 to 5) (Temporary Prohibition of Traffic) Order 2012 No. 2012/1144. - Enabling power: Road Traffic Regulation Act 1984, s. 14 (1) (a) (7). - Issued: 27.04.2012. Made: 16.04.2012. Coming into force: 23.04.2012. Effect: None. Territorial extent & classification: E. Local. - Available at http://www.legislation.gov.uk/uksi/2012/1144/contents/ma de *Non-print*

The M42 Motorway (Junctions 10 - 9) (Temporary Restriction and Prohibition of Traffic) Order 2012 No. 2012/2181. - Enabling power: Road Traffic Regulation Act 1984, s. 14 (1) (a) & S.I. 1982/1163, reg. 16 (2). - Issued: 28.08.2012. Made: 13.08.2012. Coming into force: 20.08.2012. Effect: None. Territorial extent & classification: E. Local. - Available at http://www.legislation.gov.uk/uksi/2012/2181/contents/ma de *Non-print*

The M45 Motorway (Temporary Restriction and Prohibition of Traffic) (No. 2) Order 2012 No. 2012/3305. - Enabling power: Road Traffic Regulation Act 1984, s. 14 (1) (a) (7) 7 & S.I. 1982/1163, reg. 16 (2). - Issued: 17.01.2013. Made: 24.12.2012. Coming into force: 31.12.2012. Effect: None. Territorial extent & classification: E. Local. - Available at http://www.legislation.gov.uk/uksi/2012/3305/contents/ma de *Non-print*

The M45 Motorway (Temporary Restriction and Prohibition of Traffic) Order 2012 No. 2012/575. - Enabling power: Road Traffic Regulation Act 1984, s. 14 (1) (a) (7). - Issued: 06.03.2012. Made: 13.02.2012. Coming into force: 20.02.2012. Effect: None. Territorial extent & classification: E. Local. - Available at http://www.legislation.gov.uk/uksi/2012/575/contents/mad e *Non-print*

The M45 Motorway (Thurlaston to M1 Junction 17) (Temporary Restriction and Prohibition of Traffic) (No.2) Order 2012 No. 2012/2050. - Enabling power: Road Traffic Regulation Act 1984, s. 14 (1) (a). - Issued: 09.08.2012. Made: 23.07.2012. Coming into force: 30.07.2012. Effect: None. Territorial extent & classification: E. Local. - Available at http://www.legislation.gov.uk/uksi/2012/2050/contents/ma de *Non-print*

The M48 Motorway (Junction 1 Slip Roads) (Temporary Prohibition of Traffic) Order 2012 No. 2012/1006. - Enabling power: Road Traffic Regulation Act 1984, s. 14 (1) (a). - Issued: 05.04.2012. Made: 22.03.2012. Coming into force: 30.03.2012. Effect: None. Territorial extent & classification: E. Local. - Available at http://www.legislation.gov.uk/uksi/2012/1006/contents/ma de *Non-print*

The M48 Motorway (M4 Junction 21 to M48 Junction 1) (Temporary Prohibition of Traffic) Order 2012 No. 2012/1193. - Enabling power: Road Traffic Regulation Act 1984, s. 14 (1) (a). - Issued: 04.05.2012. Made: 25.04.2012. Coming into force: 30.04.2012. Effect: None. Territorial extent & classification: E. Local. - Available at http://www.legislation.gov.uk/uksi/2012/1193/contents/ma de *Non-print*

The M48 Motorway (Severn Bridge) (Temporary Restriction of Traffic) Order 2012 No. 2012/2979. - Enabling power: Road Traffic Regulation Act 1984, s. 14 (1) (a). - Issued: 05.12.2012. Made: 21.11.2012. Coming into force: 29.11.2012. Effect: None. Territorial extent & classification: E. Local. - Available at http://www.legislation.gov.uk/uksi/2012/2979/contents/ma de *Non-print*

The M49 Motorway (Temporary Restriction of Traffic) Order 2012 No. 2012/3273. - Enabling power: Road Traffic Regulation Act 1984, s. 14 (1) (a) & S.I. 1982/1163, reg. 16 (2). - Issued: 14.01.2013. Made: 21.12.2012. Coming into force: 31.12.2012. Effect: None. Territorial extent & classification: E. Local. - Available at http://www.legislation.gov.uk/uksi/2012/3273/contents/made *Non-print*

The M50 Motorway (Junction 1) (Temporary Prohibition of Traffic) Order 2012 No. 2012/381. - Enabling power: Road Traffic Regulation Act 1984, s. 14 (1) (a). - Issued: 17.02.2012. Made: 06.02.2012. Coming into force: 13.02.2012. Effect: None. Territorial extent & classification: E. Local. - Available at http://www.legislation.gov.uk/uksi/2012/381/contents/made *Non-print*

The M50 Motorway (Junctions 1 - 2, Near Tewkesbury) (Temporary Restriction and Prohibition of Traffic) Order 2011 Variation Order 2012 No. 2012/1105. - Enabling power: Road Traffic Regulation Act 1984, s. 14 (1) (a), sch. 9, para. 27 (1). - Issued: 20.04.2012. Made: 03.04.2012. Coming into force: 10.04.2012. Effect: S.I. 2011/2969 varied. Territorial extent & classification: E. Local. - Available at http://www.legislation.gov.uk/uksi/2012/1105/contents/made *Non-print*

The M50 Motorway (Junctions 2 - 4) (Temporary Restriction and Prohibition of Traffic) Order 2012 No. 2012/2713. - Enabling power: Road Traffic Regulation Act 1984, s. 14 (1) (a) (7) & S.I. 1982/1163, reg. 16 (2). - Issued: 02.11.2012. Made: 24.09.2012. Coming into force: 01.10.2012. Effect: None. Territorial extent & classification: E. Local. - Available at http://www.legislation.gov.uk/uksi/2012/2713/contents/made *Non-print*

The M50 Motorway (Junctions 2 to 4) (Temporary Prohibition of Traffic) Order 2012 No. 2012/3309. - Enabling power: Road Traffic Regulation Act 1984, s. 14 (1) (a). - Issued: 17.01.2013. Made: 24.12.2012. Coming into force: 31.12.2012. Effect: None. Territorial extent & classification: E. Local. - Available at http://www.legislation.gov.uk/uksi/2012/3309/contents/made *Non-print*

The M50 Motorway (M5 Junction 8 to M50 Junction 2) (Temporary Restriction and Prohibition of Traffic) Order 2012 No. 2012/3164. - Enabling power: Road Traffic Regulation Act 1984, s. 14 (1) (a) & S.I. 1982/1163, reg. 16 (2). - Issued: 28.12.2012. Made: 23.11.2012. Coming into force: 30.11.2012. Effect: None. Territorial extent & classification: E. Local. - Available at http://www.legislation.gov.uk/uksi/2012/3164/contents/made *Non-print*

The M53 Motorway (Junction 1 Northbound Carriageway) (Temporary Prohibition of Traffic) Order 2012 No. 2012/1964. - Enabling power: Road Traffic Regulation Act 1984, s. 14 (1) (b). - Issued: 30.07.2012. Made: 17.07.2012. Coming into force: 22.07.2012. Effect: None. Territorial extent & classification: E. Local. - Available at http://www.legislation.gov.uk/uksi/2012/1964/contents/made *Non-print*

The M53 Motorway (Junction 1, Northbound Exit Slip Road) (Temporary Prohibition of Traffic) Order 2012 No. 2012/296. - Enabling power: Road Traffic Regulation Act 1984, s. 14 (1) (a). - Issued: 10.02.2012. Made: 31.01.2012. Coming into force: 05.02.2012. Effect: None. Territorial extent & classification: E. Local. - Available at http://www.legislation.gov.uk/uksi/2012/296/contents/made *Non-print*

The M53 Motorway (Junction 2, Southbound Entry Slip Road) (Temporary Prohibition of Traffic) Order 2012 No. 2012/1888. - Enabling power: Road Traffic Regulation Act 1984, s. 14 (1) (a). - Issued: 23.07.2012. Made: 10.07.2012. Coming into force: 15.07.2012. Effect: None. Territorial extent & classification: E. Local. - Available at http://www.legislation.gov.uk/uksi/2012/1888/contents/made *Non-print*

The M53 Motorway (Junction 4, Northbound Entry Slip Road) (Temporary Prohibition of Traffic) Order 2012 No. 2012/1706. - Enabling power: Road Traffic Regulation Act 1984, s. 14 (1) (a). - Issued: 12.07.2012. Made: 19.06.2012. Coming into force: 25.06.2012. Effect: None. Territorial extent & classification: E. Local. - Available at http://www.legislation.gov.uk/uksi/2012/1706/contents/made *Non-print*

The M53 Motorway (Junction 9, Northbound and Southbound Exit and Entry Slip Roads) (Temporary Prohibition of Traffic) Order 2012 No. 2012/1834. - Enabling power: Road Traffic Regulation Act 1984, s. 14 (1) (a). - Issued: 19.07.2012. Made: 03.07.2012. Coming into force: 08.07.2012. Effect: None. Territorial extent & classification: E. Local. - Available at http://www.legislation.gov.uk/uksi/2012/1834/contents/made *Non-print*

The M53 Motorway (Junction 10, Northbound Exit Slip Road) (Temporary Prohibition of Traffic) Order 2012 No. 2012/2061. - Enabling power: Road Traffic Regulation Act 1984, s. 14 (1) (a). - Issued: 10.08.2012. Made: 24.07.2012. Coming into force: 29.07.2012. Effect: None. Territorial extent & classification: E. Local. - Available at http://www.legislation.gov.uk/uksi/2012/2061/contents/made *Non-print*

The M53 Motorway (Junction 12) and the A55 Trunk Road (Junction 37) Northbound and Southbound Carriageways and Slip Roads) (Temporary Prohibition of Traffic) Order 2012 No. 2012/177. - Enabling power: Road Traffic Regulation Act 1984, s. 14 (1) (a). - Issued: 31.01.2012. Made: 19.01.2012. Coming into force: 05.02.2012. Effect: None. Territorial extent & classification: E. Local. - Available at http://www.legislation.gov.uk/uksi/2012/177contents/made *Non-print*

The M53 Motorway (Junctions 4-1 Northbound and Southbound Carriageways and Slip Roads) (Temporary Prohibition and Restriction of Traffic) Order 2012 No. 2012/31. - Enabling power: Road Traffic Regulation Act 1984, s. 14 (1) (a) (7). - Issued: 11.01.2012. Made: 03.01.2012. Coming into force: 08.01.2012. Effect: None. Territorial extent & classification: E. Local. - Available at http://www.legislation.gov.uk/uksi/2012/31/contents/made *Non-print*

The M53 Motorway (Junctions 6-7 Southbound Carriageway and Junction 5 Northbound Exit Slip Road) (Temporary Prohibition of Traffic) Order 2012 No. 2012/1885. - Enabling power: Road Traffic Regulation Act 1984, s. 14 (1) (a). - Issued: 23.07.2012. Made: 10.07.2012. Coming into force: 28.07.2012. Effect: None. Territorial extent & classification: E. Local. - Available at http://www.legislation.gov.uk/uksi/2012/1885/contents/made *Non-print*

The M54 and M6 Motorways (M54 Junction 1 to M6 Junction 10a) (Temporary Prohibition of Traffic) Order 2012 No. 2012/127. - Enabling power: Road Traffic Regulation Act 1984, s. 14 (1) (a). - Issued: 23.01.2012. Made: 06.01.2012. Coming into force: 13.01.2012. Effect: None. Territorial extent & classification: E. Local. - Available at http://www.legislation.gov.uk/uksi/2012/127/contents/made *Non-print*

The M54 Motorway and the A5 Trunk Road (Telford to Shrewsbury) (Temporary Prohibition of Traffic) Order 2012 No. 2012/1194. - Enabling power: Road Traffic Regulation Act 1984, s. 14 (1) (a). - Issued: 04.05.2012. Made: 23.04.2012. Coming into force: 30.04.2012. Effect: None. Territorial extent & classification: E. Local. - Available at http://www.legislation.gov.uk/uksi/2012/1194/contents/made *Non-print*

The M54 Motorway (Junction 1 and Junction 2) (Eastbound Slip Roads) (Temporary Prohibition of Traffic) Order 2012 No. 2012/654. - Enabling power: Road Traffic Regulation Act 1984, s. 14 (1) (a). - Issued: 14.03.2012. Made: 28.02.2012. Coming into force: 06.03.2012. Effect: None. Territorial extent & classification: E. Local. - Available at http://www.legislation.gov.uk/uksi/2012/654/contents/made *Non-print*

The M54 Motorway (Junction 1 to Junction 3) (Temporary Restriction and Prohibition of Traffic) Order 2012 No. 2012/1579. - Enabling power: Road Traffic Regulation Act 1984, ss. 14 (1) (a), 15 (2). - Issued: 26.06.2012. Made: 18.05.2012. Coming into force: 25.05.2012. Effect: None. Territorial extent & classification: E. Local. - Available at http://www.legislation.gov.uk/uksi/2012/1579/contents/made *Non-print*

The M54 Motorway (Junction 2) (Westbound Entry Slip Road) (Temporary Prohibition of Traffic) Order 2012 No. 2012/768. - Enabling power: Road Traffic Regulation Act 1984, s. 14 (1) (a). - Issued: 20.03.2012. Made: 05.03.2012. Coming into force: 12.03.2012. Effect: None. Territorial extent & classification: E. Local. - Available at http://www.legislation.gov.uk/uksi/2012/768/contents/made *Non-print*

The M54 Motorway (Junction 3) (Eastbound Entry Slip Road) (Temporary Prohibition of Traffic) Order 2012 No. 2012/3324. - Enabling power: Road Traffic Regulation Act 1984, s. 14 (1) (a). - Issued: 18.01.2013. Made: 31.12.2012. Coming into force: 07.01.2013. Effect: None. Territorial extent & classification: E. Local. - Available at http://www.legislation.gov.uk/uksi/2012/3324/contents/made *Non-print*

The M54 Motorway (Junction 3) (Eastbound Entry Slip Road) (Temporary Prohibition of Traffic) Order 2012 No. 2012/221. - Enabling power: Road Traffic Regulation Act 1984, s. 14 (1) (a). - Issued: 03.02.2012. Made: 20.01.2012. Coming into force: 27.01.2012. Effect: None. Territorial extent & classification: E. Local. - Available at http://www.legislation.gov.uk/uksi/2012/221/contents/made *Non-print*

The M54 Motorway (Junction 3) (Eastbound Exit Slip Road) (Temporary Prohibition of Traffic) Order 2012 No. 2012/3323. - Enabling power: Road Traffic Regulation Act 1984, s. 14 (1) (a). - Issued: 18.01.2013. Made: 31.12.2012. Coming into force: 07.01.2013. Effect: None. Territorial extent & classification: E. Local. - Available at http://www.legislation.gov.uk/uksi/2012/3323/contents/made *Non-print*

The M54 Motorway (Junction 4 to Junction 5) (Temporary Prohibition of Traffic) Order 2012 No. 2012/220. - Enabling power: Road Traffic Regulation Act 1984, s. 14 (1) (a). - Issued: 03.02.2012. Made: 20.01.2012. Coming into force: 27.01.2012. Effect: None. Territorial extent & classification: E. Local. - Available at http://www.legislation.gov.uk/uksi/2012/220/contents/made *Non-print*

Road traffic: Traffic regulation

The M54 Motorway (Junction 6) (Temporary Restriction and Prohibition of Traffic) Order 2012 No. 2012/1111. - Enabling power: Road Traffic Regulation Act 1984, s. 14 (1) (a). - Issued: 23.04.2012. Made: 03.04.2012. Coming into force: 10.04.2012. Effect: None. Territorial extent & classification: E. Local. - Available at http://www.legislation.gov.uk/uksi/2012/1111/contents/made *Non-print*

The M54 Motorway (Junction 6 to Junction 7) (Temporary Prohibition of Traffic) Order 2012 No. 2012/1106. - Enabling power: Road Traffic Regulation Act 1984, s. 14 (1) (a). - Issued: 23.04.2012. Made: 02.04.2012. Coming into force: 09.04.2012. Effect: None. Territorial extent & classification: E. Local. - Available at http://www.legislation.gov.uk/uksi/2012/1106/contents/made *Non-print*

The M54 Motorway (Junction 6 to Junction 7) (Temporary Restriction and Prohibition of Traffic) Order 2012 No. 2012/2558. - Enabling power: Road Traffic Regulation Act 1984, s. 14 (1) (a). - Issued: 11.10.2012. Made: 17.09.2012. Coming into force: 24.09.2012. Effect: None. Territorial extent & classification: E. Local. - Available at http://www.legislation.gov.uk/uksi/2012/2558/contents/made *Non-print*

The M54 Motorway (Junctions 1 to 2) (Temporary Prohibition of Traffic) (No.2) Order 2012 No. 2012/3178. - Enabling power: Road Traffic Regulation Act 1984, s. 14 (1) (a). - Issued: 31.12.2012. Made: 27.11.2012. Coming into force: 04.12.2012. Effect: None. Territorial extent & classification: E. Local. - Available at http://www.legislation.gov.uk/uksi/2012/3178/contents/made *Non-print*

The M54 Motorway (Junctions 1 to 2) (Temporary Prohibition of Traffic) Order 2012 No. 2012/1995. - Enabling power: Road Traffic Regulation Act 1984, s. 14 (1) (a). - Issued: 01.08.2012. Made: 09.07.2012. Coming into force: 16.07.2012. Effect: None. Territorial extent & classification: E. Local. - Available at http://www.legislation.gov.uk/uksi/2012/1995/contents/made *Non-print*

The M54 Motorway (Junctions 2 - 3) (Temporary Prohibition of Traffic) Order 2012 No. 2012/1677. - Enabling power: Road Traffic Regulation Act 1984, s. 14 (1) (b) (7). - Issued: 03.07.2012. Made: 06.06.2012. Coming into force: 13.06.2012. Effect: None. Territorial extent & classification: E. Local. - Available at http://www.legislation.gov.uk/uksi/2012/1677/contents/made *Non-print*

The M54 Motorway (Junctions 2 to 1) (Temporary Prohibition of Traffic) Order 2012 No. 2012/1933. - Enabling power: Road Traffic Regulation Act 1984, s. 14 (1) (a). - Issued: 26.07.2012. Made: 26.06.2012. Coming into force: 03.07.2012. Effect: None. Territorial extent & classification: E. Local. - Available at http://www.legislation.gov.uk/uksi/2012/1933/contents/made *Non-print*

The M54 Motorway (Junctions 3 to 2) (Temporary Prohibition of Traffic) Order 2012 No. 2012/2196. - Enabling power: Road Traffic Regulation Act 1984, s. 14 (1) (a). - Issued: 29.08.2012. Made: 21.08.2012. Coming into force: 28.08.2012. Effect: None. Territorial extent & classification: E. Local. - Available at http://www.legislation.gov.uk/uksi/2012/2196/contents/made *Non-print*

The M54 Motorway (Junctions 5 to 6) (Temporary Prohibition of Traffic) Order 2012 No. 2012/371. - Enabling power: Road Traffic Regulation Act 1984, s. 14 (1) (a). - Issued: 17.02.2012. Made: 30.01.2012. Coming into force: 06.02.2012. Effect: None. Territorial extent & classification: E. Local. - Available at http://www.legislation.gov.uk/uksi/2012/371/contents/made *Non-print*

The M55 Motorway (Junction 1 Eastbound and Westbound Carriageway) and the M6 (Junction 32 Northbound and Southbound Carriageways Exit Slips and Link Roads) (Temporary Prohibition and Restriction of Traffic) Order 2012 No. 2012/2869. - Enabling power: Road Traffic Regulation Act 1984, s. 14 (1) (a) (7). - Issued: 19.11.2012. Made: 11.11.2012. Coming into force: 18.11.2012. Effect: None. Territorial extent & classification: E. Local. - Available at http://www.legislation.gov.uk/uksi/2012/2869/contents/made *Non-print*

The M55 Motorway (Junction 1 Eastbound Link Road to the M6 Northbound) (Temporary Prohibition of Traffic) Order 2012 No. 2012/3235. - Enabling power: Road Traffic Regulation Act 1984, s. 14 (1) (a). - Issued: 08.01.2013. Made: 13.12.2012. Coming into force: 16.12.2012. Effect: None. Territorial extent & classification: E. Local. - Available at http://www.legislation.gov.uk/uksi/2012/3235/contents/made *Non-print*

The M55 Motorway (Junction 3 Eastbound Entry and Junction 4 Westbound Exit Slip Roads) (Temporary Prohibition of Traffic) Order 2012 No. 2012/2081. - Enabling power: Road Traffic Regulation Act 1984, s. 14 (1) (a). - Issued: 14.08.2012. Made: 01.08.2012. Coming into force: 16.08.2012. Effect: None. Territorial extent & classification: E. Local. - Available at http://www.legislation.gov.uk/uksi/2012/2081/contents/made *Non-print*

The M56 Motorway (Junction 16, Eastbound Entry Slip Road) (Temporary Prohibition of Traffic) Order 2012 No. 2012/1563. - Enabling power: Road Traffic Regulation Act 1984, s. 14 (1) (a). - Issued: 22.06.2012. Made: 06.06.2012. Coming into force: 19.06.2012. Effect: None. Territorial extent & classification: E. Local. - Available at http://www.legislation.gov.uk/uksi/2012/1563/contents/made *Non-print*

The M56 Motorway (Junctions 1-3 Westbound and Eastbound Carriageways and Slip Roads) and M60 (Temporary Prohibition of Traffic) Order 2012 No. 2012/1779. - Enabling power: Road Traffic Regulation Act 1984, s. 14 (1) (a). - Issued: 18.07.2012. Made: 26.06.2012. Coming into force: 01.07.2012. Effect: None. Territorial extent & classification: E. Local. - Available at http://www.legislation.gov.uk/uksi/2012/1779/contents/made *Non-print*

The M56 Motorway (Junctions 2-5 Westbound and Eastbound Carriageways and Slip Roads) (Temporary Prohibition of Traffic) Order 2012 No. 2012/2942. - Enabling power: Road Traffic Regulation Act 1984, s. 14 (1) (a). - Issued: 28.11.2012. Made: 14.11.2012. Coming into force: 22.11.2012. Effect: None. Territorial extent & classification: E. Local. - Available at http://www.legislation.gov.uk/uksi/2012/2942/contents/made *Non-print*

The M56 Motorway (Junctions 7-9, Westbound and Eastbound Carriageways and Junction 8 Westbound Entry Slip Road) (Temporary Prohibition and Restriction of Traffic) Order 2012 No. 2012/298. - Enabling power: Road Traffic Regulation Act 1984, s. 14 (1) (a) (7). - Issued: 10.02.2012. Made: 31.01.2012. Coming into force: 05.02.2012. Effect: None. Territorial extent & classification: E. Local. - Available at http://www.legislation.gov.uk/uksi/2012/298/contents/made *Non-print*

The M56 Motorway (Junctions 9-11 Westbound and Eastbound) and the M6 (Junction 20A Southbound Link Road to the M56 Eastbound) (Temporary Prohibition and Restriction of Traffic) Order 2012 No. 2012/2259. - Enabling power: Road Traffic Regulation Act 1984, s. 14 (1) (a) & S.I. 1982/1163, reg. 16 (2). - Issued: 10.09.2012. Made: 29.08.2012. Coming into force: 16.09.2012. Effect: None. Territorial extent & classification: E. Local. - Available at http://www.legislation.gov.uk/uksi/2012/2259/contents/made *Non-print*

The M56 Motorway (Junctions 12-15) and the M53 Motorway (Junction 11) Carriageway, Link and Slip Roads (Temporary Prohibition and Restriction of Traffic) Order 2012 No. 2012/1306. - Enabling power: Road Traffic Regulation Act 1984, s. 14 (1) (a) (7). - Issued: 22.05.2012. Made: 08.05.2012. Coming into force: 27.05.2012. Effect: None. Territorial extent & classification: E. Local. - Available at http://www.legislation.gov.uk/uksi/2012/1306/contents/made *Non-print*

The M56 Motorway (Junctions 15 - 16 Westbound and Eastbound Carriageways and Slip Road) (Temporary Prohibition of Traffic) Order 2012 No. 2012/1422. - Enabling power: Road Traffic Regulation Act 1984, s. 14 (1) (a). - Issued: 06.06.2012. Made: 22.05.2012. Coming into force: 27.05.2012. Effect: None. Territorial extent & classification: E. Local. - Available at http://www.legislation.gov.uk/uksi/2012/1422/contents/made *Non-print*

The M57 Motorway (Junction 2 Southbound Exit and Entry Slip Roads) (The Tour of Britain Cycling Event) (Temporary Prohibition of Traffic) Order 2012 No. 2012/2249. - Enabling power: Road Traffic Regulation Act 1984, s. 16A (2) (a). - Issued: 05.09.2012. Made: 21.08.2012. Coming into force: 09.09.2012. Effect: None. Territorial extent & classification: E. Local. - Available at http://www.legislation.gov.uk/uksi/2012/2249/contents/made *Non-print*

The M58 Motorway (A59 (Switch Island) to Junction 1 Eastbound and Westbound Carriageways) (Temporary Prohibition and Restriction of Traffic) Order 2012 No. 2012/1048. - Enabling power: Road Traffic Regulation Act 1984, s. 14 (1) (a) (7). - Issued: 13.04.2012. Made: 27.03.2012. Coming into force: 15.04.2012. Effect: None. Territorial extent & classification: E. Local. - Available at http://www.legislation.gov.uk/uksi/2012/1048/contents/made *Non-print*

The M58 Motorway (Junction 5, Eastbound Entry Slip Roads from the A577 Northbound and Southbound) (Temporary Prohibition of Traffic) Order 2012 No. 2012/1967. - Enabling power: Road Traffic Regulation Act 1984, s. 14 (1) (a). - Issued: 30.07.2012. Made: 17.07.2012. Coming into force: 19.07.2012. Effect: None. Territorial extent & classification: E. Local. - Available at http://www.legislation.gov.uk/uksi/2012/1967/contents/made *Non-print*

The M58 Motorway (Junction 5 Westbound Exit Slip Road) (Temporary Prohibition of Traffic) (No. 2) Order 2012 No. 2012/2314. - Enabling power: Road Traffic Regulation Act 1984, s. 14 (1) (a). - Issued: 12.09.2012. Made: 22.08.2012. Coming into force: 06.09.2012. Effect: None. Territorial extent & classification: E. Local. - Available at http://www.legislation.gov.uk/uksi/2012/2314/contents/made *Non-print*

The M58 Motorway (Junction 5 Westbound Exit Slip Road) (Temporary Prohibition of Traffic) Order 2012 No. 2012/1890. - Enabling power: Road Traffic Regulation Act 1984, s. 14 (1) (a). - Issued: 23.07.2012. Made: 10.07.2012. Coming into force: 15.07.2012. Effect: None. Territorial extent & classification: E. Local. - Available at http://www.legislation.gov.uk/uksi/2012/1890/contents/made *Non-print*

The M58 Motorway (Junctions 0-6 Eastbound and Westbound) and Slip Roads (Temporary Prohibition and Restriction of Traffic and Temporary Suspension of Statutory Provisions) Order 2012 No. 2012/2671. - Enabling power: Road Traffic Regulation Act 1984, s. 14 (1) (a) (7). - Issued: 26.10.2012. Made: 10.10.2012. Coming into force: 14.10.2012. Effect: None. Territorial extent & classification: E. Local. - Available at http://www.legislation.gov.uk/uksi/2012/2671/contents/made *Non-print*

The M58 Motorway (Junctions 4-6 Eastbound Carriageway and Slip Roads) (Temporary Prohibition and Restriction of Traffic) Order 2012 No. 2012/2430. - Enabling power: Road Traffic Regulation Act 1984, s. 14 (1) (a) & S.I. 1982/1163, reg. 16 (2). - Issued: 26.09.2012. Made: 12.09.2012. Coming into force: 27.09.2012. Effect: None. Territorial extent & classification: E. Local. - Available at http://www.legislation.gov.uk/uksi/2012/2430/contents/made *Non-print*

The M60 Motorway (Junction 3 Anticlockwise and Clockwise Exit Slip Roads to the A34 Southbound) (Temporary Prohibition of Traffic) Order 2012 No. 2012/1528. - Enabling power: Road Traffic Regulation Act 1984, s. 14 (1) (a). - Issued: 19.06.2012. Made: 29.05.2012. Coming into force: 06.06.2012. Effect: None. Territorial extent & classification: E. Local. - Available at http://www.legislation.gov.uk/uksi/2012/1528/contents/made *Non-print*

The M60 Motorway (Junction 7 Clockwise Exit and Anticlockwise Entry Slip Roads) (Greater Manchester Marathon) (Temporary Prohibition of Traffic) Order 2012 No. 2012/1165. - Enabling power: Road Traffic Regulation Act 1984, s. 16A (2) (a). - Issued: 01.05.2012. Made: 18.04.2012. Coming into force: 28.04.2012. Effect: None. Territorial extent & classification: E. Local. - Available at http://www.legislation.gov.uk/uksi/2012/1165/contents/made *Non-print*

The M60 Motorway Junction 12 (Clockwise Link Road to the M62 Westbound Carriageway) (Temporary Prohibition of Traffic) Order 2012 No. 2012/781. - Enabling power: Road Traffic Regulation Act 1984, s. 14 (1) (a). - Issued: 20.03.2012. Made: 07.03.2012. Coming into force: 11.03.2012. Effect: None. Territorial extent & classification: E. Local. - Available at http://www.legislation.gov.uk/uksi/2012/781/contents/made *Non-print*

The M60 Motorway (Junction 19 Clockwise and Anticlockwise Exit Slip Roads) (The Stone Roses Concert) (Temporary Prohibition of Traffic) Order 2012 No. 2012/1725. - Enabling power: Road Traffic Regulation Act 1984, s. 16A (2) (a). - Issued: 13.07.2012. Made: 20.06.2012. Coming into force: 28.06.2012. Effect: None. Territorial extent & classification: E. Local. - Available at http://www.legislation.gov.uk/uksi/2012/1725/contents/made *Non-print*

The M60 Motorway (Junction 23 Clockwise Entry and Exit and Anticlockwise Exit Slip Roads) (Temporary Prohibition of Traffic) Order 2012 No. 2012/2054. - Enabling power: Road Traffic Regulation Act 1984, s. 14 (1) (a). - Issued: 09.08.2012. Made: 25.07.2012. Coming into force: 29.07.2012. Effect: None. Territorial extent & classification: E. Local. - Available at http://www.legislation.gov.uk/uksi/2012/2054/contents/made *Non-print*

The M60 Motorway (Junction 27-1, Clockwise and Anticlockwise Carriageways and Slip Roads) (Temporary Prohibition of Traffic) Order 2012 No. 2012/3268. - Enabling power: Road Traffic Regulation Act 1984, s. 14 (1) (a). - Issued: 14.01.2013. Made: 18.12.2012. Coming into force: 31.12.2012. Effect: None. Territorial extent & classification: E. Local. - Available at http://www.legislation.gov.uk/uksi/2012/3268/contents/made *Non-print*

The M60 Motorway (Junctions 5-2 Anticlockwise) and the M56 (Junctions 3-1 Eastbound) (Temporary Prohibition and Restriction of Traffic) Order 2012 No. 2012/1481. - Enabling power: Road Traffic Regulation Act 1984, s. 14 (1) (a) (7). - Issued: 12.06.2012. Made: 29.05.2012. Coming into force: 06.06.2012. Effect: None. Territorial extent & classification: E. Local. - Available at http://www.legislation.gov.uk/uksi/2012/1481/contents/made *Non-print*

The M60 Motorway (Junctions 5-8 Clockwise and Anticlockwise Carriageways and Slip Roads) (Temporary Prohibition of Traffic) Order 2012 No. 2012/2808. - Enabling power: Road Traffic Regulation Act 1984, s. 14 (1) (a). - Issued: 12.11.2012. Made: 24.10.2012. Coming into force: 01.11.2012. Effect: None. Territorial extent & classification: E. Local. - Available at http://www.legislation.gov.uk/uksi/2012/2808/contents/made *Non-print*

The M60 Motorway (Junctions 6-8 Clockwise and Anticlockwise Carriageways and Entry, Exit and Dedicated Slip Roads) (Temporary Prohibition of Traffic) Order 2012 No. 2012/568. - Enabling power: Road Traffic Regulation Act 1984, s. 14 (1) (a). - Issued: 02.03.2012. Made: 22.02.2012. Coming into force: 26.02.2012. Effect: None. Territorial extent & classification: E. Local. - Available at http://www.legislation.gov.uk/uksi/2012/568/contents/made *Non-print*

The M60 Motorway (Junctions 8-6 Anticlockwise Collector-Distributor Road and Slip Roads) (Temporary Prohibition of Traffic) Order 2012 No. 2012/2623. - Enabling power: Road Traffic Regulation Act 1984, s. 14 (1) (a). - Issued: 22.10.2012. Made: 09.10.2012. Coming into force: 14.10.2012. Effect: None. Territorial extent & classification: E. Local. - Available at http://www.legislation.gov.uk/uksi/2012/2623/contents/made *Non-print*

The M60 Motorway (Junctions 13 and 14 Anticlockwise and Clockwise Exit and Entry Slip Roads) (Temporary Prohibition of Traffic) Order 2012 No. 2012/2080. - Enabling power: Road Traffic Regulation Act 1984, s. 14 (1) (a). - Issued: 14.08.2012. Made: 01.08.2012. Coming into force: 05.08.2012. Effect: None. Territorial extent & classification: E. Local. - Available at http://www.legislation.gov.uk/uksi/2012/2080/contents/made *Non-print*

Road traffic: Traffic regulation

The M60 Motorway (Junctions 15-17 Clockwise and Anti-Clockwise Carriageways and Junction 16 Slip Roads) (Temporary Prohibition and Restriction of Traffic) Order 2012 No. 2012/2493. - Enabling power: Road Traffic Regulation Act 1984, s. 14 (1) (a) (7). - Issued: 03.10.2012. Made: 26.09.2012. Coming into force: 14.10.2012. Effect: None. Territorial extent & classification: E. Local. - Available at http://www.legislation.gov.uk/uksi/2012/2493/contents/made *Non-print*

The M60 Motorway (Junctions 18-19), the M66 Motorway (Junction 4) and the M62 Motorway (Junction 18) (Temporary Prohibition of Traffic) Order 2012 No. 2012/784. - Enabling power: Road Traffic Regulation Act 1984, s. 14 (1) (a). - Issued: 20.03.2012. Made: 07.03.2012. Coming into force: 11.03.2012. Effect: None. Territorial extent & classification: E. Local. - Available at http://www.legislation.gov.uk/uksi/2012/784/contents/made *Non-print*

The M61 Motorway (Junction 3 Kearsley Spur Northbound Carriageway) (Temporary Prohibition of Traffic) Order 2012 No. 2012/1212. - Enabling power: Road Traffic Regulation Act 1984, s. 14 (1) (a). - Issued: 08.05.2012. Made: 26.04.2012. Coming into force: 11.05.2012. Effect: None. Territorial extent & classification: E. Local. - Available at http://www.legislation.gov.uk/uksi/2012/1212/contents/made *Non-print*

The M61 Motorway (Junctions 3-6 Northbound and Southbound Carriageways and Slip Roads) (Temporary Prohibition and Restriction of Traffic) Order 2012 No. 2012/1973. - Enabling power: Road Traffic Regulation Act 1984, s. 14 (1) (a) (7). - Issued: 30.07.2012. Made: 18.07.2012. Coming into force: 05.08.2012. Effect: None. Territorial extent & classification: E. Local. - Available at http://www.legislation.gov.uk/uksi/2012/1973/contents/made *Non-print*

The M61 Motorway (Junctions 3-9 Northbound and Southbound) and the M65 Motorway (Junctions 1-3 Eastbound and Westbound), Carriageways and Slip Roads (Temporary Prohibition and Restriction of Traffic) Order 2012 No. 2012/438. - Enabling power: Road Traffic Regulation Act 1984, s. 14 (1) (a) (7). - Issued: 22.02.2012. Made: 14.02.2012. Coming into force: 04.03.2012. Effect: None. Territorial extent & classification: E. Local. - Available at http://www.legislation.gov.uk/uksi/2012/438/contents/made *Non-print*

The M61 Motorway (Junctions 9 - 7 Southbound Carriageway and Slip Roads) (Temporary Prohibition and Restriction of Traffic) Order 2012 No. 2012/2253. - Enabling power: Road Traffic Regulation Act 1984, s. 14 (1) (a) & S.I. 1982/1163, reg. 16 (2). - Issued: 05.09.2012. Made: 28.08.2012. Coming into force: 16.09.2012. Effect: None. Territorial extent & classification: E. Local. - Available at http://www.legislation.gov.uk/uksi/2012/2253/contents/made *Non-print*

The M61 Motorway (Northbound Entry Slip Road from the A580 Westbound) (Temporary Prohibition of Traffic) Order 2012 No. 2012/450. - Enabling power: Road Traffic Regulation Act 1984, s. 14 (1) (a). - Issued: 24.02.2012. Made: 15.02.2012. Coming into force: 19.02.2012. Effect: None. Territorial extent & classification: E. Local. - Available at http://www.legislation.gov.uk/uksi/2012/450/contents/made *Non-print*

The M62 Motorway and the A1(M) Motorway (Holmfield Interchange) (Temporary Restriction and Prohibition of Traffic) Order 2012 No. 2012/2289. - Enabling power: Road Traffic Regulation Act 1984, s. 14 (1) (a) & S.I. 1982/1163, reg. 16 (2). - Issued: 10.09.2012. Made: 30.08.2012. Coming into force: 09.09.2012. Effect: None. Territorial extent & classification: E. Local. - Available at http://www.legislation.gov.uk/uksi/2012/2289/contents/made *Non-print*

The M62 Motorway and the M1 Motorway (Lofthouse Interchange) (Temporary Prohibition of Traffic) Order 2012 No. 2012/2293. - Enabling power: Road Traffic Regulation Act 1984, s. 14 (1) (a). - Issued: 10.09.2012. Made: 30.08.2012. Coming into force: 09.09.2012. Effect: None. Territorial extent & classification: E. Local. - Available at http://www.legislation.gov.uk/uksi/2012/2293/contents/made *Non-print*

The M62 Motorway (Junction 6, Westbound Carriageway and Link Road to the M57 Northbound) (Temporary Prohibition of Traffic) Order 2012 No. 2012/2147. - Enabling power: Road Traffic Regulation Act 1984, s. 14 (1) (a). - Issued: 22.08.2012. Made: 15.08.2012. Coming into force: 02.09.2012. Effect: None. Territorial extent & classification: E. Local. - Available at http://www.legislation.gov.uk/uksi/2012/2147/contents/made *Non-print*

The M62 Motorway (Junction 10 Eastbound and Westbound Exit Slip Roads and Links to M6 Northbound and Southbound Entry Slip Roads) (Temporary Prohibition of Traffic) Order 2012 No. 2012/2943. - Enabling power: Road Traffic Regulation Act 1984, s. 14 (1) (a). - Issued: 28.11.2012. Made: 14.11.2012. Coming into force: 02.12.2012. Effect: None. Territorial extent & classification: E. Local. - Available at http://www.legislation.gov.uk/uksi/2012/2943/contents/made *Non-print*

The M62 Motorway (Junction 20, Westbound Exit Slip Road) (Temporary Prohibition of Traffic) Order 2012 No. 2012/558. - Enabling power: Road Traffic Regulation Act 1984, s. 14 (1) (a). - Issued: 01.03.2012. Made: 21.02.2012. Coming into force: 26.02.2012. Effect: None. Territorial extent & classification: E. Local. - Available at http://www.legislation.gov.uk/uksi/2012/558/contents/made *Non-print*

The M62 Motorway (Junction 22 to Junction 23) (Temporary Restriction and Prohibition of Traffic) Order 2012 No. 2012/2155. - Enabling power: Road Traffic Regulation Act 1984, s. 14 (1) (a) & S.I. 1982/1163, reg. 16 (2). - Issued: 23.08.2012. Made: 16.08.2012. Coming into force: 27.08.2012. Effect: None. Territorial extent & classification: E. Local. - Available at http://www.legislation.gov.uk/uksi/2012/2155/contents/made *Non-print*

The M62 Motorway (Junction 23 to Junction 22) (Temporary Restriction and Prohibition of Traffic) Order 2012 No. 2012/1543. - Enabling power: Road Traffic Regulation Act 1984, s. 14 (1) (a) (7). - Issued: 20.06.2012. Made: 31.05.2012. Coming into force: 10.06.2012. Effect: None. Territorial extent & classification: E. Local. - Available at http://www.legislation.gov.uk/uksi/2012/1543/contents/made *Non-print*

The M62 Motorway (Junction 24, Ainley Top) (Temporary Prohibition of Traffic) Order 2012 No. 2012/2579. - Enabling power: Road Traffic Regulation Act 1984, s. 14 (1) (a). - Issued: 16.10.2012. Made: 04.10.2012. Coming into force: 14.10.2012. Effect: None. Territorial extent & classification: E. Local. - Available at http://www.legislation.gov.uk/uksi/2012/2579/contents/made *Non-print*

The M62 Motorway (Junction 24, Ainley Top) (Temporary Restriction and Prohibition of Traffic) Order 2012 No. 2012/1722. - Enabling power: Road Traffic Regulation Act 1984, s. 14 (1) (a) (7). - Issued: 13.07.2012. Made: 21.06.2012. Coming into force: 30.06.2012. Effect: None. Territorial extent & classification: E. Local. - Available at http://www.legislation.gov.uk/uksi/2012/1722/contents/made *Non-print*

The M62 Motorway (Junction 24, Ainley Top) (Temporary Restriction and Prohibition of Traffic) Order 2012 Amendment Order 2012 No. 2012/2624. - Enabling power: Road Traffic Regulation Act 1984, s. 14 (1) (a). - Issued: 22.10.2012. Made: 05.10.2012. Coming into force: 07.10.2012. Effect: None. Territorial extent & classification: E. Local. - Available at http://www.legislation.gov.uk/uksi/2012/2624/contents/made *Non-print*

The M62 Motorway (Junction 24 to Junction 25) (Temporary Restriction and Prohibition of Traffic) Order 2012 No. 2012/2490. - Enabling power: Road Traffic Regulation Act 1984, s. 14 (1) (a) & S.I. 1982/1163, reg. 16 (2). - Issued: 03.10.2012. Made: 27.09.2012. Coming into force: 04.10.2012. Effect: None. Territorial extent & classification: E. Local. - Available at http://www.legislation.gov.uk/uksi/2012/2490/contents/made *Non-print*

The M62 Motorway (Junction 26, Chain Bar) (Temporary Prohibition of Traffic) Order 2012 No. 2012/2489. - Enabling power: Road Traffic Regulation Act 1984, s. 14 (1) (a). - Issued: 03.10.2012. Made: 27.09.2012. Coming into force: 07.10.2012. Effect: None. Territorial extent & classification: E. Local. - Available at http://www.legislation.gov.uk/uksi/2012/2489/contents/made *Non-print*

The M62 Motorway (Junction 29) (Temporary Prohibition of Traffic) Order 2012 No. 2012/1723. - Enabling power: Road Traffic Regulation Act 1984, s. 14 (1) (a). - Issued: 03.07.2012. Made: 21.06.2012. Coming into force: 01.07.2012. Effect: None. Territorial extent & classification: E. Local. - Available at http://www.legislation.gov.uk/uksi/2012/1723/contents/made *Non-print*

The M62 Motorway (Junction 29 to Junction 28) (Temporary Prohibition of Traffic) Order 2012 No. 2012/1245. - Enabling power: Road Traffic Regulation Act 1984, s. 14 (1) (a). - Issued: 11.05.2012. Made: 03.05.2012. Coming into force: 13.05.2012. Effect: None. Territorial extent & classification: E. Local. - Available at http://www.legislation.gov.uk/uksi/2012/1245/contents/made *Non-print*

The M62 Motorway (Junction 30) (Temporary Prohibition of Traffic) Order 2012 No. 2012/2765. - Enabling power: Road Traffic Regulation Act 1984, s. 14 (1) (a). - Issued: 07.11.2012. Made: 18.10.2012. Coming into force: 28.10.2012. Effect: None. Territorial extent & classification: E. Local. - Available at http://www.legislation.gov.uk/uksi/2012/2765/contents/made *Non-print*

The M62 Motorway (Junction 31, Junction 32 and Junction 33 to Junction 34) (Temporary Restriction and Prohibition of Traffic) Order 2012 No. 2012/661. - Enabling power: Road Traffic Regulation Act 1984, s. 14 (1) (a) (7). - Issued: 14.03.2012. Made: 01.03.2012. Coming into force: 11.03.2012. Effect: None. Territorial extent & classification: E. Local. - Available at http://www.legislation.gov.uk/uksi/2012/661/contents/made *Non-print*

The M62 Motorway (Junction 32 and Junction 32a) (Temporary Restriction and Prohibition of Traffic) Order 2012 No. 2012/1179. - Enabling power: Road Traffic Regulation Act 1984, s. 14 (1) (b) (7). - Issued: 02.05.2012. Made: 20.04.2012. Coming into force: 28.04.2012. Effect: None. Territorial extent & classification: E. Local. - Available at http://www.legislation.gov.uk/uksi/2012/1179/contents/made *Non-print*

The M62 Motorway (Junction 32 to Junction 33) (Temporary Prohibition of Traffic) Order 2012 No. 2012/2644. - Enabling power: Road Traffic Regulation Act 1984, s. 14 (1) (a). - Issued: 23.10.2012. Made: 11.10.2012. Coming into force: 21.10.2012. Effect: None. Territorial extent & classification: E. Local. - Available at http://www.legislation.gov.uk/uksi/2012/2644/contents/made *Non-print*

The M62 Motorway (Junction 33, Ferrybridge) (Temporary Restriction and Prohibition of Traffic) Order 2012 No. 2012/2064. - Enabling power: Road Traffic Regulation Act 1984, s. 14 (1) (a). - Issued: 10.08.2012. Made: 26.07.2012. Coming into force: 08.08.2012. Effect: None. Territorial extent & classification: E. Local. - Available at http://www.legislation.gov.uk/uksi/2012/2064/contents/made *Non-print*

The M62 Motorway (Junction 33) (Temporary Prohibition of Traffic) (No. 2) Order 2012 No. 2012/3282. - Enabling power: Road Traffic Regulation Act 1984, s. 14 (1) (a). - Issued: 15.01.2013. Made: 27.12.2012. Coming into force: 06.01.2013. Effect: None. Territorial extent & classification: E. Local. - Available at http://www.legislation.gov.uk/uksi/2012/3282/contents/made *Non-print*

The M62 Motorway (Junction 33) (Temporary Prohibition of Traffic) Order 2012 No. 2012/1950. - Enabling power: Road Traffic Regulation Act 1984, s. 14 (1) (a). - Issued: 30.07.2012. Made: 12.07.2012. Coming into force: 22.07.2012. Effect: None. Territorial extent & classification: E. Local. - Available at http://www.legislation.gov.uk/uksi/2012/1950/contents/made *Non-print*

The M62 Motorway (Junction 34) (Temporary 50 Miles Per Hour Speed Restriction) Order 2012 No. 2012/2766. - Enabling power: Road Traffic Regulation Act 1984, s. 14 (1) (a). - Issued: 07.11.2012. Made: 18.10.2012. Coming into force: 31.10.2012. Effect: None. Territorial extent & classification: E. Local. - Available at http://www.legislation.gov.uk/uksi/2012/2766/contents/made *Non-print*

The M62 Motorway (Junction 34 to Junction 35) (Temporary 50 Miles Per Hour Speed Restriction) Order 2012 No. 2012/1072. - Enabling power: Road Traffic Regulation Act 1984, s. 14 (1) (a). - Issued: 16.04.2012. Made: 05.04.2012. Coming into force: 15.04.2012. Effect: None. Territorial extent & classification: E. Local. - Available at http://www.legislation.gov.uk/uksi/2012/1072/contents/made *Non-print*

The M62 Motorway (Junction 34 to Junction 35) (Temporary Restriction and Prohibition of Traffic) Order 2012 No. 2012/2809. - Enabling power: Road Traffic Regulation Act 1984, s. 14 (1) (a). - Issued: 12.11.2012. Made: 18.10.2012. Coming into force: 28.10.2012. Effect: None. Territorial extent & classification: E. Local. - Available at http://www.legislation.gov.uk/uksi/2012/2809/contents/made *Non-print*

The M62 Motorway (Junction 34, Whitley) (Temporary Prohibition of Traffic) Order 2012 No. 2012/2016. - Enabling power: Road Traffic Regulation Act 1984, s. 14 (1) (a). - Issued: 06.08.2012. Made: 19.07.2012. Coming into force: 29.07.2012. Effect: None. Territorial extent & classification: E. Local. - Available at http://www.legislation.gov.uk/uksi/2012/2016/contents/made *Non-print*

The M62 Motorway (Junction 35) (Temporary 50 Miles Per Hour Speed Restriction) Order 2012 No. 2012/315. - Enabling power: Road Traffic Regulation Act 1984, s. 14 (1) (a). - Issued: 15.02.2012. Made: 02.02.2012. Coming into force: 12.02.2012. Effect: None. Territorial extent & classification: E. Local. - Available at http://www.legislation.gov.uk/uksi/2012/315/contents/made *Non-print*

The M62 Motorway (Junction 36, Airmyn) (Temporary Prohibition of Traffic) Order 2012 No. 2012/2487. - Enabling power: Road Traffic Regulation Act 1984, s. 14 (1) (a). - Issued: 02.10.2012. Made: 27.09.2012. Coming into force: 06.10.2012. Effect: None. Territorial extent & classification: E. Local. - Available at http://www.legislation.gov.uk/uksi/2012/2487/contents/made *Non-print*

The M62 Motorway (Junction 36 and Junction 35) (Temporary Prohibition of Traffic) Order 2012 No. 2012/471. - Enabling power: Road Traffic Regulation Act 1984, s. 14 (1) (a). - Issued: 29.02.2012. Made: 16.02.2012. Coming into force: 26.02.2012. Effect: None. Territorial extent & classification: E. Local. - Available at http://www.legislation.gov.uk/uksi/2012/471/contents/made *Non-print*

The M62 Motorway (Junction 36 and Junction 38) (Temporary Prohibition of Traffic) Order 2012 No. 2012/2086. - Enabling power: Road Traffic Regulation Act 1984, s. 14 (1) (a). - Issued: 14.08.2012. Made: 02.08.2012. Coming into force: 12.08.2012. Effect: None. Territorial extent & classification: E. Local. - Available at http://www.legislation.gov.uk/uksi/2012/2086/contents/made *Non-print*

The M62 Motorway (Junction 37) (Temporary Prohibition of Traffic) Order 2012 No. 2012/1249. - Enabling power: Road Traffic Regulation Act 1984, s. 14 (1) (a). - Issued: 18.05.2012. Made: 03.05.2012. Coming into force: 13.05.2012. Effect: None. Territorial extent & classification: E. Local. - Available at http://www.legislation.gov.uk/uksi/2012/1249/contents/made *Non-print*

The M62 Motorway (Junction 38, North Cave) (Temporary Prohibition of Traffic) Order 2012 No. 2012/1614. - Enabling power: Road Traffic Regulation Act 1984, s. 14 (1) (a). - Issued: 28.06.2012. Made: 14.06.2012. Coming into force: 24.06.2012. Effect: None. Territorial extent & classification: E. Local. - Available at http://www.legislation.gov.uk/uksi/2012/1614/contents/made *Non-print*

The M62 Motorway (Junctions 5 - 10 Eastbound and Westbound Carriageways, Link and Slip Roads) (Temporary Prohibition and Restriction of Traffic and Temporary Suspension of Statutory Provisions) Order 2012 No. 2012/2060. - Enabling power: Road Traffic Regulation Act 1984, s. 14 (1) (a). - Issued: 10.08.2012. Made: 25.07.2012. Coming into force: 31.07.2012. Effect: None. Territorial extent & classification: E. Local. - Available at http://www.legislation.gov.uk/uksi/2012/2060/contents/made *Non-print*

Road traffic: Traffic regulation

The M62 Motorway (Junctions 7 - 8 Eastbound and Westbound Carriageways) (Temporary Prohibition and Restriction of Traffic) Order 2012 No. 2012/1448. - Enabling power: Road Traffic Regulation Act 1984, s. 14 (1) (a) (7). - Issued: 12.06.2012. Made: 23.05.2012. Coming into force: 07.06.2012. Effect: None. Territorial extent & classification: E. Local. - Available at http://www.legislation.gov.uk/uksi/2012/1448/contents/made *Non-print*

The M62 Motorway (Junctions 10-12 Eastbound and Westbound Carriageways and Slip Roads) (Temporary Prohibition and Restriction of Traffic) Order 2012 No. 2012/1830. - Enabling power: Road Traffic Regulation Act 1984, s. 14 (1) (a) (7). - Issued: 19.07.2012. Made: 04.07.2012. Coming into force: 19.07.2012. Effect: None. Territorial extent & classification: E. Local. - Available at http://www.legislation.gov.uk/uksi/2012/1830/contents/made *Non-print*

The M62 Motorway (Junctions 11 - 9 Westbound Carriageway) and the M6 (Junctions 20-22 Northbound and Southbound) (Temporary Prohibition and Restriction of Traffic) Order 2012 No. 2012/2248. - Enabling power: Road Traffic Regulation Act 1984, s. 14 (1) (a) & S.I. 1982/1163, reg. 16 (2). - Issued: 04.09.2012. Made: 21.08.2012. Coming into force: 02.09.2012. Effect: None. Territorial extent & classification: E. Local. - Available at http://www.legislation.gov.uk/uksi/2012/2248/contents/made *Non-print*

The M62 Motorway (Junctions 18 - 22 Eastbound and Westbound Carriageways and Slip Roads) and the M60 and M66 Motorways (Temporary Prohibition and Restriction of Traffic) Order 2012 No. 2012/2455. - Enabling power: Road Traffic Regulation Act 1984, s. 14 (1) (a) (7). - Issued: 28.09.2012. Made: 18.09.2012. Coming into force: 23.09.2012. Effect: None. Territorial extent & classification: E. Local. - Available at http://www.legislation.gov.uk/uksi/2012/2455/contents/made *Non-print*

The M65 Motorway (Junction 1 Eastbound Carriageway and Junction 1 Eastbound Exit Slip Road) (Temporary Prohibition of Traffic) Order 2012 No. 2012/2252. - Enabling power: Road Traffic Regulation Act 1984, s. 14 (1) (a). - Issued: 05.09.2012. Made: 28.08.2012. Coming into force: 16.09.2012. Effect: None. Territorial extent & classification: E. Local. - Available at http://www.legislation.gov.uk/uksi/2012/2252/contents/made *Non-print*

The M65 Motorway (Junction 1 Westbound Carriageway) (Temporary Prohibition of Traffic) Order 2012 No. 2012/2338. - Enabling power: Road Traffic Regulation Act 1984, s. 14 (1) (a). - Issued: 14.09.2012. Made: 30.08.2012. Coming into force: 17.09.2012. Effect: None. Territorial extent & classification: E. Local. - Available at http://www.legislation.gov.uk/uksi/2012/2338/contents/made *Non-print*

The M65 Motorway (Junction 6, Eastbound Carriageway) (Temporary Prohibition of Traffic) Order 2012 No. 2012/726. - Enabling power: Road Traffic Regulation Act 1984, s. 14 (1) (a). - Issued: 19.03.2012. Made: 01.03.2012. Coming into force: 18.03.2012. Effect: None. Territorial extent & classification: E. Local. - Available at http://www.legislation.gov.uk/uksi/2012/726/contents/made *Non-print*

The M65 Motorway (Junctions 1 - 5 Eastbound and Westbound Carriageways and Slip Roads) (Temporary Prohibition and Restriction of Traffic) Order 2012 No. 2012/2223. - Enabling power: Road Traffic Regulation Act 1984, s. 14 (1) (a) & S.I. 1982/1163, s. 16 (2). - Issued: 03.09.2012. Made: 23.08.2012. Coming into force: 09.09.2012. Effect: None. Territorial extent & classification: E. Local. - Available at http://www.legislation.gov.uk/uksi/2012/2223/contents/made *Non-print*

The M65 Motorway (Junctions 3-4 Eastbound and Westbound Carriageways) (Temporary Restriction of Traffic) Order 2012 No. 2012/968. - Enabling power: Road Traffic Regulation Act 1984, s. 14 (1) (a) (7). - Issued: 04.04.2012. Made: 01.03.2012. Coming into force: 04.03.2012. Effect: None. Territorial extent & classification: E. Local. - Available at http://www.legislation.gov.uk/uksi/2012/968/contents/made *Non-print*

The M65 Motorway (Junctions 3-4 Eastbound and Westbound Carriageways) (Temporary Restriction of Traffic) Order 2012 No. 2012/448 Cancelled. - Enabling power: Road Traffic Regulation Act 1984, s. 14 (1) (a) (7). - Made: 01.03.2012. Coming into force: 04.03.2012. Effect: None. Territorial extent & classification: E. Local. - *Cancelled see S.I. 2012/968 (Non-print) for replacement.*

The M65 Motorway (Junctions 4-3 Westbound Carriageway and Slip Roads) (Temporary Prohibition of Traffic) Order 2012 No. 2012/2474. - Enabling power: Road Traffic Regulation Act 1984, s. 14 (1) (a). - Issued: 01.10.2012. Made: 20.09.2012. Coming into force: 26.09.2012. Effect: None. Territorial extent & classification: E. Local. - Available at http://www.legislation.gov.uk/uksi/2012/2474/contents/made *Non-print*

The M65 Motorway (Junctions 5 - 6 Westbound and Eastbound Entry and Exit Slip Roads) (Temporary Prohibition of Traffic) Order 2012 No. 2012/2218. - Enabling power: Road Traffic Regulation Act 1984, s. 14 (1) (a). - Issued: 31.08.2012. Made: 23.08.2012. Coming into force: 02.09.2012. Effect: None. Territorial extent & classification: E. Local. - Available at http://www.legislation.gov.uk/uksi/2012/2218/contents/made *Non-print*

The M65 Motorway (Junctions 5-10 Eastbound and Westbound Carriageways and Slip Roads) (Temporary Prohibition and Restriction of Traffic) Order 2012 No. 2012/2021. - Enabling power: Road Traffic Regulation Act 1984, s. 14 (1) (a) (7). - Issued: 06.08.2012. Made: 19.07.2012. Coming into force: 22.07.2012. Effect: None. Territorial extent & classification: E. Local. - Available at http://www.legislation.gov.uk/uksi/2012/2021/contents/made *Non-print*

The M66 Motorway (A56 - Junction 3 Southbound and Northbound Carriageways and Slip Roads) (Temporary Prohibition of Traffic) Order 2012 No. 2012/2266. - Enabling power: Road Traffic Regulation Act 1984, s. 14 (1) (a). - Issued: 10.09.2012. Made: 29.08.2012. Coming into force: 16.09.2012. Effect: None. Territorial extent & classification: E. Local. - Available at http://www.legislation.gov.uk/uksi/2012/2266/contents/made *Non-print*

The M66 Motorway (Junction 1 Northbound Carriageway) and the A56 Trunk Road (Northbound Carriageway and Slip Roads) (Temporary Prohibition of Traffic) Order 2012 No. 2012/2222. - Enabling power: Road Traffic Regulation Act 1984, s. 14 (1) (a). - Issued: 03.09.2012. Made: 23.08.2012. Coming into force: 09.09.2012. Effect: None. Territorial extent & classification: E. Local. - Available at http://www.legislation.gov.uk/uksi/2012/2222/contents/made *Non-print*

The M66 Motorway (Junctions 3-4 Southbound Carriageway and Slip and Link Roads) (Temporary Prohibition and Restriction of Traffic) Order 2012 No. 2012/1947. - Enabling power: Road Traffic Regulation Act 1984, s. 14 (1) (a). - Issued: 30.07.2012. Made: 26.06.2012. Coming into force: 05.07.2012. Effect: None. Territorial extent & classification: E. Local. - Available at http://www.legislation.gov.uk/uksi/2012/1947/contents/made *Non-print*

The M69 Motorway (Junction 1 - A46) (Temporary Restriction and Prohibition of Traffic) Order 2012 No. 2012/375. - Enabling power: Road Traffic Regulation Act 1984, s. 14 (1) (a) (7). - Issued: 17.02.2012. Made: 03.02.2012. Coming into force: 10.02.2012. Effect: None. Territorial extent & classification: E. Local. - Available at http://www.legislation.gov.uk/uksi/2012/375/contents/made *Non-print*

The M69 Motorway (Junction 1) (Northbound Exit Slip Road) (Temporary Prohibition of Traffic) Order 2012 No. 2012/2702. - Enabling power: Road Traffic Regulation Act 1984, s. 14 (1) (a). - Issued: 01.11.2012. Made: 24.09.2012. Coming into force: 01.10.2012. Effect: None. Territorial extent & classification: E. Local. - Available at http://www.legislation.gov.uk/uksi/2012/2702/contents/made *Non-print*

The M69 Motorway (M1 Junction 21) (Link Road) (Temporary Prohibition of Traffic) (No. 2) Order 2012 No. 2012/579. - Enabling power: Road Traffic Regulation Act 1984, s. 14 (1) (a). - Issued: 06.03.2012. Made: 13.02.2012. Coming into force: 20.02.2012. Effect: None. Territorial extent & classification: E. Local. - Available at http://www.legislation.gov.uk/uksi/2012/579/contents/made *Non-print*

The M69 Motorway (M1 Junction 21) (Link Road) (Temporary Prohibition of Traffic) Order 2012 No. 2012/578. - Enabling power: Road Traffic Regulation Act 1984, s. 14 (1) (a). - Issued: 06.03.2012. Made: 13.02.2012. Coming into force: 20.02.2012. Effect: None. Territorial extent & classification: E. Local. - Available at http://www.legislation.gov.uk/uksi/2012/578/contents/made *Non-print*

The M69 Motorway (M1 Junction 21 to M69 Junction 1) (Temporary Restriction and Prohibition of Traffic) Order 2012 No. 2012/2189. - Enabling power: Road Traffic Regulation Act 1984, s. 14 (1) (a). - Issued: 29.08.2012. Made: 20.08.2012. Coming into force: 27.08.2012. Effect: None. Territorial extent & classification: E. Local. - Available at http://www.legislation.gov.uk/uksi/2012/2189/contents/made *Non-print*

The M69 Motorway (M6 Junction 2 to M69 Junction 1) (Temporary Prohibition of Traffic) Order 2012 No. 2012/627. - Enabling power: Road Traffic Regulation Act 1984, s. 14 (1) (a). - Issued: 07.03.2012. Made: 27.02.2012. Coming into force: 05.03.2012. Effect: None. Territorial extent & classification: E. Local. - Available at http://www.legislation.gov.uk/uksi/2012/627/contents/made *Non-print*

The M180 Motorway and the A180 Trunk Road (Barnetby Interchange to Stallingborough Interchange) (Temporary Prohibition of Traffic) Order 2012 No. 2012/1931. - Enabling power: Road Traffic Regulation Act 1984, s. 14 (1) (a). - Issued: 26.07.2012. Made: 05.07.2012. Coming into force: 15.07.2012. Effect: None. Territorial extent & classification: E. Local. - Available at http://www.legislation.gov.uk/uksi/2012/1931/contents/made *Non-print*

The M180 Motorway (Junction 1 to Junction 2) (Temporary Restriction of Traffic) Order 2012 No. 2012/2452. - Enabling power: Road Traffic Regulation Act 1984, s. 14 (1) (a) & S.I. 1982/1163 reg. 16 (2). - Issued: 27.09.2012. Made: 20.09.2012. Coming into force: 30.09.2012. Effect: None. Territorial extent & classification: E. Local. - Available at http://www.legislation.gov.uk/uksi/2012/2452/contents/made *Non-print*

The M180 Motorway (Junction 1 to Junction 3) (Temporary Prohibition of Traffic) Order 2012 No. 2012/1116. - Enabling power: Road Traffic Regulation Act 1984, s. 14 (1) (a). - Issued: 23.04.2012. Made: 12.04.2012. Coming into force: 22.04.2012. Effect: None. Territorial extent & classification: E. Local. - Available at http://www.legislation.gov.uk/uksi/2012/1116/contents/made *Non-print*

The M180 Motorway (Junction 2 to Junction 3) (Temporary Restriction of Traffic) Order 2012 No. 2012/2764. - Enabling power: Road Traffic Regulation Act 1984, s. 14 (1) (a) & S.I. 1982/1163, art. 16 (2). - Issued: 07.11.2012. Made: 16.10.2012. Coming into force: 21.10.2012. Effect: None. Territorial extent & classification: E. Local. - Available at http://www.legislation.gov.uk/uksi/2012/2764/contents/made *Non-print*

The M180 Motorway (Junction 2 to North Ings Interchange) (Temporary Restriction and Prohibition of Traffic) Order 2012 No. 2012/2013. - Enabling power: Road Traffic Regulation Act 1984, s. 14 (1) (a) (7). - Issued: 02.08.2012. Made: 19.07.2012. Coming into force: 29.07.2012. Effect: None. Territorial extent & classification: E. Local. - Available at http://www.legislation.gov.uk/uksi/2012/2013/contents/made *Non-print*

The M180 Motorway (Junction 3 to Junction 2) (Temporary Prohibition of Traffic) Order 2012 No. 2012/775. - Enabling power: Road Traffic Regulation Act 1984, s. 14 (1) (a). - Issued: 20.03.2012. Made: 08.03.2012. Coming into force: 18.03.2012. Effect: None. Territorial extent & classification: E. Local. - Available at http://www.legislation.gov.uk/uksi/2012/775/contents/made *Non-print*

The M180 Motorway (Junction 3 to Junction 5) (Temporary Prohibition of Traffic) Order 2012 No. 2012/1721. - Enabling power: Road Traffic Regulation Act 1984, s. 14 (1) (a). - Issued: 13.07.2012. Made: 21.06.2012. Coming into force: 01.07.2012. Effect: None. Territorial extent & classification: E. Local. - Available at http://www.legislation.gov.uk/uksi/2012/1721/contents/made *Non-print*

The M180 Motorway (Junction 4, Broughton) (Temporary Restriction and Prohibition of Traffic) Order 2012 No. 2012/404. - Enabling power: Road Traffic Regulation Act 1984, s. 14 (1) (a). - Issued: 21.02.2012. Made: 09.02.2012. Coming into force: 18.02.2012. Effect: None. Territorial extent & classification: E. Local. - Available at http://www.legislation.gov.uk/uksi/2012/404/contents/made *Non-print*

The M180 Motorway (Junction 4 to Junction 5) (Temporary 50 Miles Per Hour Speed Restriction) Order 2012 No. 2012/1564. - Enabling power: Road Traffic Regulation Act 1984, s. 14 (1) (a). - Issued: 22.06.2012. Made: 07.06.2012. Coming into force: 17.06.2012. Effect: None. Territorial extent & classification: E. Local. - Available at http://www.legislation.gov.uk/uksi/2012/1564/contents/made *Non-print*

The M180 Motorway (Junction 4 to Junction 5) (Temporary Restriction and Prohibition of Traffic) Order 2012 No. 2012/1213. - Enabling power: Road Traffic Regulation Act 1984, s. 14 (1) (a) (7). - Issued: 10.05.2012. Made: 26.04.2012. Coming into force: 05.05.2012. Effect: None. Territorial extent & classification: E. Local. - Available at http://www.legislation.gov.uk/uksi/2012/1213/contents/made *Non-print*

The M180 Motorway (North Ings Interchange to Junction 1) (Temporary Restriction and Prohibition of Traffic) Order 2012 No. 2012/3278. - Enabling power: Road Traffic Regulation Act 1984, s. 14 (1) (a) & S.I. 1982/1163, reg. 16 (2). - Issued: 15.01.2013. Made: 27.12.2012. Coming into force: 06.01.2013. Effect: None. Territorial extent & classification: E. Local. - Available at http://www.legislation.gov.uk/uksi/2012/3278/contents/made *Non-print*

The M181 Motorway (Frodingham Grange Roundabout to Midmoor Interchange) (Temporary Prohibition of Traffic) Order 2012 No. 2012/185. - Enabling power: Road Traffic Regulation Act 1984, s. 14 (1) (a). - Issued: 31.01.2012. Made: 20.01.2012. Coming into force: 29.01.2012. Effect: None. Territorial extent & classification: E. Local. - Available at http://www.legislation.gov.uk/uksi/2012/185/contents/made *Non-print*

The M181 Motorway (Midmoor Interchange to Frodingham Grange Roundabout) (Temporary Prohibition of Traffic) Order 2012 No. 2012/2434. - Enabling power: Road Traffic Regulation Act 1984, s. 14 (1) (a). - Issued: 26.09.2012. Made: 13.09.2012. Coming into force: 23.09.2012. Effect: None. Territorial extent & classification: E. Local. - Available at http://www.legislation.gov.uk/uksi/2012/2434/contents/made *Non-print*

The M271 Motorway (Romsey Road Roundabout - Redbridge Roundabout) (Temporary Prohibition of Traffic) Order 2012 No. 2012/2699. - Enabling power: Road Traffic Regulation Act 1984, s. 14 (1) (a). - Issued: 01.11.2012. Made: 22.10.2012. Coming into force: 10.11.2012. Effect: None. Territorial extent & classification: E. Local. - Available at http://www.legislation.gov.uk/uksi/2012/2699/contents/made *Non-print*

The M275 Motorway and the M27 Motorway (Tipner Lake Bridge - M27 Junction 12) (Temporary Restriction and Prohibition of Traffic) Order 2012 No. 2012/2826. - Enabling power: Road Traffic Regulation Act 1984, s. 14 (1) (a). - Issued: 14.11.2012. Made: 29.10.2012. Coming into force: 17.11.2012. Effect: None. Territorial extent & classification: E. Local. - Available at http://www.legislation.gov.uk/uksi/2012/2826/contents/made *Non-print*

Road traffic: Traffic regulation

The M602 Motorway (Junction 1 Eastbound and Westbound Carriageways and Link Road) and Link Roads to and from the M60 Motorway (Temporary Prohibition of Traffic) Order 2012 No. 2012/1942. - Enabling power: Road Traffic Regulation Act 1984, s. 14 (1) (a). - Issued: 30.07.2012. Made: 11.07.2012. Coming into force: 15.07.2012. Effect: None. Territorial extent & classification: E. Local. - Available at http://www.legislation.gov.uk/uksi/2012/1942/contents/made *Non-print*

The M602 Motorway (Junction 2 Westbound Entry Slip Road) (Temporary Prohibition of Traffic) Order 2012 No. 2012/408. - Enabling power: Road Traffic Regulation Act 1984, s. 14 (1) (a). - Issued: 21.02.2012. Made: 08.02.2012. Coming into force: 12.02.2012. Effect: None. Territorial extent & classification: E. Local. - Available at http://www.legislation.gov.uk/uksi/2012/408/contents/made *Non-print*

The M606 Motorway (Junction 1 to Junction 3) (Temporary Restriction and Prohibition of Traffic) Order 2012 No. 2012/776. - Enabling power: Road Traffic Regulation Act 1984, s. 14 (1) (a) (7). - Issued: 20.03.2012. Made: 08.03.2012. Coming into force: 18.03.2012. Effect: None. Territorial extent & classification: E. Local. - Available at http://www.legislation.gov.uk/uksi/2012/776/contents/made *Non-print*

The M606 Motorway (Junction 2, Euroway) (Temporary Prohibition of Traffic) (No. 2) Order 2012 No. 2012/2451. - Enabling power: Road Traffic Regulation Act 1984, s. 14 (1) (a). - Issued: 27.09.2012. Made: 20.09.2012. Coming into force: 30.09.2012. Effect: None. Territorial extent & classification: E. Local. - Available at http://www.legislation.gov.uk/uksi/2012/2451/contents/made *Non-print*

The M606 Motorway (Junction 2, Euroway) (Temporary Prohibition of Traffic) Order 2012 No. 2012/2292. - Enabling power: Road Traffic Regulation Act 1984, s. 14 (1) (a). - Issued: 10.09.2012. Made: 30.08.2012. Coming into force: 09.09.2012. Effect: None. Territorial extent & classification: E. Local. - Available at http://www.legislation.gov.uk/uksi/2012/2292/contents/made *Non-print*

The M621 Motorway (Gildersome Interchange) (Temporary Restriction and Prohibition of Traffic) Order 2012 No. 2012/2352. - Enabling power: Road Traffic Regulation Act 1984, s. 14 (1) (a). - Issued: 14.09.2012. Made: 06.09.2012. Coming into force: 16.09.2012. Effect: None. Territorial extent & classification: E. Local. - Available at http://www.legislation.gov.uk/uksi/2012/2352/contents/made *Non-print*

The M621 Motorway (Gildersome Interchange to Junction 1) (Temporary Restriction and Prohibition of Traffic) Order 2012 No. 2012/2291. - Enabling power: Road Traffic Regulation Act 1984, s. 14 (1) (a) & S.I. 1982/1163, reg. 16 (2). - Issued: 10.09.2012. Made: 30.08.2012. Coming into force: 06.09.2012. Effect: None. Territorial extent & classification: E. Local. - Available at http://www.legislation.gov.uk/uksi/2012/2291/contents/made *Non-print*

The M621 Motorway (Junction 1) (Temporary Prohibition of Traffic) Order 2012 No. 2012/3280. - Enabling power: Road Traffic Regulation Act 1984, s. 14 (1) (a). - Issued: 15.01.2013. Made: 27.12.2012. Coming into force: 06.01.2013. Effect: None. Territorial extent & classification: E. Local. - Available at http://www.legislation.gov.uk/uksi/2012/3280/contents/made *Non-print*

The M621 Motorway (Junction 1 to Gildersome Interchange) (Temporary Prohibition of Traffic) Order 2012 No. 2012/1362. - Enabling power: Road Traffic Regulation Act 1984, s. 14 (1) (a). - Issued: 28.05.2012. Made: 10.05.2012. Coming into force: 20.05.2012. Effect: None. Territorial extent & classification: E. Local. - Available at http://www.legislation.gov.uk/uksi/2012/1362/contents/made *Non-print*

The M621 Motorway (Junction 1 to Junction 7) (Temporary Prohibition of Traffic) Order 2012 No. 2012/1175. - Enabling power: Road Traffic Regulation Act 1984, s. 14 (1) (a). - Issued: 02.05.2012. Made: 20.04.2012. Coming into force: 28.04.2012. Effect: None. Territorial extent & classification: E. Local. - Available at http://www.legislation.gov.uk/uksi/2012/1175/contents/made *Non-print*

The M621 Motorway (Junction 2) (Temporary Prohibition of Traffic) Order 2012 No. 2012/2810. - Enabling power: Road Traffic Regulation Act 1984, s. 14 (1) (a). - Issued: 12.11.2012. Made: 18.10.2012. Coming into force: 28.10.2012. Effect: None. Territorial extent & classification: E. Local. - Available at http://www.legislation.gov.uk/uksi/2012/2810/contents/made *Non-print*

The M621 Motorway (Junction 3) (Temporary Prohibition of Traffic) Order 2012 No. 2012/2063. - Enabling power: Road Traffic Regulation Act 1984, s. 14 (1) (a). - Issued: 10.08.2012. Made: 26.07.2012. Coming into force: 05.08.2012. Effect: None. Territorial extent & classification: E. Local. - Available at http://www.legislation.gov.uk/uksi/2012/2063/contents/made *Non-print*

The M621 Motorway (Junction 3 to Junction 4) (Temporary Restriction and Prohibition of Traffic) Order 2012 No. 2012/2435. - Enabling power: Road Traffic Regulation Act 1984, s. 14 (1) (a) & S.I. 1982/1163, reg. 16 (2). - Issued: 26.09.2012. Made: 13.09.2012. Coming into force: 23.09.2012. Effect: None. Territorial extent & classification: E. Local. - Available at http://www.legislation.gov.uk/uksi/2012/2435/contents/made *Non-print*

The M621 Motorway (Junction 4) (Temporary Prohibition of Traffic) (No. 2) Order 2012 No. 2012/1840. - Enabling power: Road Traffic Regulation Act 1984, s. 14 (1) (a). - Issued: 19.07.2012. Made: 05.07.2012. Coming into force: 14.07.2012. Effect: None. Territorial extent & classification: E. Local. - Available at http://www.legislation.gov.uk/uksi/2012/1840/contents/made *Non-print*

The M621 Motorway (Junction 4) (Temporary Prohibition of Traffic) Order 2012 No. 2012/1372. - Enabling power: Road Traffic Regulation Act 1984, s. 14 (1) (a). - Issued: 28.05.2012. Made: 17.05.2012. Coming into force: 30.05.2012. Effect: None. Territorial extent & classification: E. Local. - Available at http://www.legislation.gov.uk/uksi/2012/1372/contents/made *Non-print*

The M621 Motorway (Junction 7) (Temporary Prohibition of Traffic) (No. 2) Order 2012 No. 2012/2356. - Enabling power: Road Traffic Regulation Act 1984, s. 14 (1) (a). - Issued: 17.09.2012. Made: 06.09.2012. Coming into force: 16.09.2012. Effect: None. Territorial extent & classification: E. Local. - Available at http://www.legislation.gov.uk/uksi/2012/2356/contents/made *Non-print*

The M621 Motorway (Junction 7) (Temporary Prohibition of Traffic) Order 2012 No. 2012/662. - Enabling power: Road Traffic Regulation Act 1984, s. 14 (1) (a). - Issued: 14.03.2012. Made: 01.03.2012. Coming into force: 11.03.2012. Effect: None. Territorial extent & classification: E. Local. - Available at http://www.legislation.gov.uk/uksi/2012/662/contents/made *Non-print*

Road traffic, England

The Bus Lane Contraventions (Approved Local Authorities) (England) (Amendment) and Civil Enforcement of Parking Contraventions Designation (No. 2) Order 2012 No. 2012/2659. - Enabling power: Traffic Management Act 2004, s. 89 (3), sch. 8, para. 8 (1), sch. 10, para. 3 (1) & Transport Act 2000, s. 144 (3) (b). - Issued: 06.11.2012. Made: 30.10.2012. Laid: 02.11.2012. Coming into force: 30.11.2012. Effect: S.I. 2005/2755 amended & S.I. 2001/894 revoked. Territorial extent & classification: E. General. - 20p., 10 maps: 30 cm. - 978-0-11-153033-7 £5.75

The Bus Lane Contraventions (Approved Local Authorities) (England) (Amendment) and Civil Enforcement of Parking Contraventions Designation Order 2012 No. 2012/846. - Enabling power: Traffic Management Act 2004, s. 89 (3), sch. 8, para. 8 (1), sch. 10, para. 3 (1) & Transport Act 2000, s. 144 (3) (b). - Issued: 29.03.2012. Made: 21.03.2012. Laid: 23.03.2012. Coming into force: 16.04.2012, arts. 1 to 3, and 5; 11.06.2012, art. 4. Effect: S.I. 2005/2755 amended & S.I. 2006/1445; 2007/2535 revoked. Territorial extent & classification: E. General. - 16p., 6 maps: 30 cm. - 978-0-11-152271-4 £5.75

The Protection of Freedoms Act 2012 (Consequential Amendments) Order 2012 No. 2012/2278. - Enabling power: Protection of Freedoms Act 2012, ss. 115 (3) (4). - Issued: 07.09.2012. Made: 28.08.2012. Laid: 06.09.2012. Coming into force: 01.10.2012. Effect: S.I. 1970/1958; 2008/2367 amended. Territorial extent & classification: E. General. - 2p.: 30 cm. - 978-0-11-152860-0 £4.00

The Removal and Disposal of Vehicles (Amendment) (England) Regulations 2012 No. 2012/2277. - Enabling power: Road Traffic Regulation Act 1984, s. 99. - Issued: 07.09.2012. Made: 28.08.2012. Laid: 06.09.2012. Coming into force: 01.10.2012. Effect: S.I. 1986/183 amended in relation to England. Territorial extent & classification: E. General. - 2p.: 30 cm. - 978-0-11-152859-4 £4.00

The Traffic Management Act 2004 (Amendment of Schedule 7) (City of Exeter) Regulations 2012 No. 2012/12. - Enabling power: Traffic Management Act 2004, sch. 7, para. 5 (1). - Issued: 11.01.2012. Made: 04.01.2012. Laid: 06.01.2012. Coming into force: 30.01.2012. Effect: 2004 c.18 amended. Territorial extent & classification: E. General. - 2p.: 30 cm. - 978-0-11-151895-3 £4.00

Road traffic, England: Special roads

The M1 Motorway (Junctions 10 to 13) (Actively Managed Hard Shoulder and Variable Speed Limits) Regulations 2012 No. 2012/985. - Enabling power: Road Traffic Regulation Act 1984, s. 17 (2) (3). - Issued: 05.04.2012. Made: 29.03.2012. Laid: 03.04.2012. Coming into force: 03.05.2012. Effect: S.I. 1982/1163 modified. Territorial extent & classification: E. Local. - 8p.: 30 cm. - 978-0-11-152325-4 £5.75

The M25 Motorway (Junctions 2 to 3) (Variable Speed Limits) Regulations 2012 No. 2012/104. - Enabling power: Road Traffic Regulation Act 1984, s. 17 (2) (3). - Issued: 23.01.2012. Made: 12.01.2012. Laid: 18.01.2012. Coming into force: 10.02.2012. Effect: None. Territorial extent & classification: E. Local. - 8p.: 30 cm. - 978-0-11-151929-5 £4.00

The M25 Motorway (Junctions 7 to 16) (Variable Speed Limits) Regulations 2012 No. 2012/2134. - Enabling power: Road Traffic Regulation Act 1984, s. 17 (2) (3). - Issued: 20.08.2012. Made: 15.08.2012. Laid: 20.08.2012. Coming into force: 17.09.2012. Effect: S.I. 2001/3763 revoked. Territorial extent & classification: E. Local. - 4p.: 30 cm. - 978-0-11-152827-3 £4.00

The M62 Motorway (Junctions 25 to 30) (Actively Managed Hard Shoulder and Variable Speed Limits) Regulations 2012 No. 2012/1865. - Enabling power: Road Traffic Regulation Act 1984, s. 17 (2) (3). - Issued: 23.07.2012. Made: 16.07.2012. Laid: 19.07.2012. Coming into force: 20.08.2012. Effect: S.I. 1982/1163 modified. Territorial extent & classification: E. Local. - 12p.: 30 cm. - 978-0-11-152725-2 £5.75

Road traffic, England and Wales

The Protection of Freedoms Act 2012 (Commencement No. 2) Order 2012 No. 2012/2075 (C.82). - Enabling power: Protection of Freedoms Act 2012, ss. 116 (1), 120 (1). Bringing into operation various provisions of the 2012 Act on 10.08.2012, 01.10.2012 & 01.11.2012, 25.11.2012, in accord. with arts 2 to 5. - Issued: 10.08.2012. Made: 07.08.2012. Effect: None. Territorial extent & classification: E/W/S/NI. General. - 4p.: 30 cm. - 978-0-11-152805-1 £4.00

Road traffic, Wales

The Civil Enforcement of Parking Contraventions (County Borough of Ceredigion) Designation Order 2012 No. 2012/1189 (W.146). - Enabling power: Traffic Management Act 2004, ss. 74, 84, 89, sch. 8, para. 8 (1), sch. 10, para. 3 (1). - Issued: 17.05.2012. Made: 29.04.2012. Laid before the National Assembly for Wales: 01.05.2012. Coming into force: 04.06.2012. Effect: None. Territorial extent & classification: W. General. - In English and Welsh. Welsh title: Gorchymyn Dynodi Gorfodi Sifil ar Dramgwyddau Parcio (Sir Ceredigion) 2012. - 4p.: 30 cm. - 978-0-348-10606-0 £4.00

The Civil Enforcement of Parking Contraventions (County Borough of Rhondda Cynon Taf) Designation Order 2012 No. 2012/1520 (W.202). - Enabling power: Traffic Management Act 2004, sch. 8, para. 8 (1), sch. 10, para. 3 (1). - Issued: 29.06.2012. Made: 13.06.2012. Laid before the National Assembly for Wales: 15.06.2012. Coming into force: 01.08.2012. Effect: None. Territorial extent & classification: W. General. - In English and Welsh. Welsh title: Gorchymyn Dynodi Gorfodi Sifil ar Dramgwyddau Parcio (Bwrdeistref Sirol Rhondda Cynon Taf) 2012. - 4p.: 30 cm. - 978-0-348-10629-9 £4.00

The Disabled Persons (Badges for Motor Vehicles) (Wales) (Amendment) Regulations 2012 No. 2012/309 (W.50). - Enabling power: Chronically Sick and Disabled Persons Act 1970, s. 21. - Issued: 23.02.2012. Made: 07.02.2012. Laid before the National Assembly for Wales: 02.02.2012. Coming into force: 01.03.2012. Effect: S.I. 2000/1786 (W.123) amended. Territorial extent & classification: W. General. - In English and Welsh. Welsh title: Rheoliadau Personau Anabl (Bathodynnau ar gyfer Cerbydau Modur) (Cymru) (Diwygio) 2012. - 12p.: 30 cm. - 978-0-348-10689-3 £5.75

The Protection of Freedoms Act 2012 (Commencement No. 1) (Wales) Order 2012 No. 2012/2499 (W.274) (C.98). - Enabling power: Protection of Freedoms Act 2012, s. 120 (2) (3). Bringing into operation various provisions of the 2012 Act on 01.10.2012. - Issued: 15.10.2012. Made: 01.10.2012. Effect: None. Territorial extent & classification: W. General. - In English and Welsh. Welsh title: Gorchymyn Deddf Diogelu Rhyddidau 2012 (Cychwyn Rhif 1) (Cymru) 2012. - 4p.: 30 cm. - 978-0-348-10655-8 £4.00

Road traffic, Wales: Speed limits

The A465 Trunk Road (Rhigos Roundabout, Rhondda Cynon Taf to Dowlais Top Roundabout, Merthyr Tydfil) (De-restriction) Order 2012 No. 2012/3249 (W.324). - Enabling power: Road Traffic Regulation Act 1984, ss. 82 (2), 83 (1). - Issued: 09.01.2013. Made: 14.12.2012. Coming into force: 21.12.2012. Effect: None. Territorial extent & classification: W. Local. - Available at http://www.legislation.gov.uk/wsi/2012/3249/contents/made. - In English and Welsh. Welsh title: Gorchymyn Cefnffordd yr A465 (Cylchfan y Rhigos, Rhondda Cynon Taf i Gylchfan Dowlais Top, Merthyr Tudful) (Dileu Cyfyngiadau) 2012 *Non-print*

The A470 Trunk Road (Bridge Street Interchange, Pontypridd, Rhondda Cynon Taf) (30 MPH Speed Limit and Removal of Prohibition of Pedestrians) Order 2012 No. 2012/2507 (W.276). - Enabling power: Road Traffic Regulation Act 1984, ss. 1 (1), 2 (1) (2), 84 (1) (2), 124, sch. 9, para. 27. - Issued: 05.10.2012. Made: 01.10.2012. Coming into force: 05.10.2012. Effect: S.I. 1973/947 revoked. Territorial extent & classification: W. Local. - Available at http://www.legislation.gov.uk/wsi/2012/2507/contents/made. - In English and Welsh. Welsh title: Gorchymyn Cefnffordd yr A470 (Cyfnewidfa Bridge Street, Pontypridd, Rhondda Cynon Taf) (Cyfyngiad Cyflymder 30 MYA a Diddymu Gwaharddiad ar Gerddwyr) 2012 *Non-print*

The A470 Trunk Road (Llanrwst, Gwynedd) (40 MPH Speed Limit) Order 2012 No. 2012/339 (W.56). - Enabling power: Road Traffic Regulation Act 1984, ss. 84 (1) (2), 124, sch. 9, para. 27. - Issued: 14.02.2012. Made: 09.02.2012. Coming into force: 20.02.2012. Effect: S.I. 1995/2692; 2002/2585 revoked. Territorial extent & classification: W. Local. - Available at http://www.legislation.gov.uk/wsi/2012/339/contents/made. - In English and Welsh. Welsh title: Gorchymyn Cefnffordd yr A470 (Llanrwst, Gwynedd) (Terfyn Cyflymder 40 MYA) 2012 *Non-print*

Road traffic, Wales: Traffic regulation

The A5 Trunk Road (Allt Dinas, Betws y Coed, Conwy) (Temporary Traffic Restrictions and Prohibition) Order 2012 No. 2012/464 (W.75). - Enabling power: Road Traffic Regulation Act 1984, s. 14 (1) (4). - Issued: 27.02.2012. Made: 22.02.2012. Coming into force: 27.02.2012. Effect: None. Territorial extent & classification: W. Local. - Available at http://www.legislation.gov.uk/wsi/2012/464/contents/made. - In English and Welsh. Welsh title: Gorchymyn Cefnffordd yr A5 (Allt Dinas, Betws-y-coed, Conwy) (Cyfyngu a Gwahardd Traffig Dros Dro) 2012 *Non-print*

The A5 Trunk Road (Bethesda, Gwynedd) (Temporary Prohibition of Vehicles) Order 2012 No. 2012/2818 (W.296). - Enabling power: Road Traffic Regulation Act 1984, s. 14 (1) (4). - Issued: 14.11.2012. Made: 09.11.2012. Coming into force: 19.11.2012. Effect: None. Territorial extent & classification: W. Local. - Available at http://www.legislation.gov.uk/wsi/2012/2818/contents/made. - In English and Welsh. Welsh title: Gorchymyn Cefnffordd yr A5 (Bethesda, Gwynedd) (Gwahardd Cerbydau Dros Dro) 2012 *Non-print*

The A5 Trunk Road (Betws-y-Coed, Conwy) (Prohibition of Waiting) Order 2012 No. 2012/2447 (W.265). - Enabling power: Road Traffic Regulation Act 1984, s. 1 (1), 2 (1) (2), 4 (2). - Issued: 27.09.2012. Made: 20.09.2012. Coming into force: 28.09.2012. Effect: None. Territorial extent & classification: W. Local. - Available at http://www.legislation.gov.uk/wsi/2012/2447/contents/made. - In English and Welsh. Welsh title: Gorchymyn Cefnffordd yr A5 (Betws-y-coed, Conwy) (Gwahardd Aros) 2012 *Non-print*

The A5 Trunk Road (Bron Haul, Conwy) (Temporary Traffic Restrictions and Prohibition) Order 2012 No. 2012/197 (W.32). - Enabling power: Road Traffic Regulation Act 1984, s. 14 (1) (4). - Issued: 01.02.2012. Made: 27.01.2012. Coming into force: 06.02.2012. Effect: None. Territorial extent & classification: W. Local. - Available at http://www.legislation.gov.uk/wsi/2012/197/contents/made. - In English and Welsh. Welsh title: Gorchymyn Cefnffordd yr A5 (Bron Haul, Conwy) (Cyfyngu a Gwahardd Traffig Dros Dro) 2012 *Non-print*

The A5 Trunk Road (Cerrigydrudion to Glasfryn, Conwy County Borough) (Temporary Traffic Restrictions & Prohibition) Order 2012 No. 2012/1169 (W.142). - Enabling power: Road Traffic Regulation Act 1984, s. 14 (1) (4). - Issued: 03.05.2012. Made: 27.04.2012. Coming into force: 08.05.2012. Effect: None. Territorial extent & classification: W. Local. - Available at http://www.legislation.gov.uk/wsi/2012/1169/contents/made. - In English and Welsh. Welsh title: Gorchymyn Cefnffordd yr A5 (Cerrigydrudion i Lasfryn, Bwrdeistref Sirol Conwy) (Cyfyngu a Gwahardd Traffig Dros Dro) 2012 *Non-print*

The A5 Trunk Road (Chirk Bypass, Wrexham County Borough) (Temporary Prohibition of Vehicles & Cyclists) Order 2012 No. 2012/1782 (W.226). - Enabling power: Road Traffic Regulation Act 1984, s. 14 (1) (4). - Issued: 12.07.2012. Made: 09.07.2012. Coming into force: 17.07.2012. Effect: None. Territorial extent & classification: W. Local. - Available at http://www.legislation.gov.uk/wsi/2012/1782/contents/made. - In English and Welsh. Welsh title: Gorchymyn Cefnffordd yr A5 (Ffordd Osgoi'r Waun, Bwrdeistref Sirol Wrecsam) (Gwahardd Cerbydau a Beicwyr Dros Dro) 2012 *Non-print*

The A5 Trunk Road (Corwen, Denbighshire) (Temporary Traffic Restrictions and Prohibitions) Order 2012 No. 2012/2322 (W.254). - Enabling power: Road Traffic Regulation Act 1984, s. 14 (1) (4). - Issued: 14.09.2012. Made: 11.09.2012. Coming into force: 24.09.2012. Effect: None. Territorial extent & classification: W. Local. - Available at http://www.legislation.gov.uk/wsi/2012/2322/contents/made. - In English and Welsh. Welsh title: Gorchymyn Cefnffordd yr A5 (Corwen, Sir Ddinbych) (Cyfyngiadau a Gwaharddiadau Traffig Dros Dro) 2012 *Non-print*

The A5 Trunk Road (Dolgoch, Bethesda, Gwynedd) (Temporary Traffic Restrictions & Prohibition) Order 2012 No. 2012/1521 (W.203). - Enabling power: Road Traffic Regulation Act 1984, s. 14 (1) (4). - Issued: 18.06.2012. Made: 29.05.2012. Coming into force: 11.06.2012. Effect: None. Territorial extent & classification: W. Local. - Available at http://www.legislation.gov.uk/wsi/2012/1521/contents/made. - In English and Welsh. Welsh title: Gorchymyn Cefnffordd yr A5 (Dolgoch, Bethesda, Gwynedd) (Cyfyngiadau Traffig a Gwarddiad Traffig Dros Dro) 2012 *Non-print*

The A5 Trunk Road (East of Corwen, Denbighshire) (Temporary Traffic Restrictions & Prohibition) Order 2012 No. 2012/1499 (W.197). - Enabling power: Road Traffic Regulation Act 1984, s. 14 (1) (4). - Issued: 14.06.2012. Made: 29.05.2012. Coming into force: 11.06.2012. Effect: None. Territorial extent & classification: W. Local. - Available at http://www.legislation.gov.uk/wsi/2012/1499/contents/made. - In English and Welsh. Welsh title: Gorchymyn Cefnffordd yr A5 (Man i'r Dwyrain o Gorwen, Sir Ddinbych) (Cyfyngiadau Traffig a Gwarddiad Traffig Dros Dro) 2012 *Non-print*

The A5 Trunk Road (Froncysyllte, Wrexham) (Temporary Traffic Restrictions and Prohibition) Order 2012 No. 2012/143 (W.19). - Enabling power: Road Traffic Regulation Act 1984, s. 14 (1) (4). - Issued: 25.01.2012. Made: 23.01.2012. Coming into force: 06.02.2012. Effect: None. Territorial extent & classification: W. Local. - Available at http://www.legislation.gov.uk/wsi/2012/143/contents/made. - In English and Welsh. Welsh title: Gorchymyn Cefnffordd yr A5 (Froncysyllte, Wrecsam) (Cyfyngiadau a Gwarddiad Traffig Dros Dro) 2012 *Non-print*

The A5 Trunk Road (Hendre Arddwyfaen, Cerrigydrudion, Conwy) (Temporary Traffic Restrictions and Prohibition) Order 2012 No. 2012/1545 (W.205). - Enabling power: Road Traffic Regulation Act 1984, s. 14 (1) (4). - Issued: 20.06.2012. Made: 15.06.2012. Coming into force: 25.06.2012. Effect: None. Territorial extent & classification: W. Local. - Available at http://www.legislation.gov.uk/wsi/2012/1545/contents/made. - In English and Welsh. Welsh title: Gorchymyn Cefnffordd yr A5 (Hendre Arddwyfaen, Cerrigydrudion, Conwy) (Cyfyngiadau Traffig a Gwarddiad Traffig Dros Dro) 2012 *Non-print*

The A5 Trunk Road (Swallow Falls Hotel to Ty Hyll, Betws y Coed, Conwy) (Temporary Traffic Restrictions and Prohibition) Order 2012 No. 2012/144 (W.20). - Enabling power: Road Traffic Regulation Act 1984, s. 14 (1) (4). - Issued: 25.01.2012. Made: 23.01.2012. Coming into force: 01.02.2012. Effect: None. Territorial extent & classification: W. Local. - Available at http://www.legislation.gov.uk/wsi/2012/144/contents/made . - In English and Welsh. Welsh title: Gorchymyn Cefnffordd yr A5 (Gwesty'r Swallow Falls i'r T? Hyll, Betws-y-Coed, Conwy) (Cyfyngiadau Traffig a Gwaharddiad Traffig Dros Dro) 2012 *Non-print*

The A5 Trunk Road (West of Glyndyfrdwy, Denbighshire) (Temporary Traffic Restrictions & Prohibitions) Order 2012 No. 2012/165 (W.24). - Enabling power: Road Traffic Regulation Act 1984, s. 14 (1) (4). - Issued: 27.01.2012. Made: 23.01.2012. Coming into force: 01.02.2012. Effect: None. Territorial extent & classification: W. Local. - Available at http://www.legislation.gov.uk/wsi/2012/165/contents/made . - In English and Welsh. Welsh title: Gorchymyn Cefnffordd yr A5 (Man i'r Gorllewin o Lyndyfrdwy, Sir Ddinbych) (Cyfyngu a Gwahardd Traffig Dros Dro) 2012 *Non-print*

The A5 Trunk Road (Wrexham/Denbighshire Border, West of Froncysyllte to Bryn Dethol Junction, East of Llangollen, Denbighshire) (Temporary Traffic Restrictions and Prohibitions) Order 2012 No. 2012/1497 (W.195). - Enabling power: Road Traffic Regulation Act 1984, s. 14 (1) (4). - Issued: 18.06.2012. Made: 29.05.2012. Coming into force: 11.06.2012. Effect: None. Territorial extent & classification: W. Local. - Available at http://www.legislation.gov.uk/wsi/2012/1497/contents/made . - In English and Welsh. Welsh title: Gorchymyn Cefnffordd yr A5 (Ffin Sirol Wrecsam/Sir Ddinbych, i'r Gorllewin o Froncysylltau i Gyffordd Bryn Dethol, i'r Dwyrain o Langollen, Sir Ddinbych) (Cyfyngiadau a Gwaharddiadau Traffig Dros Dro) 2012 *Non-print*

The A40, A465 and A4042 Trunk Roads (Hardwick Gyratory and approaches, Abergavenny, Monmouthshire) (Temporary Traffic Restrictions and Prohibitions) Order 2012 No. 2012/2255 (W.250). - Enabling power: Road Traffic Regulation Act 1984, s. 14 (1) (4). - Issued: 06.09.2012. Made: 03.09.2012. Coming into force: 10.09.2012. Effect: None. Territorial extent & classification: W. Local. - Available at http://www.legislation.gov.uk/wsi/2012/2255/contents/made . - In English and Welsh. Welsh title: Gorchymyn Cefnffyrdd yr A40, yr A465 a'r A4042 (System Gylchu Hardwick a'r ffyrdd sy'n arwain ati, y Fenni, Sir Fynwy) (Cyfyngiadau a Gwaharddiadau Traffig Dros Dro) 2012 *Non-print*

The A40 Trunk Road (County Border at Halfway to Tarrell Roundabout, Brecon, Powys) (Temporary Traffic Restrictions and Prohibition) Order 2012 No. 2012/1636 (W.210). - Enabling power: Road Traffic Regulation Act 1984, s. 14 (1) (4). - Issued: 28.06.2012. Made: 22.06.2012. Coming into force: 01.07.2012. Effect: None. Territorial extent & classification: W. Local. - Available at http://www.legislation.gov.uk/wsi/2012/1636/contents/made . - In English and Welsh. Welsh title: Gorchymyn Cefnffordd yr A40 (Y Ffin Sirol yn Halfway i Gylchfan Tarell, Abcrhonddu, Powys) (Cyfyngu a Gwahardd Traffig Dros Dro) 2012 *Non-print*

The A40 Trunk Road (Dolau Gwynion, Near Llandovery, Carmarthenshire) (Temporary Traffic Restrictions & Prohibition) Order 2012 No. 2012/366 (W.61). - Enabling power: Road Traffic Regulation Act 1984, s. 14 (1) (4). - Issued: 16.02.2012. Made: 14.02.2012. Coming into force: 20.02.2012. Effect: None. Territorial extent & classification: W. Local. - Available at http://www.legislation.gov.uk/wsi/2012/366/contents/made . - In English and Welsh. Welsh title: Gorchymyn Cefnffordd yr A40 (Dolau Gwynion, Ger Llanymddyfri, Sir Gaerfyrddin) (Cyfyngiadau a Gwaharddiad Dros Dro ar Draffig) 2012 *Non-print*

The A40 Trunk Road (Dryslwyn to Nantgaredig, Carmarthenshire) (Temporary Traffic Restrictions & Prohibition) Order 2012 No. 2012/367 (W.62). - Enabling power: Road Traffic Regulation Act 1984, s. 14 (1) (4). - Issued: 16.02.2012. Made: 14.02.2012. Coming into force: 20.02.2012. Effect: None. Territorial extent & classification: W. Local. - Available at http://www.legislation.gov.uk/wsi/2012/367/contents/made . - In English and Welsh. Welsh title: Gorchymyn Cefnffordd yr A40 (Dryslwyn i Nantgaredig, Sir Gaerfyrddin) (Cyfyngu a Gwahardd Traffig Dros Dro) 2012 *Non-print*

The A40 Trunk Road (East of Glangrwyney, Monmouthshire & Powys) (Temporary Traffic Restrictions & Prohibition) Order 2012 No. 2012/430 (W.72). - Enabling power: Road Traffic Regulation Act 1984, s. 14 (1) (4). - Issued: 23.02.2012. Made: 17.02.2012. Coming into force: 27.02.2012. Effect: None. Territorial extent & classification: W. Local. - Available at http://www.legislation.gov.uk/wsi/2012/430/contents/made . - In English and Welsh. Welsh title: Gorchymyn Cefnffordd yr A40 (Man i'r Dwyrain o Langrwyne, Sir Fynwy a Phowys) (Cyfyngiadau a Gwaharddiad Traffig Dros Dro) 2012 *Non-print*

The A40 Trunk Road (Gibraltar Tunnels, Monmouth, Monmouthshire) (Temporary Traffic Restriction and Prohibition) Order 2012 No. 2012/1400 (W.171). - Enabling power: Road Traffic Regulation Act 1984, s. 14 (1) (4). - Issued: 31.05.2012. Made: 28.05.2012. Coming into force: 10.06.2012. Effect: None. Territorial extent & classification: W. Local. - Available at http://www.legislation.gov.uk/wsi/2012/1400/contents/made. - In English and Welsh. Welsh title: Gorchymyn Cefnffordd yr A40 (Twnelau Gibraltar, Trefynwy, Sir Fynwy) (Gwaharddiad a Chyfyngiad Traffig Dros Dro) 2012 *Non-print*

The A40 Trunk Road (Glangwili Roundabout to Broad Oak, Carmarthenshire) (Temporary Traffic Restrictions and Prohibitions) Order 2012 No. 2012/2633 (W.285). - Enabling power: Road Traffic Regulation Act 1984, s. 14 (1) (4). - Issued: 24.10.2012. Made: 17.10.2012. Coming into force: 21.10.2012. Effect: None. Territorial extent & classification: W. Local. - Available at http://www.legislation.gov.uk/wsi/2012/2633/contents/made. - In English and Welsh. Welsh title: Gorchymyn Cefnffordd yr A40 (Cylchfan Glangwili i Dderwen-fawr, Sir Gaerfyrddin) (Cyfyngiadau a Gwaharddiadau Traffig Dros Dro) 2012 *Non-print*

The A40 Trunk Road (Haverfordwest, Pembrokeshire) (Temporary Traffic Restrictions & Prohibition) Order 2012 No. 2012/2444 (W.262). - Enabling power: Road Traffic Regulation Act 1984, s. 14 (1) (4). - Issued: 27.09.2012. Made: 20.09.2012. Coming into force: 01.10.2012. Effect: None. Territorial extent & classification: W. Local. - Available at http://www.legislation.gov.uk/wsi/2012/2444/contents/made. - In English and Welsh. Welsh title: Gorchymyn Cefnffordd yr A40 (Hwlffordd, Sir Benfro) (Cyfyngiadau a Gwaharddiad Traffig Dros Dro) 2012 *Non-print*

The A40 Trunk Road (Monmouth, Monmouthshire) (Temporary Traffic Restrictions and Prohibitions) Order 2012 No. 2012/427 (W.69). - Enabling power: Road Traffic Regulation Act 1984, s. 14 (1) (4). - Issued: 23.02.2012. Made: 17.02.2012. Coming into force: 27.02.2012. Effect: None. Territorial extent & classification: W. Local. - Available at http://www.legislation.gov.uk/wsi/2012/427/contents/made. - In English and Welsh. Welsh title: Gorchymyn Cefnffordd yr A40 (Trefynwy, Sir Fynwy) (Cyfyngu a Gwahardd Traffig Dros Dro) 2012 *Non-print*

The A40 Trunk Road (Northbound on Slip Road, Monmouth, Monmouthshire) (Temporary Prohibition of Vehicles) Order 2012 No. 2012/1505 (W.200). - Enabling power: Road Traffic Regulation Act 1984, s. 14 (1) (4). - Issued: 18.06.2012. Made: 08.06.2012. Coming into force: 18.06.2012. Effect: None. Territorial extent & classification: W. Local. - Available at http://www.legislation.gov.uk/wsi/2012/1505/contents/made. - In English and Welsh. Welsh title: Gorchymyn Cefnffordd yr A40 (Ffordd Ymuno tua'r Gogledd, Trefynwy, Sir Fynwy) (Gwahardd Cerbydau Dros Dro) 2012 *Non-print*

The A40 Trunk Road (North of Dixton Roundabout to Wye Bridge Junction, Monmouth, Monmouthshire) (Temporary 40 mph Speed Limit) Order 2012 No. 2012/2446 (W.264). - Enabling power: Road Traffic Regulation Act 1984, s. 14 (1) (4). - Issued: 27.09.2012. Made: 21.09.2012. Coming into force: 01.10.2012. Effect: None. Territorial extent & classification: W. Local. - Available at http://www.legislation.gov.uk/wsi/2012/2446/contents/made. - In English and Welsh. Welsh title: Gorchymyn Cefnffordd yr A40 (Man i'r Gogledd o Gylchfan Llandidwg i Gyffordd Pont Afon Gwy, Trefynwy, Sir Fynwy) (Terfyn Cyflymder 40 mya Dros Dro) 2012 *Non-print*

The A40 Trunk Road (Raglan Roundabout, Monmouthshire) (Temporary Traffic Restrictions and Prohibitions) Order 2012 No. 2012/676 (W.90). - Enabling power: Road Traffic Regulation Act 1984, s. 14 (1) (4). - Issued: 07.03.2012. Made: 02.03.2012. Coming into force: 12.03.2012. Effect: None. Territorial extent & classification: W. Local. - Available at http://www.legislation.gov.uk/wsi/2012/676/contents/made. - In English and Welsh. Welsh title: Gorchymyn Cefnffordd yr A40 (Cylchfan Rhaglan, Sir Fynwy) (Cyfyngiadau a Gwaharddiadau Traffig Dros Dro) 2012 *Non-print*

The A40 Trunk Road (Slebech, Pembrokeshire) (Temporary Traffic Restrictions and Prohibition) Order 2012 No. 2012/1912 (W. 234). - Enabling power: Road Traffic Regulation Act 1984, s. 14 (1) (4). - Issued: 25.07.2012. Made: 19.07.2012. Coming into force: 01.08.2012. Effect: None. Territorial extent & classification: W. Local. - Available at http://www.legislation.gov.uk/wsi/2012/1912/contents/made. - In English and Welsh. Welsh title: Gorchymyn Cefnffordd yr A40 (Slebets, Sir Benfro) (Cyfyngiadau a Gwaharddiad Traffig Dros Dro) 2012 *Non-print*

The A40 Trunk Road (Southbound Entry Slip Road at Raglan Interchange, Monmouthshire) (Temporary Prohibition of Vehicles & Cyclists) Order 2012 No. 2012/2495 (W.272). - Enabling power: Road Traffic Regulation Act 1984, s. 14 (1) (4). - Issued: 04.10.2012. Made: 28.09.2012. Coming into force: 11.10.2012. Effect: None. Territorial extent & classification: W. Local. - Available at http://www.legislation.gov.uk/wsi/2012/2495/contents/made. - In English and Welsh. Welsh title: Gorchymyn Cefnffordd yr A40 (Y Ffordd Ymuno Tua'r De wrth Gyfnewidfa Rhaglan, Sir Fynwy) (Gwahardd Cerbydau a Beicwyr Dros Dro) 2012 *Non-print*

Road traffic, Wales: Traffic regulation

The A40 Trunk Road (Tarrell Roundabout, Brecon to County Boundary, Glangrwyney, Powys) (Temporary Traffic Restrictions and Prohibition) Order 2012 No. 2012/2221 (W.248). - Enabling power: Road Traffic Regulation Act 1984, s. 14 (1) (4). - Issued: 03.09.2012. Made: 24.08.2012. Coming into force: 04.09.2012. Effect: None. Territorial extent & classification: W. Local. - Available at http://www.legislation.gov.uk/wsi/2012/2221/contents/made. - In English and Welsh. Welsh title: Gorchymyn Cefnffordd yr A40 (Cylchfan Tarrell, Aberhonddu i'r Ffin Sirol, Glangrwync, Powys) (Cyfyngiadau a Gwaharddiad Traffig Dros Dro) 2012 *Non-print*

The A44 Trunk Road (Llangurig to Eisteddfa Gurig, Powys) (Temporary Traffic Restrictions and Prohibition) Order 2012 No. 2012/1488 (W.187). - Enabling power: Road Traffic Regulation Act 1984, s. 14 (1) (4). - Issued: 14.06.2012. Made: 01.06.2012. Coming into force: 11.06.2012. Effect: None. Territorial extent & classification: W. Local. - Available at http://www.legislation.gov.uk/wsi/2012/1488/contents/made. - In English and Welsh. Welsh title: Gorchymyn Cefnffordd yr A44 (Llangurig i Eisteddfa Gurig, Powys) (Cyfyngiadau a Gwaharddiad Traffig Dros Dro) 2012 *Non-print*

The A44 Trunk Road (Nantyrarian to Cwmbrwyno, Ceredigion) (Temporary Traffic Restrictions & Prohibition) Order 2012 No. 2012/1168 (W.141). - Enabling power: Road Traffic Regulation Act 1984, s. 14 (1) (4). - Issued: 03.05.2012. Made: 27.04.2012. Coming into force: 03.05.2012. Effect: None. Territorial extent & classification: W. Local. - Available at http://www.legislation.gov.uk/wsi/2012/1168/contents/made. - In English and Welsh. Welsh title: Gorchymyn Cefnffordd yr A44 (Nantyrarian i Gwmbrwyno, Ceredigion) (Cyfyngiadau Traffig a Gwaharddiad Traffig Dros Dro) 2012 *Non-print*

The A48, A40, A487, A44 & A470 Trunk Roads (Various Locations in the Counties of Carmarthenshire, Pembrokeshire, Ceredigion and Powys) (Temporary Prohibition of Vehicles, Pedestrians & Cyclists) Order 2012 No. 2012/1166 (W.140). - Enabling power: Road Traffic Regulation Act 1984, s. 14 (1) (4). - Issued: 02.05.2012. Made: 27.04.2012. Coming into force: 09.05.2012. Effect: None. Territorial extent & classification: W. Local. - Available at http://www.legislation.gov.uk/wsi/2012/1166/contents/made. - In English and Welsh. Welsh title: Gorchymyn Cefnffyrdd yr A48, yr A40, yr A487, yr A44 a'r A470 (Lleoliadau Amrywiol yn Siroedd Caerfyrddin, Penfro, Ceredigion a Phowys) (Gwahardd Cerbydau, Cerddwyr a Beicwyr Dros Dro) 2012 *Non-print*

The A48, A40 & A4076 Trunk Roads (Pont Abraham, Carmarthenshire to Johnston, Pembrokeshire) (Temporary Prohibition of Vehicles, Pedestrians & Cyclists) Order 2012 No. 2012/2156 (W.243). - Enabling power: Road Traffic Regulation Act 1984, s. 14 (1) (4). - Issued: 23.08.2012. Made: 16.08.2012. Coming into force: 28.08.2012. Effect: None. Territorial extent & classification: W. Local. - Available at http://www.legislation.gov.uk/wsi/2012/2156/contents/made. - In English and Welsh. Welsh title: Gorchymyn Cefnffyrdd yr A48, yr A40 a'r A4076 (Pont Abraham, Sir Gacrfyrddin i Johnston, Sir Benfro) (Gwahardd Cerbydau, Cerddwyr a Beicwyr Dros Dro) 2012 *Non-print*

The A48, A40 & A4076 Trunk Roads (Pont Abraham, Carmarthenshire to Milford Haven, Pembrokeshire) (Temporary Prohibition of Vehicles, Pedestrians & Cyclists) Order 2012 No. 2012/2741 (W.293). - Enabling power: Road Traffic Regulation Act 1984, s. 14 (1) (4). - Issued: 06.11.2012. Made: 01.11.2012. Coming into force: 12.11.2012. Effect: None. Territorial extent & classification: W. Local. - Available at http://www.legislation.gov.uk/wsi/2012/2741/contents/made. - In English and Welsh. Welsh title: Gorchymyn Cefnffyrdd yr A48, yr A40 a'r A4076 (Pont Abraham, Sir Gaerfyrddin i Aberdaugleddau, Sir Benfro) (Gwahardd Cerbydau, Cerddwyr a Beicwyr Dros Dro) 2012 *Non-print*

The A48 & A483 Trunk Roads & M4 Motorway (Hendy to Cross Hands, Carmarthenshire) (Temporary Prohibition of Vehicles) Order 2012 No. 2012/1487 (W.186). - Enabling power: Road Traffic Regulation Act 1984, s. 14 (1) (4). - Issued: 14.06.2012. Made: 01.06.2012. Coming into force: 11.06.2012. Effect: None. Territorial extent & classification: W. Local. - Available at http://www.legislation.gov.uk/wsi/2012/1487/contents/made. - In English and Welsh. Welsh title: Gorchymyn Cefnffyrdd yr A48 ac A483 a Thraffordd yr M4 (Hendy i Cross Hands, Sir Gaerfyrddin) (Gwahardd Cerbydau Dros Dro) 2012 *Non-print*

The A48 & A483 Trunk Roads & M4 Motorway (Pont Abraham Roundabout and its Approaches, Carmarthenshire) (Temporary Traffic Restrictions & Prohibition) (No. 2) Order 2012 No. 2012/3218 (W.320). - Enabling power: Road Traffic Regulation Act 1984, s. 14 (1) (4). - Issued: 07.01.2013. Made: 27.12.2012. Coming into force: 07.01.2013. Effect: None. Territorial extent & classification: W. Local. - Available at http://www.legislation.gov.uk/wsi/2012/3218/contents/made. - In English and Welsh. Welsh title: Gorchymyn Cefnffyrdd yr A48 a'r A483 a Thraffordd yr M4 (Cylchfan Pont Abraham a'r ffyrdd sy'n arwain ati, Sir Gaerfyrddin) (Cyfyngiadau a Gwaharddiad Traffig Dros Dro) (Rhif 2) 2012 *Non-print*

The A48 & A483 Trunk Roads & M4 Motorway (Pont Abraham Roundabout and its Approaches, Carmarthenshire) (Temporary Traffic Restrictions & Prohibition) Order 2012 No. 2012/395 (W.64). - Enabling power: Road Traffic Regulation Act 1984, s. 14 (1) (4). - Issued: 22.02.2012. Made: 15.02.2012. Coming into force: 27.02.2012. Effect: None. Territorial extent & classification: W. Local. - Available at http://www.legislation.gov.uk/wsi/2012/395/contents/made. - In English and Welsh. Welsh title: Gorchymyn Cefnffyrdd yr A48 a'r A483 a Thraffordd yr M4 (Cylchfan Pont Abraham a'r ffyrdd sy'n arwain ati, Sir Gaerfyrddin) (Cyfyngiadau Traffig a Gwaharddiad Dros Dro) 2012 *Non-print*

The A48 and A40 Trunk Roads (St Clears to Cross Hands, Carmarthenshire) (Temporary Traffic Restrictions and Prohibition) Order 2012 No. 2012/11 (W.4). - Enabling power: Road Traffic Regulation Act 1984, s. 14 (1) (4). - Issued: 09.01.2012. Made: 03.01.2012. Coming into force: 09.01.2012. Effect: None. Territorial extent & classification: W. Local. - Available at http://www.legislation.gov.uk/wsi/2012/11/contents/made. - In English and Welsh. Welsh title: Gorchymyn Cefnffyrdd yr A48 a'r A40 (Sanclêr i Cross Hands, Sir Gaerfyrddin) (Cyfyngiadau a Gwaharddiad Traffig Dros Dro) 2012 *Non-print*

The A48 Trunk Road & M4 Motorway (Earlswood Junction and Interchange, Neath Port Talbot) (Temporary Prohibition of Vehicles) Order 2012 No. 2012/428 (W.70). - Enabling power: Road Traffic Regulation Act 1984, s. 14 (1) (4). - Issued: 23.02.2012. Made: 17.02.2012. Coming into force: 27.02.2012. Effect: None. Territorial extent & classification: W. Local. - Available at http://www.legislation.gov.uk/wsi/2012/428/contents/made. - In English and Welsh. Welsh title: Gorchymyn Cefnffordd yr A48 a Thraffordd yr M4 (Cyffordd a Chyfnewidfa Earlswood, Castell-nedd Port Talbot) (Gwahardd Cerbydau Dros Dro) 2012 *Non-print*

The A55 & A494 Trunk Roads (Westbound Carriageway between Junction 35 and Junction 33b, Flintshire) (Temporary Traffic Restriction & Prohibitions) Order 2012 No. 2012/2949 (W.303). - Enabling power: Road Traffic Regulation Act 1984, s. 14 (1) (4). - Issued: 29.11.2012. Made: 26.11.2012. Coming into force: 03.12.2012. Effect: None. Territorial extent & classification: W. Local. - Available at http://www.legislation.gov.uk/wsi/2012/2949/contents/made. - In English and Welsh. Welsh title: *Non-print*

The A55 Trunk Road (Black Bridge, Holyhead, Isle of Anglesey to Junction 11 (Llys y Gwynt Interchange), Bangor, Gwynedd) (Temporary 40 mph Speed Limit & Prohibition of Vehicles) Order 2012 No. 2012/1268 (W.159). - Enabling power: Road Traffic Regulation Act 1984, s. 14 (1) (4). - Issued: 17.05.2012. Made: 11.05.2012. Coming into force: 21.05.2012. Effect: None. Territorial extent & classification: W. Local. - Available at http://www.legislation.gov.uk/wsi/2012/1268/contents/made. - In English and Welsh. Welsh title: Gorchymyn Cefnffordd yr A55 (Black Bridge, Caergybi, Ynys Môn i Gyffordd 11 (Cyfnewidfa Llys y Gwynt), Bangor, Gwynedd) (Cyfyngiad o 40 mya a Gwahardd Cerbydau Dros Dro) 2012 *Non-print*

The A55 Trunk Road (Conwy Tunnel, Conwy) (Temporary Traffic Restriction & Prohibitions) Order 2012 No. 2012/6 (W.2). - Enabling power: Road Traffic Regulation Act 1984, s. 14 (1) (4) (7). - Issued: 09.01.2012. Made: 03.01.2012. Coming into force: 08.01.2012. Effect: None. Territorial extent & classification: W. Local. - Available at http://www.legislation.gov.uk/wsi/2012/6/contents/made. - In English and Welsh. Welsh title: Gorchymyn Cefnffordd yr A55 (Twnnel Conwy, Conwy) (Cyfyngiad a Gwaharddiadau Traffig Dros Dro) 2012 *Non-print*

The A55 Trunk Road (Conwy Tunnel, Conwy) (Temporary Traffic Restrictions & Prohibitions) (No. 2) Order 2012 No. 2012/275 (W.45). - Enabling power: Road Traffic Regulation Act 1984, s. 14 (1) (4) (7). - Issued: 09.02.2012. Made: 06.02.2012. Coming into force: 19.02.2012. Effect: None. Territorial extent & classification: W. Local. - Available at http://www.legislation.gov.uk/wsi/2012/275/contents/made. - In English and Welsh. Welsh title: Gorchymyn Cefnffordd yr A55 (Twnnel Conwy, Conwy) (Cyfyngiadau a Gwaharddiadau Traffig Dros Dro) (Rhif 2) 2012 *Non-print*

The A55 Trunk Road (Eastbound Carriageway at Junction 20 (Colwyn Bay/Rhos on Sea), Conwy County Borough) (Temporary 40 mph Speed Limit & Prohibition of Vehicles) Order 2012 No. 2012/429 (W.71). - Enabling power: Road Traffic Regulation Act 1984, s. 14 (1) (4). - Issued: 23.02.2012. Made: 20.02.2012. Coming into force: 01.03.2012. Effect: None. Territorial extent & classification: W. Local. - Available at http://www.legislation.gov.uk/wsi/2012/429/contents/made. - In English and Welsh. Welsh title: Gorchymyn Cefnffordd yr A55 (Cerbytffordd Tua'r Dwyrain yng Nghyffordd 20 (Bae Colwyn/Llandrillo-yn-Rhos), Bwrdeistref Sirol Conwy) (Terfyn Cyflymder 40 mya a Gwahardd Cerbydau Dros Dro) 2012 *Non-print*

The A55 Trunk Road (Eastbound Carriageway at Junction 36 (Warren Interchange), Flintshire) (Temporary Prohibition of Vehicles & 40 mph Speed Limit) Order 2012 No. 2012/345 (W.57). - Enabling power: Road Traffic Regulation Act 1984, s. 14 (1) (4). - Issued: 15.02.2012. Made: 10.02.2012. Coming into force: 20.02.2012. Effect: None. Territorial extent & classification: W. Local. - Available at http://www.legislation.gov.uk/wsi/2012/345/contents/made . - In English and Welsh. Welsh title: Gorchymyn Cefnffordd yr A55 (Lôn Gerbydau Tua'r Dwyrain yng Nghyffordd 36 (Cyfnewidfa Warren), Sir y Fflint) (Gwaharddiad Dros Dro ar Gerbydau a Therfyn Cyflymder 40 mya) 2012 *Non-print*

The A55 Trunk Road (Eastbound Carriageway between Junction 31 and Junction 32, Flintshire) (Temporary Traffic Restriction & Prohibitions) Order 2012 No. 2012/561 (W. 85). - Enabling power: Road Traffic Regulation Act 1984, s. 14 (1) (4). - Issued: 02.03.2012. Made: 27.02.2012. Coming into force: 06.03.2012. Effect: None. Territorial extent & classification: W. Local. - Available at http://www.legislation.gov.uk/wsi/2012/561/contents/made . - In English and Welsh. Welsh title: Gorchymyn Cefnffordd yr A55 (Cerbytffordd Tua'r Dwyrain rhwng Cyffordd 31 a Chyffordd 32, Sir y Fflint) (Cyfyngiad a Gwaharddiadau Traffig Dros Dro) 2012 *Non-print*

The A55 Trunk Road (Junction 8A, Carreg Bran, Britannia Bridge, Isle of Anglesey) (Temporary Prohibition of Vehicles and 30 MPH Speed Limit) Order 2012 No. 2012/1195 (W.147). - Enabling power: Road Traffic Regulation Act 1984, s. 14 (1) (4). - Issued: 08.05.2012. Made: 01.05.2012. Coming into force: 12.05.2012. Effect: None. Territorial extent & classification: W. Local. - Available at http://www.legislation.gov.uk/wsi/2012/1195/contents/made . - In English and Welsh. Welsh title: Gorchymyn Cefnffordd yr A55 (Cyffordd 8A, Carreg Brân, Pont Britannia, Ynys Môn) (Gwahardd Cerbydau Dros Dro a Therfyn Cyflymder 30 MYA) 2012 *Non-print*

The A55 Trunk Road (Junction 11 (Llandegai Interchange) to Junction 9 (Treborth Interchange), Bangor, Gwynedd) (Temporary Traffic Restrictions & Prohibitions) Order 2012 No. 2012/1485 (W.184). - Enabling power: Road Traffic Regulation Act 1984, s. 14 (1) (4). - Issued: 14.06.2012. Made: 29.05.2012. Coming into force: 12.06.2012. Effect: None. Territorial extent & classification: W. Local. - Available at http://www.legislation.gov.uk/wsi/2012/1485/contents/made . - In English and Welsh. Welsh title: Gorchymyn Cefnffordd yr A55 (Cyffordd 11 (Cyfnewidfa Llandygái) i Gyffordd 9 (Cyfnewidfa Treborth), Bangor, Gwynedd) (Cyfyngiadau a Gwaharddiadau Traffig Dros Dro) 2012 *Non-print*

The A55 Trunk Road (Junction 11 (Llys y Gwynt Interchange), Bangor, Gwynedd to the Wales/England Border) and The A494/A550 Trunk Road (Ewloe Interchange, Flintshire) (Temporary 40 mph Speed Limit & Prohibition of Vehicles) Order 2012 No. 2012/945 (W.124). - Enabling power: Road Traffic Regulation Act 1984, s. 14 (1) (4). - Issued: 30.03.2012. Made: 23.03.2012. Coming into force: 01.04.2012. Effect: None. Territorial extent & classification: W. Local. - Available at http://www.legislation.gov.uk/wsi/2012/945/contents/made . - In English and Welsh. Welsh title: Gorchymyn Cefnffordd yr A55 (Cyffordd 11 (Cyfnewidfa Llys y Gwynt), Bangor, Gwynedd i Ffin Cymru/Lloegr) a Chefnffordd yr A494/A550 (Cyfnewidfa Ewloe, Sir y Fflint) (Terfyn Cyflymder 40 mya a Gwahardd Cerbydau Dros Dro) 2012 *Non-print*

The A55 Trunk Road (Junction 12, Talybont to Junction 13, Abergwyngregyn, Conwy) (Temporary Traffic Prohibitions and Restrictions) Order 2012 No. 2012/2506 (W.275). - Enabling power: Road Traffic Regulation Act 1984, s. 14 (1) (4) (7). - Issued: 05.10.2012. Made: 27.09.2012. Coming into force: 08.10.2012. Effect: None. Territorial extent & classification: W. Local. - Available at http://www.legislation.gov.uk/wsi/2012/2506/contents/made . - In English and Welsh. Welsh title: Gorchymyn Cefnffordd yr A55 (Cyffordd 12, Tal-y-bont i Gyffordd 13, Abergwyngregyn, Bwrdeistref Sirol Conwy) (Cyfyngiadau a Gwaharddiadau Traffig Dros Dro) 2012 *Non-print*

The A55 Trunk Road (Junction 14, Madryn Interchange to Junction 15, Llanfairfechan Roundabout, Conwy) (Temporary Traffic Prohibitions and Restriction) Order 2012 No. 2012/2498 (W.273). - Enabling power: Road Traffic Regulation Act 1984, s. 14 (1) (4). - Issued: 04.10.2012. Made: 17.09.2012. Coming into force: 29.09.2012. Effect: None. Territorial extent & classification: W. Local. - Available at http://www.legislation.gov.uk/wsi/2012/2498/contents/made . - In English and Welsh. Welsh title: Gorchymyn Cefnffordd yr A55 (Cyffordd 14, Cyfnewidfa Madryn i Gyffordd 15, Cylchfan Llanfairfechan, Conwy) (Gwaharddiadau a Chyfyngiad Traffig Dros Dro) 2012 *Non-print*

The A55 Trunk Road (Junction 16a (Dwygyfylchi) Conwy County Borough) (Temporary Traffic Restriction & Prohibitions) Order 2012 No. 2012/365 (W.60). - Enabling power: Road Traffic Regulation Act 1984, s. 14 (1) (4) (7). - Issued: 16.02.2012. Made: 10.02.2012. Coming into force: 20.02.2012. Effect: None. Territorial extent & classification: W. Local. - Available at http://www.legislation.gov.uk/wsi/2012/365/contents/made . - In English and Welsh. Welsh title: Gorchymyn Cefnffordd yr A55 (Cyffordd 16a (Dwygyfylchi) Bwrdeistref Sirol Conwy) (Cyfyngu a Gwahardd Traffig Dros Dro) 2012 *Non-print*

The A55 Trunk Road (Junction 18 (Llandudno Junction Interchange) to Junction 16 (Puffin Roundabout), Conwy County Borough) (Temporary Traffic Restrictions & Prohibitions) Order 2012 No. 2012/163 (W.23). - Enabling power: Road Traffic Regulation Act 1984, s. 14 (1) (4) (7). - Issued: 27.01.2012. Made: 23.01.2012. Coming into force: 29.01.2012. Effect: None. Territorial extent & classification: W. Local. - Available at http://www.legislation.gov.uk/wsi/2012/163/contents/made . - In English and Welsh. Welsh title: Gorchymyn Cefnffordd yr A55 (Cyffordd 18 (Cyfnewidfa Cyffordd Llandudno) i Gyffordd 16 (Cylchfan Puffin), Bwrdeistref Sirol Conwy) (Cyfyngiadau a Gwaharddiadau Traffig Dros Dro) 2012 *Non-print*

The A55 Trunk Road (Junction 23, Llanddulas, Conwy) (Temporary Traffic Prohibitions and Restriction) Order 2012 No. 2012/2032 (W.236). - Enabling power: Road Traffic Regulation Act 1984, s. 14 (1) (4) (7). - Issued: 08.08.2012. Made: 01.08.2012. Coming into force: 09.08.2012. Effect: None. Territorial extent & classification: W. Local. - Available at http://www.legislation.gov.uk/wsi/2012/2032/contents/made. - In English and Welsh. Welsh title: Gorchymyn Cefnffordd yr A55 (Cyffordd 23, Llanddulas, Conwy) (Gwaharddiadau Traffig a Chyfyngiad Traffig Dros Dro) 2012 *Non-print*

The A55 Trunk Road (Junction 25 (Bodelwyddan) to Junction 28 (Rhuallt), Denbighshire) (Temporary Traffic Restriction & Prohibitions) Order 2012 No. 2012/49 (W.12). - Enabling power: Road Traffic Regulation Act 1984, s. 14 (1) (4). - Issued: 12.01.2012. Made: 09.01.2012. Coming into force: 16.01.2012. Effect: None. Territorial extent & classification: W. Local. - Available at http://www.legislation.gov.uk/wsi/2012/49/contents/made. - In English and Welsh. Welsh title: Gorchymyn Cefnffordd yr A55 (Cyffordd 25 (Bodelwyddan) i Gyffordd 28 (Rhuallt), Sir Ddinbych) (Cyfyngiad a Gwaharddiadau Traffig Dros Dro) 2012 *Non-print*

The A55 Trunk Road (Junction 35, Dobshill, to Junction 36A, Broughton Retail Park, Flintshire) (Temporary Prohibitions and 40 MPH Speed Limit) Order 2012 No. 2012/614 (W. 86). - Enabling power: Road Traffic Regulation Act 1984, s. 14 (1) (4). - Issued: 05.03.2012. Made: 01.03.2012. Coming into force: 12.03.2012. Effect: None. Territorial extent & classification: W. Local. - Available at http://www.legislation.gov.uk/wsi/2012/614/contents/made . - In English and Welsh. Welsh title: Gorchymyn Cefnffordd yr A55 (Cyffordd 35, Dobshill, i Gyffordd 36A, Parc Manwerthu Brychdyn, Sir y Fflint) (Gwaharddiadau Dros Dro a Therfyn Cyflymder Dros Dro o 40 MYA) 2012 *Non-print*

The A55 Trunk Road (Junction 36a, Broughton, Flintshire) (Temporary Traffic Restriction & Prohibitions) Order 2012 No. 2012/699 (W.95). - Enabling power: Road Traffic Regulation Act 1984, s. 14 (1) (4). - Issued: 09.03.2012. Made: 02.03.2012. Coming into force: 13.03.2012. Effect: None. Territorial extent & classification: W. Local. - Available at http://www.legislation.gov.uk/wsi/2012/699/contents/made . - In English and Welsh. Welsh title: Gorchymyn Cefnffordd yr A55 (Cyffordd 36a, Brychdyn, Sir y Fflint) (Cyfyngiad a Gwaharddiadau Traffig Dros Dro) 2012 *Non-print*

The A55 Trunk Road (Penmaenbach Tunnel, Conwy County Borough) (Temporary Traffic Restrictions & Prohibitions) Order 2012 No. 2012/141 (W.18). - Enabling power: Road Traffic Regulation Act 1984, s. 14 (1) (4) (7). - Issued: 25.01.2012. Made: 20.01.2012. Coming into force: 29.01.2012. Effect: None. Territorial extent & classification: W. Local. - Available at http://www.legislation.gov.uk/wsi/2012/141/contents/made . - In English and Welsh. Welsh title: Gorchymyn Cefnffordd yr A55 (Twnnel Penmaen-bach, Bwrdeistref Sirol Conwy) (Cyfyngiadau a Gwaharddiadau Traffig Dros Dro) 2012 *Non-print*

The A55 Trunk Road (Pen-y-clip Tunnel, Conwy County Borough) (Temporary Traffic Prohibitions & Restrictions) Order 2012 No. 2012/423 (W.67). - Enabling power: Road Traffic Regulation Act 1984, s. 14 (1) (4) (7). - Issued: 23.02.2012. Made: 17.02.2012. Coming into force: 26.02.2012. Effect: None. Territorial extent & classification: W. Local. - Available at http://www.legislation.gov.uk/wsi/2012/423/contents/made . - In English and Welsh. Welsh title: Gorchymyn Cefnffordd yr A55 (Twnnel Pen-y-clip, Bwrdeistref Sirol Conwy) (Gwaharddiadau a Chyfyngiadau Dros Dro) 2012 *Non-print*

The A55 Trunk Road (Westbound Carriageway between Junction 19, Llandudno Junction and Junction 23, Llanddulas, Conwy) (Temporary Traffic Restriction & Prohibitions) Order 2012 No. 2012/1086 (W.134). - Enabling power: Road Traffic Regulation Act 1984, s. 14 (1) (4) (7). - Issued: 18.04.2012. Made: 13.04.2012. Coming into force: 23.04.2012. Effect: None. Territorial extent & classification: W. Local. - Available at http://www.legislation.gov.uk/wsi/2012/1086/contents/made. - In English and Welsh. Welsh title: Gorchymyn Cefnffordd yr A55 (Cerbytffordd tua'r Gorllewin rhwng Cyffordd 19, Cyffordd Llandudno, a Chyffordd 23, Llanddulas, Conwy) (Cyfyngiad a Gwaharddiadau Traffig Dros Dro) 2012 *Non-print*

Road traffic, Wales: Traffic regulation

The A55 Trunk Road (Westbound Carriageway between Junction 32a and Junction 31, Flintshire) (Temporary Traffic Restriction & Prohibitions) Order 2012 No. 2012/1036 (W.131). - Enabling power: Road Traffic Regulation Act 1984, s. 14 (1) (4). - Issued: 12.04.2012. Made: 05.04.2012. Coming into force: 16.04.2012. Effect: None. Territorial extent & classification: W. Local. - Available at http://www.legislation.gov.uk/wsi/2012/1036/contents/made. - In English and Welsh. Welsh title: Gorchymyn Cefnffordd yr A55 (Cerbytffordd tua'r Gorllewin rhwng Cyffordd 32a a Chyffordd 31, Sir y Fflint) (Cyfyngiad a Gwaharddiadau Traffig Dros Dro) 2012 *Non-print*

The A449 Trunk Road (Coldra Interchange, Newport to Usk Interchange, Monmouthshire) (Temporary Traffic Restrictions & Prohibitions) Order 2012 No. 2012/2934 (W.299). - Enabling power: Road Traffic Regulation Act 1984, s. 14 (1) (4). - Issued: 14.11.2012. Made: 20.11.2012. Coming into force: 02.12.2012. Effect: None. Territorial extent & classification: W. Local. - Available at http://www.legislation.gov.uk/wsi/2012/2934/contents/made. - In English and Welsh. Welsh title: Gorchymyn Cefnffordd yr A449 (Cyfnewidfa Coldra, Casnewydd i Gyfnewidfa Brynbuga, Sir Fynwy) (Cyfyngiadau a Gwaharddiadau Traffig Dros Dro) 2012 *Non-print*

The A458 Trunk Road (Brigands Inn, Mallwyd, Gwynedd) (Temporary Traffic Restrictions and Prohibition) Order 2012 No. 2012/1496 (W.194). - Enabling power: Road Traffic Regulation Act 1984, s. 14 (1) (4). - Issued: 14.06.2012. Made: 07.06.2012. Coming into force: 11.06.2012. Effect: None. Territorial extent & classification: W. Local. - Available at http://www.legislation.gov.uk/wsi/2012/1496/contents/made. - In English and Welsh. Welsh title: Gorchymyn Cefnffordd yr A458 (Brigands Inn, Mallwyd, Gwynedd) (Cyfyngiadau a Gwaharddiad Traffig Dros Dro) 2012 *Non-print*

The A458 Trunk Road (Cyfronydd to Heniarth, Powys) (Temporary Traffic Restrictions & Prohibitions) Order 2012 No. 2012/2947 (W.301). - Enabling power: Road Traffic Regulation Act 1984, s. 14 (1) (4). - Issued: 29.11.2012. Made: 26.11.2012. Coming into force: 30.11.2012. Effect: None. Territorial extent & classification: W. Local. - Available at http://www.legislation.gov.uk/wsi/2012/2947/contents/made. - In English and Welsh. Welsh title: Gorchymyn Cefnffordd yr A458 (Cyfronnydd i Heniarth, Powys) (Cyfyngiadau a Gwaharddiadau Traffig Dros Dro) 2012 *Non-print*

The A458 Trunk Road (Nant yr Ehedydd, Mallwyd, Gwynedd) (Temporary Traffic Restriction & Prohibitions) Order 2012 No. 2012/2557 (W.281). - Enabling power: Road Traffic Regulation Act 1984, s. 14 (1) (4). - Issued: 11.10.2012. Made: 08.10.2012. Coming into force: 15.10.2012. Effect: None. Territorial extent & classification: W. Local. - Available at http://www.legislation.gov.uk/wsi/2012/2557/contents/made. - In English and Welsh. Welsh title: Gorchymyn Cefnffordd yr A458 (Nant yr Ehedydd, Mallwyd, Gwynedd) (Cyfyngiad a Gwaharddiadau Traffig Dros Dro) 2012 *Non-print*

The A458 Trunk Road (Powys/Shropshire Border to Middletown, Powys) (Temporary Traffic Restrictions & Prohibitions) Order 2012 No. 2012/2948 (W.302). - Enabling power: Road Traffic Regulation Act 1984, s. 14 (1) (4). - Issued: 29.11.2012. Made: 26.11.2012. Coming into force: 03.12.2012. Effect: None. Territorial extent & classification: W. Local. - Available at http://www.legislation.gov.uk/wsi/2012/2948/contents/made. - In English and Welsh. Welsh title: Gorchymyn Cefnffordd yr A458 (Ffin Powys/Swydd Amwythig i Dreberfedd, Powys) (Cyfyngiadau a Gwaharddiadau Traffig Dros Dro) 2012 *Non-print*

The A458 Trunk Road (The Powys and Shropshire County Boundary near Middletown to Buttington Roundabout, Welshpool, Powys) (Temporary Traffic Restrictions & Prohibition) Order 2012 No. 2012/2244 (W.249). - Enabling power: Road Traffic Regulation Act 1984, s. 14 (1) (4). - Issued: 05.09.2012. Made: 29.08.2012. Coming into force: 04.09.2012. Effect: None. Territorial extent & classification: W. Local. - Available at http://www.legislation.gov.uk/wsi/2012/2244/contents/made. - In English and Welsh. Welsh title: Gorchymyn Cefnffordd yr A458 (Ffin Sirol Powys a Swydd Amwythig ger Treberfedd i Gylchfan Tal-y-bont, Y Trallwng, Powys) (Cyfyngiadau a Gwaharddiad Traffig Dros Dro) 2012 *Non-print*

The A458 Trunk Road (Various Locations between Mallwyd Gwynedd and Welshpool, Powys) (Temporary Traffic Restrictions & Prohibition) Order 2012 No. 2012/1272 (W.162). - Enabling power: Road Traffic Regulation Act 1984, s. 14 (1) (4). - Issued: 17.05.2012. Made: 14.05.2012. Coming into force: 21.05.2012. Effect: None. Territorial extent & classification: W. Local. - Available at http://www.legislation.gov.uk/wsi/2012/1272/contents/made. - In English and Welsh. Welsh title: Gorchymyn Cefnffordd yr A458 (Lleoliadau Amrywiol rhwng Mallwyd, Gwynedd a'r Trallwng, Powys) (Cyfyngiadau a Gwaharddiad Traffig Dros Dro) 2012 *Non-print*

Road traffic, Wales: Traffic regulation

The A465 Trunk Road (Brynmawr, Blaenau Gwent to Gilwern, Monmouthshire) (Temporary Traffic Restrictions & Prohibitions) Order 2012 No. 2012/559 (W. 84). - Enabling power: Road Traffic Regulation Act 1984, s. 14 (1) (4). - Issued: 02.03.2012. Made: 24.02.2012. Coming into force: 05.03.2012. Effect: None. Territorial extent & classification: W. Local. - Available at http://www.legislation.gov.uk/wsi/2012/559/contents/made. - In English and Welsh. Welsh title: Gorchymyn Cefnffordd yr A465 (Brynmawr, Blaenau Gwent i Gilwern, Sir Fynwy) (Cyfyngiadau a Gwaharddiadau Traffig Dros Dro) 2012 *Non-print*

The A465 Trunk Road (Cwmgwrach Roundabout to Resolven Roundabout, Neath Port Talbot) (Temporary Prohibition of Vehicles) Order 2012 No. 2012/2820 (W.298). - Enabling power: Road Traffic Regulation Act 1984, s. 14 (1) (4). - Issued: 14.11.2012. Made: 09.11.2012. Coming into force: 19.11.2012. Effect: None. Territorial extent & classification: W. Local. - Available at http://www.legislation.gov.uk/wsi/2012/2820/contents/made. - In English and Welsh. Welsh title: Gorchymyn Cefnffordd yr A465 (Cylchfan Cwm-gwrach i Gylchfan Resolfen, Castell-nedd Port Talbot) (Gwahardd Cerbydau Dros Dro) 2012 *Non-print*

The A465 Trunk Road (Dowlais Top Roundabout, Merthyr Tydfil) (Temporary Traffic Restrictions and Prohibitions) Order 2012 No. 2012/678 (W.91). - Enabling power: Road Traffic Regulation Act 1984, s. 14 (1) (4). - Issued: 07.03.2012. Made: 02.03.2012. Coming into force: 12.03.2012. Effect: None. Territorial extent & classification: W. Local. - Available at http://www.legislation.gov.uk/wsi/2012/678/contents/made. - In English and Welsh. Welsh title: Gorchymyn Cefnffordd yr A465 (Cylchfan Dowlais Top, Merthyr Tudful) (Cyfyngiadau a Gwaharddiadau Traffig Dros Dro) 2012 *Non-print*

The A465 Trunk Road (Glynneath Interchange, Neath Port Talbot to Rhigos Roundabout, Rhondda Cynon Taf) (Temporary Traffic Restriction & Prohibition) Order 2012 No. 2012/273 (W.43). - Enabling power: Road Traffic Regulation Act 1984, s. 14 (1) (4). - Issued: 09.02.2012. Made: 03.02.2012. Coming into force: 13.02.2012. Effect: None. Territorial extent & classification: W. Local. - Available at http://www.legislation.gov.uk/wsi/2012/273/contents/made. - In English and Welsh. Welsh title: Gorchymyn Cefnffordd yr A465 (Cyfnewidfa Glyn-nedd, Castell-nedd Port Talbot i Gylchfan Rhigos, Rhondda Cynon Taf) (Cyfyngiad a Gwaharddiad Traffig Dros Dro) 2012 *Non-print*

The A465 Trunk Road (Hereford Road, North of Abergavenny, Monmouthshire) (Temporary Traffic Restrictions & Prohibitions) Order 2012 No. 2012/2525 (W. 277). - Enabling power: Road Traffic Regulation Act 1984, ss. 14 (1) (4) (7). - Issued: 09.10.2012. Made: 04.10.2012. Coming into force: 08.10.2012. Effect: None. Territorial extent & classification: W. Local. - Available at http://www.legislation.gov.uk/wsi/2012/2525/contents/made. - In English and Welsh. Welsh title: Gorchymyn Cefnffordd yr A465 (Hereford Road, Man i'r Gogledd o'r Fenni, Sir Fynwy) (Cyfyngiadau a Gwaharddiadau Traffig Dros Dro) 2012 *Non-print*

The A465 Trunk Road (Near Llangua, Monmouthshire) (Temporary Traffic Restrictions and Prohibition) Order 2012 No. 2012/426 (W.68). - Enabling power: Road Traffic Regulation Act 1984, s. 14 (1) (4). - Issued: 23.02.2012. Made: 17.02.2012. Coming into force: 27.02.2012. Effect: None. Territorial extent & classification: W. Local. - Available at http://www.legislation.gov.uk/wsi/2012/426/contents/made. - In English and Welsh. Welsh title: Gorchymyn Cefnffordd yr A465 (ger Llangiwa, Sir Fynwy) (Cyfyngiadau a Gwaharddiad Dros Dro ar Draffig) 2012 *Non-print*

The A465 Trunk Road (Neath Interchange, Neath Port Talbot) (Temporary Prohibition of Vehicles) Order 2012 No. 2012/2819 (W.297). - Enabling power: Road Traffic Regulation Act 1984, s. 14 (1) (4). - Issued: 14.11.2012. Made: 09.11.2012. Coming into force: 19.11.2012. Effect: None. Territorial extent & classification: W. Local. - Available at http://www.legislation.gov.uk/wsi/2012/2819/contents/made. - In English and Welsh. Welsh title: Gorchymyn Cefnffordd yr A465 (Cyfnewidfa Castell-nedd, Castell-nedd Port Talbot) (Gwahardd Cerbydau Dros Dro) 2012 *Non-print*

The A465 Trunk Road (Princetown to Rassau Industrial Estate Roundabout, Blaenau Gwent) (Temporary Traffic Restrictions & Prohibition) Order 2012 No. 2012/396 (W.65). - Enabling power: Road Traffic Regulation Act 1984, s. 14 (1) (4). - Issued: 20.02.2012. Made: 16.02.2012. Coming into force: 27.02.2012. Effect: None. Territorial extent & classification: W. Local. - Available at http://www.legislation.gov.uk/wsi/2012/396/contents/made. - In English and Welsh. Welsh title: Gorchymyn Cefnffordd yr A465 (Princetown i Gylchfan Ystad Ddiwydiannol Rasa, Blaenau Gwent) (Cyfyngiadau a Gwaharddiad Traffig Dros Dro) 2012 *Non-print*

Road traffic, Wales: Traffic regulation

The A465 Trunk Road (Rassau Industrial Estate Roundabout to Garnlydan, Blaenau Gwent) (Temporary Traffic Restrictions & Prohibition) Order 2012 No. 2012/394 (W.63). - Enabling power: Road Traffic Regulation Act 1984, s. 14 (1) (4). - Issued: 22.02.2012. Made: 15.02.2012. Coming into force: 27.02.2012. Effect: None. Territorial extent & classification: W. Local. - Available at http://www.legislation.gov.uk/wsi/2012/394/contents/made. - In English and Welsh. Welsh title: Gorchymyn Cefnffordd yr A465 (Cylchfan Ystad Ddiwydiannol Rasa i Garnlydan, Blaenau Gwent) (Cyfyngiadau a Gwaharddiad Traffig Dros Dro) 2012 *Non-print*

The A465 Trunk Road (Rassau Roundabout to Ebbw Vale Roundabout, Blaenau Gwent) (Temporary Traffic Restrictions & Prohibitions) Order 2012 No. 2012/2448 (W.266). - Enabling power: Road Traffic Regulation Act 1984, s. 14 (1) (4). - Issued: 27.09.2012. Made: 21.09.2012. Coming into force: 01.10.2012. Effect: None. Territorial extent & classification: W. Local. - Available at http://www.legislation.gov.uk/wsi/2012/2448/contents/made. - In English and Welsh. Welsh title: Gorchymyn Cefnffordd yr A465 (Cylchfan Rasa i Gylchfan Glynebwy, Blaenau Gwent) (Cyfyngiadau a Gwaharddiadau Traffig Dros Dro) 2012 *Non-print*

The A470, A40, A479 & A483 Trunk Roads (Various Locations in the Counties of Merthyr Tydfil, Brecon and Powys) (Temporary Prohibition of Vehicular and Non Vehicular Traffic) Order 2012 No. 2012/1130 (W.136). - Enabling power: Road Traffic Regulation Act 1984, s. 14 (1) (4). - Issued: 26.04.2012. Made: 09.04.2012. Coming into force: 16.04.2012. Effect: None. Territorial extent & classification: W. Local. - Available at http://www.legislation.gov.uk/wsi/2012/1130/contents/made. - In English and Welsh. Welsh title: Gorchymyn Cefnffyrdd yr A470, yr A40, yr A479 a'r A483 (Lleoliadau Amrywiol yn Siroedd Merthyr Tudful a Phowys) (Gwahardd Dros Dro Draffig Cerbydol a Thraffig nad yw'n Gerbydol) 2012 *Non-print*

The A470 Trunk Road (Abercynon Roundabout, Rhondda Cynon Taf, to Abercanaid Roundabout, Merthyr Tydfil) (Temporary Traffic Restriction and Prohibitions) Order 2012 No. 2012/2410 (W.260). - Enabling power: Road Traffic Regulation Act 1984, s. 14 (1) (4). - Issued: 24.09.2012. Made: 18.09.2012. Coming into force: 24.09.2012. Effect: None. Territorial extent & classification: W. Local. - Available at http://www.legislation.gov.uk/wsi/2012/2410/contents/made. - In English and Welsh. Welsh title: Gorchymyn Cefnffordd yr A470 (Cylchfan Abercynon, Rhondda Cynon Taf, i Gylchfan Abercannaid, Merthyr Tudful) (Cyfyngiadau a Gwaharddiadau Traffig Dros Dro) 2012 *Non-print*

The A470 Trunk Road (Black Cat Interchange to Glan Conwy, Conwy County Borough) (Temporary Traffic Restrictions & Prohibition) Order 2012 No. 2012/1171 (W.144). - Enabling power: Road Traffic Regulation Act 1984, s. 14 (1) (4). - Issued: 03.05.2012. Made: 27.04.2012. Coming into force: 08.05.2012. Effect: None. Territorial extent & classification: W. Local. - Available at http://www.legislation.gov.uk/wsi/2012/1171/contents/made. - In English and Welsh. Welsh title: Gorchymyn Cefnffordd yr A470 (Cyfnewidfa'r Black Cat i Lanconwy, Bwrdeistref Sirol Conwy) (Cyfyngu a Gwahardd Traffig Dros Dro) 2012 *Non-print*

The A470 Trunk Road (Brecon to Llyswen, Powys) (Temporary Traffic Restrictions & Prohibition) Order 2012 No. 2012/486 (W.81). - Enabling power: Road Traffic Regulation Act 1984, s. 14 (1) (4). - Issued: 28.02.2012. Made: 23.02.2012. Coming into force: 05.03.2012. Effect: None. Territorial extent & classification: W. Local. - Available at http://www.legislation.gov.uk/wsi/2012/486/contents/made. - In English and Welsh. Welsh title: Gorchymyn Cefnffordd yr A470 (Aberhonddu i Lys-wen, Powys) (Cyfyngiadau a Gwaharddiad Dros Dro ar Draffig) 2012 *Non-print*

The A470 Trunk Road (Caersws to Cemmaes Road Roundabout) (Temporary Traffic Restrictions and Prohibition) Order 2012 No. 2012/2219 (W.247). - Enabling power: Road Traffic Regulation Act 1984, s. 14 (1) (4). - Issued: 03.09.2012. Made: 24.08.2012. Coming into force: 04.09.2012. Effect: None. Territorial extent & classification: W. Local. - Available at http://www.legislation.gov.uk/wsi/2012/2219/contents/made. - In English and Welsh. Welsh title: Gorchymyn Cefnffordd yr A470 (Caersws i Gylchfan Glantwymyn, Powys) (Cyfyngiadau a Gwaharddiad Traffig Dros Dro) 2012 *Non-print*

The A470 Trunk Road (Coed y Celyn, Conwy) (Temporary Traffic Restrictions and Prohibition) Order 2012 No. 2012/22 (W.8). - Enabling power: Road Traffic Regulation Act 1984, s. 14 (1) (4). - Issued: 12.01.2012. Made: 06.01.2012. Coming into force: 16.01.2012. Effect: None. Territorial extent & classification: W. Local. - Available at http://www.legislation.gov.uk/wsi/2012/22/contents/made. - In English and Welsh. Welsh title: Gorchymyn Cefnffordd yr A470 (Coedycelyn, Conwy) (Cyfyngu a Gwahardd Traffig Dros Dro) 2012 *Non-print*

The A470 Trunk Road (Dolwyddelan, Conwy County Borough) (Temporary Traffic Restrictions & Prohibition) Order 2012 No. 2012/1494 (W.192). - Enabling power: Road Traffic Regulation Act 1984, s. 14 (1) (4). - Issued: 18.06.2012. Made: 01.06.2012. Coming into force: 11.06.2012. Effect: None. Territorial extent & classification: W. Local. - Available at http://www.legislation.gov.uk/wsi/2012/1494/contents/made. - In English and Welsh. Welsh title: Gorchymyn Cefnffordd yr A470 (Dolwyddelan, Bwrdeistref Sirol Conwy) (Cyfyngiadau a Gwaharddiad Traffig Dros Dro) 2012 *Non-print*

The A470 Trunk Road (Glan Conwy to Eglwysbach, Conwy County Borough) (Temporary Traffic Restrictions & Prohibition) Order 2012 No. 2012/1170 (W.143). - Enabling power: Road Traffic Regulation Act 1984, s. 14 (1) (4). - Issued: 03.05.2012. Made: 27.04.2012. Coming into force: 08.05.2012. Effect: None. Territorial extent & classification: W. Local. - Available at http://www.legislation.gov.uk/wsi/2012/1170/contents/made. - In English and Welsh. Welsh title: Gorchymyn Cefnffordd yr A470 (Glanconwy i Eglwys-bach, Bwrdeistref Sirol Conwy) (Cyfyngu a Gwahardd Traffig Dros Dro) 2012 *Non-print*

The A470 Trunk Road (Glan y Rhyd, Conwy) (Temporary Traffic Restrictions and Prohibition) Order 2012 No. 2012/422 (W.66). - Enabling power: Road Traffic Regulation Act 1984, s. 14 (1) (4). - Issued: 23.02.2012. Made: 17.02.2012. Coming into force: 27.02.2012. Effect: None. Territorial extent & classification: W. Local. - Available at http://www.legislation.gov.uk/wsi/2012/422/contents/made. - In English and Welsh. Welsh title: Gorchymyn Cefnffordd yr A470 (Glan-y-rhyd, Conwy) (Cyfyngu a Gwahardd Traffig Dros Dro) 2012 *Non-print*

The A470 Trunk Road (Llyswen, Powys) (Temporary Prohibition of Vehicles) Order 2012 No. 2012/2634 (W.286). - Enabling power: Road Traffic Regulation Act 1984, s. 14 (1) (4). - Issued: 24.10.2012. Made: 18.10.2012. Coming into force: 29.10.2012. Effect: None. Territorial extent & classification: W. Local. - Available at http://www.legislation.gov.uk/wsi/2012/2634/contents/made. - In English and Welsh. Welsh title: Gorchymyn Cefnffordd yr A470 (Llys-wen, Powys) (Gwahardd Cerbydau Dros Dro) 201 *Non-print*

The A470 Trunk Road (Maenan, Conwy County Borough) (Temporary Traffic Restrictions & Prohibition) Order 2012 No. 2012/675 (W.89). - Enabling power: Road Traffic Regulation Act 1984, s. 14 (1) (4). - Issued: 07.03.2012. Made: 02.03.2012. Coming into force: 12.03.2012. Effect: None. Territorial extent & classification: W. Local. - Available at http://www.legislation.gov.uk/wsi/2012/675/contents/made. - In English and Welsh. Welsh title: Gorchymyn Cefnffordd yr A470 (Maenan, Bwrdeistref Sirol Conwy) (Cyfyngu a Gwahardd Traffig Dros Dro) 2012 *Non-print*

The A470 Trunk Road (Maes yr Helmau to Cross Foxes, Gwynedd) (Temporary Traffic Restrictions and Prohibitions) Order 2012 No. 2012/445 (W.73). - Enabling power: Road Traffic Regulation Act 1984, s. 14 (1) (4). - Issued: 24.02.2012. Made: 21.02.2012. Coming into force: 05.03.2012. Effect: None. Territorial extent & classification: W. Local. - Available at http://www.legislation.gov.uk/wsi/2012/445/contents/made. - In English and Welsh. Welsh title: Gorchymyn Cefnffordd yr A470 (Maes yr Helmau i Cross Foxes, Gwynedd) (Cyfyngiadau a Gwaharddiadau Traffig Dros Dro) 2012 *Non-print*

The A470 Trunk Road (Nant Ddu Lodge to Llanelwedd Roundabout, Powys) (Temporary Traffic Restrictions & Prohibition) Order 2012 No. 2012/1412 (W.172). - Enabling power: Road Traffic Regulation Act 1984, s. 14 (1) (4). - Issued: 06.06.2012. Made: 22.05.2012. Coming into force: 01.06.2012. Effect: None. Territorial extent & classification: W. Local. - Available at http://www.legislation.gov.uk/wsi/2012/1412/contents/made. - In English and Welsh. Welsh title: Gorchymyn Cefnffordd yr A470 (Nant Ddu Lodge i Gylchfan Llanelwedd, Powys) (Cyfyngiadau a Gwaharddiad Traffig Dros Dro) 2012 *Non-print*

The A470 Trunk Road (Navigation Park to Abercynon Roundabout, Rhondda Cynon Taf) (Temporary Prohibition of Vehicles) Order 2012 No. 2012/1718 (W.223). - Enabling power: Road Traffic Regulation Act 1984, s. 14 (1) (4). - Issued: 05.07.2012. Made: 03.07.2012. Coming into force: 16.07.2012. Effect: None. Territorial extent & classification: W. Local. - Available at http://www.legislation.gov.uk/wsi/2012/1718/contents/made. - In English and Welsh. Welsh title: Gorchymyn Cefnffordd yr A470 (Parc Navigation i Gylchfan Abercynon, Rhondda Cynon Taf) (Gwahardd Cerbydau Dros Dro) 2012 *Non-print*

The A470 Trunk Road (Near Talerddig, Powys) (Temporary Prohibition of Vehicles) Order 2012 No. 2012/2389 (W.256). - Enabling power: Road Traffic Regulation Act 1984, s. 14 (1) (4). - Issued: 19.09.2012. Made: 14.09.2012. Coming into force: 24.09.2012. Effect: None. Territorial extent & classification: W. Local. - Available at http://www.legislation.gov.uk/wsi/2012/2389/contents/made. - In English and Welsh. Welsh title: Gorchymyn Cefnffordd yr A470 (Ger Talerddig, Powys) (Gwahardd Cerbydau Dros Dro) 2012 *Non-print*

The A470 Trunk Road (Northbound Exit & Entry Slip Roads at Nantgarw Interchange, Rhondda Cynon Taf) (Temporary Prohibition of Vehicles & Cyclists) Order 2012 No. 2012/1694 (W.219). - Enabling power: Road Traffic Regulation Act 1984, s. 14 (1) (4). - Issued: 04.07.2012. Made: 28.06.2012. Coming into force: 09.07.2012. Effect: None. Territorial extent & classification: W. Local. - Available at http://www.legislation.gov.uk/wsi/2012/1694/contents/made. - In English and Welsh. Welsh title: Gorchymyn Cefnffordd yr A470 (Ffyrdd Ymuno ac Ymadael tua'r Gogledd wrth Gyfnewidfa Nantgarw, Rhondda Cynon Taf) (Gwahardd Cerbydau a Beicwyr Dros Dro) 2012 *Non-print*

Road traffic, Wales: Traffic regulation

The A470 Trunk Road (Pontdolgoch, Powys) (Temporary Traffic Restrictions and Prohibition) Order 2012 No. 2012/777 (W.104). - Enabling power: Road Traffic Regulation Act 1984, s. 14 (1) (4). - Issued: 15.03.2012. Made: 09.03.2012. Coming into force: 19.03.2012. Effect: None. Territorial extent & classification: W. Local. - Available at http://www.legislation.gov.uk/wsi/2012/777/contents/made. - In English and Welsh. Welsh title: Gorchymyn Cefnffordd yr A470 (Pont-dôl-goch, Powys) (Cyfyngiadau a Gwaharddiad Traffig Dros Dro) 2012 *Non-print. Issued 15 March 2012 - we apologise for late appearance on the list*

The A470 Trunk Road (Rhyd-y-Creuau, Betws-y-Coed, Conwy County Borough) (Temporary Traffic Restrictions & Prohibition) Order 2012 No. 2012/162 (W.22). - Enabling power: Road Traffic Regulation Act 1984, s. 14 (1) (4). - Issued: 27.01.2012. Made: 23.01.2012. Coming into force: 01.02.2012. Effect: None. Territorial extent & classification: W. Local. - Available at http://www.legislation.gov.uk/wsi/2012/162/contents/made. - In English and Welsh. Welsh title: Gorchymyn Cefnffordd yr A470 (Rhyd-y-creuau, Betws-y-coed, Bwrdeistref Sirol Conwy) (Cyfyngiadau a Gwaharddiad Traffig Dros Dro) 2012 *Non-print*

The A470 Trunk Road (Southbound Exit Slip Road at Nantgarw Interchange, Rhondda Cynon Taf) (Temporary Prohibition of Vehicles & Cyclists) Order 2012 No. 2012/1913 (W.235). - Enabling power: Road Traffic Regulation Act 1984, s. 14 (1) (4). - Issued: 17.08.2012. Made: 13.08.2012. Coming into force: 22.08.2012. Effect: None. Territorial extent & classification: W. Local. - Available at http://www.legislation.gov.uk/wsi/2012/1913/contents/made. - In English and Welsh. Welsh title: Gorchymyn Cefnffordd yr A470 (Y Ffordd Ymadael tua'r De wrth Gyfnewidfa Nantgarw, Rhondda Cynon Taf) (Gwahardd Cerbydau a Beicwyr Dros Dro) 2012 *Non-print*

The A470 Trunk Road (Various Locations between Rhayader Quarry and Llangurig, Powys) (Temporary Traffic Restrictions & Prohibition) Order 2012 No. 2012/1417 (W.173). - Enabling power: Road Traffic Regulation Act 1984, s. 14 (1) (4). - Issued: 06.06.2012. Made: 28.05.2012. Coming into force: 06.06.2012. Effect: None. Territorial extent & classification: W. Local. - Available at http://www.legislation.gov.uk/wsi/2012/1417/contents/made. - In English and Welsh. Welsh title: Gorchymyn Cefnffordd yr A470 (Lleoliadau Amrywiol rhwng Chwarel Rhaeadr Gwy a Llangurig, Powys) (Cyfyngiadau a Gwaharddiad Traffig Dros Dro) 2012 *Non-print*

The A477 Trunk Road (Broadmoor to Redberth, Pembrokeshire) (Temporary Traffic Restrictions & Prohibition) Order 2012 No. 2012/3219 (W.321). - Enabling power: Road Traffic Regulation Act 1984, s. 14 (1) (4). - Issued: 07.01.2013. Made: 27.12.2012. Coming into force: 07.01.2013. Effect: None. Territorial extent & classification: W. Local. - Available at http://www.legislation.gov.uk/wsi/2012/3219/contents/made. - In English and Welsh. Welsh title: Gorchymyn Cefnffordd yr A477 (Broadmoor i Redberth, Sir Benfro) (Cyfyngiadau a Gwaharddiad Traffig Dros Dro) 2012 *Non-print*

The A477 Trunk Road (Killgetty, Pembrokeshire) (Temporary Traffic Restrictions and Prohibition) Order 2012 No. 2012/19 (W.6). - Enabling power: Road Traffic Regulation Act 1984, s. 14 (1) (4). - Issued: 10.01.2012. Made: 06.01.2012. Coming into force: 16.01.2012. Effect: None. Territorial extent & classification: W. Local. - Available at http://www.legislation.gov.uk/wsi/2012/19/contents/made. - In English and Welsh. Welsh title: Gorchymyn Cefnffordd yr A477 (Cilgeti, Sir Benfro) (Cyfyngiadau Traffig a Gwaharddiad Dros Dro) 2012 *Non-print*

The A477 Trunk Road (Milton to Slade Cross, Pembrokeshire) (Temporary Traffic Restrictions & Prohibition) Order 2012 No. 2012/3034 (W.309). - Enabling power: Road Traffic Regulation Act 1984, s. 14 (1) (4). - Issued: 04.01.2013. Made: 03.12.2012. Coming into force: 10.12.2012. Effect: None. Territorial extent & classification: W. Local. - Available at http://www.legislation.gov.uk/wsi/2012/3034/contents/made. - In English and Welsh. Welsh title: Gorchymyn Cefnffordd yr A477 (Milton i Slade Cross, Sir Benfro) (Cyfyngiadau a Gwaharddiad Traffig Dros Dro) 2012 *Non-print*

The A477 Trunk Road (Red Roses, Carmarthenshire) (Temporary Traffic Restriction & Prohibition) Order 2012 No. 2012/3220 (W.322). - Enabling power: Road Traffic Regulation Act 1984, s. 14 (1) (4). - Issued: 07.01.2013. Made: 27.12.2012. Coming into force: 07.01.2013. Effect: None. Territorial extent & classification: W. Local. - Available at http://www.legislation.gov.uk/wsi/2012/3220/contents/made. - In English and Welsh. Welsh title: Gorchymyn Cefnffordd yr A477 (Rhos-goch, Sir Gaerfyrddin) (Cyfyngiad a Gwaharddiad Traffig Dros Dro) 2012 *Non-print*

The A477 Trunk Road (West of Carew Roundabout to Redberth Junction, Pembrokeshire) (Temporary Traffic Restrictions and Prohibitions) Order 2012 No. 2012/2377 (W.255). - Enabling power: Road Traffic Regulation Act 1984, s. 14 (1) (4). - Issued: 18.09.2012. Made: 13.09.2012. Coming into force: 23.09.2012. Effect: None. Territorial extent & classification: W. Local. - Available at http://www.legislation.gov.uk/wsi/2012/2377/contents/made. - In English and Welsh. Welsh title: Gorchymyn Cefnffordd yr A477 (Man i'r Gorllewin o Gylchfan Caeriw i Gyffordd Redberth, Sir Benfro) (Cyfyngiadau a Gwaharddiadau Traffig Dros Dro) 2012 *Non-print*

Road traffic, Wales: Traffic regulation

The A477 Trunk Road (West of St Clears to West of Red Roses, Carmarthenshire) (Temporary Traffic Restrictions & Prohibition) Order 2012 No. 2012/944 (W.123). - Enabling power: Road Traffic Regulation Act 1984, s. 14 (1) (4). - Issued: 29.03.2012. Made: 23.03.2012. Coming into force: 01.04.2012. Effect: None. Territorial extent & classification: W. Local. - Available at http://www.legislation.gov.uk/wsi/2012/944/contents/made. - In English and Welsh. Welsh title: Gorchymyn Cefnffordd yr A477 (Man i'r Gorllewin o Sanclêr i Fan i'r Gorllewin o Ros-goch, Sir Gaerfyrddin) (Cyfyngiadau a Gwaharddiad Traffig Dros Dro) 2012 *Non-print*

The A479 Trunk Road (Marish Junction to Dderw Roundabout, South of Llyswen, Powys) (Temporary Traffic Restrictions & Prohibitions) Order 2012 No. 2012/1629 (W.208). - Enabling power: Road Traffic Regulation Act 1984, s. 14 (1) (4). - Issued: 26.06.2012. Made: 21.06.2012. Coming into force: 01.07.2012. Effect: None. Territorial extent & classification: W. Local. - Available at http://www.legislation.gov.uk/wsi/2012/1629/contents/made. - In English and Welsh. Welsh title: Gorchymyn Cefnffordd yr A479 (Cyffordd Marish i Gylchfan Dderw, i'r De o Lys-wen, Powys) (Cyfyngiadau a Gwaharddiadau Traffig Dros Dro) 2012 *Non-print*

The A483, A489, A470 & A44 Trunk Roads (Various Locations in the Counties of Powys and Ceredigion) (Temporary Prohibition of Vehicles, Pedestrians & Cyclists) Order 2012 No. 2012/1059 (W.132). - Enabling power: Road Traffic Regulation Act 1984, s. 14 (1) (4). - Issued: 16.04.2012. Made: 10.04.2012. Coming into force: 13.04.2012. Effect: None. Territorial extent & classification: W. Local. - Available at http://www.legislation.gov.uk/wsi/2012/1059/contents/made. - In English and Welsh. Welsh title: Gorchymyn Cefnffyrdd yr A483, yr A489, yr A470 a'r A44 (Lleoliadau Amrywiol yn Siroedd Powys a Cheredigion) (Gwahardd Cerbydau, Cerddwyr a Beicwyr Dros Dro) 2012 *Non-print*

The A483 Trunk Road (Bridge Street, Llandeilo, Carmarthenshire) (Temporary Waiting Restrictions & Prohibitions) Order 2012 No. 2012/2600 (W.284). - Enabling power: Road Traffic Regulation Act 1984, s. 14 (1) (4). - Issued: 18.10.2012. Made: 11.10.2012. Coming into force: 17.10.2012. Effect: None. Territorial extent & classification: W. Local. - Available at http://www.legislation.gov.uk/wsi/2012/2600/contents/made. - In English and Welsh. Welsh title: Gorchymyn Cefnffordd yr A483 (Heol y Bont, Llandeilo, Sir Gaerfyrddin) (Cyfyngiadau a Gwaharddiadau ar Aros Dros Dro) 2012 *Non-print*

The A483 Trunk Road (Cwmrhiwdre, Powys) (Temporary Traffic Restrictions & Prohibitions) Order 2012 No. 2012/1419 (W.175). - Enabling power: Road Traffic Regulation Act 1984, s. 14 (1) (4). - Issued: 14.06.2012. Made: 29.05.2012. Coming into force: 10.06.2012. Effect: None. Territorial extent & classification: W. Local. - Available at http://www.legislation.gov.uk/wsi/2012/1419/contents/made. - In English and Welsh. Welsh title: Gorchymyn Cefnffordd yr A483 (Cwmyrhiwdre, Powys) (Cyfyngiadau a Gwaharddiadau Traffig Dros Dro) 2012 *Non-print*

The A483 Trunk Road (Ffairfach Level Crossing, Ffairfach, Carmarthenshire) (Temporary Prohibition of Vehicles) Order 2012 No. 2012/2445 (W.263). - Enabling power: Road Traffic Regulation Act 1984, s. 14 (1) (4). - Issued: 27.09.2012. Made: 20.09.2012. Coming into force: 29.09.2012. Effect: None. Territorial extent & classification: W. Local. - Available at http://www.legislation.gov.uk/wsi/2012/2445/contents/made. - In English and Welsh. Welsh title: Gorchymyn Cefnffordd yr A483 (Croesfan Reilffordd Ffair-fach, Ffair-fach, Sir Gaerfyrddin) (Gwahardd Cerbydau Dros Dro) 2012 *Non-print*

The A483 Trunk Road (Junction 1, Ruabon, Wrexham) (Temporary Prohibition of Vehicles & 40 mph Speed Limit) Order 2012 No. 2012/274 (W.44). - Enabling power: Road Traffic Regulation Act 1984, s. 14 (1) (4). - Issued: 09.02.2012. Made: 03.02.2012. Coming into force: 13.02.2012. Effect: None. Territorial extent & classification: W. Local. - Available at http://www.legislation.gov.uk/wsi/2012/274/contents/made. - In English and Welsh. Welsh title: Gorchymyn Cefnffordd yr A483 (Cyffordd 1, Rhiwabon, Wrecsam) (Gwahardd Cerbydau Dros Dro a Therfyn Cyflymder 40 mya) 2012 *Non-print*

The A483 Trunk Road (Moors Straight, Welshpool, Powys) (Temporary Traffic Restrictions and Prohibition) Order 2012 No. 2012/2995 (W.305). - Enabling power: Road Traffic Regulation Act 1984, s. 14 (1) (4). - Issued: 04.12.2012. Made: 30.11.2012. Coming into force: 06.12.2012. Effect: None. Territorial extent & classification: W. Local. - Available at http://www.legislation.gov.uk/wsi/2012/2995/contents/made. - In English and Welsh. Welsh title: Gorchymyn Cefnffordd yr A483 (Moors Straight, Y Trallwng, Powys) (Cyfyngiadau a Gwaharddiad Traffig Dros Dro) 2012 *Non-print*

The A483 Trunk Road (Newbridge Bypass, Newbridge, Wrexham) (Temporary Prohibition of Vehicles) Order 2012 No. 2012/1720 (W.224). - Enabling power: Road Traffic Regulation Act 1984, s. 14 (1) (4). - Issued: 05.07.2012. Made: 03.07.2012. Coming into force: 16.07.2012. Effect: None. Territorial extent & classification: W. Local. - Available at http://www.legislation.gov.uk/wsi/2012/1720/contents/made. - In English and Welsh. Welsh title: Gorchymyn Cefnffordd yr A483 (Ffordd Osgoi Newbridge, Newbridge, Wrecsam) (Gwahardd Cerbydau Dros Dro) 2012 *Non-print*

Road traffic, Wales: Traffic regulation

The A483 Trunk Road (Newtown to Llanymynech, Powys) (Temporary Traffic Restrictions and Prohibition) Order 2012 No. 2012/1503 (W.198). - Enabling power: Road Traffic Regulation Act 1984, s. 14 (1) (4). - Issued: 18.06.2012. Made: 08.06.2012. Coming into force: 18.06.2012. Effect: None. Territorial extent & classification: W. Local. - Available at http://www.legislation.gov.uk/wsi/2012/1503/contents/made. - In English and Welsh. Welsh title: Gorchymyn Cefnffordd yr A483 (Y Drenewydd i Lanymynech, Powys) (Cyfyngiadau a Gwaharddiad Traffig Dros Dro) 2012 *Non-print*

The A483 Trunk Road (Pencerrig, Near Llanelwedd, Powys) (Temporary Prohibition of Wide Vehicles) Order 2012 No. 2012/2767 (W.295). - Enabling power: Road Traffic Regulation Act 1984, s. 14 (1) (4). - Issued: 08.11.2012. Made: 02.11.2012. Coming into force: 12.11.2012. Effect: None. Territorial extent & classification: W. Local. - Available at http://www.legislation.gov.uk/wsi/2012/2767/contents/made. - In English and Welsh. Welsh title: Gorchymyn Cefnffordd yr A483 (Pencerrig, Ger Llanelwedd, Powys) (Gwahardd Cerbydau Llydan Dros Dro) 2012 *Non-print*

The A483 Trunk Road (Various Locations between Llanwrtyd Wells and Newtown, Powys) (Temporary Traffic Restrictions & Prohibition) Order 2012 No. 2012/1484 (W.183). - Enabling power: Road Traffic Regulation Act 1984, s. 14 (1) (4). - Issued: 14.06.2012. Made: 31.05.2012. Coming into force: 06.06.2012. Effect: None. Territorial extent & classification: W. Local. - Available at http://www.legislation.gov.uk/wsi/2012/1484/contents/made. - In English and Welsh. Welsh title: Gorchymyn Cefnffordd yr A483 (Lleoliadau Amrywiol rhwng Llanwrtyd a'r Drenewydd, Powys) (Cyfyngiadau a Gwaharddiad Traffig Dros Dro) 2012 *Non-print*

The A487 Trunk Road (Aberarth, Ceredigion) (Temporary Traffic Restrictions & Prohibition) Order 2012 No. 2012/1270 (W.161). - Enabling power: Road Traffic Regulation Act 1984, s. 14 (1) (4). - Issued: 17.05.2012. Made: 08.05.2012. Coming into force: 18.05.2012. Effect: None. Territorial extent & classification: W. Local. - Available at http://www.legislation.gov.uk/wsi/2012/1270/contents/made. - In English and Welsh. Welsh title: Gorchymyn Cefnffordd yr A487 (Aber-arth, Ceredigion) (Cyfyngiadau a Gwaharddiad Traffig Dros Dro) 2012 *Non-print*

The A487 Trunk Road (Corris, Gwynedd) (Temporary Traffic Restrictions & Prohibitions) Order 2012 No. 2012/2494 (W.271). - Enabling power: Road Traffic Regulation Act 1984, s. 14 (1) (4). - Issued: 04.10.2012. Made: 28.09.2012. Coming into force: 10.10.2012. Effect: None. Territorial extent & classification: W. Local. - Available at http://www.legislation.gov.uk/wsi/2012/2494/contents/made. - In English and Welsh. Welsh title: Gorchymyn Cefnffordd yr A487 (Corris, Gwynedd) (Cyfyngiadau a Gwaharddiadau Traffig Dros Dro) 2012 *Non-print*

The A487 Trunk Road (Corris to Pantperthog, Gwynedd) (Temporary Traffic Restrictions & Prohibition) Order 2012 No. 2012/2210 (W.246). - Enabling power: Road Traffic Regulation Act 1984, s. 14 (1) (4). - Issued: 31.08.2012. Made: 24.08.2012. Coming into force: 03.09.2012. Effect: None. Territorial extent & classification: W. Local. - Available at http://www.legislation.gov.uk/wsi/2012/2210/contents/made. - In English and Welsh. Welsh title: Gorchymyn Cefnffordd yr A487 (Corris i Bantperthog, Gwynedd) (Cyfyngiadau a Gwaharddiad Traffig Dros Dro) 2012 *Non-print*

The A487 Trunk Road (Eglwyswrw, Pembrokeshire) (Temporary Traffic Restrictions & Prohibition) Order 2012 No. 2012/2179 (W.244). - Enabling power: Road Traffic Regulation Act 1984, s. 14 (1) (4). - Issued: 28.08.2012. Made: 22.08.2012. Coming into force: 01.09.2012. Effect: None. Territorial extent & classification: W. Local. - Available at http://www.legislation.gov.uk/wsi/2012/2179/contents/made. - In English and Welsh. Welsh title: Gorchymyn Cefnffordd yr A487 (Eglwyswrw, Sir Benfro) (Cyfyngiadau a Gwaharddiad Traffig Dros Dro) 2012 *Non-print*

The A487 Trunk Road (Fishguard, Pembrokeshire) (Temporary Traffic Restrictions and Prohibition) Order 2012 No. 2012/21 (W.7). - Enabling power: Road Traffic Regulation Act 1984, s. 14 (1) (4). - Issued: 11.01.2012. Made: 06.01.2012. Coming into force: 16.01.2012. Effect: None. Territorial extent & classification: W. Local. - Available at http://www.legislation.gov.uk/wsi/2012/21/contents/made. - In English and Welsh. Welsh title: Gorchymyn Cefnffordd yr A487 (Abergwaun, Sir Benfro) (Cyfyngu a Gwahardd Traffig Dros Dro) 2012 *Non-print*

The A487 Trunk Road (Gamallt Bends, Cardigan, Ceredigion) (Temporary Traffic Restrictions & Prohibition) Order 2012 No. 2012/1269 (W.160). - Enabling power: Road Traffic Regulation Act 1984, s. 14 (1) (4). - Issued: 17.05.2012. Made: 11.05.2012. Coming into force: 17.05.2012. Effect: None. Territorial extent & classification: W. Local. - Available at http://www.legislation.gov.uk/wsi/2012/1269/contents/made. - In English and Welsh. Welsh title: Gorchymyn Cefnffordd yr A487 (Troeon Gamallt, Aberteifi, Ceredigion) (Cyfyngiadau a Gwaharddiad Traffig Dros Dro) 2012 *Non-print*

The A487 Trunk Road (Glandyfi Improvement, Ceredigion) (Temporary Traffic Prohibition and Restrictions) Order 2012 No. 2012/3031 (W.308). - Enabling power: Road Traffic Regulation Act 1984, s. 14 (1) (4). - Issued: 04.01.2013. Made: 03.12.2012. Coming into force: 06.12.2012. Effect: None. Territorial extent & classification: W. Local. - Available at http://www.legislation.gov.uk/wsi/2012/3031/contents/made. - In English and Welsh. Welsh title: Gorchymyn Cefnffordd yr A487 (Gwelliant Glandyfi, Ceredigion) (Gwaharddiad a Chyfyngiadau Traffig Dros Dro) 2012 *Non-print*

Road traffic, Wales: Traffic regulation

The A487 Trunk Road (Llanarth, Ceredigion) (Temporary Traffic Restrictions and Prohibition) Order 2012 No. 2012/1235 (W.150). - Enabling power: Road Traffic Regulation Act 1984, s. 14 (1) (4). - Issued: 11.05.2012. Made: 04.05.2012. Coming into force: 14.05.2012. Effect: None. Territorial extent & classification: W. Local. - Available at http://www.legislation.gov.uk/wsi/2012/1235/contents/made. - In English and Welsh. Welsh title: Gorchymyn Cefnffordd yr A487 (Llanarth, Ceredigion) (Cyfyngiadau Traffig a Gwaharddiad Traffig Dros Dro 2012 *Non-print*

The A487 Trunk Road (North Parade, Aberystwyth, Ceredigion) (Temporary Prohibition of Vehicles) Order 2012 No. 2012/2044 (W.237). - Enabling power: Road Traffic Regulation Act 1984, s. 14 (1) (4). - Issued: 08.08.2012. Made: 03.08.2012. Coming into force: 13.08.2012. Effect: None. Territorial extent & classification: W. Local. - Available at http://www.legislation.gov.uk/wsi/2012/2044/contents/made. - In English and Welsh. Welsh title: Gorchymyn Cefnffordd yr A487 (Rhodfa'r Gogledd, Aberystwyth, Ceredigion) (Gwahardd Cerbydau Dros Dro) 2012 *Non-print*

The A487 Trunk Road (Penrhyndeudraeth to Maentwrog, Gwynedd) (Temporary Traffic Restrictions & Prohibition) Order 2012 No. 2012/1456 (W.180). - Enabling power: Road Traffic Regulation Act 1984, s. 14 (1) (4). - Issued: 11.06.2012. Made: 30.05.2012. Coming into force: 11.06.2012. Effect: None. Territorial extent & classification: W. Local. - Available at http://www.legislation.gov.uk/wsi/2012/1456/contents/made. - In English and Welsh. Welsh title: Gorchymyn Cefnffordd yr A487 (Penrhyndeudraeth i Faentwrog, Gwynedd) (Cyfyngiadau a Gwaharddiad Traffig Dros Dro) 2012 *Non-print*

The A487 Trunk Road (Pont ar Dyfi, Machynlleth, Powys) (Temporary Prohibition of Vehicles, Pedestrians and Cyclists) Order 2012 No. 2012/267 (W.42). - Enabling power: Road Traffic Regulation Act 1984, s. 14 (1) (4). - Issued: 09.02.2012. Made: 03.02.2012. Coming into force: 13.02.2012. Effect: None. Territorial extent & classification: W. Local. - Available at http://www.legislation.gov.uk/wsi/2012/267/contents/made. - In English and Welsh. Welsh title: Gorchymyn Cefnffordd yr A487 (Pont ar Ddyfi, Machynlleth, Powys) (Gwahardd Cerbydau, Cerddwyr a Beicwyr Dros Dro) 2012 *Non-print*

The A487 Trunk Road (Porthmadog Bypass, Gwynedd) (Temporary Prohibition of Vehicles, Pedestrians and Cyclists) Order 2012 No. 2012/942 (W.122). - Enabling power: Road Traffic Regulation Act 1984, s. 14 (1) (4). - Issued: 29.03.2012. Made: 23.03.2012. Coming into force: 01.04.2012. Effect: None. Territorial extent & classification: W. Local. - Available at http://www.legislation.gov.uk/wsi/2012/942/contents/made. - In English and Welsh. Welsh title: Gorchymyn Cefnffordd yr A487 (Ffordd Osgoi Porthmadog, Gwynedd) (Gwahardd Cerbydau, Cerddwyr a Beicwyr Dros Dro) 2012 *Non-print*

The A487 Trunk Road (Priory Bridge, Cardigan, Ceredigion) (Temporary Traffic Restrictions & Prohibition) Order 2012 No. 2012/1504 (W.199). - Enabling power: Road Traffic Regulation Act 1984, s. 14 (1) (4). - Issued: 18.06.2012. Made: 08.06.2012. Coming into force: 18.06.2012. Effect: None. Territorial extent & classification: W. Local. - Available at http://www.legislation.gov.uk/wsi/2012/1504/contents/made. - In English and Welsh. Welsh title: Gorchymyn Cefnffordd yr A487 (Pont y Priordy, Aberteifi, Ceredigion) (Cyfyngiadau a Gwaharddiad Traffig Dros Dro) 2012 *Non-print*

The A487 Trunk Road (Rhiw Gwgan, Corris, Gwynedd) (Temporary Traffic Restrictions & Prohibition) Order 2012 No. 2012/1457 (W.181). - Enabling power: Road Traffic Regulation Act 1984, s. 14 (1) (4). - Issued: 11.06.2012. Made: 30.05.2012. Coming into force: 11.06.2012. Effect: None. Territorial extent & classification: W. Local. - Available at http://www.legislation.gov.uk/wsi/2012/1457/contents/made. - In English and Welsh. Welsh title: Gorchymyn Cefnffordd yr A487 (Rhiw Gwgan, Corris, Gwynedd) (Cyfyngiadau a Gwaharddiad Traffig Dros Dro) 2012 *Non-print*

The A487 Trunk Road (Rhiw Staerdywyll to Rugog, Corris, Gwynedd) (Temporary Traffic Restrictions & Prohibition) Order 2012 No. 2012/1486 (W.185). - Enabling power: Road Traffic Regulation Act 1984, s. 14 (1) (4). - Issued: 14.06.2012. Made: 01.06.2012. Coming into force: 11.06.2012. Effect: None. Territorial extent & classification: W. Local. - Available at http://www.legislation.gov.uk/wsi/2012/1486/contents/made. - In English and Welsh. Welsh title: Gorchymyn Cefnffordd yr A487 (Rhiw Staerdywyll i Rugog, Corris, Gwynedd) (Cyfyngiadau a Gwaharddiad Traffig Dros Dro) 2012 *Non-print*

The A487 Trunk Road (Rhydypennau to Pwll-glas, Ceredigion) (Temporary Traffic Restrictions and Prohibition) Order 2012 No. 2012/1398 (W.170). - Enabling power: Road Traffic Regulation Act 1984, s. 14 (1) (4). - Issued: 30.05.2012. Made: 25.05.2012. Coming into force: 06.06.2012. Effect: None. Territorial extent & classification: W. Local. - Available at http://www.legislation.gov.uk/wsi/2012/1398/contents/made. - In English and Welsh. Welsh title: Gorchymyn Cefnffordd yr A487 (Rhydypennau i Bwll-glas, Ceredigion) (Cyfyngiadau a Gwaharddiad Traffig Dros Dro) 2012 *Non-print*

The A487 Trunk Road (Sarnau to Pentregat, Ceredigion) (Temporary Traffic Restrictions and Prohibition) Order 2012 No. 2012/1522 (W.204). - Enabling power: Road Traffic Regulation Act 1984, s. 14 (1) (4). - Issued: 19.06.2012. Made: 08.06.2012. Coming into force: 18.06.2012. Effect: None. Territorial extent & classification: W. Local. - Available at http://www.legislation.gov.uk/wsi/2012/1522/contents/made. - In English and Welsh. Welsh title: Gorchymyn Cefnffordd yr A487 (Sarnau i Bentregât, Ceredigion) (Cyfyngiadau Traffig a Gwaharddiad Traffig Dros Dro) 2012 *Non-print*

Road traffic, Wales: Traffic regulation

The A487 Trunk Road (Tal-y-llyn Pass, Gwynedd) (Temporary Traffic Restrictions & Prohibition) Order 2012 No. 2012/1498 (W.196). - Enabling power: Road Traffic Regulation Act 1984, s. 14 (1) (4). - Issued: 14.06.2012. Made: 01.06.2012. Coming into force: 11.06.2012. Effect: None. Territorial extent & classification: W. Local. - Available at http://www.legislation.gov.uk/wsi/2012/1498/contents/made. - In English and Welsh. Welsh title: Gorchymyn Cefnffordd yr A487 (Bwlch Tal-y-llyn, Gwynedd) (Cyfyngiadau a Gwaharddiad Traffig Dros Dro) 2012 *Non-print*

The A489 Trunk Road (Caersws to Newtown, Powys) (Temporary Traffic Restrictions and Prohibition) Order 2012 No. 2012/1490 (W.188). - Enabling power: Road Traffic Regulation Act 1984, s. 14 (1) (4). - Issued: 14.06.2012. Made: 01.06.2012. Coming into force: 11.06.2012. Effect: None. Territorial extent & classification: W. Local. - Available at http://www.legislation.gov.uk/wsi/2012/1490/contents/made. - In English and Welsh. Welsh title: Gorchymyn Cefnffordd yr A489 (Caersws i'r Drenewydd, Powys) (Cyfyngiadau a Gwaharddiad Traffig Dros Dro) 2012 *Non-print*

The A494/A550 Trunk Road (Deeside Interchange, Flintshire) (Temporary Prohibition of Vehicles) Order 2012 No. 2012/1642 (W.211). - Enabling power: Road Traffic Regulation Act 1984, s. 14 (1) (4). - Issued: 29.06.2012. Made: 25.06.2012. Coming into force: 05.07.2012. Effect: None. Territorial extent & classification: W. Local. - Available at http://www.legislation.gov.uk/wsi/2012/1642/contents/made. - In English and Welsh. Welsh title: Gorchymyn Cefnffordd yr A494/A550 (Cyfnewidfa Glannau Dyfrdwy, Sir y Fflint) (Gwahardd Cerbydau Dros Dro) 2012 *Non-print*

The A494/A550 Trunk Road (Queensferry, Flintshire) (Temporary 50 mph Speed Limit) Order 2012 No. 2012/1145 (W.138). - Enabling power: Road Traffic Regulation Act 1984, s. 14 (1) (4). - Issued: 27.04.2012. Made: 24.04.2012. Coming into force: 27.04.2012. Effect: None. Territorial extent & classification: W. Local. - Available at http://www.legislation.gov.uk/wsi/2012/1145contents/made. - In English and Welsh. Welsh title: Gorchymyn Cefnffordd yr A494/A550 (Queensferry, Sir y Fflint) (Terfyn Cyflymder 50 mya Dros Dro) 2012 *Non-print*

The A494 Trunk Road (Gwernymynydd, Flintshire to the Flintshire/Denbighshire Border) (Temporary Traffic Restrictions & Prohibition) Order 2012 No. 2012/2260 (W.251). - Enabling power: Road Traffic Regulation Act 1984, s. 14 (1) (4). - Issued: 06.09.2012. Made: 31.08.2012. Coming into force: 10.09.2012. Effect: None. Territorial extent & classification: W. Local. - Available at http://www.legislation.gov.uk/wsi/2012/2260/contents/made. - In English and Welsh. Welsh title: Gorchymyn Cefnffordd yr A494 (Gwernymynydd, Sir y Fflint i Ffin Sirol Sir y Fflint/Sir Ddinbych) (Cyfyngiadau a Gwaharddiad Traffig Dros Dro) 2012 *Non-print*

The A494 Trunk Road (Llanarmon to Clwyd Gate, Denbighshire) (Temporary Traffic Restrictions & Prohibition) Order 2012 No. 2012/1492 (W.190). - Enabling power: Road Traffic Regulation Act 1984, s. 14 (1) (4). - Issued: 18.06.2012. Made: 01.06.2012. Coming into force: 11.06.2012. Effect: None. Territorial extent & classification: W. Local. - Available at http://www.legislation.gov.uk/wsi/2012/1492/contents/made. - In English and Welsh. Welsh title: Gorchymyn Cefnffordd yr A494 (Llanarmon i Clwyd Gate, Sir Ddinbych) (Cyfyngiadau a Gwaharddiad Traffig Dros Dro) 2012 *Non-print*

The A494 Trunk Road (Llanbedr-Dyffryn-Clwyd, Denbighshire) (Temporary Traffic Restriction and Prohibitions) Order 2012 No. 2012/1648 (W.213). - Enabling power: Road Traffic Regulation Act 1984, s. 14 (1) (4). - Issued: 29.06.2012. Made: 25.06.2012. Coming into force: 02.07.2012. Effect: None. Territorial extent & classification: W. Local. - Available at http://www.legislation.gov.uk/wsi/2012/1648/contents/made. - In English and Welsh. Welsh title: Gorchymyn Cefnffordd yr A494 (Llanbedr Dyffryn Clwyd, Sir Ddinbych) (Gwaharddiadau a Chyfyngiad Traffig Dros Dro) 2012 *Non-print*

The A494 Trunk Road (Loggerheads, Denbighshire) (Temporary Traffic Restrictions & Prohibitions) Order 2012 No. 2012/346 (W.58). - Enabling power: Road Traffic Regulation Act 1984, s. 14 (1) (4). - Issued: 15.02.2012. Made: 10.02.2012. Coming into force: 21.02.2012. Effect: None. Territorial extent & classification: W. Local. - Available at http://www.legislation.gov.uk/wsi/2012/346/contents/made. - In English and Welsh. Welsh title: Gorchymyn Cefnffordd yr A494 (Loggerheads, Sir Ddinbych) (Cyfyngiadau a Gwaharddiadau Traffig Dros Dro) 2012 *Non-print*

The A494 Trunk Road (Mold Bypass, Flintshire) (Temporary Prohibition of Vehicles and Cyclists) Order 2012 No. 2012/1233 (W.149). - Enabling power: Road Traffic Regulation Act 1984, s. 14 (1) (4). - Issued: 10.05.2012. Made: 04.05.2012. Coming into force: 16.05.2012. Effect: None. Territorial extent & classification: W. Local. - Available at http://www.legislation.gov.uk/wsi/2012/1233/contents/made. - In English and Welsh. Welsh title: Gorchymyn Cefnffordd yr A494 (Ffordd Osgoi'r Wyddgrug, Sir y Fflint) (Gwahardd Cerbydau a Beicwyr Dros Dro) 2012 *Non-print*

The A494 Trunk Road (Pont Eyarth to Pwll-glâs, Denbighshire) (Temporary Traffic Restrictions & Prohibitions) Order 2012 No. 2012/1491 (W.189). - Enabling power: Road Traffic Regulation Act 1984, s. 14 (1) (4). - Issued: 14.06.2012. Made: 01.06.2012. Coming into force: 11.06.2012. Effect: None. Territorial extent & classification: W. Local. - Available at http://www.legislation.gov.uk/wsi/2012/1491/contents/made. - In English and Welsh. Welsh title: Gorchymyn Cefnffordd yr A494 (Pont Eyarth i Pwll-glâs, Sir Ddinbych) (Gwaharddiadau a Chyfyngiadau Traffig Dros Dro) 2012 *Non-print*

Road traffic, Wales: Traffic regulation

The A494 Trunk Road (Queensferry Interchange to St Davids Park, Flintshire) (Temporary Prohibitions and 40 MPH Speed Limit) Order 2012 No. 2012/446 (W.74). - Enabling power: Road Traffic Regulation Act 1984, s. 14 (1) (4). - Issued: 24.02.2012. Made: 21.02.2012. Coming into force: 05.03.2012. Effect: None. Territorial extent & classification: W. Local. - Available at http://www.legislation.gov.uk/wsi/2012/446/contents/made . - In English and Welsh. Welsh title: Gorchymyn Cefnffordd yr A494 (Cyfnewidfa Queensferry i Barc Dewi Sant, Sir y Fflint) (Gwaharddiadau a Therfyn Cyflymder 40 MYA Dros Dro) 2012 *Non-print*

The A494 Trunk Road (Ruthin, Denbighshire) (Temporary Traffic Restrictions & Prohibitions) Order 2012 No. 2012/1495 (W.193). - Enabling power: Road Traffic Regulation Act 1984, s. 14 (1) (4). - Issued: 18.06.2012. Made: 01.06.2012. Coming into force: 11.06.2012. Effect: None. Territorial extent & classification: W. Local. - Available at http://www.legislation.gov.uk/wsi/2012/1495/contents/made . - In English and Welsh. Welsh title: Gorchymyn Cefnffordd yr A494 (Rhuthun, Sir Ddinbych) (Cyfyngiad a Gwaharddiadau Traffig Dros Dro) 2012 *Non-print*

The A494 Trunk Road (South of Pwll-glas, Denbighshire) (Temporary Traffic Restrictions & Prohibition) Order 2012 No. 2012/1482 (W.182). - Enabling power: Road Traffic Regulation Act 1984, s. 14 (1) (4). - Issued: 13.06.2012. Made: 30.05.2012. Coming into force: 11.06.2012. Effect: None. Territorial extent & classification: W. Local. - Available at http://www.legislation.gov.uk/wsi/2012/1482/contents/made . - In English and Welsh. Welsh title: Gorchymyn Cefnffordd yr A494 (Man i'r De o Bwll-glas, Sir Ddinbych) (Cyfyngu a Gwahardd Traffig Dros Dro) 2012 *Non-print*

The A550 Trunk Road (Deeside Park Interchange, Flintshire) (Temporary Prohibition of Vehicles, Pedestrians and Cyclists) Order 2012 No. 2012/2408 (W.258). - Enabling power: Road Traffic Regulation Act 1984, s. 14 (1) (4). - Issued: 24.09.2012. Made: 18.09.2012. Coming into force: 01.10.2012. Effect: None. Territorial extent & classification: W. Local. - Available at http://www.legislation.gov.uk/wsi/2012/2408/contents/made . - In English and Welsh. Welsh title: Gorchymyn Cefnffordd yr A550 (Cyfnewidfa Parc Glannau Dyfrdwy, Sir y Fflint) (Gwahardd Cerbydau, Cerddwyr a Beicwyr Dros Dro) 2012 *Non-print*

The A4042 Trunk Road (Court Farm Roundabout, Pontypool, Torfaen to Penperlleni, Monmouthshire) (Temporary Traffic Restrictions & Prohibitions) Order 2012 No. 2012/2045 (W.238). - Enabling power: Road Traffic Regulation Act 1984, s. 14 (1) (4). - Issued: 08.08.2012. Made: 03.08.2012. Coming into force: 13.08.2012. Effect: None. Territorial extent & classification: W. Local. - Available at http://www.legislation.gov.uk/wsi/2012/2045/contents/made . - In English and Welsh. Welsh title: Gorchymyn Cefnffordd yr A4042 (Cylchfan Court Farm, Pont-y-pwl, Torfaen i Benperllenni, Sir Fynwy) (Cyfyngiadau a Gwaharddiadau Traffig Dros Dro) 2012 *Non-print*

The A4042 Trunk Road & M4 Motorway (Grove Park Roundabout to Caerleon Interchange, Newport) (Temporary Prohibition of Vehicles) Order 2012 No. 2012/337 (W.54). - Enabling power: Road Traffic Regulation Act 1984, s. 14 (1) (4). - Issued: 14.02.2012. Made: 09.02.2012. Coming into force: 20.02.2012. Effect: None. Territorial extent & classification: W. Local. - Available at http://www.legislation.gov.uk/wsi/2012/337/contents/made . - In English and Welsh. Welsh title: Gorchymyn Cefnffordd yr A4042 a Thraffordd yr M4 (Cylchfan Grove Park i Gyfnewidfa Caerllion, Casnewydd) (Gwaharddiad Dros Dro ar Gerbydau) 2012 *Non-print*

The A4042 Trunk Road & M4 Motorway (Junction 25A, Grove Park Roundabout, Newport) (Temporary Prohibition of Vehicles) Order 2012 No. 2012/2458 (W.268). - Enabling power: Road Traffic Regulation Act 1984, s. 14 (1) (4). - Issued: 28.09.2012. Made: 25.09.2012. Coming into force: 01.10.2012. Effect: None. Territorial extent & classification: W. Local. - Available at http://www.legislation.gov.uk/wsi/2012/2458/contents/made . - In English and Welsh. Welsh title: Gorchymyn Cefnffordd yr A4042 a Thraffordd yr M4 (Cyffordd 25A, Cylchfan Grove Park, Casnewydd) (Gwahardd Cerbydau Dros Dro) 2012 *Non-print*

The A4042 Trunk Road (North of Edlogan Way Roundabout to South of Mamhilad Roundabout, Torfaen) (Temporary Traffic Restrictions & Prohibitions) Order 2012 No. 2012/2556 (W.280). - Enabling power: Road Traffic Regulation Act 1984, s. 14 (1) (4). - Issued: 11.10.2012. Made: 05.10.2012. Coming into force: 15.10.2012. Effect: None. Territorial extent & classification: W. Local. - Available at http://www.legislation.gov.uk/wsi/2012/2556/contents/made . - In English and Welsh. Welsh title: Gorchymyn Cefnffordd yr A4042 (Man i'r Gogledd o Gylchfan Edlogan Way i Fan i'r De o Gylchfan Mamheilad, Torfaen) (Cyfyngiadau a Gwaharddiadau Traffig Dros Dro) 2012 *Non-print*

The A4042 Trunk Road (Southbound Lay-by between Court Farm Roundabout and Pontypool Roundabout, Torfaen) (Temporary Prohibition of Vehicles) Order 2012 No. 2012/3221 (W.323). - Enabling power: Road Traffic Regulation Act 1984, s. 14 (1) (4). - Issued: 07.01.2013. Made: 27.12.2012. Coming into force: 07.01.2013. Effect: None. Territorial extent & classification: W. Local. - Available at http://www.legislation.gov.uk/wsi/2012/3221/contents/made . - In English and Welsh. Welsh title: Gorchymyn Cefnffordd yr A4042 (Cilfan tua'r De rhwng Cylchfan Court Farm a Chylchfan Pont-y-P?l, Torfaen) (Gwahardd Cerbydau Dros Dro) 2012 *Non-print*

Road traffic, Wales: Traffic regulation

The A4042 Trunk Road (Turnpike Roundabout to Mamhilad Roundabout, Torfaen) (Temporary Traffic Restrictions & Prohibitions) Order 2012 No. 2012/7 (W.3). - Enabling power: Road Traffic Regulation Act 1984, s. 14 (1) (4). - Issued: 09.01.2012. Made: 03.01.2012. Coming into force: 09.01.2012. Effect: None. Territorial extent & classification: W. Local. - Available at http://www.legislation.gov.uk/wsi/2012/7/contents/made. - In English and Welsh. Welsh title: Gorchymyn Cefnffordd yr A4042 (Cylchfan y Tyrpeg i Gylchfan Mamheilad, Tor-faen) (Cyfyngu a Gwahardd Traffig Dros Dro) 2012 *Non-print*

The A4060 Trunk Road (Pentrebach, Merthyr Tydfil) (Temporary Prohibition of Vehicles) Order 2012 No. 2012/23 (W.9). - Enabling power: Road Traffic Regulation Act 1984, s. 14 (1) (4). - Issued: 11.01.2012. Made: 06.01.2012. Coming into force: 15.01.2012. Effect: None. Territorial extent & classification: W. Local. - Available at http://www.legislation.gov.uk/wsi/2012/23/contents/made. - In English and Welsh. Welsh title: Gorchymyn Cefnffordd yr A4060 (Pentre-bach, Merthyr Tudful) (Gwahardd Cerbydau Dros Dro) 2012 *Non-print*

The A4076 Trunk Road (Milford Haven, Pembrokeshire) (Temporary Traffic Restriction & Prohibitions) Order 2012 No. 2012/3217 (W.319). - Enabling power: Road Traffic Regulation Act 1984, s. 14 (1) (4). - Issued: 07.01.2013. Made: 27.12.2012. Coming into force: 07.01.2013. Effect: None. Territorial extent & classification: W. Local. - Available at http://www.legislation.gov.uk/wsi/2012/3217/contents/made. - In English and Welsh. Welsh title: Gorchymyn Cefnffordd yr A4076 (Aberdaugleddau, Sir Benfro) (Cyfyngiad a Gwaharddiadau Traffig Dros Dro) 2012 *Non-print*

The A4232 Trunk Road (Culverhouse Cross Interchange, Cardiff, Northbound On Slip Road) (Temporary Prohibition of Vehicles) Order 2012 No. 2012/338 (W.55). - Enabling power: Road Traffic Regulation Act 1984, s. 14 (1) (4). - Issued: 14.02.2012. Made: 09.02.2012. Coming into force: 20.02.2012. Effect: None. Territorial extent & classification: W. Local. - Available at http://www.legislation.gov.uk/wsi/2012/338/contents/made. - In English and Welsh. Welsh title: Gorchymyn Cefnffordd yr A4232 (Cyfnewidfa Croes Cwrlwys, Caerdydd, Y Ffordd Ymuno tua'r Gogledd) (Gwahardd Cerbydau Dros Dro) 2012 *Non-print*

The A4232 Trunk Road (St Brides Over-bridge to Ely River Viaduct, Cardiff) (Temporary 50 mph & 40 mph Speed Limits) Order 2012 No. 2012/485 (W.80). - Enabling power: Road Traffic Regulation Act 1984, s. 14 (1) (4). - Issued: 28.02.2012. Made: 23.02.2012. Coming into force: 05.03.2012. Effect: None. Territorial extent & classification: W. Local. - Available at http://www.legislation.gov.uk/wsi/2012/485/contents/made. - In English and Welsh. Welsh title: Gorchymyn Cefnffordd yr A4232 (Trosbont Llansanffraid-ar-Elái i Draphont Afon Elái, Caerdydd) (Terfynau Cyflymder 50 mya a 40 mya Dros Dro) 2012 *Non-print*

The A4232 Trunk Road (St Fagans to Drope Road Over-bridge, Cardiff) (Temporary Traffic Restrictions & Prohibition) Order 2012 No. 2012/111 (W.17). - Enabling power: Road Traffic Regulation Act 1984, s. 14 (1) (4). - Issued: 20.01.2012. Made: 16.01.2012. Coming into force: 23.01.2012. Effect: None. Territorial extent & classification: W. Local. - Available at http://www.legislation.gov.uk/wsi/2012/111/contents/made. - In English and Welsh. Welsh title: Gorchymyn Cefnffordd yr A4232 (Sain Ffagan i Drosbont Drope Road, Caerdydd) (Cyfyngiadau a Gwaharddiad Traffig Dros Dro) 2012 *Non-print*

The M4 Motorway (Brynglas Tunnels, Newport) (Temporary Restriction & Prohibitions) Order 2012 No. 2012/5 (W.1). - Enabling power: Road Traffic Regulation Act 1984, s. 14 (1) (4) (7). - Issued: 06.01.2012. Made: 03.01.2012. Coming into force: 04.01.2012. Effect: None. Territorial extent & classification: W. Local. - Available at http://www.legislation.gov.uk/wsi/2012/5/contents/made. - In English and Welsh. Welsh title: Gorchymyn Traffordd yr M4 (Twneli Bryn-glas, Casnewydd) (Cyfyngiad a Gwaharddiadau Traffig Dros Dro) 2012 *Non-print*

The M4 Motorway (Eastbound Carriageway at Junction 24, Coldra, Monmouthshire) (Temporary Prohibition of Vehicles) Order 2012 No. 2012/481 (W.79). - Enabling power: Road Traffic Regulation Act 1984, s. 14 (1) (4). - Issued: 28.02.2012. Made: 21.02.2012. Coming into force: 01.03.2012. Effect: None. Territorial extent & classification: W. Local. - Available at http://www.legislation.gov.uk/wsi/2012/481/contents/made. - In English and Welsh. Welsh title: Gorchymyn Traffordd yr M4 (Y Gerbytffordd tua'r Dwyrain wrth Gyffordd 24, Coldra, Sir Fynwy) (Gwahardd Cerbydau Dros Dro) 2012 *Non-print*

The M4 Motorway (Junction 33, Capel Llanilltern, Cardiff, Eastbound On-Slip Road) (Temporary Prohibition of Vehicles) Order 2012 No. 2012/1597 (W.207). - Enabling power: Road Traffic Regulation Act 1984, s. 14 (1) (4). - Issued: 25.06.2012. Made: 19.06.2012. Coming into force: 29.06.2012. Effect: None. Territorial extent & classification: W. Local. - Available at http://www.legislation.gov.uk/wsi/2012/1597/contents/made. - In English and Welsh. Welsh title: Gorchymyn Traffordd yr M4 (Cyffordd 33, Capel Llanilltern, Caerdydd, y Ffordd Ymuno tua'r Dwyrain) (Gwahardd Cerbydau Dros Dro) 2012 *Non-print*

The M4 Motorway (Junction 41, Pentyla, to Junction 42, Earlswood, Neath Port Talbot) (Temporary Prohibition of Vehicles) Order 2012 No. 2012/2409 (W.259). - Enabling power: Road Traffic Regulation Act 1984, s. 14 (1) (4). - Issued: 25.09.2012. Made: 18.09.2012. Coming into force: 01.10.2012. Effect: None. Territorial extent & classification: W. Local. - Available at http://www.legislation.gov.uk/wsi/2012/2409/contents/made. - In English and Welsh. Welsh title: Gorchymyn Traffordd yr M4 (Cyffordd 41, Pentyla i Gyffordd 42, Earlswood, Castell-nedd Port Talbot) (Gwahardd Cerbydau Dros Dro) 2012 *Non-print*

The M4 Motorway (Junction 46 (Llangyfelach), Swansea to Junction 49 (Pont Abraham), Carmarthenshire) (Temporary Prohibition of Vehicles) Order 2012 No. 2012/1695 (W.220). - Enabling power: Road Traffic Regulation Act 1984, s. 14 (1) (4). - Issued: 04.07.2012. Made: 28.06.2012. Coming into force: 09.07.2012. Effect: None. Territorial extent & classification: W. Local. - Available at http://www.legislation.gov.uk/wsi/2012/1695/contents/made. - In English and Welsh. Welsh title: Gorchymyn Traffordd yr M4 (Cyffordd 46 (Llangyfelach), Abertawe i Gyffordd 49 (Pont Abraham), Sir Gaerfyrddin) (Gwahardd Cerbydau Dros Dro) 2012 *Non-print*

The M4 Motorway (Slip Roads between Junction 24 (Coldra) and Junction 28 (Tredegar Park), Newport) (Temporary Prohibition of Vehicles) Order 2012 No. 2012/2209 (W.245). - Enabling power: Road Traffic Regulation Act 1984, s. 14 (1) (4). - Issued: 31.08.2012. Made: 23.08.2012. Coming into force: 01.09.2012. Effect: None. Territorial extent & classification: W. Local. - Available at http://www.legislation.gov.uk/wsi/2012/2209/contents/made. - In English and Welsh. Welsh title: Gorchymyn Traffordd yr M4 (Slipffyrdd rhwng Cyffordd 24 (Coldra) a Chyffordd 28 (Parc Tredegar), Casnewydd) (Gwahardd Cerbydau Dros Dro) 2012 *Non-print*

The M4 Motorway (Slip Roads between Junction 38 (Margam) and Junction 43 (Llandarcy), Neath Port Talbot) (Temporary Prohibition of Vehicles) Order 2012 No. 2012/2742 (W.294). - Enabling power: Road Traffic Regulation Act 1984, s. 14 (1) (4). - Issued: 06.11.2012. Made: 31.10.2012. Coming into force: 09.11.2012. Effect: None. Territorial extent & classification: W. Local. - Available at http://www.legislation.gov.uk/wsi/2012/2742/contents/made. - In English and Welsh. Welsh title: Gorchymyn Traffordd yr M4 (Slipffyrdd rhwng Cyffordd 38 (Margam) a Chyffordd 43 (Llandarsi), Castell-nedd Port Talbot) (Gwahardd Cerbydau Dros Dro) 2012 *Non-print*

The M4 Motorway (Westbound Carriageway at Junction 24 (Coldra) Newport) (Temporary Prohibition of Vehicles) Order 2012 No. 2012/2461 (W.269). - Enabling power: Road Traffic Regulation Act 1984, s. 14 (1) (4). - Issued: 05.10.2012. Made: 21.09.2012. Coming into force: 01.10.2012. Effect: None. Territorial extent & classification: W. Local. - Available at http://www.legislation.gov.uk/wsi/2012/2461/contents/made. - In English and Welsh. Welsh title: Gorchymyn Traffordd yr M4 (Y Gerbytffordd tua'r Gorllewin wrth Gyffordd 24 (Coldra), Casnewydd) (Gwahardd Cerbydau Dros Dro) 2012 *Non-print*

The M4 Motorway (Westbound Exit Slip Road at Junction 23a (Magor), Monmouthshire) (Temporary Prohibition of Vehicles) Order 2012 No. 2012/347 (W.59). - Enabling power: Road Traffic Regulation Act 1984, s. 14 (1) (4). - Issued: 15.02.2012. Made: 10.02.2012. Coming into force: 21.02.2012. Effect: None. Territorial extent & classification: W. Local. - Available at http://www.legislation.gov.uk/wsi/2012/347/contents/made. - In English and Welsh. Welsh title: Gorchymyn Traffordd yr M4 (Ffordd Ymadael Tua'r Gorllewin wrth Gyffordd 23a (Magwyr), Sir Fynwy) (Gwahardd Cerbydau Dros Dro) 2012 *Non-print*

Savings banks

The National Savings Bank (Investment Deposits) (Limits) (Amendment) Order 2012 No. 2012/795. - Enabling power: National Savings Bank Act 1971, ss. 4 (1) (2) (a) (f). - Issued: 14.03.2012. Made: 12.03.2012. Laid: 13.03.2012. Coming into force: 06.04.2012. Effect: S.I. 1977/1210 amended. Territorial extent & classification: E/W/S/NI. General. - 2p.: 30 cm. - 978-0-11-152201-1 £4.00

Sea fisheries, England

The Sea Fishing (Licences and Notices) (England) Regulations 2012 No. 2012/827. - Enabling power: Sea Fish (Conservation) Act 1967, s. 4B. - Issued: 20.03.2012. Made: 14.03.2012. Laid: 16.03.2012. Coming into force: 06.04.2012. Effect: S.I. 1994/2813 revoked in relation to England. Territorial extent & classification: E. General. - 8p.: 30 cm. - 978-0-11-152222-6 £4.00

Sea fisheries, England: Conservation of sea fish

The Scallop Fishing (England) Order 2012 No. 2012/2283. - Enabling power: Sea Fish (Conservation) Act 1967, ss. 1 (3), 3 (1) (4), 20 (1). - Issued: 10.09.2012. Made: 05.09.2012. Laid: 07.09.2012. Coming into force: 01.10.2012. Effect: S.I .2004/12 revoked. Territorial extent and classification: E. General. - 8p.: 30 cm. - 978-0-11-152863-1 £4.00

Sea fisheries, England: Sea fish industry

The Fishing Boats (Satellite-Tracking Devices and Electronic Reporting) (England) Scheme 2012 No. 2012/1375. - Enabling power: Fisheries Act 1981, s. 15 (1) (2). - Issued: 28.05.2012. Made: 21.05.2012. Laid: 24.05.2012. Coming into force: 28.05.2012. Effect: S.I. 2004/2467; 2010/1600 revoked. Territorial extent & classification: E. General. - Superseded by approved SI of the same number but different ISBN (9780111526965) issued on 16.07.2012. For approval by a resolution by each House of Parliament within forty days. EC note: This Scheme makes provision for state funding of the costs incurred by persons in charge of English fishing boats in complying with two EU obligations. - 8p.: 30 cm. - 978-0-11-152480-0 £4.00

The Fishing Boats (Satellite-Tracking Devices and Electronic Reporting) (England) Scheme 2012 No. 2012/1375. - Enabling power: Fisheries Act 1981, s. 15 (1) (2). - Issued: 16.07.2012. Made: 21.05.2012. Laid: 24.05.2012. Coming into force: 28.05.2012. Effect: S.I. 2004/2467; 2010/1600 revoked. Territorial extent & classification: E. General. - Approved by both Houses of Parliament. EC note: This Scheme makes provision for state funding of the costs incurred by persons in charge of English fishing boats in complying with two EU obligations. - 8p.: 30 cm. - 978-0-11-152696-5 £5.75

Sea fisheries, Wales

The Fishing Boats (Satellite -Tracking Devices and Electronic Transmission of Fishing Activities Data) (Wales) Scheme 2012 No. 2012/3172 (W.318). - Enabling power: Fisheries Act 1981, ss. 15 (1) (2). - Issued: 17.01.2013. Made: 21.12.2012. Laid before the National Assembly for Wales: 21.01.2012. Coming into force: 31.12.2012. Effect: S.I. 2006/2799 (W.238); 2010/2369 (W.203) revoked. Territorial extent & classification: W. General. - For approval by resolution of the National Assembly for Wales, within forty days beginning with the day on which the scheme was made, subject to extension for periods of dissolution or recess for more than four days. - In English and Welsh: Cynllun Cychod Pysgota (Dyfeisiau Olrhain Drwy Loeren a Darlledu Data Gweithgareddau Pysgota yn Electronig) (Cymru) 2012. - 16p.: 30 cm. - 978-0-348-10676-3 £5.75

The Scallop Dredging Operations (Tracking Devices) (Wales) Order 2012 No. 2012/2729 (W.292). - Enabling power: Sea Fisheries Act 1968, s. 5 (1). - Issued: 16.11.2012. Made: 30.10.2012. Laid before the National Assembly for Wales : 31.10.2012. Coming into force: 01.11.2012. Effect: None. Territorial extent & classification: W. General. - In English and Welsh. Welsh title: Gorchymyn Gweithrediadau Llusgrwydo Cregyn Bylchog (Dyfeisiau Olrhain) (Cymru) 2012. - 8p.: 30 cm. - 978-0-348-10667-1 £5.75

The Sea Fish (Specified Sea Areas) (Prohibition of Fishing Method) (Wales) Order 2012 No. 2012/2571 (W.282). - Enabling power: Sea Fish (Conservation) Act 1967, ss. 5 (1) (1B), 5A (1), 20 (1). - Issued: 29.10.2012. Made: 10.10.2012. Laid before the National Assembly for Wales: 11.10.2012. Coming into force: 01.11.2012. Effect: S.I. 2010/630 (C.42) amended & Byelaw 21 (Prohibition of Bottom Towed Fishing Gear) of the former North Western and North Wales Sea Fisheries Committee revoked in relation to Wales. Territorial extent & classification: W. General. - In English and Welsh: Gorchymyn Pysgod Môr (Ardaloedd Môr Penodedig) (Gwahardd Dull Pysgota) (Cymru) 2012. - 8p.: 30 cm. - 978-0-348-10660-2 £5.75

Sea fisheries, Wales: Shellfish

The Swansea Bay (Thomas Shellfish Limited) Mussel Fishery Order 2012 No. 2012/1689 (W.217). - Enabling power: Sea Fisheries (Shellfish) Act 1967, s. 1. - Issued: 19.07.2012. Made: 27.06.2012. Laid before the National Assembly for Wales: 29.06.2012. Coming into force: 18.09.2012. Effect: None. Territorial extent & classification: W. General. - In English and Welsh. Welsh title: Gorchymyn Pysgodfa Cregyn Gleision Bae Abertawe (Thomas Shellfish Limited) 2012. - 8p.: 30 cm. - 978-0-348-10638-1 £5.75

Security industry

The Private Security Industry Act 2001 (Exemption) (Aviation Security) (Amendment) Regulations 2012 No. 2012/1567. - Enabling power: Private Security Industry Act 2001, s. 4. - Issued: 21.06.2012. Made: 19.06.2012. Laid: 20.06.2012. Coming into force: 11.07.2012. Effect: S.I. 2010/3018 amended. Territorial extent & classification: E/W/S/NI. General. - 2p.: 30 cm. - 978-0-11-152561-6 £4.00

The Private Security Industry Act 2001 (Exemption) (Olympics Security) Regulations 2012 No. 2012/145. - Enabling power: Private Security Industry Act 2001, s. 4. - Issued: 26.01.2012. Made: 19.01.2012. Laid: 25.01.2012. Coming into force: 01.03.2012 and ceasing to have effect 30.09.2012. Effect: S.I. 2007/808, 810 amended. Territorial extent & classification: E/W/S/NI. General. - 4p.: 30 cm. - 978-0-11-151940-0 £4.00

Seeds, England

The Seed Marketing (Amendment) Regulations 2012 No. 2012/3035. - Enabling power: Plant Varieties and Seeds Act 1964, ss. 16 (1) (1A) (2) (3) (5), 36 & European Communities Act 1972, sch. 2, para. 1A. - Issued: 10.12.2012. Made: 03.12.2012. Laid: 10.12.2012. Coming into force: 31.12.2012. Effect: S.I. 2011/463 amended. Territorial extent and classification: E. General. - EC note: These regulations add Council Decision 2003/17/EC to list of EU instruments references. - 4p.: 30 cm. - 978-0-11-153181-5 £4.00

Seeds, Wales

The Seed Marketing (Wales) Regulations 2012 No. 2012/245 (W.39). - Enabling power: Plant Varieties and Seeds Act 1964, ss. 16 (1) (1A) (2) (3) (4) (5) (5A), 36 & European Communities Act 1972, sch. 2, para. 1A. - Issued: 02.03.2012. Made: 01.02.2012. Laid before the National Assembly for Wales: 02.02.2012. Coming into force: 27.02.2012. Effect: S.I. 2004/2881 (W.251); 2005/1207 (W.79), 3035 (W.223), 3036 (W.224), 3037 (W.225), 3038 (W.226); 2006/3250 (W.294); 2007/119 (W.9); 2009/1356 (W.131); 2010/1808 (W.176); 2011/994 (W.147) revoked. Territorial extent & classification: W. General. - EC note: These Regulations implement, in relation to Wales, Council/Commission Directives 66/401/EEC; 66/402/EEC; 2002/54/EC; 2002/55/EC; 2002/57/EC; 2009/74/EC ; 2010/60/EU; 2011/180/EU. The 2009 Directive amends Council Directives 66/401/EEC, 66/402/EEC, 2002/55/EC and 2002/57/EC as regards the botanical names of plants, the scientific names of other organisms and certain annexes to Directives 66/401/EEC, 66/402/EEC, and 2002/57/EC in the light of developments of scientific and technical knowledge. - In English and Welsh. Welsh title: Rheoliadau Marchnata Hadau (Cymru) 2012. - 75p.: 30 cm. - 978-0-348-10556-8 £13.75

Senior courts of England and Wales

The Civil Courts (Amendment) (No. 2) Order 2012 No. 2012/1954. - Enabling power: County Courts Act 1984, s. 2 (1) & Matrimonial and Family Proceedings Act 1984, s. 33 (1) & Senior Courts Act 1981, s. 99 (1). - Issued: 27.07.2012. Made: 23.07.2012. Laid: 26.07.2012. Coming into force: 10.09.2012. Effect: S.I. 1983/713 amended. Territorial extent & classification: E/W. General. - 2p.: 30 cm. - 978-0-11-152773-3 £4.00

The Civil Courts (Amendment) Order 2012 No. 2012/643. - Enabling power: County Courts Act 1984, s. 2 (1) & Matrimonial and Family Proceedings Act 1984, s. 33 (1) & Senior Courts Act 1981, s. 99 (1). - Issued: 05.03.2012. Made: 01.03.2012. Laid: 05.03.2012. Coming into force: 02.04.2012. Effect: S.I. 1983/713 amended. Territorial extent & classification: E/W. General. - 4p.: 30 cm. - 978-0-11-152111-3 £4.00

The Civil Procedure (Amendment No. 2) Rules 2012 No. 2012/2208 (L.8). - Enabling power: Civil Procedure Act 1997, s. 2. - Issued: 30.08.2012. Made: 07.08.2012. Laid: 29.08.2012. Coming into force: 01.10.2012, in accord. with rule 1. Effect: S.I. 1998/3132 amended. Territorial extent & classification: E/W. General. - 24p.: 30 cm. - 978-0-11-152839-6 £5.75

The Civil Procedure (Amendment) Rules 2011 No. 2012/505 (L.2). - Enabling power: Civil Procedure Act 1997, s. 2. - Issued: 02.03.2012. Made: 23.02.2012. Laid: 27.02.2012. Coming into force: 19.03.2012. Effect: S.I. 1998/3132 amended. Territorial extent & classification: E/W. General. - 4p.: 30 cm. - 978-0-11-152066-6 £4.00

The Criminal Procedure (Amendment) Rules 2012 No. 2012/3089 (L.12). - Enabling power: Courts Act 2003, s. 69 & Criminal Justice Act 2003, s. 174 (4). - Issued: 17.12.2012. Made: 11.12.2012. Laid: 13.12.2012. Coming into force: 01.04.2013. Effect: S.I. 2012/1726 amended. Territorial extent and classification: E/W. General. - 12p.: 30 cm. - 978-0-11-153218-8 £5.75

The Criminal Procedure Rules 2012 No. 2012/1726 (L.6). - Enabling power: Senior Courts Act 1981, ss. 52, 73 (2), 74 (2) (3) (4), 87 (4); Police and Criminal Evidence Act 1984, s. 81; Criminal Procedure and Investigations Act 1996, ss. 19, 20 (3), sch. 2, para. 4; Powers of Criminal Courts (Sentencing) Act 2000, s. 155 (7); Terrorism Act 2000, sch. 5, para. 10, sch. 6, para. 4, sch. 6A, para. 5; Proceeds of Crime Act 2002, ss. 91, 351 (2), 362 (2), 369 (2), 375 (1); Courts Act 2003, s. 69; & Criminal Justice Act 2003, s. 132 (4). - Issued: 16.07.2012. Made: 02.07.2012. Laid: 12.07.2012. Coming into force: 01.10.2012. Effect: S.I. 2011/1709 revoked. Territorial extent and classification: E/W. General. - 331p.: 30 cm. - 978-0-11-152633-0 £38.00

The Family Procedure (Amendment) (No. 2) Rules 2012 No. 2012/1462. - Enabling power: Courts Act 2003, s. 75. - Issued: 11.06.2012. Made: 31.05.2012. Laid: 07.06.2012. Coming into force: 01.07.2012. Effect: S.I. 2010/2955 amended. Territorial extent & classification: E/W. General. - 2p.: 30 cm. - 978-0-11-152508-1 £4.00

The Family Procedure (Amendment No. 3) Rules 2012 No. 2012/2046 (L.7). - Enabling power: Courts Act 2003, ss. 75, 76. - Issued: 08.08.2012. Made: 31.07.2012. Laid: 07.08.2012. Coming into force: 30.009.2012. Effect: S.I. 2010/2955 amended. Territorial extent & classification: E/W. General. - 4p.: 30 cm. - 978-0-11-152799-3 £4.00

The Family Procedure (Amendment No. 4) Rules 2012 No. 2012/2806 (L.10). - Enabling power: Courts Act 2003, ss. 75, 76 & Civil Jurisdiction and Judgments Act 1982, ss. 12, 48. - Issued: 12.11.2012. Made: 06.11.2012. Laid: 09.11.2012. Coming into force: 20.12.2012. Effect: S.I. 2010/2955 amended. Territorial extent & classification: E/W. General. - 12p.: 30 cm. - 978-0-11-153059-7 £5.75

The Family Procedure (Amendment No. 5) Rules 2012 No. 2012/3061. - Enabling power: Courts Act 2003, ss. 75, 76. - Issued: 13.12.2013. Made: 10.12.2012. Laid: 13.12.2012. Coming into force: 31.01.2013. Effect: S.I. 2010/2955 amended. Territorial extent & classification: E/W. General. - 12p.: 30 cm. - 978-0-11-153210-2 £5.75

The Family Procedure (Amendment) Rules 2012 No. 2012/679 (L.3). - Enabling power: Civil Jurisdiction and Judgements Act 1982, ss. 12, 48 & Adoption and Children Act 2002, ss. 102, 141 (1) & Courts Act 2003, ss. 75, 76. - Issued: 07.03.2012. Made: 01.03.2012. Laid: 06.03.2012. Coming into force: 06.04.2012. Effect: S.I. 2010/2955 amended. Territorial extent & classification: E/W. General. - 8p.: 30 cm. - 978-0-11-152133-5 £5.75

Social care

The Health and Social Care Act 2012 (Commencement No. 2 and Transitional, Savings and Transitory Provisions) Order 2012 No. 2012/1831 (C.71). - Enabling power: Health and Social Care Act 2012, ss. 304 (10), 306. Bringing into operation various provisions of the 2012 Act in accord. with art. 2. - Issued: 16.07.2012. Made: 11.07.2012. Coming into force: .- Effect: None. Territorial extent & classification: E/W. General. - 16p.: 30 cm. - 978-0-11-152699-6 £5.75

The Health and Social Care Act 2012 (Commencement No. 3, Transitional, Savings and Transitory Provisions and Amendment) Order 2012 No. 2012/2657 (C.107). - Enabling power: Health and Social Care Act 2012, ss. 304 (10), 306. Bringing into operation various provisions of the 2012 Act on 01.11.2012 in accord. with art. 2. - Issued: 25.10.2012. Made: 22.10.2012. Effect: 2012 c.7; S.I. 2912/1831 (C.71) amended. Territorial extent & classification: E. General. - 12p.: 30 cm. - 978-0-11-152990-4 £5.75

Social care, England

The Care Quality Commission (Healthwatch England Committee) Regulations 2012 No. 2012/1640. - Enabling power: Health and Social Care Act 2008, s. 161 (3) (4), sch. 1, para. 6 (1A) (5A) to (5D). - Issued: 27.06.2012. Made: 21.06.2012. Laid: 27.06.2012. Coming into force: In accord. with reg. 1. Effect: None. Territorial extent & classification: E. General. - 12p.: 30 cm. - 978-0-11-152581-4 £5.75

The Care Quality Commission (Registration) and (Additional Functions) and Health and Social Care Act 2008 (Regulated Activities) (Amendment) Regulations 2012 No. 2012/921. - Enabling power: Health and Social Care Act 2008, ss. 16 (d), 20, 59 (1), 65 (1) (3), 86 (2), 87 (1) (2), 161 (3) (4). - Issued: 27.03.2012. Made: 22.03.2012. Laid: 27.03.2012. Coming into force: In accord. with reg. 1 (2). Effect: S.I. 2009/3112; 2010/781; 2011/1551 amended & S.I. 2009/3112 partially revoked (18.06.2012) & S.I. 2010/49 revoked (18.06.2012). Territorial extent & classification: E. General. - 8p.: 30 cm. - 978-0-11-152283-7 £5.75

The Care Quality Commission (Registration and Membership) (Amendment) Regulations 2012 No. 2012/1186. - Enabling power: Health and Social Care Act 2008, ss. 20, 161 (3), sch. 1, para. 3 (4). - Issued: 03.05.2012. Made: 30.04.2012. Laid: 03.05.2012. Coming into force: 01.06.2012. Effect: S.I. 2009/3112 amended. Territorial extent & classification: E. General. - 2p.: 30 cm. - 978-0-11-152394-0 £4.00

The Health and Social Care Act 2008 (Regulated Activities) (Amendment) Regulations 2012 No. 2012/1513. - Enabling power: Health and Social Care Act 2008, ss. 8 (1), 20, 35, 161 (3) (4). - Issued: 14.06.2012. Made: 12.06.2012. Coming into force: In accord. with reg. 1 (2). Effect: S.I. 2010/781 amended. Territorial extent & classification: E. General. - Supersedes draft SI (ISBN 9780111522752) issued on 27.03.2012. - 8p.: 30 cm. - 978-0-11-152536-4 £5.75

The Health and Social Care Act 2012 (Commencement No. 1 and Transitory Provision) Order 2012 No. 2012/1319 (C.47). - Enabling power: Health and Social Care Act 2012, ss. 304 (10), 306. Bringing into operation various provisions of this Act on 01.06.2012, 01.07.2012, 01.08.2012 in accord. with art. 2. - Issued: 22.05.2012. Made: 17.05.2012. Coming into force: .- Effect: S.I. 2010/781 amended. Territorial extent & classification: E/W. General. - 8p.: 30 cm. - 978-0-11-152461-9 £4.00

Social care, Wales

The Care Council for Wales (Appointment, Membership and Procedure) (Amendment) Regulations 2012 No. 2012/3023 (W.307). - Enabling power: Care Standards Act 2000, s. 118A (1) to (3), sch.1, para. 6. - Issued: 20.012.2012. Made: 01.12.2012. Laid before the National Assembly for Wales: 05.12.2012. Coming into force: 01.01.2013. Effect: S.I. 2001/2136 (W.149) amended/partially revoked. Territorial extent & classification: W. General. - In English and Welsh. Welsh title: Rheoliadau Cyngor Gofal Cymru (Penodi, Aelodaeth a Gweithdrefn) (Diwygio) 2012. - 8p.: 30 cm. - 978-0-348-10670-1 £4.00

The Carers Strategies (Wales) (Amendment) Regulations 2012 No. 2012/282 (W.46). - Enabling power: Carers Strategies (Wales) Measure 2010, ss. 5 (1) (2), 10 (2). - Issued: 23.02.2012. Made: 03.02.2012. Laid before the National Assembly for Wales: 07.02.2012. Coming into force: 29.02.2012. Effect: S.I. 2011/2939 (W.315) amended/partially revoked. Territorial extent & classification: W. General. - In English and Welsh. Welsh title: Rheoliadau Strategaethau ar gyfer Gofalwyr (Cymru) (Diwygio) 2012. - 4p.: 30 cm. - 978-0-348-10687-9 £4.00

The Children and Families (Wales) Measure 2010 (Commencement No. 4) Order 2012 No. 2012/191 (W.30) (C.5). - Enabling power: Children and Families (Wales) Measure 2010, ss. 74 (2), 75 (3). Bringing into operation various provisions of the 2010 Measure on 27.01.2012, 31.01.2012, 28.02.2012, 31.03.2012 in accord. with arts. 2, 3, 4, 5. - Issued: 10.02.2012. Made: 26.01.2012. Effect: None. Territorial extent & classification: W. General. - In English and Welsh. Welsh title: Gorchymyn Mesur Plant a Theuluoedd (Cymru) 2010 (Cychwyn Rhif 4) 2012. - 8p.: 30 cm. - 978-0-348-10549-0 £5.75

The Integrated Family Support Teams (Composition of Teams and Board Functions) (Wales) Regulations 2012 No. 2012/202 (W.33). - Enabling power: Children and Families (Wales) Measure 2010, ss. 60 (1), 62 (2). - Issued: 23.02.2012. Made: 30.01.2012. Laid before the National Assembly for Wales: 31.01.2012. Coming into force: 28.02.2012. Effect: S.I. 2010/1690 (W.159) revoked. Territorial extent & classification: W. General. - In English & Welsh. Welsh title: Rheoliadau Timau Integredig Cymorth i Deuluoedd (Cyfansoddiad Timau a Swyddogaethau Byrddau) (Cymru) 2012. - 8p.: 30 cm. - 978-0-348-10690-9 £5.75

The Integrated Family Support Teams (Family Support Functions) (Wales) Regulations 2012 No. 2012/204 (W.34). - Enabling power: Children and Families (Wales) Measure 2010, s. 58 (2). - Issued: 16.02.2012. Made: 30.01.2012. Laid before the National Assembly for Wales: 31.01.2012. Coming into force: 28.02.2012. Effect: S.I. 2010/1701 (W.162); 2011/191 (W. 36) revoked. Territorial extent & classification: W. General. - In English & Welsh. Welsh title: Rheoliadau Timau Integredig Cymorth i Deuluoedd (Swyddogaethau Cymorth i Deuluoedd) (Cymru) 2012. - 8p.: 30 cm. - 978-0-348-10554-4 £5.75

The Integrated Family Support Teams (Review of Cases) (Wales) Regulations 2012 No. 2012/205 (W.35). - Enabling power: Children and Families (Wales) Measure 2010, ss. 63 (a), 74 (2) & Children Act 1989, ss. 26 (1) (2), 104 (4), 104A (1) (2). - Issued: 23.02.2012. Made: 30.01.2012. Laid before the National Assembly for Wales: 31.01.2012. Coming into force: 28.02.2012. Effect: S.I. 2010/1700 (W.161) partially revoked. Territorial extent & classification: W. General. - In English & Welsh. Welsh title: Rheoliadau Timau Integredig Cymorth i Deuluoedd (Adolygu Achosion) (Cymru) 2012. - 8p.: 30 cm. - 978-0-348-10691-6 £5.75

Social security

The Benefit Cap (Housing Benefit) Regulations 2012 No. 2012/2994. - Enabling power: Welfare Reform Act 2012, ss. 96 (1) (3) (4) (a) (b) (c) (g) (5) (10), 97 (1). - Issued: 03.12.2012. Made: 29.11.2012. Coming into force: 15.04.2013. Effect: S.I. 2001/1002; 2006/213 amended. Territorial extent & classification: E/W/S. General. - Supersedes draft SI (ISBN 9780111526750) issued 16.07.2012. - 8p.: 30 cm. - 978-0-11-153147-1 £5.75

The Child Benefit and Child Tax Credit (Miscellaneous Amendments) Regulations 2012 No. 2012/2612. - Enabling power: Social Security Contributions and Benefits Act 1992, s. 146 (3) & Social Security Contributions and Benefits (Northern Ireland) Act 1992, s. 142 (3) & Tax Credits Act 2002, s. 3 (7). - Issued: 18.10.2012. Made: 16.10.2012. Laid: 17.10.2012. Coming into force: 08.11.2012. Effect: S.I. 2003/654; 2006/223 amended. Territorial extent & classification: E/W/S/NI. General. - 4p.: 30 cm. - 978-0-11-152959-1 £4.00

The Child Benefit and Guardian's Allowance (Administration) (Amendment) Regulations 2012 No. 2012/1074. - Enabling power: Social Security Administration Act 1992, s. 71 (8) & Social Security Administration Act (Northern Ireland) 1992, s. 69 (8). - Issued: 17.04.2012. Made: 12.04.2012. Laid: 16.04.2012. Coming into force: 08.05.2012. Effect: S.I. 2003/492 amended. Territorial extent & classification: E/W/S/NI. General. - 2p.: 30 cm. - 978-0-11-152355-1 £4.00

The Child Benefit (General) (Amendment) Regulations 2012 No. 2012/818. - Enabling power: Social Security Contributions and Benefits Act 1992, s. 142 (2), 147 (6), sch. 9, para. 1 & Social Security Contributions and Benefits (Northern Ireland) Act 1992, s. 138 (2), 143 (6), sch. 9, para. 1. - Issued: 15.03.2012. Made: 14.03.2012. Laid: 15.03.2012. Coming into force: 06.04.2012. Effect: S.I. 2006/223 amended. Territorial extent & classification: E/W/S/NI. General. - 4p.: 30 cm. - 978-0-11-152212-7 £4.00

The Child Maintenance and Other Payments Act 2008 (Commencement No. 9) and the Welfare Reform Act 2009 (Commencement No. 9) Order 2012 No. 2012/2523 (C.101). - Enabling power: Child Maintenance and Other Payments Act 2008, s. 62 (3) & Welfare Reform Act 2009, s. 61 (3). Bringing into operation various provisions of the 2008 and 2009 Acts on 08.10.2012, in accord. with art. 2. - Issued: 05.10.2012. Made: 04.10.2012. Effect: None. Territorial extent & classification: E/W/S. General. - 8p.: 30 cm. - 978-0-11-152913-3 £4.00

The Child Maintenance and Other Payments Act 2008 (Commencement No. 10 and Transitional Provisions) Order 2012 No. 2012/3042 (C.122). - Enabling power: Child Maintenance and Other Payments Act 2008, s. 62 (3) (4). Bringing into operation various provisions of the 2008 Act on 10.12.2012, in accord. with art. 4. - Issued: 07.12.2012. Made: 05.12.2012. Effect: None. Territorial extent & classification: E/W/S. General. - 8p.: 30 cm. - 978-0-11-153190-7 £5.75

The Employment and Support Allowance (Amendment of Linking Rules) Regulations 2012 No. 2012/919. - Enabling power: Social Security Contributions and Benefits Act 1992, ss. 123 (1) (d) (e), 135 (1), 137 (1) & Social Security Act 1998, ss. 9 (1) (a), 84 & Welfare reform Act 2007, ss. 2 (4), 4 (2) (a) (6), 24 (1) (2) (b), 25 (2), sch. 2, paras. 1, 4, 9, sch. 4, paras. 1 (1), 7 (1), 8 (1). - Issued: 26.03.2012. Made: 21.03.2012. Laid: 26.03.2012. Coming into force: In accord. with reg. 1 (2). Effect: S.I. 1999/991; 2006/213, 215; 2008/794; 2010/1907 amended. Territorial extent & classification: E/W/S. General. - 8p.: 30 cm. - 978-0-11-152277-6 £5.75

The Employment and Support Allowance (Amendment) Regulations 2012 No. 2012/3096. - Enabling power: Welfare Reform Act 2007, ss. 8 (1) (2) (3) (5), 9 (1) (2) (3), 24 (1), 25 (2) (5), sch. 2, paras. 1, 9. - Issued: 17.12.2012. Made: 13.12.2012. Laid: 17.12.2012. Coming into force: 28.01.2013. Effect: S.I. 2008/794 amended. Territorial extent & classification: E/W/S General. - 8p.: 30 cm. - 978-0-11-153248-5 £5.75

The Employment and Support Allowance (Duration of Contributory Allowance) (Consequential Amendments) Regulations 2012 No. 2012/913. - Enabling power: Social Security Contributions and Benefits Act 1992, ss. 22 (5), 122 (1), 123 (1) (a) (d) (e), 124 (1) (d), 135 (1), 137 (1), 175 (1) (3) & Jobseekers Act 1995, ss. 4 (5), 35 (1), 36 (2) & Social Security Act 1998, ss. 9 (1) (a), 79 (1) (4), 84 & State Pension Credit Act 2002, s. 2 (3) (b), 17 (1) & Welfare Reform Act 2007, ss. 2 (4) (a) (6) (a), 24 (1), 25 (2), 28 (2), sch. 2, para. 2, sch. 4, paras. 1 (1), 7 (1) (2) (f). - Issued: 26.03.2012. Made: 21.03.2012. Laid: 26.03.2012. Coming into force: 01.05.2012. Effect: S.I. 1975/556; 1987/1967; 1996/207; 1999/991; 2002/1792; 2006/213, 215; 2008/794; 2010/1907 amended. Territorial extent & classification: E/W/S General. - 8p.: 30 cm. - 978-0-11-152272-1 £5.75

The Employment and Support Allowance (Sanctions) (Amendment) Regulations 2012 No. 2012/2756. - Enabling power: Welfare Reform Act 2007, ss. 12 (2) (3) (4), 13 (2) (6) (4), 16, 16A, 25 (2) (3) (5) & Social Security Act 1998, ss. 10 (6), 79 (4) (6). - Issued: 05.11.2012. Made: 02.11.2012. Laid: 05.11.2012. Coming into force: 03.12.2012. Effect: S.I. 1999/991; 2008/794; 2011/1349 amended. Territorial extent & classification: E/W/S. General. - 8p.: 30 cm. - 978-0-11-153039-9 £5.75

The Guardian's Allowance Up-rating Order 2012 No. 2012/834. - Enabling power: Social Security Administration Act 1992, ss. 150 (9) (10) (a) (i), 189 (4). - Issued: 16.03.2012. Made: 14.03.2012. Coming into force: 09.04.2012. Effect: 1992 c.4 & S.I. 2006/965 amended. Territorial extent & classification: E/W/S. General. - Supersedes draft S.I. (ISBN 9780111519943) issued on 09.02.2012. - 2p.: 30 cm. - 978-0-11-152226-4 £4.00

The Guardian's Allowance Up-rating Regulations 2012 No. 2012/845. - Enabling power: Social Security Contributions and Benefits Act 1992, ss. 113 (1), 175 (1) (3) (4) & Social Security Administration Act 1992, ss. 155 (3), 189 (1) (4) (5), 190, 191 & Social Security Contributions and Benefits (Northern Ireland) Act 1992, ss. 113 (1), 171 (1) (3) (4) & Social Security Administration (Northern Ireland) Act 1992, ss. 135 (3), 165 (1) (4) (5), 167 (1). - Issued: 19.03.2012. Made: 15.03.2012. Laid: 16.03.2012. Coming into force: 09.04.2012. Effect: S.I. 2011/1039 superseded. Territorial extent & classification: E/W/S/NI. General. - 4p.: 30 cm. - 978-0-11-152239-4 £4.00

The Housing Benefit (Amendment) Regulations 2012 No. 2012/3040. - Enabling power: Social Security Contributions and Benefits Act 1992, ss. 123 (1) (d), 130A (2) (3) (5), 137 (1), 175 (1) (3) (4) (5) & Social Security Act 1998, s. 79 (4) & Child Support, Pensions and Social Security Act 2000, sch. 7, paras 4 (4A) (6), 20 (1), 23 (1). - Issued: 07.10.2012. Made: 03.12.2012. Coming into force: In accord. with reg. 1. Effect: S.I. 2001/1002; 2006/213, 214 amended. Territorial extent & classification: E/W/S. General. - 8p.: 30 cm. - 978-0-11-153189-1 £5.75

The Industrial Injuries Benefit (Injuries arising before 5th July 1948) (Amendment) Regulations 2012 No. 2012/2812. - Enabling power: Welfare Reform Act 2012, s. 64 (3). - Issued: 09.11.2012. Made: 08.11.2012. Laid: 09.11.2012. Coming into force: 04.12.2012. Effect: S.I. 2012/2743 amended. Territorial extent & classification: E/W/S. General. - This Statutory Instrument has been made in consequence of defects in S.I. 2012/2743 (ISBN 9780111530351) and is being issued free of charge to all known recipients of that Statutory Instrument. - 2p.: 30 cm. - 978-0-11-153069-6 £4.00

The Industrial Injuries Benefit (Injuries arising before 5th July 1948) Regulations 2012 No. 2012/2743. - Enabling power: Welfare Reform Act 2012, s. 64 (3). - Issued: 05.11.2012. Made: 01.11.2012. Laid: 05.11.2012. Coming into force: 05.12.2012. Effect: None. Territorial extent & classification: E/W/S. General. - Defects in this instrument have been corrected by SI 2012/2812 (ISBN 9780111530696), published 09.11.2012, which is being issued free of charge to all known recipients of SI 2012/2743. - 4p.: 30 cm. - 978-0-11-153035-1 £4.00

The Jobseeker's Allowance (Amendment) Regulations 2012 No. 2012/1135. - Enabling power: Jobseekers Act 1995, ss. 19 (8) (b), 35 (1), 36 (2). - Issued: 25.04.2012. Made: 23.04.2012. Laid: 25.04.2012. Coming into force: 16.05.2012. Effect: S.I. 1996/207 amended. Territorial extent & classification: E/W/S. General. - 2p.: 30 cm. - 978-0-11-152379-7 £4.00

The Jobseeker's Allowance (Domestic Violence) (Amendment) Regulations 2012 No. 2012/853. - Enabling power: Jobseekers Act 1995, ss. 6 (4), 7 (4), 9 (10), 35 (1), 36 (2) (4) (a), sch. 1, para. 8B. - Issued: 23.03.2012. Made: 15.03.2012. Coming into force: 23.04.2012. Effect: S.I. 1996/207 amended. Territorial extent & classification: E/W/S. - Supersedes draft SI (ISBN 9780111519288) issued 19.01.2012. - 4p.: 30 cm. - 978-0-11-152244-8 £4.00

The Jobseeker's Allowance (Jobseeking and Work for Your Benefit) (Amendment and Revocation) Regulations 2012 No. 2012/397. - Enabling power: Social Security Contributions and Benefits Act 1992, ss. 123 (1) (d) (e), 136 (3) (5) (a) (b), 137 (1), 175 (3) (4) & Jobseekers Act 1995, ss. 6 (4), 7 (4), 12 (1) (4) (a) (b), 17A (1) (2) (5) (a) (b) (d) (f) (6) to (9), 20B (4) (5) (6), 29, 35 (1), 36 (2) (4) & Housing Grants, Construction and Regeneration Act 1996, ss. 30, 146 (1) (2). - Issued: 20.02.2012. Made: 26.01.2012. Coming into force: 01.03.2012. Effect: S.I. 1996/207; 2011/917 amended & S.I. 2010/1222 revoked. Territorial extent & classification: E/W/S. General. - Supersedes draft S.I. (ISBN 9780111517109) issued on 21.11.2011. - 4p.: 30 cm. - 978-0-11-152034-5 £4.00

The Jobseeker's Allowance (Members of the Reserve Forces) Regulations 2012 No. 2012/1616. - Enabling power: Jobseekers Act 1995, ss. 6 (4), 7 (4), 8 (2) (d), 12 (1) to (3) (4) (b), 35 (1), 36 (2) (4). - Issued: 27.06.2012. Made: 20.06.2012. Laid: 27.06.2012. Coming into force: 30.07.2012. Effect: S.I. 1996/207 amended. Territorial extent & classification: E/W/S. General. - 4p.: 30 cm. - 978-0-11-152572-2 £4.00

Social security

The Jobseeker's Allowance (Sanctions) (Amendment) Regulations 2012 No. 2012/2568. - Enabling power: Jobseekers Act 1995, ss. 8, 19 (2) (e) (3) (4) (5) (6), 19A (4) (5) (9), 19B (1) (2) (3) (4) (6) (7), 35, 36 (2) (4), sch. 1, para. 14AA. - Issued: 15.10.2012. Made: 10.10.2012. Coming into force: 22.10.2012. Effect: S.I. 1975/556; 1996/207; 1999/991 amended & S.I. 2011/688, 917 partially revoked. Territorial extent & classification: E/W/S. General. - Supersedes draft SI (ISBN 9780111526408) issued 09.07.2012. - 16p.: 30 cm. - 978-0-11-152942-3 £5.75

The Mesothelioma Lump Sum Payments (Conditions and Amounts) (Amendment) Regulations 2012 No. 2012/918. - Enabling power: Child Maintenance and Other Payments Act 2008, ss. 46 (3), 53 (1). - Issued: 27.03.2012. Made: 21.03.2012. Coming into force: 01.04.2012. Effect: S.I. 2008/1963 amended. Territorial extent & classification: E/W/S. General. - Supersedes draft S.I. (ISBN 9780111520611) issued 27.02.2012. - 4p.: 30 cm. - 978-0-11-152276-9 £4.00

The National Insurance Contributions (Application of Part 7 of the Finance Act 2004) Regulations 2012 No. 2012/1868. - Enabling power: Social Security Administration Act 1992, ss. 132A (1), 189 (4) (5). - Issued: 18.07.2012. Made: 16.07.2012. Laid: 17.07.2012. Coming into force: 01.09.2012. Effect: 1970 c.9 & S.I. 2006/1543; 2012/1836 modified & S.I. 2007/785; 2008/2678; 2009/208, 612; 2010/2927 revoked. Territorial extent & classification: E/W/S/NI. General. - With correction slip dated January 2013. - 20p.: 30 cm. - 978-0-11-152717-7 £5.75

The Pneumoconiosis etc. (Workers' Compensation) (Payment of Claims) (Amendment) Regulations 2012 No. 2012/923. - Enabling power: Pneumoconiosis etc. (Workers' Compensation) Act 1979, ss. 1 (1) (2) (4), 7 (2). - Issued: 27.02.2012. Made: 21.03.2012. Coming into force: 01.04.2012. Effect: S.I. 1988/668 amended. Territorial extent & classification: E/W/S. General. - Supersedes draft SI (ISBN 9780111520628) issued 27.02.2012. - 12p.: 30 cm. - 978-0-11-152285-1 £5.75

The Social Fund Cold Weather Payments (General) Amendment (No. 2) Regulations 2012 No. 2012/2379. - Enabling power: Social Security Contributions and Benefits Act 1992, ss. 138 (2) (4), 175 (1) (4). - Issued: 19.09.2012. Made: 17.09.2012. Laid: 18.09.2012. Coming into force: In accord. with reg. 1 (2). Effect: S.I. 1988/1724 amended. Territorial extent & classification: E/W/S. General. - This Statutory Instrument has been made in consequence of a defect in SI 2012/2280 (ISBN 9780111528624) and is being issued free of charge to all known recipients of that statutory instrument. - 2p.: 30 cm. - 978-0-11-152890-7 £4.00

The Social Fund Cold Weather Payments (General) Amendment Regulations 2012 No. 2012/2280. - Enabling power: Social Security Contributions and Benefits Act 1992, ss. 138 (2) (4), 175 (1) (4). - Issued: 11.09.2012. Made: 05.09.2012. Laid: 11.09.2012. Coming into force: 01.11.2012. Effect: S.I. 1988/1724 amended. Territorial extent & classification: E/W/S. General. - This SI has been corrected by SI 2012/2379 (ISBN 9780111528907) which if being sent free of charge to all known recipients of 2012/2280. - 8p.: 30 cm. - 978-0-11-152862-4 £5.75

The Social Fund Maternity Grant Amendment Regulations 2012 No. 2012/1814. - Enabling power: Social Security Contributions and Benefits Act 1992, ss. 138 (1) (a) (4), 175 (1) (3) (4). - Issued: 12.07.2012. Made: 11.07.2012. Laid: 12.07.2012. Coming into force: 13.08.2012. Effect: S.I. 2005/3061 amended. Territorial extent & classification: E/W/S. General. - 4p.: 30 cm. - 978-0-11-152680-4 £4.00

The Social Security (Benefit) (Members of the Forces) (Amendment) Regulations 2012 No. 2012/1656. - Enabling power: Social Security Administration Act 1992, ss. 116 (2), 175 (3) (4) & Social Security Contributions and Benefits (Northern Ireland) Act 1992, ss. 116 (2), 171 (3) (4). - Issued: 28.06.2012. Made: 25.06.2012. Laid: 27.06.2012. Coming into force: 30.07.2012. Effect: S.I. 1975/493 amended. Territorial extent & classification: E/W/S/NI. General. - 2p.: 30 cm. - 978-0-11-152594-4 £4.00

The Social Security Benefits Up-rating Order 2012 No. 2012/780. - Enabling power: Social Security Administration Act 1992, ss. 150, 150A, 151, 189 (1) (4) (5). - Issued: 19.03.2012. Made: 06.03.2012. Coming into force: In accord. with art. 1. Effect: 1965 c. 51; 1992 c. 4 & S.I. 1986/1960; 1987/1967;1991/2890; 1994/2946; 1995/310; 1996/207; 2002/1792, 2818; 2006/213, 214, 215, 216; 2008/794; 2010/1060, 2818 amended & S.I. 2011/821 revoked. Territorial extent & classification: E/W/S. General. - Supersedes draft S.I. (ISBN 9780111519486) issued 30.01.2012. - 60p.: 30 cm. - 978-0-11-152236-3 £9.75

The Social Security Benefits Up-rating Regulations 2012 No. 2012/819. - Enabling power: Social Security Contributions and Benefits Act 1992, ss. 90, 113 (1), 122 (1), 175 (1) (3) & Social Security Administration Act 1992, ss. 5 (1) (p), 155 (3), 189 (1) (4), 191. - Issued: 15.03.2012. Made: 14.03.2012. Laid: 15.03.2012. Coming into force: 09.04.2012. Effect: S.I. 1977/343; 1987/1968 amended & S.I. 2011/830 revoked. Territorial extent & classification: E/W/S. General. - 4p.: 30 cm. - 978-0-11-152213-4 £4.00

The Social Security (Categorisation of Earners) (Amendment) Regulations 2012 No. 2012/816. - Enabling power: Social Security Contributions and Benefits Act 1992, s. 2 (2) (b) (2A), 7 (2) (3), 175 (4) & Social Security Contributions and Benefits (Northern Ireland) Act 1992, ss. 2 (2) (b) (2A), 7 (2) (3), 171 (4). - Issued: 15.03.2012. Made: 13.03.2012. Laid: 14.03.2012. Coming into force: 06.04.2012. Effect: S.I. 1978/1689; S.R. 1978/401 amended. Territorial extent & classification: E/W/S/NI. General. - 4p.: 30 cm. - 978-0-11-152211-0 £4.00

The Social Security Child Support (Supersession of Appeal Decisions) Regulations 2012 No. 2012/1267. - Enabling power: Child Support Act 1991, ss. 17 (3) (5), 54; Social Security Act 1998, ss. 10 (3) (6), 84; Child Support, Pensions and Social Security Act 2000, sch. 7, paras 4 (4) (6), 23 (1) & Welfare Reform Act 2012, s. 103 (2) (b). - Issued: 14.05.2012. Made: 08.05.2012. Laid: 14.05.2012. Coming into force: 04.06.2012. Effect: S.I. 1992/1813; 1996/2907; 1999/991; 2001/1002 amended. Territorial extent & classification: E/W/S. General. - This Statutory Instrument has been printed to correct errors in S.I. 2008/2683 (ISBN 9780110846156) and is being issued free of charge to all known recipients of that Statutory Instrument. - With correction slip dated December 2012. - 4p.: 30 cm. - 978-0-11-152428-2 £4.00

The Social Security (Civil Penalties) Regulations 2012 No. 2012/1990. - Enabling power: Social Security Administration Act 1992, ss 115C (2), 115D (1) (2), 189 (1), 191. - Issued: 31.07.2012. Made: 25.07.2012. Coming into force: 01.10.2012. Effect: None. Territorial extent & classification: E/W/S. General. - Supersedes draft SI (ISBN 9780111524244) issued on 14.05.2012. - 4p.: 30 cm. - 978-0-11-152788-7 £4.00

The Social Security (Claims and Payments) Amendment Regulations 2012 No. 2012/644. - Enabling power: Social Security Administration Act 1992, ss. 15A (2) (b), 189 (1) (4). - Issued: 06.03.2012. Made: 29.02.2012. Laid: 06.03.2012. Coming into force: 01.04.2012. Effect: S.I. 1987/1968 amended. Territorial extent & classification: E/W/S. General. - 2p.: 30 cm. - 978-0-11-152121-2 £4.00

The Social Security (Contributions) (Amendment No. 2) Regulations 2012 No. 2012/817. - Enabling power: Social Security Contributions and Benefits Act 1992, ss. 1 (6) (7), 3 (2) (3), 10 (9), 19 (1) (2) (5A), 122 (1), 175 (3) (4) & Social Security Contributions and Benefits (Northern Ireland) Act 1992, ss. 1 (6) (7), 3 (2) (3), 10 (9), 19 (1) (2) (5A), 121 (1), 171 (3) (4) (10). - Issued: 15.03.2012. Made: 13.03.2012. Laid: 14.03.2012. Coming into force: 06.04.2012. Effect: S.I. 2001/1004; 2003/2085 amended. Territorial extent & classification: E/W/S/NI. General. - 8p.: 30 cm. - 978-0-11-152210-3 £5.75

The Social Security (Contributions) (Amendment No. 3) Regulations 2012 No. 2012/821. - Enabling power: Social Security Contributions and Benefits Act 1992, ss. 175 (4), sch. 1, para. 6 (1) (2) & Social Security Contributions and Benefits (Northern Ireland) Act 1992, ss. 171 (4) (10), sch. 1, para. 6 (1) (2). - Issued: 16.03.2012. Made: 14.03.2012. Laid: 15.03.2012. Coming into force: 06.04.2012. Effect: S.I. 2001/1004 amended. Territorial extent & classification: E/W/S/NI. General. - 20p.: 30 cm. - 978-0-11-152230-1 £5.75

The Social Security (Contributions) (Amendment) Regulations 2012 No. 2012/573. - Enabling power: Social Security Contributions and Benefits Act 1992, ss. 19 (1) (5A), 175 (3) & Social Security Contributions and Benefits (Northern Ireland) Act 1992, ss. 19 (1) (5A), 171 (3). - Issued: 29.02.2012. Made: 28.02.2012. Laid: 29.02.2012. Coming into force: 26.03.2012. Effect: S.I. 2001/1004 amended. Territorial extent & classification: E/W/S/NI. General. - 2p.: 30 cm. - 978-0-11-152092-5 £4.00

The Social Security (Contributions) (Limits and Thresholds) (Amendment) Regulations 2012 No. 2012/804. - Enabling power: Social Security Contributions and Benefits Act 1992, ss. 5 (1) (4) to (6), 175 (3) & Social Security Contributions and Benefits (Northern Ireland) Act 1992, ss. 5 (1) (4) to (6), 171 (3) (10). - Issued: 14.03.2012. Made: -. Coming into force: 06.04.2011. Effect: S.I. 2001/1004 amended. Territorial extent & classification: E/W/S/NI. General. - Supersedes draft S.I. (ISBN 9780111519653) issued 31.01.2012. - 4p.: 30 cm. - 978-0-11-152202-8 £4.00

The Social Security (Contributions) (Re-Rating) Consequential Amendment Regulations 2012 No. 2012/867. - Enabling power: Social Security Contributions and Benefits Act 1992, s. 175 (3) & Social Security Contributions and Benefits (Northern Ireland) Act 1992, ss. 171 (3) (10). - Issued: 20.03.2012. Made: 19.03.2012. Laid: 20.03.2012. Coming into force: 06.04.2012. Effect: S.I. 2001/1004 amended. Territorial extent & classification: E/W/S/NI. General. - 4p.: 30 cm. - 978-0-11-152248-6 £4.00

The Social Security (Contributions) (Re-Rating) Order 2012 No. 2012/807. - Enabling power: Social Security Administration Act 1992, ss. 141 (4) (5), 142 (2) (3) & Social Security Administration (Northern Ireland) Act 1992, s. 129. - Issued: 14.03.2012. Made: 12.03.2012. Coming into force: 06.04.2012. Effect: 1992 c. 4, 7 amended. Territorial extent & classification: E/W/S/NI. General. - Supersedes draft S.I. (ISBN 9780111519646) issued 31.01.2012. - 4p.: 30 cm. - 978-0-11-152203-5 £4.00

The Social Security (Credits) (Amendment) (No. 2) Regulations 2012 No. 2012/2680. - Enabling power: Social Security Contributions and Benefits Act 1992, ss. 22 (5), 122 (1), 175 (1) (3). - Issued: 31.10.2012. Made: 25.10.2012. Laid: 31.10.2012. Coming into force: 01.12.2012. Effect: S.I. 1975/556 amended. Territorial extent & classification: E/W/S. General. - 2p.: 30 cm. - 978-0-11-153008-5 £4.00

Social security

The Social Security (Credits) (Amendment) Regulations 2012 No. 2012/766. - Enabling power: Social Security Contributions and Benefits Act 1992, ss. 22 (5), 122 (1), 175 (1) (3). - Issued: 12.03.2012. Made: 08.03.2012. Laid: 12.03.2012. Coming into force: 05.04.2012. Effect: S.I. 1975/ 556 amended. Territorial extent & classification: E/W/S. General. - 2p.: 30 cm. - 978-0-11-152185-4 £4.00

The Social Security (Habitual Residence) (Amendment) Regulations 2012 No. 2012/2587. - Enabling power: Social Security Contributions and Benefits Act 1992, ss. 123 (1) (a) (d) (e), 131 (3) (b), 135 (1) (2), 137 (1), 175 (1) (3) (4) & Jobseekers Act 1995, ss. 4 (5) (12), 35 (1), 36 (2) (4) & State Pensions Credit Act 2002, ss. 1 (5) (a), 17 (1) & Welfare Reform Act 2007, ss. 4 (3), 24, 25 (2) (3) (5). - Issued: 17.10.2012. Made: 11.10.2012. Laid: 17.10.2012. Coming into force: 08.11.2012. Effect: S.I. 1987/1967; 1996/207; 2002/1792; 2006/213, 214, 215, 216; 2008/794 amended. Territorial extent & classification: E/W/S. General. - 8p.: 30 cm. - 978-0-11-152944-7 £4.00

The Social Security (Industrial Injuries) (Dependency) (Permitted Earnings Limits) Order 2012 No. 2012/823. - Enabling power: Social Security Contributions and Benefits Act 1992, sch. 7, para. 4 (5). - Issued: 15.03.2012. Made: 14.03.2012. Laid: 15.03.2012. Coming into force: 11.04.2012. Effect: 1992 c. 4 amended. Territorial extent & classification: E/W/S. General. - 2p.: 30 cm. - 978-0-11-152214-1 £4.00

The Social Security (Industrial Injuries) (Prescribed Diseases) Amendment (No. 2) Regulations 2012 No. 2012/1634. - Enabling power: Social Security Contributions and Benefits Act 1992, ss. 108 (2), 122 (1), 175 (1) (3) (4). - Issued: 02.07.2012. Made: 20.06.2012. Laid: 02.07.2012. Coming into force: 01.08.2012. Effect: S.I. 1985/967 amended. Territorial extent & classification: E/W/S. General. - This Statutory Instrument has been printed in substitution of the SI of same number and ISBN (published 27.06.2012, withdrawn 28.06.2012) and is being issued free fo charge to all known recipients of that Statutory Instrument. - 2p.: 30 cm. - 978-0-11-152576-0 £4.00

The Social Security (Industrial Injuries) (Prescribed Diseases) Amendment Regulations 2012 No. 2012/647. - Enabling power: Social Security Contributions and Benefits Act 1992, ss. 108 (2), 122 (1), 175 (1) (3). - Issued: 06.03.2012. Made: 01.03.2012. Laid: 06.03.2012. Coming into force: 30.03.2012. Effect: S.I. 1985/967 amended. Territorial extent & classification: E/W/S. General. - 4p.: 30 cm. - 978-0-11-152119-9 £4.00

The Social Security (Information-sharing in relation to Welfare Services etc.) Regulations 2012 No. 2012/1483. - Enabling power: Welfare Reform Act 2012, ss. 130 (2) (7), 131 (1) (3) (11), 132 (8), 133 (1) (2). - Issued: 11.06.2012. Made: 08.06.2012. Laid: 11.06.2012. Coming into force: 02.07.2012. Effect: None. Territorial extent & classification: E/W/S. General. - 12p.: 30 cm. - 978-0-11-152518-0 £5.75

The Social Security (Lone Parents and Miscellaneous Amendments) Regulations 2012 No. 2012/874. - Enabling power: Social Security Administration Act 1992, ss. 2A (1), 189 (1) (4) (5), 191 & Social Security Contributions and Benefits Act 1992, ss. 123 (1), 124 (1) (e), 137 (1), 175 (1) (3) to (5) & Jobseekers Act 1995, ss. 6 (4), 7 (4), 35 (1), 36 (2) & Welfare Reform Act 2007, ss. 2 (4) (a), 4 (6) (a), 24 (1). - Issued: 22.03.2012. Made: 20.03.2012. Laid: 22.03.2012. Coming into force: 21.05.2012. Effect: S.I. 1987/1967; 1996/207; 2000/1926; 2002/1703; 2008/794 amended. Territorial extent & classification: E/W/S. General. - 8p.: 30 cm. - 978-0-11-152256-1 £5.75

The Social Security (Miscellaneous Amendments) (No. 2) Regulations 2012 No. 2012/2575. - Enabling power: Social Security Contributions and Benefits Act 1992, ss. 123 (1) (a), 136 (3) (4) (5) (b), 137 (1), 175 (3) (4) & Jobseekers Act 1995, s. 12 (1) to (3), 20 (4), 35 (1), 36 (2) (4) (a), sch. 1, para. 11 (2), 14AA & Social Security Act 1998, s. 9 (1), 79 (4), 84 & Welfare Reform Act 2007, ss. 17 (1) (2) (3) (b), 24 (1), 25 (2)(3) (5). - Issued: 15.10.2012. Made: 11.10.2012. Laid: 15.10.2012. Coming into force: 05.11.2012. Effect: S.I. 1987/1967; 1996/207; 1999/991; 2008/794 amended. Territorial extent & classification: E/W/S. General. - 8p.: 30 cm. - 978-0-11-152938-6 £4.00

The Social Security (Miscellaneous Amendments) Regulations 2012 No. 2012/757. - Enabling power: Social Security Contributions and Benefits Act 1992, ss. 123 (1) (a) (d) (e), 124 (1) (d) (e), 131 (3) (b), 136 (3) (5) (b), 136A (3), 137 (1) (2) (i), 138 (2) (4), 175 (1) (3) (4) & Social Security Administration Act 1992, ss. 5 (1) (i) (m) (p), 71 (4), 189 (1) (4) (5), 191 & Jobseekers Act 1995, ss. 12 (4) (b), 35 (1), 36 (1) (2) (4) & Social Security Act 1998, ss. 10 (6), 79 (1) (4) (5), 84 & Child Support, Pensions and Social Security Act 2000, s. 68, sch. 7, paras. 4 (4), 20 (1) & State Pension Credit Act 2002, ss. 15 (1) (e) (3), 17 (1), 19 (1) & Welfare Reform Act 2007, ss. 1 (2), 24 (1), 25 (1) to (3) (5), 29, sch. 1, paras. 1 (4) (a), 6 (5), sch. 4, paras. 1 (1), 7 (1) (a). - Issued: 19.03.2012. Made: 08.03.2012. Laid: 08.03.2012. Coming into force: In accord. with reg. 1 (2) to (4). Effect: S.I. 1987/1967, 1968; 1988/664; 1996/207; 1999/991; 2000/729; 2001/1002; 2002/1792; 2006/213, 214, 215, 216; 2008/794; 2010/1907 amended. Territorial extent & classification: E/W/S. General. - 16p.: 30 cm. - 978-0-11-152235-6 £5.75

The Social Security (Notification of Deaths) Regulations 2012 No. 2012/1604. - Enabling power: Social Security Administration Act 1992, ss. 125, 189 (1) (4) (6). - Issued: 25.06.2012. Made: 20.06.2012. Laid: 25.06.2012. Coming into force: 16.07.2012. Effect: S.I. 1987/250 revoked. Territorial extent & classification: E/W/S. General. - With correction slip dated July 2012. - 8p.: 30 cm. - 978-0-11-152568-5 £5.75

The Social Security Pensions (Flat Rate Accrual Amount) Order 2012 No. 2012/189. - Enabling power: Social Security Contributions and Benefits Act 1992, s. 148AA (3) to (6). - Issued: 31.01.2012. Made: 26.01.2012. Laid: 31.01.2012. Coming into force: 06.04.2012. Effect: None. Territorial extent & classification: E/W/S. General. - 2p.: 30 cm. - 978-0-11-151957-8 £4.00

The Social Security Pensions (Low Earnings Threshold) Order 2012 No. 2012/188. - Enabling power: Social Security Administration Act 1992, s. 148A (3) (4). - Issued: 31.01.2012. Made: 26.01.2012. Laid: 31.01.2012. Coming into force: 06.04.2012. Effect: None. Territorial extent & classification: E/W/S. General. - 2p.: 30 cm. - 978-0-11-151956-1 £4.00

The Social Security (Reciprocal Agreements) Order 2012 No. 2012/360. - Enabling power: Social Security Administration Act 1992, s. 179 (1) (b) (2) (5). - Issued: 22.02.2012. Made: 15.02.2012. Coming into force: 22.02.2012. Effect: 1992 c. 4, 5; 2007 c.5 & S.I. 1958/1263; 1961/584; 1984/1817; 1992/812; 1994/2802; 1997/871 modified. Territorial extent & classification: E/W/S/NI. General. - 4p.: 30 cm. - 978-0-11-152037-6 £4.00

The Social Security (Recovery) (Amendment) Regulations 2012 No. 2012/645. - Enabling power: Social Security Administration Act 1992, ss. 71 (6) (a) (8), 75 (1) (4) (5), 76 (1), 189 (1) (4), 191. - Issued: 06.03.2012. Made: 01.03.2012. Laid: 06.03.2012. Coming into force: 01.04.2012. Effect: S.I. 1988/664; 2006/213, 214, 215, 216 amended. Territorial extent & classification: E/W/S. General. - 4p.: 30 cm. - 978-0-11-152117-5 £4.00

The Social Security Revaluation of Earnings Factors Order 2012 No. 2012/187. - Enabling power: Social Security Administration Act 1992, ss. 148 (3) (4), 189 (1) (4) (5). - Issued: 31.01.2012. Made: 26.01.2012. Laid: 31.01.2012. Coming into force: 06.04.2012. Effect: None. Territorial extent & classification: E/W/S. General. - 4p.: 30 cm. - 978-0-11-151955-4 £4.00

The Social Security (Suspension of Payment of Benefits and Miscellaneous Amendments) Regulations 2012 No. 2012/824. - Enabling power: Social Security Administration Act 1992, ss. 5 (1) (hh) (i) (3A), 6 (1) (i), 189 (1) (4) to (6), 191 & Social Security Act 1998, ss. 9 (1) (a), 22, 79 (1) (4) (6) (7), 84. - Issued: 15.03.2012. Made: 14.03.2012. Laid: 15.03.2012. Coming into force: 17.04.2012. Effect: S.I. 1987/1968; 1996/207; 1999/991; 2006/213, 214, 215, 216 amended. Territorial extent & classification: E/W/S. General. - 4p.: 30 cm. - 978-0-11-152215-8 £4.00

The Welfare Reform Act 2009 (Commencement No. 7) Order 2012 No. 2012/68 (C.3). - Enabling power: Welfare Reform Act 2009, s. 61 (3) (4). Bringing into operation various provisions of the 2009 Act on 19.01.2012, in accord. with art 2. - Issued: 17.01.2012. Made: 11.01.2012. Effect: None. Territorial extent & classification: E/W/S. General. - 4p.: 30 cm. - 978-0-11-151923-3 £4.00

The Welfare Reform Act 2009 (Commencement No. 8) Order 2012 No. 2012/1256 (C.43). - Enabling power: Welfare Reform Act 2009, s. 61 (5). Bringing into operation various provisions of the 2009 Act on 21.05.2012 & 28.05.2012, in accord. with art 2. - Issued: 14.05.2012. Made: 10.05.2012. Effect: None. Territorial extent & classification: E/W/S. General. - 4p.: 30 cm. - 978-0-11-152422-0 £4.00

The Welfare Reform Act 2012 (Commencement No. 1) Order 2012 No. 2012/863 (C.23). - Enabling power: Welfare Reform Act 2012, s. 150 (3) (4) (a). Bringing into operation various provisions of the 2012 Act on 20.03.2012, 01.05.2012, 08.05.2012, in accord. with art 2. - Issued: 20.03.2012. Made: 19.03.2012. Effect: None. Territorial extent & classification: E/W/S. General. - 4p.: 30 cm. - 978-0-11-152247-9 £4.00

The Welfare Reform Act 2012 (Commencement No. 2) (Amendment) Order 2012 No. 2012/1440 (C.55). - Enabling power: Welfare Reform Act 2012, s. 150 (3). Bringing into operation various provisions of the 2012 Act. - Issued: 06.06.2012. Made: 31.05.2012. Effect: None. Territorial extent & classification: E/W. General. - This Statutory Instrument corrects an error in S.I. 2012/1246 (ISBN 9780111524138) and is being issued free of charge to all known recipients of that Statutory Instrument. - 4p.: 30 cm. - 978-0-11-152503-6 £4.00

The Welfare Reform Act 2012 (Commencement No. 2) Order 2012 No. 2012/1246 (C.42). - Enabling power: Welfare Reform Act 2012, s. 150 (3) (4) (a). Bringing into operation various provisions of the 2012 Act on various dates in accord. with art. 2. - Issued: 10.05.2012. Made: 09.05.2012. Effect: None. Territorial extent & classification: E/W/S. General. - 8p.: 30 cm. - 978-0-11-152413-8 £4.00

The Welfare Reform Act 2012 (Commencement No. 3, Savings Provision) Order 2012 No. 2012/1651 (C.62). - Enabling power: Welfare Reform Act 2012, s. 150 (3) (4) (a) (c). Bringing into operation various provisions of the 2012 Act on 02.07.2012 in accord. with art. 2. - Issued: 29.06.2012. Made: 26.06.2012. Effect: None. Territorial extent & classification: E/W/S. General. - Partially revoked by SI 2012/2530 (C.102) (ISBN 9780111529157). - 4p.: 30 cm. - 978-0-11-152592-0 £4.00

The Welfare Reform Act 2012 (Commencement No. 4) Order 2012 No. 2012/2530 (C.102). - Enabling power: Welfare Reform Act 2012, s. 150 (3) (4) (a). Bringing into operation certain provisions of the 2012 Act on various dates in accord. with art. 2. - Issued: 05.10.2012. Made: 04.10.2012. Effect: S.I. 2012/1651 partially revoked (08.10.2012). Territorial extent & classification: E/W/S. General. - 8p.: 30 cm. - 978-0-11-152915-7 £4.00

The Welfare Reform Act 2012 (Commencement No. 5) Order 2012 No. 2012/2946 (C.118). - Enabling power: Welfare Reform Act 2012, s. 150 (3) (4) (a). Bringing into operation certain provisions of the 2012 Act on various dates in accord. with art. 2. - Issued: 27.11.2012. Made: 24.11.2012. Effect: None. Territorial extent & classification: E/W/S. General. - 4p.: 30 cm. - 978-0-11-153123-5 £4.00

The Welfare Reform Act 2012 (Commencement No. 6 and Savings Provisions) Order 2012 No. 2012/3090 (C.123). - Enabling power: Welfare Reform Act 2012, s. 150 (3) (4) (a) (c). Bringing into operation certain provisions of the 2012 Act on various dates in accord. with art. 2. - Issued: 14.12.2012. Made: 12.12.2012. Effect: None. Territorial extent & classification: E/W/S. General. - 8p.: 30 cm. - 978-0-11-153219-5 £4.00

The Workmen's Compensation (Supplementation) (Amendment) Scheme 2012 No. 2012/833. - Enabling power: Social Security Contributions and Benefits Act 1992, sch. 8, para. 2 & Social Security Administration Act 1992, sch. 9, para. 1. - Issued: 15.03.2012. Made: 14.03.2012. Laid: 15.03.2012. Coming into force: 11.04.2012. Effect: S.I. 1982/1489 amended. Territorial extent & classification: E/W/S. General. - 4p.: 30 cm. - 978-0-11-152225-7 £4.00

Social security, Northern Ireland

The Guardian's Allowance Up-rating (Northern Ireland) Order 2012 No. 2012/835. - Enabling power: Social Security Administration (Northern Ireland) Act 1992, ss. 132 (1), 165 (4). - Issued: 16.03.2012. Made: 14.03.2012. Coming into force: 09.04.2012. Effect: 1992 c. 7 amended. Territorial extent & classification: NI. General. - Supersedes draft SI (ISBN 9780111519806) issued 03.02.2012. - 2p.: 30 cm. - 978-0-11-152227-1 £4.00

The Jobseeker's Allowance (Members of the Forces) (Northern Ireland) (Amendment) Regulations 2012 No. 2012/2569. - Enabling power: S.I. 1995/2705 (NI. 15), arts 2 (2), 24 (1) (3), 36 (2). - Issued: 15.10.2012. Made: 10.10.2012. Laid: 15.10.2012. Coming into force: 05.11.2012. Effect: S.I. 1997/932 amended. Territorial extent & classification: NI. General. - 2p.: 30 cm. - 978-0-11-152935-5 £4.00

Sports grounds and sporting events, England and Wales

The Football Spectators (2012 European Championship Control Period) Order 2012 No. 2012/340. - Enabling power: Football Spectators Act 1989, ss. 14 (6), 22A (2). - Issued: 15.02.2012. Made: 09.02.2012. Laid: 14.02.2012. Coming into force: 08.03.2012. Effect: None. Territorial extent & classification: E/W. General. - 2p.: 30 cm. - 978-0-11-152019-2 £4.00

The Football Spectators (Seating) Order 2012 No. 2012/1470. - Enabling power: Football Spectators Act 1989, s. 11. - Issued: 11.06.2012. Made: 06.06.2012. Laid: 08.06.2012. Coming into force: 01.07.2012. Effect: None. Territorial extent & classification: E/W. General. - 2p.: 30 cm. - 978-0-11-152514-2 £4.00

The Safety of Sports Grounds (Designation) (No. 2) Order 2012 No. 2012/1666. - Enabling power: Safety of Sports Grounds Act 1975, s. 1 (1). - Issued: 29.06.2012. Made: 27.06.2012. Laid: 28.06.2012. Coming into force: 20.07.2012. Effect: None. Territorial extent & classification: E/W. General. - 2p.: 30 cm. - 978-0-11-152602-6 £4.00

The Safety of Sports Grounds (Designation) Order 2012 No. 2012/1133. - Enabling power: Safety of Sports Grounds Act 1975, s. 1 (1). - Issued: 25.04.2012. Made: 20.04.2012. Laid: 24.04.2012. Coming into force: 18.05.2012. Effect: None. Territorial extent & classification: E/W. General. - 2p.: 30 cm. - 978-0-11-152376-6 £4.00

Stamp duty

The British Waterways Board (Tax Consequences) Order 2012 No. 2012/1709. - Enabling power: Public Bodies Act 2011, s. 25. - Issued: 03.07.2012. Made: 02.07.2012 at 12 noon. Laid: 02.07.2012 at 3 p.m. Coming into force: 02.07.2012 at 3.30 p.m. Effect: None. Territorial extent and classification: E/W/S/NI. General. - 8p.: 30 cm. - 978-0-11-152617-0 £4.00

The Finance Act 2010, Schedule 6, Part 2 (Commencement) Order 2012 No. 2012/736 (C.18). - Enabling power: Finance Act 2010, sch. 6, para. 34 (1) (b) (2) (3). Bringing into operation various provisions of this Act on 01.04.2012. - Issued: 12.03.2012. Made: 08.03.2012. Effect: None. Territorial extent & classification: E/W/S/NI. General. - 8p.: 30 cm. - 978-0-11-152189-2 £5.75

The Postal Services Act 2011 (Taxation) Regulations 2012 No. 2012/764. - Enabling power: Postal Services Act 2011, ss. 23, 89 (2). - Issued: 12.03.2012. Made: 08.03.2012. Laid: 09.03.2012. Coming into force: In accord. with reg. 1 (1). Effect: None. Territorial extent & classification: E/W/S/NI. General. - 16p.: 30 cm. - 978-0-11-152180-9 £5.75

Stamp duty land tax

The British Waterways Board (Tax Consequences) Order 2012 No. 2012/1709. - Enabling power: Public Bodies Act 2011, s. 25. - Issued: 03.07.2012. Made: 02.07.2012 at 12 noon. Laid: 02.07.2012 at 3 p.m. Coming into force: 02.07.2012 at 3.30 p.m. Effect: None. Territorial extent and classification: E/W/S/NI. General. - 8p.: 30 cm. - 978-0-11-152617-0 £4.00

The Finance Act 2010, Schedule 6, Part 2 (Commencement) Order 2012 No. 2012/736 (C.18). - Enabling power: Finance Act 2010, sch. 6, para. 34 (1) (b) (2) (3). Bringing into operation various provisions of this Act on 01.04.2012. - Issued: 12.03.2012. Made: 08.03.2012. Effect: None. Territorial extent & classification: E/W/S/NI. General. - 8p.: 30 cm. - 978-0-11-152189-2 £5.75

The London Legacy Development Corporation (Tax Consequences) Regulations 2012 No. 2012/701. - Enabling power: Localism Act 2011, sch. 24, part 3. - Issued: 07.03.2012. Made: 06.03.2012. Laid: 07.03.2012. Coming into force: 31.03.2012. Effect: None. Territorial extent & classification: UK. General. - 4p.: 30 cm. - 978-0-11-152152-6 £4.00

The Postal Services Act 2011 (Taxation) Regulations 2012 No. 2012/764. - Enabling power: Postal Services Act 2011, ss. 23, 89 (2). - Issued: 12.03.2012. Made: 08.03.2012. Laid: 09.03.2012. Coming into force: In accord. with reg. 1 (1). Effect: None. Territorial extent & classification: E/W/S/NI. General. - 16p.: 30 cm. - 978-0-11-152180-9 £5.75

The Stamp Duty Land Tax (Amendment to the Finance Act 2003) Regulations 2012 No. 2012/1667. - Enabling power: Finance Act 2003, ss. 50 (2) (3). - Issued: 29.06.2012. Made: 27.06.2012. Laid: 28.06.2012. Coming into force: 19.07.2012. Effect: 2003 c. 14 amended. Territorial extent & classification: E/W/S/NI. General. - 2p.: 30 cm. - 978-0-11-152603-3 £4.00

The Stamp Duty Land Tax Avoidance Schemes (Prescribed Descriptions of Arrangements) (Amendment) Regulations 2012 No. 2012/2395. - Enabling power: Finance Act 2004, ss. 306 (1) (a) (b), 318. - Issued: 18.09.2012. Made: 17.09.2012. Laid: 18.09.2012. Coming into force: 01.11.2012. Effect: S.I. 2005/1868 amended. Territorial extent & classification: E/W/S/NI. General. - 4p.: 30 cm. - 978-0-11-152886-0 £4.00

The Stamp Duty Land Tax Avoidance Schemes (Specified Proposals or Arrangements) Regulations 2012 No. 2012/2396. - Enabling power: Finance Act 2004, ss. 308 (6), 317. - Issued: 18.09.2012. Made: 17.09.2012. Laid: 18.09.2012. Coming into force: 01.11.2012. Effect: 2004 c. 12 modified. Territorial extent & classification: E/W/S/NI. General. - 4p.: 30 cm. - 978-0-11-152887-7 £4.00

The Visiting Forces and International Military Headquarters (NATO and PfP) (Tax Designation) Order 2012 No. 2012/3071. - Enabling power: Finance Act 1960, s. 74A & Inheritance Tax Act 1984, s.155 & Income Tax (Earnings and Pensions) Act 2003, s. 303 & Income Tax Act 2007, s. 833. - Issued: 17.12.2012. Made: 12.12.2012. Coming into force: In accord. with art. 1 (2). Effect: S.I. 1961/580; 1960/581; 1998/1513, 1514, 1515, 1516, 1517, 1518 revoked (13.12.2012). Territorial extent & classification: E/W/S/NI. General. - [8]p.: 30 cm. - 978-0-11-153238-6 £4.00

Stamp duty reserve tax

The Child Trust Funds, Registered Pension Schemes and Stamp Duty Reserve Tax (Consequential Amendments) Regulations 2012 No. 2012/886. - Enabling power: Child Trust Funds Act 2004, ss. 13, 28 (1) (2) & Finance Act 1986, s. 98 & Finance Act 2004, ss. ss. 267 (10), 268 (10). - Issued: 21.03.2012. Made: 21.03.2012. Laid: 21.03.2012. Coming into force: 06.04.2012. Effect: S.I. 1986/1711; 2004/1450; 2005/3452 amended. Territorial extent & classification: E/W/S/NI. General. - 4p.: 30 cm. - 978-0-11-152265-3 £4.00

The Finance Act 2010, Schedule 6, Part 2 (Commencement) Order 2012 No. 2012/736 (C.18). - Enabling power: Finance Act 2010, sch. 6, para. 34 (1) (b) (2) (3). Bringing into operation various provisions of this Act on 01.04.2012. - Issued: 12.03.2012. Made: 08.03.2012. Effect: None. Territorial extent & classification: E/W/S/NI. General. - 8p.: 30 cm. - 978-0-11-152189-2 £5.75

The Postal Services Act 2011 (Taxation) Regulations 2012 No. 2012/764. - Enabling power: Postal Services Act 2011, ss. 23, 89 (2). - Issued: 12.03.2012. Made: 08.03.2012. Laid: 09.03.2012. Coming into force: In accord. with reg. 1 (1). Effect: None. Territorial extent & classification: E/W/S/NI. General. - 16p.: 30 cm. - 978-0-11-152180-9 £5.75

Statistics Board

The Statistics and Registration Service Act 2007 (Disclosure of Social Security and Revenue Information) Regulations 2012 No. 2012/1711. - Enabling power: Statistics and Registration Service Act 2007, s. 47 (1) (a) (6) (b) (7) (b). - Issued: 04.07.2012. Made: 17.05.2012. Coming into force: 18.05.2012 in accord. with reg. 1. Effect: None. Territorial extent & classification: UK. General. - Supersedes draft S.I. (ISBN 9780111520550) issued 27.02.2012. - 8p.: 30 cm. - 978-0-11-152622-4 £4.00

Statistics of trade

The Statistics of Trade (Customs and Excise) (Amendment) Regulations 2012 No. 2012/532. - Enabling power: European Communities Act 1972, s. 2 (2). - Issued: 29.02.2012. Made: 27.02.2012. Laid: 28.02.2012. Coming into force: 01.04.2012. Effect: S.I. 1992/2790 amended. Territorial extent & classification: E/W/S/NI. General. - 4p.: 30 cm. - 978-0-11-152080-2 £4.00

Tax credits

The Child Benefit and Child Tax Credit (Miscellaneous Amendments) Regulations 2012 No. 2012/2612. - Enabling power: Social Security Contributions and Benefits Act 1992, s. 146 (3) & Social Security Contributions and Benefits (Northern Ireland) Act 1992, s. 142 (3) & Tax Credits Act 2002, s. 3 (7). - Issued: 18.10.2012. Made: 16.10.2012. Laid: 17.10.2012. Coming into force: 08.11.2012. Effect: S.I. 2003/654; 2006/223 amended. Territorial extent & classification: E/W/S/NI. General. - 4p.: 30 cm. - 978-0-11-152959-1 £4.00

The Tax Credits (Miscellaneous Amendments) Regulations 2012 No. 2012/848. - Enabling power: Tax Credits Act 2002, ss. 3 (7), 4 (1) (b), 6, 7 (8), 8 (2) (3), 9, 10, 11, (7), 12 (1), 24 (7), 42 (1), 65 (1) (2) (7) (9), 67. - Issued: 19.03.2012. Made: 16.03.2012. Laid: 16.03.2012. Coming into force: 06.04.2012 for the purpose of regulations 1 (1) to 1 (3), 2 (1) (2) (b) (3) to (10) (11) (c) (12) (13) (c) (14) to (16) (17) (c) (iii) (18) (20), 3 to 9; 01.05.2012 for the purposes of regulations 1 (4), 2 (2) (a) (11) (a) to (b) (13) (a) to (b) (17) (a) to (c) (ii). Effect: S.I. 2002/2005, 2006, 2007, 2014, 2173; 2003/653, 654, 742 amended. Territorial extent & classification: E/W/S/NI. General. - 12p.: 30 cm. - 978-0-11-152242-4 £5.75

The Tax Credits Up-rating Regulations 2012 No. 2012/849. - Enabling power: Tax Credits Act 2002, ss. 7 (1) (a), 9, 11 to 13, 65 (1), 67. - Issued: 19.03.2012. Made: 14.03.2012. Coming into force: 06.04.2012. Effect: S.I. 2002/2005, 2007, 2008 amended. Territorial extent & classification: E/W/S/NI. General. - Supersedes draft S.I. (ISBN 9780111519790) issued 03.02.2012. - 4p.: 30 cm. - 978-0-11-152241-7 £4.00

Taxes

The Data-gathering Powers (Relevant Data) Regulations 2012 No. 2012/847. - Enabling power: Finance Act 2011, s. 23, para. 44 (2). - Issued: 19.03.2012. Made: 14.03.2012. Coming into force: 01.04.2012. Effect: None. Territorial extent & classification: UK. General. - Supersedes draft S.I. (ISBN 9780111520444) issued 21.02.2012. - 12p.: 30 cm. - 978-0-11-152240-0 £5.75

The Double Taxation Relief and International Tax Enforcement (Switzerland) Order 2012 No. 2012/3079. - Enabling power: Taxation (International and Other Provisions) Act 2010, s. 2 & Finance Act 2006, s. 173 (1) to (3). - Issued: 17.07.2012. Made: 12.12.2012. Effect: None. Territorial extent & classification: E/W/S/NI. General. - Supersedes draft SI (ISBN 9780111527085) issued 17.07.2012. - 8p.: 30 cm. - 978-0-11-153239-3 £5.75

The Reporting of Savings Income and Interest payments (Data-gathering) Regulations 2012 No. 2012/756. - Enabling power: Taxes Management Act 1970, s. 18B. - Issued: 12.03.2012. Made: 08.03.2012. Laid before the House of Commons: 09.03.2012. Coming into force: 31.03.2012, for the purpose of reg. 3 & 01.04.2012, for the purpose of reg. 2. Effect: S.I. 2003/3297 amended & S.I. 2011/22 partially revoked & S.I. 1992/15; 2001/405; 2008/2688 revoked. Territorial extent & classification: E/W/S/NI. General. - 4p.: 30 cm. - 978-0-11-152173-1 £4.00

The Tax Avoidance Schemes (Information) Regulations 2012 No. 2012/1836. - Enabling power: Taxes Management Act 1970, s. 98C (2A) (2B) (2C) (b) & Finance Act 1999, s. 132 & Finance Act 2002, s. 135 & Finance Act 2004, ss. 306A (6), 307 (5), 308 (1) (3), 308A (5) (6) (a), 309 (1), 310, 312 (2) (5), 312A (2) (5), 313 (1) (3), 313ZA (3) (4), 313A (4) (a), 313B (2) (a), 313C (1) (3) (a), 317 (2), 318 (1). - Issued: 16.07.2012. Made: 12.07.2012. Laid: 13.07.2012. Coming into force: 01.09.2012. Effect: S.I. 2004/1865 amended & S.I. 2004/2613 partially revoked & S.I. 2004/1864; 2005/1869; 2006/1544; 2007/2153, 3103; 2008/1947; 2009/611; 2010/410, 2928; 2011/171 revoked. Territorial extent & classification: E/W/S/NI. General. - With correction slip dated January 2013. - 12p.: 30 cm. - 978-0-11-152703-0 £5.75

Terms and conditions of employment

The Employment Rights (Increase of Limits) Order 2012 No. 2012/3007. - Enabling power: Employment Relations Act 1999, s. 34. - Issued: 06.12.2012. Made: 29.11.2012. Laid: 04.12.2012. Coming into force: 01.02.2013. Effect: S.I. 2011/3006 revoked. Territorial extent & classification: E/W/S. General. - 8p.: 30 cm. - 978-0-11-153161-7 £4.00

The Local Policing Bodies (Consequential Amendments and Transitional Provision) Order 2012 No. 2012/2733. - Enabling power: Employment Rights Act 1996, ss. 209 (1) (b), 236 & Police Act 1996, sch. 4A, para. 3 (4) & Police Reform and Social Responsibility Act 2011, sch. 15, para. 24. - Issued: 05.11.2012. Made: 30.10.2012. Laid: 01.11.2012. Coming into force: 22.11.2012. Effect: S.I. 1999/2277; 2007/1170 amended. Territorial extent & classification: E/W. General. - 4p.: 30 cm. - 978-0-11-153029-0 £4.00

The National Minimum Wage (Amendment) Regulations 2012 No. 2012/2397. - Enabling power: National Minimum Wage Act 1998, ss. 1 (3), 2, 3, 51. - Issued: 19.09.2012. Made: 15.09.2012. Coming into force: 01.10.2012. Effect: S.I. 1999/584; 2010/93 amended. Territorial extent & classification: E/W/S/NI. General. - Supersedes draft SI (ISBN 9780111525739) issued on 25.06.2012. - 4p.: 30 cm. - 978-0-11-152888-4 £4.00

The Public Interest Disclosure (Prescribed Persons) (Amendment) Order 2012 No. 2012/462. - Enabling power: Employment Rights Act 1996, s. 43F. - Issued: 28.02.2012. Made: 21.02.2012. Laid: 28.02.2012. Coming into force: 22.03.2012. Effect: S.I. 1999/1549 amended. Territorial extent & classification: E/W/S. General. - 2p.: 30 cm. - 978-0-11-152052-9 £4.00

The Social Security Benefits Up-rating Order 2012 No. 2012/780. - Enabling power: Social Security Administration Act 1992, ss. 150, 150A, 151, 189 (1) (4) (5). - Issued: 19.03.2012. Made: 06.03.2012. Coming into force: In accord. with art. 1. Effect: 1965 c. 51; 1992 c. 4 & S.I. 1986/1960; 1987/1967;1991/2890; 1994/2946; 1995/310; 1996/207; 2002/1792, 2818; 2006/213, 214, 215, 216; 2008/794; 2010/1060, 2818 amended & S.I. 2011/821 revoked. Territorial extent & classification: E/W/S. General. - Supersedes draft S.I. (ISBN 9780111519486) issued 30.01.2012. - 60p.: 30 cm. - 978-0-11-152236-3 £9.75

The Transfer of Undertakings (Protection of Employment) (RCUK Shared Services Centre Limited) Regulations 2012 No. 2012/2413. - Enabling power: Employment Relations Act 1999, s. 38. - Issued: 24.09.2012. Made: 19.09.2012 Laid: 21.09.2012. Coming into force: 01.11.2012. Effect: None. Territorial extent & classification: E/W/S/NI. General. - 4p.: 30 cm. - 978-0-11-152898-3 £4.00

The Unfair Dismissal and Statement of Reasons for Dismissal (Variation of Qualifying Period) Order 2012 No. 2012/989. - Enabling power: Employment Rights Act 1996, ss. 209 (1) (c) (5), 236 (5). - Issued: 03.04.2012. Made: 30.03.2012. Coming into force: 06.04.2012. Effect: 1996 c.18 amended & S.I. 1999/1436 revoked. Territorial extent & classification: E/W/S. General. - Supersedes draft S.I. (ISBN 9780111519974) issued 10.02.2012. - 2p.: 30 cm. - 978-0-11-152328-5 £4.00

Town and country planning, England

The Land Compensation Development (England) Order 2012 No. 2012/634. - Enabling power: Land Compensation Act 1961, s. 20 & Town and Country Planning Act 1990, ss. 59, 61 (1), 333 (7). - Issued: 06.03.2012. Made: 01.03.2012. Laid: 06.03.2012. Coming into force: 06.04.2012. Effect: S.I. 1974/539 revoked in relation to England. Territorial extent & classification: E. General. - 4p.: 30 cm. - 978-0-11-152113-7 £4.00

The Localism Act 2011 (Commencement No. 7 and Transitional, Savings and Transitory Provisions) Order 2012 No. 2012/2029 (C.80). - Enabling power: Localism Act 2011, s. 240 (2) (7). Bringing into operation various provisions of the 2011 Act on 03.08.2012, in accord. with art. 2. - Issued: 07.08.2012. Made: 02.08.2012. Effect: S.I. 2012/628 partially revoked (03.08.2012). Territorial extent & classification: E/W. General. - 8p.: 30 cm. - 978-0-11-152796-2 £4.00

The Neighbourhood Planning (General) Regulations 2012 No. 2012/637. - Enabling power: Town and Country Planning Act 1990, ss. 61E, 61F, 61G, 61K, 61L, 61M, 71A, sch. 4B, paras 1, 4, 7, 8, 1011, 12, 15, sch. 4C, paras 3, 11 & Planning and Compulsory Purchase Act 2004, ss. 38A, 38B, 122 (1). - Issued: 06.03.2012. Made: 01.03.2012. Laid: 06.03.2012. Coming into force: 06.04.2012. Effect: S.I. 2010/490 amended. Territorial extent & classification: E. General. - 28p.: 30 cm. - 978-0-11-152122-9 £5.75

The Neighbourhood Planning (Prescribed Dates) Regulations 2012 No. 2012/2030. - Enabling power: Town and Country Planning Act 1990, ss. 14 (4) (6), 15 (3), sch. 4B. - Issued: 07.08.2012. Made: 02.08.2012. Laid: 07.08.2012. Coming into force: 01.09.2012. Effect: None. Territorial extent & classification: E. General. - 2p.: 30 cm. - 978-0-11-152797-9 £4.00

The Neighbourhood Planning (Referendums) Regulations 2012 No. 2012/2031. - Enabling power: Town and Country Planning Act 1990, sch. 4B, para. 16 & Planning and Compulsory Purchase Act 2004, s. 38A (3). - Issued: 06.08.2012. Made: 02.08.2012. Coming into force: 03.08.2012, in accord. with reg. 1. Effect: 1983 c. 2; 1985 c. 50; 2000 c. 2, c. 41; 2006 c. 22; S.I. 2001/341; 2004/293, 294; 2006/3304, 3305; 2007/1024, 3541; 2012/323, 444, 1917 have effect subject to modifications. Territorial extent & classification: E. General. - Supersedes draft SI (ISBN 9780111525050) issued on 11.06.2012. - 118p.: 30 cm. - 978-0-11-152798-6 £18.50

The Planning Act 2008 (Commencement No.2) (England) Order 2012 No. 2011/601 (C.13). - Enabling power: Planning Act 2008, s. 241 (3) (8). Bringing into operation various provisions of the 2008 Act on 06.04.2012, in accord. with art. 2. - Issued: 05.03.2012. Made: 28.02.2012. Effect: None. Territorial extent & classification: E. General. - 4p.: 30 cm. - 978-0-11-152097-0 £4.00

The Planning (Listed Buildings and Conservation Areas) (Amendment) (England) Regulations 2012 No. 2012/2275. - Enabling power: Planning (Listed Buildings and Conservation Areas) Act 1990, ss. 10, 93. - Issued: 06.09.2012. Made: 04.09.2012. Laid: 06.09.2012. Coming into force: 01.10.2012. Effect: S.I. 1990/1519 amended in relation to England. Territorial extent & classification: E. General. - 2p.: 30 cm. - 978-0-11-152856-3 £4.00

The Regional Strategy for the East of England (Revocation) Order 2012 No. 2012/3046. - Enabling power: Localism Act 2011, s. 109 (3) (5) (6). - Issued: 11.12.2012. Made: 06.12.2012. Laid: 11.12.2012. Coming into force: 03.01.2013. Effect: None. Territorial extent & classification: E. General. - Revokes the regional strategy for the East of England, comprising the East of England plan (2008, ISBN 9780117539952) and revisions: Accommodation for gypsy and travellers .. (2009, ISBN 9780117540132), Thurrock key centre .. (2010, ISBN 9780117540873) and elements of the 2005 Milton Keynes and South Midlands strategy (2005, ISBN 9780117539426). - 2p.: 30 cm. - 978-0-11-153197-6 £4.00

The Town and Country Planning (Compensation) (England) Regulations 2012 No. 2012/749. - Enabling power: Town and Country Planning Act 1990, s. 108 (2A), (3C), (3D) (5) (6). - Issued: 13.03.2012. Made: 05.03.2012. Laid: 13.03.2012. Coming into force: 06.04.2012 in accord. with regulation 1. Effect: S.I. 2011/2058 revoked (06.04.2012). Territorial extent & classification: E. General. - 4p.: 30 cm. - 978-0-11-152186-1 £4.00

The Town and Country Planning (Control of Advertisements) (England) (Amendment) Regulations 2012 No. 2012/2372. - Enabling power: Town and Country Planning Act 1990, ss. 220, 221, 333 (1). - Issued: 17.09.2012. Made: 13.09.2012. Laid: 17.09.2012. Coming into force: 12.10.2012. Effect: S.I. 2007/783 amended. Territorial extent & classification: E. General. - 4p.: 30 cm. - 978-0-11-152878-5 £4.00

The Town and Country Planning (Development Management Procedure) (England) (Amendment No. 2) Order 2012 No. 2012/2274. - Enabling power: Town and Country Planning Act 1990, ss. 59, 62 (1). - Issued: 07.09.2012. Made: 04.09.2012. Laid: 06.09.2012. Coming into force: In accord, with art. 1. Effect: S.I. 2010/2184 amended. Territorial extent & classification: E. General. - 2p.: 30 cm. - 978-0-11-152857-0 £4.00

The Town and Country Planning (Development Management Procedure) (England) (Amendment No. 3) Order 2012 No. 2012/3109. - Enabling power: Town and Country Planning Act 1990, ss. 59, 62 (1), 333 (7). - Issued: 20.12.2012. Made: 17.12.2012. Laid: 20.12.2012. Coming into force: 31.01.2013. Effect: S.I. 2010/2184 amended. Territorial extent & classification: E. General. - With correction slip dated January 2013. - 4p.: 30 cm. - 978-0-11-153266-9 £4.00

The Town and Country Planning (Development Management Procedure) (England) (Amendment) Order 2012 No. 2012/636. - Enabling power: Town and Country Planning Act 1990, ss. 59, 69, 74 (1) (c), 188, sch. 4A, para 1. - Issued: 06.03.2012. Made: 01.03.2012. Laid: 06.03.2012. Coming into force: 06.04.2012. Effect: S.I. 2010/2184 amended. Territorial extent & classification: E. General. - 8p.: 30 cm. - 978-0-11-152115-1 £4.00

The Town and Country Planning (Fees for Applications, Deemed Applications, Requests and Site Visits) (England) Regulations 2012 No. 2012/2920. - Enabling power: Town and Country Planning Act 1990, ss. 303, 333 (2A). - Issued: 23.11.2012. Made: 21.11.2012. Coming into force: In accord.with reg. 1. Effect: S.I. 1989/193; 1990/2473; 1991/2735; 1992/1817, 3052; 1993/3170; 1997/37; 2001/2719; 2002/768; 2006/994; 2008/958; 2010/472 revoked in relation to England. Territorial extent & classification: E. General. - Supersedes draft SI (ISBN 9780111527290) issued 18.07.2012. - 28p.: 30 cm. - 978-0-11-153112-9 £5.75

The Town and Country Planning (General Permitted Development) (Amendment) (England) Order 2012 No. 2012/748. - Enabling power: Town and Country Planning Act 1990, ss. 59, 60, 61, 333 (7). - Issued: 13.03.2012. Made: 05.03.2012. Laid: 13.03.2012. Coming into force: In accord. with art. 1. Effect: S.I. 1995/418 amended. Territorial extent & classification: E. General. - 8p.: 30 cm. - 978-0-11-152190-8 £5.75

The Town and Country Planning (General Permitted Development) (Amendment) (No. 2) (England) Order 2012 No. 2012/2257. - Enabling power: Town and Country Planning Act 1990, ss. 59, 60, 61, 333 (7). - Issued: 06.09.2012. Made: 31.08.2012. Laid: 06.09.2012. Coming into force: 01.10.2012. Effect: S.I. 1995/418 amended. Territorial extent & classification: E. General. - 2p.: 30 cm. - 978-0-11-152844-0 £4.00

The Town and Country Planning (Local Planning) (England) (Amendment) Regulations 2012 No. 2012/2613. - Enabling power: Planning and Compulsory Purchase Act 2004, ss. 33A (9), 122 (1). - Issued: 18.10.2012. Made: 08.10.2012. Laid: 18.10.2012. Coming into force: 12.11.2012. Effect: S.I. 2012/767 amended. Territorial extent & classification: E. General. - 2p.: 30 cm. - 978-0-11-152961-4 £4.00

The Town and Country Planning (Local Planning) (England) Regulations 2012 No. 2012/767. - Enabling power: Planning and Compulsory Purchase Act 2004, ss. 17 (7), 19 (2) (j), 20 (3), 28 (9) (11), 31 (6) (7), 33A (1) (c) (9), 35 (2), 36. - Issued: 15.03.2012. Made: 08.03.2012. Laid: 15.03.2012. Coming into force: 06.04.2012. Effect: S.I. 2010/602; 2011/988, 3058 partially revoked & S.I. 2004/2204; 2008/1371; 2009/401 revoked with savings. Territorial extent & classification: E. General. - With correction slip dated June 2012. - 28p.: 30 cm. - 978-0-11-152192-2 £5.75

The Town and Country Planning (Tree Preservation) (England) Regulations 2012 No. 2012/605. - Enabling power: Town and Country Planning Act 1990, ss. 202A to 202G, 206 (1) (b), 212, 213 (1) (b), 316 (1), 323, 333 (1). - Issued: 05.03.2012. Made: 28.02.2012. Laid: 05.03.2012. Coming into force: 06.04.2012. Effect: S.I. 1999/1892; 2008/2260, 3202 revoked with savings. Territorial extent & classification: E. General. - With correction slip dated May 2012. - 24p.: 30 cm. - 978-0-11-152109-0 £5.75

Town and country planning, England and Wales

The Localism Act 2011 (Commencement No. 2 and Transitional and Saving Provision) Order 2012 No. 2012/57 (C. 2). - Enabling power: Localism Act 2011, ss. 37, 240 (2) (7) (8). Bringing into operation various provisions of the 2011 Act on 15.01.2012; 31.01.2012. - Issued: 16.01.2012. Made: 11.01.2012. Effect: None. Territorial extent & classification: E/W and S in part. General. - 12p.: 30 cm. - 978-0-11-151911-0 £5.75

The Localism Act 2011 (Commencement No. 4 and Transitional, Transitory and Saving Provisions) Order 2012 No. 2012/628 (C.14). - Enabling power: Localism Act 2011, s. 240 (2) (7). Bringing into operation various provisions of the 2011 Act in accord. with arts. 2 to 8. - Issued: 07.03.2012. Made: 01.03.2012. Effect: None. Territorial extent & classification: E/W. General. - Partially revoked by S.I. 2012/2029 (C.80) (ISBN 9780111527962). - 12p.: 30 cm. - 978-0-11-152126-7 £5.75

The Localism Act 2011 (Consequential Amendments) Order 2012 No. 2012/961. - Enabling power: Localism Act 2011, s. 236. - Issued: 30.03.2012. Made: 27.03.2012. Coming into force: 28.03.2012 except fort art. 3, sch. 2; 06.04.2012 for art. 3, sch. 2 in accord. with art. 1 (2). Effect: 1961 c.33; 1965 c.12; 1972 c.70; 1980 c.66; 2002 c.41; 2003 c.43; 2004 c.5; 2006 c.40; 2008 c.14; S.I. 2002/522; 2003/1987; 2008/239 amended. Territorial extent & classification: E/W. General. - Supersedes draft S.I. (ISBN 9780111519912) issued 09.02.2012. - 8p.: 30 cm. - 978-0-11-152306-3 £4.00

Town and country planning, Wales

The Land Compensation Development (Wales) Order 2012 No. 2012/843 (W.116). - Enabling power: Land Compensation Act 1961, s. 20 & Town and Country Planning Act 1990, ss. 59, 61 (1), 333 (7). - Issued: 03.04.2012. Made: 15.03.2012. Laid before the National Assembly for Wales: 16.03.2012. Coming into force: 06.04.2012. Effect: S.I. 1974/539 revoked with saving. Territorial extent & classification: W. General. - In English and Welsh. Welsh title: Gorchymyn Datblygu Digollediad Tir (Cymru) 2012. - 8p.: 30 cm. - 978-0-348-10584-1 £4.00

The Planning Act 2008 (Commencement No. 1) (Wales) Order 2012 No. 2012/802 (W.111)(C.20). - Enabling power: Planning Act 2008, s. 241 (3). Bringing into operation various provisions of the 2008 Act on 30.04.2012, in accord. with art. 2. - Issued: 03.04.2012. Made: 10.03.2012. Effect: None. Territorial extent & classification: W. General. - In English and Welsh. Welsh title: Gorchymyn Deddf Cynllunio 2008 (Cychwyn Rhif 1) (Cymru) 2012. - 8p.: 30 cm. - 978-0-348-10581-0 £5.75

The Planning and Compulsory Purchase Act 2004 (Commencement No. 4 and Consequential, Transitional and Savings Provisions) (Wales) (Amendment) Order 2012 No. 2012/1664 (W.214). - Enabling power: Planning and Compulsory Purchase Act 2004, ss. 121 (5), 122 (3). - Issued: 19.07.2012. Made: 27.06.2012. Coming into force: 02.07.2012. Effect: S.I. 2005/2722 (W.193) (C.110) amended. Territorial extent & classification: W. General. - In English and Welsh. Welsh title: Gorchymyn Deddf Cynllunio a Phrynu Gorfodol 2004 (Cychwyn Rhif 4 a Darpariaethau Canlyniadol a Throsiannol a Darpariaethau Arbed) (Cymru) (Diwygio) 2012. - 4p.: 30 cm. - 978-0-348-10636-7 £4.00

The Planning and Compulsory Purchase Act 2004 (Commencement No. 13) Order 2012 No. 2012/1100 (C.36). - Enabling power: Planning and Compulsory Purchase Act 2004, ss. 121 (1), 122 (3). Bringing into operation various provisions of the 2004 Act on 30.04.2012 (in relation to Wales), in accord. with art. 2. - Issued: 23.04.2012. Made: 16.04.2012. Effect: None. Territorial extent & classification: W. General. - 8p.: 30 cm. - 978-0-11-152361-2 £4.00

The Planning (Listed Buildings and Conservation Areas) (Wales) Regulations 2012 No. 2012/793 (W.108). - Enabling power: Planning (Listed Buildings and Conservation Areas) Act 1990, ss. 2, 10, 11, 19, 20, 21, 25, 28, 29, 32, 42, 74, 82, 82B, 82F, 91, 93. - Issued: 04.04.2012. Made: 10.03.2012. Laid before the National Assembly for Wales: 13.03.2012. Coming into force: 30.04.2012. Effect: 1990 c. 9 modified in relation to Wales & S.I. 1991/2804; 2006/1388 (W.138) amended in relation to Wales & S.I. 1990/1147, 1519; 2009/1026 (W.88) revoked in relation to Wales. Territorial extent & classification: W. General. - In English and Welsh. Welsh title: Rheoliadau Cynllunio (Adeiladau Rhestredig ac Ardaloedd Cadwraeth) (Cymru) 2012. - 32p.: 30 cm. - 978-0-348-10577-3 £9.75

The Planning Permission (Withdrawal of Development Order or Local Development Order) (Compensation) (Wales) Order 2012 No. 2012/210 (W.36). - Enabling power: Planning Act 2008, s. 203 (1) (6). - Issued: 23.02.2012. Made: 27.01.2012. Coming into force: 31.01.2012. Effect: 1990 c.8 amended. Territorial extent & classification: W. General. - In English and Welsh. Welsh language title: Gorchymyn Caniatâd Cynllunio (Tynnu'n ôl Orchymyn Datblygu neu Orchymyn Datblygu Lleol) (Iawndal) (Cymru) 2012. - 4p.: 30 cm. - 978-0-348-10697-8 £4.00

The Town and Country Planning (Compensation) (Wales) (No. 2) Regulations 2012 No. 2012/2319 (W. 253). - Enabling power: Town and Country Planning Act 1990, s. 108 (2A) (3C) (3D) (5) (6). - Issued: 27.09.2012. Made: 06.09.2012. Laid before the National Assembly for Wales: 11.09.2012. Coming into force: 05.10.2012 in accord. with reg. 1 (1). Effect: S.I. 2012/789 (W.105) revoked. Territorial extent & classification: W. General. - In English and Welsh. Welsh language title: Rheoliadau Cynllunio Gwlad a Thref (Digolledu) (Cymru) (Rhif 2) 2012. - 8p.: 30 cm. - 978-0-348-10652-7 £4.00

The Town and Country Planning (Compensation) (Wales) Regulations 2012 No. 2012/789 (W.105). - Enabling power: Town and Country Planning Act 1990, s. 108 (2A) (3C) (3D) (5) (6). - Issued: 03.04.2012. Made: 10.03.2012. Laid before the National Assembly for Wales: 13.03.2012. Coming into force: In accord. with reg. 1. Effect: None. Territorial extent & classification: W. General. - Revoked by WSI 2012/2319 (W.253) (ISBN 9780348106527). - In English and Welsh. Welsh language title: Rheoliadau Cynllunio Gwlad a Thref (Digoolledu) (Cymru) 2012. - 4p.: 30 cm. - 978-0-348-10582-7 £4.00

The Town and Country Planning (Control of Advertisements) (Amendment) (Wales) Regulations 2012 No. 2012/791 (W.106). - Enabling power: Town and Country Planning Act 1990, ss. 220 (1) (2a), 333 (1). - Issued: 03.04.2012. Made: 10.03.2012. Laid before the National Assembly for Wales: 13.03.2012. Coming into force: 30.04.2012. Effect: S.I. 1992/666 amended. Territorial extent & classification: W. General. - In English and Welsh. Welsh language title: Rheoliadau Cynllunio Gwlad a Thref (Rheoli Hysbysebion) (Diwygio) (Cymru) 2012. - 4p.: 30 cm. - 978-0-348-10578-0 £4.00

The Town and Country Planning (Development Management Procedure) (Wales) Order 2012 No. 2012/801 (W.110). - Enabling power: Town and Country Planning Act 1990, ss. 59, 61(1), 61A, 62, 65, 69, 71, 74, 77, 78, 79 (4), 188, 193, 196 (4), 293A, 333 (7), sch. 1A, paras 1, 2, sch. 4A & Planning and Compulsory Purchase Act 2004, ss. 88, 122 (3). - Issued: 10.04.2012. Made: 10.03.2012. Laid before the National Assembly for Wales: 13.03.2012. Coming into force: 30.04.2012. Effect: S.I. 1995/2803; 1996/525; 2004/3156 (W.273); 2006/1386 (W.136) partially revoked & S.I. 1995/419, 3336; 1996/1817; 1997/858; 2002/1877 (W.186); 2004/1434 (W.147); 2006/3390 (W.310); 2008/2336 (W.199); 2009/1024 (W.87) revoked. Territorial extent & classification: W. General. - With correction slip dated November 2012. - In English and Welsh. Welsh language title: Gorchymyn Cynllunio Gwlad a Thref (Gweithdrefn Rheoli Datblygu) (Cymru) 2012. - 92p.: 30 cm. - 978-0-348-10589-6 £15.50

The Town and Country Planning (General Permitted Development) (Amendment) (Wales) (No. 2) Order 2012 No. 2012/2318 (W.252). - Enabling power: Town and Country Planning Act 1990, ss. 59, 60, 61, 333 (7). - Issued: 27.09.2012. Made: 06.09.2012. Laid: 11.09.2012. Coming into force: 05.10.2012 in accord. with art. 1 (1). Effect: S.I. 1995/418 amended in relation to Wales. Territorial extent & classification: W. General. - In English and Welsh. Welsh language title: Gorchymyn Cynllunio Gwlad a Thref (Datblygu Cyffredinol a Ganiateir) (Diwygio) (Cymru) (Rhif 2) 2012. - 12p.: 30 cm. - 978-0-348-10651-0 £5.75

The Town and Country Planning (General Permitted Development) (Amendment) (Wales) Order 2012 No. 2012/1346 (W.167). - Enabling power: Town and Country Planning Act 1990, ss. 59, 60, 61, 333 (7). - Issued: 06.06.2012. Made: 19.05.2012. Laid: 22.05.2012. Coming into force: 18.06.2012 in accord. with art. 1 (1). Effect: S.I. 1995/418 amended in relation to Wales. Territorial extent & classification: W. General. - In English and Welsh. Welsh language title: Gorchymyn Cynllunio Gwlad a Thref (Datblygu Cyffredinol a Ganiateir) (Diwygio) (Cymru) 2012. - 12p.: 30 cm. - 978-0-348-10616-9 £5.75

The Town and Country Planning (Trees) (Amendment) (Wales) Regulations 2012 No. 2012/792 (W.107). - Enabling power: Town and Country Planning Act 1990, ss. 198 (8), 333 (1). - Issued: 03.04.2012. Made: 10.03.2012. Laid before the National Assembly for Wales: 13.03.2012. Coming into force: 30.04.2012. Effect: S.I. 1999/1892 amended. Territorial extent & classification: W. General. - In English and Welsh. Welsh language title: Rheoliadau Cynllunio Gwlad a Thref (Coed) (Diwygio) (Cymru) 2012. - 4p.: 30 cm. - 978-0-348-10583-4 £4.00

Trade marks

The Trade Marks and Trade Marks (Fees) (Amendment) Rules 2012 No. 2012/1003. - Enabling power: Trade Marks Act 1994, ss. 41 (1) (3), 78, 79. - Issued: 05.04.2012. Made: 03.04.2012. Laid: 04.04.2012. Coming into force: 01.10.2012. Effect: S.I. 2008/1958, 1797 amended. Territorial extent & classification: E/W/S/NI. General. - 4p.: 30 cm. - 978-0-11-152336-0 £4.00

Trading with the enemy

The Trading with the Enemy (Transfer of Negotiable Instruments, etc.) (Revocation) Order 2012 No. 2012/1367. - Enabling power: Trading with the Enemy Act 1939, ss. 4, 15 (5). - Issued: 25.05.2012. Made: 22.05.2012. Coming into force: 25.05.2012. Effect: S.R. & O. 1945/347, 859, 961, 1031, 1078, 1099, 1118, 1358, 1495; 1946/293, 441, 1043, 1060, 1433; 1947/665, 2088, 2204 & S.I. 1949/606; 1950/29; 1952/5 revoked. Territorial extent & classification: E/W/S/NI. General. - 4p.: 30 cm. - 978-0-11-152478-7 £4.00

Transport

The British Waterways Board (Transfer of Functions) Order 2011 No. 2012/1659. - Enabling power: Public Bodies Act 2011, ss. 5 (1), 6 (1) to (3), 35 (2). - Issued: 04.07.2012. Made: 01.07.2012. Coming into force: 02.07.2012 in accord. with art. 1. Effect: 29 Acts and 9 statutory instruments amended & S.I. 2003/1545 revoked. Territorial extent & classification: E/W/S/NI. General. - Supersedes draft S.I. (ISBN 9780111521045) issued 02.03.2012. - 32p.: 30 cm. - 978-0-11-152621-7 £5.75

The Energy Act 2004 (Amendment) Regulations 2012 No. 2012/2723. - Enabling power: European Communities Act 1972, s. 2 (2). - Issued: 05.11.2012. Made: 29.10.2012. Laid: 01.11.2012. Coming into force: 04.12.2012. Effect: 2004 c.20 amended. Territorial extent & classification: E/W/S/NI. General. - EC note: These Regulations enable effect to be given to certain requirements contained in Directive 98/707/EC. - 4p.: 30 cm. - 978-0-11-153024-5 £4.00

The Rail Vehicle Accessibility (Non-Interoperable Rail System) (London Underground Circle, District and Hammersmith & City Lines S7 Vehicles) Exemption Order 2012 No. 2012/105. - Enabling power: Equality Act 2010, ss. 183 (1) (2) (4) (b) (5), 207 (1) (4). - Issued: 23.01.2012. Made: 12.01.2012. Laid: 18.01.2012. Coming into force: 13.02.2012. Effect: None. Territorial extent & classification: E/W/S. General. - 12p.: 30 cm. - 978-0-11-151930-1 £5.75

The Road Transport (Working Time) (Amendment) Regulations 2012 No. 2012/991. - Enabling power: European Communities Act 1972, s. 2 (2). - Issued: 10.04.2012. Made: 02.04.2012. Laid: 04.04.2012. Coming into force: 11.05.2012. Effect: S.I. 2005/639 amended. Territorial extent & classification: E/W/S. General. - EC note: These Regulations amend the Road transport (Working Time) Regulations 2005 (S.I. 2005/639) ("the principal Regulations") as amended by S.I. 2007/853 to implement Directive 2002/15/EC on the organisation of the working time of persons performing mobile road transport activities in respect of self employed drivers. - 8p.: 30 cm. - 978-0-11-152329-2 £5.75

Transport and works, England

The Bridgewater Canal (Transfer of Undertaking) Order 2012 No. 2012/1266. - Enabling power: Transport and Works Act 1992, s. 3 (1) (a), 5, sch. 1, paras. 5, 7, 8, 12, 13, 15. - Issued: 18.05.2012. Made: 01.05.2012. Coming into force: 22.05.2012. Effect: None. Territorial extent & classification: E. General. - 8p.: 30 cm. - 978-0-11-152430-5 £5.75

The Chiltern Railways (Bicester to Oxford Improvements) Order 2012 No. 2012/2679. - Enabling power: Transport and Works Act 1992, ss. 1, 5, sch. 1, paras 1to 5, 7, 8, 10, 11, 15 to 17. - Issued: 01.11.2012. Made: 23.10.2012. Coming into force: 13.11.2012. Effect: None. Territorial extent & classification: E. General. - 76p.: 30 cm. - 978-0-11-153004-7 £13.75

The Hinkley Point (Temporary Jetty) (Land Acquisition) Order 2012 No. 2012/1924. - Enabling power: Transport and Works Act 1992, ss. 3, 5, sch. 1, paras 3 to 5, 7, 8, 11, 16. - Issued: 27.07.2012. Made: 20.07.2012. Coming into force: 12.08.2012. Effect: 1965 c.56; 1973 c.26; 1981 c.66 modified. Territorial extent & classification: E. Local. - 12p.: 30 cm. - 978-0-11-152767-2 £5.75

The Ipswich Barrier Order 2012 No. 2012/1867. - Enabling power: Transport and Works Act 1992, s. 3 (1) (b), 5, sch. 1, paras 1 to 5, 7, 8, 10, 11, 13, 15 to 17 & S.I. 1992/3230, art. 2. - Issued: 19.07.2012. Made: 16.07.2012. Coming into force: 07.08.2012. Effect: None. Territorial extent & classification: E. Local. - 44p.: 30 cm. - 978-0-11-152730-6 £9.75

The London Cable Car Order 2012 No. 2012/472. - Enabling power: Transport and Works Act 1992, ss. 1, 2, 5, sch. 1, paras. 1, 8, 9, 12, 13, 15. - Issued: 29.02.2012. Made: 21.02.2012. Coming into force: 13.03.2012. Effect: None. Territorial extent & classification: E. General. - 16p.: 30 cm. - 978-0-11-152059-8 £5.75

The Nene Valley Railway (Fletton Branch) Order 2012 No. 2012/1993. - Enabling power: Transport and Works Act 1992, ss. 1, 5, sch. 1, paras 1, 4, 8, 15. - Issued: 03.08.2012. Made: 26.07.2012. Coming into force: 16.08.2012. Effect: None. Territorial extent & classification: E. General. - 8p.: 30 cm. - 978-0-11-152789-4 £4.00

The River Humber (Burcom Outfall) (Transfer) Order 2012 No. 2012/2533. - Enabling power: Transport and Works Act 1992, ss. 3, 5 of, sch. 1, para. 15. - Issued: 08.11.2012. Made: 04.10.2012. Coming into force: 05.10.2012. Effect: None. Territorial extent & classification: E. General. - 4p.: 30 cm. - 978-0-11-153049-8 £4.00

The Transport for Greater Manchester (Light Rapid Transit System) (Oldham, Manchester Street Modification) Order 2012 No. 2012/2980. - Enabling power: Transport and Works Act 1992, ss. 1, 5, sch. 1, paras. 1, 2, 4, 8, 9, 13, 15. - Issued: 07.12.2012. Made: 27.11.2012. Coming into force: 18.12.2012. Effect: None. Territorial extent & classification: E. General. - 8p.: 30 cm. - 978-0-11-153138-9 £4.00

The Transport for Greater Manchester (Light Rapid Transit System) (Oldham, Mumps Modification) Order 2012 No. 2012/981. - Enabling power: Transport and Works Act 1992, ss. 1, 5, sch. 1, paras. 1, 2, 4, 8, 9, 13, 15. - Issued: 05.04.2012. Made: 29.03.2012. Coming into force: 19.04.2012. Effect: None. Territorial extent & classification: E. General. - This Statutory Instrument has been printed in substitution of the SI of the same number and ISBN (issued on 05.04.2012) and is being issued free of charge to all known recipients of the original version. - 8p.: 30 cm. - 978-0-11-152323-0 £4.00

Transport, England

The Chiltern Railways (Bicester to Oxford Improvements) Order 2012 No. 2012/2679. - Enabling power: Transport and Works Act 1992, ss. 1, 5, sch. 1, paras 1to 5, 7, 8, 10, 11, 15 to 17. - Issued: 01.11.2012. Made: 23.10.2012. Coming into force: 13.11.2012. Effect: None. Territorial extent & classification: E. General. - 76p.: 30 cm. - 978-0-11-153004-7 £13.75

The Hinkley Point (Temporary Jetty) (Land Acquisition) Order 2012 No. 2012/1924. - Enabling power: Transport and Works Act 1992, ss. 3, 5, sch. 1, paras 3 to 5, 7, 8, 11, 16. - Issued: 27.07.2012. Made: 20.07.2012. Coming into force: 12.08.2012. Effect: 1965 c.56; 1973 c.26; 1981 c.66 modified. Territorial extent & classification: E. Local. - 12p.: 30 cm. - 978-0-11-152767-2 £5.75

The London Cable Car Order 2012 No. 2012/472. - Enabling power: Transport and Works Act 1992, ss. 1, 2, 5, sch. 1, paras. 1, 8, 9, 12, 13, 15. - Issued: 29.02.2012. Made: 21.02.2012. Coming into force: 13.03.2012. Effect: None. Territorial extent & classification: E. General. - 16p.: 30 cm. - 978-0-11-152059-8 £5.75

The Nene Valley Railway (Fletton Branch) Order 2012 No. 2012/1993. - Enabling power: Transport and Works Act 1992, ss. 1, 5, sch. 1, paras 1, 4, 8, 15. - Issued: 03.08.2012. Made: 26.07.2012. Coming into force: 16.08.2012. Effect: None. Territorial extent & classification: E. General. - 8p.: 30 cm. - 978-0-11-152789-4 £4.00

The Transport for Greater Manchester (Light Rapid Transit System) (Oldham, Manchester Street Modification) Order 2012 No. 2012/2980. - Enabling power: Transport and Works Act 1992, ss. 1, 5, sch. 1, paras. 1, 2, 4, 8, 9, 13, 15. - Issued: 07.12.2012. Made: 27.11.2012. Coming into force: 18.12.2012. Effect: None. Territorial extent & classification: E. General. - 8p.: 30 cm. - 978-0-11-153138-9 £4.00

The Transport for Greater Manchester (Light Rapid Transit System) (Oldham, Mumps Modification) Order 2012 No. 2012/981. - Enabling power: Transport and Works Act 1992, ss. 1, 5, sch. 1, paras. 1, 2, 4, 8, 9, 13, 15. - Issued: 05.04.2012. Made: 29.03.2012. Coming into force: 19.04.2012. Effect: None. Territorial extent & classification: E. General. - This Statutory Instrument has been printed in substitution of the SI of the same number and ISBN (issued on 05.04.2012) and is being issued free of charge to all known recipients of the original version. - 8p.: 30 cm. - 978-0-11-152323-0 £4.00

Transport, England and Wales

The Local Policing Bodies (Consequential Amendments No. 2) Regulations 2012 No. 2012/2732. - Enabling power: Police Reform Act 2002, ss. 43, 105 (4) & Planning Act 2008, ss. 4, 7, 37, 42, 48, 51, 56, 58, 59, 127 (7), 232, sch. 6, paras 2, 4, 6. - Issued: 05.11.2012. Made: 30.10.2012. Laid: 01.11.2012. Coming into force: 22.11.2012. Effect: S.I. 2004/915; 2009/1302, 2264; 2010/102, 104; 2011/2055 amended. Territorial extent & classification: E/W. General. - 4p.: 30 cm. - 978-0-11-153032-0 £4.00

Tribunals and inquiries

The First-tier Tribunal and Upper Tribunal (Chambers) (Amendment) Order 2012 No. 2012/1673. - Enabling power: Tribunals, Courts and Enforcement Act 2007, s. 7 (9). - Issued: 29.06.2012. Made: 26.06.2012. Laid: 29.06.2012. Coming into force: 20.07.2012. Effect: S.I. 2010/2655 amended. Territorial extent & classification: E/W/S/NI. General. - 2p.: 30 cm. - 978-0-11-152604-0 £4.00

The Qualifications for Appointment of Members to the First-tier Tribunal and Upper Tribunal (Amendment) Order 2012 No. 2012/897. - Enabling power: Tribunals, Courts and Enforcement Act 2007, sch. 2, para. 2 (2), sch. 3, para. 2 (2). - Issued: 22.03.2012. Made: 15.03.2012. Laid: 22.03.2012. Coming into force: 16.04.2012. Effect: S.I. 2008/2692 amended. Territorial extent & classification: E/W/S/NI. General. - 2p.: 30 cm. - 978-0-11-152268-4 £4.00

The Revenue and Customs Appeals Order 2012 No. 2012/533. - Enabling power: Finance Act 2008, s. 124 (1) (6). - Issued: 28.02.2012. Made: 27.02.2012. Coming into force: 01.03.2012. Effect: 2002 c. 21 amended. Territorial extent & classification: E/W/S/NI. General. - Supersedes draft S.I. (ISBN 9780111519189) issued 12.01.2012. - 2p.: 30 cm. - 978-0-11-152073-4 £4.00

The Tribunal Procedure (Amendment No. 2) Rules 2012 No. 2012/1363 (L.5). - Enabling power: Tribunals, Courts and Enforcement Act 2007, s. 22, sch. 5. - Issued: 25.05.2012. Made: 22.05.2012. Laid: 24.05.2012. Coming into force: For the purposes of rules 2 &3: 01.09.2012; for all other purposes: 01.07.2012, in accord. with rule 1. Effect: S.I. 2008/2698, 2699 amended (01.09.2012). Territorial extent & classification: E/W/S/NI. General. - 4p.: 30 cm. - 978-0-11-152477-0 £4.00

The Tribunal Procedure (Amendment) Rules 2012 No. 2012/500 (L. 1). - Enabling power: Tribunals, Courts and Enforcement Act 2007, s. 22, sch. 5. - Issued: 06.03.2012. Made: 22.02.2012. Laid: 06.03.2012. Coming into force: 06.04.2012. Effect: S.I. 2008/2685, 2698, 2699; 2009/1976; 2010/2600 amended. Territorial extent & classification: E/W/S/NI. General. - 8p.: 30 cm. - 978-0-11-152070-3 £4.00

The Tribunal Procedure (Upper Tribunal) (Amendment) Rules 2012 No. 2012/2890 (L.11). - Enabling power: Tribunals, Courts and Enforcement Act 2007, s. 22, sch. 5. - Issued: 21.11.2012. Made: 13.11.2012. Laid: 19.11.2012. Coming into force: 11.12.2012. Effect: S.I. 2008/2698 amended. Territorial extent & classification: E/W/S/NI. General. - 2p.: 30 cm. - 978-0-11-153087-0 £4.00

United Nations

The Iraq (United Nations Sanctions) (Overseas Territories) (Amendment) Order 2012 No. 2012/2748. - Enabling power: United Nations Act 1946, s. 1 & Saint Helena Act 1833, s. 112 & British Settlements Act 1887 and 1945. - Issued: 14.11.2012. Made: 07.11.2012. Laid: 14.11.2012. Coming into force: 05.12.2012. Effect: S.I. 2003/1516 amended/partially revoked; S.I. 2004/1983, 2671 partially revoked & S.I. 2000/3242; 2001/395 revoked. Territorial extent & classification: Anguilla, Bermuda, British Antarctic Territory, British Indian Ocean Territory, Cayman Islands, Falkland Islands, Montserrat, Pitcairn, Henderson, Ducie and Oeno Islands, St. Helena and Dependencies, South Georgia and South Sandwich Islands, The Sovereign Base Areas of Akrotiri and Dhekelia in the Island of Cyprus, Turks and Caicos Islands, Virgin Islands. General. - 16p.: 30 cm. - 978-0-11-153068-9 £5.75

The United Nations (International Tribunals) (Former Yugoslavia and Rwanda) (Amendment) Order 2012 No. 2012/2559. - Enabling power: United Nations Act 1946, s. 1. - Issued: 19.10.2012. Made: 17.10.2012. Laid: 18.10.2012. Coming into force: 08.11.2012. Effect: S.I. 1996/716, 1296; 1997/1753 amended. Territorial extent & classification: E/W/S/NI. General. - 4p.: 30 cm. - 978-0-11-152966-9 £4.00

The United Nations Sanctions (Overseas Territories) (Revocations) Order 2012 No. 2012/2592. - Enabling power: United Nations Act 1946, s. 1. - Issued: 24.10.2012. Made: 17.10.201.2 Laid: 24.10.2012. Coming into force: 14.11.2012. Effect: S.I. 1992/1305; 1993/1195; 1994/2674; 1998/1064; 1999/281; 2000/1557, 1821 revoked. Territorial extent & classification: Anguilla, Bermuda, British Antarctic Territory, British Indian Ocean Territory, Cayman Islands, Falkland Islands, Montserrat, Pitcairn, Henderson, Ducie and Oeno Islands, St. Helena and Dependencies, South Georgia and South Sandwich Islands, The Sovereign Base Areas of Akrotiri and Dhekelia in the Island of Cyprus, Turks and Caicos Islands, Virgin Islands. General. - 4p.: 30 cm. - 978-0-11-152968-3 £4.00

Urban development

The London Legacy Development Corporation (Planning Functions) Order 2012 No. 2012/2167. - Enabling power: Local Government, Planning and Land Act 1980, s. 149 (1) (3) (11) (13) & Localism Act 2011, ss. 198 (2) (c), 235 (2) (b). - Issued: 28.08.2012. Made: 20.08.2012. Laid: 28.08.2012. Coming into force: 01.10.2012. Effect: S.I. 2005/272; 2006/2185, 2186; 2011/549 revoked. Territorial extent & classification: E. General. - 12p.: 30 cm. - 978-0-11-152833-4 £5.75

Urban development, England

The London Legacy Development Corporation (Establishment) Order 2012 No. 2012/310. - Enabling power: Localism Act 2011, s. 198. - Issued: 14.02.2012. Made: 07.02.2012. Laid: 14.02.2012. Coming into force: 09.03.2012. Effect: None. Territorial extent & classification: E. General. - 2p.: 30 cm. - 978-0-11-151995-0 £4.00

The London Thames Gateway Development Corporation (Transfer of Property, Rights and Liabilities) (Greater London Authority) (No. 2) Order 2012 No. 2012/3084. - Enabling power: Local Government, Planning and Land Act 1980, s. 165B. - Issued: 17.12.2012. Made: 11.12.2012. Laid: 17.12.2012. Coming into force: 22.01.2013. Effect: None. Territorial extent & classification: E. General. - 4p.: 30 cm. - 978-0-11-153221-8 £4.00

The London Thames Gateway Development Corporation (Transfer of Property, Rights and Liabilities) (Greater London Authority) Order 2012 No. 2012/872. - Enabling power: Local Government, Planning and Land Act 1980, s. 165B. - Issued: 23.03.2012. Made: 19.03.2012. Laid: 23.03.2012. Coming into force: 16.04.2012. Effect: None. Territorial extent & classification: E. General. - 12p.: 30 cm. - 978-0-11-152253-0 £5.75

The Milton Keynes (Urban Area and Planning Functions) (Revocation) Order 2012 No. 2012/3099. - Enabling power: Leasehold Reform, Housing and Urban Development Act 1993, s. 170 (4). - Issued: 18.12.2012. Made: 13.12.2012. Laid: 18.12.2012. Coming into force: 14.01.2013. Effect: S.I. 2004/932 revoked. Territorial extent & classification: E. General. - 4p.: 30 cm. - 978-0-11-153250-8 £4.00

The Thurrock Development Corporation (Dissolution) Order 2012 No. 2012/995. - Enabling power: Local Government, Planning and Land Act 1980, s. 166. - Issued: 05.04.2012. Made: 02.04.2012. Coming into force: 03.04.2012. Effect: None. Territorial extent & classification: E. General. - 2p.: 30 cm. - 978-0-11-152331-5 £4.00

The Thurrock Development Corporation (Transfer of Property, Rights and Liabilities) Order 2012 No. 2012/534. - Enabling power: Local Government, Planning and Land Act 1980, s. 165B. - Issued: 02.03.2012. Made: 27.02.2012. Laid: 02.03.2012. Coming into force: 31.03.2012. Effect: None. Territorial extent & classification: E. General. - 4p.: 30 cm. - 978-0-11-152098-7 £4.00

The Urban Development Corporations (Planning Functions) Order 2012 No. 2012/535. - Enabling power: Local Government, Planning and Land Act 1980, s. 149 (1) (3) (11). - Issued: 02.03.2011. Made: 27.02.2011. Laid: 02.03.2011. Coming into force: 31.03.2012. Effect: S.I. 2005/2572; 2006/616; 2011/560 revoked. Territorial extent & classification: E. General. - 4p.: 30 cm. - 978-0-11-152086-4 £4.00

Value added tax

The Finance Act 2010, Schedule 6, Part 1 (Further Consequential and Incidental Provision etc) Order 2012 No. 2012/735. - Enabling power: Finance Act 2010, sch. 6, para. 29 (1) (2). - Issued: 12.03.2012. Made: 08.03.2012. Laid: 09.03.2012. Coming into force: 01.04.2012. Effect: 2009 c.4 amended. Territorial extent & classification: E/W/S/NI. General. - 4p.: 30 cm. - 978-0-11-152181-6 £4.00

The Value Added Tax (Amendment) (No. 2) Regulations 2012 No. 2012/1899. - Enabling power: Value Added Tax Act 1994, ss. 3 (2) (4), 18B (2A), 18C (1A), 25 (1), 26 (3) (4), 26B (1), 35 (2), 39 (1) (3), 48 (4) (4A) (6), 49 (2), 54 (1) (6), sch. 1, para. 17, sch. 1A, para. 14, sch. 2, para. 9, sch. 3, para. 10, sch. 3A, para. 8, sch. 11, para. 2 (1) (3) (4) (5) (10), 2A, 7 (1) & Finance Act 1999, ss. 132, 133 & Finance Act 2002, ss. 135, 136 & Finance Act 2012, sch. 27, para. 10. - Issued: 20.07.2012. Made: 18.07.2012. Laid: 19.07.2012. Coming into force: 01.10.2012 for regs 1, 2, 3, 9, 17 & 15.10.2012 for the remaining regs. Effect: S.I. 1995/2518 amended. Territorial extent & classification: E/W/S/NI. General. - 8p.: 30 cm. - 978-0-11-152749-8 £5.75

The Value Added Tax (Amendment) (No. 3) Regulations 2012 No. 2012/2951. - Enabling power: Value Added Tax Act 1994, ss. 6 (14), 12 (3), sch. 11, paras (2A) (2B) (3) (6). - Issued: 28.11.2012. Made: 26.11.2012. Laid: 27.11.2012. Coming into force: 01.01.2013. Effect: S.I. 1995/2518 amended. Territorial extent & classification: E/W/S/NI. General. - 4p.: 30 cm. - 978-0-11-153125-9 £4.00

The Value Added Tax (Amendment) Regulations 2012 No. 2012/33. - Enabling power: Value Added Tax Act 1994, s. 25 (1), sch. 11, para. 2 (1) (11) & Finance Act 1999, ss. 132, 133 & Finance Act 2002, ss. 135, 136. - Issued: 11.01.2012. Made: 09.01.2012. Laid: 10.01.2012. Coming into force: 01.04.2012. Effect: S.I. 1995/2518 amended. Territorial extent & classification: E/W/S/NI. General. - 4p.: 30 cm. - 978-0-11-151904-2 £4.00

The Value Added Tax (Consideration for Fuel Provided for Private Use) Order 2012 No. 2012/882. - Enabling power: Value Added Tax Act 1994, s. 57 (4) to (4G). - Issued: 21.03.2012. Made: 20.03.2012. Laid: 21.03.2012. Coming into force: 01.05.2012. Effect: 1994 c. 23 amended. Territorial extent & classification: E/W/S/NI. General. - 4p.: 30 cm. - 978-0-11-152261-5 £4.00

The Value Added Tax (Increase of Registration Limits) Order 2012 No. 2012/883. - Enabling power: Value Added Tax Act 1994, sch. 1, para. 15; sch. 3, para. 9. - Issued: 21.03.2012. Made: 20.03.2012. Laid: 21.03.2012. Coming into force: 01.04.2012. Effect: 1994 c.23 amended. Territorial extent & classification: E/W/S/NI. General. - 2p.: 30 cm. - 978-0-11-152262-2 £4.00

The Value Added Tax (Land Exemption) Order 2012 No. 2012/58. - Enabling power: Value Added Tax Act 1994, s. 31 (2). - Issued: 06.02.2012. Made: 11.01.2012. Laid: 11.01.2012. Coming into force: 01.03.2012. Effect: 1994 c. 23 amended. Territorial extent & classification: E/W/S/NI. General. - Approved by the House of Commons. - 2p.: 30 cm. - 978-0-11-151985-1 £4.00

The Value Added Tax (Land Exemption) Order 2012 No. 2012/58. - Enabling power: Value Added Tax Act 1994, s. 31 (2). - Issued: 12.01.2012. Made: 11.01.2012. Laid: 11.01.2012. Coming into force: 01.03.2012. Effect: 1994 c. 23 amended. Territorial extent & classification: E/W/S/NI. General. - For approval by resolution of the House of Commons within twenty-eight days beginning with the day on which the Order was made, subject to extension for periods of dissolution, prorogation or adjournment for more than four days. Superseded by approved version issued 06.02.2012 (ISBN 9780111519851). - 2p.: 30 cm. - 978-0-11-151912-7 £4.00

The Value Added Tax (Place of Supply of Services) (Transport of Goods) Order 2012 No. 2012/2787. - Enabling power: Value Added Tax Act 1994, s. 7A (6). - Issued: 14.12.2012. Made: 06.11.2012. Laid: 07.11.2012. Coming into force: 20.12.2012. Effect: 1994 c.23 amended. Territorial extent & classification: E/W/S/NI. General. - Approved by the House of Commons. Supersedes previous version of same number but different ISBN (9780111530528) issued on 08.11.2012. - 2p.: 30 cm. - 978-0-11-153232-4 £4.00

The Value Added Tax (Place of Supply of Services) (Transport of Goods) Order 2012 No. 2012/2787. - Enabling power: Value Added Tax Act 1994, s. 7A (6). - Issued: 08.11.2012. Made: 06.11.2012. Laid: 07.11.2012. Coming into force: 20.12.2012. Effect: 1994 c.23 amended. Territorial extent & classification: E/W/S/NI. General. - Superseded by approved version (ISBN 9780111532324) issued on 14.12.2012. For approval by resolution of that House within twenty-eight days beginning with the date on which the Order was made, subject to extension for periods of dissolution, prorogation or adjournment for more than four days. - 2p.: 30 cm. - 978-0-11-153052-8 £4.00

The Value Added Tax (Refund of Tax to Museums and Galleries) (Amendment) Order 2012 No. 2012/2731. - Enabling power: Value Added Tax Act 1994, s. 33A (9). - Issued: 31.10.2012. Made: 30.10.2012. Laid: 31.10.2012. Coming into force: 01.12.2012. Effect: S.I. 2001/2879 amended. Territorial extent & classification: E/W/S/NI. General. - 8p.: 30 cm. - 978-0-11-153025-2 £5.75

The Value Added Tax (Refund of VAT to Chief Constables and the Commissioner of Police of the Metropolis) Order 2012 No. 2012/2393. - Enabling power: Value Added Tax Act 1994, s. 33 (3) (k). - Issued: 18.09.2012. Made: 17.09.2012. Laid: 18.09.2012. Coming into force: 15.11.2012. Effect: None. Territorial extent & classification: E/W. General. - With correction slip dated October 2012. - 2p.: 30 cm. - 978-0-11-152884-6 £4.00

The Value Added Tax (Relief for European Research Infrastructure Consortia) Order 2012 No. 2012/2907. - Enabling power: Value Added Tax Act 1994, ss. 30 (4), 36A, 37 (1), 96 (9). - Issued: 21.11.2012. Made: 20.11.2012. Laid: 21.11.2012. Coming into force: 01.01.2013. Effect: 1994 c. 23 amended. Territorial extent & classification: E/W/S/NI. General. - 4p.: 30 cm. - 978-0-11-153101-3 £4.00

The Value Added Tax (Removal of Goods) (Amendment) Order 2012 No. 2012/2953. - Enabling power: Value Added Tax Act 1994, s. 5 (3). - Issued: 27.11.2012. Made: 26.11.2012. Laid: 27.11.2012. Coming into force: 01.01.2013. Effect: S.I. 1992/3111 amended. Territorial extent & classification: E/W/S/NI. General. - 2p.: 30 cm. - 978-0-11-153126-6 £4.00

The Value Added Tax (Small Non-Commercial Consignments) Relief (Amendment) Order 2012 No. 2012/3060. - Enabling power: Value Added Tax Act 1994, ss. 37 (1). - Issued: 11.12.2012. Made: 10.12.2012. Laid: 11.12.2012. Coming into force: 01.01.2013. Effect: S.I. 1986/939 amended. Territorial extent & classification: E/W/S/NI. General. - EC note: The amendment is made in order to comply with Council Directive 2006/79/EC. - 2p.: 30 cm. - 978-0-11-153208-9 £4.00

Video recordings

The Digital Economy Act 2010 (Appointed Day No. 2) Order 2012 No. 2012/1164 (C.39). - Enabling power: Digital Economy Act 2010, s. 47 (3). Bringing into operation various provisions of the 2010 Act on 01.05.2012. - Issued: 02.05.2012. Made: 26.04.2012. Effect: None. Territorial extent & classification: E/W/S/NI. General. - 2p.: 30 cm. - 978-0-11-152388-9 £4.00

The Digital Economy Act 2010 (Appointed Day No. 3) Order 2012 No. 2012/1766 (C.69). - Enabling power: Digital Economy Act 2010, s. 47 (3). Bringing into operation various provisions of the 2010 Act on 30.07.2012. - Issued: 10.07.2012. Made: 04.07.2012. Effect: None. Territorial extent & classification: E/W/S/NI. General. - 2p.: 30 cm. - 978-0-11-152647-7 £4.00

The Digital Economy Act 2010 (Transitional Provision) Regulations 2012 No. 2012/1764. - Enabling power: Digital Economy Act 2010, s. 44. - Issued: 10.07.2012. Made: 04.07.2012. Laid: 06.07.2012. Coming into force: 29.07.2012. Effect: None. Territorial extent & classification: E/W/S/NI. General. - 2p.: 30 cm. - 978-0-11-152644-6 £4.00

Video recordings: Labelling

The Video Recordings (Labelling) Regulations 2012 No. 2012/1767. - Enabling power: Video Recordings Act 1984, ss. 8, 22A. - Issued: 10.07.2012. Made: 04.07.2012. Laid: 06.07.2012. Coming into force: 30.07.2012. Effect: S.I. 2010/115 revoked. Territorial extent & classification: E/W/S/NI. General. - 8p.: 30 cm. - 978-0-11-152645-3 £5.75

Water, England

The Nitrate Pollution Prevention (Amendment) Regulations 2012 No. 2012/1849. - Enabling power: European Communities Act 1972, s. 2 (2). - Issued: 17.07.2012. Made: 13.07.2012. Laid: 16.07.2012. Coming into force: 07.08.2012. Effect: S.I. 2008/2349 amended. Territorial extent & classification: E. General. - EC note: These Regulations revoke and replace certain provisions of S.I. 2008/2349 which relate to the designation of nitrate vulnerable zones. The principal regulations implement in England Council Directive 91/676/EEC concerning the protection of waters against pollution by nitrates from agricultural sources. - 4p.: 30 cm. - 978-0-11-152711-5 £4.00

The Water Act 2003 (Commencement No. 11) Order 2012 No. 2012/264 (C.8). - Enabling power: Water Act 2003, s. 105 (3) (4) (6). Bringing into operation various provisions of the 2003 Act on 06.04.2012 in accord. with art. 2. - Issued: 07.02.2012. Made: 02.02.2012. Effect: None. Territorial extent & classification: E. General. - 8p.: 30 cm. - 978-0-11-151982-0 £4.00

Water industry, England and Wales

The Flood and Water Management Act 2010 (Commencement No. 6 and Transitional Provisions) Order 2012 No. 2012/879 (C.25). - Enabling power: Flood and Water Management Act 2010, ss. 48 (2), 49 (3) (h) (i) (6). Bringing into operation various provisions of this Act on 06.04.2012, in accord. with art. 3. - Issued: 22.03.2012. Made: 19.03.2012. Effect: None. Territorial extent & classification: E/W. General. - 8p.: 30 cm. - 978-0-11-152259-2 £5.75

The Flood and Water Management Act 2010 (Commencement No. 7) Order 2012 No. 2012/2000 (C.79). - Enabling power: Flood and Water Management Act 2010, s. 49 (3) (h) (i). Bringing into operation various provisions of this Act on 01.08.2012, in accord. with art. 2. - Issued: 01.08.2012. Made: 30.07.2012. Effect: None. Territorial extent & classification: E/W. General. - 8p.: 30 cm. - 978-0-11-152791-7 £5.75

The Flood and Water Management Act 2010 (Commencement No.8 and Transitional Provisions) Order 2012 No. 2012/2048 (W.239) (C.81). - Enabling power: Flood and Water Management Act 2010, ss. 48 (2), 49 (3) (e) (6). Bringing into operation various provisions of the 2010 Act on 01.10.2012. - Issued: 20.08.2012. Made: 06.08.2012. Effect: None. Territorial extent & classification: W. General. - In English and Welsh. Welsh title: Gorchymyn Deddf Rheoli Llifogydd a Dwr 2010 (Cychwyn Rhif 8 a Darpariaethau Trosiannol) 2012. - 12p.: 30 cm. - 978-0-348-10648-0 £5.75

The Public Bodies (Water Supply and Water Quality) (Inspection Fees) Order 2012 No. 2012/3101 (W.314). - Enabling power: Public Bodies Act 2011, ss. 14 (3), 15 (1). - Issued: 17.01.2013. Made: 12.12.2012. Coming into force: 13.12.2012 in accord. with art. 1. Effect: None. Territorial extent & classification: E/W. General. - In English and Welsh. Welsh title: Gorchymyn Cyrff Cyhoeddus (Cyflenwad Dwr ac Ansawdd Dwr) (Ffioedd Arolygu) 2012. - 8p.: 30 cm. - 978-0-348-10677-0 £5.75

Water, Wales

The Nitrate Pollution Prevention (Wales) (Amendment) Regulations 2012 No. 2012/1238 (W.151). - Enabling power: European Communities Act 1972, s. 2 (2). - Issued: 24.05.2012. Made: 05.05.2012. Laid before the National Assembly for Wales: 09.05.2012. Coming into force: 01.06.2012. Effect: S.I. 2008/3143 (W.278) amended. Territorial extent & classification: W. General. - In English and Welsh. Welsh title: Rheoliadau Atal Llygredd Nitradau (Cymru) (Diwygio) 2012. - 8p.: 30 cm. - 978-0-348-10609-1 £5.75

The Water Act 2003 (Commencement No. 3) (Wales) Order 2012 No. 2012/284 (W.48) (C.9). - Enabling power: Water Act 2003, s. 105 (3) (4) (6). Bringing into operation various provisions of the 2003 Act on 06.04.2012. - Issued: 23.02.2012. Made: 03.02.2012. Effect: None. Territorial extent & classification: W. General. - In English and Welsh. Welsh title: Gorchymyn Deddf Dwr 2003 (Cychwyn Rhif 3) (Cymru) 2012. - 8p.: 30 cm. - 978-0-348-10688-6 £5.75

Welsh language, Wales

The Advisory Panel to the Welsh Language Commissioner (Appointment) Regulations 2012 No. 2012/59 (W.13). - Enabling power: Welsh Language (Wales) Measure 2011, s. 23 (4), sch. 4, para. 5. - Issued: 27.01.2012. Made: 11.01.2012. Laid before the National Assembly for Wales: 12.01.2012. Coming into force: 06.02.2012. Effect: None. Territorial extent & classification: W. General. - In English and Welsh. Welsh title: Rheoliadau Panel Cynghori Comisiynydd y Gymraeg (Penodi) 2012. - 4p.: 30 cm. - 978-0-348-10542-1 £4.00

The Welsh Language Board (Transfer of Staff, Property, Rights and Liabilities) Order 2012 No. 2012/752 (W.102). - Enabling power: Welsh Language (Wales) Measure 2011, ss. 146 and 150 (5), sch. 12, paras 1, 2. - Issued: 28.03.2012. Made: 07.03.2012. Laid before the National Assembly for Wales: 09.03.2012. Coming into force: 01.04.2012. Effect: None. Territorial extent & classification: W. General. - In English and Welsh. Welsh title: Gorchymyn Bwrdd yr Iaith Gymraeg (Trosglwyddo Staff, Eiddo, Hawliau a Rhwymedigaethau) 2012. - 8p.: 30 cm. - 978-0-348-10570-4 £5.75

The Welsh Language Measure (Registrable Interests) Regulations 2012 No. 2012/753 (W.103). - Enabling power: Welsh Language (Wales) Measure 2011, s. 138. - Issued: 28.03.2012. Made: 07.03.2012. Laid before the National Assembly for Wales: 09.03.2012. Coming into force: 01.04.2012. Effect: None. Territorial extent & classification: W. General. - In English and Welsh. Welsh title: Rheoliadau Mesur y Gymraeg (Buddiannau Cofrestradwy) 2012. - 4p.: 30 cm. - 978-0-348-10565-0 £4.00

The Welsh Language Schemes (Public Bodies) Order 2012 No. 2012/3095 (W.312). - Enabling power: Welsh Language Act 1993, s. 6 (1) (o). - Issued: 27.12.2012. Made: 13.12.2012. Laid before the National Assembly for Wales: 14.12.2012. Coming into force: 04.01.2013. Effect: None. Territorial extent & classification: W. General. - In English and Welsh. Welsh title: Gorchymyn Cynlluniau Iaith Gymraeg (Cyrff Cyhoeddus) 2012. - 4p.: 30 cm. - 978-0-348-10673-2 £4.00

The Welsh Language (Wales) Measure 2011 (Commencement No.2) Order 2012 No. 2012/46 (W.10)(C.1). - Enabling power: Welsh Language (Wales) Measure 2011, ss. 150 (5), 156 (2). Bringing into force various provisions of the 2011 Measure on 10.01.2012. - Issued: 27.01.2012. Made: 09.01.2012. Effect: None. Territorial extent & classification: W. General. - In English and Welsh. Welsh title: Gorchymyn Mesur y Gymraeg (Cymru) 2011 (Cychwyn Rhif 2) 2012. - 4p.: 30 cm. - 978-0-348-10543-8 £4.00

The Welsh Language (Wales) Measure 2011 (Commencement No.3) Order 2012 No. 2012/223 (W. 37)(C. 7). - Enabling power: Welsh Language (Wales) Measure 2011, ss. 156 (2). Bringing into force various provisions of the 2011 Measure on 05.02.2012. - Issued: 16.02.2012. Made: 30.01.2012. Effect: None. Territorial extent & classification: W. General. - In English and Welsh. Welsh title: Gorchymyn Mesur y Gymraeg (Cymru) 2011 (Cychwyn Rhif 3) 2012. - 4p.: 30 cm. - 978-0-348-10555-1 £4.00

The Welsh Language (Wales) Measure 2011 (Commencement No.4) Order 2012 No. 2012/969 (W.126)(C.31). - Enabling power: Welsh Language (Wales) Measure 2011, ss. 105 (5), 156 (2). Bringing into force various provisions of the 2011 Measure on 01.04.2012. - Issued: 17.04.2012. Made: 27.03.2012. Effect: None. Territorial extent & classification: W. General. - In English and Welsh. Welsh title: Gorchymyn Mesur y Gymraeg (Cymru) 2011 (Cychwyn Rhif 4) 2012. - 4p.: 30 cm. - 978-0-348-10595-7 £4.00

The Welsh Language (Wales) Measure 2011 (Commencement No.5) Order 2012 No. 2012/1096 (W.135)(C.35). - Enabling power: Welsh Language (Wales) Measure 2011, ss. 105 (5), 156 (2). Bringing into force various provisions of the 2011 Measure on 17.04.2012. - Issued: 09.05.2012. Made: 13.04.2012. Effect: None. Territorial extent & classification: W. General. - In English and Welsh. Welsh title: Gorchymyn Mesur y Gymraeg (Cymru) 2011 (Cychwyn Rhif 5) 2012. - 8p.: 30 cm. - 978-0-348-10601-5 £4.00

The Welsh Language (Wales) Measure 2011 (Commencement No. 6) Order 2012 No. 2012/1423 (W.176)(C.53). - Enabling power: Welsh Language (Wales) Measure 2011, ss. 150 (5), 156 (2). Bringing into force various provisions of the 2011 Measure on 01.06.2012. - Issued: 08.06.2012. Made: 29.05.2012. Effect: None. Territorial extent & classification: W. General. - In English and Welsh. Welsh title: Gorchymyn Mesur y Gymraeg (Cymru) 2011 (Cychwyn Rhif 6) 2012. - 8p.: 30 cm. - 978-0-348-10617-6 £5.75

The Welsh Language (Wales) Measure 2011 (Transfer of functions, Transitional and Consequential Provisions) Order 2012 No. 2012/990 (W.130). - Enabling power: Welsh Language (Wales) Measure 2011, ss. 105 (5), 154. - Issued: 25.04.2012. Made: 29.03.2012. Coming into force: 01.04.2012. Effect: 1998 c.38; 2000 .14, 36; 2005 c.10; 2006 c.30; 2010 c.15; 2009 nawm 2; S.I. 2007/2316 (W.187) amended. Territorial extent & classification: W. General. - In English and Welsh. Welsh title: Gorchymyn Mesur y Gymraeg (Cymru) 2011 (Trosglwyddo Swyddogaethau, Darpariaethau Trosiannol a Chanlyniadol) 2012. - 8p.: 30 cm. - 978-0-348-10598-8 £5.75

Wildlife

The Conservation of Habitats and Species (Amendment) Regulations 2012 No. 2012/1927. - Enabling power: European Communities Act 1972, s. 2 (2). - Issued: 25.07.2012. Made: 20.07.2012. Laid before Parliament & the National Assembly for Wales: 25.07.2012. Coming into force: 16.08.2012. Effect: 1949 c.97; S.I. 2010/490 amended. Territorial extent & classification: E/W/S/NI. General. - EC note: These Regulations amend the S.I. 2010/490 Regulations and transpose certain aspects of Directive 2009/147/EC on the conservation of wild birds. - 16p.: 30 cm. - 978-0-11-152765-8 £5.75

The Offshore Marine Conservation (Natural Habitats, &c.) (Amendment) Regulations 2012 No. 2012/1928. - Enabling power: European Communities Act 1972, s. 2 (2). - Issued: 25.07.2012. Made: 20.07.2012. Laid: 25.07.2012. Coming into force: 16.08.2012. Effect: S.I. 2007/1842 amended. Territorial extent & classification: E/W/S/NI. General. - EC note: These Regulations amend the Offshore Marine Conservation (Natural Habitats, &c.) Regulations 2007 which make provision for implementing Council Directive 92/43/EEC on the conservation of natural habitats and of wild flora and fauna in relation to marine areas where the United Kingdom has jurisdiction beyond its territorial sea & Directive 2009/147/EC on the conservation of wild birds. - 8p.: 30 cm. - 978-0-11-152766-5 £4.00

Statutory Instruments

Arranged by Number

1	Local government, England
2	Local government, England
3	Local government, England
4	Local government, England
5 (W.1)	Road traffic, Wales
6 (W.2)	Road traffic, Wales
7 (W.3)	Road traffic, Wales
8	Education, England
9	Education, England
10	Education, England
11 (W.4)	Road traffic, Wales
12	Road traffic, England
13	Animals, England
14 (W.5)	Education, Wales
15	London government
16	Road traffic
17	Health care and associated professions
18	Education, England
19 (W.6)	Road traffic, Wales
20	Local government, England
21 (W.7)	Road traffic, Wales
22 (W.8)	Road traffic, Wales
23 (W.9)	Road traffic, Wales
24	Rating and valuation, England
25	Rating and valuation, England
26	Road traffic
27	Road traffic
28	Road traffic
29	Road traffic
30	Road traffic
31	Road traffic
32	Road traffic
33	Value added tax
34	Road traffic
35	Road traffic
36	Road traffic
37	Road traffic
38	Road traffic
39	Road traffic
40	Road traffic
41	Road traffic
42	Road traffic
43	Road traffic
44	Road traffic
45	Road traffic
46 (W.10)(C.1)	Welsh language, Wales
47	Agriculture, England Food, England
48 (W.11)	Highways, Wales
49 (W.12)	Road traffic, Wales
50	Prisons, England
51	Local government, England
52	Education, England
53	Road traffic
54	Road traffic
55	Road traffic
56	Criminal law
57 (C. 2)	Community infrastructure levy, England and Wales Infrastructure planning Housing, England and Wales Local government, England and Wales Town and country planning, England and Wales
58	Value added tax
59 (W.13)	Welsh language, Wales
60 (W.14)	London Olympic Games and Paralympic Games, Wales
61	Police, England and Wales Animals, England Local government, England and Wales Fees and charges
62	Police, England and Wales
63	Libraries
64 (W.15)	Agriculture, Wales Food, Wales
65 (W.16)	Environmental protection, Wales
66	Agriculture
67	Countryside, England
68 (C.3)	Social security
69	Road traffic
70	Road traffic
71	Civil aviation
72	Civil aviation
73	Civil aviation
74	Civil aviation
75	Police, England and Wales
76	Road traffic
77	Road traffic
78	Road traffic

79	Road traffic	124	Road traffic
80	Road traffic	125	Road traffic
81	Road traffic	126	Road traffic
82	Road traffic	127	Road traffic
83	Civil aviation	128	Road traffic
84 (C.4)	Education, England	129	Criminal law
85	Road traffic	130	Road traffic
86	Road traffic	131	Road traffic
87	Road traffic	132	Road traffic
88	Road traffic	133	Road traffic
89	Road traffic	134	Road traffic
90	Road traffic	135	Road traffic
91	Road traffic	136	Road traffic
92	Road traffic	137	Road traffic
93	Road traffic	138	Proceeds of crime, England and Wales
94	Road traffic	139	Road traffic
95	Road traffic	140	Road traffic
96	Road traffic	141 (W.18)	Road traffic, Wales
97	Road traffic	142	Road traffic
98	Open spaces	143 (W.19)	Road traffic, Wales
99	Road traffic	144 (W.20)	Road traffic, Wales
100	Road traffic	145	Security industry
101	Road traffic	146	Criminal law, England and Wales
102	Road traffic		Criminal law, Northern Ireland
103	Plant health, England	147	Environmental protection, England and Wales
104	Road traffic, England	148	Rating and valuation, England
105	Disabled persons Transport	149	Employment tribunals
106	Road traffic	150	Civil aviation
107	Road traffic	151	Civil aviation
108	Road traffic	152	Civil aviation
109	Road traffic	153	Civil aviation
110	Road traffic	154	Civil aviation
111 (W.17)	Road traffic, Wales	155	Civil aviation
112	Road traffic	156	Civil aviation
113	Road traffic	157 (W.21)	Highways, Wales
114	Agriculture	158	Road traffic
115	Education, England	159	Local government, England
116	Immigration	160	Local government, England
117	Road traffic	161	Local government, England
118	Road traffic	162 (W.22)	Road traffic, Wales
119	Road traffic	163 (W.23)	Road traffic, Wales
120	Road traffic	164	Road traffic
121	Road traffic	165 (W.24)	Road traffic, Wales
122	Road traffic	166 (W.25)	Education, Wales
123	Road traffic	167 (W.26)	Education, Wales

168 (W.27)	Education, Wales		National Health Service, Wales
169 (W.28)	Education, Wales		Children and young persons, Wales
170 (W.29)	Education, Wales	206	Education, England
171	Legal profession, England and Wales	207	Road traffic
		208	Road traffic
172	Road traffic	209	Road traffic
173	Road traffic	210 (W.36)	Town and country planning, Wales
174	Road traffic	211	Road traffic
175	Road traffic	212	Pensions
176	Road traffic	213	Local government, England
177	Road traffic	214	Road traffic
178	Customs	215	Pensions
	Customs: Forest law: Enforcement, governance & trade	216	Education, England
179	Road traffic	217	Road traffic
180	Road traffic	218	Road traffic
181	Road traffic	219	Road traffic
182	Road traffic	220	Road traffic
183	Road traffic	221	Road traffic
184	Road traffic	222	Road traffic
185	Road traffic	223 (W. 37)(C. 7)	Welsh language, Wales
186	Road traffic	224	Road traffic
187	Social security	225	Road traffic
188	Social security	226	Road traffic
189	Social security	227	Road traffic
190	Criminal law	228	Road traffic
191 (W.30) (C.5)	Social care, Wales	229	Road traffic
	National Health Service, Wales	230	Road traffic
	Children and young persons, Wales	231	Road traffic
192	Police, England and Wales	232	Road traffic
193 (W.31) (C.6)	Local government, Wales	233	Road traffic
194	Civil aviation	234	London government
195	Civil aviation	235	Road traffic
196	Civil aviation	236	Road traffic
197 (W.32)	Road traffic, Wales	237	Road traffic
198	London government	238	Road traffic
	Representation of the people, England	239	Road traffic
		240	Road traffic
199	Health and safety	241	Road traffic
200	Road traffic	242	Road traffic
201	Road traffic	243	Road traffic
202 (W.33)	Social care, Wales	244 (W.38)	Clean air, Wales
	National Health Service, Wales	245 (W.39)	Seeds, Wales
	Children and young persons, Wales	246	Regulatory reform
203	Road traffic	247 (W.40)	Agriculture, Wales
204 (W.34)	Social care, Wales	248 (W.41)	Education, Wales
	National Health Service, Wales	249	Housing, England
	Children and young persons, Wales	250	Road traffic
205 (W.35)	Social care, Wales		

251	Road traffic	293	Electronic communications
252	Road traffic		Broadcasting
253	Road traffic	294	Road traffic
254	Road traffic	295	Road traffic
255	Road traffic	296	Road traffic
256	Road traffic	297	Road traffic
257	Road traffic	298	Road traffic
258	Road traffic	299	Road traffic
259	Road traffic	300	Road traffic
260	Road traffic	301	Road traffic
261	Road traffic	302	Road traffic
262	Road traffic	303	Road traffic
263	Environmental protection, England	304	Road traffic
264 (C.8)	Water, England	305	Road traffic
265	Local government, England	306	Public passenger transport
266	Corporation tax	307	Road traffic
	Income tax	308	Road traffic
	Insurance premium tax	309 (W.50)	Road traffic, Wales
267 (W.42)	Road traffic, Wales	310	Urban development, England
268	Road traffic	311	Road traffic
269	Road traffic	312	Road traffic
270	Road traffic	313	Road traffic
271	Road traffic	314	Road traffic
272	Road traffic	315	Road traffic
273 (W.43)	Road traffic, Wales	316	Road traffic
274 (W.44)	Road traffic, Wales	317	Road traffic
275 (W.45)	Road traffic, Wales	318	Road traffic
276 *Cancelled*	Dangerous drugs *replaced by* 2012/384	319	Road traffic
		320 (W.51) (C.10)	Education, Wales
277 *Cancelled*	Dangerous drugs *replaced by* 2012/385	321 (W.52)	Education, Wales
		322 (W.53)	Education, Wales
278	Road traffic	323	Local government, England
279	Road traffic	324	Local government, England
280	Road traffic	325	Local government, England
281	Road traffic	326	Local government, England
282 (W.46)	National Health Service, Wales	327	Local government, England
	Social care, Wales	328	Local government, England
283 (W.47)	Environmental protection, Wales	329	Local government, England
284 (W.48) (C.9)	Water, Wales	330	Local government, England
285 (W.49)	Plant health, Wales	331	Local government, England
286	Corporation tax	332	Local government, England
287	Road traffic	333	Local government, England
288	Road traffic	334	Equality
289	Road traffic	335	Education, England
290	Road traffic	336	Local government, England
291	Road traffic	337 (W.54)	Road traffic, Wales
292	Broadcasting		

338 (W.55)	Road traffic, Wales	383	Road traffic
339 (W.56)	Road traffic, Wales	384	Dangerous drugs
340	Sports grounds and sporting events, England and Wales	385	Dangerous drugs
		386	Road traffic
341	Road traffic	387	National Health Service, England and Wales
342	Road traffic		
343	Road traffic	388	Road traffic
344	Health care and associated professions	389	Road traffic
		390	Road traffic
345 (W.57)	Road traffic, Wales	391	Road traffic
346 (W.58)	Road traffic, Wales	392	Road traffic
347 (W.59)	Road traffic, Wales	393	Road traffic
348	Road traffic	394 (W.63)	Road traffic, Wales
349	Road traffic	395 (W.64)	Road traffic, Wales
350	Road traffic	396 (W.65)	Road traffic, Wales
351	Road traffic	397	Social security
352	Road traffic	398	Road traffic
353	Road traffic	399	Road traffic
354	Road traffic	400	Road traffic
355	Road traffic	401	Road traffic
356	Overseas territories	402	Road traffic
357	European Union	403	Road traffic
358	European Union	404	Road traffic
359	Pensions	405	Road traffic
360	Social security	406	Road traffic
361	Overseas territories	407	Road traffic
362	Overseas territories	408	Road traffic
363	Road traffic	409	Road traffic
364	Road traffic	410	Road traffic
365 (W.60)	Road traffic, Wales	411 (C. 11)	Fire and rescue services, England Local government, England Public passenger transport, England
366 (W.61)	Road traffic, Wales		
367 (W.62)	Road traffic, Wales		
368	Road traffic	412	Road traffic
369	Road traffic	413	Road traffic
370	Road traffic	414	Road traffic
371	Road traffic	415	Road traffic
372	Road traffic	416	Harbours, docks, piers and ferries
373	Road traffic	417	National Health Service, England
374	Road traffic	418	Road traffic
375	Road traffic	419	Road traffic
376	Road traffic	420	Road traffic
377	Road traffic	421	Education, England
378	Road traffic	422 (W.66)	Road traffic, Wales
379	Road traffic	423 (W.67)	Road traffic, Wales
380	Road traffic	424	Road traffic
381	Road traffic	425	Highways, England
382	Road traffic	426 (W.68)	Road traffic, Wales

427 (W.69)	Road traffic, Wales		Transport, England
428 (W.70)	Road traffic, Wales	473	Road traffic
429 (W.71)	Road traffic, Wales	474	Road traffic
430 (W.72)	Road traffic, Wales	475	Road traffic
431	Education, England	476	National Health Service, England
432	Bank levy	477	Road traffic
433	Education, England	478	Road traffic
434	Road traffic	479	Road traffic
435	Road traffic	480	Road traffic
436	Road traffic	481 (W.79)	Road traffic, Wales
437	Road traffic	482	Road traffic
438	Road traffic	483	Road traffic
439	Road traffic	484	Road traffic
440	Road traffic	485 (W.80)	Road traffic, Wales
441	Road traffic	486 (W.81)	Road traffic, Wales
442	Road traffic	487	Civil aviation
443	Road traffic	488	Civil aviation
444	Council tax, England	489	Pensions
445 (W.73)	Road traffic, Wales	490	Civil aviation
446 (W.74)	Road traffic, Wales	491	Road traffic
447	Road traffic	492	International development
448 Cancelled	Road traffic	493	Road traffic
449	Road traffic	494	Road traffic
450	Road traffic	495	Road traffic
451	Road traffic	496	Road traffic
452	Road traffic	497	Road traffic
453	Road traffic	498	Road traffic
454	Road traffic	499	Road traffic
455	Road traffic	500 (L. 1)	Tribunals and inquiries
456	Road traffic	501	Animals, England
457	Road traffic	502	National Health Service, England
458	Bank levy	503	Offshore installations
459	Bank levy	504	Medicines
460	Council tax, England		Fees and charges
461	Environmental protection	505 (L.2)	Senior courts of England and Wales
462	Terms and conditions of employment		County courts, England and Wales
463	Highways, England	506	Road traffic
464 (W.75)	Road traffic, Wales	507	Road traffic
465 (W.76)	Rating and valuation, Wales	508	Road traffic
466 (W.77)	Rating and valuation, Wales	509	Road traffic
467 (W.78)	Rating and valuation, Wales	510	Road traffic
468	Employment tribunals	511	Children and young persons, England
469	Insolvency, England and Wales	512	Road traffic
470	National Health Service, England	513	Education, England
471	Road traffic	514	Road traffic
472	Transport and works, England	515	National Health Service, England

516	Pensions	562	Road traffic
517	International development	563	Road traffic
518	International development	564	Road traffic
519	Corporation tax	565	Road traffic
	Income tax	566	Road traffic
520	International development	567	Road traffic
521 (W.82)	Local government, Wales	568	Road traffic
522	Income tax	569	Road traffic
523	Police, England and Wales	570	Road traffic
524	Civil aviation	571	Road traffic
525	Civil aviation	572	Road traffic
526	Road traffic	573	Social security
527	Road traffic	574	Coroners, England and Wales
528	Pensions	575	Road traffic
529	Road traffic	576	Road traffic
530	Road traffic	577	Road traffic
531 (W.83)	Housing, Wales	578	Road traffic
532	Statistics of trade	579	Road traffic
533	Tribunals and inquiries	580	Road traffic
534	Urban development, England	581	Road traffic
535	Urban development, England	582	Road traffic
536	Police, England and Wales	583	Road traffic
537	Rating and valuation, England	584 (C.12)	Police, England and Wales
538	Rating and valuation, England	585	Road traffic
539	Pensions	586	Road traffic
540	Road traffic	587	Road traffic
541	Road traffic	588	Road traffic
542	Pensions	589	Road traffic
543	Road traffic	590	Road traffic
544	Road traffic	591	Road traffic
545	Road traffic	592	Road traffic
546	Road traffic	593	Road traffic
547	Road traffic	594	Immigration
548	Road traffic	595	Road traffic
549	Road traffic	596	Road traffic
550	Road traffic	597	Road traffic
551	Road traffic	598	Road traffic
552	Road traffic	599	Road traffic
553	Road traffic	600	Road traffic
554	Road traffic	601 (C.13)	Town and country planning, England
555	Education, England and Wales	602	Road traffic
556	Road traffic	603	Road traffic
557	Road traffic	604	Road traffic
558	Road traffic	605	Town and country planning, England
559 (W. 84)	Road traffic, Wales		
560	Education, England	606	Road traffic
561 (W. 85)	Road traffic, Wales		

607	Road traffic	642	County courts, England and Wales
608	Road traffic	643	Senior courts of England and Wales
609	Road traffic		County courts, England and Wales
610	National Health Service, England and Wales	644	Social security
		645	Social security
611	Road traffic	646	Housing
612	Road traffic	647	Social security
613	Road traffic	648	Road traffic
614 (W. 86)	Road traffic, Wales	649	Road traffic
615	Road traffic	650	Road traffic
616	Road traffic	651	Road traffic
617	Road traffic	652	Road traffic
618	Road traffic	653	Road traffic
619	Education, England	654	Road traffic
620	Road traffic	655	Road traffic
621	Road traffic	656	Road traffic
622	Road traffic	657	Road traffic
623	Road traffic	658	Road traffic
624	Civil contingencies, England and Wales	659	Road traffic
	Civil contingencies, Northern Ireland	660	Road traffic
		661	Road traffic
625	Road traffic	662	Road traffic
626	Road traffic	663	National assistance services, England
627	Road traffic		
628 (C.14)	Housing, England and Wales	664	Rating and valuation, England
	Infrastructure planning	665	Road traffic
	Local government, England and Wales	666	London Government
		667	Local government, England
	London Government	668	Local government, England and Wales
	Rating and valuation, England		
	Town and country planning, England and Wales	669 (C. 15)	Defence
629 (W.87)	Local government, Wales	670	Pensions
630	Environmental protection, England and Wales	671	Electricity
		672	Council tax, England
631 (W.88)	Education, Wales	673	Education, England and Wales
632	Health and safety	674	Education, England
633	Road traffic	675 (W.89)	Road traffic, Wales
634	Town and country planning, England	676 (W.90)	Road traffic, Wales
		677	Public health, England
635	Infrastructure planning	678 (W.91)	Road traffic, Wales
636	Town and country planning, England	679 (L.3)	Family proceedings
637	Town and country planning, England		Senior courts of England and Wales
			County courts, England and Wales
638	Health and safety		Magistrates' courts, England and Wales
639	Criminal law		
640	Police, England and Wales	680	Police, England and Wales
	Pensions, England and Wales	681	Prisons, England
641	Housing, England and Wales	682 (C.16)	Pensions

683 (C.17)	Pensions	724 (W.96)	Education, Wales
684 (W.92)	National Health Service, Wales	725	Budget responsibility
685 (W.93)	Local government, Wales	726	Road traffic
686 (W.94)	Local government, Wales	727	Budget responsibility
687	Postal services	728	Road traffic
688	Postal services	729	Civil aviation
689	Revenue and customs	730	Civil aviation
690	Food, Wales	731	Road traffic
691	Pensions	732	Road traffic
692	Pensions	733	Road traffic
693	Pensions	734	Housing, England
694	Education, England and Wales	735	Charities Capital gains tax Corporation tax Income tax Value added tax
695	Housing, England		
696	Housing, England		
697	Plant health, England		
698	Environmental protection Licensing (marine)	736 (C.18)	Charities Income tax Capital gains tax Corporation tax Inheritance tax Stamp duty Stamp duty land tax Stamp duty reserve tax
699 (W.95)	Road traffic, Wales		
700	Constitutional law Devolution, Scotland Housing		
701	Corporation tax Income tax Stamp duty land tax		
		737 (W.97)	Commons, Wales
702	Housing, England	738 (W.98)	Commons, Wales
703	Road traffic	739 (W.99) (C.19)	Commons, Wales
704	Road traffic	740 (W.100)	Commons, Wales
705	Income tax Capital gains tax	741	Road traffic
		742	Marine pollution
706	Civil aviation	743	Road traffic
707	Road traffic	744	Road traffic
708	Civil aviation	745	Plant health, England
709	Pensions	746 (W.101)	Constitutional law Local government, Wales
710	Competition		
711	Local government, England	747	Education, England
712	Family law	748	Town and country planning, England
713	Road traffic	749	Town and country planning, England
714	Road traffic		
715	Road traffic	750	Legal Services Commission, England and Wales
716	Highways, England		
717	Government resources and accounts	751	Fees and charges
718	Building and buildings, England and Wales	752 (W.102)	Welsh language, Wales
		753 (W.103)	Welsh language, Wales
719	Road traffic	754	Road traffic
720	Road traffic	755	National Health Service, England
721	Road traffic	756	Taxes
722	Road traffic	757	Social security
723	Road traffic	758	Road traffic

759	Road traffic	798	Diplomatic Service
760	Registration of births, deaths and marriages, etc., England and Wales	799	Copyright Rights in performances
761	Civil partnership, England and Wales	800 (W.109)	National Health Service, Wales
		801 (W.110)	Town and country planning, Wales
762	Education, England	802 (W.111)(C.20)	Town and country planning, Wales
763	Financial services and markets	803	National Health Service, England
764	Corporation tax Income tax Stamp duty Stamp duty land tax Stamp duty reserve tax	804	Social security
		805 (W.112)	Local government, Wales
		806 (W.113) (C.21)	Commons, Wales
		807	Social security
765	Education, England and Wales	808	Police
766	Social security	809	Building and buildings, England and Wales
767	Town and country planning, England	810	Customs
768	Road traffic	811	Environmental protection, England and Wales
769	Road traffic		
770	Road traffic	812	Civil aviation
771	Immigration	813	Immigration Nationality
772	Road traffic		
773	Road traffic	814	Clean air, England
774	Road traffic	815	Clean air, England
775	Road traffic	816	Social security
776	Road traffic	817	Social security
777 (W.104)	Road traffic, Wales	818	Social security
778	Road traffic	819	Social security
779	National Health Service, England	820	Income tax Corporation tax
780	Social security Terms and conditions of employment	821	Social security
		822	Income tax
781	Road traffic	823	Social security
782	Pensions	824	Social security
783	Road traffic	825 (C.22)	Criminal law, England and Wales
784	Road traffic	826 (W.114)	Food, Wales
785	Highways, England	827	Sea fisheries, England
786	National Health Service, England	828	Licences and licensing, England and Wales
787	Infrastructure planning		
788	National Health Service, England	829	Betting, gaming and lotteries
789 (W.105)	Town and country planning, Wales	830	Road traffic
790	Civil aviation	831	Road traffic
791 (W.106)	Town and country planning, Wales	832	Road traffic
792 (W.107)	Town and country planning, Wales	833	Social security
793 (W.108)	Town and country planning, Wales	834	Social security
		835	Social security, Northern Ireland
794	Income tax	836	Education
795	Savings banks	837	Civil aviation
796	National Health Service, England	838	Education, England
797	European Union	839	Highways, England

840	Road traffic
841	Road traffic
842 (W.115)	National assistance services, Wales
843 (W.116)	Town and country planning, Wales
844	Employment and training, England
845	Social security
846	Local government, England
	Road traffic, England
847	Taxes
848	Tax credits
849	Tax credits
850	Road traffic
851	Road traffic
852	Highways, England
853	Social security
854	Government resources and accounts
855	Road traffic
856	Road traffic
857	Road traffic
858	Road traffic
859	Road traffic
860	Road traffic
861	Road traffic
862	Road traffic
863 (C.23)	Social security
864	Road traffic
865	Road traffic
866	Road traffic
867	Social security
868	Income tax
	Corporation tax
869	Civil aviation
870 (W.117)	Highways, Wales
871	Civil aviation
872	Urban development, England
873 (C.24)	Energy
874	Social security
875	Local government, England
876	Road traffic
877	Local government, England
878	Education, England
879 (C.25)	Coast protection, England and Wales
	Environmental protection, England and Wales
	Flood risk management, England and Wales
	Water industry, England and Wales
880	Road traffic
881	Capital gains tax
882	Value added tax
883	Value added tax
884	Income tax
885	Landfill tax
886	Child trust funds
	Income tax
	Stamp duty reserve tax
887 (W.118) (C.26)	Fire and rescue services, England and Wales
	Local government, Wales
	Housing, Wales
888	Road traffic
889	Road traffic
890	Road traffic
891	Civil aviation
892	Civil aviation
893	Road traffic
894	Road traffic
895	Civil aviation
896 (C.27)	Licences and licensing, England and Wales
897	Tribunals and inquiries
898 (C. 28)	Environmental protection, England and Wales
899 (W.119)	Mobile homes, Wales
900	Road traffic
901	National Health Service, England
902	Road traffic
903	Road traffic
904	Road traffic
905	Road traffic
906	Civil aviation
907	Civil aviation
908	Civil aviation
909	Civil aviation
910	Civil aviation
911 (C.29)	Pensions
912	Road traffic
913	Social security
914	Road traffic
915	Income tax
916	Financial services and markets
917	Financial services and markets
918	Social security
919	Social security
920	Gender recognition

921	National Health Service, England Social care, England Public health, England		Licences and licensing, England and Wales
922	National Health Service, England	961	Local government, England and Wales Town and country planning, England and Wales
923	Social security		
924 (C.30)	Education, England and Wales	962	Education, England
925	Criminal law	963	Criminal law, England and Wales Licences and licensing, England and Wales
926	Road traffic		
927	Road traffic	964	Public bodies
928	Road traffic	965	Local government, England
929	Customs	966	Postal services
930	Road traffic	967	Education, England
931	Road traffic	968	Road traffic
932	Road traffic	969 (W.126)(C.31)	Welsh language, Wales
933	Road traffic	970	National Health Service, England
934 (W.120)	Fire and rescue services, Wales	971	Immigration Nationality
935 (W.121)	Education, Wales	972 (W.127)	Fire and rescue services, Wales Pensions, Wales
936	Postal services		
937	Children and young persons, England	973	Dangerous drugs
938	Children and young persons, England	974 (W.128)	Fire and rescue services, Wales Pensions, Wales
939	Children and young persons, England	975 (W.129)	Food, Wales
940	Landfill tax	976	Education, England
941	Offshore installations	977	Road traffic
942 (W.122)	Road traffic, Wales	978	Civil aviation
943	Climate change levy	979	Education, England
944 (W.123)	Road traffic, Wales	980	Dangerous drugs
945 (W.124)	Road traffic, Wales	981	Transport and works, England Transport, England
946	Licences and licensing, England and Wales		
947	Horticulture, England and Wales	982	Civil aviation
948 (W.125)	Agriculture, Wales	983	Civil aviation
949	Offshore installations	984	Civil aviation
950	National Health Service, England	985	Road traffic, England
951	Education, England	986	Education, England
952	Companies	987	Education, England
953	Fire and rescue services, England Pensions, England	988	Employment tribunals
		989	Terms and conditions of employment
954	Fire and rescue services, England Pensions, England	990 (W.130)	Welsh language, Wales
		991	Transport
955	Licences and licensing, England and Wales	992	Ecclesiastical law, England
		993	Ecclesiastical law, England
956	Education, England	994	Rating and valuation, England
957	Open spaces	995	Urban development, England
958	Employment and training	996	Road traffic
959	Employment and training	997	Road traffic
960			

998	Road traffic	1041	Road traffic
999	Road traffic	1042	Road traffic
1000	Road traffic	1043	Road traffic
1001	Road traffic	1044	Road traffic
1002	Road traffic	1045	Road traffic
1003	Trade marks	1046	Education, England
1004	Road traffic	1047	Road traffic
1005	Road traffic	1048	Road traffic
1006	Road traffic	1049	Road traffic
1007	Road traffic	1050	Road traffic
1008 (C.32)	Housing, England and Wales Local government, England and Wales London Government Public bodies	1051	Road traffic
		1052	Road traffic
		1053	Road traffic
		1054	Road traffic
1009	Road traffic	1055	Road traffic
1010	Road traffic	1056	Road traffic
1011	Road traffic	1057	Road traffic
1012	Road traffic	1058	Road traffic
1013	Local government, England	1059 (W.132)	Road traffic, Wales
1014	Civil aviation	1060	Civil aviation
1015	Road traffic	1061	Civil aviation
1016	Civil aviation	1062	Road traffic
1017	Civil aviation	1063	Road traffic
1018	Civil aviation	1064	Road traffic
1019	Local government, England	1065	Road traffic
1020	Local government, England	1066	Road traffic
1021	Local government, England	1067	Road traffic
1022	Local government, England	1068	Road traffic
1023	Local government, England	1069	Road traffic
1024	Land drainage, England	1070	Road traffic
1025	Land drainage, England	1071	Road traffic
1026	Land drainage, England	1072	Road traffic
1027	Land drainage, England	1073	Road traffic
1028	Land drainage, England	1074	Social security
1029	Land drainage, England	1075	Electronic communications
1030	Land drainage, England	1076	Road traffic
1031	Land drainage, England	1077	Road traffic
1032	Land drainage, England	1078	Road traffic
1033	Education, England	1079	Road traffic
1034	Education, England	1080	Road traffic
1035	Education, England	1081	Road traffic
1036 (W.131)	Road traffic, Wales	1082	Road traffic
1037	Road traffic	1083	Road traffic
1038	Road traffic	1084	Road traffic
1039	Road traffic	1085 (W.133)	Fire precautions, Wales
1040	Road traffic	1086 (W.134)	Road traffic, Wales

1087 (C.33)	Education, England and Wales
1088	Road traffic
1089	Road traffic
1090	Road traffic
1091	Road traffic
1092	Road traffic
1093	Road traffic
1094	Road traffic
1095 (C.34)	Postal services
1096 (W.135)(C.35)	Welsh language, Wales
1097	Road traffic
1098	Road traffic
1099	Road traffic
1100 (C.36)	Town and country planning, Wales
1101	Healthcare and associated professions
1102	Consumer protection
1103	Road traffic
1104	Road traffic
1105	Road traffic
1106	Road traffic
1107	Education, England
1108	National Health Service, England
1109	National Health Service, England
1110	Defence
1111	Road traffic
1112	Road traffic
1113	Road traffic
1114	Road traffic
1115	Education, England
1116	Road traffic
1117	Road traffic
1118	Mental health, England
1119	Road traffic
1120	Road traffic
1121 (C.37)	Prevention and suppression of terrorism
1122	Road traffic
1123	Road traffic
1124	Education, England
1125	Road traffic
1126	Road traffic
1127	Postal services
1128	Postal services
1129 (C.38)	Licences and licensing, England and Wales
	Police, England and Wales
1130 (W.136)	Road traffic, Wales
1131	Road traffic
1132	Road traffic
1133	Sports grounds and sporting events, England and Wales
1134	Civil aviation
1135	Social security
1136	Road traffic
1137	Road traffic
1138	Road traffic
1139	Environmental protection
1140	Road traffic
1141	Road traffic
1142	Road traffic
1143 (W.137)	Local government, Wales
1144	Road traffic
1145 (W.138)	Road traffic, Wales
1146	Road traffic
1147	Road traffic
1148	Road traffic
1149	Road traffic
1150	Environmental protection, England
1151	Environmental protection, England
1152	Road traffic
1153	Education, England and Wales
1154	Harbours, docks, piers and ferries
1155	Food, England
1156 (W.139)	Education, Wales
1157	Education, England
1158	Education, England
1159	Road traffic
1160	Road traffic
1161	Road traffic
1162	Road traffic
1163	Road traffic
1164 (C.39)	Video recordings
1165	Road traffic
1166 (W.140)	Road traffic, Wales
1167	Education, England
1168 (W.141)	Road traffic, Wales
1169 (W.142)	Road traffic, Wales
1170 (W.143)	Road traffic, Wales
1171 (W.144)	Road traffic, Wales
1172	Civil aviation
1173	Road traffic
1174	Civil aviation
1175	Road traffic

1176	Civil aviation
1177	Civil aviation
1178	Road traffic
1179	Road traffic
1180	Road traffic
1181	Road traffic
1182	Road traffic
1183	Road traffic
1184	Road traffic
1185	Road traffic
1186	National Health Service, England Social care, England Public health, England
1187 (W.145)(C.40)	Local government, Wales
1188	Income tax
1189 (W.146)	Road traffic, Wales
1190	Road traffic
1191	Road traffic
1192	Road traffic
1193	Road traffic
1194	Road traffic
1195 (W.147)	Road traffic, Wales
1196	Road traffic
1197	Education, England
1198 (W.148)	Food, Wales
1199	Education, England
1200	Road traffic
1201	Education, England
1202	Road traffic
1203	Registration of births, deaths, marriages, etc., England and Wales
1204	Police, England and Wales
1205 (C.41)	Rights of the subject, England and Wales Rights of the subject, England and Wales Freedom of information, England and Wales Freedom of information, Northern Ireland Police, England and Wales Prevention and suppression of terrorism
1206	Public bodies
1207	Civil aviation
1208	Civil aviation
1209	Civil aviation
1210	Civil aviation
1211	Road traffic
1212	Road traffic
1213	Road traffic
1214	Road traffic
1215	Probation, England and Wales
1216	Road traffic
1217	Road traffic
1218	Highways, England
1219	Highways, England
1220	Road traffic
1221	Income tax
1222	Road traffic
1223	Dogs, England
1224	Road traffic
1225	Road traffic
1226	Road traffic
1227	Road traffic
1228	Road traffic
1229	Road traffic
1230	Civil aviation
1231	Civil aviation
1232	Civil aviation
1233 (W.149)	Road traffic, Wales
1234	Enforcement of civil penalties, England London government
1235 (W.150)	Road traffic, Wales
1236	Road traffic
1237	Road traffic
1238 (W.151)	Agriculture, Wales Water, Wales
1239	Road traffic
1240	Road traffic
1241	Road traffic
1242	Road traffic
1243	Customs
1244 (W.152)	Mental health, Wales
1245	Road traffic
1246 (C.42)	Social security
1247	Road traffic
1248 (W.153)	Education, Wales
1249	Road traffic
1250	Road traffic
1251	Road traffic
1252	Road traffic
1253	Road traffic
1254	Road traffic
1255	Road traffic

1256 (C.43)	Registration of births, deaths, marriages, etc., England and Wales Social security	1297	Road traffic
		1298	Road traffic
		1299	Road traffic
1257	Pensions	1300	Road traffic
1258	Income tax	1301	Criminal law
1259 (W.154)	Education, Wales	1302	Criminal law
1260 (W.155)	Education, Wales	1303	Road traffic
1261 (W.156)	National Health Service, Wales	1304	Road traffic
1262 (W.157)	National Health Service, Wales	1305 (W.166)	Mental health, Wales
1263 (C.44)	Immigration	1306	Road traffic
1264	Channel Tunnel	1307	Road traffic
1265 (W.158)	Mental health, Wales	1308	Road traffic
1266	Transport and works, England Canals and inland waterways, England	1309	Education
		1310	Dangerous drugs
		1311	Dangerous drugs
1267	Social security	1312 (C.46)	Charging orders, England and Wales
1268 (W.159)	Road traffic, Wales		
1269 (W.160)	Road traffic, Wales	1313	Local government, England
1270 (W.161)	Road traffic, Wales	1314	Road traffic
1271	Road traffic	1315	Road traffic
1272 (W.162)	Road traffic, Wales	1316	Road traffic
1273	National Health Service, England	1317	Road traffic
1274	Education, England	1318	Road traffic
1275 (L.4)	Magistrates' courts, England and Wales	1319 (C.47)	Health care and associated professions Licensing (liquor) Mental health, England and Wales National Health Service Social care, England
1276	Road traffic		
1277	Justices of the Peace, England and Wales		
1278	Children and young persons, England		
		1320 (C.48)	Criminal law, England and Wales
1279	Road traffic	1321	Road traffic
1280	Road traffic	1322	Highways, England
1281	Road traffic	1323	Road traffic
1282	Highways, England	1324	Local government, England
1283	Road traffic	1325	Road traffic
1284	Highways, England	1326	Road traffic
1285 (W.163)	Public health, Wales	1327	Road traffic
1286	Highways, England	1328	Civil aviation
1287 (W.164)	Public health, Wales	1329	Civil aviation
1288 (W.165)(C.45)	National Health Service, Wales	1330	Civil aviation
1289	Highways, England	1331	Civil aviation
1290	National Health Service, England	1332	Civil aviation
1291	Rating and valuation, England	1333	Civil aviation
1292	Rating and valuation, England	1334	Civil aviation
1293	Education, England	1335	Civil aviation
1294	Highways, England	1336	Civil aviation
1295	Highways, England	1337	Civil aviation
1296	Road traffic	1338	Civil aviation

1339	Civil aviation	1384	Highways, England
1340	Civil aviation	1385	Highways, England
1341	Civil aviation	1386	Climate change
1342	Civil aviation	1387 (W.168)	Animals, Wales
1343	Legal Services Commission, England and Wales	1388	Pensions
		1389	Overseas territories
1344	Criminal law, England and Wales	1390	Dangerous drugs
1345	Criminal law, England and Wales	1391	Animals, England
1346 (W.167)	Town and country planning, Wales	1392	Highways, England
1347	Civil aviation	1393	Electricity
1348	Civil aviation	1394	Local government, England
1349	Civil aviation	1395	Local government, England
1350	Civil aviation	1396	Local government, England
1351	Civil aviation	1397 (W.169) (C.52)	Mental health, England and Wales
1352	Civil aviation	1398 (W.170)	Road traffic, Wales
1353	Civil aviation	1399	National Health Service, England
1354	Civil aviation	1400 (W.171)	Road traffic, Wales
1355	Road traffic	1401	Civil aviation
1356 (C.49)	Road traffic	1402	Civil aviation
1357 (C.50)	Road traffic	1403	Civil aviation
1358 (C.51)	Local government, England and Wales	1404	Road traffic
		1405	Road traffic
1359	Income tax	1406	Road traffic
1360	Income tax	1407	Road traffic
1361	Road traffic	1408	Road traffic
1362	Road traffic	1409	Road traffic
1363 (L.5)	Tribunals and inquiries	1410	Children and young persons, England and Wales
1364	Road traffic	1411	Road traffic
1365	Road traffic	1412 (W.172)	Road traffic, Wales
1366	Road traffic	1413	Road traffic
1367	Trading with the enemy	1414	Road traffic
1368	Road traffic	1415	Road traffic
1369	Road traffic	1416	Road traffic
1370	Road traffic	1417 (W.173)	Road traffic, Wales
1371	Road traffic	1418 (W.174)	Education, Wales
1372	Road traffic	1419 (W.175)	Road traffic, Wales
1373	Road traffic	1420	Road traffic
1374	Road traffic	1421	Road traffic
1375	Sea fisheries, England	1422	Road traffic
1376	Road traffic	1423 (W.176)(C.53)	Welsh language
1377	Road traffic	1424	National Health Service, England
1378	Road traffic	1425	National Health Service, England
1379	Animals, England	1426	Consumer protection
1380	Animals, England	1427 (W. 177)	Animals, Wales
1381	Road traffic		Destructive animals
1382	Road traffic	1428 (W.178)	Mental health, Wales
1383	Road traffic		

1429 (W.179)	National Health Service, Wales	1468	Road traffic
1430	Criminal law, England and Wales	1469	Road traffic
	Police, England and Wales	1470	Sports grounds and sporting events, England and Wales
1431	Criminal law, England and Wales		
	Police, England and Wales	1471	Public bodies
1432 (C.54)	Criminal law	1472	Road traffic
1433	Police, England and Wales	1473	Road traffic
1434	Road traffic	1474	Road traffic
1435	Road traffic	1475	Road traffic
1436	Road traffic	1476	Road traffic
1437	Road traffic	1477	Pensions
1438	Road traffic	1478	Defence
1439	Companies	1479	Health care and associated professions
1440 (C.55)	Social security		
1441	Road traffic	1480	Health care and associated professions
1442	Road traffic	1481	Road traffic
1443	Road traffic	1482 (W.182)	Road traffic, Wales
1444	Road traffic	1483	Social security
1445	Road traffic	1484 (W.183)	Road traffic, Wales
1446	Road traffic	1485 (W.184)	Road traffic, Wales
1447	Road traffic	1486 (W.185)	Road traffic, Wales
1448	Road traffic	1487 (W.186)	Road traffic, Wales
1449	Road traffic	1488 (W.187)	Road traffic, Wales
1450	Road traffic	1489	Criminal law
1451	Road traffic	1490 (W.188)	Road traffic, Wales
1452	Road traffic	1491 (W.189)	Road traffic, Wales
1453	Road traffic	1492 (W.190)	Road traffic, Wales
1454	Road traffic	1493 (W.191)	Plant health, Wales
1455	Road traffic	1494 (W.192)	Road traffic, Wales
1456 (W.180)	Road traffic, Wales	1495 (W.193)	Road traffic, Wales
1457 (W.181)	Road traffic, Wales	1496 (W.194)	Road traffic, Wales
1458	Road traffic	1497 (W.195)	Road traffic, Wales
1459	Road traffic	1498 (W.196)	Road traffic, Wales
1460	Road traffic	1499 (W.197)	Road traffic, Wales
1461	Road traffic	1500	Investigatory powers, England and Wales
1462	Family proceedings		
	Senior courts of England and Wales	1501	Human tissue
	County courts, England and Wales	1502	Road traffic
	Magistrates' courts, England and Wales	1503 (W.198)	Road traffic, Wales
1463 (C.56)	Housing, England and Wales	1504 (W.199)	Road traffic, Wales
	Local government, England and Wales	1505 (W.200)	Road traffic, Wales
	London government	1506	Pensions
1464	Local government, England	1507	Criminal law
1465	Local government, England	1508	Criminal law
1466	Prevention and suppression of terrorism	1509	Criminal law
		1510	Criminal law
1467	National Health Service, England	1511	Criminal law

1512	National Health Service, England	1554	Education, England
1513	National Health Service, England Social care, England Public health, England	1555	Justices of the Peace, England and Wales
		1556	Road traffic
1514	National Health Service, England	1557	Road traffic
1515	Criminal law	1558	Road traffic
1516	Criminal law	1559	Countryside, England
1517	Criminal law	1560	Road traffic
1518 (W.201)	Education, Wales	1561	Road traffic
1519	Electromagnetic compatibility	1562	Road traffic
1520 (W.202)	Road traffic, Wales	1563	Road traffic
1521 (W.203)	Road traffic, Wales	1564	Road traffic
1522 (W.204)	Road traffic, Wales	1565	Road traffic
1523	Local government, England	1566	Road traffic
1524	Road traffic	1567	Security industry
1525	Road traffic	1568	Road traffic
1526	Road traffic	1569 (C.59)	Equality
1527	Road traffic	1570	Road traffic
1528	Road traffic	1571	Road traffic
1529	Road traffic	1572	Road traffic
1530	London government	1573	Pensions
1531 (C.57)	Immigration	1574	Offshore installations
1532	Immigration	1575	Road traffic
1533	Road traffic	1576	Road traffic
1534	Prevention and suppression of terrorism Proceeds of crime	1577	Road traffic
		1578	Road traffic
		1579	Road traffic
1535	Road traffic	1580	Road traffic
1536	Public health, England	1581	Road traffic
1537	Health and safety	1582	Road traffic
1538	Financial services and markets	1583	Road traffic
1539	Road traffic	1584	Road traffic
1540	Road traffic	1585	Road traffic
1541	Road traffic	1586	National Health Service, England
1542	Road traffic	1587	Road traffic
1543	Road traffic	1588	British nationality
1544	Parliament Insolvency	1589	Road traffic
		1590	Road traffic
1545 (W.205)	Road traffic, Wales	1591	Road traffic
1546	Road traffic	1592	Road traffic
1547	Immigration	1593	Road traffic
1548	Road traffic	1594	Road traffic
1549	Road traffic	1595	Road traffic
1550	Road traffic	1596	Road traffic
1551	Road traffic	1597 (W.207)	Road traffic, Wales
1552	Road traffic	1598	Civil aviation
1553 (W.206) (C.58)	Children and young persons, Wales	1599	Road traffic

1600	Road traffic
1601	Road traffic
1602	Road traffic
1603	Road traffic
1604	Social security
1605	Road traffic
1606	Road traffic
1607	Road traffic
1608	Road traffic
1609	Road traffic
1610	Road traffic
1611	Road traffic
1612	Road traffic
1613	Road traffic
1614	Road traffic
1615 (C.60)	Police, England and Wales
1616	Social security
1617	Road traffic
1618	Road traffic
1619	Road traffic
1620	Road traffic
1621	Road traffic
1622	Road traffic
1623	Road traffic
1624	Road traffic
1625	Road traffic
1626	Road traffic
1627	Road traffic
1628	Road traffic
1629 (W.208)	Road traffic, Wales
1630 (W.209)	Education, Wales
1631	National Health Service, England
1632	Civil aviation
1633	Betting, gaming and lotteries
1634	Social security
1635	Criminal law, England and Wales
1636 (W.210)	Road traffic, Wales
1637	Civil aviation
1638	Civil aviation
1639	Road traffic
1640	National Health Service, England Social care, England Public health, England
1641	National Health Service
1642 (W.211)	Road traffic, Wales
1643 (W.212)	Education, Wales
1644	Local government, England
1645	Infrastructure planning, England
1646	Electricity, England and Wales
1647	Local government, England
1648 (W.213)	Road traffic, Wales
1649 (C.61)	Family law
1650	National Health Service, England
1651 (C.62)	Social security
1652	Health and safety
1653	Education, England
1654	Health care and associated professions
1655	Health care and associated professions
1656	Social security
1657	Pesticides
1658	Canals and inland waterways Public bodies
1659	Canals and inland waterways Public bodies Transport
1660	Energy conservation
1661	Energy conservation
1662 (C.63)	Public bodies
1663	Immigration
1664 (W.214)	Town and country planning, Wales
1665	Public records
1666	Sports grounds and sporting events, England and Wales
1667	Stamp duty land tax
1668	Road traffic
1669	Road traffic
1670	Road traffic
1671	Road traffic
1672	Environmental protection Public sector information
1673	Tribunals and inquiries
1674 (W.215)	Children and young persons, Wales
1675 (W.216)	Education, Wales
1676	Road traffic
1677	Road traffic
1678	Road traffic
1679	Road traffic
1680	Road traffic
1681 (C.64)	Pensions
1682 (C.65)	Pensions
1683	Road traffic
1684	Road traffic
1685	Road traffic

1686	Road traffic	1724 (C.68)	Prevention and suppression of terrorism
1687	Road traffic	1725	Road traffic
1688	Pensions	1726 (L.6)	Senior courts of England and Wales
1689 (W.217)	Sea fisheries, Wales		Magistrates' courts, England and Wales
1690	Police, England and Wales	1727	Road traffic
1691	Civil aviation	1728	Road traffic
1692 (W.218)	Coast protection, Wales	1729	Road traffic
	Environmental protection, Wales	1730	Road traffic
	Flood risk management, Wales	1731	Road traffic
1693	Coast protection, England	1732	Road traffic
	Environmental protection, England	1733	Road traffic
	Flood risk management, England	1734	Charities, England and Wales
1694 (W.219)	Road traffic, Wales	1735	Road traffic
1695 (W.220)	Road traffic, Wales	1736	Education, England
1696	Criminal law, England and Wales	1737	Road traffic
1697 (C.66)	Criminal law, England and Wales	1738	Road traffic
1698	Children and young persons, England	1739	Road traffic
1699	Children and young persons, England	1740	Education, England
1700	Road traffic	1741	Companies
1701	Road traffic		Auditors
1702	Road traffic	1742	Food, England
1703 (W.221)	Education, Wales	1743	Merchant shipping
1704	Road traffic	1744	Road traffic
1705	Road traffic	1745	Consumer credit
1706	Road traffic	1746	Road traffic
1707	Road traffic	1747	Road traffic
1708	Road traffic	1748	Education, England
1709	Corporation tax	1749	Education, England
	Stamp duty	1750	Defence
	Stamp duty land tax	1751	Civil aviation
1710 (C.67)	Constitutional law	1752	Diplomatic Service
	Devolution, Scotland	1753	Copyright
1711	Statistics Board	1754	Copyright
1712 (W.222)	Children and young persons, Wales	1755	Overseas territories
1713	Police, England and Wales	1756	Overseas territories
1714	Local government, England and Wales	1757	Overseas territories
1715	Environmental protection	1758	Overseas territories
1716	Road traffic	1759	European Union
1717	Road traffic	1760	Local government, England
1718 (W.223)	Road traffic, Wales	1761	Overseas territories
1719	Road traffic	1762	Police
1720 (W.224)	Road traffic, Wales	1763	Immigration
1721	Road traffic	1764	Video recordings
1722	Road traffic	1765 (W.225)	Food, Wales
1723	Road traffic	1766 (C.69)	Video recordings

1767	Video recordings
1768	Education, England
	Education, Northern Ireland
1769	Criminal law, England and Wales
1770	Judgments
1771	Prevention and suppression of terrorism
1772	Local government, England
1773	Protection of wrecks, England
1774	Road traffic
1775	Road traffic
1776	Road traffic
1777	Harbours, docks, piers and ferries
1778	Road traffic
1779	Road traffic
1780	Road traffic
1781	Road traffic
1782 (W.226)	Road traffic, Wales
1783	Corporation tax
	Capital gains tax
1784	Road traffic
1785	Road traffic
1786	Road traffic
1787	Road traffic
1788	Road traffic
1789	Road traffic
1790	Road traffic
1791	Financial services and markets
1792	Prevention and suppression of terrorism
1793	Prevention and suppression of terrorism
1794	Prevention and suppression of terrorism
1795	Income tax
1796	Pensions
1797 (W.227)	Education, Wales
1798	Police, England and Wales
1799	Road traffic
1800	Road traffic
1801	Road traffic
1802	Road traffic
1803	Government resources and accounts
1804	Criminal law, England and Wales
1805	Court martial (appeals), England and Wales
1806	National Health Service, England
1807	Protection of wrecks, England
1808	Income tax
1809	European Union
1810 (C.70)	Prevention and suppression of terrorism
1811	Pensions
1812	Local government, England
1813	Pensions
1814	Social security
1815	Consumer protection
1816	Prices
1817	Pensions
1818	Education, England
1819 (W.228)	Coast protection, Wales
	Environmental protection, Wales
	Flood risk management, Wales
1820	Road traffic
1821	Housing, England
1822	Road traffic
1823	Road traffic
1824	National Health Service, England
1825	Education, England
1826	Juries, England and Wales
1827	Road traffic
1828	Road traffic
1829	Education, England
1830	Road traffic
1831 (C.71)	Health care and associated professions
	National Health Service, England
	Public health
	Social care
1832	Income tax
	Corporation tax
1833	Criminal law, England and Wales
1834	Road traffic
1835	Road traffic
1836	Taxes
1837	National Health Service, England
1838	Income tax
	Corporation tax
1839	Road traffic
1840	Road traffic
1841 (C.72)	Energy
1842	Electronic communications
	Broadcasting
1843	Capital gains tax
	Corporation tax
1844	Merchant shipping
1845	Education, England

1846	Ecclesiastical law, England	1887 (C.73)	Immigration
1847	Ecclesiastical law, England	1888	Road traffic
1848	Consumer protection Health and safety	1889	Environmental protection, England and Wales
1849	Agriculture, England Water, England	1890	Road traffic
		1891	Road traffic
1850	Road traffic	1892	Road traffic
1851	Betting, gaming and lotteries	1893 (W.229)	National Health Service, Wales
1852	Constitutional law Devolution, Scotland	1894	Immigration
		1895	Income tax
1853	Road traffic	1896 (C. 74)	Income tax Capital gains tax
1854	Road traffic		
1855	Road traffic	1897	Excise
1856	Road traffic	1898	Income tax
1857	Road traffic	1899	Value added tax
1858	Road traffic	1900	Excise
1859	Road traffic	1901 (C.75)	Income tax
1860	Road traffic	1902 (C.76)	National Health Service, England
1861	Road traffic	1903 (W.230)	Public bodies, Wales Environmental protection, Wales
1862	Road traffic		
1863	Road traffic	1904 (W.231)	Education, Wales
1864	Road traffic	1905 (W.232)	Children and young persons, Wales
1865	Road traffic, England	1906	Financial services
1866	Parliament	1907	Fees and charges
1867	Transport and works, England	1908	Fees and charges
1868	Social security	1909	National Health Service, England
1869	Housing, England	1910	Customs
1870	Child trust funds	1911 (W.233)	Public health, Wales
1871	Income tax Capital gains tax	1912 (W. 234)	Road traffic, Wales
		1913 (W.235)	Road traffic, Wales
1872	Local government, England	1914	Harbours, docks, piers and ferries
1873	Road traffic	1915	Council tax, England and Wales Public health, England and Wales
1874	Road traffic		
1875	Road traffic	1916	Medicines
1876	Criminal law, England and Wales	1917	Police, England and Wales
1877	National debt	1918	Police, England and Wales
1878	Competition	1919	Education, England
1879	Children and young persons, England Education, England Regulatory reform	1920	Road traffic
		1921	Road traffic
		1922	Road traffic
		1923	Environmental protection Health and safety Public bodies
1880	National debt		
1881	Income tax		
1882	National debt	1924	Transport and works, England Transport, England
1883	Criminal law, England and Wales		
1884	Road traffic	1925	Education, England
1885	Road traffic	1926	Education, England
1886	Fire and rescue services, England	1927	Wildlife

	Countryside	1969	Land registration, England and Wales
	Marine management		
1928	Wildlife	1970	Civil aviation
1929	Road traffic	1971	Civil aviation
1930	Road traffic	1972	Civil aviation
1931	Road traffic	1973	Road traffic
1932	Road traffic	1974	Civil aviation
1933	Road traffic	1975	Civil aviation
1934	Road traffic	1976	Climate change levy
1935	Road traffic	1977	Animals, England
1936	Road traffic	1978	Data protection
1937	Road traffic	1979	Road traffic
1938	Road traffic	1980	Road traffic
1939	Road traffic	1981	Road traffic
1940	Civil aviation	1982	Road traffic
1941	Road traffic	1983	Road traffic
1942	Road traffic	1984	Harbours, docks, piers and ferries
1943	Education, England and Wales	1985	Road traffic
1944	Representation of the people	1986	Road traffic
1945	Coast protection, England	1987	Road traffic
	Environmental protection, England	1988	Road traffic
	Flood risk management, England	1989	Pensions, England and Wales
1946	Civil aviation	1990	Social security
1947	Road traffic	1991	Road traffic
1948	Road traffic	1992	Road traffic
1949	Road traffic	1993	Transport and works, England
1950	Road traffic		Transport, England
1951	Road traffic	1994	Road traffic
1952	Road traffic	1995	Road traffic
1953	Road traffic	1996	Road traffic
1954	Senior courts of England and Wales	1997	Road traffic
	County courts, England and Wales	1998	Road traffic
1955	County courts, England and Wales	1999	Energy
1956 (C.77)	Criminal law, England and Wales	2000 (C.79)	Coast protection, England and Wales
1957	Rehabilitation of offenders, England and Wales		Environmental protection, England and Wales
1958	Civil aviation		Flood risk management, England and Wales
1959	Civil aviation		
1960	Police, England and Wales		Water industry, England and Wales
1961	Police, England and Wales	2001	Road traffic
1962	Road traffic	2002	Road traffic
1963	Police, England and Wales	2003	Road traffic
1964	Road traffic	2004	Road traffic
1965	Police, England and Wales	2005	Road traffic
1966 (C.78)	Prevention and suppression of terrorism	2006	Road traffic
		2007	Public bodies
1967	Road traffic		Family law
1968	Road traffic		

2008	Education, England	2048 (W.239) (C.81)	Water industry, England and Wales
2009	Road traffic	2049	Road traffic
2010	Road traffic	2050	Road traffic
2011	Road traffic	2051	Education, England and Wales
2012	Road traffic	2052	Road traffic
2013	Road traffic	2053	Road traffic
2014	Road traffic	2054	Road traffic
2015	Financial services and markets	2055	Education, England
2016	Road traffic	2056	Education, England
2017	Financial services and markets	2057	Road traffic
2018	Magistrates' courts, England and Wales	2058	Immigration
2019	Road traffic	2059	Local government, England and Wales
2020	Road traffic	2060	Road traffic
2021	Road traffic	2061	Road traffic
2022	Road traffic	2062	Road traffic
2023	Road traffic	2063	Road traffic
2024	Road traffic	2064	Road traffic
2025	Road traffic	2065	Road traffic
2026	Road traffic	2066	Road traffic
2027	Road traffic	2067	Criminal law, England and Wales
2028	Road traffic	2068	Road traffic
2029 (C.80)	Town and country planning, England Housing, England	2069	Road traffic
		2070	Road traffic
2030	Town and country planning, England	2071	Road traffic
		2072	Road traffic
2031	Town and country planning, England	2073	Road traffic
		2074	Road traffic
2032 (W.236)	Road traffic, Wales	2075 (C.82)	Children and young persons, Northern Ireland Criminal law, England and Wales Investigatory powers Protection of vulnerable adults, Northern Ireland Road traffic, England and Wales
2033	Road traffic		
2034	Road traffic		
2035	Road traffic		
2036	Road traffic		
2037	Road traffic		
2038	Road traffic	2076	Road traffic
2039	Road traffic	2077	Road traffic
2040	Road traffic	2078	Road traffic
2041	Road traffic	2079	Energy conservation
2042	Road traffic	2080	Road traffic
2043	Road traffic	2081	Road traffic
2044 (W.237)	Road traffic, Wales	2082	Road traffic
2045 (W.238)	Road traffic, Wales	2083	Road traffic
2046 (L.7)	Family proceedings Senior courts of England and Wales County courts, England and Wales Magistrates' courts, England and Wales	2084	Police, England and Wales
		2085	Police, England and Wales
		2086	Road traffic
		2087	Police, England and Wales
2047	Road traffic	2088	Police, England and Wales

2089	Local government, England	2130	Road traffic
2090 (W.240)	Housing, Wales	2131	Road traffic
2091 (W.241) (C.83)	Housing, Wales	2132	Road traffic
2092 (W.242)	Highways, Wales	2133	Road traffic
2093	Road traffic	2134	Road traffic, England
2094	Road traffic	2135	Road traffic
2095	Road traffic	2136	Road traffic
2096	Road traffic	2137	Road traffic
2097	Road traffic	2138	Road traffic
2098	Road traffic	2139	Road traffic
2099	Road traffic	2140	Energy conservation, England
2100	Road traffic	2141	Road traffic
2101	Road traffic	2142	Road traffic
2102	Road traffic	2143	Road traffic
2103	Road traffic	2144	Road traffic
2104	Road traffic	2145	Road traffic
2105	Energy conservation	2146	Road traffic
2106	Energy conservation	2147	Road traffic
2107	Police	2148	Road traffic
2108	Police	2149	Road traffic
2109	Police	2150	Road traffic
2110	Civil aviation	2151	Road traffic
2111	Housing, England	2152	Road traffic
2112	Children and young persons, England and Wales Protection of vulnerable adults, England and Wales	2153	Road traffic
		2154	Road traffic
		2155	Road traffic
2113	Children and young persons, England and Wales Protection of vulnerable adults, England and Wales	2156 (W.243)	Road traffic, Wales
		2157	Children and young persons, England and Wales Protection of vulnerable adults, England and Wales
2114	Police, England and Wales		
2115 (C.84)	Licences and licensing, England and Wales	2158	Road traffic
		2159	Road traffic
2116	Road traffic	2160	Children and young persons, England and Wales Protection of vulnerable adults, England and Wales
2117	Road traffic		
2118	Road traffic		
2119	Road traffic	2161	Road traffic
2120	Road traffic	2162	Road traffic
2121	Road traffic	2163	Road traffic
2122	Road traffic	2164	Road traffic
2123	Road traffic	2165	Education, England
2124	Road traffic	2166	Education, England
2125	Customs	2167	Urban development
2126	Road traffic	2168	Children and young persons, England
2127	Road traffic		
2128	Road traffic	2169	Road traffic
2129	Road traffic	2170	Road traffic

2171	Road traffic	2217	Road traffic
2172	Road traffic	2218	Road traffic
2173	Road traffic	2219 (W.247)	Road traffic, Wales
2174	Road traffic	2220	Road traffic
2175	Road traffic	2221 (W.248)	Road traffic, Wales
2176	Road traffic	2222	Road traffic
2177	Road traffic	2223	Road traffic
2178	Road traffic	2224	Road traffic
2179 (W.244)	Road traffic, Wales	2225	Road traffic
2180	Road traffic	2226	Road traffic
2181	Road traffic	2227	Road traffic
2182	Road traffic	2228	Road traffic
2183	Road traffic	2229	Road traffic
2184 (C.85)	Equality	2230	Road traffic
2185	Road traffic	2231 (C.88)	Children and young persons, England and Wales
2186	Electronic communications		Protection of vulnerable adults, England and Wales
2187	Electronic communications		
2188	Road traffic	2232	Road traffic
2189	Road traffic	2233	Road traffic
2190	Road traffic	2234 (C.89)	Children and young persons, England and Wales
2191	Road traffic		Children and young persons, Northern Ireland
2192	Road traffic		
2193	Road traffic		Prevention and suppression of terrorism
2194	Road traffic		
2195	Road traffic		Protection of vulnerable adults, England and Wales
2196	Road traffic		Protection of vulnerable adults, Northern Ireland
2197 (C.86)	Education, England and Wales		
2198	Road traffic		Rights of the subject, England and Wales
2199	Road traffic	2235 (C.90)	Police, England and Wales
2200	Road traffic		Police, Northern Ireland
2201	Road traffic	2236	Road traffic
2202	Road traffic	2237	Road traffic
2203	Road traffic	2238	Road traffic
2204	Road traffic	2239	Road traffic
2205	Road traffic	2240	Road traffic
2206	Road traffic	2241	Road traffic
2207	Road traffic	2242	Road traffic
2208 (L.8)	Senior courts of England and Wales	2243	Road traffic
	County courts, England and Wales	2244 (W.249)	Road traffic, Wales
2209 (W.245)	Road traffic, Wales	2245	Road traffic
2210 (W.246)	Road traffic, Wales	2246	Road traffic
2211	Road traffic	2247	Road traffic
2212	Road traffic	2248	Road traffic
2213 (C.87)	Education, England and Wales	2249	Road traffic
2214	Road traffic	2250	Road traffic
2215	Road traffic	2251	Road traffic
2216	Road traffic		

2252	Road traffic	2294	Road traffic
2253	Road traffic	2295	Road traffic
2254	Road traffic	2296	Road traffic
2255 (W.250)	Road traffic, Wales	2297	Road traffic
2256	Road traffic	2298	Financial services
2257	Town and country planning, England	2299	Prevention and suppression of terrorism
2258	Road traffic		Proceeds of crime
2259	Road traffic	2300	Fees and charges
2260 (W.251)	Road traffic, Wales	2301	Companies
2261	Education, England		Limited liability partnerships
2262	Iron and steel	2302	Civil aviation
2263	Consumer protection	2303	Civil aviation
2264	Insolvency, England and Wales	2304	Road traffic
2265	Education, England	2305	Road traffic
2266	Road traffic	2306	Road traffic
2267	Merchant shipping	2307	Road traffic
2268	Electricity	2308	Road traffic
2269	Local government, England	2309	Road traffic
2270	Education, England and Wales	2310	Road traffic
2271	Police, England and Wales	2311	Road traffic
2272	Highways, England	2312	Road traffic
2273	National Health Service, England	2313	Road traffic
2274	Town and country planning, England	2314	Road traffic
2275	Town and country planning, England	2315	Road traffic
		2316	Road traffic
2276	Immigration	2317	National Health Service, England
	Nationality	2318 (W.252)	Town and country planning, Wales
2277	Road traffic, England	2319 (W. 253)	Town and country planning, Wales
2278	Road traffic, England	2320	Environmental protection, England
2279	Rights of the subject, England and Wales	2321	Road traffic
		2322 (W.254)	Road traffic, Wales
2280	Social security	2323	Road traffic
2281	Clean air, England	2324	Road traffic
2282	Clean air, England	2325	Road traffic
2283	Sea fisheries, England	2326	Road traffic
2284	Infrastructure planning	2327	Road traffic
2285	Road traffic	2328	Road traffic
2286	Road traffic	2329	Road traffic
2287	Road traffic	2330	Civil aviation
2288	Road traffic	2331	Road traffic
2289	Road traffic	2332	Road traffic
2290	Licences and licensing, England and Wales	2333	Road traffic
		2334	Road traffic
2291	Road traffic	2335	Companies
2292	Road traffic	2336	National assistance services, England
2293	Road traffic		

2337	Civil aviation	2380	Family law
2338	Road traffic	2381	Road traffic
2339	Road traffic	2382	Road traffic
2340	Road traffic	2383	Road traffic
2341	Road traffic	2384	Road traffic
2342	Road traffic	2385	Road traffic
2343	Road traffic	2386	Road traffic
2344	Road traffic	2387	Highways, England
2345	Road traffic	2388	Road traffic
2346	Road traffic	2389 (W.256)	Road traffic, Wales
2347	Road traffic	2390	Road traffic
2348	Road traffic	2391	Road traffic
2349	Road traffic	2392	Road traffic
2350	Road traffic	2393	Value added tax
2351	Road traffic	2394	Dangerous drugs, England and Wales
2352	Road traffic		Dangerous drugs, Scotland
2353	Road traffic	2395	Stamp duty land tax
2354	Road traffic	2396	Stamp duty land tax
2355	Road traffic	2397	Terms and conditions of employment
2356	Road traffic		
2357	Road traffic	2398	Public bodies
2358	Road traffic	2399	Road traffic
2359	Road traffic	2400	Electricity
2360	Road traffic		Gas
2361	Road traffic	2401	Public bodies
2362	Road traffic	2402	Road traffic
2363	Road traffic	2403 (W.257)	Animals, Wales
2364	Road traffic	2404	Debt management and relief
2365	Road traffic	2405	Companies
2366	Road traffic	2406	Environmental protection
2367	Road traffic		Public bodies
2368	Road traffic	2407	Environmental protection
2369	Road traffic		Public bodies
2370	Civil aviation	2408 (W.258)	Road traffic, Wales
2371	National Health Service, England	2409 (W.259)	Road traffic, Wales
2372	Town and country planning, England	2410 (W.260)	Road traffic, Wales
		2411 (W.261) (C.93)	Mental health, England and Wales
2373 (C.91)	Criminal procedure, England and Wales	2412 (C.94)	Legal services, England and Wales
			Criminal law, England and Wales
2374 (C.92)	Coroners, England and Wales		Rehabilitation of offenders
	Criminal procedure, England and Wales	2413	Terms and conditions of employment
	Defence	2414	Electricity
2375	Civil aviation		Gas
2376	Civil aviation	2415	Road traffic
2377 (W.255)	Road traffic, Wales	2416	Road traffic
2378	Police, England and Wales	2417	Road traffic
2379	Social security	2418	Road traffic

2419	Road traffic	2465	Road traffic
2420 (C.95)	Local government, England	2466	Equality
2421	Local government, England	2467	Road traffic
2422	Road traffic	2468	Road traffic
2423	Road traffic	2469	Road traffic
2424	Road traffic	2470	Road traffic
2425	Road traffic	2471	Road traffic
2426	Road traffic	2472	Road traffic
2427	Road traffic	2473	Road traffic
2428	Road traffic	2474	Road traffic
2429	Road traffic	2475	Road traffic
2430	Road traffic	2476	Road traffic
2431	Road traffic	2477	Road traffic
2432	Road traffic	2478 (W.270)	Representation of the people, Wales
2433	Road traffic	2479	Police, England and Wales
2434	Road traffic	2480 (C.97)	Pensions
2435	Road traffic	2481	Road traffic
2436	Road traffic	2482	Road traffic
2437	Road traffic	2483	Road traffic
2438	Road traffic	2484	Road traffic
2439	Road traffic	2485	Road traffic
2440	Road traffic	2486	Road traffic
2441	Road traffic	2487	Road traffic
2442	Road traffic	2488	Children and young persons, England
2443	Road traffic	2489	Road traffic
2444 (W.262)	Road traffic, Wales	2490	Road traffic
2445 (W.263)	Road traffic, Wales	2491	Road traffic
2446 (W.264)	Road traffic, Wales	2492	Road traffic
2447 (W.265)	Road traffic, Wales	2493	Road traffic
2448 (W.266)	Road traffic, Wales	2494 (W.271)	Road traffic, Wales
2449	Road traffic	2495 (W.272)	Road traffic, Wales
2450	Road traffic	2496	Road traffic
2451	Road traffic	2497	Road traffic
2452	Road traffic	2498 (W.273)	Road traffic, Wales
2453 (W.267) (C.96)	Children and young persons, Wales	2499 (W.274) (C.98)	Road traffic, Wales
2454	Road traffic	2500	Excise
2455	Road traffic	2501	Road traffic
2456	Road traffic	2502	Road traffic
2457	Road traffic	2503	Road traffic
2458 (W.268)	Road traffic, Wales	2504	Police, England and Wales
2459	Road traffic	2505	Defence
2460	Road traffic	2506 (W.275)	Road traffic, Wales
2461 (W.269)	Road traffic, Wales	2507 (W.276)	Road traffic, Wales
2462	Road traffic	2508	Road traffic
2463	Children and young persons, England	2509	Road traffic
2464	Road traffic	2510	Road traffic

2511	Road traffic
2512	Road traffic
2513	Road traffic
2514	Road traffic
2515	Road traffic
2516 (C.99)	Constitutional law
	Devolution, Scotland
2517	Road traffic
2518	Road traffic
2519	Road traffic
2520	Road traffic
2521 (C.100)	Children and young persons, England and Wales
	Children and young persons, Northern Ireland
	Protection of vulnerable adults, England and Wales
	Protection of vulnerable adults, Northern Ireland
2522	Children and young persons, England and Wales
	Protection of vulnerable adults, England and Wales
2523 (C.101)	Family law
	Social security
2524	Criminal law
2525 (W. 277)	Road traffic, Wales
2526	Road traffic
2527	Road traffic
2528	Road traffic
2529	Road traffic
2530 (C.102)	Social security
2531	Road traffic
2532	Education, England
2533	Transport and works, England
2534	Road traffic
2535	Road traffic
2536	Road traffic
2537	Road traffic
2538	Road traffic
2539 (W.278)	Local government, Wales
2540	Road traffic
2541	Highways, England
2542	Road traffic
2543	Road traffic
2544	Road traffic
2545	Road traffic
2546	Medicines
	Fees and charges
2547	Highways, England
2548	Highways, England
2549	Highways, England
2550	Licences and licensing, England and Wales
2551	Licences and licensing, England and Wales
2552	Housing, England
2553	Police, England and Wales
2554	Financial services and markets
2555 (W.279)	Children and young persons, Wales
2556 (W.280)	Road traffic, Wales
2557 (W.281)	Road traffic, Wales
2558	Road traffic
2559	United Nations
2560	Immigration
2561	Road traffic
2562	Road traffic
2563 (L.19)	Magistrates' courts, England and Wales
2564	Road traffic
2565	Road traffic
2566	Road traffic
2567	Public health
2568	Social security
2569	Northern Ireland
	Social security, Northern Ireland
2570	National Health Service, England
2571 (W.282)	Sea fisheries, Wales
2572 (W.283)	National Health Service, Wales
2573	Landlord and tenant, England
2574 (C.103)	Criminal law
2575	Social security
2576	Education, England
2577	Road traffic
2578	Road traffic
2579	Road traffic
2580	Road traffic
2581	Road traffic
2582	Road traffic
2583	Road traffic
2584	Road traffic
2585	Road traffic
2586	Road traffic
2587	Social security
2588	Housing, England
2589	Geneva conventions
2590	Ministers of the Crown
2591	Police

2592	United Nations	2634 (W.286)	Road traffic, Wales
2593	Immigration	2635	Infrastructure planning
2594	Criminal law	2636	Merchant shipping
2595	Northern Ireland Constitutional law	2637	Road traffic
		2638	Road traffic
2596	Overseas territories	2639	Road traffic
2597	Education, England Children and young persons, England	2640	Road traffic
		2641	Road traffic
		2642	Road traffic
2598	Police	2643	Road traffic
2599 (C.104)	Housing, England	2644	Road traffic
2600 (W.284)	Road traffic, Wales	2645	Road traffic
2601	Housing, England	2646	Road traffic
2602	Income tax Corporation tax	2647 (C.105)	Public health, England
		2648	Road traffic
2603	Civil aviation	2649	Road traffic
2604	Civil aviation	2650	Road traffic
2605	Coroners, Wales	2651	Road traffic
2606	Police, England and Wales	2652	Road traffic
2607	Merchant shipping	2653	Road traffic
2608	Merchant shipping	2654	Public bodies
2609	Merchant shipping	2655 (W.287)	Education, Wales
2610	Merchant shipping	2656 (W.288)(C.106)	Education, Wales
2611	Merchant shipping	2657 (C.107)	Health care and associated professions National Health Service, England Social care
2612	Social security Tax credits		
2613	Town and country planning, England		
		2658	Public health, England
2614	Road traffic	2659	Local government, England Road traffic, England
2615	Road traffic		
2616	Road traffic	2660	Criminal law, England
2617	Road traffic	2661	Environmental protection
2618	Road traffic	2662	Road traffic
2619	Food, England	2663	Road traffic
2620	Road traffic	2664	Road traffic
2621	Road traffic	2665	Animals, England
2622	Road traffic	2666	Police
2623	Road traffic	2667	Police
2624	Road traffic	2668	Police
2625	Housing, England	2669	Police, England and Wales
2626	Road traffic	2670 (C.108)	Licences and licensing, England and Wales
2627	Road traffic		
2628	Road traffic	2671	Road traffic
2629	Animals, England	2672	Health care and associated professions
2630	Police, England and Wales		
2631	Police, England and Wales	2673	Road traffic
2632	Police, England and Wales	2674	Road traffic
2633 (W.285)	Road traffic, Wales	2675 (W.289)	Mobile homes, Wales

2676 (W.290)	Local government, Wales	2717	Road traffic
2677	Family law	2718	Road traffic
2678	Family law	2719	Road traffic
2679	Transport and works, England Transport, England	2720	Road traffic
		2721	Road traffic
2680	Social security	2722	Road traffic
2681	Criminal law, England and Wales	2723	Transport Energy
2682	Civil aviation		
2683	Legal aid and advice, England and Wales	2724	Road traffic
		2725	Road traffic
2684	Legal aid and advice, England and Wales	2726	Road traffic
		2727	Road traffic
2685	Health care and associated professions	2728	Road traffic
2686 (C.109)	Health care and associated professions	2729 (W.292)	Sea fisheries, Wales
		2730	Licences and licensing, England and Wales
2687	Legal aid and advice, England and Wales	2731	Value added tax
2688	Electronic communications Broadcasting	2732	Police, England and Wales Transport, England and Wales Infrastructure planning
2689	Civil aviation		
2690	Broadcasting	2733	Police, England and Wales Terms and conditions of employment
2691	Pensions		
2692	Road traffic		
2693	Road traffic	2734	Police, England and Wales
2694	Road traffic	2735	Road traffic
2695	Road traffic	2736	Road traffic
2696	Road traffic	2737	Road traffic
2697	Road traffic	2738	Road traffic
2698	Road traffic	2739	Road traffic
2699	Road traffic	2740	Electricity, England and Wales
2700	Road traffic	2741 (W.293)	Road traffic, Wales
2701	Road traffic	2742 (W.294)	Road traffic, Wales
2702	Road traffic	2743	Social security
2703	Road traffic	2744	Road traffic
2704	Road traffic	2745	Health care and associated professions
2705 (W.291)	Food, Wales	2746	Coinage
2706	Highways, England	2747	Ministers of the Crown
2707	Plant health	2748	United Nations
2708	Road traffic	2749	Overseas territories
2709	Criminal law, England and Wales	2750	Overseas territories
2710	Highways, England	2751	Overseas territories
2711	Medicines	2752	European Union
2712	Police, England and Wales	2753	Overseas territories
2713	Road traffic	2754	Health care and associated professions
2714	Road traffic		
2715	Road traffic	2755	National Health Service, England
2716	Road traffic	2756	Social security

2757	Road traffic	2800	Road traffic
2758	Road traffic	2801	Road traffic
2759	Road traffic	2802	Road traffic
2760	Road traffic	2803	Road traffic
2761	Criminal law	2804	Road traffic
2762	Road traffic	2805	Road traffic
2763	Road traffic	2806 (L.10)	Family proceedings Senior courts of England and Wales County courts, England and Wales Magistrates' courts, England and Wales
2764	Road traffic		
2765	Road traffic		
2766	Road traffic		
2767 (W.295)	Road traffic, Wales	2807	Road traffic
2768	Police, England and Wales	2808	Road traffic
2769	Local government, England	2809	Road traffic
2770 (C.110)	Criminal law	2810	Road traffic
2771	Road traffic	2811	Police, England and Wales Pensions, England and Wales
2772	Road traffic		
2773	Road traffic	2812	Social security
2774	Road traffic	2813	Children and young persons, England and Wales
2775	Road traffic		
2776	Road traffic	2814	Judgments
2777	Road traffic	2815	Road traffic
2778	Road traffic	2816	Road traffic
2779	Road traffic	2817	Electronic communications
2780	Road traffic	2818 (W.296)	Road traffic, Wales
2781	Road traffic	2819 (W.297)	Road traffic, Wales
2782	Electricity	2820 (W.298)	Road traffic, Wales
2783	Road traffic	2821	Road traffic
2784	Road traffic	2822	Criminal law, England and Wales
2785	Family law	2823	Road traffic
2786	Excise	2824	Criminal law, England and Wales Children and young persons, England and Wales Defence
2787	Value added tax		
2788	Climate change		
2789	Government resources and accounts	2825	Road traffic
2790	International development	2826	Road traffic
2791	National Health Service, England and Wales National Health Service, Scotland Health and personal social services, Northern Ireland	2827	Road traffic
		2828	Road traffic
		2829	Road traffic
		2830	Road traffic
2792	Road traffic	2831	Road traffic
2793	Road traffic	2832	Road traffic
2794	Road traffic	2833	Road traffic
2795	Road traffic	2834	Road traffic
2796	Road traffic	2835	Road traffic
2797	Road traffic	2836	Road traffic
2798	Consumer credit	2837	Road traffic
2799	Road traffic	2838	Road traffic

2839	Road traffic	2883	Road traffic
2840	Revenue and customs	2884	Land charges, England and Wales
2841	Road traffic	2885	Council tax, England
2842	Road traffic	2886	Council tax, England
2843	Road traffic	2887	Road traffic
2844	Road traffic	2888	Road traffic
2845	Road traffic	2889	Road traffic
2846	Road traffic	2890 (L.11)	Tribunals and inquiries
2847	Road traffic	2891	National Health Service, England
2848	Road traffic	2892 (C.111)	Police, England and Wales
2849	Road traffic	2893	Road traffic
2850	Road traffic	2894	Road traffic
2851	Road traffic	2895	Road traffic
2852	Road traffic	2896	Road traffic
2853	Road traffic	2897	Animals, England and Wales
2854	Local government, England	2898	Excise
2855 (S.1)	Constitutional law Devolution, Scotland Forestry	2899	Road traffic
		2900	Official secrets
		2901 (C.112)	Criminal law, England and Wales
2856	Highways, England	2902	Income tax
2857	Road traffic	2903	Inheritance tax
2858	Road traffic	2904	Prevention of nuclear proliferation
2859	Road traffic	2905 (C.113)	Criminal law, England and Wales
2860	Road traffic	2906 (C.114)	Criminal law, England and Wales Defence
2861	Road traffic		
2862	Control of Fuel and Electricity	2907	Value added tax
2863	Road traffic	2908	Road traffic
2864	Road traffic	2909	Criminal law
2865	Road traffic	2910	Land charges, England and Wales
2866	Road traffic	2911	Electricity, England and Wales
2867	Road traffic	2912	Road traffic
2868	Road traffic	2913 (C.115)	Local government, England and Wales
2869	Road traffic		
2870	Road traffic	2914	Council tax, England
2871	Road traffic	2915	Road traffic
2872	Road traffic	2916	Road traffic
2873	Road traffic	2917	Road traffic
2874	Road traffic	2918	Road traffic
2875	Road traffic	2919	Defence
2876	Immigration	2920	Town and country planning, England
2877	Road traffic	2921 (C. 116)	Defence
2878	Road traffic	2922	Plant health, England
2879	Fire and rescue services, England	2923	Road traffic
2880	Road traffic	2924	Road traffic
2881	Road traffic	2925	Road traffic
2882	Health care and associated professions	2926	Road traffic

2927	Road traffic	2972	Road traffic
2928	Road traffic	2973	Road traffic
2929	Road traffic	2974	Road traffic
2930	Road traffic	2975	Community infrastructure levy, England and Wales
2931	Road traffic		
2932	Animals, England	2976	Civil partnership
2933	Bank levy	2977	Financial services and markets
2934 (W.299)	Road traffic, Wales	2978 (W.304)	Public health, Wales
2935	Local government, England		Food contamination
2936	Road traffic	2979	Road traffic
2937	Prevention and suppression of terrorism	2980	Transport and works, England Transport, England
2938 (C.117)	Road traffic	2981	Road traffic
2939	Road traffic	2982	Road traffic
2940	Income tax	2983	Road traffic
2941 (W.300)	Animals, Wales	2984	Local government, England
2942	Road traffic	2985	Local government, England
2943	Road traffic	2986	Local government, England
2944	Road traffic	2987	Legal services, England and Wales
2945	Road traffic	2988	Fire and rescue services, England Pensions, England
2946 (C.118)	Social security		
2947 (W.301)	Road traffic, Wales	2989	Housing, England
2948 (W.302)	Road traffic, Wales	2990	Prisons, England
2949 (W.303)	Road traffic, Wales	2991	Education, England
2950	National Health Service, England	2992	Equality
2951	Value added tax	2993	Local government, England
2952	Pensions	2994	Social security
2953	Value added tax	2995 (W.305)	Road traffic, Wales
2954	Police, England and Wales Pensions, England and Wales	2996	Mental health, England National Health Service, England
2955	Road traffic	2997	Road traffic
2956	Road traffic	2998	Road traffic
2957	Road traffic	2999	Climate change levy
2958	Road traffic	3000	Road traffic
2959	Road traffic	3001 (C.119)	Public records Freedom of information
2960	Road traffic	3002	Family law
2961	Road traffic	3003	Contracting out, England
2962	Education, England	3004	Income tax
2963	Consumer protection	3005	Energy conservation
2964	Council tax, England	3006	Children and young persons, England and Wales
2965	Council tax, England		
2966	Road traffic		Children and young persons, Northern Ireland
2967	Road traffic		
2968	Road traffic		Police, England and Wales
2969	Road traffic		Protection of vulnerable adults, England and Wales
2970	Electronic communications		
2971	Road traffic		Protection of vulnerable adults, Northern Ireland

3007	Terms and conditions of employment	3049	Climate change levy
3008	Corporation tax	3050	Animals
3009	Corporation tax	3051	Civil aviation
3010	Immigration	3052	Civil aviation
3011 (C.120)	Charities, England and Wales	3053	Highways, England
3012	Charities, England and Wales	3054	Civil aviation
3013	Charities, England and Wales	3055	Excise
3014	Charities, England and Wales	3056	Excise
3015 (C.121)	Excise	3057	Police, England and Wales Pensions, England and Wales
3016	Police, England and Wales	3058	Police, England and Wales
3017	Excise	3059	Education, England
3018	Electricity Gas	3060	Value added tax
3019	Financial services and markets	3061	Family proceedings Senior courts of England and Wales County courts, England and Wales Magistrates' courts, England and Wales
3020	Excise		
3021	Energy conservation		
3022 (W.306)	Landlord and tenant, Wales	3062	Recovery of taxes
3023 (W.307)	Social care, Wales	3063	Civil partnership
3024	Corporation tax	3064	Overseas territories
3025	Health care and associated professions	3065	Overseas territories
		3066	Overseas territories
3026	Health care and associated professions	3067	Overseas territories
		3068	Overseas territories
3027	Agriculture, England	3069	Overseas territories
3028	Public records	3070	Defence
3029	Freedom of information	3071	Defence Income tax Inheritance tax Stamp duty land tax
3030	Climate change		
3031 (W.308)	Road traffic, Wales		
3032	Environmental protection		
3033	Plant health, England		
3034 (W.309)	Road traffic, Wales	3072	National Health Service, England
3035	Seeds, England	3073	Constitutional law Devolution, Scotland
3036 (W.310)	Rating and valuation, Wales		
3037	Income tax	3074	Northern Ireland
3038	Climate change	3075	Capital gains tax Corporation tax Income tax
3039	Animals		
3040	Social security		
3041	Corporation tax	3076	Capital gains tax Corporation tax Income tax
3042 (C.122)	Family law Social security		
		3077	Capital gains tax Corporation tax Income tax
3043	Corporation tax		
3044	Corporation tax		
3045	Corporation tax	3078	Capital gains tax Corporation tax Income tax
3046	Town and country planning, England		
		3079	Taxes
3047	Income tax	3080	Harbours, docks, piers and ferries
3048	Disabled persons, England	3081	National Health Service, England

3082	Environmental protection	3120	Road traffic
3083	Pensions	3121	Road traffic
3084	Urban development, England	3122	Financial services and markets
3085	Council tax, England	3123	Libraries
3086	Council tax, England	3124	Building and buildings, England
3087	Council tax, England	3125	London government
3088	Defence, England	3126	Road traffic
3089 (L.12)	Senior courts of England and Wales Magistrates' courts, England and Wales	3127	Road traffic
		3128	Justices of the Peace, England and Wales
3090 (C.123)	Social security	3129	Harbours, docks, piers and ferries
3091	Legal services, England and Wales	3130	Road traffic
3092	Legal services, England and Wales	3131	Road traffic
3093 (W.311)	Agriculture, Wales	3132	Road traffic
3094	National Health Service, England Local government, England	3133	Road traffic
		3134	Children and young persons, England
3095 (W.312)	Welsh language, Wales	3135	Government resources and accounts
3096	Social security	3136	Highways, England
3097 (W.313)	Education, Wales	3137	Road traffic
3098	Legal aid and advice, England and Wales	3138	Electronic communications
		3139	Road traffic
3099	Urban development, England	3140	Road traffic
3100	Regulatory reform	3141	Road traffic
3101 (W.314)	Public bodies, England and Wales Water industry, England and Wales Fees and charges, England and Wales	3142	Road traffic
		3143 (W.315)	Plant health, Wales
		3144 (W.316)	Council tax, Wales
		3145 (W.317)	Council tax, Wales
3102	Highways, England	3146	Road traffic
3103	Highways, England	3147	Road traffic
3104	Highways, England	3148	Road traffic
3105	Highways, England	3149	Road traffic
3106	Highways, England	3150	Local government, England
3107	Highways, England	3151	Road traffic
3108	Road traffic	3152	Merchant shipping
3109	Town and country planning, England	3153	Oil tax
		3154	Road traffic
3110	Consumer protection	3155	Road traffic
3111	Corporation tax	3156	Road traffic
3112	Employment and training, England and Wales	3157	Road traffic
3113	Local government, England	3158	Education, England
3114	Road traffic	3159	Offshore installations
3115	Road traffic	3160	Road traffic
3116	Road traffic	3161	Road traffic
3117	Road traffic	3162	Road traffic
3118	Building and buildings, England and Wales	3163	Road traffic
3119	Building and buildings, England and Wales	3164	Road traffic

3165	Road traffic	3209	Road traffic
3166	Road traffic	3210	Road traffic
3167	Road traffic	3211	Road traffic
3168	Road traffic	3212	Road traffic
3169	Road traffic	3213	Road traffic
3170	Building and buildings Energy conservation	3214	Road traffic
		3215	Road traffic
3171	Health care and associated professions	3216	Road traffic
		3217 (W.319)	Road traffic, Wales
3172 (W.318)	Sea fisheries, Wales	3218 (W.320)	Road traffic, Wales
3173 (C. 124)	Public procurement, England and Wales	3219 (W.321)	Road traffic, Wales
		3220 (W.322)	Road traffic, Wales
3174	Education, England	3221 (W.323)	Road traffic, Wales
3175	Road traffic	3222	Road traffic
3176	Road traffic	3223	Road traffic
3177	Road traffic	3224	Road traffic
3178	Road traffic	3225	Road traffic
3179	Road traffic	3226	Road traffic
3180	Road traffic	3227	Road traffic
3181	Road traffic	3228	Road traffic
3182	Road traffic	3229	Road traffic
3183	Road traffic	3230	Road traffic
3184	Road traffic	3231	Road traffic
3185	Road traffic	3232	Representation of the people
3186	Road traffic	3233	Road traffic
3187	Road traffic	3234	Road traffic
3188	Road traffic	3235	Road traffic
3189	Road traffic	3236	Road traffic
3190	Road traffic	3237	Road traffic
3191	Road traffic	3238	Road traffic
3192	Road traffic	3239	Road traffic
3193	Road traffic	3240	Road traffic
3194	Road traffic	3241	Road traffic
3195	Road traffic	3242	Road traffic
3196	Road traffic	3243	Road traffic
3197	Road traffic	3244	Road traffic
3198	Road traffic	3245	Road traffic
3199	Road traffic	3246	Road traffic
3200	Road traffic	3247	Road traffic
3201	Road traffic	3248	Road traffic
3202	Road traffic	3249 (W.324)	Road traffic, Wales
3203	Road traffic	3250	Road traffic
3204	Road traffic	3251	Road traffic
3205	Road traffic	3252	Road traffic
3206	Road traffic	3253	Road traffic
3207	Road traffic	3254	Road traffic
3208	Road traffic		

3255	Road traffic	3301	Road traffic
3256	Road traffic	3302	Road traffic
3257	Road traffic	3303	Road traffic
3258	Road traffic	3304	Road traffic
3259	Road traffic	3305	Road traffic
3260	Local government, England	3306	Road traffic
3261	Road traffic	3307	Road traffic
3262	Road traffic	3308	Road traffic
3263	Road traffic	3309	Road traffic
3264	Road traffic	3310	Road traffic
3265	Road traffic	3311	Road traffic
3266	Road traffic	3312	Road traffic
3267	Road traffic	3313	Road traffic
3268	Road traffic	3314	Road traffic
3269	Road traffic	3315	Road traffic
3270	Road traffic	3316	Road traffic
3271	Road traffic	3317	Road traffic
3272	Road traffic	3318	Road traffic
3273	Road traffic	3319	Road traffic
3274	Road traffic	3320	Road traffic
3275	Road traffic	3321	Road traffic
3276	Road traffic	3322	Road traffic
3277	Road traffic	3323	Road traffic
3278	Road traffic	3324	Road traffic
3279	Road traffic	3325	Road traffic
3280	Road traffic	3326	Road traffic
3281	Road traffic	3327	Road traffic
3282	Road traffic	3328	Road traffic
3283	Road traffic	3329	Road traffic
3284	Road traffic	Unnumbered (W.)	Animals, Wales
3285	Road traffic		Destructive animals, Wales
3286	Road traffic		
3287	Road traffic		
3288	Road traffic		
3289	Road traffic		
3290	Road traffic		
3291	Road traffic		
3292	Road traffic		
3293	Road traffic		
3294	Road traffic		
3295	Road traffic		
3296	Road traffic		
3297	Road traffic		
3298	Road traffic		
3299	Road traffic		
3300	Road traffic		

Subsidiary Numbers

Commencement orders (bring an act or part of an act into operation)

46 (W.10)(C.1)

57 (C. 2)

68 (C.3)

84 (C.4)

191 (W.30) (C.5)

193 (W.31) (C.6)

223 (W. 37)(C. 7)

264 (C.8)	1531 (C.57)
284 (W.48) (C.9)	1553 (W.206) (C.58)
320 (W.51) (C.10)	1569 (C.59)
411 (C. 11)	1615 (C.60)
584 (C.12)	1649 (C.61)
601 (C.13)	1651 (C.62)
628 (C.14)	1662 (C.63)
669 (C. 15)	1681 (C.64)
682 (C.16)	1682 (C.65)
683 (C.17)	1697 (C.66)
736 (C.18)	1710 (C.67)
739 (W.99) (C.19)	1724 (C.68)
802 (W.111)(C.20)	1766 (C.69)
806 (W.113) (C.21)	1810 (C.70)
825 (C.22)	1831 (C.71)
863 (C.23)	1841(C.72)
873 (C.24)	1887 (C.73)
879 (C.25)	1896 (C. 74)
887 (W.118) (C.26)	1901 (C.75)
896 (C.27)	1902 (C.76)
898 (C. 28)	1956 (C.77)
911 (C.29)	1966 (C.78)
924 (C.30)	2000 (C.79)
969 (W.126)(C.31)	2029 (C.80)
1008 (C.32)	2048 (W.239) (C.81)
1087 (C.33)	2075 (C.82)
1095 (C.34)	2091 (W.241) (C.83)
1096 (W.135)(C.35)	2115 (C.84)
1100 (C.36)	2184 (C.85)
1121 (C.37)	2197 (C.86)
1129 (C.38)	2213 (C.87)
1164 (C.39)	2231 (C.88)
1187 (W.145) (C.40)	2234 (C.89)
1205 (C.41)	2235 (C.90)
1246 (C.42)	2373 (C.91)
1256 (C.43)	2374 (C.92)
1263 (C.44)	2411 (W.261) (C.93)
1288 (W.165)(C.45)	2412 (C.94)
1312 (C.46)	2420 (C.95)
1319 (C.47)	2453 (W.267) (C.96)
1320 (C.48)	2480 (C.97)
1356 (C.49)	2499 (W.274) (C.98)
1357 (C.50)	2516 (C.99)
1358 (C.51)	2521 (C.100)
1397 (W.169) (C.52)	2523 (C.101)
1423 (W.176)(C.53)	2530 (C.102)
1432 (C.54)	2574 (C.103)
1440 (C.55)	2599 (C.104)
1463 (C.56)	2647 (C.105)

2656 (W.288) (C.106)
2657 (C.107)
2670 (C.108)
2686 (C.109)
2770 (C.110)
2892 (C.111)
2901 (C.112)
2905 (C.113)
2906 (C.114)
2913 (C.115)
2921 (C.116)
2938 (C.117)
2946 (C.118)
3001 (C.119)
3011 (C.120)
3015 (C.121)
3042 (C.122)
3090 (C.123)
3173 (C. 124)

Instruments relating to fees or procedure in courts in England and Wales

500 (L. 1)
505 (L.2)
679 (L.3)
1275 (L.4)
1363 (L.5)
1726 (L.6)
2046 (L.7)
2208 (L.8)
2563 (L.19)
2806 (L.10)
2890 (L.11)
3089 (L.12)

Instruments that extend only to Scotland

2855 (S.1)

Instruments that extend only to Wales

5 (W.1)
6 (W.2)
7 (W.3)
11 (W.4)
14 (W.5)
19 (W.6)
21 (W.7)
22 (W.8)
23 (W.9)

46 (W.10)(C.1)
48 (W.11)
49 (W.12)
59 (W.13)
60 (W.14)
64 (W.15)
65 (W.16)
111 (W.17)
141 (W.18)
143 (W.19)
144 (W.20)
157 (W.21)
162 (W.22)
163 (W.23)
165 (W.24)
166 (W.25)
167 (W.26)
168 (W.27)
169 (W.28)
170 (W.29)
191 (W.30) (C.5)
193 (W.31) (C.6)
197 (W.32)
202 (W.33)
204 (W.34)
205 (W.35)
210 (W.36)
223 (W. 37)(C. 7)
244 (W.38)
245 (W.39)
247 (W.40)
248 (W.41)
267 (W.42)
273 (W.43)
274 (W.44)
275 (W.45)
282 (W.46)
283 (W.47)
284 (W.48) (C.9)
285 (W.49)
309 (W.50)
320 (W.51) (C.10)
321 (W.52)
322 (W.53)
337 (W.54)
338 (W.55)
339 (W.56)
345 (W.57)

346 (W.58)	792 (W.107)
347 (W.59)	793 (W.108)
365 (W.60)	800 (W.109)
366 (W.61)	801 (W.110)
367 (W.62)	802 (W.111)(C.20)
394 (W.63)	805 (W.112)
395 (W.64)	806 (W.113) (C.21)
396 (W.65)	826 (W.114)
422 (W.66)	842 (W.115)
423 (W.67)	843 (W.116)
426 (W.68)	870 (W.117)
427 (W.69)	887 (W.118) (C.26)
428 (W.70)	899 (W.119)
429 (W.71)	934 (W.120)
430 (W.72)	935 (W.121)
445 (W.73)	942 (W.122)
446 (W.74)	944 (W.123)
464 (W.75)	945 (W.124)
465 (W.76)	948 (W.125)
466 (W.77)	969 (W.126)(C.31)
467 (W.78)	972 (W.127)
481 (W.79)	974 (W.128)
485 (W.80)	975 (W.129)
486 (W.81)	990 (W.130)
521 (W.82)	1036 (W.131)
531 (W.83)	1059 (W.132)
559 (W.84)	1085 (W.133)
561 (W.85)	1086 (W.134)
614 (W.86)	1096 (W.135)(C.35)
629 (W.87)	1130 (W.136)
631 (W.88)	1143 (W.137)
675 (W.89)	1145 (W.138)
676 (W.90)	1156 (W.139)
678 (W.91)	1166 (W.140)
684 (W.92)	1168 (W.141)
685 (W.93)	1169 (W.142)
686 (W.94)	1170 (W.143)
699 (W.95)	1171 (W.144)
724 (W.96)	1187 (W.145) (C.40)
737 (W.97)	1189 (W.146)
738 (W.98)	1195 (W.147)
739 (W.99) (C.19)	1198 (W.148)
740 (W.100)	1233 (W.149)
746 (W.101)	1235 (W.150)
752 (W.102)	1238 (W.151)
753 (W.103)	1244 (W.152)
777 (W.104)	1248 (W.153)
789 (W.105)	1259 (W.154)
791 (W.106)	1260 (W.155)

1261 (W.156)	1522 (W.204)
1262 (W.157)	1545 (W.205)
1265 (W.158)	1553 (W.206) (C.58)
1268 (W.159)	1597 (W.207)
1269 (W.160)	1629 (W.208)
1270 (W.161)	1630 (W.209)
1272 (W.162)	1636 (W.210)
1285 (W.163)	1642 (W.211)
1287 (W.164)	1643 (W.212)
1288 (W.165)(C.45)	1648 (W.213)
1305 (W.166)	1664 (W.214)
1346 (W.167)	1674 (W.215)
1387 (W.168)	1675 (W.216)
1397 (W.169) (C.52)	1689 (W.217)
1398 (W.170)	1692 (W.218)
1400 (W.171)	1694 (W.219)
1412 (W.172)	1695 (W.220)
1417 (W.173)	1703 (W.221)
1418 (W.174)	1712 (W.222)
1419 (W.175)	1718 (W.223)
1423 (W.176)(C.53)	1720 (W.224)
1427 (W.177)	1765 (W.225)
1428 (W.178)	1782 (W.226)
1429 (W.179)	1797 (W.227)
1456 (W.180)	1819 (W.228)
1457 (W.181)	1893 (W.229)
1482 (W.182)	1903 (W.230)
1484 (W.183)	1904 (W.231)
1485 (W.184)	1905 (W.232)
1486 (W.185)	1911 (W.233)
1487 (W.186)	1912 (W.234)
1488 (W.187)	1913 (W.235)
1490 (W.188)	2032 (W.236)
1491 (W.189)	2044 (W.237)
1492 (W.190)	2045 (W.238)
1493 (W.191)	2048 (W.239) (C.81)
1494 (W.192)	2090 (W.240)
1495 (W.193)	2091 (W.241) (C.83)
1496 (W.194)	2092 (W.242)
1497 (W.195)	2156 (W.243)
1498 (W.196)	2179 (W.244)
1499 (W.197)	2209 (W.245)
1503 (W.198)	2210 (W.246)
1504 (W.199)	2219 (W.247)
1505 (W.200)	2221 (W.248)
1518 (W.201)	2244 (W.249)
1520 (W.202)	2255 (W.250)
1521 (W.203)	2260 (W.251)

2318 (W.252)
2319 (W.253)
2322 (W.254)
2377 (W.255)
2389 (W.256)
2403 (W.257)
2408 (W.258)
2409 (W.259)
2410 (W.260)
2411 (W.261) (C.93)
2444 (W.262)
2445 (W.263)
2446 (W.264)
2447 (W.265)
2448 (W.266)
2453 (W.267) (C.96)
2458 (W.268)
2461 (W.269)
2478 (W.270)
2494 (W.271)
2495 (W.272)
2498 (W.273)
2499 (W.274) (C.98)
2506 (W.275)
2507 (W.276)
2525 (W.277)
2539 (W.278)
2555 (W.279)
2556 (W.280)
2557 (W.281)
2571 (W.282)
2572 (W.283)
2600 (W.284)
2633 (W.285)
2634 (W.286)
2655 (W.287)
2656 (W.288) (C.106)
2675 (W.289)

2676 (W.290)
2676 (W.290)
2705 (W.291)
2729 (W.292)
2741 (W.293)
2742 (W.294)
2767 (W.295)
2818 (W.296)
2819 (W.297)
2820 (W.298)
2934 (W.299)
2941 (W.300)
2947 (W.301)
2948 (W.302)
2949 (W.303)
2978 (W.304)
2995 (W.305)
3022 (W.306)
3023 (W.307)
3031 (W.308)
3034 (W.309)
3036 (W.310)
3093 (W.311)
3095 (W.312)
3097 (W.313)
3101 (W.314)
3143 (W.315)
3144 (W.316)
3145 (W.317)
3172 (W.318)
3217 (W.319)
3218 (W.320)
3219 (W.321)
3220 (W.322)
3221 (W.323)
3249 (W.324)
Unnumbered (W.)

Scottish Legislation

Acts of the Scottish Parliament

Property Factors (Scotland) Act 2011:2011 asp 8 (correction slip). - 1 sheet: 30 cm. - Correction slip (to ISBN 9780105901723) dated July 2012. - *Free*

Sexual Offences (Scotland) Act 2009:2009 asp 9 (correction slip). - 1 sheet: 30 cm. - Correction slip (to ISBN 9780105901426) dated July 2012. - *Free*

Acts of the Scottish Parliament 2012

Agricultural Holdings (Amendment) (Scotland) Act 2012:2012 asp 6. - [4]p.: 30 cm. - Royal assent, 12th July 2012. An Act of the Scottish Parliament to amend the law governing succession to agricultural tenancies and the review or variation of rent under such tenancies. Explanatory notes have been produced to assist in the understanding of this Act and are available separately (ISBN 9780105911685). - 978-0-10-590185-3 *£4.00*

Alcohol (Minimum Pricing) (Scotland) Act 2012:2012 asp 4. - [8]p.: 30 cm. - Royal assent, 29th June 2012. An Act of the Scottish Parliament to make provision about the price at which alcohol may be sold from licensed premises. Explanatory notes have been produced to assist in the understanding of this Act are available separately (ISBN 9780105911654). - 978-0-10-590184-6 *£4.00*

Budget (Scotland) Act 2012:2012 asp 2. - [16]p.: 30 cm. - Royal assent, 14th March 2011. An Act of the Scottish Parliament to make provision, for financial year 2012/13, for the use of resources by the Scottish Administration and certain bodies whose expenditure is payable out of the Scottish Consolidated Fund, for authorising the payment of sums out of the Fund and for the maximum amounts of borrowing by certain statutory bodies; to make provision, for financial year 2013/14, for authorising the payment of sums out of the Fund on a temporary basis. - 978-0-10-590182-2 *£5.75*

Criminal Cases (Punishment and Review) (Scotland) Act 2012:2012 asp 7. - [2], 9p.: 30 cm. - Royal assent, 26th July 2012. An Act of the Scottish Parliament to amend the rules about the punishment part of non-mandatory life sentences imposed in criminal cases and to amend the rules about the disclosure of information obtained by the Scottish Criminal Cases Review Commission. Explanatory notes have been produced to assist in the understanding of this Act and are available separately (ISBN 9780105911678). - 978-0-10-590187-7 *£5.75*

Land Registration etc. (Scotland) Act 2012:2012 asp 5. - vi, 94p.: 30 cm. - Royal assent, 10th July 2012. An Act of the Scottish Parliament to reform and restate the law on the registration of rights to land in the land register; to enable electronic conveyancing and registration of electronic documents in the land register; to provide for the closure of the Register of Sasines in due course; to make provision about the functions of the Keeper of the Registers of Scotland; to allow electronic documents to be used for certain contracts, unilateral obligations and trusts that must be constituted by writing; to provide about the formal validity of electronic documents and for their registration. Explanatory notes have been produced to assist in the understanding of this Act and are available separately (ISBN 9780105911708). - 978-0-10-590186-0 *£16.00*

Local Government Finance (Unoccupied Properties etc.) (Scotland) Act 2012:2012 asp 11. - [8]p.: 30 cm. - Royal assent, 5th December 2012. An Act of the Scottish Parliament to amend the law regarding non-domestic rates and council tax in respect of unoccupied properties; and to repeal certain provisions that allow grants to be made to local authorities to meet housing needs in their areas. Explanatory notes have been produced to assist in the understanding of this Act and are available separately (ISBN 9780105911715). - 978-0-10-590191-4 *£4.00*

Long Leases (Scotland) Act 2012:2012 asp 9. - iv, 47p.: 30 cm. - Royal assent, 7th August 2012. An Act of the Scottish Parliament to convert certain long leases into ownership; to provide for the conversion into real burdens of certain rights and obligations under such leases; to provide for payment to former owners of land of compensation for loss of it on conversion. Explanatory notes have been produced to assist in the understanding of this Act and will be available separately. - 978-0-10-590189-1 *£9.75*

National Library of Scotland Act 2012:2012 asp 3. - ii, 13p.: 30 cm. - Royal assent, 21st June 2012. An Act of the Scottish Parliament to make further provision about the name, functions and governance of the National Library of Scotland. Explanatory notes have been produced to assist in the understanding of this Act and are available separately (ISBN 9780105911647). - 978-0-10-590183-9 *£5.75*

Offensive Behaviour at Football and Threatening Communications (Scotland) Act 2012:2012 asp 1. - [2], 8p.: 30 cm. - Royal assent, 19 January 2012. An Act of the Scottish Parliament to create offences concerning offensive behaviour in relation to certain football matches, and concerning the communication of certain threatening material. Explanatory notes have been produced to assist in the understanding of this Act and are available separately (ISBN9780105911623). - 978-0-10-590181-5 *£5.75*

Police and Fire Reform (Scotland) Act 2012:2012 asp 8. - vi, 132p.: 30 cm. - Royal assent, 7th August 2012. An Act of the Scottish Parliament to make provision about policing; to make provision about fire and rescue services. Explanatory notes have been produced to assist in the understanding of this Act and will be available separately. - 978-0-10-590188-4 £20.00

Welfare Reform (Further Provision) (Scotland) Act 2012:2012 asp 10. - 3p.: 30 cm. - Royal assent, 7th August 2012. An Act of the Scottish Parliament to enable the Scottish Ministers to make provision by regulations in consequence of the Welfare Reform Act 2012 (in respect of matters other than reserved matters). Explanatory notes have been produced to assist in the understanding of this Act and are available separately (ISBN 9780105911692). - 978-0-10-590190-7 £4.00

Acts of the Scottish Parliament - Explanatory notes 2012

Alcohol (Minimum Pricing) (Scotland) Act 2012 (asp 4):explanatory notes. - [12]p.: 30 cm. - These notes relate to the Alcohol (Minimum Pricing) (Scotland) Act 2012 (asp 4) (ISBN 9780105901846) which received Royal assent on 29 June 2012. - 978-0-10-591165-4 £5.75

Agricultural Holdings (Amendment) (Scotland) Act 2012 (asp 6):explanatory notes. - [8]p.: 30 cm. - These notes relate to the Agricultural Holdings (Amendment) (Scotland) Act 2012 (asp 6) (ISBN 9780105901853) which received Royal assent on 12 July 2012. - 978-0-10-591168-5 £4.00

Criminal Cases (Punishment and Review) (Scotland) Act 2012 (asp 7):explanatory notes. - 9p.: 30 cm. - These Notes relate to the Criminal Cases (Punishment and Review) (Scotland) Act 2012 (asp 7) (ISBN 9780105901877) which received Royal assent on 26 July 2012. - 978-0-10-591167-8 £5.75

Domestic Abuse (Scotland) Act 2011 (asp 13): explanatory notes. - 8p.: 30 cm. - These Notes relate to the Domestic Abuse (Scotland) Act 2011 (asp 13) (ISBN 9780105901778) which received Royal assent on 20 April 2011. - 978-0-10-591166-1 £5.75

Land Registration etc. (Scotland) Act 2012 (asp 5): explanatory notes. - 53p.: 30 cm. - These Notes relate to the Land Registration etc. (Scotland) Act 2012 (asp 5) (ISBN 9780105901860) which received Royal assent on 10 July 2012. - 978-0-10-591170-8 £9.75

Local Government Finance (Unoccupied Properties etc.) (Scotland) Act 2012 (asp 11):explanatory notes. - [8]p.: 30 cm. - These Notes relate to the Local Government Finance (Unoccupied Properties etc.) (Scotland) Act 2012 (asp 11) (ISBN 9780105901914) which received Royal assent on 5 December 2012. - 978-0-10-591171-5 £5.75

National Library (Scotland) Act 2012 (asp 3): explanatory notes. - 13p.: 30 cm. - These Notes relate to the National Library of Scotland Act 2012 (asp 3) (ISBN 9780105901839) which received Royal assent on 21June 2012. - 978-0-10-591164-7 £5.75

Offensive Behaviour at Football and Threatening Communications (Scotland) Act 2012 (asp 1): explanatory notes. - [12]p.: 30 cm. - These notes relate to the Offensive Behaviour at Football and Threatening Communications (Scotland) Act 2012 (asp 1) (ISBN 9780105901815) which received Royal assent on 19 January 2012. - 978-0-10-591162-3 £5.75

Property Factors (Scotland) Act 2011 (asp 8): explanatory notes. - 21p.: 30 cm. - These Notes relate to the Property Factors (Scotland) Act 2011 (asp 8) (ISBN 9780105901723) which received Royal assent on 7 April 2011. - 978-0-10-591172-2 £5.75

Welfare Reform (Further Provision) (Scotland) Act 2012 (asp 10):explanatory notes. - [12]p.: 30 cm. - These notes relate to the Welfare Reform (Further Provision) (Scotland) Act 2012 (asp 10) (ISBN 9780105901907) which received Royal assent on 7 August 2012. - 978-0-10-591169-2 £5.75

Wildlife and Natural Environment (Scotland) Act 2011 (asp 6):explanatory notes. - 40p.: 30 cm. - These Notes relate to the Wildlife and Natural Environment (Scotland) Act 2011 (asp 6) (ISBN 9780105901709) which received Royal assent on 7 April 2011. - 978-0-10-591163-0 £9.75

Other statutory publications

Office of the Queen's Printer for Scotland.

The acts of the Scottish Parliament 2011: with lists of the acts, tables and index. - ix, 681p.: hdbk: 31 cm. - 978-0-11-840530-0 £97.50

Scottish Statutory Instruments

By Subject Heading

Adult support

The Community Care and Health (Scotland) Act 2002 (Incidental Provision) (Adult Support and Protection) Order 2012 No. 2012/66. Enabling power: Community Care and Health (Scotland) Act 2002, s. 24. - Issued: 02.03.2012. Made: 28.02.2012. Laid before the Scottish Parliament: 01.03.2012. Coming into force: 31.03.2012. Effect: None. Territorial extent & classification: S. General. - 4p.: 30 cm. - 978-0-11-101641-1 £4.00

Adults with incapacity

The Adults with Incapacity (Public Guardian's Fees) (Scotland) Amendment Regulations 2012 No. 2012/289. - Enabling power: Adults with Incapacity (Scotland) Act 2000, s. 7 (2). - Issued: 09.11.2012. Made: 30.10.2012. Laid before the Scottish Parliament: 31.10.2012. Coming into force: In accord. with reg. 1. Effect: S.S.I. 2008/52 amended. Territorial extent & classification: S. General. - 12p.: 30 cm. - 978-0-11-101825-5 £5.75

The Adults with Incapacity (Requirements for Signing Medical Treatment Certificates) (Scotland) Amendment Regulations 2012 No. 2012/170. - Enabling power: Adults with Incapacity (Scotland) Act 2000, s. 47 (1A) (b). - Issued: 01.06.2012. Made: 29.05.2012. Laid before the Scottish Parliament: 31.05.2012. Coming into force: 02.07.2012. Effect: S.S.I. 2007/105 amended. Territorial extent & classification: S. General. - 4p.: 30 cm. - 978-0-11-101731-9 £4.00

Agriculture

The Leader Grants (Scotland) Amendment Regulations 2012 No. 2012/182. - Enabling power: European Communities Act 1972, s. 2 (2). - Issued: 06.06.2012. Made: 29.05.2012. Laid before the Scottish Parliament: 31.05.2012. Coming into force: 02.07.2012. Effect: S.S.I. 2008/66 amended. Territorial extent & classification: S. General. - 4p.: 30 cm. - 978-0-11-101744-9 £4.00

The Less Favoured Area Support Scheme (Scotland) Amendment Regulations 2011 No. 2012/24. - Enabling power: European Communities Act 1972, s. 2 (2). - Issued: 31.01.2011. Made: 26.01.2012. Laid before the Scottish Parliament: 30.01.2012. Coming into force: 09.03.2012. Effect: S.S.I. 2010/273 amended. Territorial extent & classification: S. General. - 4p.: 30 cm. - 978-0-11-101599-5 £4.00

The Poultry Health Scheme (Fees) (Scotland) Regulations 2012 No. 2012/176. - Enabling power: Finance Act 1973, s. 56 (1) (2). - Issued: 06.06.2012. Made: 29.05.2012. Laid before the Scottish Parliament: 31.05.2012. Coming into force: 01.07.2012. Effect: None. Territorial extent & classification: S. General. - EC note: These Regulations set the fees for approvals for the purposes of the poultry health scheme established under Council Directive 2009/158/EC which is partially transposed by the Trade in Animals and Related Products (Scotland) Regs 2012, schedule 2, part 1, para. 3. - 4p.: 30 cm. - 978-0-11-101733-3 £4.00

The Rural Development Contracts (Rural Priorities) (Scotland) Amendment Regulations 2012 No. 2012/307. - Enabling power: European Communities Act 1972, s. 2 (2). - Issued: 19.11.2012. Made: 15.11.2012. Laid before the Scottish Parliament: 16.11.2012. Coming into force: 01.01.2013. Effect: S.S.I. 2008/100 amended. Territorial extent & classification: S. General. - EC note: These Regulations amend S.S.I. 2008/100 which introduce measures laying down general rules governing Community support for rural development. - 4p.: 30 cm. - 978-0-11-101844-6 £4.00

The Rural Payments (Appeals) (Scotland) Amendment Regulations 2012 No. 2012/143. - Enabling power: European Communities Act 1972, s. 2 (2), sch. 2, para. 1A. - Issued: 16.05.2012. Made: 10.05.2012. Laid before the Scottish Parliament: 14.05.2012. Coming into force: 12.06.2012. Effect: S.S.I. 2009/376 amended. Territorial extent & classification: S. General. - EC note: These Regulations amend the Rural Payments (Appeals) (Scotland) Regulations 2009 which provide for a right of review and appeal in relation to certain decisions of the Scottish Ministers. - 8p.: 30 cm. - 978-0-11-101698-5 £5.75

The Specified Products from China (Restriction on First Placing on the Market) (Scotland) Amendment Regulations 2012 No. 2012/3. - Enabling power: European Communities Act 1972, s. 2 (2). - Issued: 13.01.2012. Made: 10.01.2012. Laid before the Scottish Parliament: 12.01.2012. Coming into force: 12.01.2012. Effect: S.S.I. 2008/148 amended. Territorial extent & classification: S. General. - EC note: These Regulations amend SSI 2008/148 in order to implement Commission Implementing Decision 2011/884/EU on emergency measures regarding unauthorised genetically modified rice in rice products originating from China and repealing Decision 2008/289/EC. The Decision provides for import restrictions that previously applied to Bt 63 genetically modified rice to apply, with modifications, to all unauthorised genetically modified rice. - 4p.: 30 cm. - 978-0-11-101581-0 £4.00

The Trade in Animals and Related Products (Scotland) Amendment Order 2012 No. 2012/198. - Enabling power: European Communities Act 1972, s. 2 (2), sch. 2, para. 1A & Animal Health Act 1981, s. 72. - Issued: 25.06.2012. Made: 20.06.2012. Laid before the Scottish Parliament: 22.06.2012. Coming into force: 01.07.2012. Effect: S.S.I. 2008/11; 2012/177 amended. Territorial extent & classification: S. General. - This instrument has been made to correct defects in S.S.I. 2012/177 (ISBN 9780111017340) and is being issued free of charge to all known recipients of that instrument. Partially revoked by SSI 2012/199 (9780111017562). - 4p.: 30 cm. - 978-0-11-101758-6 £4.00

The Trade in Animals and Related Products (Scotland) Regulations 2012 No. 2012/177. - Enabling power: European Communities Act 1972, s. 2 (2), sch. 2, para. 1A & Finance Act 1973, s. 56 (1) (2). - Issued: 06.06.2012. Made: 29.05.2012. Laid before the Scottish Parliament: 31.05.2012. Coming into force: 01.07.2012. Effect: S.I. 1974/2211; 1980/14 & S.S.I. 2007/537; 2008/11; 2009/85, 173, 446 amended & S.I. 1996/3124, 3125; 1997/3023; 1999/157; S.S.I. 2001/257; 2006/450; 2007/1, 194, 304, 375; 2008/155; 2009/227, 228; 2010/225, 343 revoked. Territorial extent & classification: S. General. - This SSI has been corrected by SSI 2012/198 (ISBN 9780111017586) which is being sent free of charge to all known recipients of 2012/177. EC note: These Regulations implement four European Directives in Scotland: Council Directive 89/662/EEC; Council Directive 90/425/EEC; Council Directive 91/496/EEC (amending Directives 89/662/EEC, 90/425/EEC and 90/675/EEC) and Council Directive 97/78/EC. With correction slip dated July 2012. Partially revoked by SSI 2012/199 (9780111017562). - 30p.: 30 cm. - 978-0-11-101734-0 £5.75

Animals

The Food Protection (Emergency Prohibitions) (Radioactivity in Sheep) and the Export of Sheep (Prohibition) Revocation (Scotland) Order 2012 No. 2012/263. - Enabling power: Animal Health Act 1981, s. 11 & Food and Environment Protection Act 1985, ss. 1 (1) (2), 24 (3). - Issued: 01.10.2012. Made: 26.09.2012. Laid before the Scottish Parliament: 28.09.2012. Coming into force: 01.10.2012. Effect: S.I. 1991/20, 58, 2766; 1993/13; 1994/50; 1995/48; 1996/31; 1997/62; 1998/82; 1999/80 revoked in relation to Scotland & S.S.I. 2001/313; 2003/375; 2004/48; 2005/71; 2006/52; 2007/38; 2008/63 revoked. Territorial extent & classification: S. General. - 4p.: 30 cm. - 978-0-11-101797-5 £4.00

The Poultry Health Scheme (Fees) (Scotland) Regulations 2012 No. 2012/176. - Enabling power: Finance Act 1973, s. 56 (1) (2). - Issued: 06.06.2012. Made: 29.05.2012. Laid before the Scottish Parliament: 31.05.2012. Coming into force: 01.07.2012. Effect: None. Territorial extent & classification: S. General. - EC note: These Regulations set the fees for approvals for the purposes of the poultry health scheme established under Council Directive 2009/158/EC which is partially transposed by the Trade in Animals and Related Products (Scotland) Regs 2012, schedule 2, part 1, para. 3. - 4p.: 30 cm. - 978-0-11-101733-3 £4.00

The Prohibited Procedures on Protected Animals (Exemptions) (Scotland) Amendment Regulations 2012 No. 2012/40. - Enabling power: Animal Health and Welfare (Scotland) Act 2006, s. 20 (5) (b). - Issued: 14.02.2011. Made: 08.02.2012. Coming into force: 09.02.2012, in accord. with reg. 1. Effect: S.S.I. 2010/387 amended. Territorial extent & classification: S. General. - Supersedes draft SSI (ISBN 9780111015599) issued on 16.12.2011. - 4p.: 30 cm. - 978-0-11-101619-0 £4.00

The Trade in Animals and Related Products (Scotland) Amendment Order 2012 No. 2012/198. - Enabling power: European Communities Act 1972, s. 2 (2), sch. 2, para. 1A & Animal Health Act 1981, s. 72. - Issued: 25.06.2012. Made: 20.06.2012. Laid before the Scottish Parliament: 22.06.2012. Coming into force: 01.07.2012. Effect: S.S.I. 2008/11; 2012/177 amended. Territorial extent & classification: S. General. - This instrument has been made to correct defects in S.S.I. 2012/177 (ISBN 9780111017340) and is being issued free of charge to all known recipients of that instrument. Partially revoked by SSI 2012/199 (9780111017562). - 4p.: 30 cm. - 978-0-11-101758-6 £4.00

The Trade in Animals and Related Products (Scotland) Regulations 2012 No. 2012/177. - Enabling power: European Communities Act 1972, s. 2 (2), sch. 2, para. 1A & Finance Act 1973, s. 56 (1) (2). - Issued: 06.06.2012. Made: 29.05.2012. Laid before the Scottish Parliament: 31.05.2012. Coming into force: 01.07.2012. Effect: S.I. 1974/2211; 1980/14 & S.S.I. 2007/537; 2008/11; 2009/85, 173, 446 amended & S.I. 1996/3124, 3125; 1997/3023; 1999/157; S.S.I. 2001/257; 2006/450; 2007/1, 194, 304, 375; 2008/155; 2009/227, 228; 2010/225, 343 revoked. Territorial extent & classification: S. General. - This SSI has been corrected by SSI 2012/198 (ISBN 9780111017586) which is being sent free of charge to all known recipients of 2012/177. EC note: These Regulations implement four European Directives in Scotland: Council Directive 89/662/EEC; Council Directive 90/425/EEC; Council Directive 91/496/EEC (amending Directives 89/662/EEC, 90/425/EEC and 90/675/EEC) and Council Directive 97/78/EC. With correction slip dated July 2012. Partially revoked by SSI 2012/199 (9780111017562). - 30p.: 30 cm. - 978-0-11-101734-0 £5.75

Animals: Animal health

The African Horse Sickness (Scotland) Order 2012 No. 2012/178. - Enabling power: European Communities Act 1972, s. 2 (2) & Animal Health Act 1981, ss. 1, 7 (1), 8 (1), 15 (4), 17 (1), 23, 25, 28, 35 (1) (3), 83 (2), 87 (2), 88 (2). - Issued: 06.06.2012. Made: 29.05.2012. Laid before the Scottish Parliament: 31.05.2012. Coming into force: 01.07.2012. Effect: S.I. 1992/3159; 1996/2628 amended. Territorial extent & classification: S. General. - EC note: This Order which applies to Scotland, implements Council directive 92/35/EEC laying down control rules and measures to combat African horse sickness. - 24p.: 30 cm. - 978-0-11-101745-6 £5.75

The Animal By-Products (Miscellaneous Amendments) (Scotland) Regulations 2012 No. 2012/179. - Enabling power: European Communities Act 1972, s. 2 (2). - Issued: 06.06.2012. Made: 29.05.2012. Laid before the Scottish Parliament: 31.05.2012. Coming into force: 01.07.2012. Effect: S.S.I. 2007/61, 62; 2011/171 amended. Territorial extent & classification: S. General. - 4p.: 30 cm. - 978-0-11-101735-7 £4.00

The Bluetongue (Scotland) Amendment Order 2012 No. 2012/184. - Enabling power: European Communities Act 1972, sch. 2, para. 1A & Animal Health Act 1981, s. 72. - Issued: 07.06.2012. Made: 31.05.2012. Laid before the Scottish Parliament: 06.06.2012. Coming into force: 05.06.2012. Effect: S.S.I. 2008/11 amended. Territorial extent & classification: S. General. - EC note: In consequence of the amendment of the Commission Regulation 1266/2007 by Commission Implementing Regulation 456/2012 the obligation to report any suspicion of bluetongue is now contained in point 2.1 of Annex 1 to the Commission Regulation rather than the first indent of that point. Art. 2 of this Order substitutes a new article 8 of the principal Order containing the correct reference. Revoked by SSI 2012/199 (ISBN 9780111017562)- 4p.: 30 cm. - 978-0-11-101737-1 £4.00

The Bluetongue (Scotland) Order 2012 No. 2012/199. - Enabling power: European Communities Act 1972, sch. 2, para. 1A & Animal Health Act 1981, ss. 1, 7 (1), 8 (1), 15 (4), 17 (1), 23, 25, 28, 32 (2), 35 (3), 72, 83 (2), 87 (2), 88 (2). - Issued: 25.06.2012. Made: 20.06.2012. Laid before the Scottish Parliament: 22.06.2012. Coming into force: 24.09.2012. Effect: S.S.I. 2012/177, 198 partially revoked & S.S.I. 2008/11, 234, 327; 2012/184 revoked. Territorial extent & classification: S. General. - EC note: Implements Council Directive 2000/75/EC laying down specific provisions for the control and eradication of bluetongue and enforces Commission Regulation 1266/2007. - 16p.: 30 cm. - 978-0-11-101756-2 £5.75

The Bovine Viral Diarrhoea (Scotland) Order 2012 No. 2012/78. - Enabling power: Animal Health Act 1981, ss. 1, 8 (1), 83 (2), 88 (2). - Issued: 07.03.2012. Made: 29.02.2012. Laid before the Scottish Parliament: 02.03.2012. Coming into force: 01.04.2012. Effect: None. Territorial extent & classification: S. General. - Revoked by SSI 2013/3 (ISBN 9780111019030) with saving. - 16p.: 30 cm. - 978-0-11-101654-1 £5.75

Animals: Prevention of cruelty

The Welfare of Animals at the Time of Killing (Scotland) Amendment Regulations 2012 No. 2012/355. - Enabling power: European Communities Act 1972, s. 2 (2). - Issued: 24.12.2012. Made: 19.12.2012. Laid before the Scottish Parliament: 21.12.2012. Coming into force: 01.01.2013. Effect: S.S.I. 2012/321 amended. Territorial extent & classification: S. General. - This SSI has been made to correct defects in SSI 2012/321 (ISBN 9780111018491) and is being issued free of charge to all known recipients of that instrument. - 4p.: 30 cm. - 978-0-11-101891-0 £4.00

The Welfare of Animals at the Time of Killing (Scotland) Regulations 2012 No. 2012/321. - Enabling power: European Communities Act 1972, s. 2 (2) & Finance Act 1973, s. 56 (1). - Issued: 27.11.2012. Made: 22.11.2012. Laid before the Scottish Parliament: 23.11.2012. Coming into force: 01.01.2013. Effect: S.I. 1995/731 modified & partially revoked & 1980 c. 13; S.S.I. 2006/44, 45; 2009/262 amended & 1967 c. 24 repealed & 1980 c. 13; 1984 c. 40; 1991 c. 30; 1994 c. 40 partially repealed & S.I. 1996/2235; 1999/400, 1820 & S.S.I. 2000/62; 2006/536 partially revoked. Territorial extent & classification: S. General. - This SSI is being corrected by SSI 2012/355 (ISBN 9780111018910) which is being sent free of charge to all known recipients of 2012/321. EC note: These Regulations make provision in Scotland for the administration and enforcement of Council Regulation 1099/2009 on the protection of animals at the time of killing and certain national rules maintained under art. 26 (1) (2). - 28p.: 30 cm. - 978-0-11-101849-1 £5.75

Building and buildings

The Building (Scotland) Amendment Regulations 2012 No. 2012/209. - Enabling power: Building (Scotland) Act 2003, ss. 1, 2, 54 (2). - Issued: 29.06.2012. Made: 26.06.2012. Laid before the Scottish Parliament: 28.06.2012. Coming into force: 09.01.2013. Effect: S.S.I. 2004/406 amended. Territorial extent & classification: S. General. - 4p.: 30 cm. - 978-0-11-101763-0 £4.00

The Energy Performance of Buildings (Scotland) Amendment (No. 2) Regulations 2012 No. 2012/208. - Enabling power: European Communities Act 1972, s. 2 (2). - Issued: 29.06.2012. Made: 26.06.2012. Laid before the Scottish Parliament: 28.06.2012. Coming into force: 30.09.2012, 01.10.2012 & 09.01.2013, in accord. with reg. 1. Effect: S.S.I. 2008/309; 2012/190 amended. Territorial extent & classification: S. General. - EC note: These Regulations transpose the further provisions of Directive 2010/31//EU that require legislative changes to the 2008 Regulations (SSI 2008/309). - 12p.: 30 cm. - 978-0-11-101762-3 £5.75

The Energy Performance of Buildings (Scotland) Amendment (No. 3) Regulations 2012 No. 2012/315. - Enabling power: European Communities Act 1972, s. 2 (2). - Issued: 23.11.2012. Made: 20.11.2012. Laid before the Scottish Parliament: 22.11.2012. Coming into force: 21.12.2012. Effect: S.S.I. 2008/309; 2012/190, 208 amended. Territorial extent & classification: S. General. - 12p.: 30 cm. - 978-0-11-101846-0 £5.75

The Energy Performance of Buildings (Scotland) Amendment Regulations 2012 No. 2012/190. - Enabling power: European Communities Act 1972, s. 2 (2). - Issued: 11.06.2012. Made: 06.06.2012. Laid before the Scottish Parliament: 08.06.2012. Coming into force: 01.10.2012. Effect: S.S.I. 2008/309 amended. Territorial extent & classification: S. General. - 4p.: 30 cm. - 978-0-11-101749-4 £4.00

Charities

The Charities Reorganisation (Scotland) Amendment Regulations 2012 No. 2012/220. - Enabling power: Charities and Trustee Investment (Scotland) Act 2005, ss. 39 (2) (3), 103 (2). - Issued: 10.07.2012. Made: 04.07.2012. Laid before the Scottish Parliament: 06.07.2012. Coming into force: 01.11.2012. Effect: S.S.I. 2007/204 amended. Territorial extent & classification: S. General. - 4p.: 30 cm. - 978-0-11-101775-3 £4.00

The Charities Restricted Funds Reorganisation (Scotland) Regulations 2012 No. 2012/219. - Enabling power: Charities and Trustee Investment (Scotland) Act 2005, ss. 43A (3) (4), 43B (5), 43D, 103 (2). - Issued: 10.07.2012. Made: 04.07.2012. Laid before the Scottish Parliament: 06.07.2012. Coming into force: 01.11.2012. Effect: None. Territorial extent & classification: S. General. - With correction slip dated September 2012. - 8p.: 30 cm. - 978-0-11-101774-6 £5.75

The Public Services Reform (Scotland) Act 2010 (Commencement No. 6) Order 2012 No. 2012/218 (C.19). - Enabling power: Public Services Reform (Scotland) Act 2010, s. 134 (7). Bringing into operation various provisions of the 2010 Act on 01.11.2012. - Issued: 10.07.2012. Made: 04.07.2012. Laid before the Scottish Parliament: 06.07.2012. Effect: None. Territorial extent & classification: S. General. - 4p.: 30 cm. - 978-0-11-101773-9 £4.00

Children and young persons

The Adoption and Children (Scotland) Act 2007 (Commencement No. 4, Transitional and Savings Provisions) Amendment Order 2012 No. 2012/99. - Enabling power: Adoption and Children Act 2007, ss. 116 (1), 117 (2) (3). - Issued: 22.03.2012. Made: 20.03.2012. Laid before the Scottish Parliament: 22.03.2012. Coming into force: 07.05.2012. Effect: SSI 2009/267 (C.22) amended. Territorial extent & classification: S. General. - 4p.: 30 cm. - 978-0-11-101667-1 £4.00

The Children's Hearings (Scotland) Act 2011 (Appeals against Dismissal by SCRA) Regulations 2012 No. 2012/337. - Enabling power: Children's Hearing (Scotland) Act 2011, s. 195 (2), sch. 3, paras 8 (8), 12 (1) (3). - Issued: 12.12.2012. Made: 06.12.2012. Laid before the Scottish Parliament: 10.12.2012. Coming into force: In accord. with reg. 1. Effect: None. Territorial extent & classification: S. General. - 8p.: 30 cm. - 978-0-11-101872-9 £5.75

The Children's Hearings (Scotland) Act 2011 (Child Protection Emergency Measures) Regulations 2012 No. 2012/334. - Enabling power: Children's Hearing (Scotland) Act 2011, s. 57. - Issued: 12.12.2012. Made: 06.12.2012. Laid before the Scottish Parliament: 10.12.2012. Coming into force: In accord. with reg. 1. Effect: None. Territorial extent & classification: S. General. - 8p.: 30 cm. - 978-0-11-101869-9 £4.00

The Children's Hearings (Scotland) Act 2011 (Commencement No. 3) Order 2012 No. 2012/1 (C.1). - Enabling power: Children's Hearings (Scotland) Act 2011, s. 206 (2). Bringing into operation various provisions of the 2011 Act on 31.01.2012 and 26.03.2012, in accord. with art. 1. - Issued: 12.01.2012. Made: 09.01.2012. Laid before the Scottish Parliament: 11.01.2012. Coming into force: 31.01.2012. Effect: None. Territorial extent & classification: S. General. - With correction slip dated February 2012. - 4p.: 30 cm. - 978-0-11-101579-7 £4.00

The Children's Hearings (Scotland) Act 2011 (Commencement No. 4) Order 2012 No. 2012/23 (C.6). - Enabling power: Children's Hearings (Scotland) Act 2011, s. 206 (2). Bringing into operation various provisions of the 2011 Act on 13.02.2012, in accord. with art. 2. - Issued: 31.01.2012. Made: 26.01.2012. Laid before the Scottish Parliament: 30.01.2012. Coming into force: 13.02.2012. Effect: None. Territorial extent & classification: S. General. - 2p.: 30 cm. - 978-0-11-101598-8 £4.00

The Children's Hearings (Scotland) Act 2011 (Commencement No. 5) Order 2012 No. 2012/246 (C.20). - Enabling power: Children's Hearings (Scotland) Act 2011, s. 206 (2). Bringing into operation various provisions of the 2011 Act on 19.09.2012, in accord. with art. 2. - Issued: 07.09.2012. Made: 04.09.2012. Laid before the Scottish Parliament: 05.09.2012. Coming into force: 19.09.2012. Effect: None. Territorial extent & classification: S. General. - 4p.: 30 cm. - 978-0-11-101784-5 £4.00

The Children's Hearings (Scotland) Act 2011 (Commencement No. 6) Order 2012 No. 2012/252 (C.23). - Enabling power: Children's Hearings (Scotland) Act 2011, s. 206 (2). Bringing into operation various provisions of the 2011 Act on 19.09.2012, in accord. with art. 2. - Issued: 17.09.2012. Made: 12.09.2012. Laid before the Scottish Parliament: 14.09.2012. Effect: None. Territorial extent & classification: S. General. - 2p.: 30 cm. - 978-0-11-101788-3 £4.00

The Children's Hearings (Scotland) Act 2011 (Rights of Audience of the Principal Reporter) Regulations 2012 No. 2012/335. - Enabling power: Children's Hearing (Scotland) Act 2011, ss. 19 (1), 195 (2). - Issued: 12.12.2012. Made: 06.12.2012. Laid before the Scottish Parliament: 10.12.2012. Coming into force: In accord. with reg. 1. Effect: None. Territorial extent & classification: S. General. - 4p.: 30 cm. - 978-0-11-101870-5 £4.00

The Children's Hearings (Scotland) Act 2011 (Safeguarders: Further Provision) Regulations 2012 No. 2012/336. - Enabling power: Children's Hearing (Scotland) Act 2011, ss. 34, 195. - Issued: 12.12.2012. Made: 06.12.2012. Laid before the Scottish Parliament: 10.12.2012. Coming into force: In accord. with reg. 1. Effect: None. Territorial extent & classification: S. General. - 8p.: 30 cm. - 978-0-11-101871-2 £5.75

The Children's Hearings (Scotland) Act 2011 (Safeguarders Panel) Regulations 2012 No. 2012/54. - Enabling power: Children's Hearing (Scotland) Act 2011, s. 32 (2). - Issued: 24.02.2012. Made: 21.02.2012. Laid before the Scottish Parliament: 23.02.2012. Coming into force: 26.03.2012. Effect: None. Territorial extent & classification: S. General. - 8p.: 30 cm. - 978-0-11-101631-2 £4.00

Climate change

The Forestry Commissioners (Climate Change Functions) (Scotland) Order 2012 No. 2012/77. - Enabling power: Climate Change (Scotland) Act 2009, ss. 59 (1), 96 (2) (3). - Issued: 06.03.2012. Made: 28.02.2012. Coming into force: 01.03.2012 in accord. with art. 1. Effect: 1967 c.10 amended. Territorial extent & classification: S. General. - Supersedes draft SSI 2012 (ISBN 9780111015780) issued on 29.12.2011. - 4p.: 30 cm. - 978-0-11-101653-4 £4.00

Council tax

The Council Tax (Administration and Enforcement) (Scotland) Amendment Order 2012 No. 2012/338. - Enabling power: Local Government Finance Act 1992, ss. 113 (1), 116 (1), sch. 2, paras 1 (1), 2 (2) (4) (a) (e) (5), 4 (2) (5B). - Issued: 12.12.2012. Made: 06.12.2012. Laid before the Scottish Parliament: 10.12.2012. Coming into force: 09.02.2013. Effect: S.I. 1992/1332; amended. Territorial extent & classification: S. General. - 4p.: 30 cm. - 978-0-11-101873-6 £4.00

The Council Tax (Exempt Dwellings) (Scotland) Amendment Order 2012 No. 2012/339. - Enabling power: Local Government Finance Act 1992, ss. 72 (6) (7), 113 (2). - Issued: 12.12.2012. Made: 06.12.2012. Laid before the Scottish Parliament: 10.12.2012. Coming into force: 01.04.2012. Effect: S.I. 1997/728 amended. Territorial extent & classification: S. General. - 4p.: 30 cm. - 978-0-11-101874-3 £4.00

The Council Tax Reduction (Scotland) Regulations 2012 No. 2012/303. - Enabling power: Local Government Finance Act 1992, s. 113 (1) (2), sch. 2, para. 1. - Issued: 14.11.2012. Made: 07.11.2012. Laid before the Scottish Parliament: 09.11.2012. Coming into force: 28.01.2013. Effect: S.I. 1992/1332, 1335; 1993/355; 1994/3170; 1996/430 amended. Territorial extent & classification: S. General. - 132p.: 30 cm. - 978-0-11-101838-5 £20.00

The Council Tax Reduction (State Pension Credit) (Scotland) Regulations 2012 No. 2012/319. - Enabling power: Local Government Finance Act 1992, s. 113 (1) (2), sch. 2, para. 1. - Issued: 28.11.2012. Made: 21.11.2012. Laid before the Scottish Parliament: 23.11.2012. Coming into force: 28.01.2013. Effect: None. Territorial extent & classification: S. General. - 97p.: 30 cm. - 978-0-11-101850-7 £16.00

Court of Session

Act of Sederunt (Fees of Messengers-at-Arms) (Amendment) 2012 No. 2012/8. - Enabling power: Execution of Diligence (Scotland) Act 1926, s. 6 & Court of Session Act 1988, s. 5. - Issued: 23.01.2012. Made: 17.01.2012. Laid before the Scottish Parliament: 19.01.2012. Coming into force: 22.01.2012. Effect: S.S.I. 2011/431 amended. Territorial extent & classification: S. General. - The following statement has been omitted in error from this SI: This Order has been made in consequence of a defect in S.S.I. 2011/431 (ISBN 9780111015520) and is being issued free of charge to all known recipients of that Statutory Instrument. - 4p.: 30 cm. - 978-0-11-101586-5 £4.00

Act of Sederunt (Fees of Messengers-at-Arms) (Amendment) (No. 2) 2012 No. 2012/340. - Enabling power: Execution of Diligence (Scotland) Act 1926, s. 6 & Court of Session Act 1988, s. 5 & Debtors (Scotland) Act 1987, s. 75. - Issued: 13.12.2012. Made: 10.12.2012. Laid before the Scottish Parliament: 12.12.2012. Coming into force: 28.01.2013. Effect: S.S.I. 2002/566 amended & S.S.I. 2008/366 revoked. Territorial extent & classification: S. General. - 8p.: 30 cm. - 978-0-11-101877-4 £5.75

Act of Sederunt (Registration Appeal Court) 2012 No. 2012/245. - Enabling power: Representation of the People Act 1983, s. 57 (2). - Issued: 07.09.2012. Made: 04.09.2012. Laid before the Scottish Parliament: 06.09.2012. Coming into force: 01.10.2012. Effect: S.S.I. 2010/7 revoked. Territorial extent & classification: S. General. - 2p.: 30 cm. - 978-0-11-101783-8 £4.00

Act of Sederunt (Rules of the Court of Session Amendment) (Fees of Shorthand Writers) 2012 No. 2012/100. - Enabling power: Court of Session Act 1988, s. 5. - Issued: 23.03.2012. Made: 20.03.2012. Laid before the Scottish Parliament: 22.03.2012. Coming into force: 21.05.2012. Effect: S.I. 1994/1443 amended. Territorial extent & classification: S. General. - 4p.: 30 cm. - 978-0-11-101668-8 £4.00

Act of Sederunt (Rules of the Court of Session Amendment No. 2) (Miscellaneous) 2012 No. 2012/126. - Enabling power: Court of Session Act 1988, s. 5. - Issued: 27.04.2012. Made: 24.04.2012. Laid before the Scottish Parliament: 26.04.2012. Coming into force: 28.05.2012. Effect: S.I. 1994/1443 amended. Territorial extent & classification: S. General. - 4p.: 30 cm. - 978-0-11-101687-9 £4.00

Act of Sederunt (Rules of the Court of Session Amendment No. 3) (Miscellaneous) 2012 No. 2012/189. - Enabling power: Court of Session Act 1988, ss. 5, 5A. - Issued: 11.06.2012. Made: 06.06.2012. Laid before the Scottish Parliament: 08.06.2012. Coming into force: 09.07.2012. Effect: S.I. 1994/1443 amended. Territorial extent & classification: S. General. - 8p.: 30 cm. - 978-0-11-101748-7 £5.75

Act of Sederunt (Rules of the Court of Session Amendment No. 4) (Fees of Solicitors) 2012 No. 2012/270. - Enabling power: Court of Session Act 1988, s. 5. - Issued: 09.10.2012. Made: 04.10.2012. Laid before the Scottish Parliament: 08.10.2012. Coming into force: 05.11.2012. Effect: S.I. 1994/1443 amended. Territorial extent & classification: S. General. - 4p.: 30 cm. - 978-0-11-101805-7 £4.00

Act of Sederunt (Rules of the Court of Session Amendment No. 5) (Miscellaneous) 2012 No. 2012/275. - Enabling power: Court of Session Act 1988, s. 5. - Issued: 19.10.2012. Made: 16.10.2012. Laid before the Scottish Parliament: 18.10.2012. Coming into force: 19.11.2012. Effect: S.I. 1994/1443 amended. Territorial extent & classification: S. General. - 16p.: 30 cm. - 978-0-11-101810-1 £5.75

The Court Fees (Miscellaneous Amendments) Scotland Order 2012 No. 2012/322. - Enabling power: Court of Law Fees (Scotland) Act 1895, s. 2. - Issued: 28.11.2012. Made: 22.11.2012. Laid before the Scottish Parliament: 26.11.2012. Coming into force: 09.12.2012. Effect: S.S.I. 2012/290, 291, 293 amended. Territorial extent & classification: S. General. - This SSI has been made in consequence of defects in SSI 2012/290 (ISBN 9780111018330), 2012/291 (ISBN 9780111018323) and SSI 2012/293 (ISBN 9780111018347) and is being issued free of charge to all known recipients of those instruments. - 4p.: 30 cm. - 978-0-11-101853-8 £4.00

The Court of Session etc. Fees Amendment Order 2012 No. 2012/290. - Enabling power: Court of Law Fees (Scotland) Act 1895, s. 2. - Issued: 09.11.2012. Made: 30.10.2012. Laid before the Scottish Parliament: 31.10.2012. Coming into force: In accord. with art. 1. Effect: S.I. 1997/688 amended. Territorial extent & classification: S. General. - 24p.: 30 cm. - 978-0-11-101833-0 £5.75

Criminal law

The Criminal Cases (Punishment and Review) (Scotland) Act 2012 (Commencement, Transitional and Savings) Order 2012 No. 2012/249 (C.22). - Enabling power: Criminal Cases (Punishment and review) (Scotland) Act 2012, s. 5 (2) (3). Bringing into operation various provisions of the 2012 Act on 24.09.2012. - Issued: 13.09.2012. Made: 10.09.2012. Laid before the Scottish Parliament: 12.09.2012. Effect: None. Territorial extent & classification: S. General. - 4p.: 30 cm. - 978-0-11-101786-9 £4.00

The Criminal Justice and Licensing (Scotland) Act 2010 (Commencement No. 10 and Savings Provisions) Order 2012 No. 2012/160 (C.15). - Enabling power: Criminal Justice and Licensing (Scotland) Act 2010, ss. 201 (1) (2), 206 (1). - Issued: 24.05.2012. Made: 21.05.2012. Laid before the Scottish Parliament: 23.05.2012. Coming into force: 25.06.2012. Effect: None. Territorial extent & classification: S. General. - 8p.: 30 cm. - 978-0-11-101723-4 £5.75

The Criminal Justice and Licensing (Scotland) Act 2010 (Incidental Provisions) Order 2012 No. 2012/304. - Enabling power: Criminal Justice and Licensing (Scotland) Act 2010, ss. 204. - Issued: 14.11.2012. Made: 08.11.2012. Coming into force: 09.11.2012. Effect: 2010 asp 13 amended. Territorial extent & classification: S. General. - Supersedes draft SSI (ISBN 9780111017708) issued 04.07.2012. - [2]p.: 30 cm. - 978-0-11-101839-2 £4.00

The Criminal Proceedings etc. (Reform) (Scotland) Act 2007 (Commencement No. 10) Order 2012 No. 2012/274 (C.28). - Enabling power: Criminal Proceedings etc. (Reform) (Scotland) Act 2007, s. 84 (1) (2). Bringing various provisions of the 2007 Act into operation on 01.11.2012 in accord. with art. 2. - Issued: 17.10.2012. Made: 11.10.2012. Laid before the Scottish Parliament: 15.10.2012. Coming into force: 01.11.2012. Effect: None. Territorial extent & classification: S. General. - 16p.: 30 cm. - 978-0-11-101809-5 £5.75

The Offensive Behaviour at Football and Threatening Communications (Scotland) Act 2012 (Commencement) Order 2012 No. 2012/20 (C.4). - Enabling power: Offensive Behaviour at Football and Threatening Communications (Scotland) Act 2012, s. 12 (2). Bringing various provisions of the 2012 Act into operation on 01.03.2012 in accord. with art. 2. - Issued: 27.01.2012. Made: 24.01.2012. Laid before the Scottish Parliament: 26.01.2012. Effect: None. Territorial extent & classification: S. General. - 2p.: 30 cm. - 978-0-11-101595-7 £4.00

The Sexual Offences Act 2003 (Prescribed Police Stations) (Scotland) Amendment Regulations 2012 No. 2012/50. - Enabling power: Sexual Offences Act 2003, s. 87 (1) (a). - Issued: 22.002.2012. Made: 16.02.2012. Laid: 20.02.2012. Coming into force: 02.04.2012. Effect: S.S.I. 2008/128 amended. Territorial extent & classification: S. General. - 4p.: 30 cm. - 978-0-11-101629-9 £4.00

Crofters, cottars and small landholders

The Crofting Reform (Scotland) Act 2010 (Commencement No. 3, Transitory, Transitional and Savings Provisions) Order 2012 No. 2012/288 (C.31). - Enabling power: Crofting Reform (Scotland) Act 2010, ss. 53 (2), 57 (2) (3). Bringing into operation various provisions of the 2010 Act on 30.10.2012. - Issued: 01.11.2012. Made: 29.10.2012. Coming into force: 30.10.2012. Effect: None. Territorial extent & classification: S. General. - Supersedes draft S.S.I. (ISBN 9780111017821) issued 06.09.2012. - 16p.: 30 cm. - 978-0-11-101823-1 £5.75

The Crofting Register (Fees) (Scotland) Amendment Order 2012 No. 2012/328. - Enabling power: Crofting Reform (Scotland) Act 2010, ss. 19 (2), 53 (2) (a). - Issued: 30.11.2012. Made: 27.11.2012. Laid before the Scottish Parliament: 29.11.2012. Coming into force: 13.01.2012. Effect: S.S.I. 2012/295 amended. Territorial extent & classification: S. General. - This S.S.I. has been made in consequence of a defect in S.S.I. 2012/295 (ISBN 9780111018286) and is being issued free of charge to all known recipients of that instrument. - 2p.: 30 cm. - 978-0-11-101859-0 £4.00

The Crofting Register (Fees) (Scotland) Order 2012 No. 2012/295. - Enabling power: Crofting Reform (Scotland) Act 2010, ss. 19 (2) (3), 53 (2) (a). - Issued: 05.11.2012. Made: 30.10.2012. Laid before the Scottish Parliament: 01.11.2012. Coming into force: 30.11.2012. Effect: None. Territorial extent & classification: S. General. - This SSI has been corrected by SSI 2012/328 (ISBN 9780111018590) which is being sent free of charge to all known recipients of S.S.I. 2012/295. - 4p.: 30 cm. - 978-0-11-101828-6 £4.00

The Crofting Register (Notice of First Registration) (Scotland) Order 2012 No. 2012/296. - Enabling power: Crofting Reform (Scotland) Act 2010, ss. 12 (8) (b), 53 (2) (a). - Issued: 08.11.2012. Made: 30.10.2012. Laid before the Scottish Parliament: 01.11.2012. Coming into force: 30.11.2012. Effect: None. Territorial extent & classification: S. General. - 8p.: 30 cm. - 978-0-11-101826-2 £4.00

The Crofting Register (Scotland) Amendment Rules 2012 No. 2012/327. - Enabling power: Crofting Reform (Scotland) Act 2010, ss. 19 (1), 53 (2) (a). - Issued: 30.11.2012. Made: 27.11.2012. Laid before the Scottish Parliament: 29.11.2012. Coming into force: 13.01.2013. Effect: S.S.I. 2012/294 amended. Territorial extent & classification: S. General. - This S.S.I. has been made in consequence of a defect in S.S.I. 2012/294 (ISBN 9780111018279) and is being issued free of charge to all known recipients of that instrument. - 4p.: 30 cm. - 978-0-11-101858-3 £4.00

The Crofting Register (Scotland) Rules 2012 No. 2012/294. - Enabling power: Crofting Reform (Scotland) Act 2010, ss. 19 (1), 53 (2) (a). - Issued: 05.11.2012. Made: 30.10.2012. Laid before the Scottish Parliament: 01.11.2012. Coming into force: 30.11.2012. Effect: None. Territorial extent & classification: S. General. - This SSI has been corrected by SSI 2012/327 (ISBN 9780111018583) which is being sent free of charge to all known recipients of 2012/294. - 42p.: 30 cm. - 978-0-11-101827-9 £9.75

The Crofting Register (Transfer of Ownership) (Scotland) Regulations 2012 No. 2012/297. - Enabling power: Crofting Reform (Scotland) Act 2010, ss. 4 (8), 5 (6), 25 (4), 53 (2) (a). - Issued: 05.11.2012. Made: 30.10.2012. Laid before the Scottish Parliament: 01.11.2012. Coming into force: 30.11.2012. Effect: None. Territorial extent & classification: S. General. - 4p.: 30 cm. - 978-0-11-101829-3 £4.00

Education

The Education (Fees, Awards and Student Support) (Miscellaneous Amendments) (Scotland) Regulations 2012 No. 2012/72. - Enabling power: Education (Scotland) Act 1980, ss. 49 (3), 73 (f), 74 (1) & Education (Fees and Awards) Act 1983, ss, 1, 2. - Issued: 05.03.2012. Made: 29.02.2012. Laid before the Scottish Parliament: 02.03.2012. Coming into force: 01.04.2012. Effect: S.S.I. 2006/333; 2007/149, 151, 152, 153, 154, 156; 2011/389 amended. Territorial extent & classification: S. General. - 24p.: 30 cm. - 978-0-11-101648-0 £5.75

The Education (Provision of Information as to Schools) (Scotland) Revocation Regulations 2012 No. 2012/129. - Enabling power: Education (Scotland) Act 1980, ss. 28 (1) (4) (9). - Issued: 30.04.2012. Made: 25.04.2012. Laid before the Scottish Parliament: 27.04.2012. Coming into force: 30.05.2012. Effect: S.I. 1994/351 partially revoked & S.I. 1993/1605; S.S.I. 2000/406 revoked. Territorial extent & classification: S. General. - 4p.: 30 cm. - 978-0-11-101691-6 £4.00

The Education (School and Placing Information) (Scotland) Regulations 2012 No. 2012/130. - Enabling power: Education (Scotland) Act 1980, ss. 2, 28B (1) (a) (ii) (3). - Issued: 30.04.2012. Made: 25.04.2012. Laid before the Scottish Parliament: 27.04.2012. Coming into force: 08.12.2012. Effect: S.I. 1993/1604; 1994/351 partially revoked & S.I. 1982/950; 1990/181 & S.S.I. 2000/407; 2007/487 revoked. Territorial extent & classification: S. General. - 20p.: 30 cm. - 978-0-11-101692-3 £5.75

The Elmwood College, Oatridge College and The Barony College (Transfer and Closure) (Scotland) Order 2012 No. 2012/237. - Enabling power: Further and Higher Education (Scotland) Act 1992, ss. 3 (1) (c), 25 (1) (1A) (2) (5), 60 (3). - Issued: 03.09.2012. Made: 28.08.2012. Laid before the Scottish Parliament: 30.08.2012. Coming into force: 01.10.2012. Effect: None. Territorial extent & classification: S. General. - 4p.: 30 cm. - 978-0-11-101779-1 £4.00

The Fundable Bodies (Scotland) Order 2012 No. 2012/216. - Enabling power: Further and Higher Education (Scotland) Act 2005, s. 7 (1). - Issued: 05.07.2012. Made: 28.06.2021. Coming into force: 01.08.2012. Effect: 2005 asp 6 modified. Territorial extent & classification: S. General. - Supersedes draft S.S.I. (ISBN 9780111017227) issued 24.05.2012. - 4p.: 30 cm. - 978-0-11-101771-5 £4.00

The General Teaching Council for Scotland (Legal Assessor) Rules 2012 No. 2012/86. - Enabling power: S.S.I. 2010/215, sch. 4, para. 3 (4) (5). - Issued: 16.03.2012. Made: 13.03.2012. Laid before the Scottish Parliament: 15.03.2012. Coming into force: 02.04.2012. Effect: S.S.I. 2006/455 revoked. Territorial extent & classification: S. General. - 4p.: 30 cm. - 978-0-11-101656-5 £4.00

The Individual Learning Account (Scotland) Amendment Regulations 2012 No. 2012/172. - Enabling power: Education and Training (Scotland) Act 2000, ss. 1, 2, 3 (2). - Issued: 06.06.2012. Made: 30.05.2012. Laid before the Scottish Parliament: 31.05.2012. Coming into force: 01.07.2012. Effect: S.S.I. 2011/107 amended. Territorial extent & classification: S. General. - 4p.: 30 cm. - 978-0-11-101739-5 £4.00

The Jewel and Esk College and Stevenson College Edinburgh (Transfer and Closure) (Scotland) Order 2012 No. 2012/238. - Enabling power: Further and Higher Education (Scotland) Act 1992, ss. 3 (1) (c), 25 (1) (1A) (2) (5), 60 (3). - Issued: 03.09.2012. Made: 28.08.2012. Laid before the Scottish Parliament: 30.08.2012. Coming into force: 01.10.2012. Effect: None. Territorial extent & classification: S. General. - 4p.: 30 cm. - 978-0-11-101780-7 £4.00

The Public Services Reform (Recovery of Expenses in respect of Inspection of Independent Further Education Colleges and English Language Schools) (Scotland) Order 2012 No. 2012/102. - Enabling power: Public Services Reform (Scotland) Act 2010, s. 17 (1) (9). - Issued: 23.03.2012. Made: 20.03.2012. Coming into force: 21.03.2012 in accord. with art. 1. Effect: 1980 c. 44 amended. Territorial extent & classification: S. General. - Supersedes draft S.S.I. (ISBN 9780111016015) issued 02.02.2012. - 4p.: 30 cm. - 978-0-11-101670-1 £4.00

The Repayment of Student Loans (Scotland) Amendment Regulations 2012 No. 2012/22. - Enabling power: Education (Scotland) Act 1980, ss. 73 (f), 73B, 74 (1). - Issued: 30.01.2012. Made: 25.01.2012. Laid before the Scottish Parliament: 27.01.2012. Coming into force: 06.04.2012. Effect: S.S.I. 2000/110 amended. Territorial extent & classification: S. General. - 4p.: 30 cm. - 978-0-11-101597-1 £4.00

Energy

The Energy Act 2011 (Commencement No. 1) (Scotland) Order 2012 No. 2012/191 (C.17). - Enabling power: Energy Act 2011, s. 121 (2). Bringing into operation various provisions of the 2011 Act on 22.06.2012. - Issued: 13.06.2012. Made: 07.06.2012. Laid before the Scottish Parliament: 11.06.2012. Effect: None. Territorial extent & classification: S. General. - 2p.: 30 cm. - 978-0-11-101750-0 £4.00

Energy conservation

The Home Energy Assistance Scheme (Scotland) Amendment Regulations 2012 No. 2012/34. - Enabling power: Social Security Act 1990, s. 15 (1) (2) (a) (c) (9) (b). - Issued: 13.02.2012. Made: 08.02.2012. Laid before the Scottish Parliament: 10.02.2012. Coming into force: 01.04.2012. Effect: S.S.I. 2009/48 amended. Territorial extent & classification: S. General. - 4p.: 30 cm. - 978-0-11-101610-7 £4.00

Energy conservation, Scotland

The Green Deal (Acknowledgment) (Scotland) Regulations 2012 No. 2012/214. - Enabling power: Energy Act 2011, ss. 14 (7), 14 (8), 15 (4), 40 (1). - Issued: 03.07.2012. Made: 28.06.2012. Laid before the Scottish Parliament: 02.07.2012. Coming into force: 28.01.2012. Effect: None. Territorial extent & classification: S. General. - 4p.: 30 cm. - 978-0-11-101768-5 £4.00

Enforcement

The Diligence against Earnings (Variation) (Scotland) Regulations 2012 No. 2012/308. - Enabling power: Debtors (Scotland) Act 1987, ss. 49 (7) (a), 53 (3), 63 (6). - Issued: 20.11.2012. Made: 15.11.2012. Laid before the Scottish Parliament: 19.11.2012. Coming into force: 06.04.2012. Effect: 1987 c.18 amended. Territorial extent & classification: S. General. - 4p.: 30 cm. - 978-0-11-101845-3 £4.00

Environmental protection

The Bathing Waters (Scotland) Amendment Regulations 2012 No. 2012/243. - Enabling power: European Communities Act 1972, s. 2 (2). - Issued: 04.09.2012. Made: 30.08.2012. Laid before the Scottish Parliament: 03.09.2012. Coming into force: 02.10.2012. Effect: S.S.I. 2008/170 amended. Territorial extent & classification: S. General. - 4p.: 30 cm. - 978-0-11-101781-4 £4.00

The INSPIRE (Scotland) Amendment Regulations 2012 No. 2012/284. - Enabling power: European Communities Act 1972, s. 2 (2). - Issued: 29.10.2012. Made: 23.10.2012. Laid before the Scottish Parliament: 25.10.2012. Coming into force: 23.11.2012. Effect: S.S.I. 2009/440 amended. Territorial extent & classification: S. General. - INSPIRE = Infrastructure for Spatial Information in the European Community. EC note: These Regulations amend the principal regulations which implemented, in part, Directive 2007/2/EC which concerns the creation and operation of national and Community infrastructures relating to spatial information for the purposes of Community environmental policies and other policies or activities which may have an impact on the environment. Implementing rules of Directive 2007/2/EC as regards interoperability of spatial sets and services as amended by Reg 102/2011 have now been adopted by virtue of Reg. 1089/2010. In consequence of the adoption of the implementing rules these regulations amend the principal regulations to further implement Directive 2007/2/EC. - 8p.: 30 cm. - 978-0-11-101816-3 £4.00

The Marine Licensing (Exempted Activities) (Scottish Inshore and Offshore Regions) Amendment Order 2012 No. 2012/25. - Enabling power: Marine and Coastal Access Act 2009, ss. 74 (1) (2) (3), 316 (1) & Marine (Scotland) Act 2010, ss. 32 (1) (2) (3), 165 (1). - Issued: 07.02.2012. Made: 02.02.2012. Coming into force: 03.02.2012 in accord. with art. 1. Effect: S.S.I. 2011/57, 204 amended. Territorial extent & classification: S. General. - Supersedes draft SI (ISBN 9780111015506) issued on 09.12.2011. - 8p.: 30 cm. - 978-0-11-101603-9 £5.75

The Marine Licensing (Fees) (Scotland) Regulations 2012 No. 2012/183. - Enabling power: Marine and Coastal Access Act 2009, ss. 67 (2) (3) (b), 316 (1) (b) & Marine (Scotland) Act 2010, ss. 25 (1) (b) (2), 165 (1) (b). - Issued: 06.06.2012. Made: 30.05.2012. Laid before the Scottish Parliament: 31.05.2012. Coming into force: 29.06.2012. Effect: S.S.I. 2011/78 amended. Territorial extent & classification: S. General. - 4p.: 30 cm. - 978-0-11-101738-8 £4.00

The Pollution Prevention and Control (Scotland) Regulations 2012 No. 2012/360. - Enabling power: Pollution Prevention and Control Act 1999, s. 2, sch. 1 & European Communities Act 1972, s. 2 (2). - Issued: 07.01.2013. Made: 20.12.2012. Coming into force: 07.01.2013. Effect: 1990 c.43; 1995 c.25; 2004 asp 8 modified & SI 1991/472, 1624, 2839; 1994/2716; 1996/972, 1527; 2005/925; 2006/3289; 2007/871, 2325, 3106; 2009/890, 2037; 2010/265; 2011/2860; 2012/1715; SSI 2000/178; 2003/235; 2006/133; 2008/100, 159, 298; 2011/209, 228 amended & S.S.I. 2003/235; 2004/112, 512; 2009/247; 2011/171, 226, 418; 2012/148; S.I. 2007/2325 partially revoked & SSI 2000/323; 2002/493; 2003/170, 221; 2004/26, 110; 2005/101, 340, 510; 2008/410; 2009/336; 2010/236; 2011/285 revoked. Territorial extent & classification: S. General. - EC note: These regulations provide an integrated pollution control regime for Scotland for the purposes of implementing Directive 2010/75/EU on industrial emissions and of regulating other environmentally polluting activities not covered by the Industrial Emissions Directive. Supersedes draft SSI (ISBN 9780111018514) issued on 28.11.2012. - 128p.: 30 cm. - 978-0-11-101892-7 £18.50

The Waste (Scotland) Regulations 2012 No. 2012/148. - Enabling power: European Communities Act 1972, s. 2 (2). - Issued: 22.05.2012. Made: 16.05.2012. Coming into force: 17.05.2012. Effect: 1990 c. 43 (in relation to Scotland); S.S.I. 2000/323; 2003/235; 2011/228 amended. Territorial extent & classification: S. General. - Supersedes draft S.I. (ISBN 9780111016657) issued 21.03.2012. Partially revoked by SSI 2012/360 (ISBN 9780111018927). - 12p.: 30 cm. - 978-0-11-101713-5 £5.75

Equality

The Equality Act 2010 (Specific Duties) (Scotland) Regulations 2012 No. 2012/162. - Enabling power: Equality Act 2010, ss. 153 (3), 155 (1) (c) (2), 207 (4). - Issued: 28.05.2012. Made: 23.05.2012. Coming into force: 27.05.2012. Effect: None. Territorial extent & classification: S. General. - Supersedes draft S.I. (ISBN 9780111016718) issued 23.03.2011. - 12p.: 30 cm. - 978-0-11-101725-8 £5.75

Equal opportunities

The Equality Act 2010 (Specification of Public Authorities) (Scotland) Order 2012 No. 2012/55. - Enabling power: Equality Act 2010, s. 151 (3). - Issued: 24.02.2012. Made: 21.02.2012. Coming into force: 05.03.2012. Effect: 2010 c.15 amended. Territorial extent & classification: S. General. - Supersedes draft S.S.I. (ISBN 9780111015476) issued 07.12.2011. - 2p.: 30 cm. - 978-0-11-101632-9 £4.00

Evidence

The Evidence in Civil Partnership and Divorce Actions (Scotland) Order 2012 No. 2012/111. - Enabling power: Civil Evidence (Scotland) Act 1988, s. 8 (4). - Issued: 03.04.2012. Made: 29.03.2012. Coming into force: In accord. with art. 1. Effect: S.I. 1989/582 amended. Territorial tent & classification: S. General. - Supersedes draft S.I. (ISBN 9780111016206) issued 16.02.2012. - 4p.: 30 cm. - 978-0-11-101676-3 £4.00

Family law

The Population (Statistics) Act 1938 Modifications (Scotland) Order 2012 No. 2012/287. - Enabling power: Family Law (Scotland) Act 2006, s. 44 (1) (2) & Civil Partnership Act 2004, s. 259 (1) (2) (3). - Issued: 31.10.2012. Made: 24.10.2012. Coming into force: 01.01.2013. Effect: 1938 c.12 modified. Territorial extent & classification: S. General. - Supersedes draft SI (ISBN 9780111017616) issued on 28.06.2012. - 4p.: 30 cm. - 978-0-11-101820-0 £4.00

Fire and rescue services

The Fire and Rescue Services (Framework) (Scotland) Order 2012 No. 2012/146. - Enabling power: Fire (Scotland) Act 2005, s. 40 (4). - Issued: 21.05.2012. Made: 16.05.2012. Laid before the Scottish Parliament: 18.05.2012. Coming into force: 29.06.2012. Effect: S.S.I. 2005/453 revoked. Territorial extent & classification: S. General. - 2p.: 30 cm. - 978-0-11-101708-1 £4.00

The Police and Fire Reform (Scotland) Act 2012 (Commencement No. 1, Transitional, Transitory and Saving Provisions) Order 2012 No. 2012/253 (C.24). - Enabling power: Police and Fire Reform (Scotland) Act 2012, s. 129 (2) (3). Bringing into operation various provisions of the 2012 Act on 01.10.2012. - Issued: 18.09.2012. Made: 13.09.2012. Laid before the Scottish Parliament: 14.09.2012. Effect: 2012 asp 8 modified. Territorial extent & classification: S. General. - 8p.: 30 cm. - 978-0-11-101789-0 £5.75

The Police and Fire Reform (Scotland) Act 2012 (Commencement No. 2, Transitory and Transitional Provisions and Appointed Day) Order 2012 No. 2012/333 (C.32). - Enabling power: Police and Fire Reform (Scotland) Act 2012, s. 129 (2) (3), sch. 6, para. 1. Bringing into operation various provisions of the 2012 Act on 01.01.2013, 01.04.2013, in accord. with arts. 2, 4. - Issued: 07.12.2012. Made: 04.12.2012. Laid before the Scottish Parliament: 06.12.2012. Coming into force: 01.01.2013. Effect: None. Territorial extent & classification: S. General. - 12p.: 30 cm. - 978-0-11-101868-2 £5.75

Fire safety

The Fire (Scotland) Act 2005 (Relevant Premises) Regulations 2012 No. 2012/332. - Enabling power: Fire (Scotland) Act 2005, ss. 58, 78 (8), 88 (2). - Issued: 05.12.2012. Made: 28.11.2012. Coming into force: 29.11.2012. Effect: 2005 asp 5 & S.S.I. 2006/456 modified. Territorial extent & classification: S. General. - Supersedes draft SSI (ISBN 9780111017944) issued 27.09.2012. - 4p.: 30 cm. - 978-0-11-101867-5 £4.00

Fire services

The Firefighters' Pension Scheme (Scotland) Amendment Order 2012 No. 2012/107. - Enabling power: Fire and Rescue Services Act 2004, ss. 34, 60. - Issued: 04.04.2012. Made: 29.03.2012. Laid before the Scottish Parliament: 30.03.2012. Coming into force: 01.04.2012. Effect: S.S.I. 2007/199 amended. Territorial extent & classification: S. General. - 4p.: 30 cm. - 978-0-11-101679-4 £4.00

The Firemen's Pension Scheme Amendment (Scotland) Order 2012 No. 2012/106. - Enabling power: Fire Services Act 1947, s. 26 (1) to (5). - Issued: 04.04.2012. Made: 29.03.2012. Laid: 30.03.2012. Coming into force: 01.04.2012. Effect: S.I. 1992/129 amended in relation to Scotland. Territorial extent & classification: S. General. - With correction slip dated May 2012. - 4p.: 30 cm. - 978-0-11-101678-7 £4.00

Food

The Food Additives (Scotland) Amendment Regulations 2012 No. 2012/119. - Enabling power: Food Safety Act 1990, ss. 16 (1) (a) (f), 17 (1) (2), 48 (1) & European Communities Act 1972, sch. 2, para. 1A. - Issued: 24.04.2012. Made: 19.04.2012. Laid before the Scottish Parliament: 23.04.2012. Coming into force: 23.05.2012. Effect: S.S.I. 2009/436 amended. Territorial extent & classification: S. General. - EC note: These Regulations make certain amendments to SSI 2009/436 in order to provide for the execution and enforcement in Scotland of the following Commission regulations: no. 1129/2011; 1130/2011; 1131/2011; 231/2012. - 8p.: 30 cm. - 978-0-11-101684-8 £4.00

The Food Hygiene (Scotland) Amendment Regulations 2012 No. 2012/75. - Enabling power: European Communities Act 1972, s. 2 (2), sch. 2, para. 1A. - Issued: 06.03.2012. Made: 29.02.2012. Laid: 02.03.2012. Coming into force: 01.04.2012. Effect: S.S.I. 2006/3 amended. Territorial extent & classification: S. General. - 8p.: 30 cm. - 978-0-11-101651-0 £5.75

The Materials and Articles in Contact with Food (Scotland) Regulations 2012 No. 2012/318. - Enabling power: Food Safety Act 1990, ss. 16 (2), 17 (1) (2), 26 (1) (a) (2) (a) (3), 31, 48 (1) & European Communities Act 1972, sch. 2, para. 1A. - Issued: 27.11.2012. Made: 22.11.2012. Laid before the Scottish Parliament: 23.11.2012. Coming into force: 22.12.2012. Effect: 1990 c. 16 modified & S.I. 1990/2463; 1996/1499 amended in relation to Scotland & S.S.I. 2006/230; 2008/261; 2009/30; 2010/327; 2011/100 revoked. Territorial extent & classification: S. General. - EC note: These Regulations provide for the implementation of the following Directives and enforcement of the following Regulations: Directives 78/142/EC, 84/500/EEC, 2007/43/EC & Regulations (EC) 1935/2004, 1895/2005, 2023/2006, 450/2009, 10/2011. - 20p.: 30 cm. - 978-0-11-101848-4 £5.75

The Specified Products from China (Restriction on First Placing on the Market) (Scotland) Amendment Regulations 2012 No. 2012/3. - Enabling power: European Communities Act 1972, s. 2 (2). - Issued: 13.01.2012. Made: 10.01.2012. Laid before the Scottish Parliament: 12.01.2012. Coming into force: 12.01.2012. Effect: S.S.I. 2008/148 amended. Territorial extent & classification: S. General. - EC note: These Regulations amend SSI 2008/148 in order to implement Commission Implementing Decision 2011/884/EU on emergency measures regarding unauthorised genetically modified rice in rice products originating from China and repealing Decision 2008/289/EC. The Decision provides for import restrictions that previously applied to Bt 63 genetically modified rice to apply, with modifications, to all unauthorised genetically modified rice. - 4p.: 30 cm. - 978-0-11-101581-0 £4.00

Forestry

The Forestry Commissioners (Climate Change Functions) (Scotland) Order 2012 No. 2012/77. - Enabling power: Climate Change (Scotland) Act 2009, ss. 59 (1), 96 (2) (3). - Issued: 06.03.2012. Made: 28.02.2012. Coming into force: 01.03.2012 in accord. with art. 1. Effect: 1967 c.10 amended. Territorial extent & classification: S. General. - Supersedes draft SSI 2012 (ISBN 9780111015780) issued on 29.12.2011. - 4p.: 30 cm. - 978-0-11-101653-4 £4.00

Harbours, docks, piers and ferries

The Fraserburgh Harbour Revision (Constitution) Order 2012 No. 2012/262. - Enabling power: Harbours Act 1964, s. 14 (1) (2A). - Issued: 01.10.2012. Made: 27.09.2012. Coming into force: 28.09.2012. Effect: 1985 c.xlv amended & S.S.I. 2001/457; 2011/447 partially revoked. Territorial extent & classification: S. Local. - 8p.: 30 cm. - 978-0-11-101796-8 £5.75

The Inverness Harbour Revision (Constitution) Order 2012 No. 2012/302. - Enabling power: Harbours Act 1964, s. 14 (1) (2A). - Issued: 13.11.2012. Made: 07.11.2012. Coming into force: 08.11.2012. Effect: Inverness Harbour Revision (Constitution) Order 2002 amended. Territorial extent & classification: S. Local. - 4p.: 30 cm. - 978-0-11-101837-8 £4.00

The Mallaig Harbour Revision (Constitution) Order 2012 No. 2012/114. - Enabling power: Harbours Act 1964, s. 14 (1) (2A) (3). - Issued: 05.04.2012. Made: 29.03.2012. Coming into force: 30.03.2012. Effect: S.S.I. 1968/1202 partially revoked. Territorial extent & classification: S. Local. - 12p.: 30 cm. - 978-0-11-101680-0 £5.75

The Port of Cairnryan Harbour Revision Order 2012 No. 2012/350. - Enabling power: Harbours Act 1964, s. 14 (1) (2A) (3). - Issued: 19.12.2012. Made: 13.12.2012. Coming into force: 14.12.2012. Effect: S.S.I. 2007/308 amended. Territorial extent & classification: S. Local. - 8p.: 30 cm. - 978-0-11-101887-3 £5.75

High Court of Justiciary

Act of Adjournal (Amendment of the Criminal Procedure (Scotland) Act 1995 (Transcripts) 2012 No. 2012/272. - Enabling power: Criminal Procedure (Scotland) Act 1995, s. 305. - Issued: 15.10.2012. Made: 09.10.2012. Laid before the Scottish Parliament: 11.10.2012. Coming into force: 12.11.2012. Effect: 1995 c. 46 amended. Territorial extent & classification: S. General. - 4p.: 30 cm. - 978-0-11-101807-1 £4.00

Act of Adjournal (Criminal Procedure Rules Amendment) (Miscellaneous) 2012 No. 2012/125. - Enabling power: Criminal Procedure (Scotland) Act 1995, s. 305 & Extradition Act 2003, s. 210. - Issued: 25.04.2012. Made: 24.04.2012. Laid before the Scottish Parliament: 26.04.2012. Coming into force: 04.06.2012. Effect: S.I. 1996/513 amended. Territorial extent & classification: S. General. - 4p.: 30 cm. - 978-0-11-101686-2 £4.00

Act of Adjournal (Criminal Procedure Rules Amendment No. 2) (Miscellaneous) 2012 No. 2012/187. - Enabling power: Criminal Procedure (Scotland) Act 1995, s. 305. - Issued: 11.06.2012. Made: 06.06.2012. Laid before the Scottish Parliament: 08.06.2012. Coming into force: 16.07.2012. Effect: S.I. 1996/513 amended. Territorial extent & classification: S. General. - 4p.: 30 cm. - 978-0-11-101746-3 £4.00

Act of Adjournal (Criminal Procedure Rules Amendment No. 3) (Procedural Hearings in Appeals from Solemn Proceedings) 2012 No. 2012/300. - Enabling power: Criminal Procedure (Scotland) Act 1995, s. 305. - Issued: 08.10.2012. Made: 06.11.2012. Laid before the Scottish Parliament: 08.11.2012. Coming into force: 10.12.2012. Effect: S.I. 1996/513 amended. Territorial extent & classification: S. General. - 2p.: 30 cm. - 978-0-11-101835-4 £4.00

The Court Fees (Miscellaneous Amendments) Scotland Order 2012 No. 2012/322. - Enabling power: Court of Law Fees (Scotland) Act 1895, s. 2. - Issued: 28.11.2012. Made: 22.11.2012. Laid before the Scottish Parliament: 26.11.2012. Coming into force: 09.12.2012. Effect: S.S.I. 2012/290, 291, 293 amended. Territorial extent & classification: S. General. - This SSI has been made in consequence of defects in SSI 2012/290 (ISBN 9780111018330), 2012/291 (ISBN 9780111018323) and SSI 2012/293 (ISBN 9780111018347) and is being issued free of charge to all known recipients of those instruments. - 4p.: 30 cm. - 978-0-11-101853-8 £4.00

The High Court of Justiciary Fees Amendment Order 2012 No. 2012/291. - Enabling power: Courts of Law Fees (Scotland) Act 1895, s. 2. - Issued: 06.11.2012. Made: 30.10.2012 Laid before the Scottish Parliament: 31.10.2012. Coming into force: In accord. with art. 1. Effect: S.I. 1984/252 amended. Territorial extent & classification: S. General. - 8p.: 30 cm. - 978-0-11-101832-3 £5.75

Horticulture

The Marketing of Bananas (Scotland) Regulations 2012 No. 2012/349. - Enabling power: Food Safety Act 1990, ss. 16 (1) (e), 17 (2) & European Communities Act 1972, sch. 2, para. 1A. - Issued: 20.12.2012. Made: 13.12.2012. Laid before the Scottish Parliament: 17.12.2012. Coming into force: 01.02.2013. Effect: S.S.I. 2011/325 amended. Territorial extent & classification: S. General. - EC note: These Regulations provide for the enforcement of the EU marketing rules for bananas as provided for article 113 of Council Regulation (EC) no. 1234/2007 establishing a common organisation of agricultural markets and on specific provisions for certain agricultural products, and contained in Commission implementing Regulation (EU) no. 1333/2011 laying down marketing standards for bananas, rules on the verification of compliance with those marketing standards and requirements for notifications in banana sector. - 16p.: 30 cm. - 978-0-11-101886-6 £5.75

Housing

The Homelessness (Abolition of Priority Need Test) (Scotland) Order 2012 No. 2012/330. - Enabling power: Homelessness etc. (Scotland) Act 2003, s. 2 (1) (3). - Issued: 03.12.2012. Made: 27.11.2012. Coming into force: 31.12.2012. Effect: 1987 c.26; 2003 asp 10; 2004 asp 8 amended. Territorial extent and classification: S. General. - Supersedes draft SI (ISBN 9780111018187) issued on 30.10.2012. - 4p.: 30 cm. - 978-0-11-101861-3 £4.00

The Housing (Scotland) Act 2001 (Assistance to Registered Social Landlords and Other Persons) (Grants) Amendment Regulations 2012 No. 2012/258. - Enabling power: Housing (Scotland) Act 2001, ss. 93 (2), 109 (1) (2). - Issued: 24.09.2012. Made: 19.09.2012. Laid before the Scottish Parliament: 21.09.2012. Coming into force: 19.11.2012. Effect: S.S.I. 2004/117 amended. Territorial extent & classification: S. General. - Revoked by SSI 2012/306 (ISBN 9780111018439). - 12p.: 30 cm. - 978-0-11-101791-3 £5.75

The Housing (Scotland) Act 2001 (Assistance to Registered Social Landlords and Other Persons) (Grants) Amendment Revocation Regulations 2012 No. 2012/306. - Enabling power: Housing (Scotland) Act 2001, ss. 93 (2), 109 (1) (2). - Issued: 19.11.2012. Made: 13.11.2012. Laid before the Scottish Parliament: 15.11.2012. Coming into force: 18.11.2012. Effect: S.S.I. 2002/258 revoked. Territorial extent & classification: S. General. - 2p.: 30 cm. - 978-0-11-101843-9 £4.00

The Housing (Scotland) Act 2010 (Commencement No. 5) Order 2012 No. 2012/19 (C.3). - Enabling power: Housing (Scotland) Act 2010, s. 166 (2). Bringing various provisions of the 2010 Act into operation on 22.02.2012. - Issued: 27.01.2012. Made: 24.01.2012. Laid before the Scottish Parliament: 26.01.2012. Effect: None. Territorial extent & classification: S. General. - 4p.: 30 cm. - 978-0-11-101594-0 £4.00

The Housing (Scotland) Act 2010 (Commencement No. 6, Transitional and Savings Provisions) Order 2012 No. 2012/39 (C.8). - Enabling power: Housing (Scotland) Act 2010, ss. 161 (2) (a) (c), 166 (2). Bringing into operation various provisions of the 2010 Act on 01.04.2012. - Issued: 14.02.2012. Made: 09.02.2012. Laid before the Scottish Parliament: 13.02.2012. Effect: None. Territorial extent & classification: S. General. - 12p.: 30 cm. - 978-0-11-101618-3 £5.75

The Housing (Scotland) Act 2010 (Commencement No. 7, Transitional Provision) Order 2012 No. 2012/91 (C.10). - Enabling power: Housing (Scotland) Act 2010, ss. 161 (2) (a), 166 (2). Bringing into operation various provisions of the 2010 Act on 01.08.2012, in accord. with art. 2. - Issued: 19.03.2012. Made: 14.03.2012. Laid before the Scottish Parliament: 16.03.2012. Coming into force: 01.04.2012. Effect: S.S.I. 2012/39 amended. Territorial extent & classification: S. General. - 4p.: 30 cm. - 978-0-11-101660-2 £4.00

The Housing (Scotland) Act 2010 (Commencement No. 8 and Saving Provision) Order 2012 No. 2012/283 (C.30). - Enabling power: Housing (Scotland) Act 2010, ss. 161 (2) (a), 166 (2). Bringing into operation various provisions of the 2010 Act on 01.04.2013, 01.06.2013, in accord. with arts 2, 3. - Issued: 29.10.2012. Made: 22.10.2012. Laid before the Scottish Parliament: 25.10.2012. Coming into force: 31.12.2012. Effect: None. Territorial extent & classification: S. General. - 4p.: 30 cm. - 978-0-11-101815-6 £4.00

The Housing (Scotland) Act 2010 (Consequential Modifications) Order 2012 No. 2012/38. - Enabling power: Housing (Scotland) Act 2010, s. 163 (1) (b) (2). - Issued: 14.02.2012. Made: 09.02.2012. Laid before the Scottish Parliament: 13.02.2012. Coming into force: 01.04.2012. Effect: 1985 c. 69; 1987 c. 26; 2003 asp 2, asp 11 modified & S.S.I. 2002/312; 2004/117; 2005/558; 2006/218; 2007/92; 2009/48 modified. Territorial extent & classification: S. General. - 4p.: 30 cm. - 978-0-11-101617-6 £4.00

The Housing Support Grant (Scotland) Order 2012 No. 2012/113. - Enabling power: Housing (Scotland) Act 1987, ss. 191, 192. - Issued: 04.04.2012. Made: 29.03.2012. Coming into force: 01.04.2012. Effect: None. Territorial extent & classification: S. General. - Supersedes draft S.S.I. (ISBN 9780111016008) issued 01.02.2012. - 4p.: 30 cm. - 978-0-11-101677-0 £4.00

The Housing Support Services (Homelessness) (Scotland) Regulations 2012 No. 2012/331. - Enabling power: Housing (Scotland) Act 1987, s. 32B. - Issued: 03.12.2012. Made: 27.11.2012. Coming into force: 01.06.2013. Effect: None. Territorial extent & classification: S. General. - Supersedes draft SI (ISBN 9780111018170) issued 30.10.2012. - 4p.: 30 cm. - 978-0-11-101862-0 £4.00

The Private Landlord Registration (Information and Fees) (Scotland) Amendment Regulations 2012 No. 2012/151. - Enabling power: Antisocial Behaviour etc. (Scotland) Act 2004, ss. 83 (1) (d) (3), 88 (2C), 141 (2) (b). - Issued: 22.05.2012. Made: 17.05.2012. Laid before the Scottish Parliament: 21.05.2012. Coming into force: 01.07.2012. Effect: S.S.I. 2005/558 amended. Territorial extent & classification: S. General. - 4p.: 30 cm. - 978-0-11-101716-6 £4.00

The Private Rented Housing (Scotland) Act 2011 (Commencement No. 2 and Transitional Provision) Order 2012 No. 2012/2 (C.2). - Enabling power: Private Rented Housing (Scotland) Act 2011, s. 41 (3) (4). Bringing into operation various provisions of the 2011 Act on 31.01.2012. - Issued: 13.01.2012. Made: 10.01.2012. Laid: 12.01.2012. Effect: None. Territorial extent & classification: S. General. - 4p.: 30 cm. - 978-0-11-101580-3 £4.00

The Private Rented Housing (Scotland) Act 2011 (Commencement No. 3) Order 2012 No. 2012/150 (C.13). - Enabling power: Private Rented Housing (Scotland) Act 2011, s. 41 (3). Bringing into operation various provisions of the 2011 Act on 01.07.2012. - Issued: 22.05.2012. Made: 17.05.2012. Laid: 21.05.2012. Coming into force: 30.06.2012. Effect: None. Territorial extent & classification: S. General. - 2p.: 30 cm. - 978-0-11-101715-9 £4.00

The Private Rented Housing (Scotland) Act 2011 (Commencement No. 4) Order 2012 No. 2012/267 (C.27). - Enabling power: Private Rented Housing (Scotland) Act 2011, s. 41 (3) (4). Bringing into operation various provisions of the 2011 Act on 30.11.2012. - Issued: 04.10.2012. Made: 02.10.2012. Laid: 04.10.2012. Coming into force: 29.11.2012. Effect: None. Territorial extent & classification: S. General. - With correction slip dated November 2012. - 2p.: 30 cm. - 978-0-11-101803-3 £4.00

The Scottish Secure Tenancies (Proceedings for Possession) (Confirmation of Compliance with Pre-Action Requirements) Regulations 2012 No. 2012/93. - Enabling power: Housing (Scotland) Act 2001, s. 14 (2A) (b). - Issued: 19.03.2012. Made: 14.03.2012. Laid before the Scottish Parliament: 16.03.2012. Coming into force: 01.08.2012. Effect: None. Territorial extent & classification: S. - 2p.: 30 cm. - 978-0-11-101662-6 £4.00

The Scottish Secure Tenancies (Proceedings for Possession) (Form of Notice) Regulations 2012 No. 2012/92. - Enabling power: Housing (Scotland) Act 2001, ss. 14 (4), 109 (2). - Issued: 19.03.2012. Made: 14.03.2012. Laid before the Scottish Parliament: 16.03.2012. Coming into force: 01.08.2012. Effect: None. Territorial extent & classification: S. - 12p.: 30 cm. - 978-0-11-101661-9 £5.75

The Scottish Secure Tenancies (Proceedings for Possession) (Pre-Action Requirements) Order 2012 No. 2012/127. - Enabling power: Housing (Scotland) Act 2001, s. 14A (9). - Issued: 27.04.2012. Made: 19.04.2012. Coming into force: 01.08.2012. Effect: None. Territorial extent & classification: S. General. - Supersedes draft SSI (ISBN 9780111016336) issued on 28.02.2012. - 8p.: 30 cm. - 978-0-11-101688-6 £4.00

The Scottish Secure Tenancies (Repossession Orders) (Maximum Period) Order 2012 No. 2012/128. - Enabling power: Housing (Scotland) Act 2001, ss. 16 (5A) (c), 109 (2). - Issued: 27.04.2012. Made: 19.04.2012. Coming into force: 01.08.2012. Effect: None. Territorial extent & classification: S. General. - Supersedes draft SSI (ISBN 9780111016343) issued on 28.02.2012. - 4p.: 30 cm. - 978-0-11-101689-3 £4.00

Insolvency: Bankruptcy

The Bankruptcy Fees (Scotland) Regulations 2012 No. 2012/118. - Enabling power: Bankruptcy (Scotland) Act 1985, ss. 5 (4B) (b), 69A, 72 (1). - Issued: 23.04.2012. Made: 18.04.2012. Laid before the Scottish Parliament: 20.04.2012. Coming into force: In accord. with reg. 1 (2). Effect: S.I. 1993/486; 1999/752; S.S.I. 2007/220; 2008/5, 79; 2009/97; 2010/76; 2011/142 revoked with savings. Territorial extent & classification: S. General. - With correction slip dated July 2012. - 12p.: 30 cm. - 978-0-11-101683-1 £5.75

Judgments

The International Recovery of Maintenance (Hague Convention 2007) (Scotland) Regulations 2012 No. 2012/301. - Enabling power: European Communities Act 1972, s. 2 (2). - Issued: 12.11.2012. Made: 06.11.2012. Laid before the Scottish Parliament: 08.11.2012. Coming into force: In accord. with reg. 1 (b). Effect: 1987 c.18; 2002 asp 17; 2007 asp 3 & S.S.I. 2002/494 amended. Territorial extent & classification: S. General. - These regulations make provision in Scotland, the application of the Convention on the International Recovery of Child Support and Other Forms of Family Maintenance done at The Hague on 23 November 2007. The Convention will be concluded by the European Union on a date yet to be determined pursuant to Council Decision 2011/432/EC. - 12p.: 30 cm. - 978-0-11-101836-1 £5.75

Justice of the Peace Court

Act of Adjournal (Criminal Procedure Rules Amendment No. 2) (Miscellaneous) 2012 No. 2012/187. - Enabling power: Criminal Procedure (Scotland) Act 1995, s. 305. - Issued: 11.06.2012. Made: 06.06.2012. Laid before the Scottish Parliament: 08.06.2012. Coming into force: 16.07.2012. Effect: S.I. 1996/513 amended. Territorial extent & classification: S. General. - 4p.: 30 cm. - 978-0-11-101746-3 £4.00

The Justice of the Peace Courts Fees (Scotland) Order 2012 No. 2012/292. - Enabling power: Courts of Law Fees (Scotland) Act 1895, s. 2. - Issued: 06.11.2012. Made: 30.10.2012. Laid before the Scottish Parliament: 31.10.2012. Coming into force: In accord. with art. 1. Effect: S.I. 1984/251 revoked (10.12.2012). Territorial extent & classification: S. General. - 8p.: 30 cm. - 978-0-11-101831-6 £5.75

Landlord and tenant

The Rent (Scotland) Act 1984 (Premiums) Regulations 2012 No. 2012/329. - Enabling power: Rent (Scotland) Act 1984, s. 89A (1) (2) (a). - Issued: 30.11.2012. Made: 27.11.2012. Coming into force: 30.11.2012. Effect: None. Territorial extent & classification: S. General. - Supersedes draft SI (ISBN 9780111018026) issued 04.10.2012. - 2p.: 30 cm. - 978-0-11-101860-6 £4.00

Land registration

The Land Registration etc. (Scotland) Act 2012 (Commencement No. 1) Order 2012 No. 2012/265 (C.26). - Enabling power: Land Registration etc. (Scotland) Act 2012, s. 123 (3). Bringing into operation certain provisions of the 2012 Act on 01.11.2012. - Issued: 02.10.2012. Made: 27.09.2012. Laid before the Scottish Parliament: 01.10.2012. Coming into force: 01.11.2012. Effect: None. Territorial extent & classification: S. General. - 2p.: 30 cm. - 978-0-11-101799-9 £4.00

Legal aid and advice

The Advice and Assistance (Assistance by Way of Representation) (Scotland) Amendment Regulations 2012 No. 2012/84. - Enabling power: Legal Aid (Scotland) Act 1986, s. 9. - Issued: 08.03.2012. Made: 05.03.2012. Coming into force: In accord. with reg. 1. Effect: S.S.I. 2003/179 amended. Territorial extent & classification: S. General. - Supersedes draft S.I. (ISBN 9780111015766) issued 29.12.2011. - 4p.: 30 cm. - 978-0-11-101655-8 £4.00

The Children's Hearings (Scotland) Act 2011 (Commencement No. 3) Order 2012 No. 2012/1 (C.1). - Enabling power: Children's Hearings (Scotland) Act 2011, s. 206 (2). Bringing into operation various provisions of the 2011 Act on 31.01.2012 and 26.03.2012, in accord. with art. 1. - Issued: 12.01.2012. Made: 09.01.2012. Laid before the Scottish Parliament: 11.01.2012. Coming into force: 31.01.2012. Effect: None. Territorial extent & classification: S. General. - With correction slip dated February 2012. - 4p.: 30 cm. - 978-0-11-101579-7 £4.00

The Civil Legal Aid (Scotland) Amendment Regulations 2012 No. 2012/64. - Enabling power: Legal Aid (Scotland) Act 1986, s. 36 (1) (2) (g). - Issued: 02.03.2012. Made: 28.02.2012. Laid before the Scottish Parliament: 01.03.2012. Coming into force: 30.03.2012. Effect: S.S.I. 2002/494 amended. Territorial extent & classification: S. General. - 2p.: 30 cm. - 978-0-11-101639-8 £4.00

The Criminal Legal Aid (Scotland) (Fees) Amendment (No. 2) Regulations 2012 No. 2012/305. - Enabling power: Legal Aid (Scotland) Act 1986, ss. 33 (2) (a) (3) (a), 36 (1). - Issued: 16.11.2012. Made: 13.11.2012. Laid before the Scottish Parliament: 15.11.2012. Coming into force: 18.12.2012. Effect: S.I. 1989/1491 amended. Territorial extent & classification: S. General. - This S.S.I. has been made in consequence of a defect in S.S.I. 2012/276 (ISBN 9780111018125) and is being issued free of charge to all known recipients of that instrument. - 2p.: 30 cm. - 978-0-11-101841-5 £4.00

The Criminal Legal Aid (Scotland) (Fees) Amendment Regulations 2012 No. 2012/276. - Enabling power: Legal Aid (Scotland) Act 1986, ss. 33 (2) (a) (3) (a) (b), 36 (1). - Issued: 23.10.2012. Made: 17.10.2012. Laid before the Scottish Parliament: 19.10.2012. Coming into force: 03.12.2012. Effect: S.I. 1989/1491 amended. Territorial extent & classification: S. General. - A defect in this SSI has been corrected by SSI 2012/305 (ISBN 9780111018415) which is being sent free of charge to all known recipients of 2012/276. - 12p.: 30 cm. - 978-0-11-101812-5 £5.75

Legal profession

The Legal Services (Scotland) Act 2010 (Ancillary Provision) Regulations 2012 No. 2012/212. - Enabling power: Legal Services (Scotland) Act 2010, s. 148 (1). - Issued: 03.07.2012. Made: 27.06.2012. Coming into force: 02.07.2012. Effect: 1980 c.46; 1986 c.47; 2007 asp 5 amended. Territorial extent & classification: S. General. - Supersedes draft S.I. (ISBN 9780111017111) issued 21.05.2012. - 4p.: 30 cm. - 978-0-11-101766-1 £4.00

The Legal Services (Scotland) Act 2010 (Commencement No. 2 and Transitional Provisions) Order 2012 No. 2012/152 (C.14). - Enabling power: Legal Services (Scotland) Act 2010, ss. 150 (2) (4). Bringing into operation various provisions of this Act on 02.07.2012, in accord. with art 2. - Issued: 22.05.2012. Made: 17.05.2012. Laid before the Scottish Parliament: 21.05.2012. Coming into force: 02.07.2012. Effect: None. Territorial extent & classification: S. General. - 8p.: 30 cm. - 978-0-11-101717-3 £5.75

The Licensed Legal Services (Complaints and Compensation Arrangements) (Scotland) Regulations 2012 No. 2012/153. - Enabling power: Legal Profession and Legal Aid (Scotland) Act 2007, s. 57A (2) (b) & Legal Services (Scotland) Act 2010, ss. 26 (2), 79 (8). - Issued: 23.05.2012. Made: 17.05.2012. Laid before the Scottish Parliament: 21.05.2012. Coming into force: 02.07.2012. Effect: 2007 asp.5 modified. Territorial extent & classification: S. General. - 8p.: 30 cm. - 978-0-11-101718-0 £4.00

The Licensed Legal Services (Interests in Licensed Providers) (Scotland) Regulations 2012 No. 2012/154. - Enabling power: Legal Services (Scotland) Act 2010, ss. 67 (2) (a) (4) (c) (d), 146 (2) (a). - Issued: 23.05.2012. Made: 17.05.2012. Laid before the Scottish Parliament: 21.05.2012. Coming into force: 02.07.2012. Effect: None. Territorial extent & classification: S. General. - 8p.: 30 cm. - 978-0-11-101719-7 £4.00

The Licensed Legal Services (Maximum Penalty and Interest in respect of Approved Regulators) (Scotland) Regulations 2012 No. 2012/155. - Enabling power: Legal Services (Scotland) Act 2010, sch. 4, paras 2 (2), 11 (2). - Issued: 23.05.2012. Made: 17.05.2012. Laid before the Scottish Parliament: 21.05.2012. Coming into force: 02.07.2012. Effect: None. Territorial extent & classification: S. General. - 4p.: 30 cm. - 978-0-11-101720-3 £4.00

The Licensed Legal Services (Specification of Regulated Professions) (Scotland) Regulations 2012 No. 2012/213. - Enabling power: Legal Services (Scotland) Act 2010, s. 49 (4). - Issued: 03.07.2012. Made: 27.06.2012. Coming into force: 02.07.2012. Effect: None. Territorial extent & classification: S. General. - Supersedes draft SSI (ISBN 9780111017128) issued 21.05.2012. - 4p.: 30 cm. - 978-0-11-101767-8 £4.00

Licences and licensing

The Civic Government (Scotland) Act 1982 (Metal Dealers' Exemption Warrants) Order 2012 No. 2012/324. - Enabling power: Civic Government (Scotland) Act 1982, s. 29 (1). - Issued: 29.11.2012. Made: 26.11.2012. Laid: 28.11.2012. Coming into force: 20.02.2013. Effect: 1982 c. 45 amended. Territorial extent & classification: S. General. - 2p.: 30 cm. - 978-0-11-101855-2 £4.00

Licensing (marine)

The Marine Licensing (Exempted Activities) (Scottish Inshore and Offshore Regions) Amendment Order 2012 No. 2012/25. - Enabling power: Marine and Coastal Access Act 2009, ss. 74 (1) (2) (3), 316 (1) & Marine (Scotland) Act 2010, ss. 32 (1) (2) (3), 165 (1). - Issued: 07.02.2012. Made: 02.02.2012. Coming into force: 03.02.2012 in accord. with art. 1. Effect: S.S.I. 2011/57, 204 amended. Territorial extent & classification: S. General. - Supersedes draft SI (ISBN 9780111015506) issued on 09.12.2011. - 8p.: 30 cm. - 978-0-11-101603-9 £5.75

The Marine Licensing (Fees) (Scotland) Regulations 2012 No. 2012/183. - Enabling power: Marine and Coastal Access Act 2009, ss. 67 (2) (3) (b), 316 (1) (b) & Marine (Scotland) Act 2010, ss. 25 (1) (b) (2), 165 (1) (b). - Issued: 06.06.2012. Made: 30.05.2012. Laid before the Scottish Parliament: 31.05.2012. Coming into force: 29.06.2012. Effect: S.S.I. 2011/78 amended. Territorial extent & classification: S. General. - 4p.: 30 cm. - 978-0-11-101738-8 £4.00

Local government

The Local Government Finance (Scotland) Amendment Order 2012 No. 2012/94. - Enabling power: Local Government Finance Act 1992, sch. 12, para. 1. - Issued: 20.03.2012. Made: 15.03.2012. Coming into force: 16.03.2012 in accord. with art. 1. Effect: S.S.I. 2012/41 amended. Territorial extent & classification: S. General. - Supersedes draft S.I. (ISBN 9780111016435) issued 05.03.2012. - 4p.: 30 cm. - 978-0-11-101666-4 £4.00

The Local Government Finance (Scotland) Order 2012 No. 2012/41. - Enabling power: Local Government Finance Act 1992, sch. 12, paras. 1, 9 (4). - Issued: 16.02.2012. Made: 09.02.2012. Coming into force: 10.02.2012. Effect: S.S.I. 2011/109 partially revoked. Territorial extent & classification: S. General. - Supersedes draft S.I. (ISBN 9780111015933) issued 27.01.2012. - 8p.: 30 cm. - 978-0-11-101621-3 £4.00

Mental health

The Mental Health (Safety and Security) (Scotland) Amendment Regulations 2012 No. 2012/211. - Enabling power: Mental Health (Care and Treatment) (Scotland) Act 2003, s. 286 (1). - Issued: 03.07.2012. Made: 26.06.2012. Coming into force: 01.08.2012. Effect: S.S.I. 2005/464 amended & S.S.I. 2007/243 revoked. Territorial extent & classification: S. General. - Supersedes draft S.I. (ISBN 9780111017067) issued 18.05.2012. - 4p.: 30 cm. - 978-0-11-101765-4 £4.00

The Mental Health Tribunal for Scotland (Practice and Procedure) (No. 2) Amendment Rules 2012 No. 2012/132. - Enabling power: Mental Health (Care and Treatment) (Scotland) Act 2003, ss. 21 (4), 326, sch. 2, para. 10. - Issued: 02.05.2012. Made: 26.04.2012. Laid before the Scottish Parliament: 30.04.2012. Coming into force: 01.06.2012. Effect: S.S.I. 2005/519 amended. Territorial extent & classification: S. General. - 4p.: 30 cm. - 978-0-11-101694-7 *£4.00*

National assistance services

The National Assistance (Assessment of Resources) Amendment (Scotland) Regulations 2012 No. 2012/68. - Enabling power: National Assistance Act 1948, s. 22 (5). - Issued: 05.03.2012. Made: 28.02.2012. Laid before the Scottish Parliament: 01.03.2012. Coming into force: 09.04.2012. Effect: S.I. 1992/2977 amended in relation to Scotland & S.S.I. 2011/124 partially revoked. Territorial extent & classification: S. General. - 4p.: 30 cm. - 978-0-11-101644-2 *£4.00*

The National Assistance (Sums for Personal Requirements) (Scotland) Regulations 2012 No. 2012/67. - Enabling power: National Assistance Act 1948, s. 22 (4). - Issued: 05.03.2012. Made: 28.02.2012. Laid before the Scottish Parliament: 01.03.2012. Coming into force: 09.04.2012. Effect: S.S.I. 2011/123 revoked. Territorial extent & classification: S. General. - 4p.: 30 cm. - 978-0-11-101642-8 *£4.00*

National Health Service

The National Health Service (Charges to Overseas Visitors) (Scotland) Amendment Regulations 2012 No. 2012/87. - Enabling power: National Health Service (Scotland) Act 1987, ss. 98, 105. - Issued: 19.03.2012. Made: 13.03.2012. Laid before the Scottish Parliament: 15.03.2012. Coming into force: 01.05.2012. Effect: S.S.I. 1989/364 amended. Territorial extent & classification: S. General. - 4p.: 30 cm. - 978-0-11-101658-9 *£4.00*

The National Health Service (Free Prescriptions and Charges for Drugs and Appliances) (Scotland) Amendment Regulations 2012 No. 2012/74. - Enabling power: National Health Service (Scotland) Act 1978, ss. 69 (1) (2), 105 (7), 108 (1). - Issued: 05.03.2012. Made: 29.02.2012. Laid before the Scottish Parliament: 02.03.2012. Coming into force: 01.04.2012. Effect: S.S.I. 2011/55 amended. Territorial extent & classification: S. General. - 4p.: 30 cm. - 978-0-11-101650-3 *£4.00*

The National Health Service (General Medical Services Contracts) (Scotland) Amendment Regulations 2012 No. 2012/9. - Enabling power: National Health Service (Scotland) Act 1978, ss. 17N, 105 (7), 106 (a), 108 (1). - Issued: 20.01.2012. Made: 17.01.2012. Laid before the Scottish Parliament: 19.01.2012. Coming into force: 26.01.2012. Effect: S.S.I. 2004/115 amended. Territorial extent & classification: S. General. - 4p.: 30 cm. - 978-0-11-101589-6 *£4.00*

The National Health Service (Optical Charges and Payments) (Scotland) Amendment Regulations 2012 No. 2012/73. - Enabling power: National Health Service (Scotland) Act 1978, ss. 70 (1), 73 (a), 74 (a), 105 (7), 108 (1), sch. 11, paras. 2, 2A. - Issued: 06.03.2012. Made: 29.02.2012. Laid before the Scottish Parliament: 02.03.2012. Coming into force: 01.04.2012. Effect: S.I. 1998/642 amended. Territorial extent & classification: S. General. - 8p.: 30 cm. - 978-0-11-101649-7 *£4.00*

The National Health Service (Primary Medical Services Section 17C Agreements) (Scotland) Amendment Regulations 2012 No. 2012/10. - Enabling power: National Health Service (Scotland) Act 1978, ss. 17E, 105 (7),108 (1). - Issued: 20.01.2012. Made: 17.01.2012. Laid before the Scottish Parliament: 19.01.2012. Coming into force: 26.02.2012. Effect: S.S.I. 2004/116 amended. Territorial extent & classification: S. General. - 4p.: 30 cm. - 978-0-11-101590-2 *£4.00*

The National Health Service (Superannuation Scheme and Pension Scheme) (Scotland) Amendment Regulations 2012 No. 2012/69. - Enabling power: Superannuation Act 1972, s. 10, sch. 3. - Issued: 05.03.2012. Made: 28.02.2012. Laid before the Scottish Parliament: 01.03.2012. Coming into force: 01.04.2012. Effect: S.S.I. 2008/224, 2011/117 amended. Territorial extent & classification: S. General. - 8p.: 30 cm. - 978-0-11-101645-9 *£5.75*

The National Health Service Superannuation Scheme etc. (Miscellaneous Amendments) (Scotland) Regulations 2012 No. 2012/163. - Enabling power: Superannuation Act 1972, ss. 10, 12, sch. 3. - Issued: 28.05.2012. Made: 21.05.2012. Laid before the Scottish Parliament: 24.05.2012. Coming into force: 28.06.2012. Effect: S.I. 1998/1451, 1594; S.S.I. 2008/224, 2011/117 amended. Territorial extent & classification: S. General. - With correction slip dated July 2012. - 12p.: 30 cm. - 978-0-11-101726-5 *£5.75*

The National Health Service (Travelling Expenses and Remission of Charges) (Scotland) (No. 2) Amendment Regulations 2012 No. 2012/171. - Enabling power: National Health Service (Scotland) Act 1978, ss. 75A, 105 (7), 108 (1). - Issued: 01.06.2012. Made: 29.05.2012. Laid before the Scottish Parliament: 31.05.2012. Coming into force: 01.09.2012. Effect: S.S.I. 2003/460 amended. Territorial extent & classification: S. General. - 4p.: 30 cm. - 978-0-11-101732-6 *£4.00*

The Patient Rights (Complaints Procedure and Consequential Provisions) (Scotland) Regulations 2012 No. 2012/36. - Enabling power: Patient Rights (Scotland) Act 2011, ss. 15 (4) (a), 25 (1). - Issued: 13.02.2012. Made: 08.02.2012. Laid before the Scottish Parliament: 10.02.2012. Coming into force: 01.04.2012. Effect: S.S.I. 2004/115, 116; 2006/135, 330; 2009/183; 2010/208 amended. Territorial extent & classification: S. General. - 8p.: 30 cm. - 978-0-11-101612-1 *£5.75*

The Patient Rights (Scotland) Act 2011 (Commencement) Order 2012 No. 2012/35 (C.7). - Enabling power: Patient Rights (Scotland) Act 2011, s. 26 (3). Bringing into operation various provisions of the 2011 Act on 01.04.2012 for ss. 1 to 7, 14 to 21, 23 & 01.10.2012 for remaining provisions. - Issued: 13.02.2012. Made: 08.02.2012. Laid before the Scottish Parliament: 10.02.2012. Effect: None. Territorial extent & classification: S. General. - 2p.: 30 cm. - 978-0-11-101611-4 £4.00

The Patient Rights (Treatment Time Guarantee) (Scotland) Regulations 2012 No. 2012/110. - Enabling power: Patient Rights (Scotland) Act 2011, ss. 9 (1) (3), 25 (1). - Issued: 03.04.2012. Made: 29.03.2012. Coming into force: 01.10.2012. Effect: None. Territorial extent & classification: S. General. - Supersedes draft S.I. (ISBN 9780111016152) issued on 14.02.2012. - 8p.: 30 cm. - 978-0-11-101675-6 £5.75

The Personal Injuries (NHS Charges) (Amounts) (Scotland) Amendment Regulations 2012 No. 2012/76. - Enabling power: Health and Social care (Community Health and Standards) Act 2003, ss. 153 (2) (5), 195 (1) (2). - Issued: 06.03.2012. Made: 29.02.2012. Laid before the Scottish Parliament: 02.03.2012. Coming into force: 01.04.2012. Effect: S.S.I. 2006/588 amended. Territorial extent & classification: S. General. - 4p.: 30 cm. - 978-0-11-101652-7 £4.00

Official statistics

The Official Statistics (Scotland) Amendment Order 2012 No. 2012/196. - Enabling power: Statistics and Registration Service Act 2007, s. 6 (1) (b) (ii) (2). - Issued: 19.06.2012. Made: 31.05.2012. Coming into force: 01.06.2012 in accord. with art. 1. Effect: S.S.I. 2008/131 amended. Territorial extent & classification: S. General. - Supersedes draft SSI (ISBN 9780111016909) issued on 30.04.2012. - 4p.: 30 cm. - 978-0-11-101754-8 £4.00

Pensions

The Local Government Pension Scheme (Administration) (Scotland) Amendment Regulations 2012 No. 2012/236. - Enabling power: Superannuation Act 1972, ss. 7, 12, 24, sch. 3. - Issued: 31.08.2012. Made: 27.08.2012. Laid before the Scottish Parliament: 29.08.2012. Coming into force: 12.10.2012. Effect: S.S.I. 2008/228 amended. Territorial extent & classification: S. General. - 8p.: 30 cm. - 978-0-11-101778-4 £5.75

The Local Government Pension Scheme (Miscellaneous Amendments) (Scotland) Regulations 2012 No. 2012/347. - Enabling power: Superannuation Act 1972, ss. 7, 12, 24, sch. 3. - Issued: 19.12.2012. Made: 13.12.2012. Laid before the Scottish Parliament: 17.12.2012. Coming into force: 01.02.2013. Effect: S.S.I. 2008/228, 229, 230 amended. Territorial extent & classification: S. General. - 12p.: 30 cm. - 978-0-11-101884-2 £5.75

The Police Pensions (Contributions) Amendment (Scotland) Regulations 2012 No. 2012/71. - Enabling power: Police Pensions Act 1976, ss. 1. - Issued: 05.03.2012. Made: 28.02.2012. Laid before the Scottish Parliament: 01.03.2012. Coming into force: 01.04.2012. Effect: S.I. 1987/257, 2215; S.S.I. 2007/201 amended. Territorial extent & classification: S. General. - 8p.: 30 cm. - 978-0-11-101647-3 £4.00

The Teachers' Superannuation (Scotland) Amendment Regulations 2012 No. 2012/70. - Enabling power: Superannuation Act 1972, ss. 9, 12, sch. 3. - Issued: 05.03.2012. Made: 28.02.2012. Laid before the Scottish Parliament: 01.03.2012. Coming into force: 01.04.2012. Effect: S.S.I. 2005/393 amended. Territorial extent & classification: S. General. - With correction slip dated March 2012. - 4p.: 30 cm. - 978-0-11-101646-6 £4.00

Plant health

The Plant Health (Scotland) Amendment (No. 2) Order 2012 No. 2012/326. - Enabling power: Plant Health Act 1967, ss. 2, 3, 4 (1) & Agriculture (Miscellaneous Provisions) Act 1972, s. 20. - Issued: 30.11.2012. Made: 27.11.2012. Laid before the Scottish Parliament: 29.11.2012. Coming into force: 14.01.2013. Effect: S.S.I. 2005/613 amended. Territorial extent & classification: S. General. - 8p.: 30 cm. - 978-0-11-101857-6 £4.00

The Plant Health (Scotland) Amendment Order 2012 No. 2012/266. - Enabling power: Plant Health Act 1967, ss. 2, 3, 4 (1); Agriculture (Miscellaneous Provisions) Act 1972, s. 20 & European Communities Act 1972, s. 2 (2), sch. 2, para. 1A. - Issued: 04.10.2012. Made: 27.09.2012. Laid before the Scottish Parliament: 01.10.2012. Coming into force: 15.11.2012. Effect: S.S.I. 2005/613 amended & S.S.I 2006/474; 2008/350; 2010/342 partially revoked. Territorial extent & classification: S. General. - EC note: This Order implements Decision 2012/138/EU; 2012/219/EU; 2012/270/EU; DIR 2007/33/EC. - 16p.: 30 cm. - 978-0-11-101801-9 £5.75

The Potatoes Originating in Egypt (Scotland) Amendment Regulations 2012 No. 2012/37. - Enabling power: European Communities Act 1972, s. 2 (2), sch. 2, para 1A. - Issued: 14.02.2012. Made: 09.02.2012. Laid before the Scottish Parliament: 13.02.2012. Coming into force: 21.03.2012. Effect: S.S.I. 2004/111 amended & S.S.I. 2007/94 partially revoked. Territorial extent & classification: S. General. - EC note: These Regs, implement in Scotland Commission Implementing Decision 2011/787/EC authorising Member States temporarily to take emergency measures against the dissemination of Ralstonia solanacearum (Smith) Yabuuchi et al as regards Egypt. The Decision repeals and replaces Commission Decision 2004/4. - 4p.: 30 cm. - 978-0-11-101616-9 £4.00

Police

The Police Act 1997 (Criminal Records) (Scotland) Amendment Regulations 2012 No. 2012/354. - Enabling power: Police Act 1997, ss. 112 (3), 113A (6). - Issued: 24.12.2012. Made: 19.12.2012. Laid before the Scottish Parliament: 21.12.2012. Coming into force: 04.02.2013. Effect: S.S.I. 2010/168 amended. Territorial extent & classification: S. General. - 2p.: 30 cm. - 978-0-11-101890-3 £4.00

The Police and Fire Reform (Scotland) Act 2012 (Commencement No. 1, Transitional, Transitory and Saving Provisions) Order 2012 No. 2012/253 (C.24). - Enabling power: Police and Fire Reform (Scotland) Act 2012, s. 129 (2) (3). Bringing into operation various provisions of the 2012 Act on 01.10.2012. - Issued: 18.09.2012. Made: 13.09.2012. Laid before the Scottish Parliament: 14.09.2012. Effect: 2012 asp 8 modified. Territorial extent & classification: S. General. - 8p.: 30 cm. - 978-0-11-101789-0 £5.75

The Police and Fire Reform (Scotland) Act 2012 (Commencement No. 2, Transitory and Transitional Provisions and Appointed Day) Order 2012 No. 2012/333 (C.32). - Enabling power: Police and Fire Reform (Scotland) Act 2012, s. 129 (2) (3), sch. 6, para. 1. Bringing into operation various provisions of the 2012 Act on 01.01.2013, 01.04.2013, in accord. with arts. 2, 4. - Issued: 07.12.2012. Made: 04.12.2012. Laid before the Scottish Parliament: 06.12.2012. Coming into force: 01.01.2013. Effect: None. Territorial extent & classification: S. General. - 12p.: 30 cm. - 978-0-11-101868-2 £5.75

The Police Grant Variation (Scotland) Order 2012 No. 2012/316. - Enabling power: Police (Scotland) Act 1967, s. 32 (3) (5). - Issued: 23.11.2012. Made: 20.11.2012. Laid before the Scottish Parliament: 22.11.2012. Coming into force: 01.01.2013. Effect: S.S.I. 2012/316 varied. Territorial extent & classification: S. General. - 4p.: 30 cm. - 978-0-11-101847-7 £4.00

The Police Grant and Variation (Scotland) Order 2012 No. 2012/49. - Enabling power: Police (Scotland) Act 1967, s. 32 (3) (5). - Issued: 22.02.2012. Made: 16.02.2012. Laid before the Scottish Parliament: 20.02.2012. Coming into force: 01.04.2012. Effect: S.S.I. 2010/64 varied. Territorial extent & classification: S. General. - 4p.: 30 cm. - 978-0-11-101628-2 £4.00

Prisons

The Parole Board (Scotland) Amendment (No. 2) Rules 2012 No. 2012/197. - Enabling power: Prisoners and Criminal Proceedings (Scotland) Act 1993, s. 20 (4). - Issued: 21.06.2012. Made: 18.06.2012. Laid before the Scottish Parliament: 20.06.2012. Coming into force: 26.06.2012. Effect: S.S.I. 2001/315 amended & S.S.I. 2012/167 partially revoked. Territorial extent & classification: S. General. - This instrument has been made to correct defects in S.S.I. 2012/167 (ISBN 9780111017302) and is being issued free of charge to all known recipients of that instrument. - 4p.: 30 cm. - 978-0-11-101755-5 £4.00

The Parole Board (Scotland) Amendment Rules 2012 No. 2012/167. - Enabling power: Prisoners and Criminal Proceedings (Scotland) Act 1993, s. 20 (4). - Issued: 30.05.2012. Made: 24.05.2012. Laid before the Scottish Parliament: 28.05.2012. Coming into force: 26.06.2012. Effect: S.S.I. 2001/315 amended. Territorial extent & classification: S. General. - Partially revoked by SSI 2012/197 (ISBN 9780111017555). - 8p.: 30 cm. - 978-0-11-101730-2 £4.00

The Prisons and Young Offenders Institutions (Scotland) Amendment Rules 2012 No. 2012/26. - Enabling power: Prisons (Scotland) Act 1989, ss. 8, 11, 12, 33A, 39. - Issued: 08.02.2012. Made: 06.02.2012. Laid before the Scottish Parliament: 08.02.2012. Coming into force: 19.03.2012. Effect: S.S.I. 2011/331 amended. Territorial extent & classification: S. General. - With correction slip dated May 2012. - 8p.: 30 cm. - 978-0-11-101604-6 £4.00

Property factors

The Homeowner Housing Panel (Applications and Decisions) (Scotland) Regulations 2012 No. 2012/180. - Enabling power: Property Factors (Scotland) Act 2011, ss. 25, 30 (2). - Issued: 06.06.2012. Made: 29.05.2012. Laid before the Scottish Parliament: 31.05.2012. Coming into force: 01.10.2012. Effect: None. Territorial extent & classification: S. General. - 12p.: 30 cm. - 978-0-11-101736-4 £5.75

The Property Factors (Code of Conduct) (Scotland) Order 2012 No. 2012/217. - Enabling power: Property Factors (Scotland) Act 2011, s. 14 (3) (c). - Issued: 09.07.2012. Made: 28.06.2012. Coming into force: 29.06.2012, in accord. with art. 1. Effect: None. Territorial extent & classification: S. General. - Supersedes draft SSI (ISBN 9780111016954) issued on 02.05.2012. - 2p.: 30 cm. - 978-0-11-101772-2 £4.00

The Property Factors (Registration) (Scotland) Regulations 2012 No. 2012/181. - Enabling power: Property Factors (Scotland) Act 2011, ss. 3 (2) (f) (4), 30 (2). - Issued: 06.06.2012. Made: 29.05.2012. Laid before the Scottish Parliament: 31.05.2012. Coming into force: 01.07.2012. Effect: None. Territorial extent & classification: S. General. - 4p.: 30 cm. - 978-0-11-101743-2 £4.00

The Property Factors (Scotland) Act 2011 (Commencement No. 2 and Transitional) Order 2012 No. 2012/149 (C.12). - Enabling power: Property Factors (Scotland) Act 2011, ss. 30 (2), 33 (2) (4). Bringing into operation various provisions of the 2011 Act on 01.07.2012, in accord. with art. 2. - Issued: 22.05.2012. Made: 17.05.2012. Laid before the Scottish Parliament: 21.05.2012. Coming into force: 01.07.2012. Effect: None. Territorial extent & classification: S. General. - 4p.: 30 cm. - 978-0-11-101714-2 £4.00

The Property Factors (Scotland) Act 2011 (Modification) Order 2012 No. 2012/269. - Enabling power: Property Factors (Scotland) Act 2011, ss. 29 (1) (2), 30 (2). - Issued: 08.10.2012. Made: 02.10.2012. Coming into force: 03.10.2012. Effect: 2011 asp 8 modified. Territorial extent & classification: S. General. - Supersedes draft S.I. (ISBN 9780111017579) issued 25.06.2012. - 2p.: 30 cm. - 978-0-11-101804-0 £4.00

Public bodies

The Public Appointments and Public Bodies etc. (Scotland) Act 2003 (Treatment of Office or Body as Specified Authority) Order 2012 No. 2012/193. - Enabling power: Public Appointments and Public Bodies etc. (Scotland) Act 2003, s. 3 (3). - Issued: 15.06.2012. Made: 11.06.2012. Coming into force: 12.06.2012. Effect: None. Territorial extent & classification: S. General. - Supersedes draft SSI (ISBN 9780111016992) issued on 16.05.2012. - 4p.: 30 cm. - 978-0-11-101752-4 £4.00

Public finance and accountability

The Budget (Scotland) Act 2011 Amendment Order 2012 No. 2012/105. - Enabling power: Budget (Scotland) Act 2011, s. 7 (1). - Issued: 30.03.2012. Made: 22.03.2012. Coming into force: 23.03.2012. in accord. with art. 1 (1). Effect: 2011 asp 4 amended. Territorial extent & classification: S. General. - Supersedes draft S.S.I. (ISBN 9780111016022) issued 02.02.2012. - 4p.: 30 cm. - 978-0-11-101672-5 £4.00

The Budget (Scotland) Act 2012 Amendment Order 2012 No. 2012/346. - Enabling power: Budget (Scotland) Act 2012, s. 7 (1). - Issued: 18.12.2012. Made: 12.12.2012. Coming into force: In accord. with art. 1 (1). Effect: 2012 asp 2 amended. Territorial extent & classification: S. General. - Supersedes draft SI (ISBN 9780111018118) issued on 22.10.2012. - 4p.: 30 cm. - 978-0-11-101881-1 £4.00

Public health

The Food Protection (Emergency Prohibitions) (Radioactivity in Sheep) and the Export of Sheep (Prohibition) Revocation (Scotland) Order 2012 No. 2012/263. - Enabling power: Animal Health Act 1981, s. 11 & Food and Environment Protection Act 1985, ss. 1 (1) (2), 24 (3). - Issued: 01.10.2012. Made: 26.09.2012. Laid before the Scottish Parliament: 28.09.2012. Coming into force: 01.10.2012. Effect: S.I. 1991/20, 58, 2766; 1993/13; 1994/50; 1995/48; 1996/31; 1997/62; 1998/82; 1999/80 revoked in relation to Scotland & S.S.I. 2001/313; 2003/375; 2004/48; 2005/71; 2006/52; 2007/38; 2008/63 revoked. Territorial extent & classification: S. General. - 4p.: 30 cm. - 978-0-11-101797-5 £4.00

Public health: Contamination of food

The Food Protection (Emergency Prohibitions) (Dalgety Bay) (Scotland) Order 2012 No. 2012/135. - Enabling power: Food and Environment Protection Act 1985, ss. 1 (1) (2), 24 (3). - Issued: 11.05.2012. Made: 08.05.2012. Laid before the Scottish Parliament: 09.05.2012. Coming into force: In accord. with art. 1 (1). Effect: None. Territorial extent & classification: S. General. - For approval by resolution of the Scottish Parliament within twenty eight days. - 8p., map: 30 cm. - 978-0-11-101696-1 £4.00

Public passenger transport

The Public Service Vehicles (Registration of Local Services) (Scotland) Amendment Regulations 2012 No. 2012/32. - Enabling power: Transport Act 1985, s. 6 (2) (a) (3) (a) (8) (a) (9) & Public Passenger Vehicles Act 1981, s. 60 (1) (e) (f) (1A). - Issued: 13.02.2012. Made: 08.02.2012. Laid before the Scottish Parliament: 10.02.2012. Coming into force: 01.04.2012. Effect: S.S.I. 2001/219 amended. Territorial extent & classification: S. General. - 8p.: 30 cm. - 978-0-11-101613-8 £5.75

Public procurement

The Public Contracts and Utilities Contracts (Scotland) Amendment Regulations 2012 No. 2012/108. - Enabling power: European Communities Act 1972, s. 2 (2). - Issued: 03.04.2012. Made: 28.03.2012. Laid before the Scottish Parliament: 30.03.2012. Coming into force: 01.05.2012. Effect: S.S.I. 2012/88, 89 amended. Territorial extent & classification: S. General. - This Scottish Statutory Instrument has been made to correct errors in S.S.I. 2012/88 (ISBN 9780111016633) and S.S.I. 2012/89 (ISBN 9780111016640) and is being issued free of charge to all known recipients of those instruments. - 4p.: 30 cm. - 978-0-11-101673-2 £4.00

The Public Contracts (Scotland) Regulations 2012 No. 2012/88. - Enabling power: European Communities Act 1972, s. 2 (2), sch. 2, para. 1A. - Issued: 22.03.2012. Made: 14.03.2012. Laid before the Scottish Parliament: 16.03.2012. Coming into force: 01.05.2012. Effect: S.S.I. 2003/231; 2008/170; 2010/390; 2011/1848 amended & S.S.I. 2007/565; 2008/94, 291, 376; 2009/428, 439 revoked insofar as they extend to the Public Contracts (Scotland) Regulations 2006 (SSI. 2006/1) & S.S.I. 2006/1 revoked. Territorial extent & classification: S. General. - With correction slip dated July 2012. Partially revoked by SSI 2013/50 (ISBN 9780111019504). - 96p.: 30 cm. - 978-0-11-101663-3 £15.50

The Utilities Contracts (Scotland) Amendment Regulations 2012 No. 2012/89. - Enabling power: European Communities Act 1972, s. 2 (2), sch. 2, para 1A. - Issued: 22.03.2012. Made: 14.03.2012. Laid before the Scottish Parliament: 16.03.2012. Coming into force: 01.05.2012. Effect: SSI 2003/231; 2010/390; 2011/1848 amended; SSI 2007/565; 2008/94, 291; 2009/428, 439 revoked insofar as they extend to the Utilities Contracts (Scotland) Regulations 2006 (SSI 2006/2) & SSI 2008/376 revoked insofar as it extends to the Public Contracts (Scotland) Regulations 2006 (SSI 2006/1) & S.S.I. 2006/2 revoked. Territorial extent & classification: S. General. - With correction slip dated July 2012. Partially revoked by SSI 2013/50 (ISBN 9780111019504). - 76p.: 30 cm. - 978-0-11-101664-0 £13.75

Public sector information

The INSPIRE (Scotland) Amendment Regulations 2012 No. 2012/284. - Enabling power: European Communities Act 1972, s. 2 (2). - Issued: 29.10.2012. Made: 23.10.2012. Laid before the Scottish Parliament: 25.10.2012. Coming into force: 23.11.2012. Effect: S.S.I. 2009/440 amended. Territorial extent & classification: S. General. - INSPIRE = Infrastructure for Spatial Information in the European Community. EC note: These Regulations amend the principal regulations which implemented, in part, Directive 2007/2/EC which concerns the creation and operation of national and Community infrastructures relating to spatial information for the purposes of Community environmental policies and other policies or activities which may have an impact on the environment. Implementing rules of Directive 2007/2/EC as regards interoperability of spatial sets and services as amended by Reg 102/2011 have now been adopted by virtue of Reg. 1089/2010. In consequence of the adoption of the implementing rules these regulations amend the principal regulations to further implement Directive 2007/2/EC. - 8p.: 30 cm. - 978-0-11-101816-3 £4.00

Rating and valuation

The Non-Domestic Rate (Scotland) (No. 2) Order 2012 No. 2012/352. - Enabling power: Local Government (Scotland) Act 1975, ss. 7B (1), 37 (1). - Issued: 21.12.2012. Made: 18.12.2012. Laid before the Scottish Parliament: 20.12.2012. Coming into force: 01.04.2013. Effect: None. Territorial extent & classification: S. General. - 2p.: 30 cm. - 978-0-11-101888-0 £4.00

The Non-Domestic Rate (Scotland) Order 2012 No. 2012/27. - Enabling power: Local Government (Scotland) Act 1975, ss. 7B(1), 37(1). - Issued: 10.02.2012. Made: 07.02.2012. Laid before the Scottish Parliament: 09.02.2012. Coming into force: 01.04.2012. Effect: None. Territorial extent & classification: S. General. - 2p.: 30 cm. - 978-0-11-101606-0 £4.00

The Non-Domestic Rates (Enterprise Areas) (Scotland) Regulations 2012 No. 2012/48. - Enabling power: Local Government etc. (Scotland) Act 1994, s. 153. - Issued: 21.02.2012. Made: 16.02.2012. Laid before the Scottish Parliament: 20.02.2012. Coming into force: 01.04.2012. Effect: None. Territorial extent & classification: S. General. - 8p.: 30 cm. - 978-0-11-101627-5 £5.75

The Non-Domestic Rates (Levying) (Scotland) (No. 2) Regulations 2012 No. 2012/29. - Enabling power: Local Government etc. (Scotland) Act 1994, s. 153. - Issued: 10.02.2012. Made: 07.02.2012. Laid before the Scottish Parliament: 09.02.2012. Coming into force: 01.04.2012. Effect: None. Territorial extent & classification: S. General. - 4p.: 30 cm. - 978-0-11-101608-4 £4.00

The Non-Domestic Rates (Levying) (Scotland) (No. 3) Regulations 2012 No. 2012/353. - Enabling power: Local Government etc. (Scotland) Act 1994, s. 153. - Issued: 21.12.2012. Made: 18.12.2012. Laid before the Scottish Parliament: 20.12.2012. Coming into force: 01.04.2013. Effect: S.S.I. 2012/28 revoked with saving. Territorial extent & classification: S. General. - This SSI has been corrected by SSI 2013/34 (ISBN 9780111019306) and is being issued free of charge to all known recipients of that SSI. - [8]p.: 30 cm. - 978-0-11-101889-7 £4.00

The Non-Domestic Rates (Levying) (Scotland) Regulations 2012 No. 2012/28. - Enabling power: Local Government etc. (Scotland) Act 1994, s. 153. - Issued: 10.02.2012. Made: 07.02.2012. Laid before the Scottish Parliament: 09.02.2012. Coming into force: 01.04.2012. Effect: S.S.I. 2010/440 partially revoked with savings. Territorial extent & classification: S. General. - 8p.: 30 cm. - 978-0-11-101607-7 £4.00

Registers and records

The Crofting Register (Fees) (Scotland) Amendment Order 2012 No. 2012/328. - Enabling power: Crofting Reform (Scotland) Act 2010, ss. 19 (2), 53 (2) (a). - Issued: 30.11.2012. Made: 27.11.2012. Laid before the Scottish Parliament: 29.11.2012. Coming into force: 13.01.2012. Effect: S.S.I. 2012/295 amended. Territorial extent & classification: S. General. - This S.S.I. has been made in consequence of a defect in S.S.I. 2012/295 (ISBN 9780111018286) and is being issued free of charge to all known recipients of that instrument. - 2p.: 30 cm. - 978-0-11-101859-0 £4.00

The Crofting Register (Fees) (Scotland) Order 2012 No. 2012/295. - Enabling power: Crofting Reform (Scotland) Act 2010, ss. 19 (2) (3), 53 (2) (a). - Issued: 05.11.2012. Made: 30.10.2012. Laid before the Scottish Parliament: 01.11.2012. Coming into force: 30.11.2012. Effect: None. Territorial extent & classification: S. General. - This SSI has been corrected by SSI 2012/328 (ISBN 9780111018590) which is being sent free of charge to all known recipients of that 2012/295. - 4p.: 30 cm. - 978-0-11-101828-6 £4.00

The Crofting Register (Notice of First Registration) (Scotland) Order 2012 No. 2012/296. - Enabling power: Crofting Reform (Scotland) Act 2010, ss. 12 (8) (b), 53 (2) (a). - Issued: 08.11.2012. Made: 30.10.2012. Laid before the Scottish Parliament: 01.11.2012. Coming into force: 30.11.2012. Effect: None. Territorial extent & classification: S. General. - 8p.: 30 cm. - 978-0-11-101826-2 £4.00

The Crofting Register (Scotland) Amendment Rules 2012 No. 2012/327. - Enabling power: Crofting Reform (Scotland) Act 2010, ss. 19 (1), 53 (2) (a). - Issued: 30.11.2012. Made: 27.11.2012. Laid before the Scottish Parliament: 29.11.2012. Coming into force: 13.01.2013. Effect: S.S.I. 2012/294 amended. Territorial extent & classification: S. General. - This S.S.I. has been made in consequence of a defect in S.S.I. 2012/294 (ISBN 9780111018279) and is being issued free of charge to all known recipients of that instrument. - 4p.: 30 cm. - 978-0-11-101858-3 £4.00

The Crofting Register (Scotland) Rules 2012 No. 2012/294. - Enabling power: Crofting Reform (Scotland) Act 2010, ss. 19 (1), 53 (2) (a). - Issued: 05.11.2012. Made: 30.10.2012. Laid before the Scottish Parliament: 01.11.2012. Coming into force: 30.11.2012. Effect: None. Territorial extent & classification: S. General. - This SSI has been corrected by SSI 2012/327 (ISBN 9780111018583) which is being sent free of charge to all known recipients of 2012/294. - 42p.: 30 cm. - 978-0-11-101827-9 £9.75

The Crofting Register (Transfer of Ownership) (Scotland) Regulations 2012 No. 2012/297. - Enabling power: Crofting Reform (Scotland) Act 2010, ss. 4 (8), 5 (6), 25 (4), 53 (2) (a). - Issued: 05.11.2012. Made: 30.10.2012. Laid before the Scottish Parliament: 01.11.2012. Coming into force: 30.11.2012. Effect: None. Territorial extent & classification: S. General. - 4p.: 30 cm. - 978-0-11-101829-3 £4.00

The Public Records (Scotland) Act 2011 (Commencement No. 1) Amendment Order 2012 No. 2012/42 (C.9). - Enabling power: Public Records (Scotland) Act 2011, s. 16 (1). Bringing into operations various provisions of the 2011 Act on 23.02.2012, in accord. with art. 1. - Issued: 16.02.2012. Made: 13.02.2012. Laid before the Scottish Parliament: 15.02.2012. Coming into force: 23.03.2012. Effect: None. Territorial extent & classification: S. General. - 2p.: 30 cm. - 978-0-11-101622-0 £4.00

The Public Records (Scotland) Act 2011 (Commencement No. 1) Order 2012 No. 2012/21 (C.5). - Enabling power: Public Records (Scotland) Act 2011, s. 16 (1). Bringing into operations various provisions of the 2011 Act on 24.02.012, in accord. with art. 2. - Issued: 30.01.2012. Made: 25.01.2012. Laid before the Scottish Parliament: 27.01.2012. Effect: None. Territorial extent & classification: S. General. - 2p.: 30 cm. - 978-0-11-101596-4 £4.00

The Public Records (Scotland) Act 2011 (Commencement No. 2) Order 2012 No. 2012/247 (C.21). - Enabling power: Public Records (Scotland) Act 2011, s. 16 (1). Bringing into operations various provisions of the 2011 Act on 01.01.2013, in accord. with art. 2. - Issued: 10.09.2012. Made: 05.09.2012. Laid before the Scottish Parliament: 07.09.2012. Effect: None. Territorial extent & classification: S. General. - 2p.: 30 cm. - 978-0-11-101785-2 £4.00

Regulatory reform

The Public Services Reform (Recovery of Expenses in respect of Inspection of Independent Further Education Colleges and English Language Schools) (Scotland) Order 2012 No. 2012/102. - Enabling power: Public Services Reform (Scotland) Act 2010, s. 17 (1) (9). - Issued: 23.03.2012. Made: 20.03.2012. Coming into force: 21.03.2012 in accord. with art. 1. Effect: 1980 c. 44 amended. Territorial extent & classification: S. General. - Supersedes draft S.S.I. (ISBN 9780111016015) issued 02.02.2012. - 4p.: 30 cm. - 978-0-11-101670-1 £4.00

Representation of the people

The Local Electoral Administration (Scotland) Act 2011 (Consequential Amendments) Order 2012 No. 2012/31. - Enabling power: Local Electoral Administration (Scotland) Act 2011, s. 20 (1). - Issued: 13.02.2012. Made: 08.02.2012. Coming into force: In accord. with art. 2. Effect: 1983 c.2; 2006 asp 14 & S.S.I. 2007/263 amended. Territorial extent & classification: S. General. - Supersedes draft SI (ISBN 9780111015636) issued 16.12.2011. - 4p.: 30 cm. - 978-0-11-101609-1 £4.00

The Representation of the People (Post-Local Government Elections Supply and Inspection of Documents) (Scotland) Amendment Regulations 2012 No. 2012/61. - Enabling power: Local Electoral Administration and Registration Services (Scotland) Act 2006, ss. 5 (5). - Issued: 28.02.2012. Made: 23.02.2012. Coming into force: 03.05.2012. Effect: None. Territorial extent & classification: S. General. - Supersedes draft S.I. (ISBN 9780111015872) issued 20.01.2012. - 4p.: 30 cm. - 978-0-11-101636-7 £4.00

The Representation of the People (Variation of Limits of Candidates' Local Government Election Expenses) (Scotland) Order 2011 No. 2012/16. - Enabling power: Representation of the People Act 1983, s. 76A (1) (a). - Issued: 24.01.2012. Made: 19.01.2012. Laid before the Scottish Parliament: 23.01.2012. Coming into force: 12.03.2012. Effect: 1983 c.2 varied. Territorial extent & classification: S. General. - 4p.: 30 cm. - 978-0-11-101592-6 £4.00

The Scottish Local Government Elections Amendment (No. 2) Order 2012 No. 2012/342. - Enabling power: Local Governance (Scotland) Act 2004, ss. 3A (1) (2), 16 (2) (a). - Issued: 17.12.2012. Made: 11.12.2012. Coming into force: 07.01.2013. Effect: S.S.I. 2011/399 amended. Territorial extent & classification: S. General. - Supersedes draft SSI (ISBN 9780111018248) issued 02.11.2012. - 4p.: 30 cm. - 978-0-11-101879-8 £4.00

The Scottish Local Government Elections Amendment Order 2012 No. 2012/60. - Enabling power: Local Governance (Scotland) Act 2004, ss. 3, 3A, 16 (2). - Issued: 28.02.2012. Made: 23.02.2012. Coming into force: 24.02.2012. Effect: S.S.I. 2011/399 amended. Territorial extent & classification: S. General. - Supersedes draft S.I. (ISBN 9780111015889) issued 20.01.2012. - 4p.: 30 cm. - 978-0-11-101635-0 £4.00

River: Salmon and freshwater fisheries

The Annual Close Time (Permitted Periods of Fishing) (River Dee (Aberdeenshire) Salmon Fishery District) Order 2012 No. 2012/210. - Enabling power: Salmon and Freshwater Fisheries (Consolidation) (Scotland) Act 2003, s. 37 (3). - Issued: 02.07.2012. Made: 26.06.2012. Laid before the Scottish Parliament: 28.06.2012. Coming into force: 01.10.2012. Effect: None. Territorial extent & classification: S. General. - 8p., map: 30 cm. - 978-0-11-101764-7 £4.00

The Conservation of Salmon (River Annan Salmon Fishery District) (Scotland) Regulations 2012 No. 2012/6. - Enabling power: Salmon and Freshwater Fisheries (Consolidation) (Scotland) Act 2003, s. 38 (1) (5) (6) (b) (c), sch. 1, para. 7 (a) (i), 14 (1). - Issued: 17.01.2012. Made: 12.01.2012. Laid before the Scottish Parliament: 16.01.2012. Coming into force: 25.01.2012. Effect: None. Territorial extent & classification: S. General. - 8p., map: 30 cm. - 978-0-11-101584-1 £4.00

Roads and bridges

The A82 Trunk Road (Crianlarich Bypass) Order 2012 No. 2012/239. - Enabling power: Roads (Scotland) Act 1984, s. 5 (2) (6). - Issued: 31.08.2012. Made: 30.08.2012. Coming into force: 06.09.2012. Effect: None. Territorial extent & classification: S. Local. - Available at http://www.legislation.gov.uk/ssi/2012/239/contents/made
Non-print

The A82 Trunk Road (Crianlarich Bypass) (Side Road) Order 2012 No. 2012/240. - Enabling power: Roads (Scotland) Act 1984, ss. 12 (1) (5), 70 (1). - Issued: 31.08.2012. Made: 30.08.2012. Coming into force: 06.09.2012. Effect: None. Territorial extent & classification: S. Local. - Available at http://www.legislation.gov.uk/ssi/2012/240/contents/made
Non-print

The A82 Trunk Road (Crianlarich Western Bypass) Revocation Order 2012 No. 2012/241. - Enabling power: Roads (Scotland) Act 1984, ss. 5, 145. - Issued: 03.09.2012. Made: 30.08.2012. Coming into force: 06.09.2012. Effect: S.I. 1996/1130 revoked. Territorial extent & classification: S. Local. - Available at http://www.legislation.gov.uk/ssi/2012/241/contents/made
Non-print

The A82 Trunk Road (Crianlarich Western Bypass) (Side Roads) Revocation Order 2012 No. 2012/242. - Enabling power: Roads (Scotland) Act 1984, ss. 12, 145. - Issued: 03.09.2012. Made: 30.08.2012. Coming into force: 06.09.2012. Effect: S.I. 1996/1131 revoked. Territorial extent & classification: S. Local. - Available at http://www.legislation.gov.uk/ssi/2012/242/contents/made
Non-print

The A82 Trunk Road (Pulpit Rock Improvement) Order 2012 No. 2012/51. - Enabling power: Roads (Scotland) Act 1984, s. 5 (2). - Issued: 21.02.2012. Made: 16.02.2012. Coming into force: 23.02.2012. Effect: None. Territorial extent & classification: S. Local. - Available at http://www.legislation.gov.uk/ssi/2012/51/contents/made
Non-print

The A82 Trunk Road (Pulpit Rock Improvement) (Stopping Up) Order 2012 No. 2012/52. - Enabling power: Roads (Scotland) Act 1984, s. 68 (1). - Issued: 21.02.2012. Made: 16.02.2012. Coming into force: 23.02.2012. Effect: None. Territorial extent & classification: S. Local. - Available at http://www.legislation.gov.uk/ssi/2012/52/contents/made
Non-print

The M9/A90/M90 Trunk Road (Balmedie to Tipperty) (Side Roads) Order 2012 No. 2012/80. - Enabling power: Roads (Scotland) Act 1984, ss. 12 (1) (a) (5), 70 (1). - Issued: 06.03.2012. Made: 01.03.2012. Coming into force: 15.03.2012. Effect: None. Territorial extent & classification: S. Local. - Available at http://www.legislation.gov.uk/ssi/2012/80/contents/made
Non-print

The M9/A90/M90 Trunk Road (Balmedie to Tipperty) (Trunking and Detrunking) Order 2012 No. 2012/79. - Enabling power: Roads (Scotland) Act 1984, s. 5 (2) (6). - Issued: 06.03.2012. Made: 01.03.2012. Coming into force: 15.03.2012. Effect: None. Territorial extent & classification: S. Local. - Available at http://www.legislation.gov.uk/ssi/2012/79/contents/made
Non-print

The M9/A90/M90 Trunk Road (Easter Hatton Link) (Stopping Up of Accesses) Order 2012 No. 2012/81. - Enabling power: Roads (Scotland) Act 1984, s. 69 (1). - Issued: 06.03.2012. Made: 01.03.2012. Coming into force: 15.03.2012. Effect: None. Territorial extent & classification: S. Local. - Available at http://www.legislation.gov.uk/ssi/2012/81/contents/made
Non-print

The Road Works (Inspection Fees) (Scotland) Amendment Regulations 2012 No. 2012/250. - Enabling power: New Roads and Street Works Act 1991, s. 134. - Issued: 14.09.2012. Made: 11.09.2012. Laid before the Scottish Parliament: 13.09.2012. Coming into force: 01.11.2012. Effect: S.S.I. 2003/415 amended. Territorial extent & classification: S. General. - 2p.: 30 cm. - 978-0-11-101787-6 *£4.00*

The Road Works (Maintenance) (Scotland) Amendment Regulations 2012 No. 2012/286. - Enabling power: New Roads and Street Works Act 1991, s. 140 (4). - Issued: 31.10.2012. Made: 24.10.2012. Laid before the Scottish Parliament: 29.10.2012. Coming into force: 30.11.2012. Effect: S.S.I. 1992/1673 amended. Territorial extent & classification: S. General. - 2p.: 30 cm. - 978-0-11-101822-4 *£4.00*

The Scottish Road Works Register (Prescribed Fees) Regulations 2012 No. 2012/11. - Enabling power: New Roads and Street Works Act 1991, ss. 112A (4), 163 (1). - Issued: 23.01.2012. Made: 18.01.2012. Laid before the Scottish Parliament: 20.01.2012. Coming into force: 29.02.2012 except for Reg. 4 & 01.04.2012, for Reg. 4, in accord. with reg. 1. Effect: S.S.I. 2011/43 revoked. Territorial extent & classification: S. General. - 8p.: 30 cm. - 978-0-11-101591-9 *£4.00*

Road traffic

The A720 Edinburgh City Bypass and M8 (Hermiston Junction) (Speed Limit) Regulations 2012 No. 2012/62. - Enabling power: Road Traffic Regulation Act 1984, s. 17 (2) (3). - Issued: 29.02.2012. Made: 23.02.2012. Laid before the Scottish Parliament: 27.02.2012. Coming into force: 31.03.2012. Effect: S.I. 1989/2125 revoked. Territorial extent & classification: S. General. - 8p.: 30 cm. - 978-0-11-101637-4 *£4.00*

The A823(M) Pitreavie Spur Trunk Road (Variable Speed Limits) Regulations 2012 No. 2012/145. - Enabling power: Road Traffic Regulation Act 1984, s. 17 (2) (3). - Issued: 21.05.2012. Made: 16.05.2012. Laid before the Scottish Parliament: 18.05.2012. Coming into force: 01.09.2012. Effect: None. Territorial extent & classification: S. General. - 4p.: 30 cm. - 978-0-11-101707-4 *£4.00*

The M9/A9 Trunk Road (Newbridge to Winchburgh) (Variable Speed Limits and Actively Managed Hard Shoulder) Regulations 2012 No. 2012/344. - Enabling power: Road Traffic Regulation Act 1984, s. 17 (2) (3) (3ZA). - Issued: 19.12.2012. Made: 12.12.2012. Laid before the Scottish Parliament: 14.12.2012. Coming into force: 01.02.2013. Effect: None. Territorial extent & classification: S. General. - 8p.: 30 cm. - 978-0-11-101883-5 *£5.75*

The M9/A90/M90 Trunk Road (Humbie Rail Bridge to M9 Junction 1a) (Variable Speed Limits and Actively Managed Hard Shoulder) Regulations 2012 No. 2012/343. - Enabling power: Road Traffic Regulation Act 1984, s. 17 (2) (3) (3ZA). - Issued: 18.12.2012. Made: 12.12.2012. Laid before the Scottish Parliament: 14.12.2012. Coming into force: 01.02.2013. Effect: None. Territorial extent & classification: S. General. - 8p.: 30 cm. - 978-0-11-101882-8 *£5.75*

The M9/A90/M90 Trunk Road (Kirkliston to Halbeath) (Variable Speed Limits and Actively Managed Hard Shoulder) Regulations 2012 No. 2012/147. - Enabling power: Road Traffic Regulation Act 1984, s. 17 (2) (3). - Issued: 21.05.2012. Made: 16.05.2012. Laid before the Scottish Parliament: 18.05.2012. Coming into force: 01.09.2012. Effect: None. Territorial extent & classification: S. General. - 8p.: 30 cm. - 978-0-11-101709-8 *£5.75*

The M74 Motorway (Fullarton Road to the M8 West of Kingston Bridge) (Speed Limit) Regulations 2012 No. 2012/320. - Enabling power: Road Traffic Regulation Act 1984, s. 17 (2) (3) (3ZA). - Issued: 28.11.2012. Made: 22.11.2012. Laid before the Scottish Parliament: 23.11.2012. Coming into force: 28.12.2012. Effect: None. Territorial extent & classification: S. General. - 8p.: 30 cm. - 978-0-11-101852-1 *£5.75*

The Parking Attendants (Wearing of Uniforms) (East Ayrshire Council Parking Area) Regulations 2012 No. 2012/138. - Enabling power: Road Traffic Regulation Act 1984, s. 63A. - Issued: 16.05.2012. Made: 10.05.2012. Laid: 14.05.2012. Coming into force: 01.07.2012. Effect: None. Territorial extent & classification: S. General. - 4p.: 30 cm. - 978-0-11-101704-3 £4.00

The Parking Attendants (Wearing of Uniforms) (South Ayrshire Council Parking Area) Regulations 2012 No. 2012/141. - Enabling power: Road Traffic Regulation Act 1984, s. 63A. - Issued: 17.05.2012. Made: 10.05.2012. Laid before the Scottish Parliament: 14.05.2012. Coming into force: 01.09.2012. Effect: None. Territorial extent classification: S. General. - 4p.: 30 cm. - 978-0-11-101702-9 £4.00

The Road Traffic (Parking Adjudicators) (East Ayrshire Council) Regulations 2012 No. 2012/139. - Enabling power: Road Traffic Act 1991, s. 73 (11) (12). - Issued: 17.05.2012. Made: 10.05.2012. Laid before the Scottish Parliament: 14.05.2012. Coming into force: 01.07.2012. Effect: None. Territorial extent & classification: S. General. - 12p.: 30 cm. - 978-0-11-101705-0 £5.75

The Road Traffic (Parking Adjudicators) (South Ayrshire Council) Regulations 2012 No. 2012/142. - Enabling power: Road Traffic Act 1991, s. 73 (11) (12). - Issued: 17.05.2012. Made: 10.05.2012. Laid before the Scottish Parliament: 14.05.2012. Coming into force: 01.09.2012. Effect: None. Territorial extent & classification: S. General. - 12p.: 30 cm. - 978-0-11-101703-6 £5.75

The Road Traffic (Permitted Parking Area and Special Parking Area) (East Ayrshire Council) Designation Order 2012 No. 2012/137. - Enabling power: Road Traffic Act 1991, sch. 3, paras 1 (1), 2 (1), 3 (3). - Issued: 16.05.2012. Made: 10.05.2012. Laid before the Scottish Parliament: 14.05.2012. Coming into force: 01.06.2012. Effect: 1984 c.27; 1991 c. 40 modified. Territorial extent & classification: S. General. - 12p.: 30 cm. - 978-0-11-101700-5 £5.75

The Road Traffic (Permitted Parking Area and Special Parking Area) (South Ayrshire Council) Designation Order 2012 No. 2012/140. - Enabling power: Road Traffic Regulation Act 1991, sch. 3, paras 1 (1), 2 (1), 3 (3). - Issued: 17.05.2012. Made: 10.05.2012. Laid before the Scottish Parliament: 14.05.2012. Coming into force: 01.09.2012. Effect: 1984 c. 27; 1991 c.40 modified. Territorial extent & classification: S. General. - 12p.: 30 cm. - 978-0-11-101701-2 £5.75

Road traffic: Speed limits

The A9 Trunk Road (Inshes Junction) (30mph Speed Limit) Order 2012 No. 2012/231. - Enabling power: Road Traffic Regulation Act 1984, s. 84 (1) (a). - Issued: 20.08.2012. Made: 17.08.2012. Coming into force: 27.08.2012. Effect: None. Territorial extent & classification: S. Local. - Available at http://www.legislation.gov.uk/ssi/2012/231/contents/made
Non-print

The A77 Trunk Road (Cairnryan) (30 mph Speed Limit) Order 2012 No. 2012/115. - Enabling power: Road Traffic Regulation Act 1984, ss. 84 (1) (a), 124 (1) (d), sch. 9, para. 27. - Issued: 18.04.2012. Made: 17.04.2012. Coming into force: 30.04.2012. Effect: S.I. 1996/1362 revoked. Territorial extent & classification: S. Local. - Available at http://www.legislation.gov.uk/ssi/2012/115/contents/made
Non-print

The A720 Trunk Road (Edinburgh City Bypass) (Hermiston Junction to Calder Junction) (Speed Limit) Order 2012 No. 2012/112. - Enabling power: Road Traffic Regulation Act 1984, ss. 84 (1) (a), 124 (1) (d), sch. 9, para. 27 (1). - Issued: 02.04.2012. Made: 28.03.2012. Coming into force: 04.04.2012. Effect: S.I. 1998/1235 revoked. Territorial extent & classification: S. Local. - Available at http://www.legislation.gov.uk/ssi/2012/112/contents/made
Non-print

The A737 Trunk Road (Kilwinning) (30mph Speed Limit) and Kilwinning Academy and Abbey Primary School (Part-Time 20mph Speed Limit) Order 2012 No. 2012/268. - Enabling power: Road Traffic Regulation Act 1984, ss. 82 (2) (a), 83 (1), 84 (1) (c), 124 (1) (d), sch. 9, Part IV, para. 27. - Issued: 03.10.2012. Made: 02.10.2012. Coming into force: 15.10.2012. Effect: The Strathclyde Regional Council (Restricted Roads) (Transitional) Order 1985 amended & S.I. 2000/174; 2006/267 revoked. Territorial extent & classification: S. Local. - Available at: http://www.legislation.gov.uk/ssi/2012/268/contents/made
Non-print

Road traffic: Traffic regulation

The A9 (Olrig Street/Smith Terrace/Pennyland Terrace, Thurso) (Temporary Prohibition of Waiting, Loading and Unloading) Order 2012 No. 2012/248. - Enabling power: Road Traffic Regulation Act 1984, ss. 2 (1) (2), 4 (1), 14 (1) (a) (4). - Issued: 10.09.2012. Made: 07.09.2012. Coming into force: 17.09.2012. Effect: None. Territorial extent & classification: S. Local. - Available at http://www.legislation.gov.uk/ssi/2012/248/contents/made
Non-print

The A9 Trunk Road (Dunkeld Junction) (Temporary Prohibition of Traffic, Temporary Prohibition of Overtaking and Temporary Speed Restriction) Order 2012 No. 2012/47. - Enabling power: Road Traffic Regulation Act 1984, ss. 2 (1) (2) (3), 4 (1), 14 (1). - Issued: 17.02.2012. Made: 15.02.2012. Coming into force: 27.02.2012. Effect: None. Territorial extent & classification: S. Local. - Available at http://www.legislation.gov.uk/ssi/2012/47/contents/made
Non-print

The A9 Trunk Road (Inshes Junction) (Temporary 30mph Restriction of Speed) Order 2012 No. 2012/46. - Enabling power: Road Traffic Regulation Act 1984, ss. 2 (1), 4 (1), 14 (1) (b) (4). - Issued: 17.02.2012. Made: 15.02.2012. Coming into force: 27.02.2012. Effect: None. Territorial extent & classification: S. Local. - Available at http://www.legislation.gov.uk/ssi/2012/46/contents/made
Non-print

The A77 Trunk Road (Cairnryan) (Temporary 30 mph Speed Limit) (No. 2) Order 2012 No. 2012/103. - Enabling power: Road Traffic Regulation Act 1984, ss. 2 (1), 4 (1), 14 (1) (b) (4). - Issued: 23.03.2012. Made: 21.03.2012. Coming into force: 30.03.2012. Effect: None. Territorial extent & classification: S. Local. - Available at http://www.legislation.gov.uk/ssi/2012/103/contents/made
Non-print

The A77 Trunk Road (Cairnryan) (Temporary 30 mph Speed Limit) Order 2012 No. 2012/17. - Enabling power: Road Traffic Regulation Act 1984, ss. 2 (1), 4 (1), 14 (1) (b) (4). - Issued: 26.01.2012. Made: 23.01.2012. Coming into force: 01.02.2012. Effect: None. Territorial extent & classification: S. Local. - Available at http://www.legislation.gov.uk/ssi/2012/17/contents/made
Non-print

The A77 Trunk Road (Dalrymple Street, Girvan) (Temporary Prohibition of Traffic) Order 2012 No. 2012/317. - Enabling power: Road Traffic Regulation Act 1984, ss. 2 (1) (2), 4 (1), 16A. - Issued: 22.11.2012. Made: 19.11.2012. Coming into force: 30.11.2012. Effect: None. Territorial extent & classification: S. Local. - Available at http://www.legislation.gov.uk/ssi/2012/317/contents/made
Non-print

The A77 Trunk Road (Turnberry) (Temporary 30mph Speed Restriction) Order 2012 No. 2012/222. - Enabling power: Road Traffic Regulation Act 1984, ss. 2 (1), 4 (1), 14 (1) (b) (4). - Issued: 16.07.2012. Made: 11.07.2012. Coming into force: 23.07.2012. Effect: None. Territorial extent & classification: S. Local. - Available at http://www.legislation.gov.uk/ssi/2012/222/contents/made
Non-print

The A82 Trunk Road (Drumnadrochit to Fort Augustus) (Temporary Prohibition of Traffic) Order 2012 No. 2012/251. - Enabling power: Road Traffic Regulation Act 1984, ss. 2 (1) (2), 4 (1), 14 (1) (a) (4). - Issued: 14.09.2012. Made: 13.09.2012. Coming into force: 22.09.2012. Effect: None. Territorial extent & classification: S. Local. - Available at http://www.legislation.gov.uk/ssi/2012/251/contents/made
Non-print

The A83 Trunk Road (Poltalloch Street, Lochgilphead) (Special Event) (Temporary Prohibition of Traffic) Order 2012 No. 2012/195. - Enabling power: Road Traffic Regulation Act 1984, ss. 2 (1) (2), 4 (1), 16A. - Issued: 18.06.2012. Made: 13.06.2012. Coming into force: 23.06.2012. Effect: None. Territorial extent & classification: S. Local. - Available at http://www.legislation.gov.uk/ssi/2012/195/contents/made
Non-print

The A84 Trunk Road (Main Street and Leny Road, Callander) (Temporary Prohibition of Waiting, Loading and Unloading) Order 2012 No. 2012/18. - Enabling power: Road Traffic Regulation Act 1984, ss. 2 (1) (2), 4 (1), 14 (1) (a) (4). - Issued: 26.01.2012. Made: 24.01.2012. Coming into force: 06.02.2012. Effect: None. Territorial extent & classification: S. Local. - Available at http://www.legislation.gov.uk/ssi/2012/18/contents/made
Non-print

The A85 Trunk Road (Oban) (Temporary Prohibitions) Order 2012 No. 2012/298. - Enabling power: Road Traffic Regulation Act 1984, ss. 2 (1) (2), 4 (1), 14 (1) (a) (4). - Issued: 02.11.2012. Made: 01.11.2012. Coming into force: 11.11.2012. Effect: None. Territorial extent & classification: S. Local. - Available at http://www.legislation.gov.uk/ssi/2012/298/contents/made
Non-print

The A92 Trunk Road (Leuchars) (Temporary 30mph Speed Restriction) Order 2012 No. 2012/244. - Enabling power: Road Traffic Regulation Act 1984, ss. 2 (1), 4 (1), 14 (1) (b) (4). - Issued: 05.09.2012. Made: 03.09.2012. Coming into force: 15.09.2012. Effect: None. Territorial extent & classification: S. Local. - Available at http://www.legislation.gov.uk/ssi/2012/244/contents/made
Non-print

The A96 Trunk Road (Castle Stuart) (Temporary 30mph Speed Restriction) Order 2012 No. 2012/207. - Enabling power: Road Traffic Regulation Act 1984, ss. 2 (1), 4 (1), 14 (1) (b) (4). - Issued: 28.06.2012. Made: 27.06.2012. Coming into force: 09.07.2012. Effect: None. Territorial extent & classification: S. Local. - Available at http://www.legislation.gov.uk/ssi/2012/207/contents/made
Non-print

The A96 Trunk Road (Church Road, Keith) (Temporary Prohibition of Traffic) Order 2012 No. 2012/299. - Enabling power: Road Traffic Regulation Act 1984, ss. 2 (1) (2), 4 (1), 16A. - Issued: 05.11.2012. Made: 02.11.2012. Coming into force: 11.11.2012. Effect: None. Territorial extent & classification: S. Local. - Available at http://www.legislation.gov.uk/ssi/2012/299/contents/made
Non-print

The A96 Trunk Road (High Street, Elgin) (Special Event) (Temporary Prohibition of Traffic) Order 2012 No. 2012/168. - Enabling power: Road Traffic Regulation Act 1984, ss. 2 (1) (2), 4 (1), 16A. - Issued: 29.05.2012. Made: 24.05.2012. Coming into force: 02.06.2012. Effect: None. Territorial extent & classification: S. Local. - Available at http://www.legislation.gov.uk/ssi/2012/168/contents/made
Non-print

Road traffic: Traffic regulation

The A96 Trunk Road (High Street, Fochabers) (Temporary Prohibition of Traffic) Order 2012 No. 2012/223. - Enabling power: Road Traffic Regulation Act 1984, ss. 2 (1) (2), 4 (1), 16A. - Issued: 16.07.2012. Made: 13.07.2012. Coming into force: 22.07.2012. Effect: None. Territorial extent & classification: S. Local. - Available at http://www.legislation.gov.uk/ssi/2012/223/contents/made
Non-print

The A96 Trunk Road (Newtongarry) (Prohibition of Specified Turns) Order 2012 No. 2012/104. - Enabling power: Road Traffic Regulation Act 1984, ss. 1 (1) (a), 2 (1) (2). - Issued: 27.03.2012. Made: 23.03.2012. Coming into force: 02.04.2012. Effect: None. Territorial extent & classification: S. Local. - Available at http://www.legislation.gov.uk/ssi/2012/104/contents/made
Non-print

The A99 (South Road, Wick) (Temporary Prohibition of Waiting, Loading and Unloading) (No. 2) Order 2012 No. 2012/230. - Enabling power: Road Traffic Regulation Act 1984, ss. 2 (1) (2), 4 (1), 14 (1) (a) (4). - Issued: 06.08.2012. Made: 03.08.2012. Coming into force: 11.08.2012. Effect: None. Territorial extent & classification: S. Local. - Available at http://www.legislation.gov.uk/ssi/2012/230/contents/made
Non-print

The A99 (South Road, Wick) (Temporary Prohibition of Waiting, Loading and Unloading) Order 2012 No. 2012/186. - Enabling power: Road Traffic Regulation Act 1984, ss. 2 (1) (2), 4 (1), 14 (1) (a) (4). - Issued: 07.06.2012. Made: 06.06.2012. Coming into force: 18.06.2012. Effect: None. Territorial extent & classification: S. Local. - Available at http://www.legislation.gov.uk/ssi/2012/186/contents/made
Non-print

The A702 Trunk Road (Biggar High Street) (Temporary Prohibition of Traffic) Order 2012 No. 2012/351. - Enabling power: Road Traffic Regulation Act 1984, ss. 2 (1) (2, 4 (1), 16A. - Issued: 19.12.2012. Made: 18.12.2012. Coming into force: 31.12.2012. Effect: None. Territorial extent & classification: S. Local. - Available at: http://www.legislation.gov.uk/ssi/2012/351/contents/made
Non-print

The A702 Trunk Road (Former Petrol Filling Station, Hillend) (Prohibition of Specified Turns) Order 2012 No. 2012/133. - Enabling power: Road Traffic Regulation Act 1984, ss. 1 (1), 2 (1) (2) (a). - Issued: 09.05.2012. Made: 04.05.2012. Coming into force: 14.05.2012. Effect: None. Territorial extent & classification: S. Local. - Available at http://www.legislation.gov.uk/ssi/2012/133/contents/made
Non-print

The A830 Trunk Road (Craigag Bridge) (Temporary Prohibition of Traffic) Order 2012 No. 2012/185. - Enabling power: Road Traffic Regulation Act 1984, ss. 2 (1) (2), 4 (1), 14 (1) (a) (4). - Issued: 06.06.2012. Made: 30.05.2012. Coming into force: 11.06.2012. Effect: None. Territorial extent & classification: S. Local. - Available at http://www.legislation.gov.uk/ssi/2012/185/contents/made
Non-print

The Edinburgh and West Lothian Trunk Roads (M9/A90/M90, M9/A9 and M8/A8) Temporary Speed Limits, Regulation and Prohibitions of Traffic Order 2012 No. 2012/134. - Enabling power: Road Traffic Regulation Act 1984, ss. 2 (1) (2), 4 (1), 14 (1) (a) (4). - Issued: 09.05.2012. Made: 08.05.2012. Coming into force: 18.05.2012. Effect: S.S.I. 2011/362 revoked. Territorial extent & classification: S. Local. - Available at http://www.legislation.gov.uk/ssi/2012/134/contents/made
Non-print

The Fife Area Trunk Roads (M9/A90/M90, A823(M) and A92) Temporary 40mph Speed Restriction Order 2012 No. 2012/313. - Enabling power: Road Traffic Regulation Act 1984, ss. 2 (1) (2), 4 (1), 14 (1) (a) (4). - Issued: 21.11.2012. Made: 19.11.2012. Coming into force: 02.12.2012. Effect: None. Territorial extent & classification: S. Local. - Available at: http://www.legislation.gov.uk/ssi/2012/313/contents/made
Non-print

The Fife Area Trunk Roads (M9/A90/M90, A985, A823(M) and A92) Temporary Regulation and Prohibitions of Traffic and Pedestrians Order 2012 No. 2012/314. - Enabling power: Road Traffic Regulation Act 1984, ss. 2 (1) (2) (3), 4 (1), 14 (1) (a) (4). - Issued: 22.11.2012. Made: 19.11.2012. Coming into force: 02.12.2012. Effect: None. Territorial extent & classification: S. Local. - Available at: http://www.legislation.gov.uk/ssi/2012/314/contents/made
Non-print

The M8/A8 and A737/A738 Trunk Roads (White Cart Viaduct) (Temporary Prohibition of Traffic, Temporary Prohibition of Overtaking, and Temporary Speed Restriction) Revocation Order 2012 No. 2012/169. - Enabling power: Road Traffic Regulation Act 1984, ss. 14 (1) (a), 124 (1) (d), sch. 9, para. 27. - Issued: 30.05.2012. Made: 29.05.2012. Coming into force: 01.06.2012. Effect: S.S.I. 2010/292 revoked. Territorial extent & classification: S. Local. - Available at http://www.legislation.gov.uk/ssi/2012/169/contents/made
Non-print

The M9/A90/M90 Trunk Road (Balmedie to Tipperty) (Prohibition of Specified Turns) Order 2012 No. 2012/83. - Enabling power: Road Traffic Regulation Act 1984, ss. 1 (1), 2 (1) (2). - Issued: 06.03.2012. Made: 01.03.2012. Coming into force: 15.03.2012. Effect: None. Territorial extent & classification: S. Local. - Available at http://www.legislation.gov.uk/ssi/2012/83/contents/made
Non-print

The M9/A90/M90 Trunk Road (Easter Hatton Link) (Prohibition of Specified Turns) Order 2012 No. 2012/82. - Enabling power: Road Traffic Regulation Act 1984, ss. 1 (1), 2 (1) (2). - Issued: 06.03.2012. Made: 01.03.2012. Coming into force: 15.03.2012. Effect: None. Territorial extent & classification: S. Local. - Available at http://www.legislation.gov.uk/ssi/2012/82/contents/made
Non-print

The M9/A90/M90 Trunk Road (Gairneybridge to Milnathort) (Temporary 50mph and 30mph Speed Restrictions) Order 2012 No. 2012/200. - Enabling power: Road Traffic Regulation Act 1984, ss. 2 (1), 4 (1), 14 (1) (b) (4). - Issued: 25.06.2012. Made: 20.06.2012. Coming into force: 04.07.2012. Effect: None. Territorial extent & classification: S. Local. - Available at http://www.legislation.gov.uk/ssi/2012/200/contents/made
Non-print

The M9/A90/M90 Trunk Road (North Anderson Drive, Aberdeen) (Prohibition of U-Turns) Order 2012 No. 2012/229. - Enabling power: Road Traffic Regulation Act 1984, ss. 1 (1) (a), 2 (1) (2). - Issued: 03.08.2012. Made: 02.08.2012. Coming into force: 13.08.2012. Effect: None. Territorial extent & classification: S. Local. - Available at http://www.legislation.gov.uk/ssi/2012/229/contents/made
Non-print

The North East Scotland Trunk Roads (Temporary Prohibitions of Traffic and Overtaking and Temporary Speed Restrictions) (No. 1) Order 2012 No. 2012/15. - Enabling power: Road Traffic Regulation Act 1984, ss. 2 (1) (2), 4 (1), 14 (1) (a) (4). - Issued: 20.01.2012. Made: 18.01.2012. Coming into force: 01.02.2012. Effect: None. Territorial extent & classification: S. Local. - Available at: http://www.legislation.gov.uk/ssi/2012/15/contents/made
Non-print

The North East Scotland Trunk Roads (Temporary Prohibitions of Traffic and Overtaking and Temporary Speed Restrictions) (No. 2) Order 2012 No. 2012/58. - Enabling power: Road Traffic Regulation Act 1984, ss. 2 (1) (2), 4 (1), 14 (1) (a) (4). - Issued: 24.02.2012. Made: 20.02.2012. Coming into force: 01.03.2012. Effect: None. Territorial extent & classification: S. Local. - Available at: http://www.legislation.gov.uk/ssi/2012/58/contents/made
Non-print

The North East Scotland Trunk Roads (Temporary Prohibitions of Traffic and Overtaking and Temporary Speed Restrictions) (No. 3) Order 2012 No. 2012/98. - Enabling power: Road Traffic Regulation Act 1984, ss. 2 (1) (2), 4 (1), 14 (1) (a) (4). - Issued: 21.03.2012. Made: 19.03.2012. Coming into force: 01.04.2012. Effect: None. Territorial extent & classification: S. Local. - Available at: http://www.legislation.gov.uk/ssi/2012/98/contents/made
Non-print

The North East Scotland Trunk Roads (Temporary Prohibitions of Traffic and Overtaking and Temporary Speed Restrictions) (No. 4) Order 2012 No. 2012/122. - Enabling power: Road Traffic Regulation Act 1984, ss. 2 (1) (2), 4 (1), 14 (1) (a) (4). - Issued: 25.04.2012. Made: 23.04.2012. Coming into force: 01.05.2012. Effect: None. Territorial extent & classification: S. Local. - Available at: http://www.legislation.gov.uk/ssi/2012/122/contents/made
Non-print

The North East Scotland Trunk Roads (Temporary Prohibitions of Traffic and Overtaking and Temporary Speed Restrictions) (No. 5) Order 2012 No. 2012/159. - Enabling power: Road Traffic Regulation Act 1984, ss. 2 (1) (2), 4 (1), 14 (1) (a) (4). - Issued: 22.05.2012. Made: 18.05.2012. Coming into force: 01.06.2012. Effect: None. Territorial extent & classification: S. Local. - Available at: http://www.legislation.gov.uk/ssi/2012/159/contents/made
Non-print

The North East Scotland Trunk Roads (Temporary Prohibitions of Traffic and Overtaking and Temporary Speed Restrictions) (No. 6) Order 2012 No. 2012/204. - Enabling power: Road Traffic Regulation Act 1984, ss. 2 (1) (2), 4 (1), 14 (1) (a) (4). - Issued: 25.06.2012. Made: 21.06.2012. Coming into force: 01.07.2012. Effect: None. Territorial extent & classification: S. Local. - Available at: http://www.legislation.gov.uk/ssi/2012/204/contents/made
Non-print

The North East Scotland Trunk Roads (Temporary Prohibitions of Traffic and Overtaking and Temporary Speed Restrictions) (No. 7) Order 2012 No. 2012/227. - Enabling power: Road Traffic Regulation Act 1984, ss. 2 (1) (2), 4 (1), 14 (1) (a) (4). - Issued: 23.07.2012. Made: 18.07.2012. Coming into force: 01.08.2012. Effect: None. Territorial extent & classification: S. Local. - Available at: http://www.legislation.gov.uk/ssi/2012/227/contents/made
Non-print

The North East Scotland Trunk Roads (Temporary Prohibitions of Traffic and Overtaking and Temporary Speed Restrictions) (No. 8) Order 2012 No. 2012/235. - Enabling power: Road Traffic Regulation Act 1984, ss. 2 (1) (2), 4 (1), 14 (1) (a) (4). - Issued: 28.08.2012. Made: 23.08.2012. Coming into force: 01.09.2012. Effect: None. Territorial extent & classification: S. Local. - Available at: http://www.legislation.gov.uk/ssi/2012/235/contents/made
Non-print

The North East Scotland Trunk Roads (Temporary Prohibitions of Traffic and Overtaking and Temporary Speed Restrictions) (No. 9) Order 2012 No. 2012/257. - Enabling power: Road Traffic Regulation Act 1984, ss. 2 (1) (2), 4 (1), 14 (1) (a) (4). - Issued: 20.09.2012. Made: 18.09.2012. Coming into force: 01.10.2012. Effect: None. Territorial extent & classification: S. Local. - Available at: http://www.legislation.gov.uk/ssi/2012/257/contents/made
Non-print

The North East Scotland Trunk Roads (Temporary Prohibitions of Traffic and Overtaking and Temporary Speed Restrictions) (No. 10) Order 2012 No. 2012/278. - Enabling power: Road Traffic Regulation Act 1984, ss. 2 (1) (2), 4 (1), 14 (1) (a) (4). - Issued: 24.10.2012. Made: 22.10.2012. Coming into force: 01.11.2012. Effect: None. Territorial extent & classification: S. Local. - Available at: http://www.legislation.gov.uk/ssi/2012/278/contents/made
Non-print

Road traffic: Traffic regulation

The North East Scotland Trunk Roads (Temporary Prohibitions of Traffic and Overtaking and Temporary Speed Restrictions) (No. 11) Order 2012 No. 2012/312. - Enabling power: Road Traffic Regulation Act 1984, ss. 2 (1) (2), 4 (1), 14 (1) (a) (4). - Issued: 21.11.2012. Made: 19.11.2012. Coming into force: 01.12.2012. Effect: None. Territorial extent & classification: S. Local. - Available at: http://www.legislation.gov.uk/ssi/2012/312/contents/made
Non-print

The North East Scotland Trunk Roads (Temporary Prohibitions of Traffic and Overtaking and Temporary Speed Restrictions) (No. 12) Order 2012 No. 2012/359. - Enabling power: Road Traffic Regulation Act 1984, ss. 2 (1) (2), 4 (1), 14 (1) (a) (4). - Issued: 21.12.2012. Made: 19.12.2012. Coming into force: 01.01.2013. Effect: None. Territorial extent & classification: S. Local. - Available at: http://www.legislation.gov.uk/ssi/2012/359/contents/made
Non-print

The North West Scotland Trunk Roads (Temporary Prohibitions of Traffic and Overtaking and Temporary Speed Restrictions) (No. 1) Order 2012 No. 2012/14. - Enabling power: Road Traffic Regulation Act 1984, ss. 2 (1) (2), 4 (1), 14 (1) (a) (4). - Issued: 20.01.2012. Made: 18.01.2012. Coming into force: 01.02.2012. Effect: None. Territorial extent & classification: S. Local. - Available at: http://www.legislation.gov.uk/ssi/2012/14/contents/made
Non-print

The North West Scotland Trunk Roads (Temporary Prohibitions of Traffic and Overtaking and Temporary Speed Restrictions) (No. 2) Order 2012 No. 2012/59. - Enabling power: Road Traffic Regulation Act 1984, ss. 2 (1) (2), 4 (1), 14 (1) (a) (4). - Issued: 24.02.2012. Made: 20.02.2012. Coming into force: 01.03.2012. Effect: None. Territorial extent & classification: S. Local. - Available at: http://www.legislation.gov.uk/ssi/2012/59/contents/made
Non-print

The North West Scotland Trunk Roads (Temporary Prohibitions of Traffic and Overtaking and Temporary Speed Restrictions) (No. 3) Order 2012 No. 2012/97. - Enabling power: Road Traffic Regulation Act 1984, ss. 2 (1) (2), 4 (1), 14 (1) (a) (4). - Issued: 21.03.2012. Made: 19.03.2012. Coming into force: 01.04.2012. Effect: None. Territorial extent & classification: S. Local. - Available at: http://www.legislation.gov.uk/ssi/2012/97/contents/made
Non-print

The North West Scotland Trunk Roads (Temporary Prohibitions of Traffic and Overtaking and Temporary Speed Restrictions) (No. 4) Order 2012 No. 2012/123. - Enabling power: Road Traffic Regulation Act 1984, ss. 2 (1) (2), 4 (1), 14 (1) (a) (4). - Issued: 25.04.2012. Made: 23.04.2012. Coming into force: 01.05.2012. Effect: None. Territorial extent & classification: S. Local. - Available at: http://www.legislation.gov.uk/ssi/2012/123/contents/made
Non-print

The North West Scotland Trunk Roads (Temporary Prohibitions of Traffic and Overtaking and Temporary Speed Restrictions) (No. 5) Order 2012 No. 2012/158. - Enabling power: Road Traffic Regulation Act 1984, ss. 2 (1) (2), 4 (1), 14 (1) (a) (4). - Issued: 22.05.2012. Made: 18.05.2012. Coming into force: 01.06.2012. Effect: None. Territorial extent & classification: S. Local. - Available at: http://www.legislation.gov.uk/ssi/2012/158/contents/made
Non-print

The North West Scotland Trunk Roads (Temporary Prohibitions of Traffic and Overtaking and Temporary Speed Restrictions) (No. 6) Order 2012 No. 2012/203. - Enabling power: Road Traffic Regulation Act 1984, ss. 2 (1) (2), 4 (1), 14 (1) (a) (4). - Issued: 25.06.2012. Made: 21.06.2012. Coming into force: 01.07.2012. Effect: None. Territorial extent & classification: S. Local. - Available at: http://www.legislation.gov.uk/ssi/2012/203/contents/made
Non-print

The North West Scotland Trunk Roads (Temporary Prohibitions of Traffic and Overtaking and Temporary Speed Restrictions) (No. 7) Order 2012 No. 2012/226. - Enabling power: Road Traffic Regulation Act 1984, ss. 2 (1) (2), 4 (1), 14 (1) (a) (4). - Issued: 23.07.2012. Made: 18.07.2012. Coming into force: 01.08.2012. Effect: None. Territorial extent & classification: S. Local. - Available at: http://www.legislation.gov.uk/ssi/2012/226/contents/made
Non-print

The North West Scotland Trunk Roads (Temporary Prohibitions of Traffic and Overtaking and Temporary Speed Restrictions) (No. 8) Order 2012 No. 2012/234. - Enabling power: Road Traffic Regulation Act 1984, ss. 2 (1) (2), 4 (1), 14 (1) (a) (4). - Issued: 28.08.2012. Made: 23.08.2012. Coming into force: 01.09.2012. Effect: None. Territorial extent & classification: S. Local. - Available at: http://www.legislation.gov.uk/ssi/2012/234/contents/made
Non-print

The North West Scotland Trunk Roads (Temporary Prohibitions of Traffic and Overtaking and Temporary Speed Restrictions) (No. 9) Order 2012 No. 2012/256. - Enabling power: Road Traffic Regulation Act 1984, ss. 2 (1) (2), 4 (1), 14 (1) (4). - Issued: 20.09.2012. Made: 18.09.2012. Coming into force: 01.10.2012. Effect: None. Territorial extent & classification: S. Local. - Available at: http://www.legislation.gov.uk/ssi/2012/256/contents/made
Non-print

The North West Scotland Trunk Roads (Temporary Prohibitions of Traffic and Overtaking and Temporary Speed Restrictions) (No. 10) Order 2012 No. 2012/277. - Enabling power: Road Traffic Regulation Act 1984, ss. 2 (1) (2), 4 (1), 14 (1) (4). - Issued: 24.10.2012. Made: 22.10.2012. Coming into force: 01.11.2012. Effect: None. Territorial extent & classification: S. Local. - Available at: http://www.legislation.gov.uk/ssi/2012/277/contents/made
Non-print

The North West Scotland Trunk Roads (Temporary Prohibitions of Traffic and Overtaking and Temporary Speed Restrictions) (No. 11) Order 2012 No. 2012/311. -
Enabling power: Road Traffic Regulation Act 1984, ss. 2 (1) (2), 4 (1), 14 (1) (4). - Issued: 21.11.2012. Made: 19.11.2012. Coming into force: 01.12.2012. Effect: None. Territorial extent & classification: S. Local. - Available at: http://www.legislation.gov.uk/ssi/2012/311/contents/made
Non-print

The North West Scotland Trunk Roads (Temporary Prohibitions of Traffic and Overtaking and Temporary Speed Restrictions) (No. 12) Order 2012 No. 2012/358. -
Enabling power: Road Traffic Regulation Act 1984, ss. 2 (1) (2), 4 (1), 14 (1) (a) (4). - Issued: 21.12.2012. Made: 19.12.2012. Coming into force: 01.01.2013. Effect: None. Territorial extent & classification: S. Local. - Available at: http://www.legislation.gov.uk/ssi/2012/358/contents/made
Non-print

The South East Scotland Trunk Roads (Temporary Prohibitions of Traffic and Overtaking and Temporary Speed Restrictions) (No. 1) Order 2012 No. 2012/13. -
Enabling power: Road Traffic Regulation Act 1984, ss. 2 (1) (2), 4 (1), 14 (1) (a) (4). - Issued: 20.01.2012. Made: 18.01.2012. Coming into force: 01.02.2012. Effect: None. Territorial extent & classification: S. Local. - Available at: http://www.legislation.gov.uk/ssi/2012/13/contents/made
Non-print

The South East Scotland Trunk Roads (Temporary Prohibitions of Traffic and Overtaking and Temporary Speed Restrictions) (No. 2) Order 2012 No. 2012/56. -
Enabling power: Road Traffic Regulation Act 1984, ss. 2 (1) (2), 4 (1), 14 (1) (a) (4). - Issued: 24.02.2012. Made: 20.02.2012. Coming into force: 01.03.2012. Effect: None. Territorial extent & classification: S. Local. - Available at: http://www.legislation.gov.uk/ssi/2012/56/contents/made
Non-print

The South East Scotland Trunk Roads (Temporary Prohibitions of Traffic and Overtaking and Temporary Speed Restrictions) (No. 3) Order 2012 No. 2012/96. -
Enabling power: Road Traffic Regulation Act 1984, ss. 2 (1) (2), 4 (1), 14 (1) (a) (4). - Issued: 21.03.2012. Made: 19.03.2012. Coming into force: 01.04.2012. Effect: None. Territorial extent & classification: S. Local. - Available at: http://www.legislation.gov.uk/ssi/2012/96/contents/made
Non-print

The South East Scotland Trunk Roads (Temporary Prohibitions of Traffic and Overtaking and Temporary Speed Restrictions) (No. 4) Order 2012 No. 2012/121. -
Enabling power: Road Traffic Regulation Act 1984, ss. 2 (1) (2), 4 (1), 14 (1) (a) (4). - Issued: 25.04.2012. Made: 23.04.2012. Coming into force: 01.05.2012. Effect: None. Territorial extent & classification: S. Local. - Available at: http://www.legislation.gov.uk/ssi/2012/121/contents/made
Non-print

The South East Scotland Trunk Roads (Temporary Prohibitions of Traffic and Overtaking and Temporary Speed Restrictions) (No. 5) Order 2012 No. 2012/157. -
Enabling power: Road Traffic Regulation Act 1984, ss. 2 (1) (2), 4 (1), 14 (1) (a) (4). - Issued: 22.05.2012. Made: 18.05.2012. Coming into force: 01.06.2012. Effect: None. Territorial extent & classification: S. Local. - Available at: http://www.legislation.gov.uk/ssi/2012/157/contents/made
Non-print

The South East Scotland Trunk Roads (Temporary Prohibitions of Traffic and Overtaking and Temporary Speed Restrictions) (No. 6) Order 2012 No. 2012/202. -
Enabling power: Road Traffic Regulation Act 1984, ss. 2 (1) (2), 4 (1), 14 (1) (a) (4). - Issued: 25.06.2012. Made: 21.06.2012. Coming into force: 01.07.2012. Effect: None. Territorial extent & classification: S. Local. - Available at: http://www.legislation.gov.uk/ssi/2012/202/contents/made
Non-print

The South East Scotland Trunk Roads (Temporary Prohibitions of Traffic and Overtaking and Temporary Speed Restrictions) (No. 7) Order 2012 No. 2012/225. -
Enabling power: Road Traffic Regulation Act 1984, ss. 2 (1) (2), 4 (1), 14 (1) (a) (4). - Issued: 23.07.2012. Made: 18.07.2012. Coming into force: 01.08.2012. Effect: None. Territorial extent & classification: S. Local. - Available at: http://www.legislation.gov.uk/ssi/2012/225/contents/made
Non-print

The South East Scotland Trunk Roads (Temporary Prohibitions of Traffic and Overtaking and Temporary Speed Restrictions) (No. 8) Order 2012 No. 2012/233. -
Enabling power: Road Traffic Regulation Act 1984, ss. 2 (1) (2), 4 (1), 14 (1) (a) (4). - Issued: 28.08.2012. Made: 23.08.2012. Coming into force: 01.09.2012. Effect: None. Territorial extent & classification: S. Local. - Available at: http://www.legislation.gov.uk/ssi/2012/233/contents/made
Non-print

The South East Scotland Trunk Roads (Temporary Prohibitions of Traffic and Overtaking and Temporary Speed Restrictions) (No. 9) Order 2012 No. 2012/255. -
Enabling power: Road Traffic Regulation Act 1984, ss. 2 (1) (2), 4 (1), 14 (1) (a) (4). - Issued: 20.09.2012. Made: 18.09.2012. Coming into force: 01.10.2012. Effect: None. Territorial extent & classification: S. Local. - Available at: http://www.legislation.gov.uk/ssi/2012/255/contents/made
Non-print

The South East Scotland Trunk Roads (Temporary Prohibitions of Traffic and Overtaking and Temporary Speed Restrictions) (No. 10) Order 2012 No. 2012/280. -
Enabling power: Road Traffic Regulation Act 1984, ss. 2 (1) (2), 4 (1), 14 (1) (a) (4). - Issued: 24.10.2012. Made: 22.10.2012. Coming into force: 01.11.2012. Effect: None. Territorial extent & classification: S. Local. - Available at: http://www.legislation.gov.uk/ssi/2012/280/contents/made
Non-print

Road traffic: Traffic regulation

The South East Scotland Trunk Roads (Temporary Prohibitions of Traffic and Overtaking and Temporary Speed Restrictions) (No. 11) Order 2012 No. 2012/310. - Enabling power: Road Traffic Regulation Act 1984, ss. 2 (1) (2), 4 (1), 14 (1) (a) (4). - Issued: 21.11.2012. Made: 19.11.2012. Coming into force: 01.12.2012. Effect: None. Territorial extent & classification: S. Local. - Available at: http://www.legislation.gov.uk/ssi/2012/310/contents/made
Non-print

The South East Scotland Trunk Roads (Temporary Prohibitions of Traffic and Overtaking and Temporary Speed Restrictions) (No. 12) Order 2012 No. 2012/357. - Enabling power: Road Traffic Regulation Act 1984, ss. 2 (1) (2), 4 (1), 14 (1) (a) (4). - Issued: 21.12.2012. Made: 19.12.2012. Coming into force: 01.01.2013. Effect: None. Territorial extent & classification: S. Local. - Available at: http://www.legislation.gov.uk/ssi/2012/357/contents/made
Non-print

The South West Scotland Trunk Roads (Temporary Prohibitions of Traffic and Overtaking and Temporary Speed Restrictions) (No. 1) Order 2012 No. 2012/12. - Enabling power: Road Traffic Regulation Act 1984, ss. 2 (1) (2), 4 (1), 14 (1) (a) (4). - Issued: 20.01.2012. Made: 18.01.2012. Coming into force: 01.02.2012. Effect: None. Territorial extent & classification: S. Local. - Available at: http://www.legislation.gov.uk/ssi/2012/12/contents/made
Non-print

The South West Scotland Trunk Roads (Temporary Prohibitions of Traffic and Overtaking and Temporary Speed Restrictions) (No. 2) Order 2012 No. 2012/57. - Enabling power: Road Traffic Regulation Act 1984, ss. 2 (1) (2), 4 (1), 14 (1) (a) (4). - Issued: 24.02.2012. Made: 20.02.2012. Coming into force: 01.03.2012. Effect: None. Territorial extent & classification: S. Local. - Available at: http://www.legislation.gov.uk/ssi/2012/57/contents/made
Non-print

The South West Scotland Trunk Roads (Temporary Prohibitions of Traffic and Overtaking and Temporary Speed Restrictions) (No. 3) Order 2012 No. 2012/95. - Enabling power: Road Traffic Regulation Act 1984, ss. 2 (1) (2), 4 (1), 14 (1) (a) (4). - Issued: 21.03.2012. Made: 19.03.2012. Coming into force: 01.04.2012. Effect: None. Territorial extent & classification: S. Local. - Available at: http://www.legislation.gov.uk/ssi/2012/95/contents/made
Non-print

The South West Scotland Trunk Roads (Temporary Prohibitions of Traffic and Overtaking and Temporary Speed Restrictions) (No. 4) Order 2012 No. 2012/120. - Enabling power: Road Traffic Regulation Act 1984, ss. 2 (1) (2), 4 (1), 14 (1) (a) (4). - Issued: 25.04.2012. Made: 23.04.2012. Coming into force: 01.05.2012. Effect: None. Territorial extent & classification: S. Local. - Available at: http://www.legislation.gov.uk/ssi/2012/120/contents/made
Non-print

The South West Scotland Trunk Roads (Temporary Prohibitions of Traffic and Overtaking and Temporary Speed Restrictions) (No. 5) Order 2012 No. 2012/156. - Enabling power: Road Traffic Regulation Act 1984, ss. 2 (1) (2), 4 (1), 14 (1) (a) (4). - Issued: 22.05.2012. Made: 18.05.2012. Coming into force: 01.06.2012. Effect: None. Territorial extent & classification: S. Local. - Available at: http://www.legislation.gov.uk/ssi/2012/156/contents/made
Non-print

The South West Scotland Trunk Roads (Temporary Prohibitions of Traffic and Overtaking and Temporary Speed Restrictions) (No. 6) Order 2012 No. 2012/201. - Enabling power: Road Traffic Regulation Act 1984, ss. 2 (1) (2), 4 (1), 14 (1) (a) (4). - Issued: 25.06.2012. Made: 21.06.2012. Coming into force: 01.07.2012. Effect: None. Territorial extent & classification: S. Local. - Available at: http://www.legislation.gov.uk/ssi/2012/201/contents/made
Non-print

The South West Scotland Trunk Roads (Temporary Prohibitions of Traffic and Overtaking and Temporary Speed Restrictions) (No. 7) Order 2012 No. 2012/224. - Enabling power: Road Traffic Regulation Act 1984, ss. 2 (1) (2), 4 (1), 14 (1) (a) (4). - Issued: 23.07.2012. Made: 18.07.2012. Coming into force: 01.08.2012. Effect: None. Territorial extent & classification: S. Local. - Available at: http://www.legislation.gov.uk/ssi/2012/224/contents/made
Non-print

The South West Scotland Trunk Roads (Temporary Prohibitions of Traffic and Overtaking and Temporary Speed Restrictions) (No. 8) Order 2012 No. 2012/232. - Enabling power: Road Traffic Regulation Act 1984, ss. 2 (1) (2), 4 (1), 14 (1) (a) (4). - Issued: 28.08.2012. Made: 23.08.2012. Coming into force: 01.09.2012. Effect: None. Territorial extent & classification: S. Local. - Available at: http://www.legislation.gov.uk/ssi/2012/232/contents/made
Non-print

The South West Scotland Trunk Roads (Temporary Prohibitions of Traffic and Overtaking and Temporary Speed Restrictions) (No. 9) Order 2012 No. 2012/254. - Enabling power: Road Traffic Regulation Act 1984, ss. 2 (1) (2), 4 (1), 14 (1) (a) (4). - Issued: 20.09.2012. Made: 18.09.2012. Coming into force: 01.10.2012. Effect: None. Territorial extent & classification: S. Local. - Available at: http://www.legislation.gov.uk/ssi/2012/254/contents/made
Non-print

The South West Scotland Trunk Roads (Temporary Prohibitions of Traffic and Overtaking and Temporary Speed Restrictions) (No. 10) Order 2012 No. 2012/279. - Enabling power: Road Traffic Regulation Act 1984, ss. 2 (1) (2), 4 (1), 14 (1) (a) (4). - Issued: 24.10.2012. Made: 22.10.2012. Coming into force: 01.11.2012. Effect: None. Territorial extent & classification: S. Local. - Available at: http://www.legislation.gov.uk/ssi/2012/279/contents/made
Non-print

Road traffic: Traffic regulation

The South West Scotland Trunk Roads (Temporary Prohibitions of Traffic and Overtaking and Temporary Speed Restrictions) (No. 11) Order 2012 No. 2012/309. - Enabling power: Road Traffic Regulation Act 1984, ss. 2 (1) (2), 4 (1), 14 (1) (a) (4). - Issued: 21.11.2012. Made: 19.11.2012. Coming into force: 01.12.2012. Effect: None. Territorial extent & classification: S. Local. - Available at: http://www.legislation.gov.uk/ssi/2012/309/contents/made
Non-print

The South West Scotland Trunk Roads (Temporary Prohibitions of Traffic and Overtaking and Temporary Speed Restrictions) (No. 12) Order 2012 No. 2012/356. - Enabling power: Road Traffic Regulation Act 1984, ss. 2 (1) (2), 4 (1), 14 (1) (a) (4). - Issued: 21.12.2012. Made: 19.12.2012. Coming into force: 01.01.2013. Effect: None. Territorial extent & classification: S. Local. - Available at: http://www.legislation.gov.uk/ssi/2012/356/contents/made
Non-print

Scottish Public Services Ombudsman

The Scottish Public Services Ombudsman Act 2002 Amendment (No. 2) Order 2012 No. 2012/85. - Enabling power: Scottish Public Services Ombudsman Act 2002, s. 3 (2) (b). - Issued: 19.03.2012. Made: 14.03.2012. Coming into force: 02.04.2012. Effect: 2002 asp 11 amended. Territorial extent & classification: S. General. - Supersedes draft S.S.I. (ISBN 9780111015742) issued 29.12.2011. - 4p.: 30 cm. - 978-0-11-101657-2 *£4.00*

The Scottish Public Services Ombudsman Act 2002 Amendment Order 2012 No. 2012/43. - Enabling power: Scottish Public Services Ombudsman Act 2002, s. 3 (2) (c). - Issued: 20.02.2012. Made: 15.02.2012. Coming into force: In accord. with art. 1 (2) (3). Effect: 2002 asp 11 modified. Territorial extent & classification: S. General. - Supersedes draft SSI (ISBN 9780111015315) issued on 23.11.2011. - 4p.: 30 cm. - 978-0-11-101625-1 *£4.00*

Sea fisheries

The European Fisheries Fund (Grants) (Scotland) Amendment Regulations 2012 No. 2012/166. - Enabling power: European Communities Act 1972, s. 2 (2), sch. 2, para. 1A. - Issued: 30.05.2012. Made: 24.05.2012. Laid before the Scottish Parliament: 25.04.2012. Coming into force: 25.06.2012. Effect: S.S.I. 2007/307 amended. Territorial extent & classification: S. General. - 8p.: 30 cm. - 978-0-11-101729-6 *£5.75*

The Shetland Islands Regulated Fishery (Scotland) Order 2012 No. 2012/348. - Enabling power: Sea Fisheries Act 1967, s. 1. - Issued: 20.12.2012. Made: 13.12.2012. Laid before the Scottish Parliament: 17.12.2012. Coming into force: 01.02.2013. Effect: None. Territorial extent & classification: S. General. - 8p., map: 30 cm. - 978-0-11-101885-9 *£5.75*

Sea fisheries: Conservation of sea fish

The Sea Fish (Prohibited Methods of Fishing) (Firth of Clyde) Order 2012 No. 2012/4. - Enabling power: Sea Fish (Conservation) Act 1967, ss. 5 (1) (a) (iii), 15 (3). - Issued: 13.01.2012. Made: 10.01.2012. Laid before the Scottish Parliament: 12.01.2012. Coming into force: 14.02.2012. Effect: S.S.I. 2010/9 revoked. Territorial extent & classification: S. General. - 8p., map: 30 cm. - 978-0-11-101582-7 *£5.75*

The Sharks, Skates and Rays (Prohibition of Fishing, Trans-shipment and Landing) (Scotland) Order 2012 No. 2012/63. - Enabling power: Sea Fish (Conservation) Act 1967, ss. 5 (1) (a) (iii), 6 (1) (1A) (2) (b), 15 (3). - Issued: 02.03.2012. Made: 28.02.2012. Laid before the Scottish Parliament: 01.03.2012. Coming into force: 30.03.2012. Effect: None. Territorial extent & classification: S. General. - EC note: This Order provides for conservation measures for sharks, skates and rays in Scottish waters, pursuant to art. 10 of Council Regulation 2371/2002 on the conservation and sustainable exploitation of fisheries resources under the Common Fisheries Policy. - 8p.: 30 cm. - 978-0-11-101638-1 *£5.75*

Sea fisheries: Sea fish industry

The Fishing Boats (Satellite-tracking Devices) (Scotland) Scheme 2012 No. 2012/264. - Enabling power: Fisheries Act 1981, ss. 15 (1) (2). - Issued: 01.10.2012. Made: 25.09.2012. Laid before the Scottish Parliament: 28.09.2012. Coming into force: 29.10.2012. Effect: None. Territorial extent & classification: S. General. - For approval by resolution of the Scottish Parliament within forty days beginning with the day on which the Scheme was made, not taking into account periods of dissolution or recess for more than four days. - 8p.: 30 cm. - 978-0-11-101798-2 *£5.75*

Seeds

The Fodder Plant Seed (Scotland) Amendment Regulations 2012 No. 2012/5. - Enabling power: Plant Varieties and Seeds Act 1964, ss. 16 (1) (1A) (2) (3) (4) (5) (a), 36. - Issued: 13.01.2012. Made: 10.01.2012. Laid before the Scottish Parliament: 12.01.2012. Coming into force: 10.02.2012. Effect: S.S.I. 2005/329 amended. Territorial extent and classification: S. General. - EC note: These Regulations implement Commission Directive 2010/60/EU. - 8p.: 30 cm. - 978-0-11-101583-4 *£5.75*

Sheriff Court

Act of Adjournal (Amendment of the Criminal Procedure (Scotland) Act 1995 (Transcripts) 2012 No. 2012/272. - Enabling power: Criminal Procedure (Scotland) Act 1995, s. 305. - Issued: 15.10.2012. Made: 09.10.2012. Laid before the Scottish Parliament: 11.10.2012. Coming into force: 12.11.2012. Effect: 1995 c. 46 amended. Territorial extent & classification: S. General. - 4p.: 30 cm. - 978-0-11-101807-1 £4.00

Act of Adjournal (Criminal Procedure Rules Amendment) (Miscellaneous) 2012 No. 2012/125. - Enabling power: Criminal Procedure (Scotland) Act 1995, s. 305 & Extradition Act 2003, s. 210. - Issued: 25.04.2012. Made: 24.04.2012. Laid before the Scottish Parliament: 26.04.2012. Coming into force: 04.06.2012. Effect: S.I. 1996/513 amended. Territorial extent & classification: S. General. - 4p.: 30 cm. - 978-0-11-101686-2 £4.00

Act of Adjournal (Criminal Procedure Rules Amendment No. 2) (Miscellaneous) 2012 No. 2012/187. - Enabling power: Criminal Procedure (Scotland) Act 1995, s. 305. - Issued: 11.06.2012. Made: 06.06.2012. Laid before the Scottish Parliament: 08.06.2012. Coming into force: 16.07.2012. Effect: S.I. 1996/513 amended. Territorial extent & classification: S. General. - 4p.: 30 cm. - 978-0-11-101746-3 £4.00

Act of Adjournal (Criminal Procedure Rules Amendment No. 3) (Procedural Hearings in Appeals from Solemn Proceedings) 2012 No. 2012/300. - Enabling power: Criminal Procedure (Scotland) Act 1995, s. 305. - Issued: 08.10.2012. Made: 06.11.2012. Laid before the Scottish Parliament: 08.11.2012. Coming into force: 10.12.2012. Effect: S.I. 1996/513 amended. Territorial extent & classification: S. General. - 2p.: 30 cm. - 978-0-11-101835-4 £4.00

Act of Sederunt (Actions for removing from heritable property) 2012 No. 2012/136. - Enabling power: Sheriff Courts (Scotland) Act 1971, s. 32 & Bankruptcy and Diligence etc. (Scotland) Act 2007, s. 215. - Issued: 14.05.2012. Made: 09.05.2012. Laid before the Scottish Parliament: 11.05.2012. Coming into force: 18.06.2012. Effect: None. Territorial extent & classification: S. General. - 8p.: 30 cm. - 978-0-11-101697-8 £5.75

Act of Sederunt (Actions for removing from heritable property) (Amendment) 2012 No. 2012/273. - Enabling power: Sheriff Courts (Scotland) Act 1971, s. 32 & Bankruptcy and Diligence etc. (Scotland) Act 2007, s. 215. - Issued: 12.10.2012. Made: 09.10.2012. Laid before the Scottish Parliament: 11.10.2012. Coming into force: 12.11.2012. Effect: S.S.I. 2012/136 amended. Territorial extent & classification: S. General. - With correction slip dated November 2012. - 4p.: 30 cm. - 978-0-11-101808-8 £4.00

Act of Sederunt (Fees of Sheriff Officers) (Amendment) 2012 No. 2012/7. - Enabling power: Sheriff Courts (Scotland) Act 1907, s. 40 (1) & Execution of Diligence (Scotland) Act 1926, s. 6. - Issued: 23.01.2012. Made: 17.01.2012. Laid before the Scottish Parliament: 19.01.2012. Coming into force: 22.01.2012. Effect: S.S.I. 2011/432 amended. Territorial extent & classification: S. General. - With correction slip. The following statement has been omitted in error from this SI: This Order has been made in consequence of a defect in S.S.I. 2011/432 (ISBN 9780111015537) and is being issued free of charge to all known recipients of that Statutory Instrument. - 4p.: 30 cm. - 978-0-11-101585-8 £4.00

Act of Sederunt (Fees of Sheriff Officers) (Amendment) (No. 2) 2012 No. 2012/341. - Enabling power: Sheriff Courts (Scotland) Act 1907, s. 40 & Execution of Diligence (Scotland) Act 1926, s. 6. - Issued: 13.12.2012. Made: 10.12.2012. Laid before the Scottish Parliament: 12.12.2012. Coming into force: 28.01.2013. Effect: S.S.I. Effect: S.S.I. 2002/567 amended. Territorial extent & classification: S. General. - 8p.: 30 cm. - 978-0-11-101878-1 £5.75

Act of Sederunt (Fees of Shorthand Writers in the Sheriff Court) (Amendment) 2012 No. 2012/101. - Enabling power: Sheriff Courts (Scotland) Act 1907, s. 40 (1). - Issued: 23.03.2012. Made: 20.03.2012. Laid before the Scottish Parliament: 22.03.2012. Coming into force: 21.05.2012. Effect: S.I. 1992/1878 amended. Territorial extent & classification: S. General. - 4p.: 30 cm. - 978-0-11-101669-5 £4.00

Act of Sederunt (Sheriff Court Rules) (Miscellaneous Amendments) 2012 No. 2012/188. - Enabling power: Sheriff Courts (Scotland) Act 1971, s. 32 & Adoption and Children (Scotland) Act 2007, s. 114. - Issued: 11.06.2012. Made: 06.06.2012. Laid before the Scottish Parliament: 08.06.2012. Coming into force: 01.08.2012. Effect: 1907 c.51 & S.I. 1997/291; 1999/929 & S.S.I. 2002/132; 2012/144 amended. Territorial extent & classification: S. General. - 32p.: 30 cm. - 978-0-11-101747-0 £9.75

Act of Sederunt (Sheriff Court Rules) (Miscellaneous Amendments) (No. 2) 2012 No. 2012/221. - Enabling power: Sheriff Courts (Scotland) Act 1971, s. 32. - Issued: 17.07.2012. Made: 12.07.2012. Laid before the Scottish Parliament: 13.07.2012. Coming into force: 31.07.2012 & 01.08.2012 in accord. with para. 1 (1) (2). Effect: 1907 c.51 & S.S.I. 2012/188 amended. Territorial extent & classification: S. General. - 4p.: 30 cm. - 978-0-11-101776-0 £4.00

Act of Sederunt (Sheriff Court Rules) (Miscellaneous Amendments) (No. 3) 2012 No. 2012/271. - Enabling power: Sheriff Courts (Scotland) Act 1971, s. 32. - Issued: 09.10.2012. Made: 04.10.2012. Laid before the Scottish Parliament: 08.10.2012. Coming into force: 01.11.2012. Effect: 1907 c.51 & S.S.I. 1993/920; 1999/929 amended. Territorial extent & classification: S. General. - 16p.: 30 cm. - 978-0-11-101806-4 £5.75

Act of Sederunt (Summary Cause Rules Amendment) (Personal Injuries Actions) 2012 No. 2012/144. - Enabling power: Sheriff Courts (Scotland) Act 1971, s. 32. - Issued: 21.05.2012. Made: 16.05.2012. Laid before the Scottish Parliament: 18.05.2012. Coming into force: 01.09.2012. Effect: S.S.I. 2002/132 amended. Territorial extent & classification: S. General. - 52p.: 30 cm. - 978-0-11-101710-4 £9.75

The Court Fees (Miscellaneous Amendments) Scotland Order 2012 No. 2012/322. - Enabling power: Court of Law Fees (Scotland) Act 1895, s. 2. - Issued: 28.11.2012. Made: 22.11.2012. Laid before the Scottish Parliament: 26.11.2012. Coming into force: 09.12.2012. Effect: S.S.I. 2012/290, 291, 293 amended. Territorial extent & classification: S. General. - This SSI has been made in consequence of defects in SSI 2012/290 (ISBN 9780111018330), 2012/291 (ISBN 9780111018323) and SSI 2012/293 (ISBN 9780111018347) and is being issued free of charge to all known recipients of those instruments. - 4p.: 30 cm. - 978-0-11-101853-8 £4.00

The Sheriff Court Fees Amendment Order 2012 No. 2012/293. - Enabling power: Courts of Law Fees (Scotland) Act 1895, s. 2. - Issued: 09.11.2012. Made: 30.10.2012. Laid before the Scottish Parliament: 31.10.2012. Coming into force: In accord. with art. 1. Effect: S.I. 1997/687 amended. Territorial extent & classification: S. General. - 20p.: 30 cm. - 978-0-11-101834-7 £5.75

Social care

The Community Care and Health (Scotland) Act 2002 (Incidental Provision) (Adult Support and Protection) Order 2012 No. 2012/66. - Enabling power: Community Care and Health (Scotland) Act 2002, s. 24. - Issued: 02.03.2012. Made: 28.02.2012. Laid before the Scottish Parliament: 01.03.2012. Coming into force: 31.03.2012. Effect: None. Territorial extent & classification: S. General. - 4p.: 30 cm. - 978-0-11-101641-1 £4.00

The Community Care (Joint Working etc.) (Scotland) Amendment Regulations 2012 No. 2012/65. - Enabling power: Community Care and Health (Scotland) Act 2002, ss. 13 (1), 14, 15 (1) (2) (4), 23 (4). - Issued: 02.03.2012. Made: 28.02.2012. Laid before the Scottish Parliament: 01.03.2012. Coming into force: 30.03.2012. Effect: S.S.I. 2002/533 amended. Territorial extent & classification: S. General. - 8p.: 30 cm. - 978-0-11-101640-4 £5.75

The Community Care (Personal Care and Nursing Care) (Scotland) Amendment Regulations 2012 No. 2012/109. - Enabling power: Community Care and Health (Scotland) Act 2002, ss. 1 (2) (a), 2, 23 (4). - Issued: 03.04.2012. Made: 28.03.2012. Coming into force: 01.04.2012. Effect: S.S.I. 2002/303 amended & S.S.I. 2008/78; 2009/138; 2010/117; 2011/230 revoked. Territorial extent & classification: S. - Supersedes draft S.I. (ISBN 9780111016268) issued 21.02.2012. - 4p.: 30 cm. - 978-0-11-101674-9 £4.00

The Public Services Reform (Social Services Inspections) (Scotland) Amendment Regulations 2012 No. 2012/45. - Enabling power: Public Services Reform (Scotland) Act 2010, ss. 58 (1), 104 (1). - Issued: 16.02.2012. Made: 07.02.2012. Coming into force: In accord. with reg. 1. Effect: S.S.I 2011/185 amended. Territorial extent & classification: S. General. - Supersedes draft SI (ISBN 9780111015605) issued on 16.12.2011. - 4p.: 30 cm. - 978-0-11-101624-4 £4.00

The Social Care and Social Work Improvement Scotland (Excepted Services) Regulations 2012 No. 2012/44. - Enabling power: Public Services Reform (Scotland) Act 2010, s. 104 (1), sch. 12, paras. 1 (2) (a), 4, 13. - Issued: 16.02.2012. Made: 07.02.2012. Coming into force: In accord. with reg. 1. Effect: None. Territorial extent & classification: S. General. - 4p.: 30 cm. - 978-0-11-101623-7 £4.00

Sports grounds and sporting events

The Glasgow Commonwealth Games Act 2008 (Commencement No. 3) Order 2012 No. 2012/261 (C.25). - Enabling power: Glasgow Commonwealth Games Act 2008, s. 49 (2). Bringing into operation various provisions of the 2008 Act on 29.11.2012. - Issued: 01.10.2012. Made: 26.09.2012. Laid before the Scottish Parliament: 28.09.2012. Effect: None. Territorial extent & classification: S. General. - 4p.: 30 cm. - 978-0-11-101795-1 £4.00

The Glasgow Commonwealth Games Act 2008 (Ticket Touting Offence) (Exceptions for Use of Internet etc.) (Scotland) Regulations 2012 No. 2012/323. - Enabling power: Glasgow Commonwealth Games Act 2008, ss. 19, 43 (2) & European Communities Act 1972, s. 2 (2). - Issued: 28.11.2012. Made: 21.11.2012. Coming into force: 29.11.2012. Effect: None. Territorial extent & classification: S. General. - Supersedes draft SSI (ISBN 9780111018002) issued on 02.10.2012. - 8p.: 30 cm. - 978-0-11-101854-5 £4.00

The Sports Grounds and Sporting Events (Designation) (Scotland) Amendment Order 2012 No. 2012/164. - Enabling power: Criminal Law (Consolidation) (Scotland) Act 1995, s. 18. - Issued: 28.05.2012. Made: 23.05.2012. Laid before the Scottish Parliament: 25.05.2012. Coming into force: 23.06.2012. Effect: S.S.I. 2010/199 amended. Territorial extent & classification: S. General. - 4p.: 30 cm. - 978-0-11-101728-9 £4.00

Title conditions

The Title Conditions (Scotland) Act 2003 (Conservation Bodies) Amendment Order 2012 No. 2012/30. - Enabling power: Title Conditions (Scotland) Act 2003, s. 38 (4). - Issued: 10.02.2012. Made: 07.02.2012. Laid before the Scottish Parliament: 09.02.2012. Coming into force: 30.03.2012. Effect: S.S.I. 2003/453 amended. Territorial extent & classification: S. General. - 2p.: 30 cm. - 978-0-11-101605-3 £4.00

Town and country planning

The Planning etc. (Scotland) Act 2006 (National Parks) (Consequential Provisions) Order 2012 No. 2012/117. - Enabling power: Planning etc. (Scotland) Act 2006, ss. 58 (1) (2). - Issued: 23.04.2012. Made: 18.04.2012. Laid before the Scottish Parliament: 20.04.2012. Coming into force: 01.06.2012. Effect: SSI 2002/201; 2003/1; 2007/268 amended. Territorial extent & classification: S. General. - 4p.: 30 cm. - 978-0-11-101682-4 £4.00

The Town and Country Planning (Continuation in force of Local Plans) (Highland) (Scotland) Order 2012 No. 2012/90. - Enabling power: Town and Country Planning (Scotland) Act 1997, sch. 1, para. 7. - Issued: 19.03.2012. Made: 14.03.2012. Laid before the Scottish Parliament: 16.03.2012. Coming into force: 01.04.2012 Effect: None. Territorial extent & classification: S. General. - 16p.: 30 cm. - 978-0-11-101659-6 £5.75

The Town and Country Planning (Continuation in force of South Lanarkshire Local Plan) (Scotland) Order 2012 No. 2012/194. - Enabling power: Town and Country Planning (Scotland) Act 1997, sch. 1, para. 7. - Issued: 18.06.2012. Made: 12.06.2012. Laid before the Scottish Parliament: 14.06.2012. Coming into force: 29.06.2012 Effect: None. Territorial extent & classification: S. General. - 2p.: 30 cm. - 978-0-11-101753-1 £4.00

The Town and Country Planning (Development Management Procedure) (Scotland) Amendment Regulations 2012 No. 2012/165. - Enabling power: Town and Country Planning (Scotland) Act 1997, ss. 30 (1) (3), 43 (1) (c), 275. - Issued: 28.05.2012. Made: 23.05.2012. Laid before the Scottish Parliament: 25.05.2012. Coming into force: 01.07.2012. Effect: S.I. 2008/432 amended. Territorial extent & classification: S. General. - 4p.: 30 cm. - 978-0-11-101727-2 £4.00

The Town and Country Planning (General Permitted Development) (Fish Farming) (Scotland) Amendment (No. 2) Order 2012 No. 2012/285. - Enabling power: Town and Country Planning (Scotland) Act 1997, ss. 30, 31, 275. - Issued: 30.10.2012. Made: 25.10.2012. Laid before the Scottish Parliament: 29.10.2012. Coming into force: 01.12.2012. Effect: S.I. 1992/223 amended. Territorial extent & classification: S. General. - 4p.: 30 cm. - 978-0-11-101819-4 £4.00

The Town and Country Planning (General Permitted Development) (Fish Farming) (Scotland) Amendment Order 2012 No. 2012/131. - Enabling power: Town and Country Planning (Scotland) Act 1997, ss. 30, 31, 275. - Issued: 01.05.2012. Made: 26.04.2012. Laid before the Scottish Parliament: 30.04.2012. Coming into force: 01.06.2012. Effect: S.I. 1992/223 amended. Territorial extent & classification: S. General. - 12p.: 30 cm. - 978-0-11-101693-0 £5.75

The Town and Country Planning (Marine Fish Farming) (Scotland) Amendment Regulations 2012 No. 2012/259. - Enabling power: Town and Country Planning (Scotland) Act 1997, s. 31A (8). - Issued: 25.09.2012. Made: 20.09.2012. Laid before the Scottish Parliament: 24.09.2012. Coming into force: 10.11.2012. Effect: S.S.I. 2007/175 amended & S.S.I. 2011/145 partially revoked. Territorial extent & classification: S. General. - 4p.: 30 cm. - 978-0-11-101792-0 £4.00

The Town and Country Planning (Miscellaneous Amendments) (Scotland) Regulations 2012 No. 2012/325. - Enabling power: Town and Country Planning (Scotland) Act 1997, ss. 30, 32, 43, 43A, 275. - Issued: 30.11.2012. Made: 27.11.2012. Laid before the Scottish Parliament: 29.11.2012. Coming into force: 02.02.2013. Effect: S.S.I. 2008/432, 433 amended. Territorial extent & classification: S. General. - 4p.: 30 cm. - 978-0-11-101856-9 £4.00

The Town and Country Planning (Prescribed Date) (Scotland) Regulations 2012 No. 2012/260. - Enabling power: Town and Country Planning (Scotland) Act 1997, s. 26AA (2) (a). - Issued: 26.09.2012. Made: 20.09.2012. Laid before the Scottish Parliament: 24.09.2012. Coming into force: 10.11.2012. Effect: S.S.I. 2007/123; 2010/61 revoked. Territorial extent & classification: S. General. - 2p.: 30 cm. - 978-0-11-101793-7 £4.00

Transport

The Banchory and Crathes Light Railway Order 2012 No. 2012/345. - Enabling power: Light Railways Act 1896, ss. 7, 9, 10, 11, 12. - Issued: 18.12.2012. Made: 12.12.2012. Laid before the Scottish Parliament: 14.12.2012. Coming into force: 28.12.2012. Effect: None. Territorial extent & classification: S. General. - 8p.: 30 cm. - 978-0-11-101880-4 £5.75

The Bus Service Operators Grant (Scotland) Amendment Regulations 2012 No. 2012/33. - Enabling power: Transport (Scotland) Act 2001, ss. 38 (5), 81 (2). - Issued: 13.02.2012. Made: 08.02.2012. Laid before the Scottish Parliament: 10.02.2012. Coming into force: 01.04.2012. Effect: S.S.I. 2002/289 amended. Territorial extent & classification: S. General. - 4p.: 30 cm. - 978-0-11-101614-5 £4.00

Water

The Bathing Waters (Scotland) Amendment Regulations 2012 No. 2012/243. - Enabling power: European Communities Act 1972, s. 2 (2). - Issued: 04.09.2012. Made: 30.08.2012. Laid before the Scottish Parliament: 03.09.2012. Coming into force: 02.10.2012. Effect: S.S.I. 2008/170 amended. Territorial extent & classification: S. General. - 4p.: 30 cm. - 978-0-11-101781-4 £4.00

Water industry

The Water Services etc. (Scotland) Act 2005 (Commencement No. 6) Order 2012 No. 2012/192 (C.18). - Enabling power: Water Services etc. (Scotland) Act 2005, s. 37 (2). Bringing into operation various provisions of the 2005 Act on 22.07.2012. - Issued: 15.06.2012. Made: 11.06.2012. Laid before the Scottish Parliament: 13.06.2012. Coming into force: 22.07.2012. Effect: None. Territorial extent & classification: S. General. - 4p.: 30 cm. - 978-0-11-101751-7 £4.00

Water supply

The Water Services Charges (Billing and Collection) (Scotland) Order 2012 No. 2012/53. - Enabling power: Water Industry (Scotland) Act 2002, s. 37. - Issued: 23.02.2012. Made: 20.02.2012. Laid before the Scottish Parliament: 22.02.2012. Coming into force: 01.04.2012. Effect: None. Territorial extent & classification: S. General. - 8p.: 30 cm. - 978-0-11-101630-5 £5.75

Wildlife

The Conservation (Natural Habitats, &c.) Amendment (Scotland) Regulations 2012 No. 2012/228. - Enabling power: European Communities Act 1972, s. 2 (2). - Issued: 01.08.2012. Made: 26.07.2012. Laid before the Scottish Parliament: 31.07.2012. Coming into force: 16.08.2012. Effect: 1949 c.97; S.I. 1994/2716 (in relation to Scotland) amended & 2003 asp 2; S.I. 2007/1843; S.S.I. 2004/475; 2007/80 partially revoked & S.I. 1997/3055 revoked. Territorial extent & classification: S. General. - EC note: These Regulations amend the 1994 Regulations which make provision for the transposition of Council Directive 92/43/EEC on the conservation of natural habitats and of wild flora and fauna and certain aspects of Directive 2009/147/EC on the conservation of wild birds. - 8p.: 30 cm. - 978-0-11-101777-7 £5.75

The Snares (Identification Numbers and Tags) (Scotland) Order 2012 No. 2012/282. - Enabling power: Wildlife and Countryside Act 1981, s. 11A (8) (b) (c) (d) (e) (f) (g) (h) (i). - Issued: 25.10.2012. Made: 22.10.2012 Laid before the Scottish Parliament: 24.10.2012. Coming into force: 22.11.2012. Effect: None. Territorial extent & classification: S. General. - 8p.: 30 cm. - 978-0-11-101814-9 £5.75

The Snares (Training) (Scotland) (No. 2) Order 2012 No. 2012/161. - Enabling power: Wildlife and Countryside Act 1981, s. 11A (8) (a) (i). - Issued: 25.05.2012. Made: 22.05.2012 Laid before the Scottish Parliament: 23.05.2012. Coming into force: 21.06.2012. Effect: S.S.I. 2012/124 revoked. Territorial extent & classification: S. General. - 4p.: 30 cm. - 978-0-11-101724-1 £4.00

The Snares (Training) (Scotland) Order 2012 No. 2012/124. - Enabling power: Wildlife and Countryside Act 1981, s. 11A (8) (a) (i). - Issued: 27.04.2012. Made: 23.04.2012 Laid before the Scottish Parliament: 25.04.2012. Coming into force: 04.06.2012. Effect: None. Territorial extent & classification: S. General. - Revoked by SSI 2012/161 (ISBN 9780111017241). - 4p.: 30 cm. - 978-0-11-101685-5 £4.00

The Wildlife and Countryside Act 1981 (Exceptions to section 14) (Scotland) Amendment Order 2012 No. 2012/205. - Enabling power: Wildlife and Countryside Act 1981, s. 14 (2B) (2D) (a) (e). - Issued: 27.06.2012. Made: 21.06.2012. Laid before the Scottish Parliament: 25.06.2012. Coming into force: 02.07.2012. Effect: S.S.I. 2012/173 amended. Territorial extent & classification: S. General. - This Scottish Statutory Instrument has been made in consequence of a defect in SSI. 2012/173 (ISBN 9780111017401) and is being issued free of charge to all known recipients of that SSI. - 8p.: 30 cm. - 978-0-11-101759-3 £5.75

The Wildlife and Countryside Act 1981 (Exceptions to section 14) (Scotland) Order 2012 No. 2012/173. - Enabling power: Wildlife and Countryside Act 1981, s. 14 (2B) (2D) (a) (b) (e). - Issued: 06.06.2012. Made: 30.05.2012. Laid before the Scottish Parliament: 31.05.2012. Coming into force: 02.07.2012. Effect: None. Territorial extent & classification: S. General. - This SSI has been corrected by SSI 2012/205 (ISBN 9780111017593) which is being sent free of charge to all known recipients of SSI 2012/173. - 8p.: 30 cm. - 978-0-11-101740-1 £4.00

The Wildlife and Countryside Act 1981 (Keeping and Release and Notification Requirements) (Scotland) Amendment Order 2012 No. 2012/206. - Enabling power: Wildlife and Countryside Act 1981, s. 14 (1) (a) (ii) (2D) (a) (e), 14ZC (1) (a) (2) (a). - Issued: 27.06.2012. Made: 21.06.2012. Laid before the Scottish Parliament: 25.06.2012. Coming into force: 02.07.2012. Effect: S.S.I. 2012/174 amended. Territorial extent & classification: S. General. - This Scottish Statutory Instrument has been made in consequence of a defect in SSI. 2012/174 (ISBN 9780111017418) and is being issued free of charge to all known recipients of that SSI. - 8p.: 30 cm. - 978-0-11-101760-9 £4.00

The Wildlife and Countryside Act 1981 (Keeping and Release and Notification Requirements) (Scotland) Order 2012 No. 2012/174. - Enabling power: Wildlife and Countryside Act 1981, s. 14 (1) (a) (ii) (2D) (a) (e), 14ZC (1) (a) (2) (a), 14B (1) (a) (2) (a) (b) (d) (f) (4) (a) & Wildlife and Natural Environment (Scotland) Act 2011, s. 42 (1). - Issued: 06.06.2012. Made: 30.05.2012. Laid before the Scottish Parliament: 31.05.2012. Coming into force: 02.07.2012. Effect: S.I. 1933/106; 1937/478; 1954/927; 1975/2223; 1977/2122; 1979/1669; 1982/1883; 1987/2195, 2225; 1997/2751, 2750; S.S.I. 2000/400; 2003/528, 560; 2011/63, 172 revoked subject to art. 3 of S.S.I. 2012/175 (C.16) saving. Territorial extent & classification: S. General. - This SSI has been corrected by SSI 2012/206 (ISBN 9780111017609) which is being sent free of charge to all known recipients of SSI 2012/174. - 8p.: 30 cm. - 978-0-11-101741-8 £5.75

The Wildlife and Natural Environment (Scotland) Act 2011 (Commencement No. 2) Amendment (No. 2) Order 2012 No. 2012/281 (C.29). - Enabling power: Wildlife and Natural Environment (Scotland) Act 2011, s. 43 (1) (2) (a). Bringing into operation various provisions of the 2011 Act on 22.11.2012, in accord. with art. 1. - Issued: 25.10.2012. Made: 22.10.2012. Laid before the Scottish Parliament: 24.10.2012. Effect: S.S.I. 2011/433 C.37 amended. Territorial extent & classification: S. General. - 2p.: 30 cm. - 978-0-11-101813-2 £4.00

The Wildlife and Natural Environment (Scotland) Act 2011 (Commencement No. 3) Order 2012 No. 2012/116 (C.11). - Enabling power: Wildlife and Natural Environment (Scotland) Act 2011, s. 43 (1) (2) (a). Bringing into operation various provisions of the 2011 Act on 01.05.2012, in accord. with art. 2. - Issued: 20.04.2012. Made: 17.04.2012. Laid before the Scottish Parliament: 19.04.2012. Effect: None. Territorial extent & classification: S. General. - 8p.: 30 cm. - 978-0-11-101681-7 £4.00

The Wildlife and Natural Environment (Scotland) Act 2011 (Commencement No. 4, Savings and Transitional Provisions) Order 2012 No. 2012/175 (C.16). - Enabling power: Wildlife and Natural Environment (Scotland) Act 2011, s. 43 (1) (2). Bringing into operation various provisions of the 2011 Act on 02.07.2012, in accord. with art. 2. - Issued: 06.06.2012. Made: 30.05.2012. Laid before the Scottish Parliament: 31.05.2012. Coming into force: 02.07.2012. Effect: None. Territorial extent & classification: S. General. - 2p.: 30 cm. - 978-0-11-101742-5 £4.00

The Wildlife and Natural Environment (Scotland) Act 2011 (Consequential Modifications) Order 2012 No. 2012/215. - Enabling power: Wildlife and Natural Environment (Scotland) Act 2011, s. 42 (1) (2). - Issued: 03.07.2012. Made: 28.06.2012. Coming into force: 02.07.2012. Effect: 1995 c.46; 2010 asp 5; S.I. 1994/1404, 2716; 1997/2674 & S.S.I. 2008/100 modified & 1995 c.46 partially repealed & S.S.I. 2010/8 revoked. Territorial extent & classification: S. General. - Supersedes draft S.I. (ISBN 9780111017210) issued 24.05.2012. - 4p.: 30 cm. - 978-0-11-101769-2 £4.00

Scottish Statutory Instruments
Arranged by Number

1 (C.1)	Children and young persons
	Legal aid and advice
2 (C.2)	Housing
3	Agriculture
	Food
4	Sea fisheries
5	Seeds
6	River
7	Sheriff Court
8	Court of Session
9	National Health Service
10	National Health Service
11	Roads and bridges
12	Road traffic
13	Road traffic
14	Road traffic
15	Road traffic
16	Representation of the people
17	Road traffic
18	Road traffic
19 (C.3)	Housing
20 (C.4)	Criminal law
21 (C.5)	Registers and records
22	Education
23 (C.6)	Children and young persons
24	Agriculture
25	Environmental protection
	Licensing (marine)
26	Prisons
27	Rating and valuation
28	Rating and valuation
29	Rating and valuation
30	Title conditions
31	Representation of the people
32	Public passenger transport
33	Transport
34	Energy conservation
35 (C.7)	National Health Service
36	National Health Service
37	Plant health
38	Housing
39 (C.8)	Housing
40	Animals
41	Local government
42 (C.9)	Registers and records
43	Scottish Public Services Ombudsman
44	Social care
45	Social care
46	Road traffic
47	Road traffic
48	Rating and valuation
49	Police
50	Criminal law
51	Roads and bridges
52	Roads and bridges
53	Water supply
54	Children and young persons
55	Equal opportunities
56	Road traffic
57	Road traffic
58	Road traffic
59	Road traffic
60	Representation of the people
61	Representation of the people
62	Road traffic
63	Sea fisheries
64	Legal aid and advice
65	Social care
66	Adult support
	Social care
67	National assistance services
68	National assistance services
69	National Health Service
70	Pensions
71	Pensions
72	Education
73	National Health Service
74	National Health Service
75	Food
76	National Health Service
77	Forestry
	Climate change
78	Animals
79	Roads and bridges
80	Roads and bridges
81	Roads and bridges
82	Road traffic
83	Road traffic
84	Legal aid and advice

85	Scottish Public Services Ombudsman	129	Education
86	Education	130	Education
87	National Health Service	131	Town and country planning
88	Public procurement	132	Mental health
89	Public procurement	133	Road traffic
90	Town and country planning	134	Road traffic
91 (C.10)	Housing	135	Public health
92	Housing	136	Sheriff Court
93	Housing	137	Road traffic
94	Local government	138	Road traffic
95	Road traffic	139	Road traffic
96	Road traffic	140	Road traffic
97	Road traffic	141	Road traffic
98	Road traffic	142	Road traffic
99	Children and young persons	143	Agriculture
100	Court of Session	144	Sheriff Court
101	Sheriff Court	145	Road traffic
102	Regulatory reform Education	146	Fire and rescue services
		147	Road traffic
103	Road traffic	148	Environmental protection
104	Road traffic	149 (C.12)	Property factors
105	Public finance and accountability	150 (C.13)	Housing
106	Fire services	151	Housing
107	Fire services	152 (C.14)	Legal profession
108	Public procurement	153	Legal profession
109	Social care	154	Legal profession
110	National Health Service	155	Legal profession
111	Evidence	156	Road traffic
112	Road traffic	157	Road traffic
113	Housing	158	Road traffic
114	Harbours, docks, piers and ferries	159	Road traffic
115	Road traffic	160 (C.15)	Criminal law
116 (C.11)	Wildlife	161	Wildlife
117	Town and country planning	162	Equality
118	Insolvency	163	National Health Service
119	Food	164	Sports grounds and sporting events
120	Road traffic	165	Town and country planning
121	Road traffic	166	Sea fisheries
122	Road traffic	167	Prisons
123	Road traffic	168	Road traffic
124	Wildlife	169	Road traffic
125	High Court of Justiciary Sheriff Court	170	Adults with incapacity
		171	National Health Service
126	Court of Session	172	Education
127	Housing	173	Wildlife
128	Housing	174	Wildlife

175 (C.16)	Wildlife	216	Education
176	Animals Agriculture	217	Property factors
177	Animals Agriculture	218 (C.19)	Charities
		219	Charities
178	Animals	220	Charities
179	Animals	221	Sheriff Court
180	Property factors	222	Road traffic
181	Property factors	223	Road traffic
182	Agriculture	224	Road traffic
183	Environmental protection Licensing (marine)	225	Road traffic
		226	Road traffic
		227	Road traffic
184	Animals	228	Wildlife
185	Road traffic	229	Road traffic
186	Road traffic	230	Road traffic
187	High Court of Justiciary Sheriff Court Justice of the Peace Court	231	Road traffic
		232	Road traffic
		233	Road traffic
188	Sheriff Court	234	Road traffic
189	Court of Session	235	Road traffic
190	Building and buildings	236	Pensions
191 (C.17)	Energy	237	Education
192 (C.18)	Water industry	238	Education
193	Public bodies	239	Roads and bridges
194	Town and country planning	240	Roads and bridges
195	Road traffic	241	Roads and bridges
196	Official statistics	242	Roads and bridges
197	Prisons	243	Environmental protection Water
198	Animals Agriculture	244	Road traffic
199	Animals	245	Court of Session
200	Road traffic	246 (C.20)	Children and young persons
201	Road traffic	247 (C.21)	Registers and records
202	Road traffic	248	Road traffic
203	Road traffic	249 (C.22)	Criminal law
204	Road traffic	250	Roads and bridges
205	Wildlife	251	Road traffic
206	Wildlife	252 (C.23)	Children and young persons
207	Road traffic	253 (C.24)	Fire and rescue services Police
208	Building and buildings		
209	Building and buildings	254	Road traffic
210	River	255	Road traffic
211	Mental health	256	Road traffic
212	Legal profession	257	Road traffic
213	Legal profession	258	Housing
214	Energy conservation, Scotland	259	Town and country planning
215	Wildlife	260	Town and country planning

261 (C.25)	Sports grounds and sporting events	298	Road traffic
262	Harbours, docks, piers and ferries	299	Road traffic
263	Public health Animals	300	High Court of Justiciary Sheriff Court
264	Sea fisheries	301	Judgments
265 (C.26)	Land registration	302	Harbours, docks, piers and ferries
266	Plant health	303	Council tax
267 (C.27)	Housing	304	Criminal law
268	Road traffic	305	Legal aid and advice
269	Property factors	306	Housing
270	Court of Session	307	Agriculture
271	Sheriff Court	308	Enforcement
272	High Court of Justiciary Sheriff Court	309	Road traffic
		310	Road traffic
273	Sheriff Court	311	Road traffic
274 (C.28)	Criminal law	312	Road traffic
275	Court of Session	313	Road traffic
276	Legal aid and advice	314	Road traffic
277	Road traffic	315	Building and buildings
278	Road traffic	316	Police
279	Road traffic	317	Road traffic
280	Road traffic	318	Food
281 (C.29)	Wildlife	319	Council tax
282	Wildlife	320	Road traffic
283 (C.30)	Housing	321	Animals
284	Environmental protection Public sector information	322	Court of Session High Court of Justiciary Sheriff Court
285	Town and country planning		
286	Roads and bridges	323	Sports grounds and sporting events
287	Family law	324	Licences and licensing
288 (C.31)	Crofters, cottars and small landholders	325	Town and country planning
		326	Plant health
289	Adults with incapacity	327	Crofters, cottars and small landholders Registers and records
290	Court of Session		
291	High Court of Justiciary		
292	Justice of the Peace Court	328	Crofters, cottars and small landholders Registers and records
293	Sheriff Court		
294	Crofters, cottars and small landholders Registers and records	329	Landlord and tenant
		330	Housing
295	Crofters, cottars and small landholders Registers and records	331	Housing
		332	Fire safety
		333 (C.32)	Fire and rescue services Police
296	Crofters, cottars and small landholders Registers and records		
		334	Children and young persons
297	Crofters, cottars and small landholders Registers and records	335	Children and young persons
		336	Children and young persons
		337	Children and young persons

338	Council tax	20 (C.4)
339	Council tax	21 (C.5)
340	Court of Session	23 (C.6)
341	Sheriff Court	35 (C.7)
342	Representation of the people	39 (C.8)
343	Road traffic	42 (C.9)
344	Road traffic	91 (C.10)
345	Transport	116 (C.11)
346	Public finance and accountability	149 (C.12)
347	Pensions	150 (C.13)
348	Sea fisheries	152 (C.14)
349	Horticulture	160 (C.15)
350	Harbours, docks, piers and ferries	175 (C.16)
351	Road traffic	191 (C.17)
352	Rating and valuation	192 (C.18)
353	Rating and valuation	218 (C.19)
354	Police	246 (C.20)
355	Animals	247 (C.21)
356	Road traffic	249 (C.22)
357	Road traffic	252 (C.23)
358	Road traffic	253 (C.24)
359	Road traffic	261 (C.25)
360	Environmental protection	265 (C.26)

List of Scottish Commencement Orders

1 (C.1)
2 (C.2)
19 (C.3)

267 (C.27)
274 (C.28)
281 (C.29)
283 (C.30)
288 (C.31)
333 (C.32)

Northern Ireland Legislation

Acts of the Northern Ireland Assembly

Acts of the Northern Ireland Assembly 2012

Air Passenger Duty (Setting of Rate) Act (Northern Ireland) 2012: Chapter 5. - [4]p.: 30 cm. - Royal Assent, 11th December 2012. An Act to set the rate of air passenger duty for the purposes of section 30A (3) to (5A) of the Finance Act 1994. Explanatory notes for this Act are also available (ISBN 9780105961352). - 978-0-10-595130-8 £4.00

Budget Act (Northern Ireland) 2012: Chapter 2. - [1], 36p.: 30 cm. - Royal Assent, 20th March 2012. An Act to authorise the issue out of the Consolidated Fund of certain sums for the service of the years ending 31st March 2012 and 2013; to appropriate those sums for specified purposes; to authorise the Department of Finance and Personnel to borrow on the credit of the appropriated sums; to authorise the use for the public service of certain resources for the years ending 31st March 2012 and 2013; and to revise the limits on the use of certain accruing resources in the year ending 31st March 2012. Explanatory notes to the Act are also available (ISBN 9780105961321). - 978-0-10-595127-8 £9.75

Budget (No. 2) Act (Northern Ireland) 2012: Chapter 4. - [1], 22p.: 30 cm. - Royal Assent, 20th July 2012. An Act to authorise the issue out of the Consolidated Fund of certain sums for the service of the year ending 31st March 2013; to appropriate those sums for specified purposes; to authorise the Department of Finance and Personnel to borrow on the credit of the appropriated sums; to authorise the use for the public service of certain resources (including accruing resources) for the year ending 31st March 2013; to authorise the use for the public service of excess resources for the year ending 31st March 2011; and to repeal certain spent provisions. Explanatory notes to the Act are also available (ISBN 9780105961345). With binder holes. - 978-0-10-595129-2 £5.75

Pensions Act (Northern Ireland) 2012: Chapter 3. - [ii], 42p.: 30 cm. - Royal Assent, 1st June 2012. An Act to to make provision relating to pensions. Explanatory notes to the Act are also available (ISBN 9780105961338). - 978-0-10-595285-5 £9.75

Rates (Amendment) Act (Northern Ireland) 2012: Chapter 1. - [12]p.: 30 cm. - Royal Assent, 28th February 2012. An Act to amend the Rates (Northern Ireland) Order 1977. Explanatory notes to the Act are also available (ISBN 9780105961314). - 978-0-10-595126-1 £5.75

Acts of the Northern Ireland Assembly - Explanatory and financial memorandum 2012

Air Passenger Duty (Setting of Rate) Act (Northern Ireland) 2012: chapter 5; explanatory notes. - [1], 3p.: 30 cm. - These notes refer to the Air Passenger Duty (Setting of Rate) Act (Northern Ireland) 2012 (c.5) (ISBN 9780105951308) which received Royal Assent on 11 December 2012. - 978-0-10-596135-2 £4.00

Budget Act (Northern Ireland) 2012: chapter 2; explanatory notes. - [8]p.: 30 cm. - These Notes refer to the Budget Act (Northern Ireland) 2012 (c. 2) (ISBN 9780105951278) which received Royal Assent on 20 March 2012. - 978-0-10-596132-1 £4.00

Budget (No. 2) Act (Northern Ireland) 2012: chapter 4; explanatory notes. - [4]p.: 30 cm. - These Notes refer to the Budget (No. 2) Act (Northern Ireland) 2012 (c. 4) (ISBN 9780105951292) which received Royal Assent on 20 July 2012. - 978-0-10-596134-5 £4.00

Pensions Act (Northern Ireland) 2012: chapter 3; explanatory notes. - 27p.: 30 cm. - These Notes refer to the Pensions Act (Northern Ireland) 2012 (c. 3) (ISBN 9780105952855) which received Royal Assent on 1 June 2012. - 978-0-10-596133-8 £5.75

Rates (Amendment) Act (Northern Ireland) 2012: chapter 1; explanatory notes. - [12]p.: 30 cm. - These notes refer to the Rates (Amendment) Act (Northern Ireland) 2012 (c. 1) (ISBN 9780105951261) which received Royal Assent on 28th February 2012. - 978-0-10-596131-4 £5.75

Other statutory publications

Statutory Publications Office.

Chronological table of statutory rules Northern Ireland : covering the legislation to 31 December 2011. - 8th ed. - ca. 925 pages: looseleaf with binder holes: 30 cm. - Supersedes 7th edition (ISBN 9780337097058). - 978-0-337-09800-0 £129.00

Chronological table of the statutes Northern Ireland: covering the legislation to 31 December 2011. - 38th ed. - x, 751p.: looseleaf with binder holes: 30 cm. - 978-0-337-09849-9 £130.00

Northern Ireland statutes 2011: [binder]. - 1 binder: 31 cm. - 978-0-337-09784-3 £25.00

Northern Ireland statutes 2012: [binder]. - 1 binder: 31 cm. - 978-0-337-09864-2 £25.00

The statutes revised: Northern Ireland. - Cumulative supplement vols A-D (1537 - 1920) to 31 December 2011. - 2nd ed. - 78p.: looseleaf with binder holes: 30 cm. - The material held in the main updated Statutes revised has been integrated into the UK Statute Law Database, available online at www.statutelaw.gov.uk. However, pre-1921 legislation published in vols A to D and amended since is not currently covered by the Statute Law Database, so printed supplements will continue to be issued for amendments made to that legislation. - 978-0-337-09859-8 £11.70

Title page and index to Northern Ireland statutes volume 2011. - 20p.: looseleaf with binder holes: 30 cm. - 978-0-337-09794-2 £3.00

Statutory Rules of Northern Ireland

By Subject Heading

Agriculture

Agriculture (Student fees) (Amendment) Regulations (Northern Ireland) 2012 No. 2012/254. - Enabling power: Agriculture Act (Northern Ireland) 1949, s. 5A (1) (2). - Issued: 03.07.2012. Made: 27.06.2012. Coming into operation: 24.08.2012. Effect: S.R. 2007/54 amended & S.R. 2010/230 revoked. Territorial extent & classification: NI. General. - 2p: 30 cm. - 978-0-337-98837-0 £4.00

The Common Agricultural Policy Single Payment and Support Schemes (Cross Compliance) (Amendment) Regulations (Northern Ireland) 2012 No. 2012/452. - Enabling power: European Communities Act 1972, s. 2 (2). - Issued: 18.12.2012. Made: 14.12.2012. Coming into operation: 07.01.2012. Effect: S.R. 2005/6 amended. Territorial extent & classification: NI. General. - EC note: The Regulations make provision in Northern Ireland for the administration of Council Regulation (EC) no. 73/2009 and Commission Regulations 1120/2009 and 1122/2009. - 4p.: 30 cm. - 978-0-337-98996-4 £4.00

The Common Agricultural Policy Support Schemes (Review of Decisions) (Amendment) Regulations (Northern Ireland) 2012 No. 2012/457. - Enabling power: European Communities Act 1972, s. 2 (2). - Issued: 21.12.2012. Made: 18.12.2012. Coming into operation: 01.02.2013. Effect: S.R. 2010/220 amended. Territorial extent & classification: NI. General. - 4p.: 30 cm. - 978-0-337-99002-1 £4.00

The Less Favoured Area Compensatory Allowances Regulations (Northern Ireland) 2012 No. 2012/456. - Enabling power: European Communities Act 1972, s. 2 (2). - Issued: 20.12.2012. Made: 17.12.2012. Coming into operation: 01.02.2013. Effect: S.R. 2001/391 amended. Territorial extent & classification: NI. General. - EC note: These Regulations provide for the implementation of Articles 13(a), 14(1), 14(2) first and second indents, and 15 of Council Regulation (EC) No. 1257/1999 together with Articles 36(a)(ii) and 51(1) of Council Regulation (EC) No. 1698/2005 in so far as those Council Regulations relate to less favoured areas. - 12p.: 30 cm. - 978-0-337-99000-7 £5.75

The Specified Products from China (Restriction on First Placing on the Market) (Amendment) Regulations (Northern Ireland) 2012 No. 2012/3. - Enabling power: European Communities Act 1972, s. 2 (2). - Issued: 13.01.2012. Made: 10.01.2012. Coming into operation: 12.01.2012. Effect: S.R. 2008/171 amended. Territorial extent & classification: NI. General. - EC note: These Regulations amend SR 2008/171 in order to implement Commission Implementing Decision 2008/884/EU on emergency measures regarding the unauthorised genetically modified rice in rice products originating from China and repealing Decision 2008/289/EC. The Decision provides for import restrictions that previously applied to Bt 63 genetically modified rice to apply, with modifications, to all unauthorised GM rice. - 4p.: 30 cm. - 978-0-337-98635-2 £4.00

Air passenger duty

Air Passenger Duty (2012 Act) (Commencement) Order (Northern Ireland) 2012 No. 2012/445 (C.46). - Enabling power: Air Passenger Duty (Setting of Rates) Act (Northern Ireland) 2012, s. 3. Bringing into operation various provisions of the 2012 Act on 01.01.2013 in accord. with art. 2. - Issued: 17.12.2012. Made: 12.12.2012. Coming into operation: -. Effect: None. Territorial extent & classification: NI. General. - 2p.: 30 cm. - 978-0-337-98990-2 £4.00

Airports

The Belfast International Airport (Control Over Land) Order (Northern Ireland) 2012 No. 2012/94. - Enabling power: S.I. 1994/426 (N.I. 1), art. 8. - Issued: 08.03.2012. Made: 06.03.2012. Coming into operation: 01.05.2012. Effect: None. Territorial extent & classification: NI. General. - 4p.: 30 cm. - 978-0-337-98712-0 £4.00

Animals

The Aujeszky's Disease Order (Northern Ireland) 2012 No. 2012/65 . - Enabling power: S.I. 1981/1115 (N.I. 22), arts. 5 (1), 8A, 10 (6), 12 (1), 14, 19, 44, 46 (7A) (7B), 60 (1), sch. 2, pt. 1, para. 10. - Issued: 01.03.2012. Made: 22.02.2012. Coming into force: 19.03.2012. Effect: S.R. 1975/294; 2004/492; 2007/70; 2009/411 amended & S.R. 1994/198 revoked. Territorial extent & classification: NI. General. - 16p.: 25 cm. - 978-0-337-98686-4 £5.75

Aujeszky's Disease Scheme Order (Northern Ireland) 2012 No. 2012/66. - Enabling power: S.I. 1981/1115 (N.I. 22), art. 8 (1) (2). - Issued: 28.02.2012. Made: 23.02.2012. Coming into force: 19.03.2012. Effect: S.R. 1994/199 revoked. Territorial extent & classification: NI. General. - 8p.: 25 cm. - 978-0-337-98687-1 £4.00

The Brucellosis Control (Amendment) Order (Northern Ireland) 2012 No. 2012/315. - Enabling power: S.I. 1981/1115 (NI.22), arts. 18 (7), 60 (1), sch. 2, part 2, para. 5 (1). - Issued: 10.08.2012. Made: 08.08.2012. Coming into operation: 01.09.2012. Effect: S.R. 2004/361 amended. Territorial extent & classification: NI. General. - 4p.: 30 cm. - 978-0-337-98879-0 £4.00

The Diseases of Animals (Importation of Machinery and Vehicles) Order (Northern Ireland) 2012 No. 2012/176. - Enabling power: S.I. 1981/1115 (N.I. 22), arts 5 (1), 19, 24, 29, 60 (1). - Issued: 27.04.2012. Made: 24.04.2012. Coming into operation: 01.05.2012. Effect: S.R. 1979/281 revoked. Territorial extent & classification: NI. General. - 8p.: 30 cm. - 978-0-337-98784-7 £5.75

The Dogs (Amendment) (2011 Act) (Commencement No.3) Order (Northern Ireland) 2012 No. 2012/131 (C.13). - Enabling power: Dogs (Amendment) Act (Northern Ireland) 2011, s. 18. Bringing various provisions of the 2011 Act into operation on 09.04.2012. - Issued: 22.03.2012. Made: 16.03.2012. Coming into operation: -. Effect: None. Territorial extent & classification: NI. General. - 2p.: 30 cm. - 978-0-337-98742-7 £4.00

The Pig (Records, Identification and Movement) Order (Northern Ireland) 2012 No. 2012/67. - Enabling power: S.I. 1981/1115 (N.I. 22), arts. 5 (1), 19, 44, 51 (2), 60 (1). - Issued: 28.02.2012. Made: 22.02.2012. Coming into operation: 19.03.2012. Effect: S.R. 1975/294 amended & S.R. 1997/172, 2000/344 revoked. Territorial extent & classification: NI. General. - 12p.: 30 cm. - 978-0-337-98688-8 £5.75

The Tuberculosis Control (Amendment) Order (Northern Ireland) 2012 No. 2012/314. - Enabling power: S.I. 1981/1115 (NI.22), arts. 18 (7), 60 (1), sch. 2, part 2, para. 4. - Issued: 10.08.2012. Made: 08.08.2012. Coming into operation: 01.09.2012. Effect: S.R. 1999/263 amended. Territorial extent & classification: NI. General. - 2p.: 30 cm. - 978-0-337-98878-3 £4.00

The Welfare of Animals (2011 Act) (Commencement and Transitional Provisions No. 2) Order (Northern Ireland) 2012 No. 2012/154 (C.15). - Enabling power: Welfare of Animals Act (Northern Ireland) 2011, s. 59. Bringing various provisions of the 2011 Act into operation on 02.04.2012, in accord. with art. 2. - Issued: 03.04.2012. Made: 30.03.2012. Coming into operation: 02.04.2012. Effect: 1972 c.7 repealed to the extent specified in sch. 3. Territorial extent & classification: NI. General. - 4p.: 30 cm. - 978-0-337-98767-0 £4.00

The Welfare of Animals (2011 Act) (Commencement No. 3) Order (Northern Ireland) 2012 No. 2012/386 (C.36). - Enabling power: Welfare of Animals Act (Northern Ireland) 2011, s. 59. Bringing various provisions of the 2011 Act into operation on 01.01.2013, in accord. with art. 2. - Issued: 26.10.2012. Made: 24.10.2012. Coming into operation: -. Effect: None. Territorial extent & classification: NI. General. - 4p.: 30 cm. - 978-0-337-98933-9 £4.00

The Zoonoses (Fees) (Amendment) Regulations (Northern Ireland) 2012 No. 2012/158. - Enabling power: European Communities Act 1972, s. 2 (2) & Finance Act 1973, s. 56 (1) (2) (5). - Issued: 11.04.2012. Made: 03.04.2012. Coming into operation: 30.04.2012. Effect: S.R. 2011/71 amended. Territorial extent & classification: NI. General. - EC note: These Regulations make provision for the Department to charge fees for activities required under Commission Regulation (EC) nos 1003/2005, 1168/2006, 646/2007, 584/2008, 2160/2003 and 1237/2007. - 4p.: 30 cm. - 978-0-337-98772-4 £4.00

Animals: Animal health

The Bluetongue (Amendment) Regulations (Northern Ireland) 2012 No. 2012/383. - Enabling power: European Communities Act 1972, s. 2 (2). - Issued: 25.10.2012. Made: 22.10.2012. Coming into operation: 19.11.2012. Effect: S.R. 2008/275 revoked. - EC note: These Regulations amend the Bluetongue Regulations 2008 (S.R. 2008 No.275) by transposing Directive 2012/5/EU of 14 March 2012 amending Council Directive 2000/75/EC as regards vaccination against bluetongue- 4p: 30 cm. - 978-0-337-98928-5 £4.00

The Northern Ireland Poultry Health Assurance Scheme (Fees) Order (Northern Ireland) 2012 No. 2012/305. - Enabling power: S.I. 1981/1115 (N.I. 22), art. 8 (1) (2) (5) & European Communities Act 1972, s. 2 (2). - Issued: 31.07.2012. Made: 27.07.2012. Coming into operation: 27.08.2012. Effect: S.R. 2011/436 amended & S.R. 2011/435 revoked. Territorial extent & classification: NI. General. - 4p.: 30 cm. - 978-0-337-98870-7 £4.00

Animals: Welfare of animals

The Welfare of Animals (Docking of Working Dogs' Tails and Miscellaneous Amendments) Regulations (Northern Ireland) 2012 No. 2012/387. - Enabling power: Welfare of Animals Act (Northern Ireland) 2011, ss. 5 (5), 6 (5) (6) (10) (16), 11 (1) (2) (3). - Issued: 26.10.2012. Made: 24.10.2012. Coming into operation: 01.01.2013. Effect: S.R. 2012/153, 156 amended. Territorial extent & classification: NI. General. - Supersedes draft S.R. (ISBN 9780337988134) issued 01.06.2012. - 12p.: 30 cm. - 978-0-337-98934-6 £5.75

The Welfare of Animals (Permitted Procedures by Lay Persons) Regulations (Northern Ireland) 2012 No. 2012/153. - Enabling power: Welfare of Animals Act (Northern Ireland) 2011, s. 5 (5) (a) (iv). - Issued: 03.04.2012. Made: 30.04.2012. Coming into operation: 02.04.2012. Effect: S.R. 1987/415 repealed. Territorial extent & classification: NI. General. - Supersedes draft S.R. (ISBN 9780337986765) issued 03.04.2012. - 16p.: 30 cm. - 978-0-337-98766-3 £5.75

Aquaculture

The Alien and Locally Absent Species in Aquaculture Regulations (Northern Ireland) 2012 No. 2012/335. - Enabling power: European Communities Act 1972, s. 2 (2). - Issued: 17.09.2012. Made: 07.09.2012. Coming into operation: 15.10.2012. Effect: S.R. & O. 1972/9 & S.R. 1979/178 amended. Territorial extent & classification: NI. General. - 16p.: 30 cm. - 978-0-337-98902-5 £5.75

Building regulations

The Building (Amendment) Regulations (Northern Ireland) 2012 No. 2012/375. - Enabling power: S.I. 1979/1709 (N.I. 16), arts. 3, 18 (5). - Issued: 15.10.2012. Made: 10.10.2012. Coming into operation: 31.10.2012. Effect: S.R. 2012/192 amended. Territorial extent & classification: NI. General. - 4p.: 30 cm. - 978-0-337-98920-9 £4.00

The Building Regulations (1979 Order) (Commencement No. 3) Order (Northern Ireland) 2012 No. 2012/187 (C.17). - Enabling power: S.I. 1979/1709 (NI. 16), art. 1 (2). Bringing into operation various provisions of the 1979 Order on 15.05.2012 & 31.10.2012. - Issued: 17.05.2012. Made: 14.05.2012. Coming into operation: -. Effect: None. Territorial extent & classification: NI. General. - 2p.: 30 cm. - 978-0-337-98798-4 £4.00

The Building Regulations (2009 Amendment Act) (Commencement No. 2) Order (Northern Ireland) 2012 No. 2012/186 (C.16). - Enabling power: Building Regulations (Amendment) Act (Northern Ireland) 2009, s. 15 (4). Bringing into operation various provisions of the 2009 Act on 15.05.2012 & 31.10.2012. - Issued: 17.05.2012. Made: 14.05.2012. Coming into operation: -. Effect: None. Territorial extent & classification: NI. General. - 2p.: 30 cm. - 978-0-337-98797-7 £4.00

The Building Regulations (Northern Ireland) 2012 No. 2012/192. - Enabling power: S.I. 1979/1709 (N.I. 16), arts. 3, 5 (1) (2) (3), 5A (1), 8, 9, 12, 15, 16 (1) (2), 17 (1) (2) (2A) (5), 18 (5), 18B, 18C (1), 19, sch. 1, paras 1 to 7, 9 to 13, 17 to 22 - Issued: 18.05.2012. Made: 15.05.2012. Coming into operation: 31.10.2012. Effect: S.R. 2000/389; 2005/295; 2006/355, 440; 2008/170; 2010/1, 382 revoked (with saving). Territorial extent & classification: NI. General. - 60p.: 30 cm. - 978-0-337-98800-4 £9.75

Children and young persons

The Health (2009 Act) (Commencement No. 1) Order (Northern Ireland) 2012 No. 2012/68 (C. 9). - Enabling power: Health Act 2009, s. 40 (3). Bringing into operation various provisions of this Act on 01.03.2012, in accord. with art. 2. - Issued: 28.02.2012. Made: 23.02.2012. Coming into operation: -. Effect: None. Territorial extent & classification: NI. General. - 2p: 30 cm. - 978-0-337-98689-5 £4.00

The Protection from Tobacco (Sales from Vending Machines) Regulations (Northern Ireland) 2012 No. 2012/15. - Enabling power: S.I. 1991/2872 (N.I.25), art. 4A. - Issued: 26.01.2012. Made: 19.01.2012. Coming into operation: 01.03.2012. Effect: None. Territorial extent & classification: NI. General. - Supersedes draft S.R. (ISBN 9780337985898) issued 28.11.2011. - 2p.: 30 cm. - 978-0-337-98646-8 £4.00

Child support

The Child Support (Great Britain Reciprocal Arrangements) (Amendment) Regulations (Northern Ireland) 2012 No. 2012/374. - Enabling power: Northern Ireland Act 1998, s. 87 (5) (10). - Issued: 09.10.2012. Made: 05.10.2012. Coming into operation: 29.10.2012. Effect: S.R. 1993/117 amended. Territorial extent & classification: NI. General. - 8p.: 30 cm. - 978-0-337-98918-6 £4.00

Civil registration

The Civil Registration (2011 Act) (Commencement No. 2) Order (Northern Ireland) 2012 No. 2012/406 (C.40). - Enabling power: Civil Registration Act (Northern Ireland) 2011, s. 34. Bringing into operation various provisions of the 2011 Act on 16.11.2012 in accord. with art. 2. - Issued: 27.11.2012. Made: 15.11.2012. Coming into operation: -. Effect: None. Territorial extent & classification: NI. General. - 4p.: 30 cm. - 978-0-337-98956-8 £4.00

The Civil Registration Regulations (Northern Ireland) 2012 No. 2012/408. - Enabling power: S.I. 1976/1041 (N.I. 14), arts 10 (1) (4), 11 (1), 12 (1), 14 (3), 14ZA (3), 15 (3) (6) (7) (9), 16 (1) (2), 18 (2), 19 (2), 19A(2), 21 (1) (5), 23 (1), 25 (2), 29 (1) (2), 30 (1), 31 (2), 32, 34A (1), 35 (2) (3), 36 (3), 37 (3) (4) (4B), 39, 40, 40A, 40B (2) & S.I. 1987/2203 (N.I. 22) art. 50 (4) & S.I. 2003/413 (N.I. 3), arts 35(5), 35A(2) & Civil Partnership Act 2004, ss. 155A(2), 159 & Presumption of Death Act (Northern Ireland) 2009, sch. 1 para. 3A (1) & Civil Registration Act (Northern Ireland) 2011, s. 31 (2). - Issued: 27.11.2012. Made: 19.11.2012. Coming into operation: 17.12.2012. Effect: S.R. 1973/373 revoked. Territorial extent & classification: NI. General. - 52p.: 30 cm. - 978-0-337-98958-2 £9.75

Clean air

The Smoke Control Areas (Authorised Fuels) Regulations (Northern Ireland) 2012 No. 2012/399. - Enabling power: S.I. 1981/158 (N.I. 4), art. 2 (2). - Issued: 07.11.2012. Made: 05.11.2012. Coming into operation: 05.12.2012. Effect: S.R. 2011/374 revoked. Territorial extent & classification: NI. General. - 16p.: 30 cm. - 978-0-337-98949-0 £5.75

The Smoke Control Areas (Exempted Fireplaces) (No. 2) Regulations (Northern Ireland) 2012 No. 2012/379. - Enabling power: S.I. 1981/158 (N.I. 4), art. 17 (7). - Issued: 22.10.2012. Made: 17.10.2012. Coming into operation: 21.11.2012. Effect: S.R. 2012/250 revoked. Territorial extent & classification: NI. General. - 92p.: 30 cm. - 978-0-337-98925-4 £15.50

The Smoke Control Areas (Exempted Fireplaces) Regulations (Northern Ireland) 2012 No. 2012/250. - Enabling power: S.I. 1981/158 (N.I. 4), art. 17 (7). - Issued: 27.06.2012. Made: 22.06.2012. Coming into operation: 30.07.2012. Effect: S.R. 2010/369 revoked. Territorial extent & classification: NI. General. - Revoked by SR 2012/379 (ISBN 9780337989254). - 80p.: 30 cm. - 978-0-337-98835-6 £13.75

Construction

The Construction Contracts (2011 Act) (Commencement) Order (Northern Ireland) 2012 No. 2012/367 (C.34). - Enabling power: Construction Contracts (Amendment) Act (Northern Ireland) 2011, s. 9 (2). Bringing various provisions of the 2011 Act into operation on 14.11.2012. - Issued: 02.10.2012. Made: 20.09.2012. Coming into operation: -. Effect: -. Territorial extent & classification: NI. General. - 2p.: 30 cm. - 978-0-337-98891-2 £4.00

The Construction Contracts Exclusion Order (Northern Ireland) 2012 No. 2012/366. - Enabling power: S.I. 1997/274 (N.I. 1), art. 5 (1A). - Issued: 13.11.2012. Made: 20.09.2012. Coming into operation: 14.11.2012. Effect: S.R. 1999/33 amended. Territorial extent & classification: NI. General. - Affirmed by resolution of the Assembly on 23rd October 2012. - 4p.: 30 cm. - 978-0-337-98931-5 £4.00

The Construction Contracts Exclusion Order (Northern Ireland) 2012 No. 2012/366. - Enabling power: S.I. 1997/274 (N.I. 1), art. 5 (1A). - Issued: 02.10.2012. Made: 20.09.2012. Coming into operation: 14.11.2012. Effect: S.R. 1999/33 amended. Territorial extent & classification: NI. General. - Superseded by affirmed SR of the same number (ISBN 9780337989315) issued on 13.11.2012. - 4p.: 30 cm. - 978-0-337-98892-9 £4.00

The Scheme for Construction Contracts in Northern Ireland (Amendment) Regulations (Northern Ireland) 2012 No. 2012/365. - Enabling power: S.I. 1997/274 (N.I. 1), arts 7 (6), 13, 16 (1). - Issued: 02.10.2012. Made: 20.09.2012. Coming into operation: 14.11.2012. Effect: S.R. 1999/32 amended. Territorial extent & classification: NI. General. - Superseded by affirmed SR of the same number (ISBN 9780337989322) issued on 13.11.2012. - 8p.: 30 cm. - 978-0-337-98886-8 £4.00

The Scheme for Construction Contracts in Northern Ireland (Amendment) Regulations (Northern Ireland) 2012 No. 2012/365. - Enabling power: S.I. 1997/274 (N.I. 1), arts 7 (6), 13, 16 (1). - Issued: 13.11.2012. Made: 20.09.2012. Coming into operation: 14.11.2012. Effect: S.R. 1999/32 amended. Territorial extent & classification: NI. General. - Affirmed by resolution of the Assembly on 23rd October 2012. - 8p.: 30 cm. - 978-0-337-98932-2 £4.00

County courts

The County Court (Amendment) Rules (Northern Ireland) 2012 No. 2012/402. - Enabling power: S.I. 1980/397 (N.I. 3), art. 47 & S.I. 1996/1921 (NI. 18), s. 21A (10) & S.I. 1998/3162 (NI. 21), s.88A (10). - Issued: 12.11.2012. Made: 06.11.2012. Coming into operation: 03.12.2012. Effect: S.R. 1981/225 amended. Territorial extent & classification: NI. General. - 4p.: 30 cm. - 978-0-337-98952-0 £4.00

Court of Judicature, Northern Ireland: Procedure

The Rules of the Court of Judicature (Northern Ireland) (Amendment) 2012 No. 2012/272. - Enabling power: Judicature (Northern Ireland) Act 1978, ss. 55, 55A. - Issued: 10.07.2012. Made: 04.07.2012. Coming into operation: 01.08.2012. Effect: S.R. 1980/346 amended. Territorial extent & classification: NI. General. - 4p.: 30 cm. - 978-0-337-98855-4 £4.00

The Rules of the Court of Judicature (Northern Ireland) (Amendment No. 2) 2012 No. 2012/273. - Enabling power: Judicature (Northern Ireland) Act 1978, ss. 55, 55A. - Issued: 10.07.2012. Made: 04.07.2012. Coming into operation: 01.08.2012. Effect: S.R. 1980/346 amended. Territorial extent & classification: NI. General. - 4p.: 30 cm. - 978-0-337-98856-1 £4.00

The Rules of the Court of Judicature (Northern Ireland) (Amendment No. 3) 2012 No. 2012/431. - Enabling power: Judicature (Northern Ireland) Act 1978, ss. 55, 55A. - Issued: 10.12.2012. Made: 30.11.2012. Coming into operation: 01.01.2013. Effect: S.R. 1980/346 amended. Territorial extent & classification: NI. General. - 4p.: 30 cm. - 978-0-337-98976-6 £4.00

Criminal law

The Corporate Manslaughter and Corporate Homicide (2007 Act) (Commencement) Order (Northern Ireland) 2012 No. 2012/286 (C.26). - Enabling power: Corporate Manslaughter and Corporate Homicide Act 2007, ss. 24 (9), 27 (1) (1A). Bringing into operation various provisions of the 2007 Act on 03.09.2012. - Issued: 16.07.2012. Made: 06.07.2012. Coming into operation: -. Effect: None. Territorial extent & classification: NI. General. - Supersedes draft S.R. (ISBN 9780337987854) issued 11.05.2012. - 2p.: 30 cm. - 978-0-337-98861-5 £4.00

The Police Act 1997 (Criminal Records) (Amendment No. 2) Regulations (Northern Ireland) 2012 No. 2012/321. - Enabling power: Police Act 1997, ss. 113B (9), 113BA (1), 113BB (1), 125 (1) (5). - Issued: 20.08.2012. Made: 15.08.2012. Coming into operation: 10.09.2012. Effect: S.I. 2008/542 amended. Territorial extent & classification: NI. General. - 4p.: 30 cm. - 978-0-337-98888-2 £4.00

The Police Act 1997 (Criminal Records) (Amendment No. 3) Regulations (Northern Ireland) 2012 No. 2012/446. - Enabling power: Police Act 1997, ss. 113A (6), 125 (1) (5). - Issued: 17.12.2012. Made: 17.12.2012. Coming into operation: 14.01.2013. Effect: S.I. 2008/542 amended. Territorial extent & classification: NI. General. - 2p.: 30 cm. - 978-0-337-98991-9 £4.00

The Police Act 1997 (Criminal Records) (Amendment) Regulations (Northern Ireland) 2012 No. 2012/86. - Enabling power: Police Act 1997, ss. 113B (9), 120Z (1) (2), 120AA (1), 125 (1) (5). - Issued: 06.03.2012. Made: 29.02.2012. Coming into operation: 02.04.2012. Effect: S.I. 2007/3283; 2008/542 amended. Territorial extent & classification: NI. General. - With correction slip dated March 2012. - 4p.: 30 cm. - 978-0-337-98703-8 £4.00

The Sexual Offences Act 2003 (Prescribed Police Stations) Regulations (Northern Ireland) 2012 No. 2012/325. - Enabling power: Sexual Offences Act 2003, s. 87 (1). - Issued: 24.08.2012. Made: 13.08.2012. Coming into operation: 08.10.2012. Effect: S.R. 2010/207 partially revoked. Territorial extent & classification: NI. General. - 4p.: 30 cm. - 978-0-337-98894-3 £4.00

Dangerous drugs

The Health (2006 Act) (Commencement) Order (Northern Ireland) 2012 No. 2012/307 (C.27). - Enabling power: Health Act 2006, s. 83 (6). Bringing into operation in relation to Northern Ireland various provisions of this Act on 01.08.2012, in accord. with art. 2. - Issued: 06.08.2012. Made: 01.08.2012. Coming into operation: -. Effect: None. Territorial extent & classification: NI. General. - 2p.: 30 cm. - 978-0-337-98872-1 £4.00

The Misuse of Drugs (Amendment No. 2) Regulations (Northern Ireland) 2012 No. 2012/213. - Enabling power: Misuse of Drugs Act 1971, ss. 7, 10, 22, 31. - Issued: 25.05.2012. Made: 22.05.2012. Coming into operation: 13.06.2012. Effect: S.R. 2002/1 amended. Territorial extent & classification: NI. General. - 4p.: 30 cm. - 978-0-337-98807-3 £4.00

The Misuse of Drugs (Amendment) Regulations (Northern Ireland) 2012 No. 2012/168. - Enabling power: Misuse of Drugs Act 1971, ss. 7, 10, 22, 31. - Issued: 25.04.2012. Made: 18.04.2012. Coming into operation: 10.05.2012. Effect: S.R. 2002/1 amended. Territorial extent & classification: NI. General. - 8p.: 30 cm. - 978-0-337-98779-3 £5.75

The Misuse of Drugs (Designation) (Amendment) Order (Northern Ireland) 2012 No. 2012/212. - Enabling power: Misuse of Drugs Act 1971, s. 7 (4). - Issued: 25.05.2012. Made: 22.05.2012. Coming into operation: 13.06.2012. Effect: S.R. 2001/431 amended. Territorial extent & classification: NI. General. - 2p.: 30 cm. - 978-0-337-98806-6 £4.00

Dogs

The Dogs (Licensing and Identification) Regulations (Northern Ireland) 2012 No. 2012/132. - Enabling power: S.I. 1983/764 (N.I. 8), arts 6 (2) (3) (5), 7 (9), 8 (2) (3), 15 (1), 31 (1) (1A). - Issued: 22.03.2012. Made: 16.03.2012. Coming into operation: 09.04.2012. Effect: S.R. 2011/279 revoked. - 16p.: 30 cm. - 978-0-337-98744-1 £5.75

Dogs: Control of dogs

The Control on Dogs (Non-application to Designated Land) Order (Northern Ireland) 2012 No. 2012/34. - Enabling power: Clean Neighbourhoods and Environment Act (Northern Ireland) 2011, s. 42 (3). - Issued: 14.02.2012. Made: 07.02.2012. Coming into operation: 01.04.2012. Effect: None. Territorial extent & classification: NI. General. - 4p.: 30 cm. - 978-0-337-98663-5 £4.00

The Dog Control Orders (Prescribed Offences and Penalties, etc.) Regulations (Northern Ireland) 2012 No. 2012/114. - Enabling power: Clean Neighbourhoods and Environment Act (Northern Ireland) 2011, ss. 40 (4), 41 (1) (3). - Issued: 16.03.2012. Made: 14.03.2012. Coming into operation: 01.04.2012. Effect: None. Territorial extent & classification: NI. General. - Supersedes draft SR (ISBN 9780337986369) issued 17.01.2012. - 16p.: 30 cm. - 978-0-337-98727-4 £5.75

Dog Control Orders (Procedures) Regulations (Northern Ireland) 2012 No. 2012/39. - Enabling power: Clean Neighbourhoods and Environment Act (Northern Ireland) 2011, s. 41 (4). - Issued: 13.02.2012. Made: 07.02.2012. Coming into operation: 01.04.2012. Effect: None. Territorial extent & classification: NI. General. - 4p.: 30 cm. - 978-0-337-98668-0 £4.00

Education

The Education (Levels of Progression for Key Stages 1, 2 and 3) Order (Northern Ireland) 2012 No. 2012/444. - Enabling power: S.I. 2006/1915 (N.I. 11), arts 8 (3), 9 (2) (3), 10 (2), 43 (5). - Issued: 17.12.2012. Made: 12.12.2012. Coming into operation: 10.01.2013. Effect: S.R. 2010/135 revoked. Territorial extent & classification: NI. General. - 4p.: 30 cm. - 978-0-337-98989-6 £4.00

The Education (Student Loans) (Repayment) (Amendment) Regulations (Northern Ireland) 2012 No. 2012/136. - Enabling power: S.I. 1998/1760 (N.I. 14), arts 3 (2) to (5), 8 (4). - Issued: 28.03.2012. Made: 21.03.2012. Coming into operation: 06.04.2012. Effect: S.R. 2009/128 amended. Territorial extent & classification: NI. General. - 12p.: 30 cm. - 978-0-337-98750-2 £5.75

The Education (Student Support) (No. 2) Regulations (Northern Ireland) 2009 (Amendment) (No. 2) Regulations (Northern Ireland) 2012 No. 2012/398. - Enabling power: S.I. 1998/1760 (N.I. 14), arts 3, 8 (4). - Issued: 07.11.2012. Made: 01.11.2012. Coming into operation: 01.12.2012. Effect: S.R. 2009/373 amended. Territorial extent & classification: NI. General. - 8p.: 30 cm. - 978-0-337-98946-9 £5.75

The Education (Student Support) (No. 2) Regulations (Northern Ireland) 2009 (Amendment) Regulations (Northern Ireland) 2012 No. 2012/62. - Enabling power: S.I. 1998/1760 (N.I. 14), arts 3, 8 (4). - Issued: 01.03.2012. Made: 22.02.2012. Coming into operation: 21.03.2012. Effect: S.R. 2009/373 amended. Territorial extent & classification: NI. General. - With correction slip dated March 2012. - 8p.: 30 cm. - 978-0-337-98684-0 £4.00

The Further Education (Student Support) (Eligibility) Regulations (Northern Ireland) 2012 No. 2012/306. - Enabling power: S.I. 1998/1760 (N.I. 14), arts 3 (1) (2), 8 (4). - Issued: 02.08.2012. Made: 30.07.2012. Coming into operation: 01.09.2012. Effect: S.R. 2011/262 revoked. Territorial extent & classification: NI. General. - 12p.: 30 cm. - 978-0-337-98871-4 £5.75

Pre-School Education in Schools (Admissions Criteria) (Amendment) Regulations (Northern Ireland) 2012 No. 2012/239. - Enabling power: S.I. 1998/1759 (N.I. 13), arts 32 (6), 90 (3). - Issued: 18.06.2012. Made: 12.06.2012. Coming into operation: 06.07.2012. Effect: SR 1999/419 amended. Territorial extent & classification: NI. General. - 2p.: 30 cm. - 978-0-337-98824-0 £4.00

The Student Fees (Amounts) (Amendment) Regulations (Northern Ireland) 2012 No. 2012/184. - Enabling power: S.I. 2005/1116 (N.I. 5), arts 4 (8), 14 (4). - Issued: 16.05.2012. Made: 09.05.2012. Coming into operation: 01.09.2013. Effect: S.R. 2005/290 amended & S.R. 2011/369 revoked. Territorial extent & classification: NI. General. - 2p.: 30 cm. - 978-0-337-98794-6 £4.00

The Teachers' Superannuation (Amendment) Regulations (Northern Ireland) 2012 No. 2012/126. - Enabling power: S.I. 1972/1073 (N.I. 10), art. 11 (1) (2) (3) (3A), sch. 3, paras 1, 3, 4, 5, 6, 8, 11, 13. - Issued: 20.03.2012. Made: 16.03.2012. Coming into operation: 01.04.2012. Effect: S.R. 1998/333 amended. Territorial extent & classification: NI. General. - With correction slip dated March 2012. - 4p: 30 cm. - 978-0-337-98741-0 £4.00

Electricity

Electricity (Priority Dispatch) Regulations (Northern Ireland) 2012 No. 2012/385. - Enabling power: European Communities Act 1972, s. 2 (2). - Issued: 26.10.2012. Made: 24.10.2012. Coming into operation: 20.11.2012. Effect: S.I. 1992/231 (N.I. 1) amended. Territorial extent & classification: NI. General. - 4p.: 30 cm. - 978-0-337-98930-8 £4.00

The Electricity Safety, Quality and Continuity Regulations (Northern Ireland) 2012 No. 2012/381. - Enabling power: S.I. 1992/231 (NI. 1), arts. 32, 33 (3), 64. - Issued: 23.10.2012. Made: 18.10.2012. Coming into operation: 31.12.2012. Effect: S.R. 1991/536; 1993/21 revoked. Territorial extent & classification: NI. General. - 28p., fig: 30 cm. - 978-0-337-98927-8 £5.75

Employment

The Code of Practice (Time Off for Trade Union Duties and Activities) (Appointed Day) Order (Northern Ireland) 2012 No. 2012/138. - Enabling power: S.I. 1992/807 (N.I. 5), arts. 90 (5). - Issued: 26.03.2012. Made: 21.03.2012. Coming into operation: 19.04.2012. Effect: S.R. 2004/230 revoked with saving. - 4p.: 30 cm. - 978-0-337-98752-6 £4.00

The Employment Rights (Increase of Limits) Order (Northern Ireland) 2012 No. 2012/81. - Enabling power: S.I. 1999/2790 (N.I. 9), arts 33 (2) (3), 39 (3). - Issued: 05.03.2012. Made: 29.03.2012. Coming into operation: 04.03.2012. Effect: S.R. 2011/30 revoked. Territorial extent & classification: NI. General. - 8p: 30 cm. - 978-0-337-98698-7 £5.75

The Labour Relations Agency Arbitration Scheme (Jurisdiction) Order (Northern Ireland) 2012 No. 2012/302. - Enabling power: S.I. 1992/807 (N.I. 5), art. 84A (1) (b). - Issued: 31.07.2012. Made: 26.07.2012. Coming into operation: 27.09.2012. Effect: None. Territorial extent & classification: NI. General. - Supersedes draft S.R. (ISBN 9780337988011) issued 25.05.2012. - 4p.: 30 cm. - 978-0-337-98867-7 £4.00

The Labour Relations Agency Arbitration Scheme Order (Northern Ireland) 2012 No. 2012/301. - Enabling power: S.I. 1992/807 (N.I. 5), art. 84A (2) (6) (7) (8) & S.I. 1998/3162 (N.I. 21), art. 89 (2) (6). - Issued: 31.07.2012. Made: 26.07.2012. Coming into operation: 27.09.2012. Effect: S.R. 2002/120; 2006/206 revoked with savings. Territorial extent & classification: NI. General. - 36p.: 30 cm. - 978-0-337-98866-0 £9.75

Public Interest Disclosure (Prescribed Persons) (Amendment) Order (Northern Ireland) 2012 No. 2012/283. - Enabling power: S.I. 1996/1919 (N.I. 16), art. 67F. - Issued: 23.07.2012. Made: 09.07.2012. Coming into operation: 01.10.2012. Effect: S.R. 2010/361, 399 revoked. Territorial extent & classification: NI. General. - 8p.: 30 cm. - 978-0-337-98858-5 £5.75

The Social Security Benefits Up-rating Order (Northern Ireland) 2012 No. 2012/116. - Enabling power: Social Security Administration (Northern Ireland) Act 1992, ss. 132, 132A,165 (1) (4) (5). - Issued: 20.03.2012. Made: 14.03.2012. Coming into operation: In accord. with 1. Effect: 1966 c. 6 (N.I.); 1992 c. 7; 1993 c. 49; S.R. 1987/30, 459; 1992/32; 1994/461; 1995/35; 1996/198; 2002/380; 2003/28; 2006/405, 406; 2008/280; 2010/302, 407 amended & 2011/119 revoked (12.04.2012). Territorial extent & classification: NI. General. - For approval of the Assembly before the expiration of six months from the date of its coming into operation. Superseded by approved version (ISBN 9780337988264) issued on 15.06.2012. - 42p.: 30 cm. - 978-0-337-98731-1 £9.75

The Social Security Benefits Up-rating Order (Northern Ireland) 2012 No. 2012/116. - Enabling power: Social Security Administration (Northern Ireland) Act 1992, ss. 132, 132A, 165 (1) (4) (5). - Issued: 15.06.2012. Made: 14.03.2012. Coming into operation: In accord. with art. 1. Effect: 1966 c. 6 (N.I.); 1992 c. 7; 1993 c. 49; S.R. 1987/30, 459, 460; 1992/32; 1994/461; 1995/35; 1996/198; 2002/380; 2003/28; 2006/405, 406; 2008/280; 2010/302, 407 amended & 2011/119 revoked (12.04.2012). Territorial extent & classification: NI. General. - Approved by resolution of the Assembly on 11th June 2012. Supersedes pre-approved version (ISBN 9780337987311). - 44p.: 30 cm. - 978-0-337-98826-4 £9.75

Energy

The Renewable Heat Incentive Scheme Regulations (Northern Ireland) 2012 No. 2012/396. - Enabling power: Energy Act 2011, s. 113. - Issued: 05.11.2012. Made: 31.10.2012. Coming into operation: 01.11.2012. Effect: None. Territorial extent & classification: NI. General. - Supersedes draft SR (ISBN 9780337989193) issued 12.10.2012. - 34p.: 30 cm. - 978-0-337-98944-5 £9.75

Environment

The High Hedges (2011 Act) (Commencement) Order (Northern Ireland) 2012 No. 2012/20 (C.4). - Enabling power: High Hedges Act (Northern Ireland) 2011. Bringing in operation various provisions of the 2011 Act on 31.01.2012; 31.03.2012, in accord. with art. 2. - Issued: 03.02.2012. Made: 25.01.2012. Coming into operation: -. Effect: None. Territorial extent & classification: NI. General. - 4p.: 30 cm. - 978-0-337-98652-9 £4.00

Environment: High hedges

The High Hedges (Fee) Regulations (Northern Ireland) 2012 No. 2012/33. - Enabling power: High Hedges Act (Northern Ireland) 2011, s. 4 (1). - Issued: 10.02.2012. Made: 06.02.2012. Coming into operation: 31.03.2012. Effect: None. Territorial extent & classification: NI. General. - 2p.: 30 cm. - 978-0-337-98661-1 £4.00

The High Hedges (Fee Transfer) Regulations (Northern Ireland) 2012 No. 2012/105. - Enabling power: High Hedges Act (Northern Ireland) 2011, s. 4 (4). - Issued: 14.03.2012. Made: 07.03.2012. Coming into operation: 31.03.2012. Effect: None. Territorial extent & classification: NI. General. - Supersedes draft S.R. (ISBN 9780337986628) issued on 10.02.2012. - 2p.: 30 cm. - 978-0-337-98719-9 £4.00

Environmental protection

The Clean Neighbourhoods and Environment (2011 Act) (Commencement, Savings and Transitional Provisions) Order (Northern Ireland) 2012 No. 2012/13 (C.2). - Enabling power: Clean Neighbourhoods and Environment Act (Northern Ireland) 2011, ss. 75 (1), 78. Bringing into operation various provisions of the 2011 Act on 18.01.2012 & 01.04.2012 in accord. with art. 2. - Issued: 20.01.2012. Made: 18.01.2012. Coming into operation: -. Effect: None. Territorial extent & classification: NI. General. - 8p.: 30 cm. - 978-0-337-98644-4 £4.00

The Environmental Offences (Fixed Penalties) (Miscellaneous Provisions) Regulations (Northern Ireland) 2012 No. 2012/35. - Enabling power: S.I. 1978/1049 (N.I. 19), art. 29A (11) & S.I. 1994/1896 (N.I. 10), art. 18A (1) & Noise Act 1996, s. 8A (5) & Clean Neighbourhoods and Environment Act (Northern Ireland) 2011, ss. 4 (11), 27 (3), 44 (4), 53 (4). - Issued: 14.02.2012. Made: 07.02.2012. Coming into operation: 01.04.2012. Effect: S.R. 1995/17 revoked. Territorial extent & classification: NI. General. - 4p.: 30 cm. - 978-0-337-98664-2 £4.00

The Fluorinated Greenhouse Gases (Amendment) Regulations (Northern Ireland) 2012 No. 2012/230. - Enabling power: European Communities Act 1972, s. 2 (2). - Issued: 08.06.2012. Made: 01.06.2012. Coming into operation: 30.06.2012. Effect: S.R. 2009/184 amended and partially revoked. Territorial extent & classification: NI. General. - 4p.: 30 cm. - 978-0-337-98816-5 £4.00

The Nitrates Action Programme (Amendment) Regulations (Northern Ireland) 2012 No. 2012/231. - Enabling power: European Communities Act 1972, s. 2 (2) & S.I. 1997/2778 (N.I. 19), art. 32. - Issued: 08.06.2012. Made: 01.06.2012. Coming into operation: 22.06.2012. Effect: S.R. 2006/488; 2010/411 amended. Territorial extent & classification: NI. General. - 12p.: 30 cm. - 978-0-337-98817-2 £5.75

The Pollution Prevention and Control (Industrial Emissions) Regulations (Northern Ireland) 2012 No. 2012/453. - Enabling power: S.I. 2002/3153 (N.I. 7), art. 4 (1). - Issued: 24.12.2012. Made: 14.12.2012. Coming into operation: 06.01.2013. Effect: S.R. 1993/170; 1998/28 revoked & S.R. 2003/46, 390; 2004/35, 36, 507; 2005/229, 285, 454; 2006/98; 2007/245; 2009/403; 2010/165; 2011/2, 212, 402 revoked from 07.01.2014 & S.R. 2003/210 revoked from 01.01.2016. Territorial extent & classification: NI. General. - EC note: Regulations transpose Directive 2010/75/EU on industrial emissions. - 112p.: 30 cm. - 978-0-337-98999-5 £16.00

The Producer Responsibility Obligations (Packaging Waste) (Amendment) Regulations (Northern Ireland) 2012 No. 2012/437. - Enabling power: S.I. 1998/1762 (N.I. 16), arts 3 (1), 4 (1) (b) (c) (d). - Issued: 11.12.2012. Made: 06.12.2012. Coming into operation: 01.01.2013. Effect: S.R. 2007/198 amended. Territorial extent & classification: NI. General. - 4p.: 30 cm. - 978-0-337-98979-7 £4.00

The Quality of Bathing Water (Amendment) Regulations (Northern Ireland) 2012 No. 2012/218. - Enabling power: European Communities Act 1972, s. 2 (2). - Issued: 01.06.2012. Made: 25.05.2012. Coming into operation: 01.06.2012. Effect: S.R. 2008/231 amended. Territorial extent & classification: NI. General. - 4p.: 30 cm. - 978-0-337-98810-3 £4.00

The Removal and Disposal of Vehicles (Prescribed Periods) Regulations (Northern Ireland) 2012 No. 2012/52. - Enabling power: S.I. 1978/1049 (N.I. 19), arts 30 (2), 31 (1) (c) (ii) (5). - Issued: 28.02.2012. Made: 20.02.2012. Coming into operation: 01.04.2012. Effect: None. Territorial extent & classification: NI. General. - 2p.: 30 cm. - 978-0-337-98680-2 £4.00

The Statutory Nuisances (Appeals) Regulations (Northern Ireland) 2012 No. 2012/61. - Enabling power: Clean Neighbourhoods and Environment Act (Northern Ireland) 2011, sch. 2, para 1 (4). - Issued: 01.03.2012. Made: 22.02.2012. Coming into operation: 01.04.2012. Effect: None. Territorial extent & classification: NI. General. - 4p.: 30 cm. - 978-0-337-98683-3 £4.00

The Statutory Nuisances (Artificial Lighting) (Designation of Relevant Sports) Order (Northern Ireland) 2012 No. 2012/37. - Enabling power: Clean Neighbourhoods and Environment Act (Northern Ireland) 2011, s. 65 (15). - Issued: 14.02.2012. Made: 07.02.2012. Coming into operation: 01.04.2012. Effect: None. Territorial extent & classification: NI. General. - 4p.: 30 cm. - 978-0-337-98666-6 £4.00

The Statutory Nuisances (Insects) Regulations (Northern Ireland) 2012 No. 2012/36. - Enabling power: Clean Neighbourhoods and Environment Act (Northern Ireland) 2011, s. 63 (11) (d). - Issued: 14.02.2012. Made: 07.02.2012. Coming into operation: 01.04.2012. Effect: None. Territorial extent & classification: NI. General. - 2p.: 30 cm. - 978-0-337-98665-9 £4.00

Street Litter Control Notices (Amendment) Order (Northern Ireland) 2012 No. 2012/38. - Enabling power: S.I. 1994/1896 (N.I. 10), art. 2. - Issued: 14.02.2012. Made: 07.02.2012. Coming into operation: 01.04.2012. Effect: S.R. 1995/42 amended. Territorial extent & classification: NI. General. - 2p.: 30 cm. - 978-0-337-98667-3 £4.00

The Waste (Fees and Charges) (Amendment) Regulations (Northern Ireland) 2012 No. 2012/112. - Enabling power: European Communities Act 1972, s. 2 (2) & S.I. 1997/2778 (N.I.19), art. 39 (2) (3). - Issued: 16.03.2012. Made: 12.03.2012. Coming into operation: 09.04.2012. Effect: S.R. 1999/362; 2003/493 amended. Territorial extent & classification: NI. General. - 4p.: 30 cm. - 978-0-337-98725-0 £4.00

The Water Framework Directive (Priority Substances and Classification) (Amendment) Regulations (Northern Ireland) 2012 No. 2012/442. - Enabling power: European Communities Act 1972, s. 2 (2) & S.I. 1999/662 (NI.6), art. 5. - Issued: 11.12.2012. Made: 07.12.2012. Coming into operation: 31.12.2012. Effect: S.R. 2011/10 amended. Territorial extent & classification: NI. General. - 2p.: 30 cm. - 978-0-337-98984-1 £4.00

European Communities: Animals

Cattle Identification (Miscellaneous Amendments) Regulations (Northern Ireland) 2012 No. 2012/416. - Enabling power: European Communities Act 1972, s. 2 (2). - Issued: 23.11.2012. Made: 21.11.2012. Coming into operation: 01.01.2013. Effect: S.R. 1998/279; 1999/265, 324 amended. - 4p.: 30 cm. - 978-0-337-98960-5 £4.00

European Communities: Nature conservation

The Conservation (Natural Habitats, etc.) (Amendment) Regulations (Northern Ireland) 2012 No. 2012/368. - Enabling power: European Communities Act 1972, s. 2 (2). - Issued: 01.10.2012. Made: 26.09.2012. Coming into operation: 29.10.2012. Effect: S.R. 1995/380 amended. Territorial extent & classification: NI. General. - EC note: These Regulations amend the Conservation (Natural Habitats, etc.) Regulations (Northern Ireland) 1995 which make provision for implementing Council Directive 92/43/EEC on the conservation of natural habitats and of wild flora and fauna ("the Habitats Directive")( ) and certain aspects of Directive 2009/147/EC of the European Parliament and of the Council on the conservation of wild birds ("the Wild Birds Directive"). - 8p.: 30 cm. - 978-0-337-98913-1 £5.75

European Communities: Road traffic and vehicles

The Community Drivers' Hours Regulations (Northern Ireland) 2012 No. 2012/248. - Enabling power: European Communities Act 1972, s. 2 (2), sch. 2, para. 1A. - Issued: 28.06.2012. Made: 21.06.2012. Coming into force: 30.07.2012. Effect: None. NI. General. - 4p.: 30 cm. - 978-0-337-98833-2 £4.00

Fair employment

The Fair Employment (Specification of Public Authorities) (Amendment) Order (Northern Ireland) 2012 No. 2012/96. - Enabling power: S.I. 1998/3162 (N.I. 21), arts 50, 51. - Issued: 09.03.2012. Made: 07.03.2012. Coming into operation: 31.03.2012. Effect: S.R. 2004/494 amended & S.R. 2009/405 revoked. Territorial extent & classification: NI. General. - 8p: 30 cm. - 978-0-337-98714-4 £5.75

Family law

The Child Support (Great Britain Reciprocal Arrangements) (Amendment) Regulations (Northern Ireland) 2012 No. 2012/374. - Enabling power: Northern Ireland Act 1998, s. 87 (5) (10). - Issued: 09.10.2012. Made: 05.10.2012. Coming into operation: 29.10.2012. Effect: S.R. 1993/117 amended. Territorial extent & classification: NI. General. - 8p.: 30 cm. - 978-0-337-98918-6 £4.00

Family law: Child support

The Child Maintenance (2008 Act) (Commencement No. 9) Order (Northern Ireland) 2012 No. 2012/423 (C.43). - Enabling power: Child Maintenance Act (Northern Ireland) 2008, s. 41 (1). Bringing into operation various provisions of the 2008 Act on 03.12.2012 in accord. with art. 2. - Issued: 04.12.2012. Made: 30.11.2012. Coming into operation: -. Effect: None. Territorial extent & classification: NI. General. - 4p.: 30 cm. - 978-0-337-98968-1 £4.00

The Child Maintenance (2008 Act) (Commencement No. 10 and Transitional Provisions) Order (Northern Ireland) 2012 No. 2012/440 (C.45). - Enabling power: Child Maintenance Act (Northern Ireland) 2008, s. 41 (1) (2). Bringing into operation various provisions of the 2008 Act on 10.12.2012 in accord. with art. 2. - Issued: 11.12.2012. Made: 06.12.2012. Coming into operation: -. Effect: S.R. 2012/427 modified. Territorial extent & classification: NI. General. - 8p.: 30 cm. - 978-0-337-98982-7 £4.00

The Child Support Maintenance Calculation Regulations (Northern Ireland) 2012 No. 2012/427. - Enabling power: S.I. 1991/2628 (N.I. 23), arts, 3 (1) (b), 4 (3), 8 (3), 14 (4) (5), 16(1) (1A), 18(1) (4) (6), 19 (2) (3) (5), 28ZA (2) (b) (4) (c), 28ZB (6) (c) (8), 28A (5), 28B (2) (c), 28C (2) (b) (5), 28F (2) (b) (3) (b) (5), 28G (2) (3), 39, 47 (1) (2), 48(4), sch. 1, paras 3 (2) a(3), 4 (1) (2), 5, 5A (6) (b), 7 (3), 8 (2), 9, 10 (1) (2), 10C (2) (b), 11, sch. 4A, paras 2, 4, 5, sch. 4B, paras 2 (2) to (5), 4 to 6. - Issued: 06.12.2012. Made: 03.12.2012. Coming into operation: In accord. with reg. 1. Effect: None. Territorial extent & classification: NI. General. - For approval of the Assembly before the expiration of six months from the the date of their coming into operation. - 44p.: 30 cm. - 978-0-337-98971-1 £9.75

The Child Support Maintenance (Changes to Basic Rate Calculation and Minimum Amount of Liability) Regulations (Northern Ireland) 2012 No. 2012/428. - Enabling power: S.I. 1991/2628 (N.I. 23), sch. 1, para. 10A (1). - Issued: 06.12.2012. Made: 03.12.2012. Coming into operation: In accord. with reg. 1. Effect: S.I. 1991/2628 (N.I. 23) modified. Territorial extent & classification: NI. General. - For approval of the Assembly before the expiration of six months from the the date of their coming into operation. - 4p.: 30 cm. - 978-0-337-98972-8 £4.00

The Child Support (Management of Payments and Arrears) (Amendment) Regulations (Northern Ireland) 2012 No. 2012/439. - Enabling power: S.I. 1991/2628 (N.I. 23), arts, 16 (3), 38D (2) (3), 38E, 47 (1), 48 (4). - Issued: 11.12.2012. Made: 06.12.2012. Coming into operation: In accord. with reg. 1. Effect: S.R. 2009/422; 2008/403 amended. Territorial extent & classification: NI. General. - For approval of the Assembly before the expiration of six months from the date of their coming into operation. - 8p.: 30 cm. - 978-0-337-98981-0 £5.75

The Child Support (Meaning of Child and New Calculation Rules) (Consequential and Miscellaneous Amendments) Regulations 2012 No. 2012/438. - Enabling power: S.I. 1991/2628 (N.I. 23), arts 3 (1) (b), 16 (1), 29 (3) (3A), 47 (1) (2), 48 (4) & Child Maintenance Act (Northern Ireland) 2008, ss. 36 (2), 38 (2). - Issued: 11.12.2012. Made: 06.12.2012. Coming into operation: In accord. with art. 1. Effect: S.R. 1992/340, 390, 466; 1999/162; 2001/17, 21; 2008/403 amended & S.R. 1992/390, 466; 1993/164; 1994/37; 1995/19, 162, 475; 1996/65, 288, 289, 317, 590; 1998/8; 1999/152, 162, 246, 385; 2000/215; 2001/15, 16, 21, 23, 29, 176; 2002/164, 323; 2003/84, 91, 191, 224, 274, 469; 2004/428; 2005/46, 125, 536; 2006/273, 407; 2007/196, 347, 382; 2008/286, 403, 404, 409; 2009/133, 286, 363; 2012/163, 438 partially revoked & S.R. 1992/340 (with saving), 341; 1993/191; 1996/541; 1999/167; 2001/17, 18, 20; 2011/226 revoked. Territorial extent & classification: NI. General. - Partially revoked by S.R. 2012/438 (ISBN 9780337989803). - 16p.: 30 cm. - 978-0-337-98980-3 £5.75

The Child Support (Miscellaneous Amendments) Regulations (Northern Ireland) 2012 No. 2012/163. - Enabling power: S.I. 1991/2628 (N.I. 23), arts, 19 (3) (5), 29 (2) (3), 47 (1) (2) (i), 48 (4), sch. 1, para. 10 (1) (2). - Issued: 16.04.2012. Made: 06.04.2012. Coming into operation: 30.04.2012. Effect: S.R. 1992/340, 341, 390; 2001/18; 2009/422 amended & S.R. 2011/226 partially revoked. Territorial extent & classification: NI. General. - Partially revoked by S.R. 2012/438 (ISBN 9780337989803). - 8p.: 30 cm. - 978-0-337-98776-2 £4.00

The Welfare Reform (2010 Act) (Commencement No. 5) Order (Northern Ireland) 2012 No. 2012/424 (C.44). - Enabling power: Welfare Reform Act (Northern Ireland) 2010, s. 36 (2). Bringing into operation various provisions of the 2010 Act on 03.12.2012 in accord. with art. 2. - Issued: 05.12.2012. Made: 30.11.2012. Coming into operation: -. Effect: None. Territorial extent & classification: NI. General. - 2p.: 30 cm. - 978-0-337-98969-8 £4.00

Fees and charges

The Medicines (Products for Human Use) (Fees) Regulations 2012 No. 2012/134. - Enabling power: Medicines Act 1968, s. 1 (1) (2) & European Communities Act 1972, s. 2 (2) & Finance Act 1973, s. 56 (1) (2). - Issued: 26.03.2012. Made: 23.02.2012. Laid: 29.02.2012. Coming into operation: 01.04.2012. Effect: S.I. 2004/1031 amended & S.I. 1994/899; 2010/551 revoked with saving. - 78p.: 30 cm. - 978-0-337-98747-2 £13.75

Financial assistance

The Fuel Allowance Payments Scheme Regulations (Northern Ireland) 2012 No. 2012/159. - Enabling power: Financial Assistance Act (Northern Ireland) 2009, ss. 1 (2), 3. - Issued: 08.03.2013. Made: 20.03.2012. Coming into operation: 20.03.2012. Effect: None. Territorial extent & classification: NI. General. - 8p.: 30 cm. - 978-0-337-99045-8 £4.00

The Fuel Payments Scheme (Patients Receiving Treatment for Cancer) Regulations (Northern Ireland) 2012 No. 2012/141. - Enabling power: Financial Assistance Act (Northern Ireland) 2009, ss. 1 (2), 3. - Issued: 29.03.2012. Made: 20.03.2012. Coming into operation: 16.04.2012. Effect: None. Territorial extent & classification: NI. General. - 8p.: 30 cm. - 978-0-337-98755-7 £4.00

Fire and rescue services: Pensions

The Firefighters' Pension Scheme (Amendment) Order (Northern Ireland) 2012 No. 2012/161. - Enabling power: S.I. 1984/1821 (N.I.11), arts 10 (1) (3) (4) (5). - Issued: 11.04.2012. Made: 04.04.2012. Coming into operation: 01.04.2012. Effect: S.R. 2007/144 amended. Territorial extent & classification: NI. General. - 4p.: 30 cm. - 978-0-337-98774-8 £4.00

The Firefighters Pension Scheme (Contributions) (Amendment) Order (Northern Ireland) 2012 No. 2012/71. - Enabling power: S.I. 1984/1821 (N.I. 11), art. 10 (1) (3) (4) (5). - Issued: 02.03.2012. Made: 27.02.2012. Coming into operation: 01.04.2012. Effect: S.R. 2007/144 amended. Territorial extent & classification: NI. General. - Revoked by S.R. 2012/151 (ISBN 9780337987649). - 4p.: 30 cm. - 978-0-337-98690-1 £4.00

The Firefighters Pension Scheme (Contributions) (Revocation) Order (Northern Ireland) 2012 No. 2012/151. - Enabling power: S.I. 1984/1821 (N.I. 11), art. 10 (1) (3) (4) (5). - Issued: 02.04.2012. Made: 29.03.2012. Coming into operation: 31.03.2012. Effect: S.R. 2012/71 revoked. Territorial extent & classification: NI. General. - 2p.: 30 cm. - 978-0-337-98764-9 £4.00

The New Firefighters' Pension Scheme (Amendment) Order (Northern Ireland) 2012 No. 2012/162. - Enabling power: S.I. 1984/1821 (N.I. 11), art. 10 (1) (3) (4) (5). - Issued: 11.04.2012. Made: 04.04.2012. Coming into operation: 01.04.2012. Effect: S.R. 2007/215 amended. Territorial extent & classification: NI. General. - 4p.: 30 cm. - 978-0-337-98775-5 £4.00

The New Firefighters' Pension Scheme (Contributions) (Amendment) Order (Northern Ireland) 2012 No. 2012/72. - Enabling power: S.I. 1984/1821 (N.I. 11), art. 10 (1) (3) (4) (5). - Issued: 02.03.2012. Made: 27.02.2012. Coming into operation: 01.04.2012. Effect: S.R. 2007/215 amended. Territorial extent & classification: NI. General. - Revoked by S.R. 2012/152 (ISBN 9780337987656). - 4p.: 30 cm. - 978-0-337-98691-8 £4.00

The New Firefighters' Pension Scheme (Contributions) (Revocation) Order (Northern Ireland) 2012 No. 2012/152. - Enabling power: S.I. 1984/1821 (N.I. 11), art. 10 (1) (3) (4) (5). - Issued: 02.04.2012. Made: 29.03.2012. Coming into operation: 31.03.2012. Effect: S.R. 2012/72 revoked. Territorial extent & classification: NI. General. - 2p.: 30 cm. - 978-0-337-98765-6 £4.00

Firearms and ammunition

The Firearms (Northern Ireland) Order 2004 (Amendment) Regulations 2012 No. 2012/395. - Enabling power: European Communities Act 1972, s. 2 (2). - Issued: 06.11.2012. Made: 30.10.2012. Coming into operation: 29.11.2012. Effect: S.I. 2004/704 (NI. 3) amended. Territorial extent & classification: NI. General. - 2p.: 30 cm. - 978-0-337-98943-8 £4.00

Fisheries

Fisheries (Amendment) Regulations (Northern Ireland) 2012 No. 2012/397. - Enabling power: Fisheries Act (Northern Ireland) 1996, s. 26 (1). - Issued: 02.11.2012. Made: 29.10.2012. Coming into operation: 01.12.2012. Effect: S.R. 2003/525 amended. Territorial extent & classification: NI. General. - 4p.: 30 cm. - 978-0-337-98945-2 £4.00

The Foyle and Carlingford Fisheries (2007 Order) (Commencement No. 2) Order (Northern Ireland) 2012 No. 2012/336 (C.31). - Enabling power: S.I. 2007/915 (N.I. 9), art. 1 (3). Bringing into operation various provisions of the 2007 Order on 17.09.2012. - Issued: 17.09.2012. Made: 07.09.2012. Coming into operation: -. Effect: None. Territorial extent & classification: NI. General. - 2p.: 30 cm. - 978-0-337-98906-3 £4.00

The Foyle Area and Carlingford Area (Angling) (Amendment) Regulations 2012 No. 2012/458. - Enabling power: Foyle Fisheries Act 1952, s. 13 (1) & Foyle Fisheries Act (Northern Ireland) 1952, s. 13 (1). - Issued: 21.12.2012. Made: 12.12.2012. Coming into operation: 31.01.2013. Effect: S.R. 2001/158 amended. Territorial extent & classification: NI. General. - 8p.: 30 cm. - 978-0-337-99003-8 £5.75

The Foyle Area (Control of Fishing) (Amendment) Regulations 2012 No. 2012/459. - Enabling power: Foyle Fisheries Act 1952, s. 13 (1) & Foyle Fisheries Act (Northern Ireland) 1952, s. 13 (1). - Issued: 21.12.2012. Made: 12.12.2012. Coming into operation: 31.01.2013. Effect: S.R. 2010/199 amended. Territorial extent & classification: NI. General. - 4p.: 30 cm. - 978-0-337-99004-5 £4.00

The Foyle Area (Greenbraes Fishery Angling Permits) Regulations 2012 No. 2012/95. - Enabling power: Foyle Fisheries Act 1952, s. 13 (1) (k), 14B (1) (b) & Foyle Fisheries Act (Northern Ireland) 1952, s. 13 (1) (k), 14B (1) (b). - Issued: 09.03.2012. Made: 01.03.2012. Coming into operation: 26.03.2012. Effect: None. Territorial extent & classification: NI. General. - 4p.: 30 cm. - 978-0-337-98713-7 £4.00

Food

The Food Additives (Amendment) and the Extraction Solvents in Food (Amendment) Regulations (Northern Ireland) 2012 No. 2012/180. - Enabling power: S.I. 1991/762 (N.I. 7), arts 15 (1) (a) (c) (f), 16 (1) (2), 47 (2). - Issued: 30.04.2012. Made: 24.04.2012. Coming into operation: 23.05.2012. Effect: S.R. 1993/330; 2009/416 amended. Territorial extent & classification: NI. General. - EC note: These Regulations make certain amendments to the 2009 Regulations (S.R. 2009/416) in order to provide for the execution and enforcement of Commission Regulation 1129/2011 (amending Annex II to Regulation 1333/2008); Commission Regulation 1130/2011 (amending Annex III to Regulation 1333/2008); Commission Regulation 1131/2011 (amending Annex II to Regulation 1333/2008); Commission Regulation 231/2012 laying down specifications for food additives listed in Annexes II and III to Regulation 1333/2008. These Regulations also amended S.R. 1993/330 in order to rectify an omission from the Extraction Solvents in Food (Amendment) Regulation (Northern Ireland) 2011 (S.R. 2011/284). - 4p.: 30 cm. - 978-0-337-98789-2 £4.00

The Food Hygiene (Amendment) (No. 2) Regulations (Northern Ireland) 2012 No. 2012/280. - Enabling power: European Communities Act 1972, s. 2 (2), sch. 2, para. 1A. - Issued: 11.07.2012. Made: 06.07.2012. Coming into operation: 30.07.2012. Effect: S.R. 2006/3 amended. Territorial extent & classification: NI. General. - EC note: These Regulations amend the 2006 Regulations by updating the definitions of certain EU instruments that are referred to in those Regulations. - 8p: 30 cm. - 978-0-337-98857-8 £5.75

The Food Hygiene (Amendment) Regulations (Northern Ireland) 2012 No. 2012/130. - Enabling power: European Communities Act 1972, s. 2 (2). - Issued: 22.03.2012. Made: 16.03.2012. Coming into operation: 10.04.2012. Effect: S.R. 2006/3 amended. Territorial extent & classification: NI. General. - 4p: 30 cm. - 978-0-337-98743-4 £4.00

The Materials and Articles in Contact with Food Regulations (Northern Ireland) 2012 No. 2012/384. - Enabling power: S.I. 1991/762 (N.I.7), arts 15 (2), 16 (1) (2), 25 (1) (a), 2 (a) (3), 32, 47 (2). - Issued: 25.10.2012. Made: 22.10.2012. Coming into operation: 20.11.2012. Effect: S.R. 1991/198; 1996/383 amended & S.R. 2006/217; 2009/56; 2010/321; 2011/28 revoked. Territorial extent & classification: NI. General. - EC note: These Regulations provide for the implementation of the following Directives and the enforcement of the following EU Regulations - Council Directives 78/142/EEC; 84/500/EEC; Commission Directive 2007/42/EC; Regulation 1935/2004 and Commission Regulations 1895/2005; 2023/2006; 450/2009; 10/2011. - 20p.: 30 cm. - 978-0-337-98929-2 £5.75

The Specified Products from China (Restriction on First Placing on the Market) (Amendment) Regulations (Northern Ireland) 2012 No. 2012/3. - Enabling power: European Communities Act 1972, s. 2 (2). - Issued: 13.01.2012. Made: 10.01.2012. Coming into operation: 12.01.2012. Effect: S.R. 2008/171 amended. Territorial extent & classification: NI. General. - EC note: These Regulations amend SR 2008/171 in order to implement Commission Implementing Decision 2008/884/EU on emergency measures regarding the unauthorised genetically modified rice in rice products originating from China and repealing Decision 2008/289/EC. The Decision provides for import restrictions that previously applied to Bt 63 genetically modified rice to apply, with modifications, to all unauthorised GM rice. - 4p.: 30 cm. - 978-0-337-98635-2 £4.00

Gas

Gas (Meter Testing and Stamping) Regulations (Northern Ireland) 2012 No. 2012/454. - Enabling power: S.I. 1996/275 (NI 2), art. 22 (13). - Issued: 18.12.2012. Made: 14.12.2012. Coming into operation: 17.01.2013. Effect: None. Territorial extent & classification: NI. General. - With correction slip dated December 2012. - 2p.: 30 cm. - 978-0-337-98997-1 £4.00

Government resources and accounts

The Whole of Government Accounts (Designation of Bodies) Order (Northern Ireland) 2012 No. 2012/173. - Enabling power: Government Resources and Accounts Act (Northern Ireland) 2001, s. 15 (1). - Issued: 26.04.2012. Made: 23.04.2012. Coming into operation: 21.05.2012. Effect: None. Territorial extent & classification: NI. General. - 8p.: 30 cm. - 978-0-337-98783-0 £5.75

Health and personal social services

The Health and Personal Social Services (Superannuation), Health and Social Care (Pension Scheme) (Amendment) Regulations (Northern Ireland) 2012 No. 2012/78. - Enabling power: S.I. 1972/1073 (N.I. 10), arts 12 (1) (2), 14 (1) (2) (3), sch. 3. - Issued: 08.03.2012. Made: 29.02.2012. Coming into operation: 01.04.2012. Effect: S.R. 1995/95; 2008/256 amended. Territorial extent & classification: NI. General. - 12p.: 30 cm. - 978-0-337-98696-3 £5.75

The Health and Personal Social Services (Superannuation Scheme, Injury Benefits and Additional Voluntary Contributions), Health and Social Care (Pension Scheme) (Amendment) Regulations (Northern Ireland) 2012 No. 2012/42. - Enabling power: S.I. 1972/1073 (N.I. 10), arts 12 (1) (2), 14 (1) (2) (3), sch. 3. - Issued: 23.02.2012. Made: 10.02.2012. Coming into operation: 14.03.2012. Effect: S.R. 1995/95; 1999/294; 2001/367; 2008/256 amended. Territorial extent & classification: NI. General. - 16p.: 30 cm. - 978-0-337-98671-0 £5.75

The Health Care (Reimbursement of the Cost of EEA Services etc.) Regulations (Northern Ireland) 2012 No. 2012/167. - Enabling power: European Communities Act 1972, s. 2 (2). - Issued: 20.04.2012. Made: 18.04.2012. Coming into operation: 10.05.2012. Effect: 2009 c. 1 (N.I.); S.I. 1972/1265 (N.I. 14) amended. Territorial extent & application: NI. General. - EC note: These Regulations give effect to the judgement of the European Court of Justice in Case C-372/04 The Queen, on the application of Yvonne Watts v Bedford Primary Care Trust and Secretary of State for Health ([2006]ECR I-4325). It held that the obligation under Article 49 of the EC Treaty to reimburse the cost of hospital treatment provided in another member State also applies to a tax-funded health service, such as in Northern Ireland, which provides such treatment free of charge. - 8p.: 30 cm. - 978-0-337-98777-9 £5.75

Optical Charges and Payments (Amendment) Regulations (Northern Ireland) 2010 No. 2012/259. - Enabling power: S.I 1972/1265 (N.I. 14), arts 62, 98, 106, 107 (6), sch. 15. - Issued: 02.07.2012. Made: 28.06.2012. Coming into operation: 01.08.2012. Effect: S.R. 1997/191 amended. Territorial extent & classification: NI. General. - 8p.: 30 cm. - 978-0-337-98842-4 £4.00

The Travelling Expenses and Remission of Charges (Amendment No. 2) Regulations (Northern Ireland) 2012 No. 2012/378. - Enabling power: S.I. 1972/1265 (N.I. 14), arts 45, 98, 106, 107 (6), sch. 15, paras 1 (b), 1B. - Issued: 18.10.2012. Made: 16.10.2012. Coming into operation: 07.11.2012. Effect: S.R. 2004/91 amended. Territorial extent & classification: NI. General. - 4p.: 30 cm. - 978-0-337-98924-7 £4.00

The Travelling Expenses and Remission of Charges (Amendment) Regulations (Northern Ireland) 2012 No. 2012/73. - Enabling power: S.I. 1972/1265 (N.I. 14), arts 45, 98, 106, 107 (6), sch. 15, paras 1 (b), 1B. - Issued: 07.03.2012. Made: 28.02.2012. Coming into operation: 28.03.2012. Effect: S.R. 2004/91 amended. Territorial extent & classification: NI. General. - 4p.: 30 cm. - 978-0-337-98692-5 £4.00

Health and safety

The Carriage of Explosives (Amendment) Regulations (Northern Ireland) 2012 No. 2012/177. - Enabling power: S.I. 1978/1039 (N.I. 9), arts. 17 (1) to (6), 20 (2), 54, 55 (2), sch. 3, paras. 1 (1) (4), 2, 3 (1), 5, 14. - Issued: 03.05.2012. Made: 25.04.2012. Coming into operation: 28.05.2012. Effect: S.R. 1993/488; 1995/87; 1996/262; 2002/147; 2003/152; 2010/1554 amended & S.R. 2010/59 amended & partially revoked & S.R. 1991/516 revoked. - EC note: These Regulations make fairly minor amendments to The Carriage of Explosives Regulations (Northern Ireland) 2010 as a result of Directive 2010/35/EU on transportable pressure equipment and repealing Council Directives 76/767/EEC, 84/525/EEC, 84/526/EEC, 84/527/EEC and 1999/36/EC. - 8p.: 30 cm. - 978-0-337-98786-1 £5.75

The Control of Asbestos Regulations (Northern Ireland) 2012 No. 2012/179. - Enabling power: European Communities Act 1972, s. 2 (2) & S.I. 1978/1039 (N.I. 9), arts. 17 (1) to (6), 20 (2), 54 (1), 55 (2), sch. 3. paras 1 (1) to (4), 2 (2), 3, 5, 7 to 10, 12 (1) (3), 13, 14 (1), 15, 19. - Issued: 30.04.2012. Made: 25.04.2012. Coming into operation: 28.05.2012. Effect: S.R. 1993/20; 1999/90, 305; 2003/34; 2007/291; 2010/60 amended & S.R. 2007/31; 2010/187 revoked. Territorial extent & classification: NI. General. - EC note: These Regulations revoke and replace the Control of Asbestos Regulations (S.R. 2007/31) and the Control of Asbestos (Amendment) Regulations 2010 (S.R. 2010/187). These Regs implement as respects Northern Ireland Council Directive 2009/148/EC (repealed and replaced Council Directive 83/477/EEC as amended by Council Directive 91/382/EEC and Directive 2003/18/EC. Also Council Directive90/394/EEC insofar as it relates to asbestos and also Council Directive 98/24/EC insofar as it relates to risks to health from exposure to asbestos. With correction slip dated April 2012. - 32p.: 30 cm. - 978-0-337-98788-5 £9.75

The Health and Safety (Fees) Regulations (Northern Ireland) 2012 No. 2012/255. - Enabling power: European Communities Act 1972, s. 2 (2) & S.I. 1978/1039 (N.I. 9), arts. 40 (2) (4), 49, 55 (2). - Issued: 02.07.2012. Made: 27.06.2012. Coming into operation: 30.07.2012. Effect: S.R. 2010/60 revoked with savings. Territorial extent & classification: NI. General. - 24p: 30 cm. - 978-0-337-98838-7 £5.75

The Health and Safety (Miscellaneous Revocations) Regulations (Northern Ireland) 2012 No. 2012/450. - Enabling power: SI 1978/1039 (NI 9), arts 17 (1) (3), 45 (1) (2), 55 (2). - Issued: 18.12.2012. Made: 13.12.2012. Coming into operation: 14.01.2013. Effect: S.R. & O. 1913/2 & S.R. 1979/187; 1982/185; 1964/46 revoked. Territorial extent & classification: NI. General. - 2p.: 30 cm. - 978-0-337-98993-3 £4.00

The Identification and Traceability of Explosives (Amendment) (Northern Ireland) Regulations 2012 No. 2012/123. - Enabling power: S.I. 1978/1039 (N.I. 9), arts. 17 (1) (2) (3) (c), 4 (b) (5), 55 (2), sch. 3, paras. 1 (1) (4), 2, 5 (1), 14 (1), 15. - Issued: 21.03.2012. Made: 14.03.2012. Laid: 15.03.2012. Coming into operation: 05.04.2012. Effect: S.R. 2010/143 amended. Territorial extent & classification: NI. General. - EC note: These Regulations amend the 2010 Regulations which implement, as regards Northern Ireland, Commission Directive 2008/43/EC setting up, pursuant to Council Directive 93/15/EC, a system for the identification and traceability of explosives for civil uses. - 4p.: 30 cm. - 978-0-337-98738-0 £4.00

The Petroleum (Consolidation) Act (Amendment of Licensing Provisions) Regulations (Northern Ireland) 2012 No. 2012/11. - Enabling power: S.I. 1978/1039 (N.I. 9), arts 17 (1) (2) (3), 40, 54 (1), 55 (2), sch. 3, paras 1 (1), 2 (2), 3. - Issued: 19.01.2012. Made: 17.01.2012. Coming into operation: 19.03.2012. Effect: 1929 c. 13 amended. Territorial extent & classification: NI. General. - 4p.: 30 cm. - 978-0-337-98641-3 £4.00

Health and social care

The Children's Homes (Amendment) Regulations (Northern Ireland) 2012 No. 2012/182. - Enabling power: S.I. 2003/431 (N.I. 9), art. 23 (2) (c) (d) (f) (7) (a) (c) (d) (j). - Issued: 09.05.2012. Made: 03.05.2012. Coming into operation: 01.06.2012. Effect: S.R. 2005/176 amended. Territorial extent & classification: NI. General. - 4p.: 30 cm. - 978-0-337-98792-2 £4.00

The Foster Placement (Children) (Amendment) Regulations (Northern Ireland) 2012 No. 2012/229. - Enabling power: S.R. 1995/755 (N.I. 2), art. 27 (2) (a), 28 (1), 75 (2), 77 (3), 183. - Issued: 13.06.2012. Made: 31.05.2012. Coming into operation: 01.07.2012. Effect: S.R. 1996/467 amended. Territorial extent & classification: NI. General. - 2p.: 30 cm. - 978-0-337-98815-8 £4.00

The Health (2006 Act) (Commencement) Order (Northern Ireland) 2012 No. 2012/307 (C.27). - Enabling power: Health Act 2006, s. 83 (6). Bringing into operation in relation to Northern Ireland various provisions of this Act on 01.08.2012, in accord. with art. 2. - Issued: 06.08.2012. Made: 01.08.2012. Coming into operation: -. Effect: None. Territorial extent & classification: NI. General. - 2p.: 30 cm. - 978-0-337-98872-1 £4.00

The Safeguarding Board (2011 Act) (Commencement No. 1) Order (Northern Ireland) 2012 No. 2012/338 (C.32). - Enabling power: Safeguarding Board Act (Northern Ireland) 2011, s. 17 (2). Bringing into operation various provisions of the 2011 Act on 14.09.2012. - Issued: 18.09.2012. Made: 14.09.2012. Laid before Parliament: -. Coming into operation: -. Effect: None. Territorial extent & classification: NI. General. - 2p.: 30 cm. - 978-0-337-98908-7 £4.00

The Safeguarding Board for Northern Ireland (Membership, Procedure, Functions and Committee) Regulations (Northern Ireland) 2012 No. 2012/324. - Enabling power: Safeguarding Board Act (Northern Ireland) 2011, ss. 1 (2) (b) (3) (j) (5), 3 (4), 5 (1), 6 (1), 7 (1) (a), 7 (4) (5), 8 (1), 9, 12 (1) (j). - Issued: 24.08.2012. Made: 20.08.2012. Laid before Parliament: -. Coming into operation: 17.09.2012. Effect: None. Territorial extent & classification: NI. General. - 28p.: 30 cm. - 978-0-337-98893-6 £5.75

Health services charges

The Recovery of Health Services Charges (Amounts) (Amendment) Regulations (Northern Ireland) 2012 No. 2012/111. - Enabling power: S.I. 2006/1944 (N.I. 13), arts 5 (2) (5), 19 (3). - Issued: 23.03.2012. Made: 09.03.2012. Coming into operation: 01.04.2012. Effect: S.R. 2006/507 amended. - 4p: 30 cm. - 978-0-337-98748-9 £4.00

Horticulture

The Marketing of Fresh Horticulture Produce (Amendment) Regulations (Northern Ireland) 2012 No. 2012/299. - Enabling power: European Communities Act 1972, s. 2 (2). - Issued: 25.07.2012. Made: 20.07.2012. Coming into operation: 27.08.2012. Effect: S.R. 2010/198 amended. Territorial extent & classification: NI. General. - EC note: These Regulations implement Commission Implementing Regulation (EU) No 543/2011 laying down detailed rules for the application of Council Regulation (EC) No 1234/2007 in respect of the fruit and vegetables and processed fruit and vegetables sector. The EU Regulation consolidated with amendments Commission Regulation (EC) No 1580/2007 laying down implementing rules of Council Regulations (EC) No 2200/96, (EC) No 2201/96 and (EC) No 1182/2007 in the fruit and vegetable sector- 8p.: 30 cm. - 978-0-337-98865-3 £5.75

Housing

Allocation of Housing and Homelessness (Eligibility) (Amendment) Regulations (Northern Ireland) 2012 No. 2012/429. - Enabling power: S.I. 1981/156 (NI. 3), art. 22A (3) & S.I. 1988/1990 (NI. 23), art. 7A (2). - Issued: 10.12.2012. Made: 02.12.2012. Coming into operation: 14.01.2013. Effect: S.R. 2006/397 amended. Territorial extent & classification: NI. General. - 4p.: 30 cm. - 978-0-337-98974-2 £4.00

The Housing Benefit (Executive Determinations) (Amendment) Regulations (Northern Ireland) 2012 No. 2012/157. - Enabling power: Social Security Contributions and Benefits (Northern Ireland) Act 1992, ss. 122 (1) (d), 129A (2), 171 (1) (3) to (5). - Issued: 04.04.2012. Made: 30.03.2012. Coming into operation: 02.04.2012. Effect: S.R. 2008/100 amended. Territorial extent & classification: NI. General. - 4p.: 30 cm. - 978-0-337-98770-0 £4.00

The Jobseeker's Allowance (Sanctions for Failure to Attend) Regulations (Northern Ireland) 2012 No. 2012/44. - Enabling power: Social Security Contributions and Benefits (Northern Ireland) Act 1992, ss. 22 (5), 122 (1) (d), 171 (1) (3); S.I. 1995/2705 (N.I. 15), arts 10, 36 (2), sch. 1, para. 15; S.I. 1998/1506 (N.I. 10), arts 10 (1), 11 (3) (6), 74 (1). - Issued: 16.02.2012. Made: 13.02.2012. Coming into operation: 06.03.2012. Effect: S.R. 1996/198; 1975/113; 1999/162; 2001/216; 2006/405 amended & S.R. 1999/145; 2000/350 partially revoked. Territorial extent & classification: NI. General. - 8p.: 30 cm. - 978-0-337-98672-7 £5.75

The Social Security Benefits Up-rating Order (Northern Ireland) 2012 No. 2012/116. - Enabling power: Social Security Administration (Northern Ireland) Act 1992, ss. 132, 132A,165 (1) (4) (5). - Issued: 20.03.2012. Made: 14.03.2012. Coming into operation: In accord. with 1. Effect: 1966 c. 6 (N.I.); 1992 c. 7; 1993 c. 49; S.R. 1987/30, 459; 1992/32; 1994/461; 1995/35; 1996/198; 2002/380; 2003/28; 2006/405, 406; 2008/280; 2010/302, 407 amended & 2011/119 revoked (12.04.2012). Territorial extent & classification: NI. General. - For approval of the Assembly before the expiration of six months from the date of its coming into operation. Superseded by approved version (ISBN 9780337988264) issued on 15.06.2012. - 42p.: 30 cm. - 978-0-337-98731-1 £9.75

The Social Security Benefits Up-rating Order (Northern Ireland) 2012 No. 2012/116. - Enabling power: Social Security Administration (Northern Ireland) Act 1992, ss. 132, 132A, 165 (1) (4) (5). - Issued: 15.06.2012. Made: 14.03.2012. Coming into operation: In accord. with art. 1. Effect: 1966 c. 6 (N.I.); 1992 c. 7; 1993 c. 49; S.R. 1987/30, 459, 460; 1992/32; 1994/461; 1995/35; 1996/198; 2002/380; 2003/28; 2006/405, 406; 2008/280; 2010/302, 407 amended & 2011/119 revoked (12.04.2012). Territorial extent & classification: NI. General. - Approved by resolution of the Assembly on 11th June 2012. Supersedes pre-approved version (ISBN 9780337987311). - 44p.: 30 cm. - 978-0-337-98826-4 £9.75

The Social Security (Habitual Residence) (Amendment) Regulations (Northern Ireland) 2012 No. 2012/380. - Enabling power: Social Security Contributions and Benefits (Northern Ireland) Act 1992, ss. 122 (1) (a) (d), 131 (1) (2), 171 (1) (3) (4) & S.I. 1995/2705 (N.I. 15), arts 6 (5) (12), 36 (2) & State Pension Credit Act (Northern Ireland) 2002, ss. 1 (5) (a), 19 (1) (2) (a) (3) & Welfare Reform Act (Northern Ireland) 2007, ss. 4 (3), 25 (2). - Issued: 22.10.2012. Made: 17.10.2012. Coming into operation: 08.11.2012. Effect: S.R. 1987/459; 1996/198; 2003/28; 2006/405, 406; 2008/280 amended. Territorial extent & classification: NI. General. - 8p.: 30 cm. - 978-0-337-98926-1 £4.00

The Social Security (Miscellaneous Amendments) Regulations (Northern Ireland) 2012 No. 2012/121. - Enabling power: Social Security Contributions and Benefits (Northern Ireland) Act 1992, ss. 122 (1) (a) (d), 123 (1) (d) (e), 132 (3) (4) (b), 132A (3), 133 (2) (i), 134 (2), 171 (1) (3) (4) & Social Security Administration (Northern Ireland) Act 1992, ss. 5 (1) (j) (n), 69 (4), 165 (1) (4) (5) & S.I. 1995/2705 (N.I.15), arts 14 (4) (b), 36 (1) (2) & S.I. 1998/1506 (N.I.10), arts 11 (6), 74 (1) (3) (4) & Child Support, Pensions and Social Security Act (Northern Ireland) 2000, s. 59, sch. 7 paras 4 (3), 20 (1) & State Pension Credit Act (Northern Ireland) 2002, ss. 15 (1) (e) (3), 19 (1) to (3) & Welfare Reform Act (Northern Ireland) 2007, ss. 1 (2), 25 (1) (2), 28 (2), 29, sch. 1, paras 1 (4) (a), 6 (5). sch. 4, paras 1 (1), 7 (1) (a). - Issued: 20.03.2012. Made: 14.03.2012. Coming into operation: In accord. with reg. 1. Effect: S.R. 1982/263; 1987/459, 465; 1988/142; 1996/198; 1999/162; 2000/91; 2001/213; 2003/28; 2006/405, 406; 2008/280; 2010/312 amended & S.R. 1987/465; 2003/421; 2006/168; 2008/280; 2009/92, 338; 2010/69; 2011/357 partially revoked (01.04.2012). Territorial extent & classification: NI. General. - 12p.: 30 cm. - 978-0-337-98736-6 £5.75

The Social Security (Recovery) (Amendment) Regulations (Northern Ireland) 2012 No. 2012/108. - Enabling power: Social Security Administration (Northern Ireland) Act 1992, ss. 69 (6) (a) (8), 73 (1) (4) (5), 165 (1) (4). - Issued: 13.03.2012. Made: 09.03.2012. Coming into operation: 01.04.2012. Effect: S.R. 1988/142 amended. Territorial extent & classification: NI. General. - 4p.: 30 cm. - 978-0-337-98722-9 £4.00

The Social Security (Suspension of Payment of Benefits and Miscellaneous Amendments) Regulations (Northern Ireland) 2012 No. 2012/140. - Enabling power: Social Security Administration (Northern Ireland) Act 1992, ss. 5 (1) (hh) (j) (2A), 165 (1) (4) to (6) & S.I. 1998/1506 (N.I. 10), arts 10 (1) (a), 22, 74 (1) (3) (5) (6). - Issued: 29.03.2012. Made: 26.03.2012. Coming into operation: 17.04.2012. Effect: S.R. 1987/465; 1996/198; 1999/162; 2006/405, 406 amended & S.R. 2000/350; 2003/421; 2008/262 partially revoked. Territorial extent & classification: NI. General. - 4p.: 30 cm. - 978-0-337-98754-0 £4.00

Industrial training

The Industrial Training Levy (Construction Industry) Order (Northern Ireland) 2012 No. 2012/245. - Enabling power: S.I. 1984/1159 (N.I. 9), arts 23 (2) (3), 24 (3) (4). - Issued: 03.07.2012. Made: 18.06.2012. Coming into operation: 31.08.2012. Effect: None. Territorial extent & classification: NI. General. - 8p.: 30 cm. - 978-0-337-98830-1 £5.75

Judgments

The International Recovery of Maintenance (Hague Convention 2007 etc.) Regulations (Northern Ireland) 2012 No. 2012/413. - Enabling power: European Communities Act 1972, s. 2 (2). - Issued: 04.12.2012. Made: 16.11.2012. Coming into operation: In accord. with reg. 1. Effect: 1966 c.35; 1992 c.8 & SI 1981/1675 (NI. 26); 1995/755 (NI 2) amended. Territorial extent & classification: NI. General. - 16p.: 30 cm. - 978-0-337-98959-9 £5.75

Juries

The Juries (Amendment) Regulations (Northern Ireland) 2012 No. 2012/407. - Enabling power: S.I. 1996/141 (N.I. 6), art. 30 (1). - Issued: 23.11.2012. Made: 15.11.2012. Coming into operation: 01.01.2013. Effect: S.R. 1996/269 amended. Territorial extent & classification: NI. General. - 4p.: 30 cm. - 978-0-337-98957-5 £4.00

Justice

The Justice (2011 Act) (Commencement No. 3) Order (Northern Ireland) 2012 No. 2012/142 (C.14). - Enabling power: Justice Act (Northern Ireland) 2011, ss. 111 (3). Bringing into operation various provisions of the 2011 Act on 01.04.2012 , in accord. with art. 2. - Issued: 29.03.2012. Made: 26.03.2012. Coming into operation: -. Effect: None. - 4p.: 30 cm. - 978-0-337-98756-4 £4.00

The Justice (2011 Act) (Commencement No. 4 and Transitory Provision) Order (Northern Ireland) 2012 No. 2012/214 (C.18). - Enabling power: Justice Act (Northern Ireland) 2011, ss. 111 (3) (4). Bringing into operation various provisions of the 2011 Act on 06.06.2012; 11.06.2012; 01.09.2012. - Issued: 28.05.2012. Made: 21.05.2012. Coming into operation: -. Effect: None. NI. General. - 4p.: 30 cm. - 978-0-337-98808-0 £4.00

The Justice (2011 Act) (Commencement No. 5) Order (Northern Ireland) 2012 No. 2012/449 (C.47). - Enabling power: Justice Act (Northern Ireland) 2011, ss. 111 (3). Bringing into operation various provisions of the 2011 Act on 07.01.2013 in accord. with art. 2. - Issued: 18.12.2012. Made: 12.12.2012. Coming into operation: -. Effect: None. Territorial extent & classification: NI. General. - 4p.: 30 cm. - 978-0-337-98992-6 £4.00

Landlord and tenant

Registered Rents (Increase) Order (Northern Ireland) 2012 No. 2012/139. - Enabling power: S.I. 2006/1459 (N.I. 10), art. 55 (5) (6). - Issued: 28.03.2012. Made: 23.03.2012. Coming into operation: 08.05.2012. Effect: None. Territorial extent & classification: NI. General. - 2p.: 30 cm. - 978-0-337-98753-3 £4.00

The Tenancy Deposit Schemes Regulations (Northern Ireland) 2012 No. 2012/373. - Enabling power: S.I. 2006/1459 (N.I. 10), arts 5A (1) (3), 5B (5) (6), 73 (1). - Issued: 12.10.2012. Made: 03.10.2012. Coming into operation: 01.11.2012. Effect: None. Territorial extent & classification: NI. General. - Supersedes draft SR (ISBN 9780337988752) issued on 14.08.2012. - 20p.: 30 cm. - 978-0-337-98916-2 £5.75

Legal aid and advice

The Criminal Aid Certificates Rules (Northern Ireland) 2012 No. 2012/135. - Enabling power: S.I. 1981/228 (N.I. 8), art. 36 (3). - Issued: 24.03.2012. Made: 14.03.2012. Coming into operation: 16.04.2012. Effect: S.R. & O. (N.I.) 1966/52, 53, 54; S.R. 2003/513 revoked- 28p.: 30 cm. - 978-0-337-98749-6 £5.75

The Criminal Legal Aid (Recovery of Defence Costs Orders) Rules (Northern Ireland) 2012 No. 2012/268. - Enabling power: S.I. 1981/228 (N.I. 8), arts. 33A, 36 (3). - Issued: 05.07.2012. Made: 02.07.2012. Coming into operation: 15.10.2012. Effect: None. Territorial extent & classification: NI. General. - With correction slip dated July 2012. - 8p.: 30 cm. - 978-0-337-98851-6 £4.00

The Legal Advice and Assistance (Amendment) Regulations (Northern Ireland) 2012 No. 2012/419. - Enabling power: S.I. 1981/228 (N.I. 8), arts 4, 5, 22, 27. - Issued: 27.11.2012. Made: 22.11.2012. Coming into operation: 01.01.2013. Effect: S.R. 1981/366 amended. Territorial extent & classification: NI. General. - 4p.: 30 cm. - 978-0-337-98964-3 £4.00

Legal Aid (General) (Amendment) Regulations (Northern Ireland) 2012 No. 2012/391. - Enabling power: S.I. 1981/228 (N.I. 8), arts 12 (5), 22, 27. - Issued: 31.10.2012. Made: 25.10.2012. Coming into operation: 10.12.2012. Effect: S.R & O.(NI) 1965/217 amended. Territorial extent & classification: NI. General. - 4p.: 30 cm. - 978-0-337-98940-7 £4.00

Licensing

Licensing and Registration of Clubs (Amendment) (2011 Act) (Commencement No.1) Order (Northern Ireland) 2012 No. 2012/9 (C.1). - Enabling power: Licensing and Registration of Clubs (Amendment) Act (Northern Ireland) 2011, s. 18. Bringing into operation various provisions of the 2011 Act on 01.03.2012, in accord. with art. 2. - Issued: 19.01.2012. Made: 13.01.2012. Coming into operation: -. Effect: None. Territorial extent & classification: NI. General. - 2p.: 30 cm. - 978-0-337-98639-0 £4.00

Licensing and Registration of Clubs (Amendment) (2011 Act) (Commencement No.2) Order (Northern Ireland) 2012 No. 2012/28 (C.6). - Enabling power: Licensing and Registration of Clubs (Amendment) Act (Northern Ireland) 2011, s. 18. Bringing into operation various provisions of the 2011 Act on 01.05.2012, in accord. with art. 2. - Issued: 03.02.2012. Made: 30.01.2012. Coming into operation: -. Effect: None. Territorial extent & classification: NI. General. - 4p.: 30 cm. - 978-0-337-98660-4 £4.00

Licensing and Registration of Clubs (Amendment) (2011 Act) (Commencement No.3) Order (Northern Ireland) 2012 No. 2012/48 (C.8). - Enabling power: Licensing and Registration of Clubs (Amendment) Act (Northern Ireland) 2011, s. 18. Bringing into operation various provisions of the 2011 Act on 01.05.2012, in accord. with art. 2. - Issued: 21.02.2012. Made: 15.02.2012. Coming into operation: -. Effect: None. Territorial extent & classification: NI. General. - 4p.: 30 cm. - 978-0-337-98675-8 £4.00

Licensing and Registration of Clubs (Amendment) (2011 Act) (Commencement No.4) Order (Northern Ireland) 2012 No. 2012/405 (C.39). - Enabling power: Licensing and Registration of Clubs (Amendment) Act (Northern Ireland) 2011, s. 18. Bringing into operation various provisions of the 2011 Act on 01.01.2013, in accord. with art. 2. - Issued: 20.11.2012. Made: 15.11.2012. Coming into operation: -. Effect: None. Territorial extent & classification: NI. General. - 4p.: 30 cm. - 978-0-337-98955-1 £4.00

Licensing and Registration of Clubs (Amendment) (2011 Act) (Commencement No.5) Order (Northern Ireland) 2012 No. 2012/420 (C.42). - Enabling power: Licensing and Registration of Clubs (Amendment) Act (Northern Ireland) 2011, s. 18. Bringing into operation various provisions of the 2011 Act on 10.12.2012, in accord. with art. 2. - Issued: 29.11.2012. Made: 26.11.2012. Coming into operation: -. Effect: None. Territorial extent & classification: NI. General. - 4p.: 30 cm. - 978-0-337-98965-0 £4.00

The Licensing (Form of Licence) (Amendment) Regulations (Northern Ireland) 2012 No. 2012/22. - Enabling power: S.I. 1996/3158 (N.I.22), art. 33. - Issued: 03.02.2012. Made: 30.01.2012. Coming into operation: 01.05.2012. Effect: S.R. 1997/20 amended. Territorial extent & classification: NI. General. - 2p.: 30 cm. - 978-0-337-98654-3 £4.00

The Licensing (Irresponsible Drinks Promotions) Regulations (Northern Ireland) 2012 No. 2012/435. - Enabling power: S.I. 1996/3158 (N.I. 22), art. 57A (1) to (3). - Issued: 11.12.2012. Made: 06.12.2012. Coming into operation: 01.01.2013. Effect: None. Territorial extent & classification: NI. General. - Supersedes draft SR (ISBN 9780337989476) issued 07.12.2012. - 2p.: 30 cm. - 978-0-337-98977-3 £4.00

The Licensing (Notice relating to Age) Regulations (Northern Ireland) 2012 No. 2012/24. - Enabling power: S.I. 1996/3158 (N.I.22), art. 60B (2) (3). - Issued: 03.02.2012. Made: 30.01.2012. Coming into operation: 01.05.2012. Effect: None. Territorial extent & classification: NI. General. - 4p.: 30 cm. - 978-0-337-98656-7 £4.00

The Licensing (Register of Licences) (Amendment) Regulations (Northern Ireland) 2012 No. 2012/23. - Enabling power: S.I. 1996/3158 (N.I.22), art. 34 (1). - Issued: 03.02.2012. Made: 30.01.2012. Coming into operation: 01.05.2012. Effect: S.R. 1997/75 amended. Territorial extent & classification: NI. General. - 2p.: 30 cm. - 978-0-337-98655-0 £4.00

The Licensing (Requirements for Conference Centre) (Amendment) Regulations (Northern Ireland) 2012 No. 2012/249. - Enabling power: S.I. 1996/3158 (N.I.22), art. 2 (2). - Issued: 27.06.2012. Made: 21.06.2012. Coming into operation: 01.09.2012. Effect: S.R. 1997/26 amended. Territorial extent & classification: NI. General. - 4p.: 30 cm. - 978-0-337-98834-9 £4.00

Local government

The Local Government (2005 Order) (Commencement No. 3) Order (Northern Ireland) 2012 No. 2012/417 (C.41). - Enabling power: S.I. 2005/1968 (NI 18), art. 1 (2). Bringing into operation various provisions of the 2005 Order on 26.11.2012, in accord. with art. 2. - Issued: 26.11.2012. Made: 21.11.2012. Coming into operation: -. Effect: None.Territorial extent & classification: NI. General. - 2p: 30 cm. - 978-0-337-98963-6 £4.00

Local Government Best Value (Exclusion of Non-commercial Considerations) Order (Northern Ireland) 2012 No. 2012/271. - Enabling power: Local Government (Best Value) Act (Northern Ireland) 2002, s. 2 (1) (2). - Issued: 09.07.2012. Made: 04.07.2012. Coming into operation: 04.07.2012. Effect: None. Territorial extent & classification: NI. General. - Supersedes draft S.R. (ISBN 9780337987465) issued 30.03.2012. - 2p.: 30 cm. - 978-0-337-98853-0 £4.00

Local Government (Boundaries) Order (Northern Ireland) 2012 No. 2012/421. - Enabling power: Local Government Act (Northern Ireland) 1972, s. 50 (10). - Issued: 04.12.2012. Made: 30.11.2012. Coming into operation: In accord. with art. 1. Effect: S.R. 1992/303 revoked. Territorial extent & classification: NI. General. - Supersedes draft SI (ISBN 9780337987786) issued 26.04.2012. - 12p.: 30 cm. - 978-0-337-98967-4 £5.75

The Local Government (Constituting Joint Committees as Bodies Corporate) Order (Northern Ireland) 2012 No. 2012/10. - Enabling power: Local Government Act (Northern Ireland) 1972, s. 19 (9). - Issued: 30.01.2012. Made: 17.01.2012. Coming into operation: 02.04.2012. Effect: S.R. 2004/49; 2007/505; 2008/310 revoked. Territorial extent & classification: NI. General. - 4p.: 30 cm. - 978-0-337-98640-6 £4.00

Local Government (Councillors' Remuneration Panel) Regulations (Northern Ireland) 2012 No. 2012/279. - Enabling power: Local Government Finance Act (Northern Ireland) 2011, s. 35. - Issued: 10.07.2012. Made: 05.07.2012. Coming into operation: 10.09.2012. Effect: None. Territorial extent & classification: NI. General. - 4p.: 30 cm. - 978-0-337-98854-7 £4.00

Local Government (Indemnities for Members and Officers) Order (Northern Ireland) 2012 No. 2012/422. - Enabling power: S.I. 2005/1968 (N.I. 18), art. 33. - Issued: 04.12.2012. Made: 27.11.2012. Coming into operation: 27.11.2012. Effect: None. Territorial extent & classification: NI. General. - Laid before the Assembly in draft (ISBN 9780337989179) issued on 08.10.2012. - 4p.: 30 cm. - 978-0-337-98966-7 £4.00

Local Government (Payments to Councillors) Regulations (Northern Ireland) 2012 No. 2012/85. - Enabling power: Local Government Finance Act (Northern Ireland) 2011, ss. 31 (1) (3) (4), 43 (2). - Issued: 06.03.2012. Made: 02.03.2012. Coming into operation: 01.04.2012. Effect: S.R. 2009/32 amended & S.R. & O. (N.I.) 1973/366; 1979/25; 1981/114; 1997/431; 1999/449; 2003/125; 2007/168 revoked with savings. Territorial extent & classification: NI. General. - 12p: 30 cm. - 978-0-337-98702-1 £5.75

Local Government Pension Scheme (Amendment) Regulations (Northern Ireland) 2012 No. 2012/183. - Enabling power: S.I. 1972/1073 (N.I. 10), arts 9, 14, sch. 3. - Issued: 08.05.2012. Made: 03.05.2012. Coming into operation: 01.04.2009, 09.05.2011 and 01.06.2012, in accord. with art. 2. Effect: S.R. 2009/32, 33 amended. Territorial extent & classification: NI. General. - With correction slip dated May 2012. - 8p.: 30 cm. - 978-0-337-98793-9 £5.75

The Local Government (Specified Bodies) Regulations (Northern Ireland) 2012 No. 2012/8. - Enabling power: Local Government Finance Act (Northern Ireland) 2011, s. 28 (6). - Issued: 20.01.2012. Made: 13.01.2012. Coming into operation: 01.04.2012. Effect: S.R. 2007/85 revoked. Territorial extent & classification: NI. General. - 4p.: 30 cm. - 978-0-337-98638-3 £4.00

Magistrates' courts

The Magistrates' Courts (Amendment No. 2) Rules (Northern Ireland) 2012 No. 2012/415. - Enabling power: S.I. 1981/1675 (N.I. 26), art. 13. - Issued: 26.11.2012. Made: 20.11.2012. Coming into operation: 20.12.2012. Effect: S.R. 1984/225 amended. Territorial extent & classification: NI. General. - 8p.: 30 cm. - 978-0-337-98962-9 £4.00

The Magistrates' Courts (Amendment) Rules (Northern Ireland) 2012 No. 2012/189. - Enabling power: S.I. 1981/1675 (N.I. 26), art. 13. - Issued: 23.05.2012. Made: 16.05.2012. Coming into operation: 06.06.2012 & 11.06.2012. In accord. with rule 1. Effect: S.R. 1984/225 amended. Territorial extent & classification: NI. General. - With correction slip dated August 2012. - 20p.: 30 cm. - 978-0-337-98805-9 £5.75

The Magistrates' Courts (Civil Jurisdiction and Judgments Act 1982) (Amendment) Rules (Northern Ireland) 2012 No. 2012/414. - Enabling power: S.R. 1981/1675 (N.I. 26), art. 13 & Civil Jurisdiction and Judgments Act 1982, s. 48. - Issued: 26.11.2012. Made: 20.11.2012. Coming into operation: In accord. with rule 1. Effect: S.R. 1986/359 amended. Territorial extent & classification: NI. General. - 8p.: 30 cm. - 978-0-337-98961-2 £4.00

The Magistrates' Courts (Costs in Criminal Cases) (Amendment) Rules (Northern Ireland) 2012 No. 2012/430. - Enabling power: S.I. 1981/1675 (N.I.26), art. 13 & Costs in Criminal Cases Act (Northern Ireland) 1968, s. 7. - Issued: 10.12.2012. Made: 03.12.2012. Coming into operation: 01.01.2013. Effect: S.R. 1988/136 amended. Territorial extent & classification: NI. General. - 8p.: 30 cm. - 978-0-337-98975-9 £5.75

The Magistrates' Courts (Declarations of Parentage) (Amendment) Rules (Northern Ireland) 2012 No. 2012/190. - Enabling power: S.R. 1981/1675 (N.I. 26), art. 13. - Issued: 22.05.2012. Made: 16.05.2012. Coming into operation: 06.06.2012. Effect: S.R. 2002/158 amended. Territorial extent & classification: NI. General. - 4p.: 30 cm. - 978-0-337-98802-8 £4.00

Medicines

The Medicines (Products for Human Use) (Fees) Regulations 2012 No. 2012/134. - Enabling power: Medicines Act 1968, s. 1 (1) (2) & European Communities Act 1972, s. 2 (2) & Finance Act 1973, s. 56 (1) (2). - Issued: 26.03.2012. Made: 23.02.2012. Laid: 29.02.2012. Coming into operation: 01.04.2012. Effect: S.I. 2004/1031 amended & S.I. 1994/899; 2010/551 revoked with saving. - 78p.: 30 cm. - 978-0-337-98747-2 £13.75

Mental health services

The Mental Health (1986 Order) (Commencement No. 5) Order (Northern Ireland) 2012 No. 2012/349 (C.33). - Enabling power: S.I. 1986/595 (NI.4), art. 1 (2). Bringing into operation in relation to Northern Ireland various provisions of the 1986 Order on 01.11.2012; 31.03.2013, in accord. with art. 2. - Issued: 24.09.2012. Made: 20.09.2012. Coming into operation: -. Effect: None. Territorial extent & classification: NI. General. - 4p.: 30 cm. - 978-0-337-98910-0 £4.00

Mental health services: Private hospitals

Mental Health (Private Hospitals) (Fees) Regulations (Northern Ireland) 2012 No. 2012/401. - Enabling power: S.I. 1986/595 (N.I. 4), arts. 91 (1), 135 (1). - Issued: 12.11.2012. Made: 07.11.2012. Coming into operation: 31.03.2013. Effect: None. Territorial extent & classification: NI. General. - 2p.: 30 cm. - 978-0-337-98950-6 £4.00

Mental Health (Private Hospitals) Regulations (Northern Ireland) 2012 No. 2012/403. - Enabling power: S.I. 1986/595 (N.I. 4), art. 95. - Issued: 16.11.2012. Made: 13.11.2012. Coming into operation: 31.03.2013. Effect: S.I. 1986/595 (N.I. 14) amended. Territorial extent & classification: NI. General. - Subject to affirmative resolution procedure of the Assembly. - 8p.: 30 cm. - 978-0-337-98954-4 £5.75

Northern Ireland Assembly

The Assembly Members (Independent Financial Review and Standards) (2011 Act) (Commencement) Order (Northern Ireland) 2012 No. 2012/334 (C.30). - Enabling power: Assembly Members (Independent Financial Review and Standards) Act (Northern Ireland) 2011, s. 38 (2), 30. Bringing into operation various provisions of the 2011 Act on 17.09.2012. - Issued: 21.09.2012. Made: 10.09.2012. Coming into operation: -. Effect: None. Territorial extent & classification: NI. General. - 2p.: 30 cm. - 978-0-337-98901-8 £4.00

Official statistics

The Official Statistics Order (Northern Ireland) 2012 No. 2012/2. - Enabling power: Statistics and Registration Service Act 2007, s. 6 (1) (b) (2). - Issued: 16.01.2012. Made: 05.01.2012. Coming into operation: In accord.with art. 1. Effect: None. Territorial extent & classification: NI. General. - Superseded by Affirmed version (ISBN 9780337986826) issued on 24.02.2012. Subject to affirmative resolution procedure of the Assembly. - 4p.: 30 cm. - 978-0-337-98632-1 £4.00

The Official Statistics Order (Northern Ireland) 2012 No. 2012/2. - Enabling power: Statistics and Registration Service Act 2007, s. 6 (1) (b) (2). - Issued: 24.02.2012. Made: 05.01.2012. Coming into operation: 01.04.2012 in accord. with art. 1. Effect: None. Territorial extent & classification: NI. General. - Affirmed by resolution of the Assembly on 21st February 2012. Supersedes version issued 16.01.2012 (ISBN 9780337986321). - 4p.: 30 cm. - 978-0-337-98682-6 £4.00

The Statistics and Registration Service Act 2007 (Disclosure of Social Security Information) Regulations (Northern Ireland) 2012 No. 2012/215. - Enabling power: Statistics and Registration Service Act 2007, s. 49 (1) (2) (5) (b) (6) (b). - Issued: 07.06.2012. Made: 23.05.2012. Coming into operation: In accord. with reg. 1. Effect: None. Territorial extent & classification: NI. General. - Superseded by affirmed SR of same number but different ISBN (9780337988363) issued on 27.06.2012. Subject to affirmative resolution procedure of the Assembly. - 4p.: 30 cm. - 978-0-337-98812-7 £4.00

The Statistics and Registration Service Act 2007
(Disclosure of Social Security Information) Regulations
(Northern Ireland) 2012 No. 2012/215. - Enabling
power: Statistics and Registration Service Act 2007, s. 49
(1) (2) (5) (b) (6) (b). - Issued: 27.06.2012. Made:
23.05.2012. Coming into operation: 20.06.2012 in accord.
with reg. 1. Effect: None. Territorial extent &
classification: NI. General. - Affirmed by resolution of the
Assembly on 19th June 2012. - 4p.: 30 cm. -
978-0-337-98836-3 £4.00

Older people

Commissioner for Older People Act 2011
(Commencement) Order (Northern Ireland) 2012 No.
2012/388 (C.37). - Enabling power: Commissioner for
Older People Act (Northern Ireland) 2011, s. 28 (2).
Bringing into operation various provisions of the 2011 Act
on 01.12.2012, in accord. with art. 2. - Issued: 30.10.2012.
Made: 25.10.2012. Coming into operation: -. Effect: None.
Territorial extent & classification: NI. General. - 4p.: 30
cm. - 978-0-337-98936-0 £4.00

Pensions

The Automatic Enrolment (Earnings Trigger and
Qualifying Earnings Band) Order (Northern Ireland)
2012 No. 2012/240. - Enabling power: Pensions (No. 2)
Act (Northern Ireland) 2008, ss. 14, 15A(1). - Issued:
18.06.2012. Made: 14.06.2012. Coming into operation:
15.06.2012. Effect: 2008 c. 13 (N.I.) amended. Territorial
extent & classification: NI. General. - 2p.: 30 cm. -
978-0-337-98827-1 £4.00

The Automatic Enrolment (Miscellaneous
Amendments) Regulations (Northern Ireland) 2012 No.
2012/232. - Enabling power: Pension Schemes (Northern
Ireland) Act 1993, ss. 107A (15) (b), 177 (2) to (4) & S.I.
1995/3213 (N.I. 22), arts 49 (8), 166 (1) to (3) & Pensions
(No. 2) Act (Northern Ireland) 2008, ss. 2 (3), 3 (2) (5) (6),
4 (1) to (3) (5) , 5 (4) (6) (8), 6 (1) (b) (2), 7 (5), 10, 11, 12,
15 (1) (2), 16 (2), 22 (4), 23 (1) (b) (c) (3) (6), 24 (1), 29
(2) (4), 30 (5) (7A) (8), 37 (3), 38 (2) to (4), 40 (4), 41 (4)
(5), 43 (3), 52 (3), 54 (3), 59, 78, 113 (2). - Issued:
11.06.2012. Made: 06.06.2012. Coming into operation:
07.06.2012. & 01.07.2012. In accord. with reg. 1 (1).
Effect: S.R. 2010/122 amended /partially revoked
(01.07.2012) & S.R. 2010/123,186 amended. Territorial
extent & classification: NI. General. - Partially revoked by
SR 2012/332 (ISBN 9780337989001). - 16p.: 30 cm. -
978-0-337-98818-9 £5.75

The Employers' Duties (Implementation) (Amendment)
Regulations (Northern Ireland) 2012 No. 2012/332. -
Enabling power: Pensions (No. 2) Act (Northern Ireland)
2008, ss. 12, 29 (2), 30 (8), 113 (2). - Issued: 10.09.2012.
Made: 05.09.2012. Coming into operation: 01.10.2012.
Effect: S.R. 2010/123 amended & S.R. 2012/232 partially
revoked. Territorial extent & classification: NI. General. -
8p.: 30 cm. - 978-0-337-98900-1 £4.00

The Guaranteed Minimum Pensions Increase Order
(Northern Ireland) 2012 No. 2012/97. - Enabling power:
Pension Schemes (Northern Ireland) Act 1993, s. 109 (4). -
Issued: 15.03.2012. Made: 07.03.2012. Coming into
operation: 06.04.2012. Effect: None. Territorial extent &
classification: NI. General. - 2p.: 30 cm. -
978-0-337-98715-1 £4.00

The Hybrid Schemes Quality Requirements Rules
(Northern Ireland) 2012 No. 2012/267. - Enabling
power: Pensions (No. 2) Act (Northern Ireland) 2008, s. 24
(2) to (4). - Issued: 04.07.2012. Made: 29.06.2012.
Coming into operation: 01.07.2012. Effect: None.
Territorial extent & classification: NI. General. - 4p.: 30
cm. - 978-0-337-98850-9 £4.00

The Occupational and Personal Pension Schemes
(Automatic Enrolment) (Amendment No. 2)
Regulations (Northern Ireland) 2012 No. 2012/238. -
Enabling power: S.I. 2005/255(N.I. 1), art. 268A (a). -
Issued: 13.06.2012. Made: 11.06.2012. Coming into
operation: 02.07.2012. Effect: S.R. 2010/122 amended.
Territorial extent & classification: NI. General. - 2p.: 30
cm. - 978-0-337-98823-3 £4.00

The Occupational and Personal Pension Schemes
(Automatic Enrolment) (Amendment No. 3)
Regulations (Northern Ireland) 2012 No. 2012/390. -
Enabling power: Pensions (No. 2) Act (Northern Ireland)
2008, ss. 16 (3) (c), 113 (2). - Issued: 30.10.2012. Made:
26.10.2012. Coming into operation: 01.11.2012. Effect:
S.R. 2010/122 amended. Territorial extent & classification:
NI. General. - For approval of the Assembly before the
expiration of six months from the date of their coming into
operation. Superseded by approved version of SR
2012/390 (ISBN 9780337989872) issued 14.12.2012. -
2p.: 30 cm. - 978-0-337-98938-4 £4.00

The Occupational and Personal Pension Schemes
(Automatic Enrolment) (Amendment No. 3)
Regulations (Northern Ireland) 2012 No. 2012/390. -
Enabling power: Pensions (No. 2) Act (Northern Ireland)
2008, ss. 16 (3) (c), 113 (2). - Issued: 14.12.2012. Made:
26.10.2012. Coming into operation: 01.11.2012. Effect:
S.R. 2010/122 amended. Territorial extent & classification:
NI. General. - Approved by resolution of the Assembly on
10th December 2012. Supersedes pre-approved version
(ISBN 9780337989384) issued on 30.10.2012. - 2p.: 30
cm. - 978-0-337-98987-2 £4.00

The Occupational and Personal Pension Schemes (Automatic Enrolment) (Amendment) Regulations (Northern Ireland) 2012 No. 2012/237. - Enabling power: Pension Schemes (Northern Ireland) Act 1993, ss. 107A (15) (b), 177 (2) to (4) & S.I. 1995/3213 (N.I. 22), arts 49 (8), 166 (1) to (3) & Pensions (No. 2) Act (Northern Ireland) 2008, ss. 2 (3), 3 (2) (5) (6), 5 (2) (4) (6) (7) (8), 6 (1) (b) (2), 7 (4) to (6), 8 (2) (b) (3) to (6), 9 (3), 10, 15 (1) (2), 16 (2) (3) (c), 17 (1) (c), 18 (c), 22 (4) to (7), 23 (1) (b) (c) (3) (6), 24 (1), 25, 27, 28 (1) (2) (b) (3A) (4) to (7), 30 (5) (6) (c) (7A), 33 (2), 37 (3), 59, 113 (2). - Issued: 13.06.2012. Made: 08.06.2012. Coming into operation: 01.07.2012. Effect: S.R. 2010/122 amended. Territorial extent & classification: NI. General. - For approval of the Assembly. Superseded by approved version SR 2012/237 (ISBN 9780337989858) issued 14.12.2012. - 16p.: 30 cm. - 978-0-337-98822-6 £5.75

The Occupational and Personal Pension Schemes (Automatic Enrolment) (Amendment) Regulations (Northern Ireland) 2012 No. 2012/237. - Enabling power: Pension Schemes (Northern Ireland) Act 1993, ss. 107A (15) (b), 177 (2) to (4) & S.I. 1995/3213 (N.I. 22), arts 49 (8), 166 (1) to (3) & Pensions (No. 2) Act (Northern Ireland) 2008, ss. 2 (3), 3 (2) (5) (6), 5 (2) (4) (6) (7) (8), 6 (1) (b) (2), 7 (4) to (6), 8 (2) (b) (3) to (6), 9 (3), 10, 15 (1) (2), 16 (2) (3) (c), 17 (1) (c), 18 (c), 22 (4) to (7), 23 (1) (b) (c) (3) (6), 24 (1), 25, 27, 28 (1) (2) (b) (3A) (4) to (7), 30 (5) (6) (c) (7A), 33 (2), 37 (3), 59, 113 (2). - Issued: 14.12.2012. Made: 08.06.2012. Coming into operation: 01.07.2012. Effect: S.R. 2010/122 amended. Territorial extent & classification: NI. General. - Approved by resolution of the Assembly on 10th December 2012. Supersedes pre-approved version (ISBN 9780337988226) issued on 13.06.2012. - 16p.: 30 cm. - 978-0-337-98985-8 £5.75

The Occupational and Personal Pension Schemes (Levies) (Amendment) Regulations (Northern Ireland) 2012 No. 2012/98. - Enabling power: Pension Schemes (Northern Ireland) Act 1993, ss. 170, 177 (2). - Issued: 14.09.2012. Made: 07.03.2012. Coming into operation: 01.04.2012. Effect: S.R. 2005/92, 147 amended. Territorial extent & classification: NI. General. - Approved by resolution of the Assembly on 11th September 2012. - 4p: 30 cm. - 978-0-337-98903-2 £4.00

The Occupational and Personal Pension Schemes (Levies) (Amendment) Regulations (Northern Ireland) 2012 No. 2012/98. - Enabling power: Pension Schemes (Northern Ireland) Act 1993, ss. 170, 177 (2). - Issued: 12.03.2012. Made: 07.03.2012. Coming into operation: 01.04.2012. Effect: S.R. 2005/92, 147 amended. Territorial extent & classification: NI. General. - Superseded by SR of same number but different ISBN (9780337989032) approved by the Assembly on 14.09.2012. For approval of the Assembly before the expiration of six months from the date of their coming into operation. - 4p: 30 cm. - 978-0-337-98716-8 £4.00

The Occupational Pension Schemes (Contracting-out and Modification of Schemes) (Amendment) Regulations (Northern Ireland) 2012 No. 2012/125. - Enabling power: Pension Schemes (Northern Ireland) Act 1993, ss. 12 (3), 177 (4). - Issued: 20.03.2012. Made: 16.03.2012. Coming into operation: 06.04.2012. Effect: S.R.1996/493 amended. Territorial extent & classification: NI. General. - 2p.: 30 cm. - 978-0-337-98740-3 £4.00

The Occupational Pension Schemes (Disclosure of Information) (Amendment) Regulations (Northern Ireland) 2012 No. 2012/331. - Enabling power: Pension Schemes (Northern Ireland) Act 1993, ss. 109 (1) (2) (e) (3), 177 (2) to (4). - Issued: 10.09.2012. Made: 05.09.2012. Coming into operation: 01.10.2012. Effect: S.R. 1997/98 amended & S.R. 1997/544; 2010/373 partially revoked. Territorial extent & classification: NI. General. - 4p.: 30 cm. - 978-0-337-98899-8 £4.00

The Occupational Pension Schemes (Employer Debt and Miscellaneous Amendments) Regulations (Northern Ireland) 2012 No. 2012/1. - Enabling power: S.I. 1995/3213 (N.I. 22), arts 75 (5) (10), 75A (1) to (4) (5) (a), 122 (3), 166 (1) to (3) & S.I. 2005/255 (N.I. 1), arts 2 (5) (a), 64 (2) (a), 110 (5), 211, 280 (1) (b) (2) (b), 287 (3). - Issued: 10.01.2012. Made: 04.01.2012. Coming into operation: 27.01.2012. Effect: S.R. 2005/91, 126, 168, 378, 568 amended & S.R. 2010/111 partially revoked. Territorial extent & classification: NI. General. - 12p.: 30 cm. - 978-0-337-98631-4 £5.75

The Occupational Pensions (Revaluation) Order (Northern Ireland) 2012 No. 2012/426. - Enabling power: Pension Schemes (Northern Ireland) Act 1993, sch. 2, para. 2 (1). - Issued: 10.12.2012. Made: 03.12.2012. Coming into operation: 01.01.2013. Effect: None. Territorial extent & classification: NI. General. - 4p.: 30 cm. - 978-0-337-98970-4 £4.00

The Pension Protection Fund and Occupational Pension Schemes (Levy Ceiling and Compensation Cap) Order (Northern Ireland) 2012 No. 2012/99. - Enabling power: S.I. 2005/255 (N.I.1), arts 161, 287 (3), sch. 6, paras. 26 (7), 27. - Issued: 12.03.2012. Made: 07.03.2012. Coming into operation: In accord. with art. 1(1). Effect: S.R. 2011/122. 123 revoked. Territorial extent & classification: NI. General. - 4p.: 30 cm. - 978-0-337-98717-5 £4.00

The Pension Protection Fund (Miscellaneous Amendments) Regulations (Northern Ireland) 2012 No. 2012/270. - Enabling power: S.I. 2005/255 (N.I.1), arts 127 (3) to (5), 127A (5), 135 (4), 140 (1), 168 (4) (a), 185 (1), 189 (1) (2) (5) (a), 192 (1) (2) (b), 280 (1) (b) (2) (b), 287 (2) (3). - Issued: 05.07.2012. Made: 02.07.2012. Coming into operation: 23.07.2012. Effect: S.R. 2005/91, 126, 129, 131, 138, 344, 381; 2007/186 amended. Territorial extent & classification: NI. General. - For approval by Assembly. Superseded by approved version of SR 2012/270 (ISBN 9780337989865) issued 14.12.2012. - 16p.: 30 cm. - 978-0-337-98852-3 £5.75

The Pension Protection Fund (Miscellaneous Amendments) Regulations (Northern Ireland) 2012 No. 2012/270. - Enabling power: S.I. 2005/255 (N.I. 1), arts 127(3) to (5), 127A (5), 135 (4), 140 (1), 168 (4) (a), 185 (1), 189 (1), (2) (5)(a), 192 (1) (2)(b), 280 (1) (b) (2)(b), 287 (2) (3). - Issued: 14.12.2012. Made: 02.07.2012. Coming into operation: 23.07.2012. Effect: S.R. 2005/91, 126, 129, 131, 138, 344, 381; 2007/186 amended. Territorial extent & classification: NI. General. - Approved by resolution of the Assembly on 10th December 2012. Supersedes pre-approved version (ISBN 9780337988523) issued on 05.07.2012. - 16p.: 30 cm. - 978-0-337-98986-5 £5.75

The Pensions (2005 Order) (Disclosure of Restricted Information by the Pensions Regulator) (Amendment) Order (Northern Ireland) 2012 No. 2012/110. - Enabling power: S.I. 2005/255 (N.I. 1), art. 81 (2) (a) (iii). - Issued: 15.03.2011. Made: 09.03.2012. Coming into operation: 06.04.2012. Effect: S.I. 2005/255 (N.I. 1) amended. Territorial extent: NI. General. - 2p.: 30 cm. - 978-0-337-98724-3 £4.00

The Pensions (2008 Act) (Abolition of Contracting-out for Defined Contribution Pension Schemes) (Consequential Provisions) Regulations (Northern Ireland) 2012 No. 2012/120. - Enabling power: Pensions Act (Northern Ireland) 2008, s. 13 (5) (6). - Issued: 20.03.2012. Made: 14.03.2012. Coming into operation: In accord. with reg. 1. Effect: 1992 c. 8; 2008 c. 13 (NI); S.R.1987/288; 1991/37; 1996/493, 618; 1997/98, 139, 140; 2000/144, 146, 262 amended & S.R 1997/56 partially revoked (06.04.2012) & S.R. 1996/509; 1997/167 revoked (06.04.2012). Territorial extent & classification: NI. General. - Superseded by SR of same number but different ISBN (9780337989049) approved by the Assembly on 14.09.2012. For approval of the Assembly before the expiration of 6 months from the date of their coming into operation. - 16p: 30 cm. - 978-0-337-98735-9 £5.75

The Pensions (2008 Act) (Abolition of Contracting-out for Defined Contribution Pension Schemes) (Consequential Provisions) Regulations (Northern Ireland) 2012 No. 2012/120. - Enabling power: Pensions Act (Northern Ireland) 2008, s. 13 (5) (6). - Issued: 14.09.2012. Made: 14.03.2012. Coming into operation: In accord. with reg. 1. Effect: 1992 c. 8; 2008 c. 13 (NI); S.R.1987/288; 1991/37; 1996/493, 618; 1997/98, 139, 140; 2000/144, 146, 262 amended & S.R 1997/56 partially revoked (06.04.2012) & S.R. 1996/509; 1997/167 revoked (06.04.2012). Territorial extent & classification: NI. General. - Approved by resolution of the Assembly on 11th September 2012. - 16p: 30 cm. - 978-0-337-98904-9 £5.75

The Pensions (2008 Act) (Commencement No. 3) Order (Northern Ireland) 2012 No. 2012/115 (C.11). - Enabling power: Pensions Act (Northern Ireland) 2008, s. 21 (1). Bringing into operation various provisions of the 2008 Act on 06.04.2012; 06.04.2015, in accord. with art. 2. - Issued: 20.03.2012. Made: 14.03.2012. Coming into operation: -. Effect: None. Territorial extent & classification: NI. General. - 4p.: 30 cm. - 978-0-337-98730-4 £4.00

The Pensions (2008 Act) (Commencement No. 4) Order (Northern Ireland) 2012 No. 2012/234 (C.20). - Enabling power: Pensions Act (Northern Ireland) 2008, s. 21 (1). Bringing into operation various provisions of the 2008 Act on 07.06.2012 & 06.04.2015, in accord. with art. 2. - Issued: 11.06.2012. Made: 06.06.2012. Coming into operation: -. Effect: None. Territorial extent & classification: NI. General. - 2p.: 30 cm. - 978-0-337-98820-2 £4.00

The Pensions (2008 No. 2 Act) (Abolition of Protected Rights) (Consequential Provisions) Order (Northern Ireland) 2012 No. 2012/124. - Enabling power: Pensions (No. 2) Act (Northern Ireland) 2008, s. 114 (1) (2). - Issued: 20.03.2012. Made: 15.03.2012. Coming into operation: In accord. with art. 1. Effect: 1993 c.8, c. 49; S.I. 1989/2405 (NI.19); 1995/3213 (NI. 22); 2005/255 (NI.1); S.R. 1987/288, 290, 291; 1991/37; 1996/493, 618, 619, 621; 1997/8, 94, 98, 139; 1998/208; 2000/262; 2005/193; 2006/149, 155, 261 amended & S.R. 1988/449; 1996/94; 1997/95 revoked (06.04.2012) & S.R. 1997/56 revoked (06.04.2013). Territorial extent & classification: NI. General. - Superseded by SR of same title (ISBN 9780337989056) approved by the Assembly on 14.09.2012. For approval of the Assembly before the expiration of six months from the date of its coming into operation. - 20p: 30 cm. - 978-0-337-98739-7 £5.75

The Pensions (2008 No. 2 Act) (Abolition of Protected Rights) (Consequential Provisions) Order (Northern Ireland) 2012 No. 2012/124. - Enabling power: Pensions (No. 2) Act (Northern Ireland) 2008, s. 114 (1) (2). - Issued: 14.09.2012. Made: 15.03.2012. Coming into operation: In accord. with art. 1. Effect: 1993 c.8, c. 49; S.I. 1989/2405 (NI.19); 1995/3213 (NI. 22); 2005/255 (NI.1); S.R. 1987/288, 290, 291; 1991/37; 1996/493, 618, 619, 621; 1997/8, 94, 98, 139; 1998/208; 2000/262; 2005/193; 2006/149, 155, 261 amended & S.R. 1997/56 partially revoked & S.R. 1988/449; 1996/94; 1997/95 revoked (06.04.2012) & S.R. 1997/56 revoked (06.04.2013). Territorial extent & classification: NI. General. - Approved by resolution of the Assembly on 11th September 2012. - 20p: 30 cm. - 978-0-337-98905-6 £5.75

The Pensions (2008 No. 2 Act) (Commencement No. 7) Order (Northern Ireland) 2012 No. 2012/119 (C.12). - Enabling power: Pensions (No. 2) Act (Northern Ireland) 2008, s. 118 (1). Bringing into operation various provisions of the 2008 Act on 06.04.2012, in accord. with art. 2. - Issued: 20.03.2012. Made: 14.03.2012. Coming into operation: -. Effect: None. Territorial extent & classification: NI. General. - 4p.: 30 cm. - 978-0-337-98734-2 £4.00

The Pensions (2008 No. 2 Act) (Commencement No. 8) Order (Northern Ireland) 2012 No. 2012/236 (C.21). - Enabling power: Pensions (No. 2) Act (Northern Ireland) 2008, s. 118 (1). Bringing into operation various provisions of the 2008 Act on 08.06.2012, in accord. with art. 2. - Issued: 12.06.2012. Made: 07.06.2012. Coming into operation: -. Effect: None. Territorial extent & classification: NI. General. - 4p.: 30 cm. - 978-0-337-98821-9 £4.00

The Pensions (2008 No. 2 Act) (Commencement No. 9) Order (Northern Ireland) 2012 No. 2012/266 (C.25). - Enabling power: Pensions (No. 2) Act (Northern Ireland) 2008, s. 118 (1). Bringing into operation various provisions of the 2008 Act on 30.06.2012, in accord. with art. 2. - Issued: 04.07.2012. Made: 29.06.2012. Coming into operation: -. Effect: None. Territorial extent & classification: NI. General. - 8p.: 30 cm. - 978-0-337-98849-3 £4.00

The Pensions (2008 No. 2 Act) (Commencement No. 10 and Supplementary Provisions) Order (Northern Ireland) 2012 No. 2012/372 (C.35). - Enabling power: Pensions (No. 2) Act (Northern Ireland) 2008, ss. 113 (2) (a), 118 (1). Bringing into operation various provisions of the 2008 Act on 01.10.2012, in accord. with art. 2. - Issued: 03.10.2012. Made: 28.09.2012. Coming into operation: -. Effect: None. Territorial extent & classification: NI. General. - 4p.: 30 cm. - 978-0-337-98915-5 £4.00

The Pensions (2012 Act) (Commencement No. 1) Order (Northern Ireland) 2012 No. 2012/233 (C.19). - Enabling power: Pensions Act (Northern Ireland) 2012, s. 34 (3). Bringing into operation various provisions of the 2012 Act on 07.06.2012, in accord. with art. 2. - Issued: 11.06.2012. Made: 06.06.2012. Coming into operation: -. Effect: None. Territorial extent & classification: NI. General. - 4p.: 30 cm. - 978-0-337-98819-6 £4.00

The Pensions (2012 Act) (Commencement No. 2) Order (Northern Ireland) 2012 No. 2012/265 (C.24). - Enabling power: Pensions Act (Northern Ireland) 2012, s. 34 (3). Bringing into operation various provisions of the 2012 Act on 30.06.2012, 23.07.2012 in accord. with art. 2. - Issued: 04.07.2012. Made: 29.06.2012. Coming into operation: -. Effect: None. Territorial extent & classification: NI. General. - 4p.: 30 cm. - 978-0-337-98848-6 £4.00

The Pensions (Financial Reporting Council) (Amendment) Regulations (Northern Ireland) 2012 No. 2012/294. - Enabling power: Pension Schemes (Northern Ireland) Act 1993, ss. 8A (4) (5), 109 (1) (3A) & S.I. 1995/3213 (NI.22), arts 41 (1) (6), 67D (4) (5), 73B (4) (a), 75 (5), 75A (4) (5), 116 & S.I. 2005/255 (NI. 1), arts 127 (3) (4), 135 (8) (b) (9) (b), 140 (2), 209 (3). - Issued: 24.07.2012. Made: 19.07.2012. Coming into operation: 09.08.2012. Effect: S.R. 1987/288; 1996/493, 585, 621; 1997/40, 98; 2000/262; 2005/126, 131, 168, 568; 2006/149; 2007/186 amended & S.R. 2007/64; 2008/132; 2010/108 partially revoked. Territorial extent & classification: NI. General. - 8p.: 30 cm. - 978-0-337-98864-6 £5.75

Pensions Increase (Review) Order (Northern Ireland) 2012 No. 2012/137. - Enabling power: S.I. 1975/1503 (N.I. 15), art. 69 (1) (2) (5) (5ZA). - Issued: 26.03.2012. Made: 21.03.2012. Coming into operation: 09.04.2012. Effect: None. - 8p.: 30 cm. - 978-0-337-98751-9 £5.75

The Pensions (Institute and Faculty of Actuaries and Consultation by Employers) (Amendment) Regulations (Northern Ireland) 2012 No. 2012/113. - Enabling power: Pensions Schemes (Northern Ireland) Act 1993, ss. 15 (4) (c), 69 (4) (b), 93 (1), 97AF (1), 97D (4) (b), 177 (2) to (4) & S.I. 1995/3212 (N.I. 22), arts. 37 (3) (a), 47 (5) (b), 67C (7) (a) (ii), 75 (5), 166 (1) to (3) & S.I. 2005/255 (N.I. 1), arts, 19 (10), 127 (11) (a) (ii) (a), 140 (6), 162 (2), 236 (1) (2), 237 (1), 287 (2) (3). - Issued: 15.03.2012. Made: 12.03.2012. Coming into operation: 06.04.2012. Effect: S.R. 1991/37; 1996/585, 619; 1997/94, 159; 2000/146; 2005/114, 131; 2006/48, 49, 149, 161; 2007/186 amended. Territorial extent & classification: NI. General. - 4p.: 30 cm. - 978-0-337-98726-7 £4.00

Superannuation (Charity Commission for Northern Ireland) Order (Northern Ireland) 2012 No. 2012/285. - Enabling power: S.I. 1972/1073 (N.I. 10), art. 3 (4) (7). - Issued: 23.07.2012. Made: 09.07.2012. Coming into operation: 01.09.2012. Effect: None. Territorial extent & classification: NI. General. - 2p.: 30 cm. - 978-0-337-98860-8 £4.00

Superannuation (Chief Inspector of Criminal Justice in Northern Ireland) Order (Northern Ireland) 2012 No. 2012/49. - Enabling power: S.I. 1972/1073 (N.I. 10), art. 3 (4) (7). - Issued: 24.02.2012. Made: 17.02.2012. Coming into operation: 14.03.2012. Effect: S.I. 1972/1073 (N.I. 10) amended. Territorial extent & classification: NI. General. - 2p.: 30 cm. - 978-0-337-98677-2 £4.00

Superannuation (Commissioner for Victims and Survivors for Northern Ireland) Order (Northern Ireland) 2012 No. 2012/393. - Enabling power: S.I. 1972/1073 (N.I. 10), art. 3 (4) (7). - Issued: 13.11.2012. Made: 29.10.2012. Coming into operation: 17.12.2012. Effect: S.I. 1972/1073 (N.I. 10) amended. Territorial extent & classification: NI. General. - 2p.: 30 cm. - 978-0-337-98941-4 £4.00

Superannuation (Commissioner of the Northern Ireland Law Commission) Order (Northern Ireland) 2012 No. 2012/51. - Enabling power: S.I. 1972/1073 (N.I. 10), art. 3 (4) (7). - Issued: 24.02.2012. Made: 17.02.2012. Coming into operation: 14.03.2012. Effect: S.I. 1972/1073 (N.I. 10) amended. Territorial extent & classification: NI. General. - 2p.: 30 cm. - 978-0-337-98679-6 £4.00

Superannuation (Police Ombudsman for Northern Ireland) Order (Northern Ireland) 2012 No. 2012/50. - Enabling power: S.I. 1972/1073 (N.I. 10), art. 3 (4) (7). - Issued: 24.02.2012. Made: 17.02.2012. Coming into operation: 14.03.2012. Effect: S.I. 1972/1073 (N.I. 10) amended. Territorial extent & classification: NI. General. - 2p.: 30 cm. - 978-0-337-98678-9 £4.00

Superannuation (Victims and Survivors Service Limited) Order (Northern Ireland) 2012 No. 2012/455. - Enabling power: S.I. 1972/1073 (N.I. 10), art. 3 (4) (7). - Issued: 31.12.2012. Made: 14.12.2012. Coming into operation: 11.02.2013. Effect: S.I. 1972/1073 (N.I. 10) amended. Territorial extent & classification: NI. General. - 2p.: 30 cm. - 978-0-337-98998-8 £4.00

Pesticides

Plant Protection Products (Amendment) Regulations (Northern Ireland) 2012 No. 2012/12. - Enabling power: European Communities Act 1972, s. 2 (2). - Issued: 23.01.2012. Made: 16.01.2012. Coming into operation: 29.02.2012. Effect: S.R. 2011/295 amended. Territorial extent & classification: NI. General. - 4p.: 30 cm. - 978-0-337-98642-0 £4.00

Pharmacy

The Council of the Pharmaceutical Society of Northern Ireland (Appointments and Procedure) Regulations (Northern Ireland) 2012 No. 2012/309. - Enabling power: S.I. 1976/1213 (N.I. 22), art. 4 (2), sch. 2, para. 3. - Issued: 14.08.2012. Made: 07.08.2012. Coming into operation: 01.10.2012. Effect: None. Territorial extent & classification: NI. General. - 8p.: 30 cm. - 978-0-337-98877-6 £5.75

The Council of the Pharmaceutical Society of Northern Ireland (Continuing Professional Development) Regulations (Northern Ireland) 2012 No. 2012/312. - Enabling power: S.I. 1976/1213 (N.I. 22), arts 4A (9) (10), 5 (1) (ff) (fff) (ffg), sch. 3, paras 5 (1) (2) (b), 15 (1) (b) (2) (3). - Issued: 16.08.2012. Made: 08.08.2012. Coming into operation: 01.06.2013. Effect: None. Territorial extent & classification: NI. General. - 12p.: 30 cm. - 978-0-337-98883-7 £5.75

The Council of the Pharmaceutical Society of Northern Ireland (Fitness to Practise and Disqualification) Regulations (Northern Ireland) 2012 No. 2012/311. - Enabling power: S.I. 1976/1213 (N.I. 22), art. 5 (1) (fff), sch. 3, paras 1 (1) (b), 4 (5), 5 (1) (2), 9 (3), 14 (1), 15 (1) to (3) (5), 17 (4), 18 (8). - Issued: 16.08.2012. Made: 08.08.2012. Coming into operation: 01.10.2012. Effect: None. Territorial extent & classification: NI. General. - 36p.: 30 cm. - 978-0-337-98882-0 £9.75

The Council of the Pharmaceutical Society of Northern Ireland (Statutory Committee, Scrutiny Committee and Advisers) Regulations (Northern Ireland) 2012 No. 2012/310. - Enabling power: S.I. 1976/1213 (N.I. 22), art. 19 (8), sch. 2, para 2 (5), sch. 3, paras 17 (4), 18 (8). - Issued: 16.08.2012. Made: 08.08.2012. Coming into operation: 01.10.2012. Effect: None. Territorial extent & classification: NI. General. - 12p.: 30 cm. - 978-0-337-98881-3 £5.75

The Pharmacy (Order 1976) (Amendment) Order (Northern Ireland) 2012 No. 2012/308. - Enabling power: Health and Personal Social Services Act (Northern Ireland) 2001, s. 56, sch. 4. - Issued: 09.08.2012. Made: 03.08.2012. Coming into operation: In accord. with art. 1. Effect: S.I. 1976/1213 (N.I. 22) amended. Territorial extent & classification: NI. - Supersedes draft S.R. (ISBN 9780337986338) issued 11.01.2012. - 28p.: 30 cm. - 978-0-337-98873-8 £5.75

Planning

The Planning (Environmental Impact Assessment) Regulations (Northern Ireland) 2012 No. 2012/59. - Enabling power: European Communities Act 1972, s. 2 (2). - Issued: 08.03.2012. Made: 21.02.2012. Coming into operation: 13.03.2012. Effect: S.R. 1993/278 amended & S.R. 2006/218, 276 partially revoked & S.R. 1999/73; 2008/17, 372 revoked. Territorial extent & classification: NI. General. - This Statutory Rule has been printed in substitution of the SR of the same number & ISBN (issued 24.02.2012) and is being issued free of charge to all known recipients of that Statutory Rule. - 36p.: 30 cm. - 978-0-337-98681-9 £9.75

The Planning (Fees) (Amendment) Regulations (Northern Ireland) 2012 No. 2012/293. - Enabling power: S.I. 1991/1220 (N.I. 11), art. 127. - Issued: 20.07.2012. Made: 17.07.2012. Coming into operation: 22.10.2012. Effect: S.R. 2005/222 amended. Territorial extent & classification: NI. General. - 8p.: 30 cm. - 978-0-337-98863-9 £5.75

The Planning (General Development) (Amendment) Order (Northern Ireland) 2012 No. 2012/329. - Enabling power: S.I. 1991/1220 (N.I. 11), arts 13, 20 (1) (3). - Issued: 30.08.2012. Made: 28.08.2012. Coming into operation: 19.09.2012. Effect: S.R. 1993/278 amended. Territorial extent & classification: NI. General. - 16p.: 30 cm. - 978-0-337-98896-7 £5.75

Plant health

The Plant Health (Amendment No. 2) Order (Northern Ireland) 2012 No. 2012/241. - Enabling power: Plant Health Act (Northern Ireland) 1967, ss. 2, 3, 4 (1). - Issued: 21.06.2012. Made: 18.06.2012. Coming into operation: 16.07.2012. Effect: S.R. 2006/82 amended. Territorial extent & classification: NI. General. - EC note: Makes amendments to the Plant Health Order (Northern Ireland) 2006 to enforce Decision 1/2010 which relates to plant health controls on trade in plant material with Switzerland. - 4p.: 30 cm. - 978-0-337-98828-8 £4.00

The Plant Health (Amendment No. 3) Order (Northern Ireland) 2012 No. 2012/392. - Enabling power: Plant Health Act (Northern Ireland) 1967, ss. 2, 3 (1), 4 (1) & European Communities Act 1972, sch. 2, para. 1A. - Issued: 01.11.2012. Made: 26.10.2012. Coming into operation: 26.10.2012. Effect: S.R. 2006/82 amended. Territorial extent & classification: NI. General. - EC note: This Order amends S.R. 2006/82 (ISBN) to introduce emergency measures to prevent the introduction and spread of Chalara fraxinea T. Kowalski, including its teleomorph Hymenoscyohus psuedoalbidux, a cause of ash dieback. This Order also implements Commission Directive 2008/61/EC which replaced Commission Directive 95/44/EC. - 4p.: 30 cm. - 978-0-337-98939-1 £4.00

The Plant Health (Amendment) Order (Northern Ireland) 2012 No. 2012/133. - Enabling power: Plant Health Act (Northern Ireland) 1967, s. 3 (1). - Issued: 23.03.2012. Made: 21.03.2012. Coming into operation: 26.04.2012. Effect: S.R. 2006/82 amended. Territorial extent & classification: NI. General. - 2p.: 30 cm. - 978-0-337-98745-8 £4.00

The Plant Health (Wood and Bark) (Amendment) Order (Northern Ireland) 2012 No. 2012/400. - Enabling power: Plant Health Act (Northern Ireland) 1967, ss. 2, 3 (1), 3A, 3B (1), 4 (1) & European Communities Act 1972, sch. 2, para. 1A. - Issued: 12.11.2012. Made: 06.11.2012. Coming into operation: 06.11.2012. Effect: S.R. 2006/66 amended. Territorial extent & classification: NI. General. - EC note: This Order amends SR 2006/66 to introduce emergency measures to prevent the introduction and spread of Chalara fraxinea T. Kowlaski, including its telemorph Hymenoscyphus pseudoalbidus, a cause of Ash dieback. This order also implements Commission Directive 2008/61/EC which replaced Commission Directive 95/44/EC. - 8p.: 30 cm. - 978-0-337-98951-3 £4.00

Police

The Police and Criminal Evidence (1989 Order) (Codes of Practice) (Temporary Modification to Code A) Order (Northern Ireland) 2012 No. 2012/226. - Enabling power: S.I. 1989/1341 (N.I.12), art. 66 (6A). - Issued: 15.06.2012. Made: 25.05.2012. Coming into operation: 30.07.2012. Effect: None. Territorial extent & classification: NI. General. - 4p.: 30 cm. - 978-0-337-98814-1 £4.00

The Police and Criminal Evidence (Northern Ireland) Order 1989 (Codes of Practice) (Revision of Codes C, E, F and H) Order 2012 No. 2012/376. - Enabling power: S.I. 1989/1341 (N.I.12), arts 60, 60A, 65, 66 (6). - Issued: 18.10.2012. Made: 11.10.2012. Coming into operation: 22.11.2012. Effect: None. Territorial extent & classification: NI. General. - 2p.: 30 cm. - 978-0-337-98922-3 £4.00

Police Service of Northern Ireland (Amendment) Regulations 2012 No. 2012/178. - Enabling power: Police (Northern Ireland) Act 1998, s. 25. - Issued: 03.05.2012. Made: 25.04.2012. Coming into operation: 27.05.2012. Effect: S.R. 2005/547 amended. Territorial extent & classification: NI. General. - 2p.: 30 cm. - 978-0-337-98787-8 £4.00

Police Service of Northern Ireland and Police Service of Northern Ireland Reserve (Injury Benefit) (Amendment) Regulations 2012 No. 2012/82. - Enabling power: Police (Northern Ireland) Act 1998, ss, 25 (1) (2) (k), 26 (1) (2) (g), 72 (2) & Police (Northern Ireland) Act 2000, s. 49. - Issued: 08.03.2012. Made: 01.03.2012. Coming into operation: 31.03.2012. Effect: S.R. 2006/268 amended. Territorial extent & classification: NI. General. - 4p: 30 cm. - 978-0-337-98699-4 £4.00

Police Service of Northern Ireland Pensions (Amendment) Regulations 2012 No. 2012/64. - Enabling power: Police (Northern Ireland) Act 1998, ss. 25 (2) (k), 26 (2) (g). - Issued: 29.02.2012. Made: 22.02.2012. Coming into operation: 01.04.2012. Effect: S.R. 1988/374, 379; 2009/79 amended. Territorial extent & classification: NI. General. - 4p.: 30 cm. - 978-0-337-98685-7 £4.00

Prisons

The Prison Service (Pay Review Body) Regulations (Northern Ireland) 2012 No. 2012/191. - Enabling power: Criminal Justice and Public Order Act 1994, s. 128A. - Issued: 28.05.2012. Made: 09.05.2012. Coming into operation: 15.06.2012. Effect: None. Territorial extent & classification: NI. General. - 2p.: 30 cm. - 978-0-337-98799-1 £4.00

Procedure

The Penalty Notices (Justice Act (Northern Ireland) 2011) (Enforcement of Fines) Regulations (Northern Ireland) 2012 No. 2012/188. - Enabling power: Justice Act (Northern Ireland) 2011, s. 67 (4). - Issued: 21.05.2012. Made: 14.05.2012. Coming into operation: In accord. with rule 1. Effect: None. Territorial extent & classification: NI. General. - 8p.: 30 cm. - 978-0-337-98803-5 £5.75

Public health

The Health (2009 Act) (Commencement No. 2) Order (Northern Ireland) 2012 No. 2012/389 (C.38). - Enabling power: Health Act 2009, s. 40 (3) (4). Bringing into operation various provisions of this Act on 31.10.2012; 06.04.2015, in accord. with art. 2. - Issued: 31.10.2012. Made: 25.10.2012. Coming into operation: -. Effect: None. Territorial extent & classification: NI. General. - 4p.: 30 cm. - 978-0-337-98937-7 £4.00

The Sunbeds (2011 Act) (Commencement No. 1) Order (Northern Ireland) 2012 No. 2012/41 (C.7). - Enabling power: Sunbeds Act (Northern Ireland) 2011, s. 18 (2). Bringing into operation various provisions of this Act on 13.02.2012, in accord. with art. 2. - Issued: 13.02.2012. Made: 09.02.2012. Coming into operation: -. Effect: None. Territorial extent & classification: NI. General. - 2p.: 30 cm. - 978-0-337-98670-3 £4.00

The Sunbeds (2011 Act) (Commencement No. 2) Order (Northern Ireland) 2012 No. 2012/90 (C.10). - Enabling power: Sunbeds Act (Northern Ireland) 2011, s. 18 (2). Bringing into operation various provisions of this Act on 01.05.2012, in accord. with art. 2. - Issued: 08.03.2012. Made: 05.03.2012. Coming into operation: -. Effect: None. Territorial extent & classification: NI. General. - 2p.: 30 cm. - 978-0-337-98708-3 £4.00

The Sunbeds (Fixed Penalty) (Amount) Regulations (Northern Ireland) 2012 No. 2012/92. - Enabling power: Sunbeds Act (Northern Ireland) 2012, ss. 12 (3), 16 (1), sch. 2, para. 4. - Issued: 08.03.2012. Made: 05.03.2012. Coming into operation: 01.05.2012-. Effect: None. Territorial extent & classification: NI. General. - Supersedes draft S.R. (ISBN 9780337986147) issued 06.12.2011. With correction slip dated April 2012. - 8p.: 30 cm. - 978-0-337-98711-3 £4.00

The Sunbeds (Fixed Penalty) (General) Regulations (Northern Ireland) 2012 No. 2012/93. - Enabling power: Sunbeds Act (Northern Ireland) 2011, ss. 12 (3), 16 (1), sch. 2, para. 14. - Issued: 13.03.2012. Made: 05.03.2012. Coming into operation: 01.05.2012-. Effect: None. Territorial extent & classification: NI. General. - 8p.: 30 cm. - 978-0-337-98710-6 £5.75

The Sunbeds (Information) Regulations (Northern Ireland) 2012 No. 2012/91. - Enabling power: Sunbeds Act (Northern Ireland) 2011, ss. 4 (11), 5 (4), 16 (1). - Issued: 13.03.2012. Made: 05.03.2012. Coming into operation: 01.05.2012. Effect: None. Territorial extent & classification: NI. General. - With correction slip dated April 2012. - 8p.: 30 cm. - 978-0-337-98709-0 £5.75

The Tobacco Advertising and Promotion (Display of Prices) Regulations (Northern Ireland) 2012 No. 2012/341. - Enabling power: Tobacco Advertising and Promotion Act 2002, ss. 7C, 19 (2). - Issued: 21.09.2012. Made: 18.09.2012. Coming into operation: 31.10.2012 for the purposes of large shops; 06.04.2015 for all other purposes. Effect: None. Territorial extent & classification: NI. General. - Supersedes draft S.R. (ISBN 9780337988257) issued 18.06.2012. - 8p.: 30 cm. - 978-0-337-98909-4 £5.75

The Tobacco Advertising and Promotion (Display) Regulations (Northern Ireland) 2012 No. 2012/246. - Enabling power: Tobacco Advertising and Promotion Act 2002, ss. 4 (3), 7A (2), 7B (3), 19 (2). - Issued: 25.06.2012. Made: 20.06.2012. Coming into operation: 31.10.2012 for the purpose of large shops other than bulk tobacconists; 06.04.2015 for all other purposes. Effect: S.I. 2004/765 revoked in so far as they apply to Northern Ireland. Territorial extent & classification: NI. General. - 8p.: 30 cm. - 978-0-337-98831-8 £5.75

The Tobacco Advertising and Promotion (Specialist Tobacconists) Regulations (Northern Ireland) 2012 No. 2012/244. - Enabling power: Tobacco Advertising and Promotion Act 2002, ss. 6 (A1), 7B (3), 19 (2). - Issued: 25.06.2012. Made: 20.06.2012. Coming into operation: 06.04.2015. Effect: S.I. 2004/1277 revoked in so far as they apply to Northern Ireland. Territorial extent & classification: NI. General. - 4p.: 30 cm. - 978-0-337-98829-5 £4.00

Race relations

The Race Relations Order 1997 (Amendment) Order (Northern Ireland) 2012 No. 2012/263. - Enabling power: European Communities Act 1972, s. 2 (2) & S.I. 1997/869 (N.I. 6), art. 69 (1) (b). - Issued: 03.07.2012. Made: 26.06.2012. Coming into operation: 09.07.2012. Effect: S.I. 1997/869 (N.I. 6) amended. Territorial extent & classification: NI. General. - Laid before the Assembly in draft. Supersedes draft S.I. (ISBN 9780337987717) issued 11.04.2012. - 4p: 30 cm. - 978-0-337-98846-2 £4.00

Rates

The Jobseeker's Allowance (Sanctions for Failure to Attend) Regulations (Northern Ireland) 2012 No. 2012/44. - Enabling power: Social Security Contributions and Benefits (Northern Ireland) Act 1992, ss. 22 (5), 122 (1) (d), 171 (1) (3); S.I. 1995/2705 (N.I. 15), arts 10, 36 (2), sch. 1, para. 15; S.I. 1998/1506 (N.I. 10), arts 10 (1), 11 (3) (6), 74 (1). - Issued: 16.02.2012. Made: 13.02.2012. Coming into operation: 06.03.2012. Effect: S.R. 1996/198; 1975/113; 1999/162; 2001/216; 2006/405 amended & S.R. 1999/145; 2000/350 partially revoked. Territorial extent & classification: NI. General. - 8p.: 30 cm. - 978-0-337-98672-7 £5.75

The Rates (Deferment) (Revocation and Savings) Regulations (Northern Ireland) 2012 No. 2012/147. - Enabling power: S.I. 1977/2157 (N.I. 28), art. 29A. - Issued: 29.03.2012. Made: 27.03.2012. Coming into operation: 01.04.2012. Effect: S.R. 2010/63 revoked with savings. Territorial extent & classification: NI. General. - Supersedes draft S.R. (ISBN 9780337987076) issued 07.03.2012. - 4p.: 30 cm. - 978-0-337-98760-1 £4.00

The Rates (Microgeneration) Order (Northern Ireland) 2012 No. 2012/47. - Enabling power: S.I. 1977/2157 (N.I. 28), art. 39 (2) (3), sch. 12, part III, para. 4. - Issued: 21.02.2012. Made: 16.02.2012. Coming into operation: 01.04.2012. Effect: S.I. 1977/2157 (N.I. 28) amended. Territorial extent and classification: NI. General. - Subject to the affirmative resolution procedure of the Assembly. Superseded by affirmed version (ISBN 9780337987274) issued 16.03.2012. - 4p.: 30 cm. - 978-0-337-98674-1 £4.00

The Rates (Microgeneration) Order (Northern Ireland) 2012 No. 2012/47. - Enabling power: S.I. 1977/2157 (N.I. 28), art. 39 (2) (3), sch. 12, part 3, para. 4. - Issued: 16.03.2012. Made: 16.02.2012. Coming into operation: 01.04.2012. Effect: S.I. 1977/2157 (N.I. 28) amended. Territorial extent and classification: NI. General. - Affirmed by resolution of the Assembly on 12th March 2012. - 4p.: 30 cm. - 978-0-337-98728-1 £4.00

The Rates (Regional Rates) Order (Northern Ireland) 2012 No. 2012/46. - Enabling power: S.I. 1977/2157 (N.I. 28), art. 7 (1) (3). - Issued: 16.03.2012. Made: 16.02.2012. Coming into operation: In accord. with art. 1. Effect: None. Territorial extent and classification: NI. General. - Affirmed by resolution of the Assembly on 12th March 2012. - 2p.: 30 cm. - 978-0-337-98729-8 £4.00

The Rates (Regional Rates) Order (Northern Ireland) 2012 No. 2012/46. - Enabling power: S.I. 1977/2157 (N.I. 28), art. 7 (1) (3). - Issued: 21.02.2012. Made: 16.02.2012. Coming into operation: In accord. with art. 1. Effect: None. Territorial extent and classification: NI. General. - Subject to the affirmative resolution procedure of the Assembly. Superseded by affirmed version (ISBN 9780337987298) issued 16.03.2012. - 2p.: 30 cm. - 978-0-337-98673-4 *£4.00*

Rates (Small Business Hereditament Relief) (Amendment) Regulations (Northern Ireland) 2012 No. 2012/106. - Enabling power: S.I. 1977/2157 (N.I. 28), art 31C. - Issued: 13.03.2012. Made: 09.03.2012. Coming into operation: 01.04.2012. None. Territorial extent & classification: NI. General. - 4p: 30 cm. - 978-0-337-98720-5 *£4.00*

The Rates (Social Sector Value) (Amendment) Regulations (Northern Ireland) 2012 No. 2012/79. - Enabling power: S.I. 1977/2157 (N.I. 28), art. 23A. - Issued: 05.03.2012. Made: 29.02.2012. Coming into operation: 01.04.2012. Effect: S.R. 2010/21 revoked. Territorial extent & classification: NI. General. - 4p: 30 cm. - 978-0-337-98697-0 *£4.00*

The Social Security Benefits Up-rating Order (Northern Ireland) 2012 No. 2012/116. - Enabling power: Social Security Administration (Northern Ireland) Act 1992, ss. 132, 132A,165 (1) (4) (5). - Issued: 20.03.2012. Made: 14.03.2012. Coming into operation: In accord. with 1. Effect: 1966 c. 6 (N.I.); 1992 c. 7; 1993 c. 49; S.R. 1987/30, 459; 1992/32; 1994/461; 1995/35; 1996/198; 2002/380; 2003/28; 2006/405, 406; 2008/280; 2010/302, 407 amended & 2011/119 revoked (12.04.2012). Territorial extent & classification: NI. General. - For approval of the Assembly before the expiration of six months from the date of its coming into operation. Superseded by approved version (ISBN 9780337988264) issued on 15.06.2012. - 42p.: 30 cm. - 978-0-337-98731-1 *£9.75*

The Social Security Benefits Up-rating Order (Northern Ireland) 2012 No. 2012/116. - Enabling power: Social Security Administration (Northern Ireland) Act 1992, ss. 132, 132A, 165 (1) (4) (5). - Issued: 15.06.2012. Made: 14.03.2012. Coming into operation: In accord. with art. 1. Effect: 1966 c. 6 (N.I.); 1992 c. 7; 1993 c. 49; S.R. 1987/30, 459, 460; 1992/32; 1994/461; 1995/35; 1996/198; 2002/380; 2003/28; 2006/405, 406; 2008/280; 2010/302, 407 amended & 2011/119 revoked (12.04.2012). Territorial extent & classification: NI. General. - Approved by resolution of the Assembly on 11th June 2012. Supersedes pre-approved version (ISBN 9780337987311). - 44p.: 30 cm. - 978-0-337-98826-4 *£9.75*

The Social Security (Habitual Residence) (Amendment) Regulations (Northern Ireland) 2012 No. 2012/380. - Enabling power: Social Security Contributions and Benefits (Northern Ireland) Act 1992, ss. 122 (1) (a) (d), 131 (1) (2), 171 (1) (3) (4) & S.I. 1995/2705 (N.I. 15), arts 6 (5) (12), 36 (2) & State Pension Credit Act (Northern Ireland) 2002, ss. 1 (5) (a), 19 (1) (2) (a) (3) & Welfare Reform Act (Northern Ireland) 2007, ss. 4 (3), 25 (2). - Issued: 22.10.2012. Made: 17.10.2012. Coming into operation: 08.11.2012. Effect: S.R. 1987/459; 1996/198; 2003/28; 2006/405, 406; 2008/280 amended. Territorial extent & classification: NI. General. - 8p.: 30 cm. - 978-0-337-98926-1 *£4.00*

The Social Security (Miscellaneous Amendments) Regulations (Northern Ireland) 2012 No. 2012/121. - Enabling power: Social Security Contributions and Benefits (Northern Ireland) Act 1992, ss. 122 (1) (a) (d), 123 (1) (d) (e), 132 (3) (4) (b), 132A (3), 133 (2) (i), 134 (2), 171 (1) (3) (4) & Social Security Administration (Northern Ireland) Act 1992, ss. 5 (1) (j) (n), 69 (4), 165 (1) (4) (5) & S.I. 1995/2705 (N.I.15), arts 14 (4) (b), 36 (1) (2) & S.I. 1998/1506 (N.I.10), arts 11 (6), 74 (1) (3) (4) & Child Support, Pensions and Social Security Act (Northern Ireland) 2000, s. 59, sch. 7 paras 4 (3), 20 (1) & State Pension Credit Act (Northern Ireland) 2002, ss. 15 (1) (e) (3), 19 (1) to (3) & Welfare Reform Act (Northern Ireland) 2007, ss. 1 (2), 25 (1) (2), 28 (2), 29, sch. 1, paras 1 (4) (a), 6 (5). sch. 4, paras 1 (1), 7 (1) (a). - Issued: 20.03.2012. Made: 14.03.2012. Coming into operation: In accord. with reg. 1. Effect: S.R. 1982/263; 1987/459, 465; 1988/142; 1996/198; 1999/162; 2000/91; 2001/213; 2003/28; 2006/405, 406; 2008/280; 2010/312 amended & S.R. 1987/465; 2003/421; 2006/168; 2008/280; 2009/92, 338; 2010/69; 2011/357 partially revoked (01.04.2012). Territorial extent & classification: NI. General. - 12p.: 30 cm. - 978-0-337-98736-6 *£5.75*

The Social Security (Recovery) (Amendment) Regulations (Northern Ireland) 2012 No. 2012/108. - Enabling power: Social Security Administration (Northern Ireland) Act 1992, ss. 69 (6) (a) (8), 73 (1) (4) (5), 165 (1) (4). - Issued: 13.03.2012. Made: 09.03.2012. Coming into operation: 01.04.2012. Effect: S.R. 1988/142 amended. Territorial extent & classification: NI. General. - 4p.: 30 cm. - 978-0-337-98722-9 *£4.00*

The Social Security (Suspension of Payment of Benefits and Miscellaneous Amendments) Regulations (Northern Ireland) 2012 No. 2012/140. - Enabling power: Social Security Administration (Northern Ireland) Act 1992, ss. 5 (1) (hh) (j) (2A), 165 (1) (4) to (6) & S.I. 1998/1506 (N.I. 10), arts 10 (1) (a), 22, 74 (1) (3) (5) (6). - Issued: 29.03.2012. Made: 26.03.2012. Coming into operation: 17.04.2012. Effect: S.R. 1987/465; 1996/198; 1999/162; 2006/405, 406 amended & S.R. 2000/350; 2003/421; 2008/262 partially revoked. Territorial extent & classification: NI. General. - 4p.: 30 cm. - 978-0-337-98754-0 *£4.00*

The Valuation Tribunal (Amendment No. 2) Rules (Northern Ireland) 2012 No. 2012/217. - Enabling power: S.I. 1977/2157 (N.I. 28), art. 36A (3), sch. 9B, para. 7. - Issued: 29.05.2012. Made: 23.05.2012. Coming into operation: 25.06.2012. Effect: S.R. 2007/182 amended. Territorial extent & classification: NI. General. - 4p.: 30 cm. - 978-0-337-98809-7 £4.00

Rates: High hedges

The Valuation Tribunal (Amendment) Rules (Northern Ireland) 2012 No. 2012/122. - Enabling power: High Hedges Act (Northern Ireland) 2011, s. 7 (7) & S.I. 1977/2157 (N.I. 28), art. 36A (3), sch. 9B, paras 7 to 13. - Issued: 20.03.2012. Made: 12.03.2012. Coming into operation: 16.04.2012. Effect: S.R. 2007/182 amended. Territorial extent & classification: NI. General. - 8p.: 30 cm. - 978-0-337-98737-3 £5.75

Registration of clubs

The Registration of Clubs (Certificate of Registration) (Amendment) Regulations (Northern Ireland) 2012 No. 2012/26. - Enabling power: S.I. 1996/3159 (N.I. 23), art. 6 (1). - Issued: 03.02.2012. Made: 30.01.2012. Coming into operation: 01.05.2012. Effect: S.R. 1997/78 amended. Territorial extent & classification: NI. General. - 2p.: 30 cm. - 978-0-337-98658-1 £4.00

The Registration of Clubs (Irresponsible Drinks Promotions) Regulations (Northern Ireland) 2012 No. 2012/436. - Enabling power: S.I. 1996/3159 (N.I. 23), art. 31A (1) (2). - Issued: 11.12.2012. Made: 06.12.2012. Coming into operation: 01.01.2013. Effect: None. Territorial extent & classification: NI. General. - Supersedes draft SI (ISBN 9780337989483) issued 07.11.2012. - 2p.: 30 cm. - 978-0-337-98978-0 £4.00

The Registration of Clubs (Notice relating to Age) Regulations (Northern Ireland) 2012 No. 2012/27. - Enabling power: S.I. 1996/3159 (N.I. 23), art. 34 (a) (2) (3). - Issued: 03.02.2012. Made: 30.01.2012. Coming into operation: 01.05.2012. Effect: None. Territorial extent & classification: NI. General. - 4p.: 30 cm. - 978-0-337-98659-8 £4.00

Registration of vital events

General Register Office (Fees) Order (Northern Ireland) 2012 No. 2012/443. - Enabling power: S.I. 1976/1041 (N.I. 14), art. 47 (1) (2) & S.I. 2003/413 (N.I. 3), arts 3 (3) (b), 19 (1) (a), 35 (3), 36 (1) (b) (3), 37 & Civil Partnership Act 2004, s. 157 (1). - Issued: 17.12.2012. Made: 12.12.2012. Coming into operation: 17.12.2012. Effect: S.R. 2010/409 revoked. Territorial extent & classification: NI. General. - Supersedes draft SI (ISBN 9780337989353) issued 05.11.2012. - 8p.: 30 cm. - 978-0-337-98988-9 £4.00

Rehabilitation of offenders

Rehabilitation of Offenders (Exceptions) (Amendment) Order (Northern Ireland) 2012 No. 2012/318. - Enabling power: S.I. 1978/1908 (N.I. 27), arts. 5 (4), 8 (4). - Issued: 16.08.2012. Made: 13.08.2012. Coming into operation: 10.09.2012. Effect: S.R. 1979/195 amended. Territorial extent & classification: NI. General. - 4p.: 30 cm. - 978-0-337-98884-4 £4.00

Roads

The A3 Northway, Portadown (Abandonment) Order (Northern Ireland) 2012 No. 2012/296. - Enabling power: S.I. 1993/3160 (N.I. 15), art. 68 (1) (5). - Issued: 25.07.2012. Made: 23.07.2012. Coming into force: 10.10.2012. Effect: None. Territorial extent & classification: NI. Local. - Available at http://www.legislation.gov.uk/nisr/2012/296/contents/made *Non-print*

The Ballydogherty Road (U5003), Loughgilly (Abandonment) Order (Northern Ireland) 2012 No. 2012/30. - Enabling power: S.I. 1993/3160 (N.I. 15), art. 68 (1). - Issued: 08.02.2012. Made: 06.02.2012. Coming into force: 14.03.2012. Effect: None. Territorial extent & classification: NI. Local. - Available at http://www.legislation.gov.uk/nisr/2012/30/contents/made *Non-print*

The Browning Drive, Londonderry (Abandonment) Order (Northern Ireland) 2012 No. 2012/211. - Enabling power: S.I. 1993/3160 (N.I. 15), art. 68 (1) (5). - Issued: 24.05.2012. Made: 22.05.2012. Coming into force: 04.07.2012. Effect: None. Territorial extent & classification: NI. Local. - Available at http://www.legislation.gov.uk/nisr/2012/211/contents/made *Non-print*

The C156 (Unnamed road), Moyraverty, Craigavon (Abandonment) Order (Northern Ireland) 2012 No. 2012/361. - Enabling power: S.I. 1993/3160 (N.I. 15), art. 68 (1). - Issued: 26.09.2012. Made: 24.09.2012. Coming into force: 07.11.2012. Effect: None. Territorial extent & classification: NI. Local. - Available at http://www.legislation.gov.uk/nisr/2012/361/contents/made *Non-print*

The College Avenue, Belfast (Stopping-Up) Order (Northern Ireland) 2012 No. 2012/129. - Enabling power: S.I. 1993/3160 (N.I. 15), art. 68 (1) (3) (5). - Issued: 20.03.2012. Made: 16.03.2012. Coming into force: 16.05.2012. Effect: None. Territorial extent & classification: NI. Local. - Available at http://www.legislation.gov.uk/nisr/2012/129/contents/made *Non-print*

The Drumlin Road, Donaghcloney (Abandonment) Order (Northern Ireland) 2012 No. 2012/295. - Enabling power: S.I. 1993/3160 (N.I. 15), art. 68 (1) (5). - Issued: 24.07.2012. Made: 20.07.2012. Coming into force: 10.10.2012. Effect: None. Territorial extent & classification: NI. Local. - Available at http://www.legislation.gov.uk/nisr/2012/295/contents/made *Non-print*

The Durham Street and Hamill Street - Killen Street, Belfast (Stopping-Up) Order (Northern Ireland) 2012 No. 2012/196. - Enabling power: S.I. 1993/3160 (N.I. 15), art. 68 (1) (3) (5). - Issued: 18.05.2012. Made: 16.05.2012. Coming into force: 04.07.2012. Effect: None. Territorial extent & classification: NI. Local. - Available at http://www.legislation.gov.uk/nisr/2012/196/contents/made *Non-print*

The Grange Lodge, Antrim (Abandonment) Order (Northern Ireland) 2012 No. 2012/101. - Enabling power: S.I. 1993/3160 (N.I. 15), art. 68 (1) (5). - Issued: 12.03.2012. Made: 08.03.2012. Coming into force: 02.05.2012. Effect: None. Territorial extent & classification: NI. Local. - Available at http://www.legislation.gov.uk/nisr/2012/101/contents/made *Non-print*

The Greystone Road, Limavady (Abandonment) Order (Northern Ireland) 2012 No. 2012/448. - Enabling power: S.I. 1993/3160 (N.I. 15), art. 68 (1) (5). - Issued: 17.12.2012. Made: 13.12.2012. Coming into force: 13.02.2012. Effect: None. Territorial extent & classification: NI. Local. - Available at http://www.legislation.gov.uk/nisr/2012/448/contents/made *Non-print*

The Longlands Avenue, Newtownabbey (Abandonment) Order (Northern Ireland) 2012 No. 2012/210. - Enabling power: S.I. 1993/3160 (N.I. 15), art. 68 (1) (5). - Issued: 24.05.2012. Made: 22.05.2012. Coming into force: 04.07.2012. Effect: None. Territorial extent & classification: NI. Local. - Available at http://www.legislation.gov.uk/nisr/2012/210/contents/made *Non-print*

The Loopland Court, Belfast (Abandonment) Order (Northern Ireland) 2012 No. 2012/104. - Enabling power: S.I. 1993/3160 (N.I. 15), art. 68 (1) (5). - Issued: 12.03.2012. Made: 08.03.2012. Coming into force: 02.05.2012. Effect: None. Territorial extent & classification: NI. Local. - Available at http://www.legislation.gov.uk/nisr/2012/104/contents/made *Non-print*

The M2 Motorway at Whitla Street, Belfast (Abandonment) Order (Northern Ireland) 2012 No. 2012/235. - Enabling power: S.I. 1993/3160 (N.I. 15), art. 68 (1) (5). - Issued: 11.06.2012. Made: 07.06.2012. Coming into force: 12.09.2012. Effect: None. Territorial extent & classification: NI. Local. - Available at http://www.legislation.gov.uk/nisr/2012/235/contents/made, Plan *Non-print*

The M3 Motorway at Titanic Quarter Railway Station, Belfast (Abandonment) Order (Northern Ireland) 2012 No. 2012/274. - Enabling power: S.I. 1993/3160 (N.I. 15), art. 68 (1) (5). - Issued: 10.07.2012. Made: 06.07.2012. Coming into force: 30.07.2012. Effect: None. Territorial extent & classification: NI. Local. - Available at http://www.legislation.gov.uk/nisr/2012/274/contents/made, Plan *Non-print*

The Malone Beeches, Belfast (Abandonment) Order (Northern Ireland) 2012 No. 2012/60. - Enabling power: S.I. 1993/3160 (N.I. 15), art. 68 (1) (5). - Issued: 23.02.2012. Made: 21.02.2012. Coming into force: 18.04.2012. Effect: None. Territorial extent & classification: NI. Local. - Available at http://www.legislation.gov.uk/nisr/2012/60/contents/made *Non-print*

The Marine Highway, Carrickfergus (Abandonment) Order (Northern Ireland) 2012 No. 2012/209. - Enabling power: S.I. 1993/3160 (N.I. 15), art. 68 (1). - Issued: 24.05.2012. Made: 22.05.2012. Coming into force: 04.07.2012. Effect: None. Territorial extent & classification: NI. Local. - Available at http://www.legislation.gov.uk/nisr/2012/209/contents/made *Non-print*

The North Circular Road and Tarry Lane, Lurgan (Abandonment) Order (Northern Ireland) 2012 No. 2012/31. - Enabling power: S.I. 1993/3160 (N.I. 15), art. 68 (1). - Issued: 08.02.2012. Made: 06.02.2012. Coming into force: 14.03.2012. Effect: None. Territorial extent & classification: NI. Local. - Available at http://www.legislation.gov.uk/nisr/2012/31/contents/made *Non-print*

The Off-Street Parking (Amendment) Order (Northern Ireland) 2012 No. 2012/216. - Enabling power: S.I. 1997/276 (N.I. 2), art. 13 (1) (2). - Issued: 28.05.2012. Made: 24.05.2012. Coming into force: 18.06.2012. Effect: S.R. 2000/384 amended. Territorial extent & classification: NI. Local. - Available at http://www.legislation.gov.uk/nisr/2012/216/contents/made *Non-print*

The Old Church Road, Newtownabbey (Abandonment) Order (Northern Ireland) 2012 No. 2012/43. - Enabling power: S.I. 1993/3160 (N.I. 15), art. 68 (1) (5). - Issued: 15.02.2012. Made: 13.02.2012. Coming into force: 27.03.2012. Effect: None. Territorial extent & classification: NI. Local. - Available at http://www.legislation.gov.uk/nisr/2012/43/contents/made *Non-print*

The Private Accesses (A8 Belfast to Larne Dual Carriageway (Coleman's Corner to Ballyrickard Road)) Stopping-Up Order (Northern Ireland) 2012 No. 2012/174. - Enabling power: S.I. 1993/3160 (N.I. 15), art. 69 (1), sch. 5, para. 5. - Issued: 26.04.2012. Made: 24.04.2012. Coming into force: 06.06.2012. Effect: None. Territorial extent & classification: NI. Local. - Available at http://www.legislation.gov.uk/nisr/2012/174/contents/made *Non-print*

The Private Accesses at A55 Knock Road, Belfast (Stopping-Up) Order (Northern Ireland) 2012 No. 2012/340. - Enabling power: S.I. 1993/3160 (N.I.15), art. 69 (1). - Issued: 19.09.2012. Made: 17.09.2012. Coming into operation: 01.11.2012. Effect: None. Territorial extent & classification: NI. Local. - Available at http://www.legislation.gov.uk/nisr/2012/340/contents/made *Non-print*

The Private Accesses on the A5 Western Transport Corridor (Stopping-Up) Order (Northern Ireland) 2012 No. 2012/304. - Enabling power: S.I. 1993/3160 (N.I. 15), art. 69 (1). - Issued: 27.07.2012. Made: 25.07.2012. Coming into force: 09.10.2012. Effect: None. Territorial extent & classification: NI. Local. - Available at http://www.legislation.gov.uk/nisr/2012/304/contents/made *Non-print*

The Road Races (Circuit of Ireland International Rally) Order (Northern Ireland) 2012 No. 2012/128. - Enabling power: S.I. 1986/1887 (N.I. 17), art. 3. - Issued: 20.03.2012. Made: 16.03.2012. Coming into force: 04.04.2012. Effect: None. Territorial extent & classification: NI. Local. - Available at http://www.legislation.gov.uk/nisr/2012/128/contents/made *Non-print*

The Road Races (Cookstown 100) Order (Northern Ireland) 2012 No. 2012/144. - Enabling power: S.I. 1986/1887 (N.I. 17), art. 3. - Issued: 29.03.2012. Made: 27.03.2012. Coming into force: 26.04.2012. Effect: None. Territorial extent & classification: NI. Local. - Available at http://www.legislation.gov.uk/nisr/2012/144/contents/made *Non-print*

The Road Races (Croft Hill Climb) Order (Northern Ireland) 2012 No. 2012/127. - Enabling power: S.I. 1986/1887 (N.I. 17), art. 3. - Issued: 20.03.2012. Made: 16.03.2012. Coming into force: 13.04.2012. Effect: None. Territorial extent & classification: NI. Local. - Available at http://www.legislation.gov.uk/nisr/2012/127/contents/made *Non-print*

The Road Races (Spamount Hill Climb) Order (Northern Ireland) 2012 No. 2012/164. - Enabling power: S.I. 1986/1887 (N.I. 17), art. 3. - Issued: 18.04.2012. Made: 16.04.2012. Coming into force: 25.05.2012. Effect: None. Territorial extent & classification: NI. Local. - Available at http://www.legislation.gov.uk/nisr/2012/164/contents/made *Non-print*

The Road Races (Tandragee 100) Order (Northern Ireland) 2012 No. 2012/145. - Enabling power: S.I. 1986/1887 (N.I. 17), art. 3. - Issued: 29.03.2012. Made: 27.03.2012. Coming into force: 03.05.2012. Effect: None. Territorial extent & classification: NI. Local. - Available at http://www.legislation.gov.uk/nisr/2012/145/contents/made *Non-print*

The Road Races (Ulster Grand Prix Bike Week) Order (Northern Ireland) 2012 No. 2012/291. - Enabling power: S.I. 1986/1887 (N.I. 17), art. 3. - Issued: 16.07.2012. Made: 11.07.2012. Coming into force: 07.08.2012. Effect: None. Territorial extent & classification: NI. Local. - Available at http://www.legislation.gov.uk/nisr/2012/291/contents/made *Non-print*

The Route B30 Newry Road, Crossmaglen (Abandonment) Order (Northern Ireland) 2012 No. 2012/208. - Enabling power: S.I. 1993/3160 (N.I. 15), art. 68 (1) (5). - Issued: 24.05.2012. Made: 22.05.2012. Coming into force: 04.07.2012. Effect: None. Territorial extent & classification: NI. Local. - Available at http://www.legislation.gov.uk/nisr/2012/208/contents/made *Non-print*

The Route U5160, Carnbane Industrial Estate, Newry (Abandonment) Order (Northern Ireland) 2012 No. 2012/207. - Enabling power: S.I. 1993/3160 (N.I. 15), art. 68 (1) (5). - Issued: 24.05.2012. Made: 22.05.2012. Coming into force: 04.07.2012. Effect: None. Territorial extent & classification: NI. Local. - Available at http://www.legislation.gov.uk/nisr/2012/207/contents/made *Non-print*

The Shankbridge Road, Ballymena (Abandonment) Order (Northern Ireland) 2012 No. 2012/58. - Enabling power: S.I. 1993/3160 (N.I. 15), art. 68 (1) (5). - Issued: 23.02.2012. Made: 21.02.2012. Coming into force: 18.04.2012. Effect: None. Territorial extent & classification: NI. Local. - Available at http://www.legislation.gov.uk/nisr/2012/58/contents/made *Non-print*

The Shore Road and Northwood Parade, Belfast (Abandonment) Order (Northern Ireland) 2012 No. 2012/103. - Enabling power: S.I. 1993/3160 (N.I. 15), art. 68 (1) (5). - Issued: 12.03.2012. Made: 08.03.2012. Coming into force: 02.05.2012. Effect: None. Territorial extent & classification: NI. Local. - Available at http://www.legislation.gov.uk/nisr/2012/103/contents/made *Non-print*

The Templemore Street, Belfast (Abandonment) Order (Northern Ireland) 2012 No. 2012/360. - Enabling power: S.I. 1993/3160 (N.I. 15), art. 68 (1). - Issued: 26.09.2012. Made: 24.09.2012. Coming into force: 07.11.2012. Effect: None. Territorial extent & classification: NI. Local. - Available at http://www.legislation.gov.uk/nisr/2012/360/contents/made *Non-print*

The Trunk Road T3 (Western Transport Corridor) Order (Northern Ireland) 2012 No. 2012/303. - Enabling power: S.I. 1993/3160 (N.I. 15), arts 14 (1), 68 (1) (3), sch. 8, para. 5. - Issued: 27.07.2012. Made: 25.07.2012. Coming into force: 09.10.2012. Effect: None. Territorial extent & classification: NI. Local. - Available at http://www.legislation.gov.uk/nisr/2012/303/contents/made. - col. plan *Non-print*

The Trunk Road T9 (Coleman's Corner to Ballyrickard Road) Order (Northern Ireland) 2012 No. 2012/172. - Enabling power: S.I. 1993/3160 (N.I. 15), arts 14 (1), 68 (1) (3) (5), sch. 8, para. 5. - Issued: 25.04.2012. Made: 23.04.2012. Coming into force: 06.06.2012. Effect: None. Territorial extent & classification: NI. Local. - Available at http://www.legislation.gov.uk/nisr/2012/172/contents/made. - col. plan *Non-print*

The Trunk Road T14 (A55 Knock Road, Belfast) Order (Northern Ireland) 2012 No. 2012/339. - Enabling power: S.I. 1993/3160 (N.I.15), arts 14 (1), 68 (1) (3). - Issued: 19.09.2012. Made: 17.09.2012. Coming into operation: 01.11.2012. Effect: None. Territorial extent & classification: NI. Local. - Available at http://www.legislation.gov.uk/nisr/2012/339/contents/made *Non-print*

The Tullynacross Road, Lisburn (Abandonment) Order (Northern Ireland) 2012 No. 2012/359. - Enabling power: S.I. 1993/3160 (N.I. 15), art. 68 (1) (5). - Issued: 26.09.2012. Made: 24.09.2012. Coming into force: 07.11.2012. Effect: None. Territorial extent & classification: NI. Local. - Available at http://www.legislation.gov.uk/nisr/2012/359/contents/made *Non-print*

The University Terrace, Belfast (Abandonment) Order (Northern Ireland) 2012 No. 2012/57. - Enabling power: S.I. 1993/3160 (N.I. 15), art. 68 (1) (5). - Issued: 23.02.2012. Made: 21.02.2012. Coming into force: 18.04.2012. Effect: None. Territorial extent & classification: NI. Local. - Available at http://www.legislation.gov.uk/nisr/2012/57/contents/made *Non-print*

The Upper Dunmurry Lane, Dunmurry (Abandonment) Order (Northern Ireland) 2012 No. 2012/275. - Enabling power: S.I. 1993/3160 (N.I. 15), art. 68 (1) (5). - Issued: 10.07.2012. Made: 06.07.2012. Coming into force: 10.10.2012. Effect: None. Territorial extent & classification: NI. Local. - Available at http://www.legislation.gov.uk/nisr/2012/275/contents/made *Non-print*

The Westbourne Avenue, Ballymena (Abandonment) Order (Northern Ireland) 2012 No. 2012/70. - Enabling power: S.I. 1993/3160 (N.I. 15), art. 68 (1). - Issued: 29.02.2012. Made: 27.02.2012. Coming into force: 25.04.2012. Effect: None. Territorial extent & classification: NI. Local. - Available at http://www.legislation.gov.uk/nisr/2012/70/contents/made *Non-print*

Road traffic and vehicles

The Bus Lanes (Belfast City Centre) Order (Northern Ireland) 2012 No. 2012/198. - Enabling power: S.I. 1997/276 (N.I. 2), art. 4 (1) (2) (3). - Issued: 21.05.2012. Made: 17.05.2012. Coming into operation: 08.06.2012. Effect: S.R. 2002/173 amended. Territorial extent & classification: NI. Local. - Available at http://www.legislation.gov.uk/nisr/2012/198/contents/made *Non-print*

The Bus Lanes (East Bridge Street and Cromac Street, Belfast) (Amendment) Order (Northern Ireland) 2012 No. 2012/412. - Enabling power: S.I. 1997/276 (N.I. 2), art. 4 (1) (2) (3). - Issued: 21.11.2012. Made: 19.11.2012. Coming into operation: 10.12.2012. Effect: S.R. 2012/55 amended. Territorial extent & classification: NI. Local. - Available at http://www.legislation.gov.uk/nisr/2012/412/contents/made *Non-print*

The Bus Lanes (East Bridge Street and Cromac Street, Belfast) Order (Northern Ireland) 2012 No. 2012/55. - Enabling power: S.I. 1997/276 (N.I. 2), art. 4 (1) (2) (3). - Issued: 22.02.2012. Made: 20.02.2012. Coming into operation: 12.03.2012. Effect: None. Territorial extent & classification: NI. Local. - Available at http://www.legislation.gov.uk/nisr/2012/55/contents/made *Non-print*

The Control of Traffic (Apsley Street, Belfast) Order (Northern Ireland) 2012 No. 2012/411. - Enabling power: S.I. 1997/276 (NI. 2), art. 4 (1) (2) (3). - Issued: 21.11.2012. Made: 19.11.2012. Coming into operation: 10.12.2012. Effect: S.R. 2009/49 amended. Territorial extent & classification: NI. Local. - Available at http://www.legislation.gov.uk/nisr/2012/411/contents/made *Non-print*

The Control of Traffic (Belfast City Centre) Order (Northern Ireland) 2012 No. 2012/197. - Enabling power: S.I. 1997/276 (NI. 2), art. 4 (1) (2) (3). - Issued: 21.05.2012. Made: 17.05.2012. Coming into operation: 08.06.2012. Effect: S.R. 1980/114; 1995/327; 2009/49 amended. Territorial extent & classification: NI. Local. - Available at http://www.legislation.gov.uk/nisr/2012/197/contents/made *Non-print*

The Control of Traffic (Belfast) Order (Northern Ireland) 2012 No. 2012/32. - Enabling power: S.I. 1997/276 (NI. 2), art. 4 (1) (2) (3). - Issued: 08.02.2012. Made: 06.02.2012. Coming into operation: 29.02.2012. Effect: S.R. 2009/49 amended. Territorial extent & classification: NI. Local. - Available at http://www.legislation.gov.uk/nisr/2012/32/contents/made *Non-print*

The Control of Traffic (Carrickfergus) Order (Northern Ireland) 2012 No. 2012/45. - Enabling power: S.I. 1997/276 (NI. 2), art. 4 (1) (2) (3). - Issued: 16.02.2012. Made: 14.02.2012. Coming into operation: 29.02.2012. Effect: S.R. 1982/152 amended. Territorial extent & classification: NI. Local. - Available at http://www.legislation.gov.uk/nisr/2012/45/contents/made *Non-print*

The Cycle Routes (Amendment No. 2) Order (Northern Ireland) 2012 No. 2012/193. - Enabling power: Enabling power: S.I. 1997/276 (N.I. 2), art. 4 (1) (2) (3). - Issued: 18.05.2012. Made: 16.05.2012. Coming into force: 07.06.2012. Effect: S.R. 2008/317 amended. Territorial extent & classification: NI. Local. - Available at http://www.legislation.gov.uk/nisr/2012/193/contents/made *Non-print*

The Cycle Routes (Amendment No. 3) Order (Northern Ireland) 2012 No. 2012/200. - Enabling power: Enabling power: S.I. 1997/276 (N.I. 2), art. 4 (1) (2) (3). - Issued: 21.05.2012. Made: 17.05.2012. Coming into force: 08.06.2012. Effect: S.R. 2008/317 amended. Territorial extent & classification: NI. Local. - Available at http://www.legislation.gov.uk/nisr/2012/200/contents/made *Non-print*

The Cycle Routes (Amendment No. 4) Order (Northern Ireland) 2012 No. 2012/342. - Enabling power: Enabling power: S.I. 1997/276 (N.I. 2), art. 4 (1) (2) (3). - Issued: 21.09.2012. Made: 19.09.2012. Coming into force: 11.10.2012. Effect: S.R. 2008/317 amended. Territorial extent & classification: NI. Local. - Available at http://www.legislation.gov.uk/nisr/2012/342/contents/made *Non-print*

The Cycle Routes (Amendment No. 5) Order (Northern Ireland) 2012 No. 2012/353. - Enabling power: Enabling power: S.I. 1997/276 (N.I. 2), art. 4 (1) (2) (3). - Issued: 24.09.2012. Made: 20.09.2012. Coming into force: 12.10.2012. Effect: S.R. 2008/317 amended. Territorial extent & classification: NI. Local. - Available at http://www.legislation.gov.uk/nisr/2012/353/contents/made *Non-print*

The Cycle Routes (Amendment No. 6) Order (Northern Ireland) 2012 No. 2012/418. - Enabling power: Enabling power: S.I. 1997/276 (N.I. 2), art. 4 (1) (2) (3). - Issued: 26.11.2012. Made: 22.11.2012. Coming into force: 14.12.2012. Effect: S.R. 2008/317 amended. Territorial extent & classification: NI. Local. - Available at http://www.legislation.gov.uk/nisr/2012/418/contents/made *Non-print*

The Cycle Routes (Amendment) Order (Northern Ireland) 2012 No. 2012/54. - Enabling power: Enabling power: S.I. 1997/276 (NI. 2), art. 4 (1) (2) (3). - Issued: 22.02.2012. Made: 20.02.2012. Coming into force: 12.03.2012. Effect: S.R. 2008/317 amended. Territorial extent & classification: NI. Local. - Available at http://www.legislation.gov.uk/nisr/2012/54/contents/made *Non-print*

The Goods Vehicles (Enforcement Powers) Regulations (Northern Ireland) 2012 No. 2012/258. - Enabling power: Goods Vehicles (Licensing of Operators) Act (Northern Ireland) 2010, s. 44 & sch. 2. - Issued: 02.07.2012. Made: 28.06.2012. Coming into operation: 01.07.2012. Effect: None. Territorial extent & classification: NI. General. - 12p.: 30 cm. - 978-0-337-98841-7 £5.75

The Goods Vehicles (Licensing of Operators) (2010 Act) (Commencement No. 1) Order (Northern Ireland) 2012 No. 2012/247 (C. 22). - Enabling power: Goods Vehicles (Licensing of Operators) Act (Northern Ireland) 2010, s. 60 (2). Bringing into operation various provisions of this Act on 22.06.2012, in accord. with art. 2. - Issued: 28.06.2012. Made: 21.06.2012. Coming into operation: -. Effect: None. Territorial extent & classification: NI. General. - 4p.: 30 cm. - 978-0-337-98832-5 £4.00

The Goods Vehicles (Licensing of Operators) (2010 Act) (Commencement No. 2 and Transitional Provisions) Order (Northern Ireland) 2012 No. 2012/262 (C.23). - Enabling power: Goods Vehicles (Licensing of Operators) Act (Northern Ireland) 2010, s. 60 (2). Bringing into operation various provisions of this Act on 01.07.2012, in accord. with art. 2. - Issued: 03.07.2012. Made: 28.06.2012. Coming into operation: -. Effect: None. Territorial extent & classification: NI. General. - 8p.: 30 cm. - 978-0-337-98845-5 £4.00

The Goods Vehicles (Licensing of Operators) (Exemption) Regulations (Northern Ireland) 2012 No. 2012/256. - Enabling power: Goods Vehicles (Licensing of Operators) Act (Northern Ireland) 2010, s. 1 (2) (d) (3) (b). - Issued: 02.07.2012. Made: -. Coming into operation: 01.07.2012 in accord. with art. 1. Effect: None. Territorial extent & classification: NI. General. - Supersedes draft S.I. (ISBN 9780337987915) issued 10.05.2012. - 8p.: 30 cm. - 978-0-337-98839-4 £5.75

The Goods Vehicles (Licensing of Operators) (Fees) Regulations (Northern Ireland) 2012 No. 2012/260. - Enabling power: Goods Vehicles (Licensing of Operators) Act (Northern Ireland) 2010, ss. 47 (1) (4), 49 (3). - Issued: 02.07.2012. Made: 28.06.2012. Coming into operation: 01.07.2012. Effect: None. Territorial extent & classification: NI. General. - 4p.: 30 cm. - 978-0-337-98843-1 £4.00

The Goods Vehicles (Licensing of Operators) Regulations (Northern Ireland) 2012 No. 2012/261. - Enabling power: Goods Vehicles (Licensing of Operators) Act (Northern Ireland) 2010, ss. 4 (3), 7 (3) (4), 8 (1), 9 (1), 10 (2), 11 (3) (6) (7), 13 (5) (c), 16 (2), 17 (3), 18 (9) (c) (10), 20 (1) (d), 27 (1), 28 (5) (a), 31 (1), 32 (3), 34 (2) (a), 48 (2) (3) (4), 52, 53, 57, sch. 1, paras 1 (7) (b), 3 (7) (b). - Issued: 03.07.2012. Made: 28.06.2012. Coming into operation: 01.07.2012. Effect: None. Territorial extent & classification: NI. General. - 24p.: 30 cm. - 978-0-337-98844-8 £5.75

The Goods Vehicles (Qualifications of Operators) Regulations (Northern Ireland) 2012 No. 2012/257. - Enabling power: European Communities Act 1972, s. 2 (2). - Issued: 02.07.2012. Made: 28.06.2012. Coming into operation: 01.07.2012. Effect: 2010 c.2 (NI) amended. Territorial extent & classification: NI. General. - EC note: These Regulations give effect to Regulation 1071/2009 which establishes common rules concerning the conditions to be complied with to pursue the occupation of road transport operator and repeals Council Directive 96/26/EC. - 12p.: 30 cm. - 978-0-337-98840-0 £5.75

The Goods Vehicles (Testing) (Amendment) Regulations (Northern Ireland) 2012 No. 2012/149. - Enabling power: S.I. 1995/2994 (N.I. 18), arts 65 (1) (2), 110 (2). - Issued: 03.04.2012. Made: 28.03.2012. Coming into operation: 01.05.2012. Effect: S.R. 2003/304 amended. Territorial extent & classification: NI. General. - 2p.: 30 cm. - 978-0-337-98762-5 £4.00

The Goods Vehicles (Testing) (Fees) (Amendment) Regulations (Northern Ireland) 2012 No. 2012/328. - Enabling power: S.I. 1995/2994 (N.I. 18), arts 65 (1) (2), 67 (1) (h), 110 (2). - Issued: 04.09.2012. Made: 23.08.2012. Coming into operation: 01.10.2012. Effect: S.R. 2003/304 amended. Territorial extent & classification: NI. General. - 4p.: 30 cm. - 978-0-337-98895-0 £4.00

The Loading Bays and Parking Places on Roads (Amendment No. 2) Order (Northern Ireland) 2012 No. 2012/371. - Enabling power: S.I. 1997/276 (N.I. 2), arts 10 (4), 13 (1). - Issued: 02.10.2012. Made: 28.09.2012. Coming into force: 22.10.2012. Effect: S.R. 2008/308 amended. Territorial extent & classification: NI. Local. - Available at http://www.legislation.gov.uk/nisr/2012/371/contents/made *Non-print*

The Loading Bays and Parking Places on Roads (Amendment) Order (Northern Ireland) 2012 No. 2012/225. - Enabling power: S.I. 1997/276 (N.I. 2), arts 10 (4), 13 (1). - Issued: 01.06.2012. Made: 30.05.2012. Coming into operation: 20.06.2012. Effect: S.R. 2007/270; 2008/308 amended. Territorial extent & classification: NI. Local. - Available at http://www.legislation.gov.uk/nisr/2012/225/contents/made *Non-print*

The Loading Bays on Roads (Amendment No. 2) Order (Northern Ireland) 2012 No. 2012/251. - Enabling power: S.I. 1997/276 (N.I. 2), arts 10 (4), 13 (1). - Issued: 28.06.2012. Made: 26.06.2012. Coming into force: 18.07.2012. Effect: S.R. 2007/270 amended. Territorial extent & classification: NI. Local. - Available at http://www.legislation.gov.uk/nisr/2012/251/contents/made *Non-print*

The Loading Bays on Roads (Amendment No. 3) Order (Northern Ireland) 2012 No. 2012/357. - Enabling power: S.I. 1997/276 (N.I. 2), arts 10 (4), 13 (1). - Issued: 25.09.2012. Made: 21.09.2012. Coming into force: 15.10.2012. Effect: S.R. 2007/270 amended. Territorial extent & classification: NI. Local. - Available at http://www.legislation.gov.uk/nisr/2012/357/contents/made *Non-print*

The Loading Bays on Roads (Amendment No. 4) Order (Northern Ireland) 2012 No. 2012/363. - Enabling power: S.I. 1997/276 (N.I. 2), arts 10 (4), 13 (1). - Issued: 27.09.2012. Made: 25.09.2012. Coming into force: 17.10.2012. Effect: S.R. 2007/270 amended. Territorial extent & classification: NI. Local. - Available at http://www.legislation.gov.uk/nisr/2012/363/contents/made *Non-print*

The Loading Bays on Roads (Amendment No. 5) Order (Northern Ireland) 2012 No. 2012/432. - Enabling power: S.I. 1997/276 (N.I. 2), arts 10 (4), 13 (1). - Issued: 10.12.2012. Made: 06.12.2012. Coming into force: 28.12.2012. Effect: S.R. 2007/270 amended. Territorial extent & classification: NI. Local. - Available at http://www.legislation.gov.uk/nisr/2012/432/contents/made *Non-print*

The Loading Bays on Roads (Amendment) Order (Northern Ireland) 2012 No. 2012/75. - Enabling power: S.I. 1997/276 (N.I. 2), arts 10 (4), 13 (1). - Issued: 02.03.2012. Made: 29.02.2012. Coming into force: 21.03.2012. Effect: S.R. 2007/270 amended. Territorial extent & classification: NI. Local. - Available at http://www.legislation.gov.uk/nisr/2012/75/contents/made *Non-print*

The Motor Vehicles (Construction and Use) (Amendment) Regulations (Northern Ireland) 2012 No. 2012/150. - Enabling power: S.I. 1995/2994 (N.I. 18), arts 55 (1) (2), 110 (2). - Issued: 03.04.2012. Made: 28.03.2012. Coming into operation: 01.05.2012. Effect: S.R. 1999/454 amended. Territorial extent & classification: NI. General. - 2p.: 30 cm. - 978-0-337-98763-2 £4.00

The Motor Vehicles (Driving Licences) (Amendment No. 2) Regulations (Northern Ireland) 2012 No. 2012/355. - Enabling power: S.I. 1981/154 (N.I. 1), arts 9 (2) (4) (b), 218 (1). - Issued: 02.10.2012. Made: 20.09.2012. Coming into operation: 29.10.2012. Effect: S.R. 1996/542 amended & S.R. 1999/358 partially revoked & S.R. 1998/415; 2001/267 revoked. Territorial extent & classification: NI. General. - EC note: These Regulations implement the minimum standards of medical fitness required for diabetes milletus as specified in Directive 2009/112/EC and 2009/113/EC. - 4p: 30 cm. - 978-0-337-98912-4 £4.00

The Motor Vehicles (Driving Licences) (Amendment No. 3) Regulations (Northern Ireland) 2012 No. 2012/451. - Enabling power: European Communities Act 1972, s. 2 (2) & S.I. 1981/154 (NI 1), arts 5 (3), 13 (3A) (3B), 218 (1). - Issued: 18.12.2012. Made: 13.12.2012. Coming into operation: 19.01.2013. Effect: S.I. 1981/154 (NI 1) & S.R. 1996/542 amended. Territorial extent & classification: NI. General. - EC note: These Regulations accommodate the requirements of Directive 2006/126/EC on driving licences. - 8p.: 30 cm. - 978-0-337-98994-0 £5.75

The Motor Vehicles (Driving Licences) (Amendment) Regulations (Northern Ireland) 2012 No. 2012/170. - Enabling power: European Communities Act 1972, s. 2 (2) & S.I. 1981/154 (N.I. 1), arts 5 (3) (4), 13 (3), 14 (4), 19C (1A) (2), 218 (1). - Issued: 30.04.2012. Made: 19.04.2012. Coming into operation: In accord. with reg. 1 (1) to (3). Effect: S.I. 1981/154 (N.I. 1); S.R. 1996/542 amended. Territorial extent & classification: NI. General. - EC note: Implements Directive 2006/126/EC and part of Annex II to 91/439/EEC. - 28p: 30 cm. - 978-0-337-98781-6 £5.75

The Motor Vehicles (Driving Licences) (Fees) (Amendment) Regulations (Northern Ireland) 2012 No. 2012/354. - Enabling power: S.I. 1981/154 (N.I. 1), arts 13 (1), 19C (1), 218 (1). - Issued: 25.09.2012. Made: 20.09.2012. Coming into operation: 15.10.2012. Effect: S.R. 1996/542 amended & S.R. 2009/344 revoked. Territorial extent & classification: NI. General. - 8p.: 30 cm. - 978-0-337-98911-7 £4.00

The Motor Vehicles (Taxi Drivers' Licences) (Amendment) Regulations (Northern Ireland) 2012 No. 2012/7. - Enabling power: S.I. 1981/154 (N.I. 1), arts 79A (3), 218 (1). - Issued: 17.01.2012. Made: 12.01.2012. Coming into operation: 30.04.2012. Effect: S.R. 1991/454 amended & S.R. 1994/363 revoked. Territorial extent & classification: NI. General. - 4p.: 30 cm. - 978-0-337-98637-6 £4.00

The Motor Vehicle Testing (Amendment) Regulations (Northern Ireland) 2012 No. 2012/148. - Enabling power: S.I. 1995/2994 (N.I. 18), arts. 61 (2) (6), 110 (2). - Issued: 05.04.2012. Made: 28.03.2012. Coming into operation: 01.05.2012. Effect: S.R. 2003/303 amended. Territorial extent & classification: NI. General. - 2p.: 30 cm. - 978-0-337-98761-8 £4.00

The Off-Street Parking (Amendment No. 2) Order (Northern Ireland) 2012 No. 2012/253. - Enabling power: S.I. 1997/276 (N.I. 2), art. 13 (14) (15). - Issued: 28.06.2012. Made: 26.06.2012. Coming into force: 18.07.2012. Effect: S.R. 2000/384 amended. Territorial extent & classification: NI. Local. - Available at http://www.legislation.gov.uk/nisr/2012/253/contents/made *Non-print*

The Off-Street Parking (Amendment No. 3) Order (Northern Ireland) 2012 No. 2012/289. - Enabling power: S.I. 1997/276 (N.I. 2), arts 11 (1) (b), 13 (1). - Issued: 16.07.2012. Made: 11.07.2012. Coming into force: 01.08.2012. Effect: S.R. 2000/384 amended. Territorial extent & classification: NI. Local. - Available at http://www.legislation.gov.uk/nisr/2012/289/contents/made *Non-print*

The Off-Street Parking (Amendment No. 4) Order (Northern Ireland) 2012 No. 2012/333. - Enabling power: S.I. 1997/276 (N.I. 2), art. 13 (1) (2). - Issued: 12.09.2012. Made: 10.09.2012. Coming into force: 12.10.2012. Effect: S.R. 2000/384 amended. Territorial extent & classification: NI. Local. - Available at http://www.legislation.gov.uk/nisr/2012/333/contents/made *Non-print*

The Off-Street Parking (Amendment No. 5) Order (Northern Ireland) 2012 No. 2012/382. - Enabling power: S.I. 1997/276 (N.I. 2), art. 13 (1). - Issued: 11.01.2013. Made: 19.10.2012. Coming into force: 09.11.2012. Effect: S.R. 2000/384 amended. Territorial extent & classification: NI. Local. - Available at http://www.legislation.gov.uk/nisr/2012/382/contents/made *Non-print*

The Off-Street Parking (Amendment No. 6) Order (Northern Ireland) 2012 No. 2012/409. - Enabling power: S.I. 1997/276 (N.I. 2), art. 13 (1) (2). - Issued: 21.11.2012. Made: 19.11.2012. Coming into force: 10.12.2012. Effect: S.R. 2000/384 amended. Territorial extent & classification: NI. Local. - Available at http://www.legislation.gov.uk/nisr/2012/409/contents/made *Non-print*

The On-Street Parking (Amendment No. 2) Order (Northern Ireland) 2012 No. 2012/327. - Enabling power: S.I. 1997/276 (N.I. 2), arts 15 (1), 16 (1). - Issued: 28.08.2012. Made: 22.08.2012. Coming into operation: 26.09.2012. Effect: S.R. 2000/383 amended. Territorial extent & classification: NI. Local. - Available at http://www.legislation.gov.uk/nisr/2012/327/contents/made *Non-print*

The On-Street Parking (Amendment No. 3) Order (Northern Ireland) 2012 No. 2012/348. - Enabling power: S.I. 1997/276 (N.I. 2), art. 15 (1) (4). - Issued: 21.09.2012. Made: 19.09.2012. Coming into operation: 11.10.2012. Effect: S.R. 2000/383 amended. Territorial extent & classification: NI. Local. - Available at http://www.legislation.gov.uk/nisr/2012/348/contents/made *Non-print*

The On-Street Parking (Amendment) Order (Northern Ireland) 2012 No. 2012/288. - Enabling power: S.I. 1997/276 (NI. 2), art. 15 (1) (4). - Issued: 16.07.2012. Made: 11.07.2012. Coming into operation: 01.08.2012. Effect: S.R. 2000/383 amended. Territorial extent & classification: NI. Local. - Available at http://www.legislation.gov.uk/nisr/2012/288/contents/made *Non-print*

The Parking and Waiting Restrictions (Ballymena) (Amendment No. 2) Order (Northern Ireland) 2012 No. 2012/461. - Enabling power: S.I. 1997/276 (N.I. 2), arts 4 (1) (2) (3), 10 (4), 13 (1). - Issued: 24.12.2012. Made: 20.12.2012. Coming into force: 10.01.2013. Effect: S.R. 2009/54 amended. Territorial extent & classification: NI. Local. - Available at http://www.legislation.gov.uk/nisr/2012/461/contents/made *Non-print*

The Parking and Waiting Restrictions (Ballymena) (Amendment) Order (Northern Ireland) 2012 No. 2012/447. - Enabling power: S.I. 1997/276 (N.I. 2), arts 4 (1) (2) (3), 10 (4), 13 (1). - Issued: 17.12.2012. Made: 13.12.2012. Coming into force: 03.01.2013. Effect: S.R. 2009/54 amended. Territorial extent & classification: NI. Local. - Available at http://www.legislation.gov.uk/nisr/2012/447/contents/made *Non-print*

The Parking and Waiting Restrictions (Ballymoney) (Amendment) Order (Northern Ireland) 2012 No. 2012/4. - Enabling power: S.I. 1997/276 (NI. 2), art. 4 (1) (2) (3)- Issued: 16.01.2012. Made: 12.01.2012. Coming into force: 06.02.2012. Effect: S.R. 2008/5 amended. Territorial extent & classification: NI. Local. - Available at http://www.legislation.gov.uk/nisr/2012/4/contents/made *Non-print*

The Parking and Waiting Restrictions (Belfast) (Amendment No. 2) Order (Northern Ireland) 2012 No. 2012/317. - Enabling power: S.I. 1997/276 (N.I. 2), arts 4 (1) (2) (3), 10 (4), 13 (1), sch. 1, para. 5, sch. 4, para. 5. - Issued: 14.08.2012. Made: 10.08.2012. Coming into force: 23.08.2012. Effect: S.R. 2008/180 amended. Territorial extent & classification: NI. Local. - Available at http://www.legislation.gov.uk/nisr/2012/317/contents/made *Non-print*

The Parking and Waiting Restrictions (Belfast) (Amendment) Order (Northern Ireland) 2012 No. 2012/5. - Enabling power: S.I. 1997/276 (N.I. 2), arts 4 (1) (2) (3), sch. 1, para. 5. - Issued: 16.01.2012. Made: 12.01.2012. Coming into force: 06.02.2012. Effect: S.R. 2008/180 amended. Territorial extent & classification: NI. Local. - Available at http://www.legislation.gov.uk/nisr/2012/5/contents/made *Non-print*

The Parking and Waiting Restrictions (Newtownards) Order (Northern Ireland) 2012 No. 2012/356. - Enabling power: S.I. 1997/276 (N.I. 2), arts 4 (1) (2) (3), 10 (4), 13 (1) (13) (16), sch. 1 & 4, para .5. - Issued: 25.09.2012. Made: 21.09.2012 Coming into force: 15.10.2012. Effect: None. Territorial extent & classification: NI. Local. - Available at http://www.legislation.gov.uk/nisr/2012/356/contents/made *Non-print*

The Parking and Waiting Restrictions (Omagh) (No. 2) Order (Amendment) Order (Northern Ireland) 2012 No. 2012/29. - Enabling power: S.I. 1997/276 (N.I. 2), arts 4 (1) (2) (3). - Issued: 08.02.2012. Made: 06.02.2012. Coming into force: 29.02.2012. Effect: S.R. 2010/393 amended. Territorial extent & classification: NI. Local. - Available at http://www.legislation.gov.uk/nisr/2012/29/contents/made *Non-print*

The Parking and Waiting Restrictions (Rathfriland) Order (Northern Ireland) 2012 No. 2012/143. - Enabling power: S.I. 1997/276 (N.I. 2), arts 4 (1) (2) (3), 10 (4), 13 (1) (13) (16). - Issued: 29.03.2012. Made: 27.03.2012 Coming into force: 19.04.2012. Effect: S.R. 2008/334 revoked. Territorial extent & classification: NI. Local. - Available at http://www.legislation.gov.uk/nisr/2012/143/contents/made *Non-print.*

The Parking and Waiting Restrictions (Strabane) (Amendment No. 2) Order (Northern Ireland) 2012 No. 2012/224. - Enabling power: S.I. 1997/276 (N.I. 2), arts 4 (1) (2) (3), 10 (4), 13 (1). - Issued: 01.06.2012. Made: 30.05.2012 Coming into force: 20.06.2012. Effect: S.R. 2011/400 amended. Territorial extent & classification: NI. Local. - Available at http://www.legislation.gov.uk/nisr/2012/224/contents/made *Non-print*

The Parking and Waiting Restrictions (Strabane) (Amendment) Order (Northern Ireland) 2012 No. 2012/102. - Enabling power: S.I. 1997/276 (N.I. 2), arts 10 (4), 13 (1). - Issued: 12.03.2012. Made: 08.03.2012. Coming into force: 30.03.2012. Effect: S.R. 2011/400 amended. Territorial extent & classification: NI. Local. - Available at http://www.legislation.gov.uk/nisr/2012/102/contents/made *Non-print*

The Parking Places and Loading Bays on Roads (Londonderry) (Amendment No. 2) Order (Northern Ireland) 2012 No. 2012/346. - Enabling power: S.I. 1997/276 (N.I. 2), arts 10 (4), 13 (1). - Issued: 21.09.2012. Made: 19.09.2012. Coming into operation: 11.10.2012. Effect: S.R. 2008/10 amended. Territorial extent & classification: NI. Local. - Available at http://www.legislation.gov.uk/nisr/2012/346/contents/made *Non-print*

The Parking Places and Loading Bays on Roads (Londonderry) (Amendment) Order (Northern Ireland) 2012 No. 2012/80. - Enabling power: S.I. 1997/276 (N.I. 2), arts 10 (4), 13 (1). - Issued: 05.03.2012. Made: 01.03.2012. Coming into operation: 22.03.2012. Effect: S.R. 2008/10 amended. Territorial extent & classification: NI. Local. - Available at http://www.legislation.gov.uk/nisr/2012/80/contents/made *Non-print*

The Parking Places (Disabled Persons' Vehicles) (Amendment No. 2) Order (Northern Ireland) 2012 No. 2012/56. - Enabling power: S.I. 1997/276 (NI. 2), arts 10 (4), 13 (1) (16). - Made: 22.02.2012. Coming into operation: 20.02.2012. Effect: S.R. 2006/201, 327 amended. Territorial extent & classification: NI. Local. - Available at http://www.legislation.gov.uk/nisr/2012/56/contents/made *Non-print*

The Parking Places (Disabled Persons' Vehicles) (Amendment No. 3) Order (Northern Ireland) 2012 No. 2012/194. - Enabling power: S.I. 1997/276 (N.I. 2), arts 10 (4), 13 (1) (16), sch. 4, para. 5. - Issued: 18.05.2012 Made: 16.05.2012. Coming into operation: 07.06.2012. Effect: S.R. 2006/201, 327 amended. Territorial extent & classification: NI. Local. - Available at http://www.legislation.gov.uk/nisr/2012/194/contents/made *Non-print*

The Parking Places (Disabled Persons' Vehicles) (Amendment No. 4) Order (Northern Ireland) 2012 No. 2012/227. - Enabling power: S.I. 1997/276 (N.I. 2), arts 10 (4), 13 (1) (16), sch. 4, para. 5. - Issued: 06.06.2012. Made: 31.05.2012. Coming into operation: 21.06.2012. Effect: S.R. 2006/201, 327 amended. Territorial extent & classification: NI. Local. - Available at http://www.legislation.gov.uk/nisr/2012/227/contents/made *Non-print*

The Parking Places (Disabled Persons' Vehicles) (Amendment No. 5) Order (Northern Ireland) 2012 No. 2012/347. - Enabling power: S.I. 1997/276 (N.I. 2), arts 10 (4), 13 (1) (16), sch. 4, para. 5. - Issued: 21.09.2012. Made: 19.09.2012. Coming into operation: 11.10.2012. Effect: S.R. 2006/201, 327 amended. Territorial extent & classification: NI. Local. - Available at http://www.legislation.gov.uk/nisr/2012/347/contents/made *Non-print*

The Parking Places (Disabled Persons' Vehicles) (Amendment No. 6) Order (Northern Ireland) 2012 No. 2012/370. - Enabling power: S.I. 1997/276 (N.I. 2), arts 10 (4), 13 (1) (16). - Issued: 02.10.2012. Made: 28.09.2012. Coming into force: 22.10.2012. Effect: S.R. 2006/201, 327 amended. Territorial extent & classification: NI. Local. - Available at http://www.legislation.gov.uk/nisr/2012/370/contents/made *Non-print*

The Parking Places (Disabled Persons' Vehicles) (Amendment) Order (Northern Ireland) 2012 No. 2012/6. - Enabling power: S.I. 1997/276 (NI. 2), arts 10 (4), 13 (1) (16). - Made: 16.01.2012. Coming into operation: 06.02.2012. Effect: S.R. 2006/201, 327 amended. Territorial extent & classification: NI. Local. - Available at http://www.legislation.gov.uk/nisr/2012/6/contents/made *Non-print*

The Parking Places, Loading Bay and Waiting Restrictions (Randalstown) Order (Northern Ireland) 2012 No. 2012/433. - Enabling power: S.I. 1997/276 (N.I. 2), arts 4 (1) (2) (3), 10 (4), 13 (1) (13) (16). - Issued: 10.12.2012. Made: 06.12.2012. Coming into operation: 28.12.2012. Effect: S.R. 2009/420 revoked. Territorial extent & classification: NI. Local. - Available at http://www.legislation.gov.uk/nisr/2012/433/contents/made *Non-print*

The Parking Places on Roads (Armagh) (Amendment) Order (Northern Ireland) 2012 No. 2012/276. - Enabling power: S.I. 1997/276 (N.I. 2), arts 10 (4), 13 (1). - Issued: 10.07.2012. Made: 06.07.2012. Coming into operation: 30.07.2012. Effect: S.R. 2009/293 amended. Territorial extent & classification: NI. Local. - Available at http://www.legislation.gov.uk/nisr/2012/276/contents/made *Non-print*

The Parking Places on Roads (Belfast City Centre) Order (Northern Ireland) 2012 No. 2012/202. - Enabling power: S.I. 1997/276 (N.I. 2), arts 10 (4), 13 (1) (9) (10) (12) (13) (16), 15 (1), sch. 4, para. 5. - Issued: 21.05.2012. Made: 17.05.2012. Coming into operation: 08.06.2012. Effect: S.R. 2000/383; 2006/201, 327; 2007/270; 2011/132 amended. Territorial extent & classification: NI. Local. - Available at http://www.legislation.gov.uk/nisr/2012/202/contents/made *Non-print*

The Parking Places on Roads (Belfast) Order (Northern Ireland) 2012 No. 2012/404. - Enabling power: S.I. 1997/276 (N.I. 2), arts 10 (4), 13 (1) (13) (16). - Issued: 15.11.2012. Made: 13.11.2012. Coming into operation: 05.12.2012. Effect: None. Territorial extent & classification: NI. Local. - Available at http://www.legislation.gov.uk/nisr/2012/404/contents/made *Non-print*

The Parking Places on Roads (Coaches) Order (Northern Ireland) 2012 No. 2012/201. - Enabling power: S.I. 1997/276 (N.I. 2), arts 10 (4), 13 (1) (13) (16), sch. 4, para. 5. - Issued: 21.05.2012. Made: 17.05.2012. Coming into operation: 08.06.2012. Effect: S.R. 1997/510; 2005/237; 2006/490; 2009/44; 2010 /239 revoked. Territorial extent & classification: NI. Local. - Available at http://www.legislation.gov.uk/nisr/2012/201/contents/made *Non-print*

The Parking Places on Roads (Donaghmore) Order (Northern Ireland) 2012 No. 2012/434. - Enabling power: S.I. 1997/276 (N.I. 2), arts 10 (4), 13 (1) (13) (16). - Issued: 10.12.2012. Made: 06.12.2012. Coming into operation: 28.12.2012. Effect: None. Territorial extent & classification: NI. Local. - Available at http://www.legislation.gov.uk/nisr/2012/434/contents/made *Non-print*

The Parking Places on Roads (Electric Vehicles) Order (Northern Ireland) 2012 No. 2012/290. - Enabling power: S.I. 1997/276 (N.I. 2), arts 10 (4), 13 (1) (13) (16). - Issued: 16.07.2012. Made: 11.07.2012. Coming into operation: 01.08.2012. Effect: None. Territorial extent & classification: NI. Local. - Available at http://www.legislation.gov.uk/nisr/2012/290/contents/made *Non-print*

The Parking Places on Roads (Kilkeel) (No. 2) Order (Northern Ireland) 2012 No. 2012/358. - Enabling power: S.I. 1997/276 (N.I. 2), arts 10 (4), 13 (1) (13) (16). - Issued: 25.09.2012. Made: 21.09.2012. Coming into operation: 15.10.2012. Effect: S.R. 2012/69 revoked. Territorial extent & classification: NI. Local. - Available at http://www.legislation.gov.uk/nisr/2012/358/contents/made *Non-print*

The Parking Places on Roads (Kilkeel) Order (Northern Ireland) 2012 No. 2012/69. - Enabling power: S.I. 1997/276 (N.I. 2), arts 10 (4), 13 (1) (13) (16). - Issued: 29.02.2012. Made: 27.02.2012. Coming into operation: 20.03.2012. Effect: None. Territorial extent & classification: NI. Local. - Available at http://www.legislation.gov.uk/nisr/2012/69/contents/made. Revoked by S.R. 2012/358 (Non-print) *Non-print*

The Parking Places on Roads (Larne) (Amendment) Order (Northern Ireland) 2012 No. 2012/222. - Enabling power: S.I. 1997/276 (N.I. 2), arts 10 (4), 13 (1). - Issued: 31.05.2012. Made: 29.05.2012. Coming into operation: 19.06.2012. Effect: S.R. 2011/202 amended. Territorial extent & classification: NI. Local. - Available at http://www.legislation.gov.uk/nisr/2012/222/contents/made *Non-print*

The Parking Places on Roads (Toome) Order (Northern Ireland) 2012 No. 2012/223. - Enabling power: S.I. 1997/276 (N.I. 2), arts 10 (4), 13 (1) (13) (16). - Issued: 01.06.2012. Made: 30.05.2012. Coming into operation: 20.06.2012. Effect: None. Territorial extent & classification: NI. Local. - Available at http://www.legislation.gov.uk/nisr/2012/223/contents/made *Non-print*

The Penalty Charges (Prescribed Amounts) (Amendment) Regulations (Northern Ireland) 2012 No. 2012/203. - Enabling power: S.I. 2005/1964 (N.I. 14), art. 4 (4). - Issued: 22.05.2012. Made: 17.05.2012. Coming into operation: 04.07.2012. Effect: S.R. 2006/338 amended. Territorial extent & classification: NI. General. - 2p.: 30 cm. - 978-0-337-98804-2 £4.00

The Prohibition of Right-Hand Turn (Enniskillen) Order (Northern Ireland) 2012 No. 2012/277. - Enabling power: S.I. 1997/276 (N.I. 2), art. 4 (1) (2) (3). - Issued: 10.07.2012. Made: 06.07.2012. Coming into operation: 30.07.2012. Effect: None. Territorial extent & classification: NI. Local. - Available at http://www.legislation.gov.uk/nisr/2012/277/contents/made *Non-print*

The Prohibition of Traffic (Lenadoon, Belfast) Order (Northern Ireland) 2012 No. 2012/63. - Enabling power: S.I. 1997/276 (N.I. 2), art. 4 (1) (2). - Issued: 24.02.2012. Made: 22.02.2012. Coming into force: 14.03.2012. Effect: None. Territorial extent & classification: NI. Local. - Available at http://www.legislation.gov.uk/nisr/2012/63/contents/made *Non-print*

The Prohibition of Traffic (Lower Windsor, Belfast) Order (Northern Ireland) 2012 No. 2012/76. - Enabling power: S.I. 1997/276 (N.I. 2), art. 4 (1) (2). - Issued: 02.03.2012. Made: 29.02.2012. Coming into operation: 21.03.2012. Effect: None. Territorial extent & classification: NI. Local. - Available at http://www.legislation.gov.uk/nisr/2012/76/contents/made *Non-print*

The Prohibition of Traffic (Rosemount Gardens, Londonderry) Order (Northern Ireland) 2012 No. 2012/326. - Enabling power: S.I. 1997/276 (N.I. 2), art. 4 (1) (2) (4A). - Issued: 28.08.2012. Made: 22.08.2012. Coming into operation: 12.09.2012. Effect: None. Territorial extent & classification: NI. Local. - Available at http://www.legislation.gov.uk/nisr/2012/326/contents/made *Non-print*

The Prohibition of Waiting (Amendment) Order (Northern Ireland) 2012 No. 2012/364. - Enabling power: S.I. 1997/276 (N.I. 2), art. 4 (1) (2) (3). - Issued: 27.09.2012. Made: 25.09.2012. Coming into force: 17.10.2012. Effect: S.R. 2001/59 amended. Territorial extent & classification: NI. Local. - Available at http://www.legislation.gov.uk/nisr/2012/364/contents/made *Non-print*

The Road Races (Armoy Motorcycle Race) Order (Northern Ireland) 2012 No. 2012/242. - Enabling power: S.I. 1986/1887 (N.I. 17), art. 3. - Issued: 25.06.2012. Made: 19.06.2012. Coming into force: 26.07.2012. Effect: None. Territorial extent & classification: NI. Local. - Available at http://www.legislation.gov.uk/nisr/2012/242/contents/made *Non-print*

The Road Races (Bush, Dungannon) Order (Northern Ireland) 2012 No. 2012/206. - Enabling power: S.I. 1986/1887 (N.I. 17), art. 3. - Issued: 23.05.2012. Made: 21.05.2012. Coming into force: 21.06.2012. Effect: None. Territorial extent & classification: NI. Local. - Available at http://www.legislation.gov.uk/nisr/2012/206/contents/made *Non-print*

The Road Races (Cairncastle Hill Climb) Order (Northern Ireland) 2012 No. 2012/205. - Enabling power: S.I. 1986/1887 (N.I. 17), art. 3. - Issued: 23.05.2012. Made: 21.05.2012. Coming into force: 21.06.2012. Effect: None. Territorial extent & classification: NI. Local. - Available at http://www.legislation.gov.uk/nisr/2012/205/contents/made *Non-print*

The Road Races (Craigantlet Hill Climb) Order (Northern Ireland) 2012 No. 2012/278. - Enabling power: S.I. 1986/1887 (N.I. 17), art. 3. - Issued: 10.07.2012. Made: 06.07.2012. Coming into force: 03.08.2012. Effect: None. Territorial extent & classification: NI. Local. - Available at http://www.legislation.gov.uk/nisr/2012/278/contents/made *Non-print*

The Road Races (Down Special Stages Rally) Order (Northern Ireland) 2012 No. 2012/228. - Enabling power: S.I. 1986/1887 (N.I. 17), art. 3. - Issued: 06.06.2012. Made: 31.05.2012. Coming into force: 06.07.2012. Effect: None. Territorial extent & classification: NI. Local. - Available at http://www.legislation.gov.uk/nisr/2012/228/contents/made *Non-print*

The Road Races (Drumhorc Hill Climb) Order (Northern Ireland) 2012 No. 2012/171. - Enabling power: S.I. 1986/1887 (N.I. 17), art. 3. - Issued: 24.04.2012. Made: 20.04.2012. Coming into force: 11.05.2012. Effect: None. Territorial extent & classification: NI. Local. - Available at http://www.legislation.gov.uk/nisr/2012/171/contents/made *Non-print*

The Road Races (Eagles Rock Hill Climb) Order (Northern Ireland) 2012 No. 2012/269. - Enabling power: S.I. 1986/1887 (N.I. 17), art. 3. - Issued: 04.07.2012. Made: 02.07.2012. Coming into force: 20.07.2012. Effect: None. Territorial extent & classification: NI. Local. - Available at http://www.legislation.gov.uk/nisr/2012/269/contents/made *Non-print*

The Road Races (Garron Point Hill Climb) Order (Northern Ireland) 2012 No. 2012/281. - Enabling power: S.I. 1986/1887 (N.I. 17), art. 3. - Issued: 11.07.2012. Made: 09.07.2012. Coming into force: 10.08.2012. Effect: None. Territorial extent & classification: NI. Local. - Available at http://www.legislation.gov.uk/nisr/2012/281/contents/made *Non-print*

The Road Races (Mid-Antrim 150) Order (Northern Ireland) 2012 No. 2012/204. - Enabling power: S.I. 1986/1887 (N.I. 17), art. 3. - Issued: 23.05.2012. Made: 21.05.2012. Coming into force: 14.06.2012. Effect: None. Territorial extent & classification: NI. Local. - Available at http://www.legislation.gov.uk/nisr/2012/204/contents/made *Non-print*

The Road Races (North West 200) Order (Northern Ireland) 2012 No. 2012/175. - Enabling power: S.I. 1986/1887 (N.I. 17), art. 3. - Issued: 26.04.2012. Made: 24.04.2012. Coming into force: 14.05.2012. Effect: None. Territorial extent & classification: NI. Local. - Available at http://www.legislation.gov.uk/nisr/2012/175/contents/made *Non-print*

The Road Races (Spelga Hill Climb) Order (Northern Ireland) 2012 No. 2012/282. - Enabling power: S.I. 1986/1887 (N.I. 17), art. 3. - Issued: 11.07.2012. Made: 09.07.2012. Coming into force: 24.08.2012. Effect: None. Territorial extent & classification: NI. Local. - Available at http://www.legislation.gov.uk/nisr/2012/282/contents/made *Non-print*

The Road Races (Ulster Rally) Order (Northern Ireland) 2012 No. 2012/300. - Enabling power: S.I. 1986/1887 (N.I. 17), art. 3. - Issued: 26.07.2012. Made: 24.07.2012. Coming into force: 16.08.2012. Effect: None. Territorial extent & classification: NI. Local. - Available at http://www.legislation.gov.uk/nisr/2012/300/contents/made *Non-print*

The Roads (Speed Limit) (No. 2) Order (Northern Ireland) 2012 No. 2012/221. - Enabling power: S.I. 1997/276 (NI. 2), arts 37 (3) (4), 38 (1) (a), sch. 5, para. 5. - Issued: 31.05.2012. Made: 29.05.2012. Coming into force: 19.06.2012. Effect: S.R. 1981/207, 208; 1991/315; 1997/263, 285 partially revoked. Territorial extent & classification: NI. Local. - Available at http://www.legislation.gov.uk/nisr/2012/221/contents/made *Non-print*

The Roads (Speed Limit) (No. 3) Order (Northern Ireland) 2012 No. 2012/345. - Enabling power: S.I. 1997/276 (N.I. 2), arts 37 (3) (4), 38 (1) (a). - Issued: 21.09.2012. Made: 19.09.2012. Coming into force: 11.10.2012. Effect: S.R. 1977/40; 1984/126; 1990/165; 1995/432; 1996/2; 1997/263, 348; 1998/87 partially revoked. Territorial extent & classification: NI. Local. - Available at http://www.legislation.gov.uk/nisr/2012/345/contents/made *Non-print*

The Roads (Speed Limit) (No. 4) Order (Northern Ireland) 2012 No. 2012/410. - Enabling power: S.I. 1997/276 (N.I. 2), art 38 (1) (a). - Issued: 21.11.2012. Made: 19.11.2012. Coming into force: 10.12.2012. Effect: S.R. 1987/164; 1992/498; 1997/263 partially revoked. Territorial extent & classification: NI. Local. - Available at http://www.legislation.gov.uk/nisr/2012/410/contents/made *Non-print*

The Roads (Speed Limit) Order (Northern Ireland) 2012 No. 2012/166. - Enabling power: S.I. 1997/276 (NI. 2), arts 37 (3) (4), 38 (1) (a). - Issued: 18.04.2012. Made: 16.04.2012. Coming into force: 08.05.2012. Effect: S.R. & O. (NI) 1966/160; 1967/59; S.R. 1976/182; 1980/205; 1984/126, 127; 1987/164; 1990/165, 166; 1991/76; 1992/320; 1997/263, 285, 348; 2003/327; 2004/210; 2009/285 partially revoked. Territorial extent & classification: NI. Local. - Available at http://www.legislation.gov.uk/nisr/2012/166/contents/made *Non-print*

The Road Traffic (2007 Order) (Commencement No. 5) (Amendment) Order (Northern Ireland) 2012 No. 2012/337. - Enabling power: S.I. 2007/916 (N.I. 10), art. 1 (3). - Issued: 20.09.2012. Made: 13.09.2012. Coming into operation: 13.09.2012. Effect: S.R. 2010 No. 226 (C. 13) amended. Territorial extent & classification: NI. General. - 2p.: 30 cm. - 978-0-337-98907-0 *£4.00*

The Road Traffic (2007 Order) (Commencement No. 9) Order (Northern Ireland) 2012 No. 2012/16 (C.3). - Enabling power: S.I. 2007/916 (N.I. 10), art. 1 (3). Bringing into operation various provisions of the 2007 Order on 23.04.2012. - Issued: 31.01.2012. Made: 26.01.2012. Coming into operation: -. Effect: None. Territorial extent & classification: NI. General. - 8p.: 30 cm. - 978-0-337-98648-2 *£4.00*

The Road Traffic (Financial Penalty Deposit) (Appropriate Amount) Order (Northern Ireland) 2012 No. 2012/18. - Enabling power: S.I. 1996/1320 (N.I. 10), art. 91C (2). - Issued: 03.02.2012. Made: 26.01.2012. Coming into operation: 23.04.2012. Effect: None. Territorial extent & classification: NI. General. - 20p.: 30 cm. - 978-0-337-98650-5 *£5.75*

The Road Traffic (Financial Penalty Deposit) (Interest) Order (Northern Ireland) 2012 No. 2012/74. - Enabling power: S.I. 1996/1320 (N.I. 10), art. 91D (10). - Issued: 02.03.2012. Made: 28.02.2012. Coming into operation: 23.04.2012. Effect: None. Territorial extent & classification: NI. General. - 2p.: 30 cm. - 978-0-337-98693-2 *£4.00*

The Road Traffic (Financial Penalty Deposit) Order (Northern Ireland) 2012 No. 2012/17. - Enabling power: S.I. 1996/1320 (N.I. 10), arts 91B (2) (b), 91C (1) (a), 91D (9). - Issued: 03.02.2012. Made: 26.01.2012. Coming into operation: 23.04.2012. Effect: None. Territorial extent & classification: NI. General. - 12p.: 30 cm. - 978-0-337-98649-9 £5.75

The Road Traffic (Immobilisation, Removal and Disposal of Vehicles) (Amendment) Regulations (Northern Ireland) 2012 No. 2012/146. - Enabling power: S.I. 2007/916 (N.I. 10), art. 13, sch. 1. - Issued: 30.03.2012. Made: 26.03.2012. Coming into operation: 23.04.2012. Effect: S.R. 2012/19 amended. Territorial extent & classification: NI. General. - 2p.: 30 cm. - 978-0-337-98757-1 £4.00

The Road Traffic (Immobilisation, Removal and Disposal of Vehicles) Regulations (Northern Ireland) 2012 No. 2012/19. - Enabling power: S.I. 2007/916 (N.I. 10), art. 13, sch. 1. - Issued: 03.02.2012. Made: 26.01.2012. Coming into operation: 23.04.2012. Effect: None. Territorial extent & classification: NI. General. - 12p.: 30 cm. - 978-0-337-98651-2 £5.75

The Road Traffic Offenders (Prescribed Devices) Order (Northern Ireland) 2012 No. 2012/77. - Enabling power: S.I. 1996/1320 (N.I. 10), art. 23 (9). - Issued: 09.03.2012. Made: 29.02.2012. Coming into operation: 02.04.2012. Effect: None. Territorial extent & classification: NI. General. - 4p.: 30 cm. - 978-0-337-98695-6 £4.00

The Taxi Operators Licensing Regulations (Northern Ireland) 2012 No. 2012/316. - Enabling power: Taxis Act (Northern Ireland) 2008, ss. 1 (4), 2 (4) (5) (7), 3 (2) (3) (6) (7), 28 (3), 30 (1) (a) (b) (2) (3), 33 (1) (e), 56. - Issued: 10.08.2012. Made: 08.08.2012. Coming into operation: 01.09.2012. Effect: None. Territorial extent & classification: NI. General. - 12p.: 30 cm. - 978-0-337-98880-6 £5.75

The Taxis (2008 Act) (Commencement No. 2) Order (Northern Ireland) 2012 No. 2012/313 (C.28). - Enabling power: Taxis Act (Northern Ireland) 2008, s. 59. Bringing into operation various provisions of the 2008 Act on 08.08.2012 & 01.09.2012. - Issued: 15.08.2012. Made: 07.08.2012. Coming into operation: -. Effect: None. Territorial extent & classification: NI. General. - 4p.: 30 cm. - 978-0-337-98876-9 £4.00

The Taxis (Bushmills) Order (Northern Ireland) 2012 No. 2012/298. - Enabling power: S.I. 1997/276 (N.I. 2), art. 27A (1). - Issued: 25.07.2012. Made: 23.07.2012. Coming into force: 13.08.2012. Effect: S.R. 2010/270 amended. Territorial extent & classification: NI. Local. - Available at http://www.legislation.gov.uk/nisr/2012/298/contents/made *Non-print*

The Traffic Weight Restriction (Amendment) Order (Northern Ireland) 2012 No. 2012/252. - Enabling power: S.I. 1997/276 (NI. 2), art. 4 (1) (2). - Issued: 28.06.2012. Made: 26.06.2012. Coming into operation: 18.07.2012. Effect: S.R. 2004/231 amended. Territorial extent & classification: NI. Local. - Available at http://www.legislation.gov.uk/nisr/2012/252/contents/made *Non-print*

The Waiting Restrictions (Ahoghill) Order (Northern Ireland) 2012 No. 2012/425. - Enabling power: S.I. 1997/276 (N.I. 2), art. 4 (1) (2) (3). - Issued: 05.12.2012. Made: 03.12.2012. Coming into force: 27.12.2012. Effect: None. Territorial extent & classification: NI. Local. - Available at http://www.legislation.gov.uk/nisr/2012/425/contents/made *Non-print*

The Waiting Restrictions (Bangor) Order (Northern Ireland) 2012 No. 2012/165. - Enabling power: S.I. 1997/276 (N.I. 2), arts 4 (1) (2) (3). - Issued: 18.04.2012. Made: 16.04.2012. Coming into force: 08.05.2012. Effect: None. Territorial extent & classification: NI. Local. - Revoked by SR 2013/20 (Non-print). - Available at http://www.legislation.gov.uk/nisr/2012/165/contents/made. Revoked by S.R. 2013/20 (non-print) *Non-print*

The Waiting Restrictions (Belfast City Centre) Order (Northern Ireland) 2012 No. 2012/199. - Enabling power: S.I. 1997/276 (N.I. 2), arts 4 (1) (2) (3). - Issued: 21.05.2012. Made: 17.05.2012. Coming into force: 08.06.2012. Effect: None. Territorial extent & classification: NI. Local. - Available at http://www.legislation.gov.uk/nisr/2012/199/contents/made *Non-print*

The Waiting Restrictions (Bushmills) Order (Northern Ireland) 2012 No. 2012/297. - Enabling power: S.I. 1997/276 (N.I. 2), art. 4 (1) (2) (3). - Issued: 25.07.2012. Made: 23.07.2012. Coming into force: 13.08.2012. Effect: S.R. 2008/443; 2011/197 revoked. Territorial extent & classification: NI. Local. - Available at http://www.legislation.gov.uk/nisr/2012/297/contents/made *Non-print*

The Waiting Restrictions (Dundonald) Order (Northern Ireland) 2012 No. 2012/350. - Enabling power: S.I. 1997/276 (N.I. 2), art. 4 (1) (2) (3), sch. 1, para. 5. - Issued: 24.09.2012. Made: 20.09.2012. Coming into force: 12.10.2012. Effect: SR 2011/310 revoked. Territorial extent & classification: NI. Local. - Available at http://www.legislation.gov.uk/nisr/2012/350/contents/made *Non-print*

The Waiting Restrictions (Dungannon) (Amendment No. 2) Order (Northern Ireland) 2012 No. 2012/460. - Enabling power: S.I. 1997/276 (N.I. 2), art. 4 (1) (2) (3). - Issued: 24.12.2012. Made: 20.12.2012. Coming into force: 10.01.2013. Effect: S.R. 2010/209 amended. Territorial extent & classification: NI. Local. - Available at http://www.legislation.gov.uk/nisr/2012/460/contents/made *Non-print*

The Waiting Restrictions (Dungannon) (Amendment) Order (Northern Ireland) 2012 No. 2012/351. - Enabling power: S.I. 1997/276 (N.I. 2), art. 4 (1) (2) (3). - Issued: 25.09.2012. Made: 20.09.2012. Coming into force: 12.10.2012. Effect: SR 2010/209 amended. Territorial extent & classification: NI. Local. - Available at http://www.legislation.gov.uk/nisr/2012/351/contents/made *Non-print*

The Waiting Restrictions (Holywood) Order (Northern Ireland) 2012 No. 2012/287. - Enabling power: S.I. 1997/276 (N.I. 2), art. 4 (1) (2) (3). - Issued: 16.07.2012. Made: 10.07.2012. Coming into force: 01.08.2012. Effect: S.R. 2010/315 revoked. Territorial extent & classification: NI. Local. - Available at http://www.legislation.gov.uk/nisr/2012/287/contents/made *Non-print*

The Waiting Restrictions (John Street, Castlederg) Order (Northern Ireland) 2012 No. 2012/343. - Enabling power: S.I. 1997/276 (N.I. 2), art. 4 (1) (2) (3), sch. 1, para. 5. - Issued: 21.09.2012. Made: 19.09.2012. Coming into force: 11.10.2012. Effect: None. Territorial extent & classification: NI. Local. - Available at http://www.legislation.gov.uk/nisr/2012/343/contents/made *Non-print*

The Waiting Restrictions (Larne) Order (Northern Ireland) 2012 No. 2012/220. - Enabling power: S.I. 1997/276 (N.I. 2), arts 4 (1) (2) (3). - Issued: 31.05.2012. Made: 29.05.2012. Coming into force: 19.06.2012. Effect: None. Territorial extent & classification: NI. Local. - Available at http://www.legislation.gov.uk/nisr/2012/220/contents/made *Non-print*

The Waiting Restrictions (Lisburn) (No. 2) Order (Northern Ireland) 2012 No. 2012/362. - Enabling power: S.I. 1997/276 (N.I. 2), art. 4 (1) (2) (3). - Issued: 27.09.2012. Made: 25.09.2012. Coming into force: 17.10.2012. Effect: None. Territorial extent & classification: NI. Local. - Available at http://www.legislation.gov.uk/nisr/2012/362/contents/made *Non-print*

The Waiting Restrictions (Lisburn) Order (Northern Ireland) 2012 No. 2012/195. - Enabling power: S.I. 1997/276 (N.I. 2), arts 4 (1) (2) (3). - Issued: 18.05.2012. Made: 16.05.2012. Coming into force: 07.06.2012. Effect: S.R. 2009/372 revoked. Territorial extent & classification: NI. Local. - Available at http://www.legislation.gov.uk/nisr/2012/195/contents/made *Non-print*

The Waiting Restrictions (Londonderry) (Amendment No. 2) Order (Northern Ireland) 2012 No. 2012/352. - Enabling power: S.I. 1997/276 (N.I. 2), art. 4 (1) (2) (3). - Issued: 24.09.2012. Made: 20.09.2012. Coming into force: 12.10.2012. Effect: SR 2010/256 amended. Territorial extent & classification: NI. Local. - Available at http://www.legislation.gov.uk/nisr/2012/352/contents/made *Non-print*

The Waiting Restrictions (Londonderry) (Amendment) Order (Northern Ireland) 2012 No. 2012/243. - Enabling power: S.I. 1997/276 (N.I. 2), art. 4 (1) (2) (3). - Issued: 25.06.2012. Made: 19.06.2012. Coming into force: 11.07.2012. Effect: S.R. 2010/256 amended. Territorial extent & classification: NI. Local. - Available at http://www.legislation.gov.uk/nisr/2012/243/contents/made *Non-print*

The Waiting Restrictions (Ormeau Road, Belfast) Order (Northern Ireland) 2012 No. 2012/53. - Enabling power: S.I. 1997/276 (N.I. 2), arts 4 (1) (2) (3). - Issued: 22.02.2012. Made: 20.02.2012. Coming into force: 12.03.2012. Effect: None. Territorial extent & classification: NI. Local. - Available at http://www.legislation.gov.uk/nisr/2012/53/contents/made *Non-print*

The Waiting Restrictions (Springfield Road, Belfast) Order (Northern Ireland) 2012 No. 2012/344. - Enabling power: S.I. 1997/276 (N.I. 2), art. 4 (1) (2) (3). - Issued: 21.09.2012. Made: 19.09.2012. Coming into force: 11.10.2012. Effect: None. Territorial extent & classification: NI. Local. - Available at http://www.legislation.gov.uk/nisr/2012/344/contents/made *Non-print*

Safeguarding vulnerable groups

The Safeguarding Vulnerable Groups (2007 Order) (Commencement No. 7) Order (Northern Ireland) 2012 No. 2012/330 (C.29). - Enabling power: S.I. 2007/1351 (N.I. 11), art. 1 (3). Bringing into operation various provisions of the 2007 Order on 10.09.2012 and on the day on which Protection of Freedoms Act 2012, sch. 7, para. 9 comes into force. - Issued: 05.09.2012. Made: 28.08.2012. Coming into operation: -. Effect: None. Territorial extent & classification: NI. General. - 8p.: 30 cm. - 978-0-337-98897-4 *£4.00*

The Safeguarding Vulnerable Groups (Miscellaneous Amendments) Order (Northern Ireland) 2012 No. 2012/320. - Enabling power: S.I. 2007/1351 (N.I. 11), arts 3 (11), 61 (1) (2) (3), sch. 2, paras 6, 9. - Issued: 21.08.2012. Made: 14.08.2012. Laid before Parliament: 17.08.2012. Coming into operation: 10.09.2012. Effect: S.R. 2009/304, 305 amended. Territorial extent & classification: NI. General. - 4p.: 30 cm. - 978-0-337-98887-5 *£4.00*

The Safeguarding Vulnerable Groups (Miscellaneous Provisions) Order (Northern Ireland) 2012 No. 2012/322. - Enabling power: S.I. 2007/1351 (N.I. 11), arts 45 (7), 50 (6), 51(6), sch. 2, para. 9. - Issued: 20.08.2012. Made: 14.08.2012. Laid before Parliament: 17.08.2012. Coming into operation: 10.09.2012. In accord. with art. 1. Effect: None. Territorial extent & classification: NI. General. - 4p.: 30 cm. - 978-0-337-98889-9 *£4.00*

The Safeguarding Vulnerable Groups (Miscellaneous Provisions) Regulations (Northern Ireland) 2012 No. 2012/323. - Enabling power: S.I. 2007/1351 (N.I. 11), arts 6 (5), 37 (1), 38 (1), 39 (2), 41 (1) (5), 43 (1), 44 (2), 47 (1) (5), 48 (1) (2), 52A (1) (d), sch. 1, para. 15, sch. 2, para. 7 (1) (f) (g). - Issued: 20.08.2012. Made: 14.08.2012. Laid before Parliament: 17.08.2012. Coming into operation: 10.09.2012. In accord. with art. 1 (2) (3). Effect: S.I.2008/202, 203; 2009/40, 306 amended. Territorial extent & classification: NI. General. - 8p.: 30 cm. - 978-0-337-98890-5 £4.00

The Safeguarding Vulnerable Groups (Prescribed Criteria and Miscellaneous Provisions) (Amendment) Regulations (Northern Ireland) 2012 No. 2012/319. - Enabling power: S.I. 2007/1351 (N.I. 11), art. 61 (1) (a) (3), sch. 1, paras 1 (1), 2 (1), 7 (1), 8 (1), 24 (1) (2). - Issued: 21.08.2012. Made: 14.08.2012. Laid before Parliament: 17.08.2012. Coming into operation: 10.09.2012. Effect: S.R. 2009/39 amended. Territorial extent & classification: NI. General. - 8p.: 30 cm. - 978-0-337-98885-1 £4.00

Sea fisheries

The Strangford Lough (Sea Fishing Exclusion Zones) Regulations (Northern Ireland) 2012 No. 2012/441. - Enabling power: Fisheries Act (Northern Ireland) 1966, ss. 19 (1), 124 (1) (2) (2A). - Issued: 13.12.2012. Made: 07.12.2012. Coming into operation: 08.01.2013. Effect: None. Territorial extent & classification: NI. General. - 4p.: 30 cm. - 978-0-337-98983-4 £4.00

Seeds

The Potatoes Originating in Egypt (Amendment) Regulations (Northern Ireland) 2012 No. 2012/185. - Enabling power: European Communities Act 1972, s. 2 (2). - Issued: 15.05.2012. Made: 10.05.2012. Coming into operation: 11.06.2012. Effect: S.R. 2004/183 amended. Territorial extent & classification: NI. General. - EC note: These regulations implement Commission Implementing Decision 2011/787/EU which repeals Commission Decision 2004/4/EC and as amended. They authorise Member States temporarily to take additional measures against the dissemination of Ralstonia solanacearum (Smith) Yabuuchi et al. as regards Egypt. With correction slip dated May 2012. - 4p.: 30 cm. - 978-0-337-98795-3 £4.00

Sex discrimination

The Sex Discrimination Order 1976 (Amendment) Regulations (Northern Ireland) 2012 No. 2012/462. - Enabling power: European Communities Act 1972, s. 2 (2). - Issued: 08.01.2013. Made: 21.12.2012. Coming into operation: 21.12.2012. Effect: S.I. 1976/1042 (N.I. 15) amended. Territorial extent & classification: NI. General. - EC note: These Regulations amend the Sex Discrimination (Northern Ireland) Order 1976 to reflect a change to EU law consequent on the ruling by the Court of Justice of the EU in case C-236/09 of 1 March 2011. In that case, the Court ruled that art. 5 (2) of Council Directive 2004/113/EC implementing the principle of equal treatment between men and women in the access to and supply of goods and services is invalid with effect from 21 December 2012. - 4p.: 30 cm. - 978-0-337-99005-2 £4.00

Social security

The Employment and Support Allowance (Amendment of Linking Rules) Regulations (Northern Ireland) 2012 No. 2012/160. - Enabling power: Welfare Reform Act (Northern Ireland) 2007, ss. 2(4), 4 (6), 24 (2) (b), 25 (2), 28 (2), sch. 2, paras 1, 4, 9, sch. 4, paras 1 (1), 7 (1), 8. - Issued: 11.04.2012. Made: 04.04.2012. Coming into operation: 01.05.2012. Effect: S.R. 2008/280; 2010/312 amended & S.R. 2010/200 partially revoked. Territorial extent & classification: NI. General. - 4p.: 30 cm. - 978-0-337-98773-1 £4.00

The Jobseeker's Allowance (Amendment) Regulations (Northern Ireland) 2012 No. 2012/181. - Enabling power: S.I. 1995/2705 (N.I. 15), art. 21 (8) (b). - Issued: 01.05.2012. Made: 26.04.2012. Coming into operation: 16.05.2012. Effect: S.R. 1996/198 amended. Territorial extent & classification: NI. General. - 2p.: 30 cm. - 978-0-337-98790-8 £4.00

The Jobseeker's Allowance (Domestic Violence) (Amendment) Regulations (Northern Ireland) 2012 No. 2012/155. - Enabling power: S.I. 1995/2705 (N.I. 15), arts 8 (4), 9 (4), 11 (10), 36 (2) (a), sch. 1, para. 8B. - Issued: 15.10.2012. Made: 30.03.2012. Coming into operation: 23.04.2012. Effect: S.R. 1996/198 amended. Territorial extent & classification: NI. General. - Approved by resolution of the Assembly on 9th October 2012. Supersedes pre-approval version (ISBN 9780337987687). - 8p.: 30 cm. - 978-0-337-98921-6 £4.00

The Jobseeker's Allowance (Domestic Violence) (Amendment) Regulations (Northern Ireland) 2012 No. 2012/155. - Enabling power: S.I. 1995/2705 (N.I. 15), arts 8 (4), 9 (4), 11 (10), 36 (2) (a), sch. 1, para. 8B. - Issued: 03.04.2012. Made: 30.03.2012. Coming into operation: 23.04.2012. Effect: S.R. 1996/198 amended. Territorial extent & classification: NI. General. - For approval of the Assembly before the expiration of 6 months from the date of their coming into operation. Superseded by approved version (ISBN 9780337989216). - 8p.: 30 cm. - 978-0-337-98768-7 £4.00

The Jobseeker's Allowance (Members of the Reserve Forces) Regulations (Northern Ireland) 2012 No. 2012/284. - Enabling power: S.I. 1995/2705 (N.I. 15), arts 8 (4), 9 (4), 10 (2) (d), 14 (1) to (3) (4) (b), 36 (2). - Issued: 06.12.2012. Made: 09.07.2012. Coming into operation: 30.07.2012. Effect: S.R. 1996/198 amended. Territorial extent & classification: NI. General. - Approved by the Assembly on 03.12.2012. Supersedes pre-approval version (ISBN 9780337988592). - 4p.: 30 cm. - 978-0-337-98973-5 £4.00

The Jobseeker's Allowance (Members of the Reserve Forces) Regulations (Northern Ireland) 2012 No. 2012/284. - Enabling power: S.I. 1995/2705 (N.I. 15), arts 8 (4), 9 (4), 10 (2) (d), 14 (1) to (3) (4) (b), 36 (2). - Issued: 11.07.2012. Made: 09.07.2012. Coming into operation: 30.07.2012. Effect: S.R. 1996/198 amended. Territorial extent & classification: NI. General. - For approval of the Assembly before the expiration of 6 months from the date of their coming into operation. Superseded by version approved 03.12.2012 (ISBN 9780337989735). - 4p.: 30 cm. - 978-0-337-98859-2 £4.00

The Jobseeker's Allowance (Sanctions for Failure to Attend) Regulations (Northern Ireland) 2012 No. 2012/44. - Enabling power: Social Security Contributions and Benefits (Northern Ireland) Act 1992, ss. 22 (5), 122 (1) (d), 171 (1) (3); S.I. 1995/2705 (N.I. 15), arts 10, 36 (2), sch. 1, para. 15; S.I. 1998/1506 (N.I. 10), arts 10 (1), 11 (3) (6), 74 (1). - Issued: 16.02.2012. Made: 13.02.2012. Coming into operation: 06.03.2012. Effect: S.R. 1996/198; 1975/113; 1999/162; 2001/216; 2006/405 amended & S.R. 1999/145; 2000/350 partially revoked. Territorial extent & classification: NI. General. - 8p.: 30 cm. - 978-0-337-98672-7 £5.75

The Jobseeker's Allowance (Work Experience) (Amendment) Regulations (Northern Ireland) 2012 No. 2012/14. - Enabling power: S.I. 1995/2705 (N.I. 15), arts 9 (4), 21 (8) (10) (c), 36 (2), sch. 1, para. 1 (2) (b). - Issued: 24.01.2012. Made: 20.01.2012. Coming into operation: 13.02.2012. Effect: S.R. 1996/198 amended. Territorial extent & classification: NI. General. - 4p.: 30 cm. - 978-0-337-98645-1 £4.00

The Jobseeker's Allowance (Work Experience) (Amendment) Regulations (Northern Ireland) 2012 No. 2012/14. - Enabling power: S.I. 1995/2705 (N.I. 15), arts 9 (4), 21 (8) (10) (c), 36 (2), sch. 1, para. 1 (2) (b). - Issued: 31.07.2012. Made: 20.01.2012. Coming into operation: 13.02.2012. Effect: S.R. 1996/198 amended. Territorial extent & classification: NI. General. - Approved by resolution of the Assembly on 2nd July 2012. - 4p.: 30 cm. - 978-0-337-98869-1 £4.00

The Mesothelioma Lump Sum Payments (Conditions and Amounts) (Amendment) Regulations (Northern Ireland) 2012 No. 2012/83. - Enabling power: Mesothelioma, etc., Act (Northern Ireland) 2008, s. 1 (3). - Issued: 29.03.2012. Made: 01.03.2012. Coming into operation: 01.04.2012. Effect: S.R. 2008/354 amended. Territorial extent & classification: NI. General. - Approved by resolution of the Assembly on 26th March 2012. - 8p.: 30 cm. - 978-0-337-98758-8 £4.00

The Mesothelioma Lump Sum Payments (Conditions and Amounts) (Amendment) Regulations (Northern Ireland) 2012 No. 2012/83. - Enabling power: Mesothelioma, etc., Act (Northern Ireland) 2008, s. 1 (3). - Issued: 06.03.2012. Made: 01.03.2012. Coming into operation: 01.04.2012. Effect: S.R. 2008/354 amended. Territorial extent & classification: NI. General. - For approval of the Assembly before the expiration of six months from the date of their coming into operation. - 8p.: 30 cm. - 978-0-337-98700-7 £4.00

The Pneumoconiosis, etc., (Workers' Compensation) (Payment of Claims) (Amendment) Regulations (Northern Ireland) 2012 No. 2012/84. - Enabling power: S.I. 1979/925 (N.I.9), arts. 3 (3), 4 (3), 11 (1) (4). - Issued: 06.03.2012. Made: 01.03.2012. Coming into operation: In accord. with reg. 1 (1). Effect: S.R. 1988/242 amended. Territorial extent & classification: NI. General. - Subject to affirmative by resolution of the Assembly. Superseded by affirmed version (ISBN 9780337987595) issued 29.03.2012. - 8p.: 30 cm. - 978-0-337-98701-4 £5.75

The Pneumoconiosis, etc., (Workers' Compensation) (Payment of Claims) (Amendment) Regulations (Northern Ireland) 2012 No. 2012/84. - Enabling power: S.I. 1979/925 (N.I.9), arts. 3 (3), 4 (3), 11 (1) (4). - Issued: 29.03.2012. Made: 01.03.2012. Coming into operation: In accord. with reg. 1 (1). Effect: S.R. 1988/242 amended. Territorial extent & classification: NI. General. - Affirmed by resolution of the Assembly on 26th March 2012. - 8p.: 30 cm. - 978-0-337-98759-5 £5.75

The Social Fund (Cold Weather Payments) (General) (Amendment) Regulations (Northern Ireland) 2012 No. 2012/369. - Enabling power: Social Security Contributions and Benefits (Northern Ireland) Act 1992, ss. 134 (2), 171 (1) (3) (4). - Issued: 02.10.2012. Made: 27.09.2012. Coming into operation: 01.11.2012. Effect: S.R. 1988/368 amended. Territorial extent & classification: NI. General. - 4p.: 30 cm. - 978-0-337-98914-8 £4.00

The Social Fund Maternity and Funeral Expenses (General) (Amendment) Regulations (Northern Ireland) 2012 No. 2012/292. - Enabling power: Social Security Contributions and Benefits (Northern Ireland) Act 1992, ss. 134 (1) (a), 171 (1), (3) (4). - Issued: 19.07.2012. Made: 16.07.2012. Coming into operation: 13.08.2012. Effect: S.R. 2005/506 amended & S.R. 2011/130 partially revoked. Territorial extent & classification: NI. General. - 4p.: 30 cm. - 978-0-337-98862-2 £4.00

The Social Security Benefits Up-rating Order (Northern Ireland) 2012 No. 2012/116. - Enabling power: Social Security Administration (Northern Ireland) Act 1992, ss. 132, 132A,165 (1) (4) (5). - Issued: 20.03.2012. Made: 14.03.2012. Coming into operation: In accord. with 1. Effect: 1966 c. 6 (N.I.); 1992 c. 7; 1993 c. 49; S.R. 1987/30, 459; 1992/32; 1994/461; 1995/35; 1996/198; 2002/380; 2003/28; 2006/405, 406; 2008/280; 2010/302, 407 amended & 2011/119 revoked (12.04.2012). Territorial extent & classification: NI. General. - For approval of the Assembly before the expiration of six months from the date of its coming into operation. Superseded by approved version (ISBN 9780337988264) issued on 15.06.2012. - 42p.: 30 cm. - 978-0-337-98731-1 £9.75

The Social Security Benefits Up-rating Order (Northern Ireland) 2012 No. 2012/116. - Enabling power: Social Security Administration (Northern Ireland) Act 1992, ss. 132, 132A, 165 (1) (4) (5). - Issued: 15.06.2012. Made: 14.03.2012. Coming into operation: In accord. with art. 1. Effect: 1966 c. 6 (N.I.); 1992 c. 7; 1993 c. 49; S.R. 1987/30, 459, 460; 1992/32; 1994/461; 1995/35; 1996/198; 2002/380; 2003/28; 2006/405, 406; 2008/280; 2010/302, 407 amended & 2011/119 revoked (12.04.2012). Territorial extent & classification: NI. General. - Approved by resolution of the Assembly on 11th June 2012. Supersedes pre-approved version (ISBN 9780337987311). - 44p.: 30 cm. - 978-0-337-98826-4 £9.75

The Social Security Benefits Up-rating Regulations (Northern Ireland) 2012 No. 2012/117. - Enabling power: Social Security Contributions and Benefits (Northern Ireland) Act 1992, ss. 90, 113 (1) (a), 171 (1) (3) & Social Security Administration (Northern Ireland) Act 1992, ss. 5 (1) (q), 135 (3), 165 (1) (4). - Issued: 20.03.2012. Made: 14.03.2012. Coming into operation: 09.04.2012. Effect: S.R. 1977/74; 1987/465 amended & S.R. 2011/120 revoked. Territorial extent & classification: NI. General. - 4p.: 30 cm. - 978-0-337-98732-8 £4.00

The Social Security (Claims and Payments) (Amendment) Regulations (Northern Ireland) 2012 No. 2012/107. - Enabling power: Social Security Administration (Northern Ireland) Act 1992, ss. 13A (2) (b), 165 (1). - Issued: 13.03.2012. Made: 09.03.2012. Coming into operation: 01.04.2012. Effect: S.R. 1987/465 amended. Territorial extent & classification: NI. General. - 2p.: 30 cm. - 978-0-337-98721-2 £4.00

The Social Security (Credits) (Amendment No. 2) Regulations (Northern Ireland) 2012 No. 2012/394. - Enabling power: Social Security Contributions and Benefits (Northern Ireland) Act 1992, ss. 22 (5), 171 (1) (3). - Issued: 01.11.2012. Made: 29.10.2012. Coming into force: 01.12.2012. Effect: S.R. 1975/113 amended. Territorial extent: NI. General. - 2p.: 30 cm. - 978-0-337-98942-1 £4.00

The Social Security (Credits) (Amendment) Regulations (Northern Ireland) 2012 No. 2012/109. - Enabling power: Social Security Contributions and Benefits (Northern Ireland) Act 1992, ss. 22 (5), 171 (1) (3). - Issued: 13.03.2012. Made: 09.03.2012. Coming into force: 05.04.2012. Effect: S.R. 1975/113 amended. Territorial extent: NI. General. - 2p.: 30 cm. - 978-0-337-98723-6 £4.00

The Social Security (Habitual Residence) (Amendment) Regulations (Northern Ireland) 2012 No. 2012/380. - Enabling power: Social Security Contributions and Benefits (Northern Ireland) Act 1992, ss. 122 (1) (a) (d), 131 (1) (2), 171 (1) (3) (4) & S.I. 1995/2705 (N.I. 15), arts 6 (5) (12), 36 (2) & State Pension Credit Act (Northern Ireland) 2002, ss. 1 (5) (a), 19 (1) (2) (a) (3) & Welfare Reform Act (Northern Ireland) 2007, ss. 4 (3), 25 (2). - Issued: 22.10.2012. Made: 17.10.2012. Coming into operation: 08.11.2012. Effect: S.R. 1987/459; 1996/198; 2003/28; 2006/405, 406; 2008/280 amended. Territorial extent & classification: NI. General. - 8p.: 30 cm. - 978-0-337-98926-1 £4.00

The Social Security (Industrial Injuries) (Dependency) (Permitted Earnings Limits) Order (Northern Ireland) 2012 No. 2012/118. - Enabling power: Social Security Contributions and Benefits (Northern Ireland) Act 1992, sch. 7, para. 4 (5). - Issued: 20.03.2012. Made: 14.03.2012. Coming into operation: 11.04.2012. Effect: 1992 c. 7 amended & S.R. 2011/121 revoked. Territorial extent & classification: NI. General. - 2p.: 30 cm. - 978-0-337-98733-5 £4.00

The Social Security (Industrial Injuries) (Prescribed Diseases) (Amendment No. 2) Regulations (Northern Ireland) 2012 No. 2012/264. - Enabling power: Social Security Contributions and Benefits (Northern Ireland) Act 1992, ss. 108 (2), 171 (1) (3) (4). - Issued: 03.07.2012. Made: 28.06.2012. Coming into operation: 01.08.2012. Effect: S.R. 1986/179 amended. Territorial extent & classification: NI. General. - 2p.: 30 cm. - 978-0-337-98847-9 £4.00

The Social Security (Industrial Injuries) (Prescribed Diseases) (Amendment) Regulations (Northern Ireland) 2012 No. 2012/100. - Enabling power: Social Security Contributions and Benefits (Northern Ireland) Act 1992, ss. 108 (2), 171 (1) (3) (4). - Issued: 12.03.2012. Made: 07.03.2012. Coming into operation: 30.03.2011. Effect: S.R. 1986/179 amended. Territorial extent & classification: NI. General. - 2p.: 30 cm. - 978-0-337-98718-2 £4.00

The Social Security (Miscellaneous Amendments No. 2) Regulations (Northern Ireland) 2012 No. 2012/377. - Enabling power: Social Security Contributions and Benefits (Northern Ireland) Act 1992, ss. 122 (1) (a), 132 (3) (4) (b), 171 (3) (4) & S.I. 1995/2705 (N.I.15), arts 14 (1) to (3), 36 (2), sch. 1, para. 11 (2) & Welfare Reform Act (Northern Ireland) 2007, ss. 17 (1) (2) (3) (b), 25 (2), 28 (2). - Issued: 18.10.2012. Made: 15.10.2012. Coming into operation: 05.11.2012. Effect: S.R. 1987/459; 1996/198; 2008/280 amended & S.R. 1996/405 partially revoked. Territorial extent & classification: NI. General. - 8p.: 30 cm. - 978-0-337-98923-0 £4.00

The Social Security (Miscellaneous Amendments) Regulations (Northern Ireland) 2012 No. 2012/121. - Enabling power: Social Security Contributions and Benefits (Northern Ireland) Act 1992, ss. 122 (1) (a) (d), 123 (1) (d) (e), 132 (3) (4) (b), 132A (3), 133 (2) (i), 134 (2), 171 (1) (3) (4) & Social Security Administration (Northern Ireland) Act 1992, ss. 5 (1) (j) (n), 69 (4), 165 (1) (4) (5) & S.I. 1995/2705 (N.I.15), arts 14 (4) (b), 36 (1) (2) & S.I. 1998/1506 (N.I.10), arts 11 (6), 74 (1) (3) (4) & Child Support, Pensions and Social Security Act (Northern Ireland) 2000, s. 59, sch. 7 paras 4 (3), 20 (1) & State Pension Credit Act (Northern Ireland) 2002, ss. 15 (1) (e) (3), 19 (1) to (3) & Welfare Reform Act (Northern Ireland) 2007, ss. 1 (2), 25 (1) (2), 28 (2), 29, sch. 1, paras 1 (4) (a), 6 (5). sch. 4, paras 1 (1), 7 (1) (a). - Issued: 20.03.2012. Made: 14.03.2012. Coming into operation: In accord. with reg. 1. Effect: S.R. 1982/263; 1987/459, 465; 1988/142; 1996/198; 1999/162; 2000/91; 2001/213; 2003/28; 2006/405, 406; 2008/280; 2010/312 amended & S.R. 1987/465; 2003/421; 2006/168; 2008/280; 2009/92, 338; 2010/69; 2011/357 partially revoked (01.04.2012). Territorial extent & classification: NI. General. - 12p.: 30 cm. - 978-0-337-98736-6 £5.75

The Social Security Pensions (Flat Rate Accrual Amount) Order (Northern Ireland) 2012 No. 2012/89. - Enabling power: Social Security Administration (Northern Ireland) Act 1992, s. 130AA. - Issued: 07.03.2012. Made: 02.03.2012. Coming into operation: 06.04.2012. Effect: None. Territorial extent & classification: NI. General. - 2p.: 30 cm. - 978-0-337-98706-9 £4.00

The Social Security Pensions (Flat Rate Introduction Year) Order (Northern Ireland) 2012 No. 2012/40. - Enabling power: Social Security Contributions and Benefits (Northern Ireland) Act 1992, ss. 121 (1), 171 (1). - Issued: 10.02.2012. Made: 07.02.2012. Coming into operation: 07.02.2012. Effect: None. Territorial extent & classification: NI. General. - 2p.: 30 cm. - 978-0-337-98669-7 £4.00

The Social Security Pensions (Low Earnings Threshold) Order (Northern Ireland) 2012 No. 2012/88. - Enabling power: Social Security Administration (Northern Ireland) Act 1992, s. 130A. - Issued: 07.03.2012. Made: 02.03.2012. Coming into operation: 06.04.2012. Effect: None. Territorial extent & classification: NI. General. - 2p.: 30 cm. - 978-0-337-98705-2 £4.00

The Social Security (Recovery) (Amendment) Regulations (Northern Ireland) 2012 No. 2012/108. - Enabling power: Social Security Administration (Northern Ireland) Act 1992, ss. 69 (6) (a) (8), 73 (1) (4) (5), 165 (1) (4). - Issued: 13.03.2012. Made: 09.03.2012. Coming into operation: 01.04.2012. Effect: S.R. 1988/142 amended. Territorial extent & classification: NI. General. - 4p.: 30 cm. - 978-0-337-98722-9 £4.00

The Social Security Revaluation of Earnings Factors Order (Northern Ireland) 2012 No. 2012/87. - Enabling power: Social Security Administration (Northern Ireland) Act 1992, ss. 130, 165 (1) (4) (5). - Issued: 07.03.2012. Made: 02.03.2012. Coming into operation: 06.04.2012. Effect: None. Territorial extent & classification: NI. General. - 4p.: 30 cm. - 978-0-337-98704-5 £4.00

The Social Security (Suspension of Payment of Benefits and Miscellaneous Amendments) Regulations (Northern Ireland) 2012 No. 2012/140. - Enabling power: Social Security Administration (Northern Ireland) Act 1992, ss. 5 (1) (hh) (j) (2A), 165 (1) (4) to (6) & S.I. 1998/1506 (N.I. 10), arts 10 (1) (a), 22, 74 (1) (3) (5) (6). - Issued: 29.03.2012. Made: 26.03.2012. Coming into operation: 17.04.2012. Effect: S.R. 1987/465; 1996/198; 1999/162; 2006/405, 406 amended & S.R. 2000/350; 2003/421; 2008/262 partially revoked. Territorial extent & classification: NI. General. - 4p.: 30 cm. - 978-0-337-98754-0 £4.00

Sports grounds

The Safety of Sports Grounds (Fees and Appeals) (Amendment) Regulations (Northern Ireland) 2012 No. 2012/219. - Enabling power: SI 2006/313 (N.I. 2), arts 19 (1) (b), 27 (1) (2). - Issued: 31.05.2012. Made: 28.05.2012. Coming into operation: 31.07.2012. Effect: S.R. 2009/289 amended. Territorial extent & classification: NI. General. - 4p.: 30 cm. - 978-0-337-98811-0 £4.00

Statutory maternity pay

The Social Security Benefits Up-rating Order (Northern Ireland) 2012 No. 2012/116. - Enabling power: Social Security Administration (Northern Ireland) Act 1992, ss. 132, 132A,165 (1) (4) (5). - Issued: 20.03.2012. Made: 14.03.2012. Coming into operation: In accord. with 1. Effect: 1966 c. 6 (N.I.); 1992 c. 7; 1993 c. 49; S.R. 1987/30, 459; 1992/32; 1994/461; 1995/35; 1996/198; 2002/380; 2003/28; 2006/405, 406; 2008/280; 2010/302, 407 amended & 2011/119 revoked (12.04.2012). Territorial extent & classification: NI. General. - For approval of the Assembly before the expiration of six months from the date of its coming into operation. Superseded by approved version (ISBN 9780337988264) isssued on 15.06.2012. - 42p.: 30 cm. - 978-0-337-98731-1 £9.75

The Social Security Benefits Up-rating Order (Northern Ireland) 2012 No. 2012/116. - Enabling power: Social Security Administration (Northern Ireland) Act 1992, ss. 132, 132A, 165 (1) (4) (5). - Issued: 15.06.2012. Made: 14.03.2012. Coming into operation: In accord. with art. 1. Effect: 1966 c. 6 (N.I.); 1992 c. 7; 1993 c. 49; S.R. 1987/30, 459, 460; 1992/32; 1994/461; 1995/35; 1996/198; 2002/380; 2003/28; 2006/405, 406; 2008/280; 2010/302, 407 amended & 2011/119 revoked (12.04.2012). Territorial extent & classification: NI. General. - Approved by resolution of the Assembly on 11th June 2012. Supersedes pre-approved version (ISBN 9780337987311). - 44p.: 30 cm. - 978-0-337-98826-4 £9.75

Statutory sick pay

The Social Security Benefits Up-rating Order (Northern Ireland) 2012 No. 2012/116. - Enabling power: Social Security Administration (Northern Ireland) Act 1992, ss. 132, 132A,165 (1) (4) (5). - Issued: 20.03.2012. Made: 14.03.2012. Coming into operation: In accord. with 1. Effect: 1966 c. 6 (N.I.); 1992 c. 7; 1993 c. 49; S.R. 1987/30, 459; 1992/32; 1994/461; 1995/35; 1996/198; 2002/380; 2003/28; 2006/405, 406; 2008/280; 2010/302, 407 amended & 2011/119 revoked (12.04.2012). Territorial extent & classification: NI. General. - For approval of the Assembly before the expiration of six months from the date of its coming into operation. Superseded by approved version (ISBN 9780337988264) isssued on 15.06.2012. - 42p.: 30 cm. - 978-0-337-98731-1 £9.75

The Social Security Benefits Up-rating Order (Northern Ireland) 2012 No. 2012/116. - Enabling power: Social Security Administration (Northern Ireland) Act 1992, ss. 132, 132A, 165 (1) (4) (5). - Issued: 15.06.2012. Made: 14.03.2012. Coming into operation: In accord. with art. 1. Effect: 1966 c. 6 (N.I.); 1992 c. 7; 1993 c. 49; S.R. 1987/30, 459, 460; 1992/32; 1994/461; 1995/35; 1996/198; 2002/380; 2003/28; 2006/405, 406; 2008/280; 2010/302, 407 amended & 2011/119 revoked (12.04.2012). Territorial extent & classification: NI. General. - Approved by resolution of the Assembly on 11th June 2012. Supersedes pre-approved version (ISBN 9780337987311). - 44p.: 30 cm. - 978-0-337-98826-4 £9.75

Transport

The Road Transport (Working Time) (Amendment) Regulations (Northern Ireland) 2012 No. 2012/169. - Enabling power: European Communities Act 1972, s. 2 (2). - Issued: 24.04.2012. Made: 19.04.2012. Coming into operation: 11.05.2012. Effect: S.R. 2005/241 amended. Territorial extent & classification: NI. General. - EC note: These Regulations relate to the implementation of Council Directive 2002/15/EC concerning the organisation of the working time of persons performing mobile road transport activities. - 8p.: 30 cm. - 978-0-337-98780-9 £5.75

Welfare of animals

Welfare of Farmed Animals Regulations (Northern Ireland) 2012 No. 2012/156. - Enabling power: Welfare of Animals Act (Northern Ireland) 2011, s. 11 (1) (2) (3). - Issued: 04.04.2012. Made: 30.03.2012. Coming into operation: 02.04.2012. Effect: S.R. 2000/270 revoked. Territorial extent & classification: NI. General. - Supersedes draft S.R. (ISBN 9780337986475) issued 31.01.2012. - 24p.: 30 cm. - 978-0-337-98769-4 £5.75

Wildlife

The Spring Traps Approval Order (Northern Ireland) 2012 No. 2012/25. - Enabling power: S.I. 1985 No.171 (N.I.2), art. 12A (2) (3). - Issued: 03.02.2012. Made: 31.01.2012. Coming into operation: 12.03.2012. Effect: S.R. 1996/515 revoked. Territorial extent & classification: NI. General. - 8p.: 30 cm. - 978-0-337-98657-4 £5.75

The Wildlife and Natural Environment (2011 Act) (Commencement No.3) Order (Northern Ireland) 2012 No. 2012/21 (C.5). - Enabling power: Wildlife and Natural Environment Act (Northern Ireland) 2011, s. 40. Bringing into operation various provisions of the 2011 Act on 30.01.2012 & 12.03.2012 in accord. with art. 2. - Issued: 01.02.2012. Made: 27.01.2012. Coming into operation: -. Effect: None. Territorial extent & classification: NI. General. - 4p.: 30 cm. - 978-0-337-98653-6 £4.00

Statutory Rules of Northern Ireland

Arranged by Number

1	Pensions
2	Official statistics
3	Agriculture
	Food
4	Road traffic and vehicles
5	Road traffic and vehicles
6	Road traffic and vehicles
7	Road traffic and vehicles
8	Local government
9 (C.1)	Licensing
10	Local government
11	Health and safety
12	Pesticides
13 (C.2)	Environmental protection
14	Social security
15	Children and young persons
16 (C.3)	Road traffic and vehicles
17	Road traffic and vehicles
18	Road traffic and vehicles
19	Road traffic and vehicles
20 (C.4)	Environment
21 (C.5)	Wildlife
22	Licensing
23	Licensing
24	Licensing
25	Wildlife
26	Registration of clubs
27	Registration of clubs
28 (C.6)	Licensing
29	Road traffic and vehicles
30	Roads
31	Roads
32	Road traffic and vehicles
33	Environment
34	Dogs
35	Environmental protection
36	Environmental protection
37	Environmental protection
38	Environmental protection
39	Dogs
40	Social security
41 (C.7)	Public health
42	Health and personal social services
43	Roads
44	Housing
	Rates
	Social security
45	Road traffic and vehicles
46	Rates
47	Rates
48 (C.8)	Licensing
49	Pensions
50	Pensions
51	Pensions
52	Environmental protection
53	Road traffic and vehicles
54	Road traffic and vehicles
55	Road traffic and vehicles
56	Road traffic and vehicles
57	Roads
58	Roads
59	Planning
60	Roads
61	Environmental protection
62	Education
63	Road traffic and vehicles
64	Police
65	Animals
66	Animals
67	Animals
68 (C. 9)	Children and young persons
69	Road traffic and vehicles
70	Roads
71	Fire and rescue services
72	Fire and rescue services
73	Health and personal social services
74	Road traffic and vehicles
75	Road traffic and vehicles
76	Road traffic and vehicles
77	Road traffic and vehicles
78	Health and personal social services
79	Rates
80	Road traffic and vehicles
81	Employment
82	Police
83	Social security
84	Social security
85	Local government

86	Criminal law	125	Pensions
87	Social security	126	Education
88	Social security	127	Roads
89	Social security	128	Roads
90 (C.10)	Public health	129	Roads
91	Public health	130	Food
92	Public health	131 (C.13)	Animals
93	Public health	132	Dogs
94	Airports	133	Plant health
95	Fisheries	134	Medicines Fees and charges
96	Fair employment	135	Legal aid and advice
97	Pensions	136	Education
98	Pensions	137	Pensions
99	Pensions	138	Employment
100	Social security	139	Landlord and tenant
101	Roads	140	Social security Housing Rates
102	Road traffic and vehicles		
103	Roads	141	Financial assistance
104	Roads	142 (C.14)	Justice
105	Environment	143	Road traffic and vehicles
106	Rates	144	Roads
107	Social security	145	Roads
108	Social security Housing Rates	146	Road traffic and vehicles
109	Social security	147	Rates
110	Pensions	148	Road traffic and vehicles
111	Health services charges	149	Road traffic and vehicles
112	Environmental protection	150	Road traffic and vehicles
113	Pensions	151	Fire and rescue services
114	Dogs	152	Fire and rescue services
115 (C.11)	Pensions	153	Animals
116	Social security Statutory maternity pay Statutory sick pay Employment Housing Rates	154 (C.15)	Animals
		155	Social security
		156	Welfare of animals
		157	Housing
		158	Animals
117	Social security	159	Financial assistance
118	Social security	160	Social security
119 (C.12)	Pensions	161	Fire and rescue services
120	Pensions	162	Fire and rescue services
121	Housing Rates Social security	163	Family law
		164	Roads
		165	Road traffic and vehicles
122	Rates	166	Road traffic and vehicles
123	Health and safety	167	Health and personal social services
124	Pensions	168	Dangerous drugs

169	Transport	215	Official statistics
170	Road traffic and vehicles	216	Roads
171	Road traffic and vehicles	217	Rates
172	Roads	218	Environmental protection
173	Government resources and accounts	219	Sports grounds
174	Roads	220	Road traffic and vehicles
175	Road traffic and vehicles	221	Road traffic and vehicles
176	Animals	222	Road traffic and vehicles
177	Health and safety	223	Road traffic and vehicles
178	Police	224	Road traffic and vehicles
179	Health and safety	225	Road traffic and vehicles
180	Food	226	Police
181	Social security	227	Road traffic and vehicles
182	Health and social care	228	Road traffic and vehicles
183	Local government	229	Health and social care
184	Education	230	Environmental protection
185	Seeds	231	Environmental protection
186 (C.16)	Building regulations	232	Pensions
187 (C.17)	Building regulations	233 (C.19)	Pensions
188	Procedure	234 (C.20)	Pensions
189	Magistrates' courts	235	Roads
190	Magistrates' courts	236 (C.21)	Pensions
191	Prisons	237	Pensions
192	Building regulations	238	Pensions
193	Road traffic and vehicles	239	Education
194	Road traffic and vehicles	240	Pensions
195	Road traffic and vehicles	241	Plant health
196	Roads	242	Road traffic and vehicles
197	Road traffic and vehicles	243	Road traffic and vehicles
198	Road traffic and vehicles	244	Public health
199	Road traffic and vehicles	245	Industrial training
200	Road traffic and vehicles	246	Public health
201	Road traffic and vehicles	247 (C. 22)	Road traffic and vehicles
202	Road traffic and vehicles	248	European Communities
203	Road traffic and vehicles	249	Licensing
204	Road traffic and vehicles	250	Clean air
205	Road traffic and vehicles	251	Road traffic and vehicles
206	Road traffic and vehicles	252	Road traffic and vehicles
207	Roads	253	Road traffic and vehicles
208	Roads	254	Agriculture
209	Roads	255	Health and safety
210	Roads	256	Road traffic and vehicles
211	Roads	257	Road traffic and vehicles
212	Dangerous drugs	258	Road traffic and vehicles
213	Dangerous drugs	259	Health and personal social services
214 (C.18)	Justice	260	Road traffic and vehicles

261	Road traffic and vehicles	306	Education
262 (C.23)	Road traffic and vehicles	307 (C.27)	Dangerous drugs
263	Race relations		Health and social care
264	Social security	308	Pharmacy
265 (C.24)	Pensions	309	Pharmacy
266 (C.25)	Pensions	310	Pharmacy
267	Pensions	311	Pharmacy
268	Legal aid and advice	312	Pharmacy
269	Road traffic and vehicles	313 (C.28)	Road traffic and vehicles
270	Pensions	314	Animals
271	Local government	315	Animals
272	Court of Judicature, Northern Ireland	316	Road traffic and vehicles
		317	Road traffic and vehicles
273	Court of Judicature, Northern Ireland	318	Rehabilitation of offenders
		319	Safeguarding vulnerable groups
274	Roads	320	Safeguarding vulnerable groups
275	Roads	321	Criminal law
276	Road traffic and vehicles	322	Safeguarding vulnerable groups
277	Road traffic and vehicles	323	Safeguarding vulnerable groups
278	Road traffic and vehicles	324	Health and social care
279	Local government	325	Criminal law
280	Food	326	Road traffic and vehicles
281	Road traffic and vehicles	327	Road traffic and vehicles
282	Road traffic and vehicles	328	Road traffic and vehicles
283	Employment	329	Planning
284	Social security	330 (C.29)	Safeguarding vulnerable groups
285	Pensions	331	Pensions
286 (C.26)	Criminal law	332	Pensions
287	Road traffic and vehicles	333	Road traffic and vehicles
288	Road traffic and vehicles	334 (C.30)	Northern Ireland Assembly
289	Road traffic and vehicles	335	Aquaculture
290	Road traffic and vehicles	336 (C.31)	Fisheries
291	Roads	337	Road traffic and vehicles
292	Social security	338 (C.32)	Health and social care
293	Planning	339	Roads
294	Pensions	340	Roads
295	Roads	341	Public health
296	Roads	342	Road traffic and vehicles
297	Road traffic and vehicles	343	Road traffic and vehicles
298	Road traffic and vehicles	344	Road traffic and vehicles
299	Horticulture	345	Road traffic and vehicles
300	Road traffic and vehicles	346	Road traffic and vehicles
301	Employment	347	Road traffic and vehicles
302	Employment	348	Road traffic and vehicles
303	Roads	349 (C.33)	Mental health services
304	Roads	350	Road traffic and vehicles
305	Animals	351	Road traffic and vehicles

352	Road traffic and vehicles	396	Energy
353	Road traffic and vehicles	397	Fisheries
354	Road traffic and vehicles	398	Education
355	Road traffic and vehicles	399	Clean air
356	Road traffic and vehicles	400	Plant health
357	Road traffic and vehicles	401	Mental health services
358	Road traffic and vehicles	402	County courts
359	Roads	403	Mental health services
360	Roads	404	Road traffic and vehicles
361	Roads	405 (C.39)	Licensing
362	Road traffic and vehicles	406 (C.40)	Civil registration
363	Road traffic and vehicles	407	Juries
364	Road traffic and vehicles	408	Civil registration
365	Construction	409	Road traffic and vehicles
366	Construction	410	Road traffic and vehicles
367 (C.34)	Construction	411	Road traffic and vehicles
368	European Communities	412	Road traffic and vehicles
369	Social security	413	Judgments
370	Road traffic and vehicles	414	Magistrates' courts
371	Road traffic and vehicles	415	Magistrates' courts
372 (C.35)	Pensions	416	European Communities
373	Landlord and tenant	417 (C.41)	Local government
374	Family law Child support	418	Road traffic and vehicles
		419	Legal aid and advice
375	Building regulations	420 (C.42)	Licensing
376	Police	421	Local government
377	Social security	422	Local government
378	Health and personal social services	423 (C.43)	Family law
379	Clean air	424 (C.44)	Family law
380	Housing Rates Social security	425	Road traffic and vehicles
		426	Pensions
		427	Family law
381	Electricity	428	Family law
382	Road traffic and vehicles	429	Housing
383	Animals	430	Magistrates' courts
384	Food	431	Court of Judicature, Northern Ireland
385	Electricity		
386 (C.36)	Animals	432	Road traffic and vehicles
387	Animals	433	Road traffic and vehicles
388 (C.37)	Older people	434	Road traffic and vehicles
389 (C.38)	Public health	435	Licensing
390	Pensions	436	Registration of clubs
391	Legal aid and advice	437	Environmental protection
392	Plant health	438	Family law
393	Pensions	439	Family law
394	Social security	440 (C.45)	Family law
395	Firearms and ammunition	441	Sea fisheries

442	Environmental protection	119 (C.12)
443	Registration of vital events	131 (C.13)
444	Education	142 (C.14)
445 (C.46)	Air passenger duty	154 (C.15)
446	Criminal law	186 (C.16)
447	Road traffic and vehicles	187 (C.17)
448	Roads	214 (C.18)
449 (C.47)	Justice	233 (C.19)
450	Health and safety	234 (C.20)
451	Road traffic and vehicles	236 (C.21)
452	Agriculture	247 (C.22)
453	Environmental protection	262 (C.23)
454	Gas	265 (C.24)
455	Pensions	266 (C.25)
456	Agriculture	286 (C.26)
457	Agriculture	307 (C.27)
458	Fisheries	313 (C.28)
459	Fisheries	330 (C.29)
460	Road traffic and vehicles	334 (C.30)
461	Road traffic and vehicles	336 (C.31)
462	Sex discrimination	338 (C.32)

List of Commencement Orders

9 (C.1)
13 (C.2)
16 (C.3)
20 (C.4)
21 (C.5)
28 (C.6)
41 (C.7)
48 (C.8)
68 (C.9)
90 (C.10)
115 (C.11)
349 (C.33)
367 (C.34)
372 (C.35)
386 (C.36)
388 (C.37)
389 (C.38)
405 (C.39)
406 (C.40)
417 (C.41)
420 (C.42)
423 (C.43)
424 (C.44)
440 (C.45)
445 (C.46)
449 (C.47)

Welsh Assembly Legislation

Measures of the National Assembly for Wales

Issued on 3rd March 2013

Measures of the National Assembly for Wales

Learning and Skills (Wales) Measure 2009: 2009 nawm 1 (correction slip). - 1 sheet: 30 cm. - Correction slip to (ISBN 9780105636052), issued 08.06.2009. Dated March 2012. Parallel texts in English and Welsh. Welsh title: Mesur Dysgu a Sgiliau (Cymru) 2009. 2009 mccc 1. - *Free*

Acts of the National Assembly for Wales

Acts of the National Assembly for Wales

Local Government Byelaws (Wales) Act 2012: 2012 anaw 2. - ii, ii, 23, 23p.: 30 cm. - Royal assent on 29 November 2012. An Act of the National Assembly for Wales to make provision for the powers of county councils, county borough councils, community councils and other public bodies to make byelaws; the procedure for making byelaws; the enforcement of byelaws. Explanatory notes to assist in the understanding of this Act are available separately (ISBN 9780348105292). - Parallel texts in English and Welsh. Welsh title: Deddf Is-ddeddfau Llywodraeth Leol (Cymru) 2012: (dccc 2). - 978-0-348-10501-8 £9.75

National Assembly for Wales (Official Languages) Act 2012: 2012 anaw 1. - ii, ii, 4, 4p.: 30 cm. - Royal assent on 12 November 2012. An Act of the National Assembly for Wales to make provision about the use of the English and Welsh languages in proceedings of the National Assembly for Wales and in the discharge of the functions of the Assembly Commission. Explanatory notes to assist in the understanding of this Act are available separately, 2012 anaw 1 (ISBN 9780105456285). - Corrected reprint, replacing that published on 16 November 2012, which is being sent free of charge to all known recipients of the original version. - Parallel texts in English and Welsh. Welsh title: Deddf Cynulliad Cenedlaethol Cymru (Ieithoedd Swyddogol) 2012: (dccc 1). - 978-0-10-545618-6 £5.75

Acts of the National Assembly for Wales - Explanatory Notes

Local Government Byelaws (Wales) Act 2012: 2012 anaw 2: explanatory notes. - [24]p.: 30 cm. - These notes refer to the Local Government Byelaws (Wales) Act 2012 (anaw 2) which received Royal assent on 29 November 2012 (ISBN 9780348105018). - Parallel texts in English and Welsh. Welsh title: Deddf Is-ddeddfau Llywodraeth Leol (Cymru) 2012: 2012 dccc 2: nodiadau esboniadol. - 978-0-348-10529-2 £5.75

National Assembly for Wales (Official Languages) Act 2012: 2012 anaw 1: explanatory notes. - [16]p.: 30 cm. - These notes refer to the National Assembly for Wales (Official Languages) Act 2012 (anaw 1) which received Royal assent on 12 November 2012 (ISBN 9780105456186). - Parallel texts in English and Welsh. Welsh title: Deddf Cynulliad Cenedlaethol Cymru (Ieithoedd Swyddogol) 2012: (dccc 1): nodiadau esboniadol. - 978-0-10-545628-5 £5.75

Alphabetical Index

A

A3 Northway, Portadown: Abandonment: Northern Ireland. 431
A55 Knock Rd, Belfast: Private accesses: Stopping-up: Roads: Northern Ireland 433
A55 Knock Rd, Belfast: Trunk road T14: Roads: Northern Ireland 434
Aberdeen: Port security: Merchant shipping. 104
Abergavenny Improvement Act 1854: Partial repeal 99
Abuse: Domestic: Acts: Explanatory notes: Scotland 362
Academies: Alternative provision academies: Consequential amendments: England. 48, 49
Academies: Land transfer schemes: England 48
Academies: School behaviour: Measures: Determination & publicising: England 53
Access: Countryside: Coastal margin: Weymouth Bay. 38
Accident reporting & investigation: Merchant shipping. 104
Accounting standards: Prescribed bodies: United States & Japan: Companies 31
Act of Adjournal: Criminal Procedure (Scotland) Act 1995: Transcripts: Amendments: Scotland 373, 394
Act of Adjournal: Criminal procedure rules: Scotland 373, 375, 394
Act of Sederunt: Court of Session: Messengers-at-Arms: Fees: Scotland 367
Act of Sederunt: Court of Session: Miscellaneous: Scotland 367, 368
Act of Sederunt: Court of Session: Registration Appeal Court: Scotland 367
Act of Sederunt: Court of Session: Rules: Solicitor's fees: Scotland 368
Act of Sederunt: Court of Session: Shorthand writers: Fees: Scotland 367
Act of Sederunt: Sheriff Court: Heritable property: Actions for removing: Scotland 394
Act of Sederunt: Sheriff Court: Rules: Scotland 394
Act of Sederunt: Sheriff Court: Sheriff officers: Fees: Scotland 394
Act of Sederunt: Sheriff Court: Shorthand writers: Fees: Scotland 394
Addicts supply: Misuse of drugs 45
Additional voluntary contributions: Health & personal social services: Northern Ireland. 416
Additives: Food: England 71
Additives: Food: Northern Ireland 415
Additives: Food: Wales 72
Adoption & Children Act 2007: Commencements: Scotland 366
Adoption agencies: Panel & consequential amendments: England & Wales 17
Adoption agencies: Wales. 18
Adult support & protection: Community Care & Health (Scotland) Act 2002: Scotland 362, 395
Adults with incapacity: Medical treatment certificates: Signing: Requirements: Scotland 363
Adults with incapacity: Public Guardian: Fees: Amendments: Scotland 363
Adults: Safeguarding Vulnerable Groups: 2007 Order: Commencements: Northern Ireland . . . 443
Advertisements: Control: Town & country planning: England 306
Advertising & trading: London Olympic & Paralympic Games: Wales. 101
Advice & assistance: Representation: Scotland 376
Advisory Committee on Hazardous Substances (ACHS): Abolition. 61, 74, 129
Aerodromes see also Airports 28
Afghanistan: United Nations: Measures: Overseas territories 113
African horse sickness: England 10
African horse sickness: Scotland. 364
Agricultural holdings: Amendments: Acts: Explanatory notes: Scotland 362
Agricultural holdings: Amendments: Acts: Scotland 361
Agricultural holdings: Units of production: England 90
Agricultural holdings: Units of production: Wales 90
Agriculture: Amendments 8
Agriculture: Animals: Trade in: Related products: Scotland 363, 364
Agriculture: Beef & pigs: Carcase classification: Wales. 9
Agriculture: Common Agricultural Policy: Single payment & support schemes: Cross-compliance: Northern Ireland. . . 405
Agriculture: Common Agricultural Policy: Single payment & support schemes: England. 9
Agriculture: Common Agricultural Policy: Single payment & support schemes: Wales. 9
Agriculture: Common Agricultural Policy: Support schemes: Decisions: Review: Northern Ireland 405
Agriculture: International Fund for Agricultural Development: Eighth replenishment 88
Agriculture: Leader grants: Scotland. 363

Entry	Page
Agriculture: Less favoured area support schemes: Scotland	363
Agriculture: Less favoured areas: Compensatory allowances: Northern Ireland	405
Agriculture: Miscellaneous amendments: England & Wales	11
Agriculture: Nitrate pollution: Prevention.	9, 313
Agriculture: Nitrate pollution: Prevention: Wales.	9, 314
Agriculture: Northern Ireland Poultry Health Assurance Scheme: Fees: Northern Ireland	406
Agriculture: Plant protection products: Sustainable use	119
Agriculture: Poultry: Health scheme: Fees: Scotland.	363, 364
Agriculture: Red meat industry: Slaughterers & exporters: Designation: Wales	9
Agriculture: Rural development contracts: Rural priorities: Scotland	363
Agriculture: Rural payments: Appeals: Scotland	363
Agriculture: Specified products: From China: Marketing: Restrictions: England	9, 71
Agriculture: Specified products: From China: Marketing: Restrictions: Northern Ireland	405, 416
Agriculture: Specified products: From China: Marketing: Restrictions: Scotland	363, 372
Agriculture: Specified products: From China: Marketing: Restrictions: Wales.	10, 72
Agriculture: Student fees: Northern Ireland	405
Agriculture: Uplands: Transitional payments.	9
Ahoghill: Waiting restrictions: Road traffic & vehicles: Northern Ireland	442
Air Force: Disablement & death: Service pensions	116
Air navigation: Amendments	19
Air navigation: Dangerous goods	19
Air navigation: Flying restrictions: Abingdon Air & Country Show	20
Air navigation: Flying restrictions: Balado	20
Air navigation: Flying restrictions: Biggin Hill	20
Air navigation: Flying restrictions: Bournemouth.	20
Air navigation: Flying restrictions: Breighton Airfield	20
Air navigation: Flying restrictions: Brentwood	20
Air navigation: Flying restrictions: Burton Bradstock, Dorset	20
Air navigation: Flying restrictions: Chelmsford.	20
Air navigation: Flying restrictions: Cheltenham Festival	20
Air navigation: Flying restrictions: Cholmondeley Castle	20
Air navigation: Flying restrictions: Diamond Jubilee Concert	20
Air navigation: Flying restrictions: Dunsfold	20
Air navigation: Flying restrictions: Duxford	21
Air navigation: Flying restrictions: Eastbourne	21
Air navigation: Flying restrictions: Elgin offshore installation	21
Air navigation: Flying restrictions: Elgin Offshore Installation.	21
Air navigation: Flying restrictions: Exeter	21
Air navigation: Flying restrictions: Fair Isle	21
Air navigation: Flying restrictions: Farnborough Air Show.	21
Air navigation: Flying restrictions: Fillingham	22
Air navigation: Flying restrictions: Folkestone	22
Air navigation: Flying restrictions: Frogham	22
Air navigation: Flying restrictions: Guildford.	22
Air navigation: Flying restrictions: Her Majesty The Queen's Birthday Flypast	22
Air navigation: Flying restrictions: Her Majesty The Queen's Diamond Jubilee flypast	22
Air navigation: Flying restrictions: Her Majesty The Queen's Diamond Jubilee flypast rehearsal	22
Air navigation: Flying restrictions: Jet formation display teams	22, 23
Air navigation: Flying restrictions: Kemble.	23
Air navigation: Flying restrictions: Kensington.	23
Air navigation: Flying restrictions: London 2012 Olympic & Paralympic Games, Lee Valley White Water Centre, Broxbourne, Hertfordshire	24
Air navigation: Flying restrictions: London 2012 Olympic & Paralympic Games, Road Cycle Event, Leatherhead, Surrey	24
Air navigation: Flying restrictions: London 2012 Olympic & Paralympic Games: Brands Hatch, Kent	23
Air navigation: Flying restrictions: London 2012 Olympic & Paralympic Games: City of Coventry Stadium, Coventry	23
Air navigation: Flying restrictions: London 2012 Olympic & Paralympic Games: Egham, Surrey	23
Air navigation: Flying restrictions: London 2012 Olympic & Paralympic Games: Eton Dorney, Buckinghamshire.	24
Air navigation: Flying restrictions: London 2012 Olympic & Paralympic Games: Hadleigh Farm, Essex.	24
Air navigation: Flying restrictions: London 2012 Olympic & Paralympic Games: Hampden Park, Glasgow	24
Air navigation: Flying restrictions: London 2012 Olympic & Paralympic Games: Lee Valley White Water Centre, Broxbourne, Hertfordshire	24
Air navigation: Flying restrictions: London 2012 Olympic & Paralympic Games: London Prohibited Zone EGP111.	24
Air navigation: Flying restrictions: London 2012 Olympic & Paralympic Games: London Prohibited Zone EGP114.	24
Air navigation: Flying restrictions: London 2012 Olympic & Paralympic Games: London Restricted Zone EGR112.	24
Air navigation: Flying restrictions: London 2012 Olympic & Paralympic Games: Millennium Stadium, Cardiff	24

Air navigation: Flying restrictions: London 2012 Olympic & Paralympic Games: Old Trafford, Manchester 24
Air navigation: Flying restrictions: London 2012 Olympic & Paralympic Games: St James' Park, Newcastle 25
Air navigation: Flying restrictions: London 2012 Olympic & Paralympic Games: Weymouth Restricted Zone EGR005 . . 25
Air navigation: Flying restrictions: London Remembrance Commemorations 25
Air navigation: Flying restrictions: Lowestoft 25
Air navigation: Flying restrictions: Machynlleth 25
Air navigation: Flying restrictions: Northampton Sywell 25
Air navigation: Flying restrictions: Northern Ireland International Air Show 25
Air navigation: Flying restrictions: Old Warden 25
Air navigation: Flying restrictions: Plymouth 25
Air navigation: Flying restrictions: Portsmouth 25
Air navigation: Flying restrictions: RNAS Yeovilton 25
Air navigation: Flying restrictions: Royal Air Force Cosford 25
Air navigation: Flying restrictions: Royal Air Force Leuchars 26
Air navigation: Flying restrictions: Royal Air Force Waddington 26
Air navigation: Flying restrictions: Royal International Air Tattoo RAF Fairford 26
Air navigation: Flying restrictions: Saltburn-by-the-Sea, Durham 26
Air navigation: Flying restrictions: Shivering Sands 26
Air navigation: Flying restrictions: Shoreham-by-Sea 26
Air navigation: Flying restrictions: Silverstone & Turweston 26
Air navigation: Flying restrictions: Southend-on-Sea 26, 27
Air navigation: Flying restrictions: Southport 27
Air navigation: Flying restrictions: State opening of Parliament 27
Air navigation: Flying restrictions: Stonehenge 27
Air navigation: Flying restrictions: Stratford 27
Air navigation: Flying restrictions: Sunderland 27
Air navigation: Flying restrictions: Thames Diamond Jubilee Pageant 27
Air navigation: Flying restrictions: Tottenham Court Road, London 27
Air navigation: Flying restrictions: Trooping the Colour 27
Air navigation: Flying restrictions: Wales Rally GB 27
Air navigation: Flying restrictions: West Wales 28
Air navigation: Flying restrictions: Weston Park 27
Air navigation: Flying restrictions: Wimbeldon 28
Air passenger duty 65
Air Passenger Duty 2012 Act: Commencements: Northern Ireland 405
Air passenger duty: Setting of rate: Acts: Explanatory notes: Northern Ireland 404
Air passenger duty: Setting of rate: Acts: Northern Ireland 404
Air travel organisers: Licensing: Civil aviation 28
Aircraft operators: Accounts & records 65
Airports: Aviation security: Policing: Belfast International Airport 28
Airports: Belfast International Airport: Land control: Northern Ireland 405
Alcohol: Children: Persistent selling to: Closure Notices: Prescribed forms: Licensing Act 2003 . . . . 42, 92
Alcohol: Minimum pricing: Acts: Explanatory notes: Scotland 362
Alcohol: Minimum pricing: Acts: Scotland 361
Alien & locally absent species: Aquaculture: Northern Ireland 407
Al-Qaida: United Nations: Measures: Overseas territories 113
Anglesey, Isle of: Local authorities: Ordinary elections 99
Anglesey, Isle: Local authorities: Electoral arrangements 99
Animal by-products: Scotland 364
Animal health: African horse sickness: England 10
Animal health: Animal by-products: Scotland 364
Animal health: Bluetongue: England 10
Animal health: Bluetongue: Northern Ireland 406
Animal health: Bluetongue: Scotland 365
Animal health: Bluetongue: Wales 11
Animal health: Bovine viral diarrhoea: Scotland 365
Animal health: Cattle compensation: England 10
Animal health: Tuberculosis: England 11
Animal health: Value: Individual ascertainment: England 11
Animals (Scientific Procedures) Act 1986: Amendments 10
Animals (Scientific Procedures) Act 1986: Fees 10
Animals: Animal health: African horse sickness: Scotland 364
Animals: Aujeszky's Disease scheme: Northern Ireland 406
Animals: Aujeszky's Disease: Pigs: Northern Ireland 406
Animals: Badgers: Control areas: Wales 11

Animals: Brucellosis: Control: Northern Ireland 406
Animals: Cattle compensation: England 10
Animals: Cattle: Identification: Northern Ireland 412
Animals: Diseases: Machinery & vehicles: Importation: Northern Ireland 406
Animals: Dogs: 2011 Amendment Act: Commencements: Northern Ireland 406
Animals: Health & welfare: Miscellaneous amendments: England & Wales. 11
Animals: Local policing bodies 10, 67, 99, 122
Animals: Mink keeping: Prohibition: Wales 11, 47
Animals: Northern Ireland Poultry Health Assurance Scheme: Fees: Northern Ireland 406
Animals: Pigs: Records, identification & movement: Northern Ireland 406
Animals: Poultry: Health scheme: Fees: Scotland 363, 364
Animals: Prevention of cruelty: Spring traps: Approval: England 11
Animals: Prevention of cruelty: Welfare: At time of killing: Scotland 365
Animals: Protected animals: Prohibited procedures: Exemptions: Scotland. 364
Animals: Sheep: Export: Prohibition: Scotland. 364, 381
Animals: Spring traps: Approval: Wales 11
Animals: Trade in: Related products: Scotland. 363, 364
Animals: Tuberculosis: Control: Northern Ireland. 406
Animals: Tuberculosis: England 11
Animals: Value: Individual ascertainment: England 11
Animals: Welfare: 2011 Act: Commencements: Northern Ireland. 406
Animals: Welfare: At time of killing: Scotland 365
Animals: Welfare: Dogs (working): Tail docking: Northern Ireland 407
Animals: Welfare: Northern Ireland 448
Animals: Welfare: Permitted procedures: Lay persons: Northern Ireland 407
Animals: Welfare: Slaughter or killing: England 11
Animals: Wild animals: Travelling circuses: Welfare: England 10
Animals: Zoonoses: Fees: Northern Ireland 406
Animals: Zootechnical standards: England 10
Annuities: Purchased: Income tax. 86
Annuities: Relevant: Registered pension schemes: Income tax 87
Anti-terrorism, Crime & Security Act 2001: Modifications 126
Apprenticeships, Skills, Children & Learning Act 2009: Consequential amendments 60
Apprenticeships: Agreement form 60
Apprenticeships: Alternative English completion conditions 49
Aquaculture: Alien & locally absent species: Northern Ireland 407
Armagh: Parking places: Northern Ireland. 439
Armed Forces Act 2011: Commencements 45, 46
Armed Forces Act: Continuation 46
Armed Forces: Compensation schemes 116
Armed forces: Enhanced Learning Credit Scheme: Further & Higher Education Commitment Scheme 116
Armed forces: Housing: Additional preference: England. 81
Armed forces: Housing: Allocation: Qualification criteria: England 80
Armed Forces: Powers of stop & search, search, seizure & retention. 46
Armorial bearings: Local authorities 95
Army: Disablement & death: Service pensions 116
Artificial lighting: Statutory nuisances: Environmental protection: Relevant sports: Northern Ireland 412
Asbestos: Control. 74
Asbestos: Control: Northern Ireland. 417
Ash dieback: Wood & bark: Plant health: Northern Ireland 428
Assembly Members (Independent Financial Review and Standards) Act (Northern Ireland) 2011: Commencements: Northern Ireland 422
Asylum: Immigration & asylum: Jersey. 82
Asylum: Immigration, Asylum & Nationality Act 2006: Commencements. 83
Asylum: Nationality, Immigration & Asylum Act 2002: Authority to carry 84
Asylum: Nationality, Immigration & Asylum Act 2002: Commencements. 84
Auditors: Statutory auditors: Companies Act 2006: Amendment & delegation of functions 12, 32
Aujeszky's Disease scheme: Northern Ireland. 406
Aujeszky's Disease: Pigs: Northern Ireland 406
Authorised Investment Funds: Taxes 14, 35, 84
Automatic enrolment: Pensions: Earnings trigger & qualifying earnings band 116
Automatic enrolment: Pensions: Earnings trigger & qualifying earnings band: Northern Ireland. 423
Automatic enrolment: Pensions: Northern Ireland. 423
Aviation security: Policing: Belfast International Airport. 28
Aviation: Civil: Acts 4

Aviation: Civil: Acts: Explanatory notes 7
Aviation: Civil: Air navigation: Amendments 19
Aviation: Civil: Air passenger duty 65
Axe Brue Internal Drainage Board 89

B

Badgers: Control areas: Wales 11
Bahrain: Double taxation: Relief & international enforcement 14, 35, 85
Ballydogherty Road (U5003), Loughgilly: Abandonment: Roads: Northern Ireland 431
Ballymena: Parking & waiting restrictions: Road traffic & vehicles: Northern Ireland 437
Ballymoney: Road traffic & vehicles: Northern Ireland 438
Bananas: Green: Quality standards: England & Wales 80
Bananas: Marketing: Scotland 374
Banchory & Cranthes Light Railway: Scotland 396
Bangor: Waiting restrictions: Road traffic & vehicles: Northern Ireland 442
Bank levy: Double taxation: Arrangements: Germany 12
Bank levy: Double taxation: Relief 12
Bank levy: International tax enforcement: Arrangements: Germany 12
Bank levy: Taxes: Double taxation: Relief: Germany 12
Bank of Ireland (UK) plc: Local acts 7
Bankruptcy: Fees: Scotland 375
Barbados: Double taxation: Relief & international enforcement 14, 35, 85
Barnsley Metropolitan Borough Council: Permit schemes: Traffic management 78
Barony College: Transfer & closures: Scotland 369
Barts Health, The London, Newham University Hospital & Whipps Cross Hospital: National Health Service Trust 106
Bathing water: Quality: Northern Ireland 412
Batteries & accumulators: Market: Placing: Environmental protection 61
Bedford Borough Council: Permit schemes: Traffic management 78
Bedfordshire Fire Services: Combination scheme 69
Beef: Carcase classification: Wales 9
Behaviour improvement: Educational provision England 50
Belarus: Asset-freezing 39
Belfast city centre: Parking places: Northern Ireland 439
Belfast city centre: Traffic control: Northern Ireland 434
Belfast city centre: Waiting restrictions: Road traffic & vehicles: Northern Ireland 438, 442
Belfast International Airport: Land control: Northern Ireland 405
Belfast: Apsley St.: Traffic control: Northern Ireland 434
Belfast: International Airport: Policing 28
Belfast: Parking & waiting restrictions: Road traffic & vehicles: Northern Ireland 438
Belfast: Roads: Parking places: Northern Ireland 439
Belfast: Traffic control: Northern Ireland 434
Betting, gaming & lotteries: Gambling Act 2005: Schedule 6: Amendments 12
Betting, gaming & lotteries: Gambling: Licence fees: Amendments 12
Betting, gaming & lotteries: Gambling: Operating licences & single-machine permit fees 12
Bexley, London Borough: Permit schemes: Traffic management 79
Biometric registration: Immigration 83
Birmingham, City: Mayoral referendum 93
Births & deaths: Registration: England & Wales 134
Births, deaths & marriages, etc.: Registration: Fees: Amendments 134
Blaby, District: Electoral changes 94
Bluetongue: Animal health: England 10
Bluetongue: Animal health: Northern Ireland 406
Bluetongue: Animal health: Scotland 365
Bluetongue: Animal health: Wales 11
Bonds: Regulated covered bonds 69
Bovine viral diarrhoea: Scotland 365
Bradford, City: Mayoral referendum 93
Bridgewater Canal: Transfer of undertaking 14, 309
Bristol, City: Mayoral referendum 93
British nationality 12
British Waterways Board: Tax consequences 35, 302
British Waterways Board: Transfer of functions 14, 129, 308
Broadcasting: Communications: Guernsey 12, 59
Broadcasting: Community radio: Guernsey 13

Broadcasting: Local digital television programme services. 13
Broadcasting: Local digital television programme services: Independent productions 12, 59
Broadcasting: Wireless Telegraphy Act 2006: OFCOM: Directions 13, 59
Browning Drive, Londonderry: Abandonment: Roads: Northern Ireland 431
Broxbourne: Electoral changes 93
Brucellosis: Control: Animals: Northern Ireland 406
Buckinghamshire: Electoral changes 93
Budget (Scotland) Act 2010: Amendments: Scotland 381
Budget Responsibility & National Audit Act 2011: Appointed days 13
Budget Responsibility & National Audit Act 2011: Consequential amendments. 13
Budget: Acts: Explanatory notes: Northern Ireland 404
Budget: Acts: Northern Ireland 404
Budget: Acts: Scotland. 361
Building & buildings: Energy Act 2011: Energy performance 13, 61
Building & buildings: Energy performance: Certificates & inspections: England & Wales 13
Building & buildings: Energy performance: England & Wales. 14
Building & buildings: Energy performance: Scotland 365
Building & buildings: Scotland 365
Building regulations: 1979 Order: Commencements: Northern Ireland 407
Building regulations: 2009 Amendment Act: Commencements: Northern Ireland 407
Building regulations: England & Wales. 13
Building regulations: Northern Ireland. 407
Buildings: Listed: Conservation areas: Planning: England 305
Burma & Syria: Export control: Sanctions 44
Burma/Myanmar: European Communities: Financial restrictions: Suspension 39
Burma: Restrictive measures: Overseas territories. 113
Bus lane contraventions: Approved local authorities 93, 272
Bus lanes: Belfast city centre: Northern Ireland 434
Bus lanes: East Bridge St. & Cromac St., Belfast: Northern Ireland. 434
Bus Service Operators Grant: Scotland 396
Buses: Bus Service Operators Grant: Scotland 396
Bushmills: Waiting restrictions: Road traffic & vehicles: Northern Ireland. 442
Business investment relief. 84
Business rate supplements: Non-domestic rating: Deferred payments: England 133

C

C156 (Unnamed road), Moyraverty, Craigavon: Abandonment: Northern Ireland 431
Cable car: London 309, 310
Caernarfon Harbour Trust: Constitution: Harbour revision 74
Canals & inland waterways: Bridgewater Canal: Transfer of undertaking 14, 309
Canals & inland waterways: British Waterways Board: Transfer of functions. 14, 129, 308
Cancer patients: Treatment: Fuel payments scheme: Northern Ireland 414
Capital allowances: Energy-saving plant & machinery. 35, 84
Capital allowances: Environmentally beneficial plant & machinery 35, 84
Capital gains tax: Annual exempt amount. 14
Capital gains tax: Authorised Investment Funds 14, 35
Capital gains tax: Chargeable gains: Gilt-edged securities 15, 36
Capital gains tax: Finance Act 2010: Schedule 6, part 1: Consequential & incidental provisions. 15, 36, 85, 312
Capital gains tax: Finance Act 2012: Enterprise investment scheme: Appointed day. 15, 85
Capital gains tax: Financial Services Act 2010: Schedule 6: Part 2: Commencements. 15, 36, 85, 88, 302, 303
Capital gains tax: Individual savings accounts 15, 86
Capital requirements: Financial services & markets 68
Car & van fuel: Benefit: Income tax 84
Car fuel: Benefit: Income tax 84
Carbon dioxide: Storage: Inspections 62
Carbon reduction commitment: CRC energy efficiency scheme: Allocation of allowances 30
Care Council for Wales: Appointment, membership & procedure. 295
Care Quality Commission: Healthwatch England Committee. 106, 131, 295
Care Quality Commission: Registration & additional functions 106, 131, 295
Care Quality Commission: Registration & membership 106, 131, 295
Carers Strategies: Wales 110, 295
Carers: Disabled children: Breaks: Wales. 18
Carlingford area: Fisheries: Angling: Northern Ireland 415
Carlingford fisheries: Foyle & Carlingford Fisheries: 2007 Order: Commencements: Northern Ireland 415

Carrickfergus: Traffic control: Northern Ireland. 435
Cars: Motor cars: Driving instruction: Compensation schemes 136
Cash: Detention & forfeiture: Magistrates' courts: England & Wales. 102
Cattle compensation: England. 10
Cattle: Identification: Northern Ireland 412
Cattle: Slaughter: Value: Individual ascertainment: England 11
Caversfield Service Family Accommodation Byelaws 46
Central rating list: England 133
Ceredigion: Parking contraventions: Civil enforcement: Wales. 273
Channel Tunnel: International arrangements 15
Charging orders: Tribunals, Courts & Enforcement Act 2007: Commencements. 15
Charitable incorporated organisations. 16
Charities Act 2011: Commencements. 16
Charities Restricted Funds Reorganisation: Scotland 366
Charities: Charitable incorporated organisations 15, 16
Charities: Charitable incorporated organisations: Insolvency & dissolution 16
Charities: Charities reorganisation: Amendments: Scotland. 366
Charities: Charities Restricted Funds Reorganisation: Scotland. 366
Charities: Finance Act 2010: Schedule 6, part 1: Consequential & incidental provisions 15, 36, 85, 312
Charities: Financial Services Act 2010: Schedule 6: Part 2: Commencements. 15, 36, 85, 88, 302, 303
Charities: Public Services Reform (Scotland) Act 2010: Commencements: Scotland. 366
Charities: Registration: Exceptions 16
Charities: Small donations: Taxation: Acts. 6
Charities: Small donations: Taxation: Acts: Explanatory notes 7
Charity Commission for Northern Ireland: Superannuation: Northern Ireland 426
Chemical agents: Health & safety: At work: Merchant shipping & fishing vessels 104
Chief constables & the Commissioner of the Police of the Metropolis: Value added tax: Refunds 312
Chief Inspector of Criminal Justice in Northern Ireland: Superannuation: Northern Ireland 426
Child benefit: Child tax credits. 296, 304
Child benefit: General 296
Child benefit: Guardian's allowance: Administration 296
Child Maintenance & Enforcement Commission: Abolition. 67, 130
Child Maintenance & Other Payments Act 2008: Commencements. 66, 296
Child Maintenance Act 2008 Act: Commencements: Northern Ireland 413
Child maintenance: Welfare reform: Acts 7
Child maintenance: Welfare reform: Acts: Explanatory notes 7
Child support 67
Child support maintenance: Basic rate calculation: Changes: Liability: Minimum amounts 66
Child support maintenance: Calculation 66
Child support: Appeal decisions: Supersession 299
Child support: Child Maintenance & Other Payments Act 2008: Commencements. 66, 296
Child support: Family law: Northern Ireland 414
Child support: Family law: Payments & arrears: Management: Northern Ireland. 413
Child support: Maintenance calculation: Family law: Northern Ireland. 413
Child support: Maintenance: Basic rate calculation & minimum liability: Changes: Family law: Northern Ireland 413
Child support: New calculation rules 67
Child support: New calculation rules: Northern Ireland. 414
Child support: Northern Ireland 407, 413
Child support: Payments & arrears: Management: Amendments 67
Child support: Public bodies: Child Maintenance & Enforcement Commission: Abolition 67, 130
Child support: Reciprocal arrangements: Northern Ireland 67
Child support: Welfare Reform Act 2009: Commencements 66, 296
Child support: Welfare Reform Act 2010: Commencements: Northern Ireland. 414
Child tax credit: Up-rating. 304
Child trust funds. 19
Childcare: Early years register 16
Childcare: Fees: England 16
Childcare: General childcare register 16
Childcare: Inspections. 16
Children & Families (Wales) Measure: Commencements 18, 19, 110, 295
Children & Young Persons Act 2008: Commencements: Wales 19
Children & young persons: Adoption & Children Act 2007: Commencements: Scotland. 366
Children & young persons: Adoption agencies: Panel & consequential amendments: England & Wales 17
Children & young persons: Adoption agencies: Wales 18
Children & young persons: Childcare: Early years register. 16

Children & young persons: Childcare: Fees: England 16
Children & young persons: Childcare: General childcare register 16
Children & young persons: Childcare: Inspections 16
Children & young persons: Children & Families (Wales) Measure: Commencements. 18, 19, 110, 295
Children & young persons: Children Act 2004: Information database: England 16
Children & young persons: Children's Hearings (Scotland) Act 2011: Appeals against Dismissal by SCRA: Scotland . . 366
Children & young persons: Children's Hearings (Scotland) Act 2011: Child protection emergency measures: Scotland. . 366
Children & young persons: Children's Hearings (Scotland) Act 2011: Commencements: Scotland. 366, 376
Children & young persons: Children's Hearings (Scotland) Act 2011: Rights of audience: Principal reporter: Scotland. . 366
Children & young persons: Children's Hearings (Scotland) Act 2011: Safeguarders Panel: Scotland 367
Children & young persons: Children's Hearings (Scotland) Act 2011: Safeguarders: Further Provision: Scotland. . . . 366
Children & young persons: Disabled children: Carers: Breaks: Wales 18
Children & young persons: Disclosure & Barring Service: Core functions 17, 128
Children & young persons: Early Years Foundation Stage: Learning & development requirements 16
Children & young persons: Early Years Foundation Stage: Learning & development requirements: Exemptions 16
Children & young persons: Early Years Foundation Stage: Welfare requirements 16
Children & young persons: Family support teams: Composition & board functions: Wales. 19, 111, 296
Children & young persons: Family support teams: Family support functions: Wales 19, 111, 296
Children & young persons: Family support teams: Review of cases: Wales 19, 111, 296
Children & young persons: Health: 2009 Act: Commencements: Northern Ireland. 407
Children & young persons: Her Majesty's Inspector of Education, Children's Services & Skills 17, 52
Children & young persons: Her Majesty's Inspector of Education, Children's Services & Skills: Children's homes etc.: Fees
& frequency of inspections 17
Children & young persons: Legal Aid, Sentencing & Punishment of Offenders Act 2012: Consequential & savings
provisions 17, 42, 46
Children & young persons: Legal Aid, Sentencing & Punishment of Offenders Act 2012: Youth detention. 17
Children & young persons: Legislative reform: Local authorities: Annual review 17, 52, 135
Children & young persons: Local authorities: Early years provision: Free: Duty. 17
Children & young persons: Local Safeguarding Children Boards: Wales 19
Children & young persons: Play sufficiency assessment: Wales 19
Children & young persons: Protection of Freedoms Act 2012 . . . . 17, 18, 125, 128, 129
Children & young persons: Protection of Freedoms Act 2012: Commencements . . . 17, 18, 43, 89, 126, 128, 129, 136, 273
Children & young persons: Safeguarding Vulnerable Groups Act 2006: Commencements. 17, 128
Children & young persons: Safeguarding Vulnerable Groups Act 2006: Controlled activity & prescribed criteria: England &
Wales. 18, 128
Children & young persons: Safeguarding Vulnerable Groups Act 2006: Miscellaneous amendments 18, 128
Children & young persons: Safeguarding Vulnerable Groups Act 2006: Miscellaneous provisions 18, 128
Children & young persons: Secure accommodation: Amendments. 16
Children & young persons: Tobacco: Sale: Vending machines: Northern Ireland. 407
Children Act 2004: Information database: England. 16
Children: Alcohol: Persistent selling to: Closure Notices: Prescribed forms: Licensing Act 2003 . . . . 42, 92
Children: Safeguarding Vulnerable Groups: 2007 Order: Commencements: Northern Ireland 443
Children: Secure accommodation: Amendments 16
Children's Hearings (Scotland) Act 2011: Appeals against Dismissal by SCRA: Scotland. 366
Children's Hearings (Scotland) Act 2011: Child protection emergency measures: Scotland 366
Children's Hearings (Scotland) Act 2011: Commencements: Scotland 366, 376
Children's Hearings (Scotland) Act 2011: Rights of audience: Principal reporter: Scotland 366
Children's Hearings (Scotland) Act 2011: Safeguarders Panel: Scotland 367
Children's Hearings (Scotland) Act 2011: Safeguarders: Further Provision: Scotland 366
Children's homes: Health & social care: Northern Ireland 417
Children's homes: Her Majesty's Inspector of Education, Children's Services & Skills 17, 52
Children's homes: Her Majesty's Inspector of Education, Children's Services & Skills: Fees & frequency of inspections . 17
Chiltern Railways: Bicester to Oxford improvement 309
Chronological tables: Statutes 8
Church of England: General Synod: Measures. 8
Church of England: General Synod: Measures: Bound volumes. 8
Church of England: General Synod: Measures: Tables & index 8
Citizenship: Freedoms: Protection: Acts 6
Citizenship: Freedoms: Protection: Acts: Explanatory notes. 7
Civic Government (Scotland) Act 1982: Metal Dealers': Exemption Warrants: Scotland. 377
Civil aviation: Acts. 4
Civil aviation: Acts: Explanatory notes. 7
Civil aviation: Air navigation: Amendments 19
Civil aviation: Air navigation: Dangerous goods 19
Civil aviation: Air passenger duty. 65

Civil aviation: Air travel organisers: Licensing 28
Civil aviation: Flying restrictions 20, 21, 22, 23, 24, 25, 26, 27, 28
Civil Contingencies Act 2004: Contingency planning 28
Civil contingencies: Acts 4
Civil courts: England & Wales. 38, 294
Civil defence: Civil contingencies: Acts 4
Civil Jurisdiction & Judgments Act 1982: Magistrates' courts: Rules: Northern Ireland 422
Civil legal aid: Amendments: Scotland 376
Civil legal aid: England & Wales 90
Civil legal aid: Environment: Pollution: Prescribed types 91
Civil legal aid: Immigration interviews: Exceptions 91
Civil legal aid: Procedure: England & Wales 91
Civil partnership: Registration abroad & certificates 28
Civil Partnerships Act 2004: Overseas relationships 28
Civil partnerships: Divorce actions: Scotland 371
Civil partnerships: Registration: Fees: Amendments 28
Civil penalties: Penalty charges enforcement: London 61, 101
Civil penalties: Social security 299
Civil procedure: Rules: England & Wales 38, 294
Civil Registration Act (Northern Ireland) 2011: Commencements : Northern Ireland 407
Civil registration: Northern Ireland 408
Clean air: Smoke control areas: Authorised fuels: England 29
Clean air: Smoke control areas: Authorised fuels: Northern Ireland 408
Clean air: Smoke control areas: Fireplaces: Exempt: England 29
Clean air: Smoke control areas: Fireplaces: Exempt: Northern Ireland 408
Clean air: Smoke control areas: Fireplaces: Exempt: Wales 29
Clean Neighbourhoods & Environment Act (Northern Ireland) 2011: Commencements: Northern Ireland . . . 411
Climate change agreements: Administration 30
Climate change agreements: Eligible facilities 30
Climate change levy: Climate change agreements: Administration 30
Climate change levy: Climate change agreements: Eligible facilities 30
Climate change levy: General 30
Climate change: CRC Energy efficiency scheme: Allocation of allowances 30
Climate change: Forestry Commissioners: Functions: Scotland 367, 373
Climate change: Greenhouse gas emissions trading scheme 29
Climate change: Greenhouse gas emissions trading scheme: Charging schemes: Amendments 29
Climate change: Motor fuel: Road vehicle & mobile machinery: Greenhouse gas emissions reporting 29
Clinical commissioning groups: National Health Service: England 107
Coaches: Parking places: Northern Ireland 439
Coast protection: Features: Designation: Appeals: England 30, 63, 70
Coast protection: Features: Designation: Appeals: Wales 30, 64, 71
Coast protection: Features: Designation: Notices: England 30, 63, 70
Coast protection: Features: Designation: Notices: Wales 30, 64, 71
Coast protection: Flood & Water Management Act 2010: Commencements 30, 63, 71, 313
Code of practice: Trade union duties & activities: Time off: Appointed day: Northern Ireland 410
Coinage: Pyx: Trial of 30
Cold weather payments: General: Social fund: Northern Ireland 445
Cold weather payments: Social fund 298
Coleg Menai Further Education Corporation: Dissolution 55
College Avenue, Belfast: Stopping-up: Northern Ireland 431
Commission for Architecture & the Built Environment: Dissolution: England & Wales 63
Commission for Rural Communities: Abolition 130
Commissioner for older People Act 2011: Commencements: Northern Ireland 423
Commissioner for Victims & Survivors for Northern Ireland: Superannuation: Northern Ireland 426
Commissioner of the Northern Ireland Law Commission: Superannuation: Northern Ireland 426
Committee systems: Local authorities: England 96
Committees: Overview & scrutiny: Local authorities: England 96
Common Agricultural Policy: Single payment & support schemes: Cross-compliance: Northern Ireland . . . 405
Common Agricultural Policy: Single payment & support schemes: England 9
Common Agricultural Policy: Single payment & support schemes: Wales 9
Common Agricultural Policy: Support schemes: Decisions: Review: Northern Ireland 405
Commons Act 2006: Commencements 31
Commons: Deregistration & exchange orders: Interim arrangements 31
Commons: Deregistration & exchange: Common land & greens: Procedure: Wales 31
Commons: Works: Procedure: Wales 31

Commonwealth games: Glasgow Commonwealth Games Act 2008: Ticket touting offence: England, Wales & Northern Ireland 32, 47
Communications: Guernsey 12, 59
Communities: Localism: Acts 4
Community Care & Health (Scotland) Act 2002 : Adult support & protection: Scotland 362, 395
Community care: Adult support & protection: Scotland 362, 395
Community care: Joint working: Scotland 395
Community care: Personal care & nursing care: Scotland 395
Community drivers: Hours & recording equipment 136
Community emissions trading scheme: Allocation of allowances for payment 62
Community infrastructure levy: Amendments 31
Community infrastructure levy: Localism Act 2011: Commencements 31, 81, 87, 98, 306
Community interest companies 31
Community radio: Guernsey 13
Companies Act 2006: Amendment & delegation of functions: Statutory auditors 12, 32
Companies Act 2006: Commencements 31
Companies: Accounting standards: Prescribed bodies: United States & Japan 31
Companies: Accounts & reports: Prescribed body: Supervision 32
Companies: Community interest 31
Companies: Defective accounts & directors' reports: Authorised person 32
Companies: European public limited-liability companies: Fees 67
Companies: Limited liability partnerships: Accounts & audit exemptions 32, 93
Competition Act 1998: Public policy exclusion 32
Competition: Enterprise Act 2002: Merger fees 32
Compromise agreements: Automatic enrolment 116
Congo (Democratic Republic): Asset-freezing 39
Congo (Democratic Republic): Restrictive measures: Overseas territories 114
Conservation areas: Listed buildings: Planning: England 305
Conservation areas: Wales 307
Conservation of sea fish: Sharks, skates & rays: Fishing, trans-shipment & landing: Prohibitions: Scotland 393
Conservation: Habitats: Species 38, 102, 315
Conservation: Natural habitats: Northern Ireland 413
Conservation: Natural habitats: Scotland 397
Constitutional law: Forestry Commissioners (Climate Change Functions) (Scotland) Order 2012: Consequential modifications 32, 47, 72
Constitutional law: Glasgow Commonwealth Games Act 2008: Ticket touting offence: England, Wales & Northern Ireland 32, 47
Constitutional law: Housing (Scotland) Act 2006: Consequential provisions 32, 47, 80
Constitutional law: Partnership Council for Wales: Local health boards & National Health Service trusts: Wales . . . 33, 100
Constitutional law: Scotland Act 2012: Commencements 33, 47
Constitutional law: Scottish Administration: Offices 33, 47
Constitutional Reform & Governance Act 2010: Commencements 73, 133
Construction contracts: 2011 Act: Commencements: Northern Ireland 408
Construction industry scheme: Income tax: Amendments 36, 85
Construction Industry Training Board: Industrial training levy 59
Construction industry: Industrial training levy: Northern Ireland 419
Construction: Contracts exclusion: Northern Ireland 408
Construction: Contracts scheme: Northern Ireland 408
Consular fees 47
Consumer credit: Green deal 33
Consumer credit: Total charges 33
Consumer insurance: Disclosure & representations: Acts 4
Consumer protection: Consumer rights: Payment surcharges 33
Consumer protection: Cosmetic products: Safety 33
Consumer protection: Customs: Disclosure of information: Miscellaneous amendments 33, 75
Consumer protection: Enterprise Act 2002: Merger fees 32
Consumer protection: Medical devices 33
Consumer protection: Product safety 34
Consumer protection: Product safety: Amendments & revocations 34
Consumer protection: Textile products: Labelling & fibre composition 34
Consumer rights: Payment surcharges 33
Contaminated land: England 62
Contaminated land: Wales 64
Contracting out: Social services functions: England 34
Control of fuel & electricity: Oil stocking 34

Controlled foreign companies: Excluded banking business profits 35
Controlled foreign companies: Excluded territories. 35
Controlled waste: England 63
Controlled waste: England & Wales 63
Copyright & performances: Application to other countries 34, 136
Copyright Act 2011: Jersey: Repeal. 34
Coroners & Justice Act 2009: Commencements 34, 43, 46, 126
Coroners' districts: Lincolnshire: England & Wales 34
Coroners' districts: North Wales (East & Central) 34
Corporate manslaughter & homicide: 2007 Act: Commencements: Northern Ireland. 409
Corporation tax: Authorised Investment Funds 14, 35, 84
Corporation tax: British Waterways Board: Tax consequences 35, 302
Corporation tax: Business premises renovation allowances 35, 84
Corporation tax: Capital allowances: Energy-saving plant & machinery 35, 84
Corporation tax: Capital allowances: Environmentally beneficial plant & machinery 35, 84
Corporation tax: Chargeable gains: Gilt-edged securities. 15, 36
Corporation tax: Controlled foreign companies: Excluded banking business profits 35
Corporation tax: Controlled foreign companies: Excluded territories. 35
Corporation tax: Extra-statutory concessions: Enactments 36, 85, 88
Corporation tax: Finance Act 2010: Schedule 6, part 1: Consequential & incidental provisions 15, 36, 85, 312
Corporation tax: Financial Services Act 2010: Schedule 6: Part 2: Commencements 15, 36, 85, 88, 302, 303
Corporation tax: Financing costs & income: Treatment: Mismatches correction: Partnerships & pensions 36
Corporation tax: Insurance companies: Controlled Foreign Companies (CFCs): Double charge: Avoidance 36
Corporation tax: Insurance companies: Transitional provisions 36
Corporation tax: London Legacy Development Corporation: Tax consequences 36, 86, 303
Corporation tax: Postal Services Act 2011: Taxation. 36, 86, 302, 303
Corporation tax: Research & development: Qualifying bodies 36
Corporation tax: Tax Acts: Modification: Friendly societies 36
Corporation tax: Taxation (International and Other Provisions) Act 2010: Part 7: Amendments. 36
Cosmetic products: Safety. 33
Cote d'Ivoire: Sanctions: Overseas territories 113
Cotonou agreement: European Communities: Definition of treaties 65
Council tax: Administration & enforcement: England 37
Council tax: Administration & enforcement: Scotland 367
Council tax: Base: Calculation: Local authorities: England 37
Council tax: Demand notices: England 37, 133
Council tax: Dwellings: Prescribed classes: England 37
Council tax: Exempt dwellings: England 37
Council tax: Exempt dwellings: Scotland 367
Council tax: Health & Social Care Act 2008 . . . . 37, 132
Council tax: Increases: Referendums: Conduct: England 37
Council tax: Increases: Referendums: England 37
Council tax: Reduction schemes & prescribed requirements: Wales 38
Council tax: Reduction schemes: Default scheme: England 37
Council tax: Reduction schemes: Default scheme: Wales. 38
Council tax: Reduction schemes: Prescribed requirements: Default scheme: England 37
Council tax: Reduction schemes: Prescribed requirements: England 37
Council tax: Reduction: Scotland 367
Council tax: Reduction: State pension credit: Scotland 367
Counter-terrorism Act 2008: Commencements 126
Counter-terrorism Act 2008: Video recording with sound of post-charge questioning: Codes of practice 126
Countryside: Access: Coastal margin: Weymouth Bay 38
Countryside: Access: Works notices: Appeals: England 38
Countryside: Conservation: Habitats: Species 38, 102, 315
County courts: Civil courts: England & Wales 38, 294
County courts: Civil procedure: Rules: England & Wales. 38, 294
County courts: Family procedure 38, 39, 67, 101, 102, 294
County courts: Family proceedings: Allocation: England & Wales. 38
County courts: Rules: Northern Ireland 408
Court fees: Scotland 368, 373, 395
Court Martial Appeal Court: Costs 39
Court of Judicature, Northern Ireland: Procedure: Rules: Northern Ireland 408, 409
Court of Session: Court Fees: Scotland 368, 373, 395
Court of Session: Fees: Scotland. 368
Court of Session: Messengers-at-Arms: Fees: Act of Sederunt: Scotland 367

Court of Session: Miscellaneous: Act of Sederunt: Scotland 367, 368
Court of Session: Registration Appeal Court: Act of Sederunt: Scotland 367
Court of Session: Rules: Solicitor's fees: Scotland 368
Court of Session: Shorthand writers: Fees: Act of Sederunt: Scotland 367
Courts: Boards: Abolition 129
Courts: Magistrates' courts: Civil Jurisdiction & Judgments Act 1982: Rules: Northern Ireland 422
Courts: Magistrates' courts: Declarations of parentage: Rules: Northern Ireland 422
Covanta Ince Parl Limited: Electricity: Licence requirement: Exemption: England & Wales 58
Coventry, City: Mayoral referendum 94
Cowes Harbour: Revision 74
Cowick & Snaith Internal Drainage Board 90
Craven, District: Electoral changes 95
CRC energy efficiency scheme: Allocation of allowances 30
Crime & Disorder Act 1998: Prosecution evidence: Service 41
Crime & disorder: Strategy: Formulation & implementation: England 41
Crime & Security Act 2010: Commencements 121
Crime (International Co-operation) Act 2003: Prosecuting authorities: Designation 41, 43
Crime (Sentences) Act 1997: Commencements 41
Crime: Domestic violence, crime & victims: Acts 4
Crime: Domestic violence, crime & victims: Acts: Explanatory notes 7
Crime: Police & crime commissioners: Disqualification 123
Crime: Police & crime commissioners: Elections 123
Crime: Police & crime commissioners: Elections: Local authorities: Designation 123
Crime: Police & crime commissioners: Elections: Police area returning officers: Designation 123
Crime: Police & crime commissioners: Elections: Returning officers: Area designation: England & Wales 123
Crime: Police & crime commissioners: Elections: Returning officers: Functions 123
Crime: Police & crime commissioners: Elections: Returning officers' accounts 123
Crime: Police & crime commissioners: Elections: Welsh forms 123
Crime: Police & crime panels: Functions: Modifications: England & Wales 124
Crime: Police & crime panels: Local authority enactments: Application 123
Crime: Police & crime panels: Nominations, appointments & notifications: England & Wales 124
Crime: Police & crime panels: Precepts & Chief Constable appointments: England & Wales 124
Crime: Proceeds of Crime Act 2002: External requests & orders: England & Wales 128
Criminal aid certificates: Rules: Northern Ireland 420
Criminal cases: Costs: England & Wales 41
Criminal cases: Costs: Magistrates' courts: Northern Ireland 422
Criminal cases: Punishment & review: Acts: Explanatory notes: Scotland 362
Criminal cases: Punishment & review: Acts: Scotland 361
Criminal cases: Punishment & review: Commencements: Scotland 368
Criminal Defence Service: Funding: England & Wales 91
Criminal Justice & Licensing (Scotland) Act 2010: Commencements: Scotland 368
Criminal Justice & Licensing (Scotland) Act 2010: Incidental provisions: Scotland 368
Criminal Justice & Police Act 2001: Amendments: England & Wales 42, 121
Criminal Justice Act 1988: Sentencing: Reviews: England & Wales 41
Criminal Justice Act 2003: Commencements 39, 42
Criminal Justice Act 2003: Surcharge 42
Criminal justice: Acts 4
Criminal justice: Sexual offences: Acts 4
Criminal law: Belarus: Asset-freezing 39
Criminal law: Burma/Myanmar: European Communities: Financial restrictions: Suspension 39
Criminal law: Corporate manslaughter & homicide: 2007 Act: Commencements: Northern Ireland 409
Criminal law: Crime & Disorder Act 1998: Prosecution evidence: Service 41
Criminal law: Crime & disorder: Strategy: Formulation & implementation: England 41
Criminal law: Crime (International Co-operation) Act 2003: Prosecuting authorities: Designation 41, 43
Criminal law: Crime (Sentences) Act 1997: Commencements 41
Criminal law: Criminal cases: Costs: England & Wales 41
Criminal law: Criminal cases: Punishment & review: Commencements: Scotland 368
Criminal law: Criminal Justice & Police Act 2001: Amendments: England & Wales 42, 121
Criminal law: Criminal Justice Act 1988: Sentencing: Reviews: England & Wales 41
Criminal law: Criminal Justice Act 2003: Commencements 39, 42
Criminal law: Criminal Justice Act 2003: Surcharge 42
Criminal law: Criminal Proceedings etc. (Reform) (Scotland) Act 2007: Commencements: Scotland 368
Criminal law: Democratic Republic of the Congo: Asset-freezing 39
Criminal law: Disorderly behaviour: Penalties: Amount: England & Wales 42, 122
Criminal law: Domestic Violence, Crime & Victims (Amendment) Act 2012: Commencements 39

Criminal law: Domestic Violence, Crime & Victims Act 2004: Commencements 42
Criminal law: Eritrea: Asset-freezing 39
Criminal law: Guinea-Bissau: Asset-freezing 39
Criminal law: International Criminal Tribunal for the former Yugoslavia: Indictees: Financial sanctions 40
Criminal law: Iran: European Communities: Financial sanctions 40
Criminal law: Iraq: Asset-freezing 40
Criminal law: Lebanon: Syria: Asset-freezing 40
Criminal law: Legal Aid, Sentencing & Punishment of Offenders Act 2012: Commencements 40, 42, 46, 91, 135
Criminal law: Legal Aid, Sentencing & Punishment of Offenders Act 2012: Consequential & savings provisions . 17, 42, 46
Criminal law: Legal Aid, Sentencing & Punishment of Offenders Act 2012: Youth detention 17
Criminal law: Liberia: Asset-freezing 40
Criminal law: Libya: Asset-freezing 40
Criminal law: Licensing Act 2003: Children: Alcohol: Persistent selling to: Closure Notices: Prescribed forms 42, 92
Criminal law: Offences: Prosecution: Custody time limits: England & Wales 43
Criminal law: Offensive Behaviour at Football & Threatening Communications (Scotland) Act 2012: Commencements:
Scotland 368
Criminal law: Police Act 1997: Criminal records: Northern Ireland 409
Criminal law: Prosecution of Offences Act 1985: Specified proceedings 42, 43
Criminal law: Protection of Freedoms Act 2012: Commencements 18, 43, 89, 129, 273
Criminal law: Republic of Guinea: Asset-freezing 41
Criminal law: Serious Organised Crime & Police Act 2005: Designated sites: Section 128: Amendments 43
Criminal law: Sexual Offences Act 2003: Notification requirements 43
Criminal law: Sexual Offences Act 2003: Prescribed police stations: Northern Ireland 409
Criminal law: Sexual Offences Act 2003: Prescribed police stations: Scotland 368
Criminal law: Sexual Offences Act 2003: Remedial 43
Criminal law: Sudan: Asset-freezing 41
Criminal law: Syria: European Union financial sanctions 41
Criminal law: United Nations: Personnel: Isle of Man 41
Criminal law: Youth detention accommodation: Remand: Recovery of costs 43
Criminal legal aid: Defence costs orders: Recovery: Northern Ireland 420
Criminal legal aid: Fees: Scotland 376
Criminal Procedure (Scotland) Act 1995: Transcripts: Act of Adjournal: Amendments: Scotland 373, 394
Criminal procedure rules: Act of Adjournal: Scotland 373, 375, 394
Criminal procedure: Coroners & Justice Act 2009: Commencements 34, 43, 46
Criminal procedure: Police & Justice Act 2006: Commencements 43
Criminal procedure: Rules: England & Wales 101, 294
Criminal Proceedings etc. (Reform) (Scotland) Act 2007: Commencements: Scotland 368
Criminal records & registration: Police Act 1997: Guernsey 121
Criminal records & registration: Police Act 1997: Isle of Man 121
Criminal records & registration: Police Act 1997: Jersey 121
Criminal records: Police Act 1997 122
Criminal records: Police Act 1997: Amendments: Scotland 380
Criminal records: Police Act 1997: Guernsey 121
Criminal records: Police Act 1997: Isle of Man 121
Crofters, cottars & small landholders: Crofting Reform (Scotland). Act 2010: Commencements: Scotland 368
Crofters, cottars & small landholders: Crofting register: Fees: Scotland 369, 383
Crofters, cottars & small landholders: Crofting register: First registration: Scotland 369, 383
Crofters, cottars & small landholders: Crofting register: Scotland 369, 383
Crofters, cottars & small landholders: Crofting register: Transfer of ownership: Scotland 369, 383
Crofting Reform (Scotland). Act 2010: Commencements: Scotland 368
Crofting register: Fees: Scotland 369, 383
Crofting register: First registration: Scotland 369, 383
Crofting register: Scotland 369, 383
Crofting register: Transfer of ownership: Scotland 369, 383
Crown Court Rule Committee: Abolition 130
Cumbria: Electoral changes 94
Curen: Electricity: Licence requirement: Exemption: England & Wales 58
Curriculum: National: Key stage 2: Assessment arrangements: England 50
Curriculum: National: Key stage 4: Amendments: England 50
Customs & excise: Air passenger duty 65
Customs & excise: Trade: Statistics 303
Customs: Disclosure of information: Miscellaneous amendments 33, 75
Customs: Export control 44
Customs: Export control: Sanctions: Iran 44
Customs: Export control: Sanctions: Syria 44

Customs: Export control: Sanctions: Syria & Burma 44
Customs: Forest law: Enforcement, governance & trade 44
Customs: Inspections: HM Inspectors of Constabulary & Scottish Inspectors 136
Cycle routes: Road traffic & vehicles: Northern Ireland 435

D

Dalgety Bay: Food protection: Emergency prohibitions: Scotland 381
Dangerous drugs: Health: 2006 Act: Commencements: Northern Ireland 409, 417
Dangerous drugs: Misuse of drugs 45
Dangerous drugs: Misuse of Drugs Act 1971: Amendments 44, 45
Dangerous drugs: Misuse of drugs: Addicts supply 45
Dangerous drugs: Misuse of drugs: Designation 45
Dangerous drugs: Misuse of drugs: Designation: Northern Ireland 409
Dangerous drugs: Misuse of drugs: Northern Ireland 409
Dangerous goods: Air navigation 19
Danvm Drainage Commissioners 90
Dartford - Thurrock Crossing charging scheme: A282 77
Data protection: Sensitive personal data: Processing 45
Data-gathering powers: Relevant data 304
Daventry: Electoral changes 94
Death & disablement: Navy, Army & Air Force: Service pensions 116
Deaths & births: Registration: England & Wales 134
Debt management & relief: Tribunals, Courts & Enforcement Act 2007: Consequential amendments 45
Defence: Armed Forces Act 2011: Commencements 45, 46
Defence: Armed Forces: Powers of stop & search, search, seizure & retention 46
Defence: Caversfield Service Family Accommodation Byelaws 46
Defence: Coroners & Justice Act 2009: Commencements 34, 43, 46
Defence: Legal Aid, Sentencing & Punishment of Offenders Act 2012: Commencements 42, 46
Defence: Legal Aid, Sentencing & Punishment of Offenders Act 2012: Consequential & savings provisions 17, 42, 46
Defence: Ot Moor Range 46
Defence: Police & Criminal Evidence Act 1984: Armed Forces 46
Defence: Protection of Military Remains Act 1986: Vessels & controlled sites: Designations 46
Defence: Visiting forces: International Military Headquarters: EU SOFA: Tax Designation 46
Defence: Visiting forces: International Military Headquarters: NATO & PfP: Tax Designation 46, 87, 88, 303
Democratic People's Republic of Korea: Sanctions: Overseas territories 114
Democratic Republic of the Congo: Asset-freezing 39
Denbighshire County Council: Foryd Harbour Walking & Cycling Bridge: Construction: Scheme 2011 Confirmation instrument 79
Dental charges: National Health Service: Wales 111
Dental services: National Health Service: Wales 111
Dental services: Primary: England 108
Dental services: Primary: Related units: Amendments: England 108
Dentists: General Dental Council: Constitution 75, 77
Derbyshire: Electoral changes 94
Destructive animals: Mink keeping: Prohibition: Wales 11, 47
Devolution, Scotland: Forestry Commissioners (Climate Change Functions) (Scotland) Order 2012: Consequential modifications 32, 47, 72
Devolution, Scotland: Glasgow Commonwealth Games Act 2008: Ticket touting offence: England, Wales & Northern Ireland 32, 47
Devolution, Scotland: Housing (Scotland) Act 2006: Consequential provisions 32, 47, 80
Devolution, Scotland: Scotland Act 2012: Commencements 33, 47
Devolution: Scotland: Policies: Acts 6
Devolution: Scotland: Policies: Acts: Explanatory notes 7
Devolution: Scottish Administration: Offices 33, 47
Devon, North: Electoral changes 97
Devon: Torbay & Southern Devon Health & Care: National Health Service Trust 110
Diamond Jubilee: Licensing hours: Licensing Act 2003 92
Digital Economy Act 2010: Appointed days 313
Digital Economy Act 2010: Transitional provisions 313
Digital television: Local programme services 13
Digital television: Local programme services: Independent productions 12, 59
Diligence against earnings: Variation: Scotland 370
Diocese of Leicester: Educational endowments 49
Diocese of St. Albans: Educational endowments 49

Diocese of St. Albans: Radlett Church of England School: Educational endowments 49
Diocese of Swansea & Brecon: Llandegley: Educational endowments: Wales 56
Diplomatic Service: Consular fees 47
Disabled children: Carers: Breaks: Wales 18
Disabled people: Welfare reform: Acts. 7
Disabled people: Welfare reform: Acts: Explanatory notes 7
Disabled persons: Motor vehicles: Badges. 273
Disabled persons: Rail vehicles: Accessibility: Non-interoperable rail system 47, 309
Disabled persons: Right to control: Pilot scheme: England 48
Disabled persons' vehicles: Parking places: Northern Ireland 438, 439
Disablement & death: Navy, Army & Air Force: Service pensions 116
Disclosure & Barring Service: Core functions. 17, 128
Disorderly behaviour: Penalties: Amount: England & Wales 42, 122
District electoral areas: Commissioner: Northern Ireland 112
Doctors: General Medical Council: Constitution 76
Doctors: General Medical Council: Licence to practise. 76
Doctors: Postgraduate medical education & training 76
Dogs (working): Tail docking: Animals: Welfare: Northern Ireland 407
Dogs: 2011 Amendment Act: Commencements: Northern Ireland 406
Dogs: Control orders: Prescribed offences & penalties: Northern Ireland 410
Dogs: Control orders: Procedures: Northern Ireland 410
Dogs: Control: Designated land: Northern Ireland. 409
Dogs: Controls: City of London Common Council: Secondary authority. 48
Dogs: Licensing & identification: Northern Ireland 409
Domestic abuse: Acts: Explanatory notes: Scotland 362
Domestic Violence, Crime & Victims (Amendment) Act 2012: Commencements 39
Domestic Violence, Crime & Victims Act 2004: Commencements. 42
Domestic violence, crime & victims: Acts 4
Domestic violence, crime & victims: Acts: Explanatory notes. 7
Domestic violence: Jobseeker's allowance 297
Donaghmore: Roads: Parking places: Northern Ireland 439
Doncaster Borough Council: Permit schemes: Traffic management 78
Doncaster East: Internal drainage Board 90
Double taxation: Arrangements: Germany 12
Double taxation: Relief: Bank levy 12
Dover harbour: Revision 74
Drink: Rehabilitation courses: Relevant drink offences 137
Drivers: Community drivers: Hours & recording equipment 136
Drivers: Hours: Northern Ireland 413
Driving instruction: Compensation schemes. 136
Driving instruction: Suspension & exemption powers: Commencements 136
Driving licences: Motor vehicles: Fees: Northern Ireland 437
Driving licences: Motor vehicles: Northern Ireland 436, 437
Driving licences: Taxis: Northern Ireland 437
Drugs & appliances: Charges: National Health Service: England 107
Drugs & appliances: Charges: National Health Service: Scotland. 378
Drugs: Misuse of drugs 45
Drugs: Misuse of Drugs Act 1971: Amendments 44
Drugs: Misuse of Drugs Act 1971: Temporary class drugs 44, 45
Drugs: Misuse of drugs: Addicts supply 45
Drugs: Misuse of drugs: Designation 45
Drugs: Misuse of drugs: Designation: Northern Ireland 409
Drugs: Misuse of drugs: Northern Ireland 409
Drumlin Road, Donaghcloney: Abandonment: Northern Ireland 432
Dundonald: Waiting restrictions: Road traffic & vehicles: Northern Ireland 442
Dungannon: Waiting restrictions: Road traffic & vehicles: Northern Ireland 442, 443
Dunham Bridge: Tolls: Revision 77
Durham Street & Hamill Street - Killen Street, Belfast: Stopping-up: Northern Ireland 432
Durham: Electoral changes 95
Dwellings: Exempt: Council tax: Scotland 367

E

Early Years Foundation Stage: Learning & development requirements 16
Early Years Foundation Stage: Learning & development requirements: Exemptions 16

Early Years Foundation Stage: Welfare requirements 16
Early years: Education: Charges 50
East Ayrshire Council: Parking adjudicators: Scotland 386
East Ayrshire Council: Parking attendants: Wearing of uniforms: Scotland 386
East Ayrshire Council: Road traffic: Permitted & special parking area: Scotland 386
Easton & Otley College: Government 49
Easton & Otley College: Incorporation 49
Ecclesiastical law: Ecclesiastical offices: Terms of service 48
Ecclesiastical law: Judges, legal officers & others: Fees 48
Ecclesiastical law: Legal officers: Annual fees 48
Ecclesiastical law: Parochial fees: Scheduled matters amending 48
Ecclesiastical offices: Terms of service 48
Ecodesign: Energy-related products & energy information 60
Education & Skills Act 2008: Commencements: England & Wales 54
Education (Wales) Measure 2009: Commencements 56
Education (Wales) Measure 2009: Pilot 56
Education (Wales) Measure 2011: Commencements 56
Education Act 2011: Commencements: England 49, 54
Education Act 2011: GTCE consequential amendments & revocations: England 54
Education Act 2011: Subordinate legislation: Consequential amendments: England 54
Education bodies: Collaboration: Wales 55
Education, children's services & skills: Inspectors 17, 52
Education: Academies: Alternative provision academies: Consequential amendments: England 48, 49
Education: Academies: Land transfer schemes: England 48
Education: Academies: School behaviour: Measures: Determination & publicising: England 53
Education: Apprenticeships: Alternative English completion conditions 49
Education: Behaviour improvement: Provision: England 50
Education: Coleg Menai Further Education Corporation: Dissolution 55
Education: Diocese of Leicester: Educational endowments 49
Education: Diocese of St. Albans: Educational endowments 49
Education: Diocese of St. Albans: Radlett Church of England School: Educational endowments 49
Education: Early years: Charges 50
Education: Easton & Otley College: Government 49
Education: Easton & Otley College: Incorporation 49
Education: Education bodies: Collaboration: Wales 55
Education: Educational Endowments: Diocese of Swansea & Brecon: Llandegley: Wales 56
Education: Elmwood, Oatridge & The Barony Colleges: Transfer & closures: Scotland 369
Education: Fees, awards & student support: Scotland 369
Education: Filton College & Stroud College of Further Education: Dissolution 51
Education: Financial reporting: Consistent 49
Education: Fundable bodies: Scotland 369
Education: Further education corporations: Dissolution: Prescribed bodies 49
Education: Further education corporations: Publication of proposals 51
Education: Further education institutions: 16 to 19 academies: Specification & disposal of articles: England 51
Education: Further education institutions: Exemption from inspection: England 51
Education: Further education: Student support: Eligibility: Northern Ireland 410
Education: Further education: Teachers' qualifications: England 52
Education: Further: Loans: England 51
Education: Further: Teachers' qualifications, continuing professional development & registration: England 51, 52
Education: General Teaching Council for Wales: Additional functions: Wales 56
Education: General Teaching Council for Wales: Amendments: Wales 57
Education: General Teaching Council for Wales: Constitution: Wales 57
Education: General Teaching Council for Wales: Disciplinary functions: Wales 57
Education: General Teaching Council for Wales: Functions: Wales 57
Education: Head teachers: Qualifications: England 50
Education: Her Majesty's Inspector of Education, Children's Services & Skills 17, 52
Education: Her Majesty's Inspector of Education, Children's Services & Skills: Children's homes etc.: Fees & frequency of inspections 17
Education: Higher Education Funding Council for Wales 57
Education: Higher education: Assembly learning grants & loans: Wales 55
Education: Higher education: Student loans: Living costs liability: Cancellation 55
Education: Independent further education colleges & English language schools: Inspections: Recovery of expenses: Scotland 370, 383
Education: Independent schools: Standards: England 50
Education: Individual learning accounts: Scotland 370

Education: Information: Individual pupils: England 50
Education: Jewel & Esk College: Transfer & closure: Scotland 370
Education: Key Stages 1, 2 & 3: Levels of progression: Northern Ireland 410
Education: Legislative reform: Local authorities: Annual review 17, 52, 135
Education: Middle schools: Wales 56
Education: National curriculum: Foundation phase: Entry: Assessment arrangements: Wales 57
Education: National curriculum: Key stage 1, 2, 3, 4: Exceptions: England 52
Education: National curriculum: Key stage 2: Assessment arrangements: England 50
Education: National curriculum: Key stage 4: Curriculum: Amendments: England 50
Education: Office of Qualifications & Examinations Regulation: Monetary penalties: Turnover determination 52, 55
Education: Penalty notices: England 50
Education: Pre-school education: Schools: Admissions criteria: Northern Ireland 410
Education: Provision: Information 52
Education: Public services reform: General Teaching Council for Scotland: Legal assessors: Scotland 369
Education: Pupil referral units: Amendments: England 52
Education: Pupil referral units: Application of enactments: England 50
Education: Recognised bodies: Wales 56
Education: Recognised persons: Monetary penalties: Determination of turnover: Wales 57
Education: Rural primary schools: Designation: England 49
Education: School & early years finance: England 53
Education: School & placing information: Scotland 369
Education: School day & school year: Wales 56
Education: School discipline: Pupil exclusions & reviews: England 53
Education: School governance: Constitution: England 53
Education: School governance: Federations: England 53
Education: School government: Terms of reference: England 50
Education: School premises 55
Education: Schools forums: England 53
Education: Schools: Admission: Appeals arrangements: England 52
Education: Schools: Admission: Arrangements: England 52
Education: Schools: Admission: Infant class sizes: England 52
Education: Schools: Admissions appeals code: Appointed day: England 52
Education: Schools: Articles: Specification & disposal: England 53
Education: Schools: Finance: England 53
Education: Schools: Governance: England 53
Education: Schools: Governance: Transition from Interim Executive Board: Wales 57
Education: Schools: Independent: Religious character: Designation: England 49
Education: Schools: Information: England 53
Education: Schools: Information: Provision: Scotland 369
Education: Schools: Inspections: Exemptions: England 50
Education: Schools: Performance information: England 51
Education: Schools: Staffing: England 53
Education: Sixth form college corporations: Dissolution: Prescribed bodies 49
Education: Sixth form college corporations: Publication of proposals: England 53
Education: Special Educational Needs Tribunal for Wales 57, 58
Education: Special educational needs: Direct payments: Pilot scheme: England 54
Education: Specified work: Amendments: England 51
Education: Stevenson College, Edinburgh: Transfer & closure: Scotland 370
Education: Student fees: Amounts: Northern Ireland 410
Education: Student fees: Basic & higher amounts: Approved plans: England 54
Education: Student fees: Qualifying courses & persons: Wales 58
Education: Student loans: Repayment 48
Education: Student loans: Repayment: Northern Ireland 410
Education: Student loans: Repayment: Scotland 370
Education: Student support: European University Institute 51
Education: Student support: Financial: Amendments: Northern Ireland 410
Education: Student support: Wales 56
Education: Students: Fees, awards & support: England 51
Education: Teachers: Appraisal: England 51
Education: Teachers: Discipline 54
Education: Teachers: Incentive payments: England 53
Education: Teachers: Induction arrangements: England 50
Education: Teachers: Induction arrangements: Wales 56
Education: Teachers: Pay & conditions: England & Wales 55
Education: Teachers: Pensions: England & Wales 55

Education: Teachers: Professional qualifications: England 55
Education: Teachers: Qualifications & appraisal: Amendments: England 51
Education: Teachers: Qualifications & specified work: Amendments: England 51
Education: Teachers: Qualifications: Wales. 57
Education: Teachers: Student loans: Repayment 55
Education: Teachers: Superannuation: Northern Ireland. 410
Education: Wiltshire Council: Suitable education: Provision for: Arrangements: England. 54
Education: Young People's Learning Agency: Abolition. 54
EEA Services: Health care: Costs: Reimbursement: Northern Ireland. 416
Egypt: Potatoes: Originating in Egypt: Scotland. 379
Election expenses: Local government: Limits: Variation: Scotland 384
Elections: Local government: Declaration of acceptance of office 96
Elections: Mayoral: Local authorities: England. 96
Elections: Mayoral: Local authorities: England & Wales. 98
Electoral areas: District: Commissioner: Northern Ireland 112
Electoral changes: Blaby, District. 94
Electoral changes: Broxbourne 93
Electoral changes: Buckinghamshire 93
Electoral changes: Cumbria 94
Electoral changes: Daventry. 94
Electoral changes: Derbyshire. 94
Electoral changes: District of Craven 95
Electoral changes: Durham 95
Electoral changes: Gloucestershire 95
Electoral changes: Hart 95
Electoral changes: Hartlepool 95
Electoral changes: Huntingdonshire. 95
Electoral changes: King's Lynn & West Norfolk 95
Electoral changes: North Devon. 97
Electoral changes: Oxfordshire 97
Electoral changes: Rugby 97
Electoral changes: Rushmoor 97
Electoral changes: Shropshire. 94
Electoral changes: Slough 97
Electoral changes: Somerset. 97
Electoral changes: Staffordshire. 97
Electoral changes: Surrey 98
Electoral changes: Swale 98
Electoral changes: Swindon 98
Electoral changes: West Lindsey 98
Electoral changes: West Oxfordshire 95
Electoral data schemes 135
Electric vehicles: Parking places: Northern Ireland 439
Electrical & electronic equipment: Hazardous substances: Restrictions on use. 62
Electricity safety, quality & continuity: Northern Ireland 410
Electricity: Control of fuel & electricity: Oil stocking 34
Electricity: Energy companies obligation 58, 73
Electricity: Feed-in tariffs 58
Electricity: Feed-in tariffs: Maximum capacity & functions 58
Electricity: Generation: Licence requirement: Exemption: Covanta Ince Parl Limited: England & Wales. 58
Electricity: Generation: Licence requirement: Exemption: Curen: England & Wales 58
Electricity: Generation: Licence requirement: Exemption: MVV Environment Devonport Ltd: England & Wales 58
Electricity: Priority dispatch: Northern Ireland 410
Electricity: Smart meters: Communication licences: Competitive tenders 58, 73
Electricity: Smart meters: Licensable activity. 58, 73
Electromagnetic compatibility: Wireless telegraphy: London Olympic Games & Paralympic Games: Apparatus: Interference control 59
Electronic communications: Guernsey 12, 59
Electronic communications: Local digital television programme services: Independent productions 12, 59
Electronic communications: Wireless Telegraphy Act 2006: OFCOM: Directions. 13, 59
Electronic communications: Wireless telegraphy: Interference: Prisons: Acts 6
Electronic communications: Wireless telegraphy: Licence award 59
Electronic communications: Wireless telegraphy: Licence charges. 59
Electronic communications: Wireless telegraphy: Licences: Limitation of number 59
Electronic communications: Wireless telegraphy: Register 59

Electronic communications: Wireless telegraphy: Spectrum trading 59
Elmwood College: Transfer & closures: Scotland 369
Emergency planning: Civil contingencies: Acts 4
Emissions trading: Community scheme: Allocation of allowances for payment 62
Emissions trading: CRC energy efficiency scheme: Allocation of allowances 30
Employees' capabilities: Fire safety: Fire precautions: Wales 70
Employers' duties: Pensions: Implementation 116
Employment & support allowance 296
Employment & support allowance: Contributory allowance 297
Employment & support allowance: Linking rules 296
Employment & support allowance: Linking rules: Northern Ireland 444
Employment & support allowance: Sanctions 297
Employment & training: Apprenticeships, Skills, Children & Learning Act 2009: Consequential amendments 60
Employment & training: Apprenticeships: Agreement form 60
Employment & training: Industrial training levy: Construction Industry Training Board 59
Employment & training: Industrial training levy: Engineering Construction Industry Training Board 59
Employment rights: Increase of limits: Northern Ireland 410
Employment rights: Limits: Increase 304, 305
Employment tribunals: Constitution: Rules of procedure 60
Employment tribunals: Maximum deposits: Increases 60
Employment tribunals: Tribunal composition 60
Employment: Labour Relations Agency Arbitration Scheme: Jurisdiction: Northern Ireland 411
Employment: Labour Relations Agency Arbitration Scheme: Northern Ireland 411
Employment: Occupational & personal pension schemes: Prescribed bodies 117
Employment: Protection: Transfer of undertakings: RCUK Shared Services Centre Limited 305
Employment: Public interest disclosure: Prescribed persons: Northern Ireland 411
Employment: Social security: Benefits: Up-rating: Northern Ireland 411, 418, 430, 446, 447, 448
Employment: Trade union duties & activities: Time off: Code of practice: Appointed day: Northern Ireland 410
Energy Act 2004: Amendment 60, 308
Energy Act 2010: Commencements 60
Energy Act 2011: Buildings: Energy performance 13, 61
Energy Act 2011: Commencements 60
Energy Act 2011: Commencements: Scotland 370
Energy companies obligation: Electricity & gas 58, 73
Energy conservation: Buildings: Energy Act 2011: Energy performance 13, 61
Energy conservation: Ecodesign: Energy-related products & energy information 60
Energy conservation: Green deal framework: Disclosure, acknowledgment, redress 61
Energy conservation: Green deal: Acknowledgment 61
Energy conservation: Green deal: Acknowledgment: Scotland 370
Energy conservation: Green deal: Disclosure 61
Energy conservation: Green deal: Energy efficiency improvements 61
Energy conservation: Green deal: Qualifying energy improvements 61
Energy conservation: Home energy assistance schemes: Amendments: Scotland 370
Energy conservation: Home energy efficiency scheme: England 61
Energy conservation: Miscellaneous amendments: England & Wales 11
Energy performance: Building & buildings: England & Wales 14
Energy performance: Buildings: Scotland 365
Energy performance: Certificates & inspections: Building & buildings: England & Wales 13
Energy: Acts 4
Energy: Electricity: Priority dispatch: Northern Ireland 410
Energy: Gas & electricity: Smart meters: Communication licences: Competitive tenders 58, 73
Energy: Renewable heat incentive schemes: Northern Ireland 411
Energy: Renewable heat incentives 60
Enforcement of civil penalties: Penalty charges enforcement: London 61, 101
Enforcement: Diligence against earnings: Variation: Scotland 370
Engineering Construction Industry Training Board: Industrial training levy 59
Enhanced Learning Credit Scheme: Further & Higher Education Commitment Scheme: Armed forces 116
Enniskillen: Right-hand turns: Prohibition: Road traffic & vehicles: Northern Ireland 440
Enterprise Act 2002: Merger fees 32
Enterprise management: Incentives: Income tax: Limits 86
Entertainers & sportsmen: Income tax 85
Environment Protection Advisory Committees: Abolition: Public bodies 62, 130
Environment protection: Marine licensing: Fees: Scotland 371, 377
Environment: High Hedges Act 2011: Northern Ireland 411
Environment: High hedges: Fee transfer: Northern Ireland 411

Environment: High hedges: Fees: Northern Ireland 411
Environment: Natural: Acts: Explanatory notes: Scotland. 362
Environment: Taxes: Landfill tax 90
Environment: Taxes: Landfill tax: Qualifying materials 90
Environmental impact assessment: Infrastructure planning. 87
Environmental impact assessment: Planning: Northern Ireland 427
Environmental offences: Fixed penalties: England 63
Environmental offences: Fixed penalties: Northern Ireland 412
Environmental permitting: England & Wales. 63
Environmental Protection Act 1990: Commencement: England & Wales 63
Environmental Protection Act 1990: Fixed penalty amount 63
Environmental protection: Advisory Committee on Hazardous Substances (ACHS): Abolition 61, 74, 129
Environmental protection: Bathing water: Quality: Northern Ireland 412
Environmental protection: Bathing waters: Scotland. 370, 396
Environmental protection: Batteries & accumulators: Market: Placing. 61
Environmental protection: Carbon dioxide: Storage: Inspections. 62
Environmental protection: Commission for Architecture & the Built Environment: Dissolution: England & Wales 63
Environmental protection: Contaminated land: England 62
Environmental protection: Contaminated land: Wales 64
Environmental protection: Controlled waste: England 63
Environmental protection: Controlled waste: England & Wales 63
Environmental protection: Environment Protection Advisory Committees: Abolition: Public bodies 62, 130
Environmental protection: Environmental offences: Fixed penalties: England 63
Environmental protection: Environmental offences: Fixed penalties: Northern Ireland 412
Environmental protection: Environmental permitting: England & Wales. 63
Environmental Protection: Features: Designation: Appeals: England. 30, 63, 70
Environmental protection: Features: Designation: Appeals: Wales 30, 64, 71
Environmental Protection: Features: Designation: Notices: England 30, 63, 70
Environmental protection: Features: Designation: Notices: Wales 30, 64, 71
Environmental protection: Flood & Water Management Act 2010: Commencements 30, 63, 71, 313
Environmental protection: Greenhouse gases: Fluorinated: Northern Ireland 412
Environmental protection: Hazardous substances: Restrictions on use: Electrical & electronic equipment 62
Environmental protection: Infrastructure for Spatial Information in the European Community (INSPIRE) 62, 133
Environmental protection: Infrastructure for Spatial Information in the European Community (INSPIRE): Scotland   370, 382
Environmental protection: Landfill allowances scheme: Wales. 64
Environmental protection: Marine & Coastal Access Act 2009: Transitional provisions: England. 62, 93
Environmental protection: Marine licensing: Exempted activities: Scottish inshore & offshore regions: Scotland . . 371, 377
Environmental protection: Miscellaneous amendments: England & Wales. 11
Environmental protection: Natural Resources Body for Wales: Establishment 64, 131
Environmental protection: Nitrates Action Programme: Northern Ireland. 412
Environmental protection: Pollution: Prevention & control: Northern Ireland 412
Environmental protection: Pollution: Prevention & control: Scotland. 371
Environmental protection: Producer responsibility & obligations: Packaging waste 62
Environmental protection: Producer responsibility & obligations: Packaging waste: Northern Ireland. 412
Environmental protection: Public bodies: Regional & local fisheries advisory committees: Abolition 62, 130
Environmental protection: Statutory nuisances: Appeals: Northern Ireland 412
Environmental protection: Statutory nuisances: Artificial lighting: Relevant sports: Northern Ireland 412
Environmental protection: Statutory nuisances: Insects: Northern Ireland 412
Environmental protection: Street litter: Control notices: Amendments: Northern Ireland. 412
Environmental protection: Vehicles: Removal & disposal: Prescribed periods: Northern Ireland. 412
Environmental protection: Volatile organic compounds: Paints, varnishes & vehicle refinishing products 62
Environmental protection: Waste: England & Wales. 64
Environmental protection: Waste: Fees & charges: Northern Ireland 412
Environmental protection: Waste: Scotland 371
Environmental protection: Water: Priority substances & classification: EC directive: Northern Ireland 412
Equality Act 2010: Age exceptions 64
Equality Act 2010: Amendment. 64
Equality Act 2010: Commencements 64, 65
Equality Act 2010: Public authorities: Specifications: Scotland. 371
Equality Act 2010: Specific duties: Scotland 371
Eritrea: Asset-freezing. 39
Eritrea: Sanctions: Overseas territories 114
Estimates & accounts: Government Resources & Accounts Act 2000 . . . . 73, 74
Euro: Payments: Credit transfers & direct debits 69
Europe: Economic interest grouping & public limited-liability companies: Registrar of Companies: Fees & charges. . . . 68

Europe: Economic interest grouping: Fees 67
European Administrative Co-operation: Taxation 134
European Championship: Football spectators: 2012 control period 302
European Communities: Animals: Cattle: Identification: Northern Ireland 412
European Communities: Burma/Myanmar: Financial restrictions: Suspension 39
European Communities: Conservation: Natural habitats: Northern Ireland 413
European Communities: Definition of treaties: Cotonou agreement 65
European Communities: Definition of treaties: Korea: Framework agreements 65
European Communities: Definition of treaties: Korea: Free trade agreements 65
European Communities: Designation 65
European Communities: Iran: Financial sanctions 40
European Communities: Iron & steel: Employees: Re-adaption benefits scheme. 89
European Communities: Road traffic: Drivers: Hours: Northern Ireland 413
European Communities: Treaty of Lisbon: Terminology & numbering: Changes 65
European Court of Human Rights: Judicial pensions 116
European Economic Area: Homelessness: Allocation of housing & homelessness: Eligibility: Northern Ireland 418
European Economic Area: Immigration. 83
European economic interest grouping: Fees. 67
European economic interest grouping: Registrar of Companies: Fees & charges. 68
European Fisheries Fund: Grants: Scotland 393
European public limited-liability companies: Fees 67
European public limited-liability companies: Registrar of Companies: Fees & charges 68
European Research Infrastructure Consortia: Value added tax: Relief 313
European Union: Approval of Treaty Amendment Decision: Acts. 5
European Union: Approval of Treaty Amendment Decision: Acts: Explanatory notes 7
Evidence: Civil Partnerships: Divorce actions: Scotland 371
Evidence: Police & criminal evidence: Code of practice A: Modification: Northern Ireland 428
Evidence: Police & criminal evidence: Code of practice C, E, F & H: Revision: Northern Ireland 428
Excise: Air passenger duty 65
Excise: Aircraft operators: Accounts & records. 65
Excise: Duties: Surcharges or rebates: Hydrocarbon oils 65
Excise: Finance Act 1994: Section 30A (9): Appointed days. 66
Excise: Gaming: Duty. 66
Excise: Goods: Holding, movement & duty point. 65
Excise: Machine games: Duty. 66
Excise: Machine games: Duty: Exemptions. 66
Excise: Remote gambling: Double taxation relief. 66
Excise: Road fuel gas: Reliefs. 65
Exeter: Traffic Management Act 2004. 272
Explosives: Carriage: Health & safety: Northern Ireland 416
Explosives: Identification & traceability 75
Explosives: Identification & traceability: Northern Ireland 417
Export control. 44
Export control: Sanctions: Iran 44
Export control: Sanctions: Syria. 44
Export control: Sanctions: Syria & Burma 44
Extraction solvents: Food: Northern Ireland 415

F

Fair employment: Public authorities: Specification: Northern Ireland. 413
Family law: Child Maintenance & Other Payments Act 2008: Commencements 66, 296
Family law: Child support. 67
Family law: Child support maintenance: Basic rate calculation: Changes: Liability: Minimum amounts 66
Family law: Child support maintenance: Calculation 66
Family law: Child support: Child Maintenance Act 2008 Act: Commencements: Northern Ireland 413
Family law: Child support: Maintenance calculation: Northern Ireland. 413
Family law: Child support: Maintenance: Basic rate calculation & minimum liability: Changes: Northern Ireland 413
Family law: Child support: New calculation rules 67
Family law: Child support: New calculation rules: Northern Ireland 414
Family law: Child support: Northern Ireland 407, 413, 414
Family law: Child support: Payments & arrears: Management 67
Family law: Child support: Payments & arrears: Management: Northern Ireland. 413
Family law: Child support: Reciprocal arrangements: Northern Ireland 67
Family law: Population (Statistics) Act 1938: Modifications: Scotland 371

Family law: Public bodies: Child Maintenance & Enforcement Commission: Abolition 67, 130
Family law: Welfare Reform Act 2009: Commencements. 66, 296
Family law: Welfare Reform Act 2010: Commencements: Northern Ireland 414
Family procedure 38, 39, 67, 101, 102, 294
Family proceedings: Allocation: England & Wales. 38
Family proceedings: Family procedure 38, 39, 67, 101, 102, 294
Family support teams: Composition & board functions: Wales 19, 111, 296
Family support teams: Family support functions: Wales. 19, 111, 296
Family support teams: Review of cases: Wales. 19, 111, 296
Fees & charges: European economic interest grouping 67
Fees & charges: Local policing bodies. 10, 67, 99, 122
Fees & charges: Measuring instruments: EEC requirements: Fees 68
Fees & charges: Medicines: Human use: Fees 68, 102
Fees & charges: Medicines: Human use: Products: Northern Ireland 414, 422
Fees & charges: Registrar of Companies: Companies, overseas companies & limited liability partnerships. 68
Fees & charges: Registrar of Companies: European economic interest grouping & European public limited-liability
companies 68
Fees & charges: Water supply & water quality: Inspection fees 68, 130, 314
Filton College & Stroud College of Further Education: Dissolution 51
Finance Act 1994: Section 30A (9): Appointed days 66
Finance Act 2003: Stamp duty land tax 303
Finance Act 2004: Part 7: Application: National insurance: Contributions 298
Finance Act 2004: Section 180 (5): Modifications 85
Finance Act 2010: Schedule 6, part 1: Consequential & incidental provisions 15, 36, 85, 312
Finance Act 2012. 5
Finance Act 2012: Enterprise investment scheme: Appointed day 15, 85
Finance Act 2012: Explanatory notes 7
Finance Act 2012: Venture capital trusts: Appointed days: Income tax. 85
Finance: Budget Responsibility & National Audit Act 2011: Appointed days 13
Finance: Budget Responsibility & National Audit Act 2011: Consequential amendments 13
Financial assistance: Fuel allowance payments scheme: Northern Ireland 414
Financial assistance: Fuel payments scheme: Cancer patients: Treatment: Northern Ireland 414
Financial restrictions: Iran 127
Financial Services & Markets Act 2000: Confidential information: Disclosure 68
Financial Services & Markets Act 2000: Exemptions. 69
Financial Services & Markets Act 2000: Gibraltar: Amendments 69
Financial Services & Markets Act 2000: Regulated activities: Amendments. 68
Financial Services & Markets Act 2000: Short selling 69
Financial services & markets: Capital requirements 68
Financial services & markets: Payment services 69
Financial services & markets: Payments: Euros: Credit transfers & direct debits 69
Financial services & markets: Prospectus: Regulations 69
Financial services & markets: Regulated covered bonds 69
Financial services & markets: Undertakings for collective investment in transferable securities. 69
Financial Services Act 2010: Schedule 6: Part 2: Commencements 15, 36, 85, 88, 302, 303
Financial services: Acts. 5
Financial services: Money laundering. 68
Financial services: Omnibus 1 Directive 69
Fire & police reform: Acts: Scotland 362
Fire & rescue authorities: Expressions of interest: Community challenge: England 94
Fire & rescue authorities: Improvement plans: Wales. 99
Fire & rescue authorities: National framework: England 69
Fire & rescue service: Localism Act 2011: Commencements 70, 96, 132
Fire & rescue services: Bedfordshire Fire Services: Combination scheme 69
Fire & rescue services: Fire & rescue authorities: National framework: England 69
Fire & rescue services: Firefighters: Pension schemes: Contributions: Northern Ireland 414
Fire & rescue services: Firefighters: Pension schemes: Contributions: Wales. 70, 119
Fire & rescue services: Firefighters: Pension schemes: England. 69, 70, 119
Fire & rescue services: Firefighters: Pension schemes: Northern Ireland 414
Fire & rescue services: Firefighters' pension schemes: England 70, 119
Fire & rescue services: Framework: Scotland 371
Fire & rescue services: Localism Act 2011: Commencements: England & Wales 70, 82, 100
Fire & rescue services: National framework: Wales 70
Fire & rescue services: Pension schemes: Contributions: Wales 70, 119
Fire & rescue services: Police & Fire Reform (Scotland) Act 2012: Commencements: Scotland 372, 380

Fire (Scotland) Act 2005: Relevant premises: Scotland 372
Fire precautions: Fire safety: Employees' capabilities: Wales 70
Fire safety: Employees' capabilities: Fire precautions: Wales 70
Fire services: Firefighters: Pension schemes: Scotland 372
Fire services: Firemen: Pension schemes: Scotland 372
Firearms & ammunition: 2004 Order: Amendments: Northern Ireland 415
Firefighters: Pension schemes: Contributions: Northern Ireland 414
Firefighters: Pension schemes: Contributions: Wales 70, 119
Firefighters: Pension schemes: England 69, 70, 119
Firefighters: Pension schemes: Northern Ireland 414
Firefighters: Pension schemes: Scotland 372
Firemen: Pension schemes: Scotland 372
Fireplaces: Exempt: Smoke control areas: England 29
Fireplaces: Exempt: Smoke control areas: Northern Ireland 408
Fireplaces: Exempt: Smoke control areas: Wales 29
First-tier & Upper tribunals: Members: Appointment: Qualifications 310
Fish farming: Marine: Town & country planning: Scotland 396
Fish farms: General permitted development: Town & country planning: Scotland 396
Fish: Conservation: Salmon: River Annan salmon fishery district: Scotland 384
Fisheries: Amendments: Northern Ireland 415
Fisheries: Control: Foyle area: Northern Ireland 415
Fisheries: European Fisheries Fund: Grants: Scotland 393
Fisheries: Foyle & Carlingford areas: Angling: Northern Ireland 415
Fisheries: Foyle & Carlingford Fisheries: 2007 Order: Commencements: Northern Ireland 415
Fisheries: Foyle area: Greenbraes Fishery: Angling permits: Northern Ireland 415
Fisheries: Salmon & freshwater: River Dee, Aberdeenshire: Salmon Fishery District: Annual close time: Scotland 384
Fishing boats: EU electronic reporting: Scotland 393
Fishing boats: Satellite-tracking devices 293
Fishing vessels: Health & safety: At work: Chemical agents 104
Fishing vessels: Satellite-tracking devices: Electronic reporting: Scheme 293
Fishing: Prohibited methods: Firth of Clyde: Scotland 393
Fishing: Scallop fishing: England 292
Fishing: Sharks, skates & rays: Fishing, trans-shipment & landing: Prohibitions: Scotland 393
Fishing: Strangford Lough: Sea fishing exclusion zones: Northern Ireland 444
Flexible tenancies: Review procedures 80
Flood & Water Management Act 2010: Commencements 30, 63, 71, 313
Flood & Water Management Act 2010: Commencements: Wales 313
Flood risk management: Features: Designation: Appeals: England 30, 63, 70
Flood risk management: Features: Designation: Appeals: Wales 30, 64, 71
Flood risk management: Features: Designation: Notices: England 30, 63, 70
Flood risk management: Features: Designation: Notices: Wales 30, 64, 71
Flood risk management: Flood & Water Management Act 2010: Commencements 30, 63, 71, 313
Fluorinated greenhouse gases: Northern Ireland 412
Fodder plant seeds: Scotland 393
Food 71
Food contamination: Emergency prohibitions: Sheep: Radioactivity: Wales 71, 132
Food hygiene: Wales 72
Food protection: Emergency prohibitions: Dalgety Bay: Scotland 381
Food protection: Emergency prohibitions: Sheep: Radioactivity: England 132
Food protection: Emergency prohibitions: Sheep: Radioactivity: Scotland 364, 381
Food: Additives: England 71
Food: Additives: Northern Ireland 415
Food: Additives: Scotland 372
Food: Additives: Wales 72
Food: Extraction solvents: Northern Ireland 415
Food: Hygiene: England 71
Food: Hygiene: Northern Ireland 415
Food: Hygiene: Scotland 372
Food: Materials & articles: Contact: England 71
Food: Materials & articles: Contact: Northern Ireland 415
Food: Materials & articles: Contact: Scotland 372
Food: Materials & articles: Contact: Wales 72
Food: Meat: Inspection: Authorised officers: Revocation 72
Food: Meat: Inspection: Authorised officers: Wales 72
Food: Miscellaneous amendments: England & Wales 11

Food: Solvents: Extraction: England 71
Food: Solvents: Extraction: Wales 72
Food: Specified products: From China: Marketing: Restrictions: England. 9, 71
Food: Specified products: From China: Marketing: Restrictions: Northern Ireland 405, 416
Food: Specified products: From China: Marketing: Restrictions: Scotland 363, 372
Food: Specified products: From China: Marketing: Restrictions: Wales 10, 72
Football spectators: 2012 European Championship control period 302
Football spectators: Seating: Sports grounds & sporting events 302
Football: Offensive behaviour: Threatening communications: Acts: Explanatory notes: Scotland 362
Football: Offensive behaviour: Threatening communications: Acts: Scotland 361
Forest law: Enforcement, governance & trade 44
Forestry Commissioners (Climate Change Functions) (Scotland) Order 2012: Consequential modifications 32, 47, 72
Forestry Commissioners: Functions: Climate change: Scotland 367, 373
Forestry: Plant health: Amendments: Ash dieback 120
Foryd Harbour Walking & Cycling Bridge: Construction: Scheme 2011 Confirmation instrument 79
Foundation phase: Entry: Assessment arrangements: Wales 57
Foyle & Carlingford Fisheries: 2007 Order: Commencements: Northern Ireland 415
Foyle area: Control of fishing: Northern Ireland. 415
Foyle area: Fisheries: Angling: Northern Ireland 415
Foyle area: Greenbraes Fishery: Angling permits: Northern Ireland 415
Fraserburgh: Harbour revision: Scotland 373
Freedom of information: Constitutional Reform & Governance Act 2010: Commencements. 73, 133
Freedom of information: Historical records: Definition. 73
Freedom of information: Protection of Freedoms Act 2012: Commencements 73, 125, 126, 136
Freedoms: Protection: Acts. 6
Freedoms: Protection: Acts: Explanatory notes 7
Friendly Societies: Tax Acts: Modification 36
Fruit: Bananas: Green: Quality standards: England & Wales 80
Fuel allowance payments scheme: Northern Ireland. 414
Fuel payments scheme: Cancer patients: Treatment: Northern Ireland 414
Fuel: Car & van fuel: Benefit: Income tax 84
Fuel: Car fuel: Benefit: Income tax 84
Fuel: Control of fuel & electricity: Oil stocking 34
Fuel: Motor fuel: Composition & content: Amendments 131
Fuel: Motor fuel: Road vehicle & mobile machinery: Greenhouse gas emissions reporting 29
Fuel: Private use: Consideration: Value added tax. 312
Fuels: Authorised fuels: Smoke control areas: England. 29
Fuels: Authorised fuels: Smoke control areas: Northern Ireland. 408
Fuels: Sustainable & renewable fuels: Energy Act 2004: Amendment 60, 308
Fundable bodies: Education: Scotland 369
Funeral expenses: Social Fund: Northern Ireland 445
Further & Higher Education Commitment Scheme: Enhanced Learning Credit Scheme: Armed forces 116
Further education corporations: Dissolution: Prescribed bodies 49
Further education corporations: Publication of proposals. 51
Further education institutions: 16 to 19 academies: Specification & disposal of articles: England 51
Further education institutions: Exemption from inspection: England 51
Further education loans: England 51
Further education: Filton College & Stroud College of Further Education: Dissolution 51
Further education: Student support: Eligibility: Northern Ireland 410
Further education: Teachers' qualifications, continuing professional development & registration: England 51, 52
Further education: Teachers' qualifications: England. 52

G

Gambling Act 2005: Schedule 6: Amendments 12
Gambling: Licence fees: Amendments 12
Gambling: Operating licences & single-machine permit fees 12
Gambling: Remote gambling: Double taxation relief 66
Gaming: Duty 66
Gas: Energy companies obligation 58, 73
Gas: Meters: Testing & stamping: Northern Ireland. 416
Gas: Oil & gas: Installation & pipelines: Abandonment fees 112
Gas: Smart meters: Communication licences: Competitive tenders 58, 73
Gas: Smart meters: Licensable activity 58, 73
Gender Recognition: Application fees 73

General Dental Council: Constitution 75, 77
General Medical Council: Constitution 76
General Medical Council: Licence to practise 76
General medical services: National Health Service: Contracts: Scotland 378
General Optical Council: Continuing education & training 76
General Osteopathic Council: Registration & fees: Applications 76
General permitted development: Fish farms: Town & country planning: Scotland 396
General Pharmaceutical Council: Constitution: Miscellaneous provisions 77
General Register Office: Fees: Northern Ireland 431
General Social Care Council: Transfer of register & abolition: Transitional & saving provisions 77
General Synod of the Church of England: Measures 8
General Synod of the Church of England: Measures: Bound volumes 8
General Synod of the Church of England: Measures: Tables & index 8
General Teaching Council for Scotland: Legal assessors: Public services reform: Scotland 369
General Teaching Council for Wales: Additional functions: Wales 56
General Teaching Council for Wales: Amendments: Wales 57
General Teaching Council for Wales: Constitution: Wales 57
General Teaching Council for Wales: Disciplinary functions: Wales 57
General Teaching Council for Wales: Functions: Wales 57
Generation: Electricity: Licence requirement: Exemption: MVV Environment Devonport Ltd: England & Wales 58
Geneva Conventions Act: Jersey 73
Germany: Double taxation: Arrangements 12
Germany: Double taxation: Relief 12
Germany: International tax enforcement: Arrangements 12
Gilt-edged securities: Chargeable gains: Capital gains tax 15, 36
Glasgow Commonwealth Games Act 2008: Commencements: Scotland 395
Glasgow Commonwealth Games Act 2008: Ticket touting offence: England, Wales & Northern Ireland 32, 47
Glasgow Commonwealth Games Act 2008: Ticket touting offences: Exceptions: Scotland 395
Gloucestershire: Electoral changes 95
Goods vehicles: Enforcement powers: Northern Ireland 435
Goods vehicles: Operators: Licensing: Commencements: Northern Ireland 435
Goods vehicles: Operators: Licensing: Exemptions: Northern Ireland 435
Goods vehicles: Operators: Licensing: Fees 136
Goods vehicles: Operators: Licensing: Fees: Northern Ireland 435
Goods vehicles: Operators: Licensing: Northern Ireland 435
Goods vehicles: Operators: Qualifications: Northern Ireland 436
Goods vehicles: Plating & testing 137
Goods vehicles: Testing: Fees: Northern Ireland 436
Goods vehicles: Testing: Northern Ireland 436
Government Resources & Accounts Act 2000: Audit of public bodies 73
Government Resources & Accounts Act 2000: Estimates & accounts 73, 74
Government resources & accounts: NHS bodies: Summarised accounts 74
Government resources & accounts: Whole of government accounts: Bodies: Designation 74
Government resources & accounts: Whole of government accounts: Bodies: Designation: Northern Ireland 416
Grange Lodge, Antrim: Abandonment: Roads: Northern Ireland 432
Greater London Authority Act 1999: Amendments 100
Greater London Authority: Council tax: Requirement procedure 100
Greater London Authority: Elections: Rules 100, 135
Greater London Authority: Salaries: Limitation 101
Green deal framework: Disclosure, acknowledgment, redress 61
Green deal: Acknowledgment 61
Green deal: Acknowledgment: Scotland 370
Green deal: Disclosure 61
Green deal: Energy efficiency improvements 61
Green deal: Qualifying energy improvements 61
Greenbraes Fishery: Angling permits: Northern Ireland 415
Greenhouse gas emissions reporting: Motor fuel: Road vehicle & mobile machinery 29
Greenhouse gas emissions trading scheme 29
Greenhouse gas emissions trading scheme: Charging schemes: Amendments 29
Greenhouse gases: Fluorinated: Northern Ireland 412
Greystone Road, Limavady: Abandonment: Northern Ireland 432
Guardian's allowance: Child benefit: Administration 296
Guardian's allowance: Up-rating 297
Guardian's allowance: Up-rating: Northern Ireland 302
Guernsey: Broadcasting 12, 59

Guernsey: Communications 12, 59
Guernsey: Community radio 13
Guinea (Republic): Asset-freezing 41
Guinea-Bissau: Asset-freezing 39
Guinea-Bissau: Sanctions: Overseas territories 114

H

Habitats: Species: Conservation 38, 102, 315
Habitual residence: Social security: Northern Ireland. 418, 430, 446
Hague Convention: International recovery: Maintenance: Northern Ireland 419
Hammersmith Hospitals: National Health Service Trust. 107
Harassment: Domestic abuse: Acts: Explanatory notes: Scotland 362
Harbours, docks, piers & ferries: Caernarfon Harbour Trust: Constitution: Harbour revision 74
Harbours, docks, piers & ferries: Cowes Harbour revision 74
Harbours, docks, piers & ferries: Dover: Harbour revision 74
Harbours, docks, piers & ferries: Fraserburgh: Harbour revision: Scotland 373
Harbours, docks, piers & ferries: Hinkley Point Harbour: Empowerment 74
Harbours, docks, piers & ferries: Inverness: Harbour revision: Scotland 373
Harbours, docks, piers & ferries: Mallaig: Harbour revision: Scotland 373
Harbours, docks, piers & ferries: Milford Haven Port Authority: Harbour revision 74
Harbours, docks, piers & ferries: Poole Harbour revision. 74
Harbours, docks, piers & ferries: Port of Cairnryan: Harbour revision: Scotland 373
Harbours, docks, piers & ferries: Port of Ipswich: Harbour revision 74
Hart: Electoral changes 95
Hartlepool: Electoral changes 95
Havering, London Borough: Permit schemes: Traffic management 79
Hazardous substances: Advisory Committee on Hazardous Substances (ACHS): Abolition 61, 74, 129
Hazardous substances: Restrictions on use: Electrical & electronic equipment. 62
Head teachers: Qualifications: England. 50
Health & personal social services: Health care: EEA Services: Costs: Reimbursement: Northern Ireland 416
Health & personal social services: Optical charges & payments: Northern Ireland 416
Health & personal social services: Superannuation scheme, injury benefits, additional voluntary contributions & health & social care pension scheme: Northern Ireland 416
Health & personal social services: Superannuation: Northern Ireland. 416
Health & personal social services: Travelling expenses & remission of charges: Northern Ireland 416
Health & safety: Advisory Committee on Hazardous Substances (ACHS): Abolition 61, 74, 129
Health & safety: Asbestos: Control 74
Health & safety: Asbestos: Control: Northern Ireland. 417
Health & safety: At work: Chemical agents: Merchant shipping & fishing vessels 104
Health & safety: Customs: Disclosure of information: Miscellaneous amendments 33, 75
Health & safety: Explosives: Carriage: Northern Ireland 416
Health & safety: Explosives: Identification & traceability 75
Health & safety: Explosives: Identification & traceability: Northern Ireland 417
Health & safety: Fees 75
Health & safety: Fees: Northern Ireland. 417
Health & safety: Injuries, diseases & dangerous occurrences: Reporting. 75
Health & safety: Miscellaneous revocations 75
Health & safety: Miscellaneous revocations: Northern Ireland 417
Health & safety: Offshore installations: Safety zones 112
Health & safety: Petroleum (Consolidation) Act: Licensing provisions: Amendment: Northern Ireland 417
Health & Social Care Act 2008: Council tax 37, 132
Health & Social Care Act 2008: Regulated activities 106, 131, 295
Health & Social Care Act 2012: Commencements. 75, 93, 103, 106, 131, 295
Health & Social Care Act 2012: Professional Standards Authority for Health & Social Care: Consequential amendments . 75
Health & Social Care Act 2012: Social workers 77
Health & social care: Children's homes: Northern Ireland 417
Health & social care: Health: 2006 Act: Commencements: Northern Ireland 409, 417
Health & social care: Pension schemes: Northern Ireland 416
Health & social care: Safeguarding Board for Northern Ireland: Membership, procedure, functions & committees: Northern Ireland 417
Health & social care: Safeguarding Board: 2011 Act: Commencements: Northern Ireland 417
Health Act 2006: Commencements: Northern Ireland 409, 417
Health Act 2009: Commencements: England. 106, 131
Health Act 2009: Commencements: Wales 110

Health and Social Care Act 2012: Consequential amendments 106
Health care & associated professions: General Dental Council: Constitution. 75, 77
Health care & associated professions: General Medical Council: Constitution 76
Health care & associated professions: General Medical Council: Licence to practise 76
Health care & associated professions: General Optical Council: Continuing education & training rules. 76
Health care & associated professions: General Social Care Council: Transfer of register & abolition: Transitional & saving
provisions 77
Health care & associated professions: Health & Social Care Act 2012: Commencements 75, 93, 103, 106, 131, 295
Health care & associated professions: Health & Social Care Act 2012: Professional Standards Authority for Health & Social
Care: Consequential amendments. 75
Health care & associated professions: Medical Profession (Miscellaneous Amendments) Order 2008: Commencements. . 76
Health care & associated professions: Nurse & midwives: Nursing & Midwifery Council: Constitution 76
Health care & associated professions: Nursing & Midwifery Council: Education, registration & appeals 76
Health care & associated professions: Nursing & Midwifery Council: Fees 76
Health care & associated professions: Nursing & Midwifery Council: Fitness to practise: Amendments 76
Health care & associated professions: Nursing & Midwifery Council: Midwives: Rules. 76
Health care & associated professions: Pharmacy: General Pharmaceutical Council: Miscellaneous provisions 77
Health care & associated professions: Postgraduate medical education & training. 76
Health care: EEA Services: Costs: Reimbursement: Northern Ireland. 416
Health Education England 107
Health Education England: Establishment & constitution 107
Health Research Authority: England. 107
Health Research Authority: Establishment & constitution: England 107
Health Service Commissioner for England: Special health authorities 107
Health service: Medicines: Branded medicines: Prices control: Information supply 74, 110
Health Service: National Health Service Development Authority: Establishment & constitution. 108
Health Service: National Trusts. 74, 106, 107, 109, 110, 111
Health services: Charges: Recovery: Amounts: Northern Ireland 417
Health: 2009 Act: Commencements: Northern Ireland. 407, 428
Health: Acts. 5
Health: Acts: Explanatory notes 7
Health: Cancer patients: Treatment: Fuel payments scheme: Northern Ireland 414
Healthcare & associated professions: General Osteopathic Council: Registration & fees: Application 76
Her Majesty's Inspector of Education, Children's Services & Skills 17, 52
Her Majesty's Inspector of Education, Children's Services & Skills: Children's homes etc.: Fees & frequency of inspections
. . . . 17
Her Majesty's Inspectorate of Courts Administration: Abolition 130
Heritable property: Actions for removing: Sheriff Court: Act of Sederunt: Scotland 394
Hertfordshire County Council: Permit schemes: Traffic management 78
High Court of Justiciary: Act of Adjournal: Criminal Procedure (Scotland) Act 1995: Transcripts: Amendments: Scotland
. . . . 373, 394
High Court of Justiciary: Act of Adjournal: Criminal procedure rules: Scotland 373, 375, 394
High Court of Justiciary: Court Fees: Amendments: Scotland 368, 373, 395
High Court of Justiciary: Fees: Scotland. 373
High Hedges Act 2011: Northern Ireland 411
High hedges: Fee transfer: Northern Ireland. 411
High hedges: Fees: Northern Ireland. 411
High hedges: Rates: Valuation Tribunal: Rules: Northern Ireland. 431
Higher Education Funding Council for Wales 57
Higher education: Assembly learning grants & loans: Wales. 55
Higher education: Student loans: Living costs liability: Cancellation. 55
Highways, England: River Tyne: Tunnels: Revision of tolls 78
Highways, Wales 80
Highways: A282: Dartford - Thurrock Crossing charging scheme 77
Highways: A30: Turks Head Link 77
Highways: A470. 79
Highways: A477: Wales. 80
Highways: Dunham Bridge: Tolls: Revision 77
Highways: England 77, 78
Highways: England: Sunderland City Council: New Wear Bridge scheme. 78
Highways: Humber Bridge Board: Membership 77
Highways: Humber Bridge: Debts 77
Highways: Portsmouth City Council: M275 Motorway slip roads: Tipner Interchange: Confirmation. 78
Highways: Severn Bridges: Tolls 78
Highways: Street works: Charges for occupation: England. 78

Highways: Street works: Unreasonably prolonged occupation: Charges: England 78
Highways: Traffic management: Permit schemes: Barnsley Metropolitan Borough Council. 78
Highways: Traffic management: Permit schemes: Bedford Borough Council 78
Highways: Traffic management: Permit schemes: Bexley, London Borough. 79
Highways: Traffic management: Permit schemes: Council of the Borough of Kirklees 79
Highways: Traffic management: Permit schemes: Doncaster Borough Council 78
Highways: Traffic management: Permit schemes: Havering, London Borough 79
Highways: Traffic management: Permit schemes: Hertfordshire County Council 78
Highways: Traffic management: Permit schemes: Kingston upon Thames, Royal Borough 79
Highways: Traffic management: Permit schemes: Leeds City Council. 78
Highways: Traffic management: Permit schemes: Luton Borough Council 79
Highways: Traffic management: Permit schemes: Merton, London Borough 79
Highways: Traffic management: Permit schemes: Rotherham Borough Council. 79
Highways: Traffic management: Permit schemes: Sheffield City Council 79
Highways: Traffic management: Permit schemes: Southend-on-Sea Borough Council 79
Highways: Traffic management: Permit schemes: St Helens Borough Council 79
Highways: Traffic management: Permit schemes: Sutton, London Borough 79
Highways: Traffic management: Permit schemes: Tower Hamlets, London Borough 79
Highways: Wales 79
Hinkley Point Harbour: Empowerment 74
Hinkley Point: Temporary jetty: Land acquisition. 309
Historical records: Definition: Freedom of information. 73
Holywood: Waiting restrictions: Road traffic & vehicles: Northern Ireland. 443
Home energy assistance schemes: Amendments: Scotland 370
Home energy efficiency scheme: England 61
Homelessness: Allocation of housing & homelessness: Eligibility: England 80
Homelessness: Allocation of housing & homelessness: Eligibility: Northern Ireland. 418
Homelessness: Priority need test: Abolition: Scotland. 374
Homelessness: Suitability of accommodation: England. 80
Homelessness: Support services: Scotland. 374
Homeowner housing panel: Application & decisions: Scotland 380
Horse sickness: African: Scotland 364
Horticulture: Bananas: Green: Quality standards: England & Wales 80
Horticulture: Bananas: Marketing: Scotland. 374
Horticulture: Fresh produce: Marketing: Northern Ireland 418
House of Commons Members' Fund: Resolutions. 116
Housing & Regeneration Act 2008: Consequential provisions: England 81
Housing (Scotland) Act 2001: Registered social landlords & other persons: Assistance to: Grants: Scotland 374
Housing (Scotland) Act 2006: Consequential provisions 32, 47, 80
Housing (Scotland) Act 2010: Commencements: Scotland 374
Housing (Scotland) Act 2010: Consequential modifications: Scotland 374
Housing (Wales) Measure 2011: Commencements: Wales 82
Housing (Wales) Measure 2011: Consequential amendments: Wales 82
Housing benefit 297
Housing benefit: Benefit cap. 296
Housing benefit: Executive determinations: Northern Ireland 418
Housing benefit: Functions: Rent officers: Amendments 80
Housing: Allocation of housing & homelessness: Eligibility: England 80
Housing: Allocation of housing & homelessness: Eligibility: Northern Ireland 418
Housing: Allocation: Qualification criteria for armed forces: England 80
Housing: Armed forces: Additional preference: England 81
Housing: Empty dwelling management orders: Prescribed exceptions & requirements: England 81
Housing: Flexible tenancies: Review procedures 80
Housing: Homelessness: Priority need test: Abolition: Scotland 374
Housing: Homelessness: Suitability of accommodation: England 80
Housing: Homeowner housing panel: Application & decisions: Scotland. 380
Housing: Houses in multiple occupation: Specified educational establishments 81
Housing: Jobseeker's allowance: Failure to attend: Sanctions: Northern Ireland 418, 429, 445
Housing: Landlords: Private: Registration: Information & fees: Scotland. 375
Housing: Licensing & management. 81
Housing: Localism Act 2011: Commencements. 31, 81, 82, 87, 98, 99, 101, 129, 133, 305, 306, 307
Housing: Localism Act 2011: Commencements: Wales 70, 82, 100
Housing: Localism Act 2011: Greater London: Housing & regeneration functions 81
Housing: Localism Act 2011: Social housing: Regulation: Consequential provisions 82
Housing: Localism: Acts 4

Housing: Mobile Homes Act 1983: Residential property tribunals: Jurisdiction: Wales 105
Housing: Mobile homes: Written statement: Wales 105
Housing: Private Rented Housing (Scotland) Act 2011: Commencements: Scotland 375
Housing: Property factors: Acts: Explanatory notes: Scotland 362
Housing: Property factors: Acts: Scotland 361
Housing: Residential property tribunal procedures & fees 82
Housing: Right to buy: Discount limits 81
Housing: Right to manage: England. 81
Housing: Scottish secure tenancies: Proceedings for possession: Scotland 375
Housing: Scottish secure tenancies: Repossession orders: Scotland. 375
Housing: Social security: Benefits: Payment suspensions: Miscellaneous amendments: Northern Ireland. . . . 419, 430, 447
Housing: Social security: Benefits: Up-rating: Northern Ireland 411, 418, 430, 446, 447, 448
Housing: Social security: Habitual residence: Northern Ireland 418, 430, 446
Housing: Social security: Northern Ireland 419, 430, 447
Housing: Social security: Recovery: Northern Ireland 419, 430, 447
Housing: Support grants: Scotland. 374
Housing: Support services: Homelessness: Scotland 374
Housing: Tenancies: Transfer: Right to acquire: Exclusion. 81
Housing: Tenancy deposit schemes: Northern Ireland. 420
Human tissue: Transplantation: Organs: Quality & safety 82
Humber Bridge Board: Membership 77
Humber Bridge: Debts 77
Huntingdonshire: Electoral changes. 95
Hydrocarbon oils: Excise: Duties: Surcharges or rebates 65

I

Immigration & asylum: Jersey 82
Immigration & nationality: Cost recovery fees 82, 83, 112
Immigration & nationality: Fees 83, 112
Immigration, Asylum & Nationality Act 2006: Commencements 83
Immigration: Appeals: Family visitor. 83
Immigration: Biometric registration. 83
Immigration: European Economic Area. 83
Immigration: Jersey 83
Immigration: Nationality, Immigration & Asylum Act 2002: Authority to carry. 84
Immigration: Nationality, Immigration & Asylum Act 2002: Commencements 84
Immigration: Passenger transit: Visas. 83, 84
Immigration: Travel bans: Designation 83
Immigration: UK Borders Act 2007: Border & immigration inspectorate: Joint working 84
Imperial College Healthcare: National Health Service Trust 107
Incapacity: Adults with incapacity: Medical treatment certificates: Signing: Requirements: Scotland 363
Incapacity: Adults with incapacity: Public Guardian: Fees: Amendments: Scotland 363
Income & interest payments: Reporting: Data gathering 304
Income tax: Amendments 19, 84, 303
Income tax: Authorised Investment Funds 35, 84
Income tax: Business investment relief 84
Income tax: Business premises renovation allowances 35, 84
Income tax: Capital allowances: Energy-saving plant & machinery 35, 84
Income tax: Capital allowances: Environmentally beneficial plant & machinery. 35, 84
Income tax: Car & van fuel: Benefit: Rates. 84
Income tax: Car fuel: Benefit: Rates 84
Income tax: Construction industry scheme: Amendments 36, 85
Income tax: Entertainers & sportsmen 85
Income tax: Extra-statutory concessions: Enactments. 36, 85, 88
Income tax: Finance Act 2010: Schedule 6, part 1: Consequential & incidental provisions 15, 36, 85, 312
Income tax: Finance Act 2012: Enterprise investment scheme: Appointed day. 15, 85
Income tax: Finance Act 2012: Venture capital trusts: Appointed days. 85
Income tax: Financial Services Act 2010: Schedule 6: Part 2: Commencements. 15, 36, 85, 88, 302, 303
Income tax: Indexation 85
Income tax: Individual savings accounts 15, 86
Income tax: Limits: Enterprise management: Incentives 86
Income tax: London Legacy Development Corporation: Tax consequences 36, 86, 303
Income tax: Minor benefits: Exemptions 85
Income tax: PAYE 86

Income tax: Pension schemes: Application of UK provisions: Non-UK schemes 86
Income tax: Pension schemes: Categories of country & requirements for overseas schemes & recognised overseas schemes 86
Income tax: Pension schemes: Registered & overseas: Amendments 86
Income tax: Postal Services Act 2011: Taxation 36, 86, 302, 303
Income tax: Professional fees 86
Income tax: Purchased life annuities 86
Income tax: Qualifying care relief: Specified social care schemes 86
Income tax: Registered pension schemes: Authorised payments 86, 87
Income tax: Registered pension schemes: Relevant annuities 87
Income tax: Skipton Fund Limited 87
Income tax: Visiting forces: International Military Headquarters: NATO & PfP: Tax Designation 46, 87, 88, 303
Indication of prices: Beds 127
Individual learning accounts: Education: Scotland 370
Individual savings accounts: Income tax 15, 86
Industrial injuries benefit 297
Industrial injuries: Dependency: Permitted earnings limits 300
Industrial injuries: Dependency: Permitted earnings limits: Northern Ireland 446
Industrial injuries: Prescribed diseases 300
Industrial injuries: Prescribed diseases: Northern Ireland 446
Industrial training levy: Construction Industry Training Board 59
Industrial training levy: Construction industry: Northern Ireland 419
Industrial training levy: Engineering Construction Industry Training Board 59
Information database: Children Act 2004: England 16
Information: Access: Executive arrangements: Local authorities: England 96
Infrastructure for Spatial Information in the European Community (INSPIRE) 62, 133
Infrastructure for Spatial Information in the European Community (INSPIRE): Scotland 370, 382
Infrastructure planning: Environmental impact assessment 87
Infrastructure planning: Local policing bodies 87, 122, 310
Infrastructure planning: Localism Act 2011: Amendments 87
Infrastructure planning: Localism Act 2011: Commencements 31, 81, 87, 98, 101, 133, 306, 307
Infrastructure planning: Network Rail: Ipswich Chord 87
Infrastructure planning: Network Rail: North Doncaster Chord 87
Infrastructure planning: Waste water transfer & storage 87
Infrastructure: Financial Assistance: Acts 5
Infrastructure: Financial Assistance: Acts: Explanatory notes 7
Inheritance tax: Financial Services Act 2010: Schedule 6: Part 2: Commencements 15, 36, 85, 88, 302, 303
Inheritance tax: Market makers & discount houses 88
Inheritance tax: Visiting forces: International Military Headquarters: NATO & PfP: Tax Designation 46, 87, 88, 303
Injuries, diseases & dangerous occurrences: Reporting 75
Injury benefit: Police Service & Police Service Reserve: Northern Ireland 428
Injury benefits: Health & personal social services: Northern Ireland 416
Inland Waterways Advisory Council: Abolition 14, 129
Insects: Statutory nuisances: Environmental protection: Northern Ireland 412
Insolvency 88
Insolvency Act 1986: Parliament: Disqualification from 88, 116
Insolvency: Practitioners & services account: Fees 88
INSPIRE see Infrastructure for Spatial Information in the European Community
Institute & Faculty of Actuaries: Employers' consultation: Pensions: Northern Ireland 426
Insurance companies: Controlled Foreign Companies (CFCs): Double charge: Avoidance 36
Insurance companies: Transitional provisions 36
Insurance premium tax: Extra-statutory concessions: Enactments 36, 85, 88
Insurance: Consumer: Disclosure & representations: Acts 4
International Bank for Reconstruction & Development: General capital increase 88
International Bank for Reconstruction & Development: Selective capital increase 88
International Criminal Tribunal for the former Yugoslavia: Indictees: Financial sanctions 40
International Development Association: Multilateral debt relief initiative 88
International Development Association: Sixteenth replenishment 88
International development: International Bank for Reconstruction & Development: General capital increase 88
International development: International Bank for Reconstruction & Development: Selective capital increase 88
International development: International Development Association: Multilateral debt relief initiative 88
International development: International Fund for Agricultural Development: Eighth replenishment 88
International Fund for Agricultural Development: Eighth replenishment 88
International Military Headquarters: EU SOFA: Visiting forces: Tax Designation 46
International Military Headquarters: NATO & PfP: Visiting forces: Tax Designation 46, 87, 88, 303
International recovery of maintenance: Hague Convention 2007: Rules of Court 89

International recovery of maintenance: Hague Convention 2007: Scotland 375
International tax enforcement: Arrangements: Germany 12
Inverness: Harbour revision: Scotland 373
Investigatory powers: Protection of Freedoms Act 2012: Commencements 18, 43, 89, 129, 273
Investigatory powers: Regulation of investigatory powers: Covert human intelligence sources 89
Investigatory powers: Regulation of investigatory powers: Directed surveillance 89
Investigatory Powers: Regulation: Magistrates' courts: England & Wales 102
Ipswich Barrier: Transport & works 309
Ipswich Chord: Network Rail 87
Iran: European Communities: Financial sanctions 40
Iran: Export control: Sanctions 44
Iran: Financial restrictions 127
Iran: Restrictive measures: Overseas territories 114
Iraq: Asset-freezing 40
Iraq: Sanctions 311
Iron & steel: Employees: Re-adaption benefits scheme: European Communities 89
Isle of Man: United Nations: Personnel: Criminal law 41
Isle of Wight: National Health Service Trust 107

J

Japan: Accounting standards: Prescribed bodies: Companies 31
Jersey: Geneva Conventions Act 73
Jersey: Immigration 83
Jersey: Immigration & asylum 82
Jewel & Esk College: Transfer & closure: Scotland 370
Jobcentres: Welfare reform: Acts 7
Jobcentres: Welfare reform: Acts: Explanatory notes 7
Jobseeker's allowance 297
Jobseeker's allowance: Domestic violence 297
Jobseeker's allowance: Domestic violence: Northern Ireland 444
Jobseeker's allowance: Failure to attend: Sanctions: Northern Ireland 418, 429, 445
Jobseeker's allowance: Forces: Members : Northern Ireland 112, 302
Jobseeker's allowance: Northern Ireland 444
Jobseeker's allowance: Reserve forces: Members 297
Jobseeker's allowance: Reserve forces: Members: Northern Ireland 445
Jobseeker's allowance: Sanctions 298
Jobseeker's allowance: Work experience: Northern Ireland 445
Jobseeker's allowance: Work for Your Benefit 297
John Street, Castlederg: Waiting restrictions: Road traffic & vehicles: Northern Ireland 443
Judges, legal officers & others: Fees: Ecclesiastical law 48
Judgments: International recovery of maintenance: Hague Convention 2007: Rules of Court 89
Judgments: International recovery of maintenance: Hague Convention 2007: Scotland 375
Judgments: International recovery: Maintenance: Hague Convention: Northern Ireland 419
Judicial pensions: Contributions 116
Judicial pensions: European Court of Human Rights 116
Juries: Allowances: Amendments: England & Wales 89
Juries: Northern Ireland 419
Justice Act (Northern Ireland) 2011: Commencements: Northern Ireland 419
Justice of the Peace Court: Act of Adjournal: Criminal procedure rules: Scotland 373, 375, 394
Justice of the Peace Court: Fees: Scotland 376
Justice: Criminal: Acts 4
Justices of the Peace: Local justice areas 89

K

Key Stages 1, 2 & 3: Levels of progression: Education: Northern Ireland 410
Kilkeel: Roads: Parking places: Northern Ireland 439
King's Lynn & West Norfolk: Electoral changes 95
Kingston upon Thames, Royal Borough: Permit schemes: Traffic management 79
Kirklees: Council of the Borough of Kirklees: Permit schemes: Traffic management 79
Korea: Democratic People's Republic of Korea: Sanctions: Overseas territories 114
Korea: European Communities: Definition of treaties: Framework agreements 65
Korea: European Communities: Definition of treaties: Free trade agreements 65

L

Labour Relations Agency Arbitration Scheme: Jurisdiction: Northern Ireland 411
Labour Relations Agency Arbitration Scheme: Northern Ireland 411
Lancaster Castle: Prisons: Closure. 127
Land charges: Fees: Rules. 89
Land charges: Rules. 89
Land compensation development: England 305
Land compensation development: Wales 307
Land drainage: Axe Brue Internal Drainage Board 89
Land drainage: Cowick & Snaith Internal Drainage Board 90
Land drainage: Danvm Drainage Commissioners. 90
Land drainage: Doncaster East: Internal drainage Board 90
Land drainage: Needham & Laddus Internal Drainage Board 90
Land drainage: North Level District (2010): Internal drainage Board 90
Land drainage: Ouse & Humber Drainage Board. 90
Land drainage: Swale & Ure: Drainage Board 90
Land drainage: Trent Valley: Internal drainage Board 90
Land Registration etc. (Scotland) Act 2012: Commencements: Scotland 376
Land registration: Acts: Explanatory notes: Scotland 362
Land registration: Acts: Scotland 361
Land registration: Fees: England & Wales 90
Land: Common land & greens: Deregistration & exchange: Procedure: Wales. 31
Land: Contaminated land: England 62
Land: Value added tax: Exemption 312
Landfill allowances scheme: Wales. 64
Landfill tax 90
Landfill tax: Qualifying materials. 90
Landlord & tenant: Agricultural holdings: Units of production: England. 90
Landlord & tenant: Agricultural holdings: Units of production: Wales. 90
Landlord & tenant: Registered rents: Increases: Northern Ireland 419
Landlord & tenant: Rent (Scotland) Act 1984: Premiums: Scotland. 376
Landlord & tenant: Tenancy deposit schemes: Northern Ireland 420
Landlord & tenants: Long leases: Acts: Scotland 361
Landlords: Private: Registration: Information & fees: Scotland. 375
Landlords: Registered social landlords & other persons: Assistance to: Grants: Housing (Scotland) Act 2001: Scotland . 374
Larne: Parking places: Northern Ireland. 440
Larne: Waiting restrictions: Road traffic & vehicles: Northern Ireland 443
Latchmere House: Prisons: Closure 127
Late night levy: Application & administration 92
Late night levy: Expenses, exemptions & reductions: England & Wales 92
Law Society: Modification of functions: Legal Services Act 2007 91
Law: Criminal cases: Punishment & review: Acts: Explanatory notes: Scotland 362
Law: Criminal Justice: Acts 4
Law: Family proceedings: Allocation: England & Wales. 38
Law: Football: Offensive behaviour: Threatening communications: Acts: Explanatory notes: Scotland 362
Law: Football: Offensive behaviour: Threatening communications: Acts: Scotland 361
Law: Forest law: Enforcement, governance & trade 44
Law: Sexual offences: Acts: Scotland 361
Leader grants: Agriculture: Scotland. 363
Learning & skills: Measures: National Assembly for Wales. 455
Learning accounts: Individual: Education: Scotland. 370
Lebanon: Syria: Asset-freezing 40
Leeds City Council: Permit schemes: Traffic management 78
Leeds, City: Mayoral referendum 94
Legal advice & assistance: Northern Ireland. 420
Legal aid & advice: Advice & assistance: Representation: Scotland 376
Legal aid & advice: Civil legal aid: Amendments: Scotland. 376
Legal aid & advice: Civil legal aid: England & Wales 90, 91
Legal aid & advice: Civil legal aid: Environment: Pollution: Prescribed types. 91
Legal aid & advice: Civil legal aid: Immigration interviews: Exceptions. 91
Legal aid & advice: Criminal aid certificates: Rules: Northern Ireland 420
Legal aid & advice: Criminal legal aid: Defence costs orders: Recovery: Northern Ireland. 420
Legal aid & advice: Criminal legal aid: Fees: Scotland 376
Legal aid & advice: General: Northern Ireland 420

Legal aid & advice: Legal advice & assistance: Northern Ireland 420
Legal Aid, Sentencing & Punishment of Offenders Act 2012: Children: Consequential & savings provisions. . . . 17, 42, 46
Legal Aid, Sentencing & Punishment of Offenders Act 2012: Children: Youth detention 17
Legal Aid, Sentencing & Punishment of Offenders Act 2012: Commencements 40, 42, 46, 91, 135
Legal officers: Annual fees: Ecclesiastical law 48
Legal profession: Legal Services (Scotland) Act 2010: Ancillary provisions: Scotland. 376
Legal profession: Legal Services (Scotland) Act 2010: Commencement: Scotland 376
Legal profession: Licensed legal services: Approved Regulations: Maximum penalty & interest in respect of: Scotland . 377
Legal profession: Licensed legal services: Complaints & compensation arrangements: Scotland. 377
Legal profession: Licensed legal services: Licensed providers: Interests: Scotland 377
Legal profession: Licensed legal services: Regulated professions: Specification: Scotland. 377
Legal profession: Solicitors: Non-contentious business: England & Wales. 91
Legal Services (Scotland) Act 2010: Ancillary provisions: Scotland 376
Legal Services (Scotland) Act 2010: Commencement: Scotland 376
Legal Services Act 2007: Alteration of Limit. 91
Legal Services Act 2007: Law Society: Modification of functions 91
Legal Services Act 2007: Legal complaints: Parties 91
Legal Services Commission: Criminal Defence Service: Funding: England & Wales 91
Legal services: Licensed: Approved Regulations: Maximum penalty & interest in respect of: Scotland 377
Legal services: Licensed: Complaints & compensation arrangements: Scotland 377
Legal services: Licensed: Licensed providers: Interests: Scotland. 377
Legislative & regulatory reform: Civil partnership 135
Legislative reform: Local authorities: Annual review 17, 52, 135
Lenadoon, Belfast: Traffic prohibition: Road traffic & vehicles: Northern Ireland 440
Liberia: Asset-freezing 40
Liberia: Restrictive measures: Overseas territories 114
Libraries: National Library of Scotland: Acts: Explanatory notes: Scotland 362
Libraries: National Library of Scotland: Acts: Scotland. 361
Libraries: Public Lending Right Scheme 1982: Variation: Commencements. 91
Libya: Asset-freezing 40
Libya: Restrictive measures: Overseas territories 115
Licences & licensing: Late night levy: Application & administration 92
Licences & licensing: Late night levy: Expenses, exemptions & reductions: England & Wales 92
Licences & licensing: Live Music Act 2012: Commencements. 92
Licences & licensing: Police Reform & Social Responsibility Act 2011: Commencements 92, 125
Licensed legal services: Approved Regulations: Maximum penalty & interest in respect of: Scotland 377
Licensed legal services: Complaints & compensation arrangements: Scotland 377
Licensed legal services: Licensed providers: Interests: Scotland 377
Licensed legal services: Regulated professions: Specification: Scotland 377
Licenses & licensing: Civic Government (Scotland) Act 1982: Metal Dealers': Exemption Warrants: Scotland 377
Licensing & Registration of Clubs (Amendment) Act (Northern Ireland) 2011: Commencements: Northern Ireland . . . 420
Licensing (liquor): Health & Social Care Act 2012: Commencements 75, 93, 103, 106, 295
Licensing Act 2003: Children: Alcohol: Persistent selling to: Closure Notices: Prescribed forms 42, 92
Licensing Act 2003: Diamond Jubilee licensing hours 92
Licensing Act 2003: Early morning alcohol restriction orders: England & Wales 92
Licensing Act 2003: Forms & notices. 92
Licensing Act 2003: Live music: Performance of: Acts 5
Licensing Act 2003: Live music: Performance of: Acts: Explanatory notes 7
Licensing Act 2003: Permitted temporary activities: Notices. 92
Licensing Act 2003: Personal licences 92
Licensing Act 2003: Premises licences & club premises: Certificates 92
Licensing: Conference centres: Requirements: Northern Ireland 421
Licensing: Form of licence: Northern Ireland 420
Licensing: Irresponsible drinks promotions: Northern Ireland. 420
Licensing: Marine licensing: Exempted activities: Scottish inshore & offshore regions: Scotland 371, 377
Licensing: Marine licensing: Fees: Scotland 371, 377
Licensing: Marine: Marine & Coastal Access Act 2009: Transitional provisions: England 62, 93
Licensing: Notice relating to age: Northern Ireland 421
Licensing: Register of licences: Northern Ireland 421
Liechtenstein: Double taxation: Relief & international enforcement 14, 35, 85
Limited liability partnerships: Accounts & audit exemptions. 32, 93
Lincolnshire: Coroners' districts: England & Wales 34
Lisburn: Waiting restrictions: Road traffic & vehicles: Northern Ireland 443
Listed buildings & conservation areas: Planning: England 305
Listed buildings: Wales 307

Litter: Street litter: Control notices: Amendments: Environmental protection: Northern Ireland 412
Live Music Act 2012: Commencements 92
Live music: Performance of: Licensing Act 2003: Acts 5
Live music: Performance of: Licensing Act 2003: Acts: Explanatory notes 7
Llandegley: Diocese of Swansea & Brecon: Educational endowments: Wales. 56
Loading bays & parking places: Roads: Northern Ireland 436
Local authorities see also Local government 96, 97, 98
Local authorities: Armorial bearings 95
Local authorities: Capital finance & accounting: England 95, 96
Local authorities: Committee systems: England 96
Local authorities: Council tax base: Calculation: England 37
Local authorities: Council tax: Increases: Referendums: Conduct: England 37
Local authorities: Council tax: Increases: Referendums: England 37
Local authorities: Discharge of functions: Arrangements: England. 95
Local authorities: Early years provision: Free: Duty 17
Local authorities: Elected mayors: Elections, terms of office. 96
Local authorities: Executive arrangements: Meetings & access to information: England 96
Local authorities: London: Local acts 7
Local authorities: Mayoral elections: England & Wales 98
Local authorities: Overview & scrutiny committees: England 96
Local authorities: Partnership: National Health Service bodies 97, 109
Local authorities: Political restrictions: Exemption. 96
Local authorities: Property factors: Acts: Explanatory notes: Scotland 362
Local authorities: Property factors: Acts: Scotland 361
Local authorities: Referendums: Conduct of: England 96
Local authorities: Requisite calculations: Alteration: Wales. 100
Local authorities: Social services functions: Contracting out: England. 34
Local Better Regulation Office: Dissolution & transfer of functions 135
Local digital television programme services 13
Local election survey: Wales 99
Local Electoral Administration (Scotland) Act 2011: Consequential amendments: Scotland 384
Local Government (Wales) Measure 2011: Commencements: Wales. 100
Local government Act 2000: Commencements 98
Local government election expenses: Limits: Variation: Scotland 384
Local government finance: Unoccupied properties: Acts: Explanatory notes: Scotland. 362
Local government finance: Unoccupied properties: Acts: Scotland 361
Local government see also Local authorities. 37, 95, 96, 97, 98, 100
Local government: 2005 Order: Commencements: Northern Ireland 421
Local government: Abergavenny Improvement Act 1854: Partial repeal. 99
Local government: Assets of community value: England. 93
Local government: Best value: Exclusions: Non-commercial considerations: Northern Ireland 421
Local government: Boundaries: Northern Ireland 421
Local government: Bus lane contraventions: Approved local authorities 93, 272
Local government: Byelaws: Acts. 455
Local government: Byelaws: Acts: Explanatory notes. 455
Local government: City of Birmingham: Mayoral referendum 93
Local government: City of Bradford: Mayoral referendum 93
Local government: City of Bristol: Mayoral referendum 93
Local government: City of Coventry: Mayoral referendum. 94
Local government: City of Leeds: Mayoral referendum 94
Local government: City of Manchester: Mayoral referendum 94
Local government: City of Newcastle-upon-Tyne: Mayoral referendum. 94
Local government: City of Nottingham: Mayoral referendum 94
Local government: City of Sheffield: Mayoral referendum. 94
Local government: City of Wakefield: Mayoral referendum 94
Local government: Councillors: Payments: Northern Ireland 421
Local government: Councillors' Remuneration Panels: Northern Ireland 421
Local government: Elections: Declaration of acceptance of office 96
Local government: Elections: Scotland 384
Local government: Electoral changes: Blaby, District 94
Local government: Electoral changes: Broxbourne. 93
Local government: Electoral changes: Buckinghamshire 93
Local government: Electoral changes: Cumbria. 94
Local government: Electoral changes: Daventry 94
Local government: Electoral changes: Derbyshire 94

Local government: Electoral changes: District of Craven. 95
Local government: Electoral changes: Durham 95
Local government: Electoral changes: Gloucestershire 95
Local government: Electoral changes: Hart 95
Local government: Electoral changes: Hartlepool 95
Local government: Electoral changes: Huntingdonshire 95
Local government: Electoral changes: King's Lynn & West Norfolk. 95
Local government: Electoral changes: North Devon 97
Local government: Electoral changes: Oxfordshire. 97
Local government: Electoral changes: Rugby. 97
Local government: Electoral changes: Rushmoor. 97
Local government: Electoral changes: Shropshire 94
Local government: Electoral changes: Slough 97
Local government: Electoral changes: Somerset 97
Local government: Electoral changes: Staffordshire 97
Local government: Electoral changes: Swale 98
Local government: Electoral changes: Swindon 98
Local government: Electoral changes: West Lindsey 98
Local government: Electoral changes: West Oxfordshire 95
Local government: Expressions of interest: Community challenge: England. 94
Local government: Finance: Acts. 5
Local government: Finance: Acts: Explanatory notes 7
Local government: Finance: Scotland 377
Local government: Fire & rescue authorities: Expressions of interest: Community challenge: England 94
Local government: Fire & rescue authorities: Improvement plans: Wales 99
Local government: Isle of Anglesey: Electoral arrangements. 99
Local government: Isle of Anglesey: Local authorities: Ordinary elections 99
Local government: Joint Committees: Constituting as bodies corporate: Northern Ireland 421
Local government: Local authorities: Capital finance & accounting: England 95, 96
Local government: Local authorities: Committee systems: England 96
Local government: Local authorities: Discharge of functions: Arrangements: England 95
Local government: Local authorities: Executive arrangements: Meetings & access to information: England 96
Local government: Local authorities: Political restrictions: Exemption 96
Local government: Local authorities: Referendums: Conduct of: England 96
Local government: Local election survey: Wales 99
Local government: Local policing bodies 10, 67, 99, 122
Local government: Localism Act 2011: Commencements. 31, 70, 81, 82, 87, 96, 98, 99, 101, 129, 132, 133, 306, 307
Local government: Localism Act 2011: Commencements: Wales. 70, 82, 100
Local government: Localism Act 2011: Consequential amendments 99, 307
Local government: Localism Act 2011: Local Authority governance: Transitional provisions. 96
Local government: Localism: Acts 4
Local government: Members & officers: Indemnities: Northern Ireland 421
Local government: National Health Service bodies: Partnership 97, 109
Local government: Officers: Political restrictions: Amendments: England. 96
Local government: Overview & scrutiny: Reference by councillors: Excluded matters: England 97
Local government: Parish councils: General power of competence: Prescribed conditions 97
Local government: Parking contraventions: Civil enforcement 93, 272
Local government: Partnership Council for Wales: Local health boards & National Health Service trusts: Wales . . . 33, 100
Local government: Pension schemes. 119
Local government: Pension schemes: Administration: Scotland. 379
Local government: Pension schemes: Amendments: Scotland. 379
Local government: Pension schemes: Northern Ireland 421
Local government: Performance indicators: Wales 100
Local government: Relevant authorities: Disclosable pecuniary interests: England 97
Local government: Specified bodies: Northern Ireland 421
Local government: St Albans & Welwyn Hatfield: Boundary changes. 97
Local government: St. Mary Out Liberty & Tenby Communities: Pembrokeshire: Wales 100
Local government: Standards Board for England: Abolition 99
Local government: Structural changes: Finance: Amendments 98
Local government: Sustainable communities 98
Local government: Transport levying bodies 98
Local health boards: National Health Service trusts: Partnership Council for Wales 33, 100
Local justice areas. 89
Local pharmaceutical services: National Health Service: England 107
Local planning: Town & country planning: England 306

Local policing bodies.. 87, 122, 310
Localism Act 2011: Commencements 31, 70, 81, 82, 87, 96, 98, 99, 101, 129, 132, 133, 305, 306, 307
Localism Act 2011: Commencements: Wales 70, 82, 100
Localism Act 2011: Consequential amendments... 99, 307
Localism Act 2011: Greater London: Housing & regeneration functions.. 81
Localism Act 2011: Housing: Regeneration functions: Greater London... 101
Localism Act 2011: Infrastructure planning: Amendments... 87
Localism Act 2011: Local Authority governance: Transitional provisions...................................... 96
Localism Act 2011: Social housing: Regulation: Consequential provisions 82
Localism: Acts 4
London cable car 309, 310
London government: Greater London Authority Act 1999: Amendments... 100
London government: Greater London Authority: Elections: Rules.. 100, 135
London Government: Localism Act 2011: Commencements 81, 82, 87, 98, 99, 101, 129, 133, 307
London Government: Localism Act 2011: Housing: Regeneration functions: Greater London..................... 101
London government: Penalty charges enforcement 61, 101
London Legacy Development Corporation: Establishment 311
London Legacy Development Corporation: Planning functions.. 311
London Legacy Development Corporation: Tax consequences 36, 86, 303
London Olympic & Paralympic Games: Sunday trading: Acts... 6
London Olympic Games & Paralympic Games: Advertising & trading: Wales.................................... 101
London Thames Gateway Development Corporation: Transfer of property, rights & liabilities 311
London: Local authorities: Local acts 7
London: Penalty charges enforcement 61, 101
Londonderry: Roads: Parking places & loading bays: Northern Ireland....................................... 438
Londonderry: Waiting restrictions: Road traffic & vehicles: Northern Ireland 443
Long leases: Acts: Scotland 361
Longlands Avenue, Newtownabbey: Abandonment: Roads: Northern Ireland 432
Loopland Court, Belfast : Abandonment: Roads: Northern Ireland 432
Lower Windsor, Belfast: Traffic prohibition: Road traffic & vehicles: Northern Ireland 440
Luton Borough Council: Permit schemes: Traffic management 79

M

M2: Whitla Street, Belfast: Abandonment: Roads: Northern Ireland 432
M275 Motorway slip roads: Tipner Interchange: Confirmation... 78
M3: Titanic Quarter Railway Station, Belfast: Abandonment: Roads: Northern Ireland 432
Machine games: Duty... 66
Machine games: Duty: Exemptions... 66
Magistrates' Courts Rule Committee: Abolition.. 130
Magistrates' courts: Cash: Detention & forfeiture: England & Wales.. 102
Magistrates' courts: Civil Jurisdiction & Judgments Act 1982: Rules: Northern Ireland 422
Magistrates' courts: Criminal cases: Costs: Northern Ireland 422
Magistrates' courts: Criminal procedure: Rules: England & Wales 101, 294
Magistrates' courts: Declarations of parentage: Rules: Northern Ireland 422
Magistrates' courts: Family procedure 38, 39, 67, 101, 102, 294
Magistrates' courts: Investigatory Powers: Regulation: England & Wales 102
Magistrates' courts: Procedure: Sexual Offences Act 2003: Amendments: England & Wales 102
Magistrates' courts: Rules: Northern Ireland 421
Mallaig: Harbour revision: Scotland.. 373
Malone Beeches, Belfast: Abandonment: Roads: Northern Ireland 432
Manchester (Greater): Light rapid transit systems: Oldham, Manchester St. modification............... 309, 310
Manchester (Greater): Light rapid transit systems: Oldham, Mumps modification 309, 310
Manchester, City: Mayoral referendum.. 94
Manslaughter & homicide: Corporate: 2007 Act: Commencements: Northern Ireland 409
Marine & Coastal Access Act 2009: Transitional provisions: England 62, 93
Marine fish farming: Town & country planning: Scotland 396
Marine Highway, Carrickfergus: Abandonment: Roads: Northern Ireland 432
Marine licensing: Exempted activities: Scottish inshore & offshore regions: Scotland 371, 377
Marine licensing: Fees: Scotland.. 371, 377
Marine management: Conservation: Habitats: Species.. 38, 102, 315
Marine pollution: Merchant shipping: Ship-to-ship transfers 102
Marine: Offshore marine conservation: Natural habitats 315
Materials & articles: Food: Contact: Northern Ireland.. 415
Materials & articles: Food: Contact: Scotland.. 372

Maternity expenses: Social Fund: Northern Ireland 445
Maternity grant: Social Fund. 298
Mayoral referendum: City of Birmingham 93
Mayoral referendum: City of Bradford 93
Mayoral referendum: City of Bristol 93
Mayoral referendum: City of Coventry 94
Mayoral referendum: City of Leeds 94
Mayoral referendum: City of Manchester 94
Mayoral referendum: City of Newcastle-upon-Tyne 94
Mayoral referendum: City of Nottingham 94
Mayoral referendum: City of Sheffield 94
Mayoral referendum: City of Wakefield 94
Measuring instruments: EEC requirements: Fees 68
Meat: Inspection: Authorised officers: Revocation 72
Meat: Inspection: Authorised officers: Wales 72
Medical devices: Consumer protection 33
Medical Profession (Miscellaneous Amendments) Order 2008: Commencements 76
Medical services: General: National Health Service: Contracts: Scotland 378
Medical services: Primary: National Health Service: Section 17C agreements: Scotland 378
Medicines: Branded medicines: Prices control: Information supply: National Health Service 74, 110
Medicines: Human use 102
Medicines: Human use: Fees 68, 102
Medicines: Human use: Fees: Northern Ireland 414, 422
Medicines: Veterinary medicines 103
Mental Health (Wales) Measure 2010: Commencements 103
Mental health services: Mental health: 1986 Order: Commencements: Northern Ireland 422
Mental health services: Private hospitals: Fees: Northern Ireland 422
Mental health services: Private hospitals: Northern Ireland 422
Mental Health Tribunal for Scotland: Practice & procedure: Scotland 378
Mental health: 1986 Order: Commencements: Northern Ireland 422
Mental health: Approval functions: Acts 6
Mental health: Approval functions: Acts: Explanatory notes 7
Mental health: Care co-ordination: Treatment & planning: Wales 103
Mental health: Health & Social Care Act 2012: Commencements 75, 93, 103, 106, 295
Mental health: Hospitals, guardianship & treatment: England 103
Mental health: Hospitals, guardianship, community treatment & consent to treatment 103
Mental health: National Health Service: Commissioning Board & clinical commissioning groups: Responsibilities &
standing rules: England 103, 107
Mental health: Primary care referrals & eligibility to conduct primary mental health assessments 103
Mental health: Safety & security: Scotland 377
Mental health: Secondary mental health services 103
Merchant shipping: Accident reporting & investigation 104
Merchant shipping: Health & safety: At work: Chemical agents 104
Merchant shipping: Motor fuel: Composition & content: Amendments 131
Merchant shipping: Passengers: Carriage by sea 104
Merchant shipping: Port security: Aberdeen 104
Merchant shipping: Port security: Port of Grangemouth 104
Merchant shipping: Port security: Port of Portland 104
Merchant shipping: Port security: Port of Workington 104
Merchant shipping: Port security: Tees & Hartlepool 104
Merchant shipping: Safety: Passenger ships: Domestic voyages 105
Merchant shipping: Shipowners: Compulsory insurance: Maritime claims 104
Merchant shipping: Ship-to-ship transfers: Marine pollution 102
Merton, London Borough: Permit schemes: Traffic management 79
Mesothelioma: Lump sum payments: Conditions & amounts 298
Mesothelioma: Lump sum payments: Conditions & amounts: Northern Ireland 445
Messengers-at-Arms: Fees: Court of Session: Act of Sederunt: Scotland 367
Metal Dealers': Exemption Warrants: Licensing: Civic Government (Scotland) Act 1982: Scotland 377
Midwives: Nursing & Midwifery Council: Constitution 76
Midwives: Nursing & Midwifery Council: Education: Registration & appeals 76
Midwives: Nursing & Midwifery Council: Fees 76
Midwives: Nursing & Midwifery Council: Fitness to practise: Amendments 76
Midwives: Nursing & Midwifery Council: Rules 76
Milford Haven Port Authority: Revision 74
Military lands: Ot Moor Range 46

Milton Keynes: Urban areas & planning functions 311
Ministers of the Crown: Transfer of functions: Culture, Media & Sport: Secretary of State 105
Ministers of the Crown: Transfer of functions: Sea fisheries 105
Ministry of Defence: Police: Performance. 120
Mink keeping: Prohibition: Wales. 11, 47
Misuse of drugs 45
Misuse of Drugs Act 1971: Amendments. 44
Misuse of Drugs Act 1971: Temporary class drugs 44, 45
Misuse of drugs: Designation 45
Mobile Homes Act 1983: Residential property tribunals: Jurisdiction: Wales. 105
Mobile homes: Written statement: Wales 105
Money laundering. 68
Motor fuel: Composition & content: Amendments 131
Motor fuel: Road vehicle & mobile machinery: Greenhouse gas emissions reporting 29
Motor vehicles: Construction & use: Northern Ireland 436
Motor vehicles: Disabled persons: Badges. 273
Motor vehicles: Driving licences. 137
Motor vehicles: Driving licences: Fees: Northern Ireland 437
Motor vehicles: Driving licences: Northern Ireland 436, 437
Motor vehicles: Removal & disposal: England 272
Motor vehicles: Taxi drivers: Licences: Northern Ireland 437
Motor vehicles: Testing: Northern Ireland 437
Motor vehicles: Tests: Amendments 137
Motorways: A1(M) 140, 141, 142, 143, 144, 145
Motorways: A1(M)/A1 . . . . 140, 141, 145
Motorways: A1(M)/A1(M) Spur 145
Motorways: A1(M)/A1/A47 141
Motorways: A1(M)/A194(M)/A184 140
Motorways: A1(M)/M1 226
Motorways: A1(M)/M25 253
Motorways: A1(M)/M62 265
Motorways: A194(M) 210
Motorways: A194(M)/A184/A1(M) 140
Motorways: A3(M) 154, 155
Motorways: A3(M)/A27/M27/M275 175
Motorways: A3(M)/A3 154
Motorways: A404(M) 213
Motorways: A404(M)/M4 230
Motorways: A627(M) 219
Motorways: A66(M) 204, 205
Motorways: M1 . . . . 222, 223, 224, 225, 226, 227, 228, 254
Motorways: M1/A1(M) 226
Motorways: M1/A42 221
Motorways: M1/A43 221
Motorways: M1/A453 222
Motorways: M1/A50/A453 221
Motorways: M1/A631 225
Motorways: M1/M18 . . . . 222, 224
Motorways: M1/M25 222
Motorways: M1/M45 221
Motorways: M1/M6 221
Motorways: M1/M62 . . . . 222, 265
Motorways: M1/M69/A46 221
Motorways: M1: Junction 10 to 13: Actively managed hard should & variable speed limits 272
Motorways: M11 249
Motorways: M11/A120 250
Motorways: M11/A14 . . . . 166, 249
Motorways: M11/M25 . . . . 248, 249, 254
Motorways: M18 . . . . 250, 251
Motorways: M18/M1 . . . . 222, 224
Motorways: M180 . . . . 269, 270
Motorways: M180/A180 269
Motorways: M181 270
Motorways: M2 228
Motorways: M2/A2 . . . . 153, 228

Motorways: M2/A2/A282	253
Motorways: M20	251, 252
Motorways: M20/A20	172, 251
Motorways: M23/A23	252
Motorways: M23/M25	254
Motorways: M23/M25/M3	256
Motorways: M25	252, 253, 254, 255, 256
Motorways: M25/A1(M)	253
Motorways: M25/A13/A282	253
Motorways: M25/A2/A282	253
Motorways: M25/A21	172
Motorways: M25/A282	253
Motorways: M25/A3	253
Motorways: M25/A40	253
Motorways: M25/M1	222
Motorways: M25/M11	248, 249, 254
Motorways: M25/M23	254, 256
Motorways: M25/M26	253
Motorways: M25/M26/A20	252
Motorways: M25/M3	254, 256
Motorways: M25/M3/M23	256
Motorways: M25/M4/M40	256
Motorways: M25/M40	253
Motorways: M25: Junctions 2 to 3: Variable speed limits	272
Motorways: M25: Junctions 7 to 16: Variable speed limits	272
Motorways: M26	254, 256
Motorways: M26/A20/M25	252
Motorways: M26/M25	253
Motorways: M27	256, 257
Motorways: M27/A27	175
Motorways: M27/M275	270
Motorways: M27/M275/A3(M)/A27	175
Motorways: M27/M3	229
Motorways: M271	270
Motorways: M275/A3(M)/A27/M27	175
Motorways: M275/M27	270
Motorways: M3	229, 230, 254
Motorways: M3/A316	229
Motorways: M3/A34	182
Motorways: M3/M23/M25	256
Motorways: M3/M25	254
Motorways: M3/M27	229
Motorways: M32	235, 257
Motorways: M4	230, 231, 232, 233, 234, 235, 277, 291, 292
Motorways: M4/A404(M)	230
Motorways: M4/A4042	290
Motorways: M4/A419	230
Motorways: M4/A48	278
Motorways: M4/A48/A483	277, 278
Motorways: M4/M40/M25	256
Motorways: M4/M5	236
Motorways: M40	257
Motorways: M40/M25	253
Motorways: M40/M25/M4	256
Motorways: M40/M4/M25	256
Motorways: M40/M42	258
Motorways: M42	258, 259
Motorways: M42/A45	192
Motorways: M42/M40	258
Motorways: M42/M5	235
Motorways: M42/M5/M6	235
Motorways: M42/M6	241, 257
Motorways: M42/M6 Toll	258
Motorways: M42/M6/M6 Toll	258
Motorways: M45	259

Entry	Pages
Motorways: M45/M1	221
Motorways: M48	235, 259
Motorways: M49	260
Motorways: M5	235, 236, 237, 238, 239, 240, 241
Motorways: M5/M4	236
Motorways: M5/M42	235
Motorways: M5/M6	235
Motorways: M5/M6/M42	235
Motorways: M50	260
Motorways: M53	201, 260, 261
Motorways: M54	261, 262
Motorways: M54/A5	261
Motorways: M54/M6	245, 261
Motorways: M54/M6/A5/A449	243
Motorways: M54: Junction 2 improvements	77, 78
Motorways: M55	262
Motorways: M55/M6	244, 262
Motorways: M56	262, 263
Motorways: M56/A556	217
Motorways: M56/M6	244, 263
Motorways: M56/M60	263, 264
Motorways: M57	263
Motorways: M58	263, 264
Motorways: M6	241, 242, 243, 244, 245, 246, 247, 248
Motorways: M6 Toll	248
Motorways: M6 Toll/A5	157
Motorways: M6/A500	241
Motorways: M6/A590	217, 218
Motorways: M6/M1	221
Motorways: M6/M42	241, 257
Motorways: M6/M42/M5	235
Motorways: M6/M5	235
Motorways: M6/M54	245, 261
Motorways: M6/M54/A5/A449	243
Motorways: M6/M55	244, 262
Motorways: M6/M56	244, 263
Motorways: M6/M6 Toll	241
Motorways: M6/M6 Toll/M69/M42	248
Motorways: M6/M61	246
Motorways: M6/M69	241
Motorways: M60	264, 265
Motorways: M60/M56	264
Motorways: M60/M66/M62	265, 268
Motorways: M602	271
Motorways: M606	271
Motorways: M61	265
Motorways: M61/M6	246
Motorways: M61/M65	265
Motorways: M62	226, 265, 266, 267, 268
Motorways: M62/A1(M)	265
Motorways: M62/M1	222, 265
Motorways: M62/M60/M66	265, 268
Motorways: M62: Junction 25 to 30: Actively managed hard should & variable speed limits	272
Motorways: M621	226, 271, 272
Motorways: M65	201, 268, 269
Motorways: M65/M61	265
Motorways: M66	201, 269
Motorways: M66/A56	269
Motorways: M66/M62/M60	265, 268
Motorways: M69	269
Motorways: M69/A46/ M1	221
Motorways: M69/M6	241
Motorways: M74: Fullarton Rd., to M8 west of Kingston Bridge: Scotland	385
Motorways: M8/A8: Scotland	388
Motorways: M9/A90/M90: Scotland	385, 388

Motorways: M90/M9/A90: Scotland 385, 388
Museums & galleries: Value added tax: Refunds 312
Music: Live Music Act 2012: Commencements 92
Music: Live: Performance of: Licensing Act 2003: Acts. 5
Music: Live: Performance of: Licensing Act 2003: Acts: Explanatory notes 7
Mussel Fishery: Thomas Shellfish Ltd: Swansea Bay 293
Myanmar/Burma: European Communities: Financial restrictions: Suspension 39

N

National Assembly for Wales: Acts 455
National Assembly for Wales: Acts: Explanatory notes 455
National Assembly for Wales: Measures 455
National Assembly for Wales: Returning officers' charges 135
National assistance services: Personal requirements: Sums: England 105
National assistance services: Personal requirements: Sums: Scotland 378
National assistance services: Personal requirements: Sums: Wales 105
National assistance services: Resources: Assessment: England 105
National assistance services: Resources: Assessment: Scotland 378
National assistance services: Resources: Assessment: Wales 105
National curriculum: Foundation phase: Entry: Assessment arrangements: Wales 57
National curriculum: Key stage 1, 2, 3, 4: Exceptions: England 52
National curriculum: Key stage 2: Assessment arrangements: England 50
National curriculum: Key stage 4: Curriculum: Amendments: England 50
National debt: National Savings Stock Register: Amendments 105
National debt: Savings certificates 105
National debt: Savings certificates: Children's bonus bonds 105
National Endowment for Science, Technology & the Arts: Abolition 130
National Health Service bodies: Partnership: Local authorities 97, 109
National Health Service Commissioning Board Authority: Abolition & transfer of staff, property & liabilities 106
National Health Service Development Authority: Establishment & constitution 108
National Health Service Foundation Trusts: Trust funds: Trustees appointment: England 109
National Health Service Trust Development Authority 108
National Health Service Trusts: Barts Health, The London, Newham University Hospital & Whipps Cross Hospital . . . 106
National Health Service Trusts: Hammersmith Hospitals 107
National Health Service Trusts: Imperial College Healthcare 107
National Health Service Trusts: Isle of Wight 107
National Health Service Trusts: Originating capital: England 108
National Health Service Trusts: Oxfordshire Learning Disability 109
National Health Service Trusts: Royal Brompton & Harefield NHS Foundation: Transfer of property 109
National Health Service Trusts: Royal Wolverhampton Hospitals 109
National Health Service Trusts: Scarborough & North East Yorkshire Health Care 109
National Health Service Trusts: Shropshire Community 109
National Health Service Trusts: South London Healthcare 109, 110
National Health Service Trusts: St Mary's 107
National Health Service Trusts: Torbay & Southern Devon Health & Care 110
National Health Service Trusts: Trafford Healthcare 110
National Health Service Trusts: Velindre 111
National Health Service Trusts: Velindre: Shared Services Committee 111
National Health Service: Acts 5
National Health Service: Acts: Explanatory notes 7
National Health Service: Care Quality Commission: Healthwatch England Committee 106, 131, 295
National Health Service: Care Quality Commission: Membership 106, 131, 295
National Health Service: Care Quality Commission: Registration & additional functions 106, 131, 295
National Health Service: Carers strategies: Wales 110, 295
National Health Service: Charges: Personal injuries: Amounts: England & Wales 110
National Health Service: Children & Families (Wales) Measure: Commencements 18, 110, 295
National Health Service: Clinical commissioning groups: England 107
National Health Service: Commissioning Board & clinical commissioning groups: Responsibilities & standing rules:
England 103, 107
National Health Service: Dental charges: Wales 111
National Health Service: Drugs & appliances: Charges: England 107
National Health Service: Drugs & appliances: Charges: Free prescriptions: Scotland 378
National Health Service: Family support teams: Composition & board functions: Wales 19, 111, 296
National Health Service: Family support teams: Family support functions: Wales 19, 111, 296

National Health Service: Family support teams: Review of cases: Wales 19, 111, 296
National Health Service: General medical services: Contracts: Scotland 378
National Health Service: Health & Social Care Act 2008: Regulated activities 106, 131, 295
National Health Service: Health & Social Care Act 2012: Commencements 75, 106, 131, 295
National Health Service: Health Act 2009: Commencements: England 106
National Health Service: Health Act 2009: Commencements: Wales 110
National Health Service: Health Education England 107
National Health Service: Health Education England: Establishment & constitution 107
National Health Service: Health Research Authority: England 107
National Health Service: Health Research Authority: Establishment & constitution: England 107
National Health Service: Health Service Commissioner for England: Special health authorities 107
National Health Service: Local pharmaceutical services: England 107
National Health Service: Medicines: Branded medicines: Prices control: Information supply 74, 110
National Health Service: National Patient Safety Agency: Amendments: England 109
National Health Service: National Patient Safety Agency: Establishment & constitution: Amendments: England 109
National Health Service: Optical charges & payments: England 108
National Health Service: Optical charges & payments: Scotland 378
National Health Service: Optical charges & payments: Wales 111
National Health Service: Overseas visitors: Charges 107
National Health Service: Overseas visitors: Charges: Scotland 378
National Health Service: Patient Rights (Scotland) Act 2011: Commencements: Scotland 379
National Health Service: Patient rights: Complaints procedure: Consequential provisions: Scotland 378
National Health Service: Pension scheme, injury benefits & additional voluntary contributions 110
National Health Service: Personal injuries: Charges: Amounts: Scotland 379
National Health Service: Pharmaceutical services: England 108
National Health Service: Primary dental services: England 108
National Health Service: Primary dental services: Related units: Amendments: England 108
National Health Service: Primary dental services: Wales 111
National Health Service: Primary medical services 108
National Health Service: Primary medical services: Section 17C agreements: Scotland 378
National Health Service: Quality accounts 108
National Health Service: Special Health Authorities: Establishment & Constitution 110
National Health Service: Strategic health authorities & primary care trusts: Functions: England 107
National Health Service: Superannuation schemes: Pension schemes: Scotland 378
National Health Service: Travelling expenses & remission of charges: England 108
National Health Service: Travelling expenses & remission of charges: Scotland 378
National Health Service: Travelling expenses & remission of charges: Wales 111
National Health Service: Treatment time guarantee: Scotland 379
National Health Service: Welsh Ministers & Local Health Boards: Transfer of property, rights & liabilities: Wales . . . 111
National insurance: Contributions: Application of part 7 of the Finance Act 2004 298
National Library of Scotland: Acts: Explanatory notes: Scotland 362
National Library of Scotland: Acts: Scotland 361
National minimum wage: Regulations: Amendments 304
National Patient Safety Agency: Amendments: England 109
National Patient Safety Agency: Establishment & constitution: Amendments: England 109
National Savings Bank: Investment deposits: Limits 292
National Savings Stock Register: Amendments 105
Nationality & immigration: Cost recovery fees 82, 83, 112
Nationality & immigration: Fees 83, 112
Nationality, Immigration & Asylum Act 2002: Authority to carry 84
Nationality, Immigration & Asylum Act 2002: Commencements 84
Nationality: Immigration, Asylum & Nationality Act 2006: Commencements 83
Natural environment: Acts: Explanatory notes: Scotland 362
Natural habitats: Conservation: Northern Ireland 413
Natural habitats: Conservation: Wildlife: Scotland 397
Natural habitats: Offshore marine conservation 315
Natural Resources Body for Wales: Establishment 64, 131
Navy: Disablement & death: Service pensions 116
Needham & Laddus Internal Drainage Board 90
Neighbourhood planning: General: England 305
Neighbourhood planning: Prescribed dates: England 305
Neighbourhood planning: Referendums: England 305
Nene Valley Railway: Fletton Branch: England 309, 310
Network Rail: Ipswich Chord 87
Network Rail: North Doncaster Chord 87

New Wear Bridge scheme. 78
New Wear Bridge scheme: Temporary works. 78
Newcastle-upon-Tyne, City: Mayoral referendum 94
Newham University Hospital: National Health Service Trust 106
Newtownards: Parking & waiting restrictions: Road traffic & vehicles: Northern Ireland 438
NHS bodies: Summarised accounts 74
NHS bodies: Transfer of property 109
Nitrate pollution: Agriculture: Water: Prevention. 9, 313
Nitrate pollution: Prevention: Wales 9, 314
Nitrates Action Programme: Environmental protection: Northern Ireland. 412
Non-domestic rates: Enterprise areas: Scotland 382
Non-domestic rates: Levying: Scotland 382
Non-domestic rates: Scotland 382
Non-domestic rating: Backdated liabilities: Cancellation 133
Non-domestic rating: Business rate supplements: Deferred payments: England 133
Non-domestic rating: Collection & enforcement: England 133
Non-domestic rating: Contributions: England 133
Non-domestic rating: Contributions: Wales 134
Non-domestic rating: Deferred payments: Wales 134
Non-domestic rating: Demand notices: England. 133
Non-domestic rating: Demand notices: Wales 134
Non-domestic rating: Electronic communications: England. 134
Non-domestic rating: Small business rate relief: England 134
Non-domestic rating: Small business rate relief: Wales 134
Non-domestic rating: Waterways: England 134
North Circular Road & Tarry Lane, Lurgan: Abandonment: Roads: Northern Ireland 432
North Devon: Electoral changes. 97
North Doncaster Chord: Network Rail 87
North Level District (2010): Internal drainage Board. 90
North Wales (East & Central): Coroners' districts 34
Northern Ireland Act 1998: Devolution: Policing & Justice functions. 32, 112
Northern Ireland Assembly: Assembly Members (Independent Financial Review and Standards) Act (Northern Ireland)
2011: Commencements: Northern Ireland 422
Northern Ireland Poultry Health Assurance Scheme: Fees: Northern Ireland 406
Northern Ireland: Jobseeker's allowance: Forces: Members 112, 302
Northern Ireland: Statutes 404, 405
Northern Ireland: Statutes: Chronological tables 404
Northern Ireland: Statutory rules: Chronological tables 404
Nottingham, City: Mayoral referendum. 94
Nurses: Nursing & Midwifery Council: Constitution 76
Nurses: Nursing & Midwifery Council: Education, registration & appeals 76
Nurses: Nursing & Midwifery Council: Fees 76
Nurses: Nursing & Midwifery Council: Fitness to practise: Amendments 76
Nursing & Midwifery Council: Constitution 76
Nursing & Midwifery Council: Education, registration & appeals 76
Nursing & Midwifery Council: Fees 76
Nursing & Midwifery Council: Fitness to practise: Amendments 76
Nursing & Midwifery Council: Midwives: Rules. 76
Nursing care & personal care: Community care: Scotland. 395

O

Oatridge College: Transfer & closures: Scotland 369
Occupational & personal pension schemes: Automatic enrolment 117
Occupational & personal pension schemes: Levies 117
Occupational & personal pension schemes: Levies: Northern Ireland. 424
Occupational & personal pension schemes: Prescribed bodies 117
Occupational pension schemes: Automatic enrolment: Northern Ireland 423, 424
Occupational pension schemes: Contracting-out. 117
Occupational pension schemes: Contracting-out: Northern Ireland 424
Occupational pension schemes: Disclosure of information 117
Occupational pension schemes: Disclosure of information: Northern Ireland. 424
Occupational pension schemes: Employer debt: Amendments: Northern Ireland 424
Occupational pension schemes: Northern Ireland 424
Occupational pension schemes: Pension Protection Fund 117

Occupational pensions: Revaluation 117
Occupational pensions: Revaluation: Northern Ireland 424
Offences: Prosecution: Custody time limits: England & Wales. 43
Offences: Sexual: Acts: Scotland 361
Offender Management Act 2007: Probation trusts: Establishment 127
Offenders: Rehabilitation of Offenders Act 1974: Exceptions: Amendments: England & Wales. 135
Offenders: Rehabilitation of offenders: Exceptions: Northern Ireland. 431
Offenders: Road traffic: Prescribed devices: Northern Ireland 442
Offenders: Sentencing & punishment: Acts 5
Offenders: Sentencing & punishment: Acts: Explanatory notes 7
Offensive Behaviour at Football & Threatening Communications (Scotland) Act 2012: Commencements: Scotland . . . 368
Office of Qualifications & Examinations Regulation: Monetary penalties: Turnover determination. 52, 55
Official languages: National Assembly for Wales: Acts. 455
Official languages: National Assembly for Wales: Acts: Explanatory notes 455
Official Secrets Act 1989: Prescription 112
Official statistics: Northern Ireland 422
Official statistics: Statistics & Registration Service Act 2007: Social security information: Disclosure: Northern Ireland   422, 423
Offshore employment: Pensions: Automatic enrolment: Offshore employment. 116
Offshore installations: Oil & gas: Installation & pipelines: Abandonment fees 112
Offshore installations: Safety zones 112
Offshore marine conservation: Natural habitats 315
Off-street parking: Northern Ireland 432, 437
Ofsted: Children's homes etc.: Fees & frequency of inspections 17
Oil & gas: Installation & pipelines: Abandonment fees 112
Oil fields: Qualifying: Oil tax 113
Oil stocking 34
Oil tax: Oil fields: Qualifying 113
Old Church Road, Newtownabbey: Abandonment: Roads: Northern Ireland 432
Older people: Commissioner for older People Act 2011: Commencements: Northern Ireland 423
Olympic & Paralympic Games: London: Advertising & trading: Wales 101
Olympic Games: London Legacy Development Corporation: Establishment 311
Omagh: Parking & restrictions: Road traffic & vehicles: Northern Ireland 438
On-street parking: Northern Ireland 437
Open spaces: Royal Parks & other open spaces 113
Optical charges & payments: National Health Service: England 108
Optical charges & payments: National Health Service: Scotland 378
Optical charges & payments: National Health Service: Wales 111
Optical charges & payments: Northern Ireland 416
Opticians: General Optical Council: Continuing education & training rules 76
Ormeau Road, Belfast: Waiting restrictions: Road traffic & vehicles: Northern Ireland 443
Osteopaths: General Osteopathic Council: Registration & fees: Applications 76
Ot Moor Range 46
Ouse & Humber Drainage Board 90
Overseas territories: Afghanistan: Measures. 113
Overseas territories: Al-Qaida: Measures 113
Overseas territories: Burma: Restrictive measures. 113
Overseas territories: Congo (Democratic Republic): Restrictive measures 114
Overseas territories: Cote d'Ivoire: Sanctions 113
Overseas territories: Democratic People's Republic of Korea: Sanctions 114
Overseas territories: Eritrea: Sanctions 114
Overseas territories: Guinea-Bissau: Sanctions 114
Overseas territories: Iran: Restrictive measures 114
Overseas territories: Liberia: Restrictive measures 114
Overseas territories: Libya: Restrictive measures 115
Overseas territories: Restrictive measures 115
Overseas territories: Somalia: Sanctions. 115
Overseas territories: Sudan & South Sudan: Restrictive measures. 115
Overseas territories: Syria: Restrictive measures 115
Overseas territories: Syria: Sanctions 115
Overseas territories: United Nations: Sanctions: 311
Overseas territories: Zimbabwe: Sanctions: 115
Overseas visitors: Charges: National Health Service: Scotland 378
Overview & scrutiny: Reference by councillors: Excluded matters: England 97
Oxfordshire Learning Disability: National Health Service Trust 109

Oxfordshire: Electoral changes 97

P

PACE: Codes of practice: Revisions to codes C, G & 124
Packaging waste: Producer responsibility & obligations 62
Packaging waste: Producer responsibility & obligations: Northern Ireland 412
Parentage: Declarations: Magistrates' courts: Rules: Northern Ireland 422
Parents: Lone: Social security 300
Parish councils: General power of competence: Prescribed conditions 97
Parking contraventions: Civil enforcement 93, 272
Parking contraventions: Civil enforcement: Ceredigion: Wales 273
Parking contraventions: Civil enforcement: Rhondda Cynon Taf: Wales 273
Parking places & loading bays: Roads: Northern Ireland 436
Parks: Royal Parks & other open spaces 113
Parliament: House of Commons: Members' Fund: Resolutions 116
Parliament: Insolvency Act 1986: Disqualification from 88, 116
Parochial fees: Scheduled matters amending 48
Parole Board: Rules: Scotland 380
Partnership Council for Wales: Local health boards & National Health Service trusts: Wales 33, 100
Passenger ships: Domestic voyages: Merchant shipping: Safety 105
Passengers: Carriage by sea: Merchant shipping. 104
Patient Rights (Scotland) Act 2011: Commencements: Scotland 379
Pay as You Earn see PAYE
PAYE: Income tax 86
Payment services: Financial services & markets 69
Pembrokeshire: St. Mary Out Liberty & Tenby Communities: Wales. 100
Penalties: Amount: Disorderly behaviour: England & Wales 42, 122
Penalty charges enforcement: London 61, 101
Penalty notices: Justice Act (Northern Ireland) 2011: Enforcement of fines: Northern Ireland 428
Pension Protection Fund 117, 118
Pension Protection Fund: Northern Ireland 424, 425
Pension Protection Fund: Occupational pension schemes 117
Pension schemes: Application of UK provisions: Non-UK schemes 86
Pension schemes: Categories of country & requirements for overseas schemes & recognised overseas schemes 86
Pension schemes: Firefighters: Contributions: Wales 70, 119
Pension schemes: Health & social care: Northern Ireland 416
Pension schemes: Registered & overseas: Amendments 86
Pension schemes: Registered pension schemes: Authorised payments 86, 87
Pension schemes: Registered: Amendments 19, 84, 303
Pensions 2008 Act: Pension schemes: Defined contribution : Contracting-out: Abolition: Northern Ireland 425
Pensions Act 2004: Pension Regulator: Restricted information: Disclosure 118
Pensions Act 2007: Commencements 118
Pensions Act 2008: Commencements 118
Pensions Act 2008: Protected rights: Abolition: Consequential amendments 118
Pensions Act 2011: Commencements 118
Pensions see also Pension Protection Fund 117, 118
Pensions: 2005 Order: Restricted information: Disclosure by the Pensions Regulator: Northern Ireland 425
Pensions: 2008 (No.2) Act: Commencements: Northern Ireland 425, 426
Pensions: 2008 Act: Commencements: Northern Ireland 425
Pensions: 2008 No. 2 Act: Protected rights: Abolition: Consequential provisions: Northern Ireland . . . 425
Pensions: 2012 Act: Commencements: Northern Ireland 426
Pensions: Acts: Explanatory notes: Northern Ireland 404
Pensions: Acts: Northern Ireland. 404
Pensions: Armed Forces: Reserve Forces: Compensation schemes 116
Pensions: Automatic enrolment 116
Pensions: Automatic enrolment: Earnings trigger & qualifying earnings band 116
Pensions: Automatic enrolment: Earnings trigger & qualifying earnings band: Northern Ireland 423
Pensions: Automatic enrolment: Northern Ireland 423
Pensions: Automatic enrolment: Offshore employment 116
Pensions: Compromise agreements: Automatic enrolment 116
Pensions: Contributions: Police: Scotland 379
Pensions: Employers' duties: Implementation 116
Pensions: Employers' duties: Implementation: Northern Ireland 423
Pensions: Financial Reporting Council: Northern Ireland 426

Pensions: Firefighters: Pension schemes: Contributions: Northern Ireland 414
Pensions: Firefighters: Pension schemes: England. 69, 70, 119
Pensions: Firefighters: Pension schemes: Northern Ireland 414
Pensions: Firefighters: Pension schemes: Scotland 372
Pensions: Firefighters' pension schemes: England. 70, 119
Pensions: Firemen: Pension schemes: Scotland 372
Pensions: Guaranteed minimum increase 116
Pensions: Guaranteed minimum increase: Northern Ireland. 423
Pensions: Hybrid schemes: Requirement rules: Northern Ireland 423
Pensions: Increase: Review 118
Pensions: Increase: Review: Northern Ireland 426
Pensions: Institute & Faculty of Actuaries: Employers' consultation 118
Pensions: Institute & Faculty of Actuaries: Employers' consultation: Northern Ireland 426
Pensions: Judicial pensions: Contributions 116
Pensions: Judicial pensions: European Court of Human Rights 116
Pensions: Local government pension schemes: Administration: Scotland. 379
Pensions: Local government pension schemes: Amendments: Scotland. 379
Pensions: Local government pension schemes: Northern Ireland 421
Pensions: Local government: Pension schemes 119
Pensions: National Health Service: Pension scheme, injury benefits & additional voluntary contributions. 110
Pensions: Navy, army & air force: Disablement & death: Service pensions. 116
Pensions: Occupational & personal pension schemes: Automatic enrolment 117
Pensions: Occupational & personal pension schemes: Automatic enrolment: Northern Ireland 423, 424
Pensions: Occupational & personal pension schemes: Levies 117
Pensions: Occupational & personal pension schemes: Levies: Northern Ireland 424
Pensions: Occupational & personal pension schemes: Prescribed bodies 117
Pensions: Occupational pension schemes & Pension Protection Fund. 117
Pensions: Occupational pension schemes: Contracting-out 117
Pensions: Occupational pension schemes: Contracting-out: Northern Ireland. 424
Pensions: Occupational pension schemes: Disclosure of information 117
Pensions: Occupational pension schemes: Employer debt: Amendments: Northern Ireland 424
Pensions: Occupational pensions: Revaluation 117
Pensions: Occupational pensions: Revaluation: Northern Ireland 424
Pensions: Occupational, personal & stakeholder schemes: Disclosure of information: Northern Ireland 424
Pensions: Pension Protection Fund & occupational pension schemes: Northern Ireland 424
Pensions: Pension Protection Fund: Northern Ireland 424, 425
Pensions: Personal injuries: Civilians 118
Pensions: Police. 119, 124
Pensions: Police Service: Northern Ireland 428
Pensions: Police: Service descriptions 119, 124
Pensions: Registered pension schemes: Relevant annuities 87
Pensions: Social security: Flat rate accrual amount 301
Pensions: Social security: Flat rate accrual amounts: Northern Ireland 447
Pensions: Social security: Flat rate introduction year: Northern Ireland. 447
Pensions: Social security: Low earnings threshold 301
Pensions: Social security: Low earnings threshold: Northern Ireland 447
Pensions: Superannuation: Charity Commission for Northern Ireland. 426
Pensions: Superannuation: Chief Inspector of Criminal Justice in Northern Ireland 426
Pensions: Superannuation: Commissioner of the Northern Ireland Law Commission. 426
Pensions: Superannuation: Police Ombudsman for Northern Ireland 426
Pensions: Teachers: Superannuation: Scotland 379
Pensions: Teachers' pensions: England & Wales 55
Performance indicators: Local government: Wales 100
Personal care & nursing care: Community care: Scotland. 395
Personal injuries actions: Summary cause: Rules: Act of Sederunt: Scotland 395
Personal injuries: Charges: Amounts: National Health Service: Scotland 379
Personal injuries: Civilians 118
Personal injuries: NHS charges: Amounts: England & Wales 110
Personal pension schemes: Automatic enrolment: Northern Ireland 423, 424
Personal pension schemes: Disclosure of information: Northern Ireland 424
Pesticides: Plant protection products: Northern Ireland 427
Pesticides: Plant protection products: Sustainable use 119
Petroleum (Consolidation) Act: Licensing provisions: Amendment: Northern Ireland 417
Pharmaceutical services: Local: National Health Service: England 107
Pharmaceutical services: National Health Service: England. 108

Pharmaceutical Society of Northern Ireland: Council: Appointments & procedure: Northern Ireland 427
Pharmaceutical Society of Northern Ireland: Council: Continuing professional development: Northern Ireland 427
Pharmaceutical Society of Northern Ireland: Council: Fitness to practise & disqualification: Northern Ireland 427
Pharmaceutical Society of Northern Ireland: Council: Statutory Committee, Scrutiny Committee & advisors: Northern Ireland 427
Pharmacy: General Pharmaceutical Council: Miscellaneous provisions 77
Pharmacy: Northern Ireland: Northern Ireland. 427
Pigs: Aujeszky's Disease: Northern Ireland 406
Pigs: Carcase classification: Wales. 9
Pigs: Records, identification & movement: Northern Ireland 406
Pitcairn Islands: Court of Appeal 115
Planning & Compulsory Purchase Act 2004: Commencements: Wales. 307
Planning Act 2008: Commencements 305
Planning Act 2008: Commencements: Wales 307
Planning etc. (Scotland) Act 2006: National parks: Consequential provisions: Scotland 396
Planning see also Infrastructure planning
Planning see also Town & country planning
Planning: Environmental impact assessment: Northern Ireland 427
Planning: Fees: Northern Ireland. 427
Planning: General development: Northern Ireland. 427
Planning: Infrastructure planning: Environmental impact assessment 87
Planning: Infrastructure planning: Localism Act 2011: Amendments 87
Planning: Infrastructure planning: Waste water transfer & storage 87
Plant & machinery: Environmentally beneficial: Capital allowances. 35, 84
Plant health: Ash Dieback: Northern Ireland 427
Plant health: England 120
Plant health: Fees: England 120
Plant health: Forestry: Amendments: Ash dieback 120
Plant health: Import inspection fees: England 120
Plant health: Import inspection fees: Wales 120
Plant health: Northern Ireland 427, 428
Plant health: Potatoes: Originating in Egypt: Scotland 379
Plant health: Scotland 379
Plant health: Wood & bark: Ash dieback: Northern Ireland 428
Plant protection products. 119
Plant protection products: Northern Ireland 427
Play sufficiency assessment: Wales. 19
Pneumoconiosis etc.: Workers' compensation: Claims: Payments 298
Pneumoconiosis etc.: Workers' compensation: Claims: Payments: Northern Ireland 445
Police & crime commissioners: Disqualification 123
Police & crime commissioners: Elections 123
Police & crime commissioners: Elections: Acceptance of office: Declaration: England & Wales 123
Police & crime commissioners: Elections: Local authorities designation: England & Wales 123
Police & crime commissioners: Elections: Local authorities: Designation 123
Police & crime commissioners: Elections: Local returning officers': Police area returning officers's: Charges: England & Wales. 123
Police & crime commissioners: Elections: Police area returning officers: Designation 123
Police & crime commissioners: Elections: Returning officers: Area designation: England & Wales 123
Police & crime commissioners: Elections: Returning officers: Functions 123
Police & crime commissioners: Elections: Returning officers' accounts 123
Police & crime commissioners: Elections: Welsh forms. 123
Police & crime panels: Functions: Modifications: England & Wales 124
Police & crime panels: Local authority enactments: Application 123
Police & crime panels: Nominations, appointments & notifications: England & Wales. 124
Police & crime panels: Precepts & Chief Constable appointments: England & Wales 124
Police & Criminal Evidence Act 1984: Armed Forces 46
Police & Criminal Evidence Act 1984: Codes of practice: Revisions to codes C, G & H. 124
Police & criminal evidence: Code of practice A: Modification: Northern Ireland. 428
Police & criminal evidence: Code of practice C, E, F & H: Revision: Northern Ireland 428
Police & Fire Reform (Scotland) Act 2012: Commencements: Scotland. 372, 380
Police & fire reform: Acts: Scotland. 362
Police & Justice Act 2006: Commencements 43
Police & justice: Acts. 4
Police Act 1997: Criminal records. 122
Police Act 1997: Criminal records & registration: Guernsey 121

Police Act 1997: Criminal records & registration: Isle of Man 121
Police Act 1997: Criminal records & registration: Jersey 121
Police Act 1997: Criminal records: Amendments: Scotland 380
Police Act 1997: Criminal records: Guernsey 121
Police Act 1997: Criminal records: Isle of Man 121
Police Act 1997: Criminal records: Northern Ireland 409
Police Authority: Amendments 124
Police names: Welsh language 125
Police Ombudsman for Northern Ireland: Superannuation: Northern Ireland 426
Police Reform & Social Responsibility Act 2011: Commencements 92, 125
Police Service & Police Service & Reserve: Injury benefit: Northern Ireland 428
Police Service: Amendments: Northern Ireland 428
Police Service: Pensions: Northern Ireland 428
Police: Appeals tribunals 124
Police: Complaints & conduct: Acts 6
Police: Complaints & misconduct: Metropolitan Police 124
Police: Conduct 124
Police: Crime & Security Act 2010: Commencements 121
Police: Criminal Justice: Acts 4
Police: Disorderly behaviour: Penalties: Amount: England & Wales 42, 122
Police: Elected local bodies: Complaints & misconduct 121
Police: Elected local bodies: Specified information 122
Police: England & Wales 122, 123, 124
Police: Grants & variations: Scotland 380
Police: Local policing bodies 10, 67, 87, 99, 122, 304, 310
Police: Ministry of Defence: Performance 120
Police: National records: Recordable offences: Amendments 122
Police: Pensions 119, 124
Police: Pensions: Contributions: Scotland 379
Police: Pensions: Service descriptions 119, 124
Police: Performance 124
Police: Policing & Crime Act 2009: Commencements 125
Police: Prescribed police stations: Sexual Offences Act 2003: Northern Ireland 409
Police: Protection of Freedoms Act 2012: Commencements 73, 125, 126, 136
Police: Protection of Freedoms Act 2012: Disclosure & barring service: Functions transfer 17, 18, 125, 128, 129
Police: Special constables 125
Policing & Crime Act 2009: Commencements 125
Policing & Justice functions: Devolution: Northern Ireland Act 1998 . . . . 32, 112
Policing: Aviation security: Belfast International Airport 28
Political restrictions: Exemption: Local authorities 96
Pollution: Nitrate pollution: Prevention: Wales 9, 314
Pollution: Nitrate: Agriculture: Water: Prevention 9, 313
Pollution: Nitrates Action Programme: Northern Ireland 412
Pollution: Prevention & control: Industrial emissions: Northern Ireland 412
Pollution: Prevention & control: Scotland 371
Poole Harbour: Revision 74
Population (Statistics) Act 1938: Modifications: Scotland 371
Port of Cairnryan: Harbour revision: Scotland 373
Port of Grangemouth: Port security: Merchant shipping 104
Port of Ipswich: Harbour revision 74
Port of Portland: Port security: Merchant shipping 104
Port of Workington: Port security: Merchant shipping 104
Port security: Merchant shipping: Aberdeen 104
Port security: Merchant shipping: Port of Grangemouth 104
Port security: Merchant shipping: Port of Portland 104
Port security: Merchant shipping: Port of Workington 104
Port security: Merchant shipping: Tees & Hartlepool 104
Portsmouth City Council: M275 Motorway slip roads: Tipner Interchange: Confirmation 78
Postal Services Act 2011: Assets: Transfers 126
Postal Services Act 2011: Commencements 125
Postal Services Act 2011: Disclosure of Information 125
Postal Services Act 2011: Penalties: Calculation of turnover: Rules 125
Postal Services Act 2011: Pension rights: Accrued: Transfers 126
Postal Services Act 2011: Specified day 125
Postal Services Act 2011: Taxation 36, 86, 302, 303

Postal services: Universal postal service. 126
Postgraduate medical education & training 76
Potatoes: Originating in Egypt: Northern Ireland 444
Potatoes: Originating in Egypt: Scotland 379
Poultry: Health scheme: Fees: Scotland 363, 364
Poultry: Northern Ireland Poultry Health Assurance Scheme: Fees: Northern Ireland 406
PPF *see* Pension Protection Fund
Premises licences & club premises: Certificates 92
Pre-school education: Schools: Admissions criteria: Northern Ireland 410
Prescriptions: Free: National Health Service: Scotland 378
Prevention & suppression of terrorism: Anti-terrorism, Crime & Security Act 2001: Modifications 126
Prevention & suppression of terrorism: Coroners & Justice Act 2009: Commencements 126
Prevention & suppression of terrorism: Counter-Terrorism Act 2008: Commencements 126
Prevention & suppression of terrorism: Counter-Terrorism Act 2008: Video recording with sound of post-charge questioning: Codes of practice. 126
Prevention & suppression of terrorism: Protection of Freedoms Act 2012: Commencements . 17, 18, 73, 125, 126, 128, 129, 136
Prevention & suppression of terrorism: Terrorism Act 2000 & Proceeds of Crime Act 2002: Regulated sector . 126, 127, 128
Prevention & suppression of terrorism: Terrorism Act 2000: Proscribed organisations 127
Prevention & suppression of terrorism: Terrorism Act 2000: Stop & search powers: Codes of practice 126
Prevention & suppression of terrorism: Terrorism Act 2000: Video recording with sound of interviews & associated code of practice. 127
Prevention of nuclear proliferation: Financial restrictions: Iran 127
Prices: Indication of: Beds 127
Primary care trusts & strategic health authorities: Functions: National Health Service 107
Primary medical services: National Health Service 108
Primary medical services: National Health Service: Section 17C agreements: Scotland 378
Primary schools: Rural: Designation: England 49
Prison Service: Pay Review Body: Northern Ireland 428
Prisons: Closure 127
Prisons: Closure: Latchmere House 127
Prisons: Closure: Wellingborough 127
Prisons: Parole Board: Rules: Scotland 380
Prisons: Wireless telegraphy: Interference: Acts 6
Prisons: Young offender institutions: Scotland 380
Private hospitals: Mental health services: Fees: Northern Ireland 422
Private hospitals: Mental health services:: Northern Ireland 422
Private Rented Housing (Scotland) Act 2011: Commencements: Scotland 375
Private Security Industry Act 2001: Aviation security: Exemptions 293
Private Security Industry Act 2001: Olympics security: Exemption 293
Probation: Offender Management Act 2007: Probation trusts: Establishment 127
Procedure: Penalty notices: Justice Act (Northern Ireland) 2011: Enforcement of fines: Northern Ireland 428
Proceeds of Crime Act 2002: Amendments 126, 127, 128
Proceeds of Crime Act 2002: External requests & orders: England & Wales 128
Producer responsibility & obligations: Packaging waste 62
Producer responsibility & obligations: Packaging waste: Northern Ireland 412
Properties: Unoccupied properties: Local government finance: Acts: Explanatory notes: Scotland 362
Properties: Unoccupied properties: Local government finance: Acts: Scotland 361
Property Factors (Scotland) Act 2011: Commencements: Scotland 381
Property Factors (Scotland) Act 2011: Modifications: Scotland 381
Property factors: Acts: Explanatory notes: Scotland 362
Property factors: Acts: Scotland 361
Property Factors: Code of conduct: Scotland 380
Property factors: Homeowner housing panel: Application & decisions: Scotland 380
Property factors: Registration: Scotland 380
Prosecution evidence: Service: Crime & Disorder Act 1998 41
Prosecution of Offences Act 1985: Specified proceedings 42, 43
Prospectus: Regulations: Financial services & markets 69
Protection of Freedoms Act 2012 272
Protection of Freedoms Act 2012: Commencements 17, 18, 43, 73, 89, 125, 126, 128, 129, 136, 273
Protection of Freedoms Act 2012: Commencements: Wales 273
Protection of Freedoms Act 2012: Official records 136
Protection of freedoms: Acts 6
Protection of freedoms: Acts: Explanatory notes 7
Protection of Military Remains Act 1986: Vessels & controlled sites: Designations 46

Protection of vulnerable adults: Protection of Freedoms Act 2012: Commencements . 17, 18, 43, 89, 126, 128, 129, 136, 273
Protection of vulnerable adults: Protection of Freedoms Act 2012: Disclosure & barring service: Functions transfer. . . 17, 18, 125, 128, 129
Protection of vulnerable adults: Safeguarding Vulnerable Groups Act 2006: Commencements 17, 128
Protection of vulnerable adults: Safeguarding Vulnerable Groups Act 2006: Controlled activity & prescribed criteria: England & Wales 18, 128
Protection of vulnerable adults: Safeguarding Vulnerable Groups Act 2006: Miscellaneous amendments 18, 128
Protection of vulnerable adults: Safeguarding Vulnerable Groups Act 2006: Miscellaneous provisions 18, 128
Protection of wrecks: Designation: England 129
Public & utilities contracts: Scotland 381
Public Appointments & Public Bodies etc. (Scotland) Act 2003: Specified authorities: Treatment of office or body: Scotland 381
Public authorities: Equality Act 2010: Specifications: Scotland 371
Public authorities: Fair employment: Specification: Northern Ireland 413
Public Bodies Act 2011: Commencements 130
Public Bodies Act 2011: Transitional Provisions 130
Public bodies: Advisory Committee on Hazardous Substances (ACHS): Abolition 61, 74, 129
Public bodies: Audit: Government Resources & Accounts Act 2000 73
Public bodies: British Waterways Board: Transfer of functions 14, 129, 308
Public bodies: Child Maintenance & Enforcement Commission: Abolition 67, 130
Public bodies: Commission for Rural Communities: Abolition 130
Public bodies: Courts boards: Abolition 129
Public bodies: Crown Court Rule Committee & Magistrates' Courts Rule Committee: Abolition 130
Public bodies: Environment Protection Advisory Committees: Abolition 62, 130
Public bodies: Her Majesty's Inspectorate of Courts Administration & Public Guardian Board: Abolition 130
Public bodies: Inland Waterways Advisory Council: Abolition 14, 129
Public bodies: Localism Act 2011: Commencements 82, 98, 101, 129
Public bodies: National Endowment for Science, Technology & the Arts: Abolition 130
Public bodies: Natural Resources Body for Wales: Establishment 64, 131
Public bodies: Regional & local fisheries advisory committees: Abolition 62, 130
Public bodies: Water supply & water quality: Inspection fees 68, 130, 314
Public bodies: Welsh language: Schemes 314
Public contracts: Scotland 382
Public finance & accountability: Budget (Scotland) Act 2011: Amendments: Scotland 381
Public general acts: Bound volumes 8
Public general acts: Tables & index 8
Public Guardian Board: Abolition 130
Public Guardian: Fees: Amendments: Scotland 363
Public health: Care Quality Commission: Healthwatch England Committee 106, 131, 295
Public health: Care Quality Commission: Membership 106, 131, 295
Public health: Care Quality Commission: Registration & additional functions 106, 131, 295
Public health: Contamination of food 132
Public health: Contamination of food: Food protection: Emergency prohibitions: Dalgety Bay: Scotland 381
Public health: Contamination of food: Scotland 364, 381
Public health: Food protection: Emergency prohibitions: Sheep: Radioactivity: Wales 71, 132
Public health: Health & Social Care Act 2008: Council tax 37, 132
Public health: Health & Social Care Act 2008: Regulated activities 106, 131, 295
Public health: Health & Social Care Act 2012: Commencements 75, 106, 131, 295
Public health: Health Act 2009: Commencements: England 131
Public health: Health: 2009 Act: Commencements: Northern Ireland 428
Public health: Miscellaneous amendments: England & Wales 11
Public health: Motor fuel: Composition & content: Amendments 131
Public health: Smoke-free signs: England 131
Public health: Sunbeds: Act 2011: Commencements: Northern Ireland 428
Public health: Sunbeds: Information: Northern Ireland 429
Public health: Tobacco: Advertising & promotion: Display: England 131
Public health: Tobacco: Advertising & promotion: Display: Northern Ireland 429
Public health: Tobacco: Advertising & promotion: Display: Wales 132
Public health: Tobacco: Advertising & promotion: Prices: Display: Northern Ireland 429
Public health: Tobacco: Advertising & promotion: Prices: Display: Wales 132
Public health: Tobacco: Advertising & promotion: Specialist tobacconists: England 131
Public health: Tobacco: Advertising & promotion: Specialist tobacconists: Northern Ireland 429
Public health: Tobacco: Advertising & promotion: Specialist tobacconists: Wales 132
Public interest disclosure: Prescribed persons 305
Public interest disclosure: Prescribed persons: Northern Ireland 411

Public Lending Right Scheme 1982: Variation: Commencements 91
Public passenger transport: Localism Act 2011: Commencements 70, 96, 132
Public passenger transport: Public service vehicles: Local services: Registration: Scotland 381
Public passenger transport: Public service vehicles: Operators' licences: Fees 132
Public policy exclusion: Competition Act 1998. 32
Public procurement: Public & utilities contracts: Scotland. 381, 382
Public procurement: Public contracts: Scotland 382
Public procurement: Public Services (Social Value) Act 2012: Commencement 132
Public Record Office: Fees. 133
Public Records (Scotland) Act 2011: Commencements: Scotland. 383
Public records: Constitutional Reform & Governance Act 2010: Commencements. 73, 133
Public records: Public Record Office: Transfer 133
Public sector information: Infrastructure for Spatial Information in the European Community (INSPIRE). 62, 133
Public sector information: Infrastructure for Spatial Information in the European Community (INSPIRE): Scotland. 370, 382
Public service vehicles: Local services: Registration: Scotland 381
Public service vehicles: Operators' licences: Fees. 132
Public Services (Social Value) Act 2012: Commencement 132
Public Services Reform (Scotland) Act 2010: Commencements: Scotland 366
Public services reform: General Teaching Council for Scotland: Legal assessors: Scotland 369
Public services reform: Independent further education colleges & English language schools: Inspections: Recovery of expenses: Scotland 370, 383
Public services reform: Social services inspections: Scotland. 395
Public services: Social enterprise & social value: Acts. 6
Public services: Social enterprise & social value: Acts: Explanatory notes 7
Pupil exclusions & reviews: School discipline: England 53
Pupil referral units: Amendments: England. 52
Pupil referral units: Application of enactments: England 50
Pupils: Education: Information: Individual pupils: England 50
Purchased life annuities 86
Pyx: Trial of: Coinage. 30

Q

Qualifying care relief: Specified social care schemes: Income tax 86

R

Race relations: Order: Amendments: Northern Ireland 429
Racial hatred: Acts 4
Radio: Community radio: Guernsey. 13
Rail vehicles: Accessibility: Non-interoperable rail system 47, 309
Railways: Channel Tunnel: International arrangements. 15
Railways: Chiltern Railways: Bicester to Oxford improvement 309
Railways: Nene Valley Railway: Fletton Branch: England. 309, 310
Randalstown: Roads: Parking places, loading bay & waiting restrictions: Northern Ireland 439
Rates: Acts: Explanatory notes: Northern Ireland 404
Rates: Acts: Northern Ireland 404
Rates: Deferments: Northern Ireland. 429
Rates: Jobseeker's allowance: Failure to attend: Sanctions: Northern Ireland 418, 429, 445
Rates: Microgeneration: Northern Ireland 429
Rates: Regional rates: Northern Ireland 429, 430
Rates: Small business hereditament relief: Northern Ireland 430
Rates: Social sector value: Northern Ireland. 430
Rates: Social security: Benefits: Payment suspensions: Miscellaneous amendments: Northern Ireland 419, 430, 447
Rates: Social security: Benefits: Up-rating: Northern Ireland. 411, 418, 430, 446, 447, 448
Rates: Social security: Habitual residence: Northern Ireland 418, 430, 446
Rates: Social security: Northern Ireland. 419, 430, 447
Rates: Social security: Recovery: Northern Ireland 419, 430, 447
Rates: Valuation Tribunal: Rules: High hedges: Northern Ireland. 431
Rates: Valuation Tribunal: Rules: Northern Ireland 431
Rathfriland: Parking & waiting restrictions: Road traffic & vehicles: Northern Ireland. 438
Rating & valuation: Central rating list: England. 133
Rating & valuation: Council tax & non-domestic rating: Demand notices: England 133
Rating & valuation: Localism Act 2011: Commencements 81, 87, 98, 101, 133, 307
Rating & valuation: Non-domestic rates: Enterprise areas: Scotland 382

Rating & valuation: Non-domestic rates: Levying: Scotland 382
Rating & valuation: Non-domestic rates: Scotland 382
Rating & valuation: Non-domestic rating: Backdated liabilities: Cancellation 133
Rating & valuation: Non-domestic rating: Business rate supplements: Deferred payments: England. 133
Rating & valuation: Non-domestic rating: Collection & enforcement: England. 133
Rating & valuation: Non-domestic rating: Contributions: England 133
Rating & valuation: Non-domestic rating: Contributions: Wales 134
Rating & valuation: Non-domestic rating: Electronic communications: England 134
Rating & valuation: Non-domestic rating: Small business rate relief: England 134
Rating & valuation: Non-domestic rating: Small business rate relief: Wales 134
Rating & valuation: Non-domestic rating: Waterways: England 134
Rating: Non-domestic: Deferred payments: Wales 134
Rating: Non-domestic: Demand notes: Wales 134
RCUK Shared Services Centre Limited: Employment: Protection: Transfer of undertakings 305
Red meat industry: Slaughterers & exporters: Designation: Wales. 9
Referendums: Conduct of: Local authorities: England 96
Referendums: Conduct: Council tax: Increases: England 37
Referendums: Council tax: Increases: England 37
Regional & local fisheries advisory committees: Public bodies: Abolition 62, 130
Regional strategy: East of England 305
Registered pension schemes: Relevant annuities 87
Registers & records: Crofting register: Fees: Scotland 369, 383
Registers & records: Crofting register: First registration: Scotland 369, 383
Registers & records: Crofting register: Scotland 369, 383
Registers & records: Crofting register: Transfer of ownership: Scotland. 369, 383
Registers & records: Public Records (Scotland) Act 2011: Commencements: Scotland 383
Registrar of Companies: Companies, overseas companies & limited liability partnerships: Fees 68
Registration Appeal Court: Act of Sederunt: Scotland. 367
Registration of births, deaths & marriages, etc.: Births & deaths: England & Wales 134
Registration of births, deaths & marriages, etc.: Civil partnerships: Fees: Amendments 28
Registration of births, deaths & marriages, etc.: Fees: Amendments 134
Registration of births, deaths & marriages, etc.: Welfare Reform Act 2009: Commencements 135, 301
Registration of clubs: Certificates of registration: Northern Ireland 431
Registration of clubs: Irresponsible drinks promotions: Northern Ireland 431
Registration of clubs: Notice relating to age: Northern Ireland 431
Registration of vital events: General Register Office: Fees: Northern Ireland 431
Regulation of investigatory powers: Covert human intelligence sources 89
Regulation of investigatory powers: Directed surveillance 89
Regulatory reform: Legislative & regulatory reform: Civil partnership 135
Regulatory reform: Legislative reform: Local authorities: Annual review 17, 52, 135
Regulatory reform: Local Better Regulation Office: Dissolution & transfer of functions 135
Regulatory reform: Public services reform: Independent further education colleges & English language schools: Inspections:
Recovery of expenses: Scotland 370, 383
Rehabilitation courses: Relevant drink offences 137
Rehabilitation of Offenders Act 1974: Exceptions: Amendments: England & Wales 135
Rehabilitation of offenders: Exceptions: Northern Ireland. 431
Rehabilitation of offenders: Legal Aid, Sentencing & Punishment of Offenders Act 2012: Commencements . . . 42, 91, 135
Relevant authorities: Disclosable pecuniary interests: England. 97
Religious hatred: Acts 4
Remand: Youth detention accommodation: Recovery of costs 43
Remote gambling: Double taxation relief 66
Renewable heat incentive schemes: Northern Ireland 411
Renewable heat incentives 60
Rent (Scotland) Act 1984: Premiums: Scotland 376
Rent officers: Housing benefit functions: Amendments. 80
Rents: Registered rents: Increases: Northern Ireland 419
Representation of the people: Electoral data schemes 135
Representation of the people: Greater London Authority: Elections: Rules 100, 135
Representation of the people: Local Electoral Administration (Scotland) Act 2011: Consequential amendments: Scotland 384
Representation of the people: Local government election expenses: Limits: Variation: Scotland. 384
Representation of the people: Local government: Elections: Scotland 384
Representation of the people: National Assembly for Wales: Returning officers' charges 135
Representation of the people: Post-local government elections: Documents: Supply & inspection: Scotland. 384
Republic of Guinea: Asset-freezing 41
Research & development: Qualifying bodies: Tax 36

Reserve Forces: Compensation schemes. 116
Residential property tribunal procedures & fees 82
Residential property tribunals: Jurisdiction: Mobile Homes Act 1983: Wales. 105
Restrictive measures: Overseas territories 115
Revenue & customs: HM Inspectors of Constabulary & Scottish Inspectors 136
Revenue & customs: Taxes: Payment by telephone: Fees. 136
Revenue & customs: Tribunals & inquiries 310
Rhondda Cynon Taf: Parking contraventions: Civil enforcement: Wales 273
Rice products: Specified products: From China: Marketing: Restrictions: England 9, 71
Rice products: Specified products: From China: Marketing: Restrictions: Northern Ireland. 405, 416
Rice products: Specified products: From China: Marketing: Restrictions: Scotland 363, 372
Rice products: Specified products: From China: Marketing: Restrictions: Wales 10, 72
Rights in performances: Copyright & performances: Application to other countries 34, 136
Rights of the subject: Protection of Freedoms Act 2012: Commencements 17, 18, 73, 125, 126, 128, 129, 136
Rights of the subject: Protection of Freedoms Act 2012: Official records 136
River Annan salmon fishery district: Conservation: Scotland 384
River Dee, Aberdeenshire: Salmon Fishery District: Annual close time: Scotland 384
River Humber: Burcom outfall: Transfer 309
River Tyne: Tunnels: Revision of tolls 78
River: Salmon & freshwater fisheries: Conservation: River Annan salmon fishery district: Scotland 384
River: Salmon & freshwater fisheries: River Dee, Aberdeenshire: Salmon Fishery District: Annual close time: Scotland . 384
Road fuel gas: Excise: Reliefs. 65
Road races: Armoy Motorcycle Race: Northern Ireland. 440
Road races: Bush, Dungannon: Northern Ireland 440
Road races: Cairncastle Hill Climb: Northern Ireland 440
Road races: Circuit of Ireland International Rally: Northern Ireland 433
Road races: Cookstown 100: Northern Ireland 433
Road races: Craigantlet Hill Climb: Northern Ireland 440
Road races: Croft Hill Climb: Northern Ireland 433
Road races: Down Special Stages Rally: Northern Ireland 440
Road races: Drumhorc Hill Climb: Northern Ireland 440
Road races: Eagles Rock Hill Climb: Northern Ireland 441
Road races: Garron Point Hill Climb: Northern Ireland 441
Road races: Mid-Antrim 150: Northern Ireland 441
Road races: North West 200: Northern Ireland 441
Road races: Spamount Hill Climb: Northern Ireland 433
Road races: Spelga Hill Climb: Northern Ireland 441
Road races: Tandragee 100: Northern Ireland 433
Road races: Ulster Grand Prix Bike Week: Northern Ireland 433
Road races: Ulster Rally: Northern Ireland 441
Road Safety Act 2006: Commencements 137
Road traffic & vehicles: Ahoghill: Waiting restrictions: Northern Ireland 442
Road traffic & vehicles: Apsley St., Belfast: Traffic control: Northern Ireland 434
Road traffic & vehicles: Armagh: Parking places: Northern Ireland. 439
Road traffic & vehicles: Ballymena: Parking & waiting restrictions: Northern Ireland 437
Road traffic & vehicles: Ballymoney: Parking & waiting restrictions: Northern Ireland 438
Road traffic & vehicles: Bangor: Waiting restrictions: Northern Ireland 442
Road traffic & vehicles: Belfast city centre: Parking places: Northern Ireland 439
Road traffic & vehicles: Belfast city centre: Traffic control: Northern Ireland 434
Road traffic & vehicles: Belfast city centre: Waiting restrictions: Northern Ireland 438, 442
Road traffic & vehicles: Belfast: Parking & waiting restrictions: Northern Ireland 438
Road traffic & vehicles: Belfast: Roads: Parking places: Northern Ireland 439
Road traffic & vehicles: Belfast: Traffic control: Northern Ireland 434
Road traffic & vehicles: Bus lanes: Belfast city centre: Northern Ireland 434
Road traffic & vehicles: Bus lanes: East Bridge St. & Cromac St., Belfast: Northern Ireland 434
Road traffic & vehicles: Bushmills: Waiting restrictions: Northern Ireland 442
Road traffic & vehicles: Carrickfergus: Traffic control: Northern Ireland 435
Road traffic & vehicles: Cycle routes: Northern Ireland. 435
Road traffic & vehicles: Donaghmore: Roads: Parking places: Northern Ireland 439
Road traffic & vehicles: Dundonald: Waiting restrictions: Northern Ireland 442
Road traffic & vehicles: Dungannon: Waiting restrictions: Northern Ireland 442, 443
Road traffic & vehicles: Enniskillen: Right-hand turns: Prohibition: Northern Ireland 440
Road traffic & vehicles: Financial penalty deposit: Interest: Northern Ireland 441
Road traffic & vehicles: Financial penalty deposit: Northern Ireland 441, 442
Road traffic & vehicles: Goods vehicles: Enforcement powers: Northern Ireland. 435

Road traffic & vehicles: Goods vehicles: Operators: Licensing: Commencements: Northern Ireland. 435
Road traffic & vehicles: Goods vehicles: Operators: Licensing: Exemptions: Northern Ireland 435
Road traffic & vehicles: Goods vehicles: Operators: Licensing: Fees: Northern Ireland 435
Road traffic & vehicles: Goods vehicles: Operators: Licensing: Northern Ireland 435
Road traffic & vehicles: Goods vehicles: Operators: Qualifications: Northern Ireland 436
Road traffic & vehicles: Goods vehicles: Testing: Fees: Northern Ireland 436
Road traffic & vehicles: Goods vehicles: Testing: Northern Ireland. 436
Road traffic & vehicles: Holywood: Waiting restrictions: Northern Ireland. 443
Road traffic & vehicles: Immobilisation, removal & disposal: Northern Ireland 442
Road traffic & vehicles: John Street, Castlederg: Waiting restrictions: Northern Ireland 443
Road traffic & vehicles: Kilkeel: Roads: Parking places: Northern Ireland 439
Road traffic & vehicles: Larne: Parking places: Northern Ireland 440
Road traffic & vehicles: Larne: Waiting restrictions: Northern Ireland 443
Road traffic & vehicles: Lenadoon, Belfast: Traffic prohibition: Northern Ireland 440
Road traffic & vehicles: Lisburn: Waiting restrictions: Northern Ireland 443
Road traffic & vehicles: Loading bays & parking places: Northern Ireland. 436
Road traffic & vehicles: Londonderry: Roads: Parking places & loading bay: Northern Ireland 438
Road traffic & vehicles: Londonderry: Roads: Parking places & loading bays: Northern Ireland. 438
Road traffic & vehicles: Londonderry: Waiting restrictions: Northern Ireland 443
Road traffic & vehicles: Lower Windsor, Belfast: Traffic prohibition: Northern Ireland 440
Road traffic & vehicles: Motor vehicles: Construction & use: Northern Ireland 436
Road traffic & vehicles: Motor vehicles: Driving licences: Fees: Northern Ireland 437
Road traffic & vehicles: Motor vehicles: Driving licences: Northern Ireland 436, 437
Road traffic & vehicles: Motor vehicles: Taxi drivers: Licences: Northern Ireland 437
Road traffic & vehicles: Motor vehicles: Testing: Northern Ireland. 437
Road traffic & vehicles: Newtownards: Parking & waiting restrictions: Northern Ireland 438
Road traffic & vehicles: Northern Ireland 438, 439
Road traffic & vehicles: Off-street parking: Northern Ireland 432, 437
Road traffic & vehicles: Omagh: Parking & restrictions: Northern Ireland 438
Road traffic & vehicles: On-street parking: Northern Ireland 437
Road traffic & vehicles: Ormeau Road, Belfast: Waiting restrictions: Northern Ireland 443
Road traffic & vehicles: Parking places: Coaches: Northern Ireland 439
Road traffic & vehicles: Parking places: Electric vehicles: Northern Ireland 439
Road traffic & vehicles: Randalstown: Roads: Parking places, loading bay & waiting restrictions: Northern Ireland . . . 439
Road traffic & vehicles: Rathfriland: Parking & waiting restrictions: Northern Ireland. 438
Road traffic & vehicles: Road races: Armoy Motorcycle Race: Northern Ireland. 440
Road traffic & vehicles: Road races: Bush, Dungannon: Northern Ireland 440
Road traffic & vehicles: Road races: Cairncastle Hill Climb: Northern Ireland 440
Road traffic & vehicles: Road races: Circuit of Ireland International Rally: Northern Ireland 433
Road traffic & vehicles: Road races: Cookstown 100: Northern Ireland 433
Road traffic & vehicles: Road races: Craigantlet Hill Climb: Northern Ireland 440
Road traffic & vehicles: Road races: Croft Hill Climb: Northern Ireland 433
Road traffic & vehicles: Road races: Down Special Stages Rally: Northern Ireland 440
Road traffic & vehicles: Road races: Drumhorc Hill Climb: Northern Ireland 440
Road traffic & vehicles: Road races: Eagles Rock Hill Climb: Northern Ireland 441
Road traffic & vehicles: Road races: Garron Point Hill Climb: Northern Ireland 441
Road traffic & vehicles: Road races: Mid-Antrim 150: Northern Ireland 441
Road traffic & vehicles: Road races: North West 200: Northern Ireland 441
Road traffic & vehicles: Road races: Spamount Hill Climb: Northern Ireland 433
Road traffic & vehicles: Road races: Spelga Hill Climb: Northern Ireland 441
Road traffic & vehicles: Road races: Tandragee 100: Northern Ireland 433
Road traffic & vehicles: Road races: Ulster Grand Prix Bike Week: Northern Ireland 433
Road traffic & vehicles: Road races: Ulster Rally: Northern Ireland 441
Road traffic & vehicles: Road traffic: 2007 Order: Commencements: Northern Ireland 441
Road traffic & vehicles: Roads: Loading bays: Northern Ireland 436
Road traffic & vehicles: Roads: Speed limits: Northern Ireland. 441
Road traffic & vehicles: Rosemount Gardens, Londonderry: Traffic prohibitions: Northern Ireland 440
Road traffic & vehicles: Springfield Road, Belfast: Waiting restrictions: Northern Ireland. 443
Road traffic & vehicles: Strabane: Parking & waiting restrictions: Northern Ireland 438
Road traffic & vehicles: Taxi operators licensing: Northern Ireland 442
Road traffic & vehicles: Taxis: 2008 Act: Commencements: Northern Ireland 442
Road traffic & vehicles: Taxis: Bushmills: Northern Ireland 442
Road traffic & vehicles: Toome: Parking places: Northern Ireland 440
Road traffic & vehicles: Traffic management: Penalty charges: Prescribed amounts: Northern Ireland 440
Road traffic & vehicles: Traffic: Weight restriction: Northern Ireland 442

Road traffic & vehicles: Waiting: Prohibitions: Northern Ireland 440
Road traffic offenders: Prescribed devices: Northern Ireland 442
Road traffic: 2007 Order: Commencements: Northern Ireland 441
Road traffic: A720 Edinburgh City bypass: Speed limits: Scotland 385
Road traffic: Bus lane contraventions: Approved local authorities 93, 272
Road traffic: Community drivers: Hours & recording equipment 136
Road traffic: Disabled persons: Motor vehicles: Badges. 273
Road traffic: Drivers: Hours: Northern Ireland 413
Road traffic: Driving instruction: Compensation schemes. 136
Road traffic: Driving instruction: Suspension & exemption powers: Commencements 136
Road traffic: Financial penalty deposit: Northern Ireland 442
Road traffic: Goods vehicles: Operators: Licensing: Fees 136
Road traffic: Goods vehicles: Plating & testing: Amendments 137
Road traffic: Motor vehicles: Driving licences 137
Road traffic: Motor vehicles: Tests: Amendments. 137
Road traffic: Motorways: M8: Speed limits: Scotland. 385
Road traffic: Parking adjudicators: East Ayrshire Council: Scotland 386
Road traffic: Parking adjudicators: South Ayrshire Council: Scotland 386
Road traffic: Parking attendants: Wearing of uniforms: East Ayrshire Council parking area: Scotland. 386
Road traffic: Parking attendants: Wearing of uniforms: South Ayrshire Council parking area: Scotland 386
Road traffic: Parking contraventions: Civil enforcement 93, 272
Road traffic: Parking contraventions: Civil enforcement: Ceredigion: Wales 273
Road traffic: Parking contraventions: Civil enforcement: Rhondda Cynon Taf: Wales 273
Road traffic: Permitted & special parking areas: East Ayrshire Council: Scotland 386
Road traffic: Protection of Freedoms Act 2012 272
Road traffic: Protection of Freedoms Act 2012: Commencements 18, 43, 89, 129, 273
Road traffic: Protection of Freedoms Act 2012: Commencements: Wales 273
Road traffic: Rehabilitation courses: Relevant drink offences 137
Road traffic: Road Safety Act 2006: Commencements 137
Road traffic: Road vehicles: Construction & use 137
Road traffic: Road vehicles: Individual approval: Fees 137
Road traffic: Road vehicles: Registration & licensing: Amendments 137
Road traffic: Scotland 388, 389, 390, 391, 392, 393
Road traffic: South Ayrshire Council parking areas: Scotland. 386
Road traffic: Special roads: England. 272
Road traffic: Speed limits 137, 138, 139, 140, 273
Road traffic: Speed limits: Scotland 386
Road traffic: Traffic Management Act 2004: Exeter. 272
Road traffic: Traffic regulation . . . . 139 to 292
Road traffic: Traffic regulation: Scotland. 385, 386, 387, 388, 389
Road traffic: Vehicles: Removal & disposal: England. 272
Road transport: Working time: Amendments 309
Road transport: Working time: Northern Ireland 448
Road vehicle & mobile machinery: Greenhouse gas emissions reporting: Motor fuel 29
Road vehicles: Construction & use 137
Road vehicles: Individual approval: Fees 137
Road vehicles: Registration & licensing: Amendments 137
Road works: Inspection fees: Scotland. 385
Road works: Maintenance: Scotland. 385
Roads & bridges: Road works: Inspection fees: Scotland 385
Roads & bridges: Road works: Maintenance: Scotland 385
Roads & bridges: Scotland. 384
Roads & bridges: Scottish Road Works Register: Prescribed fees: Scotland 385
Roads traffic: Trunk roads: A823(M): Pitreavie Spur: Scotland. 385
Roads: A3 Northway, Portadown: Abandonment: Northern Ireland. 431
Roads: A5: Western Transport Corridor: Stopping-up: Northern Ireland 433
Roads: A55 Knock Rd, Belfast: Private accesses: Stopping-up: Northern Ireland 433
Roads: A8 Belfast to Larne Dual Carriageway: Stopping-up: Northern Ireland. 432
Roads: Ballydogherty Road (U5003), Loughgilly: Abandonment: Northern Ireland 431
Roads: Browning Drive, Londonderry: Abandonment: Northern Ireland 431
Roads: C156 (Unnamed road), Moyraverty, Craigavon: Abandonment: Northern Ireland 431
Roads: College Avenue, Belfast: Stopping-up: Northern Ireland 431
Roads: Drumlin Road, Donaghcloney: Abandonment: Northern Ireland 432
Roads: Durham Street & Hamill Street - Killen Street, Belfast: Stopping-up: Northern Ireland 432
Roads: Grange Lodge, Antrim: Abandonment: Northern Ireland 432

Roads: Greystone Road, Limavady: Abandonment: Northern Ireland. 432
Roads: Longlands Avenue, Newtownabbey: Abandonment: Northern Ireland 432
Roads: Loopland Court, Belfast : Abandonment: Northern Ireland 432
Roads: M2 Motorway at Whitla Street, Belfast: Abandonment: Northern Ireland 432
Roads: M3 Motorway, Titanic Quarter Railway Station, Belfast: Abandonment: Northern Ireland. 432
Roads: Malone Beeches, Belfast: Abandonment: Northern Ireland 432
Roads: Marine Highway, Carrickfergus: Abandonment: Northern Ireland 432
Roads: North Circular Road & Tarry Lane, Lurgan: Abandonment: Northern Ireland 432
Roads: Old Church Road, Newtownabbey: Abandonment: Northern Ireland 432
Roads: Route B30 Newry Road, Crossmaglen: Abandonment: Northern Ireland 433
Roads: Route U5160, Carnbane Industrial Estate, Newry : Abandonment: Northern Ireland 433
Roads: Shankbridge Road, Ballymena: Abandonment: Northern Ireland 433
Roads: Shore Rd & Northwood Pde, Belfast : Abandonment: Northern Ireland 433
Roads: Templemore Street, Belfast: Abandonment: Northern Ireland. 433
Roads: Trunk roads: T14: A55 Knock Rd, Belfast: Northern Ireland 434
Roads: Trunk roads: T3: Western Transport Corridor: Northern Ireland 433
Roads: Trunk roads: T9: Coleman's Corner to Ballyrickard Road: Northern Ireland 434
Roads: Tullynacross Road, Lisburn: Abandonment: Northern Ireland 434
Roads: University Terrace, Belfast: Abandonment: Northern Ireland 434
Roads: Upper Dunmurry Lane, Dunmurry: Abandonment: Northern Ireland 434
Roads: Westbourne Avenue, Ballymena: Abandonment: Northern Ireland 434
Rosemount Gardens, Londonderry: Traffic prohibitions: Road traffic & vehicles: Northern Ireland 440
Rotherham Borough Council: Permit schemes: Traffic management 79
Route B30 Newry Road, Crossmaglen: Abandonment: Roads: Northern Ireland 433
Route U5160, Carnbane Industrial Estate, Newry: Abandonment: Roads: Northern Ireland 433
Royal Brompton & Harefield NHS Foundation Trust: Transfer of property. 109
Royal Parks & other open spaces 113
Royal Wolverhampton Hospitals: National Health Service Trust 109
Rugby: Electoral changes 97
Rural development contracts: Rural priorities: Scotland. 363
Rural payments: Appeals: Scotland 363
Rural primary schools: Designation: England. 49
Rushmoor: Electoral changes 97
Rwanda: International tribunals: United Nations 311

S

Safeguarding Board for Northern Ireland: 2011 Act: Commencements: Northern Ireland 417
Safeguarding Board for Northern Ireland: Membership, procedure, functions & committees: Northern Ireland 417
Safeguarding Vulnerable Groups Act 2006: Commencements 17, 128
Safeguarding Vulnerable Groups Act 2006: Controlled activity & prescribed criteria: England & Wales 18, 128
Safeguarding Vulnerable Groups Act 2006: Miscellaneous amendments 18, 128
Safeguarding Vulnerable Groups Act 2006: Miscellaneous provisions 18, 128
Safeguarding Vulnerable Groups: 2007 Order: Commencements: Northern Ireland 443
Safeguarding vulnerable groups: Miscellaneous amendments: Northern Ireland 443
Safeguarding vulnerable groups: Miscellaneous provisions: Northern Ireland 443, 444
Safeguarding vulnerable groups: Prescribed criteria & miscellaneous provisions: Northern Ireland 444
Safety: Merchant shipping: Passenger ships: Domestic voyages 105
Salmon & freshwater fisheries: Conservation: River Annan salmon fishery district: Scotland 384
Salmon & freshwater fisheries: River Dee, Aberdeenshire: Salmon Fishery District: Annual close time: Scotland 384
Sanctions: Iraq 311
Savings banks: National Savings Bank: Investment deposits: Limits 292
Savings certificates. 105
Savings certificates: Children's bonus bonds 105
Scallop fishing: England 292
Scallops: Dredging operations: Tracking devices: Wales 293
Scarborough & North East Yorkshire Health Care: National Health Service Trust 109
School & early years finance: England 53
School & placing information: Scotland 369
School day & school year: Wales 56
School discipline: Pupil exclusions & reviews: England 53
School governance: Constitution: England 53
School governance: Federations: Education: England 53
School premises: Education 55
School teachers: Incentive payments: England 53

School teachers: Induction arrangements: Wales 56
School teachers: Pay & conditions: England & Wales 55
Schools forums: England 53
Schools: Academies: School behaviour: Measures: Determination & publicising: England 53
Schools: Admission: Appeals arrangements: England 52
Schools: Admission: Arrangements: England. 52
Schools: Admission: Infant class sizes: England 52
Schools: Admissions appeals code: Appointed day: England. 52
Schools: Articles: Specification & disposal: England. 53
Schools: Finance: England 53
Schools: Governance: England 53
Schools: Governance: Transition from Interim Executive Board: Wales 57
Schools: Government: Terms of reference: England 50
Schools: Independent: Religious character: Designation: England 49
Schools: Independent: Standards: Education: England 50
Schools: Information: England 53
Schools: Information: Provision: Scotland. 369
Schools: Inspections: Exemptions: England. 50
Schools: Middle schools: Wales. 56
Schools: Performance information: England 51
Schools: Pre-school education: Admissions criteria: Northern Ireland 410
Schools: Rural primary schools: Designation: England. 49
Schools: Staffing: England 53
Schools: Teachers: Appraisal: England 51
Schools: Teachers: Discipline. 54
Schools: Teachers: Incentive payments: England 53
Schools: Teachers: Induction arrangements: England. 50
Schools: Teachers: Induction arrangements: Wales. 56
Schools: Teachers: Pay & conditions: England & Wales 55
Schools: Teachers: Pensions: England & Wales 55
Schools: Teachers: Professional qualifications: England 55
Schools: Teachers: Qualifications & appraisal: Amendments: England 51
Schools: Teachers: Qualifications & specified work: Amendments: England 51
Schools: Teachers: Qualifications: Wales. 57
Schools: Teachers: Superannuation: Northern Ireland. 410
Schools: Teachers: Superannuation: Scotland 379
Scotland Act 2012: Commencements 33, 47
Scotland: Devolution: Policies: Acts 6
Scotland: Devolution: Policies: Acts: Explanatory notes. 7
Scotland: Education: School & placing information: Scotland 369
Scottish Administration: Offices 33, 47
Scottish Parliament: Acts: Bound volumes 362
Scottish Parliament: Constituencies: Acts 4
Scottish Public Services Ombudsman Act 2002: Scotland. 393
Scottish Public Services Ombudsman: Scottish Public Services Ombudsman Act 2002: Amendments: Scotland 393
Scottish Road Works Register: Prescribed fees: Scotland. 385
Scottish secure tenancies: Proceedings for possession: Scotland 375
Scottish secure tenancies: Repossession orders: Scotland. 375
Sea fish industry: Fishing vessels: Satellite-tracking devices: Electronic reporting: Scheme 293
Sea fisheries: Conservation of sea fish: Scallop fishing: England. 292
Sea fisheries: Conservation of sea fish: Sharks, skates & rays: Fishing, trans-shipment & landing: Prohibitions: Scotland 393
Sea fisheries: European Fisheries Fund: Grants: Scotland. 393
Sea fisheries: Fishing boats: Satellite-tracking devices 293
Sea fisheries: Fishing vessels: Satellite-tracking devices: Electronic reporting: Scheme 293
Sea fisheries: Prohibited methods of fishing: Firth of Clyde: Scotland 393
Sea fisheries: Scallops: Dredging operations: Tracking devices: Wales. 293
Sea fisheries: Shetland Islands Regulated Fishery: Scotland 393
Sea fisheries: Specified sea areas: Prohibition. 293
Sea fisheries: Strangford Lough: Sea fishing exclusion zones: Northern Ireland 444
Sea fisheries: Transfer of functions: Ministers of the Crown 105
Sea fishing: Fishing boats: EU electronic reporting: Scotland. 393
Sea fishing: Licences & notices: England 292
Secure tenancies: Proceedings for possession: Scotland. 375
Secure tenancies: Scottish: Repossession orders: Scotland 375
Securities: Transferable: Collective investment: Undertakings 69

Security industry: Private Security Industry Act 2001: Aviation security: Exemptions 293
Security industry: Private Security Industry Act 2001: Olympics security: Exemption 293
Seeds: Fodder plant seeds: Scotland 393
Seeds: Marketing: Amendments: England 293
Seeds: Marketing: Wales 294
Seeds: Potatoes: Originating in Egypt: Northern Ireland 444
Senior courts of England & Wales: Civil procedure: Rules 38, 294
Senior courts of England & Wales: Criminal procedure: Rules 101, 294
Senior courts: Civil courts: England & Wales 38, 294
Senior courts: Family procedure 38, 39, 67, 101, 102, 294
Sentencing & punishment: Offenders: Acts 5
Sentencing & punishment: Offenders: Acts: Explanatory notes 7
Serious Organised Crime & Police Act 2005: Designated sites: Section 128: Amendments 43
Severn Bridges: Tolls 78
Sex discrimination: 1976 Order: Amendments: Northern Ireland 444
Sexual Offences Act 2003: Amendments: Magistrates' courts: Procedure: England & Wales 102
Sexual Offences Act 2003: Notification requirements 43
Sexual Offences Act 2003: Prescribed police stations: Northern Ireland 409
Sexual Offences Act 2003: Prescribed police stations: Scotland 368
Sexual Offences Act 2003: Remedial 43
Sexual offences: Acts 4
Sexual offences: Acts: Scotland 361
Shankbridge Road, Ballymena: Abandonment: Roads: Northern Ireland 433
Sharks, skates & rays: Fishing, trans-shipment & landing: Prohibitions: Scotland 393
Sheep: Export: Prohibition: Scotland 364, 381
Sheep: Food protection: Emergency prohibitions: Radioactivity: England 132
Sheep: Radioactivity: Food protection: Scotland 364, 381
Sheep: Radioactivity: Food protection: Wales 71, 132
Sheffield City Council: Permit schemes: Traffic management 79
Sheffield, City: Mayoral referendum 94
Sheriff Court: Act of Adjournal: Criminal Procedure (Scotland) Act 1995: Transcripts: Amendments: Scotland . . . 373, 394
Sheriff Court: Act of Adjournal: Criminal procedure rules: Scotland 373, 375, 394
Sheriff Court: Act of Sederunt: Heritable property: Actions for removing: Scotland 394
Sheriff Court: Court Fees: Amendments: Scotland 368, 373, 395
Sheriff Court: Fees: Scotland 395
Sheriff Court: Personal injuries actions: Summary cause: Rules: Act of Sederunt: Scotland 395
Sheriff Court: Rules: Amendments: Act of Sederunt: Scotland 394
Sheriff Court: Sheriff officers: Fees: Act of Sederunt: Scotland 394
Sheriff Court: Shorthand writers: Fees: Act of Sederunt: Scotland 394
Shetland Islands Regulated Fishery: Scotland 393
Shipowners: Compulsory insurance: Maritime claims: Merchant shipping 104
Shore Rd & Northwood Pde, Belfast: Abandonment: Roads: Northern Ireland 433
Shorthand writers: Fees: Court of Session: Act of Sederunt: Scotland 367
Shorthand writers: Fees: Sheriff Court: Act of Sederunt: Scotland 394
Shropshire Community: National Health Service Trust 109
Shropshire: Electoral changes 94
Signs: Smoke-free: Public health: England 131
Singapore: Double taxation: Relief & international enforcement 14, 36, 85
Sixth form college corporations: Dissolution: Prescribed bodies 49
Sixth form college corporations: Publication of proposals: England 53
Skipton Fund Limited: Income tax 87
Slough: Electoral changes 97
Small business hereditament relief: Northern Ireland 430
Small Charitable donations: Taxation: Acts 6
Small Charitable donations: Taxation: Acts: Explanatory notes 7
Smart meters: Communication licences: Competitive tenders 58, 73
Smart meters: Licensable activity: Electricity & gas 58, 73
Smoke control areas: Authorised fuels: England 29
Smoke control areas: Authorised fuels: Northern Ireland 408
Smoke control areas: Fireplaces: Exempt: England 29
Smoke control areas: Fireplaces: Exempt: Wales 29
Smoke control areas: Fireplaces: Exemptions: Northern Ireland 408
Smoke-free signs: Public health: England 131
Snares: Identification numbers & tags: Scotland 397
Snares: Training: Wildlife: Scotland 397

Social Care & Social Work Improvement Scotland: Excepted services: Scotland. 395
Social care: Acts 5
Social care: Acts: Explanatory notes 7
Social care: Adult support & protection: Community Care & Health (Scotland) Act 2002: Scotland 362, 395
Social care: Care Council for Wales: Appointment, membership & procedure 295
Social care: Care Quality Commission: Healthwatch England Committee 106, 131, 295
Social care: Care Quality Commission: Membership 106, 131, 295
Social care: Care Quality Commission: Registration & additional functions 106, 131, 295
Social care: Carers strategies: Wales 110, 295
Social care: Children & Families (Wales) Measure: Commencements. 18, 110, 295
Social care: Community care: Joint working: Scotland 395
Social care: Community care: Personal care & nursing care: Scotland 395
Social care: Family support teams: Composition & board functions: Wales 19, 111, 296
Social care: Family support teams: Family support functions: Wales 19, 111, 296
Social care: Family support teams: Review of cases: Wales 19, 111, 296
Social care: Health & Social Care Act 2008: Regulated activities 106, 131, 295
Social care: Health & Social Care Act 2012: Commencements 75, 93, 103, 106, 131, 295
Social care: Public services reform: Social services inspections: Scotland 395
Social enterprise & social value: Public services: Acts. 6
Social enterprise & social value: Public services: Acts: Explanatory notes 7
Social fund: Cold weather payments. 298
Social fund: Cold weather payments: General: Northern Ireland 445
Social Fund: Maternity & funeral expenses: Northern Ireland. 445
Social Fund: Maternity grant. 298
Social security 300
Social security information: Disclosure: Statistics & Registration Service Act 2007: Northern Ireland. 422
Social security: Amendments: Northern Ireland. 446
Social security: Appeal decisions: Supersession. 299
Social security: Benefits: Members of the Armed Forces 298
Social security: Benefits: Payment suspensions: Miscellaneous amendments: Northern Ireland 419, 430, 447
Social security: Benefits: Payment: Suspension 301
Social security: Benefits: Up-rating 298, 305
Social security: Benefits: Up-rating: Northern Ireland 411, 418, 430, 446, 447, 448
Social security: Categorisation of earners 299
Social security: Child benefit & guardian's allowance: Administration 296
Social security: Child benefit: Child tax credits 296, 304
Social security: Child benefit: General. 296
Social security: Civil penalties. 299
Social security: Claims & payments 299
Social security: Claims & payments: Northern Ireland 446
Social security: Contributions 299
Social security: Contributions: Re-rating 299
Social security: Credits 299, 300
Social security: Credits: Northern Ireland 446
Social security: Deaths: Notification. 300
Social security: Earnings factors: Revaluation. 301
Social security: Earnings factors: Revaluations: Northern Ireland. 447
Social security: Employment & support allowance 296
Social security: Employment & support allowance: Contributory allowance 297
Social security: Employment & support allowance: Linking rules 296
Social security: Employment & support allowance: Linking rules: Northern Ireland 444
Social security: Employment & support allowance: Sanctions 297
Social security: Guardian's allowance: Up-rating 297
Social security: Guardian's allowance: Up-rating: Northern Ireland 302
Social security: Habitual residence 300
Social security: Habitual residence: Northern Ireland. 418, 430, 446
Social security: Housing benefit. 297
Social security: Housing benefit: Benefit cap 296
Social security: Industrial injuries benefit 297
Social security: Industrial injuries: Dependency: Permitted earnings limits. 300
Social security: Industrial injuries: Dependency: Permitted earnings limits: Northern Ireland 446
Social security: Industrial injuries: Prescribed diseases 300
Social security: Industrial injuries: Prescribed diseases: Northern Ireland. 446
Social security: Jobseeker's allowance 297
Social security: Jobseeker's allowance: Domestic violence 297

Social security: Jobseeker's allowance: Domestic violence: Northern Ireland 444
Social security: Jobseeker's allowance: Failure to attend: Sanctions: Northern Ireland 418, 429, 445
Social security: Jobseeker's allowance: Forces: Members: Northern Ireland 112, 302
Social security: Jobseeker's allowance: Northern Ireland 444
Social security: Jobseeker's allowance: Reserve forces: Members 297
Social security: Jobseeker's allowance: Reserve Forces: Members: Northern Ireland. 445
Social security: Jobseeker's allowance: Sanctions. 298
Social security: Jobseeker's allowance: Work experience: Northern Ireland 445
Social security: Jobseeker's allowance: Work for Your Benefit. 297
Social security: Lone parents 300
Social security: Mesothelioma: Lump sum payments: Conditions & amounts 298
Social security: Mesothelioma: Lump sum payments: Conditions & amounts: Northern Ireland 445
Social security: National insurance: Contributions: Application of part 7 of the Finance Act 2004. 298
Social security: Northern Ireland 419, 430, 447
Social security: Pensions: Flat rate accrual amount 301
Social security: Pensions: Flat rate accrual amounts: Northern Ireland 447
Social security: Pensions: Flat rate introduction year: Northern Ireland. 447
Social security: Pensions: Low earnings threshold 301
Social security: Pensions: Low earnings threshold: Northern Ireland 447
Social security: Pneumoconiosis etc.: Workers' compensation: Claims: Payments 298
Social security: Reciprocal agreements 301
Social security: Recovery 301
Social security: Recovery: Northern Ireland 419, 430, 447
Social security: Rent officers: Housing benefit functions: Amendments 80
Social security: Revenue information: Disclosures: Statistics & Registration Service Act 2007 303
Social security: Social fund: Cold weather payments 298
Social security: Social fund: Cold weather payments: General: Northern Ireland. 445
Social security: Social Fund: Maternity grant 298
Social security: Welfare Reform Act 2009: Commencements 66, 135, 296, 301
Social security: Welfare Reform Act 2012: Commencements 301, 302
Social security: Welfare reform: Acts 5, 6, 7
Social security: Welfare reform: Acts: Explanatory notes 7
Social security: Welfare services: Information sharing 300
Social security: Workers' compensation: Pneumoconiosis etc.: Claims: Payments: Northern Ireland 445
Social security: Workers' compensation: Supplementation 302
Social services functions: Local authorities: Contracting out: England 34
Social work: Social Care & Social Work Improvement Scotland: Excepted services: Scotland 395
Social workers: General Social Care Council: Transfer of register & abolition: Transitional & saving provisions 77
Solicitors: Non-contentious business: England & Wales 91
Solvents: Extraction: Food: England 71
Solvents: Extraction: Food: Wales 72
Somalia: Sanctions: Overseas territories 115
Somerset: Electoral changes. 97
South Ayrshire Council: Parking adjudicators: Scotland 386
South Ayrshire Council: Parking areas: Scotland 386
South Ayrshire Council: Parking attendants: Wearing of uniforms: Scotland 386
South London Healthcare: National Health Service Trust 109, 110
Southend-on-Sea Borough Council: Permit schemes: Traffic management. 79
Special constables: Police 125
Special Educational Needs Tribunal for Wales 57, 58
Special educational needs: Direct payments: Pilot scheme: England 54
Special Health Authorities: Establishment & Constitution 110
Special health authorities: Health Service Commissioner for England 107
Species: Habitats: Conservation 38, 102, 315
Specified social care schemes: Qualifying care relief: Income tax 86
Spectrum trading: Wireless telegraphy: Electronic communications 59
Sport: Football: Offensive behaviour: Threatening communications: Acts: Explanatory notes: Scotland. 362
Sport: Football: Offensive behaviour: Threatening communications: Acts: Scotland 361
Sports grounds & sporting events: Designations: Scotland 395
Sports grounds & sporting events: Football spectators: 2012 European Championship control period 302
Sports grounds & sporting events: Football spectators: Seating 302
Sports grounds & sporting events: Glasgow Commonwealth Games Act 2008: Commencements: Scotland 395
Sports grounds & sporting events: Glasgow Commonwealth Games Act 2008: Ticket touting offences: Exceptions: Scotland
. . . . 395
Sports grounds: Safety: Designation 302

Sports grounds: Safety: Fees & appeals: Northern Ireland. 447
Sportsmen & Entertainers: Income tax 85
Spring traps: Animals: Approval: Prevention of cruelty: England 11
Spring traps: Approval: Animals: Wales 11
Spring traps: Approval: Northern Ireland 448
Springfield Road, Belfast: Waiting restrictions: Road traffic & vehicles: Northern Ireland. 443
St Albans & Welwyn Hatfield: Boundary changes: Local government 97
St Helens Borough Council: Permit schemes: Traffic management. 79
St Mary's: National Health Service Trust 107
St. Mary Out Liberty & Tenby Communities: Pembrokeshire: Wales. 100
Staffordshire: Electoral changes. 97
Stakeholder pension schemes: Disclosure of information: Northern Ireland 424
Stamp duty land tax: British Waterways Board: Tax consequences 35, 302
Stamp duty land tax: Finance Act 2003 303
Stamp duty land tax: Financial Services Act 2010: Schedule 6: Part 2: Commencements 15, 36, 85, 88, 302, 303
Stamp duty land tax: London Legacy Development Corporation: Tax consequences 36, 86, 303
Stamp duty land tax: Postal Services Act 2011: Taxation 36, 86, 302, 303
Stamp duty land tax: Visiting forces: International Military Headquarters: NATO & PfP: Tax Designation . . 46, 87, 88, 303
Stamp duty reserve tax: Amendments 19, 84, 303
Stamp duty reserve tax: Financial Services Act 2010: Schedule 6: Part 2: Commencements 15, 36, 85, 88, 302, 303
Stamp duty reserve tax: Postal Services Act 2011: Taxation 36, 86, 302, 303
Stamp duty: British Waterways Board: Tax consequences 35, 302
Stamp duty: Financial Services Act 2010: Schedule 6: Part 2: Commencements 15, 36, 85, 88, 302, 303
Stamp duty: Land tax: Tax avoidance schemes: Arrangements 303
Stamp duty: Land tax: Tax avoidance schemes: Arrangements: Prescribed descriptions 303
Stamp duty: Postal Services Act 2011: Taxation 36, 86, 302, 303
Standards Board for England: Abolition 99
Statistics & Registration Service Act 2007: Social security information: Disclosure: Northern Ireland 422, 423
Statistics & Registration Service Act 2007: Social security: Revenue information: Disclosures 303
Statistics Board: Statistics & Registration Service Act 2007: Social security: Revenue information: Disclosures 303
Statistics of trade: Customs & excise 303
Statistics: Official statistics: Scotland 379
Statutes: Chronological tables 8
Statutes: Chronological tables: Northern Ireland 404
Statutes: Northern Ireland 404, 405
Statutes: Title page & index: Northern Ireland 405
Statutory auditors: Companies Act 2006: Amendment & delegation of functions 12, 32
Statutory concessions: Extra: Enactments. 36, 85, 88
Statutory instruments: Annual volumes 8
Statutory maternity pay: Social security: Benefits: Up-rating: Northern Ireland 411, 418, 430, 446, 447, 448
Statutory nuisances: Appeals: Environmental protection: Northern Ireland 412
Statutory nuisances: Artificial lighting: Environmental protection: Relevant sports: Northern Ireland 412
Statutory nuisances: Insects: Environmental protection: Northern Ireland 412
Statutory rules (Northern Ireland): Chronological tables: Northern Ireland 404
Statutory sick pay: Social security: Benefits: Up-rating: Northern Ireland 411, 418, 430, 446, 447, 448
Stevenson College, Edinburgh: Transfer & closure: Scotland. 370
Strabane: Parking & waiting restrictions: Road traffic & vehicles: Northern Ireland 438
Strangford Lough: Sea fishing exclusion zones: Northern Ireland. 444
Strategic health authorities & primary care trusts: Functions: National Health Service 107
Street litter: Control notices: Amendments: Environmental protection: Northern Ireland. 412
Street works: Charges for occupation: England 78
Street works: Unreasonably prolonged occupation: Charges: England 78
Stroud College: Filton College & Stroud College Further Education: Dissolution 51
Student fees: Agriculture: Northern Ireland 405
Student fees: Amounts: Northern Ireland 410
Student fees: Basic & higher amounts: Approved plans: England 54
Student fees: Qualifying courses & persons: Wales. 58
Student loans: Living costs liability: Cancellation 55
Student loans: Repayment. 48
Student loans: Repayment: Northern Ireland 410
Student support: Eligibility: Further education: Northern Ireland 410
Student support: European University Institute 51
Student support: Financial: Amendments: Education: Northern Ireland. 410
Students: Fees, awards & support: England. 51
Sudan & South Sudan: Restrictive measures: Overseas territories. 115

Sudan: Asset-freezing 41
Sunbeds: Act 2011: Commencements: Northern Ireland 428
Sunbeds: Fixed penalty: Amount: Northern Ireland 429
Sunbeds: Fixed penalty: Northern Ireland 429
Sunbeds: Information: Northern Ireland 429
Sunday trading: London Olympic & Paralympic Games: Acts. 6
Sunderland City Council: Sunderland Strategic Transport Corridor: New Wear Bridge scheme. 78
Sunderland City Council: Sunderland Strategic Transport Corridor: New Wear Bridge scheme: Temporary works. 78
Superannuation schemes: Health & personal social services: Northern Ireland 416
Superannuation: Charity Commission for Northern Ireland: Northern Ireland 426
Superannuation: Chief Inspector of Criminal Justice in Northern Ireland: Northern Ireland 426
Superannuation: Commissioner for Victims & Survivors for Northern Ireland: Northern Ireland 426
Superannuation: Commissioner of the Northern Ireland Law Commission: Northern Ireland 426
Superannuation: Firemen: Pension schemes: Scotland. 372
Superannuation: Health & personal social services: Northern Ireland. 416
Superannuation: Police Ombudsman for Northern Ireland: Northern Ireland 426
Superannuation: Teachers: Northern Ireland. 410
Superannuation: Victims & Survivors Service Ltd: Northern Ireland: Northern Ireland 426
Supply & appropriation: Anticipation & adjustments: Acts 6
Supply & appropriation: Main estimates: Acts 6
Surrey: Electoral changes 98
Sustainable & renewable fuels: Energy Act 2004: Amendment 60, 308
Sustainable communities: Local government 98
Sutton, London Borough: Permit schemes: Traffic management 79
Swale & Ure: Drainage Board. 90
Swale: Electoral changes 98
Swansea Bay: Thomas Shellfish Ltd: Mussel Fishery 293
Swindon: Electoral changes 98
Switzerland: Double taxation: Relief & international enforcement 304
Syria & Burma: Export control: Sanctions 44
Syria: European Union financial sanctions 41
Syria: Export control: Sanctions. 44
Syria: Lebanon: Asset-freezing 40
Syria: Restrictive measures: Overseas territories 115
Syria: Sanctions: Overseas territories 115

T

Tarry Lane & North Circular Road, Lurgan: Abandonment: Roads: Northern Ireland 432
Tax avoidance schemes: Stamp duty: Land tax: Arrangements 303
Tax avoidance schemes: Stamp duty: Land tax: Arrangements: Prescribed descriptions 303
Tax credits 304
Tax credits: Child benefit: Child tax credits 296, 304
Tax credits: Up-rating 304
Tax credits: Welfare reform: Acts 6, 7
Tax credits: Welfare reform: Acts: Explanatory notes 7
Taxation (International and Other Provisions) Act 2010: Part 7: Amendments. 36
Taxation: Charities: Small donations: Acts. 6
Taxation: Charities: Small donations: Acts: Explanatory notes 7
Taxes *see also* Corporation tax
Taxes *see also* Income tax
Taxes *see also* Insurance premium tax
Taxes *see also* Landfill tax
Taxes *see also* Oil tax
Taxes *see also* Value added tax
Taxes: Authorised Investment Funds 14, 35, 84
Taxes: British Waterways Board: Tax consequences 35, 302
Taxes: Business premises renovation allowances 35, 84
Taxes: Capital gains tax: Annual exempt amount. 14
Taxes: Chargeable gains: Gilt-edged securities 15, 36
Taxes: Data-gathering powers: Relevant data 304
Taxes: Double taxation: Relief & international enforcement: Bahrain 14, 35, 85
Taxes: Double taxation: Relief & international enforcement: Barbados 14, 35, 85
Taxes: Double taxation: Relief & international enforcement: Liechtenstein 14, 35, 85
Taxes: Double taxation: Relief & international enforcement: Singapore 14, 36, 85

Taxes: Double taxation: Relief & international enforcement: Switzerland 304
Taxes: Double taxation: Relief: Germany. 12
Taxes: European Administrative Co-operation 134
Taxes: Finance At 2012: Enterprise investment scheme: Appointed day 15, 85
Taxes: Income & interest payments: Reporting: Data gathering. 304
Taxes: Inheritance tax: Market makers & discount houses 88
Taxes: Payment by telephone: Fees 136
Taxes: Purchased life annuities 86
Taxes: Registered pension schemes: Relevant annuities 87
Taxes: Remote gambling: Double taxation relief 66
Taxes: Research & development: Qualifying bodies 36
Taxes: Stamp duty land tax: Finance Act 2003 303
Taxes: Tax avoidance schemes: Information 304
Taxi operators licensing: Northern Ireland. 442
Taxis: 2008 Act: Commencements: Northern Ireland 442
Taxis: Bushmills: Road traffic & vehicles: Northern Ireland 442
Taxis: Driving licences: Northern Ireland 437
Teacher student loans: Repayment 55
Teachers: Appraisal: England 51
Teachers: Discipline. 54
Teachers: Incentive payments: England. 53
Teachers: Induction arrangements: England 50
Teachers: Induction arrangements: Wales. 56
Teachers: Pay & conditions: England & Wales 55
Teachers: Pensions: England & Wales 55
Teachers: Professional qualifications: England 55
Teachers: Qualifications & appraisal: Amendments: England 51
Teachers: Qualifications & specified work: Amendments: England 51
Teachers: Qualifications: Wales. 57
Teachers: Student loans: Repayment 55
Teachers: Superannuation: Northern Ireland. 410
Teachers: Superannuation: Scotland 379
Tees & Hartlepool: Port security: Merchant shipping 104
Television: Local digital television programme services 13
Television: Local digital television programme services: Independent productions 12, 59
Templemore Street, Belfast: Abandonment: Northern Ireland. 433
Tenancies: Flexible tenancies: Review procedures 80
Tenancies: Scottish secure tenancies: Proceedings for possession: Scotland 375
Tenancies: Scottish secure tenancies: Repossession orders: Scotland 375
Tenancies: Transfer: Right to acquire: Exclusion 81
Tenancy deposit schemes: Northern Ireland 420
Terms & conditions of employment: Employment rights: Limits: Increase 304, 305
Terms & conditions of employment: Local policing bodies 122, 304
Terms & conditions of employment: National minimum wage: Regulations: Amendments 304
Terms & conditions of employment: Occupational & personal pension schemes: Prescribed bodies 117
Terms & conditions of employment: Public interest disclosure: Prescribed persons 305
Terms & conditions of employment: Social security: Benefits: Up-rating 298, 305
Terms & conditions of employment: Transfer of undertakings: Protection of employment: RCUK Shared Services Centre
Limited. 305
Terrorism Act 2000: Amendments 126, 127, 128
Terrorism Act 2000: Proscribed organisations. 127
Terrorism Act 2000: Stop & search powers: Codes of practice 126
Terrorism Act 2000: Video recording with sound of interviews & associated code of practice 127
Terrorism: Counter-Terrorism Act 2008: Video recording with sound of post-charge questioning: Codes of practice . . . 126
Textile products: Labelling & fibre composition 34
Thames: London Thames Gateway Development Corporation: Transfer of property, rights & liabilities. 311
The London: National Health Service Trust 106
Thomas Shellfish Ltd: Mussel Fishery: Swansea Bay 293
Thurrock Development Corporation: Dissolution 311
Thurrock Development Corporation: Transfer of property, rights & liabilities 311
Title Conditions (Scotland) Act 2003: Conservation bodies: Scotland 395
Tobacco: Advertising & promotion: Display: England 131
Tobacco: Advertising & promotion: Display: Northern Ireland. 429
Tobacco: Advertising & promotion: Display: Wales 132
Tobacco: Advertising & promotion: Prices: Display: Northern Ireland 429

Tobacco: Advertising & promotion: Prices: Display: Wales 132
Tobacco: Advertising & promotion: Specialist tobacconists: England 131
Tobacco: Advertising & promotion: Specialist tobacconists: Northern Ireland 429
Tobacco: Advertising & promotion: Specialist tobacconists: Wales. 132
Tobacco: Sale: Vending machines: Children & young persons: Northern Ireland. 407
Tolls: Severn Bridges 78
Toome: Parking places: Northern Ireland 440
Torbay & Southern Devon Health & Care: National Health Service Trust 110
Tower Hamlets, London Borough: Permit schemes: Traffic management 79
Town & country planning: Advertisement controls: Wales 308
Town & country planning: Advertisements: Control: England 306
Town & country planning: Amendments: Scotland 396
Town & country planning: Applications, deemed applications, requests & site visits: Fees: England 306
Town & country planning: Compensation: England. 306
Town & country planning: Compensation: Wales 307
Town & country planning: Development management procedure: England. 306
Town & country planning: Development management procedure: Scotland 396
Town & country planning: Development management procedure: Wales. 308
Town & country planning: General permitted development: England. 306
Town & country planning: General permitted development: Fish farms: Scotland 396
Town & country planning: General permitted development: Wales 308
Town & country planning: Highland: Local plans: Continuation: Scotland 396
Town & country planning: Land compensation development: England 305
Town & country planning: Land compensation development: Wales 307
Town & country planning: Listed buildings & conservation areas: England 305
Town & country planning: Listed buildings & conservation areas: Wales 307
Town & country planning: Local planning: England 306
Town & country planning: Localism Act 2011: Commencements 31, 81, 87, 98, 101, 133, 305, 306, 307
Town & country planning: Localism Act 2011: Consequential amendments 99, 307
Town & country planning: Localism: Acts. 4
Town & country planning: Marine fish farming: Scotland 396
Town & country planning: Neighbourhood planning: General: England 305
Town & country planning: Neighbourhood planning: Prescribed dates: England. 305
Town & country planning: Neighbourhood planning: Referendums: England 305
Town & country planning: Planning & Compulsory Purchase Act 2004: Commencements: Wales 307
Town & country planning: Planning Act 2008: Commencements 305
Town & country planning: Planning Act 2008: Commencements: Wales 307
Town & country planning: Planning etc. (Scotland) Act 2006: National parks: Consequential provisions: Scotland. . . . 396
Town & country planning: Planning permission: Withdrawal of development or local development order: Compensation :
Wales. 307
Town & country planning: Prescribed date: Scotland 396
Town & country planning: Regional strategy: East of England 305
Town & country planning: South Lanarkshire: Local plans: Continuation: Scotland 396
Town & country planning: Tree preservation: England 306
Town & country planning: Trees: Wales 308
Trade marks: Fees 308
Trade union duties & activities: Time off: Code of practice: Appointed day: Northern Ireland. 410
Trade: Animals: Trade in: Related products: Scotland 363, 364
Trade: Statistics: Customs & excise 303
Trading with the enemy: Negotiable instruments etc.: Transfer: Revocation 308
Trading: Advertising & trading: London Olympic & Paralympic Games: Wales 101
Trading: London Olympic & Paralympic Games: Acts 6
Traffic Management Act 2004: Exeter. 272
Traffic management: Penalty charges: Prescribed amounts: Northern Ireland 440
Traffic management: Permit schemes: Barnsley Metropolitan Borough Council. 78
Traffic management: Permit schemes: Bedford Borough Council 78
Traffic management: Permit schemes: Bexley, London Borough. 79
Traffic management: Permit schemes: Council of the Borough of Kirklees 79
Traffic management: Permit schemes: Doncaster Borough Council 78
Traffic management: Permit schemes: Havering, London Borough 79
Traffic management: Permit schemes: Hertfordshire County Council 78
Traffic management: Permit schemes: Kingston upon Thames, Royal Borough 79
Traffic management: Permit schemes: Leeds City Council 78
Traffic management: Permit schemes: Luton Borough Council 79
Traffic management: Permit schemes: Merton, London Borough 79

Traffic management: Permit schemes: Rotherham Borough Council. 79
Traffic management: Permit schemes: Sheffield City Council 79
Traffic management: Permit schemes: Southend-on-Sea Borough Council. 79
Traffic management: Permit schemes: St Helens Borough Council. 79
Traffic management: Permit schemes: Sutton, London Borough 79
Traffic management: Permit schemes: Tower Hamlets, London Borough 79
Trafford Healthcare: National Health Service Trust 110
Transfer of functions: Culture, Media & Sport: Secretary of State 105
Transplantation: Organs: Quality & safety 82
Transport & works: Greater Manchester: Light rapid transit systems: Oldham, Manchester St. modification. 309, 310
Transport & works: Greater Manchester: Light rapid transit systems: Oldham, Mumps modification. 309, 310
Transport & works: Hinkley Point: Temporary jetty: Land acquisition 309
Transport & works: Ipswich Barrier 309
Transport & works: Railways: Chiltern Railways: Bicester to Oxford improvement 309
Transport & works: Railways: Nene Valley Railway: Fletton Branch: England 309, 310
Transport & works: River Humber: Burcom outfall: Transfer 309
Transport levying bodies: Local government 98
Transport: Banchory & Cranthes Light Railway: Scotland 396
Transport: Bridgewater Canal: Transfer of undertaking 14, 309
Transport: British Waterways Board: Transfer of functions 14, 129, 308
Transport: Bus Service Operators Grant: Scotland. 396
Transport: Energy Act 2004: Amendment 60, 308
Transport: Local policing bodies 87, 122, 310
Transport: Rail vehicles: Accessibility: Non-interoperable rail system 47, 309
Transport: Road transport: Working time: Amendments 309
Transport: Road transport: Working time: Northern Ireland 448
Transports & works: London cable car 309, 310
Travelling circuses: Wild animals: Welfare: England 10
Travelling expenses & remission of charges: Health & personal social services: Northern Ireland 416
Travelling expenses & remission of charges: National Health Service: England 108
Travelling expenses & remission of charges: National Health Service: Scotland 378
Travelling expenses & remission of charges: National Health Service: Wales 111
Treaty of Lisbon: Terminology & numbering: Changes 65
Tree preservation: Town & country planning: England 306
Trent Valley: Internal drainage Board. 90
Tribunals & inquiries: First-tier & Upper tribunals: Chambers 310
Tribunals & inquiries: First-tier & Upper tribunals: Members: Appointment: Qualifications 310
Tribunals & inquiries: Revenue & customs 310
Tribunals & inquiries: Tribunal procedure 310
Tribunals & inquiries: Tribunal procedure: Upper Tribunal 310
Tribunals, Courts & Enforcement Act 2007: Commencements 15
Tribunals, Courts & Enforcement Act 2007: Consequential amendments 45
Trunk roads: A1 . . . . 140, 145, 146, 147, 148, 149, 150, 151, 152
Trunk roads: A1/A1(M) 140, 141, 145
Trunk roads: A1/A428 152
Trunk roads: A1/A47/A1(M) 141
Trunk roads: A1/A66 146
Trunk roads: A1/A69 146
Trunk roads: A1: Elkesley junctions improvement 77
Trunk roads: A1033 220
Trunk roads: A1053 220
Trunk roads: A1089/A13 164
Trunk roads: A11 . . . . 161, 162, 165
Trunk roads: A11/A14 165
Trunk roads: A12 . . . . 162, 163, 164
Trunk roads: A12/A120 162
Trunk roads: A120 . . . . 139, 208, 209
Trunk roads: A120/A12 162
Trunk roads: A120/M11 250
Trunk roads: A13 . . . . 164, 165
Trunk roads: A13/A1089 164
Trunk roads: A13/A282/M25 253
Trunk roads: A14 . . . . 165, 166, 167, 168, 169
Trunk roads: A14/A11 165
Trunk roads: A14/A428 165

Trunk roads: A14/M11	166, 249
Trunk roads: A160	209
Trunk roads: A174	209
Trunk roads: A180	209, 210
Trunk roads: A180/M180	269
Trunk roads: A184	210
Trunk roads: A184/A1(M)/A194(M)	140
Trunk roads: A19	169, 170, 171
Trunk roads: A19/A66	169
Trunk roads: A2	153, 154
Trunk roads: A2/A282/M2	253
Trunk roads: A2/A282/M25	253
Trunk roads: A2/M2	153, 228
Trunk roads: A20	172, 251, 252
Trunk roads: A20/M20	172, 251
Trunk roads: A20/M25/M26	252
Trunk roads: A2070	220
Trunk roads: A21	172, 173, 174
Trunk roads: A21/M25	172
Trunk roads: A23	174
Trunk roads: A23/A26	172
Trunk roads: A23/A27	174, 175
Trunk roads: A23/M23	252
Trunk roads: A24/A27	175
Trunk roads: A249	210
Trunk roads: A259	139, 140, 210, 211
Trunk roads: A26	175
Trunk roads: A26/A23	172
Trunk roads: A27	175, 176, 177, 178
Trunk roads: A27/A23	174, 175
Trunk roads: A27/A24	175
Trunk roads: A27/M27	175
Trunk roads: A27/M27/M275/A3(M)	175
Trunk roads: A282	211
Trunk roads: A282/M2/A2	253
Trunk roads: A282/M25	253
Trunk roads: A282/M25/A13	253
Trunk roads: A282/M25/A2	253
Trunk roads: A3	137, 155, 156
Trunk roads: A3/A3(M)	154
Trunk roads: A3/M25	253
Trunk roads: A30	178, 179, 180, 181
Trunk roads: A30/A38	178
Trunk roads: A303	140, 211, 212, 213
Trunk roads: A31	138, 181, 182
Trunk roads: A316	254
Trunk roads: A316/M3	229
Trunk roads: A34	182, 183, 184
Trunk roads: A34/M3	182
Trunk roads: A35	138, 184
Trunk roads: A36	184, 185
Trunk roads: A38	137, 138, 139, 185, 186, 187, 188, 189, 190, 221
Trunk roads: A38/A30	178
Trunk roads: A38/A5148	185
Trunk roads: A4	156
Trunk roads: A4/A46	156
Trunk roads: A40	190, 191, 275, 276, 277
Trunk roads: A40/A4076/A48	277
Trunk roads: A40/A465/A4042	275
Trunk roads: A40/A479/A483/A470	283
Trunk roads: A40/A48	278
Trunk roads: A40/M25	253
Trunk roads: A404	213
Trunk roads: A4042	290, 291
Trunk roads: A4042/A40/A465	275

Trunk roads: A4042/M4 290
Trunk roads: A405 213
Trunk roads: A4060 291
Trunk roads: A4060/A470/A465 80
Trunk roads: A4076 291
Trunk roads: A4076/A48/A40 277
Trunk roads: A417 213
Trunk roads: A419 . . . . 213, 214
Trunk roads: A419/M4 230
Trunk roads: A42 191
Trunk roads: A42/M1 221
Trunk roads: A421 214
Trunk roads: A4232 291
Trunk roads: A4253 215
Trunk roads: A428 214
Trunk roads: A428/A1 152
Trunk roads: A428/A14 165
Trunk roads: A43 191
Trunk roads: A43/M1 221
Trunk roads: A44 277
Trunk roads: A44/A483/A489/A470 286
Trunk roads: A446 . . . . 140, 215
Trunk roads: A446/A452 215
Trunk roads: A449 . . . . 215, 281
Trunk roads: A449/A5 215
Trunk roads: A449/A5/M6/M54 243
Trunk roads: A45 . . . . 139, 192, 193
Trunk roads: A45/M42 192
Trunk roads: A452 215
Trunk roads: A452/A446 215
Trunk roads: A453 215
Trunk roads: A453/A50/M1 221
Trunk roads: A453/A52 215
Trunk roads: A453/M1 222
Trunk roads: A453: Birmingham to Nottingham 77
Trunk roads: A456 140
Trunk roads: A458 . . . . 216, 281
Trunk roads: A46 . . . . 139, 193, 194, 195, 196
Trunk roads: A46/ M1/M69 221
Trunk roads: A46/A4 156
Trunk roads: A465 . . . . 273, 282, 283
Trunk roads: A465/A4042/A40 275
Trunk roads: A465/A4060/A470 80
Trunk roads: A47 . . . . 196, 197
Trunk roads: A47/A1(M)/A1 141
Trunk roads: A470 . . . . 79, 273, 277, 282, 283, 284, 285
Trunk roads: A470/A40/A479/A483 283
Trunk roads: A470/A44/A483/A489 286
Trunk roads: A470/A465/A4060 80
Trunk roads: A477 . . . . 80, 285, 286
Trunk roads: A479 286
Trunk roads: A479/A483/A470/A40 283
Trunk roads: A48 277
Trunk roads: A48/A40 278
Trunk roads: A48/A40/A4076 277
Trunk roads: A48/A483/M4 . . . . 277, 278
Trunk roads: A48/M4 278
Trunk roads: A483 . . . . 140, 216, 277, 286, 287
Trunk roads: A483/A470/A40/A479 283
Trunk roads: A483/A48/M4 277
Trunk roads: A483/A489/A470/A44 286
Trunk roads: A483/M4/A48 278
Trunk roads: A487 . . . . 277, 287, 288, 289
Trunk roads: A489 289
Trunk roads: A489/A470/A44/A483 286

Trunk roads: A49	139, 197, 198, 199
Trunk roads: A49/A5	156
Trunk roads: A494	216, 289, 290
Trunk roads: A494/A55	278
Trunk roads: A494/A550	289
Trunk roads: A5	137, 138, 156, 157, 158, 159, 160, 161, 273, 274, 275
Trunk roads: A5/A449	215
Trunk roads: A5/A449/M6/M54	243
Trunk roads: A5/A483	156
Trunk roads: A5/A49	156
Trunk roads: A5/M54	261
Trunk roads: A5/M6 Toll	157
Trunk roads: A50	199, 200
Trunk roads: A50/A453/M1	221
Trunk roads: A50/A500	199
Trunk roads: A500	216, 217
Trunk roads: A500/A50	199
Trunk roads: A500/M6	241
Trunk roads: A5006	220
Trunk roads: A5036	220
Trunk roads: A5103	221
Trunk roads: A5111/A52	200, 201, 221
Trunk roads: A5121	138
Trunk roads: A5148	221
Trunk roads: A5148/A38	185
Trunk roads: A52	139, 201
Trunk roads: A52/A453	215
Trunk roads: A52/A5111	200, 201, 221
Trunk roads: A55	201, 261, 278, 279, 280, 281
Trunk roads: A55/A494	278
Trunk roads: A550	217, 290
Trunk roads: A550/A494	289
Trunk roads: A550/A5117/A494	217
Trunk roads: A556	217
Trunk roads: A556/M56	217
Trunk roads: A56	201
Trunk roads: A56/M66	269
Trunk roads: A57	201
Trunk roads: A585	217
Trunk roads: A590	218
Trunk roads: A590/M6	217, 218
Trunk roads: A595	218
Trunk roads: A6	161
Trunk roads: A616	219
Trunk roads: A628	219
Trunk roads: A63	201, 202
Trunk roads: A631	219
Trunk roads: A631/M1	225
Trunk Roads: A631/M1	225
Trunk roads: A64	142, 202, 203, 204
Trunk roads: A66	205, 206, 207, 208
Trunk roads: A66/A1	146
Trunk roads: A66/A19	169
Trunk roads: A663	219, 220
Trunk roads: A69	208
Trunk roads: A69/A1	146
Trunk roads: A696	220
Trunk roads: A702: Scotland	388
Trunk roads: A720: Scotland	386
Trunk roads: A737/A738: Scotland	388
Trunk roads: A738/A737: Scotland	388
Trunk roads: A77: Scotland	386, 387
Trunk roads: A8/M8: Scotland	388
Trunk roads: A82: Scotland	384, 387
Trunk roads: A823(M): Pitreavie Spur: Scotland	385

Trunk roads: A83: Scotland 387
Trunk roads: A830: Scotland 388
Trunk roads: A84: Scotland 387
Trunk roads: A85: Scotland 387
Trunk roads: A9/M9: Newbridge to Winchburgh: Scotland 385
Trunk roads: A9: Scotland 386, 387
Trunk roads: A90/M90/M9: Humbie Rail Bridge to M9 junction 1a: Scotland 385
Trunk roads: A90/M90/M9: Kirkliston to Halbeath: Scotland 385
Trunk roads: A90/M90/M9: Scotland 385, 388
Trunk roads: A90: Scotland 389
Trunk roads: A92: Scotland 387
Trunk roads: A96: Scotland. 387, 388
Trunk roads: A99: Scotland 388
Trunk roads: Fife area trunk roads: Scotland 388
Trunk roads: M8/A8: Scotland. 388
Trunk roads: M9/A9: Newbridge to Winchburgh: Scotland 385
Trunk roads: M9/A9: Scotland. 388
Trunk roads: M9/A90/M90, A823(M) & A92: Fife area: Scotland 388
Trunk roads: M9/A90/M90, A985, A823(M) & A92: Fife area: Scotland. 388
Trunk roads: M9/A90/M90: Humbie Rail Bridge to M9 junction 1a: Scotland 385
Trunk roads: M9/A90/M90: Kirkliston to Halbeath: Scotland. 385
Trunk roads: M9/A90/M90: Scotland 388, 389
Trunk roads: M9: Scotland. 389
Trunk roads: M90/A90/M9: Humbie Rail Bridge to M9 junction 1a: Scotland 385
Trunk roads: M90/A90/M9: Kirkliston to Halbeath: Scotland. 385
Trunk roads: M90: Scotland 389
Trunk roads: North east trunk roads area: Scotland 389, 390
Trunk roads: North west trunk roads area: Scotland 390, 391
Trunk roads: South east trunk roads area: Scotland 391, 392
Trunk roads: South west trunk roads area: Scotland 386, 392, 393
Tuberculosis: Control: Animals: Northern Ireland. 406
Tuberculosis: England. 11
Tullynacross Road, Lisburn: Abandonment: Northern Ireland 434
Tunnels: Revision of tolls: River Tyne 78
Turks Head Link: A30. 77

U

UK Borders Act 2007: Border & immigration inspectorate: Joint working. 84
Undertakings for collective investment in transferable securities. 69
United Nations: International tribunals: Former Yugoslavia & Rwanda. 311
United Nations: Personnel: Isle of Man: Criminal law 41
United Nations: Sanctions: Iraq 311
United Nations: Sanctions: Overseas territories 311
United States: Accounting standards: Prescribed bodies: Companies. 31
Universal Credit: Welfare reform: Acts 6, 7
Universal Credit: Welfare reform: Acts: Explanatory notes 7
University Terrace, Belfast: Abandonment: Roads: Northern Ireland 434
Uplands: Transitional payments 9
Upper Dunmurry Lane, Dunmurry: Abandonment: Roads: Northern Ireland 434
Urban Development Corporations: Planning functions 311
Urban development: London Legacy Development Corporation: Establishment 311
Urban development: London Legacy Development Corporation: Planning functions. 311
Urban development: London Thames Gateway Development Corporation: Transfer of property, rights & liabilities . . . 311
Urban development: Milton Keynes: Urban areas & planning functions 311
Urban development: Thurrock Development Corporation: Dissolution 311
Urban development: Thurrock Development Corporation: Transfer of property, rights & liabilities 311
Urban development: Urban Development Corporations: Planning functions 311
Utilities contracts: Scotland 382

V

Valuation Tribunal: Rules: High hedges: Northern Ireland 431
Valuation Tribunal: Rules: Northern Ireland. 431
Value added tax 312

Value added tax: European Research Infrastructure Consortia: Relief 313
Value added tax: Finance Act 2010: Schedule 6, part 1: Consequential & incidental provisions 15, 36, 85, 312
Value added tax: Fuel: Private use: Consideration. 312
Value added tax: Land exemption 312
Value added tax: Refunds: Chief constables & the Commissioner of the Police of the Metropolis 312
Value added tax: Refunds: Museums & galleries 312
Value added tax: Registration limits: Increase 312
Value added tax: Removal of goods 313
Value added tax: Small non-commercial consignments: Relief: Amendments 313
Value added tax: Supply of services: Transport of goods 312
Vehicles: Goods vehicles: Enforcement powers: Northern Ireland 435
Vehicles: Goods vehicles: Operators: Licensing: Commencements: Northern Ireland 435
Vehicles: Goods vehicles: Operators: Licensing: Exemptions: Northern Ireland 435
Vehicles: Goods vehicles: Operators: Licensing: Fees. 136
Vehicles: Goods vehicles: Operators: Licensing: Fees: Northern Ireland 435
Vehicles: Goods vehicles: Operators: Licensing: Northern Ireland 435
Vehicles: Goods vehicles: Operators: Qualifications: Northern Ireland 436
Vehicles: Goods vehicles: Plating & testing: Amendments 137
Vehicles: Goods vehicles: Testing: Fees: Northern Ireland 436
Vehicles: Goods vehicles: Testing: Northern Ireland 436
Vehicles: Motor vehicles: Construction & use: Northern Ireland 436
Vehicles: Motor vehicles: Driving licences 137
Vehicles: Motor vehicles: Driving licences: Fees: Northern Ireland. 437
Vehicles: Motor vehicles: Driving licences: Northern Ireland 436, 437
Vehicles: Motor vehicles: Taxi drivers: Licences: Northern Ireland. 437
Vehicles: Motor vehicles: Testing: Northern Ireland 437
Vehicles: Motor vehicles: Tests: Amendments 137
Vehicles: Public service vehicles: Operators' licences: Fees 132
Vehicles: Removal & disposal: Prescribed periods: Northern Ireland 412
Vehicles: Road vehicles: Individual approval: Fees 137
Vehicles: Road vehicles: Registration & licensing: Amendments 137
Velindre: National Health Service Trust 111
Velindre: Shared Services Committee: National Health Service Trust 111
Veterinary medicines. 103
Victims & Survivors for Northern Ireland: Commissioner for: Superannuation: Northern Ireland 426
Victims & Survivors Service Ltd: Superannuation: Northern Ireland: Northern Ireland 426
Victims: Domestic violence, crime & victims: Acts 4
Victims: Domestic violence, crime & victims: Acts: Explanatory notes 7
Video recordings: Digital Economy Act 2010: Appointed days 313
Video recordings: Digital Economy Act 2010: Transitional provisions 313
Video recordings: Labelling 313
Violence: Domestic: Crime & victims: Acts 4
Violence: Domestic: Crime & victims: Acts: Explanatory notes 7
Visas: Passenger transit: Immigration 83, 84
Visiting forces: International Military Headquarters: EU SOFA: Tax Designation 46
Visiting forces: International Military Headquarters: NATO & PfP: Tax Designation 46, 87, 88, 303
Volatile organic compounds: Paints, varnishes & vehicle refinishing products. 62
Vulnerable adults: Protection: Disclosure & Barring Service: Core functions. 17, 128
Vulnerable adults: Safeguarding Vulnerable Groups Act 2006: Commencements 17, 128
Vulnerable adults: Safeguarding Vulnerable Groups Act 2006: Controlled activity & prescribed criteria: England & Wales
. . . . 18, 128
Vulnerable adults: Safeguarding Vulnerable Groups Act 2006: Miscellaneous amendments 18, 128
Vulnerable adults: Safeguarding Vulnerable Groups Act 2006: Miscellaneous provisions 18, 128
Vulnerable groups: Safeguarding Vulnerable Groups: 2007 Order: Commencements: Northern Ireland 443

W

Wakefield, City: Mayoral referendum 94
Wales: Local government: Byelaws: Acts 455
Wales: Local government: Byelaws: Acts: Explanatory notes 455
Wales: National Assembly for Wales: Official languages: Acts 455
Wales: National Assembly for Wales: Official languages: Acts: Explanatory notes 455
Wales: Police & Crime Commissioners: Elections: Welsh forms 123
Waste water transfer & storage: Infrastructure planning 87
Waste: Controlled: England 63

Waste: Controlled: England & Wales	63
Waste: England & Wales	64
Waste: Fees & charges: Northern Ireland	412
Waste: Information: Climate change: Scotland	371
Waste: Landfill tax	90
Waste: Landfill tax: Qualifying materials	90
Waste: Packaging waste: Producer responsibility & obligations	62
Water Act 2003: Commencements	313
Water Act 2003: Commencements: Wales	314
Water industry: Financial assistance: Acts	6
Water industry: Financial assistance: Acts: Explanatory notes	7
Water industry: Flood & Water Management Act 2010: Commencements	30, 63, 71, 313
Water industry: Water Services etc. (Scotland) Act 2005: Commencements: Scotland	397
Water Services etc. (Scotland) Act 2005: Commencements: Scotland	397
Water supply & water quality: Inspection fees	68, 130, 314
Water supply: Services: Charges: Billing & collection: Scotland	397
Water: Bathing water: Quality: Northern Ireland	412
Water: Bathing waters: Scotland	370, 396
Water: Nitrate pollution: Prevention	9, 313
Water: Nitrate pollution: Prevention: Wales	9, 314
Water: Priority substances & classification: EC directive: Northern Ireland	412
Water: Services: Charges: Billing & collection: Scotland	397
Waterways: Non-domestic rating: England	134
Welfare Reform Act 2009: Commencements	66, 135, 296, 301
Welfare Reform Act 2010: Commencements: Northern Ireland	414
Welfare Reform Act 2012: Commencements	301, 302
Welfare reform: Acts	7
Welfare reform: Acts: Explanatory notes	7
Welfare reform: Further provisions: Acts: Explanatory notes: Scotland	362
Welfare reform: Further provisions: Acts: Scotland	362
Welfare services: Information sharing	300
Wellingborough Prison: Closure	127
Welsh Language (Wales) Measure 2011: Commencements	314, 315
Welsh Language (Wales) Measure 2011: Transfer of functions & consequential provisions	315
Welsh Language Board: Transfer of staff, property, rights & liabilities	314
Welsh Language Commissioner: Advisory Panel: Appointments	314
Welsh Language Measure: Registrable interests	314
Welsh language: Police names	125
Welsh language: Schemes: Public bodies	314
Welsh Ministers & Local Health Boards: Transfer of property, rights & liabilities: Wales	111
Welwyn Hatfield: St Albans & Welwyn Hatfield: Boundary changes: Local government	97
West Lindsey: Electoral changes	98
West Oxfordshire: Electoral changes	95
Westbourne Avenue, Ballymena: Abandonment: Roads: Northern Ireland	434
Whipps Cross University Hospital: National Health Service Trust	106
Wild animals: Travelling circuses: Welfare: England	10
Wildlife & Countryside Act 1981: Keeping & release & notification requirements: Scotland	397, 398
Wildlife & Countryside Act 1981: Section 14: Exceptions: Scotland	397
Wildlife & Natural Environment (Scotland) Act 2011: Commencements: Scotland	398
Wildlife & Natural Environment (Scotland) Act 2011: Consequential modifications: Scotland	398
Wildlife & Natural Environment Act (Northern Ireland) 2011: Commencements: Northern Ireland	448
Wildlife: Acts: Explanatory notes: Scotland	362
Wildlife: Conservation: Habitats: Species	38, 102, 315
Wildlife: Conservation: Natural habitats: Scotland	397
Wildlife: Offshore marine conservation: Natural habitats	315
Wildlife: Snares: Identification numbers & tags: Scotland	397
Wildlife: Spring traps: Approval: Northern Ireland	448
Wildlife: Training: Snares: Scotland	397
Wiltshire Council: Suitable education: Provision for: Arrangements: England	54
Wireless Telegraphy Act 2006: OFCOM: Directions	13, 59
Wireless telegraphy: Interference: Prisons: Acts	6
Wireless telegraphy: Licence awards	59
Wireless telegraphy: Licence charges	59
Wireless telegraphy: Licences: Limitation of number	59
Wireless telegraphy: London Olympic Games & Paralympic Games: Apparatus: Interference control	59

Wireless telegraphy: Register 59
Wireless telegraphy: Spectrum trading 59
Wolverhampton: Royal Wolverhampton Hospitals: National Health Service Trust 109
Wood & bark: Ash dieback: Plant health: Northern Ireland 428
Workers' compensation: Claims: Payments: Pneumoconiosis etc. 298
Workers' compensation: Pneumoconiosis etc.: Claims: Payments: Northern Ireland 445
Workers' compensation: Supplementation 302
Working tax credit: Up-rating 304
Working time: Road transport: Northern Ireland 448
Working time: Road transport: Working time: Amendments 309
Wrecks: Protection: Designation: England 129

Y

Yorkshire: Scarborough & North East Yorkshire Health Care: National Health Service Trust 109
Young offender institutions: Prisons: Scotland 380
Young People's Learning Agency: Abolition 54
Youth detention accommodation: Remand: Recovery of costs 43
Yugoslavia, Former: International tribunals: United Nations 311
Yugoslavia: International Criminal Tribunal: Indictees: Financial sanctions 40

Z

Zimbabwe: Sanctions: Overseas territories 115
Zoonoses: Fees: Northern Ireland 406
Zootechnical standards: England 10